ATLAS OF MORAL PSYCHOLOGY

ATLAS
OF MORAL
PSYCHOLOGY

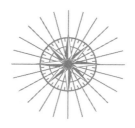

Edited by
Kurt Gray
Jesse Graham

THE GUILFORD PRESS
New York   London

Paperback edition 2020

Printed in the United States of America

This book is printed on acid-free paper.

Last digit is print number: 9   8   7   6   5   4   3   2

Library of Congress Cataloging-in-Publication Data

Names: Gray, Kurt James, editor. | Graham, Jesse, 1975- editor.
Title: Atlas of moral psychology / edited by Kurt Gray, Jesse Graham.
Description: New York, NY : The Guilford Press, 2018. | Includes
   bibliographical references and index.
Identifiers: LCCN 2017050335 | ISBN 9781462532568 (hardback) |
   ISBN 9781462541225 (paperback)
Subjects: LCSH: Social psychology. | Ethics—Psychological aspects. |
   Psychology—Philosophy. | BISAC: PSYCHOLOGY / Social Psychology. | SOCIAL
   SCIENCE / Sociology / General. | PHILOSOPHY / Ethics & Moral Philosophy.
Classification: LCC HM1033 .A86 2018 | DDC 302—dc23
LC record available at *https://lccn.loc.gov/2017050335*

About the Editors

Kurt Gray, PhD, is Assistant Professor of Psychology and Neuroscience at the University of North Carolina at Chapel Hill. He studies moral psychology, mind perception, and agent-based modeling. Dr. Gray has been named a Rising Star by the Association for Psychological Science, which awarded him the Janet Spence Award for Transformative Early Career Research. He has also received the Sage Young Scholar Award, the Wegner Theoretical Innovation Prize from the Society for Personality and Social Psychology, and the Early Career Award and Best Social Cognition Paper Award from the International Social Cognition Network, and is a Fellow of the Society of Experimental Social Psychology. Widely cited in the media, Dr. Gray has spoken at two TED events and is coauthor (with Daniel M. Wegner) of a book for general readers, *The Mind Club: Who Thinks, What Feels, and Why It Matters.* His website is *www.mpmlab.org.*

Jesse Graham, PhD, is Associate Professor of Management at the Eccles School of Business, University of Utah. He studies people's core moral, political, and religious convictions. Dr. Graham is a Fellow of the Society of Experimental Social Psychology and of the Moral Psychology Research Group. He has been named a Rising Star by the Association for Psychological Science and also has been honored with the Sage Young Scholar Award, the General Education Teacher of the Year Award from University of Southern California, the Award for Excellence in Scholarship in the Sciences from the University of Virginia, and the Morton Deutsch Award for best paper published in *Social Justice Research.* Dr. Graham is coeditor (with Piercarlo Valdesolo) of *Social Psychology of Political Polarization.*

Contributors

Mark D. Alicke, PhD,
Department of Psychology, Ohio University,
Athens, Ohio

Karl Aquino, PhD,
UBC Sauder School of Business,
University of British Columbia, Vancouver,
British Columbia, Canada

Brock Bastian, PhD,
Melbourne School of Psychological Sciences,
University of Melbourne, Melbourne, Australia

Roy F. Baumeister, PhD,
Department of Psychology,
Florida State University, Tallahassee, Florida

C. Daryl Cameron, PhD, Department of
Psychology, The Pennsylvania State University,
University Park, Pennsylvania

Nate C. Carnes, PhD, Department of
Psychological and Brain Sciences,
University of Massachusetts Amherst,
Amherst, Massachusetts

Hanah A. Chapman, PhD,
Department of Psychology, Brooklyn College,
Brooklyn, New York

Mina Cikara, PhD, Department of Psychology,
Harvard University, Cambridge, Massachusetts

Paul Conway, PhD, Department of Psychology,
Florida State University, Tallahassee, Florida

Jason M. Cowell, PhD,
Department of Psychology,
The University of Chicago, Chicago, Illinois

Clayton R. Critcher, PhD,
Haas School of Business,
University of California, Berkeley,
Berkeley, California

Fiery Cushman, PhD,
Department of Psychology, Harvard University,
Cambridge, Massachusetts

Audun Dahl, PhD, Department of Psychology,
University of California, Santa Cruz,
Santa Cruz, California

Jean Decety, PhD, Department of Psychology,
The University of Chicago, Chicago, Illinois

Morteza Dehghani, PhD,
Department of Psychology,
University of Southern California,
Los Angeles, California

Peter DeScioli, PhD,
Department of Political Science,
Stony Brook University, Stony Brook, New York

Anton J. M. Dijker, PhD,
Department of Health Promotion,
Maastricht University,
Maastricht, The Netherlands

Peter H. Ditto, PhD, Department of Psychology and Social Behavior, University of California, Irvine, Irvine, California

Susan T. Fiske, PhD, Department of Psychology, Princeton University, Princeton, New Jersey

Jeremy A. Frimer, PhD, Department of Psychology, University of Winnipeg, Winnipeg, Manitoba, Canada

Adam D. Galinsky, PhD, Columbia Business School, Columbia University, New York, New York

Roger Giner-Sorolla, PhD, School of Psychology, Keynes College, University of Kent, Canterbury, United Kingdom

Francesca Gino, PhD, Harvard Business School, Harvard University, Cambridge, Massachusetts

Geoffrey P. Goodwin, PhD, Department of Psychology, University of Pennsylvania, Philadelphia, Pennsylvania

Sara Gottlieb, PhD, Department of Psychology, University of California, Berkeley, Berkeley, California

Aner Govrin, PhD, Department of Psychology, Bar Ilan University, Tel Aviv, Israel

Jesse Graham, PhD, Eccles School of Business, University of Utah, Salt Lake City, Utah

Kurt Gray, PhD, Department of Psychology and Neuroscience, University of North Carolina at Chapel Hill, Chapel Hill, North Carolina

Jeff Greenberg, PhD, Department of Psychology, The University of Arizona, Tucson, Arizona

Joshua D. Greene, PhD, Department of Psychology, Harvard University, Cambridge, Massachusetts

Jonathan Haidt, PhD, New York University Stern School of Business, New York University, New York, New York

J. Kiley Hamlin, PhD, Department of Psychology, University of British Columbia, Vancouver, British Columbia, Canada

Eric G. Helzer, PhD, Johns Hopkins Carey Business School, Johns Hopkins University, Baltimore, Maryland

Joseph Hoover, MS, Department of Psychology, University of Southern California, Los Angeles, California

Rumen Iliev, PhD, Ford School of Public Policy, University of Michigan, Ann Arbor, Michigan

Yoel Inbar, PhD, Department of Psychology, University of Toronto Scarborough, Scarborough, Ontario, Canada

Carol Iskiwitch, MA, Department of Psychology, University of Southern California, Los Angeles, California

Ronnie Janoff-Bulman, PhD, Department of Psychological and Brain Sciences, University of Massachusetts Amherst, Amherst, Massachusetts

Kate Johnson, MA, Department of Psychology, University of Southern California, Los Angeles, California

Adam Kay, PhD, Sauder School of Business, University of British Columbia, Vancouver, British Columbia, Canada

Justin J. Kelly, BSc, Melbourne School of Psychological Sciences, University of Melbourne, Parkville, Victoria, Australia

Melanie Killen, PhD, Department of Human Development and Quantitative Methodology, University of Maryland, College Park, College Park, Maryland

Joshua Knobe, PhD, Departments of Philosophy, Psychology, and Linguistics, Yale University, New Haven, Connecticut

Robert Kurzban, PhD, Department of Psychology, University of Pennsylvania, Philadelphia, Pennsylvania

Simon M. Laham, PhD, Melbourne School of Psychological Sciences, University of Melbourne, Parkville, Victoria, Australia

Justin F. Landy, PhD, The University of Chicago Booth School of Business, The University of Chicago, Chicago, Illinois

Julia J. Lee, PhD, Stephen M. Ross School of Business, University of Michigan, Ann Arbor, Michigan

Brittany S. Liu, PhD, Department of Psychology, Kalamazoo College, Kalamazoo, Michigan

Tania Lombrozo, PhD, Department of Psychology, University of California, Berkeley, Berkeley, California

Stephen Loughnan, PhD, Department of Psychology, The University of Edinburgh, Edinburgh, United Kingdom

Jackson G. Lu, MPhil, Columbia Business School, Columbia University, New York, New York

Edouard Machery, PhD, Department of History and Philosophy of Science, University of Pittsburgh, Pittsburgh, Pennsylvania

Bertram F. Malle, PhD, Department of Cognitive, Linguistic and Psychological Sciences, Brown University, Providence, Rhode Island

Katherine McAuliffe, PhD, Department of Psychology, Boston College, Chestnut Hill, Massachusetts

Peter Meindl, PhD, Department of Psychology, University of Pennsylvania, Philadelphia, Pennsylvania

Brett Mercier, MS, Department of Psychology and Social Behavior, University of California, Irvine, Irvine, California

Ryan Miller, BA, Department of Psychology, Harvard University, Cambridge, Massachusetts

Marlon Mooijman, PhD, Kellogg School of Management, Northwestern University, Evanston, Illinois

Matt Motyl, PhD, Department of Psychology, University of Illinois at Chicago, Chicago, Illinois

Darcia Narvaez, PhD, Department of Psychology, University of Notre Dame, Notre Dame, Indiana

David T. Newman, JD, USC Marshall School of Business, University of Southern California, Los Angeles, California

Shaun Nichols, PhD, Department of Philosophy, The University of Arizona, Tucson, Arizona

Gabriela Pavarini, PhD, Department of Psychology, University of Cambridge, Cambridge, United Kingdom

Jared Piazza, PhD, Department of Psychology, Lancaster University, Lancaster, United Kingdom

Jesse L. Preston, PhD, Department of Psychology, University of Warwick, Coventry, United Kingdom

Jesse J. Prinz, PhD, Department of Philosophy, City University of New York Graduate Center, New York, New York

Tom Pyszczynski, PhD, Department of Psychology, University of Colorado Colorado Springs, Colorado Springs, Colorado

Tage S. Rai, PhD, MIT Sloan School of Management, Massachusetts Institute of Technology, Cambridge, Massachusetts

Ross Rogers, MS, Department of Psychology, Ohio University, Athens, Ohio

Derek D. Rucker, PhD, Kellogg School of Management, Northwestern University, Evanston, Illinois

Laurie R. Santos, PhD, Department of Psychology, Yale University, New Haven, Connecticut

Julian A. Scheffer, BSc, Department of Psychological and Brain Sciences, University of Iowa, Iowa City, Iowa

Chelsea Schein, BA, Department of Psychology and Neuroscience, University of North Carolina at Chapel Hill, Chapel Hill, North Carolina

Kate C. S. Schmidt, MA, Department of Philosophy, Washington University in St. Louis, St. Louis, Missouri

Simone Schnall, PhD, Department of Psychology, University of Cambridge, Cambridge, United Kingdom

Azim Shariff, PhD, Department of Psychology, University of Oregon, Eugene, Oregon

Walter Sinnott-Armstrong, PhD, Department of Philosophy, Duke University, Durham, North Carolina

Jessica A. Sommerville, PhD, Department of Psychology, University of Washington, Seattle, Washington

Victoria L. Spring, BA, Department of Psychological and Brain Sciences, University of Iowa, Iowa City, Iowa

Stephen Stich, PhD, Department of Philosophy and the Center for Cognitive Science, Rutgers, The State University of New Jersey, New Brunswick, New Jersey

Nina Strohminger, PhD, The Wharton School, University of Pennsylvania, Philadelphia, Pennsylvania

Sarah Taylor, MA, Department of Psychology, Ohio University, Athens, Ohio

Elliot Turiel, PhD, Graduate School of Education, University of California, Berkeley, Berkeley, California

Eric Luis Uhlmann, PhD, INSEAD, Singapore

Piercarlo Valdesolo, PhD, Department of Psychology, Claremont McKenna College, Claremont, California

Julia W. Van de Vondervoort, MA, Department of Psychology, University of British Columbia, Vancouver, British Columbia, Canada

Kees van den Bos, MA, Department of Social and Organizational Psychology, Utrecht University, Utrecht, The Netherlands

John Voiklis, PhD, Department of Cognitive, Linguistic and Psychological Sciences, Brown University, Providence, Rhode Island

Felix Warneken, PhD, Department of Psychology, University of Michigan, Ann Arbor, Michigan

Adam Waytz, PhD, Kellogg School of Management, Northwestern University, Evanston, Illinois

Scott S. Wiltermuth, PhD, USC Marshall School of Business, University of Southern California, Los Angeles, California

Sean P. Wojcik, PhD, Data and Analytics, Upworthy, New York, New York

Andrea M. Yetzer, MA, Department of Psychology, Northwestern University, Evanston, Illinois

Liane Young, PhD, Department of Psychology, Boston College, Chestnut Hill, Massachusetts

Jamil Zaki, PhD, Department of Psychology, Stanford University, Stanford, California

Ting Zhang, PhD, Columbia Business School, Columbia University, New York, New York

Talee Ziv, PhD, Department of Psychology, University of Washington, Seattle, Washington

Preface

Cartography used to be tricky business. In mapping out the oceans and land-masses of the world, mapmakers had to endure attacks from animals, attacks from other people, starvation, hypothermia, and even worse. Mapping out the moral domain is no less challenging: The researchers who have written chapters in this volume have had to endure uncertainty and scientific challenges on the path to reviewing truths in moral psychology. In this volume, we present 57 chapters from the freshest minds in moral psychology. These chapters provide an overview of the strikingly large terrain of the field. Welcome to the *Atlas of Moral Psychology*.

When we conceived of the idea of the atlas, we asked contributors to take a stand on a number of questions that we had developed, including whether morality was intuitive or deliberative; whether morality involved one, two, or many processes; whether morality was domain general or domain specific; and whether morality was the same across cultures. These questions reflected our own theoretical leanings, and it quickly became clear that moral psychology had more—and bigger—questions than we had ever imagined.

This volume is so exciting because you can see just how big morality is and how many other fields it intersects with. Moral psychology started as a small offshoot of philosophy many years ago, but now it is a microcosm of the entire field of psychology, with debates about thinking and reasoning, new understandings of social cognition and the self, questions about animals and God, and even critical introspection.

This book is structured into 12 sections, each of which explores a continent of moral psychology: morality and thinking, morality and feeling, morality and social cognition, morality and intergroup conflict, morality and culture, morality and the body, morality and beliefs, dynamic moral judgment, developmental and evolutionary roots of morality, moral behavior, studying moral judgment, and clarifying morality. Each chapter can be thought of as a different country, with its own unique perspective on the world. Some chapters are very close to one another in content, whereas others are quite far apart. Like real countries, some chapters are very consonant with one another, while others have clear disagreements.

Despite the diversity of chapters, they are united by a common desire: to understand the answer to an important question. We have structured the opening of each chapter to be two simple sentences. The first sentence is the question we seek to answer, and the second sentence is the answer provided by the authors. In this way, readers can tailor their reading to whatever questions they seek to be answered. The questions are listed on the part-opening pages.

Contents

PART I. MORALITY AND THINKING

1. Can We Understand Moral Thinking without Understanding Thinking?   3
   Joshua D. Greene

2. Reasoning at the Root of Morality   9
   Elliot Turiel

3. Moral Judgment: Reflective, Interactive, Spontaneous, Challenging,   20
   and Always Evolving
   Melanie Killen and Audun Dahl

4. On the Possibility of Intuitive and Deliberative Processes Working   31
   in Parallel in Moral Judgment
   Kees van den Bos

5. The Wrong and the Bad   40
   Shaun Nichols

PART II. MORALITY AND FEELING

6. Empathy Is a Moral Force   49
   Jamil Zaki

 7. Moral Values and Motivations: How Special Are They?   59
    Ryan Miller and Fiery Cushman

 8. A Component Process Model of Disgust, Anger, and Moral Judgment   70
    Hanah A. Chapman

 9. A Functional Conflict Theory of Moral Emotions   81
    Roger Giner-Sorolla

10. Getting Emotions Right in Moral Psychology   88
    Piercarlo Valdesolo

PART III. MORALITY, SOCIAL COGNITION, AND IDENTITY

11. What Do We Evaluate When We Evaluate Moral Character?   99
    Erik G. Helzer and Clayton R. Critcher

12. Moral Cognition and Its Basis in Social Cognition and Social Regulation   108
    John Voiklis and Bertram F. Malle

13. Morality Is Personal   121
    Justin F. Landy and Eric Luis Uhlmann

14. A Social Cognitive Model of Moral Identity   133
    Karl Aquino and Adam Kay

15. Identity Is Essentially Moral   141
    Nina Strohminger

16. The Core of Morality Is the Moral Self   149
    Paul Conway

17. Thinking Morally about Animals   165
    Steve Loughnan and Jared Piazza

PART IV. MORALITY AND INTERGROUP CONFLICT

18. Morality Is for Choosing Sides   177
    Peter DeScioli and Robert Kurzban

19. Morality for Us versus Them   186
    Adam Waytz and Liane Young

20. Pleasure in Response to Outgroup Pain as a Motivator   193
    of Intergroup Aggression
    Mina Cikara

ATLAS OF MORAL PSYCHOLOGY

PART I
MORALITY AND THINKING

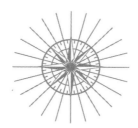

QUESTIONS ANSWERED IN PART I

CHAPTER 1 Can we understand moral thinking without understanding thinking?

CHAPTER 2 What is the role of reasoning in morality?

CHAPTER 3 Why is moral reasoning fundamental to an explanation of the development of morality?

CHAPTER 4 Is moral judgment intuitive or deliberative?

CHAPTER 5 How can a theory of moral judgment explain why people think certain actions are wrong, not simply bad?

Can We Understand Moral Thinking without Understanding Thinking?

Joshua D. Greene

Can we understand moral thinking without understanding thinking?

Only up to a point; to understand morality well enough to put it into a flexibly behaving machine, we must first learn more about how our brains compose and manipulate structured thoughts.

Nerds of a certain age will recall Commander Data from *Star Trek: The Next Generation*, the humanoid android on a personal quest to become more human. Data's positronic brain features an "ethical subroutine," a computational add-on designed to enhance his capacity for moral judgment. The field of moral cognition has bad news for Commander Data. His ethical subroutine may be wonderful, but it's not making him more human.

As far as we can tell, there is nothing in our brains specifically dedicated to moral thinking (Greene, 2014; Parkinson et al., 2011; Ruff & Fehr, 2014; Young & Dungan, 2012). (But see Hauser, 2006, and Mikhail, 2011, for a dissenting view). Observe human brains engaged in moral judgment and you'll see neural activity representing the values of available alternatives (Blair, 2007; Hutcherson et al., 2015; Moll et al., 2006; Shenhav & Greene, 2010, 2014; Zaki & Mitchell, 2011; Hutcherson et al., 2015), explicit decision rules (Greene et al., 2004; Greene &

Paxton, 2009), structured behavioral events (Frankland & Greene, 2015), and people's intentions (Young, Cushman, Hauser, & Saxe, 2007; Young, Camprodon, Hauser, Pascual-Leone, & Saxe, 2010). Critically, these neural pathways, when engaged in moral cognition, appear to be doing the same things they do in other contexts that have nothing in particular to do with morality, such as making trade-offs between risk and reward (Knutson, Taylor, Kaufman, Peterson, & Glover, 2005), overriding automatic responses based on explicit task demands (Miller & Cohen, 2001), imagining distal events (Buckner, Andrews-Hanna, & Schacter, 2008; De Brigard, Addis, Ford, Schacter, & Giovanello, 2013), understanding who did what to whom (Wu, Waller, & Chatterjee, 2007), and keeping track of who believes what (Mitchell, 2009; Saxe, Carey, & Kanwisher, 2004). It's not just that neuroscientific data are too coarse-grained to distinguish the distinctively moral patterns of thinking from the rest. Behavioral studies indicate that moral and nonmoral thinking follow similar patterns and make use of shared computational resources when we evaluate options (Crockett, 2013, 2016; Cushman, 2013; Krajbich, Hare, Bartling, Morishima, & Fehr, 2015), reason (Paxton, Ungar, & Greene, 2012), imagine (Amit & Greene, 2012), and understand the minds of others (Moran et al., 2011). Cognitively speaking, morality does not appear to be special.

If morality isn't "a thing" in the brain, then what exactly are researchers who specialize in moral psychology trying to understand? I believe that morality can be a meaningful scientific topic even if moral cognition has no distinctive cognitive mechanisms of its own. An analogy: Motorcycles and sailboats have very little in common at the mechanistic level, respectively resembling nonvehicles such as lawn mowers and kites more than they resemble each other. Nevertheless, they are both vehicles in good standing. They rightly belong to the same category because of what they do, not how they do it. In the same way, the various kinds of thinking we call moral may be bound together, not by their engagement of distinctive cognitive mechanisms but by the common function they serve: enabling otherwise selfish individuals to reap the benefits of social existence (Frank, 1988; Gintis, 2005; Greene, 2013; Haidt, 2012). If this functional account of morality is correct, then moral cognition, as a field or subfield, is best understood as a bridge. It's an attempt to connect the concepts of everyday moral life—right and wrong, good and bad, virtue and vice—to the subpersonal mechanisms of the mind and brain. Bridges are exciting to build and useful once completed, but they are rarely destinations of their own. What happens after the bridge opens? Where does the traffic go?

On the neuroscientific side, the field of moral cognition has focused on implicating rather general cognitive functions and corresponding neural regions and networks. For example, there has been some debate concerning the relative roles of intuitive and affective processes on the one hand and more controlled, rule-based reasoning on the other (Greene, 2013; Greene, Sommerville, Nystrom, Darley, & Cohen, 2001;

Haidt, 2001, 2012; Kohlberg, 1969; Turiel, 2006). This debate has featured evidence implicating brain regions associated primarily with emotion (Ciaramelli, Muccioli, Ladàvas, & di Pellegrino, 2007; Koenigs et al., 2007; Shenhav & Greene, 2014), along with other brain regions associated primarily with cognitive control (Cushman, Murray, Gordon-McKeon, Wharton, & Greene, 2012; Greene et al., 2004; Paxton & Greene, 2009; Shenhav & Greene, 2014). More recently, this contrast has been recast in terms of more basic computational principles (Crockett, 2013; Cushman, 2013), a welcome development. But in nearly all of our attempts to explain moral judgment and behavior in terms of neural mechanisms, the explanations have featured very general processes, not detailed content. For example, we may explain people's responses to the classic *footbridge* dilemma (Thomson, 1985) in terms of affective responses enabled by the amygdala and the ventromedial prefrontal cortex (vmPFC), along with a competing cost–benefit decision rule supported by the dorsolateral prefrontal cortex (DLPFC), but nowhere in the neural data is there anything specifically related to a trolley, train tracks, a footbridge, pushing one person, or saving the lives of five. We know this information is in there, but we've only the most coarse-grained theories about how these details are represented and transformed in the process of moral judgment.

In behavioral research, detailed content plays a more prominent role. We distinguish between different ways of causing harm (Cushman, Young, & Hauser, 2006; Greene et al., 2009; Spranca, Minsk, & Baron, 1991), different kinds of moral violations and norms (Graham et al., 2011; Janoff-Bulman, Sheikh, & Hepp, 2009; Young & Saxe, 2011), different moral roles (Gray & Wegner, 2009), and much more besides. But these content-based distinctions and effects, however interesting and useful they may be, seem more like hints—intriguing products of the underlying cognitive mechanisms, rather than descriptions of those mechanisms. If Commander Data ever learns to think about moral questions like a human, he'll be sensitive to the act/omission distinction, care less about people's intentions when they do things that are disgusting, and so on. But we currently have no idea how we would actually program or train in these features.

The problem, I believe, is that we're trying to understand moral thinking in the absence of a more general understanding of thinking. When you hear about a moral dilemma, involving, say, a trolley headed for five unsuspecting people and a footbridge, your brain responds to this string of words by activating a set of conceptual representations (TROLLEY, FOOTBRIDGE, FIVE, MAN, etc.). These representations are not merely activated to form a semantic stew of trolleyness, footbridgeness, and so forth. Rather, they are combined in a precise way to yield a highly specific structured representation of the situation in question, such that it's the five on the tracks, the man on the footbridge, the trolley headed toward the five, and you with the option to push the man in the name of the greater good. What's more, our brains naturally construct a representation of the situation so as to fill in countless unstated facts, such as the fact that the man, if pushed, will fall quickly through the air rather than gently floating to the ground like a feather. Our understanding of how all of this cognitive infrastructure works is rather limited. In saying this, I do not mean to discount the great strides made by philosophers (e.g., Fodor, 1975; Frege, 1976), linguists (e.g., Fillmore, 1982; Talmy, 2000), psychologists (e.g., Johnson-Laird, 1983; Johnson-Laird, Khemlani, & Goodwin, 2015; Kriete, Noelle, Cohen, & O'Reilly, 2013; Marcus, 2001; Pinker, 1994, 2007), and neuroscientists (e.g., Fedorenko, Behr, & Kanwisher, 2011; Friederici et al., 2003; Hagoort, Hald, Bastiaansen, & Petersson, 2004; Huth, de Heer, Griffiths, Theunissen, & Gallant, 2016; Pallier, Devauchell, & Dehaene, 2011) in addressing this large problem. What I mean is that we still lack a systematic understanding of what David Hume (1739/1978) and other Enlightenment philosophers called "the Understanding" and what Fodor (1975) called the "language of thought."

How well can we understand moral thinking—or any other kind of high-level thinking—without understanding the underlying mechanics of thought? Pretty well, some might say. This worry about underlying mechanisms could just be fetishistic re-ductionism. If "really" understanding moral thinking requires deciphering the language of thought, why stop there? To "really" understand the language of thought, don't we need to understand how populations of neurons represent things more generally? And to "really" understand that, don't we need a better of understanding of neurophysiology? And beneath that, must we not understand organic chemistry, chemical physics, and so on? Does this not lead to the absurd conclusion that the only "real" understanding of anything comes from particle physics?

I sympathize with this objection, but I think it goes too far. How far down the reductionist hierarchy we must go depends on what we're trying to do and what we get for our deeper digging. If you're a sailor, you need to understand the weather, but understanding the physics and chemistry of the atmosphere probably won't do you much additional good. By contrast, if you're developing models of weather and climate, pushing the bounds of long-range prediction, a detailed knowledge of the underlying mechanics is surely essential. Today, much of psychology, including moral psychology, looks more like sailing than cutting-edge atmospheric modeling. We isolate a specific variable in a specific and somewhat artificial context, and, if all goes well, we can say something about the general direction and size of the effect of manipulating that variable in that context. But if our long-term goal is to understand and predict real human behavior in complex circumstances, with many behaviorally significant variables operating simultaneously, we'll probably have to understand the thinking behind that behavior in a more encompassing way, not just in terms of "effects" but in terms of the underlying cognitive causes of those effects. I doubt that we'll need to descend into particle physics, but I suspect that we'll have to go significantly deeper than we currently do. In the best case, we'll understand the infrastructure of high-level cognition in sufficient detail that we could program or train Commander Data to think as we do—morally and otherwise.

Following this hunch, I and my collaborators have begun to pursue more basic questions about the nature of high-level cognition and its neural basis: How does the brain combine concepts to form thoughts (Frankland & Greene, 2015)? How are thoughts manipulated in the process of reasoning? How do thoughts presented in words get translated into mental images? And how do our brains distinguish the things we believe from the things we desire or merely think about? I don't know whether these investigations will bear fruit for moral psychology, sometime soon or ever. But this kind of research seems to me worth pursuing for its own sake, and there's a chance that it will teach us things about morality that we can't learn any other way.

REFERENCES

Amit, E., & Greene, J. D. (2012). You see, the ends don't justify the means: Visual imagery and moral judgment. *Psychological Science, 23*(8), 861–868.

Blair, R. J. (2007). The amygdala and ventromedial prefrontal cortex in morality and psychopathy. *Trends in Cognitive Sciences, 11,* 387–392.

Buckner, R. L., Andrews-Hanna, J. R., & Schacter, D. L. (2008). The brain's default network. *Annals of the New York Academy of Sciences, 1124*(1), 1–38.

Ciaramelli, E., Muccioli, M., Ladàvas, E., & di Pellegrino, G. (2007). Selective deficit in personal moral judgment following damage to ventromedial prefrontal cortex. *Social Cognitive and Affective Neuroscience, 2,* 84–92.

Crockett, M. J. (2013). Models of morality. *Trends in Cognitive Sciences, 17*(8), 363–366.

Crockett, M. J. (2016). How formal models can illuminate mechanisms of moral judgment and decision making. *Current Directions in Psychological Science, 25*(2), 85–90.

Cushman, F. (2013). Action, outcome, and value a dual-system framework for morality. *Personality and Social Psychology Review, 17*(3), 273–292.

Cushman, F., Murray, D., Gordon-McKeon, S., Wharton, S., & Greene, J. D. (2012). Judgment before principle: Engagement of the frontoparietal control network in condemning harms of omission. *Social Cognitive and Affective Neuroscience, 7*(8), 888–895.

Cushman, F., Young, L., & Hauser, M. (2006). The role of conscious reasoning and intuition in moral judgment: Testing three principles of harm. *Psychological Science, 17*(12), 1082–1089.

De Brigard, F., Addis, D. R., Ford, J. H., Schacter, D. L., & Giovanello, K. S. (2013). Remembering what could have happened: Neural correlates of episodic counterfactual thinking. *Neuropsychologia, 51*(12), 2401–2414.

Fedorenko, E., Behr, M. K., & Kanwisher, N. (2011). Functional specificity for high-level linguistic processing in the human brain. *Proceedings of the National Academy of Sciences of the USA, 108*(39), 16428–16433.

Fillmore, C. (1982). Frame semantics. In The Linguistic Society of Korea (Ed.), *Linguistics in the morning calm* (pp. 111–137). Seoul: Hanshin.

Fodor, J. A. (1975). *The language of thought* (Vol. 5). Cambridge, MA: Harvard University Press.

Frank, R. H. (1988). *Passions within reason: The strategic role of the emotions.* New York: Norton.

Frankland, S. M., & Greene, J. D. (2015). An architecture for encoding sentence meaning in left mid-superior temporal cortex. *Proceedings of the National Academy of Sciences of the USA, 112*(37), 11732–11737.

Frege, G. (1976). *Logische untersuchungen* (2nd suppl. ed.). Göttingen, Germany: Vandenhoeck und Ruprecht.

Friederici, A. D., Rueschemeyer, S. A., Hahne, A., & Fiebach, C. J. (2003). The role of left inferior frontal and superior temporal cortex in sentence comprehension: Localizing syntactic and semantic processes. *Cerebral Cortex, 13*(2), 170–177.

Gintis, H. (Ed.). (2005). *Moral sentiments and material interests: The foundations of cooperation in economic life.* Cambridge, MA: MIT Press.

Graham, J., Nosek, B. A., Haidt, J., Iyer, R., Koleva, S., & Ditto, P. H. (2011). Mapping the moral domain. *Journal of Personality and Social Psychology, 101*(2), 366–385.

Gray, K., & Wegner, D. M. (2009). Moral typecasting: Divergent perceptions of moral agents and moral patients. *Journal of Personality and Social Psychology, 96*(3), 505.

Greene, J. (2013). *Moral tribes: Emotion, reason, and the gap between us and them.* New York: Penguin.

Greene, J. D. (2014). The cognitive neuroscience of moral judgment and decision-making. In M. S. Gazzaniga (Ed.), *The cognitive neurosciences V* (pp. 1013–1023). Cambridge, MA: MIT Press.

Greene, J. D., Cushman, F. A., Stewart, L. E., Lowenberg, K., Nystrom, L. E., & Cohen, J. D. (2009). Pushing moral buttons: The interaction between personal force and intention in moral judgment. *Cognition, 111*(3), 364–371.

Greene, J. D., Nystrom, L. E., Engell, A. D., Darley, J. M., & Cohen, J. D. (2004). The neural bases of cognitive conflict and control in moral judgment. *Neuron, 44,* 389–400.

Greene, J. D., & Paxton, J. M. (2009). Patterns of neural activity associated with honest and dishonest moral decisions. *Proceedings of the National Academy of Sciences of the USA, 106*(30), 12506–12511.

Greene, J. D., Sommerville, R. B., Nystrom, L. E., Darley, J. M., & Cohen, J. D. (2001). An fMRI investigation of emotional engagement in moral judgment. *Science, 293,* 2105–2108.

Hagoort. P., Hald, L., Bastiaansen, M., & Petersson, K. M. (2004). Integration of word meaning and world knowledge in language comprehension. *Science, 304*(5669), 438–441.

Haidt, J. (2001). The emotional dog and its rational tail: A social intuitionist approach to moral judgment. *Psychological Review, 108*(4), 814–834.

Haidt, J. (2012). *The righteous mind: Why good people are divided by religion and politics.* New York: Pantheon.

Hauser, M. D. (2006). The liver and the moral organ. *Social Cognitive and Affective Neuroscience, 1*(3), 214–220.

Hume, D. (1978). *A treatise of human nature* (L. A. Selby-Bigge & P. H. Nidditch, Eds.). Oxford, UK: Oxford University Press. (Original work published 1739)

Hutcherson, C. A., Montaser-Kouhsari, L., Woodward, J., & Rangel, A. (2015). Emotional and utilitarian appraisals of moral dilemmas are encoded in separate areas and integrated in ventromedial prefrontal cortex. *Journal of Neuroscience, 35*(36), 12593–12605.

Huth, A. G., de Heer, W. A., Griffiths, T. L., Theunissen, F. E., & Gallant, J. L. (2016). Natural speech reveals the semantic maps that tile human cerebral cortex. *Nature, 532*(7600), 453–458.

Janoff-Bulman, R., Sheikh, S., & Hepp, S. (2009). Proscriptive versus prescriptive morality: Two faces of moral regulation. *Journal of Personality and Social Psychology, 96*(3), 521–537.

Johnson-Laird, P. N. (1983). *Mental models: Towards a cognitive science of language, inference, and consciousness (No. 6).* Cambridge, MA: Harvard University Press.

Johnson-Laird, P. N., Khemlani, S. S., & Goodwin, G. P. (2015). Logic, probability, and human reasoning. *Trends in Cognitive Sciences, 19*(4), 201–214.

Knutson, B., Taylor, J., Kaufman, M., Peterson, R., & Glover, G. (2005). Distributed neural representation of expected value. *Journal of Neuroscience, 25*(19), 4806–4812.

Koenigs, M., Young, L., Adolphs, R., Tranel, D., Cushman, F., Hauser, M., & Damasio, A. (2007). Damage to the prefrontal cortex increases utilitarian moral judgments. *Nature, 446,* 908–911.

Kohlberg, L. (1969). Stage and sequence: The cognitive-developmental approach to socialization. In D. A. Goslin (Ed.), *Handbook of socialization theory and research* (pp. 347–480). Chicago: Rand McNally.

Krajbich, I., Hare, T., Bartling, B., Morishima, Y., & Fehr, E. (2015). A common mechanism underlying food choice and social decisions. *PLOS Computational Biology, 11*(10), e1004371.

Kriete, T., Noelle, D. C., Cohen, J. D., & O'Reilly, R. C. (2013) Indirection and symbol-like processing in the prefrontal cortex and basal ganglia. *Proceedings of the National Academy of Sciences of the USA, 110*(41), 16390–16395.

Marcus, G. F. (2001). *The algebraic mind: Integrating connectionism and cognitive science.* Cambridge, MA: MIT Press.

Mikhail, J. (2011). *Elements of moral cognition: Rawls' linguistic analogy and the cognitive science of moral and legal judgment.* New York: Cambridge University Press.

Miller, E. K., & Cohen, J. D. (2001). An integrative theory of prefrontal cortex function. *Annual Review of Neuroscience, 24,* 167–202.

Mitchell, J. P. (2009). Inferences about mental states. *Philosophical Transactions of the Royal Society of London Series B: Biological Sciences, 364*(1521), 1309–1316.

Moll, J., Krueger, F., Zahn, R., Pardini, M., de Oliveira-Souza, R., & Grafman, J. (2006). Human fronto-mesolimbic networks guide decisions about charitable donation. *Proceedings of the National Academy of Sciences of the USA, 103,* 15623–15628.

Moran, J. M., Young, L. L., Saxe, R., Lee, S. M., O'Young, D., Mavros, P. L., & Gabrieli, J. D. (2011). Impaired theory of mind for moral judgment in high-functioning autism. *Proceedings of the National Academy of Sciences of the USA, 108*(7), 2688–2692.

Pallier, C., Devauchelle, A. D., & Dehaene, S. (2011). Cortical representation of the constituent structure of sentences. *Proceedings of the National Academy of Sciences of the USA, 108*(6), 2522–2527.

Parkinson, C., Sinnott-Armstrong, W., Koralus, P. E., Mendelovici, A., McGeer, V., & Wheatley, T. (2011). Is morality unified?: Evidence that distinct neural systems underlie moral judgments of harm, dishonesty, and disgust. *Journal of Cognitive Neuroscience, 23*(10), 3162–3180.

Paxton, J. M., Ungar, L., & Greene, J. D. (2012). Reflection and reasoning in moral judgment. *Cognitive Science, 36*(1), 163–177.

Pinker, S. (1994). *The language instinct.* New York: Harper Perennial Modern Classics.

Pinker, S. (2007). *The stuff of thought: Lan-*

guage as a window into human nature. New York: Viking.

Ruff, C. C., & Fehr, E. (2014). The neurobiology of rewards and values in social decision making. *Nature Reviews Neuroscience, 15*(8), 549–562.

Saxe, R., Carey, S., & Kanwisher, N. (2004). Understanding other minds: Linking developmental psychology and functional neuroimaging. *Annual Review of Psychology, 55,* 87–124.

Shenhav, A., & Greene, J. D. (2010). Moral judgments recruit domain-general valuation mechanisms to integrate representations of probability and magnitude. *Neuron, 67*(4), 667–677.

Shenhav, A., & Greene, J. D. (2014). Integrative moral judgment: Dissociating the roles of the amygdala and ventromedial prefrontal cortex. *Journal of Neuroscience, 34*(13), 4741–4749.

Spranca, M., Minsk, E., & Baron, J. (1991). Omission and commission in judgment and choice. *Journal of Experimental Social Psychology, 27*(1), 76–105.

Talmy, L. (2000). *Toward a cognitive semantics: Concept structuring systems* (Vols. 1–2). Cambridge, MA: MIT Press.

Thomson, J. (1985). The trolley problem. *Yale Law Journal, 94,* 1395–1415.

Turiel, E. (2006). Thought, emotions and social interactional processes in moral development. In M. Killen & J. Smetana (Eds.), *Handbook of moral development* (pp. 1–30). Mahwah, NJ: Erlbaum,

Wu, D. H., Waller, S., & Chatterjee, A. (2007). The functional neuroanatomy of thematic role and locative relational knowledge. *Journal of Cognitive Neuroscience, 19*(9), 1542–1555.

Young, L., Camprodon, J. A., Hauser, M., Pascual-Leone, A., & Saxe, R. (2010). Disruption of the right temporoparietal junction with transcranial magnetic stimulation reduces the role of beliefs in moral judgments. *Proceedings of the National Academy of Sciences of the USA, 107*(15), 6753–6758.

Young, L., Cushman, F., Hauser, M., & Saxe, R. (2007). The neural basis of the interaction between theory of mind and moral judgment. *Proceedings of the National Academy of Sciences of the USA, 104*(20), 8235–8240.

Young, L., & Dungan, J. (2012). Where in the brain is morality?: Everywhere and maybe nowhere. *Social Neuroscience, 7*(1), 1–10.

Young, L., & Saxe, R. (2011). When ignorance is no excuse: Different roles for intent across moral domains. *Cognition, 120*(2), 202–214.

Zaki, J., & Mitchell, J. P. (2011). Equitable decision making is associated with neural markers of intrinsic value. *Proceedings of the National Academy of Sciences of the USA, 108*(49), 19761–19766.

CHAPTER 2

Reasoning at the Root of Morality

Elliot Turiel

> **What is the role of reasoning in morality?**
>
> Moral decisions involve reasoning about different considerations and goals, including moral goals of welfare, justice, and rights, and nonmoral goals, including social coordination.

In psychological writings on the topic of morality, there is sometimes, though not often enough, an effort to link research and theory to philosophical approaches. In my view, such linkages are positive, because it is important for research to be guided by substantive definitions of the domain of study. Given the contested positions often seen in the field of psychology, it is not surprising that consensus does not exist as to which philosophical–epistemological positions are supported by evidence from psychological research nor as to which philosophical traditions to utilize.

My approach is associated, in a general way, with philosophical conceptions of morality centrally involving judgment or reasoning (e.g., Dworkin, 1977, 1993; Gewirth, 1978, 1982; Habermas, 1993; Nussbaum, 1999, 2000; Okin, 1989; Rawls, 1971, 1993; Sen, 1999, 2006, 2009). The substantive aspects of morality formulated in these philosophical traditions include welfare of persons, justice, rights, civil liberties, and equalities—as connected with judgment, thought, and reflection. As put

by Nussbaum (1999, p. 71): "human beings are above all reasoning beings, and . . . the dignity of reason is the primary source of human equality." Promoting the same perspective, Sen (1999, p. 272) maintained that "it is the power of reason that allows us to consider our obligations and ideals as well as our interests and advantages. To deny this freedom of thought would amount to a severe constraint on the reach of our rationality." Part of human reasoning is choice and reflection upon social conditions: "Central to leading a human life . . . are the responsibilities of choice and reasoning" (Sen, 2006, p. xiii).

However, an emphasis on reasoning should not be taken to mean, as sometimes is mistakenly done, that emotions are regarded as unimportant. Emotions are important in the context of reasoning, but they need to be seen not as forces driving judgments or decisions, nor as independent of thought: "Emotions are not just the fuel that powers the psychological mechanisms of a reasoning creature, they are parts, highly complex and messy parts, of this creature's reasoning itself" (Nussbaum, 2001, p. 3). The inter-connections referred to by Nussbaum take the form of evaluative appraisals: "I shall argue that emotions always involve thought of an object combined with thought of the object's salience or importance; in that sense they always involve appraisal or evaluation" (Nussbaum, 2001, p. 23). The proposition that emotions entail evaluative appraisals is also present in psychological theory and re-search (Frijda, 1986; Lazarus; 1991; Moors & Scherer, 2013; see also Turiel & Dahl, in press).

There are several broad questions that need to be addressed in psychological per-spectives associated with the philosophical perspectives on judgment, reasoning, and reflection. As already noted, one question bears on the nature of morality, that is, how to define the moral domain. A ques-tion related to such definitions is whether morality is a category substantively differ-ent from other categories of judgment about social relationships. In turn, questions arise regarding how morality develops in onto-genesis, how to explain processes of moral decision making, which in turn are associ-ated with the place of cultural practices in moral development and decision making. In this chapter, I briefly outline a position on a definition of morality and its distinc-tion from other social domains, as well as on processes of development. In the main, I consider explanations of decision making and their connection with cultural practices.

The Development of Morality and Other Social Domains

There are, indeed, correspondences between philosophical conceptions of the realm of morality and the psychology of morality as documented by a large number of studies conducted over many years in many cultural settings. The research has shown that, by fairly early ages (4–6 years), children form complex configurations of judgments about welfare, justice, and rights that differ from their judgments about other aspects of social interactions. Young children's moral think-ing is mainly focused on issues of welfare, whereas older children's judgments, while including concerns with welfare, also have

developed increased concerns with justice and rights (for reviews, see Smetana, 2006, and Turiel, 1983, 2002, 2015). The con-figuration of moral judgments differs from the configuration of judgments about social organizations, with their systems of norms and conventions, as well as from judgments about the domain of personal jurisdiction. To state it briefly, judgments in the moral domain are not contingent on rules, author-ity dictates, or existing practices. By con-trast, conventional norms are judged to be dependent on existing rules, the dictate of those in authority, and common practices in a social system. The personal domain per-tains to concepts regarding areas of freedom of choice and autonomy. (These rather brief characterizations derive from much more extensive and detailed discussions and re-search documentation.)

As it has been proposed and found that these domains of social judgment are formed by children in many cultures, the question arises as to how it can be that children grow-ing up with different cultural practices form similar judgments. The answer to this ques-tion is twofold. One part has to do with the theoretical proposition that children *con-struct* thinking through their interactions with the world (Kohlberg, 1969, 1971; Piag-et, 1932, 1970; Turiel, 1983, 2002; Werner, 1957). In this perspective, development is neither genetically nor environmentally de-termined but involves constructions in ef-forts to make sense of experiences, social rules, roles of authorities, social institutions, and cultural practices.

The second part of the answer to the ques-tion is that, with regard to morality, a major source of development is children's everyday experiences with others of the same ages and of different ages (younger and older children, adults) having to do with harm, benefits, fairness, equality, and adjudication of disagreements and conflicts. Concrete-ly, these types of experiences include, as a few examples, children hurting each other (physically and emotionally), helping and failing to help, sharing and failing to share, including and excluding others, cooperating and failing to cooperate, and treating people equally and unequally. Moreover, children are not solely recipients of "moral" messages from adults. They interact with adults over many of the same issues and observe adults interacting with each other harmoniously and with conflicts—and sometimes around matters of harm, helping, sharing, cooperating, and equality.

These types of experiences, social interactions, and observations might be connected with the formation of judgments about persons, but they are also centrally involved in the formation of moral judgments. A number of observational studies with preschoolers (Nucci & Turiel, 1978; Nucci, Turiel, & Encarnacion-Gawrych, 1983; Nucci & Weber, 1995) and older children (Nucci & Nucci, 1982a, 1982b; Turiel, 2008) have documented that children's social interactions around events classified as moral differ from social interactions around events in the conventional and personal domains. Interactions around moral transgressions typically do not involve commands or communications about rules and expectations of adults. Interactions around moral transgressions are about the effects of actions on people, the perspectives of others, the need to avoid harm, and the pain experienced, as well as communications about welfare and fairness. By contrast, interactions around conventional events revolve around adherence to rules, commands from those in authority, and an emphasis on social order.

Processes of Social and Moral Decision Making

It might appear that the findings that the moral judgments of children and adults are not contingent on adherence to rules nor based on authority dictates and common practices are inconsistent with a set of still well-known findings from classic social psychological experiments of about 40–60 years ago. I am referring to experiments on so-called conformity (Asch, 1952, 1956), bystander intervention (Latané & Darley, 1968, 1970), and obedience to authority (Milgram, 1963, 1974). In common portrayals (e.g., textbooks, essays, and the media), the experiments are said to show that individuals (adults) conform to the group even in solutions of simple tasks (comparing lengths of lines), fail to intervene to help another in distress in group settings, and obey the commands of authority to inflict pain and harm on others.

In actuality, the findings are not as straightforward as often portrayed. An important set of findings, often overlooked, in each of the studies is that variations were found in behaviors by experimental conditions. For instance, it was found that participants went along with the groups (confederates of the researchers) in erroneously judging the length of lines in some conditions and not others (e.g., depending on the number of others giving correct and incorrect responses; see also Ross, Bierbrauer, & Hoffman, 1976). These experiments did not clearly involve moral issues, but they most likely involved judgments and reflection on the part of most participants and not simple conformity. Asch's (1952) own interpretation of the finding in the condition in which most went along with the group was that participants were attempting to understand what appeared to them as a perplexing social situation that involved a conflict between their own perceptions and those of the rest in the group. They were, therefore, led to question their own perceptions and give credibility to the judgments of the others. The studies on bystander intervention, which involved moral issues pertaining to helping others in distress (Latané & Darley, 1968), also obtained variations by social contexts. It was found that participants were more likely to intervene and help another when alone than when others were present.

The contextual variations evident in the body of research from the social psychological studies do not simply reflect that individuals are pushed and pulled by situational factors. Rather, they strongly suggest that individuals do reason about social situations in ways that lead them to perceive the varying facets of the social situations and that, in the process, they apply and attempt to coordinate or weigh and balance different considerations in the decision-making process. Such different considerations can include conflicting moral goals or conflicting moral and nonmoral goals. The Milgram experiments provide us with an illustrative example of how behavioral choices can involve processes of coordination. To review briefly, the central components of the experiments are that participants were placed in situations in which they were instructed by an experimenter (usually wearing a white lab coat) to administer increasing levels of electric shocks (which were not real) to another person (who was an accomplice of the researcher) in the guise of the learning of word associations. Participants were told that it was a study of the effects of punishment on learning and memory. In one experimental condition, the experimenter gave instructions directly to the participant, who was in the same room, while the so-called learner, who had been strapped to the electric shock apparatus, was not visible but within hearing range in an adjacent room. It is in that condition that approximately 65% of participants continued administering the shocks to the end of the scale in spite of loud protest from the victim (learner).

The common interpretation that large numbers of people obey authority even when commanded to inflict severe pain on another fails to consider that the experimental situations included multiple components that participants attempted to take into account. The most obvious are considerations of the conflict between inflicting physical pain on another and adhering to the instructions established by the goals of the experimenter as conveyed to participants, coupled with the exhortations to continue the experiment because that is what is required (Turiel, 2002; Turiel & Smetana, 1984). Milgram's (1974) descriptions of the details of what occurred in the experiment indicate that most participants, regardless of their ultimate decision, were experiencing conflict about the two considerations (e.g., even when continuing to administer the shocks, participants displayed a good deal of anxiety and would stop to tell the experimenter that the "learner" was in pain and danger, that the experimenter should look to see if he was all right, that they did not want to harm the learner). Unfortunately, the reactions of participants were not systematically analyzed. Such analyses should have examined the emotional reactions of the participants, the verbal interactions of participants with the experimenter, and comments from participants to the person (supposedly) receiving the electric shocks. It seems likely from the way Milgram (1974) described what

went on that such analyses would have revealed that participants were attending both to the harm experienced by the other while wishing to prevent it and to the goals of the scientific enterprise, which they wished to maintain. These two goals were in conflict, and participants were most likely trying to coordinate the two.

The findings of different experimental conditions in the research (Milgram, 1974) are congruent with the idea that participants were coordinating different considerations and goals. In contrast with the finding in one experimental condition that the majority of participants continued administering electric shocks to another person, in several other conditions most defied the instructions of the "authority" and refused to continue administering the shocks (Milgram, 1974). In some experimental conditions, the location and proximity of the person receiving the shocks were varied in ways that increased the salience of the harm (e.g., the learner was in the same room; the participant was told to place the learner's hand on a shock plate). In other conditions, the place and role of the experimenter was varied in ways that decreased the significance of the scientific enterprise and the role of the experimenter (e.g., instructions given by telephone; authority delegated to someone who was not part of the team of researchers). In most of these other conditions, the large majority of participants decided to stop shocking the learner and thus defied the experimenter's instructions (for more details, see Turiel, 2002, and Turiel & Smetana, 1984).

If we also put into the mix—as explained by Baumrind (1964, 2013)—the decisions of the researcher (i.e., Milgram) and those who assisted him in carrying out the studies, the coordination becomes further multilayered. Milgram engaged in deception by placing newspaper advertisements to recruit participants that stated the study was on memory and learning. Those who chose to participate were deceived again by Milgram and his associates (i.e., the persons in the roles of experimenter and learner) when they were told face-to-face that the study was on learning and memory, that the person given the role of learner was another participant who had chosen to be in the study, and that they would be administering electric shocks (all falsehoods). At least in the case of the researcher himself, the acts of deception were based on the decision that deceiving others should be given less priority than the goals of a scientific enterprise on what they regarded as important questions of whether people obey authority in carrying out acts that inflict physical pain on others[1].

Consequently, the actions of both the researchers and the study participants involve coordination of moral goals (preventing harm), honesty, and the role of authority or experts in achieving scientific goals. This interpretation is connected with the findings of distinct domains of thinking, including morality, social conventions, and personal jurisdiction. Processes of coordination are often involved in social and moral decisions, as individuals form different types of judgments, which they can apply in reflective and flexible ways, and because many social situations are multifaceted in that they include more than one component. Moreover, the different components in social situations can be in conflict with each other. Conflicts are sometimes between moral and nonmoral considerations and sometimes between different moral considerations. When making decisions, individuals perceive multiple components and often have to give priority to one over another—not always to the moral considerations and goals (as was the case for some in the Milgram experiments).

From the perspective of the development of distinct developmental pathways within domains and processes of coordination in decision making, it is not necessarily the case that morality is given priority over other substantive considerations. It is sometimes assumed that individuals will give priority to morality and that, insofar as they do not, it is because psychological factors other than judgment or reasoning take hold. Those assumptions include (1) that one has insufficient self-control to live up to one's ideals (Mischel & Mischel, 1976); (2) that disengagement with morality has occurred (Bandura, 2002); (3) that a sufficient moral identity has not been formed (Blasi, 1984); or (4) that the development of moral judgments has not progressed to a sufficiently advanced stage (Kohlberg, 1971).

A contrasting proposition is that decision making involves processes of coordination of different types of substantive judgments. The evidence for this proposition is not limited to the social psychological studies I have mentioned. Research directly examining judgments in the moral domain bearing on rights, social inclusion and exclusion, and honesty, trust, and deception shows that coordination between different social goals is central in decision making. For example, it has been found in several cultures that children, adolescents, and adults endorse freedoms of speech, religion, and literacy as rights in response to general questions and in some situations. However, in some situations they also give lesser priority to the expression of these rights when they are in conflict with other moral considerations, such as physical harm (Day, 2014; Helwig, 1995, 1997; Helwig, Ruck, & Peterson-Badila, 2014; Helwig & Turiel, 2017; Ruck, Abramovitch, & Keating, 1998; Turiel & Wainryb, 1998). A similar pattern of findings was obtained in research on concepts of the fairness of social inclusion (Horn, 2003; Killen, Lee-Kim, McGlothlin, & Stagnor, 2002; Killen, Pisacane, Lee-Kim, & Ardila-Rey, 2001). Children and adolescents judged exclusion based on race or gender as wrong, but they also judged exclusion to be acceptable when in conflict with other considerations, such as the legitimacy of achieving group goals (e.g., in sport or academic competitions).

Research on honesty or trust with children and adolescents has yielded comparable results. Honesty is particularly interesting with regard to coordination because it is often assumed that it is an obviously moral good that ought to be unwaveringly maintained. As illustrated in philosophical discussions, however, honesty is not always straightforward and does not necessarily dictate the moral course of action. Some philosophical discussions have centered on Kant's contention that it is always wrong to lie (Bok, 1978/1999), posing the example of someone passing a bystander who is soon thereafter asked by a murderer where his intended victim has gone. It has been argued that in such a situation the moral prescription to save a life should take precedence over the moral prescription to tell the truth and that there is even a moral obligation for the bystander to engage in deception.

Research on honesty and deception with adolescents and adults clearly shows that individuals attempt to coordinate different moral goals, as well as moral and nonmoral goals. In one study (Perkins & Turiel, 2007), groups of 12- to 13-year-olds and 16- to 17-year-olds made judgments about hypothetical situations in which parents and peers give directives to an adolescent regarding moral (directives to hit another or to engage in racial discrimination), personal (which club to join, whom to date), and prudential (homework, riding a motorcycle) activities. The actor in the situation does not comply with the directive and lies about it. It was found that the large majority of the adolescents in both age groups judged it acceptable to deceive parents about demands considered morally wrong on the grounds of preventing injustice or harm. The majority of adolescents also judged that deception was justified when parents directed personal choices, although the older adolescents were more likely to judge deception of parents regarding personal choices as acceptable than the younger ones (92 vs. 62%). However, adolescents do not simply regard deception as acceptable, because they gave priority to honesty regarding the prudential acts, with the large majority judging that it is not right to deceive parents in those situations (such directives were seen as within parents' legitimate authority to place restrictions bearing on the potential harm to their children).

Adolescents, therefore, coordinate judgments about the value of honesty or trust with moral, personal, and prudential considerations in different ways. By the age of 12 or 13 years, they make decisions upholding moral judgments about harm and fairness over honesty in some situations. Similarly, judgments about the importance of maintaining certain personal choices are balanced against the value of honesty—though more uniformly in late than early adolescence. Similar findings have been obtained in research with adults on their judgments about deception when aimed at promoting well-being and preventing harm in the context of marital relationship with power differences (Turiel, Perkins, & Mensing, 2009).

Research also shows that physicians accept the legitimacy of deception as a means of preventing physical harm to patients (Freeman, Rathore, Weinfurt, Schulman, & Sulmasy, 1999).

Decision Making and Cultural Practices

A significant component in processes of decision making regarding social situations is disparities in power and control—which was seen in the study with the adolescents (Perkins & Turiel, 2007). The relevant finding is that fewer of the adolescents judged deception of peers acceptable than deception of parents for the morally relevant and personal issues. Although the adolescents thought that the restrictions directed by peers were not legitimate, they were less likely to accept deception of peers than of parents. The difference between how adolescents perceived the acceptability of deception of parents and friends points to another element of the coordination of different considerations in moral and social decision making. The reason that deception of friends is considered less acceptable is that such relationships are seen as based on equality and mutuality, whereas relationships with parents involve greater inequality in power.

Although there are differences in power and status between parents and adolescents, adolescents did not always accept parental directives. They distinguished between activities that they saw as within legitimate parental authority and those they regarded as not within legitimate parental authority. Those judgments, along with the judgments about deception of parents, reflect both acceptance of and opposition to authority (see also research on adolescents' disclosure and nondisclosure with parents; e.g., Finkenauer, Engels, & Meeus, 2002; Kerr & Stattin, 2000; Smetana, Metzger, Gettman, & Campione-Barr, 2006; Smetana, Villalobos, Tasopoulos-Chan, Gettman, & Campione-Barr, 2009).

Social opposition and moral resistance are not restricted to adolescents or adults living in Western cultures. A number of psychological and anthropological studies have shown that opposition and resistance stem from reasoning and reflection about fairness, personal choices, social organization, and cultural practices. The psychological studies were conducted in patriarchal cultures with social inequalities between males and females as part of the social organization and cultural practices. The studies, conducted in the Middle East (Guvenc, 2011; Wainryb & Turiel, 1994), India (Neff, 2001), Colombia (Mensing, 2002), and Benin (Conry-Murray, 2009), assessed the judgments of adolescent and adult males and females regarding practices of inequality in matters pertaining to education, work, recreational activities, and decision making in the family. For the present purposes, I highlight several features of the findings.

- Males and females are cognizant of the inequalities. Males assert their independence and freedom of choice and their right to exert control over females (in keeping with cultural practices).
- Females are aware of cultural practices granting independence and control to males, in some respects accepting social roles (often due to fear of consequences of defiance).
- Females strive for freedoms and equality, evaluating many cultural practices involving inequalities between males and females as *unfair*.

The findings of those studies indicate that moral and social judgments within cultures are heterogeneous in that there are orientations to personal entitlements and independence, as well as morality and interdependence. Moreover, people reflect on cultural practices and are able to take critical perspectives on social organization and coordinate commitments to cultural norms with moral judgments of unfairness. Hence, there can be relationships of both harmony and conflict within cultures. These orientations are not limited to people's judgments. Fieldwork by anthropologists, such as Abu-Lughod's (1993) work among Bedouins in rural areas of Egypt and Wikan's (1996) with people living in conditions of poverty in Cairo, documents that females in patriarchal cultures act on their judgments. Another feature of the research findings is, therefore, that:

- Females act to assert freedoms and avoid undue control.

Both Abu-Lughod and Wikan have documented that females, in their everyday lives, engage in overt and covert actions (including the use of deception) designed to combat restrictions placed on them and thereby subvert cultural practices of gender inequality (see Turiel, 2015, for more extensive discussion).

Some Conclusions about Moral Thought and Cultures

As already noted, orientations to social relationships and persons are heterogeneous within individuals and within cultures. Moral judgments about welfare, justice, and rights and about independence are not specific to cultures or to regions, such as Western and non-Western parts of the world (e.g., Oyserman, Coon, & Kemmelmeier, 2002; Raeff, 2006; Spiro, 1993; Turiel, 2002; Turiel & Wainryb, 1994, 2000). However, moral judgments are not applied in absolutistic ways, as individuals do attempt to coordinate their moral judgments with social, personal, and pragmatic judgments in social situations with multiple components. We can consider moral and social judgments in the patriarchal cultures studied. Whereas females are critical of the fairness of cultural practices of inequality, males are more likely to accept a hierarchical system that places males in dominant positions and females in subordinate positions. This does not mean that males do not hold concepts of fairness and equality, as they would apply such moral concepts to many relationships with other males and in some instances to females (Sen, 1997).

Cultures also undergo transformations over time. Such transformations may be a consequence of the types of tensions and conflicts over inequalities, rights, and domination of one group over another evident in the psychological and anthropological studies in the patriarchal cultures. Conflicts, inequalities, and domination are not restricted to gender and do include differences between racial, ethnic, and social class groups. The philosopher Gregory Vlastos articulated the possible sources of cultural and societal changes as follows: "The great historical struggles for social justice have centered about some demand for equal rights: the struggle against slavery, political absolutism, economic exploitation, the disfranchisement of women, colonialism, racial oppression" (1962, p. 31).

The conclusions drawn by Vlastos are consistent with findings that indicate that there are "collective practices" that are at the same time contested practices. This seeming contradiction occurs because practices can appear to be collective in that they are part of public pronouncements and/or public documents and endorsed by those in positions of power and authority. Yet those in lower positions in the social hierarchy who regard them as unfair contest those practices.

The findings of differences in perspectives of different groups (e.g., females and males) in social hierarchies have implications for how to characterize differences and similarities among cultures. In addition to commonalities between cultures (such as in moral judgments) and differences between cultures (such as in ways moral judgments are applied), there can be some commonalities in social perspectives between those in different cultures who occupy similar positions in their respective social hierarchies and which, in turn, make for differences in perspectives of those of different positions within their own culture. Figure 2.1 outlines such relations of perspectives. The general proposition is that there are multiple layers of similarities and differences between and within cultures. In some respects—not all by any means—there are more commonalities in perspectives of those in similar positions in different cultures than between those in different positions in the same culture.

NOTE

1. In an interesting twist, Baumrind (2013) explained how the actions of the associates could be construed as "obedience to authority" by their adherence to the instructions of the person in a position of authority who recruited them to play roles entailing deception in the research they carried out. They went along with the "legitimate authority" who instructed them to engage in acts that resulted in emotional distress to the participants, and thereby gave priority to the perceived worthy scientific goals over preventing harm.

REFERENCES

Abu-Lughod, L. (1993). *Writing women's worlds: Bedouin stories*. Berkeley: University of California Press.

Asch, S. E. (1952). *Social psychology*. Englewood Cliffs, NJ: Prentice-Hall.

Asch, S. E. (1956). Studies of independence and conformity: A minority of one against a unanimous majority. *Psychological Monographs*, *70*(9).

Bandura, A. (2002). Selective moral disengagement in the exercise of moral agency. *Journal of Moral Education*, *31*, 101–119.

Baumrind, D. (1964). Some thoughts on the ethics of research: After reading Milgram's "Behavioral Study of Obedience." *American Psychologist*, *19*, 421–423.

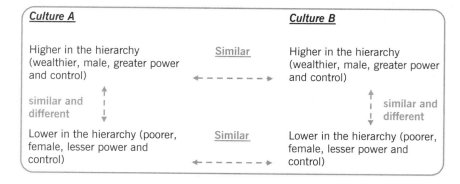

FIGURE 2.1. A schematic view of cultural comparisons.

Baumrind, D. (2013). Is Milgram's deceptive research ethically acceptable? *Theoretical and Applied Ethics, 2,* 1–18.

Blasi, A. (1984). Moral identity: Its role in moral functioning. In J. L. Gewirtz & W. M. Kurtines (Eds.), *Morality, moral behavior, and moral development* (pp. 128–139). New York: Wiley.

Bok, S. (1999). *Lying: Moral choice in public and private life.* New York: Vintage Books. (Original work published 1979)

Conry-Murray, C. (2009). Adolescent and adult reasoning about gender roles and fairness in Benin, West Africa. *Cognitive Development, 24,* 207–219.

Day, K. (2014). The right to literacy and cultural change: Zulu adolescents in post-apartheid rural South Africa. *Cognitive Development, 29,* 81–94.

Dworkin, R. (1977). *Taking rights seriously.* Cambridge, MA: Harvard University Press.

Dworkin, R. (1993). *Life's dominion: An argument about abortion, euthanasia, and individual freedom.* New York: Knopf.

Finkenauer, C., Engels, R. C. M. E., & Meeus, W. (2002). Keeping secrets from parents: Advantages and disadvantages of secrecy in adolescence. *Journal of Youth and Adolescence, 2,* 123–136.

Freeman, V. G., Rathore, S. S., Weinfurt, K. P., Schulman, K. A., & Sulmasy, D. P. (1999). Lying for patients: Physician deception of third-party payers. *Archives of Internal Medicine, 159,* 2263–2270.

Frijda, N. (1986). *The emotions.* New York: Cambridge University Press.

Gewirth, A. (1978). *Reason and morality.* Chicago: University of Chicago Press.

Gewirth, A. (1982). *Human rights: Essays on justification and applications.* Chicago: University of Chicago Press.

Guvenc, G. (2011). *Women's construction of familial-gender identities and embodied subjectivities in Saraycik, Turkey.* Unpublished manuscript, Isik University, Istanbul, Turkey.

Habermas, J. (1993). *Justification and application.* Cambridge, MA: MIT Press.

Helwig, C. C. (1995). Adolescents' and young adults' conceptions of civil liberties: Freedom of speech and religion. *Child Development, 66,* 152–166.

Helwig, C. C. (1997). The role of agent and social context in judgments of freedom of speech and religion. *Child Development, 68,* 484–495.

Helwig, C. C., Ruck, M., & Peterson-Badali, M. (2014). Rights, civil liberties, and democracy. In M. Killen & J. G. Smetana (Eds.), *Handbook of moral development* (2nd ed., pp. 46–69). Mahwah, NJ: Taylor & Francis.

Helwig, C. C., & Turiel, E. (2017). The psychology of children's rights. In M. Ruck, M. Peterson-Badali, & M. Freeman (Eds.), *Handbook of children's rights: Global and multidisciplinary perspectives* (pp. 132–148). New York: Routledge.

Horn, S. S. (2003). Adolescents reasoning about exclusion from social groups. *Developmental Psychology, 39,* 71–84.

Kerr, M., & Stattin, H. (2000). What parents know, how they know it, and several forms of adolescent adjustment: Further support for a reinterpretation of monitoring. *Developmental Psychology, 36,* 366–380.

Killen, M., Lee-Kim, J., McGlothlin, H., & Stagnor, C. (2002). How children and adolescents value gender and racial exclusion. *Monographs of the Society for Research in Child Development, 67*(4, Serial No. 271).

Killen, M., Pisacane, K., Lee-Kim, J., & Ardila-Rey, A. (2001). Fairness or stereotypes?: Young children's priorities when evaluating group exclusion and inclusion. *Developmental Psychology, 37,* 587–596.

Kohlberg, L. (1969). Stage and sequence: The cognitive-developmental approach to socialization. In D. Goslin (Ed.), *Handbook of socialization theory and research* (pp. 347–480). Chicago: Rand McNally.

Kohlberg, L. (1971). From is to ought: How to commit the naturalistic fallacy and get away with it in the study of moral development. In T. Mischel (Ed.), *Psychology and genetic epistemology* (pp. 151–235). New York: Academic Press.

Latané, B., & Darley, J. M. (1968). Group inhibition of bystander intervention in emergencies. *Journal of Personality and Social Psychology, 10,* 215–221.

Latané, B., & Darley, J. M. (1970). *The unresponsive bystander: Why doesn't he help?* New York: Appleton-Crofts.

Lazarus, N. (1991). *Emotion and adaptation.* New York: Oxford University Press.

Mensing, J. F. (2002). *Collectivism, individualism, and interpersonal responsibilities in families: Differences and similarities in social reasoning between individuals in poor, urban families in Colombia and the United States.* Unpublished doctoral dissertation, University of California, Berkeley, CA.

Milgram, S. (1963). Behavioral study of obedience. *Journal of Abnormal and Social Psychology, 67,* 371–378.

Milgram, S. (1974). *Obedience to authority.* New York: Harper & Row.

Mischel, W., & Mischel, H. (1976). A cognitive social-learning approach to morality and self-regulation. In T. Lickona (Ed.), *Moral devel-*

opment and behavior: Theory, research, and social issues (pp. 84–107). New York: Holt, Rinehart & Winston.

Moors, A., & Scherer, K. R. (2013). The role of appraisal in emotion. In M. D. Robinson, E. R. Watkins, & E. Harmon-Jones (Eds.), *Handbook of cognition and emotion* (pp. 131–155). New York: Guilford Press.

Neff, K. D. (2001). Judgments of personal autonomy and interpersonal responsibility in the context of Indian spousal relationships: An examination of young people's reasoning in Mysore, India. *British Journal of Developmental Psychology, 19,* 233–257.

Nucci, L. P., & Nucci, M. S. (1982a). Children's responses to moral and social conventional transgressions in free-play settings. *Child Development, 53,* 1337–1342.

Nucci, L. P., & Nucci, M. S. (1982b). Children's social interactions in the context of moral and conventional transgressions. *Child Development, 53,* 403–412.

Nucci, L. P., & Turiel, E. (1978). Social interactions and the development of social concepts in preschool children. *Child Development, 49,* 400–407.

Nucci, L. P., Turiel, E., & Encarnacion-Gawrych, G. (1983). Children's social interactions and social concepts: Analyses of morality and convention in the Virgin Islands. *Journal of Cross-Cultural Psychology, 14,* 469–487.

Nucci, L. P., & Weber, E. (1995). Social interactions in the home and the development of young children's conceptions of the personal. *Child Development, 66,* 1438–1452.

Nussbaum, M. C. (1999). *Sex and social justice.* New York: Oxford University Press.

Nussbaum, M. C. (2000). *Women and human development: The capabilities approach.* Cambridge, UK: Cambridge University Press.

Nussbaum, M. C. (2001). *Upheavals of thought: The intelligence of emotions.* Cambridge, UK: Cambridge University Press.

Okin, S. M. (1989). *Justice, gender, and the family.* New York: Basic Books.

Oyserman, D., Coon, H. M., & Kemmelmeier, M. (2002). Rethinking individualism and collectivism: Evaluation of theoretical assumptions and meta-analyses. *Psychological Bulletin, 128,* 3–72.

Perkins, S. A., & Turiel, E. (2007). To lie or not to lie: To whom and under what circumstances. *Child Development, 78,* 609–621.

Piaget, J. (1932). *The moral judgment of the child.* London: Routledge & Kegan Paul.

Piaget, J. (1970). *Psychology and epistemology.* New York: Viking Press.

Raeff, C. (2006). Multiple and inseparable: Conceptualizing the development of independence and interdependence. *Human Development, 49,* 96–121.

Rawls, J. (1971). *A theory of justice.* Cambridge, MA: Harvard University Press.

Rawls, J. (1993). *Political liberalism.* New York: Columbia University Press.

Ross, L., Bierbrauer, G., & Hoffman, S. (1976). The role of attributional processes in conformity and dissent: Revisiting the Asch situation. *American Psychologist, 31,* 148–157.

Ruck, M. D., Abramovitch, R., & Keating, D. P. (1998). Children's and adolescents' understandings of rights: Balancing nurturance and self-determination. *Child Development, 69,* 404–417.

Sen, A. (1997, July 14, 21). Human rights and Asian values. *The New Republic,* pp. 33–39.

Sen, A. (1999). *Development as freedom.* New York: Knopf.

Sen, A. (2006). *Identity and violence: The illusion of destiny.* New York: Norton.

Sen, A. (2009). *The idea of justice.* Cambridge, MA: Harvard University Press.

Smetana, J. G. (2006). Social domain theory: Consistencies and variations in children's moral and social judgments. In M. Killen & J. G. Smetana (Eds.), *Handbook of moral development* (pp. 119–153). Mahwah, NJ: Erlbaum.

Smetana, J. G., Metzger, A., Gettman, D. C., & Campione-Barr, N. (2006). Disclosure and secrecy in adolescent–parent relationships. *Child Development, 77,* 201–217.

Smetana, J. G., Villalobos, M., Tasopoulos-Chan, M., Gettman, D. C., & Campione-Barr, N. (2009). Early and middle adolescents' disclosure to parents about activities in different domains. *Journal of Adolescence, 32,* 693–713.

Spiro, M. (1993). Is the Western conception of the self "peculiar" within the context of the world cultures? *Ethos, 21,* 107–153.

Turiel, E. (1983). *The development of social knowledge: Morality and convention.* Cambridge, UK: Cambridge University Press.

Turiel, E. (2002). *The culture of morality: Social development, context, and conflict.* Cambridge, UK: Cambridge University Press.

Turiel, E. (2008). Thought about actions in social domains: Morality, social conventions, and social interactions. *Cognitive Development, 23,* 126–154.

Turiel, E. (2015). Moral development. In W. F. Overton & P. C. Molenaar (Eds.), *Handbook of child psychology: Vol. 1. Theory and method* (7th ed., pp. 484–522). Hoboken, NJ: Wiley.

Turiel, E., & Dahl, A. (in press). The development of domains of moral and conventional norms, coordination in decision-making, and the implications of social opposition. In K. Bayertz & N. Roughley (Eds.), *The normative animal: On the anthropological significance of social, moral, and linguistic norms.* Oxford, UK: Oxford University Press.

Turiel, E., Perkins, S. A., & Mensing, J. F. (2009). *Judgments about deception in marital relationships.* Unpublished manuscript, University of California, Berkeley, CA.

Turiel, E., & Smetana, J. G. (1984). Social knowledge and social action: The coordination of domains. In W. M. Kurtines & J. L. Gewirtz (Eds.), *Morality, moral behavior, and moral development: Basic issues in theory and research* (pp. 261–282). New York: Wiley.

Turiel, E., & Wainryb, C. (1994). Social reasoning and the varieties of social experience in cultural contexts. In H. W. Reese (Ed.), *Advances in child development and behavior* (Vol. 25, pp. 289–326). New York: Academic Press.

Turiel, E., & Wainryb, C. (1998). Concepts of freedoms and rights in a traditional hierarchically organized society. *British Journal of Developmental Psychology, 16,* 375–395.

Turiel, E., & Wainryb, C. (2000) Social life in cultures: Judgments, conflicts, and subversion. *Child Development, 71,* 250–256.

Vlastos, G. (1962). Justice and equality. In R. B. Brandt (Ed.), *Social justice* (pp. 31–72). Englewood Cliffs, NJ: Prentice-Hall.

Wainryb, C., & Turiel, E. (1994). Dominance, subordination, and concepts of personal entitlements in cultural contexts. *Child Development, 65,* 1701–1722.

Werner, H. (1957). *Comparative psychology of mental development.* New York: International Universities Press.

Wikan, U. (1996). *Tomorrow, God willing: Self-made destinies in Cairo.* Chicago: University of Chicago Press.

CHAPTER 3

Moral Judgment
Reflective, Interactive, Spontaneous, Challenging, and Always Evolving

Melanie Killen
Audun Dahl

> **Why is moral reasoning fundamental to an explanation of the development of morality?**
>
> Reasoning is the process by which humans create and apply principles for how individuals ought to treat one another; it is neither innate nor inculcated, but constructed through everyday interactions over the course of development.

A Conceptualization of Morality

The psychological study of morality investigates how people relate to moral issues by applying, endorsing, enforcing, defending, coordinating, and giving priority to moral principles. By moral principles, we mean principles protecting others' welfare, rights, fairness, and justice. This definition of morality implies that moral considerations affect people's lives in numerous ways: People condemn violence, are outraged by injustice, applaud selflessness, are torn by dilemmas, and often seek to promote the well-being of others. Across these diverse situations, people retain their moral concerns even though the elicited thoughts, emotions, and behaviors that accompany such moral concerns often vary with the changing morally relevant circumstances (Nussbaum, 2013).

In fact, most people in all communities are concerned with the moral issues of others' welfare, rights, and fairness (Appiah, 2005; Gewirth, 1978; Nussbaum, 1999; Sen, 2009; Turiel, 2006). Moreover, the denial of just and fair treatment of others prevents the full capacities of human cooperation, cognition, and culture to flourish. As has been proposed and well documented, the decline of violence among humankind over the past several millennia can be attributed to changes in societal organizations that have promoted increases in moral reasoning (Pinker, 2011). Without a doubt, morality is a core feature of humanity.

How moral principles arise, where they come from, the biological correlates and moral orientations of the construction of such principles is at the center of current moral psychological inquiry (Schein & Gray, 2017;

Turiel, 2014). In this chapter, we discuss the developmental origins of morality, drawing on theories and empirical research in developmental science. Understanding the origins and developmental changes of any phenomenon provides insights into sources of influence, change, and evolution throughout the life course. Although morality was once thought to be the province of adulthood (children were viewed as selfish, antagonistic, or as a blank slate), a large body of research has demonstrated that children are social beings, oriented toward others, motivated to help others and to cooperate, and, beginning in early childhood, capable of drawing categorical distinctions between moral considerations and other social organizational norms (Killen & Smetana, 2015). Moreover, starting at preschool age, children justify moral judgments by reference to fairness, rights, or others' welfare, whereas they justify conventional judgments by reference to rules, authority, and social traditions. Over several decades, empirical evidence has demonstrated that the developmental emergence of morality stems out of social interactions, both with peers and through adult–child exchanges, and changes slowly over the life course (Killen & Smetana, 2015). Morality is constructed through social interactions and observations of events in the world, involving evaluation, reflection, and judgments about the fair treatment of others (Dahl & Killen, 2017; Piaget, 1932; Turiel, 2006).

The application of moral judgments to social life is not always easy, however, and many different theories have been proposed about what makes it difficult, why apparent discrepancies between judgments and action exist, and why atrocities are committed. The question of why humans do not always uphold moral codes is a very complex issue and necessitates providing a clear definition of morality and its relation to thought, emotion, and behavior. In this short chapter we address these issues through our discussion of two substantial points about morality, based on developmental science theory and data. These points are: (1) children's first moral concerns and understandings are constructed from early social orientations through everyday interactions established in infancy, through observations of helping and responding to the distress of others;

and (2) affiliations with groups and the development of group identity are important for the development of the individual and for becoming part of a community but also contribute to challenges to morality with the emergence of prejudicial (unfair) judgments, discriminatory behavior, and social inequalities.

With these points in mind, we aim to explain why individuals both uphold deeply felt moral principles yet, at the same time, give priority to nonmoral concerns in certain contexts. Developmental research provides the basis for identifying the complexity of morality throughout the lifespan, how morality can be fostered or hindered, and the role of social cognition and group affiliation as part of the acquisition and development of morality.

Defining Morality

We begin with our definition of morality, the criteria that have been generated and empirically validated, and how morality is a central part of psychological functioning and development. To define morality for psychological science means situating it within the broader realm of social considerations that are brought to bear on decision making, which includes societal concerns about group functioning, traditions, and conventions, as well as psychological concerns about autonomy, personal choice, and individual prerogatives. Our model is a social science one, drawing on philosophical categories to define morality as prescriptive norms about how others ought to treat one another with respect to justice, fairness, others' welfare, equality, and rights (see Gewirth, 1978; Scheffler, 2015; Sen, 2009).

These norms, though, are not coded in the DNA, nor solely transmitted by adults, nor learned exclusively through explicit teaching. Instead, a large body of developmental science research has documented how evaluations of moral transgressions (violations of fair and equal treatment of others) evolve throughout childhood as children become more capable of making inferences about their own and others' social experiences, reading emotional cues of others, and determining what makes an act wrong.

In general, the findings have revealed that children, beginning around 3–4 years of age and becoming more systematic over the next 7–8 years, use criteria such as impartiality, generalizability, and autonomy from authority when evaluating decisions about fairness, equality, and rights and refer to an alternative set of criteria, such as rule contingency, alterability, and group norms, when evaluating decisions involving cultural traditions, practices, and conventions (Killen & Smetana, 2015; Malti & Ongley, 2014; Nucci, 2001; Smetana, Jambon, & Ball, 2014; Turiel, 2006). As one brief example, when asked about the rule "Do not hit others," children view unprovoked hitting as wrong even when told that a teacher said it was all right ("It's still wrong because it would be mean, and you could get a bruise which would hurt"), conveying their understanding that the act is not contingent on authority mandates (e.g., autonomy from authority). These data indicate that assessing children's moral evaluations by coding whether they state that an act is "good" or "bad" does little to convey the depth of their moral knowledge; nor does it provide critical and unique evidence for moral judgments in childhood, given that many acts that are "good" or "bad" have little to do with morality.

Moreover, around the globe, children and adolescents formulate obligatory expectations that apply across individuals and groups, such as those pertaining to the right to be treated with fairness, protection of welfare, and equality (Helwig, Ruck, & Peterson-Badali, 2014; Wainryb, Shaw, & Maianu, 1998). Acts of unprovoked harm, the denial of resources, property destruction, and lack of free speech are viewed as violations of moral principles about fairness and protection of others' welfare that require an impartial perspective, independence from authority jurisdiction, and an application across contexts.

Autonomous decision making is a necessary aspect of morality because authority expectations are not always consistent with principles of morality. Providing autonomous evaluations of authority mandates with respect to fairness and equality becomes a way of determining whether cultural norms, laws, and customs are unfair, creating the context for victimization and harassment that could result from compliance with unfair authority practices. Generalizability enables morality to be those sets of norms and expectations that apply to individuals and groups from different communities, cultures, and nationalities, as has been shown with expectations regarding the wrongfulness of child abuse, for example.

Thus the criteria that individuals use indicate that morality is more than an arbitrary set of rules agreed upon by individuals in a culture, even though this might be what some individuals articulate when asked "What is morality?" Conventions that structure groups and make groups work well do not necessarily provide the foundation necessary for fair and just treatment of others. Many examples of cultural norms that perpetuate harassment, victimization, and the unfair and unjust treatment of its members exist throughout history and continue to be pervasive in current societies around the world. To effect change and improve the quality of life for individuals across the globe, conflicts between cultural conventions and moral principles are debated, evaluated and rectified. Extensive developmental data reveal that children and adolescents, just as adults do, spend much of their social life debating, evaluating, reflecting, and determining how best to resolve conflicts that entail concerns of unfairness and unequal treatment of others.

Why Do Otherwise Rational Individuals Give Priority to Nonmoral Considerations?

From infancy to adulthood, moral knowledge emerges and becomes complex, reflecting underlying criteria that reveal a systematic capacity for reasoning about morality. At the same time, children's awareness and knowledge about other aspects of social life—such as self-identity, group identity, social institutions, social group goals, personal projects and ambitions, others' intentions, and the facts of the world—become more enriched, providing a greater level of connections to others in social life (Killen, Mulvey, & Hitti, 2013). This increased awareness and knowledge of social complexity, however, also generates norms, values, and judgments that potentially challenge an emerging understanding and valuing of moral principles.

Aspects of human psychological functioning that reflect moral issues are sometimes coordinated and coherent and, at other times, contradictory and antagonistic. Importantly, disagreement does not undermine morality but often helps individuals to understand just what makes an act right or wrong and to determine what aspects of the context need to be considered to make a moral judgment. This is true not only in adult life but during childhood as well, during which peer-focused discussions serve a particularly powerful role for the facilitation and acquisition of moral concepts. Discussion, debate, and engagement enable individuals to understand different perspectives of a complex system embodied by moral principles. An adequate explanation of how people grapple with such dilemmas, sometimes giving priority to nonmoral considerations, requires an adequate account of the moral concerns and understandings that individuals bring into such situations pertaining to others' welfare, rights, equality, and fairness.

Social Cognitive Development: A Developmental Science Approach to Morality

Thus a general tenet of a social cognitive developmental approach is that children, adolescents, and adults are thinking, reasoning beings who reflect on social experiences and social events in everyday life. Social cognitive developmental research, with specific variants of this approach that have been formulated within this broad perspective, such as social domain theory (Dahl, 2014; Smetana et al., 2014; Turiel, 2006) and the social reasoning developmental model (Killen & Rutland, 2011; Rutland & Killen, 2017), has reflected a broad research program designed to analyze the origins, acquisition, and developmental trajectory of morality from infancy to adulthood. To do this, morality has to be measured using a wide range of assessments, documenting individuals' behavior, emotion attributions, judgments, and reasoning in multiple contexts (Malti, Gasser, & Buchmann, 2009; Malti & Ongley, 2014; Rizzo & Killen, 2016). A developmental science approach addresses fundamental questions about how early in development humans are capable of moral

decision making, whether and how external sources of influence change the course of moral development, and how conceptions of morality change as human cognitive and social capacities develop concurrently. What do we know about how morality emerges?

The Constructive Origins of Morality: It's Neither Innate *nor* Learned

The origin of morality is a fundamental issue with implications for psychological accounts of morality. An abundance of evidence indicates that morality is neither innate nor learned, nor is it "both"; morality is constructed through social interactions and cognitive reflection (see Dahl, 2014; Spencer et al., 2009). In abandoning the innate–learned dichotomy, we adopt a fundamentally different—constructivist—framework for understanding how moral capabilities emerge. Our proposition is that the first moral concerns and understandings are constructed from earlier, nonmoral capabilities through social interactions. During the first 2 years, infants observe and engage in morally relevant behaviors, such as helping and harming others, without yet viewing such actions as morally right or wrong. However, through repeated experiences in such interactions, children eventually form explicit judgments reflecting moral evaluations, usually around the 2nd birthday and into the 3rd year (Dahl, 2014).

Infants demonstrate social orientations soon after birth (Trevarthen, 1979). The reciprocal nature of their interactions with caregivers become particularly pronounced with the onset of the social smile, around 4–6 weeks after birth (Lavelli & Fogel, 2002). Through their observations of and interactions with others, they gradually acquire an understanding of others and a sensitivity to the emotional signals of others (Barrett & Campos, 1987; Dunn, 1988; Hoffman, 2000).

From a constructivist point of view, these early orientations, understandings, and sensitivities form the foundations for subsequent moral acquisitions. They guide children's interactions with others and how they make sense of others' signals and actions. Gradually, children go from simply being curious or distressed when others are distressed to comforting others; they become increasingly competent helpers; they become aware of others' expectations of them; and their use of physical aggression declines from late infancy to school age (Dunn, 2014; Hastings, Zahn-Waxler, & McShane, 2006; Schmidt & Sommerville, 2011). However, it is not until around the 3rd year of life that children's social and cognitive experiences and abilities enable them to express and justify moral judgments, protest against moral violations, distribute resources with concerns for equality and fairness, and show clear signs of guilt or shame (Smetana et al., 2012; Vaish, Missana, & Tomasello, 2011).

Why Is Morality Not Innate?

The constructivist approach, which argues that there are qualitative changes in children's orientations toward others' welfare, differs from nativist theories, which argue that at least some components of morality are innate. Importantly, nativists are not denying that infants lack certain moral capabilities. For instance, infants do things that—in older children—would be considered distinctly immoral. In one study, over 80% of 1-year-olds used force against another person, by hitting, biting, or kicking, without any provocation or sign of frustration (Dahl, 2015). And although infants show some responsiveness to signals of distress in others, only a minority of such signals elicit concerned or comforting behavior until well into the 2nd year (Hay, Nash, & Pedersen, 1981; Roth-Hanania, Davidov, & Zahn-Waxler, 2011; Zahn-Waxler, Radke-Yarrow, Wagner, & Chapman, 1992). For these and other reasons, most researchers appear to agree that morality *as a whole* is not innate (Hamlin, 2015).

A controversial question is whether infants at least have innate moral concepts or innate capabilities of forming moral evaluations (Bloom, 2013; Hamlin, 2015). The debate has focused on a series of experiments in which 3- to 5-month-old infants show looking and reaching preferences for puppets that help, rather than hinder, the goal acquisition of another puppet (Hamlin, 2015). Importantly, infants' responses in these studies differ from moral capabilities in older children. So far, research has only found infants to have relative preferences (i.e. preference

for one over the other), not categorical judgments (e.g. "this puppet is bad and should not hit the other puppet"), and to apply such preferences to puppets, not to themselves or other people (Dahl, Schuck, & Campos, 2013; Dahl, 2014). Infants' puppet preferences are, by most definitions, precursors to moral judgments. This is because these responses do not reflect an obligation to act in a prescriptive manner toward others.

Contemporary nativist theo.ries propose that infants' experiences are insufficient to explain these social preferences. However, there is no research on whether the emergence of looking and reaching preferences is tied to specific social experiences. What we do know is that most infants are involved in reciprocal social interactions with their caregivers from the earliest periods of life (Trevarthen, 1979; Tronick, 1989). There is currently no evidence to suggest that infants would develop the documented social preferences without engaging in and observing social interactions in everyday life over the course of several months. More generally, given the constant interplay of environments, organisms, and genes at all stages of development (prenatal, perinatal, and postnatal), some researchers have questioned whether we can meaningfully distinguish between "innate" and "non-innate" psychological characteristics (e.g. Spencer et al., 2009).

In sum, infants from a very early age show complex sensitivities to social interactions, some of which are reflected in their preferential looking and reaching toward helpful puppets. Yet we do not think these sensitivities are properly characterized as innate (as they are observed after months of social interactions), nor do we consider these sensitivities to reflect fully formed moral judgments.

Why Are We Also Saying That Morality Is Not Learned?

Learning theory has a long history in research on moral and social development (Aronfreed, 1968; Bandura & Walters, 1963). Its basic tenet, reflected in contemporary characterizations of non-nativist positions, as well as in statements of socialization theories, is that children acquire moral concerns and understandings because adults teach the children to be moral. Children are thought to adopt parental teachings through acceptance of explicit instruction, punishments, rewards, or imitation.

Within most learning-based approaches to morality, there is little distinction between compliance and morality. As long as children follow the commands of their parents in the absence of supervision, they are taken to be showing adaptive moral development (Kochanska & Aksan, 2006). The conflation of compliance and morality is problematic for, at least, two reasons. First, most children do not uncritically accept parental commands. Infants and toddlers show high rates of noncompliance (Kuczynski, Kochanska, Radke-Yarrow, & Girnius-Brown, 1987), while older children challenge parental authority on issues they consider to be under personal jurisdiction. Moreover, children do not give parents or teachers the authority to alter basic moral prohibitions against hitting or stealing (Killen & Smetana, 2015; Smetana & Braeges, 1990). Thus children do not seem to acquire moral judgments solely through compliance with adult mandates. Rather, children evaluate caregiver messages within the context of their own moral and nonmoral concerns and understandings (Grusec & Goodnow, 1994). Second, compliance can lead to distinctly immoral actions, whereas resistance to immoral commands is, in some cases, the morally better course of action (Turiel, 2002).

Thus our constructivist view of the emergence of morality differs from both the nativist and the learning perspectives. Moral considerations do not emerge independently of social experiences, nor are they acquired by simply accepting messages received from parents. We argue that genuine moral concerns and understandings are constructed over the course of the first years of life through reciprocal interactions taking place in the everyday lives of children. In the 2 first years, children display many skills that lay the foundations for morality, such as helping, empathy, and emotion understanding. Still, children at this age do not demonstrate the categorical evaluations based on concerns of others' welfare, rights, and fairness we consider to be necessary components of morality. We now turn to research on how these moral considerations, once acquired, operate in the increasingly multifaceted social worlds in which children find themselves.

Moral Judgments: Application of Moral Concepts to Social Life

Much effort has recently been invested in determining whether moral evaluations are best described as the result of unconscious, automatic intuitions, deliberative reasoning from explicit principles, or some combination of these (see Dahl & Killen, in press). In order to adequately answer this debate, however, it would be necessary to have some way of deciding with some certainty whether a given moral judgment is intuitive, deliberate, or both. Unfortunately, operationalization of these three terms has proven extremely difficult. For instance, although intuitive judgments are sometimes defined as judgments made without awareness of going through steps of reasoning, researchers who claim to study intuitive judgments typically do not assess whether people have such awareness. From our viewpoint, a more fruitful research agenda focuses on the concepts involved in the generation of moral and other social judgments, revealed by patterns of reasoning, emotion attributions, and justifications that guide individuals' decision making and behavior in morally relevant situations.

By the 3rd year of life children consistently and inconsistently apply their emerging moral judgments to their everyday interactions with others, as well as those witnessed and unwitnessed (events described to children by others). An important part of the research program is to determine what factors contribute to inconsistent application of moral judgments and how morality is applied (or not applied) in social interactions. Research has determined that children weigh multiple considerations, which does not mean that children are not moral but, rather, that humans have competing concerns; morality does not always "win out." Thus an interesting question is to determine the circumstances under which children give priority to fairness and what adults can do to enable them to become capable of and aware of the necessity of moral priority.

Constructing Morality in the Context of Intergroup Relationships

A challenging context for the application of morality is one that arises as groups become increasingly salient to identity during childhood and throughout adolescence and adulthood (Nesdale et al., 2010). According to social identity development theories, group identity generates ingroup preferences that have the potential to lead to outgroup dislike in order to enhance the ingroup affiliation. Ingroup bias, as well as outgroup dislike, often (but not necessarily) lead to unfair and unequal treatment of others. Research findings reveal that group affiliation both facilitates moral concerns for others due to an attachment to one's ingroup and the need to belong and increases ingroup bias and a heightened concern for effective group functioning (Olson, Dweck, Spelke, & Banaji, 2011; Rutland, Killen, & Abrams, 2010; Weller & Lagattuta, 2014).

As with moral judgments, prejudice in the form of intergroup bias in childhood does not begin as an automatic, uncontrolled, intuitive process, despite extensive research with adults conducted to show it being an automatic process. Instead, prejudicial attitudes in the form of outgroup dislike emerge slowly over childhood as children's experiences either encourage or hinder negative attitudes about the outgroup (Baron, 2015; Nesdale et al., 2010; Rutland & Killen, 2015). How groups are defined, how ingroup bias and outgroup threat emerge, and when children view it as unfair to act in a prejudicial manner toward others are evolving, developmental processes, with both coordinated and uncoordinated deliberations about what constitutes as fair and equal treatment of others in the context of group dynamics. Further, social experiences and contact with members of outgroups plays a significant role in decreasing negative attitudes about others based on group membership.

What we know is that young children inconsistently reveal an ingroup bias, and which group is defined as the ingroup is also highly variable, depending in large part on the messages about group membership received from adults, peers, and other sources (such as the media) in society (Hitti & Killen, 2015). For example, schools in which gender is made extremely salient, with gender-specific toys and activities (often done stereotypically), children group themselves by gender and often use stereotypic information to exclude others (Bigler & Liben, 2007; Brown, Bigler, & Chu, 2010). Yet, even in such contexts, young children are also likely to reject gender-stereotypical bases for exclusion (Horn & Sinno, 2014)

As illustrated with data regarding morality and intergroup contexts, children often fluctuate, sometimes giving priority to stereotypical norms associated with group identity, and other times recognizing that the fair decision overrides other concerns. This portrayal of moral reasoning does not fit the definition of automatic, uncontrolled intuitions or conscious deliberations (when defined as some sort of logical deductive process). These judgments are not uncontrolled in the sense that children are consciously expressing their desires to be fair to others or to adhere to group norms. At the same time, the conceptual systems implicated in this process are not logically or hierarchically ordered but, instead, reflect qualitatively different domains of reasoning, moral, societal, and psychological (Turiel, 2014).

One way to investigate how individuals weigh different considerations is to assess judgments about a complex issue that reflects moral as well as nonmoral decisions. Social exclusion based on group membership (such as gender, race, nationality, and ethnicity) has been the focus of a number of studies because of its multifaceted dimensions. Individuals often view it as unfair to exclude someone from a group activity solely because of their gender, race, or ethnicity (such as excluding black women from living in an all-white sorority house at a university). However, individuals often view it as legitimate to exclude someone from a group when inclusion would be viewed as having a negative impact on the effective functioning of the group (such as excluding men from living in an all-female sorority house at a university). In a series of studies with children about intergroup social exclusion, the findings have indicated that children consistently give priority to morality (and fairness) in straightforward exclusion contexts but often rely on stereotypical expectations in complex or ambiguous contexts (Killen, Pisacane, Lee-Kim, & Ardila-Rey, 2001).

Morality Requires Weighing Multiple Considerations

It is not the case that everyone uses moral reasons to reject intergroup exclusion, for example, even when asked about it explicitly. Some individuals condone racial exclusion, for example, based on a perception of peer discomfort and parental disapproval ("Your friends might not be comfortable sitting next to someone who is a different race, and you don't want to upset your friends"; "Your parents might not want you to invite someone to your house who is a different race because they think that they do not have any manners") (Killen, 2007; Killen, Henning, Kelly, Crystal, & Ruck, 2007).

In contrast, other individuals reject intergroup exclusion using reasons based on challenging exclusionary group norms ("Of course you should let them sit next to you. How will you find out what you have in common? Your friends need to learn not to be like that.") and fairness ("If you aren't friends with them just because of their skin color, then how will we learn to get along? You know it's kind of like not fair to be like that."; "Sometimes you have to teach your parents not to be racist"). The factors that determine which types of reasons and explanations children use to reject intergroup exclusion appear to be social relational (cross-group friendships), messages from authority (adult use of markers to reduce group differences and to encourage peer integration), and the power of group norms (when groups have norms of inclusion rather than exclusion). The evidence does not support an intuitive, automatic process but a social constructivist trajectory that includes interaction, discussion, affiliations, and reasoning.

Studies in which decisions about fairness have to be made in the context of group dynamics reveal the increasing coordination, with age, of intergroup attitudes and moral judgments. To some extent, it appears that young children are more "moral" than older children because they often apply moral principles of equality without consideration for group dynamics or group identity concerns. Young children will challenge group norms, often at the expense of a benefit to their own group, to ensure equal treatment of others. With age, children develop strong affiliations with groups and understand group dynamics, which is essential as a member of any community. However, this affiliation, when turned into unquestioning loyalty, has the potential to fly in the face of deeply held moral principles.

Rectifying Social Inequalities: Cognitive Complexity and Effort

Fortunately, with age, children begin to take disadvantaged status and inequalities into account when making decisions about the allocation of resources, a central moral decision throughout social life. Rectifying preexisting inequalities, however, requires unequal allocation of resources to balance out existing inequities; children are capable of doing this spontaneously as early as 8–10 years of age (Elenbaas & Killen, 2016; Olson et al., 2011).

In a study by Elenbaas and Killen (2016), increasing awareness of overarching economic inequalities combined with increasingly negative moral judgments of the resource disparity led children, with age, to endorse actions taken to attenuate the inequality by giving more to an institution serving African Americans that had received less in the past. These judgments reveal the effort that children go through to preserve fair treatment of others, taking into account social inequalities, and disadvantaged status.

Across a number of studies, children use reasons to identify who owns what for ensuring fair allocation of resources, to assert the necessity of individual rights, and to avoid harm to others in contexts of competing considerations (Blake, Ganea, & Harris, 2012; Helwig, 1998; Jambon & Smetana, 2014). These judgments require effort, reflection, and evaluation. As children get older and move into adolescence, the construction of moral judgments is evident in their navigation of social networks, cliques, and peer groups. Adolescents reject parental expectations to refrain from cross-group friendships but recognize that their peers may provide pressure to conform to ingroup norms, viewing deviations as a form of group disloyalty. These conflicts provide lifelong challenges to morality. But the fact that children are grappling with it and making efforts to rectify inequalities is important (and encouraging). These examples provide evidence for the assertion that the application of morality to complex social contexts reflects a developmental and constructive process.

Conclusions: Morality Is Developing across the Lifespan

Morality is constructed through social interactions and involves reflection, evaluation, and abstraction about social events in the world. By early childhood, children formulate prescriptive norms about how individuals ought to treat one another. Morality is neither innate nor learned; nor an intuitive judgment; nor a form of conscious deliberation independent of social experience. Children, adolescents, and adults make meaningful decisions about how to treat others fairly and justly. This process is not easy, however, and moral development through the lifespan reflects debate, dialogue, discussion, and argument. Without prescriptive norms of how individuals ought to treat one another, humans would not have codes to live by or develop obligatory ways of interacting with one another that reflect fairness, kindness, and justice.

Throughout history, humankind has committed horrific atrocities and has also generated codes of conduct to live by, and to prevent, rectify, and address social inequalities and maltreatment, including the Magna Carta, the U.N. Declaration of Human Rights, the U.S. Bill of Rights, and the Bill of Rights for a New South Africa, to name a few. In fact, many countries in the world have constitutions that include a bill of rights. These codified moral laws were created, constructed, and formulated by individuals to prevent the reoccurrence of prior violations of rights, as well as previous authoritarian practices that contributed to past atrocities. Morality exists despite these laws, and oftentimes laws reflect unfair practices, which leads morality to necessarily be independent of laws themselves. Codifying moral norms is not reifying them but providing a basis by which to remind individuals of the necessity of giving priority to principles of fairness, justice, others' welfare, and rights, even in the context of salient and deeply held conflicting beliefs and social norms.

The fact that violations of such rights are pervasive throughout the world is not to deny that these constitutional rights are deeply held. As we have discussed in our developmental analysis, other factors in social life become salient, and conflict with moral codes, creating debate but often resulting in acts of extreme aggression. Humans spontaneously construct moral codes in early development, and, with age, they coordinate such considerations with other issues to rectify social inequalities and distribute resources fairly, taking multiple factors into account. The fact that young children make moral judgments provides an important window of opportunity for the facilitation of morality to create a more just world.

ACKNOWLEDGMENTS

We are grateful for our discussions, debates, and reflections about morality with our colleagues and graduate students. We thank Laura Elenbaas and Michael Rizzo for very helpful feedback on the manuscript. We extend our appreciation to the editors for their inclusion of diverse perspectives in a moral atlas.

REFERENCES

Appiah, K. A. (2005). *The ethics of identity*. Princeton, NJ: Princeton University Press.

Aronfreed, J. (1968). *Conduct and conscience: The socialization of internalized control over behavior*. Oxford, UK: Academic Press.

Bandura, A., & Walters, R. H. (1963). *Social learning and personality development*. New York: Holt, Rinehart & Winston.

Baron, A. S. (2015). Constraints on the development of implicit intergroup attitudes. *Child Development Perspectives, 9,* 50–54.

Barrett, K. C., & Campos, J. J. (1987). Perspectives on emotional development: II. A functionalist approach to emotions. In J. D. Osofsky (Ed.), *Handbook of infant development* (2nd ed., pp. 555–578). Oxford, UK: Wiley.

Bigler, R. S., & Liben, L. S. (2007). Developmental intergroup theory: Explaining and reducing children's social stereotyping and prejudice. *Current Directions in Psychological Science, 16,* 162–166.

Blake, P. R., Ganea, P. A., & Harris, P. L. (2012). Possession is not always the law: With age, preschoolers increasingly use verbal information to identify who owns what. *Journal of Experimental Child Psychology, 113,* 259–272.

Bloom, P. (2013). *Just babies: The origins of good and evil*. New York: Crown.

Brown, C. S., Bigler, R. S., & Chu, H. (2010). An experimental study of the correlates and consequences of perceiving oneself to be the target of gender discrimination. *Journal of Experimental Child Psychology, 107,* 100–117.

Dahl, A. (2014). Definitions and developmental processes in research on infant morality. *Human Development, 57,* 241–249.

Dahl, A. (2015). Infants' unprovoked acts of force toward others. *Developmental Science, 19,* 1049–1057.

Dahl, A., & Killen, M. (in press). The development of moral reasoning from infancy to adulthood. In J. Wixted (Ed.), *The Stevens' handbook of experimental psychology and cognitive neuroscience, volume 3: Developmental and social psychology.* New York: Wiley.

Dahl, A., Schuck, R. K., & Campos, J. J. (2013). Do young toddlers act on their social preferences? *Developmental Psychology, 49,* 1964–1970.

Dunn, J. (1988). *The beginnings of social understanding.* Cambridge, MA: Harvard University Press.

Dunn, J. (2014). Moral development in early childhood and social interaction in the family. In M. Killen & J. G. Smetana (Eds.), *Handbook of moral development* (2nd ed., pp. 135–159). New York: Psychology Press.

Elenbaas, L., & Killen, M. (2016). Children rectify inequalities for disadvantaged groups. *Developmental Psychology, 52,* 1318–1329.

Gewirth, A. (1978). *Reason and morality.* Chicago: University of Chicago Press.

Grusec, J. E., & Goodnow, J. J. (1994). Impact of parental discipline methods on the child's internalization of values: A reconceptualization of current points of view. *Developmental Psychology, 30,* 4–19.

Hamlin, J. K. (2015). Does the infant possess a moral concept? In E. Margolis & S. Laurence (Eds.), *The conceptual mind: New directions in the study of concepts* (pp. 477–518). Cambridge, MA: MIT Press.

Hastings, P. D., Zahn-Waxler, C., & McShane, K. (2006). We are, by nature, moral creatures: Biological bases of concern for others. In M. Killen & J. G. Smetana (Eds.), *Handbook of moral development* (pp. 411–434). Mahwah, NJ: Erlbaum.

Hay, D. F., Nash, A., & Pedersen, J. (1981). Responses of six-month-olds to the distress of their peers. *Child Development, 52,* 1071–1075.

Helwig, C. C. (1998). Children's conceptions of fair government and freedom of speech. *Child Development, 69,* 518–531.

Helwig, C. C., Ruck, M. D., & Peterson-Badali, M. (2014). Rights, civil liberties, and democracy. In M. Killen & J. G. Smetana (Eds.), *Handbook of moral development* (2nd ed., pp. 46–69). New York: Psychology Press.

Hitti, A., & Killen, M. (2015). Expectations about ethnic peer group inclusivity: The role of shared interests, group norms, and stereotypes. *Child Development, 86,* 1522–1537.

Hoffman, M. L. (2000). *Empathy and moral development: Implications for caring and justice.* New York: Cambridge University Press.

Horn, S. S., & Sinno, S. (2014). Gender, sexual orientation, and discrimination based on gender and sexual orientation. In M. Killen & J. S. Smetana (Eds.), *Handbook of moral development* (2nd ed., pp. 317–339). New York: Psychology Press.

Jambon, M., & Smetana, J. G. (2014). Moral complexity in middle childhood: Children's evaluations of necessary harm. *Developmental Psychology, 50,* 22–33.

Killen, M. (2007). Children's social and moral reasoning about exclusion. *Current Directions in Psychological Science, 16,* 32–36.

Killen, M., Henning, A., Kelly, M. C., Crystal, D., & Ruck, M. (2007). Evaluations of interracial peer encounters by majority and minority U.S. children and adolescents. *International Journal of Behavioral Development, 31,* 491–500.

Killen, M., Mulvey, K. L., & Hitti, A. (2013). Social exclusion in childhood: A developmental intergroup perspective. *Child Development, 84,* 772–790.

Killen, M., Pisacane, K., Lee-Kim, J., & Ardila-Rey, A. (2001). Fairness or stereotypes?: Young children's priorities when evaluating group exclusion and inclusion. *Developmental Psychology, 37,* 587–596.

Killen, M., & Rutland, A. (2011). *Children and social exclusion: Morality, prejudice, and group identity.* New York: Wiley-Blackwell.

Killen, M., & Smetana, J. G. (2015). Origins and development of morality. In M. Lamb (Ed.), *Handbook of child psychology* (7th ed., Vol. 3, pp. 701–749). New York: Wiley-Blackwell.

Kochanska, G., & Aksan, N. (2006). Children's conscience and self-regulation. *Journal of Personality, 74,* 1587–1617.

Kuczynski, L., Kochanska, G., Radke-Yarrow, M., & Girnius-Brown, O. (1987). A developmental interpretation of young children's noncompliance. *Developmental Psychology, 23,* 799–806.

Lavelli, M., & Fogel, A. (2002). Developmental changes in mother–infant face-to-face communication: Birth to 3 months. *Developmental Psychology, 38,* 288–305.

Malti, T., Gasser, L., & Buchmann, M. (2009). Aggressive and prosocial children's emotion attributions and moral reasoning. *Aggressive Behavior, 35,* 90–102.

Malti, T., & Ongley, S. F. (2014). The development of moral emotions and moral reasoning.

In M. Killen & J. G. Smetana (Eds.), *Handbook of moral development* (2nd ed., pp. 163–183). New York: Psychology Press.

Nesdale, D., Durkin, K., Maass, A., Kiesner, J., Griffiths, J., Daly, J., & McKenzie, D. (2010). Peer group rejection and children's outgroup prejudice. *Journal of Applied Developmental Psychology, 31,* 134–144.

Nucci, L. P. (2001). *Education in the moral domain.* Cambridge, UK: Cambridge University Press.

Nussbaum, M. C. (1999). *Sex and social justice.* Oxford, UK: University of Oxford Press.

Nussbaum, M. C. (2013). *Political emotions: Why love matters for justice.* Cambridge, MA: Harvard University Press.

Olson, K. R., Dweck, C. S., Spelke, E. S., & Banaji, M. R. (2011). Children's responses to group-based inequalities: Perpetuation and rectification. *Social Cognition, 29,* 270–287.

Piaget, J. (1932). *The moral judgment of the child.* New York: Free Press.

Pinker, S. (2011). *The better angels of our nature: Why violence has declined.* New York: Viking.

Rizzo, M. T., & Killen, M. (2016). Children's understanding of equity in the context of inequality. *British Journal of Developmental Psychology, 34,* 569–581.

Roth-Hanania, R., Davidov, M., & Zahn-Waxler, C. (2011). Empathy development from 8 to 16 months: Early signs of concern for others. *Infant Behavior and Development, 34,* 447–458.

Rutland, A., & Killen, M. (2015). A developmental science approach to reducing prejudice and social exclusion: Intergroup processes, social-cognitive development, and moral reasoning. *Social Issues and Policy Review, 9,* 121–154.

Rutland, A., & Killen, M. (2017). Fair resource allocation among children and adolescents: The role of group and developmental processes. *Child Development Perspectives, 11,* 56–62.

Rutland, A., Killen, M., & Abrams, D. (2010). A new social-cognitive developmental perspective on prejudice: The interplay between morality and group identity. *Perspectives on Psychological Science, 5,* 279–291.

Schein, C., & Gray, K. (in press). The theory of dyadic morality: Reinventing moral judgment by redefining harm. *Personality and Social Psychology Review.*

Schmidt, M. F. H., & Sommerville, J. A. (2011). Fairness expectations and altruistic sharing in 15-month-old human infants. *PLOS ONE, 6*(10), e23223.

Sen, A. K. (2009). *The idea of justice.* Cambridge, MA: Harvard University Press.

Smetana, J. G., & Braeges, J. L. (1990). The development of toddlers' moral and conventional judgments. *Merrill–Palmer Quarterly, 36,* 329–346.

Smetana, J. G., Jambon, M., & Ball, C. (2014). The social domain approach to children's moral and social judgments. In M. Killen & J. G. Smetana (Eds.), *Handbook of moral development* (2nd ed., pp. 23–45). New York: Taylor & Francis.

Smetana, J. G., Rote, W. M., Jambon, M., Tasopoulos-Chan, M., Villalobos, M., & Comer, J. (2012). Developmental changes and individual differences in young children's moral judgments. *Child Development, 83,* 683–696.

Spencer, J. P., Blumberg, M. S., McMurray, B., Robinson, S. R., Samuelson, L. K., & Tomblin, J. B. (2009). Short arms and talking eggs: Why we should no longer abide the nativist–empiricist debate. *Child Development Perspectives, 3,* 79–87.

Trevarthen, C. (1979). Communication and cooperation in early infancy: A description of primary intersubjectivity. In M. Bullowa (Ed.), *Before speech: The beginning of human communication* (pp. 321–348). Cambridge, UK: Cambridge University Press.

Tronick, E. Z. (1989). Emotions and emotional communication in infants. *American Psychologist, 44,* 112–119.

Turiel, E. (2002). *The culture of morality: Social development, context, and conflict.* Cambridge, UK: Cambridge University Press.

Turiel, E. (2006). The development of morality. In W. Damon (Ed.), *Handbook of child psychology* (6th ed., Vol. 3, pp. 789–857). Hoboken, NJ: Wiley.

Turiel, E. (2014). Morality: Epistemology, development, and social opposition. In M. Killen & J. G. Smetana (Eds.), *Handbook of moral development* (2nd ed., pp. 3–22). New York: Psychology Press.

Vaish, A., Missana, M., & Tomasello, M. (2011). Three-year-old children intervene in third-party moral transgressions. *British Journal of Developmental Psychology, 29,* 124–130.

Wainryb, C., Shaw, L. A., & Maianu, C. (1998). Tolerance and intolerance: Children's and adolescents' judgments of dissenting beliefs, speech, persons, and conduct. *Child Development, 69,* 1541–1555.

Weller, D., & Lagattuta, K. H. (2014). Children's judgments about prosocial decisions and emotions: Gender of the helper and recipient matters. *Child Development, 85,* 2011–2028.

Zahn-Waxler, C., Radke-Yarrow, M., Wagner, E., & Chapman, M. (1992). Development of concern for others. *Developmental Psychology, 28,* 126–136.

CHAPTER 4

On the Possibility of Intuitive and Deliberative Processes Working in Parallel in Moral Judgment

Kees van den Bos

Is moral judgment intuitive or deliberative?

The parallel morality hypothesis suggests that the answer is both, such that intuitive and deliberative processes operate in parallel to drive moral judgment, and there is an asymmetry such that deliberative processes are more easily impaired than intuitive processes (the former needing more cognitive resources and motivated correction than the latter).

In this chapter, I focus on the issue of how people form judgments of morality and social justice. That is, how do people come to ascertain that something is right or wrong? An important issue pertaining to this question is the debate about whether people primarily rely on their gut feelings, automatic affective reactions, and other intuitive processes to assess what they think is right and wrong or whether morality and justice judgments are derived by careful conscious reasoning, rationalistic thought, and other deliberative processes (see, e.g., Beauchamp, 2001). A main aim of the current chapter is to argue that both intuitive and deliberative processes are important in understanding the psychology of moral judgment.

More precisely, I argue that, when people form moral judgments, there is a good pos-

sibility that intuitive and deliberative processes tend to operate in parallel. That is, the parallel morality hypothesis that I put forward here suggests that intuitive and deliberative processes simultaneously influence the construction of moral judgments. However, there is an asymmetry such that it may be more likely that deliberative processes are impaired to some extent than intuitive processes are. This asymmetry is proposed because it can be assumed that intuitive processes are more automatic and need fewer cognitive resources and are less affected by motivation to correct for self-interested impulses than deliberative processes do. This suggests that people's capability and motivation to reason should have strong effects on the exact moral judgments that people construct.

One way to test the parallel morality hypothesis is to examine people's reactions in situations in which they are suddenly better off than comparable other persons. For example, imagine that you are a student who had a job last summer, together with a fellow student. The two of you worked together in a pair. You and your fellow student have worked equally hard and performed equally well. On the last day of summer, you receive a bonus of $500 U.S. Your fellow student receives a bonus of $250 U.S. How satisfied are you with the bonus you received?

Or imagine that you are going to live in a new rented house. The rent of this house has yet to be determined. To decide on the rent, each individual tenant has to appear before a rent tribunal. The rent tribunal will decide on the monthly rent that you will have to pay. To determine this rent, your neighbor, who will rent a comparable house, also has to appear before the rent tribunal. A week after you and your neighbor have been at the tribunal, you are informed that the rent that you will have to pay is $750. Your neighbor will have to pay $1,000. How satisfied are you with the rent that you will have to pay?

Last example: Consider yourself participating in a study on how people perform tasks. In the experiment, you work on certain tasks for 10 minutes. You participate in the experiment with another person, who completes a similar amount of tasks within the 10 minutes. At the end of the study the experimenter gives you three lottery tickets with which you can win $200. The other participant receives only one lottery ticket. How satisfied are you with your lottery tickets?

These examples represent cases in which people react to situations in which they are overpaid, as their outcomes are better than the outcomes of comparable other persons (Adams, 1965; Austin, McGinn, & Susmilch, 1980; Buunk & Van Yperen, 1989). People's levels of satisfaction with these arrangements of advantageous inequity represent a combination of conflicting social motives (Van den Bos, Peters, Bobocel, & Ybema, 2006). A positive source of affect is derived from the egoism-based pleasure of receiving a relatively good outcome. A source of negative affect is provided by the fairness-based feeling of being unfairly advantaged (Van den Bos, Lind, Vermunt, &

Wilke, 1997). Thus both (self-oriented) preferences and (other-oriented) fairness considerations are influencing satisfaction with advantageous inequity (Van den Bos, Wilke, Lind, & Vermunt, 1998).

People usually will know whether their outcome gives them pleasure before they have insight into the fairness aspects of the outcome distribution (e.g., Epley & Caruso, 2004; Epley, Morewedge, & Keysar, 2004; Messick & Sentis, 1979, 1983; Moore & Loewenstein, 2004; Van den Bos et al., 2006). For example, Messick and Sentis (1979, 1983), state that people generally have more immediate access to or knowledge of their preferences than of what is fair, and they usually know their preferences before they know what is fair. In other words, preference is primary (Zajonc, 1980) and people assess whether and how fairness is relevant in a later phase (possibly almost immediately). Related to this, Moore and Loewenstein (2004) argue that self-interest is automatic, viscerally compelling, and typically unconscious, whereas paying attention to fairness concerns is usually a more thoughtful process. Similarly, Epley and Caruso (2004) propose that people automatically interpret objects and events egocentrically and only subsequently correct or adjust that interpretation when necessary. The automatic default occurs rapidly, but correction requires time and attentional resources (Epley et al., 2004).

Extending this line of reasoning one step further, what I am proposing here is that self-oriented preferences tend to influence people's reactions spontaneously and constantly, whereas other-oriented fairness concerns demand (at least somewhat) more deliberation and hence more cognitive resources and more motivation to correct for self-oriented intuitions than preferences do. Thus I am suggesting that self-oriented preferences and other-oriented fairness concerns may work in parallel, with the former being more automatic and more continuously influencing of people's reactions than the latter.

Historical Context

The parallel morality hypothesis reflects the broad debate between intuition and deliberation in morality and justice. Ever since the days of Aristotle, Aristippus, and Plato, there have been arguments in moral philosophy and philosophical ethics that either intuitionist or rationalist conceptions of justice are true (for an overview, see, e.g., Beauchamp, 2001). For example, on the one hand, there are theorists who argue that morality and justice judgments are derived from feelings, not from reasoning (e.g., Hume, 1739/1951). On the other hand, there are ethicists who conceive of morality and justice as predominantly principles that can be defined by reference to objective standards of right and wrong (e.g., Hare, 1981; Rawls, 1971/1992) and who develop rationalistic ethical theories that attempt to deduce a foundation for ethics from the meaning of rationality itself (e.g., Kant, 1785/1959).

Similarly, in the literature on moral psychology, there are debates between intuitionists, who argue that people's intuitive feelings about what is right or wrong cause moral judgments and that moral reasoning is usually a post hoc construction generated after moral judgments have been reached (e.g., Haidt, 2001; Kagan, 1984; Wilson, 1993), and rationalists, who state that moral judgments are caused primarily by processes of cognitive reasoning (e.g., Kohlberg, 1969; Piaget, 1932/1975; Turiel, 1983).

In short, in the history of morality and social justice, there tend to be two broad ways of thinking about morality and the justice concept that encompass many elements of the essence of moral judgment and social justice: Intuitionist notions suggest that morality and justice concerns are mainly the result of spontaneous or even automatic evaluations and are strongly influenced by subjective and affective factors, whereas rationalist theories emphasize that reasoning causes morality and justice judgments to be constructed primarily in a deliberate, objective, and cognitive way (for an overview, see Beauchamp, 2001).

The parallel morality hypothesis is important, I argue, because it reflects a more modern approach to how people form judgments of morality and justice (Strack & Deutsch, 2003). That is, rather than continuing the age-old and ongoing controversy between intuitive and deliberative models of morality and justice, focusing on whether morality and justice are best characterized by *either* spontaneous affective reactions *or* careful conscious reasoning, the view I propose adopts an integrative approach focusing on the simultaneous operation of both intuitive *and* deliberative processes in the formation of moral judgment and justice and fairness concerns. Examining the possibility that intuitive and deliberative processes may work in parallel may help to overcome, solve, or perhaps sidestep important aspects of the ancient and ongoing impasse of believing in either intuitionist or rationalist conceptions (see, e.g., Haidt, 2003, vs. Pizarro & Bloom, 2003).

The hypothesis that I put forward here argues that it makes more sense and that it is scientifically more exciting to adopt an integrative approach, in which social conditions are studied that affect the relative importance of intuitive and deliberative conceptions. Viewed in this way, the parallel morality hypothesis constitutes a modern, process-oriented approach to the interplay of social psychological factors that, combined, are likely to have an impact on the formation of moral and justice judgments and examines how these concerns affect people's reactions and how individuals interact with other people and how they behave in society.

Theoretical Stance

The parallel morality hypothesis is related to approaches that focus on initial self-centered gut reactions to unfair situations followed by controlled attempts to correct these first reactions. In this respect, the hypothesis is similar to earlier work on people's responses to various outcome distributions (see, e.g., Epley & Caruso, 2004; Epley et al., 2004; Knoch, Pascual-Leone, Meyer, Treyer, & Fehr, 2006; Messick & Sentis, 1979, 1983; Moore & Loewenstein, 2004). The hypothesis is differentiated from these earlier dual-process studies by its emphasis on the possibility that intuitive and deliberative processes may work in parallel.

The parallel quality of intuitive and deliberative processes is also present in more general models on how people process information that have noted that intuitive and deliberative processes operate in parallel as two independent systems that can be concurrently active and compete for dominance in overt responses (see, e.g., Strack & Deutsch,

2004; see also Gilovich & Griffin, 2002; Kahneman & Frederick, 2002). The parallel morality hypothesis differs somewhat from these other two-systems models in its proposition that intuitive and deliberative processes tend to be consequently invoked such that intuitive processes in general are more spontaneously invoked than deliberative processes are. The parallel morality hypothesis is also differentiated from these more general psychological models by its focus on morality and justice concerns.

The hypothesis that I put forward is different from notions that suggest that prosocial reactions are spontaneous and intuitive (e.g., Rand, Greene, & Nowak, 2012). The hypothesis also differs from ideas ventilated in the literature that justice concerns are genuine and have nothing to do with or outweigh egocentric responses (see, e.g., Lerner, 2003; Lerner & Goldberg, 1999). The hypothesis is also different from theories that adopt either an intuitionist (see, e.g., Haidt, 2001) or a rationalistic (Kant, 1785/1959) approach to the study of morality and social justice.

Evidence

There are important research findings that support important components of the hypothesis put forward here. Some components of the hypothesis are yet to be tested thoroughly (which is the primary reason that I put forward the parallel morality hypothesis as a "hypothesis," not as a "model" and certainly not as a "theory"). And some evidence reported in the literature seems to be inconsistent with the hypothesis. This section reviews very briefly some evidence for the hypothesis and also indicates evidence that is as yet missing, as well as suggestions that contradict my line of reasoning.

Data that support important components of the hypothesis put forward here come from various sources. Here, I focus on reactions to advantageous inequity, acceptance or rejection of unfair offers in ultimatum games, and what information children and adults look at during a perspective-taking task.

Van den Bos et al. (2006) examined how satisfied people are with outcomes that are better than the outcomes of comparable other persons. Building on classical and modern social psychological theories, we argued that when individuals are reacting to these arrangements of advantageous inequity, judging the advantage is quick and easy, as self-interested preferences are primary (Messick & Sentis, 1983; see also Zajonc, 1980). We further proposed that adjusting this appraisal requires cognitive resources, as it entails integrating fairness concerns with the initial preference appraisal. We investigated this hypothesis in a number of different experiments using different paradigms and different manipulations. Common elements in our experiments were that we varied whether participants' cognitive processing was either strongly or weakly limited while responding to the stimulus materials (see, e.g., Gilbert, Pelham, & Krull, 1988; Gilbert & Osborne, 1989; see also Wegner & Erber, 1992). Furthermore, in all experiments, advantageous inequity conditions were included in which participants received an outcome that was better than the outcome of a comparable other person, and the main dependent variable was participants' outcome satisfaction evaluations. Findings thus obtained indeed showed that participants are more satisfied with advantageous inequity when they are under high (as opposed to low) cognitive load.

Knoch et al. (2006) examined whether people accept or reject unfair offers made to them by other participants in ultimatum games. The authors argued that people's first reactions to the unfair offers are such that they are inclined to satisfy their self-interested needs, and controlling this self-interested impulse overrides this primary impulse. The dorsolateral prefrontal cortex (DLPFC) is involved in the control of impulsive reactions. Thus impairing the DLPFC by low-frequency repetitive transcranial magnetic stimulation (rTMS) will inhibit the control function of the DLPFC and thus strengthen the self-interest motive. Knoch et al. (2006) indeed showed that inhibiting the right DLPFC substantially reduced people's willingness to reject their partners' intentionally unfair offers in ultimatum bargaining games. These findings suggest that control is needed to fight or resist unfairness.

Epley et al. (2004) tested a related line of reasoning by tracking children's and adults' eye movements as they completed a perspective-taking task. Results obtained from an experiment conducted in the Children's Museum of Boston suggested that both children and adults automatically interpret objects and events egocentrically and only subsequently correct or adjust that interpretation when necessary. These findings indicate that the automatic default occurs rapidly but that correction requires time and attentional resources. Furthermore, children generally behave more egocentrically than adults when assessing another's perspective. This difference does not, however, indicate that adults process information less egocentrically than children, but rather that adults are better able to subsequently correct an initial egocentric interpretation.

A line of reasoning that ostensibly contradicts what I am proposing here comes from some aspects of Lerner's just-world theory that suggest that genuine justice concerns outweigh more egocentric responses (e.g., Lerner, 2003; Lerner & Goldberg, 1999). I think that this, indeed, may be the case in some circumstances—for example, when someone sacrifices his or her own life to safe the life of another person who is completely unrelated to him or her, in an act of true altruism (see also Batson, 1991, 1998). However, please note that although the findings briefly reviewed here suggest that people's primitive core may sometimes (e.g., when their cognitive capacities have been severely limited) push them in an egocentric direction, it may well be the case that frequently people try to free cognitive resources to do the right thing. Thus morality, fairness, and justice concerns are frequently a very real concern to people (Van den Bos et al., 2006; see also Staub, 1989, 2011). Furthermore, it may well be that for the majority of people, the genuine self seems to be a prosocial self (Van den Bos, Van Lange, et al., 2011). Thus my hypothesis is that genuine concerns for fairness tend to correct self-interested impulses most of the time (but not always) among most (but not all) individuals (Van den Bos, 2015; see also Miller, 1999).

Data that could truly falsify the line of reasoning put forward here would need to indicate that fairness and morality concerns are more primary than egocentric tendencies are. Rand et al. (2012) presented some findings that exactly tested this alternative prediction. These authors argued that coop-

eration is central to human social behavior and that cooperation is intuitive because cooperative heuristics are developed in daily life, in which cooperation is typically advantageous. Findings obtained from different economic games suggest that forcing participants to decide quickly increases cooperative behavior, whereas instructing them to reflect and forcing them to decide slowly decreases cooperation. Furthermore, priming participants to trust their intuitions increases cooperation with primes that induce deliberative reflection. According to the authors of this intriguing paper, these results suggest that intuition supports cooperation in social dilemmas and that reflection can undermine these cooperative impulses. These findings are, indeed, very interesting. However, the notion that reflection can undermine cooperative impulses can be explained by Miller's (1999) notion that, upon reflection, people tend to adhere to a norm of self-interest because they think their culture (and perhaps especially a North American culture; see, e.g., Henrich, Heine, & Norenzayan, 2010a, 2010b) tends to value self-interest over fairness and morality concerns.

Moreover, data that well could falsify an important component of the parallel morality hypothesis include findings from recent studies that suggest that people can engage in successful response inhibition of hedonistic impulses. For example, Veling, Aarts, and Papies (2011) show that stop signals can inhibit chronic dieters' responses toward palatable foods. Furthermore, Veling and Van Knippenberg (2006) note that forming intentions can inhibit responses to distracting stimuli, and recent evidence suggests that arousal can modulate response inhibition (Weinbach, Kalanthroff, Avnit, & Henik, 2015) and that medial prefrontal cortical regions contribute in important ways to conditioned inhibition (Meyer & Bucci, 2014). Importantly, when people are able to inhibit spontaneous egocentric responses to such an extent that these responses are not really there anymore for a long time, this would falsify the claim of my hypothesis that both self-centered and fairness/morality concerns tend to operate in parallel. Indeed, successful response inhibition of self-centered intuitions in the morality and justice domains would suggest that a dual-process account of intuitive and deliberative concerns is more appropriate than a framework that suggests that these concerns work in parallel. In fact, I ground important components of my line of reasoning on earlier studies that explicitly can be viewed as instances of a dual-process approach to self-centered and deliberate correction processes (see, e.g., Epley et al., 2004). Furthermore, precisely because conclusive evidence for the "parallel" component of the parallel morality hypothesis is missing, I explicitly put forward the prediction as it is, a hypothesis. Clearly, tight data need to be collected to show or falsify the parallel component of the hypothesis.

Personally, I think that full and constant inhibition such that self-centered preferences are not active anymore for a long time is rather unlikely. That is, I think that self-centered reactions can be inhibited, but to me it seems likely that these reactions will also kick back and start affecting people's reactions once more. For example, we can inhibit hedonistic responses to palatable food (Veling et al., 2011), but dieters will also tell that it is hard to constantly inhibit the responses to eat all those many things that we like but that are bad for us and our diet. Thus, I note that definitely more research is needed to sort out the strength and long-term effects of response inhibition of self-centered impulses, including egocentric intuitions in the morality and justice domains. This aspect and other aspects of the hypothesis put forward here can now be tested in detail in future research.

Extension and Expansion

The real-world implications of the parallel morality hypothesis are such that people's responses and behaviors may indeed often reflect both intuitive and deliberative processes. These processes may or may not be related to self-centered and other-oriented reactions, respectively. Thus, intuitive processes may not always reflect self-interested responses, and deliberative processes may not necessarily reflect other-oriented concerns. Future research can and should test the various components of the parallel morality hypothesis in detail.

One area to which this line of reasoning could be extended is the domain of psychol-

ogy and law. For example, intuition and deliberation may simultaneously influence the decisions of judges. Research could try to test the possible parallel operation of emotion-driven impulses to what is described in legal files and rationalistic, deliberative thoughts about how laws and legal rules apply precisely to what happened in the legal issues at hand.

In the last two decades or so, psychology has moved away from rationalistic and deliberative thinking and paid much attention to intuitive and fast decision making. This has yielded great developments in the field of psychological science. However, now is the time, I argue, to start paying more attention to the unique reasoning capabilities that humans have. Coupled with the ideals of the Enlightenment (and associated prescriptive assumptions present in Kantian philosophy), this could reveal the positive aspects of careful and deliberative thought about right and wrong and the important role that conscious processes play in this (see also Baumeister & Masicampo, 2010), quite possibly in addition or parallel to more intuitive and affect-driven processes (such as initial egocentric responses to advantageous injustice).

Studying these issues could perhaps also reveal that moral judgments derived by deliberate reasoning are qualitatively different from impressions of what is right or wrong derived from relying on gut feelings. Interestingly, work in other domains seems to be related to this issue, such as research on more automatic and more controlled components of stereotypes and prejudice (see, e.g., Devine, 1989; see also Gilbert et al., 1988; Kawakami, Dovidio, Moll, Hermsen, & Russin, 2000). The domain of psychology and law could yield good testing ground to examine the interplay between intuitive and deliberative, as well as spontaneous and controlled, processes in detail.

Another domain that may or may not be related to intuitive and deliberative parallel processes as discussed here is the area of behavioral activation and inhibition systems. Many psychologists had good reasons to consider behavioral activation and inhibition as constituting independent systems (e.g., Carver & White, 1994; Gable, Reis, & Elliot, 2000; Gray & McNaughton, 2000), but current cognitive psychologists also tend to focus on the interaction between activating and inhibitory processes (e.g., Knyazev, Schutter, & Van Honk, 2006). Related to this is work on moral disengagement that examines the deactivation of self-regulatory processes that can inhibit unethical behavior (e.g., Bandura, 1990, 1996). Processes of moral disengagement can lead people to convince themselves that certain ethical standards do not apply to themselves in particular situations, for instance, by disabling cognitive mechanisms of self-condemnation (but see Reynolds, Dang, Yam, & Leavitt, 2014). Whether behavioral activation and inhibition can operate in parallel ways when responding to issues of morality and social justice is a topic that needs further conceptual exploration and empirical examination (Van den Bos & Lind, 2013).

Importantly, other issues of right and wrong besides the topics briefly reviewed here need to be examined in detail. These issues include, but are not limited to, research on moral dilemmas (e.g., Van den Bos, Müller, & Damen, 2011) and the belief in a just world (e.g., Bal & Van den Bos, 2012; Van den Bos & Maas, 2009). The moderating effects of culture (e.g., Van den Bos et al., 2010; Van den Bos, Brockner, Van den Oudenalder, Kamble, & Nasabi, 2013; Van den Bos, Van Veldhuizen, & Au, 2015), social value orientations (e.g., Van den Bos, Van Lange, et al., 2011), and social psychological concepts such as ego depletion (Loseman & Van den Bos, 2012) need to be taken into consideration as well.

In conclusion, the current chapter argues that moral judgment may be an intuitive and a deliberative phenomenon, best characterized by two processes working in parallel. In delineating some thoughts about these issues, I hope to have conveyed that it may be conducive to the fields of morality and social justice (broadly defined) to start examining the intriguing possibility that intuitive and deliberative processes work in parallel in moral judgment.

REFERENCES

Adams, J. S. (1965). Inequity in social exchange. In L. Berkowitz (Ed.), *Advances in experimental social psychology* (Vol. 2, pp. 267–299). New York: Academic Press.

Austin, W., McGinn, N. C., & Susmilch, C. (1980). Internal standards revisited: Effects of social comparisons and expectancies on judgments of fairness and satisfaction. *Journal of Experimental Social Psychology, 16,* 426–441.

Bal, M., & Van den Bos, K. (2012). Blaming for a better future: Future orientation and associated intolerance of personal uncertainty lead to harsher reactions toward innocent victims. *Personality and Social Psychology Bulletin, 38,* 835–844.

Bandura, A. (1990). Selective activation and disengagement of moral control. *Journal of Social Issues, 46,* 27–46.

Bandura, A. (1996). Mechanisms of moral disengagement in the exercise of moral agency. *Journal of Personality and Social Psychology, 71,* 364–374.

Batson, C. D. (1991). *The altruism question: Toward a social psychological answer.* Hillsdale, NJ: Erlbaum.

Batson, C. D. (1998). Altruism and prosocial behavior. In D. T. Gilbert, S. T. Fiske, & G. Lindzey (Eds.), *The handbook of social psychology* (4th ed., Vol. 2, pp. 282–316). Boston: McGraw-Hill.

Baumeister, R. F., & Masicampo, E. J. (2010). Conscious thought is for facilitating social and cultural interactions: How mental simulations serve the animal–culture interface. *Psychological Review, 117,* 945–971.

Beauchamp, T. L. (2001). *Philosophical ethics: An introduction to moral philosophy* (3rd ed.). Boston: McGraw-Hill.

Buunk, B. P., & Van Yperen, N. W. (1989). Social comparison, equality, and relationship satisfaction: Gender differences over a ten-year period. *Social Justice Research, 3,* 157–180.

Carver, C. S., & White, T. L. (1994). Behavioral inhibition, behavioral activation, and affective responses to impending reward and punishment: The BIS/BAS scales. *Journal of Personality and Social Psychology, 67,* 319–333.

Devine, P. G. (1989). Stereotypes and prejudice: Their automatic and controlled components. *Journal of Personality and Social Psychology, 56,* 5–18.

Epley, N., & Caruso, E. M. (2004). Egocentric ethics. *Social Justice Research, 17,* 171–188.

Epley, N., Morewedge, C. K., & Keysar, B. (2004). Perspective taking in children and adults: Equivalent egocentrism but differential correction. *Journal of Experimental Social Psychology, 40,* 760–768.

Gable, S. L., Reis, H. T., & Elliot, A. J. (2000). Behavioral activation and inhibition in everyday life. *Journal of Personality and Social Psychology, 78,* 1135–1149.

Gilbert, D. T., & Osborne, R. E. (1989). Thinking backward: Some curable and incurable consequences of cognitive busyness. *Journal of Personality and Social Psychology, 57,* 940–949.

Gilbert, D. T., Pelham, B. W., & Krull, D. S. (1988). On cognitive busyness: When person perceivers meet persons perceived. *Journal of Personality and Social Psychology, 54,* 733–740.

Gilovich, T., & Griffin, D. (2002). Introduction—Heuristics and biases: Then and now. In T. Gilovich, D. Griffin, & D. Kahneman (Eds.), *Heuristics and biases: The psychology of intuitive judgment* (pp. 1–18). New York: Cambridge University Press.

Gray, J. A., & McNaughton, N. (2000). *The neuropsychology of anxiety: An enquiry into the functions of the septo-hippocampal system.* Oxford, UK: Oxford University Press.

Haidt, J. (2001). The emotional dog and its rational tail: A social intuitionist approach to moral judgment. *Psychological Review, 108,* 814–834.

Haidt, J. (2003). The emotional dog does learn new tricks: A reply to Pizarro and Bloom (2003). *Psychological Review, 110,* 197–198.

Hare, R. M. (1981). *Moral thinking: Its levels, method, and point.* Oxford, UK: Clarendon Press.

Henrich, J., Heine, S. J., & Norenzayan, A. (2010a). Most people are not WEIRD. *Nature, 466,* 29.

Henrich, J., Heine, S. J., & Norenzayan, A. (2010b). The weirdest people in the world? *Behavioral and Brain Sciences, 33,* 61–83.

Hume, D. (1951). *A treatise of human nature.* Oxford, UK: Clarendon. (Original work published 1739)

Kagan, J. (1984). *The nature of the child.* New York: Basic Books.

Kahneman, D., & Frederick, S. (2002). Representativeness revisited: Attribute substitution in intuitive judgment. In T. Gilovich, D. Griffin, & D. Kahneman (Eds.), *Heuristics and biases: The psychology of intuitive judgment* (pp. 49–81). New York: Cambridge University Press.

Kant, I. (1959). *Foundation of the metaphysics of morals.* Indianapolis, IN: Bobbs-Merrill. (Original work published 1785)

Kawakami, K., Dovidio, J. F., Moll, J., Hermsen, S., & Russin, A. (2000). Just say no (to stereotyping): Effects of training in negation of stereotypic associations on stereotype activation. *Journal of Personality and Social Psychology, 78,* 871–888.

Knoch, D., Pascual-Leone, A., Meyer, K., Treyer, V., & Fehr, E. (2006). Diminishing reciprocal fairness by disrupting the right prefrontal cortex. *Science, 314,* 829–832.

Knyazev, G. G., Schutter, D. J. L. G., & Van Honk, J. (2006). Anxious apprehension increases coupling of delta and beta oscillations. *International Journal of Psychophysiology, 61,* 283–287.

Kohlberg, L. (1969). Stage and sequence: The cognitive-developmental approach to socialization. In D. A. Goslin (Ed.), *Handbook of socialization theory and research* (pp. 347–480). Chicago: Rand McNally.

Lerner, M. J. (2003). The justice motive: Where social psychologists found it, how they lost it, and why they may not find it again. *Personality and Social Psychology Review, 7,* 388–399.

Lerner, M. J., & Goldberg, J. H. (1999). When do decent people blame victims?: The differing effects of the explicit/rational and implicit/experiential cognitive systems. In S. Chaiken & Y. Trope (Eds.), *Dual-process theories in social psychology* (pp. 627–640). New York: Guilford Press.

Loseman, A., & Van den Bos, K. (2012). A self-regulation hypothesis of coping with an unjust world: Ego-depletion and self-affirmation as underlying aspects of blaming of innocent victims. *Social Justice Research, 25,* 1–13.

Messick, D. M., & Sentis, K. (1979). Fairness and preference. *Journal of Experimental Social Psychology, 15,* 418–434.

Messick, D. M., & Sentis, K. (1983). Fairness, preference, and fairness biases. In D. M. Messick & K. S. Cook (Eds.), *Equity theory: Psychological and sociological perspectives* (pp. 61–94). New York: Praeger.

Meyer, H. C., & Bucci, D. J. (2014). The contribution of medial prefrontal cortical regions to conditioned inhibition. *Behavioral Neuroscience, 128,* 644–653.

Miller, D. T. (1999). The norm of self-interest. *American Psychologist, 54,* 1053–1060.

Moore, D. A., & Loewenstein, G. (2004). Self-interest, automaticity, and the psychology of conflict of interest. *Social Justice Research, 17,* 189–202.

Piaget, J. (1975). *The moral judgment of the child.* London: Routledge & Kegan Paul. (Original work published 1932)

Pizarro, D. A., & Bloom, P. (2003). The intelligence of the moral intuitions: Comment on Haidt (2001). *Psychological Review, 110,* 193–196.

Rand, D. G., Greene, J. D., & Nowak, M. A. (2012). Spontaneous giving and calculated greed. *Nature, 489,* 427–430.

Rawls, J. (1992). *A theory of justice.* Oxford, UK: Oxford University Press. (Original work published 1971)

Reynolds, S. J., Dang, C. T., Yam, K. C., & Leavitt, K. (2014). The role of moral knowledge in everyday immorality: What does it matter if I know what is right? *Organizational Behavior and Human Decision Processes, 123,* 124–137.

Staub, E. (1989). *The roots of evil: The origins of genocide and other group violence.* New York: Cambridge University Press.

Staub, E. (2011). Uncertainty, and the roots and prevention of genocide and terrorism. In M. A. Hogg & D. L. Blaylock (Eds.), *Extremism and the psychology of uncertainty* (pp. 263–280). Oxford, UK: Wiley-Blackwell.

Strack, F., & Deutsch, R. (2003). The two sides of social behavior: Modern classics and overlooked gems on the interplay between automatic and controlled processes. *Psychological Inquiry, 14,* 209–215.

Strack, F., & Deutsch, R. (2004). Reflective and impulsive determinants of social behavior. *Personality and Social Psychology Review, 8,* 220–247.

Turiel, E. (1983). *The development of social knowledge: Morality and convention.* Cambridge, UK: Cambridge University Press.

Van den Bos, K. (2015). Genuine concerns for fairness tend to correct self-interested impulses. *Social Justice Research, 28,* 230–232.

Van den Bos, K., Brockner, J., Stein, J. H., Steiner, D. D., Van Yperen, N. W., & Dekker, D. M. (2010). The psychology of voice and performance capabilities in masculine and feminine cultures and contexts. *Journal of Personality and Social Psychology, 99,* 638–648.

Van den Bos, K., Brockner, J., Van den Oudenalder, M., Kamble, S. V., & Nasabi, A. (2013). Delineating a method to study cross-cultural differences with experimental control: The voice effect and countercultural contexts regarding power distance. *Journal of Experimental Social Psychology, 49,* 624–634.

Van den Bos, K., & Lind, E. A. (2013). On sense-making reactions and public inhibition of benign social motives: An appraisal model of prosocial behavior. In J. M. Olson & M. P. Zanna (Eds.), *Advances in experimental social psychology* (Vol. 48, pp. 1–58). San Diego, CA: Academic Press.

Van den Bos, K., Lind, E. A., Vermunt, R., & Wilke, H. A. M. (1997). How do I judge my outcome when I do not know the outcome of others?: The psychology of the fair process effect. *Journal of Personality and Social Psychology, 72,* 1034–1046.

Van den Bos, K., & Maas, M. (2009). On the psychology of the belief in a just world: Exploring experiential and rationalistic paths to victim blaming. *Personality and Social Psychology Bulletin, 35,* 1567–1578.

Van den Bos, K., Müller, P. A., & Damen, T. (2011). A behavioral disinhibition hypothesis of interventions in moral dilemmas. *Emotion Review, 3,* 281–283.

Van den Bos, K., Peters, S. L., Bobocel, D. R., & Ybema, J. F. (2006). On preferences and doing the right thing: Satisfaction with advantageous inequity when cognitive processing is limited. *Journal of Experimental Social Psychology, 42,* 273–289.

Van den Bos, K., Van Lange, P. A. M., Lind, E. A., Venhoeven, L. A., Beudeker, D. A., Cramwinckel, F. M., . . . Van der Laan, J. (2011). On the benign qualities of behavioral disinhibition: Because of the prosocial nature of people, behavioral disinhibition can weaken pleasure with getting more than you deserve. *Journal of Personality and Social Psychology, 101,* 791–811.

Van den Bos, K., Van Veldhuizen, T. S., & Au, A. K. C. (2015). Counter cross-cultural priming and relative deprivation: The role of individualism–collectivism. *Social Justice Research, 28,* 52–75.

Van den Bos, K., Wilke, H. A. M., Lind, E. A., & Vermunt, R. (1998). Evaluating outcomes by means of the fair process effect: Evidence for different processes in fairness and satisfaction judgments. *Journal of Personality and Social Psychology, 74,* 1493–1503.

Veling, H., Aarts, H., & Papies, E. K. (2011). Using stop signals to inhibit chronic dieters' responses toward palatable foods. *Behaviour Research and Therapy, 11,* 771–780.

Veling, H., & Van Knippenberg, A. (2006). Shielding intentions from distraction: Forming an intention induces inhibition of distracting stimuli. *Social Cognition, 24,* 409–425.

Wegner, D. M., & Erber, R. (1992). The hyperaccessibility of suppressed thoughts. *Journal of Personality and Social Psychology, 63,* 903–912.

Weinbach, N., Kalanthroff, E., Avnit, A., & Henik, A. (2015). Can arousal modulate response inhibition? *Journal of Experimental Psychology: Learning, Memory, and Cognition, 41,* 1873–1877.

Wilson, J. Q. (1993). *The moral sense.* New York: Free Press.

Zajonc, R. B. (1980). Feeling and thinking: Preferences need no inferences. *American Psychologist, 35,* 151–175.

CHAPTER 5

The Wrong and the Bad

Shaun Nichols

> **How can a theory of moral judgment explain why people think certain actions are wrong, not simply bad?**
>
> By incorporating rules.

It is bad when a puppy falls off a cliff. It is wrong when a person throws a puppy off a cliff. Both of these events are morally unfortunate. But many moral systems maintain that there is a critical distinction between bad and wrong events (see, e.g., Aquinas, Kant, Ross). Accidents and natural disasters can have morally bad consequences, but only actions can be *wrong*. This distinction isn't merely the province of philosophy. Ordinary people frequently condemn actions as wrong, not merely bad. An adequate theory of human morality must explain these kinds of judgments.

The moral reactions of infants (see, e.g., Hamlin, Wynn, & Bloom, 2007) and non-human animals (see, e.g., de Waal, Leimgruber, & Greenberg, 2008) are naturally interpreted in terms of moral *badness* (or *goodness*). Kiley Hamlin and colleagues showed babies events in which one agent either helps or hinders another agent. They found that babies preferred helpers to hinderers. A plausible explanation of the phenomenon is that the babies assign a negative valence to hinderers. But it is a further question whether babies judge that it was *wrong* for the agent to hinder, and Hamlin does not argue for that richer interpretation of the data. By contrast, much moral psychology on children and adults has focused explicitly on judgments of wrongness (Blair, 1995; Cushman, Young, & Hauser, 2006; Greene & Sinnott-Armstrong, 2008; Turiel, 1983). Research on the moral–conventional distinction explores how children and adults distinguish between different *kinds* of wrongness (Turiel, 1983). Children judge that it is wrong—impermissible—to stand up during story time. They also judge that it is wrong to pull hair. The former kind of case is taken to be a *conventional* violation; the latter a *moral* violation. And these different kinds of violations exhibit systematically different patterns of responses in children and adults. Importantly, though, all of these involve judgments of wrongness. Similarly, in the moral dilemma tradition, participants are presented with scenarios—such as throwing a person in front of a train—and asked about the permissibility of such an action (Cushman et al., 2006; Mikhail, 2011).

Our account of wrongness judgments is traditional: These judgments involve structured representations of rules that invoke abstract notions such as *harm, knowledge,* and *innocence* to proscribe certain actions (e.g., Mallon & Nichols, 2010; Nichols, 2004; Nichols & Mallon, 2006; Nichols, Kumar, Lopez, Ayars, & Chan, 2016; see also Mikhail, 2011). People judge that it is wrong to throw a puppy off of a cliff because they have a rule that proscribes intentionally causing harm to an innocent creature, and they recognize that the event counts as a violation of that rule since a puppy is an innocent creature and bouncing down a mountain is a harm.

Theoretical Context

We favor an account of moral judgment that depends on structured rules defined over abstract concepts (Nichols & Mallon, 2006; Nichols et al., 2016). But many theories of moral judgment try to make do with a much more austere set of resources. It is a familiar pattern in cognitive science to seek low-level explanations for apparently high-level cognitive phenomena. This is perhaps most apparent in disputes about symbolic processing. Some influential connectionist approaches attempt to explain cognition with no recourse to symbols (McClelland, Rumelhart, & Hinton, 1986). There is a related trend in accounts of moral judgment that eschew rules in favor of lower level factors.

In low-level accounts of moral judgment, the primitive ingredient is typically some kind of aversion. Blair's account of the moral–conventional distinction is based on the distress associated with seeing others in distress (Blair, 1995). Greene's account of nonutilitarian responses to dilemma cases is based on alarm-like reactions of ancient emotions systems (Greene, Sommerville, Nystrom, Darley, & Cohen, 2008). Cushman (2013) and Crockett (2013) explain key aspects of nonutilitarian judgment by adverting to reinforcement learning, especially habit learning.

Low-level accounts are often attractive because they build on processes that are uncontroversially present in the organism. In the present case, few dispute that humans find it aversive to witness suffering; similarly, it's widely acknowledged that humans learn to find certain kinds of actions aversive through habit learning. Thus, if we can explain moral judgment in terms of some such widely accepted low-level processes, then we have no need to appeal to such cognitive extravagances as richly structured rules defined over abstract categories.

Arguments

Despite its tough-minded appeal, the race to lower levels can neglect the very phenomena we want to understand. Trying to explain human cognition without adverting to symbolic processing makes it difficult to capture core phenomena such as the systematicity and inferential potential of thought (Fodor & Pylyshyn, 1988). Similarly, it is difficult to capture the distinctive nature and specificity of wrongness judgments without adverting to structured rules.

Humans naturally find certain things aversive, including such varied phenomena as electric shock and suffering in others (see, e.g., Blair, 1999). Furthermore, like other animals, we can acquire aversions through habit learning (Crockett, 2013; Cushman, 2013). If grasping a green apple frequently leads to being shocked, then I will develop an aversion to grasping green apples. These are uncontroversial components of the human mind. But finding something aversive is not the same as judging it wrong. I find cleaning the litter box extremely aversive. But I do not judge it to be wrong to clean the litter box. By contrast, I judge that it is wrong to eat beef (for various reasons), but I find eating beef very appealing. My behavior often conforms to my aversions and attractions—I often avoid cleaning the litter box, and I frequently eat beef. But insofar as we are trying to understand our judgments of *wrongness,* we need to capture the fact that the litter box aversion does not involve a judgment of wrongness. We need something more than aversion to explain the wrongness judgment.

Aversion alone does not discriminate between the wrong and the bad. Furthermore, simple aversions seem not to have the requisite level of precision to capture moral judgment. Natural aversions tend to be triggered by concrete cues—we find a crying face aversive, but not a simple statement that someone, somewhere, is crying. Normative judgments, however, often involve not concrete cues but abstract categories such as *harm*. Often our feelings of aversion track specific cues, whereas our moral judgments track the abstract category. Consider the famous line attributed to Stalin, that a single death is a tragedy, but a million deaths is a statistic. We might well find it more aversive to imagine a single person being murdered than to acknowledge the murders of a million. But we would certainly not make the moral judgment that the murder of one is more wrong or worse than the murder of a million. Our judgments about the wrongness of the action are defined over the abstract category *murder,* not the aversion.

Indeed, in many cases, the relevant categories are clearly not perceptually available. Consider, for instance, moral judgments surrounding cousin marriage. In some cultures (parts of Korea and India), it is absolutely forbidden to marry one's first cousin; in other cultures (e.g., in Saudi Arabia), it is permitted; in other cultures, it is forbidden to marry one's *parallel cousin* (i.e., the child of a parent's same-sex sibling), but not a *cross-cousin* (i.e., the child of a parent's opposite-sex sibling). This is just one kind of norm, but norm systems in general have determinative proscriptions surrounding marriage, sex, and insults. This also holds for harm-based norm systems. Norm systems determine *what* can be harmed (e.g., cattle, outsiders, children), *how* they can be harmed (e.g., slaughtering, swindling, spanking), and *when* they can be harmed (e.g., for food, for advantage, for punishment).

It is very important for members of each community to learn the local system. To get it wrong can mean punishment, ostracism, even death. And people do generally get these things right. A rule-based account is obviously well suited to explain why people can get it right, because such an account draws on concepts that offer the greatest precision available. If people systematically judge that it is wrong to marry parallel cousins, then this is because they encode a rule defined over the concept PARALLEL

COUSIN. If people systematically judge that it is wrong to slaughter cattle, then this is because they encode a rule defined over the concept CATTLE. If people systematically judge that it is wrong to spank your child except for punishment, then this is because they encode a rule defined over the concept PUNISHMENT. A system built on natural aversion or habit learning that *does not* exploit such concepts as PARALLEL COUSIN and CATTLE will be poorly equipped to explain how it is that people seem to know and abide by these norm systems so effectively.

Accounts of moral judgment based solely on aversion thus have difficulties with both the specificity of moral judgments and the fact that the judgments are of impermissibility. By contrast, a rule-based system easily accommodates both of these core phenomena of moral judgment. At a minimum, it is hard to see how anything but a rule-based system can accommodate cases such as the norm systems surrounding cousin marriage. And a rule-based system can easily extend to such cases as prohibitions on murder, theft, and so forth. That is, once we grant that judgments about wrongful marriage are guided by rules defined over abstract categories such as *parallel cousin,* it is natural to grant that judgments about wrongful harm are guided by rules defined over such abstract categories as *harm, knowledge,* and *intention.*

From this perspective, it seems unparsimonious to hold that wrongness judgments in the harm domain count as a special island of wrongness judgments that does *not* involve rules.

None of this is to deny that natural aversions and habit learning play an important role in moral judgments of wrongness. Moral judgments that involve actions that produce intrinsically aversive outcomes (such as cues of suffering) might well be treated as distinctively wrong *because* of the aversion (Nichols, 2004). The rule in this case might take on special salience because of its close ties to aversive outcomes. In addition, even if we allow that rules play a role in moral judgment, it's a further question how the rules become internalized. Some kind of reinforcement learning might well be key here. That is, reinforcement learning might explain why we attach value to certain rules. In these ways, the low-level accounts might be used to supplement rule-based accounts rather than displace them.

Extension and Expansion

The foregoing provides reason to believe that structured rules play an essential role in moral judgment. However, a major limitation of rule-based theories is that it has been unclear how the rules are acquired. This problem is especially salient given the apparent complexity of the rules revealed in studies on moral dilemmas. In the standard "footbridge" dilemma, participants are presented with an agent who intentionally kills an innocent person for a greater good; participants regard this action as wrong. In the standard "switch" dilemma, participants are presented with an agent whose action produces, as a side effect, the death of an innocent person for a greater good; participants regard this action as permissible (Cushman et al., 2006; Mikhail, 2011). Even children reveal this kind of pattern in reasoning about dilemmas (reported in Mikhail, 2011). On a rule-based explanation of this pattern of responses, the rule against killing forbids *intentionally* killing but not *knowingly* killing in the service of a greater good (Mikhail, 2011). That is a subtle distinction to acquire, and children are presumably never given any explicit instruction on the matter. Few parents tell children "It is wrong to intend to hurt someone but sometimes okay to hurt someone as a side effect, depending on the value of the intended effect." So if we are to explain children's facility at moral distinctions in terms of structured rules, we need some explanation for how children arrive at such complex rules despite scant instruction.

One way to explain the acquisition of such rules is to posit innate biases. A number of theorists have accordingly suggested that there is an innate moral grammar that guides the acquisition of these complex rules (e.g., Dwyer, Huebner, & Hauser, 2010: Mikhail, 2007). In particular, theorists have suggested that a poverty of the stimulus argument applies for learning these moral distinctions. The idea is that the evidence the child receives is too impoverished to explain the complex set of moral distinctions that she acquires. A key part of the problem is the lack of *negative* evidence in the moral domain (Dwyer et al., 2010, p. 492). Children are generally not told what actions are *not impermissible,* as reflected by the fact noted above that children are not told that it is sometimes okay to produce an unintended but foreseen harm. The poverty of the stimulus argument here is supposed to parallel Chomsky's argument for an innate language acquisition device: Just as the child ends up with complex syntactic rules that outstrip the available evidence, so too the child ends up with moral rules that outstrip the available evidence.

The moral grammar hypothesis provides one explanation for how complex rules might be acquired. We have been pursuing an alternative, learning-theoretic approach to these issues. Recent work in Bayesian learning provides a novel account of how people learn from negative evidence (Xu & Tenenbaum, 2007). To see the idea, consider trying to determine whether a deck of cards is a pinochle deck (which has no cards numbered under 9) or a regular deck. You observe a sequence of random draws from the deck. The draws unfold as follows: Jack, King, 10, Ace, Queen, Jack, 10, 10, Ace. With each of these successive draws, you should start becoming more confident that it is a pinochle deck. Why? Because if it were a regular deck, it would be a *suspicious co-incidence* that none of the cards is under 9. That provides evidence that there are no cards under 9 in the deck.

Now consider the fact that many moral rules apply to what an agent intentionally does, but not to what an agent allows to happen. Again, parents don't give children explicit instructions on the matter. They don't say such things as "it's wrong to produce this outcome, but it's not wrong to allow the outcome to persist." But it's possible that the children can infer this based on the kinds of examples of violations they receive. If all of the observed examples of violations are examples in which the agent intentionally produced the outcome, this might count as evidence that the operative rule does not say that it is impermissible to allow the outcomes to persist. Imagine getting the following random sample of violations of a school rule: John violated the rule by putting a truck on the shelf, Jill violated the same rule by putting a ball on the shelf, and Mike violated the rule by putting a doll on the shelf. Now, is Mary violating the rule when she sees a puzzle on the shelf and doesn't remove it? The sample violations were all examples of a person *intentionally* producing the outcome. If these samples are representative, then this suggests that the rule applies to what a person *does* and not to what a person *allows to happen* (or persist). Otherwise it would be surprising that none of the sample violations included a person allowing the outcome to happen or persist. In recent experiments, we find that when given only intended-outcome examples such as those above, adult participants do *not* generalize to say that the person who *allowed* the outcome to persist violated the rule (Nichols et al., 2016). By contrast, when given two examples in which a person allows the outcome to persist (e.g., leaving the puzzle on the shelf), participants immediately generalize to other such cases. This suggests that people are sensitive to evidence that bears on whether the rule applies only to what an agent does, or also to what an agent allows.

These early results suggest new directions for rule-based theorists to investigate. But the results are preliminary, and most of the important questions remain completely open. For instance, in the learning studies, participants show a strong bias in favor of intention-based rules, even when they have only one example to learn from (Nichols et al., 2016). Why do people have such a strong bias in favor of intention-based rules? Does that require a nativist account? Furthermore, all of this work on novel rule learning has been done on adults, and we don't know whether children, too, will make these kinds of inferences. It is also unclear how the child thinks about the hypothesis space. Do children naturally think in terms of intention-based versus outcome-based rules? If so, why do they settle on this particular hypothesis space? Advocates of rule-based theories of moral judgment have a lot of territory to explore.

ACKNOWLEDGMENTS

I'd like to thank Alisabeth Ayars for comments on an earlier draft of this chapter. Research for this chapter was supported by Office of Naval Research Grant No. 11492159.

REFERENCES

Blair, R. J. R. (1995). A cognitive developmental approach to morality: Investigating the psychopath. *Cognition, 57*(1), 1–29.

Blair, R. J. R. (1999). Psychophysiological responsiveness to the distress of others in children with autism. *Personality and Individual Differences, 26*(3), 477–485.

Crockett, M. J. (2013). Models of morality. *Trends in Cognitive Sciences, 17*(8), 363–366.

Cushman, F. (2013). Action, outcome, and value: A dual-system framework for morality. *Personality and Social Psychology Review, 17*(3), 273–292.

Cushman, F., Young, L., & Hauser, M. (2006). The role of conscious reasoning and intuition in moral judgment: Testing three principles of harm. *Psychological Science, 17*(12), 1082–1089.

de Waal, F. B., Leimgruber, K., & Greenberg, A. R. (2008). Giving is self-rewarding for monkeys. *Proceedings of the National Academy of Sciences of the USA, 105*(36), 13685–13689.

Dwyer, S., Huebner, B., & Hauser, M. D. (2010). The linguistic analogy: Motivations, results, and speculations. *Topics in Cognitive Science, 2*(3), 486–510.

Fodor, J. A., & Pylyshyn, Z. W. (1988). Connectionism and cognitive architecture: A critical analysis. *Cognition, 28*(1), 3–71.

Greene, J. D., & Sinnott-Armstrong, W. (2008). The secret joke of Kant's soul. In W. Sinnott-Armstrong (Ed.), *Moral psychology: Vol. 3. The neuroscience of morality: Emotion, disease, and development* (pp. 35–79). Cambridge, MA: MIT Press.

Greene, J. D., Sommerville, R. B., Nystrom, L. E., Darley, J. M., & Cohen, J. D. (2008). An fMRI investigation of emotional engagement in moral judgment. *Science, 293*(5537), 2105–2108.

Hamlin, J. K., Wynn, K., & Bloom, P. (2007). Social evaluation by preverbal infants. *Nature, 450*(7169), 557–559.

Mallon, R., & Nichols, S. (2010). Rules. In J. Doris (Ed.), *The moral psychology handbook* (pp. 297–320). Oxford, UK: Oxford University Press.

McClelland, J. L., Rumelhart, D. E., & Hinton, G. E. (1986). The appeal of parallel distributed processing. In D. E. Rumelhart, J. L. McClelland, & the PDP Research Group (Eds.), *Parallel distributed processing* (Vol. 1, pp. 3–44). Cambridge, MA: MIT Press/Bradford Books.

Mikhail, J. (2007). Universal moral grammar: Theory, evidence and the future. *Trends in Cognitive Sciences, 11*(4), 143–152.

Mikhail, J. (2011). *Elements of moral cognition: Rawls' linguistic analogy and the cognitive science of moral and legal judgment.* Cambridge, UK: Cambridge University Press.

Nichols, S. (2004). *Sentimental rules: On the natural foundations of moral judgment.* New York: Oxford University Press.

Nichols, S., Kumar, S., Lopez, T., Ayars, A., & Chan, H. (2016). Rational learners and moral rules. *Mind and Language, 31*(5), 530–554.

Nichols, S., & Mallon, R. (2006). Moral dilemmas and moral rules. *Cognition, 100*(3), 530–542.

Turiel, E. (1983). *The development of social knowledge: Morality and convention.* Cambridge, UK: Cambridge University Press.

Xu, F., & Tenenbaum, J. B. (2007). Word learning as Bayesian inference. *Psychological Review, 114*(2), 245.

PART II
MORALITY AND FEELING

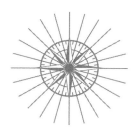

QUESTIONS ANSWERED IN PART II

CHAPTER 6 What is empathy's role in driving moral behavior?

CHAPTER 7 Does morality have specialized cognitive and neural processes?

CHAPTER 8 What is the role of disgust in morality?

CHAPTER 9 What makes some emotions *moral* emotions?

CHAPTER 10 How can moral psychology use more nuanced and developed theories of emotion to inform its process models?

CHAPTER 6

Empathy Is a Moral Force

Jamil Zaki

What is empathy's role in driving moral behavior?

Here I argue that empathy is a noisy but useful moral compass and, in particular, that (1) empathy's limits in guiding morality often reflect an empathizer's motives, not his or her capacities; (2) motivating people to empathize can overcome these limits; and (3) empathy lends affective "force" to morality, such that empathy-based moral behavior produces benefits that other forms of moral action do not.

People share each other's emotional lives. We react not only to events that befall us, but also to the experiences of those around us. The tendency to share, understand, and care about others' inner lives constitutes *empathy* (Davis, 1994; Decety & Jackson, 2004; Zaki & Ochsner, 2016).

Psychologists and neuroscientists have produced a deluge of research on empathy in recent decades. This trend reflects interest not only in empathy's characteristics but also in its power to encourage prosocial and moral action. Individuals help the targets of their empathy (Batson, 1991, 2011) and "humanize" those targets, for instance by resisting stereotypes about them or treating them fairly (Galinsky & Moskowitz, 2000). These behaviors likely reflect empathy's effects in prompting aversion to others' pain and pleasure in others' success (Lamm, Decety, & Singer, 2011; Morelli, Lieberman, & Zaki, 2015; Morelli, Sacchet, & Zaki,

2014), which in turn provide an intuitive "compass" that guides moral action. Individuals with psychopathy, who often lack empathy, provide a striking example of how important this compass is (Blair, 2005).

Does empathy's compass always guide people toward ideal moral behavior? Probably not. Like other affective responses involved in moral decision making (Haidt, 2001), empathy is noisy and biased. It can spur concern for the well-being of some people but not others, for instance, skewing prosocial behavior unfairly toward ingroup members. Empathy can even generate clearly immoral choices—for instance, when empathy for one's own community encourages aggression toward other groups (Lickel, Miller, Stenstrom, Denson, & Schmader, 2006).

These biases and constraints have led theorists to propose that empathy constitutes a suboptimal, and even dangerous, source of moral behavior (Bloom, 2013; Prinz, 2011a). For instance, Bloom (2013) highlights the case of "Baby Jessica," who became trapped in a well. Her case was captured on television and subsequently produced a worldwide outpouring of empathy. Donors provided hundreds of thousands of dollars to support Baby Jessica, while ignoring the simultaneous suffering of countless others.

How could an emotional state that produces such misguided moral behavior ever be trusted? Critics of empathy suggest that morality can better serve the greater good if it is guided by utilitarian principles (i.e., doing the most good for the most people), as opposed to emotion. This viewpoint is important and clearly right in many cases. It is also incomplete and risks discarding the baby with the proverbial well water.

Here I offer a counterpoint to recent criticisms of empathy, in two parts. First, I suggest that the limits of empathy are not stable and instead reflect individuals' motivation to connect with or avoid others' experiences. These motives shift dynamically across situations, and strategies that increase empathic motivation can also reduce biases associated with empathy. Second, although utilitarian principles best guide the behavior of large groups, individuals who act morally "with feeling" are likely to be more committed to and fulfilled by their behaviors. Thus, to the extent that people can align their principles and affect, empathy can lend emotional meaning to moral actions.

Historical Context

The modern concept of empathy is tied at the roots to moral philosophy. Adam Smith, in *The Theory of Moral Sentiments* (1790/2002), famously described the "fellow feeling"—vicarious experience of others' emotions—as a source of civilizing and moral action. In the intervening centuries, empirical data have borne out Smith's insight. In particular, Batson systematically demonstrated that empathy encourages moral actions, including the maintenance of equity and kindness to people in need (e.g., Batson, 2011; Batson et al., 2003; Batson & Shaw, 1991). At a macro level, key moments in a culture's moral development often follow a shift in popular empathy. For instance, Harriet Beecher Stowe's novel *Uncle Tom's Cabin*, which prompted widespread empathy for the struggles of slaves, also intensified support for the abolitionist movement of the 19th century (Appiah, 2010).

This and other work has inspired scientific accounts under which empathy provides a vital, evolutionarily old emotional foundation for moral action (De Waal, 2010) and the expansion of moral values (Pinker, 2011). On such accounts, social turmoil, such as political polarization, reflects people's failure to empathize with members of other groups (Trout, 2009), and remedying such problems requires either reinstating lost empathy or building empathic concern for ever wider swaths of the population (Krznaric, 2014; Rifkin, 2009; Singer, 2011).

More recently, however, a growing countercurrent has questioned the utility of empathy in driving moral action. This argument builds on the broader idea that emotions provide powerful but noisy inputs to people's moral calculus (Haidt, 2001). Affective reactions often tempt people to make judgments that are logically and morally indefensible. Such emotional static famously includes moral dumbfounding, under which people's experience of disgust causes them to judge others' actions as wrong when they have no rational basis for doing so (Cushman, Young, & Hauser, 2006). Emotion drives other irrational moral judgments, such as people's tendency to privilege physical force (a "hot" factor) over more important dimensions, such as harm, when judging the moral status of an action (Greene, 2014; Greene et al., 2009). Even incidental, morally irrelevant feelings alter moral judgment, further damaging the credibility of emotion in guiding a sense of right and wrong (Wheatley & Haidt, 2005).

In sum, although emotions play a *powerful* role in moral judgment, they need not play a *useful* role. Instead, capricious emotion-driven intuitions often attract people toward internally inconsistent and wrongheaded judgments. From a utilitarian perspective aimed at maximizing well-being, these biases render emotion a fundamentally mistaken moral engine (cf. Greene, 2014).

Does this criticism apply to empathy? In many ways, it does. Like other affective states, empathy arises in response to evocative experiences, often in noisy ways that hamper objectivity. For instance, people experience more empathy, and thus the moral obligation to help, in response to the *visible* suffering of others, as in the case of Baby Jessica described above. This empathy leads people to donate huge sums of money to help individuals whose stories they read about or see on television, while ignoring widespread misery that they could more efficaciously relieve (Genevsky, Västfjäll, Slovic, & Knutson, 2013; Slovic, 2007; Small & Loewenstein, 2003). Empathy also collapses reliably when sufferers and would-be empathizers differ along dimensions of race, politics, age, or even meaningless *de novo* group assignments (Cikara, Bruneau, & Saxe, 2011; Zaki & Cikara, 2015).

Even when people experience empathy, the causal link between affect and moral action can be circuitous and noisy. At an interindividual level, empathy fails to predict sensitivity to just versus unjust outcomes (Decety & Yoder, 2015). Worse, in some cases empathy inspires expressly unjust behavior. For instance, close connection with ingroup members can prompt aggression toward outgroup members (Gilead & Liberman, 2014; Waytz & Epley, 2012). Even when empathy generates rapport across group boundaries, it can do so at the cost of justice. Low-status group members who empathize with higher status individuals grow reticent to criticize unfair structural norms, such as unequal access to education and resources (Dixon, Tropp, Durrheim, & Tredoux, 2010; Saguy, Tausch, Dovidio, & Pratto, 2009). In these cases, empathy improves surface-level relations between groups at the cost of more meaningful social change (Zaki & Cikara, 2015).

Empathy thus falls prey to the same limitations as other emotions in driving moral behavior: It is hot-headed, short-sighted, and parochial. We would begrudge these qualities in policy makers trying to render the most good for the largest number of people. So why should people ever rely on empathy when making moral judgments?

Theoretical Stance

Empathy is not a perfect source of moral choice, but I think its recent critics have dis-

missed it too readily. I believe this for two reasons.

Empathy Is Motivated, and Limits on Empathy Are Not Stable

Critics of empathy characterize it as biased: responding to morally irrelevant content (e.g., visibility) while missing morally relevant content (e.g., total suffering). Must moral "mistakes" like these always characterize empathy? In order to answer this question, we must first ask another: To what extent can people control their experience of empathy? Psychological theory and lay intuition converge to suggest that empathy tends to fall out of our control. Imagine, for instance, witnessing someone suffer a horrific industrial accident. In cases such as this, it doesn't seem as though observers select their level of empathy; vicarious distress simply *happens to* them. The assertion that empathy is automatic runs through the philosophy (Goldman, 2006), psychology (Hatfield, Forbes, & Rapson, 2013), and neuroscience (Gallese, 2007) of empathy (for a comprehensive review of this account, see Zaki, 2014).

If empathy is automatic, then people can control neither when they feel empathy nor when they do not. Under such a state of affairs, the biases that characterize empathy—such as ingroup favoritism—are as uncontrollable as the experience of empathy itself. This assumption underlies arguments for minimizing the role of empathy in moral decision making. For instance, Greene (2014) suggests that "automatic empathy programs" lead people toward poor moral choices and that "it would be foolish to let the inflexible operating characteristics of our empathy gizmos serve as foundational moral principles" (p. 264).

This take on empathy reflects a broader view of emotions as fundamentally distinct from and inaccessible to cognition. This model is at least as old as Plato's account of reason and passion. It is also incorrect. Decades of data from affective science demonstrate that logic and emotion interact pervasively. Moral theorists focus largely on one side of this interaction: ways that emotions inadvertently color thinking, producing irrational but strongly held judgments. The opposite causal direction—from thinking to affect—matters just as much. Cognition takes part in "constructing" the emotions that people feel (Barrett, 2013; Schachter & Singer, 1962) and judge others to feel (Ong, Zaki, & Goodman, 2015). Cognition–affect interactions also characterize emotion regulation, through which people alter their feelings in response to their goals (Gross, 2015; Inzlicht, Bartholow, & Hirsh, 2015; Ochsner, Silvers, & Buhle, 2012).

Emotion regulation often comprises people's attempts to feel better by reducing negative affect or maximizing positive affect, but people sometimes want to feel bad. For instance, prior to conflicts, people up-regulate their experience of anger, and, prior to making a request for support, they up-regulate sadness (Tamir, 2009). In these contexts, negative emotions help people accomplish their goals and thus become the target of regulation strategies. "Social" emotions such as gratitude, righteous anger, and guilt are particularly useful in driving interpersonal outcomes such as cooperation (DeSteno, 2015; Trivers, 1971). As such, people regulate their experience of these states in response to social goals.

I propose that empathy follows suit. Instead of succumbing to their experience (or nonexperience) of empathy, people often *choose* to engage with or avoid others' emotions. This choice can be conscious or not, and—like other forms of emotion regulation—it (1) reflects people's goals in a given context and (2) can be carried out through multiple strategies (for a thorough review of this model, see Zaki, 2014).

A motivated account recasts the "empathic failures" described earlier. When people exhibit blunted empathy to strangers or outgroup members, this does not mean that they are *incapable* of empathizing; instead they might be *unmotivated* to do so (Keysers & Gazzola, 2014). This is important because it suggests that limits of empathy are not "baked in" to the nature of empathy itself. Instead, they signal local features of a situation that reduce people's propensity to empathize. To the extent that this is the case, empathic limits can be overcome by increasing motivation to empathy, and empathy can be harnessed to build moral concern on a broad scale (this is discussed further in the later section on extension and expansion).

Empathy-Based Action Confers Unique Benefits

If empathy is motivated, people should be capable of empathizing in "smarter" ways that supersede group boundaries and other morally irrelevant factors. Still, empathy will always be subject to some noise and cannot match the optimal moral principles that emerge from a utilitarian approach (Singer, 2015). Empathy will never provide anyone with a perfect moral compass. As such, even if empathic limits can be overcome, why bother?

One important reason is that prosocial and moral action driven by empathy might differ from action based solely on principle. These differences confer at least some advantages to empathy-based action, many of which reflect the added force emotions lend to action.

First, emotional goals often take precedent over nonemotional goals, and people pursue such goals with urgency and immediacy. Principles are difficult to abide on an empty stomach or under other states that tax people's psychological energy. For instance, cognitive load interferes with utilitarian moral judgments (Greene, Morelli, Lowenberg, Nystrom, & Cohen, 2008). Emotions, by contrast, guide behavior efficiently and in ways that are robust to limits on people's cognitive bandwith. As such, to the extent that people can tune empathy to match their principles, they gain access to a "hot," emotional engine for powering prosocial behavior (DeSteno, 2009).

Second, emotion-based moral behavior might confer benefits that other moral behaviors do not. Prosocial actions "help the helper," such that acting kindly renders people healthier and longer-lived (Dunn, Aknin, & Norton, 2014; Thoits & Hewitt, 2001). These benefits likely reflect boosts in subjective well being—such as increased happiness and decreased stress—that prosociality provides (Dunn, Aknin, & Norton, 2008; Zaki & Mitchell, 2013). I propose that these boosts most often follow prosocial acts driven by passion, not principle. The benefits of emotion-driven moral action likely transcend single individuals. Recipients of others' support, for instance, benefit most from emotion-driven help, and emotion strengthens the reputational and relational benefits associated with helping others.

In sum, emotions in general—and empathy in particular—add weight both to the efficiency of prosocial actions and to their benefits. If this is the case, then cultivating empathy-based morality stands as a worthwhile goal.

Evidence

Decades of research support a motivated model of empathy (see Zaki, 2014, for review). In particular, it is clear that situational factors reliably increase and decrease people's desire to empathize. This is reflected across self-reports, behavior, and brain activity (Cameron & Payne, 2011; Keysers & Gazzola, 2014; Tamir, 2013). When empathy is goal-inconsistent—for instance, when it carries heavy financial or emotional costs or interferes with people's ability to compete with others—people avoid empathy-provoking situations and cues (Davis et al., 1999; Pancer, McMullen, Kabatoff, Johnson, & Pond, 1979; Shaw, Batson, & Todd, 1994).

By contrast, manipulations that render empathy more goal-relevant cause people to expand their empathic experience. People who are lonely or desire social connection, as compared with people who are more socially "sated," play closer attention to others' internal states (Gump & Kulik, 1997; Pickett, Gardner, & Knowles, 2004). Likewise, people who believe that empathy is socially desirable or common among their peers also act empathically themselves, even toward outgroup members (Nook, Ong, Morelli, Mitchell, & Zaki, 2017; Tarrant, Dazeley, & Cottom, 2009; Thomas & Maio, 2008). In these cases, goal relevance increases *empathic effort,* or the extent to which people pursue empathy. Empathy and its consequences—including prosocial and kind action—follow suit.

Interestingly, the very notion that empathy is out of people's control might hinder empathic effort. This follows from the broader idea of "lay theories," or beliefs people hold about psychological constructs.

Dweck (2006; Dweck & Leggett, 1988) has demonstrated that people vary in their beliefs about whether characteristics such as intelligence, prejudice, and personality are "fixed" and out of their control or "malleable" and within their control. People who hold malleable, as compared with fixed, theories embrace challenges and difficulties as opportunities to grow valued psychological skills (Blackwell, Trzesniewski, & Dweck, 2007; Dweck, Chiu, & Hong, 1995; Rattan & Dweck, 2010; Yeager, Trzesniewski, & Dweck, 2012).

Recently, we found that lay theories concerning empathy likewise affect empathic motivation (Schumann, Zaki, & Dweck, 2014). People who held a malleable empathic theory—or in whom we induced such a theory—exhibited more willingness to empathize than people holding a fixed lay theory. This difference was especially stark in cases in which people might not otherwise feel motivated to empathize, such as intergroup settings or when empathy promises to be painful.

These data dovetail to support the idea that empathy is far from automatic and often reflects people's motives to connect with or avoid others' emotions. This further suggests, crucially, that features of empathy that often render it a poor moral compass can be reversed. Increasing empathic motives can also expand the *scope* of empathy, even to cases in which it typically fails.

Evidence also supports the contention that empathy lends weight to moral actions and the benefits they confer. Consider the effect of prosociality on well-being (Dunn et al., 2014; Thoits et al., 2001). Kindness pays dividends to those who engage in it, but more recent work suggests that such benefits are strongest for individuals who are affectively engaged in their prosocial acts. For instance, volunteering decreases mortality risks in older adults, but only if their service is driven by "other-oriented" motives, such as empathic concern for people in need (Konrath, Fuhrel-Forbis, Lou, & Brown, 2012). Likewise, college students experience increased happiness and reduced stress after providing practical help to others, but these effects are strongest in people who empathically engage with the targets of their help (Morelli, Lee, Arnn, & Zaki, 2015).

Empathy-based prosociality maximally benefits not only helpers but also the recipients of their help. When people turn to each other under both difficult and happy circumstances, they seek out not only concrete help but also emotional connection (Rimé, 2007; Zaki & Williams, 2013). As such, people feel closer to support providers who experience and exhibit empathy, as opposed to those who provide less emotionally responsive support (Gable, Gonzaga, & Strachman, 2006; Gable & Reis, 2010).

Finally, emotion serves as a broader social signal about the meaning of prosocial actions. Groups elevate the moral status of people who act prosocially (Hardy & Van Vugt, 2006). Here, too, emotion matters. Individuals who express emotion when acting prosocially are perceived by others as more genuinely motivated to help others, further building the social capital kindness provides (Barasch, Levine, Berman, & Small, 2014).

Broadly, this work demonstrates that people benefit most not from moral acts alone, but rather from those that are imbued with affective force. Empathy is a messy source of prosociality, and at a broad policy level utilitarian principles provide a clearer moral compass than affect. But at an individual level, not only can people flexibly align empathy with their principles, but doing so also renders their subsequent moral action more powerful.

Extension and Expansion

Former President Obama routinely refers to an "empathy deficit" that threatens the cohesion of our social fabric (Obama, 2006). Consistent with his view, college students' self-reported empathy has dwindled over the last 30 years (Konrath, O'Brien, & Hsing, 2011). Empathy deficits pervade crucial social problems, such as the increasing polarization that characterizes our political system (Prior, 2013), the rise of bullying among adolescents (Wang, Iannotti, & Nansel, 2009), and medical professionals' lack of connection to their patients (Haque & Waytz, 2012).

The ideas laid out above offer two broad points about this state of affairs. First, they make novel suggestions about *how* we can address the empathy deficit (cf. Zaki & Cikara, 2015). A small but growing number of interventions focus on building empathy across settings including medical training (Riess, Kelley, Bailey, Dunn, & Phillips, 2012), education (Şahin, 2012), conflict resolution (Todd & Galinsky, 2014), and the treatment of clinical populations in which empathy is impaired, such as in autism spectrum disorders (Golan & Baron-Cohen, 2006; Hadwin, Baron-Cohen, Howlin, & Hill, 1996). The majority of these interventions focus on two strategies: building empathic skills, such as emotion recognition, and inducing people to think more about social targets. This strategy is effective overall (van Berkhout & Malouff, 2016), but a motivated model of empathy suggests that it is also incomplete. In many cases, people fail to empathize not because they are incapable of doing so but because they are unmotivated to share, understand, or generate concern for others' internal lives. As such, interventions should complement training in empathic skills with "psychological levers" (Miller & Prentice, 2010) that can build people's desire to empathize in the first place.

Second, the work covered here offers evidence about *why* we should care about empathic deficits. On some accounts, a lack of empathy—although alarming—might be inconsequential. This conclusion is predicated on the idea that empathy is at best a dubious source of moral behavior and at worst a barrier to broad moral progress (Bloom, 2014; Greene, 2014; Prinz, 2011b). Here I propose that this perspective obscures both people's flexibility to grow their empathy beyond its typical limits and also the unique power of empathy in rendering moral acts more beneficial.

Empathy is noisy, but scientists should not be so quick to dismiss it as a moral force. Although unstable when compared with principles, emotion can lend those principles deeper psychological meaning.

REFERENCES

Appiah, A. (2010). *The honor code: How moral revolutions happen.* New York: Norton.
Barasch, A., Levine, E. E., Berman, J. Z., & Small, D. A. (2014). Selfish or selfless?: On the signal value of emotion in altruistic behavior.

Journal of Personality and Social Psychology, 107(3), 393.

Barrett, L. F. (2013). Psychological construction: The Darwinian approach to the science of emotion. *Emotion Review, 5*(4), 379–389.

Batson, C. D. (1991). *The altruism question: Toward a social-psychological answer* Hillsdale, NJ: Erlbaum.

Batson, C. D. (2011). *Altruism in humans.* Oxford, UK: Oxford University Press.

Batson, C. D., Lishner, D. A., Carpenter, A., Dulin, L., Harjusola-Webb, S., Stocks, E. L., . . . Sampat, B. (2003). " . . . As you would have them do unto you": Does imagining yourself in the other's place stimulate moral action? *Personality and Social Psychology Bulletin, 29*(9), 1190–1201.

Batson, C. D., & Shaw, L. (1991). Evidence for altruism: Toward a pluralism of prosocial motives. *Psychological Inquiry, 2*(2), 107–122.

Blackwell, L. S., Trzesniewski, K. H., & Dweck, C. S. (2007). Implicit theories of intelligence predict achievement across an adolescent transition: A longitudinal study and an intervention. *Child Development, 78*(1), 246–263.

Blair, R. J. (2005). Responding to the emotions of others: Dissociating forms of empathy through the study of typical and psychiatric populations. *Consciousness and Cognition, 14*(4), 698–718.

Bloom, P. (2013, May 20). The baby in the well: The case against empathy. *The New Yorker,* p. 20.

Bloom, P. (2014, September 10). Against empathy. *Boston Review.*

Cameron, C. D., & Payne, B. K. (2011). Escaping affect: How motivated emotion regulation creates insensitivity to mass suffering. *Journal of Personality and Social Psychology, 100*(1), 1.

Cikara, M., Bruneau, E., & Saxe, R. (2011). Us and them: Intergroup failures in empathy. *Current Directions in Psychological Science, 20,* 149–153.

Cushman, F., Young, L., & Hauser, M. (2006). The role of conscious reasoning and intuition in moral judgment: Testing three principles of harm. *Psychological Science, 17*(12), 1082–1089.

Davis, M. (1994). *Empathy: A social psychological approach.* New York: Westview Press.

Davis, M., Mitchell, K. V., Hall, J. A., Lothert, J., Snapp, T., & Meyer, M. (1999). Empathy, expectations, and situational preferences: Personality influences on the decision to participate in volunteer helping behaviors. *Journal of Personality, 67*(3), 469–503.

De Waal, F. (2010). *The age of empathy: Nature's lessons for a kinder society.* New York: Random House.

Decety, J., & Jackson, P. L. (2004). The functional architecture of human empathy. *Behavioral and Cognitive Neuroscience Reviews, 3*(2), 71–100.

Decety, J., & Yoder, K. J. (2015). Empathy and motivation for justice: Cognitive empathy and concern, but not emotional empathy, predict sensitivity to injustice for others. *Social Neuroscience, 11*(1), 1–14.

DeSteno, D. (2009). Social emotions and intertemporal choice, "hot" mechanisms for building social and economic capital. *Current Directions in Psychological Science, 18*(5), 280–284.

DeSteno, D. (2015). Compassion and altruism: How our minds determine who is worthy of help. *Current Opinion in Behavioral Sciences, 3,* 80–83.

Dixon, J., Tropp, L. R., Durrheim, K., & Tredoux, C. (2010). "Let them eat harmony": Prejudice-reduction strategies and attitudes of historically disadvantaged groups. *Current Directions in Psychological Science, 19*(2), 76–80.

Dunn, E., Aknin, L. B., & Norton, M. I. (2008). Spending money on others promotes happiness. *Science, 319*(5870), 1687–1688.

Dunn, E., Aknin, L., & Norton, M. (2014). Prosocial spending and happiness: Using money to benefit others pays off. *Current Directions in Psychological Science, 23*(2), 41–47.

Dweck, C. S. (2006). *Mindset: The new psychology of success.* New York: Random House.

Dweck, C. S., Chiu, C. Y., & Hong, Y. (1995). Implicit theories and their role in judgments and reactions: A word from two perspectives. *Psychological Inquiry, 6*(4), 267–285.

Dweck, C. S., & Leggett, E. L. (1988). A social-cognitive approach to motivation and personality. *Psychological Review, 95*(2), 256–273.

Gable, S. L., Gonzaga, G. C., & Strachman, A. (2006). Will you be there for me when things go right?: Supportive responses to positive event disclosures. *Journal of Personality and Social Psychology, 91*(5), 904.

Gable, S. L., & Reis, H. T. (2010). Good news!: Capitalizing on positive events in an interpersonal context. *Advances in Experimental Social Psychology, 42,* 195–257.

Galinsky, A. D., & Moskowitz, G. B. (2000). Perspective-taking: Decreasing stereotype expression, stereotype accessibility, and in-group favoritism. *Journal of Personality and Social Psychology, 78*(4), 708.

Gallese, V. (2007). Before and below "theory of mind": Embodied simulation and the neural correlates of social cognition. *Philosophical Transactions of the Royal Society of London B: Biological Sciences, 362*(1480), 659–669.

Genevsky, A., Västfjäll, D., Slovic, P., & Knutson, B. (2013). Neural underpinnings of the identifiable victim effect: Affect shifts preferences for giving. *Journal of Neuroscience, 33*(43), 17188–17196.

Gilead, M., & Liberman, N. (2014). We take care of our own: Caregiving salience increases out-group bias in response to out-group threat. *Psychological Science, 25*(7), 1380–1387.

Golan, O., & Baron-Cohen, S. (2006). Systemizing empathy: Teaching adults with Asperger syndrome or high-functioning autism to recognize complex emotions using interactive multimedia. *Development and Psychopathology, 18*(2), 591–617.

Goldman, A. I. (2006). *Simulating minds: The philosophy, psychology, and neuroscience of mindreading.* New York: Oxford University Press.

Greene, J. (2014). *Moral tribes: Emotion, reason and the gap between us and them.* New York: Penguin Press.

Greene, J., Cushman, F. A., Stewart, L. E., Lowenberg, K., Nystrom, L. E., & Cohen, J. D. (2009). Pushing moral buttons: The interaction between personal force and intention in moral judgment. *Cognition, 111*(3), 364–371.

Greene, J., Morelli, S. A., Lowenberg, K., Nystrom, L. E., & Cohen, J. D. (2008). Cognitive load selectively interferes with utilitarian moral judgment. *Cognition, 107*(3), 1144–1154.

Gross, J. J. (2015). Emotion regulation: Current status and future prospects. *Psychological Inquiry, 26*(1), 1–26.

Gump, B. B., & Kulik, J. A. (1997). Stress, affiliation, and emotional contagion. *Journal of Personality and Social Psychology, 72*(2), 305.

Hadwin, J., Baron-Cohen, S., Howlin, P., & Hill, K. (1996). Can we teach children with autism to understand emotion, belief, or pretense? *Development and Psychopathology, 8,* 345–365.

Haidt, J. (2001). The emotional dog and its rational tail: A social intuitionist approach to moral judgment. *Psychological Review, 108*(4), 814–834.

Haque, O. S., & Waytz, A. (2012). Dehumanization in medicine: Causes, solutions, and functions. *Perspectives on Psychological Science, 7*(2), 176–186.

Hardy, C. L., & Van Vugt, M. (2006). Nice guys finish first: The competitive altruism hypothesis. *Personality and Social Psychology Bulletin, 32*(10), 1402–1413.

Hatfield, E., Forbes, M., & Rapson, R. (2013). Emotional contagion as a precursor to collective emotions. In C. von Scheve & M. Salmela (Eds.), *Collective emotions.* Oxford, UK: Oxford University Press.

Inzlicht, M., Bartholow, B. D., & Hirsh, J. B. (2015). Emotional foundations of cognitive control. *Trends in Cognitive Sciences, 19*(3), 126–132.

Keysers, C., & Gazzola, V. (2014). Dissociating the ability and propensity for empathy. *Trends in Cognitive Sciences, 18*(4), 163–166.

Konrath, S., Fuhrel-Forbis, A., Lou, A., & Brown, S. (2012). Motives for volunteering are associated with mortality risk in older adults. *Health Psychology, 31*(1), 87.

Konrath, S., O'Brien, E., & Hsing, C. (2011). Changes in dispositional empathy in American college students over time: A meta-analysis. *Personality and Social Psychology Review, 15*(2), 180–198.

Krznaric, R. (2014). *Empathy: A handbook for revolution.* New York: Random House.

Lamm, C., Decety, J., & Singer, T. (2011). Meta-analytic evidence for common and distinct neural networks associated with directly experienced pain and empathy for pain. *NeuroImage, 54*(3), 2492–2502.

Lickel, B., Miller, N., Stenstrom, D. M., Denson, T. F., & Schmader, T. (2006). Vicarious retribution: The role of collective blame in intergroup aggression. *Personality and Social Psychology Review, 10*(4), 372–390.

Miller, D., & Prentice, D. (2010). Psychological levers of behavior change. In E. Shafir (Ed.), *Behavioral foundations of policy.* New York: Russell Sage Foundation.

Morelli, S., Lee, I., Arnn, M., & Zaki, J. 2015). Emotional and instrumental support provision interact to predict well-being. *Emotion, 15*(4), 484–493.

Morelli, S., Lieberman, M., & Zaki, J. (2015). The emerging study of positive empathy. *Social and Personality Psychology Compass, 9*(2), 57–68.

Morelli, S., Sacchet, M. D., & Zaki, J. (2014). Common and distinct neural correlates of personal and vicarious reward: A quantitative meta-analysis. *NeuroImage, 112,* 244–253.

Nook, E., Ong, D., Morelli, S., Mitchell, J., & Zaki, J. (2017). *Prosocial conformity: Social norms motivate broad generosity and empathy.* Manuscript submitted for publication.

Obama, B. (2006). *Commencement address.* Northwestern University, Evanston, IL.

Ochsner, K., Silvers, J., & Buhle, J. (2012). Functional imaging studies of emotion regulation: A synthetic review and evolving model of the cognitive control of emotion. *Annals of the New York Academy of Sciences, 1251,* E1–E24.

Ong, D., Zaki, J., & Goodman, N. (2015). Affective cognition: Exploring lay theories of emotion. *Cognition, 143,* 141–162.

Pancer, S. M., McMullen, L. M., Kabatoff, R.

A., Johnson, K. G., & Pond, C. A. (1979). Conflict and avoidance in the helping situation. *Journal of Personality and Social Psychology, 37*(8), 1406–1411.

Pickett, C. L., Gardner, W. L., & Knowles, M. (2004). Getting a cue: The need to belong and enhanced sensitivity to social cues. *Personality and Social Psychology Bulletin, 30*(9), 1095–1107.

Pinker, S. (2011). *The better angels of our nature: Why violence has declined.* New York: Viking.

Prinz, J. (2011a). Against empathy. *Southern Journal of Philosophy, 49*(1), 214–233.

Prinz, J. (2011b). Is empathy necessary for morality? In A. Coplan & P. Goldie (Eds.), *Empathy: Philosophical and psychological perspectives* (pp. 211–229). New York: Oxford University Press.

Prior, M. (2013). Media and political polarization. *Annual Review of Political Science, 16,* 101–127.

Rattan, A., & Dweck, C. S. (2010). Who confronts prejudice?: The role of implicit theories in the motivation to confront prejudice. *Psychological Science, 21*(7), 952–959.

Riess, H., Kelley, J. M., Bailey, R. W., Dunn, E. J., & Phillips, M. (2012). Empathy training for resident physicians: A randomized controlled trial of a neuroscience-informed curriculum. *Journal of General Internal Medicine, 27*(10), 1280–1286.

Rifkin, J. (2009). *The empathic civilization: The race to global consciousness in a world in crisis.* New York: Penguin Press.

Rimé, B. (2007). Interpersonal emotion regulation. In J. Gross (Ed.), *Handbook of emotion regulation* (pp. 466–485). New York: Guilford Press.

Saguy, T., Tausch, N., Dovidio, J. F., & Pratto, F. (2009). The irony of harmony: Intergroup contact can produce false expectations for equality. *Psychological Science, 20*(1), 114–121.

Şahin, M. (2012). An investigation into the efficiency of empathy training program on preventing bullying in primary schools. *Children and Youth Services Review, 34*(7), 1325–1330.

Schachter, S., & Singer, J. E. (1962). Cognitive, social, and physiological determinants of emotion state. *Psychological Review, 69,* 379–399.

Schumann, K., Zaki, J., & Dweck, C. S. (2014). Addressing the empathy deficit: Beliefs about the malleability of empathy predict effortful responses when empathy is challenging. *Journal of Personality and Social Psychology, 107*(3), 475–493.

Shaw, L., Batson, C. D., & Todd, R. M. (1994). Empathy avoidance: Forestalling feeling for another in order to escape the motivational consequences. *Journal of Personality and Social Psychology, 67*(5), 879–887.

Singer, P. (2011). *The expanding circle: Ethics, evolution, and moral progress.* Princeton, NJ: Princeton University Press.

Singer, P. (2015). *The most good you can do: How effective altruism is changing ideas about living ethically.* New Haven, CT: Yale University Press.

Slovic, P. (2007). If I look at the mass I will never act: Psychic numbing and genocide. *Judgment and Decision Making, 2*(2), 79–95.

Small, D. A., & Loewenstein, G. (2003). Helping a victim or helping the victim: Altruism and identifiability. *Journal of Risk and Uncertainty, 26*(1), 5–16.

Smith, A. (2002). *The theory of moral sentiments.* Cambridge, UK: Cambridge University Press. (Original work published 1790)

Tamir, M. (2009). What do people want to feel and why?: Pleasure and utility in emotion regulation. *Current Directions in Psychological Science, 18*(2), 101–105.

Tamir, M. (2013). *What do people want to feel in intractable conflicts?* Paper presented at the meeting of the Society for Experimental Social Psychology, Berkeley, CA.

Tarrant, M., Dazeley, S., & Cottom, T. (2009). Social categorization and empathy for outgroup members. *British Journal of Social Psychology, 48*(3), 427–446.

Thoits, P. A., & Hewitt, L. N. (2001). Volunteer work and well-being. *Journal of Health and Social Behavior, 42*(2), 115–131.

Thomas, G., & Maio, G. R. (2008). Man, I feel like a woman: When and how gender-role motivation helps mind-reading. *Journal of Personality and Social Psychology, 95*(5), 1165.

Todd, A. R., & Galinsky, A. D. (2014). Perspective-taking as a strategy for improving intergroup relations: Evidence, mechanisms, and qualifications. *Social and Personality Psychology Compass, 8*(7), 374–387.

Trivers, R. (1971). The evolution of reciprocal altruism. *Quarterly Review of Biology, 46,* 35–57.

Trout, J. (2009). *The empathy gap: Building bridges to the good life and the good society.* New York: Penguin Press.

van Berkhout, E., & Malouff, J. (2016). The efficacy of empathy training: A meta-analysis of randomized controlled trials. *Journal of Counseling Psychology, 63*(1), 32–41.

Wang, J., Iannotti, R. J., & Nansel, T. R. (2009). School bullying among adolescents in the United States: Physical, verbal, relational, and cyber. *Journal of Adolescent Health, 45*(4), 368–375.

Waytz, A., & Epley, N. (2012). Social connection

enables dehumanization. *Journal of Experimental Social Psychology, 48*(1), 70–76.

Wheatley, T., & Haidt, J. (2005). Hypnotic disgust makes moral judgments more severe. *Psychological Science, 16*(10), 780–784.

Yeager, D. S., Trzesniewski, K. H., & Dweck, C. S. (2012). An implicit theories of personality intervention reduces adolescent aggression in response to victimization and exclusion. *Child Development, 84*(3), 970–988.

Zaki, J. (2014). Empathy: A motivated account. *Psychological Bulletin, 140*(6), 1608–1647.

Zaki, J., & Cikara, M. (2015). Addressing empathic failures. *Current Directions in Psychological Science, 24*(6), 471–476.

Zaki, J., & Mitchell, J. P. (2013). Intuitive prosociality. *Current Directions in Psychological Science, 22*(6), 466–470.

Zaki, J., & Ochsner, K. (2016). Empathy. In L. F. Barrett, M. Lewis, & J. Haviland-Jones (Eds.), *Handbook of emotions* (4th ed., pp. 871–884). New York: Guilford Press.

Zaki, J., & Williams, W. C. (2013). Interpersonal emotion regulation. *Emotion, 13*(5), 803–810.

CHAPTER 7

Moral Values and Motivations
How Special Are They?

Ryan Miller
Fiery Cushman

Does morality have specialized cognitive and neural processes?

Moral cognition—including the value of moral actions, outcomes, and their integration—is supported by domain-general cognitive and neural architecture tied to reward processing and economic decision making.

Moral values are central to human identity. Charles Darwin considered the human moral sense, or "conscience," to be the single most important attribute distinguishing us from other animals (1872), and recent research suggests that the particular constellation of moral traits you possess is a big part of what makes you "you" (Strohminger & Nichols, 2014). Given this privileged status, we ask a simple question: Is there something special that makes moral value different from other kinds of values that humans hold? Is the way it is acquired, stored, or implemented in the brain fundamentally special? Or might the difference be less sharp, with a common system (or systems) handling value of all kinds?

In many ways, the moral value we attach to particular behaviors or social outcomes, such as generosity, honesty, or fairness, can be contrasted with other types of values, such as a love of money, chocolate cake, or Mozart. We expect others to have particular moral values—and punish them when they don't. In contrast, we don't punish them for hating Mozart (at least not often). Similarly, we feel guilt or shame when our own actions are inconsistent with our moral values, but we don't usually feel guilt or shame when we violate our food preferences and try a new dish. Moral values also tend to be sacred, meaning people are unwilling to place a material price tag on them or openly trade them against secular goods (Tetlock, Kristel, Beth, Green, & Lerner, 2000).

A closer look, however, reveals broad similarities between moral and nonmoral value. Both motivate us to obtain certain goals or desirable outcomes—such as the welfare of sick children or the newest technological gadget—and we experience pleasure in both cases when we succeed. Both types of value are also heavily influenced by the specific culture in which we live; just as local customs shape our tastes in music, food, or beauty, they also shape how we view harm, fairness, and charitable obligations (Henrich et al., 2001; Lamba & Mace, 2013). Our valuation of morally laden acts, such as sacrificing one individual to save others, also appears to be susceptible to many of the same biases that plague the valuation of monetary goods during economic decision making (Rai & Holyoak, 2010). And, as it happens, moral values *can* be traded off against each other and, with the right rhetorical gloss, even against material interests (Tetlock, 2003). Many individuals are also perfectly willing to bargain sacred values for monetary gain in practice (especially when they think no one is watching), as scandal-prone politicians often remind us.

Drawing on evidence from cognitive neuroscience, neuroeconomics, and social psychology, we argue that these similarities are more than superficial coincidences. Rather, they reflect a shared cognitive and neural architecture underlying moral and nonmoral value. This is not to say, of course, that there is *nothing* special about moral values. The basic claim is that the *motivational,* and perhaps affective, aspects of moral value— those intrinsic feelings that make you *want* to help a charity and feel pleasure when you do or to avoid harming someone and feel bad when you don't—are encoded by a domain-general system that also represents and processes a host of nonmoral rewards and punishments. Furthermore, the process of moral learning, whereby we update the moral value that we assign to particular actions or behaviors, is likely to be supported by domain-general learning processes that have been consistently identified as important in learning the value of nonmoral goods and actions.

In the first part of this chapter, we look at four basic lines of research supporting this claim. First, we examine evidence that the subjective value (and disvalue) of morally relevant, prosocial (and antisocial) *outcomes* is encoded in the same brain regions as nonmoral rewards and punishments. We then consider how moral *action* values—such as those placed on generosity or nonviolence— might rely on the same cognitive and neural processes that support action valuation in nonmoral domains. Third, we look at how social reinforcers that are important to learning moral norms (such as average group behavior or expressions of approval and disgust) appear to update value representations in the brain via the same processes as nonsocial rewards and punishments. Fourth, we consider how these values influence moral judgment, including research that they are traded against each other in a way that resembles economic decision making. In the final section of the chapter, we highlight several important questions that should be addressed by future research.

Moral Value and Nonmoral Machinery

Outcome Value

The subjective values of a wide variety of pleasurable and aversive outcomes appear to be encoded in a common network of neural structures. The receipt of positive stimuli, such as food, sex, and money, is most prominently associated with activity in the ventral striatum (VS) and the medial orbitofrontal cortex (mOFC; Bartra, McGuire, & Kable, 2013; Kable & Glimcher, 2007; Liu, Hairston, Schrier, & Fan, 2011). Activity in the VS has been found to correlate with self-reported ratings of pleasure (Salimpoor, Benovoy, Larcher, Dagher, & Zatorre, 2011; Sescousse, Li, & Dreher, 2015), and activity in both the VS and mOFC during the passive viewing of items predicts subsequent choice of those same items (Levy, Lazzaro, Rutledge, & Glimcher, 2011). Aversive outcomes, on the other hand, are more often associated with activity in the anterior insula (AI) and anterior cingulate cortex (ACC). A large meta-analysis of reward-related studies found that the value of "negative rewards" (i.e., punishments) is preferentially encoded in the AI and ACC (Bartra et al., 2013), and activation in the AI correlates with the self-reported intensity of affective states (Zaki, Davis, & Ochsner, 2012). Both these regions are also central components of what has been dubbed the "pain matrix," a network of regions consistently involved in the subjective experience of pain (Davis, 2000).

Notably, a variety of social concerns (often referred to as "social preferences"; Fehr & Fischbacher, 2002) are also encoded in these very same regions (see Ruff & Fehr, 2014, for a review). For instance, the way that we value others' well-being looks very similar to the way we value our own. When good things happen to others—especially if we like them, or if they're similar to us—we show increased activity in overlapping regions of the VS (Mobbs et al., 2009). Watching others in pain, on the other hand, is associated with activity in the AI and ACC (Jackson, Brunet, Meltzoff, & Decety, 2006; Lamm, Nusbaum, Meltzoff, & Decety, 2007; Singer et al., 2004), and the magnitude of AI response predicts the willingness to reduce an ingroup member's pain by enduring pain oneself (Hein, Silani, Preuschoff, Batson, & Singer, 2010). Interestingly, and perhaps troublingly, the decision *not* to help an outgroup member is best predicted by VS activity, suggesting that taking pleasure in others' pain may be an important inhibitor of prosocial action.

The moral value of fairness is associated with similar neural signatures. One of the tools most commonly used to study fairness preferences in the lab is the Ultimatum Game. In this game, one player, the Decider, is endowed with an initial sum of money, and she has to decide how much of it to share with a second player, the Responder. If the Responder doesn't like the offer, he can reject it, and neither player gets anything. Responders who are offered a fair share are more likely to accept the offer, feel happier about it, and show increased activity in both mOFC and VS (Tabibnia, Satpute, & Lieberman, 2008). Unfair offers lead to increased AI activation, and the magnitude of this neural response predicts rejection of the offer (Sanfey, Rilling, Aronson, Nystrom, & Cohen, 2003). Of course, a fair offer is better than a low offer for the Responder, so preferences for fairness are necessarily confounded with self-interest in the Ultimatum Game.

A variety of other tasks provide even stronger evidence for the involvement of domain-general valuation mechanisms in the pure fairness motive. Individuals who passively view a series of variable monetary allocations to themselves and another study participant show increased reward-related activity in mOFC and VS when the two totals are brought closer together, regardless of who is getting the money that turn (Tricomi, Rangel, Camerer, & O'Doherty, 2010).

When making unilateral decisions about how to distribute money among themselves and others, participants show increased mOFC activity for equitable distributions and increased AI activation when making inequitable distributions (Zaki & Mitchell, 2011). Furthermore, the AI response during these trials predicts overall unwillingness to make inequitable decisions. Finally, and perhaps most pertinent to a discussion on morality, disinterested third parties making decisions about how to distribute money among *other* individuals also show insula activity when the proposed distribution is unfair, and this is related to both its rejection rate (Civai, Crescentini, Rustichini, & Rumiati, 2012; Corradi-Dell'Acqua, Civai, Rumiati, & Fink, 2013) and a willingness to pay money to create equality among the group (Dawes et al., 2012).

Researchers have also studied how the subjective value of mutual cooperation might be encoded in the brain. The standard method used in this literature is the Prisoner's Dilemma game, in which two partners are each privately faced with the decision to either "cooperate" or "defect." Cooperation, which involves giving up a little so that your partner gains a lot, is obviously costly for the cooperator, but it leads to the greatest group benefit if both partners do it. On any given trial, however, an individual can do even better for herself if she defects (i.e. contributes nothing) while her partner cooperates. Out of the four possible combinations of cooperation and defection, mutual cooperation leads to the highest activity in reward-related regions (including the VS and mOFC; Rilling et al., 2002). Interestingly, finding out that the other person cooperated when you defected is associated with the lowest activity in these regions, despite the fact that it provides the highest monetary payout, underscoring the power of social consequences to modulate neural representations of reward.

Action Value

In the previous section, we covered several instances in which the subjective value of morally relevant outcomes appears to be represented in domain-general regions that also process nonmoral rewards. Many times when we talk about moral values, however, we do not simply mean the value that we place on states of affairs out in the world, such as whether two people have an equal amount of money or whether a friend is experiencing pleasure or pain. Rather, we refer to the value (or disvalue) we place on particular *actions* with social consequences, such as charitable giving or not harming others. Is there reason to believe that these moral "action values" might also supported by a more domain-general cognitive and neural architecture?

To answer this question, we should first clarify what nonmoral action values are and how they might be derived by learning processes in a normal environment of rewards and punishments. An action value is a motivational construct that represents the expected future reward conditioned upon choosing an action, and it is often based on the reward history of prior choices in relevantly similar circumstances. For instance, if a rat receives cheese every time it presses a lever, it will come to assign a high action value to lever-pressing, and it will be more likely to press the lever in the future. (The magnitude of this value will, of course, depend on just how much the rat likes the cheese.)

In environments in which action—outcome contingencies are relatively stable, this type of learning is very useful and can lead to benefits in computational efficiency and speed during future decision making. By storing values directly on actions, the actor doesn't need to reference an internal model of the relationships between actions and the particular outcomes they lead to. Instead, it simply performs the action with the highest value. For this reason, learning and decision-making programs that rely on cached action values are often referred to as "model free," whereas those that choose actions by searching over an internal model of the world are referred to as "model-based" (Dayan & Niv, 2008). There is good evidence that humans naturally employ both of types of decision making (Daw, Gershman, Seymour, Dayan, & Dolan, 2011), and they seem to be supported at least in part by dissociable neural systems (Gläscher, Daw, Dayan, & O'Doherty, 2010).

One interesting feature of action values is that, under the right circumstances, they can continue to influence behavior *even when the associated outcome is no longer valuable*. For instance, rats who learn to press a lever for food will continue to press the lever even after they are full, provided training has been extensive enough (Dickinson, 1985). Though this insensitivity to devaluation is typically discussed in the context of drug addiction and compulsive behaviors in humans (Gillan et al., 2014; Schwabe, Dickinson, & Wolf, 2011), it has also been demonstrated in healthy adults using a task analogous to rat devaluation paradigms (Tricomi, Balleine, & O'Doherty, 2009).

Intriguingly, we also see instances of a similar phenomenon in the domain of morality. Consider the act of charitable giving, which has been found to be driven by a mix of two motives (Andreoni, 1990). On the one hand, you may give money because you value the welfare of the charity, often referred to as altruistic giving. On the other hand, you may give money because you value (or derive utility from) the act of giving itself. This motive has been termed "warm glow" because of the positive feelings it engenders in the giver. How do we know warm glow exists? Individuals feel better when they are actively giving the money themselves rather than passively transferring it (Harbaugh, Mayr, & Burghart, 2007), personal giving is not crowded out by external sources of aid (Eckel, Grossman, & Johnston, 2005), and individuals continue to give even when they know their donation is completely ineffectual (Crumpler & Grossman, 2008). This insensitivity to changes in the utility of the donation mirrors what we see in devaluation paradigms and hints at the influence of a positive "action value" attached to charitable giving.

Where might this action value come from? One possibility is that being embedded in a generally cooperative society teaches us that prosocial, cooperative behavior is actually in our long-term best interest (Peysakhovich & Rand, 2015; Rand et al., 2014). By continually having our cooperative acts positively reinforced, we come to place a high value on prosocial action, just like the cheese-loving rat places a high value on lever pressing. In a study testing this idea, participants who were first assigned to a cooperative environment in which it paid to be nice were subsequently more likely to donate money to an anonymous individual (with no possibility of reciprocation) than participants who were first assigned to a more competitive environment in which few people cooperated (Peysakhovich & Rand, 2015). This suggests that the high value these cooperative individuals learned to place on prosocial action in the first phase "spilled over" into the second phase, even though there was no longer any rational self-benefit.

We also find evidence of the same dissociation between action and outcome values in cases of aversion to antisocial action. Cushman, Gray, Gaffey, and Mendes (2012) brought participants into the lab and asked them to perform several pseudo-violent actions, such as slamming the head of a lifelike baby doll against a table or hitting a realistic-looking artificial leg with a hammer. Despite knowledge that these actions could cause no harm, participants showed significant signs of physiological aversion (measured by peripheral vasoconstriction) when simply thinking about performing these actions. Furthermore, these physiological changes were greater than in either a control group that performed metabolically matched actions or a witness group that watched someone else perform the same actions. People also report that they would feel uncomfortable performing pseudo-violent actions in more natural contexts, such as stabbing a fellow actor in the neck with a retractable stage knife as part of a play (Miller, Hannikainen, & Cushman, 2014). These data suggest that the motoric properties of canonically violent actions (such as hitting, stabbing, and shooting), which usually cause substantial harm, can acquire a negative value that is sufficient to trigger an aversive response even after the harmful outcome has been removed.

Although multiple theoretical accounts have emerged in recent years detailing how model-free learning algorithms might shape both prosocial (Gęsiarz & Crockett, 2015) and antisocial (Crockett, 2013; Cushman, 2013) behavior and moral judgment, few, if any, studies have attempted to directly compare the neural circuits involved in the model-free learning of both moral and nonmoral action values. Several studies do, however, suggest that the positive values attached to prosocial actions and the negative values attached to antisocial actions are represented in many of the same reward-related brain regions that we have previously discussed. The warm glow associated with the prosocial act of giving to a charity, for instance, appears to be localized to the VS (Harbaugh et al., 2007). Studies on violent behaviors are a bit more difficult to interpret, in part because they have not isolated the violent act from its harmful outcomes. Nevertheless, one study found that the aversiveness of imagined harmful actions, such as forcibly removing organs from a young child, was encoded in (mid-)insula and the ACC, and functional connectivity analyses suggest that the information in the ACC was passed to the mOFC during moral judgment (Hutcherson, Montaser-Kouhsari, Woodward, & Rangel, 2015). In another study, the aversiveness of up-close-and-personal harmful actions tracked activity in the amygdala, and this appraisal was integrated into an overall moral value representation in the mOFC (Shenhav & Greene, 2014). The amygdala is important in learning to avoid negative outcomes (Delgado, Jou, LeDoux, & Phelps, 2009) and could here represent the learned association between violent actions and the harm that they typically cause (Blair, 2007). Future studies will be necessary to obtain a more fine-grained picture of how action and outcome values are independently represented in these regions.

Feedback and Learning

So far, we have discussed the various cognitive and neural substrates of moral value, but we have not said much about the reinforcers that create or modify these values. Given the consistency of moral norms within cultures and variability of moral norms between cultures (Henrich et al., 2001; Lamba & Mace, 2013), one of the primary ways to learn the specific values of your culture is via social feedback. This is likely to come in one of two forms: prescriptive (involving direct signals of approval and disapproval) or descriptive (involving information about others' behavior). If moral values are encoded in domain-general regions, we might expect the feedback that comes from these two sources to operate over the same domain-general circuitry as nonmoral feedback.

Consistent with this hypothesis, the sight of faces signaling disapproval elicits activity in the ACC (Burklund, Eisenberger, & Lieberman, 2007), and this same region, along with the AI, is activated in individuals who are subject to social exclusion (Eisenberger, Lieberman, & Williams, 2003). Facial expressions of disgust (another potential form of disapproval) also appear to amplify error processing in the ACC (Boksem, Ruys, & Aarts, 2011). Indicators of social approval, on the other hand, are associated with increased activity in more reward-related regions, including the VS and mOFC (Jones et al., 2011).

Descriptive norms also have a powerful effect on behavior—thanks to the human desire to conform—and this influence can be seen playing out in the same brain regions. When one finds out his or her behavior or preferences match the group norm, it elicits activity in the VS; when they deviate from the norm, it leads to increased activity in the AI and ACC (Wu, Luo, & Feng, 2016). Furthermore, the magnitude of response in these latter regions predicts the likelihood that the individual will change his or her behaviors or preferences to match those of the group (e.g., Klucharev, Hytönen, Rijpkema, Smidts, & Fernández, 2009; Zaki, Schirmer, & Mitchell, 2011). Interestingly, this change in preference is often accompanied by a commensurate change in reward-related striatal activity, suggesting conformity involves an updating of intrinsic preferences, rather than a superficial acquiescence to social pressures (Wu et al., 2016).

From Value to Judgment

We have discussed several ways in which the hedonic and motivational properties of morally relevant outcomes and actions mirror those of their nonmoral cousins, both cognitively and neurally. And it is easy to see how these properties might promote moral behavior. Just as we are more likely to order an entrée that our brain finds pleasing, we are more likely to donate money to a charity if we find it intrinsically rewarding. But what about the relation of these prosocial values to moral *judgment*? Does a desire to act charitably toward others influence your judgment that it is morally required? Does an aversion to harm influence your judgment that it is morally prohibited?

To address this question, Shenhav and Greene (2010) asked participants to judge the moral acceptability of killing one individual in order to save others, varying both the number of people saved and the probability that they would die if nothing was done. Not only was the expected value of action (number saved × probability) encoded in the VS, but sensitivities to this value in the brain showed up as sensitivities in moral judgment. In other words, the more this reward-related region tracked the value of lives saved when reading scenarios, the more the participant incorporated the value into his or her ratings of acceptability, suggesting that reward was indeed modulating perceptions of wrongness. There is also evidence for action values (as opposed to outcome values) influencing moral judgment. In a previously mentioned study, Cushman and colleagues (2012) found that performing pseudo-violent (harmless) actions generated signs of aversive arousal. The magnitude of this physiological aversion also predicted how wrong participants thought it would be to kill one individual to save many others. Similarly, how uncomfortable you *think* it would make you to perform pseudo-violent actions predicts your condemnation of harmful actions, even when controlling for such things as empathy and emotional reactivity (Miller et al., 2014).

Two recent neuroimaging studies have provided a window into how exactly these action and outcome values might be influencing moral judgment. In economic decision making, the values of two or more goods have to be compared with each other in order to make a choice, but often their values are not on the same scale (e.g., choosing a cake now or your health in 20 years). To perform this feat, the brain transforms these values into a "common currency" that appears to be encoded in mOFC (Chib, Rangel, Shimojo, & O'Doherty, 2009; Kable & Glimcher, 2007; Plassmann, O'Doherty, & Rangel, 2007). Interestingly, this same process seems to be occurring during moral judgment. Using tasks that pit an aversive action (such as killing) against a utilitarian justification (such as saving lives), Shenhav and Greene (2014) and Hutcherson and colleagues (2015) have found evidence that the appraisal values of each individual option, as well as the integrative moral judgment, are represented in mOFC in the moments before a judgment is made.

A common thread running through these studies is that they involve conflict, or competing moral concerns. We believe that this may tell us something about the circumstances in which value (as a potentially affect-laden, motivational construct) is most likely to influence judgment. Many moral propositions, such as "Murder is wrong," are likely to be stored in semantic memory and easily referenced. This is presumably the reason that psychopaths are able to recognize simple moral violations, despite having reduced motivation to comply with them (Aharoni, Sinnott-Armstrong, & Kiehl, 2012; Blair, 1995). However, we may lack clear propositional knowledge concerning which moral rules are more important than others. In a situation in which two moral norms—for example, *do not kill* versus *save the most lives*—are in competition, it might be necessary to reference the affective or motivational associations you have with each norm in order to render a judgment. It is precisely these circumstances in which the judgments of psychopaths appear to diverge most from those of healthy adults (Koenigs, Kruepke, Zeier, & Newman, 2012).

Conclusion and Future Directions

The fingerprint of domain-general reward and valuation processes can be seen in several key components of moral cognition. The hedonic and motivational value attached to prosocial and antisocial outcomes, the actions that lead to them, and the social feedback that shapes them all seem to be reflected in regions that have been implicated in generic reward-learning tasks. Furthermore, the values of competing moral concerns appear to be translated into a "common currency" in the mOFC during moral judgment, just as we see in economic decision making. This shared neural architecture may reflect the outsized role social cooperation plays in human fitness and survival. Cooperative ventures can lead to great personal benefits in both the short term and long term, and

placing intrinsic value on prosocial actions may facilitate their success. Indeed, humans are extremely sensitive to whether their partners *want* to cooperate for its own sake or whether they only do so after calculating the costs (Hoffman, Yoeli, & Nowak, 2015).

Several important questions remain, however, concerning the nature of these value representations. First, it is currently unclear to what extent we can truly interpret activity in reward-related regions such as the VS as "intrinsic" valuation (or "private acceptance"), divorced from social expectations and pressures. Some studies looking at conformity-induced changes in these regions have favored this view (Berns, Capra, Moore, & Noussair, 2010; Klucharev et al., 2009; Zaki et al., 2011), but the evidence is mixed. Brain regions involved in theory of mind, for instance, can modulate value representations in the mOFC (Hare, Camerer, Knoepfle, O'Doherty, & Rangel, 2010; Strombach et al., 2015), and knowledge of others' presence can amplify activity in the VS during charitable donations (Izuma, Saito, & Sadato, 2008). These studies highlight the context-dependent nature of value construction and demonstrate that anticipated social rewards (such as reputation) might simultaneously contribute to reward-related activity in these regions. Future neuroimaging studies might consider using alternative techniques such as multivoxel pattern analysis (MVPA) to dissociate multiple sources of reward.

We also lack clear evidence on the degree of specialization for moral stimuli within the reward system. Though the bulk of research comparing social and nonsocial rewards have found extensive overlap, a growing number of studies hint at some degree of regional specificity (Ruff & Fehr, 2014). For instance, the values of money (nonsocial) and erotic (social) stimuli are encoded in distinct regions of the mOFC (Sescousse, Redouté, & Dreher, 2010), and learning about the reliability of nonsocial cues versus human advisors in predicting reward seems to rely on computationally similar yet neurally adjacent processing streams (Behrens, Hunt, Woolrich, & Rushworth, 2008). Few, if any, studies, however, have directly compared moral learning with nonsocial reward learning, and even fewer have compared moral learning with nonmoral *social* learning. These are two areas that are ripe for investigation.

Finally, further research is needed to understand how exactly moral *action* values are learned. Some scholars have rightly questioned whether we have the requisite reinforcement history to form robust action values by personal experiential learning, particularly when it comes to relatively rare antisocial actions such as hitting, stabbing, or shooting (Ayars, 2016; also similar to the "poverty of the stimulus" argument, see Mikhail, 2007).

There are several potential solutions to this problem. First, we can dynamically adjust learning rates, or how fast action values are updated, depending on perceived certainty of the outcome (Behrens, Woolrich, Walton, & Rushworth, 2007). In other words, actions that are known to reliably cause harm may acquire strong negative values after very little experience. Second, watching others, also known as *observational* or *vicarious* learning, activates the same neural pathways as firsthand experience and can be an efficient way of learning actions that one is unlikely to perform oneself (Burke, Tobler, Baddeley, & Schultz, 2010; Olsson, Nearing, & Phelps, 2007). Third, instructional learning can lead to top-down modulation of reinforcement learning pathways (Doll, Jacobs, Sanfey, & Frank, 2009; Li, Delgado, & Phelps, 2011), resulting in neural responses that mirror firsthand learning. Lastly, mental simulation can play an important role in shaping action values (Gershman, Markman, & Ross, 2014); by using our model-based system to simulate various actions and their likely rewards and punishments, we can "train up" the cached action values in our model-free system so that learning occurs much more quickly and efficiently. Which of these explanations best describes how moral action values form is an open question, but we hope this chapter provides several fruitful avenues for future research.

REFERENCES

Aharoni, E., Sinnott-Armstrong, W., & Kiehl, K. A. (2012). Can psychopathic offenders discern moral wrongs?: A new look at the moral/conventional distinction. *Journal of Abnormal Psychology, 121,* 484–497.

Andreoni, J. (1990). Impure altruism and donations to public goods: A theory of warm-glow giving. *Economic Journal, 100,* 464–477.

Ayars, A. (2016). Can model-free reinforcement learning explain deontological moral judgments? *Cognition, 150,* 232–242.

Bartra, O., McGuire, J. T., & Kable, J. W. (2013). The valuation system: A coordinate-based meta-analysis of BOLD fMRI experiments examining neural correlates of subjective value. *NeuroImage, 76,* 412–427.

Behrens, T. E. J., Hunt, L. T., Woolrich, M. W., & Rushworth, M. F. S. (2008). Associative learning of social value. *Nature, 456,* 245–249.

Behrens, T. E. J., Woolrich, M. W., Walton, M. E., & Rushworth, M. F. S. (2007). Learning the value of information in an uncertain world. *Nature Neuroscience, 10,* 1214–1221.

Berns, G. S., Capra, C. M., Moore, S., & Noussair, C. (2010). Neural mechanisms of the influence of popularity on adolescent ratings of music. *NeuroImage, 49,* 2687–2696.

Blair, R. J. R. (1995). A cognitive developmental approach to morality: Investigating the psychopath. *Cognition, 57,* 1–29.

Blair, R. J. R. (2007). The amygdala and ventromedial prefrontal cortex in morality and psychopathy. *Trends in Cognitive Sciences, 11,* 387–392.

Boksem, M. A. S., Ruys, K. I., & Aarts, H. (2011). Facing disapproval: Performance monitoring in a social context. *Social Neuroscience, 6,* 360–368.

Burke, C. J., Tobler, P. N., Baddeley, M., & Schultz, W. (2010). Neural mechanisms of observational learning. *Proceedings of the National Academy of Sciences of the USA, 107,* 14431–14436.

Burklund, L. J., Eisenberger, N. I., & Lieberman, M. D. (2007). The face of rejection: Rejection sensitivity moderates dorsal anterior cingulate activity to disapproving facial expressions. *Social Neuroscience, 2,* 238–253.

Chib, V. S., Rangel, A., Shimojo, S., & O'Doherty, J. P. (2009). Evidence for a common representation of decision values for dissimilar goods in human ventromedial prefrontal cortex. *Journal of Neuroscience, 29,* 12315–12320.

Civai, C., Crescentini, C., Rustichini, A., & Rumiati, R. I. (2012). Equality versus self-interest in the brain: Differential roles of anterior insula and medial prefrontal cortex. *NeuroImage, 62,* 102–112.

Corradi-Dell'Acqua, C., Civai, C., Rumiati, R. I., & Fink, G. R. (2013). Disentangling self- and fairness-related neural mechanisms involved in the ultimatum game: An fMRI study. *Social *Cognitive and Affective Neuroscience, 8,* 424–431.

Crockett, M. J. (2013). Models of morality. *Trends in Cognitive Sciences, 17,* 363–366.

Crumpler, H., & Grossman, P. J. (2008). An experimental test of warm glow giving. *Journal of Public Economics, 92,* 1011–1021.

Cushman, F. (2013). Action, outcome, and value: A dual-system framework for morality. *Personality and Social Psychology Review, 17,* 273–292.

Cushman, F., Gray, K., Gaffey, A., & Mendes, W. B. (2012). Simulating murder: The aversion to harmful action. *Emotion, 12,* 2–7.

Darwin, C. (1872). *The descent of man, and selection in relation to sex.* London: Murray.

Davis, K. D. (2000). The neural circuitry of pain as explored with functional MRI. *Neurological Research, 22,* 313–317.

Daw, N. D., Gershman, S. J., Seymour, B., Dayan, P., & Dolan, R. J. (2011). Model-based influences on humans' choices and striatal prediction errors. *Neuron, 69,* 1204–1215.

Dawes, C. T., Loewen, P. J., Schreiber, D., Simmons, A. N., Flagan, T., McElreath, R., . . . Paulus, M. P. (2012). Neural basis of egalitarian behavior. *Proceedings of the National Academy of Sciences of the USA, 109,* 6479–6483.

Dayan, P., & Niv, Y. (2008). Reinforcement learning: The good, the bad and the ugly. *Current Opinion in Neurobiology, 18,* 185–196.

Delgado, M. R., Jou, R. L., LeDoux, J., & Phelps, L. (2009). Avoiding negative outcomes: Tracking the mechanisms of avoidance learning in humans during fear conditioning. *Frontiers in Behavioral Neuroscience, 3,* 1–9.

Dickinson, A. (1985). Actions and habits: The development of behavioural autonomy. *Philosophical Transactions of the Royal Society B: Biological Sciences, 308,* 67–78.

Doll, B. B., Jacobs, W. J., Sanfey, A. G., & Frank, M. J. (2009). Instructional control of reinforcement learning: A behavioral and neurocomputational investigation. *Brain Research, 1299,* 74–94.

Eckel, C. C., Grossman, P. J., & Johnston, R. M. (2005). An experimental test of the crowding out hypothesis. *Journal of Public Economics, 89,* 1543–1560.

Eisenberger, N. I., Lieberman, M. D., & Williams, K. D. (2003). Does rejection hurt?: An fMRI study of social exclusion. *Science, 302,* 290–292.

Fehr, E., & Fischbacher, U. (2002). Why social preferences matter: The impact of non-selfish motives on competition, cooperation and incentives. *Economic Journal, 112,* C1–C33.

Gershman, S. J., Markman, A. B., & Ross, A. (2014). Retrospective revaluation in sequential decision making: A tale of two systems. *Journal of Experimental Psychology: General, 143,* 182–194.

Gęsiarz, F., & Crockett, M. J. (2015). Goal-directed, habitual and Pavlovian prosocial behavior. *Frontiers in Behavioral Neuroscience, 9,* 1–18.

Gillan, C. M., Morein-Zamir, S., Urcelay, G. P., Sule, A., Voon, V., Apergis-Schoute, A. M., . . . Robbins, T. W. (2014). Enhanced avoidance habits in obsessive–compulsive disorder. *Biological Psychiatry, 75,* 631–638.

Gläscher, J., Daw, N., Dayan, P., & O'Doherty, J. P. (2010). States versus rewards: Dissociable neural prediction error signals underlying model-based and model-free reinforcement learning. *Neuron, 66,* 585–595.

Harbaugh, W. T., Mayr, U., & Burghart, D. R. (2007). Neural responses to taxation and voluntary giving reveal motives for charitable donations. *Science, 316,* 1622–1625.

Hare, T. A., Camerer, C. F., Knoepfle, D. T., O'Doherty, J. P., & Rangel, A. (2010). Value computations in ventral medial prefrontal cortex during charitable decision making incorporate input from regions involved in social cognition. *Journal of Neuroscience, 30,* 583–590.

Hein, G., Silani, G., Preuschoff, K., Batson, C. D., & Singer, T. (2010). Neural responses to ingroup and outgroup members' suffering predict individual differences in costly helping. *Neuron, 68,* 149–160.

Henrich, J., Boyd, R., Bowles, S., Camerer, C., Fehr, E., Gintis, H., & McElreath, R. (2001). In search of *Homo economicus*: Behavioral experiments in 15 small-scale societies. *American Economic Review, 91,* 73–78.

Hoffman, M., Yoeli, E., & Nowak, M. A. (2015). Cooperate without looking: Why we care what people think and not just what they do. *Proceedings of the National Academy of Sciences of the USA, 112,* 1727–1732.

Hutcherson, C. A., Montaser-Kouhsari, L., Woodward, J., & Rangel, A. (2015). Emotional and utilitarian appraisals of moral dilemmas are encoded in separate areas and integrated in ventromedial prefrontal cortex. *Journal of Neuroscience, 35,* 12593–12605.

Izuma, K., Saito, D. N., & Sadato, N. (2008). Processing of social and monetary rewards in the human striatum. *Neuron, 58,* 284–294.

Jackson, P. L., Brunet, E., Meltzoff, A. N., & Decety, J. (2006). Empathy examined through the neural mechanisms involved in imagining how I feel versus how you feel pain. *Neuropsychologia, 44,* 752–761.

Jones, R. M., Somerville, L. H., Li, J., Ruberry, E. J., Libby, V., Glover, G., . . . Casey, B. J. (2011). Behavioral and neural properties of social reinforcement learning. *Journal of Neuroscience, 31,* 13039–13045.

Kable, J. W., & Glimcher, P. W. (2007). The neural correlates of subjective value during intertemporal choice. *Nature Neuroscience, 10,* 1625–1633.

Klucharev, V., Hytönen, K., Rijpkema, M., Smidts, A., & Fernández, G. (2009). Reinforcement learning signal predicts social conformity. *Neuron, 61,* 140–151.

Koenigs, M., Kruepke, M., Zeier, J., & Newman, J. P. (2012). Utilitarian moral judgment in psychopathy. *Social Cognitive and Affective Neuroscience, 7,* 708–714.

Lamba, S., & Mace, R. (2013). The evolution of fairness: Explaining variation in bargaining behaviour. *Proceedings of the Royal Society of London B: Biological Sciences, 280,* 2012–2028.

Lamm, C., Nusbaum, H. C., Meltzoff, A. N., & Decety, J. (2007). What are you feeling?: Using functional magnetic resonance imaging to assess the modulation of sensory and affective responses during empathy for pain. *PLOS ONE, 2,* e1292.

Levy, I., Lazzaro, S. C., Rutledge, R. B., & Glimcher, P. W. (2011). Choice from non-choice: Predicting consumer preferences from blood oxygenation level-dependent signals obtained during passive viewing. *Journal of Neuroscience, 31,* 118–125.

Li, J., Delgado, M. R., & Phelps, E. A. (2011). How instructed knowledge modulates the neural systems of reward learning. *Proceedings of the National Academy of Sciences of the USA, 108,* 55–60.

Liu, X., Hairston, J., Schrier, M., & Fan, J. (2011). Common and distinct networks underlying reward valence and processing stages: A meta-analysis of functional neuroimaging studies. *Neuroscience and Biobehavioral Reviews, 35,* 1219–1236.

Mikhail, J. (2007). Universal moral grammar: Theory, evidence and the future. *Trends in Cognitive Sciences, 11,* 143–152.

Miller, R., Hannikainen, I., & Cushman, F. (2014). Bad actions or bad outcomes?: Differentiating affective contributions to the moral condemnation of harm. *Emotion, 14*(3), 573–587.

Mobbs, D., Yu, R., Meyer, M., Passamonti, L., Seymour, B., Calder, A. J., . . . Dalgleish, T. (2009). A key role for similarity in vicarious reward. *Science, 324,* 900.

Olsson, A., Nearing, K. I., & Phelps, E. A. (2007). Learning fears by observing others: The neural systems of social fear transmission. *Social Cognitive and Affective Neuroscience, 2,* 3–11.

Peysakhovich, A., & Rand, D. G. (2015). Habits of virtue: Creating norms of cooperation and defection in the laboratory. *Management Science, 62,* 631–647.

Plassmann, H., O'Doherty, J., & Rangel, A. (2007). Orbitofrontal cortex encodes willingness to pay in everyday economic transactions. *Journal of Neuroscience, 27,* 9984–9988.

Rai, T. S., & Holyoak, K. J. (2010). Moral principles or consumer preferences?: Alternative framings of the trolley problem. *Cognitive Science, 34,* 311–321.

Rand, D. G., Peysakhovich, A., Kraft-Todd, G. T., Newman, G. E., Wurzbacher, O., Nowak, M. A., & Greene, J. D. (2014). Social heuristics shape intuitive cooperation. *Nature Communications, 5,* 3677.

Rilling, J. K., Gutman, D. A., Zeh, T. R., Pagnoni, G., Berns, G. S., & Kilts, C. D. (2002). A neural basis for social cooperation. *Neuron, 35,* 395–405.

Ruff, C. C., & Fehr, E. (2014). The neurobiology of rewards and values in social decision making. *Nature Reviews Neuroscience, 15,* 549–562.

Salimpoor, V. N., Benovoy, M., Larcher, K., Dagher, A., & Zatorre, R. J. (2011). Anatomically distinct dopamine release during anticipation and experience of peak emotion to music. *Nature Neuroscience, 14,* 257–262.

Sanfey, A. G., Rilling, J. K., Aronson, J. A., Nystrom, L. E., & Cohen, J. D. (2003). The neural basis of economic decision-making in the ultimatum game. *Science, 300,* 1755–1758.

Schwabe, L., Dickinson, A., & Wolf, O. T. (2011). Stress, habits, and drug addiction: A psychoneuroendocrinological perspective. *Experimental and Clinical Psychopharmacology, 19,* 53–63.

Sescousse, G., Li, Y., & Dreher, J.-C. (2015). A common currency for the computation of motivational values in the human striatum. *Social Cognitive and Affective Neuroscience, 10,* 467–473.

Sescousse, G., Redouté, J., & Dreher, J.-C. (2010). The architecture of reward value coding in the human orbitofrontal cortex. *Journal of Neuroscience, 30,* 13095–13104.

Shenhav, A., & Greene, J. D. (2010). Moral judgments recruit domain-general valuation mechanisms to integrate representations of probability and magnitude. *Neuron, 67,* 667–677.

Shenhav, A., & Greene, J. D. (2014). Integrative moral judgment: Dissociating the roles of the amygdala and ventromedial prefrontal cortex. *Journal of Neuroscience, 34,* 4741–4749.

Singer, T., Seymour, B., O'Doherty, J., Kaube, H., Dolan, R. J., & Frith, C. D. (2004). Empathy for pain involves the affective but not sensory components of pain. *Science, 303,* 1157–1162.

Strohminger, N., & Nichols, S. (2014). The essential moral self. *Cognition, 131,* 159–171.

Strombach, T., Weber, B., Hangebrauk, Z., Kenning, P., Karipidis, I. I., Tobler, P. N., & Kalenscher, T. (2015). Social discounting involves modulation of neural value signals by temporoparietal junction. *Proceedings of the National Academy of Sciences of the USA, 112,* 1619–1624.

Tabibnia, G., Satpute, A. B., & Lieberman, M. D. (2008). The sunny side of fairness: Preference for fairness activates reward circuitry (and disregarding unfairness activates self-control circuitry). *Psychological Science, 19,* 339–347.

Tetlock, P. E. (2003). Thinking the unthinkable: Sacred values and taboo cognitions. *Trends in Cognitive Sciences, 7,* 320–324.

Tetlock, P. E., Kristel, O. V., Beth, S., Green, M. C., & Lerner, J. S. (2000). The psychology of the unthinkable: Taboo trade-offs, forbidden base rates, and heretical counterfactuals. *Journal of Personality and Social Psychology, 78,* 853–870.

Tricomi, E., Balleine, B. W., & O'Doherty, J. P. (2009). A specific role for posterior dorsolateral striatum in human habit learning. *European Journal of Neuroscience, 29,* 2225–2232.

Tricomi, E., Rangel, A., Camerer, C. F., & O'Doherty, J. P. (2010). Neural evidence for inequality-averse social preferences. *Nature, 463,* 1089–1091.

Wu, H., Luo, Y., & Feng, C. (2016). Neural signatures of social conformity: A coordinate-based activation likelihood estimation meta-analysis of functional brain imaging studies. *Neuroscience and Biobehavioral Reviews, 71,* 101–111.

Zaki, J., Davis, J. I., & Ochsner, K. N. (2012). Overlapping activity in anterior insula during interoception and emotional experience. *NeuroImage, 62,* 493–499.

Zaki, J., & Mitchell, J. P. (2011). Equitable decision making is associated with neural markers of intrinsic value. *Proceedings of the National Academy of Sciences of the USA, 108,* 19761–19766.

Zaki, J., Schirmer, J., & Mitchell, J. P. (2011). Social influence modulates the neural computation of value. *Psychological Science, 22,* 894–900.

CHAPTER 8

A Component Process Model
of Disgust, Anger, and Moral Judgment

Hanah A. Chapman

> **What is the role of disgust in morality?**
>
> The component process model of morality proposed in this chapter suggests that moral disgust is driven primarily by negative character evaluations, explaining why both purity and nonpurity transgressions trigger disgust and why purity transgressions are morally condemned.

The emotion of disgust has played an out-sized role in moral psychology over the past 15 years. As described below, research on moral disgust has informed such key debates as whether moral judgment is rational or intuitive; whether morality consists of one process or many; and whether morality is culturally uniform or variable. What, then, is the role of disgust in morality? As noted by Tybur and colleagues (Tybur, Lieberman, Kurzban, & DeScioli, 2012), it is critical to break this question into smaller pieces to avoid confusion.

1. *What kinds of immoral things are disgusting?* One perspective is that only disgusting immoral things can evoke disgust (Horberg, Oveis, Keltner, & Cohen, 2009; Rozin, Lowery, Imada, & Haidt, 1999; Russell & Giner-Sorolla, 2013). "Disgusting immoral things" are often referred to as

"purity" or "divinity" transgressions, meaning acts that violate sexual or bodily norms (Graham, Haidt, & Nosek, 2009; Rozin et al., 1999). Purity transgressions raise a number of important questions, which I return to shortly. However, for the current question—what kinds of immoral things are disgusting—they are not very interesting: It is hardly surprising that purity transgressions evoke disgust, given that they involve prototypical disgust elicitors such as body products and biologically disadvantageous sex.

More interesting, and more controversial, is the question of whether immoral things that are *not* intrinsically disgusting, such as harm, unfairness, and disloyalty, can evoke disgust. People certainly report disgust toward nonpurity transgressions, but there has been debate about whether this disgust is synonymous with anger (Cameron, Lindquist, & Gray, 2015; Chapman

& Anderson, 2013; Royzman, Atanasov, Landy, Parks, & Gepty, 2014; Rozin, Haidt, & Fincher, 2009; Russell & Giner-Sorolla, 2013). This issue is fraught with methodological pitfalls, and the evidence is evolving very rapidly, but at present there is reason to think that nonpurity transgressions can indeed evoke disgust that is meaningfully distinct from anger (see the discussion of evidence later in the chapter). Thus, to answer the first question, *both purity and nonpurity transgressions can be disgusting.*

2. *Why are nonpurity transgressions disgusting?* Contemporary theories of disgust propose that disgust's original function was to facilitate disease avoidance (Oaten, Stevenson, & Case, 2009; Tybur et al., 2012). It is therefore not clear why nonpurity transgressions, which do not involve disease vectors, can evoke disgust. The explanation may lie in the opposing behavioral tendencies associated with disgust and anger. In particular, whereas anger is linked to approach motivation and may be aimed at changing the target's future behavior (Carver & Harmon-Jones, 2009; Fischer & Roseman, 2007), disgust is associated with withdrawal and avoidance (Rozin, Haidt, & McCauley, 1999). Therefore, *disgust in response to nonpurity transgressions may subserve withdrawal motivation in the moral domain* (Chapman & Anderson, 2013; Hutcherson & Gross, 2011). Withdrawal/avoidance might be useful under a number of different circumstances. Most prominently, it may be futile to try to influence a transgressor's future behavior when his or her actions stem from bad character (Fischer & Roseman, 2007). Thus *nonpurity transgressions that stem from or signal bad character may be especially likely to elicit disgust* (Giner-Sorolla & Chapman, 2017; Hutcherson & Gross, 2011).

3. *Why are purity transgressions immoral?* In other words, why is it wrong to do something disgusting, if doing so does not violate any other moral rules? One explanation, derived from the social intuitionist model (Haidt, 2001), is that the strong feelings of disgust evoked by purity transgression directly cause negative moral judgments. However, a recent meta-analysis

suggests that incidental disgust has at best a weak effect on moral judgments (Landy & Goodwin, 2015). Thus it is unlikely that the disgust associated with purity transgressions is sufficient to cause moral condemnation.

Another explanation is that purity concerns may constitute a distinct moral module: that is, for some people, it may be intrinsically wrong to do something disgusting, perhaps because doing so contaminates the purity or sanctity of the soul (Graham et al., 2009; Rozin, Lowery, et al., 1999). This may explain wrongness judgments for some purity transgressions. However, the vignettes used as stimuli in moral judgment studies are heterogeneous and psychologically complex, which admits the possibility of alternative explanations. For example, people may perceive that some purity transgressions have harmful consequences even when the scenarios are constructed so as to be free from explicit harm (Gray, Schein, & Ward, 2014; Royzman, Leeman, & Baron, 2009). Perhaps more importantly, *doing something disgusting (i.e. committing a purity transgression) may be an especially strong signal that the transgressor has bad character* (Uhlmann & Zhu, 2013; Uhlmann, Pizarro, & Diermeier, 2015). Here, moral judgments may reflect condemnation of the transgressor as a person as much as condemnation of the person's acts.

4. *Are there other differences between purity and nonpurity transgressions?* Researchers have suggested that moral judgments about purity and nonpurity transgressions may rely on different cognitive processes. For example, two studies have found that the transgressor's malignant versus innocent intent matters less for condemnation of purity transgressions compared with nonpurity transgressions (Chakroff, Dungan, & Young, 2013; Young & Saxe, 2011). Such findings have been taken as evidence for distinct moral modules for purity and nonpurity transgressions (Chakroff & Young, 2015). However, close examination of the data reveals that evidence is actually mixed (see the later section on evidence). Moreover, the complexity and heterogeneity of moral transgression stimuli once again opens up the possibility of alternative explanations. *Many differences could arise*

because purity transgressions may primarily activate—and could even derive their wrongness from—character judgments rather than consequence judgments (Uhlmann et al., 2015; Uhlmann & Zhu, 2013). That said, this idea cannot account for all of the reported differences between purity and nonpurity transgressions, suggesting that purity-related moral cognition may be at least partially distinct from non-purity-related moral cognition.

Figure 8.1 summarizes this perspective on moral judgment and emotion, which I call the component process model (CPM).[1] According to the CPM, a number of component cognitive processes contribute to disgust, anger, and moral judgments. For harmless purity transgressions (e.g. consensual incest), disgust can stem from core disgust evaluations triggered by stimuli such as biologically disadvantageous sex or contact with contaminants. Purity transgressions also trigger disgust by activating negative character evaluations ("only a messed-up person would do something like that"). Nonpurity transgressions (e.g., unprovoked violence) can trigger negative character judgments as well, which similarly lead to disgust. In turn, disgust motivates avoidance-related responses. Negative character judgments also contribute to moral condemnation, which

explains why harmless purity transgressions are condemned. For nonpurity transgressions, perception of negative consequences triggers moral condemnation and anger in parallel; anger then motivates approach-related responses. Not shown in Figure 8.1 is the idea that purity transgressions that are perceived to have negative consequences will also trigger anger and approach-related behaviors. Many cognitive differences between purity and nonpurity transgressions could arise because harmless purity transgressions activate character judgments to a greater extent than consequence judgments, whereas harmful nonpurity transgressions typically activate both consequence judgments and character judgments. Some differences cannot be easily accounted for in this way, however; thus the CPM allows for purity-specific and non-purity-specific moral evaluations to influence judgments.

Historical Context

Research on disgust has informed a number of the broader debates in moral psychology. These include whether there are one or two or many moral processes; whether morality is primarily intuitive or rational; and whether morality is culturally uniform or varied.

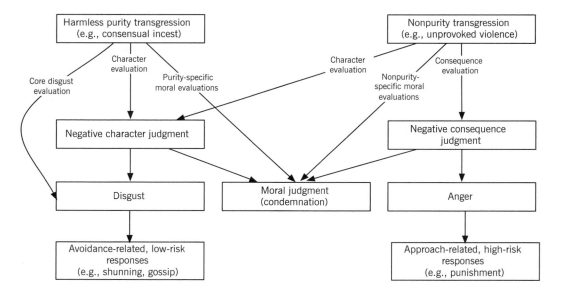

FIGURE 8.1. The component process model (CPM) of moral judgment and emotion.

• *"One or two or many processes?,"* informed by *"What kinds of immoral things are disgusting?"; "Why are disgusting things immoral?";* and *"Are there other differences between purity and nonpurity transgressions?"* One of the earliest multiprocess models of moral judgment in the field of psychology is the CAD triad hypothesis (Rozin, Lowery, et al., 1999). The CAD hypothesis takes as its starting point the three moral processes described by anthropologist Richard Shweder, namely, community, autonomy, and divinity (Shweder, Much, Mahaprata, & Park, 1997). According to the CAD hypothesis, these codes are linked to the emotions of contempt, anger, and disgust, respectively. The CAD hypothesis was a precursor to moral foundations theory, which reduces the emphasis on distinct emotions but retains the idea that divinity (a.k.a. purity) is a distinct moral process (Graham et al., 2009). Other work has also developed the idea that purity violations, and the disgust associated with them, represent a distinct moral process (Chakroff & Young, 2015; Russell & Giner-Sorolla, 2013). In sum, one historical trend has been to take evidence for a selective relationship between particular emotions (especially disgust) and particular types of transgressions (especially purity) as evidence for multiple moral processes.

Recently, the opposite approach has emerged: If purity transgressions and nonpurity transgressions evoke similar emotions (e.g., if both can evoke disgust), then this may provide evidence against the idea of multiple moral processes and in favor of single-process models such as the dyadic model (Cameron et al., 2015; Gray, Waytz, & Young, 2012). According to the dyadic model, moral judgment depends primarily on the evaluation of negative consequences, which leads to an undifferentiated negative emotional response. The dyadic model thus explains the wrongness of seemingly harmless purity transgressions by suggesting that they are implicitly perceived as having negative consequences, that is, as being harmful (Gray et al., 2014).

The alternative suggested by the CPM is that moral judgment relies on a number of component cognitive processes that may be activated to different degrees by different types of transgressions. Thus the CPM is a multiprocess model. According to the CPM, both character evaluations and consequence evaluations contribute to moral judgment; other processes may also contribute, but they are not considered here. Both purity and nonpurity transgressions can trigger character evaluations, which explains why both types of transgressions can evoke disgust. Purity transgressions may often activate character judgments to a greater extent than consequence judgments, perhaps because most purity transgressions do not have obvious negative consequences (Uhlmann & Zhu, 2013). In a strong version of the CPM, there are no qualitative differences in the processes that contribute to judgments about purity and nonpurity transgressions; all of the apparent cognitive differences between these transgression types can be accounted for by quantitative differences in the degree to which character and consequence judgments are activated. However, a weaker version of the theory (shown in Figure 8.1) allows cognitive processes that are unique to purity and nonpurity transgressions. Note that the weaker version of the CPM still maintains that both types of transgressions can activate character and consequence judgments.

• *"Intuitive versus deliberative,"* informed by *"Why are disgusting things immoral?"* The original description of the social intuitionist model (SIM; Haidt, 2001) opens with a vignette that depicts consensual incest. Consensual incest is often morally condemned, even though there appears to be no harm. If there is no harm, then where does the wrongness judgment come from? The answer, according to the SIM, is the powerful feelings of disgust evoked by incest. Thus the fact that disgusting things are sometimes immoral has been taken as evidence that emotion is what causes moral judgment. Experimental work showing that incidental disgust can increase condemnation of moral transgressions has also been taken as support for the idea that emotion causes moral judgment (Eskine, Kacinik, & Prinz, 2011; Schnall, Haidt, Clore, & Jordan, 2008; Wheatley & Haidt, 2005). However, a recent meta-analysis of disgust induction studies suggests that incidental disgust has at best a small effect on moral judgment

(Landy & Goodwin, 2015). In contrast to the SIM, the CPM puts character evaluation upstream of disgust. Such evaluations could be either implicit or explicit; thus the CPM is ambivalent as to the intuitive-versus-deliberative nature of morality.

• *"Culturally uniform or variable?," informed by "Why are disgusting things immoral?"* Some cultures judge that purity transgressions are immoral, whereas others do not. For example, American conservatives condemn purity transgressions much more than American liberals (Graham et al., 2009). According to moral foundations theory, disgusting things are immoral to such people because these individuals have a distinct moral process for purity; this process is absent in individuals who do not condemn disgusting things (Graham et al., 2009; Graham et al., 2011). In other words, differences of opinion about purity transgressions provide evidence that morality is culturally variable. By contrast, the CPM draws on social domain theory (Turiel, Killen, & Helwig, 1987) to suggest an alternative explanation for cultural variability in condemnation of purity transgressions. Specifically, different cultures may make different informational assumptions about purity transgressions (Turiel, Hildebrandt, Wainryb, & Saltzstein, 1991). For example, to the extent that a particular culture assumes that a disgusting act is harmful (to the self, others, the community, or the natural order), it will be moralized by that culture. Similarly, to the extent that a particular culture assumes that a disgusting act indicates bad character, it will be moralized. American liberals, for example, believe that homosexual sex is neither harmful nor indicative of bad character; therefore, American liberals do not moralize homosexuality. The CPM thus accounts for cultural variability in moralization of purity transgressions by pointing to variability in the component processes of character and consequence evaluation.

Theoretical Stance

The CPM differs substantially from some major theories of morality. First, according to the CPM, both purity and nonpurity transgressions can evoke disgust. Thus the CPM differs from theories in which disgust is linked uniquely to purity transgressions, such as the CAD triad hypothesis (Rozin, Lowery, et al., 1999), work by Young and colleagues (Chakroff & Young, 2015; Young & Saxe, 2011), and older work by Giner-Sorolla, Russell, and their colleagues (Russell & Giner-Sorolla, 2013). The strong version of the CPM also diverges from modular theories such as moral foundations theory (Graham et al., 2009) insofar as it denies that the cognitive processes associated with purity transgressions are fully distinct from those underlying nonpurity transgressions. (The weak version of the CPM does allow for distinct, in addition to common, processes). Finally, the CPM differs from SIM (Haidt, 2001) in that it places evaluations of character and consequences upstream of moral judgment and emotion.

By contrast, the CPM is very much allied with and indebted to a number of other theories. Specifically, the CPM attempts to combine elements of several existing theories in a novel way so as to produce a unified account of the moral judgments and emotions elicited by purity and nonpurity transgressions. The CPM borrows from person-centric models of morality (Uhlmann et al., 2015) the idea that character evaluations are critical to moral judgment, and that they can at least partly explain why harmless purity transgressions are judged as wrong. The person-centric model does not specifically address emotions, however, whereas the CPM does. The idea that moral disgust might be related to character judgments has its origins in the work of Giner-Sorolla and colleagues (Giner-Sorolla & Chapman, 2017), and in Hutcherson and colleagues' social–functionalist model (Hutcherson & Gross, 2011). Hutcherson and colleagues were also among the first to suggest that moral disgust might be associated with withdrawal motivation. However, Hutcherson and colleagues were primarily interested in disgust evoked by nonpurity transgressions and did not address the link between purity transgressions and character evaluations that the CPM includes.

Finally, the CPM has a mixed relationship with some other theories. The CPM agrees with the dyadic model of morality

(Gray et al., 2012) as to the importance of consequence (a.k.a. harm) judgments for moral condemnation. However, the CPM also emphasizes the role of character and suggests that character judgment as well as harm judgments may contribute to condemnation of purity transgressions. The dyadic model is, more broadly, an example of a constructivist model of morality (Cameron et al., 2015), with which the CPM shares the general idea that moral cognition consists of several different cognitive processes that can be combined in different ways. However, constructivist models tend to favor an undifferentiated negative emotional response to transgressions, whereas the CPM proposes that different component cognitive processes trigger different emotions. Finally, constructivist models typically favor cultural–cognitive explanations for emotion differentiation, in which distinct emotions such as anger and fear arise from an individual's culturally driven conceptualization of what is fundamentally an undifferentiated affective experience (Barrett, 2006). By contrast, the CPM is more inspired by biological–evolutionary reasoning, in which distinct emotions represent unique adaptations to particular kinds of opportunities and threats in the ancestral environment (Cosmides & Tooby, 2000; Ekman, 1992; Frijda, 1987).

Evidence

The CPM's first claim is that both purity and nonpurity transgressions can evoke disgust that is distinct from anger. This is a methodologically treacherous area, because disgust and anger evoked by moral transgressions share considerable variance (Chapman & Anderson, 2013; Russell & Giner-Sorolla, 2013). However, a small body of evidence does support the idea that moral disgust evoked by nonpurity transgressions is distinct from anger. First, endorsement of disgust words (e.g., *repulsed, sickened*) in response to nonpurity transgressions is predicted by endorsement of facial expressions of disgust but not facial expressions of anger (Gutierrez, Giner-Sorolla, & Vasiljevic, 2011). In other words, describing nonpurity transgressions as "disgusting" is not fully the same as describing them as "angering."

As well, nonpurity transgressions trigger facial movements associated with disgust, namely, activity of the levator labii muscle, which wrinkles the nose and/or raises the upper lip (Cannon, Schnall, & White, 2011; Chapman, Kim, Susskind, & Anderson, 2009). Finally, trait disgust predicts condemnation of nonpurity transgressions even when controlling for trait anger (Chapman & Anderson, 2014; Jones & Fitness, 2008).

The CPM's second claim is that disgust evoked by nonpurity transgressions subserves withdrawal/avoidance motivation in the moral domain. The logic here is that active, approach-related behaviors are not always the best way to deal with a transgression. Indeed, game-theoretic modeling shows that active punishment (which may entail a cost to the punisher) is almost always a less efficient strategy than rejection or avoidance (Ohtsuki, Iwasa, & Nowak, 2009). There is, however, only indirect support for the idea that withdrawal in the moral domain is tied to disgust. Nonmoral disgust in general is associated with withdrawal motivation (Rozin, Haidt, & McCauley, 2000), in contrast to the approach motivation linked to anger (Carver & Harmon-Jones, 2009). However, only one study has directly tested the potential link between moral disgust and withdrawal motivation, by asking participants whether they would be "willing to go to some effort" to avoid a transgressor (Hutcherson & Gross, 2011). This research actually found that anger, but not disgust, predicted avoidance, although the question wording may have suggested an active response more closely allied with anger than disgust. Thus more research is needed to test the claim that moral disgust is associated with withdrawal motivation. Such work should be careful to give participants an opportunity to actually express their behavioral tendencies, as perceived ability to attain a behavioral goal influences motivational intensity (Brehm & Self, 1989; Harmon-Jones, Sigelman, Bohlig, & Harmon-Jones, 2003).

A challenge for work seeking to link moral disgust to withdrawal is that most transgressions probably evoke both anger and disgust and hence will probably activate both approach and withdrawal tendencies. Here, the solution may be to use transgression stimuli that isolate the cognitive processes hypothesized to lead to disgust and anger. This leads to the CPM's third claim: Disgust is linked to character judgments, whereas anger is linked to consequence judgments. In principle, it should be possible to dissociate the action tendencies associated with moral disgust and anger by using stimuli that primarily activate character or consequence judgments, respectively. This is also tricky, however, because it is easy to confound bad character and negative consequences. For example, given a stripped-down scenario such as hitting someone's finger with a hammer (Chakroff & Young, 2015) or slapping someone in the face (Chapman & Anderson, 2014), participants may default to the assumption that the negative consequences occurred because the transgressor is a bad person (Giner-Sorolla & Chapman, 2017).

One way to disentangle character and consequence judgments is to cross the presence or absence of the desire to cause harm, which indicates bad character, with the presence or absence of negative consequences (Giner-Sorolla & Chapman, 2017). For example, an individual might desire to cause harm but never act on it, or an individual may not desire harm but something bad happens anyway. Research in this vein has found that desire to commit harm predicts disgust and that this effect is mediated by the perception of bad character. By contrast, negative consequences predict anger but not disgust. These findings are consistent with the CPM's claim that moral disgust is driven by negative character evaluations, whereas moral anger is driven by negative consequence evaluations.

The CPM's third claim is that purity transgressions are judged to be immoral at least in part because they signal bad character. At present, there is only partial evidence for this claim. In general, behaviors that are statistically rare (Ditto & Jemmott, 1989; Fiske, 1980; McKenzie & Mikkelsen, 2007; Snyder, Kleck, Strenta, & Mentzer, 1979) and low in attributional ambiguity (Snyder et al., 1979) are perceived as highly informative about character traits. Purity transgressions, such as drinking urine or engaging in consensual incest, certainly satisfy these conditions (Uhlmann et al., 2015). By contrast, nonpurity transgressions such as theft may be more common and easier to attribute to circumstances. Indeed, individuals who commit purity transgressions (e.g., having sex with a dead chicken) are judged to have worse character than those who commit nonpurity transgressions (e.g., stealing a dead chicken), even though nonpurity transgressions are judged to be more immoral (Uhlmann & Zhu, 2013). Thus there is good evidence that purity transgressions signal bad character. Still missing, however, is evidence that purity transgressions are judged to be immoral *because* of the character judgments that they engender, as hypothesized by the CPM.

Finally, the CPM claims that at least some of the apparent cognitive differences between purity and nonpurity transgressions are due to differential activation of the same underlying cognitive processes, namely character and consequence judgments. This stands in contrast to the claim that qualitatively different cognitive processes underlie judgments about purity and nonpurity transgressions (Chakroff & Young, 2015; Graham et al., 2009).

Here it is critical to distinguish between the cognitive processes that influence moral judgments and the cognitive processes that influence feelings of disgust. According to the CPM, disgust evoked by purity transgressions has two sources: a core disgust evaluation (triggered by the presence of pathogens, biologically disadvantageous sex, etc.) and a character evaluation. The core disgust evaluation likely dominates the disgust response to most purity transgressions and is probably insensitive to the factors that influence wrongness judgments. For example, previous work has shown that disgust in response to purity transgressions is unaffected by whether or not the victim consented to the transgression (Russell & Piazza, 2014). This makes sense: Core disgust evaluations will be triggered whether or not the victim consented, because either way a core disgust stimulus was present. By contrast, wrongness judgments are attenuated when the victim consents to a purity transgression (Russell & Piazza, 2014). Thus the cognitive processes that influence disgust are not necessarily the same as those that influence moral judgments. In what follows, my focus is on the cognitive processes that influence moral judgments and whether they might differ between purity and nonpurity transgressions.

First, some differences between purity and nonpurity transgressions can be easily explained by the idea that purity transgressions tend to activate character judgments to a greater extent than nonpurity transgressions. For example, people are more likely to make person-based attributions for purity transgressions than for nonpurity transgressions (Chakroff & Young, 2015). This fits nicely with the idea that purity transgressions may be an especially strong signal of bad character because of their statistical infrequency and low attributional ambiguity (Uhlmann et al., 2015). Note that nonpurity transgressions also trigger person-based attributions, albeit to a lesser extent, consistent with the idea that both transgression types can involve character judgments.

A related finding is that self-directed transgressions evoke more disgust (controlling for anger) than do other-directed transgressions (Chakroff et al., 2013). Self-directed transgressions were also associated with more negative character judgments than other-directed transgressions, consistent with the idea that disgust is related to character judgments. This suggests that what a person does to him- or herself may reveal character more than what he or she does to others. Indeed, whereas there could be situational reasons for doing something to someone else, we usually only do things to ourselves when we want to, and desires speak strongly to character.

Some differences between purity and nonpurity transgressions are difficult to explain using character and consequence judgments, and thus they could present a challenge to a strong version of the CPM in which character and consequence judgments are the *only* cognitive processes that contribute to differences between transgression types. For example, two studies have reported that the transgressor's intent matters less for moral judgments about purity transgressions than for judgments about nonpurity transgressions (Chakroff et al., 2013; Young & Saxe, 2011). It is difficult to see how this difference could be accounted for by the idea that purity transgressions tend to activate character judgments to a greater extent than do nonpurity transgressions. That said, the

evidence for a difference in the role of intent across purity and nonpurity domains is actually somewhat mixed. For example, one study found no interaction between transgression type and intent for wrongness judgments (Russell & Giner-Sorolla, 2011b). Critics have also argued that the purity transgressions used in many studies are novel and bizarre (Gray & Keeney, 2015), to which I would add psychologically complex and potentially rife with confounds. Indeed, unintentional disgusting behaviors that are more everyday and innocuous (e.g., getting dog feces on one's hands when trying to clean it off one's shoes) are not judged as morally wrong at all (Chapman, 2017). In sum, it is currently not clear whether the role of intent really differs between purity and nonpurity transgressions.

One final difference between purity and nonpurity transgressions is also challenging for a strong version of the CPM. Specifically, generating reasons why someone might justifiably commit a purity transgression reduces wrongness ratings to a lesser extent than generating reasons why someone might commit a nonpurity transgression (Russell & Giner-Sorolla, 2011a). On the one hand, this could be because it is difficult to come up with *good* reasons for committing a purity transgression. Consistent with this idea, participants produce less elaborated justifications for their feelings of disgust compared with anger (Russell & Giner-Sorolla, 2011c). On the other hand, even when the scenario explicitly provides external reasons for committing the transgression, people judge that purity transgressions are more voluntary than nonpurity transgressions (Chakroff & Young, 2015). For example, a person who hits his sister in a game of truth or dare is judged to have acted more freely than a person who kisses his sister. This could suggest a genuine difference in the cognitive processes that underlie moral judgments about purity and nonpurity transgressions, which would be compatible with the weaker version of the CPM.

Extension and Expansion

The CPM is part of a new wave of research that emphasizes that character and consequence judgments are distinct aspects of moral cognition (Uhlmann et al., 2015). An important future direction for this line of work will be to determine whether character and consequence judgments might be associated with different behavioral responses to moral transgressions. Most research on how people respond to transgressions has focused on punishment, especially punishment that entails a cost to the punisher (Carlsmith, Darley, & Robinson, 2002; Henrich et al., 2006). Costly punishment is just that, however: costly at worst, risky at best. In the grand scheme, therefore, punishment may be less important than rejection and avoidance, which fall under the umbrella of "partner choice" (Bull & Rice, 1991; Kuhlmeier, Dunfield, & O'Neill, 2014).

In spite of its potential importance, partner choice remains extremely understudied. For example, we do not know when people might opt for partner choice over punishment or what the motivational underpinnings of partner choice might be. The CPM points at potential answers to such questions. First, negative character evaluations may be a major reason for selecting partner choice over punishment. If a person transgresses because he or she has a fundamentally bad character, then he or she is likely to transgress again in the future, and efforts to deter such behavior (e.g., through punishment) are likely to be ineffective (Fischer & Roseman, 2007; Hutcherson & Gross, 2011). Second, given that disgust is hypothesized to subserve withdrawal and avoidance in the moral domain (Chapman & Anderson, 2013; Hutcherson & Gross, 2011), disgust may provide the motivation for partner choice. In sum, the CPM predicts that character evaluations should be a major predictor of partner choice and that disgust provides the motivation to reject and avoid transgressors.

To summarize, the CPM proposes that character and consequence evaluations both contribute to moral judgments and that these moral cognitive processes trigger the emotions of disgust and anger, respectively. In turn, disgust and anger motivate avoidance- and approach-related behavioral responses. This model parsimoniously explains why both purity and nonpurity transgressions trigger disgust and why pu-

rity transgressions are morally condemned; it can also account for at least some of the cognitive differences between purity and nonpurity transgressions. More evidence is certainly needed to shore up the CPM's claims, and the model must ultimately be expanded to include other important moral cognitive processes such as judgments of intent. Nonetheless, the CPM holds the promise of making sense of two decades' worth of work on moral disgust and of informing the fundamental debates about morality that this volume seeks to address.

NOTE

1. The CPM as depicted in Figure 8.1 focuses on the causes of moral disgust and anger rather than trying to provide a complete model of moral judgment. Thus, for simplicity, the model omits other critical moral cognitive processes, such as the role of intent judgments.

REFERENCES

Barrett, L. F. (2006). Solving the emotion paradox: Categorization and the experience of emotion. *Personality and Social Psychology Review, 10*(1), 20–46.

Brehm, J. W., & Self, E. A. (1989). The intensity of motivation. *Annual Review of Psychology, 40,* 109–131.

Bull, J. J., & Rice, W. R. (1991). Distinguishing mechanisms for the evolution of co-operation. *Journal of Theoretical Biology, 149*(1), 63–74.

Cameron, C. D., Lindquist, K. A., & Gray, K. (2015). A constructionist review of morality and emotions: No evidence for specific links between moral content and discrete emotions. *Personality and Social Psychology Review, 19*(4), 371–394.

Cannon, P. R., Schnall, S., & White, M. (2011). Transgressions and expressions: Affective facial muscle activity predicts moral judgments. *Social Psychological and Personality Science, 2*(3), 325–331.

Carlsmith, K. M., Darley, J. M., & Robinson, P. H. (2002). Why do we punish?: Deterrence and just deserts as motives for punishment. *Journal of Personality and Social Psychology, 83*(2), 284.

Carver, C. S., & Harmon-Jones, E. (2009). Anger is an approach-related affect: Evidence and implications. *Psychological Bulletin, 135*(2), 183–204.

Chakroff, A., Dungan, J., & Young, L. (2013). Harming ourselves and defiling others: What determines a moral domain? *PLOS ONE*, *8*(9). Available at *www.ncbi.nlm.nih.gov/pmc/articles/PMC3770666*.

Chakroff, A., & Young, L. (2015). Harmful situations, impure people: An attribution asymmetry across moral domains. *Cognition, 136*, 30–37.

Chapman, H. (2017). *The moral psychology of ordinary purity transgressions*. Manuscript in preparation.

Chapman, H., & Anderson, A. K. (2013). Things rank and gross in nature: A review and synthesis of moral disgust. *Psychological Bulletin, 139*(2), 300–327.

Chapman, H., & Anderson, A. K. (2014). Trait physical disgust is related to moral judgments outside of the purity domain. *Emotion, 14*(2), 341–348.

Chapman, H., Kim, D. A., Susskind, J. M., & Anderson, A. K. (2009). In bad taste: Evidence for the oral origins of moral disgust. *Science, 323*(5918), 1222–1226.

Cosmides, L., & Tooby, J. (2000). Evolutionary psychology and the emotions. In M. Lewis & J. Haviland-Jones (Eds.), *Handbook of emotions* (2nd ed., pp. 91–115). New York: Guilford Press.

Ditto, P. H., & Jemmott, J. B. (1989). From rarity to evaluative extremity: Effects of prevalence information on evaluations of positive and negative characteristics. *Journal of Personality and Social Psychology, 57*(1), 16–26.

Ekman, P. (1992). An argument for basic emotions. *Cognition and Emotion, 6*(3/4), 169–200.

Eskine, K. J., Kacinik, N. A., & Prinz, J. J. (2011). A bad taste in the mouth: Gustatory disgust influences moral judgment. *Psychological Science, 22*(3), 295–299.

Fischer, A. H., & Roseman, I. J. (2007). Beat them or ban them: The characteristics and social functions of anger and contempt. *Journal of Personality and Social Psychology, 93*(1), 103–115.

Fiske, S. T. (1980). Attention and weight in person perception: The impact of negative and extreme behavior. *Journal of Personality and Social Psychology, 38*(6), 889–906.

Frijda, N. (1987). Emotion, cognitive structure, and action tendency. *Cognition and Emotion, 1*(1), 15–143.

Giner-Sorolla, R. S., & Chapman, H. A. (2017). Beyond purity: Moral disgust toward bad character. *Psychological Science, 28*(1), 80–91.

Graham, J., Haidt, J., & Nosek, B. A. (2009). Liberals and conservatives rely on different sets of moral foundations. *Journal of Personality and Social Psychology, 96*(5), 1029–1046.

Graham, J., Nosek, B. A., Haidt, J., Iyer, R., Koleva, S., & Ditto, P. H. (2011). Mapping the moral domain. *Journal of Personality and Social Psychology, 101*(2), 366.

Gray, K., & Keeney, J. E. (2015). Impure, or just weird?: Scenario sampling bias raises questions about the foundation of morality. *Social Psychological and Personality Science, 6*(8), 859–868.

Gray, K., Schein, C., & Ward, A. (2014). The myth of harmless wrongs in moral cognition: Automatic dyadic completion from sin to suffering. *Journal of Experimental Psychology: General, 143*, 1600–1615.

Gray, K., Waytz, A., & Young, L. (2012). The moral dyad: A fundamental template unifying moral judgment. *Psychological Inquiry, 23*(2), 206–215.

Gutierrez, R., Giner-Sorolla, R. S., & Vasiljevic, M. (2011). Just an anger synonym?: Moral context influences predictors of disgust word use. *Cognition and Emotion, 26*(1), 53–64.

Haidt, J. (2001). The emotional dog and its rational tail: A social intuitionist approach to moral judgment. *Psychological Review, 108*(4), 814–834.

Harmon-Jones, E., Sigelman, J., Bohlig, A., & Harmon-Jones, C. (2003). Anger, coping, and frontal cortical activity: The effect of coping potential on anger-induced left frontal activity. *Cognition and Emotion, 17*(1), 1–24.

Henrich, J., McElreath, R., Barr, A., Ensminger, J., Barrett, C., Bolyanatz, A., . . . Ziker, J. (2006). Costly punishment across human societies. *Science, 312*(5781), 1767–1770.

Horberg, E. J., Oveis, C., Keltner, D., & Cohen, A. B. (2009). Disgust and the moralization of purity. *Journal of Personality and Social Psychology, 97*(6), 963–976.

Hutcherson, C. A., & Gross, J. J. (2011). The moral emotions: A social-functionalist account of anger, disgust, and contempt. *Journal of Personality and Social Psychology, 100*(4), 719–737.

Jones, A., & Fitness, J. (2008). Moral hypervigilance: The influence of disgust sensitivity in the moral domain. *Emotion, 8*(5), 613–627.

Kuhlmeier, V. A., Dunfield, K. A., & O'Neill, A. C. (2014). Selectivity in early prosocial behavior. *Frontiers in Psychology, 5*, 836.

Landy, J. F., & Goodwin, G. P. (2015). Does incidental disgust amplify moral judgment?: A meta-analytic review of experimental evidence. *Perspectives on Psychological Science, 10*(4), 518–536.

McKenzie, C. R., & Mikkelsen, L. A. (2007). A

Bayesian view of covariation assessment. *Cognitive Psychology, 54*(1), 33–61.

Oaten, M., Stevenson, R., & Case, T. (2009). Disgust as a disease-avoidance mechanism. *Psychological Bulletin, 135*(2), 303.

Ohtsuki, H., Iwasa, Y., & Nowak, M. A. (2009). Indirect reciprocity provides only a narrow margin of efficiency for costly punishment. *Nature, 457*(7225), 79–82.

Royzman, E., Atanasov, P., Landy, J. F., Parks, A., & Gepty, A. (2014). CAD or MAD?: Anger (not disgust) as the predominant response to pathogen-free violations of the divinity code. *Emotion, 14*, 892–907.

Royzman, E., Leeman, R., & Baron, J. (2009). Unsentimental ethics: Towards a content-specific account of the moral–conventional distinction. *Cognition, 112*(1), 159–174.

Rozin, P., Haidt, J., & Fincher, K. (2009). From oral to moral. *Science, 323*(5918), 1179.

Rozin, P., Haidt, J., & McCauley, C. (1999). Disgust: The body and soul emotion. In T. Dalgleish & M. J. Power (Eds.), *Handbook of cognition and emotion* (pp. 429–445). New York: Wiley.

Rozin, P., Haidt, J., & McCauley, C. (2000). Disgust. In M. Lewis & J. Haviland-Jones (Eds.), *Handbook of emotions* (2nd ed., pp. 637–653). New York: Guilford Press.

Rozin, P., Lowery, L., Imada, S., & Haidt, J. (1999). The CAD triad hypothesis: A mapping between three moral emotions (contempt, anger, disgust) and three moral codes (community, autonomy, divinity). *Journal of Personality and Social Psychology, 76*(4), 574–586.

Russell, P. S., & Giner-Sorolla, R. S. (2011a). Moral anger is more flexible than moral disgust. *Social Psychological and Personality Science, 2*(4), 360–364.

Russell, P. S., & Giner-Sorolla, R. S. (2011b). Moral anger, but not moral disgust, responds to intentionality. *Emotion, 11*(1), 233–240.

Russell, P. S., & Giner-Sorolla, R. S. (2011c). Social justifications for moral emotions: When reasons for disgust are less elaborated than for anger. *Emotion, 11*(3), 637.

Russell, P. S., & Giner-Sorolla, R. S. (2013). Bodily moral disgust: What it is, how it is different from anger, and why it is an unreasoned emotion. *Psychological Bulletin, 139*(2), 328.

Russell, P. S., & Piazza, J. (2014). Consenting to counter-normative sexual acts: Differential effects of consent on anger and disgust as a function of transgressor or consenter. *Cognition and Emotion, 29*(4), 634–653.

Schnall, S., Haidt, J., Clore, G. L., & Jordan, A. H. (2008). Disgust as embodied moral judgment. *Personality and Social Psychology Bulletin, 34*(8), 1096–1109.

Shweder, R. A., Much, N., Mahaprata, M., & Park, L. (1997). The "big three" of morality (autonomy, community, divinity) and the "big three" explanations of suffering. In A. Brandt & P. Rozin (Eds.), *Morality and health* (pp. 119–169). New York: Psychology Press.

Snyder, M. L., Kleck, R. E., Strenta, A., & Mentzer, S. J. (1979). Avoidance of the handicapped: An attributional ambiguity analysis. *Journal of Personality and Social Psychology, 37*(12), 2297–2306.

Turiel, E., Hildebrandt, C., Wainryb, C., & Saltzstein, H. (1991). Judging social issues: Difficulties, inconsistencies, and consistencies. *Monographs of the Society for Research in Child Development, 56*, 35–116.

Turiel, E., Killen, M., & Helwig, C. (1987). Morality: Its structure, functions, and vagaries. In J. Kagan (Ed.), *The emergence of morality in young children* (pp. 155–243). Chicago: University of Chicago Press.

Tybur, J. M., Lieberman, D., Kurzban, R., & DeScioli, P. (2012). Disgust: Evolved function and structure. *Psychological Review, 120*(1), 65–84.

Uhlmann, E. L., Pizarro, D. A., & Diermeier, D. (2015). A person-centered approach to moral judgment. *Perspectives on Psychological Science, 10*(1), 72–81.

Uhlmann, E. L., & Zhu, L. (2013). Acts, persons, and intuitions: Person-centered cues and gut reactions to harmless transgressions. *Social Psychological and Personality Science, 5*, 279–285.

Wheatley, T., & Haidt, J. (2005). Hypnotic disgust makes moral judgments more severe. *Psychological Science, 16*(10), 780–784.

Young, L., & Saxe, R. (2011). When ignorance is no excuse: Different roles for intent across moral domains. *Cognition, 120*, 202–214.

CHAPTER 9

A Functional Conflict Theory of Moral Emotions

Roger Giner-Sorolla

What makes some emotions *moral* emotions?

Emotions are moral in nature when they regulate the interests of a higher level of social organization than the currently focal one by means of four functions that sometimes dysfunctionally conflict: appraisal, association, self-regulation, and communication.

My theory tries to explain why people have emotional reactions to moral situations. It is thus a theory of moral emotions. However, it is important to keep in mind the sometimes-noted distinction between a criminal lawyer (one who deals in criminal cases) and a *criminal* lawyer (one who is a criminal him- or herself; Gilligan et al., 2010). Likewise, an emotion that deals with moral situations is not necessarily one that possesses the essence of moral virtue. In fact, there are very few emotions that are elicited only by moral situations—by "moral" here, I mean concerns that respond to the interest of another over and above one's own. Among the negative emotions, only guilt seems to be "moral" in this sense; even shame sometimes works selfishly to protect one's own reputation. Among the positive emotions, we can count sympathy, the rather rarefied construct of elevation (which by definition responds to an example of moral virtue in

another), and possibly gratitude. Shame, anger, pride, disgust: All of these are moral emotions, but they serve other functions as well. It is that ambiguity that makes them so interesting.

The key constructs here are emotions: mental and sometimes physiological phenomena consisting of eliciting perceptions, subjective feelings, and expressions through several channels, action motivations, and verbal labels to refer to the whole thing: not perfectly, but functionally. Emotions are distinguished from other states and from each other in several ways. They are activated by concerns about oneself or about values and people close to oneself (unlike perception, reasoning, curiosity, etc.). They are hard to control upon activation, so that they serve as an authentic signal of motivations for oneself and others (unlike language, decisions, etc.). And distinct emotions are culturally constructed from underlying biological elements to communicate and motivate individually and socially adaptive behavior. The more socially adaptive the function of an emotion, the more we can say it is moral.

I see four specific overlapping functions of emotions as bearing potential relevance to morality (Giner-Sorolla, 2012).

1. In the *appraisal* function, people assess stimuli in relation to goals (here, moral ones); the outcome of this assessment promotes an emotional response, which prepares and motivates an adaptive behavior. For example, you see a baby crying, you feel bad for it (sympathy, or empathy) and run over to help; if nobody had done that for us when we were little, none of us would be here.

2. *Associative* learning is often seen as irrational, but I see it as functional, too, and perhaps even morally functional. For example, children often learn to associate a national song and symbols with pride. Unlike appraisal, this connection between an arbitrary signifier and a signified emotion arises without purpose or goal, but its easy and unquestioning availability later in life can coordinate large groups of people to action. In some ways, what we consider core moral values depend on unreasoned, basic affective associations (Maio & Olson, 1998).

3. Emotions also have a *regulatory* role to play, some more than others; for example, shame, pride, and guilt seem to be partially internalized anticipations of our reactions to the social effect of our own actions. Anticipating emotional appraisals and associations helps us behave accordingly, without needing to feel or express the full weight of the emotion. There are also motivations and concerns that regulate emotions, undercutting the full weight of guilt and shame in particular by deploying excuses and rationalizations.

4. Finally, emotions *communicate* these states to others in a more trustworthy way than language, or other representations, can. Facial expressions, vocal timbre, and positions and attitudes of the body do this work.

Particularly interesting phenomena arise when these functions conflict with each other. Unlike appraisal theories (e.g., Lazarus, 1991), which attribute dysfunctional side effects of emotion to inaccurate input into an otherwise working system, my functional conflict theory proposes that dysfunction arises when an emotion activated to serve one function falls foul of another. For example, expressing moral anger may be a way to communicate one's moral character or to regulate and externalize one's own insecurities, without necessarily corresponding to the actual situation in a way that would accurately serve appraisal's function.

Historical Context

This is an integrative theory that calls up four strands of functional theorizing about emotions in general and moral emotions in particular. The theory invites them all to a party hosted by the underlying adaptive principle of exaptation, in which a single structure can serve multiple functions (Gould, 2010). Let's stroll around the party and ask the four functions about their historical roots.

Some theories, in the tradition of David Hume and Jonathan Haidt, expect emotions to be functional guides to moral behavior, and these historical perspectives find kinship in today's appraisal theory. This has taken on many forms since it was prefigured by the work of Magda Arnold (1960), developed by Lazarus and Folkman (1984) in the context of coping, and further split into many different schemes over the two decades hence (e.g., Lazarus, 1991; Ortony, Clore, & Collins, 1990; Roseman, 1984; Smith & Ellsworth, 1985; Weiner, 1985). Moral appraisals are fundamentally social, even if internalized in the self, and motivate such behaviors as punishment of wrongdoers (anger), ostracism and avoidance (disgust and contempt), and praise and support of virtuous persons (elevation).

But not all appraisals are sensitive to context, and soon enough the associative function appears to state its case. Regardless of whether or not these context-insensitive, stimulus-triggered emotional associations are classified as a special kind of appraisal (as Moors, Ellsworth, Scherer, & Frijda [2013] do), it is undeniable that they form a large part of the case for morally relevant emotions being irrational, unhelpful, and even in some cases immoral. The underlying template for the irrationality of emotions comes from Freud and other psychodynamic theorists, who see affective associations as partaking of primary-process wish fulfillment, more to do with people's past internal drama than their present external situation (e.g. Freud, 1900/2008). In moral psychology, Nussbaum (2004) has argued that disgust, in particular, as an associative emotion is more supportive of irrational prejudice than of wise and fair moral judgment. However, one can see many examples of other emotions, such as anger, also being activated out of proportion to the situation based on simmering provocations in the recent or distant past. Even emotions such as sympathy can backfire, as when news footage of unclothed children in faraway parts prompts donations of used clothing that, en masse, undercut local producers and further impoverish the economy (cf. Bloom, 2016).

As the shoving match between association and appraisal gets more heated, self-regulation and communication step in and try to mediate. The self-regulation function in my theory draws on fairly recent ideas about the use of emotions as checks or feedbacks to behavior, rather than as motivators of it (e.g., Carver, Lawrence, & Scheier, 1996; Higgins, 1987; Baumeister, Vohs, DeWall, & Zhang, 2007). In some sense, appraisal and self-regulation belong to the same family when it comes to moral emotions. Because moral concerns are ultimately social, each self-regulatory emotion can be seen as the internalization of an appraisal that would be rational in a directly social context. For example, when we accidentally harm someone we care about, we feel both empathic distress at their overt expression of pain and anxiety at their overt disapproval. Guilt and shame preempt this direct perception and invite us to become distressed at our own bad behavior. Thus, when guilt, shame, and other emotions act preemptively on the self, they lose their character of appraisal and become regulatory. In this way, they may even seem irrational.

Certainly, in survivor guilt, the reaction to having kept one's life while someone else has lost it for no good reason shows that guilt has left its original function of resource distribution far behind and reacts to inequality even when there is no hope of restoring it. Thus the regulatory function bridges the apparent gap between associative and appraisal modes by showing how a relatively more internalized, automatized, and mysterious moral feeling is just a rational social appraisal that has taken on a life of its own.

Likewise, the communication function steps in from the other side and reminds the associative and appraisal functions of how it, too, draws on both of them. Communicating emotions regulates the social environment, just as feeling them regulates action. This notion, too, is relatively recent in psychological theory but by now well supported (Parkinson, Fischer & Manstead, 2004; Parkinson & Manstead, 2015; van Kleef, 2009). Social regulation of emotions, too, is a very recently devised and studied topic (Totterdell, Hershcovis, Niven, Reich, & Stride, 2012). The full complexity of how a network of people show their emotions to others, how these emotions as well as actions and utterances seek to influence the feelings *of* others, and how these changes reflect back on us—all of this is perhaps a topic for a more complex and computational model than the simple lab experiment in psychology can reveal.

It may seem that this is a disjunctive theory, but in fact I tie these four functions together in the construct of the emotion and declare that the promise and problem of human emotions comes from the fact that the four functions are jammed together in this party, whose metaphorical usefulness is rapidly outstaying its welcome. What would happen if we could be completely rational and exert executive control over the input to our appraisals, and so turn off our emotions at will? Then our representations of emotions would be worthless as a signal of true intentions, just as they would be worthless as commitments to our own longer term causes. It is in fact this insight of the economist Robert Frank (1988) that underscores how the conflict between reason and unreason has a meaning, and unreason is not to be dismissed lightly. This, ultimately, is my view of morality. Moral feelings are the currency tying us to other individuals, to our groups and our culture, without really giving us the option of leaving them—or, at least, ensuring that leaving them will be done with pain and dislocation.

Another aspect of history that I wish to address is the long debate about whether emotions are necessary for moral judgment and action. Made famous by the contrast of the philosophers Hume and Kant (Nichols, 2004), the debate has been resurrected in recent times by social emotionalist theory (e.g., Greene & Haidt, 2002) and some of its critics (e.g., Huebner, Dwyer, & Hauser, 2009; Monin, Pizarro, & Beer, 2007). Much of this debate is still being worked out empirically, but it is clear to me that the vagueness of the terms *emotion, affect,* and *passion* needs to be sharpened if we are to continue it productively (Giner-Sorolla, 1999). Clearly, there can be no moral considerations without a basic sense of value, of good or bad, a simple level of evaluation sometimes labeled as *affect*. However, most uses of this term imply something deeper, a subjective sense of motivation and importance that is not necessarily arousal, for both the lethargy of sadness and the excitation of anger can compel us.

In previous writing (Giner-Sorolla, 2012), I have waved away the question of whether any given state is an emotion by advocating the term *emotional* to apply to this combination of valence and importance. I am not so sure about this usage now, because it seems an emotion is also more than a motivation. Emotions, or components of them, have the tendency to linger on and affect subsequent states. They have expressive elements, too. From this point of view, moral judgment needs only the simple valence judgment, as when one judges a hypothetical act as right or wrong. Moral action that is persistent and motivated to overcome self-interests and other obstacles, however, I would think needs to be facilitated by feeling a sense of relevance. And beyond mere motivation, moral emotions contribute the ability to communicate this sincere motivation to other people, and to facilitate.

Finally, although it may not stand up as part of the formal definition of an emotion,

one characteristic of many of the most interesting moral emotions is that they can be activated in response to a number of different conceptual inputs and carry through from one context to another. Only some of these may be morally relevant. For example, pride can result from viewing one's own highly competent technical accomplishments or from a basic, unconditional acceptance of oneself; anger can result from personally relevant goal blockage, a threat to one's person or group, or the violation of a moral principle (cf. Kuppens, Mechelen, Smits, & Boeck, 2003). From this point of view, moral emotions per se might be said to be outright dangerous to valid moral decision making because they accept prejudicial, incidental influence from unrelated factors. Although nonemotional judgments are also subject to carryover effects from context, a particular feature of emotions is that they create their own motivation and reality. In both self-deception and self-presentation, moral reasons for having an emotion are the most acceptable, morality being the predominant attribute when judging persons, oneself, and groups (Ellemers & van den Bos, 2012; Wojciszke, 2005). The danger in moral emotions, then, is not that they exist, but that emotions activated by selfish concerns can be given a veneer of moral reasons. The honesty of emotion, backed by its uncontrollability, does not, however, extend to a guarantee of its truly moral nature.

Theoretical Stance

Theories of moral emotions per se are actually few in social psychology, although there have been schemes distinguishing pairs or triads of moral emotions internally, such as the ideas of Tangney (Tangney & Dearing, 2002) and many others on the difference between guilt and shame, and various ideas about what distinguishes anger from disgust and (sometimes) from the Contempt/Anger/Disgust (CAD) triad (Russell & Giner-Sorolla, 2013). I believe that the theory I offer in Giner-Sorolla (2012) is the only specific general theory of the morally relevant nature of emotions, although there have been taxonomies of moral emotions (Haidt,

2003) and general statements of emotionalism (Haidt, 2001).

One idea that has been very influential on my theory is the social–functional emotions theory of Keltner and Haidt (1999). This opened my eyes to the possibility that, unlike the usual claims of "one appraisal = one emotion" prevalent at the time, categorical emotions can arise from more than one input and serve more than one function. A main difference is that Keltner and Haidt base their differing functions on analyses of different levels of social organization, from individual to cultural; they do not integrate multiple emotion theories as I do. This is actually a complementary perspective that, if included, would lead to a truly complicated two-dimensional categorization in which individuals consider the four functions on four different levels of social organization— so that people can appraise national as well as individual concerns, for example, or communicate emotions about family concerns to a family.

Other than that, my functional theory is fairly independent of other controversies in moral psychology, such as how many individual principles govern moral judgment (Cameron, Lindquist, & Gray, 2015; Graham, Haidt, & Nosek, 2009; Kugler, Jost, & Noorbaloochi, 2014). Even if it could be conclusively shown that there is only one basis of moral judgment, the different emotion experiences could underpin different ways of perceiving and communicating this moral material. For example, shame could represent a way of dealing with one's own moral failures that is character-focused, while guilt is more situation-focused (e.g. Tracy & Robins, 2006). The attempt to map specific emotions onto specific moral or immoral acts, although it has some support, is not the only factor feeding into the experience of feelings in morally relevant situations. The relevance of acts to appraising moral character (Giner-Sorolla & Chapman, 2016) and the utility of emotion expressions according to different social goals (Kupfer & Giner-Sorolla, 2016), for example, bear on which of two linked emotions (anger vs. disgust) predominates, even when the acts in question violate the same underlying principle of moral judgment, that is, direct harm to others.

Evidence

Mainly, the evidence supporting my theory has been collected as support for the four individual perspectives that it integrates, and an account of the state of these literatures as of a few years ago can be found in Chapter 2 of Giner-Sorolla (2012). But more than stating that these functions coexist and promoting a distal just-so explanation to integrate them, this theory does present a number of falsifiable statements that can in principle be tested.

Perhaps the most testable claim I propose is that the same construct of emotion serves all four functions. One could easily conceive of a rival argument that the four functions are served by modular, independent psychological and physiological structures. To give just one example of an adversarial test of these ideas, my theory would state that communicative aspects of emotions are activated by the other functions, such that facial expressions and other expressive elements occur even when a person does not think he or she is being observed. This would be falsified strongly by evidence that there is no facial communication in nonsocial situations (or that the facial grimaces produced in such situations have some other purpose, such as embodying feedback or regulating air flow, e.g., facial feedback hypotheses; McIntosh, 1996); and challenged more weakly by evidence that expressive elements of emotion come forth much more strongly in social than nonsocial situations. Likewise, the theory would be falsified to some degree by evidence that associative activation of a particular emotion from memory differs in its effects and output from creation of "fresh" emotions through new appraisal of experience.

Extension and Expansion

The theory generates a number of implications, the most important of which being that emotions are neither to be celebrated nor despised as inputs to moral decision making. With this comes the suggestion that we can gain understanding of emotions by carefully considering in what way they are functioning in the current moral situations. For example, is your disgust at a criminal defendant really due to moral disapproval or to his or her physical unattractiveness? These functional considerations tie into legal concepts of admissible and inadmissible evidence, into clinical considerations of self-deceptive and accurate knowledge, and into the tug-of-war between certainty and open-mindedness that characterizes most processes of persuasion.

As for expanding the theory: Is this not complicated enough? In all seriousness, I have tried to provide a comprehensive theory of moral emotions, and I think the next step is not to further accessorize it but to get more solid evidence for some of the large-scale implications, as outlined herein.

REFERENCES

Arnold, M. B. (1960). *Emotion and personality.* New York: Columbia University Press.

Baumeister, R. F., Vohs, K. D., DeWall, C. N., & Zhang, L. (2007). How emotion shapes behavior: Feedback, anticipation, and reflection, rather than direct causation. *Personality and Social Psychology Review, 11*(2), 167–203.

Bloom, P. (2016). *Against empathy: The case for rational compassion.* New York: Ecco.

Cameron, C. D., Lindquist, K. A., & Gray, K. (2015). A constructionist review of morality and emotions: No evidence for specific links between moral content and discrete emotions. *Personality and Social Psychology Review, 19*(4), 371–394.

Carver, C. S., Lawrence, J. W., & Scheier, M. F. (1996). A control-process perspective on the origins of affect. In L. L. Martin & A. Tesser (Eds.), *Striving and feeling: Interactions among goals, affect, and self-regulation* (pp. 11–52). Mahwah, NJ: Erlbaum.

Ellemers, N., & van den Bos, K. (2012). Morality in groups: On the social-regulatory functions of right and wrong. *Social and Personality Psychology Compass, 6*(12), 878–889.

Frank, R. H. (1988). *Passions within reason: The strategic role of the emotions.* New York: Norton.

Freud, S. (2008). *The interpretation of dreams* (R. Robertson, Ed.; J. Crick, Trans.). Oxford, UK: Oxford University Press. (Original work published 1900)

Gilligan, V., Moore, K., Porter, D., Cranston, B., Gunn, A., Mitte, R. J., . . . Sony Pictures Home Entertainment. (2010). *Breaking bad:* *The complete second season* [Television series]. Culver City, CA: Sony Pictures Home Entertainment.

Giner-Sorolla, R. (1999). Affect in attitude: Immediate and deliberative perspectives. In S. Chaiken & Y. Trope (Eds.), *Dual process theories in social psychology* (pp. 441–461). New York: Guilford Press.

Giner-Sorolla, R. (2012). *Judging passions: Moral emotions in persons and groups.* Hove, UK: Psychology Press.

Giner-Sorolla, R., & Chapman, H. A. (2016). Beyond purity: Moral disgust toward bad character. *Psychological Science, 28*(1), 80–91.

Gould, S. J. (2010). *The panda's thumb: More reflections in natural history.* New York: Norton.

Graham, J., Haidt, J., & Nosek, B. A. (2009). Liberals and conservatives rely on different sets of moral foundations. *Journal of Personality and Social Psychology, 96*(5), 1029.

Greene, J., & Haidt, J. (2002). How (and where) does moral judgment work? *Trends in Cognitive Sciences, 6*(12), 517–523.

Haidt, J. (2001). The emotional dog and its rational tail: A social intuitionist approach to moral judgment. *Psychological Review, 108*(4), 814–834.

Haidt, J. (2003). The moral emotions. In R. J. Davidson, K. R. Sherer, & H. H. Goldsmith (Eds.), *Handbook of affective sciences* (pp. 852–870). New York: Oxford University Press.

Higgins, E. T. (1987). Self-discrepancy: A theory relating self and affect. *Psychological Review, 94*(3), 319–340.

Huebner, B., Dwyer, S., & Hauser, M. (2009). The role of emotion in moral psychology. *Trends in Cognitive Sciences, 13*(1), 1–6.

Keltner, D., & Haidt, J. (1999). Social functions of emotions at four levels of analysis. *Cognition and Emotion, 13*(5), 505–521.

Kugler, M., Jost, J. T., & Noorbaloochi, S. (2014). Another look at moral foundations theory: Do authoritarianism and social dominance orientation explain liberal–conservative differences in "moral" intuitions? *Social Justice Research, 27*(4), 413–431.

Kupfer, T. R., & Giner-Sorolla, R. (2016). Communicating moral motives: The social signaling function of disgust. *Social Psychological and Personality Science.* [Epub ahead of print]

Kuppens, P., Mechelen, I. V., Smits, D. J. M., & Boeck, P. D. (2003). The appraisal basis of anger: Specificity, necessity and sufficiency of components. *Emotion, 3*(3), 254–269.

Lazarus, R. S. (1991). Progress on a cognitive–motivational–relational theory of emotion. *American Psychologist, 46*(8), 819–834.

Lazarus, R. S., & Folkman, S. (1984). *Stress, appraisal, and coping*. New York: Springer.

Maio, G. R., & Olson, J. M. (1998). Values as truisms: Evidence and implications. *Journal of Personality and Social Psychology, 74*(2), 294.

McIntosh, D. N. (1996). Facial feedback hypotheses: Evidence, implications, and directions. *Motivation and Emotion, 20*(2), 121–147.

Monin, B., Pizarro, D. A., & Beer, J. S. (2007). Deciding versus reacting: Conceptions of moral judgment and the reason–affect debate. *Review of General Psychology, 11*(2), 99–111.

Moors, A., Ellsworth, P. C., Scherer, K. R., & Frijda, N. H. (2013). Appraisal theories of emotion: State of the art and future development. *Emotion Review, 5*(2), 119–124.

Nichols, S. (2004). *Sentimental rules: On the natural foundations of moral judgment*. Oxford, UK: Oxford University Press.

Nussbaum, M. C. (2004). *Hiding from humanity: Disgust, shame, and the law*. Princeton, NJ: Princeton University Press.

Ortony, A., Clore, G. L., & Collins, A. (1990). *The cognitive structure of emotions*. Cambridge, UK: Cambridge University Press.

Parkinson, B., Fischer, A. H., & Manstead, A. S. R. (2004). *Emotions in social life: Cultural, group and interpersonal processes*. New York: Taylor & Francis.

Parkinson, B., & Manstead, A. S. R. (2015). Current emotion research in social psychology: Thinking about emotions and other people. *Emotion Review, 7*(4), 371–380.

Roseman, I. J. (1984). Cognitive determinants of emotion: A structural theory. In P. Shaver (Ed.), *Review of personality and social psychology* (Vol. 5, pp. 11–36). Beverly Hills, CA: SAGE.

Russell, P. S., & Giner-Sorolla, R. (2013). Bodily moral disgust: What it is, how it is different from anger, and why it is an unreasoned emotion. *Psychological Bulletin, 139*(2), 328.

Smith, C. A., & Ellsworth, P. C. (1985). Patterns of cognitive appraisal in emotion. *Journal of Personality and Social Psychology, 48*(4), 813–838.

Tangney, J. P., & Dearing, R. L. (2002). *Shame and guilt*. New York: Guilford Press.

Totterdell, P., Hershcovis, M. S., Niven, K., Reich, T. C., & Stride, C. (2012). Can employees be emotionally drained by witnessing unpleasant interactions between coworkers?: A diary study of induced emotion regulation. *Work and Stress, 26*(2), 112–129.

Tracy, J. L., & Robins, R. W. (2006). Appraisal antecedents of shame and guilt: Support for a theoretical model. *Personality and Social Psychology Bulletin, 32*(10), 1339–1351.

Van Kleef, G. A. (2009). How emotions regulate social life: The emotions as social information (EASI) model. *Current Directions in Psychological Science, 18*(3), 184–188.

Weiner, B. (1985). An attributional theory of achievement motivation and emotion. *Psychological Review, 92*(4), 548–573.

Wojciszke, B. (2005). Morality and competence in person- and self-perception. *European Review of Social Psychology, 16*, 155–188.

CHAPTER 10

Getting Emotions Right in Moral Psychology

Piercarlo Valdesolo

How can moral psychology use more nuanced and developed theories of emotion to inform its process models?

Close attention to how modern affective science has divided the landscape of emotions can not only help more accurately map the moral domain, but also help solve current theoretical debates.

Over the past two decades, theorists have begun to emphasize the importance of emotion to moral judgment. But moral psychology continues to be in need of more nuanced and developed theories of emotion to inform its process models. This chapter argues that (1) as models of moral judgment afford increasingly prominent roles to emotion, any attempt at mapping the moral domain requires closer attention to the state of cutting-edge affective science and (2) in doing so, theorists will be able to learn from some of the problems associated with dominant competing theories of emotion and avoid co-opting them into competing theories of what best defines morality. I highlight one way in which this may be happening in current popular theories of morality and adopt a particular critique from affective science to offer a potential theoretical resolution.

Specifically, this chapter focuses on how the modern debate between "construction-

ist" (Barrett, 2006; Clore & Ortony, 2013; Cunningham, Dunfield, & Stillman, 2013; Lindquist, 2013; Russell, 2003) and "basic" (Ekman & Cordaro, 2011; Izard, 2011; Keltner, Haidt, & Shiota, 2006; Levenson, 2011; Panksepp & Watt, 2011) theories of emotion has crept into debates over taxonomies of moral concerns (Cameron, Lindquist, & Gray, 2015; Graham et al., 2013; Gray, Young, & Waytz, 2012). Arguments as to whether emotions are best described as distinct causal mechanisms that demonstrate consistent and specific relationships with outputs (e.g., innate and universal affect programs for disgust, anger, fear) or as arising from more general combinatorial processes (e.g., core affect and conceptual knowledge) have been adapted to argue for mapping morality as either specific correspondences between moral content and psychological experiences (e.g., innate and universal responses to violations of purity or loyalty) or as involving a combination of more elemental affective responses and conceptual knowledge relevant to moral concerns (e.g., core affect and knowledge about dyadic harm).

In doing so, however, important lingering questions associated with these theories of emotion have also been borrowed. Most crucially for this debate in moral psychology is the question of what version of basic emotion theory (BET) moral psychologists are adopting. Recent constructionist critiques pose fatal problems for some versions of BET (Lindquist, Wager, Kober, Bliss-Moreau, & Barrett, 2012) but are only questionably relevant to others (cf. Scarantino & Griffiths, 2011; Scarantino, 2012a, 2012b). Therefore, the viability of categorical approaches to mapping the moral domain rests at least in part on where their allegiances lie in affective science.

This chapter argues for more specificity on the part of moral psychologists on both sides of this debate. Those adopting the theoretical approach of basic emotion theory to argue for pluralist models ought to be clearer on the version of BET to which they subscribe, and those adopting a constructionist approach to argue for primitivist models ought to acknowledge the current limitations of their critique to only certain versions of moral pluralism.

The Role of Emotions in Modern Moral Psychology

Although few theorists now cling to models of morality that do not posit important causal roles for emotions, the complexity with which these models define the relationship between emotions and morality varies substantially. Early theories were mostly concerned with demonstrating simply *that* emotional processes are causally related to moral judgments, and so were understandably vague as to precisely *how* this relationship unfolded and as to the particular definition of emotion they adopted. For example, the two articles largely credited for ushering in a surge of interest in the role of emotions in moral decision making (Greene, Sommerville, Nystrom, Darley, & Cohen, 2001; Haidt, 2001) seemed to focus solely on the role of affect. In the social intuitionist model (SIM), Haidt (2001) offered the following account of a *moral intuition*:

> . . . can be defined as the sudden appearance in consciousness of a moral judgment, including an affective valence (good–bad, like–dislike), without any conscious awareness of having gone through steps of searching, weighing evidence, or inferring a conclusion. . . . One sees or hears about a social event and one instantly feels approval or disapproval. (p. 818)

Similarly, the affective route in Greene's dual-process model is defined by an intuitive *good–bad* or *like–dislike* feeling state. Throughout much of the research that built upon these theories, it remained unclear how emotional states beyond mere valence might influence moral judgments and what theories of emotion the researchers might be adopting.

Other models of morality have posited more specific relationships between the kinds of eliciting situations people encounter, the discrete emotions they experience, and the moral judgments they subsequently make (Graham et al., 2013; Horberg, Oveis, Keltner, & Cohen, 2009; Russell & Giner-Sorolla, 2013; Rozin, Lowery, Imada, & Haidt, 1999). These theories argue that discrete emotional states are preferentially linked with specific categories of moral concerns (e.g., anger with harm, disgust with purity) and emphasize the specificity and consistency of this link.

These kinds of categorical approaches to linking moral concerns with emotional responses have been labeled *whole-number* accounts of morality (Cameron, Payne, & Doris, 2013), the most well known of which is moral foundations theory (MFT; Haidt & Joseph, 2004; Graham, Haidt, & Nosek, 2009; Graham et al., 2011; Graham et al., 2013). MFT was specifically developed as an elaboration on the SIM. Graham et al. (2013) offer the following explanation:

> There is not just one moral intuition—a general flash of "wrongness"—just as there is not one taste receptor on the tongue whose output tells us "delicious!" Rather, we posit that there are a variety of rapid, automatic reactions to patterns in the social world. When we detect such patterns, moral modules fire, and a fully en-

culturated person has an affectively-valenced experience. Not just a feeling of 'good!' or 'bad!', but an experience with a more specific 'flavor' to it, such as 'cruel!', 'unfair!', 'betrayal!', 'subversive!', or 'sick!' (pp. 109–110).

But what theory of emotion takes you from the SIM, identifying the role of mere pleasure or displeasure at an eliciting situation, to MFT, in which the more specific affective flavors such as *compassion, anger,* or *disgust* are linked to specific concerns such as harm and purity? Either implicitly or explicitly, these whole-number approaches ground their view of emotion in some version of BET.

Basic Emotions and Moral Foundations

MFT argues for the existence of moral foundations composed of innate cognitive mechanisms that are responsive to a set of particular adaptive concerns relevant to social living (e.g., protecting children, forming coalitions). These mechanisms are triggered by particular social cues (e.g., distress, cheating, uncleanliness), and in turn they trigger psychological responses, including characteristic emotional states, geared toward motivating adaptive behavioral responses. In keeping with BET, these characteristic emotions represent distinct biological mechanisms thought to "prompt us in a direction that, in the course of our evolution, has done better than other solutions in recurring circumstances" (Ekman & Cordaro, 2011, p. 364).

Critics of whole-number approaches to morality, however, have argued that it is precisely this conceptual reliance on BET that is problematic (Cameron et al., 2013; Schein & Gray, 2015; Gray & Keeney 2015a; Gray, Young, & Waytz, 2012; Cheng, Ottati, & Price, 2013). These researchers argue that in adopting this theory of emotions, any theory of distinct moral domains rests on an empirically untenable basis. Specifically, given that there is no good evidence showing that discrete emotions reflect "affect programs" or any other kind of *consistent* and *coordinated* affective response specific to particular kinds of adaptive challenges, then there will likely be no solid empirical basis for accepting the existence of consistent and coordinated psychological responses to discrete moral concerns.

What Defines a Whole-Number Approach?

Cameron, Lindquist, and Gray (2015) describe whole-number accounts as positing "a core number of evolved and encapsulated mental mechanisms corresponding to 'foundational' moral content . . . and 'basic' emotions" (p. 372). This views MFT as predicting an *exclusive* and *local* relationship between moral content and discrete emotions. Discrete emotions should be consistently and specifically evoked by distinct moral domains. For example, disgust should be evoked for *every* instance of a purity violation, and disgust should be evoked *only* for instances of purity violations. This is what is meant by a *one-to-one* mapping between psychological responses and moral foundations. Importantly, this characterization implies that even if specific emotions are preferentially linked with moral foundations (e.g., purity corresponds with disgust *more* than with anger, and harm corresponds with anger *more* than with disgust), this would still "contradict the fundamental assumptions underlying whole number accounts" (Cameron et al., p. 8). Such "softer" theories are dismissed as predicting an exclusivity that is "far from the exclusivity posited by whole-number accounts" (p. 9).

In short, constructionists argue that whole-number frameworks by definition cannot explain any meaningful overlap between moral content and emotional responding. If harm and purity violations are found to trigger both anger and disgust, even if there may be meaningful differences in effect sizes in the direction predicted by whole-number theories, then such variability must be treated as error and cannot be accommodated by the theory. Put simply, "moral infractions are thought to activate one moral concern and not others" (Schein & Gray, 2015, p. 1151).

Constructionism Defeats This Whole-Number Approach

On this characterization of MFT, constructionists only need to demonstrate that some meaningful amount of within-domain variability in emotional responding exists; that, for example, "harm and purity . . . involve substantial internal variability and large overlap with other kinds of moral content" (Cameron et al., 2015, p. 7). This has been the approach of the constructionist critique in emotion research, and it has largely been successful in accumulating relevant evidence (Barrett, 2006; Barrett, Mesquita, Ochsner, & Gross, 2007; Kassam, Markey, Cherkassky, Loewenstein, & Just, 2013; Lindquist, 2013; Lindquist et al., 2012). Constructionist models, at their core, are "inspired by the observation of variability in emotional responding and the failure of basic emotion approaches to account for this variability" (Barrett, 2009, p. 1290). Similarly, moral constructionists successfully adopt this rhetorical and empirical strategy by amassing a substantial body of research arguing against one-to-one mapping of moral content and emotional responding (cf. Cameron et al., 2013; Cheng, Ottati, & Price, 2013; Gray & Keeney, 2015a; Schein & Gray, 2015). Indeed, if whole-number approaches to morality are committed to theoretical assumptions predicting one-to-one mapping, then their empirical prognosis is grim, and they likely need revision.

But Is This the Whole Number Approach Adopted by MFT?

But of central importance to applying this critique to theories such as MFT is whether whole-number models of morality are indeed of the sort that constructionists describe. Whole-number approaches have not been particularly clear on the extent to which they adopt traditional BET as a theoretical framework. At times, moral modules are conceived of in similar ways to traditional BET—that is, as "little switches in the brains of all animals," triggered by specific moral inputs (Haidt, 2012, p. 123). But there is at least some indication that the theory might not entail the strong view constructionists ascribe to it. Writing about the link between the content of particular sociomoral concerns and subsequent emotional responses, Horberg, Oveis, and Keltner (2011) write: "We therefore expect to observe domain specificity effects, wherein a distinct emotion

predominantly influences moral judgments about issues that express the associated concern" (p. 239; emphasis added). Graham et al. (2013) describe moral foundations as adaptive modules but resist saying that this entails a view of "fully encapsulated entities with fixed neural localizations" (p. 62). And most recently, Graham (2015) acknowledges that "evidence for cognitive differences does not preclude there also being similarities, and evidence for cognitive similarities does not preclude there also being differences" (p. 872).

These statements suggest that the theory allows for overlap in emotional responding to moral concerns and that it might not be committed to the kind of one-to-one mapping of traditional BET. But if this is the case, would it indeed contradict the fundamental assumptions involved in whole-number accounts? Constructionists certainly think so: "Cognitive modules are *by definition* opposed to domain general processes that cut across content" (Gray & Keeney, 2015b, p. 875), and any whole-number account that acknowledges meaningful variability must be "internally inconsistent" (2015b, p. 876).

On this account, the only theoretical framework that can accommodate variability between moral content and emotional responding is constructionism. But what are the fundamental assumptions constructionists take whole-number accounts to be making? And might constructionist critiques be hasty in concluding that all whole-number accounts are bound by them?

If so, there may be versions of whole-number theories that can retain the central theoretical commitments of a basic emotions approach, defined by an emphasis on the specific correspondences between moral content and emotional responding, even in the face of evidence of within-domain variability. Such an approach to mapping the moral landscape would both acknowledge the modern constructionist critique and still predict meaningfully specific, consistent, and ontologically distinct cognitive mechanisms underlying moral domains and discrete emotional responses.

A consideration of how modern affective scientists have been attempting to reconcile constructionist and basic theories of emotion can highlight a more productive path forward for moral psychologists. I highlight one such way in the remainder of this chapter.

A Revised BET as a Foundation for MFT

Constructionist critiques assume commitment to what Scarantino has termed radical locationism (2012c). Specifically, that is that "discrete emotions consistently and specifically correspond to distinct brain regions. A brain region corresponds to an emotion *consistently* just in case it shows increased activation for every instance of that emotion, and *specifically* just in case it shows increased activation only for instances of that emotion" (2012c, p. 161). And for good reason. These are precisely the kinds of claims traditional basic emotion theorists have made. Ekman and Cordero (2011) argue that basic emotions are evolutionarily shaped, biologically prewired, and psychologically primitive responses that are elicited by automatic appraisals and generate automatic and mandatory response patterns in the brain.

But the viability of a theory of basic emotions, and therefore any theory of morality rooted in BET, need not be yoked to only *this particular version* of BET. Basic emotion approaches can come in different flavors, some more vulnerable to constructionist critiques than others. And a revised BET, not committed to radical locationism, might well provide a strong empirical basis for theories positing ontologically distinct content–emotion links in moral psychology. Therefore, the viability of categorical approaches to morality rests at least in part on where their allegiances lie in affective science. What might such a revised BET look like? And do whole-number approaches in morality seem amenable to adopting such a revision?

Essentialist versus Anti-Essentialist Assumptions in Whole-Number Theories

When constructionists argue against radical locationism, they are resisting the modeling of discrete emotions as *natural kinds*:

Natural kind models of emotion not only assume that there are distinct profiles of responses to characterize each kind of emotion, but they also assume that these responses are caused by distinct emotion mechanisms. The causal mechanism for *anger* is presumed responsible for the coordinated package or correlated set of features that constitute an anger response. (Barrett, 2006, p. 31)

This same resistance drives constructionist critiques of morality: "harm and purity are not unique moral mechanisms" (Cameron et al., 2015, p. 377). And a lack of evidence for these kinds of distinct causal mechanisms for emotions and moral domains prompts constructionists toward the *primitivist* conclusion: "that there are no natural kinds of emotion/anger/fear/etc.," and, therefore, researchers should "search for natural kinds at the level of primitive components of discrete emotions" (Scarantino, 2012a, p. 364). Constructionists see whole-number categories as merely descriptively different but nonetheless unified by an underlying psychological mechanism (e.g., concerns about harm) and warn against confusing "practically useful categories with ontologically distinct cognitive processes" (Cameron et al., 2015, p. 377). For example, just as ice and steam are descriptively distinct but nonetheless unified by the same underlying essence (water), distinctions between discrete emotions and moral domains may be practically useful, but they do not reflect ontologically distinct processes and therefore do not qualify as natural kinds (cf. Gray, Young, & Waytz, 2012, p. 102.).

But this is an *essentialist* view of what constitutes a natural kind, and, at least according to some theorists, it may be well suited for the chemical and physical sciences but not necessarily the biological and social sciences (Boyd, 1999; Machery, 2005; Samuels, 2009; Wilson, Barker, & Brigandt, 2007). The latter are best described by an *antiessentialist* approach in which "variability among kind members is the norm, borderline cases often emerge, and generalizations tend to be exception-ridden and only locally valid" (Scarantino, 2012a, p. 365).

Adopting an antiessentialist definition of natural kinds renders the lack of evidence for one-to-one mapping of emotions to underlying mechanism, and moral content to emotion, irrelevant to the question of the viability of all whole-number approaches to emotions or morality. On this approach, there is no good reason for predicting exclusive and local causal mechanisms, either for discrete emotions or for moral domains. The only criteria that need be demonstrated in order to qualify as a natural kind are that the categories in question have "demonstrable explanatory and predictive value in their respective domains" (Scarantino & Griffiths, 2011, p. 451). This view allows whole-number theories to account for within-category variability while still predicting the existence of natural kinds that reflect domain-specific, as opposed to domain-general, mechanisms.

This reconceptualization also allows for the existence of natural kinds at multiple levels of analysis. The essentialist commitment of constructionists compels them to search for natural kinds solely at the level of "the most basic psychological descriptions that cannot be further reduced to anything else mental" (Lindquist et al., 2012, p. 124). But antiessentialism allows for the existence of natural kinds at any level of analysis so long as they satisfy the criterion of predictive power.

So important questions for moral psychologists assessing the viability of whole-number theories become not whether moral domains consistently and specifically activate unique psychological responses; nor whether perceptions of a more general concern, such as harm (Gray, Schein & Ward, 2014; Schein & Gray, 2015), superordinate all judgments of moral wrongness; nor what kind of process constitutes the true "essence" of morality (Gray, Young, & Waytz, 2012; Graham & Iyer, 2012). Rather, the focus becomes solely whether categories of moral concerns can provide explanatory value above and beyond domain-general processes. Such categories can, in theory, be both practically useful and ontologically distinct. Domains such as harm and purity can both reflect unique moral mechanisms and demonstrate meaningful overlap with other kinds of moral content. If this is the kind of framework within which modern whole-number theorists in morality operate, then the constructionist critique can be accommodated.

Conclusion

As theories of moral psychology afford greater causal roles to emotions, the need to specify a theoretical framework for emotions has increased. This is particularly true for researchers interested in the question of how to best scientifically define and search for evidence of whole-number models of morality. The debate in modern affective science between constructionist and BET models can guide such a pursuit, not only by providing insight into that state of empirical support for such kinds of whole-number theories but also by recommending a way forward that avoids some of the conceptual ambiguities associated with advocating for one view or another.

Whole-number advocates ought to be clearer on their fundamental assumptions and situate their theory with respect to current models of emotion. If it is committed to traditional BET and an essentialist view of natural kinds, then the constructionist critique applies, and MFT needs to be revised in light of the compelling evidence from both affective science and moral psychology against the kind of radical locationism it would predict. However, if whole-number theories adopt a revised version of BET built on antiessentialist assumptions, then they can predict a level of functional specialization for domain-specific mechanisms that does not involve radical locationism and allows meaningful variability. On this account, finding significant overlap between different moral content and discrete emotions would not contradict the fundamental assumptions underlying whole-number accounts. Indeed, it would be precisely the level of exclusivity such accounts would expect. Most important, clarifying this theoretical issue could shift the focus of empirical research entirely toward testing this revised view of functional specialization, as opposed to arguing against a framework that moral psychologists may not be adopting.

REFERENCES

Barrett, L. (2006). Are emotions natural kinds? *Perspectives on Psychological Science, 1*(1), 28–58.

Barrett, L. F. (2009). Variety is the spice of life: A psychological construction approach to understanding variability in emotion. *Cognition and Emotion, 23*(7), 1284–1306.

Barrett, L. F., Mesquita, B., Ochsner, K. N., & Gross, J. J. (2007). The experience of emotion. *Annual Review of Psychology, 58,* 373–403.

Boyd, R. (1999). Homeostasis, species, and higher taxa. In R. A. Wilson (Ed.), *Species: New interdisciplinary essays* (pp. 141–185). Cambridge, MA: MIT Press.

Cameron, C. D., Lindquist, K. A., & Gray, K. (2015). A constructionist review of morality and emotions: No evidence for specific links between moral content and discrete emotions. *Personality and Social Psychology Review, 19*(4), 371–394.

Cameron, C. D., Payne, B. K., & Doris, J. M. (2013). Morality in high definition: Emotion differentiation calibrates the influence of incidental disgust on moral judgments. *Journal of Experimental Social Psychology, 49*(4), 719–725.

Cheng, J. S., Ottati, V. C., & Price, E. D. (2013). The arousal model of moral condemnation. *Journal of Experimental Social Psychology, 49*(6), 1012–1018.

Clore, G. L., & Ortony, A. (2013). Psychological construction in the OCC model of emotion. *Emotion Review, 5*(4), 335–343.

Cunningham, W. A., Dunfield, K. A., & Stillman, P. E. (2013). Emotional states from affective dynamics. *Emotion Review, 5*(4), 344–355.

Ekman, P., & Cordaro, D. (2011). What is meant by calling emotions basic. *Emotion Review, 3*(4), 364–370.

Graham, J. (2015). Explaining away differences in moral judgment: Comment on Gray & Keeney (2015). *Social Psychological and Personality Science, 6*(8), 869–873.

Graham, J., Haidt, J., Koleva, S., Motyl, M., Iyer, R., Wojcik, S. P., & Ditto, P. H. (2013). Moral foundations theory: The pragmatic validity of moral pluralism. *Advances in Experimental Social Psychology, 47,* 55–130.

Graham, J., Haidt, J., & Nosek, B. A. (2009). Liberals and conservatives rely on different sets of moral foundations. *Journal of Personality and Social Psychology, 96*(5), 1029.

Graham, J., & Iyer, R. (2012). The unbearable vagueness of "essence": Forty-four clarification questions for Gray, Young, and Waytz. *Psychological Inquiry, 23*(2), 162–165.

Graham, J., Nosek, B. A., Haidt, J., Iyer, R., Koleva, S., & Ditto, P. H. (2011). Mapping the moral domain. *Journal of Personality and Social Psychology, 101*(2), 366.

Gray, K., & Keeney, J. (2015a). Impure, or just weird?: Scenario sampling bias raises questions about the foundation of morality. *Social Psychological and Personality Science, 6*(8), 859–868.

Gray, K., & Keeney, J. E. (2015b). Disconfirming moral foundations theory on its own terms: Reply to Graham (2015). *Social Psychological and Personality Science, 6*(8), 874–877.

Gray, K., Schein, C., & Ward, A. F. (2014). The myth of harmless wrongs in moral cognition: Automatic dyadic completion from sin to suffering. *Journal of Experimental Psychology: General, 143,* 1600–1615.

Gray, K., Young, L., & Waytz, A. (2012). Mind perception is the essence of morality. *Psychological Inquiry, 23*(2), 101–124.

Greene, J. D., Sommerville, R. B., Nystrom, L. E., Darley, J. M., & Cohen, J. D. (2001). An fMRI investigation of emotional engagement in moral judgment. *Science, 293*(5537), 2105–2108.

Haidt, J. (2001). The emotional dog and its rational tail: A social intuitionist approach to moral judgment. *Psychological Review, 108*(4), 814–834.

Haidt, J. (2012). *The righteous mind: Why good people are divided by politics and religion.* New York: Vintage.

Haidt, J., & Joseph, C. (2004). Intuitive ethics: How innately prepared intuitions generate culturally variable virtues. *Daedalus, 133*(4), 55–66.

Horberg, E. J., Oveis, C., & Keltner, D. (2011). Emotions as moral amplifiers: An appraisal tendency approach to the influences of distinct emotions upon moral judgment. *Emotion Review, 3*(3), 237–244.

Horberg, E. J., Oveis, C., Keltner, D., & Cohen, A. B. (2009). Disgust and the moralization of purity. *Journal of Personality and Social Psychology, 97*(6), 963.

Izard, C. E. (2011). Forms and functions of emotions: Matters of emotion–cognition interactions. *Emotion Review, 3*(4), 371–378.

Kassam, K. S., Markey, A. R., Cherkassky, V. L., Loewenstein, G., & Just, M. A. (2013). Identifying emotions on the basis of neural activation. *PLOS ONE, 8,* 1–12.

Keltner, D., Haidt, J., & Shiota, L. (2006). Social functionalism and the evolution of emotions. In M. Schaller, D. Kenrick, & J. Simpson (Eds.), *Evolution and social psychology* (pp. 115–142). New York: Psychology Press.

Levenson, R. W. (2011). Basic emotion questions. *Emotion Review, 3*(4), 379–386.

Lindquist, K. A. (2013). Emotions emerge from more basic psychological ingredients: A modern psychological constructionist model. *Emotion Review, 5*(4), 356–368.

Lindquist, K. A., Wager, T. D., Kober, H., Bliss-Moreau, E., & Barrett, L. F. (2012). The brain basis of emotion: A meta-analytic review. *Behavioral and Brain Sciences, 35*(3), 121–143.

Machery, E. (2005). Concepts are not a natural kind. *Philosophy of Science, 72*(3), 444–467.

Panksepp, J., & Watt, D. (2011). What is basic about basic emotions?: Lasting lessons from affective neuroscience. *Emotion Review, 3*(4), 387–396.

Rozin, P., Lowery, L., Imada, S., & Haidt, J. (1999). The CAD triad hypothesis: A mapping between three moral emotions (contempt, anger, disgust) and three moral codes (community, autonomy, divinity). *Journal of Personality and Social Psychology, 76*(4), 574–586.

Russell, J. A. (2003). Core affect and the psychological construction of emotion. *Psychological Review, 110*(1), 145–172.

Russell, P. S., & Giner-Sorolla, R. (2013). Bodily moral disgust: What it is, how it is different from anger, and why it is an unreasoned emotion. *Psychological Bulletin, 139*(2), 328–351.

Samuels, R. (2009). Delusion as a natural kind. In M. Broome & L. Bortolotti (Eds.), *Psychiatry as cognitive neuroscience: Philosophical perspectives* (pp. 49–82). Oxford, UK: Oxford University Press.

Scarantino, A. (2012a). How to define emotions scientifically. *Emotion Review, 4*(4), 358–368.

Scarantino, A. (2012b). Some further thoughts on emotions and natural kinds. *Emotion Review, 4*(4), 391–393.

Scarantino, A. (2012c). Functional specialization does not require one-to-one mapping between brain regions and emotions. *Behavioral and Brain Sciences, 35*(3), 161–162.

Scarantino, A., & Griffiths, P. (2011). Don't give up on basic emotions. *Emotion Review, 3*(4), 444–454.

Schein, C., & Gray, K. (2015). The unifying moral dyad: Liberals and conservatives share the same harm-based moral template. *Personality and Social Psychology Bulletin, 41*(8), 1147–1163.

Wilson, R. A., Barker, M. J., & Brigandt, I. (2007). When traditional essentialism fails: Biological natural kinds. *Philosophical Topics, 35*, 189–215.

PART III
MORALITY, SOCIAL COGNITION, AND IDENTITY

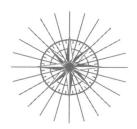

QUESTIONS ANSWERED IN PART III

CHAPTER 11 What do people evaluate when they assess another person's moral character?

CHAPTER 12 What is the basis of moral cognition?

CHAPTER 13 What is the purpose of moral judgment?

CHAPTER 14 Is moral behavior the product of intuitive psychological processes that can show both flexibility and cross-situational stability?

CHAPTER 15 What explains the deep connection between morality and the folk concept of personal identity?

CHAPTER 16 What is the best way to characterize morality?

CHAPTER 17 Why are we comfortable with eating animals, but uncomfortable with hurting them?

CHAPTER 11

What Do We Evaluate When We Evaluate Moral Character?

Erik G. Helzer
Clayton R. Critcher

What do people evaluate when they assess another person's moral character?

In this chapter, we define moral character in novel social cognitive terms and offer empirical support for the idea that the central qualities of moral character are those deemed essential for social relationships.

The notion of moral character is central to the way that people think about and evaluate one another (Landy & Uhlmann, Chapter 13, this volume; Pizarro & Tannenbaum, 2011). People prioritize moral character traits when judging the overall favorability of a person (Goodwin, Piazza, & Rozin, 2014) and define personal identity largely in terms of moral characteristics (Strohminger & Nichols, 2014). Moreover, assessments of moral character seem to be rooted in a shared social reality: People's self-rated standing on a variety of moral character traits tends to be associated with the way that others view them (Cohen, Panter, Turan, Morse, & Kim, 2013), and different observers tend to agree with one another about a target's character (Helzer et al., 2014).

We approach this chapter from the theoretical standpoint that the centrality of char-acter evaluation is due to its function in social life. Evaluation of character is, we think, inherently a judgment about a person's qualifications for being a solid long-term social investment. That is, people attempt to suss out moral character because they want to know whether a particular agent is the type of person who likely possesses the necessary (even if not sufficient) qualities they expect in a social relationship. In developing these ideas theoretically and empirically, we consider what form moral character takes, discuss what this proposal suggests about how people may and do assess others' moral character, and identify an assortment of qualities that our perspective predicts will be central to moral character evaluation.

We begin by putting forward a new idea of what we think moral character means, rooted in a social-cognitive view of the person as a moral being. We introduce the idea that a person's moral character takes the form of moral cognitive machinery—essentially a processor that accepts inputs that, if the processor functions well, should output morally relevant judgments and behavior. Because our perspective suggests that moral judgment is ultimately an exercise in evaluating character, we argue that many inputs that are assumed to change people's moral thinking—even inputs that are not themselves moral in nature—should change how people are judged for what morally relevant actions they take. We illustrate these implications by drawing on our own recent empirical work that has investigated how people engage in moral character evaluation—what we see as an exercise in identifying whether a person possesses the "right" kind of moral-cognitive machinery to produce sound moral decisions.

We next take on the question of content: What are the more specific characteristics of a person with good moral character? That is, instead of considering the abstract form that moral character may take, we ask what qualities define moral character. In this section, we present several forms of preliminary evidence suggesting that moral qualities are those that describe necessary conditions of social investment. In so doing, we engage with two questions. First, we consider how our perspective is compatible with both moral pluralism and moral universalism—how moral codes may show variety and consistency across cultural contexts. Second, we consider in what circumstances people should be more or less likely to assume that others' character is more or less upstanding.

A Social Cognition Conception of Moral Character

In determining whether someone has good moral character, the most intuitive place to start might be with outward behavior. Certain actions (e.g., kicking puppies, donating an organ), in and of themselves, would seem to offer a diagnostic view of the agent's character. However, in most cases, outward behavior alone is insufficient for character evaluation because such information fails to fully characterize what an actor has done. Is

John a bad guy if he does not tell the truth to his boss? Possibly, but to know for sure, most perceivers would want to know *why* John lied. Even kicking a puppy or donating an organ may be, with reflection, more properly characterized as saving a life or abusing a loved one, respectively, when one learns that the dog was being moved out of oncoming traffic or that the donor refused to honor the wishes of a suffering, terminally ill family member. Stated differently, if one does not know why others behaved as they did, then in most circumstances one cannot properly characterize their actions. Indeed, a plethora of research on the use of intentions, motives, desires, metadesires, beliefs, and other mental states in moral evaluation (Critcher, Inbar, & Pizarro, 2013; Fedotova, Fincher, Goodwin, & Rozin, 2011; Gray, Young, & Waytz, 2012; Monroe & Reeder, 2011; Pizarro, Uhlmann, & Salovey, 2003; Reeder, 2009) collectively highlights the idea that others' inferred or stated mental contents provide the proper context in which to evaluate the deeper meaning, and thus moral significance, of their actions.

If outwardly observed behavior alone is insufficient for classifying most moral behaviors, it is all the more insufficient for evaluating character. Moral character resides not in behaviors themselves, but in the person and his or her cross-temporal, cross-situational proclivity to make morally relevant decisions in either upstanding or disreputable ways. We propose that good moral character can be thought of as a well-functioning moral-cognitive processor, one that translates relevant inputs (e.g., situational cues, emotional impulses) into morally appropriate outputs (judgment and behavior). And by *relevant,* we do not mean cues that normatively *should* influence one's judgment and behavior. Instead, we identify cues as relevant if they are seen as likely to influence one's moral thinking and thus provide information about the soundness of the agent's processor. For example, if a woman donates to a cleft lip charity after seeing emotionally evocative pictures of those with this birth defect, we gain reassuring information that she responds in such uncomfortable situations with empathy and compassion instead of by putting on her blinders, and this tells us something favorable about her character.

That said, the worthiness of donating to the charity certainly does not depend on whether a donor has seen such pictures.

By analogy, consider what it means for a car to function properly. On the one hand, one could merely assess its "behavior": Does the car do the things that a "good" car does, namely, travel from its origin to its intended destination? But note that even a broken-down jalopy may pass this test. The driver might want to get the car from the top of a mountain to a valley below. If this were accomplished only by pushing the car over a ledge, we would hardly say this car was in good working order (and most likely would not be anytime soon). If the car's outward "behavior" is insufficient, what might we use to determine whether the car is a good, safe investment? We know a car functions well when it responds appropriately to input from the driver: a turn of the key, of the wheel, or of the radio volume knob should have predictable consequences for the engine, the car's trajectory, and the stereo. If those inputs do not prompt the relevant outputs, we say the car is broken. We would be reluctant to ride in such a car, let alone purchase it, and we would likely keep our loved ones away, as well.

We argue that assessments of moral character—the *moral-cognitive machinery* inside a person that responds to influencing inputs with potentially appropriate outputs—operate similarly. Thus, in judging others' character, people want to know whether agents attend to relevant cues, process those cues appropriately, and arrive at their moral decisions in light of those cues in the way that a good moral decision maker— that is, one who has good moral-cognitive machinery—would do. If moral judgment is indeed in the service of determining who is a good candidate for social investment, it makes sense that perceivers are concerned not merely with an agent's specific actions or motives, but with whether the agent can be trusted to make sound moral decisions in light of the many inputs and contexts that he or she may face.

It follows, then, that moral judgments (serving as a read-off of perceived moral character) should be sensitive to the demonstrated link between inputs and outputs. Consider the following scenario: A military commander must decide whether to order an air strike against an al-Qaeda terrorist cell, which would kill several top al-Qaeda leaders and thwart an imminent 9/11-style attack, but would also sacrifice one innocent person. In recent research, we (Critcher, Helzer, Tannenbaum, & Pizarro, 2017) asked people to assess the moral character of a commander who orders this strike or chooses not to under one of two conditions. In one condition, the commander can see a terrorist leader through the window of the building as he decides whether to strike. In the other condition, the commander can see the innocent person. On a strict act-based account of moral judgment, and according to several normative ethical theories (including both deontology and utilitarianism), the commander's vantage point should be irrelevant to the evaluation of the commander's actions or character. That is, his vantage point does not change his actions' consonance with these ethical theories' prescriptions. However, we found that the commander's point of view *did* matter: On average, people saw him as having less praiseworthy character if he ordered the strike with the innocent person, rather than the terrorist, in view.

The reason this seemingly irrelevant variation in context mattered to people's judgments is that it revealed something about the goodness of the agent's moral-cognitive machinery, its response to triggering inputs with appropriate (or inappropriate) outputs. When the terrorist was in view, participants assumed that utilitarian concerns about preventing future large-scale destruction would loom large in the commander's mind. But when the innocent translator loomed large in the commander's visual field, it was assumed that deontological prohibitions against taking life would weigh heavily on his conscience. The commander was seen as possessing more praiseworthy character if he then acted on the thoughts that were believed to be prompted by his context. The contextual dependency we observed in this and other studies suggests that people were looking for evidence of a well-functioning moral-cognitive machinery—one that responds to environmental inputs that are assumed to inspire morally relevant cognitions with the matching behavioral outputs. In so doing, perceivers are observing moral character that accelerates when the pedal is depressed and that stops short when the brake is slammed.

From General to Specific: What Defines Moral Character?

To say that agents have good moral character is to say their moral-cognitive machinery works soundly; it predictably translates inputs into morally appropriate outputs. But what qualities are people looking for when they are assessing another's moral character? In moral psychologists' quest to understand what differentiates *actions* that people deem morally acceptable versus those considered unacceptable, they have spent most of their efforts examining people's reactions to moral dilemmas. Such dilemmas afford the opportunity to isolate various features of actions and examine their effects on resulting moral judgments, providing a crisp picture of the features of action to which moral judgments are responsive.

In this effort to locate the fine line between right and wrong, however, moral psychologists have not paid as much attention to more prototypical, everyday examples of morality and immorality (cf. Hofmann, Wisneski, Brandt, & Skitka, 2014). This neglect poses a problem for applying our character-based perspective. Without more clearly understanding the domains that are more or less typical of lay conceptions of morality, we do not know precisely what it is that people are trying to assess or comment on when they consider others' moral character. To return to the car example, one might be comfortable investing long term in a car, even if it needs a new sound system, because sound systems are inessential features (for most of us) and are thus only somewhat relevant to the car's overall value. Most would say a car still works even when the radio's volume knob does not. However, the same person would be reluctant to invest in a car with an engine that does not always start. In the same way, although a variety of qualities or domains could be argued to be moral in nature, we consider which qualities are more or less essential to the definition.

The question of what qualities define good moral character is ultimately a ques-

tion about what constitutes morality. That is, to understand what traits define those with good and bad character, one must stipulate the boundaries of morality. On the one hand, some have balked at the notion that morality is a unified construct (Sinnott-Armstrong & Wheatley, 2012; Stich, Chapter 55, this volume). And, as such, it might seem intractable to clearly delineate what behavioral domains are or are not relevant to morality. On the other hand, if one takes a functionalist approach to defining morality by answering what morality (and, in turn, moral character judgment) is for, the boundaries of what is and is not relevant to morality may come into sharper focus. Taking such a functionalist approach, Haidt and Kesebir (2010) argue that moral systems have the ultimate goal of keeping individuals' immoral impulses in check so as to make social systems function. But even those who have taken more of a micro approach on morality by considering what characterizes morally relevant behaviors have also concluded that morality resides in one person's relationship to another (see Rai, Chapter 24, this volume). For example, Gray et al. (2012) argue that moral infractions are understood through a common schema, a dyadic template that involves an agentic wrongdoer and a passive victim. Combining both perspectives, one understands morality as an inherently social concern that offers normative prescriptions for how people should and should not relate to one another.

But even if morality's broader purpose is social, many have been quick to note that not all (im)moral actions exist in social contexts (e.g., Alicke, 2012). If so, it may call into question the degree to which moral character is understood through a social lens. For example, urinating on a holy book, masturbating with an American flag, or sprinkling a former pet's ashes over one's meal are all actions that strike many as immoral, even if the social victims are difficult to identify in such solitary activities. Although observing such victimless wrongs may still entail an automatic identification of a victim (Gray, Schein, & Ward, 2014), our character-based perspective on morality suggests that the social victims need not be found directly in the consequences of the actions. That is, we stress that moral evaluation is not merely in the service of prescribing and proscribing specific actions. Instead, it is a concern with identifying morally trustworthy and untrustworthy people. As such, some actions may be labeled as immoral not because they directly victimize someone but because they reflect a flawed moral-cognitive machinery that is likely to bring harm to others in the future. In other words, we suspect that even those who override the initial impulse to see harm in victimless wrongs may be reluctant to place social trust in the perpetrators. Few would see "Bible-urinater" as evaluatively neutral when it comes to selecting a babysitter (cf., Doris, 2002). It is for a similar reason that attempted (but unrealized) harms are morally vilified. A terrorist whose plot was foiled may have caused no one any harm, but the probability of his doing so in the future is likely perceived to be relatively high.

Combining these character-focused and social perspectives on morality, we argue that what differentiates moral dimensions from other dimensions of personality—and thus what people focus on in their assessments of moral character—are those characteristics deemed to be *socially essential*. Positive personality characteristics can range from those that are essential and nonnegotiable for long-term social investment to those that are merely preferable or optional. Although many of us would gravitate toward potential friends who are attractive, talented, or funny, we are willing to form close friendships even with those who do not meet one or all of these criteria. These are pluses, but not musts. In contrast, most of us would not be willing to invest in people who are callous, insulting, or conniving. This is because people likely have thresholds for others' compassion, empathy, and trustworthiness, below which they would rather abandon such relationships instead of investing in them further.

If it is the case that assessments of moral character are determinations of whether a person is worthy of long-term social investment, then our perspective suggests that there should be a strong overlap between what traits are most moral and what traits are most socially essential. We describe three preliminary efforts to examine empirically what qualities are central, peripheral, or un-

related to moral character and whether what differentiates such qualities is the degree to which they are socially essential in nature. In one study, we exposed 186 undergraduates at the University of California, Berkeley, to 40 positive personality traits. Participants rated all traits on several dimensions, two of which are relevant to our current interests. They indicated to what extent each trait was morally relevant and how *essential* each trait was by indicating their willingness to pursue a relationship with a person, even if he or she was *not* characterized by the trait. As expected, the two dimensions were extremely tightly correlated, $r(38) = .87$. A trait's moral connotation and social essentialism were nearly one and the same.

In another study, we experimentally manipulated the perceived morality of traits. We identified 13 traits that were relatively ambiguous in their moral connotation. For example, people differ in whether they think *reasonable* is or is not indicative of someone's moral character. We first presented people with 13 traits that were clearly moral (e.g., *honorable*) or clearly nonmoral (e.g., *imaginative*) and explicitly labeled the traits as such. Participants then saw the 13 ambiguous traits, to which we gave the contrasting label—*moral* for those who had first viewed the nonmoral traits and *nonmoral* for those who had first viewed the moral traits. Framing the same trait as moral prompted people to see it as more socially essential than when it was framed as nonmoral.

In a third investigation, community participants were given 60 traits and asked to rate how characteristic each was of someone they liked—that is, someone in whom they would invest time and interpersonal resources (Hartley et al., 2017). What was first notable was that moral traits and corresponding immoral traits clustered at the top and bottom of the list, respectively; traits that were instead related to competence and affability filled in the middle ranks. Looking more carefully at which moral traits tended to be at the top or bottom of the list, we gain a clearer picture of what moral dimensions are indeed most socially essential. Traits related to interpersonal trust (honesty, fairness, trusting) and interpersonal distrust (unfaithful, cruel) were at the top and bottom of the rankings, respectively. Other moral traits that did not relate to how people treat others but instead people's more general dispositions (e.g., grateful, wholesome) were more middling in their perceived necessity.

This suggests that moral traits related to trustworthiness—a quality of those who can be counted on to behave in fair and predictable ways—may be the most socially essential and, as such, most core to conceptions of moral character. If so, we might expect to see evidence that people are particularly attuned to the trustworthiness of others. We see three distinct lines of work as promoting this conclusion. First, trustworthiness is a core component of one of two primary dimensions underlying social cognition and person perception broadly (Fiske, Cuddy, & Glick, 2007). Second, people automatically assess others' trustworthiness from brief exposure to targets' faces (Engell, Haxby, & Todorov, 2007), an efficiency that highlights the importance of such assessments to social relations. Third, people reason quite efficiently when others fail to display untrustworthy behavior—overcoming the fundamental attribution error (Fein, 1996) and the confirmation bias (Brown & Moore, 2000)—leading some to posit an evolved cheater detection system (Cosmides & Tooby, 1992). In other words, effectively identifying who is versus who is not trustworthy may be sufficiently important to have been selected for evolutionarily. Of course, what form such trustworthiness takes, whether its concrete instantiation is universal or culturally variable, and what characterizes the circumstances in which breaking trust is acceptable (or even morally advisable) is not answered by this perspective. But by understanding that trust is seen as a core feature of worthwhile social targets, it suggests that understanding the details of how we determine others' trustworthiness (as opposed to, say, their gratitude) will give us a clearer picture of what contributes to assessments of moral character.

Implications of and Questions Raised by the Present Account

Viewing moral judgment as an exercise in determining whether others have socially essential character traits offers a lens through which to consider a number of questions in more detail. We discuss four here. First, the socially essential account accommodates both universalism and pluralism in people's moral codes. Although there is a core set of qualities that describe those who make dependable social relationship partners (e.g., trustworthiness, fairness), social groups may vary in how such qualities are properly enacted. For example, although most people will agree that fairness is a core value to promote within societies, people may vary in whether they believe a respect for authority or ability is *the fair* way to define social hierarchy. Of course, there is also likely to be some variability in different cultures' conceptions of what qualities are socially essential. One question for future research is whether there exists a relationship—either positive or negative—between the degree of cross-cultural variability in the perceived essentialness of a trait and the likelihood that the trait is seen as essential in any given culture. For example, those from interdependent cultures may be more likely to see pridefulness as socially dangerous and guilt-proneness as an encourager of social harmony than are those from independent cultures (Mesquita, De Leersnyder, & Albert, 2014). Does the cultural variability surrounding these prescriptions suggest that prescriptive norms encouraging or discouraging such traits are likely to be less strong than those governing moral universals? Or, instead, in light of such cultural variability, are such qualities moralized more because they are diagnostic of one's commitment to one's ingroup and its norms?

Second, if the task of moral judgment is to deduce whether a person has socially essential traits, then qualities that are not themselves socially essential—but that signal the presence or absence of such essential properties—may become moralized as well. For example, although hedonism need not interfere with the quality of social relationships (Schwartz, 2006) some people—especially conservatives (Iyer, Koleva, Graham, Ditto, & Haidt, 2012)—pass moral judgment on those who prioritize the pursuit of pleasure. At first blush, this appears to be at odds with our account. But once one considers that many hedonists actually are socially disagreeable—those identified by Ksendzova,

Iyer, Hill, Wojcik, and Howell (2015) as *maladaptive hedonists*—and that even those hedonists who are not disagreeable tend to reject conservative, group-binding moral ideals such as respect for authority and in-group loyalty, it becomes apparent that hedonists are likely to lack a number of these qualities that many find socially essential. By accepting that acts are judged on the basis of what they imply about moral character, not necessarily on the moral consequences that they directly cause, it is easier to understand why acts that merely signal the potential absence of socially essential personality characteristics will themselves become moralized.

Third, if good moral character is deemed essential for pursuing a relationship with someone but one does not know another's moral character before interacting with him or her, then this would seem to offer up a conundrum. Wouldn't people be constantly discouraged from expanding their social networks if candidates for such expansion are of unknown moral character? Of course, there are steps that people can take to reduce the risk inherent in wading into novel social territory. People can find out others' opinions of a potential social investment or test them in smaller ways. But people must be motivated to explore new opportunities and seek out this potentially reassuring information to begin with or decide whether to give someone a chance when trusted social networks cannot provide this information.

One way out of this conundrum is to approach new individuals with an optimistic outlook on their moral character (Critcher & Dunning, 2014). In recent work, people say that they "assume the best" about certain positive traits in others until such high hopes are proven wrong. More important, people tend to endorse this strategy more for moral traits than for nonmoral ones (Critcher & Dunning, 2015). But when it comes to actually giving others the benefit of the doubt, it seems that people apply such hopeful expectations when considering specific individuals but not when pondering humanity in general. This bias may be functional: Given that social relationships are pursued with individuals (instead of all of humanity), optimism about their moral character may be a helpful nudge in pushing one to at least preliminarily test out the goodness of a prospective friend.

Fourth, if people are interested in investing only in individuals who have sufficiently solid moral character, just how strong a moral character is it necessary for them to have? Note that one's social interactions do not merely involve other people; they also involve oneself. Furthermore, the self provides a useful and omnipresent comparison standard by which we make sense of others (Dunning & Cohen, 1992; Dunning & Hayes, 1996). People who do not donate to charity are likely to find a $150 check to the American Cancer Society to be generous, whereas those who give away 20% of their income may be less impressed. Given that self-views offer a natural context by which to evaluate others, it is likely that judgments of others' social investment value will be determined by how their credentials compare to one's own.

The trick is that people often possess inflated, rather than accurate, perceptions of their own strengths and weaknesses (Critcher, Helzer, & Dunning, 2010; Dunning, 2005). Given that others are unlikely to stack up well against this aggrandized standard, the same psychological tactics that make people feel worthy in their own eyes may diminish their perceptions of others' worthiness. These self-enhancing views, writ large, might lead people to unnecessarily dismiss others as having insufficient moral character. But research suggests a moderator of self-enhancement that may alleviate such a tendency. Alicke, Klotz, Breitenbecher, Yurak, and Vredenburg (1995) first documented that people compare themselves more humbly against a specific individual (e.g., an unknown student seated nearby) than against a population of others from which that individual was drawn (e.g., all students). So, although the typical college student is likely to see herself as more studious than her peers, she will not necessarily see herself as more studious than any particular peer against whom she compares herself. Furthermore, people rate themselves more humbly when offering ratings of themselves and another individual at the same time compared to making those self and social judgments at different points in time (Critcher & Dunning, 2015). Highlighting how such humility is functional in light of the socially essential account, both tendencies were stronger for moral traits (Critcher & Dunning, 2014, 2015). In other words, people temper their own moral self-views so as to avoid preemptively dismissing specific individuals as unworthy of social investment.

Conclusions

Judgments of moral character provide rich information about others' likely reactions and behaviors across a range of situations, ultimately informing decisions about whether to invest in social relationships with them. In this chapter, we have brought forth empirical evidence in support of this functionalist view of moral evaluation and have reviewed recent research illuminating the process and focus of that search. We argue that moral character evaluation involves both a general assessment of the soundness of a person's moral-cognitive machinery and a more specific assessment of the appropriateness of the outputs of that machinery. By appreciating that the study of moral evaluation must move beyond the question of "What makes acts moral or immoral?" to "What characterizes those of high or low moral character?", we expect that future research will be able to uncover additional strategies that social perceivers use to determine whether others are morally good people and thus worthy of social investment.

REFERENCES

Alicke, M. D. (2012). Self-injuries, harmless wrongdoing, and morality. *Psychological Inquiry, 23,* 125–128.

Alicke, M. D., Klotz, M. L., Breitenbecher, D. L., Yurak, T. J., & Vredenburg, D. S. (1995). Personal contact, individuation, and the better-than-average effect. *Journal of Personality and Social Psychology, 68,* 804–825.

Brown, W. M., & Moore, C. (2000). Is prospective altruist-detection an evolved solution to the adaptive problem of subtle cheating in cooperative ventures?: Supportive evidence using the Wason selection task. *Evolution and Human Behavior, 21,* 25–37.

Cohen, T. R., Panter, A. T., Turan, N., Morse, L., & Kim, Y. (2013). Agreement and similarity in self–other perceptions of moral character. *Journal of Research in Personality, 47,* 816–830.

Cosmides, L., & Tooby, J. (1992). Cognitive adaptations for social exchange. In J. H. Barkow, L. Cosmides, & J. Tooby (Eds.), *The adapted mind: Evolutionary psychology and the generation of culture* (pp. 163–228). Oxford, UK: Oxford University Press.

Critcher, C. R., & Dunning, D. (2014). Thinking about others vs. another: Three reasons judgments about collectives and individuals differ. *Social and Personality Psychology Compass, 8,* 687–698.

Critcher, C. R., & Dunning, D. (2015). *When and why I think I'm better than them, but not him.* Unpublished manuscript.

Critcher, C. R., Helzer, E. G., & Dunning, D. (2010). Self-enhancement via redefinition: Defining social concepts to ensure positive views of the self. In M. Alicke & C. Sedikides (Ed.), *Handbook of self-enhancement and self-protection* (pp. 69–91). New York: Guilford Press.

Critcher, C. R., Helzer, E. G., Tannenbaum, D., & Pizarro, D. A. (2017). *Moral evaluations depend upon mindreading moral occurrent beliefs.* Unpublished manuscript.

Critcher, C. R., Inbar, Y., & Pizarro, D. A. (2013). How quick decisions illuminate moral character. *Social Psychological and Personality Science, 4,* 308–315.

Doris, J. M. (2002). *Lack of character: Personality and moral behavior.* New York: Cambridge University Press.

Dunning, D. (2005). *Self-insight: Roadblocks and detours on the path to knowing thyself.* New York: Psychology Press.

Dunning, D., & Cohen, G. L. (1992). Egocentric definitions of traits and abilities in social judgment. *Journal of Personality and Social Psychology, 63,* 341–355.

Dunning, D., & Hayes, A. F. (1996). Evidence for egocentric comparison in social judgment. *Journal of Personality and Social Psychology, 71,* 213–229.

Engell, A. E., Haxby, J. V., & Todorov, A. (2007). Implicit trustworthiness decisions: Automatic coding of face properties in the human amygdala. *Journal of Cognitive Neuroscience, 19,* 1508–1519.

Fedotova, N. O., Fincher, K. M., Goodwin, G. P., & Rozin, P. (2011). How much do thoughts count?: Preference for emotion versus principle in judgments of antisocial and prosocial behavior. *Emotion Review, 3,* 316–317.

Fein, S. (1996). Effects of suspicion on attributional thinking and the correspondence bias. *Journal of Personality and Social Psychology, 70,* 1164–1184.

Fiske, S. T., Cuddy, A. J. C., & Glick, P. (2007). Universal dimensions of social cognition: Warmth and competence. *Trends in Cognitive Science, 11,* 77–83.

Goodwin, G. P., Piazza, J., & Rozin, P. (2014). Moral character predominates in person perception and evaluation. *Journal of Personality and Social Psychology, 106,* 148–168.

Gray, K., Schein, C., & Ward, A. F. (2014). The myth of harmless wrongs in moral cognition: Automatic dyadic completion from sin to suffering. *Journal of Experimental Psychology: General, 143,* 1600–1615.

Gray, K., Young, L., & Waytz, A. (2012). Mind perception is the essence of morality. *Psychological Inquiry, 23,* 101–124.

Haidt, J., & Kesebir, S. (2010). Morality. In S. Fiske, D. Gilbert, & G. Lindzey (Eds.), *Handbook of social psychology* (5th ed., pp. 797–832). Hoboken, NJ: Wiley.

Hartley, A. G., Furr, R. M., Helzer, E. G., Jayawickreme, E., Velasquez, K. R., & Fleeson, W. (2016). Morality's centrality to liking, respecting, and understanding others. *Social Psychological and Personality Science, 7*(7), 648–657.

Helzer, E. G., Furr, R. M., Hawkins, A., Barranti, M., Blackie, L. E. R., & Fleeson, W. (2014). Agreement on the perception of moral character. *Personality and Social Psychology Bulletin, 40,* 1698–1710.

Hofmann, W., Wisneski, D. C., Brandt, M. J., & Skitka, L. J. (2014). Morality in everyday life. *Science, 345,* 1340–1343.

Iyer, R., Koleva, S., Graham, J., Ditto, P., & Haidt, J. (2012). Understanding libertarian morality: The psychological dispositions of self-identified libertarians. *PLOS ONE, 7,* e42366.

Ksendzova, M., Iyer, R., Hill, G., Wojcik, S. P., & Howell, R. T. (2015). The portrait of a hedonist: The personality and ethics behind the value and maladaptive pursuit of pleasure. *Personality and Individual Differences, 79,* 68–74.

Mesquita, B., Deleersnyder, J., & Albert, D. (2014). The cultural regulation of emotions. In J. J. Gross (Ed.), *The handbook of emotion regulation* (2nd ed., pp. 284–301). New York: Guilford Press.

Monroe, A. E., & Reeder, G. D. (2011). Motive-matching: Perceptions of intentionality for coerced action. *Journal of Experimental Social Psychology, 47,* 1255–1261.

Pizarro, D. A., & Tannenbaum, D. (2011). Bringing character back: How the motivation to evaluate character influences judgments of moral blame. In P. Shaver & M. Mikulincer (Eds.), *The social psychology of morality: Exploring the causes of good and evil* (pp. 91–108). Washington, DC: American Psychological Association.

Pizarro, D. A., Uhlmann, E., & Salovey, P. (2003). Asymmetries in judgments of moral blame and praise: The role of perceived meta-desires. *Psychological Science, 14,* 267–272.

Reeder, G. D. (2009). Mindreading and dispositional inference: MIM revised and extended. *Psychological Inquiry, 20,* 73–83.

Schwartz, S. H. (2006). Basic human values: Theory, measurement, and applications. *French Review of Sociology, 47,* 929–968.

Sinnott-Armstrong, W., & Wheatley, T. (2012). The disunity of morality and why it matters to philosophy. *The Monist, 95,* 355–377.

Strohminger, N., & Nichols, S. (2014). The essential moral self. *Cognition, 131,* 159–171.

CHAPTER 12

Moral Cognition and Its Basis in Social Cognition and Social Regulation

John Voiklis
Bertram F. Malle

What is the basis of moral cognition?

Moral judgments are grounded in a number of cognitive and social cognitive processes, which guide the social regulation of behavior and are, in turn, constrained by such regulation to be fair and evidence-based.

Human beings live complex social lives, composed of various types of relationships across nested social hierarchies, all structured by rights, rules, and obligations. However, selfish goals persist, and keeping individuals' goals in line with community interests has become the primary challenge of modern morality. To meet this challenge, human societies have developed two major social-cultural tools: a vast network of rules, norms, and values (Sripada & Stich, 2006; Ullmann-Margalit, 1977) and complex social practices of norm enforcement, such as blame, praise, apology, and reconciliation (Semin & Manstead, 1983).

This kind of social-cultural morality has to be taught, learned, and enforced by community members, even by the youngest among them (Göckeritz, Schmidt, & Tomasello, 2014). Acquiring norms likely benefits from early-appearing preferences for prosocial agents over antisocial agents (Hamlin, 2014), but socially mature moral capacities rely heavily on nonmoral capacities: those of *social cognition* (Guglielmo, Monroe, & Malle, 2009).

Social cognition encompasses a hierarchy of interdependent concepts, processes, and skills that allow individuals to perceive, understand, and—most important for the present topic—evaluate one another. For example, norm enforcers infer the mental processes that generated a transgressive behavior (e.g., motive, belief, intention) before blaming the transgressor (Malle, Guglielmo, & Monroe, 2014). The transgressor must likewise infer the mental processes that generated the social act of blaming (e.g., the norm enforcer's goals, knowledge, and power of enforcing sanctions) when deciding to deny or admit, maintain or correct the norm-violating behavior.

These, then, are the phenomena this chapter aims to illuminate. We show how the elements of *social cognition* ground people's *moral cognition* and how social and moral cognition together guide the *social regulation of behavior by moral norms*. We aim to identify the concepts, mechanisms, and practices that go into making various kinds of moral judgments and the forms and functions of socially expressing those judgments.

Historical Context

The most prominent debates in moral philosophy grapple with dichotomies. Perhaps the oldest of these concerns the relative influences of *reason* and *passion* on human behavior (Hume, 1751/1998; Kant, 1785/2012). Moral *psychology,* too, has been heavily influenced by this dichotomy. During an early phase, scholars expressed great confidence in the human capacity to reason about moral matters—albeit a capacity that needs time to develop (Piaget, 1932; Kohlberg, 1981). During a later phase, scholars expressed sometimes fierce skepticism toward such reasoning capacities and offered emphatic claims about the primacy of affect in moral judgment (Alicke, 2000; Greene, 2008), about people's inability to access the cognitive basis of their judgments (Nisbett & Wilson, 1977; Haidt, 2001), and about the many biases from which these judgments suffer (Ditto, Pizarro, & Tannenbaum, 2009).

Dichotomies often suffer from exaggerations and simplifications. We hope to present a framework that goes beyond extreme positions and relies instead on theoretical analysis, existing empirical evidence, and predictions about new phenomena. We believe that drawing a line and designating two opposing sides—reason versus passion, cognition versus emotion, deliberation versus intuition—is an unproductive way to tackle a multifaceted phenomenon. We should, rather, survey the landscape and acknowledge the complex terrain of social life so as to discover the different psychological adaptations and social practices that have allowed people to navigate the terrain—imperfectly, but not in as bumbling and blundering a way as is sometimes portrayed. What enables such adaptive navigation, we try to show, is the interactive system of moral cognition, social cognition, and social regulation.

This system is schematically illustrated in Figure 12.1, in which the parts both inform one another (e.g., mental state inferences informing a blame judgment) and also justify one another (e.g., a wrongness judgment providing justification for an act of social regulation).

Two aspects of this schematic deserve comment. First, when we use the term *social cognition,* we are not pitching our tent on the "reason" side of a dichotomy but rather conceiving of social cognition as a large toolbox that contains both fast and automatic mechanisms as well as slow and controlled mechanisms, both automatic and

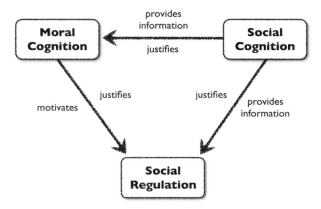

FIGURE 12.1. Schematic relationship between social cognition, moral cognition, and social regulation.

both intuition and deliberation, both affect and thought. Second, whereas the relationship between social cognition and moral cognition has been discussed before (e.g., Shaver, 1985; Weiner, 1995), the appeal to *social regulatory* mechanisms of morality goes beyond the parameters of existing debates. Highlighting the social function of moral cognition can reveal much about how that process operates. We discuss both of these issues shortly.

Theoretical Framework

To achieve the promised survey of the moral landscape and to elucidate how moral cognition, social cognition, and social regulation are related, we address three questions: (1) What makes moral cognition moral?; (2) What social cognitive processes are involved in it?; and (3) How does moral cognition interact with social regulation?

What Makes Moral Cognition Moral?

The moral domain is that of regulating individual behavior in the context of community interests. Rules, norms, and values set the standards that, if fulfilled, serve community goals and allow the community and its individuals to succeed. The broader literature sometimes distinguishes moral from conventional rules or moral from social norms (Brennan, Eriksson, Goodin, & Southwood, 2013; Kohlberg, 1981). But for many purposes, it is best to assume a continuum of norms—defined as standards and instructions that guide people in what they should do. We can then identify prototypes at each end. Moral norms, on one end, are part of a hierarchy in which moral "principles" and "values" are the most abstract instructions; social-conventional norms, at the other end, can often stand alone in regulating just one particular behavior or in solving a coordination problem. What the elements of this continuum have in common is that, in representing an instruction as a *norm* (as opposed to a goal or habit), people keenly take into account that (1) a sufficient number of individuals in the community in fact follow the instruction, and (2) a sufficient number of individuals in the community expect and demand of each

other to follow the instruction and may be willing to enforce it through sanctions (Bicchieri, 2006; Brennan et al., 2013).

We can now conceptualize *moral cognition* as the set of capacities that allow people to properly engage with social and moral norms. People have to (1) *learn, store, activate,* and *deploy* norms; (2) make *judgments* (e.g., of permissibility, wrongness, blame) about these norms; (3) make *decisions* in light of these norms; and (4) *communicate* about the norms and their violations (e.g., prescribe, justify, apologize).[1]

How Is Social Cognition Involved in Moral Cognition?

What is social cognition? We endorse an inclusive definition that subsumes under the term all conceptual and cognitive tools that serve the overarching goal of making sense of other human agents. Figure 12.2 displays many of these tools arranged in tree-like hierarchy (for a glossary and detailed discussion, see Malle, 2008, 2015). On the bottom are those that have evolved earlier in phylogeny, develop earlier in ontogeny, and are generally simpler and faster processes; on the top are those that have evolved more recently, develop later in childhood, and are generally more complex and slower processes. The tools often rely on the output of tools below them, and in concert these tools perform important tasks in social life, such as explanation, prediction, and moral judgment (depicted outside the tree itself). Moreover, several of the processes at once presuppose and shape fundamental concepts, such as intentionality, belief, desire, and emotion categories.

Against this background it is now easy to illustrate how social cognition supports and interacts with the four capacities of moral cognition.

In *norm learning*, social cognition contributes some of the learning mechanisms: Mimicry and imitation provide powerful tools of adopting norms through action, and face processing and goal identification allow people to read others' evaluations of a given behavior and thereby infer the norms that the behavior conformed to or violated. For example, a scowl toward somebody who asks a new acquaintance too many private

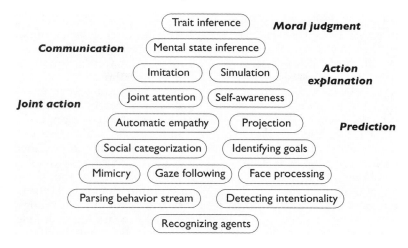

FIGURE 12.2. Broad conceptualization of social cognition as a tree-like, hierarchical collection of cognitive tools.

questions can teach and enforce norms of privacy and autonomy.

Moral judgment would be impossible without the basic tools of recognizing agents, parsing the behavior stream to identify (un)intentional norm violations, as well as empathy (often with the victim), simulation, and mental state inference to gauge the agent's specific reasons for committing the violation. Moreover, social categorization can influence judgments through prejudice (Eberhardt, Davies, Purdie-Vaughns, & Johnson, 2006) and also help assign specific norms to people in particular roles, groups, and positions. Often overlooked is the fact that different moral judgments require different levels of social-cognitive involvement: Gauging the permissibility of an action is largely a matter of analyzing an action category relative to a norm system; the agent's specific mental states are less important. Wrongness appears to be judged more on the basis of the agent's mental state (Cushman, 2008), whereas blame incorporates all these information inputs (Malle et al., 2014).

Moral decisions and actions rely in part on the tools of self-awareness, simulation of one's own future guilt, empathy with potential victims, and others' moral sanctions. Such decisions and actions also involve social categorization of one's roles and obligations and accumulated trait inferences of one's virtues (or lack thereof).

Moral communication, finally, includes such phenomena as expressing moral judgments either to the alleged violator or to another community member (Dersley & Wootton, 2000; Traverso, 2009); negotiating blame through justification and excuses (Antaki, 1994); and apology, compensation, or forgiveness to repair social estrangement after a norm violation (McKenna, 2012; Walker, 2006). People rely on mental state inferences during communicative interactions, and especially during social–moral interactions, to accurately assess the other's goals and knowledge, because the stakes of maintaining relationships are high and under the threat of sanctions. Trait inferences may be formed through observation or gossip, especially when norm violators do not respond to social regulation attempts by their community. Also, low-level tools of gaze and face processing, empathy, and goal inference are needed to gauge the honesty of justifications, the genuineness of apologies, and the seriousness of threatened sanctions.

How Does Social Regulation Interact with Moral Cognition?

We claimed earlier that heeding the social regulatory function of moral cognition can benefit our understanding of how moral cognition itself operates. We now illustrate one such benefit by reconsidering the debate over how accurate or biased people are in forming moral judgments (Alicke, 2000; Ditto, 2009; Malle et al., 2014; Nadler & McDonnell, 2011).

The accuracy or bias of a given moral judgment is difficult to measure, because the laboratory rarely offers an objective criterion for the correct judgment. Typically, researchers offer information to participants that they "should not" take into account, and when some of them do, a "bias" is diagnosed. For example, many researchers have argued that outcome severity, the motives and character of the norm violator, or the likeability of the victim must not be part of an unbiased moral judgment. But it is unclear who gets to decide, and on what basis, what people should or should not take into account (Malle et al., 2014; Nadler, 2012). Moreover, the potential arbiters, "philosophers, legal theorists and psychologists" (Alicke, 2008, p. 179), often do not agree with one another.

In the absence of objective criteria, an appealing alternative is to consider a moral judgment's function of regulating social behavior as a suitable standard—the socially shared criteria that people use to accept, question, criticize, or reject moral judgments. For example, what do people accept as the grounds of intense blame? They consider that the behavior violated an important norm, that the violation was intentional, that the agent had no justifying reasons to perform the behavior, and so forth (Malle et al., 2014). When would people reject intense blame? They do so when the behavior violated a merely insignificant norm, when the violation was unintentional and unavoidable but the norm enforcer treated it as if it were intentional, and so forth. Bias is then diagnosed when norm enforcers *overblame* or *underblame* relative to what is acceptable in the community (Kim, Voiklis, Cusimano, & Malle, 2015).

These standards of blame put pressure on people to keep their biases in check. Severe violations sometimes elicit powerful emotional responses that can lead to premature accusations or unfair punishment; further, an observer's quick moral evaluation sometimes taints subsequent inferences about whether the violation was intentional, justi-

fied, or preventable (Alicke, 2000; Knobe, 2010). Nevertheless, community members help correct these expressions of premature, biased, or inaccurate moral judgments by challenging those who blurt out allegations and by demanding warrant from those who overblame, thereby calming and slowing the processes of accusation and punishment.[2] Communities could not survive if their members blamed and punished one another without evidence or without differentiating between, say, mild and severe, intentional and unintentional violations. The regulatory functions of moral judgment, and the required warrant for such judgments, therefore push those judgments to be more reasonable, accurate, and fair, by the standards of the community in which they occur.[3]

Relating Social Cognition, Moral Cognition, and Social Regulation

We can now offer a more detailed schematic of the relationships between social cognition, moral cognition, and social regulation. In choosing the pictorial language of a flow diagram (Figure 12.3), we naturally leave out some complexity, but it forces us to make explicit certain theoretical commitments, which can be tested experimentally.

The flow of processes begins with a negative event, which prompts the perceiver to assess whether the event was caused by an agent who violated norms. If "yes," social cognitive processes analyze the violator's mental states (including intentions and goals). This information feeds into moral cognition, which generates judgments about wrongness or blame. The outputs of moral and social cognition, along with preceding information about the event and the norms that were violated, feed into a decision about whether public moral criticism is warranted. If warrant exceeds threshold, the perceiver is likely to deliver public moral criticism (though many other considerations may inhibit criticism, such as role constraints, fear of retaliation, etc.). This moral criticism may prompt a timely change in the violator's behavior or, if not, the perceiver may consider renewed criticism or alternative responses, including gossip or retreat.

The full stop with which we break off the flow diagram conceals a more complex,

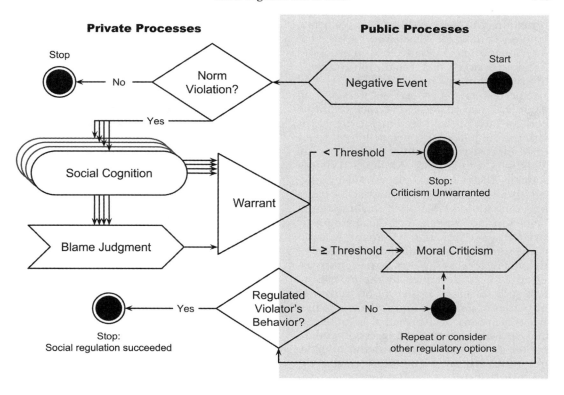

FIGURE 12.3. Flow diagram of processes of social and moral cognition in the context of social regulation of norm violations.

finely tuned social dynamic between norm enforcers and norm violators: They negotiate levels of blame, meet accusation with justification, criticism with remorse, remorse with forgiveness, all in the service of rebuilding and maintaining social relationships (Walker, 2006).

Evidence

Empirical evidence for the social cognitive basis of moral judgment has been accumulating over the past several years. In many studies, lay people clearly rely on social cognitive inferences of intentionality when judging everyday moral actions (Lagnado & Channon, 2008) and when mastering fine distinctions between willingly, knowingly, intentionally, and purposefully violating a norm (Guglielmo & Malle, 2010)—distinctions that also inform legal classifications of negligence and recklessness. Likewise, lay people judge

goal-directed harm as less permissible and more often as wrong than they judge harm as a side effect (Cushman & Young, 2011). Thus moral and legal distinctions overlap with (and perhaps derive from) more general purpose social cognitive judgments. This derivative relationship is corroborated by results from functional magnetic resonance imaging and lesion studies showing that the processing involved in either social or moral judgment activate many of the same regions in the prefrontal cortex (Forbes & Grafman, 2010).

People's cognitive system also makes distinctions between types of moral judgments that vary by the objects they judge: *Badness* judges mere events, *wrongness* judges intentional actions, and *blame* judges an agent's specific relationship to a norm violation, whether intentional or unintentional (Malle et al., 2014; Monin, Pizarro, & Beer, 2007; Sher, 2006). These judgments also differ in their sensitivity to causal and mental state information (Cushman, 2008; Malle, Scheutz, Arnold, Voiklis, & Cusimano, 2015), but experiments on the detailed causal processes that flow between social cognition and these differing judgments remain lacking.

Experiments on social expressions of blame are also scarce. Nevertheless, initial work in our lab has demonstrated that, as with private judgments, people have a finely tuned map of public acts of moral criticism (Voiklis, Cusimano, & Malle, 2014). For example, the rich vocabulary used by English speakers to describe such acts—ranging from chiding violators to lashing out at them—do not merely represent linguistic variations but pick out systematic features of the underlying moral judgment and of the social context. When participants assessed 28 acts (described by the most common verbs of moral criticism) on numerous properties of judgment and context, the first two dimensions of a principal components analysis were intensity of expression and direction of expression (toward the offender or toward others). Figure 12.4 depicts the quadrants of this space and four verbs that mark the prototypical acts in each quadrant. In a subsequent series of studies, we tested the hypothesis that people likely follow "norms of blaming" when scaling the intensity of moral criticism to the severity of transgressions (Kim et al., 2015). Indeed, when judging the appropriateness of various levels of moral criticism in response to a range of mild to severe transgressions, participants displayed a norm against "overblaming" (i.e., overly intense criticism for mild violations) but were more tolerant of "underblaming."

Individual and Situational Variability in Social and Moral Cognition

So far, we have addressed social and moral cognition at the level of cognitive system components that exist in all neurotypical adults. Nevertheless, social cognitive performance can vary as a function of maturation, neurological damage, and psychopathology (Frith & Frith, 2003) and can also be due to motivation (Klein & Hodges, 2001) and task difficulty (Birch & Bloom, 2007). Often these deficits are presented as evidence that people are reflexively egocen-

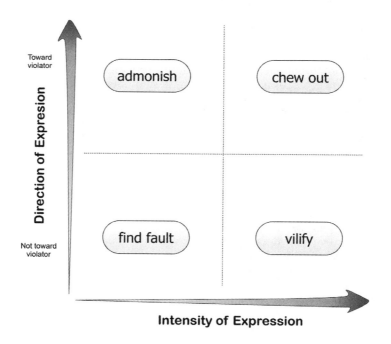

FIGURE 12.4. Four prototypes of public acts of moral criticism amidst variation of intensity of expression and direction of expression.

tric in their perception of other minds (Lin, Keysar, & Epley, 2010). An alternative interpretation is that people are dispositionally or situationally unprepared for attending to the full range of social information. In fact, preliminary evidence suggests that "warming up" social cognition with a practice task facilitates spontaneously unbiased predictions (in a mixed-motive game) and spontaneously subtle assessments of intentions and intentionality (Knobe, 2003), especially for those scoring on the lower end of a social cognitive performance measure (Voiklis, in preparation). So even though shallow processing and bias may predominate in states of disengagement, the correct situational cues can bring most individuals to their full social cognitive potential. Among these situational cues, the community's demand for warrant in moral criticism (especially blame) must rank very high, but direct tests of this hypothesis remain lacking.

There is, however, evidence for the malleability and the social shaping of moral reasoning more generally. As with other forms of (public) reasoning (Crowell & Kuhn, 2012; Kuhn, Zillmer, Crowell, & Zavala, 2013), moral judgment can improve with practice and feedback. Much as habitual reliance on heuristics (e.g., confirmation seeking) can be overcome with deliberate practice (Kuhn, 2011), people might likewise overcome any habitual neglect of social cognitive information. Howe (1991), for example, showed in an experimental context that circuit judges adjusted their blame judgments to mitigating information twice as strongly as students did. Applying one's social cognitive abilities might also be a matter of mindset. When induced to believe in the malleability, as opposed to the fixedness, of empathy, people appear more willing to expend empathic effort toward challenging targets (Schumann, Zaki, & Dweck, 2014). Moreover, people with a malleable mindset appear to seek out these challenges in order to improve their empathy; the challenge provides the learning opportunity, and the motivation to learn helps them meet that challenge.

Beyond skill learning, the vast developmental literature on changes in moral judgment and decision making support the claim of malleability. Gradual differentiation in moral cognition, according to our framework, is in good part the result of gradual differentiation in social cognition (Baird & Astington, 2004). For example, norm learning becomes more sophisticated as mental state inferences improve, and blame judgments become more sophisticated as the conceptual framework of mind grows. Specifically, as mental state concepts of belief and desire mature by ages 4–5 (Wellman, 1990), outcome considerations in blame are balanced by mental state considerations (Nelson-Le Gall, 1985). And as further differentiations of the intentionality concept emerge (Baird & Moses, 2001), the distinction between justified and unjustified violations and between preventable and unpreventable outcomes emerge as well (Fincham, 1982; Shaw & Sulzer, 1964).

What Data Would Falsify Our Proposal?

The strongest evidence against our proposal would show that early moral evaluations or emotions in response to norm violations precede and swamp subsequent social cognitive processing (Alicke, 2000; Knobe, 2010), a reversal of what our framework suggests. Confirmation of this claim requires methods for assessing temporal and causal relations between processes (millisecond by millisecond), but such methods have yet to be introduced into moral psychology. Furthermore, confirmation of this claim requires measuring a perceiver's affective responses after the perceiver recognizes an event as norm violating but before the perceiver determines the agent's causal involvement, intentionality, mental states, and so forth. Given the evidence for very early and automatic processing of agency and intentionality (Barrett, Todd, Miller, & Blythe, 2005; Decety, Michalska, & Kinzler, 2012), it would be difficult, both theoretically and experimentally, to fit any kind of graded affect into this tight early time window. Nevertheless, people are likely to perceive some kind of preconceptual badness before they process all the details of a norm-violating event. Arguably, such an undifferentiated sense of badness does not represent a moral judgment (e.g., of blame), so arriving at such a judgment would require additional social cognitive processing. If this processing were systematically biased in favor of confirming the initial negative assessment (Alicke, 2000), moral judgments would still be fundamentally reliant on social cognition—but on less accurate social cognition.

A second major challenge to our proposal would be that social regulation of norm enforcement does not, as we propose, push social (and moral) cognition toward systematic information processing and accuracy. Evidence would have to show that the demand for warrant of moral judgments can be easily satisfied by biased and inaccurate social cognitive information. It would not be enough to show that under some circumstances demand for warrant is ineffective but, rather, that widespread demand for warrant either does not exist or, even if it exists as a social practice, does not predict quality of social and moral processing.

Extension and Expansion

Social Regulation of Moral Judgments

Our hypothesis that social regulation is not only the expression of moral judgment but a mechanism that keeps moral judgments honest has yet to be tested. A first requirement of testing it will be to design suitable experimental manipulations of community members putting demands for warrant on a perceiver who is expressing a moral judgment. A second requirement will be to devise reliable measures of accuracy in moral judgments and the perceiver's systematic responsiveness to evidence.

Our theoretical model predicts that the impact of demands for warrant varies by moral judgment type. Permissibility judgments are primarily reflections of shared norms, so the presence of a community member should simply increase reliability and collective agreement in these kinds of judgments, whereas the more complex blame judgments should become more deliberate and evidence-based (taking into account intentionality, mental states, etc.) in the presence of a community representative. There is also a reverse prediction—that an overwhelming need to be accepted by one's community can lead to more biased information processing if the community has strong expectations (e.g., about the guilt or innocence of a norm violator or about

the appropriate level of punishment). The fine balance between these different forces may be examined with agent-based modeling methods (Elsenbroich & Gilbert, 2014). "Societies" that balance socially demanded accuracy against socially demanded unanimity should be most successful because they keep the costs of false accusations and exaggerated punishment in check. However, stratified societies in which some subgroups have more power may shift these costs to the less powerful groups. The current incarceration rates of minorities in the United States is an example of such a dynamic. As a counterforce, however, recently increasing public scrutiny of aggressive policing of minorities signals a renewed demand for warrant for social–moral blame and punishment.

Institutional mechanisms of regulation, such as the state and the law, were long believed to be the dominant forms of regulation. But evidence from the fields of anthropology, psychology, sociology, and legal studies suggests that informal, interpersonal moral regulation is evolutionarily and culturally old, arises developmentally early, and is the predominant way, even today, of keeping individual community members in line with collective interests. Referring back to our flow diagram (Figure 12.3), ordinary social regulation sometimes fails; an enticing research direction might be to examine when institutional mechanisms take over social regulation and when these mechanisms are more effective than interpersonal ones.

Affect and Emotion as Social–Moral Signals

Although the exact causal roles of affect and emotion in the information-processing phase of moral cognition are still under debate, their involvement in public expressions of moral criticism may be more readily apparent (Wolf, 2011). Affect intensity—in words, face, and posture—scales such expressions (Voiklis et al., 2014) so that others recognize one's degree of outrage (McGeer, 2012; de Melo, Carnevale, Read, & Gratch, 2014). These expressions signal how important the violated norm is to the blamer, teach young community members about such importance rankings, and also communicate to norm violators what possible other sanctions might follow if they show no insight or atonement. Evidence for this social function of moral emotions might come from physiological studies that show a ramping up of negative arousal from early violation detection to late public expression. That is, the very opportunity to express one's judgment publicly may increase the involvement of affect that was previously, during mere "in the head" judgments, quite modest. Additional support might come from evidence that perceivers have less differentiated emotions when they cognitively form their moral judgments than when they publicly express them, because anticipating public scrutiny leads to more attentive information appraisals. Here, too, perceivers' perception of a community's strong expectations may sometimes unduly modulate their public judgments, such as offering exaggerated expressions of outrage; this, in turn, can fuel even stronger expressions by other community members and escalate collective moral condemnation beyond what perceivers felt in private.

Artificial Morality

Work on moral psychology has recently expanded into artificial morality—the study and design of computational models of moral competence (Mao & Gratch, 2012; Tomai & Forbus, 2008) and implementation in social robots (Wallach & Allen, 2008; Malle & Scheutz, 2014). Social robots—embodied machines that are able to interact with humans—play an increasing role in contemporary society. Around a decade ago there were no robots in private homes, whereas in 2014, 4.7 million service robots for personal and domestic use were sold worldwide (International Federation of Robotics, 2015). These robots rarely posses extensive social cognitive capacities but are improving rapidly (Nourbakhsh, 2013), and robots may soon function as social companions or assistants in health care, education, security, and emergency response. In such applications, however, robots will need to have basic moral competence to ensure physically and psychologically safe interactions with humans (Malle & Scheutz, 2014). Designing such robots offers appealing new avenues for research, by testing more precise, formally specified models of both social cognitive capacities (e.g., making in-

tentionality inferences in live interactions) and moral capacities (e.g., recognizing norm violations and forming evidence-based judgments). In addition, research will need to identify the conditions under which humans ascribe features such as intentionality, free will, or blame to artificial agents (Malle et al., 2015; Meltzoff, Brooks, Shon, & Rao, 2010; Monroe, Dillon, & Malle, 2014), because such ascriptions fundamentally alter human–machine interactions. Integrating robots into research will enable a better understanding of social and moral cognition, and integrating robots into society will require such understanding to achieve beneficial human–robot coexistence.

Summary

Returning from social cognitive science fiction, we close by recapping our theoretical framework for understanding the processes of moral cognition. We argue that a hierarchy of social cognitive tools ground moral cognition and that social and moral cognition together guide the social regulation of behavior. The practice of social–moral regulation, in turn, puts pressure on community members to engage in reasonably fair and evidence-based moral criticism. With the help of these cognitive adaptations and social practices, people are able to navigate the terrain of morality, accruing bumps and bruises along the way but surviving as the most sophisticated social creature currently roaming the earth.

ACKNOWLEDGMENTS

We are grateful for the collective work and insights by all members of our lab (*http://research.clps.brown.edu/SocCogSci/Personnel/personnel.html*). This project was supported by grants from the Office of Naval Research (Nos. N00014-14-1-0144 and N00014-13-1-0269).

NOTES

1. Perhaps a helpful term for this set of capacities would be *moral competence* (Malle, 2016; Malle & Scheutz, 2014). A complete rendering of this competence would include both

positive and negative behaviors, but here we focus, in keeping with the literature, on negative behaviors.

2. These socially corrective strategies are not inventions of modern legal institutions; rather, they are successful informal practices that have persisted throughout history (Boehm, 1999; Pospisil, 1971).

3. There are well-known limits to this shaping process: For example, members of a given group may demand fair and accurate norm enforcement for one another but not for members of disliked or lower status outgroups.

REFERENCES

Alicke, M. D. (2000). Culpable control and the psychology of blame. *Psychological Bulletin, 126,* 556–574.

Alicke, M. D. (2008). Blaming badly. *Journal of Cognition and Culture, 8,* 179–186.

Antaki, C. (1994). *Explaining and arguing: The social organization of accounts.* London: SAGE.

Baird, J. A., & Astington, J. W. (2004). The role of mental state understanding in the development of moral cognition and moral action. *New Directions for Child and Adolescent Development, 2004,* 37–49.

Baird, J. A., & Moses, L. J. (2001). Do preschoolers appreciate that identical actions may be motivated by different intentions? *Journal of Cognition and Development, 2,* 413–448.

Barrett, H. C., Todd, P. M., Miller, G. F., & Blythe, P. W. (2005). Accurate judgments of intention from motion cues alone: A cross-cultural study. *Evolution and Human Behavior, 26,* 313–331.

Bicchieri, C. (2006). *The grammar of society: The nature and dynamics of social norms.* New York: Cambridge University Press.

Birch, S. A. J., & Bloom, P. (2007). The curse of knowledge in reasoning about false beliefs. *Psychological Science, 18,* 382–386.

Boehm, C. (1999). *Hierarchy in the forest: The evolution of egalitarian behavior.* Cambridge, MA: Harvard University Press.

Brennan, G., Eriksson, L., Goodin, R. E., & Southwood, N. (2013). *Explaining norms.* New York: Oxford University Press.

Crowell, A., & Kuhn, D. (2012). Developing dialogic argumentation skills: A 3-year intervention study. *Journal of Cognition and Development, 15,* 363–381.

Cushman, F. (2008). Crime and punishment: Distinguishing the roles of causal and intentional analyses in moral judgment. *Cognition, 108,* 353–380.

Cushman, F., & Young, L. (2011). Patterns of moral judgment derive from nonmoral psychological representations. *Cognitive Science, 35,* 1052–1075.

de Melo, C. M., Carnevale, P. J., Read, S. J., & Gratch, J. (2014). Reading people's minds from emotion expressions in interdependent decision making. *Journal of Personality and Social Psychology, 106,* 73–88.

Decety, J., Michalska, K. J., & Kinzler, K. D. (2012). The contribution of emotion and cognition to moral sensitivity: A neurodevelopmental study. *Cerebral Cortex, 22,* 209–220.

Dersley, I., & Wootton, A. (2000). Complaint sequences within antagonistic argument. *Research on Language and Social Interaction, 33,* 375–406.

Ditto, P. H. (2009). Passion, reason, and necessity: A quantity-of-processing view of motivated reasoning. In T. Bayne & J. Fernández (Eds.), *Delusion and self-deception: Affective and motivational influences on belief formation.* (pp. 23–53). New York: Psychology Press.

Ditto, P. H., Pizarro, D. A., & Tannenbaum, D. (2009). Motivated moral reasoning. In D. M. Bartels, C. W. Bauman, L. J. Skitka, & D. L. Medin (Eds.), *Moral judgment and decision making* (pp. 307–338). San Diego, CA: Elsevier Academic Press.

Eberhardt, J. L., Davies, P. G., Purdie-Vaughns, V. J., & Johnson, S. L. (2006). Looking deathworthy: Perceived stereotypicality of black defendants predicts capital-sentencing outcomes. *Psychological Science, 17,* 383–386.

Elsenbroich, C., & Gilbert, G. N. (2014). *Modelling norms.* Dordrecht, The Netherlands: Springer.

Fincham, F. D. (1982). Moral judgment and the development of causal schemes. *European Journal of Social Psychology, 12,* 47–61.

Forbes, C. E., & Grafman, J. (2010). The role of the human prefrontal cortex in social cognition and moral judgment. *Annual Review of Neuroscience, 33,* 299–324.

Frith, U., & Frith, C. D. (2003). Development and neurophysiology of mentalizing. *Philosophical Transactions of the Royal Society of London, Series B: Biological Sciences, 358,* 459–473.

Göckeritz, S., Schmidt, M. F. H., & Tomasello, M. (2014). Young children's creation and transmission of social norms. *Cognitive Development, 30,* 81–95.

Greene, J. D. (2008). The secret joke of Kant's soul. In W. Sinnott-Armstrong (Ed.), *Moral psychology: Vol. 3. The neuroscience of morality: Emotion, brain disorders, and development* (pp. 35–80). Cambridge, MA: MIT Press.

Guglielmo, S., & Malle, B. F. (2010). Can unintended side effects be intentional?: Resolving a controversy over intentionality and morality.

Personality and Social Psychology Bulletin, 36, 1635–1647.

Guglielmo, S., Monroe, A. E., & Malle, B. F. (2009). At the heart of morality lies folk psychology. *Inquiry: An Interdisciplinary Journal of Philosophy, 52,* 449–466.

Haidt, J. (2001). The emotional dog and its rational tail: A social intuitionist approach to moral judgment. *Psychological Review, 108,* 814–834.

Hamlin, J. K. (2014). The origins of human morality: Complex socio-moral evaluations by preverbal infants. In J. Decety & Y. Christen (Eds.), *New frontiers in social neuroscience* (Vol. 21, pp. 165–188). New York: Springer International.

Howe, E. S. (1991). Integration of mitigation, intention, and outcome damage information, by students and circuit court judges. *Journal of Applied Social Psychology, 21,* 875–895.

Hume, D. (1998). *An enquiry concerning the principles of morals* (T. L. Beauchamp, Ed.). Oxford, UK: Oxford University Press. (Original work published 1751)

International Federation of Robotics. (2015). *World robotics: Service robots 2015.* Frankfurt, Germany: Author. Available at *www.ifr.org/worldrobotics.*

Kant, I. (2012). *Groundwork of the metaphysics of morals* (M. Gregor & J. Timmermann, Trans.; rev. ed.). Cambridge, UK: Cambridge University Press. (Original work published 1785)

Kim, B., Voiklis, J., Cusimano, C., & Malle, B. F. (2015, February). *Norms of moral criticism: Do people prohibit underblaming and overblaming?* Poster presented at the annual meeting of the Society of Personality and Social Psychology, Long Beach, CA.

Klein, K. J. K., & Hodges, S. D. (2001). Gender differences, motivation, and empathic accuracy: When it pays to understand. *Personality and Social Psychology Bulletin, 27,* 720–730.

Knobe, J. (2003). Intentional action and side effects in ordinary language. *Analysis, 63,* 190–194.

Knobe, J. (2010). Person as scientist, person as moralist. *Behavioral and Brain Sciences, 33,* 315–329.

Kohlberg, L. (1981). *The philosophy of moral development: Moral stages and the idea of justice.* San Francisco: Harper & Row.

Kuhn, D. (2011). What people may do versus can do. *Behavioral and Brain Sciences, 34,* 83.

Kuhn, D., Zillmer, N., Crowell, A., & Zavala, J. (2013). Developing norms of argumentation: Metacognitive, epistemological, and social dimensions of developing argumentive competence. *Cognition and Instruction, 31,* 456–496.

Lagnado, D. A., & Channon, S. (2008). Judgments of cause and blame: The effects of intentionality and foreseeability. *Cognition, 108,* 754–770.

Lin, S., Keysar, B., & Epley, N. (2010). Reflexively mindblind: Using theory of mind to interpret behavior requires effortful attention. *Journal of Experimental Social Psychology, 46,* 551–556.

Malle, B. F. (2008). The fundamental tools, and possibly universals, of social cognition. In R. M. Sorrentino & S. Yamaguchi (Eds.), *Handbook of motivation and cognition across cultures* (pp. 267–296). New York: Elsevier/Academic Press.

Malle, B. F. (2015). Social robots and the tree of social cognition. In Y. Nagai & S. Lohan (Eds.), *Proceedings of the Workshop "Cognition: A bridge between robotics and interaction"* at HRI'15, Portland, Oregon (pp. 13–14). Available at *www.macs.hw.ac.uk/~kl360/HRI2015W/proceedings.html.*

Malle, B. F. (2016). Integrating robot ethics and machine morality: The study and design of moral competence in robots. *Ethics and Information Technology, 18*(4), 243–256.

Malle, B. F., Guglielmo, S., & Monroe, A. E. (2014). A theory of blame. *Psychological Inquiry, 25,* 147–186.

Malle, B. F., & Scheutz, M. (2014). Moral competence in social robots. *Proceedings of the IEEE International Symposium on Ethics in Engineering, Science, and Technology* (pp. 30–35). Chicago: Institute of Electrical and Electronics Engineers.

Malle, B. F., Scheutz, M., Arnold, T., Voiklis, J., & Cusimano, C. (2015). Sacrifice one for the good of many?: People apply different moral norms to human and robot agents. *Proceedings of the Tenth Annual ACM/IEEE International Conference on Human-Robot Interaction,* HRI '15 (pp. 117–124). New York,: Association for Computing Machinery.

Mao, W., & Gratch, J. (2012). Modeling social causality and responsibility judgment in multi-agent interactions. *Journal of Artificial Intelligence Research, 44,* 223–273.

McGeer, V. (2012). Civilizing blame. In D. J. Coates & N. A. Tognazzini (Eds.), *Blame: Its nature and norms* (pp. 162–188). New York: Oxford University Press.

McKenna, M. (2012). Directed blame and conversation. In D. J. Coates & N. A. Tognazzini (Eds.), *Blame: Its nature and norms* (pp. 119–140). New York: Oxford University Press.

Meltzoff, A. N., Brooks, R., Shon, A. P., & Rao, R. P. N. (2010). "Social" robots are psychological agents for infants: A test of gaze following. *Neural Networks, 23,* 966–972.

Monin, B., Pizarro, D. A., & Beer, J. S. (2007).

Deciding versus reacting: Conceptions of moral judgment and the reason–affect debate. *Review of General Psychology, 11,* 99–111.

Monroe, A. E., Dillon, K. D., & Malle, B. F. (2014). Bringing free will down to Earth: People's psychological concept of free will and its role in moral judgment. *Consciousness and Cognition, 27,* 100–108.

Nadler, J. (2012). Blaming as a social process: The influence of character and moral emotion on blame. *Law and Contemporary Problems, 75,* 1–31.

Nadler, J., & McDonnell, M.-H. (2011). Moral character, motive, and the psychology of blame. *Cornell Law Review, 97,* 255–304.

Nelson-Le Gall, S. A. (1985). Motive–outcome matching and outcome foreseeability: Effects on attribution of intentionality and moral judgments. *Developmental Psychology, 21,* 323–337.

Nisbett, R. E., & Wilson, T. D. (1977). Telling more than we can know: Verbal reports on mental processes. *Psychological Review, 84,* 231–259.

Nourbakhsh, I. R. (2013). *Robot futures.* Cambridge, MA: MIT Press.

Piaget, J. (1932). *The moral judgment of the child.* London: Kegan Paul, Trench, Trubner.

Pospisil, L. (1971). *Anthropology of law: A comparative theory.* New York: Harper & Row.

Schumann, K., Zaki, J., & Dweck, C. S. (2014). Addressing the empathy deficit: Beliefs about the malleability of empathy predict effortful responses when empathy is challenging. *Journal of Personality and Social Psychology, 107,* 475–493.

Semin, G. R., & Manstead, A. S. R. (1983). *The accountability of conduct: A social psychological analysis.* London: Academic Press.

Shaver, K. G. (1985). *The attribution of blame: Causality, responsibility, and blameworthiness.* New York: Springer Verlag.

Shaw, M. E., & Sulzer, J. L. (1964). An empirical test of Heider's levels in attribution of responsibility. *Journal of Abnormal and Social Psychology, 69,* 39–46.

Sher, G. (2006). *In praise of blame.* New York: Oxford University Press.

Sripada, C. S., & Stich, S. (2006). A framework for the psychology of norms. In P. Carruthers, S. Laurence, & S. Stich (Eds.), *The innate mind: Vol. 2. Culture and cognition* (pp. 280–301). New York: Oxford University Press.

Tomai, E., & Forbus, K. (2008). Using qualitative reasoning for the attribution of moral responsibility. In B. C. Love, K. McRae, & V. M. Sloutsky (Eds.), *Proceedings of the Thirtieth Annual Conference of the Cognitive Science Society* (pp.149–154). Austin, TX: Cognitive Science Society.

Traverso, V. (2009). The dilemmas of third-party complaints in conversation between friends. *Journal of Pragmatics, 41,* 2385–2399.

Ullmann-Margalit, E. (1977). *The emergence of norms.* Oxford, UK: Clarendon Press.

Voiklis, J. (in preparation). *A little "mindreading" practice facilitates later social-cognitive inferences.* Manuscript in preparation.

Voiklis, J., Cusimano, C., & Malle, B. F. (2014). A social-conceptual map of moral criticism. In P. Bello, M. Guarini, M. McShane, & B. Scassellati (Eds.), *Proceedings of the 36th annual meeting of the Cognitive Science Society* (pp. 1700–1705). Austin, TX: Cognitive Science Society.

Walker, M. U. (2006). *Moral repair: Reconstructing moral relations after wrongdoing.* New York: Cambridge University Press.

Wallach, W., & Allen, C. (2008). *Moral machines: Teaching robots right from wrong.* New York: Oxford University Press.

Weiner, B. (1995). *Judgments of responsibility: A foundation for a theory of social conduct.* New York: Guilford Press.

Wellman, H. M. (1990). *The child's theory of mind.* Cambridge, MA: MIT Press.

Wolf, S. (2011). Blame, Italian style. In R. J. Wallace, R. Kumar, & S. Freeman (Eds.), *Reason and recognition: Essays on the philosophy of T. M. Scanlon* (pp. 332–347). New York: Oxford University Press.

CHAPTER 13

Morality Is Personal

Justin F. Landy
Eric Luis Uhlmann

What is the purpose of moral judgment?

We argue that the basic goal of moral cognition is often not to praise or condemn specific actions but, rather, to try to understand other people's dispositional moral character via their actions, and that incorporating lay virtue ethics into psychological theory helps to paint a more complete picture of people's moral psychology.

In 2007, the Atlanta Falcons' star quarterback Michael Vick was exposed for bankrolling a dog-fighting ring. Details about the fights were grim; dogs that proved insufficiently violent in test fights, for example, were brutally hanged or drowned. Vick was criminally prosecuted and sentenced to 23 months in prison, even though prosecutors had recommended a maximum sentence of only 18 months (McCann, 2007). He also lost his $130 million contract with the Falcons, who ruled out his ever returning to the team, and team owner Arthur Blank told reporters he felt personally betrayed (King, 2007).

What underlies the public outrage over Vick's actions, and the Falcons' finality in cutting their ties to him? Although few observers would argue that killing a pit bull is more morally blameworthy than killing a human being, Vick's behavior suggests a callous and sadistic personal character that

even premeditated murder might not. While gratuitous animal cruelty may not rise to the level of murder in American jurisprudence, in everyday moral psychology it points to severe deficits in empathy and moral character.

In the present chapter, we argue that the goal of moral cognition is often not to praise or condemn specific actions but, rather, to try to understand other people's moral character *via* their actions (Pizarro & Tannenbaum, 2011; Uhlmann, Pizarro, & Diermeier, 2015). Human beings often act as intuitive virtue ethicists who view behaviors as signals of underlying moral traits such as trustworthiness and compassion. In making this argument, we first briefly review historical approaches to the philosophy and psychology of ethics before introducing our theoretical perspective, which we term person-centered morality. We then explore two lines of empirical evidence supporting our argument that moral judgment is often about evaluating people, not acts: first, character assessments are automatic, yet nuanced, and serve an important functional purpose. Second, character information can outweigh information about objective harm, and judgments of character can often diverge from evaluations of acts. Next, we present evidence that results supporting the person-centered view of morality are highly replicable. To close, we argue that recognizing that human beings have a preoccupation with moral virtues leads to the insight that our moral judgments can be both rational and intuitive, in meaningful senses.

Historical Perspectives on Morality

Since the Enlightenment, moral philosophy has been dominated by two opposing perspectives on ethics. On one side stand consequentialist philosophers, who view the outcomes resulting from an action as the only meaningful criterion for evaluating its morality or immorality. The most prominent consequentialist theory is utilitarianism, which judges as morally right the action that maximizes good outcomes across all morally relevant beings (Bentham, 1823/1970; Mill, 1861/1998; Smart & Williams, 1973). Standing in opposition to consequentialist theories of ethics are deontological theories, which evaluate the rightness or wrongness of an action according to whether it adheres to a moral rule or duty (Kant, 1785). There are several forms of deontology, some of which view the consequences of an act as one morally important feature among many, and some of which emphasize strict adherence to moral rules, regardless of the consequences (see Bartels, 2008; Kagan, 1998), but all of which deny that maximizing good outcomes, by any means necessary, is the only meaningful ethical principle.

Moral psychologists have inherited this preoccupation with deontological and utilitarian approaches to ethics from their philosophically minded counterparts. Decision researchers have commonly treated utilitarian theory as normatively correct and proceeded to document systematic departures from this ethical standard (Baron, 1994,

2008; Sunstein, 2005). Similarly, Greene and colleagues (Greene, Morelli, Lowenberg, Nystrom, & Cohen, 2008; Greene, Sommerville, Nystrom, Darley, & Cohen, 2001) have advanced a dual-process model of moral judgment, in which automatic, System 1 processes are said to produce deontological moral judgments, and deliberative, System 2 processes can sometimes override these System 1 processes and produce utilitarian judgments. In response to this line of work, some researchers have argued that deliberate reasoning is associated with *neither* deontological nor utilitarian judgment (Royzman, Landy, & Leeman, 2015), and others have suggested that, rather than resulting from System 2 overruling System 1, utilitarian judgments are a product of dispositional thinking styles (Baron, Scott, Fincher, & Metz, 2015). Still others have empirically disputed the presumed optimality of utilitarian judgments (Bartels & Pizarro, 2011).

Despite the myriad theoretical and empirical disputes, scholarship on deontology and consequentialism is united by one commonality: It takes discrete actions to be of primary concern in moral judgment. That is, both deontological and consequentialist ethical theories are focused on what makes particular actions right or wrong, and empirical studies of deontological and utilitarian judgment are focused on when and why people judge particular actions to be permissible or impermissible. There is, however, a "third voice" in ethical philosophy that takes a different approach: *Virtue ethics* places the focus on the character of moral actors. In other words, the driving question in virtue ethics is not "What is the right thing to do?" but rather "How can I be a good person?" Virtue ethics may actually be the oldest philosophical approach to normative ethics (Aristotle, trans. 1998), though it has only reemerged as a prominent alternative to deontology and utilitarianism comparatively recently (Anscombe, 1958).

Person-Centered Morality

Just as normative theories of virtue ethics contend that people's chief moral concern ought to be with cultivating moral virtues, we argue that, descriptively, moral cognition is often more concerned with evaluating others' character than the rightness or wrongness of their actions, a view that we call *person-centered morality* (PCM; Pizarro & Tannenbaum, 2011; Uhlmann et al., 2015). Rather than a stand-alone model in its own right, PCM is more of a needed corrective to descriptive theories that have focused on judgments of acts. We believe that a complete theory of moral cognition cannot neglect characterological evaluations of people.

Why would moral judgment be oriented toward character assessments, rather than praise and condemnation for particular actions? We see a functionalist reason why moral judgment so often focuses on the person. Many researchers have argued that it is vitally important to be able to predict other people's likely intentions toward us—will this person be benevolent or malevolent, trustworthy or treacherous (e.g., Abele & Wojciszke, 2007; Cottrell, Neuberg, & Li, 2007; Cuddy, Fiske, & Glick, 2008; Fiske, Cuddy, & Glick, 2007; Pizarro & Tannenbaum, 2011; Wojciszke, Bazinska, & Jaworski, 1998; Wojciszke, Dowhyluk, & Jaworski, 1998)? We agree; indeed, this seems to us to be the most important piece of information we can know about another person with whom we may interact (Goodwin, 2015; Goodwin, Piazza, & Rozin, 2014), and it is a person's moral character that should be informative about their good or bad intentions (Landy, Piazza, & Goodwin, 2016). Consistent with this perspective, judgments of character are largely determined by information about a person's intentions, rather than other considerations, such as the outcomes they have caused (Martin & Cushman, 2015, 2016). Judgments of character are even influenced by inferences about the sorts of intentions a person *would* have, under other circumstances (Landy, Linder, & Caruso, 2017). Furthermore, information about a person's moral character has been found to dominate in impression formation—Goodwin et al. (2014), using correlational, experimental, and archival research designs, demonstrated that overall impressions of both real and hypothetical targets are best predicted by their morality across a wide range of contexts. Perhaps their most striking result is that impressions of real individuals, based on their obituaries, were best predicted by the morality information the obituaries conveyed, even though they contained more information about their achievements and ability, overall. Participants learned more about the competence and ability of the deceased individuals, but primarily attended to their morality when forming opinions of them.

In fact, moral character is so fundamentally important in social evaluation that good character may be among the only unambiguously positive attributes that a person can possess. This point is illustrated by a study in which participants expressed preferences for the presence or absence of trait characteristics in others. When they considered an acquaintance who had a reputation for being competent, sociable, incompetent, or unsociable, they always preferred this person to be moral, rather than immoral, and they preferred moral acquaintances to be sociable and competent. However, they preferred immoral acquaintances to be unsociable and incompetent (Landy et al., 2016; see also Peeters, 1992; Wojciszke, Bazinska, & Jaworski, 1998). We argue that positive attributes such as intelligence and friendliness are considered negative and undesirable in the wicked, because they make it more likely that such people can successfully carry out their ill intentions toward us. People even seem to consider understanding the "intentions" of nonhuman animals to be of great importance. Although it seems unlikely that we make full-blown judgments of moral character for animals, people readily make attributions about an animal's dispositional harmfulness, which contribute to beliefs about whether the animal is worthy of moral protection (Piazza, Landy, & Goodwin, 2014).

From this functionalist perspective, discrete moral and immoral acts are informative of another's likely future intentions insofar as they provide information about that person's underlying character. Or, as Helzer and Critcher (Chapter 11, this volume) phrase it, discrete acts are "outputs" that respond to situational "inputs" and provide information about the "moral cognitive machinery" a person possesses. To possess sound moral cognitive machinery is precisely to possess good moral character, which they define as those personality traits most necessary for cooperative social relationships, particularly traits relating to how one treats other people.

Given their functional importance, we would expect assessments of character to come naturally to people. Indeed, this is the case. Incredibly, infants as young as 6 months old show a preference for a "helper" character who aided another character in reaching a goal over a "hinderer" character, who prevented them from reaching the goal (Hamlin, Wynn, & Bloom, 2007). Moreover, judgments of trustworthiness and aggression can be made by adults after as little as 100 milliseconds of exposure to a human face, and these judgments are highly correlated with analogous judgments made with no time constraints (Willis & Todorov, 2006). This result is also supported by neurological evidence: Amygdala activation in response to faces correlates with the presence of features that are thought to indicate dishonesty, even when the task at hand does not require one to assess the target's character (Engell, Haxby, & Todorov, 2007). This suggests that we automatically assess trustworthiness in others, even with only minimal information, and even when we are not consciously motivated to do so.

Of course, we do not evaluate a person's character solely on the basis of his or her facial features; we typically rely on behavior to inform our judgments, and, in such cases, assessments of character can be quite nuanced, responding to a variety of behavioral features. One widely studied feature has been called diagnosticity (Skowronski & Carlston, 1989). Immoral behaviors are seen as more diagnostic of character than moral behaviors, because, by definition, moral people rarely engage in immoral behaviors, but immoral people sometimes strategically engage in moral behaviors. Thus moral behaviors are often not particularly informative as to underlying character, whereas immoral behaviors are highly diagnostic (see also Reeder & Brewer, 1979).

Further, even the same action can seem like a better or a worse indicator of moral character, depending on how it is performed. For instance, when faced with an opportunity to do something clearly immoral, an actor who immediately gives in to temptation is seen as having worse character than an actor who does so only after deliberation. Conversely, an actor who immediately decides to do the right thing is seen as having better character than an actor who deliberates first. Faster decisions indicate less internal conflict about what to do, and therefore more extreme (good or bad) character (Critcher, Inbar, & Pizarro, 2013). Yet, in more complex situations with multiple, competing moral concerns, deliberation and careful reflection are seen as indicative of good moral character (Landy, Herzog, & Bartels, 2017). This illustrates how judgments of character can respond to quite subtle aspects of behaviors.

It should be obvious by now that inferences about character are a frequent part of social and moral cognition. But what exactly do these inferences consist of? That is, what trait attributes do people see as relevant to assessments of character, or, phrased differently, what are the constituent elements of the lay concept of "good character"? Several attempts have been made to answer this question, with somewhat disparate results, but aggregating across them, trustworthiness and compassion seem to be viable candidates for "core" elements of moral character.[1] Walker and Hennig (2004) identified three types of moral exemplar—just, caring, and brave—and found that traits ascribed to each varied considerably. However, those traits ascribed to all three were largely related to honesty and integrity (e.g., truthful, honest) and to compassion toward others (e.g., helpful, empathic). Similarly, Walker and Pitts (1998) used hierarchical cluster analysis to organize traits ascribed to a moral person. They found that traits related to being caring and honest clustered together and that other elements of trustworthiness (integrity, dependability) formed their own clusters. Other clusters related to being principled, loyal, fair, and confident. Lapsley and Lasky (2001) elicited traits that participants thought were aspects of "good character," then had a separate sample rate how characteristic each trait was of a person with good character. The majority of the traits rated as most characteristic related to trustworthiness (e.g., *sincere, honest*) or compassion (e.g., *understanding, kind*), though some were not closely related to these virtues (e.g., *loyal, fair*). Using a similar procedure, Aquino and Reed (2002) had participants generate traits that are characteristic of a moral person. Most of the traits produced related to trustworthiness or compassion. Lastly, Piazza, Goodwin, Rozin, and Royzman (2014) introduced a conceptual distinction between "core goodness traits" that should be desirable in anyone and "value commitment traits" (e.g., *committed, hardworking*) that contribute to good character in good or neutral people but make the character of bad people (e.g., a "dedicated Nazi") even worse. Half of the core goodness traits related to trustworthiness (e.g., *honest, trustworthy*) or compassion (e.g., *kind, charitable*), though others did not (e.g., *just, humble*).[2] Across all of these studies, trustworthiness and compassion emerge as central elements of good character. Other traits appear as well, but none so often and so consistently. We take this as evidence that people think of the "good person" as someone who can be trusted and who will treat others kindly.

Evaluations of character are a fundamental part of social cognition. They are functionally important and automatic, though they can also respond to subtle aspects of behaviors in quite nuanced ways. The person-centered approach to moral judgment also contributes unique and testable predictions (Pizarro & Tannenbaum, 2011; Uhlmann et al., 2015). For instance, acts that provide clear signals of poor moral character elicit moral condemnation completely out of proportion to the objective harm that they cause (Pizarro, Tannenbaum, & Uhlmann, 2012). Furthermore, striking dissociations can emerge between moral evaluations of an act and the person who performs the act. Such *act–person dissociations* suggest that *neither type of judgment can be subsumed into the other*. That is, judgments of character cannot merely be aggregations of act judgments, and judgments of acts cannot merely be inputs into character judgments. These findings provide some of the strongest available evidence that moral virtues are necessary to account for the full scope of human moral cognition.

Some Anecdotes and Some Evidence

A perfect example of person-centered moral judgment is public outrage over frivolous executive perks. Why do such perks elicit widespread condemnation, notwithstanding the fact that they may waste relatively few organizational resources and do little concrete harm? Merrill Lynch Chief Executive Officer John Thain, for instance, provoked outrage when—in the midst of laying off thousands of employees—he spent lavishly redecorating his personal office. Extravagances included $28,000 curtains, a $1,400 garbage can, and an $87,000 area rug. After the spending was reported in the media, Thain promptly lost his position as CEO. Interestingly, Thain's compensation of more than $80 million a year elicited no such vitriol (Gasparino, 2009). In cases such as this, the issue seems not to be the objective degree of waste but, rather, what these frivolous expenses say about the executives as people.

Empirical support for this idea comes from Tannenbaum, Uhlmann, and Diermeier (2011, Study 2), who asked their participants which of two candidates they would hire as CEO of a manufacturing company. The candidates were comparable in their qualifications and differed only in their requested compensation. One candidate requested a salary of $2 million, whereas the other requested a salary of $1 million plus an additional benefit that would cost $40,000. In one condition, this benefit was a cash signing bonus, and participants quite reasonably preferred the low-salary candidate. However, in another condition, the requested benefit was a marble table for the CEO's office, and in yet another, it was a marble table with the candidate's portrait carved into it. In both of these conditions, participants preferred to hire the candidate who requested $2 million in salary over the candidate who requested $1 million and the perk. Participants indicated that the request for the table indicated poor character (specifically, low integrity), and that the candidate who requested it would make less sound business decisions than the candidate who requested the higher salary. Thus, when a job candidate requested a frivolous, self-indulgent perk, participants inferred poor moral character, and this inference led to their rejecting the candidate, paralleling the public outrage directed at John Thain and his $87,000 area rug.

Interestingly, this result seems to stem from the perceived informational value of the requested perk. Participants did not just see the table requester as having worse character than the high-salary requester; they felt that they *knew more* about his underlying moral character. A more direct demonstration that objectively less harmful acts can be seen as more informative of poor character comes from a study about two unfriendly managers, a "misanthropic" manager who was rude to all of his employees and a "bigoted" manager who was rude only to his black employees (Uhlmann, Tannenbaum, Zhu, & Diermeier, 2009). Though the bigoted manager harmed fewer people, participants strongly preferred the misanthropic manager to the bigoted manager and saw the bigot's behavior as more informative about his character than the misanthrope's. Another study on this topic examined the informational value regarding character provided by tipping behavior (Uhlmann, Tannenbaum, & Diermeier, 2010). Participants considered a restaurant patron who tipped $15 in pennies to be a worse person than a patron who tipped $14 in bills, despite being materially more generous, and this effect was mediated by the perceived informational value of his act rather than the immorality of the act itself. All of this research converges on the conclusion that an act that does objectively less harm (or more good) can nonetheless signal worse moral character.

Let us now return to the sordid tale of Michael Vick recounted earlier. We argued that the cruelty he enacted upon animals led to inferences of severe character deficits, more so than some harmful actions directed at humans may have. Evidence for this assertion comes from studies involving two jilted lovers (Tannenbaum et al., 2011, Studies 1a and 1b). Participants read about two men who learned that their girlfriends were cheating on them. Both men flew into a rage; one beat up his unfaithful girlfriend, the other beat up her cat. Participants judged the former action to be more immoral but judged the cat beater as having worse character (specifically, as having less empathy) than his wom-

an-beating counterpart. This is an example of an act–person dissociation.

A similar study compared judgments of another pair of unlikable managers. The "violent" manager expressed his displeasure at a coworker by punching him in the face, whereas the "racist" manager did so by muttering a racial slur about the coworker to himself (Uhlmann, Zhu, & Diermeier, 2014). The violent manager's action was seen as more immoral, probably due to the obvious physical harm that it caused. Yet the racist manager was seen as having worse moral character, again showing a dissociation between judgments of the immorality of acts and the character of actors.

Both of these studies concerned inferences of character from actions that, though less immoral than focal comparisons, are still clearly morally negative (i.e., animal cruelty and racial epithets). However, there may be some circumstances in which even a morally *praiseworthy* act can be indicative of bad moral character. In an initial test of this idea, participants read about two target persons: a medical research assistant whose duties involved inducing tumors in mice and then administering painful injections of experimental cancer drugs and a pet store assistant whose job involved giving gerbils a grooming shampoo and then tying bows on them. Even though the medical research assistant's acts were seen as more praiseworthy than those of the pet store assistant, she was simultaneously perceived as more cold-hearted and aggressive (Uhlmann, Tannenbaum, & Diermeier, 2009). Strikingly, these results were found even among participants who strongly supported animal testing. This demonstrates a pattern of dissociation complementary to that of the cat-beater and racial-slur studies: An act can be objectively praiseworthy, yet still signal poor character.

This finding has since been replicated in the context of utilitarian dilemmas. In one study, participants read about a group of people who were stranded on a sinking life raft but could throw one injured passenger overboard to save everyone else (Uhlmann, Zhu, & Tannenbaum, 2013). When they elected to do this, their action was rated as more morally right than when they elected not to. Yet the passengers who sacrificed one life to save many were seen as having worse moral character than the passengers who did not. In two follow-up studies, participants read about a hospital administrator who had to choose between funding an expensive surgical procedure to save one sick boy or purchasing a new piece of hospital equipment that would save 500 lives in the future. As in the "life raft" study, the administrator who chose to save more people by sacrificing one was seen as having done the morally right thing but as having worse moral character. Also, as in the "frivolous perk" study discussed above, these results were attributable to the informational value ascribed to the person's action. The utilitarian administrator's choice to buy the new equipment was seen as diagnostic of a lack of empathy, which mediated the effect of his decision on overall assessments of his character. Interestingly, though, he was also seen as a better leader for having made the more pragmatic choice. In some cases, it seems, doing the right thing requires a bad person.

We have reviewed evidence supporting two novel hypotheses derived from PCM. First, information about an actor's character can outweigh information about objective harm in social judgments. Furthermore, judgments of the morality of acts can diverge from judgments of an actor's character, suggesting that neither type of judgment can fully explain the other and that both are important aspects of moral cognition. Character matters.

Person-Centered Morality Is Robust and Replicable

The field of psychology (and science more broadly) currently finds itself in the midst of a crisis of confidence in the replicability of our findings (Pashler & Wagenmakers, 2012; Nosek, Spies, & Motyl, 2012), with many high-profile failures of replication emerging recently (e.g., Klein et al., 2014; Open Science Collaboration, 2015). One approach to addressing this concern is to replicate research findings in independent laboratories before, rather than after, they are published. In a large-scale prepublication independent replication (PPIR) project, Schweinsberg et al. (2016) attempted to replicate 10 unpublished moral judgment ef-

fects, originally found by Uhlmann and his colleagues, at 25 partner universities. The 10 effects included 6 that explicitly tested predictions derived from PCM, many of which we have discussed in the present chapter.

The replication effect sizes for these six effects were all statistically significant in the expected direction, although the bad-tipper effect described earlier replicated only for samples in the United States. Perhaps the most theoretically crucial effect was the act–person dissociation such that carrying out medical tests on animals was seen as a praiseworthy act, but also led to negative character inferences. Across numerous replication sites, standardized mean difference (d) associated with this finding was over 2, indicating an extremely large and robust effect. In contrast, two out of four original effects that involved topics *other than* person-centered moral judgments entirely failed to replicate. The overall results of the PPIR suggest that PCM is reliable and replicable. Given this, we now consider how the psychological importance of moral virtues can best be integrated into prevailing models of moral judgment.

Moral Judgment Can Be Both Intuitive and Rational

Modern moral psychology is divided over the root of moral judgments. Some researchers (Landy & Royzman, in press; Royzman, Landy, & Goodwin, 2014) support variants of traditional rationalist models (e.g., Turiel, 1983) that emphasize the role of reasoning and cognitive deliberation in producing moral judgments. Many others claim instead that moral judgments are the result of rapid, automatic evaluations, often called intuitions (Haidt, 2001, 2007). We argue that moral judgment can be both rational and intuitive[3] in important senses and that PCM can provide the bridge to unite these approaches.

As we argued above, character judgments serve an important functional purpose. We think that this makes them, in an important sense, rational, in that they meet the fundamental need to understand others' likely intentions toward us. Importantly, participants themselves do not appear to view person-centered judgments as irrational. Research shows that when targets are judged simultaneously (joint evaluation), participants think more carefully and are less likely to make judgments that they themselves consider unjustified (Gaertner & Dovidio, 1986; Hsee, Loewenstein, Blount, & Bazerman, 1999; Pizarro & Uhlmann, 2005). In our empirical investigations, perceived informational value regarding character can outweigh objective harm in eliciting condemnation in both joint and separate evaluation (Tannenbaum et al., 2011; Uhlmann, Tannenbaum, Zhu, & Diermeier, 2009; Zhu, Uhlmann, & Diermeier, 2014), and act–person dissociations readily emerge under conditions of either joint or separate evaluation (e.g., Tannenbaum et al., 2011; Uhlmann & Zhu, 2014; Uhlmann, Tannenbaum, & Diermeier, 2009; Uhlmann et al., 2013). Thus PCM appears compatible with a subjective sense of making rational judgments.

We noted earlier that, in addition to being functional, character judgments are often automatic—that is, they are intuitive. Haidt and colleagues have demonstrated the role of automatic intuitions in moral judgment in their widely cited studies of "moral dumbfounding." They show that people condemn harmless transgressions such as eating a dead dog or fornicating with a chicken carcass but cannot provide explanations for their condemnation (Haidt, Bjorklund, & Murphy, 2011; Haidt, 2001; Haidt, Koller, & Dias, 1993; though see Royzman, Kim, & Leeman, 2015). These studies all examined evaluations of acts, however.

Applying the PCM perspective to the moral dumbfounding paradigm demonstrates our point that moral judgment can be both rational and intuitive. In another example of an act–person dissociation, participants rated harmless but offensive actions—copulating with a dead chicken and eating a dead dog—as less morally wrong than theft, which directly causes harm. However, the chicken-lover and the dog-eater were seen as having worse moral character than the thief (Uhlmann & Zhu, 2014). Importantly, this characterological assessment seems rationally defensible—such acts as masturbating into poultry have high informational value for judging character (Nelson, 2005; Nelson, McKenzie, Cottrell, & Sejnowski,

2010) because they are exceptionally statistically rare (Ditto & Jemmott, 1989; Fiske, 1980), because they represent extreme deviations from normative behavior (Chakroff & Young, 2015), and because there is almost no conceivable reason to commit them that is external to the person, making them low in attributional ambiguity (Snyder, Kleck, Strenta, & Mentzer, 1979; see also Gray & Keeney, 2015). Therefore, it is quite reasonable to draw strong character inferences from them. Indeed, when participants made character judgments, they were *less* morally dumbfounded when they were asked about offenses that are rare, deviant, and unambiguous, yet harmless, than when they were asked about prototypically harmful offenses (Uhlmann & Zhu, 2014, Study 3). Haidt and colleagues' participants were not able to articulate why a harmless act is wrong, but they probably could have roughly articulated why it indicates bad character.

Integrating these theoretical perspectives and relevant bodies of empirical evidence, we propose that the person-centered nature of moral cognition can unite rationalist and intuitionist perspectives on human morality. Moral judgment is rational and adaptive because social perceivers effectively exploit the informational value of social behaviors to draw reasonable inferences about the underlying vices and virtues of other agents. Moral judgment is intuitive because inferences about other people often must be made quickly and efficiently for reasons of basic survival. The ancient notion that morality is fundamentally concerned with human virtues is supported by a growing body of empirical evidence and has much to add to contemporary models of moral judgment.

NOTES

1. Insofar as trustworthiness can be seen as the likelihood that one will keep one's promises and will not cheat others, these two core elements of character bear resemblances to Kohlberg's (1969) ethics of justice and Gilligan's (1982) ethics of care, as well as Turiel's (1983) definition of the moral domain, which, he argues, involves "justice, rights, and welfare" (p. 3). All of these theories of morality are fundamentally act-centered, but their convergence with the study of character speaks to

our point that PCM must be a part of any integrated theory of moral cognition. Haidt and Graham (2007; Graham, Haidt, & Nosek, 2009) argue for additional, widely important virtues or "moral foundations," including respect for and obedience to authority, loyalty to one's ingroup, and bodily and sexual purity. However, across cultures and subcultures, only virtues relating to fairness (which include honesty and integrity) and caring for others are endorsed universally. Therefore, we see our assertion that trustworthiness and compassion are core elements of moral character as largely consistent with their work.

2. It is worth noting that the purpose of this study was to illustrate the distinction between core goodness and value commitment traits and to explore the importance of this distinction in impression formation, not to produce a complete catalog of all traits of each type. We suspect that a complete list of core goodness virtues would be dominated by trustworthiness and compassion traits.

3. The precise nature of these automatic intuitions is not relevant here, and PCM does not speak to this issue. They could be affective evaluations (Haidt, 2001; Haidt & Joseph, 2004), cognitive computations that have been automatized and can be run without conscious involvement under normal circumstances (Aarts & Custers, 2009; Kahneman & Klein, 2009; Stanovich, West, & Toplak, 2011), or some combination of both.

REFERENCES

Aarts, H., & Custers, R. (2009), Habit, action, and consciousness. In W. P. Banks, (Ed.), *Encyclopedia of consciousness* (Vol. 1, pp. 315–328). Oxford, UK: Elsevier.

Abele, A. E., & Wojciszke, B. (2007). Agency and communion from the perspective of self versus others. *Journal of Personality and Social Psychology, 93,* 751–763.

Anscombe, G. E. M. (1958). Modern moral philosophy. *Philosophy, 33,* 1–19.

Aquino, K., & Reed, A., II. (2002). The self-importance of moral identity. *Journal of Personality and Social Psychology, 83,* 1423–1440.

Aristotle. (1998). *The Nicomachean ethics* (W. D. Ross, trans.). Oxford, UK: Oxford University Press.

Baron, J. (1994). Nonconsequentialist decisions. *Behavioral and Brain Sciences, 17,* 1–10

Baron, J. (2008). *Thinking and deciding.* New York: Cambridge University Press.

Baron, J., Scott, S., Fincher, K., & Metz, S. E. (2015). Why does the Cognitive Reflection Test (sometimes) predict utilitarian moral judgment (and other things)? *Journal of Applied Research in Memory and Cognition, 4,* 265–284.

Bartels, D. (2008). Principled moral sentiment and the flexibility of moral judgment and decision making. *Cognition, 108,* 381–417.

Bartels, D. M., & Pizarro, D. A. (2011). The mismeasure of morals: Antisocial personality traits predict utilitarian responses to moral dilemmas. *Cognition, 121,* 154–161.

Bentham, J. (1970). *An introduction to the principles of morals and legislation.* London: Althone Press. (Original work published 1823)

Chakroff, A., & Young, L. (2015). Harmful situations, impure people: An attribution asymmetry across moral domains. *Cognition, 136,* 30–37.

Cottrell, C. A., Neuberg, S. L., & Li, N. P. (2007). What do people desire in others?: A sociofunctional perspective on the importance of different valued characteristics. *Journal of Personality and Social Psychology, 92,* 208–231.

Critcher, C. R., Inbar, Y., & Pizarro, D. A. (2013). How quick decisions illuminate moral character. *Social Psychological and Personality Science, 4,* 308–315.

Cuddy, A. J. C., Fiske, S. T., & Glick, P. (2008). Warmth and competence as universal dimensions of social perception: The stereotype content model and the BIAS map. *Advances in Experimental Social Psychology, 40,* 61–149.

Ditto, P. H., & Jemmott, J. B., III. (1989). From rarity to evaluative extremity: Effects of prevalence information on evaluations of positive and negative characteristics. *Journal of Personality and Social Psychology, 57,* 16–26.

Engell, A. E., Haxby, J. V., & Todorov, A. (2007). Implicit trustworthiness decisions: Automatic coding of face properties in the human amygdala. *Journal of Cognitive Neuroscience, 19,* 1508–1519.

Fiske, S. T. (1980). Attention and weight in person perception: The impact of negative and extreme behavior. *Journal of Personality and Social Psychology, 38,* 889–906.

Fiske, S. T., Cuddy, A. J. C., & Glick, P. (2007). Universal dimensions of social cognition: Warmth and competence. *Trends in Cognitive Sciences, 11,* 77–83.

Gaertner, S. L., & Dovidio, J. F. (1986). The aversive form of racism. In J. F. Dovidio & S. L. Gaertner (Eds.), *Prejudice, discrimination, and racism* (pp. 61–89). Orlando, FL: Academic Press.

Gasparino, C. (2009, January 22). John Thain's $87,000 rug. *The Daily Beast.* Retrieved from *www.thedailybeast.com.*

Gilligan, C. (1982). *In a different voice.* Cambridge, MA: Harvard University Press.

Goodwin, G. P. (2015). Moral character in person perception. *Current Directions in Psychological Science, 24,* 38–44.

Goodwin, G. P., Piazza, J., & Rozin, P. (2014). Moral character predominates in person perception and evaluation. *Journal of Personality and Social Psychology, 106,* 148–168.

Graham, J., Haidt, J., & Nosek, B. A. (2009). Liberals and conservatives rely on different sets of moral foundations. *Journal of Personality and Social Psychology, 96,* 1029–1046.

Gray, K., & Keeney, J. E. (2015). Impure or just weird?: Scenario sampling bias raises questions about the foundations of morality. *Social Psychological and Personality Science, 6,* 859–868.

Greene, J. D., Morelli, S. A., Lowenberg, K., Nystrom, L. E., & Cohen, J. D. (2008). Cognitive load selectively interferes with utilitarian moral judgment. *Cognition, 107,* 1144–1154.

Greene, J. D., Sommerville, R. B., Nystrom, L. E., Darley, J. M., & Cohen, J. D. (2001). An fMRI investigation of emotional engagement in moral judgment. *Science, 293,* 2105–2108.

Haidt, J. (2001). The emotional dog and its rational tail: A social intuitionist approach to moral judgment. *Psychological Review, 108,* 814–834.

Haidt, J. (2007). The new synthesis in moral psychology. *Science, 316,* 998–1002.

Haidt, J., Bjorklund, F., & Murphy, S. (2011). *Moral dumbfounding: When intuition finds no reason.* Unpublished manuscript.

Haidt, J., & Graham, J. (2007). When morality opposes justice: Conservatives have moral intuitions that liberals may not recognize. *Social Justice Research, 20,* 98–116.

Haidt, J., & Joseph, C. (2004). Intuitive ethics: How innately prepared intuitions generate culturally variable virtues. *Daedalus, 133,* 55–66.

Haidt, J., Koller, S., & Dias, M. (1993). Affect, culture, and morality, or is it wrong to eat your dog? *Journal of Personality and Social Psychology, 65,* 613–628.

Hamlin, J., Wynn, K., & Bloom, P. (2007). Social evaluation by preverbal infants. *Nature, 450,* 557–559.

Hsee, C. K., Loewenstein, G. F., Blount, S., & Bazerman, M. H. (1999). Preference reversals between joint and separate evaluation of options: A review and theoretical analysis. *Psychological Bulletin, 125,* 576–590.

Kagan, S. (1998). *Normative ethics.* Boulder, CO: Westview Press.

Kahneman, D., & Klein, G. (2009). Conditions for intuitive expertise: A failure to disagree. *American Psychologist, 64,* 515–526.

Kant, I. (2002). *Groundwork for the metaphysics of morals* (A. Zweig, Trans.). New York: Oxford University Press. (Original work published 1785)

King, P. (2007, August 20). A boss betrayed: Falcons' Blank deeply saddened by Vick's demise. *Sports Illustrated.* Retrieved from *http://sportsillustrated.cnn.com.*

Klein, R. A., Ratliff, K. A., Vianello, M., Adams, R. B., Jr., Bahník, Š., Bernstein, M. J., . . ., & Nosek, B. A. (2014). Investigating variation in replicability: A "many labs" replication project. *Social Psychology, 45,* 142–152.

Kohlberg, L. (1969). Stage and sequence: The cognitive-developmental approach to socialization. In D. A. Goslin (Ed.), *Handbook of socialization theory and research* (pp. 347–480). Chicago: Rand McNally.

Landy, J. F., Herzog, N. R., & Bartels, D. M. (2017). *Moral thoughtfulness: Thinking carefully about complex moral problems is a virtue.* Manuscript in preparation.

Landy, J. F., Linder, J. N., & Caruso, E. M. (2017). *Latent intentions: Why over-justifying innocence makes you seem like a worse person.* Manuscript in preparation.

Landy, J. F., Piazza, J., & Goodwin, G. P. (2016). When it's bad to be friendly and smart: The desirability of sociability and competence depends on morality. *Personality and Social Psychology Bulletin, 42,* 1272–1290.

Landy, J. F., & Royzman, E. B. (in press). Moral reasoning. In G. Pennycook (Ed.), *The new reflectionism in cognitive psychology: Why reason matters.* East Sussex, UK: Psychology Press.

Lapsley, D. K., & Lasky, B. (2001). Prototypic moral character. *Identity, 1,* 345–363.

Martin, J. W., & Cushman, F. (2015). To punish or to leave: Distinct cognitive processes underlie partner control and partner choice behaviors. *PLOS ONE, 10*(4), e0125193.

Martin, J. W., & Cushman, F. (2016). Why we forgive what can't be controlled. *Cognition, 147,* 133–143.

McCann, M. (2007, December 10). Analyzing the Vick sentence: The reason behind ruling, how long he'll serve, more. *Sports Illustrated.* Retrieved from *http://sportsillustrated.cnn.com.*

Mill, J. S. (1998). *Utilitarianism.* New York: Oxford University Press. (Original work published 1861)

Nelson, J. D. (2005). Finding useful questions: On Bayesian diagnosticity, probability, impact, and information gain. *Psychological Review, 112,* 979–999.

Nelson, J. D., McKenzie, C. R. M., Cottrell, G. W., & Sejnowski, T. J. (2010). Experience matters: Information acquisition optimizes probability gain. *Psychological Science, 21*(7), 960–969.

Nosek, B. A., Spies, J. R., & Motyl, M. (2012). Scientific utopia: II. Restructuring incentives and practices to promote truth over publishability. *Perspectives on Psychological Science, 7,* 615–631.

Open Science Collaboration. (2015). Estimating the reproducibility of psychological science. *Science, 349,* 6251.

Pashler, H., & Wagenmakers, E.-J. (2012). Editors' introduction to the special section on replicability in psychological science: A crisis of confidence? *Perspectives on Psychological Science, 7,* 528–530.

Peeters, G. (1992). Evaluative meanings of adjectives in vitro and in context: Some theoretical implications and practical consequences of positive negative asymmetry and behavioural-adaptive concepts of evaluation. *Psychologia Belgica, 32,* 211–231.

Piazza, J., Goodwin, G., Rozin, P., & Royzman, E. (2014). When a virtue is not a virtue: Conditional virtues in moral evaluation. *Social Cognition, 32,* 528–558.

Piazza, J., Landy, J. F., & Goodwin, G. P. (2014). Cruel nature: Harmfulness as an important, overlooked dimension in judgments of moral standing. *Cognition, 131,* 108–124.

Pizarro, D. A., & Tannenbaum, D. (2011). Bringing character back: How the motivation to evaluate character influences judgments of moral blame. In P. Shaver & M. Mikulincer (Eds.), *The social psychology of morality: Exploring the causes of good and evil* (pp. 91–108). New York: APA Books.

Pizarro, D. A., Tannenbaum, D., & Uhlmann, E. L. (2012). Mindless, harmless, and blameworthy. *Psychological Inquiry, 23,* 185–188.

Pizarro, D. A., & Uhlmann, E. L. (2005). Do normative standards advance our understanding of moral judgment? *Behavioral and Brain Sciences, 28,* 558–559.

Reeder, G. D., & Brewer, M. B. (1979). A schematic model of dispositional attribution in interpersonal perception. *Psychological Review, 86,* 61–79.

Royzman, E. B., Kim, K., & Leeman, R. F. (2015). The curious tale of Julie and Mark: Unraveling the moral dumbfounding effect. *Judgment and Decision Making, 10,* 296–313.

Royzman, E. B., Landy, J. F., & Goodwin, G. P. (2014). Are good reasoners more incest-friendly?: Trait cognitive reflection predicts selective moralization in a sample of American adults. *Judgment and Decision Making, 9,* 175–190.

Royzman, E. B., Landy, J. F., & Leeman, R. F. (2015). Are thoughtful people more utilitarian?: CRT as a unique predictor of moral minimalism in the dilemmatic context. *Cognitive Science, 39,* 325–352.

Schweinsberg, M., Madan, N., Vianello, M., Sommer, A., Jordan, J., Zhu, L., . . . Uhlmann, E. L. (2016). The pipeline project: Pre-publication independent replications of a single laboratory's research pipeline. *Journal of Experimental Social Psychology, 66,* 55–67.

Skowronski, J. J., & Carlston, D. E. (1989). Negativity and extremity biases in impression formation: A review of explanations. *Psychological Bulletin, 105,* 131–142.

Smart, J. J. C., & Williams, B. (1973). *Utilitarianism: For and against.* Cambridge, UK: Cambridge University Press.

Snyder, M. L., Kleck, R. E., Strenta, A., & Mentzer, S. J. (1979). Avoidance of the handicapped: An attributional ambiguity analysis. *Journal of Personality and Social Psychology, 37,* 2297–2306.

Stanovich, K. E., West, R. F., & Toplak, M. E. (2011). The complexity of developmental predictions from dual process models. *Developmental Review, 31,* 103–118.

Sunstein, C. R. (2005). Moral heuristics. *Behavioral and Brain Sciences, 28,* 531–541.

Tannenbaum, D., Uhlmann, E. L., & Diermeier, D. (2011). Moral signals, public outrage, and immaterial harms. *Journal of Experimental Social Psychology, 47,* 1249–1254.

Turiel, E. (1983). *The development of social knowledge: Morality and convention.* Cambridge, UK: Cambridge University Press.

Uhlmann, E. L., Pizarro, D., & Diermeier, D. (2015). A person-centered approach to moral judgment. *Perspectives on Psychological Science, 10,* 72–81.

Uhlmann, E. L., Tannenbaum, D., & Diermeier, D. (2009). *The cold-hearted prosociality effect.* Unpublished finding selected for replication in the Pipeline Project (Schweinsberg et al., in press). Full study report available in the online supplement for Schweinsberg et al. (in press).

Uhlmann, E. L., Tannenbaum, D., & Diermeier, D. (2010). *The bad tipper effect.* Unpublished finding selected for replication in the Pipeline Project (Schweinsberg et al., in press). Full study report available in the online supplement for Schweinsberg et al. (in press).

Uhlmann, E. L., Tannenbaum, D., Zhu, L., & Diermeier, D. (2009). *The bigot–misanthrope effect.* Unpublished finding selected for replication in the Pipeline Project (Schweinsberg et al., in press). Full study report available in the online supplement of Schweinsberg et al. (in press).

Uhlmann, E. L., & Zhu, L. (2014). Acts, persons, and intuitions: Person-centered cues and gut reactions to harmless transgressions. *Social Psychological and Personality Science, 5,* 279–285.

Uhlmann, E. L., Zhu, L., & Diermeier, D. (2014). When actions speak volumes: The role of inferences about moral character in outrage over racial bigotry. *European Journal of Social Psychology, 44,* 23–29.

Uhlmann, E. L., Zhu, L., & Tannenbaum, D. (2013). When it takes a bad person to do the right thing. *Cognition, 126,* 326–334.

Walker, L. J., & Hennig, K. H. (2004). Differing conceptions of moral exemplarity: Just, brave, and caring. *Journal of Personality and Social Psychology, 86,* 629–647.

Walker, L. J., & Pitts, R. C. (1998). Naturalistic conceptions of moral maturity. *Developmental Psychology, 34,* 403–419.

Willis, J., & Todorov, A. (2006). First impressions: Making up your mind after a 100-ms exposure to a face. *Psychological Science, 17,* 592–598.

Wojciszke, B., Bazinska, R., & Jaworski, M. (1998). On the dominance of moral categories in impression formation. *Personality and Social Psychology Bulletin, 24,* 1251–1263.

Wojciszke, B., Dowhyluk, M., & Jaworski, M. (1998). Moral and competence-related traits: How do they differ? *Polish Psychological Bulletin, 29,* 283–294.

Zhu, L., Uhlmann, E. L., & Diermeier, D. (2014). Moral evaluations of bigots and misanthropes. Available at *https://osf.io/a4uxn.*

CHAPTER 14

A Social Cognitive Model of Moral Identity

Karl Aquino
Adam Kay

Is moral behavior the product of intuitive psychological processes that can show both flexibility and cross-situational stability?

Yes, if we conceptualize moral identity as a highly accessible mental representation that mediates between people's internal states, situational cues and contingencies, and subsequent behavior.

In this chapter we explain how Aquino and Reed's (2002) social cognitive model of moral identity contributes to our understanding of moral behavior. We present their definition of moral identity, the assumptions of their model, and the underlying principles that link moral identity as they conceptualize it to moral functioning. But first, we present a brief historical review of how other scholars have defined moral identity so we can situate Aquino and Reed's (2002) model within the broader family of related concepts and theories that have been widely discussed in the literature.

The concept of moral identity first captured the interest of moral psychologists after Blasi (1983) introduced the term in his *self model* of moral functioning. According to Blasi, moral identity is an individual difference reflecting the degree to which commitment to moral goals and ideals is characteristic of a person's sense of self. Blasi suggested that what connects moral identity to behavior is the desire for self-

consistency. A number of scholars followed suit by proffering similar definitions that equated having a moral identity with a sustained commitment to moral action in line with a person's moral beliefs or values (e.g., Bergman, 2004; Colby & Damon, 1992; Damon, 1984). More recently, Blasi (2005) proposed a three-component model that lays out the theoretical requirements for having a moral identity: (1) willpower, (2) integrity, and (3) moral desire—which he described thus: "willpower is necessary to deal with internal and external obstacles in pursuing one's long-term objectives; integrity relates to one's commitments to the sense of self; moral desires guide willpower and integrity and provide them with their moral significance" (Blasi, 2005, p. 72). Blasi (2005) argued that these three virtues possess a trait-like stability and are cultivated through conscious effort.

Although sound theoretical arguments exist for treating moral identity as a combination of trait-like properties and conscious deliberation, there are also limitations to applying this perspective broadly to explain moral behavior. There is little doubt that moral behavior is at least partly regulated by conscious effort, but numerous theorists have argued that this fails to fully account for the fact that much, perhaps even most, of what constitutes "everyday morality" is the result of automatic, intuitive, or habitual processes outside of conscious awareness (Haidt, 2001; Lapsley & Narvaez, 2004). A second limitation of treating moral identity as having durable, trait-like properties is that it fails to account for the multifaceted and protean nature of identity (Aquino, Freeman, Reed, Lim, & Felps, 2009). A social cognitive framework of moral identity can address these limitations and is the basis for Aquino and Reed's (2002) model.

Social cognitive theory (SCT) is a general framework that takes into account the joint and reciprocal influence of dispositional variables and environmental factors on behavior (e.g., Bandura, 2001; Cervone & Shoda, 1999; Mischel & Mischel, 1976). SCT draws from principles of social cognition to capture the stability and accessibility of knowledge structures such as identity, as well as their dependence on situational influences. Drawing from SCT, Aquino and Reed (2002) proposed a conceptualization of moral identity as a mental representation organized around a set of moral trait associations. Their definition rests on the assumption that some knowledge structures, such as the traits people ascribe to themselves, are more closely connected to one another within the associative network of concepts in long- and short-term memory than others. In their model, the traits that constitute the mental representation of a person's moral identity are those that correspond to lay construals of what it means to be a moral person (e.g., honesty, kindness, compassion).

Aquino and Reed's (2002) model accepts the notion that moral identity can motivate behavior through the desire to maintain self-consistency (Mulder & Aquino, 2013). But it also allows for the possibility of other, more generic processes that are not connected to moral functioning, do not require conscious deliberation, and are not driven by a consistency motive to explain moral behavior. These processes are generic insofar as the cognitive operations that mediate between moral identity and behavior are built into the architecture of all functioning human brains. They are part of an interrelated set of processes that constitute what dual-process models of human cognition refer to as System 1 (e.g., Haidt & Bjorklund, 2007; Stanovich & West, 2000). System 1 consists of functions in the brain from which emotions and quick, automatic, valenced judgments arise. It is distinguished and dissociated from System 2, which consists of the "higher executive functions" of the brain, such as those involved in planning, reasoning, and regulating impulses (for reviews of dual-processing theory, see Evans, 2008; Kahneman, 2011).

In addition to being associated with System 1 processing, Aquino and Reed's (2002) conception of moral identity is distinguished by a number of features that are in accord with social cognitive principles. First, the schema of traits that constitutes a person's moral identity is presumed to vary in its accessibility in long-term memory. When this schema is *chronically accessible,* it is readily and easily made available for processing social information and is therefore experienced as being a more essential aspect of a person's sense of self. The chronic accessibility of moral identity can also be referred to as its "strength" or "centrality" (Aquino et al., 2009). In SCT, knowledge accessibility is a general principle of cognitive functioning, and it is assumed that more readily accessible mental constructs have a stronger influence on behavior than less accessible ones (Higgins, 1996). Because the accessibility of knowledge structures varies across individuals (Higgins, 1996; Higgins, King, & Mavin, 1982), a social cognitive model of moral identity allows us to treat it as having disposition-like properties (Higgins, 1996).

A second defining characteristic of Aquino and Reed's (2002) model is that regardless of its level of chronic accessibility, a moral identity can also be activated (or deactivated) by situational cues. A social cognitive model treats moral identity as a construct that can be made *more* or *less salient* at any given time. Accordingly, a person whose moral identity *is not* chronically accessible can still be prompted by situational cues to temporarily experience a strong moral identity. This, in turn, can motivate the person to behave more morally (Bargh, Bond,

Lombardi, & Tota, 1986). Conversely, a person whose moral identity *is* chronically accessible may be influenced by situational factors to momentarily lose sense of this identity, which diminishes its motivational power (Stryker, 1980). Because people must balance multiple and sometimes competing identities, of which only a subset known as the "working self-concept" is activated at any given time (Markus & Kunda, 1986), the influence of any one of these identities on behavior is strongest when that particular identity is relatively more salient (Carver & Scheier, 1998; Skitka, 2003). Together, the accessibility of moral identity and its responsiveness to situational cues allows this social cognitive conception to account for both the intraindividual stability and coherence of a moral character and the variability of moral behavior across situations (Aquino et al., 2009; Lapsley & Narvaez, 2004). It also allows for the possibility of conceptualizing moral identity as a state that exhibits within-person variation, which is consistent with how some scholars have described personality (Fleeson, 2004).

A final defining feature of Aquino and Reed's (2002) social cognitive model is that it conforms to notions of the self proposed by other identity theorists, who suggest that it has both a private and a public aspect (e.g., Fenigstein, Scheier, & Buss, 1975; James, 1890/1950; Schlenker, 1980). Aquino and Reed (2002) refer to these dimensions of moral identity as *internalization* and *symbolization*, respectively. Internalization is closest to what Blasi and like-minded theorists mean by moral identity because it reflects people's subjective experience that it is central to their overall self-concept. It is this relatively enduring association between people's sense of self and the mental representation of their moral character that links the internalized aspect of moral identity to moral action. The symbolization dimension reflects people's tendency to express their moral identity through outward actions in the world. Although such expressions have been considered an indicator of having a particular identity (e.g., Erikson, 1964) or a means of self-verifying an identity (Swann, 1983), Aquino and Reed (2002) are agnostic about whether symbolization reveals anything about the "authenticity" of moral identity. Indeed, it has been suggested that moral

identity symbolization can sometimes be driven by impression management or instrumental motives (Winterich, Aquino, Mittal, & Schwartz, 2013), and therefore may not validly represent a person's phenomenological experience of "having" a moral identity.

The distinction between moral identity internalization and symbolization is consistent with the view that people are simultaneously both agents and actors (Frimer, Schaefer, & Oakes, 2014). Whereas the agentic self is private and therefore more prone to being driven by selfish motives that increase a person's chances for survival, the self as actor recognizes that survival is also facilitated by being accepted into social groups and gaining the benefits of mutually beneficial exchange (Frimer et al., 2014). Thus the self as actor is motivated to behave prosocially and to support goals to enhance social attractiveness, even if the self as agent might want to do otherwise. We can incorporate Aquino and Reed's (2002) two-dimensional model of moral identity into this dualistic description to suggest that, although the agentic self may indeed be primarily egoistic, a highly accessible mental representation of a private moral self in working memory (e.g., being high in moral identity internalization) can moderate this tendency for selfishness (Winterich, Mittal, & Aquino, 2014). Similarly, the motivation to engage in moral identity symbolization can lead to prosocial behaviors (Winterich et al., 2014), although in this case the underlying goal of increasing one's chances of being accepted into and gaining status within groups may be more egoistic. Thus, moral identity symbolization and the self as actor may be seen as conceptually coterminous.

Aquino and Reed's (2002) social cognitive model is situated within a broader literature that can be divided into three general categories. These categories range from "flexible" to "firm" to "strong" views of what moral identity is and how it influences moral behavior. A *flexible* view recognizes the role of individual differences, yet places significant emphasis on the effect of situational factors on the processes that motivate moral behavior. A *firm* view gives relatively less attention to situational cues, placing primary emphasis on individual differences in moral identity to explain moral behavior. Nevertheless, it leaves open the possibility that situational factors can sometimes lead people to exhibit behavior that is the product of nondeliberative, unconscious processes that are partly driven by moral identity. Finally, a *strong* view also places primary emphasis on individual differences, yet unlike the firm view it places considerably more importance on the conscious, deliberative processes that lead people to have a moral identity in the first place.

Since Aquino and Reed's (2002) social cognitive model assumes that behavior is the product of an interplay between dispositional traits and situational cues, resulting in different behaviors in different contexts, it fits into the *flexible* category. Another model that falls into this category is Lapsley and Narvaez's (2004) model of "moral personality," which is substantially similar to Aquino and Reed's (2002), although it does not explicitly recognize the internalization and symbolization dimensions of moral identity. Both models draw from the notion that people hold prototypes (Walker & Pitts, 1998) of the moral character.

From a social cognitive perspective, these prototypes help people evaluate new stimuli (Kahneman & Frederick, 2005) and make sense of their moral landscape. Aquino and Reed (2002) suggest that when a distinct image of a moral prototype is brought to mind, it can lead people to act as this prototype would in the same situation (Kihlstrom & Klein, 1994). This idea raises the possibility that moral identity may function as a *heuristic* (O'Reilly, Aquino, & Skarlicki, 2016). Heuristics are cognitive shortcuts that facilitate "fast and frugal" ways of thinking, and it has been suggested that they can elicit intuitive judgments about moral "wrongness" (Gigerenzer, 2010; Sinnott-Armstrong, Young, & Cushman, 2010; Sunstein, 2005). If moral identity is indeed a form of moral prototype (Walker & Pitts, 1998), then, like other prototypes, it can influence how people behave at the neurochemical level (Reynolds, 2006). Reynolds (2006) proposed that prototypes are not mere metaphors but, rather, actual neurochemical imprints used to form quick, intuitive judgments. Yet, however prototypes are conceived, what binds *flexible* theories of moral identity is a recognition that moral behavior is often the result of automatic, intuitive processes that lie outside of conscious awareness.

Firm views of moral identity place primary emphasis on individual differences and less on the conscious, deliberative processes that lead to its emergence. Most representative of this perspective is the work of Walker and Frimer (2007), who contend that moral judgment is necessary but ultimately inadequate in accounting for moral behavior. Instead, they argue that individual-difference variables have considerably more explanatory power. Their view is firm insofar as the personality traits upon which they place such heavy reliance are relatively fixed and stable; however, it falls short of being *strong* to the extent that it does not emphasize how moral identity becomes incorporated into personality.

Strong conceptions of moral identity provide this explanation. *Strong* views also place great emphasis on the role of reflection, reasoning about morality, and the construction of narratives that give meaning and coherence to people's behavior over time. For example, Blasi (2005)—whose work we consider emblematic of the strong view—contends that moral action is a function of the extent to which morality is important to the self-concept, which, in turn, he saw as an individual difference with trait-like properties. Similarly, Colby and Damon (1992) recognize four developmental processes that combine personality traits and a strong "commitment" to moral advancement: (1) a continuing capacity for change; (2) certainty about moral values and principles, balanced by open-mindedness and truth seeking; (3) positivity, humility, love, and faith; and (4) an identity that fuses the personal with the moral and emphasizes the importance of integrity. Finally, McAdams (2008) unites dispositional traits, characteristic adaptations (e.g., motivational, developmental, and strategic aspects of personality evidenced in particular situations), and life narratives to explain moral behavior. Life narratives are seen as psychosocial constructions of personal identity over which people have a substantial amount of conscious dominion.

Rather than seeing the *firm* and *strong* views as competing or incompatible with Aquino and Reed's (2002) more *flexible* model, we suggest that they can be reconciled by recognizing the role and explanatory value of each. A *flexible* view captures moral identity's fluidity, malleability, and computational efficiency. We maintain that this is the default operative mechanism for how moral identity influences behavior for the *typical* person in *most* situations. A *firm* view, by contrast, may be appropriate in considering the morally gifted, who are dispositionally wired by a combination of natural endowments, life experiences, and intentional practice to be more concerned about morality. These people may take their predisposition toward moral behavior for granted and therefore act morally in most situations without necessarily working consciously to enhance their moral orientation toward the world. Finally, we maintain that *strong* views of moral identity may be more efficacious for explaining the behavior of true moral exemplars whose commitment to moral goals and projects is enduring and consistent. These people have a natural predisposition to act morally, but they also place a considerable amount of value and effort on developing their moral selves.

Although we see each of these conceptions as having its own place, it must be recognized that a significant body of empirical evidence is growing to support the *flexible* social cognitive model put forth by Aquino and Reed (2002). Since they proposed their model of moral identity over a decade ago, numerous studies have been conducted that show relationships between the chronic accessibility of moral identity, its temporary activation, and a host of morally relevant outcomes. Extensive reviews have been conducted on this body of research elsewhere (e.g., Boegershausen, Aquino, & Reed, 2015; Shao, Aquino, & Freeman, 2008), so we shall canvass only a select sample of the empirical evidence that supports their view.

Studies show that the chronic accessibility of moral identity, as measured by Aquino and Reed's (2002) scale, is positively related to a host of prosocial behaviors. For example, it has been linked to higher levels of volunteerism (Aquino & Reed, 2002; Winterich et al., 2013), charitable giving (Reed, Aquino, & Levy, 2007), and organizational citizenship behavior (McFerran, Aquino, & Duffy, 2010). It has also been associated with higher levels of honesty in economic games (Mulder & Aquino, 2013). Most recently, it has been shown to reduce people's aversion to giving time over money to prosocial causes, even as the psychological costs

of doing so increase (Reed, Kay, Finnel, Aquino, & Levy, 2016).

Similar effects have also been found when moral identity is made temporarily salient by situational cues. For example, activating moral identity leads people to be more willing to sacrifice their own financial interests for the benefit of others (Aquino et al., 2009) and be less aversive to donating time over money to prosocial causes, even when doing so is subjectively unpleasant (Reed et al., 2016). Conversely, it has been shown that making moral identity less salient increases the likelihood of self-interested behavior. For example, in one study, financial performance incentives reduced moral identity salience and led people to be more deceitful in business negotiations (Aquino et al., 2009).

Finally, moral identity has also been shown to influence moral and immoral behavior by amplifying or dampening the effects of other motivators. For example, people whose moral identity is either chronically accessible or temporarily activated are more likely to act prosocially after experiencing a state of moral elevation (Aquino, McFerran, & Laven, 2011). Moral identity centrality has also been shown to motivate potential donors to give more money to charities when they are perceived to be in alignment with the donors' political identity (Winterich, Zhang, & Mittal, 2012). Conversely, it has been found that moral identity salience decreases the tendency of strong adherents to binding ingroup values (e.g., obedience, loyalty, and purity) to reduce their support for the torture of outgroup members (Smith, Aquino, Koleva, & Graham, 2014).

Although there is significant empirical support for Aquino and Reed's (2002) social cognitive model of moral identity, a few inconsistent findings in the literature cast doubt on the universality of some of its underlying premises. For example, activating moral identity has been shown to both increase *and* decrease moral behavior. Although the preponderance of the evidence suggests that priming moral identity *increases* prosocial behavior (Aquino et al., 2009; Reed et al., 2007), at least one study has found that it generates a moral licensing effect that leads to a *decrease* in prosocial behavior (Sachdeva, Iliev, & Medin, 2009). One recent study further showed an inconsistency in moral priming, with a heightened salience of moral identity leading to higher intentions to donate time over money to charitable causes, yet no significant difference when it comes to donation behavior (Reed et al., 2016). Accordingly, it is still unclear when and under what circumstances activating moral identity in the working self-concept increases or decreases prosocial behavior, or when it has any effect at all. Future research is required to explain these inconsistencies and clarify the conditions under which moral priming *is* and *is not* effective.

Further questions have been raised with respect to the association of moral identity centrality and behaviors following deceit. For example, one study showed that high moral identifiers prefer to compensate for lying with subsequent truth telling, as opposed to behaving consistently with their prior deceit (Mulder & Aquino, 2013). However, this was shown to be the case only with subsequent behaviors that are qualitatively different from past behaviors, and only when it involved actively lying as opposed to concealing a truth. Moreover, such compensatory behavior was demonstrated only with respect to lying and failed to replicate in the case of cheating (Mulder & Aquino, 2013). A host of questions therefore remain about the effects of prior immoral behavior on subsequent moral behavior when moral identity has high centrality. Further research is required to answer these questions and clarify the impact of moral identity centrality on different types of moral behavior.

We contend that Aquino and Reed's (2002) model is well suited for investigating such questions, as it allows researchers to work with moral identities not only of different *degrees* but also of different *types*. For example, bifurcating each dimension of moral identity suggests a four-part typology of moral identity profiles: (1) low internalization and low symbolization; (2) low internalization and high symbolization; (3) high internalization and low symbolization; and (4) high internalization and high symbolization. Each profile represents a different arrangement of goals and motivations, and therefore suggests a different orientation toward acting morally. For example, individuals who are high (low) in both moral identity internalization and symbolization may be consistently more (less) concerned with morality in their internal thoughts and private actions,

as well as in their external words and public behaviors. Such individuals may be thought of as having "congruent" moral identities. By contrast, those who are high (low) in internalization and low (high) in symbolization may be concerned (indifferent) about morality in their internal thoughts and private actions yet indifferent (concerned) about it in their external words and public behaviors. Such individuals may be thought of as having "incongruent" moral identities. Researchers in this field are starting to recognize the important difference these moral identity profiles can make. For example, Rupp, Shao, Thornton, and Skarlicki (2013) theorized that morally imbued actions such as corporate social responsibility may have a more profound influence on people higher in internalization than symbolization. In addition, Winterich and colleagues (2013) showed that a promise of public recognition can serve to motivate people high in symbolization to volunteer their time, but only when internalization is low.

In the future, researchers should continue to explore what different combinations of moral identity internalization and symbolization reveal about underlying goals and motivations, as well as the behaviors that flow from them. Indeed, this more nuanced approach may help shed light on some of the inconsistencies in the literature. For example, whether priming moral identity increases or decreases prosocial behavior may depend not only on the nature of the moral identity profile being primed but also on the behavior in question (e.g., whether or not it yields public recognition).

To summarize, with a framework that recognizes moral cognition and behavior to be the product of the intuitive, generic psychological processes described in this chapter, Aquino and Reed's (2002) social cognitive model of moral identity is uniquely suited to explain how moral behavior is characterized both by cross-situational stability and coherence and by dynamic flexibility. It is unique insofar as it recognizes that moral behavior is the result of a complex interplay of individual differences, situational contingencies, and prior behavior. This *flexible* model of moral cognition and behavior is likely to prove helpful in resolving some of the lingering issues in the still-nascent moral identity literature. At the same time, as researchers continue to work with the model, they are sure to reveal further inconsistencies and raise more questions. These would be positive developments for the scientific study of morality, for if the foundational assumptions of Aquino and Reed's (2002) model are falsified or otherwise brought into question, then refinements can be made to enhance its explanatory power. Until then, the data thus far suggest that it continues to be a valuable model for exploring how human beings navigate the fuzzy moral terrain of everyday life.

REFERENCES

Aquino, K., Freeman, D., Reed, A., II, Lim, V. K. G., & Felps, W. (2009). Testing a social-cognitive model of moral behavior: The interactive influence of situations and moral identity centrality. *Journal of Personality and Social Psychology, 97*(1), 123–141.

Aquino, K., McFerran, B., & Laven, M. (2011). Moral identity and the experience of moral elevation in response to acts of uncommon goodness. *Journal of Personality and Social Psychology, 100,* 703–718.

Aquino, K., & Reed, A., II. (2002). The self-importance of moral identity. *Journal of Personality and Social Psychology, 83,* 1423–1440.

Bandura, A. (2001). Social cognitive theory: An agentic perspective. *Annual Review of Psychology, 52,* 1–26.

Bargh, J. A., Bond, R. N., Lombardi, W. J., & Tota, M. E. (1986). The additive nature of chronic and temporary sources of construct accessibility. *Journal of Personality and Social Psychology, 50*(5), 869–878.

Bergman, R. (2004). Identity as motivation: Toward a theory of the moral self. In D. K. Lapsley & D. Narvaez (Eds.), *Moral development, self, and identity* (pp. 21–46). Mahwah, NJ: Erlbaum.

Blasi, A. (1983). Moral cognition and moral action: A theoretical perspective. *Developmental Review, 3,* 178–210.

Blasi, A. (2005). Moral character: A psychological approach. In D. K. Lapsley & F. C. Power (Eds.), *Character psychology and character education* (pp. 67–100). Notre Dame, IN: University of Notre Dame Press.

Boegershausen, J., Aquino, K., Reed, A., II. (2015). Moral identity. *Current Opinion in Psychology, 6,* 162–166.

Carver, C. S., & Scheier, M. F. (1998). *On the self-regulation of behavior.* New York: Cambridge University Press.

Cervone, D., & Shoda, Y. (1999). Social-cognitive theories and the coherence of personality. In D. Cervone & Y. Shoda (Eds.), *The coherence of personality: Social-cognitive bases of consistency, variability, and organization* (pp. 3–33). New York: Guilford Press.

Colby, A., & Damon, W. (1992). *Some do care: Contemporary lives of moral commitment.* New York: Free Press.

Damon, W. (1984). Self-understanding and moral development from childhood to adolescence. In W. M. Kurtines & J. L. Gewirtz (Eds.), *Morality, moral behavior, and moral development* (pp. 109–127). New York: Wiley.

Erikson, E. H. (1964). *Insight and responsibility.* New York: Norton.

Evans, J. B. T. (2008). Dual-processing accounts of reasoning, judgment, and social cognition. *Annual Review of Psychology, 59,* 255–278.

Fenigstein, A., Scheier, M. F., & Buss, A. H. (1975). Public and private self-consciousness: Assessment and theory. *Journal of Consulting and Clinical Psychology, 43,* 522–527.

Fleeson, W. (2004). Moving personality beyond the person–situation debate: The challenge and opportunity of within-person variability. *Current Directions in Psychological Science, 13*(2), 83–87.

Frimer, J. A., Schaefer, N. K., & Oakes, H. (2014). Moral actor, selfish agent. *Journal of Personality and Social Psychology, 106*(5), 790–802.

Gigerenzer, G. (2010). Moral satisficing: Rethinking moral behavior as bounded rationality. *Topics in Cognitive Science, 2,* 528–554.

Haidt, J. (2001). The emotional dog and its rational tail: A social intuitionist approach to moral judgment. *Psychological Review, 108*(4), 814–834.

Haidt, J., & Bjorklund, F. (2007). Social intuitionists answer six questions about morality. In W. Sinnott-Armstrong (Ed.), *Moral psychology: Vol. 2. The cognitive science of morality* (pp. 181–217). Cambridge, MA: MIT Press.

Higgins, E. T. (1996). The "self-digest": Self-knowledge serving self-regulatory functions. *Journal of Personality and Social Psychology, 71*(6), 1062–1083.

Higgins, E. T., King, G. A., & Mavin, G. H. (1982). Individual construct accessibility and subjective impressions and recall. *Journal of Personality and Social Psychology, 43,* 35–47.

James, W. (1950). *The principles of psychology.* New York: Dover. (Original work published 1890)

Kahneman, D. (2011). *Thinking fast and slow.* Toronto, Ontario: Random House Canada.

Kahneman, D., & Frederick, S. (2005). A model of heuristic judgment. In K. J. Holyoak & R. G. Morrison (Eds.), *The Cambridge handbook of thinking and reasoning* (pp. 109–127). Cambridge, UK: Cambridge University Press.

Kihlstrom, J. F., & Klein, S. B. (1994). The self as a knowledge structure. In R. S. Wyer, Jr. & K. Thomas (Eds.), *Handbook of socialization theory and research* (pp. 347–480). Chicago: Rand McNally.

Lapsley, D. K., & Narvaez, D. (2004). A social-cognitive approach to the moral personality. In D. K. Lapsley & D. Narvaez (Eds.), *Moral development, self, and identity* (pp. 189–212). Mahwah, NJ: Erlbaum.

Markus, H., & Kunda, Z. (1986). Stability and malleability of the self-concept. *Journal of Personality and Social Psychology, 51,* 858–866.

McAdams, D. P. (2008). Personal narratives and the life story. In O. P. John, R. W. Robins, & L. A. Pervin (Eds.), *Handbook of personality: Theory and research* (3rd ed., pp. 242–262). New York: Guilford Press.

McFerran, B., Aquino, K., & Duffy, M. (2010). How personality and moral identity relate to individuals' ethical ideology. *Business Ethics Quarterly, 20*(1), 35–56.

Mischel, W., & Mischel, H. N. (1976). A cognitive social-learning approach to morality and self-regulation. In T. Lickona (Ed.), *Moral development and behavior* (pp. 84–107). New York: Holt, Rinehart & Winston.

Mulder, L. B., & Aquino, K. A. (2013). The role of moral identity in the aftermath of dishonesty. *Organizational Behavior and Human Decision Processes, 121,* 219–230.

O'Reilly, J., Aquino, K., & Skarlicki, D. P. (2016). The lives of others: Third parties' responses to others' injustice. *Journal of Applied Psychology, 101*(2), 171–189.

Reed, A., II, Aquino, K., & Levy, E. (2007). Moral identity and judgments of charitable behaviors. *Journal of Marketing, 71,* 178–193.

Reed, A., II, Kay, A., Finnel, S., Aquino, K., & Levy, E. (2016). I don't want the money, I just want your time: How moral identity overcomes the aversion to giving time to pro-social causes. *Journal of Personality and Social Psychology, 110*(3), 435–457.

Reynolds, S. J. (2006). A neurocognitive model of the ethical decision-making process: Implications for study and practice. *Journal of Applied Psychology, 91*(4), 737–748.

Rupp, D. H., Shao, R., Thornton, M. A., & Skarlicki, D. P. (2013). Applicants' and employees' reactions to corporate social responsibility: The moderating effects of first-party justice perceptions and moral identity. *Personnel Psychology, 66,* 895–933.

Sachdeva, S., Iliev, R., & Medin, D. L. (2009). Sinning saints and saintly sinners: The paradox of moral self-regulation. *Psychological Science, 20*(4), 523–528.

Schlenker, B. R. (1980). *Impression management: The self-concept, social identity and interpersonal relations.* Monterey, CA: Brooks/Cole.

Shao, R., Aquino, K., & Freeman, D. (2008). Beyond moral reasoning: A review of moral identity research and its implications for business ethics. *Business Ethics Quarterly, 18*(4), 513–540.

Sinnott-Armstrong, W., Young, L., & Cushman, F. (2010). Moral intuitions. In J. M. Doris & the Moral Psychology Research Group (Eds.), *The moral psychology handbook* (pp. 246–272). Oxford, UK: Oxford University Press.

Skitka, L. J. (2003). Of different minds: An accessible identity model of justice reasoning. *Personality and Social Psychology Review, 7,* 286–297.

Smith, I. H., Aquino, K., Koleva, S., & Graham, J. (2014). The moral ties that bind . . . Even to out-groups: The interactive effect of moral identity and the binding moral foundations. *Psychological Science, 25*(8), 1554–1562.

Stanovich, K. E., & West, R. F. (2000). Individual differences in reasoning: Implications for the rationality debate. *Behavioral and Brain Sciences, 23,* 645–665.

Stryker, S. (1980). *Symbolic interactionism: A social structural version.* Menlo Park, CA: Benjamin/Cummings.

Sunstein, C. R. (2005). Moral heuristics. *Behavioral and Brain Sciences, 28*(4), 531–573.

Swann, W. B., Jr. (1983). Self-verification: Bringing social reality into harmony with the self. In J. Suls & A. G. Greenwald (Eds.), *Social psychological perspectives on the self* (Vol. 2, pp. 33–66). Hillsdale, NJ: Erlbaum.

Walker, L. J., & Frimer, J. A. (2007). Moral personality of brave and caring exemplars. *Personality Processes and Individual Differences, 93*(5), 845–860.

Walker, L. J., & Pitts, R. C. (1998). Naturalistic conceptions of moral maturity. *Developmental Psychology, 34,* 403–419.

Winterich, K. P., Aquino, K., Mittal, V., & Schwartz, R. (2013). When moral identity symbolization motivates prosocial behavior: The role of recognition and moral identity internalization. *Journal of Applied Psychology, 98*(5), 759–770.

Winterich, K. P., Mittal, V., & Aquino, K. (2013). When does recognition increase charitable behavior?: Toward a moral identity-based model. *Journal of Marketing, 77*(3), 121–134.

Winterich, K. P., Zhang, Y., & Mittal, V. (2012). How political identity and charity positioning increase donations: Insights from moral foundations theory. *International Journal of Research in Marketing, 29,* 346–354.

CHAPTER 15

Identity Is Essentially Moral

Nina Strohminger

What explains the deep connection between morality and the folk concept of personal identity?

This relationship may seem mysterious, until we recognize that identity perception is primarily a process for tracking moral agents, rather than differentiating individuals.

Identity takes up a vast amount of real estate in the field of psychology. Broadly speaking, identity is how you think of yourself and other people. It concerns what features go into, collectively, making someone who they are. The term *identity* often evokes categories of social membership: gender, race, class, sexual orientation, and so on. But it's a big space; a lot goes into our identities. There is also, for instance, our bodies and life histories and intellect and character.

The focus of this chapter is one aspect of identity in particular: the puzzle of diachronic identity. Something maintains diachronic identity if it continues to be the same with itself over time. The puzzle is this: How is it that a person can change radically over time, yet seem to be the same person as before? And how is it that relatively minor tweaks can lead a person to seem fundamentally altered, even unrecognizable?

By some lights, this is a philosophical question, but it is also a psychological one. The factors that give rise to the sense of identity continuity over time—and the factors that break it—are crucial for understanding how people think about personal identity.

The puzzle of diachronic identity is well illustrated by conflicting accounts of what happens to identity in the wake of brain damage. Consider the infamous case of Phineas Gage, who survived a freak accident that saw a metal rod the size of a javelin perforate his skull. Though his intellectual abilities remained intact, Gage became so intemperate and volatile that his friends said "Gage was no longer Gage" (Macmillan, 2000). Contrast this with the actor Gene Wilder, who passed away of Alzheimer's disease in 2016. His nephew insisted that the illness "never stole his ability to recognize those that were closest to him, nor took command of his central-gentle-life affirming core personality. It took enough, but not that" (Miller, 2016). Wilder, even at his most incapacitated, remained Wilder until his dying day.

There is no reason to be coy about our punchline, particularly as it is embedded in the title and preamble of this chapter. Emerging research suggests that the greatest factor in establishing diachronic personal identity is the continuity of moral capacities. In this chapter, I go over the evidence for this claim and suggest a possible explanation.

Some History

For the past few hundred years, most discussions of diachronic personal identity have revolved around the putative importance of memory. Under this view, identity unwinds from the spool of continuous experience, with autobiographical memory as its most obvious manifestation.

John Locke (1690/2009), generally considered the progenitor of this view, provides the following thought experiment: "Should the soul of a prince, carrying with it the consciousness of the prince's past life, enter and inform the body of a cobbler everyone sees he [the cobbler] would be the same person with the prince, accountable only for the prince's actions" (Book II, Ch. 27, Sec. 15). *Everyone sees* this, he says: It is not only self-evident, but a view widely shared. This is a common rhetorical device in philosophy. The problem is, when phrased this way—as a matter of universally held human intuition—the claim ceases being only a metaphysical one and becomes a scientific one as well. Is this really how the typical person understands identity?

Not one to sit out on the important debates, William James (1891) arrived at a similar conclusion: "If a man wakes up one fine day unable to recall any of his past experiences, so that he has to learn his biography afresh he feels, and he says, that he is a changed person" (p. 336). A century later, the neurologist Oliver Sacks (1985) ponders this question when documenting a patient with Korsakov's syndrome. The man's amnesia was so severe that he had lost not only his entire past life but also his ability to add new memories. He was bereft of any narrative structure to hold the arc of his existence together. "One tended to speak of him, instinctively, as a spiritual casualty—a 'lost soul': was it possible that he had been 'de-souled' by a disease?" (p. 37).[1] To rob someone of his memories is to snuff out his personhood, indeed his very existence. Less

grandiose versions of this idea show up in modern psychology, in the form of theories that identity emerges from a complex interplay between narrative structure and disposition (McAdams & Manczak, 2015).

Meanwhile, the past century of social psychology has been grappling with a very different notion of personal identity, one that understands it in contrast with the group (Festinger, 1954; Erikson, 1959; Diener, 1979; Brewer, 1991). Whereas group identity consists of the properties that bind us to others, individual identity is what sets us apart: our unique set of hobbies, preferences, quirks, and dispositions. What makes you you is what allows you to be picked out of the crowd (Nelson & Miller, 1995; Vignoles, Chryssochoou, & Breakwell, 2000; Blanton & Christie, 2003). This view is nicely captured by the old *Far Side* cartoon where a penguin stands in a sea of indistinguishable penguins, belting out "I just gotta be me-ee-eee!" For humans, to be robbed of individuating characteristics is to be thrown into an unmitigated identity disaster (Erikson, 1959).

The idea that morality might be at the heart of personal identity is both new and profoundly ancient. Hints of it permeate everyday thinking under a variety of guises. Perhaps the most compelling of these is how various religious traditions characterize the self. In Abrahamic religions, the pith of the self is commonly known as the soul. The soul is the immaterial, eternal essence of a person that survives the body after death and lends each person their unique identity. It also happens to be the seat of the moral conscience. (In an old episode of *The Simpsons*, Bart sells his soul for $5. He soon discovers that automatic doors fail to open for him, jokes no longer elicit mirth, and pets recoil at his touch, as if he were a monster.) Certain Eastern religions (such as Hinduism and Jainism) have a similar concept, the atman. The atman represents the true self of a person, in spiritual form. It is not just any part of a person's essence, but their moral center especially. The atman is the part of the self that gets reincarnated from one life to the next. Personal enlightenment determines whether the atman will be reincarnated into something great, like a goddess, or something punitive, like a slug. The atman is thus strongly associated with moral and spiritual wisdom.

When social psychologists first began looking at person perception several decades ago, they noticed a curious pattern. The most salient properties of a person—the ones that leave the strongest impression on observers—are those that relate to interpersonal warmth (Anderson, 1968; Wojciszke, Bazinska, & Jaworski, 1998). More detailed analyses reveal that, within the wide umbrella of warmth traits (a category that includes sense of humor and extroversion), it is moral traits, like honesty and compassion, that are pulling most of that weight (Brambilla, Rusconi, Sacchi, & Cherubini, 2011; Goodwin, Piazza, & Rozin, 2014).

Of course, what makes us like someone is not interchangeable with diachronic identity and need not draw on the same set of personal features. Likewise, cross-cultural religious texts offer only the broadest insinuations about folk intuitions of identity. Ultimately, we must turn to direct empirical evidence.

A Brief Detour: Essentialism

Before continuing, it is worth taking a moment to consider the cognitive mechanism that allows us to make sense of identity transformations in the first place: essentialism.

Psychological essentialism refers to the tendency to infer underlying, often hidden, properties in an object that explain its behavior and confer its underlying nature or "essence" (Medin & Ortony, 1989; Gelman, 2003). Although essentialism was originally used to explain how people reason about natural kinds (Keil, 1989; Gelman & Wellman, 1991), it permeates reasoning about social categories (Taylor, 1996; Hirschfeld, 1995), artifacts (Newman, Diesendruck, & Bloom, 2011), and personality (Haslam, Bastian, & Bissett, 2004). Essentialism is what explains our ability to see that an ugly duckling and the swan it turns into are the same individual.

As it is with cygnets, so it is with humans. Persons seem to have an essence that endures across time and physical changes. We consider baby Nina Strohminger to be the same

as adult Nina Strohminger, even though she looks quite different and is not even made of the same cellular matter (Buchholz, Druid, & Frisén, 2005). And while the bloated Elvis of the 1970s bore little resemblance to the dreamboat Elvis of 20 years prior, we perceive them to be the same person, in a way that even the most uncanny Elvis impersonator can't match (Sternberg, Chawarski, & Allbritton, 1998). The persisting essence of persons underlies the superstition that the psychological traits of organ donors can manifest in transplant recipients (Sylvia & Novak, 1997; Inspector, Kutz, & David, 2004; Meyer, Leslie, Gelman, & Stilwell, 2013) and seeps into beliefs about how souls are reincarnated into new bodies (Bloom & Gelman, 2008).

The principle of psychological essentialism, therefore, yields two important points. It shows that we can perceive underlying constancy in spite of apparent change, and it suggests a mechanism for doing so (i.e., by positing an underlying essence). Further, if psychological essentialism is applied to individual persons, this suggests that some personal traits will be treated as identity conferring, whereas others will be more ancillary.

Some Empirical Evidence

One way of getting at folk conceptions of identity is to plumb folk intuitions about the soul. As noted above, the Western notion of the soul represents a kind of placeholder for the concept of the self. When asked about which traits would transfer when a soul switches bodies, participants rank moral traits as more likely to survive the transition than memories or individuating preferences like musical taste and career ambitions, as well as other mental and physical features (Strohminger & Nichols, 2014). Similarly, when asked about which traits would be reincarnated into the next life, participants select moral traits (like honesty, trustworthiness, and generosity) more often than personality traits (like intelligence, sense of humor, and creativity; Strohminger & Nichols, 2014). This effect holds cross-culturally. When Hindu Indians are asked which traits would transfer with the soul, they consistently rate moral traits more likely than other mental traits (Garfield, Nichols, Rai, & Strohminger, 2015; Nichols, Strohminger, Rai, & Garfield, 2016). Even Buddhist Tibetans, who expressly deny the existence of the self or atman, believe that moral traits are most likely to survive a soul switch. And while there are some systematic cross-cultural differences in characterizing the underlying self, the belief that it is fundamentally moral appears to be cross-culturally robust (Kung, Eibach, & Grossman, 2016; De Freitas et al., in press).

Nor is this intuition limited to religious beliefs about the nature of the soul. When asked how different someone would be if they took a pill that altered one of a variety of mental traits—memories, personality, preferences, perceptual abilities, and so on—participants responded that a person would be the most fundamentally changed if he or she took a drug that altered moral traits or behaviors, such as a pill that cured psychopathy or made someone into a thief (Strohminger & Nichols, 2014). This judgment is just as true for assessments of one's own identity as it is for that of others (Heiphetz, Strohminger, & Young, 2017). The privileging of moral traits emerges in childhood. Eight- to 10-year-olds report that a person would be most radically changed if they took a pill that altered universally held moral beliefs than other sorts of beliefs or preferences (Heiphetz, Strohminger, Young, & Gelman, 2016). Morality is not only central to identity; it is also seen as the most causally central feature of the mind (Chen, Urminsky, & Bartels, 2016). This is consistent with the more general rule that the essential properties of a concept tend to be causally central (Sloman, Love, & Ahn, 1998).

Nowhere is the evidence for the moral self more unequivocal than in actual cases of psychological change. Strohminger and Nichols (2015) surveyed family members of people with different forms of neurodegenerative disease, asking them questions about identity change across the disease progression—for instance, whether the patient ever seems like a stranger to them, or whether the patient seems like a fundamentally changed person. They found that patients whose principal symptoms are moral impairment (from frontotemporal dementia) are seen as having a more altered identity than those with Alzheimer's, whose impairments are primarily memory-based; both result in more perceived identity change than amyotrophic lateral sclerosis (ALS), a neurodegenerative disease whose symptoms are primarily motor and noncognitive. Not only that, but deterioration of the moral faculty across all three of these diseases was nearly the only impairment that altered perceived identity. Even in real cases of psychological change, morality has a singular impact on perceived identity continuity.

There is a twist here. Diachronic identity is not simply *moral,* but appears to be especially biased toward the morally *good* (Newman, Knobe, & Bloom, 2014; Strohminger, Newman, & Knobe, in press). For example, Tobia (2016) finds that a Phineas Gage-type person is seen as more radically transformed when an accident robs him of a moral compass than when it bequeaths him with one. People seem to incorporate this into their naive beliefs about how personal growth happens over the lifespan. Whereas negative moral changes give rise to a dramatic identity rupture, positive changes are seen as merely revealing an underlying capacity that was there all along (Molouki & Bartels, 2017). Perhaps this is why improvements to the self are so often seen as "discoveries" (Schlegel, Vess, & Arndt, 2012).

Some Certain Uncertainties

Earlier, we stated that essentialism is what allows us to perceive stasis in the face of change. But when the sense of diachronic identity breaks—most often, and most easily, when moral features change—very little is known about this mechanism. One possibility is that, in determining what matters for the identity of others, people draw on what they personally value most. This account would be consistent with the more general tendency to project internal knowledge onto external targets, such as the false consensus effect (Krueger & Clement, 1994). A projective account is supported by the finding that individuals scoring high in psychopathy weight morality less heavily when judging identity in others. (I will note that, as the author of many of the studies cited in this chapter, this is the only time I have ever failed to find the moral self effect; Strohminger & Nichols, 2016.)

The astute reader will rightly observe that there is a difference between how a person experiences their own sense of identity and how they perceive the identity of others. And while studies find that people report that moral changes would affect their own identity more than other types of mental change (Heiphetz et al., in press), one could further level the charge that what one predicts would happen need not reflect what one would actually experience.[2] This poses both a practical and a logical challenge for the experimentalist. It may well be the case that a sudden, complete loss of autobiographical memories would lead a person to feel so unmoored they would report being completely different from their previous self, as William James (1891) surmised. But this may be difficult to measure, given that a judgment of whether one has changed must inevitably be based on the memory of what has been lost. It doesn't help that anosognosia (a lack of awareness of one's illness) is comorbid with many brain diseases (Prigatano & Schacter, 1991). Another factor may be the severity of the deficit—perhaps a mild or moderate memory lapse does not change experienced identity continuity, but a total disappearance does (Eustache et al., 2013). This would explain the inconsistency of the studies that have attempted to answer this question (Klein, Cosmides, & Costabile, 2003; Rose Addis & Tippett, 2004; Duval et al., 2012; Levitin, 2012). More work will be required to disentangle these possibilities.

Some Expansions

The basic finding that diachronic identity is essentially moral has several broader implications. It has long been recognized that the more central morality is to one's sense of identity, the more morally one behaves (Blasi, 1983; Aquino & Reed, 2002; Hardy & Carlo, 2005; Aquino, Freeman, Reed, Lim, & Felps, 2009; Monin & Jordan, 2009). This suggests that self-identity is a driving force in regulating moral behavior, along with moral reasoning and emotions. Given that we think of other selves as good

deep down, this could be a valuable tool in mitigating intergroup conflict (De Freitas & Cikara, 2016). Identity change in dementia patients—largely brought on by moral degeneration—predicts relationship deterioration between caregiver and patient (Strohminger & Nichols, 2015). Unfortunately, the flip side of this is that people also report an unwillingness to take psychopharmaceuticals to cure moral deficits because of a reluctance to interfere with the innermost parts of the self (Riis, Simmons, & Goodwin, 2008). Finally, in an odd phenomenon that seems to reflect the tendency of humans to anthropomorphize with reckless abandon, even corporate identity appears to be essentially moral, with corporate integrity edging out other factors such as product quality and profits (Strohminger, Pizarro, & Ariely, 2017). Such findings may ultimately bear on legal issues relating to corporate personhood and corporate social responsibility.

There is, however, a deeper intellectual puzzle here. We have shown that morality plays the most powerful role in shaping judgments of diachronic identity. The evidence for this conclusion is overwhelming, and the effect is remarkably robust across contexts and testing procedures. The centrality of morality even shades into other, related concepts, like impression formation and personhood. A natural question to ask at this juncture is, *Why?* Why does morality appear at this nexus, again and again, no matter how we slice it?

To answer this question, it may be helpful to step back and consider the reason people keep track of persons in the first place. Few animals, it turns out, have individual recognition for conspecifics in the way that humans do. Those that do all have something in common: They are social (Tibbetts & Dale, 2007; Sheehan & Tibbetts, 2011). They rely on one another to survive.

Evolutionary biologists have pointed out that, in order for the building blocks of morality to emerge, animals must be able to keep track of individuals in the environment (Nowak, 2006). Reciprocal altruism requires that agents keep tabs on who has helped in the past, in order to know whom to help in the future (Trivers, 1971). Likewise, the most effective cooperation strategy requires that one keep track of offenders in order to punish them in future interactions (Axelrod, 1980).

Indeed, the whole reason that Locke and other enlightenment philosophers were so concerned with personal identity in the first place was that they recognized it to be a forensic concept, foundational to any coherent theory of personal responsibility (Locke, 1690/2009; Hume, 1739/2003; Reid, 1785/1850). If a person's identity is ever-changing, how can we hold them accountable for the deeds of their past self?

So perhaps this puzzle has been arranged backward. It is not that morality is central to diachronic identity. Rather, it's that identity is a cog within the larger machinery of the moral cognitive system. What we 're doing when we're trying to figure out who someone is "deep down," or when we're trying to pin down their essence, is to determine what they'll be like as a social partner—whether they'll cheat or be nice, help us or hurt us. We really want to know what kind of moral being they are. And maybe this is what personal identity is all about.

A Certain Irony

Embedded within this conclusion is a certain understated irony. Diachronic identity is not chiefly about identification. It is not even about *differentiation*. Nearly everyone has empathy, yet this is more important to identity than distinctive traits like one's appearance or talents or musical preferences.

Our understanding of a person's identity has much more to do with how this individual will operate within the larger group. What they'll be like to cooperate with. What they'll be like as romantic partners. As business partners. Identity is about fitting in, not standing out.

We are such social creatures that even that most autonomous concept—the individual person—still ultimately reflects our dependence on others.

NOTES

1. Sacks's case study has a twist ending, one that is consistent with the thesis of the present chapter. The curious reader is encouraged to read his essay in full.

2. Prevailing evidence suggests that future and past selves are treated as friendly strangers, rather than as numerically identical with the present self (Bartels & Rips, 2010). Perhaps the hypothetical self works the same way.

REFERENCES

Anderson, N. H. (1968). Likableness ratings of 555 personality-trait words. *Journal of Personality and Social Psychology, 9*(3), 272–279.

Aquino, K., Freeman, D., Reed, A., II, Lim, V. K., & Felps, W. (2009). Testing a social-cognitive model of moral behavior: The interactive influence of situations and moral identity centrality. *Journal of Personality and Social Psychology, 97*(1), 123–141.

Aquino, K., & Reed, A., II. (2002). The self-importance of moral identity. *Journal of Personality and Social Psychology, 83*(6), 1423–1440.

Axelrod, R. (1980). Effective choice in the prisoner's dilemma. *Journal of Conflict Resolution, 24*(1), 3–25.

Bartels, D. M., & Rips, L. J. (2010). Psychological connectedness and intertemporal choice. *Journal of Experimental Psychology: General, 139*(1), 49–69.

Blanton, H., & Christie, C. (2003). Deviance regulation: A theory of action and identity. *Review of General Psychology, 7*(2), 115–149.

Blasi, A. (1983). Moral cognition and moral action: A theoretical perspective. *Developmental Review, 3*(2), 178–210.

Bloom, P., & Gelman, S. (2008). Psychological essentialism in selecting the 14th Dalai Lama. *Trends in Cognitive Sciences, 12*(7), 243–243.

Brambilla, M., Rusconi, P., Sacchi, S., & Cherubini, P. (2011). Looking for honesty: The primary role of morality (vs. sociability and competence) in information gathering. *European Journal of Social Psychology, 41*(2), 135–143.

Brewer, M. B. (1991). The social self: On being the same and different at the same time. *Personality and Social Psychology Bulletin, 17*(5), 475–482.

Buchholz, B., Druid, H., & Frisén, J. (2005). Retrospective birth dating of cells in humans. *Cell, 122*, 133–143.

Chen, S. Y., Urminsky, O., & Bartels, D. M. (2016). Beliefs about the causal structure of the self-concept determine which changes disrupt personal identity. *Psychological Science, 27*(10), 1398–1406.

De Freitas, J., & Cikara, M. (2016). *Deep down my enemy is good: Thinking about the true self reduces intergroup bias.* Unpublished manuscript.

De Freitas, J., Sarkissian, H., Grossman, I., De

Brigard, F., Luco, A., Newman, G., & Knobe, J. (in press). Consistent belief in a good true self in misanthropes and three interdependent cultures. *Cognitive Science.*

Diener, E. (1979). Deindividuation, self-awareness, and disinhibition. *Journal of Personality and Social Psychology, 37*(7), 1160–1171.

Duval, C., Desgranges, B., de La Sayette, V., Belliard, S., Eustache, F., & Piolino, P. (2012). What happens to personal identity when semantic knowledge degrades?: A study of the self and autobiographical memory in semantic dementia. *Neuropsychologia, 50*(2), 254–265.

Erikson, E. H. (1959). *Identity and the life cycle.* New York: Norton.

Eustache, M.-L., Laisney, M., Juskenaite, A., Letortu, O., Platel, H., Eustache, F., & Desgranges, B. (2013). Sense of identity in advanced Alzheimer's dementia: A cognitive dissociation between sameness and selfhood? *Consciousness and Cognition, 22*(4), 1456–1467.

Festinger, L. (1954). A theory of social comparison processes. *Human Relations, 7*(2), 117–140.

Garfield, J. L., Nichols, S., Rai, A. K., & Strohminger, N. (2015). Ego, egoism and the impact of religion on ethical experience: What a paradoxical consequence of Buddhist culture tells us about moral psychology. *Journal of Ethics, 19*(3–4), 293–304.

Gelman, S. (2003). *The essential child: Origins of essentialism in everyday thought.* New York: Oxford University Press.

Gelman, S., & Wellman, H. (1991). Insides and essences: Early understandings of the non-obvious. *Cognition, 38*(3), 213–244.

Goodwin, G. P., Piazza, J., & Rozin, P. (2014). Moral character predominates in person perception and evaluation. *Journal of Personality and Social Psychology, 106*(1), 148–168.

Hardy, S. A., & Carlo, G. (2005). Identity as a source of moral motivation. *Human Development, 48*(4), 232–256.

Haslam, N., Bastian, B., & Bissett, M. (2004). Essentialist beliefs about personality and their implications. *Personality and Social Psychology Bulletin, 30*(12), 1661–1673.

Heiphetz, L., Strohminger, N., & Young, L. (2017). The role of moral beliefs, memories, and preferences in representations of identity. *Cognitive Science, 41*(3),744–767.

Heiphetz, L., Strohminger, N., Young, L., & Gelman, S. A. (2016). *Who am I?: The role of moral beliefs in children's and adults' understanding of identity.* Unpublished manuscript.

Hirschfeld, L. (1995). Do children have a theory of race? *Cognition, 54*(2), 209–252.

Hume, D. (2003). *A treatise of human nature.* New York: Courier. (Original work published 1739)

Inspector, Y., Kutz, I., & David, D. (2004). Another person's heart: Magical and rational thinking in the psychological adaptation to heart transplantation. *Israel Journal of Psychiatry and Related Sciences, 41*(3), 161–173.

James, W. (1891). *The principles of psychology* (Vol. 1). London: Macmillan.

Keil, F. (1989). *Concepts, kinds, and cognitive development.* Cambridge, MA: MIT Press.

Klein, S. B., Cosmides, L., & Costabile, K. A. (2003). Preserved knowledge of self in a case of Alzheimer's dementia. *Social Cognition, 21*(2), 157–165.

Krueger, J., & Clement, R. W. (1994). The truly false consensus effect: An ineradicable and egocentric bias in social perception. *Journal of Personality and Social Psychology, 67*(4), 596–610.

Kung, F. Y. H., Eibach, R., & Grossman, I. (2016). Culture, fixed-world beliefs, relationships and perception of identity change. *Social Psychological and Personality Science, 7*(7), 631–639.

LaCour, M. J., & Green, D. P. (2014). When contact changes minds: An experiment on transmission of support for gay equality. *Science, 346*(6215), 1366–1369.

Levitin, D. (2012, December). Amnesia and the self that remains when memory is lost. *Atlantic Monthly.*

Locke, J. (2009). *An essay concerning human understanding.* New York: WLC Books. (Original work published 1690)

Macmillan, M. (2000). Restoring Phineas Gage: A 150th retrospective. *Journal of the History of the Neurosciences, 9*(1), 46–66.

McAdams, D. P., & Manczak, E. (2015). Personality and the life story. In M. Mikulincer, P. R. Shaver, M. L. Cooper, & R. J. Larsen (Eds.), *APA handbook of personality and social psychology: Vol. 4. Personality processes and individual differences* (pp. 425–446). Washington, DC: American Psychological Association.

Medin, D., & Ortony, A. (1989). Psychological essentialism. In S. Vosniadou & A. Ortony (Eds.), *Similarity and analogical reasoning* (pp. 179–195). Cambridge, UK: Cambridge University Press.

Meyer, M., Leslie, S.-J., Gelman, S. A., & Stilwell, S. M. (2013). Essentialist beliefs about bodily transplants in the United States and India. *Cognitive Science, 37*(4), 668–710.

Miller, J. (2016, August 29). Gene Wilder, comic actor and *Willy Wonka* star, is dead at 83. *Vanity Fair.*

Molouki, S., & Bartels, D. M. (2017). Personal change and the continuity of identity. *Cognitive Psychology.*

Monin, B., & Jordan, A. H. (2009). The dynamic moral self: A social psychological perspective.

In D. Narvaez & D. K. Lapsley (Eds.), *Personality, identity, and character: Explorations in moral psychology* (pp. 341–354). New York: Cambridge University Press.

Nelson, L. J., & Miller, D. T. (1995). The distinctiveness effect in social categorization: You are what makes you unusual. *Psychological Science, 6*(4), 246–249.

Newman, G., Diesendruck, G., & Bloom, P. (2011). Celebrity contagion and the value of objects. *Journal of Consumer Research, 38*(2), 215–228.

Newman, G., Knobe, J., & Bloom, P. (2014). Value judgments and the true self. *Personality and Social Psychology Bulletin, 40*(2), 203–216.

Nichols, S., Strohminger, N., Rai, A. K., & Garfield, J. L. (2016). *Death and the self.* Unpublished manuscript.

Nowak, M. (2006). Five rules for the evolution of cooperation. *Science, 314*(5805), 1560–1563.

Prigatano, G. P., & Schacter, D. L. (1991). *Awareness of deficit after brain injury: Clinical and theoretical issues.* Oxford, UK: Oxford University Press.

Reid, T. (1850). *Essays on the intellectual powers of man* (Abridged ed.; J. Walker, Ed.). Cambridge, MA: John Bartlett. (Original work published 1785)

Riis, J., Simmons, J. P., & Goodwin, G. P. (2008). Preferences for enhancement pharmaceuticals: The reluctance to enhance fundamental traits. *Journal of Consumer Research, 35*(3), 495–508.

Rose Addis, D., & Tippett, L. (2004). Memory of myself: Autobiographical memory and identity in Alzheimer's disease. *Memory, 12*(1), 56–74.

Sacks, O. (1985). The lost mariner. In *The man who mistook his wife for a hat* (pp. 23–42). New York: Touchstone.

Schlegel, R. J., Vess, M., & Arndt, J. (2012). To discover or to create: Metaphors and the true self. *Journal of Personality, 80*(4), 969–993.

Sheehan, M. J., & Tibbetts, E. A. (2011). Specialized face learning is associated with individual recognition in paper wasps. *Science, 334*(6060), 1272–1275.

Sloman, S. A., Love, B. C., & Ahn, W.-K. (1998). Feature centrality and conceptual coherence. *Cognitive Science, 22*(2), 189–228.

Sternberg, R., Chawarski, M., & Allbritton, D. (1998). If you changed your name and appearance to those of Elvis Presley, who would you be?: Historical features in categorization. *American Journal of Psychology, 111*(3), 327–351.

Strohminger, N., Newman, G., & Knobe, J. (in press). The true self: A psychological concept distinct from the self. *Perspectives on Psychological Science.*

Strohminger, N., & Nichols, S. (2014). The essential moral self. *Cognition, 131*(1), 159–171.

Strohminger, N., & Nichols, S. (2015). Neurodegeneration and identity. *Psychological Science, 26*(9), 1468–1479.

Strohminger, N., & Nichols, S. (2016). *Psychopathy and the moral self.* Unpublished manuscript.

Strohminger, N., Pizarro, D., & Ariely, D. (2017). *Are corporations people?: The case of corporate identity.* Unpublished manuscript.

Sylvia, C., & Novak, W. (1997). *A change of heart.* Boston, MA: Little, Brown.

Taylor, M. (1996). The development of children's beliefs about social and biological aspects of gender differences. *Child Development, 67*(4), 1555–1571.

Tibbetts, E. A., & Dale, J. (2007). Individual recognition: It is good to be different. *Trends in Ecology and Evolution, 22*(10), 529–537.

Tobia, K. P. (2016). Personal identity, direction of change, and neuroethics. *Neuroethics, 9*(1), 37–43.

Trivers, R. L. (1971). The evolution of reciprocal altruism. *Quarterly Review of Biology, 46*(1), 35–57.

Vignoles, V. L., Chryssochoou, X., & Breakwell, G. M. (2000). The distinctiveness principle: Identity, meaning, and the bounds of cultural relativity. *Personality and Social Psychology Review, 4*(4), 337–354.

Wojciszke, B., Bazinska, R., & Jaworski, M. (1998). On the dominance of moral categories in impression formation. *Personality and Social Psychology Bulletin, 24*(12), 1251–1263.

CHAPTER 16

The Core of Morality Is the Moral Self

Paul Conway

What is the best way to characterize morality?

Morality entails integrating emotions and cognition through the universal evolved mechanisms of self and social perceptions, embedded within various cultural contexts, that functionally motivate and regulate behavior to balance self-interest against group needs and maintain successful societies.

Theories of moral psychology should be capable of explaining moral behavior across the world and throughout history. For example, how can moral psychology explain the behavior of Consul Manlius, leader of the Roman army in 340 B.C.E.? Manlius insisted that no one engage the enemy without his orders, but before battle, an enemy mocked and challenged Manlius's son, Titus. Titus fought the enemy and won. When Titus brought the enemy's sword to honor his father, Manlius said, "I am moved, not only by a man's instinctive love for his children, but by this instance you have given of your bravery, perverted though it was by an idle show of honor. But since the authority of the consuls must either be established by your death, or by your impunity be forever abrogated . . . go and bind him to the stake." Manlius then ordered his son executed. According to the historian Livy, the "orders of Manlius" horrified the other soldiers but also tightened discipline, making them more obedient and careful in their duties, result-ing in successful battle the next day (Hastings, 1985, p. 26).

Moral psychology provides many lenses through which to view Manlius's brutal action, from cognitive-developmentalism (Kohlberg, 1969) to moral intuitionism (Haidt, 2001) to moral convictions (Skitka, Bauman, & Mullen, 2008) to cognitive templates of harm (Gray, Young, & Waytz, 2012) to dual-process models (Greene, Sommerville, Nystrom, Darley, & Cohen, 2001). Although each of these perspectives highlights a different facet of human morality, each struggles to integrate the wide array of moral psychology findings, because they tend to focus on specific social cognitive processes, such as intuitions, reasoning, or mind perception. Undoubtedly such processes play important roles in moral psychology—but the best way to integrate them is through the lens of the moral self. That is, *moral self-perceptions* and *social perceptions* are the key to motivating and regulating moral behavior and the key to moral judgments and decision making.

149

Moral self-perceptions subsume and transcend the constructs of *moral identity*—individual differences in the centrality of morality to the self-concept (Aquino & Reed, 2002; Blasi, 1984)—and *moral self-regard*—contextual fluctuations in moral self-perceptions based on recent behavior (Monin & Jordan, 2009). Moral self-perceptions also entail a meta-cognitive component: considering others' perceptions of one's moral standing in light of perceptions of those same others' own moral standing. Hence moral self-perceptions are inherently comparative: People think not only *How moral am I?* but *How moral do my colleagues/family/neighbors think I am?* and *How moral are my colleagues/family/ neighbors?* Thus the real question of moral self perceptions is *How moral am I compared to (specific) other people?* Answering these questions entails considering evidence regarding one another's character, so one's perceived moral standing exists in relation to others' perceived moral standing.

Moral self-perceptions are inherently relative because morally superior people may pronounce moral judgment over morally inferior people, but not vice versa. Imagine a courtroom in which the defendant accuses the judge of crimes and is taken seriously! Not only does accusing someone of a moral violation degrade the person's moral standing, but expressing the right to judge others also demonstrates the judges' own high perceived standing. Hence, moral judgments amount to a power play: They imply that one holds moral superiority over those one is judging.

Moral self-perceptions serve to functionally regulate behavior in order to balance personal interests against the needs of one's social group. Increasing moral self-perceptions requires investing in activities that benefit others, such as prosocial behavior or altruistic punishment. People who have earned high standing may either invest in further prosociality or "cash in" by relaxing moral strivings to reap the selfish benefits (e.g., avoiding prosocial behavior, nepotism). Hence, moral self-perceptions can paradoxically sometimes increase and other times reduce prosociality (Mullen & Monin, 2016). People with lower moral standing must attempt moral repair via further group investment or else abandon moral striving altogether and thus relinquish claims to group resources.

One wrinkle to moral self-perception theory is that perceivers may disagree—so people must consider both public and private and moral self-perceptions. Imagine someone stole money that you raised for charity. You may feel higher moral standing than the selfish thief—but the charity director who accuses you of taking the money degrades your public moral status. Nonetheless, you may personally retain high private moral standing (righteous innocence). Upon encountering another member of the charity board, your socially optimal behavior (contrition vs. defiance) may depend on that person's perception of your guilt or innocence. If the person assumes you are guilty, he or she may expect contrition. Conversely, if the person believes your innocence, he or she may expect defiance. Conflict can emerge from differing perceptions of moral status among different parties.

The self model of morality is both functionalist and integrative: The moral self integrates other psychological processes into a holistic judgment of moral selfhood that serves to functionally regulate behavior. If this theory is correct, morality should form the core of self-perceptions and social perceptions, and moral judgments should track perceptions of character and drive behavior. Moral self-perceptions should motivate and regulate the "give" and "take" of social relations, and threatening or affirming the moral self should affect judgments and behavior. Finally, moral self-perceptions should reflect and regulate relations with others, such as rights and duties. Yet the content of moral self-perceptions may vary across history and culture, depending on the contextually normative relation between self and group—the moral duties of an ancient soldier are different from those of a modern nurse. Considering these points may help elucidate Manlius's thinking.

Historical Context

Moral self-theory emerges out of the cognitive-developmental literature. Building on Piaget (1965), Kohlberg (e.g., 1969) argued for a stage model of moral reasoning that culminates in Platonic rationalism (Plato, trans. 1949). However, the link between moral reasoning and moral behavior is weak at best (Blasi, 1980), leading theorists to propose a series of models (e.g., Rest, 1984; Damon, 1984; Colby & Damon, 1992) that increasingly focused on the moral self (see Bergman, 2002), culminating in Blasi's (1995) argument that moral judgments carry motivational weight due to a desire for self-consistency: When people apply moral reasoning to themselves, failure to act morally *betrays oneself*. Such inconsistency is aversive (Bem, 1972; Festinger, 1957) and existentially threatening (Schlegel, Hicks, Arndt, & King, 2009). Hence identity as a moral person powerfully motivates moral behavior (Hardy & Carlo, 2005).

Concurrently, developments in evolutionary theory increasingly suggested that morality evolved to regulate social relations (Alexander, 1987). Although some scholars scoffed at this idea (Dawkins, 1989), it traces all the way back to Darwin (1874/1998). The evolutionary pathway toward genuine morality begins with caring for kin (Hamilton, 1964) and reciprocal exchange with non-kin (Trivers, 1971), moving toward broader indirect reciprocity in which group members help one another, keeping track of group investment via image scoring (Nowak & Sigmund, 1998) and gossip (Feinberg, Willer, Stellar, & Keltner, 2012). Additionally, sexual selection (Hardy & Van Vugt, 2006; Miller, 2007) and group-level selection (Sober & Wilson, 1998) would have accelerated moral behavior under conditions consistent with early human lifestyles (Lee & DeVore, 1968). Such processes are impossible without tracking each party's sociality and selfishness: the moral selves of oneself and one's compatriots. Hence, psychological mechanisms motivating morality—moral self and social perceptions—derived from evolutionary pressure (Gintis, Bowles, Boyd, & Fehr, 2003; DeScioli & Kurzban, 2013; Haidt, 2001; Wright, 1994).

Meanwhile, social cognitive research clarified the psychology of self- and person perception. The self is rich and complex, and people balance many, sometimes competing, identities, with only a subset active at any one time (Markus & Kunda, 1986). Thus central aspects of the self remain chronically accessible, but context can influence which other self-attributes people consider (e.g., Forehand, Deshpandé, & Reed, 2002). Aquino and Reed (2002) applied these insights to Blasi's (1995) view of the moral self (see also Lapsley & Narvaez, 2004) to argue that the moral self operates as but one aspect of the overall self. For some people, it is more chronically active than for others, and context may either activate or suppress it— for example, reminders of one's good deeds may inflate moral self-perceptions, whereas reminders of misdeeds may deflate them. Likewise, as selves are inherently social (Tajfel & Turner, 1985), group memberships may reflect on individual morality (Ellemers, Pagliaro, Barreto, & Leach, 2008). Finally, recent advances in person perception outline the powerful and previously underappreciated role of morality in forming perceptions of others (e.g., Goodwin, Piazza, & Rozin, 2014). The moral self-perspective incorporates insights from all of these literatures.

Theoretical Stance

The moral self model is *functionalist* and *integrative*: It draws on evolutionary theory to posit the function of morality, to propose a parsimonious account, and to consiliently explain a disparate set of findings.

Functionalist

The moral self integrates moral emotions with reasoning to motivate situationally appropriate behavior. Keltner and Haidt (1999) argued that moral emotions (e.g., moral disgust) *exapted* (developed out of) from evolutionarily prior processes (e.g., physical disgust) and are shaped by culture and development to solve particular adaptive problems (e.g., appraisals of rule violations; Nichols & Mallon, 2006; Wondra & Ellsworth, 2015). Moral emotions serve multiple functions, including associative learning and communication, but most importantly self- and social regulation (Giner-Sorolla, 2012). For example, gratitude motivates repaying social debts (McCullough, Kilpatrick, Emmons, & Larson, 2001), guilt motivates repairing damaged relationships

(Baumeister, Stillwell, & Heatherton, 1994), anger motivates aggression toward moral violators (Skitka, Bauman, & Sargis, 2005), and distress motivates avoiding harm (Cushman, Gray, Gaffey, & Mendes, 2012)—but for an alternative view, see Cameron, Lindquist, and Gray (2015). Moral emotions may have deep evolutionary roots (de Waal, 1996), but moral reasoning serves to formalize morality into principles (Rest, 1984). The moral self unites moral emotions with reasoning through development (Frimer & Walker, 2009).

Although people perceive objectivity as a core feature of moral judgments (Skitka et al., 2008), there is pressure for both accuracy and self-enhancement (Krebs, 2008). Accuracy is important for calibrating metaperceptions of one's moral character in order to maintain effective cooperation (Boyd & Richerson, 2005), protecting low-power from high-power individuals (Boehm, 1999) and preventing conflict escalation along kin lines (DeScioli & Kurzban, 2013). People must demonstrate morality through costly signaling, such as donating to charity—especially when monitored by the ingroup (van Nunspeet, Gray, Gaffey, & Mendes, 2015). Yet people use a variety of strategies to feel sufficiently moral, whether earned or not (Effron, 2014). People apply different moral standards to themselves than to others (Lammers, 2012), pick moral standards that favor ingroups (Brandt, 2013; Skitka & Tetlock, 1992), apply different standards when they benefit than when they suffer (Bocian & Wojciszka, 2014), and strategically "forget" moral rules (Shu, Gino, & Bazerman, 2010). Accordingly, many conceptualizations of the moral self contrast a shallow, image-focused moral self with a deeper, purer, inner moral self, or "true self" (Aquino & Reed, 2002; Frimer, Schaefer, & Oakes, 2014; Newman, De Freitas, & Knobe, 2014).

Although aspects of morality are culturally universal (Fessler, 1999; Midgley, 1991), there is also room for cultural variability (Haidt & Joseph, 2004; Shweder, Much, & Park, 1997). To the degree that social groups face similar problems, moral judgments are universal. For example, intentionally hurting innocents is universally abhorred (Sousa, Holbrook, & Piazza, 2009; Turiel, 1983). Yet different environments may "evoke" different moral values because different social strategies were historically most successful in those environments (Gangestad, Haselton, & Buss, 2006)—for example, harsh environments particularly favor strong cooperation (Smaldino, Schank, & McElreath, 2013). Political differences in morality (Haidt & Graham, 2007) may likewise stem from differences in successful strategies: Conservative morality emphasizes group regulation of individuals, which may be optimal in traditional tight-knit communities, whereas liberal morality emphasizes freeing individuals to pursue enlightened self-interest, which may be optimal in large, globalized societies (Lakoff, 2010). Similarly, group characteristics such as power distance, inequality, centralization, threat, and entitativity may all influence moral norms.

Integrative

The self perspective seeks to integrate rather than overturn other theories of morality. Morality has many facets—for example, emotions, behaviors, judgments, domains—differentially emphasized by each theory. For example, regarding Manlius's decision, one might postulate that he engaged in weak moral reasoning (Kohlberg, 1969), lacked empathy (Hoffman, 2000), or aimed to uphold group cooperation (Fehr & Gächter, 2002). It appears he felt *morally convicted* about his decision—that it was objectively true, universal, obligatory, autonomous, motivational, and affective and (most important) that it reflected his core moral values and beliefs (Skitka et al., 2008). Perhaps a *moral intuition*—"the sudden appearance in consciousness of a moral judgment . . . without any conscious awareness of having gone through steps of searching, weighing evidence, or inferring a conclusion"—drove Manlius's decision, which he buttressed via post hoc reasoning to persuade others to share this intuition (Haidt, 2001, p. 817). Manlius's intuitions appear to favor the conservative moral domains of *loyalty, purity,* and *respect for authority* more than the liberal domains of *harm* and *fairness,* as he prioritized obedience, group objectives, and an unblemished reputation over aversion to killing his son or matching punishment with the crime (Graham, Haidt, & Nosek, 2009).

Regardless, participants and observers likely filtered this event through a dyadic cognitive template of moral transgressions (Gray, Young, & Waytz, 2012), assigning roles of victim and perpetrator, and ascribing more *agency* (capacity for action) to the former and *experience* (capacity for perception) to the latter (Gray, Gray, & Wegner, 2007). Accordingly, observers should have been particularly sensitive to Titus's pain and viewed Manlius as particularly capable of action (Gray & Wegner, 2009)—although Manlius may have perceived *himself* as victimized by his son's rash action. Victims and perpetrators often view transgressions differently (Baumeister, Stillwell, & Wotman, 1994).

Moreover, Manlius's situation is similar to moral dilemmas in which causing harm maximizes outcomes (Foot, 1967). Livy argues that Manlius's action increased battle success, hence making the world better (through Roman eyes). Therefore, Manlius's action was moral according to utilitarian philosophical positions, in which morality entails maximizing outcomes (e.g., Mill, 1861/1998). Conversely, Manlius's action was immoral according to deontological philosophical positions, in which morality entails adhering to universal moral rules (Kant, 1785/1959)—assuming the rule in question is *do no harm*.[1] Greene and colleagues' (2001) dual-process model of moral judgment suggests that deontological decisions (to avoid harm) are driven by affective reactions to harm, whereas utilitarian decisions (to maximize outcomes) are driven by cognitive evaluations of outcomes. According to this model, Manlius's decision may have been driven by a deficit of affect, as in psychopathy (e.g., Bartels & Pizarro, 2011), and/or a surfeit of cognitive processing (e.g., Moore, Clarke, & Kane, 2008), each of which might facilitate carrying out a brutal action that improves outcomes.

Each of these perspectives highlights a different facet of the inordinate complexity of human morality. Yet, merely touring different explanations is unsatisfying. Is moral psychology doomed to theory proliferation? The self model integrates these perspectives. Moral reasoning fails to motivate behavior unless applied to the self (Blasi, 1995), empathy may be destructive when decoupled

from moral goals (Sutton, Smith, & Swettenham, 1999), and "altruistic" punishment seems partially motivated by demonstrating one's moral status (Kurzban, DeScioli, & O'Brien, 2007). Moral convictions serve to uphold the moral self: Expressing moral convictions demonstrates that one has "an authentic moral point of view" (Skitka, 2002, p. 594). Likewise, moral intuitions uphold the moral self: Although such intuitions drive condemnation of harmless taboos (e.g., Haidt, Koller, & Dais, 1993), validating the self reduces such condemnation (Mooijman & van Dijk, 2014). Similarly, the moral cognitive template is fundamentally tied to the self. Was Manlius the perpetrator or the victim? The answer depends on his relation to oneself. Finally, even moral dilemma judgments reflect the moral self: Conway and Gawronski (2013) found that people with stronger moral identities experience stronger inclinations to *both* avoid causing harm *and* maximize outcomes. Yet different dilemma answers have different social costs (Lucas & Galinsky, 2015). Accordingly, people's answers are sensitive to social circumstances (Kundu & Cummins, 2012; Lucas & Livingstone, 2014), and people justify their answers by integrating these perspectives (Liu & Ditto, 2012).

Evidence

Morality Is Central to Self- and Person Perception

Lay people perceive morality as the essence of the self (Strohminger & Nichols, 2014; Newman et al., 2014). Morality is *identify defining*: Adhering to moral standards shared with group members signals group membership (Ellemers & van den Bos, 2012). People prefer to join (Leach, Ellemers, & Barreto, 2007), and remain in (Boezeman & Ellemers, 2014) moral groups. Suppressing self-interest to uphold group norms is key for maintaining a self-image as a good group member (Leach, Biliali, & Pagliaro, 2013) who deserves respect (Pagliaro, Ellemers, & Barreto, 2011). Accordingly, moral values are central to identity (Rokeach, 1973), and people are motivated to uphold these values in order to maintain their sense of identity (Hardy, 2006). Making moral decisions activates the self-concept (Christy & Schlegel, 2015), and the brain regions involved in moral processing overlap with regions that process the self (Moll et al., 2007). Engaging in either immoral or inauthentic behavior—both of which violate the self—makes people feel impure and immoral (Gino, Kouchaki, & Galinsky, 2015).

Moreover, judgments of morality are paramount for assessing the character of individuals (Goodwin et al., 2014) and groups (Ellemers et al., 2008). Perceivers care more about targets' morality than about their sociability or competence (Brambilla, Rusconi, Sacchi, & Cherubini, 2011). When evaluating others, people track more than mere outcomes (Cushman, 2008)—outcomes offer a window into *intentions* (Pizarro & Tannenbaum, 2011). Indeed, people infer nefarious intentions upon encountering a moral violation and vice versa (Gray, Waytz, & Young, 2012), and moral evaluations reflect perceived intentions (Guglielmo, Monroe, & Malle, 2009), even among young children (Hamlin, 2013). Immoral behaviors are more diagnostic of personality than moral behaviors (Skowronski & Carlston, 1987), because people view refraining from evil as more obligatory than engaging in prosociality (Janoff-Bulman, Sheikh, & Hepp, 2009). Hence, immoral behavior clearly indicates bad character.

Perceived moral character, in turn, drives important social decisions, from judgments of legal responsibility (Darley, 2009; Feather & Atchison, 1998; Skitka & Housten, 2001), to desired social distance (Skitka et al., 2005) to trust (Delgado, Frank, & Phelps, 2005; Simpson, Harrel, & Willer, 2013). People prefer leaders who embody moral values (Haslam, Reicher, & Platow, 2010) and policies buttressed by moral justifications—unless such policies appear insincere (Van Zant & Moore, 2015). People treat others in line with perceived *deservingness*: a "state of compatibility in valence between a target's actions or traits and his or her outcomes" (Olson, Hafer, Cheung, & Conway, 2009, p. 127). People are highly motivated to uphold deservingness (Lerner, 1980) and react to violations both emotionally (Feather & Sherman, 2002) and behaviorally (Callan, Shead, & Olson, 2011). Deservingness judgments stem primarily from

perceptions of the target's past controllable behavior (Shaver, 1985; Weiner, 1993), so socially useful targets deserve better treatment (Olson, Cheung, Conway, Hutchison, & Hafer, 2011). Accordingly, people often engage in *costly signaling* (e.g., prosocial behavior) to demonstrate usefulness (e.g., Krebs, 2008). Together, these findings suggest that people aim to determine others' "true selves"—whether their core motivations are selfish or laudable—and treat them accordingly.

Moral Self-Perceptions Motivate and Regulate Prosocial Behavior

In addition to defining the core of self- and social perception, the moral self regulates behavior. Moral exemplars treat moral and personal goals as interchangeable (Colby & Damon, 1992), and moral identity predicts prosocial behaviors (e.g., Aquino, Freeman, Reed, Felps, & Lim, 2009; Reed & Aquino, 2003) in everyday contexts (Hofmann, Wisneski, Brandt, & Skitka, 2014). Invoking the moral self can increase these effects (Jennings, Mitchell, & Hannah, 2014): Priming moral identity increases generosity (Reed, Aquino, & Levy, 2007), invoking the self ("don't be a cheater") reduces cheating (Bryan, Adams, & Monin, 2013), and signing documents reduces dishonesty (Shu, Mazar, Gino, Ariely, & Bazerman, 2012). Recalling childhood activates the true self (Baldwin, Biernat, & Landau, 2015), increasing prosociality (Gino & Desai, 2012). Labeling donors as *charitable people* increases subsequent donations, whereas labeling nondonors *uncharitable* reduces donations (Kraut, 1973); likewise with the label *caring* (Burger & Caldwell, 2003). Conversely, providing extrinsic incentives for prosociality backfires by undermining the motivation to demonstrate one's morality (Ariely, Bracha, & Meier, 2009).

In addition to *whether* the moral self is active, the *way* one conceptualizes the moral self matters. People are typically moral satisficers—they require only *sufficient* evidence of their morality (Skitka, 2002) to feel permitted to relax moral strivings (Miller & Effron, 2010). Hence demonstrating egalitarianism licenses discrimination (e.g., Effron, Cameron, & Monin, 2009), and recalling prosociality reduces donations (for reviews, see Miller & Effron, 2010; Zhong, Liljenquist, & Cain, 2009; Effron & Conway, 2015). Conversely, feeling insufficiently moral motivates increased prosociality to restore moral self-perceptions (Jordan, Mullen, & Murnighan, 2011). Thus moral standing signals when one's investment levels are sufficient that one may indulge in selfishness. Selfishness may also arise from perceived victimization, to restore balance between deprived personal interest and group outcomes (Zitek, Jordan, Monin, & Leach, 2010).

Recently, researchers have begun to disentangle the complex issue of when moral self-perceptions motivate versus relax moral strivings (Blanken, van de Ven, & Zeelenberg, 2014; Mullen & Monin, 2016). Moral consistency—acting moral when feeling moral—appears most likely when people abstractly consider the implications of past good deeds for their current identity rather than temptations (Conway & Peetz, 2012), view past moral behavior as reflecting commitment to (rather than progress toward) moral goals (Susewind & Hoelzl, 2014), and recall costly (vs. costless) prosocial behavior, which implies greater commitment to moral action (Gneezy, Imas, Brown, Nelson, & Norton, 2012). Effron and Conway (2015) suggested that consistency may result from affirming the moral self, whereas relaxed strivings may result from disconfirming an immoral self (e.g., disconfirming a racist identity). This possibility meshes with multiple-layer models of the moral self (e.g., Frimer et al., 2014). Yet more work remains to be done to unravel the paradox of when moral self-perceptions increase versus reduce moral strivings.

Threatening and Affirming the Moral Self Affects Judgments and Behavior

Unsurprisingly, people are highly motivated to perceive themselves as moral (Eply & Dunning, 2001; Monin & Jordan, 2009). Discrepancies between current self-perceptions and one's moral obligations are psychologically uncomfortable (Higgins, 1987). Accordingly, people are motivated to bolster and protect moral self-perceptions (Effron, Miller, & Monin, 2012)—unless there is a

good reason not to. People engage in a variety of justifications for unethical behavior (Shalvi, Gino, Barkan, & Ayal, 2015), such as minimizing moral failings through denial and motivated forgetting (Shu et al., 2010), distancing the self from moral failing (Bandura, 1990), and perceiving moral rules as flexible (lest they take a hit to the moral self; Cameron & Payne, 2012). People tend to avoid both tiny and large lies—the former because they are not worth the cost of lying, and the latter because they threaten moral integrity (Mazar, Amir, & Ariely, 2008). Unethical behavior increases when the role of the self is diminished because justifications are more available (Shalvi, Handgraaf, & De Dreu, 2011) and when people feel anonymous (Zhong, Bohns, & Gino, 2010), lack free will (Vohs & Schooler, 2007), or do not need others (Gino & Pierce, 2009). People also tend to avoid contemplating (even sensible) trade-offs that sacrifice moral values (Tetlock, Kristel, Elson, Green, & Lerner, 2000), and, when they are exposed to intense suffering, people strategically suppress their emotions to protect the self (Cameron & Payne, 2011), which is taxing and may increase burnout (Omdahl & O'Donnell, 1999).

Threatening and affirming the moral self influences moral judgments and behavior. People tend to intermix physical and psychological elements of morality, likely due to the evolutionary origins of moral emotions (Rozin, Haidt, & Fincher, 2009). Hence, recalling immoral behavior or exposure to other's immorality induces a sense of contamination (Eskine, Kacinik, & Webster, 2012), which motivates a desire to punish (Inbar, Pizarro, & Bloom, 2012; Schnall, Haidt, Clore, & Jordan, 2008)—which in turn restores the moral self (Kurzban et al., 2007). Conversely, feeling clean reduces the perceived severity of transgressions and hence reduces guilt (Zhong & Liljenquist, 2006) and general judgment harshness (Schnall, Benton, & Harvey, 2008), but also elevates one's moral status relative to the transgressor, allowing harsher judgments of them specifically (Zhong, Strejcek, & Sivanathan, 2010). Additionally, feeling immoral motivates the desire to physically cleanse oneself (Zhong & Liljenquist, 2006), which is modality specific (Lee & Schwarz,

2010), and motivates reconnection to high-density social networks (Lee, Im, Parmar, & Gino, 2015)—unless one has experienced self-affirmation (Steele, 1988). Moreover, affirming the true self allows for shame-free guilt in response to minor infractions (Vess, Schlegel, Hicks, & Arndt, 2013) and allows people to admit past immorality, thereby increasing reparations (Ĉehajić-Clancy, Effron, Halperin, Liberman, & Ross, 2011; Schumann, 2014). Finally, exposure to moral exemplars increases prosocial behavior (Schnall, Roper, & Fessler, 2010) when people identify with them (Nelson & Norton, 2005)—but people resent moral exemplars when a direct comparison of behavior reveals their moral inferiority (Cramwinckel, Van Dijk, Scheepers, & Van den Bos, 2013; Monin, Sawyer, & Marquez, 2008).

Although past immoral behavior often motivates people to restore their threatened moral self through prosociality (Carlsmith & Gross, 1969; Conway & Peetz, 2012), sometimes people incorporate moral failings into the self-concept: *moral injury,* which is a serious problem for veterans and distinct from PTSD (Maguen & Litz, 2012). Morality and self-control are related (Baumeister & Exline, 1999), and when people interpret self-control failure as a global self-deficit, they often give up self-regulating, inviting further failure (Baumeister & Heatherton, 1996). Similarly, people who incorporate immorality into the self-concept may give up on morality: Recalling immoral behavior can reduce prosociality (Conway & Peetz, 2012); perceiving oneself as unethical increases unethical behavior (Gino, Norton, & Ariely, 2010); and perceiving global moral defects increases defensiveness, not improvement (Gausel & Leach, 2011).

Moral Self-Perceptions Allow Judging Others

Normally, people refrain from sharing their inner thoughts regarding issues that do not affect them (Ratner & Miller, 2001), but moralizing an issue—by construing it as a reflection of one's core values and beliefs (Skitka, 2002)—frees people to express their thoughts regardless of personal stake (Effron & Miller, 2012). In turn, expressing one's moral values in this way validates the moral self (Skitka, 2003), thereby per-

mitting one to judge morally inferior others. When one lacks moral standing, attempting to regulate others may come across as hypocritical—the pot calling the kettle black—so those who wish to judge others must first establish moral selfhood (Effron & Monin, 2010).

An important implication of this view is that moral judgments are inherently social and relative: They are made by a moral self, regarding another moral self, both of whom are members of reference groups populated by yet more moral selves. Making moral judgments invokes power over the target by increasing relative moral distance: Those who judge must be more moral than those they judge. Accordingly, people view judges as moral exemplars (Walker & Hennig, 2004) and view people who make moral judgments as trustworthy (Simpson et al., 2013). Conversely, people often view targets of harm as deserving negative treatment due to their poor moral character (Olson et al., 2009), rather than somehow outside the "scope of justice" (Opotow, 1993; Olson et al., 2009). Hence, harm is morally justifiable if the target has violated important standards (Tangney, Stuewig, & Mashek, 2007). In such cases, morality motivates harm: *moralistic aggression,* in which aggressors exert physical superiority over the morally inferior victim (Rai & Fiske, 2011). Note that such aggression may appear immoral from the victim's but not the perpetrator's perspective (Giner-Sorolla, 2012).

Extension and Expansion

There are several important implications of the moral self view. First, moral judgments (e.g., dilemma decisions, blame judgments) are based not only on basic psychological processes (e.g., affect) but also on metaperceptions regarding what these judgments suggest about one's character. Engaging in morally relevant behavior affects not only one's moral self-perceptions but also one's moral standing in relation to others—one is always gaining or losing the moral high ground. Few theorists have fully appreciated how making moral judgments amounts to exerting power. More empirical work should clarify these ramifications.

Second, a better understanding of the moral self is crucial for improving society. As moral self-perceptions can both increase and relax moral strivings, researchers need to clarify moderators—when does feeling moral actually make one a better person? Resolving this paradox may suggest simple behavioral "nudges" to increase prosociality. For example, considering how past moral deeds reflect one's identity may motivate prosociality. Likewise, it is paramount to better understand negative moral self-perceptions. Considering immorality part of one's self-concept may lead to moral injury (Maguen & Litz, 2012), reducing subsequent prosociality (Conway & Peetz, 2012), thereby creating a downward spiral (Baumeister & Heatherton, 1996). On the other hand, a redemptive narrative is possible if people share their stories of immoral behavior to help others (McAdams, 1993) or aim to restore standing via prosocial acts (Baumeister, Stillwell, & Heatherton, 1994). Perhaps increasing perceptions of self-malleability (Schumann & Dweck, 2014) may influence whether people accept or reject an immoral self. Researchers should clarify how and when negative moral self-perceptions are useful versus destructive.

Finally, returning to our original question: From the moral self perspective, Manlius's decision makes (brutal) sense. Simply put, Titus's "idle show of honor" prioritized personal honor over group interests when group cohesion was paramount. Had Manlius compounded Titus's selfishness by engaging in blatant nepotism (i.e., punishing Titus less than others), this hypocrisy would have compromised Manlius's moral self. Army leadership would have appeared corrupt, motivating others to shift priority away from group goals to self-interest, diminishing group cohesion and thereby increasing the chance of disastrous defeat. Instead, by sacrificing his son, Manlius clearly demonstrated his priority of group over selfish interests, inspiring others to do the same. Manlius also demonstrated the moral clarity of a dispassionate judge, suggesting he would use his position of moral superiority to punish anyone who violated their duty. In doing so, Manlius enhanced group cohesion, resulting in success over rivals. Manlius's decision was driven by a need to uphold his moral self and social perceptions in the context of an ancient military order.

NOTE

1. Unless the deontological rule is *obey thy father and commander,* in which case rules would entail harm. The dual-process model fails to specify which moral rules are paramount (Mikhail, 2007).

REFERENCES

Alexander, R. D. (1987). *The biology of moral systems.* New York: Aldine de Gruyter.

Aquino, K., Freeman, D., Reed, A., II, Felps, W., & Lim, V. (2009). Testing a social-cognitive model of moral behavior: The interactive influence of situations and moral identity centrality. *Journal of Personality and Social Psychology, 97,* 123–141.

Aquino, K., & Reed, A., II. (2002). The self-importance of moral identity. *Journal of Personality and Social Psychology, 83,* 1423–1440.

Ariely, D., Bracha, A., & Meier, S. (2009). Doing good or doing well?: Image motivation and monetary incentives in behaving prosocially. *American Economic Review, 99,* 544–555.

Baldwin, M. W., Biernat, M., & Landau, M. J. (2015). Remembering the real me: Nostalgia offers a window to the intrinsic self. *Journal of Personality and Social Psychology, 108,* 128–147.

Bartels, D. M., & Pizarro, D. A. (2011). The mismeasure of morals: Antisocial personality traits predict utilitarian responses to moral dilemmas. *Cognition, 121,* 154–161.

Baumeister, R. F., & Exline, J. J. (1999). Virtue, personality and social relations: Self-control as the moral muscle. *Journal of Personality, 67,* 1165–1194.

Baumeister, R. F., & Heatherton, T. F. (1996). Self-regulation failure: An overview. *Psychological Inquiry, 7,* 1–15.

Baumeister, R. F., Stillwell, A. M., & Heatherton, T. F. (1994). Guilt: An interpersonal approach. *Psychological Bulletin, 115,* 243–267.

Baumeister, R. F., Stillwell, A. M., & Wotman, S. R. (1994). Victim and perpetrator accounts of interpersonal conflict: Autobiographical narratives about anger. *Journal of Personality and Social Psychology, 59,* 994–1005.

Bem, D. J. (1972). Self-perception theory. In L. Berkowitz (Ed.), *Advances in experimental social psychology* (Vol. 6, pp. 1–62). New York: Academic Press.

Bergman, R. (2002). Why be moral?: A conceptual model from developmental psychology. *Human Development, 45,* 104–124.

Blanken, I., van de Ven, N., & Zeelenberg, M. (2014). A meta-analytic review of moral licensing. *Personality and Social Psychology Bulletin, 41,* 540–558.

Blasi, A. (1980). Bridging moral cognition and moral action: A critical review of the literature. *Psychological Bulletin, 88,* 1–45.

Blasi, A. (1984). Moral identity: Its role in moral functioning. In W. M. Kurtines & J. L. Gewirtz (Eds.), *Morality, moral behavior, and moral development* (pp. 128–139). New York: Wiley.

Blasi, A. (1995). Moral understanding and the moral personality: The process of moral integration. In W. M. Kurtines & J. L. Gewirtz (Eds.), *Moral development: An introduction* (p. 78). Boston: Allyn & Bacon.

Bocian, K., & Wojciszka, B. (2014). Self-interest bias in moral judgments of others' actions. *Personality and Social Psychology Bulletin, 40,* 898–909.

Boehm, C. H. (1999). *Hierarchy in the forest: The evolution of egalitarian behavior.* Cambridge, MA: Harvard University Press.

Boezeman, E. J., & Ellemers, N. (2014). Volunteer leadership: The role of pride and respect in organizational identification and leadership satisfaction. *Leadership, 10,* 160–173.

Boyd, R., & Richerson, P. J. (2005). Solving the puzzle of human cooperation. In S. C. Levinson & P. Jaisson (Eds.), *Evolution and culture: A Fyssen Foundation Symposium* (pp. 105–132). Cambridge, MA: MIT Press.

Brambilla, M., Rusconi, P. P., Sacchi, S., & Cherubini, P. (2011). Looking for honesty: The primary role of morality (vs. sociability and competence) in information gathering. *European Journal of Social Psychology, 41,* 135–143.

Brandt, M. J. (2013). Onset and offset deservingness: The case of home foreclosures. *Political Psychology, 34,* 221–238.

Bryan, C. J., Adams, G. S., & Monin, B. (2013). When cheating would make you a cheater: Implicating the self prevents unethical behavior. *Journal of Experimental Psychology: General, 142,* 1001–1005.

Burger, J. M., & Caldwell, D. F. (2003). The effects of monetary incentives and labeling on the foot-in-the-door effect: Evidence for a self-perception process. *Basic and Applied Social Psychology, 25,* 235–241.

Callan, M. J., Shead, N. W., & Olson, J. M. (2011). Personal relative deprivation, delay discounting, and gambling. *Journal of Personality and Social Psychology, 101,* 955.

Cameron, C. D., Lindquist, K. A., & Gray, K. (2015). A constructionist review of morality and emotions: No evidence for specific relationships between moral content and discrete emotions. *Personality and Social Psychology Review, 19,* 1–24.

Cameron, C. D., & Payne, D. K. (2011). Escaping affect: How motivated emotion regulation creates insensitivity to mass suffering. *Journal of Personality and Social Psychology, 100,* 1–15.

Cameron, C. D., & Payne, B. K. (2012). The cost of callousness: Regulating compassion influences the moral self-concept. *Psychological Science, 23,* 225–229.

Ĉehajić-Clancy, S., Effron, D., Halperin, E., Liberman, V., & Ross, L. D. (2011). Affirmation, acknowledgement of in-group responsibility, group-based guilt, and support for reparative measures. *Journal of Personality and Social Psychology, 101*(2), 256–270.

Christy, A. G., & Schlegel, R. J. (2015, February). *Moral decisions and the true-self concept.* Poster presented at the annual meeting of the Society for Personality and Social Psychology, Long Beach, CA.

Colby, A., & Damon, W. (1992). *Some do care: Contemporary lives of moral commitment.* New York: Free Press.

Conway, P., & Gawronski, B. (2013). Deontological and utilitarian inclinations in moral decision-making: A process dissociation approach. *Journal of Personality and Social Psychology, 104,* 216–235.

Conway, P., & Peetz, J. (2012). When does feeling moral actually make you a better person?: Conceptual abstraction moderates whether past moral deeds motivate consistency or compensatory behavior. *Personality and Social Psychology Bulletin, 38,* 907–919.

Cramwinckel, F. M., Van Dijk, E., Scheepers, D. T., & Van den Bos, K. (2013). The threat of moral refusers for one's self-concept and the protective function of physical cleansing. *Journal of Experimental Social Psychology, 49,* 1049–1058.

Cushman, F. (2008). Crime and punishment: Distinguishing the roles of causal and intentional analyses in moral judgment. *Cognition, 108,* 353–380.

Cushman, F., Gray, K., Gaffey, A., & Mendes, W. B. (2012). Simulating murder: The aversion to harmful actions. *Emotion, 12,* 2–7.

Damon, W. (1984). Self-understanding and moral development from childhood to adolescence. In W. M. Kurtines & J. L. Gewirtz (Eds.), *Morality, moral behavior, and moral development* (pp. 109–127). New York: Wiley.

Darley, J. M. (2009). Morality in the law: The psychological foundations of citizens' desires to punish transgressions. *Annual Review of Law and Social Science, 5,* 1–23.

Darwin, C. (1998). *The descent of man.* Amherst, NY: Prometheus Books. (Original work published 1874)

Dawkins, R. (1989). *The selfish gene*. Oxford, UK: Oxford University Press.

de Waal, F. (1996). *Good natured: The origins of right and wrong in humans and other animals*. Cambridge, MA: Harvard University Press.

Delgado, M. R., Frank, R. H., & Phelps, E. A. (2005). Perceptions of moral character modulate the neural systems of reward during the trust game. *Nature Neuroscience, 8*, 1611–1618.

DeScioli, P., & Kurzban, R. (2013). A solution to the mysteries of morality. *Psychological Bulletin, 139*, 477–496.

Effron, D. A. (2014). Making mountains of morality from molehills of virtue: Threat causes people to overestimate their moral credentials. *Personality and Social Psychology Bulletin, 40*, 972–985.

Effron, D. A., Cameron, J. S., & Monin, B. (2009). Endorsing Obama licenses favoring whites. *Journal of Experimental Psychology, 45*, 590–593.

Effron, D. A., & Conway, P. (2015). When virtue leads to villainy: Advances in research on moral self-licensing. *Current Opinion in Psychology, 6*, 32–35.

Effron, D. A., & Miller, D. T. (2012). How the moralization of issues grants social legitimacy to act on one's attitudes. *Personality and Social Psychology Bulletin, 38*, 690–701.

Effron, D. A., Miller, D. T., & Monin, B. (2012). Inventing racist roads not taken: The licensing effect of immoral counterfactual behaviors. *Journal of Personality and Social Psychology, 103*, 916–932.

Effron, D. A., & Monin, B. (2010). Letting people off the hook: When do good deeds excuse transgressions? *Personality and Social Psychology Bulletin, 36*, 1618–1634.

Ellemers, N., Pagliaro, S., Barreto, M., & Leach, C. W. (2008). Is it better to be moral than smart?: The effects of morality and competence norms on the decision to work at group status improvement. *Journal of Personality and Social Psychology, 95*, 1397–1410.

Ellemers, N., & Van den Bos, K. (2012). Morality in groups: On the social-regulatory functions of right and wrong. *Social and Personality Psychology Compass, 6*, 878–889.

Epley, N., & Dunning, D. (2000). Feeling "holier than thou": Are self-serving assessments produced by errors in self-or social prediction? *Journal of Personality and Social Psychology, 79*, 861.

Eskine, K. J., Kacinik, N. A., & Webster, G. D. (2012). The bitter truth about morality: Virtue, not vice, makes a bland beverage taste nice. *PLOS ONE 7*, e41159.

Feather, N. T., & Atchison, L. (1998). Reactions to an offence in relation to the status and perceived moral character of the offender. *Australian Journal of Psychology, 50*, 119–127.

Feather, N. T., & Sherman, R. (2002). Envy, resentment, schadenfreude, and sympathy: Reactions to deserved and undeserved achievement and subsequent failure. *Personality and Social Psychology Bulletin, 28*, 953–961.

Fehr, E., & Gächter, S. (2002). Altruistic punishment in humans. *Nature, 415*, 137–140.

Feinberg, M., Willer, R., & Schultz, M. (2014). Gossip and ostracism promote cooperation in groups. *Psychological Science, 25*, 656–664.

Fessler, D. (1999). Toward an understanding of the universality of second order emotions. In A. Hinton (Ed.), *Beyond nature or nurture: Biocultural approaches to the emotions* (pp. 75–116). New York: Cambridge University Press.

Festinger, L. (1957). *A theory of cognitive dissonance*. Stanford, CA: Stanford University Press.

Foot, P. (1967). The problem of abortion and the doctrine of double effect. *Oxford Review, 5*, 5–15.

Forehand, M. R., Deshpandé, R., & Reed, A., II. (2002). Identity salience and the influence of differential activation of the social self-schema on advertising response. *Journal of Applied Psychology, 87*, 1086–1099.

Frimer, J. A., Schaefer, N. K., & Oakes, H. (2014). Moral actor, selfish agent. *Journal of Personality and Social Psychology, 106*, 790–802.

Frimer, J. A., & Walker, L. J. (2009). Reconciling the self and morality: An empirical model of moral centrality development. *Developmental Psychology, 45*, 1669–1681.

Gangestad, S. W., Haselton, M. G., & Buss, D. M. (2006). Evolutionary foundations of cultural variation: Evoked culture and mate preferences. *Psychological Inquiry, 17*, 75–95.

Gausel, N., & Leach, C. W. (2011). Concern for self-image and social-image in the management of moral failure: Rethinking shame. *European Journal of Social Psychology, 41*, 468–478.

Giner-Sorolla, R. (2012). *Judging passions: Moral emotions in persons and groups*. New York: Psychology Press.

Gino, F., & Desai, S. (2012). Memory lane and morality: How childhood memories promote prosocial behavior. *Journal of Personality and Social Psychology, 102*, 743–758.

Gino, F., Kouchaki, M., & Galinsky, A. D. (2015). The moral virtue of authenticity: How inauthenticity produces feelings of immorality and impurity. *Psychological Science, 26*, 983–996.

Gino, F., Norton, M., & Ariely, D. (2010). The counterfeit self: The deceptive costs of faking it. *Psychological Science, 21,* 712–720.

Gino, F., & Pierce, L. (2009) The abundance effect: Unethical behavior in the presence of wealth. *Organizational Behavior and Human Decision Processes, 109,* 142–155.

Gintis, H., Bowles, S., Boyd, R., & Fehr, E. (2003). Explaining altruistic behavior in humans. *Evolution and Human Behavior, 24,* 153–172.

Gneezy, A., Imas, A., Brown, A., Nelson, L. D., & Norton, M. I. (2012). Paying to be nice: Consistency and costly prosocial behavior. *Management Science, 58,* 179–187.

Goodwin, G. P., Piazza, J., & Rozin, P. (2014). Moral character predominates in person perception and evaluation. *Journal of Personality and Social Psychology, 106,* 148–168.

Graham, J., Haidt, J., & Nosek, B. A. (2009). Liberals and conservatives rely on different sets of moral foundations. *Journal of Personality and Social Psychology, 96,* 1029–1046.

Gray, H. M., Gray, K., & Wegner, D. M. (2007). Dimensions of mind perception. *Science, 315,* 619.

Gray, K., Waytz, A., & Young, L. (2012). The moral dyad: A fundamental template unifying moral judgment. *Psychological Inquiry, 23,* 206–215.

Gray, K., & Wegner, D. M. (2009). Moral typecasting: Divergent perceptions of moral agents and moral patients. *Journal of Personality and Social Psychology, 96,* 505–520.

Gray, K., Young, L., & Waytz, A. (2012). Mind perception is the essence of morality. *Psychological Inquiry, 23,* 101–124.

Greene, J. D., Sommerville, R. B., Nystrom, L. E., Darley, J. M., & Cohen, J. D. (2001). An fMRI investigation of emotional engagement in moral judgment. *Science, 293,* 2105–2108.

Guglielmo, S., Monroe, A. E., & Malle, B. F. (2009). At the heart of morality lies folk psychology. *Inquiry, 5,* 449–466.

Haidt, J. (2001). The emotional dog and its rational tail: A social intuitionist approach to moral judgment. *Psychological Review, 108,* 814–834.

Haidt, J., & Graham, J. (2007). When morality opposes justice: Conservatives have moral intuitions that liberals may not recognize. *Social Justice Research, 20,* 98–116.

Haidt, J., & Joseph, C. (2004). Intuitive ethics: How innately prepared intuitions generate culturally variable virtues. *Daedalus, 133,* 55–66.

Haidt, J., Koller, S., & Dias, M. (1993). Affect, culture, and morality, or is it wrong to eat your dog? *Journal of Personality and Social Psychology, 65,* 613–628.

Hamilton, W. D. (1964). The evolution of social behavior. *Journal of Theoretical Biology, 7,* 1–52.

Hamlin, J. K. (2013). Moral judgment and action in preverbal infants and toddlers: Evidence for an innate moral core. *Current Directions in Psychological Science, 22,* 186–193.

Hardy, C. L., & Van Vugt, M. (2006). Nice guys finish first: The competitive altruism hypothesis. *Personality and Social Psychology Bulletin, 32,* 1402–1413.

Hardy, S. A. (2006). Identity, reasoning, and emotion: An empirical comparison of three sources of moral motivation. *Motivation and Emotion, 30,* 207–215.

Hardy, S. A., & Carlo, G. (2005). Identity as a source of moral motivation. *Human Development, 48,* 232–256.

Haslam, S. A., Reicher, S. D., & Platow, M. J. (2010). *The new psychology of leadership: Identity, influence and power.* London: Psychology Press.

Hastings, M. (1985). *The Oxford book of military anecdotes.* Oxford, UK: Oxford University Press.

Higgins, T. (1987). Self-discrepancy: A theory relating self and affect. *Psychological Review, 94,* 319–340.

Hoffman, M. L. (2000). *Empathy and moral development: Implications for caring and justice.* New York: Cambridge University Press

Hofmann, W., Wisneski, D. C., Brandt, M. J., & Skitka, L. J. (2014). Morality in everyday life. *Science, 345,* 1340–1343.

Inbar, Y., Pizarro, D. A., & Bloom, P. (2012). Disgusting smells cause decreased liking of gay men. *Emotion, 12,* 23–27.

Janoff-Bulman, R., Sheikh, S., & Hepp, S. (2009). Proscriptive versus prescriptive morality: Two faces of moral regulation. *Journal of Personality and Social Psychology, 96,* 521–537.

Jennings, P. L., Mitchell, M. S., & Hannah, S. T. (2014). The moral self: A review and integration of the literature. *Journal of Organizational Behavior, 36,* S104–S168.

Jordan, J., Mullen, E., & Murnighan, J. K. (2011). Striving for the moral self: The effects of recalling past moral actions on future moral behavior. *Personality and Social Psychology Bulletin, 37,* 701–713.

Kant, I. (1959). *Foundation of the metaphysics of morals* (L. W. Beck, Trans.). Indianapolis, IN: Bobbs-Merrill. (Original work published 1785)

Keltner, D., & Haidt, J. (1999). Social functions of emotions at four levels of analysis. *Cognition and Emotion, 13,* 505–522.

Kohlberg, L. (1969). Stage and sequence: The cognitive-developmental approach to socialization. In D. A. Goslin (Ed.), *Handbook of socialization theory and research* (pp. 347–480). Chicago: Rand McNally.

Kraut, R. E. (1973). Effects of social labeling on giving to charity. *Journal of Experimental Social Psychology, 9,* 551–562.

Krebs, D. (2008). Morality: An evolutionary account. *Perspectives on Psychological Science, 3,* 149–172.

Kundu, P., & Cummins, D. D. (2012). Morality and conformity: The Asch paradigm applied to moral decisions. *Social Influence, 8,* 268–279.

Kurzban, R., DeScioli, P., & O'Brien, E. (2007). Audience effects on moralistic punishment. *Evolution and Human Behavior, 28,* 75–84.

Lakoff, G. (2010). *How liberals and conservatives think.* Chicago: University of Chicago Press.

Lammers, J. (2012). Abstraction increases hypocrisy. *Journal of Experimental Social Psychology, 48,* 475–480.

Lapsley, D. K., & Narvaez, D. (2004). A social-cognitive approach to the moral personality. In D. K. Lapsley & D. Narvaez (Eds.), *Moral development, self, and identity* (pp. 189–212). Mahwah, NJ: Erlbaum.

Leach, C. W., Bilali, R., & Pagliaro, S. (2013). Groups and morality. In J. Simpson & J. F. Dovidio (Eds.), *APA handbook of personality and social psychology: Vol. 2. Interpersonal relationships and group processes* (pp. 2–61). Washington, DC: American Psychological Association.

Leach, C. W., Ellemers, N., & Barreto, M. (2007). Group virtue: The importance of morality (vs. competence and sociability) in the positive evaluation of in-groups. *Journal of Personality and Social Psychology, 93,* 234–249.

Lee, J. J., Im, D. K., Parmar, B. L., & Gino, F. (2015). *Thick as thieves?: Dishonest behavior and egocentric social networks.* Harvard Business School Working Paper No. 15-064. Available at *http://ssrn.com/abstract=2563196 orhttp://dx.doi.org/10.2139/ssrn.2563196*

Lee, R. B., & DeVore, I. (Eds.). (1968). *Man the hunter.* Oxford, UK: Aldine.

Lee, S. W. S., & Schwarz, N. (2010). Dirty hands and dirty mouths: Embodiment of the moral-purity metaphor is specific to the motor modality involved in moral transgression. *Psychological Science, 21,* 1423–1425.

Lerner, M. J. (1980). *The belief in a just world: A fundamental delusion.* New York: Plenum Press.

Liu, B. S., & Ditto, P. H. (2012). What dilemma?: Moral evaluation shapes factual belief. *Social Psychological and Personality Science, 4,* 316–323.

Lucas, B. J., & Galinsky, A. D. (2015). Is utilitarianism risky?: How the same antecedents and mechanism produce both utilitarian and risky choices. *Perspectives on Psychological Science, 10*(4), 541–548.

Lucas, B. L., & Livingstone, R. W. (2014). Feeling socially connected increases utilitarian choices in moral dilemmas. *Journal of Experimental Social Psychology, 53,* 1–4.

Maguen, S., & Litz, B. (2012). Moral injury in veterans of war. *PTSD Research Quarterly, 23,* 1–3.

Markus, H., & Kunda, Z. (1986). Stability and malleability of the self-concept. *Journal of Personality and Social Psychology, 51,* 858–866.

Mazar, N., Amir, O., & Ariely, D. (2008). The dishonesty of honest people: A theory of self-concept maintenance. *Journal of Marketing Research, 45,* 633–644.

McAdams, D. P. (1993). *The stories we live by: Personal myths and the making of the self.* New York: Guilford Press.

McCullough, M. E., Kilpatrick, S. D., Emmons, R. A., & Larson, D. B. (2001). Is gratitude a moral affect? *Psychological Bulletin, 127,* 249–266.

Midgley, M. (1991). The origin of ethics. In P. Singer (Ed.), *A companion guide to ethics* (pp. 1–13). Oxford, UK: Blackwell Reference.

Mikhail, J. (2007). Universal moral grammar: Theory, evidence and the future. *Trends in Cognitive Sciences, 11,* 143–152.

Mill, J. S. (1998). *Utilitarianism.* New York: Oxford University Press. (Original work published 1861)

Miller, D. T., & Effron, D. A. (2010). Psychological license: When it is needed and how it functions. In M. P. Zanna & J. M. Olson (Eds.), *Advances in experimental social psychology* (Vol. 43, pp. 117–158). San Diego, CA: Academic Press/Elsevier.

Miller, G. F. (2007). The sexual selection of moral virtues. *Quarterly Review of Biology, 82,* 97–125.

Moll, J., de Oliveira-Souza, R., Garrido, G. J., Bramanti, I. E., Caparelli, E. M., Pavia, M. L., . . ., & Grafman, J., (2007). The self as moral agent: Linking the neural bases of social agency and moral sensitivity. *Social Neuroscience, 2,* 336–352.

Monin, B., & Jordan, A. H. (2009). The dynamic moral self: A social psychological perspective. In D. Narvaez & D. Lapsley (Eds.), *Personality, identity, and character: Explorations in moral psychology* (pp. 341–354). New York: Cambridge University Press.

Monin, B., Sawyer, P. J., & Marquez, M. J. (2008). The rejection of moral rebels: Resenting those who do the right thing. *Journal of Personality and Social Psychology, 95,* 76–93.

Mooijman, M., & van Dijk, W. W. (2014). The self in moral judgment: How self-affirmation affects the moral condemnation of harmless sexual taboos. *Cognition and Emotion, 29,* 1326–1334.

Moore, A. B., Clark, B. A., & Kane, M. J. (2008). Who shalt not kill?: Individual differences in working memory capacity, executive control, and moral judgment. *Psychological Science, 19,* 549–557.

Mullen, E., & Monin, B. (2016). Consistency versus licensing effects of past moral behavior. *Annual Review of Psychology, 67,* 363–385.

Nelson, L. D., & Norton, M. I. (2005). From student to superhero: Situational primes shape future helping. *Journal of Experimental Social Psychology, 41,* 423–430.

Newman, G. E., De Freitas, J., & Knobe, J. (2014). Beliefs about the true self explain asymmetries based on moral judgment. *Cognitive Science, 39,* 96–125.

Nichols, S., & Mallon, R. (2006). Moral dilemmas and moral rules. *Cognition, 100,* 530–542.

Nowak, M. A., & Sigmund, K. (1998). Evolution of indirect reciprocity by image scoring. *Nature, 393,* 573–577.

Olson, J. M., Cheung, I., Conway, P., Hutchison, J., & Hafer, C. L. (2011). Distinguishing two meanings of moral exclusion: Irrelevance of fairness vs. rationalized harm-doing. *Social Justice Research, 24,* 1–26.

Olson, J. M., Hafer, C. L., Cheung, I., & Conway, P. (2009). Deservingness, the scope of justice, and actions toward others. In A. C. Kay, D. R. Bobocel, M. P. Zanna, & J. M. Olson (Eds.), *The psychology of justice and legitimacy: The Ontario symposium* (Vol. 11, pp. 125–149). New York: Psychology Press.

Omdahl, B. L., & O'Donnell, C. (1999). Emotional contagion, empathic concern and communicative responsiveness as variables affecting nurses' stress and occupational commitment. *Journal of Advanced Nursing, 29,* 1351–1359.

Opotow, S. (1993). Animals and the scope of justice. *Journal of Social Issues, 49,* 71–85.

Pagliaro, S., Ellemers, N., & Barreto, M. (2011). Sharing moral values: Anticipated ingroup respect as a determinant of adherence to morality-based (but not competence-based) group norms. *Personality and Social Psychology Bulletin, 37,* 1117–1129.

Piaget, J. (1965). *The moral judgment of the child* (M. Gabain, Trans.). New York: Free Press. (Original work published 1932).

Pizarro, D. A., & Tannenbaum, D. (2011). Bringing character back: How the motivation to evaluate character influences judgments of moral blame. In M. Mikulincer & P. R. Shaver (Eds.), *The social psychology of morality: Exploring the causes of good and evil* (pp. 91–108). Washington, DC: American Psychological Association.

Plato. (1949). *Timaeus* (B. Jowett, Trans.). Indianapolis, IN: Bobbs-Merrill.

Rai, T. S., & Fiske, A. P. (2011). Moral psychology is relationship regulation: Moral motives for unity, hierarchy, equality, and proportionality. *Psychological Review, 118,* 57–75.

Ratner, R. K., & Miller, D. T. (2001). The norm of self-interest and its effects on social action. *Journal of Personality and Social Psychology, 81,* 5–16.

Reed, A., II, & Aquino, K. F. (2003). Moral identity and the expanding circle of moral regard toward out-groups. *Journal of Personality and Social Psychology, 84,* 1270–1286.

Reed, A., II, Aquino, K., & Levy, E. (2007). Moral identity and judgments of charitable behaviors. *Journal of Marketing, 71*(1), 178–193.

Rest, J. R. (1984). The major components of morality. In W. M. Kurtines & J. L. Gewirtz (Eds.), *Morality, moral behavior, and moral development* (pp. 24–38) New York: Wiley.

Rokeach, M. (1973). *The nature of human values.* New York: Free Press.

Rozin, P., Haidt, J., & Fincher, K. (2009). From oral to moral. *Science, 323,* 1179–1180.

Schlegel, R. J., Hicks, J. A., Arndt, J., & King, L. A. (2009). Thine own self: True self-concept accessibility and meaning in life. *Journal of Personality and Social Psychology, 96,* 473–490.

Schnall, S., Benton, J., & Harvey, S. (2008). With a clean conscience: Cleanliness reduces the severity of moral judgments. *Psychological Science, 19,* 1219–1222.

Schnall, S., Haidt, J., Clore, G. L., & Jordan, A. H. (2008). Disgust as embodied moral judgment. *Personality and Social Psychology Bulletin, 34,* 1096–1109.

Schnall, S., Roper, J., & Fessler, D. M. T. (2010). Elevation leads to altruism, above and beyond general positive affect. *Psychological Science, 21,* 315–320.

Schumann, K. (2014). An affirmed self and a better apology: The effect of self-affirmation on transgressors' responses to victims. *Journal of Experimental Social Psychology, 54,* 89–96.

Schumann, K., & Dweck, C. S. (2014). Who accepts responsibility for their transgressions? *Personality and Social Psychology Bulletin, 60,* 1598–1610.

Shalvi, S., Gino, F., Barkan, R., & Ayal, S. (2015). Self-serving justifications: Doing wrong and feeling moral. *Current Directions in Psychological Science, 24,* 125–130.

Shalvi, S., Handgraaf, M. J. J., & De Dreu, C. K. W. (2011). Ethical manoeuvring: Why people avoid both major and minor lies. *British Journal of Management, 22,* S16–S27.

Shaver, K. G. (1985). *The attribution of blame: Causality, responsibility, and blameworthiness.* New York: Springer-Verlag.

Shu, L. L., Gino, F., & Bazerman, M. (2010). Dishonest deed, clear conscience: When cheating leads to moral disengagement and motivated forgetting. *Personality and Social Psychology Bulletin, 37,* 330–349.

Shu, L. L., Mazar, N., Gino, F., Ariely, D., & Bazerman, M. (2012). Signing at the beginning makes ethics salient and decreases dishonest self-reports in comparison to signing at the end. *Proceedings of the National Academy of Sciences of the USA, 109,* 15197–15200.

Shweder, R. A., Much, N. C., Mahapatra, M., & Park, L. (1997). The "big three" of morality (autonomy, community, and divinity), and the "big three" explanations of suffering. In A. Brandt & P. Rozin (Eds.), *Morality and health* (pp. 119–169). New York: Routledge.

Simpson, B., Harrell, A., & Willer, R. (2013). Hidden paths from morality to cooperation: Moral judgments promote trust and trustworthiness. *Social Forces, 91,* 1529–1548.

Skitka, L. J. (2002). Do the means always justify the ends, or do the ends sometimes justify the means?: A value protection model of justice reasoning. *Personality and Social Psychology Bulletin, 28,* 588–597.

Skitka, L. J. (2003). Of different minds: An accessibility identity model of justice reasoning. *Personality and Social Psychology Review, 7,* 286–297.

Skitka, L. J., Bauman, C. W., & Mullen, E. (2008). Morality and justice: An expanded theoretical perspective and review. In K. A. Hedgvedt & J. Clay-Warner (Eds.), *Advances in group processes: Vol. 25. Justice* (pp. 1–27). Bingley, UK: Emerald Group.

Skitka, L. J., Bauman, C. W., & Sargis, E. G. (2005). Moral conviction: Another contributor to attitude strength or something more? *Journal of Personality and Social Psychology, 88,* 895–917.

Skitka, L. J., & Houston, D. A. (2001). When due process is of no consequence: Moral mandates and presumed defendant guilt or innocence. *Social Justice Research, 14,* 305–326.

Skitka, L. J., & Tetlock, P. E. (1992). Allocating scarce resources: A contingency model of distributive justice. *Journal of Experimental Social Psychology, 28,* 491–522.

Skowronski, J. J., & Carlston, D. E. (1987). Social judgment and social memory: The role of cue diagnosticity in negativity, positivity, and extremity biases. *Journal of Personality and Social Psychology, 52*(4), 689.

Smaldino, P. E., Schank, J. C., & McElreath, R. (2013). Increased costs of cooperation help cooperators in the long run. *American Naturalist, 181,* 451–463.

Sober, E., & Wilson, D. S. (1998). *Unto others: The evolution and psychology of unselfish behavior.* Cambridge, MA: Harvard University Press.

Sousa, P., Holbrook, C., & Piazza, J. (2009). The morality of harm. *Cognition, 113,* 80–92.

Steele, C. M. (1988). The psychology of self-affirmation: Sustaining the integrity of the self. *Advances in Experimental Social Psychology, 21,* 261–302

Strohminger, N., & Nichols, S. (2014). The essential moral self. *Cognition, 131,* 159–171.

Susewind, M., & Hoelzl, E. (2014). A matter of perspective: Why past moral behavior can sometimes encourage and other times discourage future moral striving. *Journal of Applied Social Psychology, 44,* 201–209.

Sutton, J., Smith, P. K., & Swettenham, J. (1999). Bullying and "theory of mind": A critique of the "social skills deficit" view of antisocial behaviour. *Social Development, 8,* 117–127.

Tajfel, H., & Turner, J. C. (1985). The social identity theory of intergroup behavior. In S. Worschel & W. G. Austin (Eds.), *Psychology of intergroup relations* (pp. 7–24). Chicago: Nelson-Hall.

Tangney, J. P., Stuewig, J., & Mashek, D. J. (2007). Moral emotions and moral behavior. *Annual Review of Psychology, 58,* 345–372.

Tetlock, P. E., Kristel, O. V., Elson, S., Green, M. C., & Lerner, J. S. (2000). The psychology of the unthinkable: Taboo trade-offs, forbidden base rates, and heretical counterfactuals. *Journal of Personality and Social Psychology, 78,* 853–870.

Trivers, R. (1971). The evolution of reciprocal altruism. *Review of Biology, 46,* 35–57.

Turiel, E. (1983). *The development of social knowledge: Morality and convention.* Cambridge, UK: Cambridge University Press.

van Nunspeet, F., Derks, B., Ellemers, N., & Nieuwenhuis, S. (2015). Moral impression management: Evaluation by an in-group member during a moral IAT affects perceptual attention and conflict and response monitoring. *Social Psychological and Personality Science, 6,* 183–192.

Van Zant, A. B., & Moore, D. A. (2015). Leaders' use of moral justifications increases policy support. *Psychological Science, 26,* 934–943.

Vess, M., Schlegel, R. J., Hicks, J. A., & Arndt, J. (2013). Guilty, but not ashamed: "True" self-conceptions influence affective responses to personal shortcomings. *Journal of Personality, 83,* 213–224.

Vohs, K. D., & Schooler, J. (2008). The value of believing in free will: Encouraging a belief in determinism increases cheating. *Psychological Science, 19,* 49–54.

Walker, L. J., & Hennig, K. H. (2004). Differing conceptions of moral exemplarity: Just, brave, and caring. *Journal of Personality and Social Psychology, 86,* 629–647.

Weiner, B. (1993). On sin versus sickness: A theory of perceived responsibility and social motivation. *American Psychologist, 48,* 957.

Wondra, J. D., & Ellsworth, P. C. (2015). An appraisal theory of empathy and other vicarious emotional experiences. *Psychological Review, 122,* 411–428.

Wright, R. (1994). *The moral animal: The new science of evolutionary psychology.* New York: Pantheon Books.

Zhong, C.-B., Bohns, V. K., & Gino, F. (2010). A good lamp is the best police: Darkness increases self-interested behavior and dishonesty. *Psychological Science, 21,* 311–314.

Zhong, C.-B., & Liljenquist, K. A. (2006). Washing away your sins: Threatened morality and physical cleansing. *Science, 313,* 1451–1452.

Zhong, C.-B., Liljenquist, K., & Cain, D. M. (2009). Moral self-regulation: Licensing and compensation. In D. De Cremer (Ed.), *Psychological perspectives on ethical behavior and decision making* (pp. 75–89). Charlotte, NC: Information Age.

Zhong, C.-B., Strejcek, K., & Sivanathan, N. (2010). A clean self can render harsh moral judgment. *Journal of Experimental Social Psychology, 46,* 859–862.

Zitek, E. M., Jordan, A. H., Monin, B., & Leach, F. R. (2010). Victim entitlement to behave selfishly. *Journal of Personality and Social Psychology, 98,* 245–255.

CHAPTER 17

Thinking Morally about Animals

Steve Loughnan
Jared Piazza

Why are we comfortable with eating animals, but uncomfortable with hurting them?

A blend of attributions, emotions, and identity processes combine to help us evade this moral dilemma.

It is difficult to think morally about animals. The category *animal* itself is sufficiently vast and variable as to be almost psychologically meaningless, stretching from the near-human capacities of great apes to the alien simplicity of microscopic organisms. This objective variability is compounded by a subjective variability; different people, in different places, at different times, think about the same animals differently (Amiot & Bastian, 2015). Crossing this biological diversity among the animal kingdom with the psychological diversity among people results in an explosion of complexity.

The great anthropologist Claude Levi-Strauss recognized this when he wrote that animals are both "good to eat" and "good to think" (Levi-Strauss, 1962). Although the authors of this chapter are divided on whether animals are good to eat, we agree that they are good to think with, especially where morality is concerned. Animals reside in a moral gray area between artifacts and humans, shared with spirits, gods, and robots (Haslam, Kashima, Loughnan, Shi, &

Suitner, 2008). Among these unusual cases, we would suggest that animals are the most long-standing. Whether as predator, prey, pest, or pet, both ancestral and modern humans spend their days surrounded by animals and animal products. Unlike the tools and artifacts that also surround us, our treatment of animals has a decidedly moral flavor. Yet the extent of our moral responsibilities toward animals has been and will continue to be a matter of dispute.

In this chapter, we attempt to map how people think morally about animals, particularly when thinking about the suffering of animals. The main way in which people harm animals is by eating them (in terms of the scale of suffering); however, our work is not limited to the psychology of meat. We argue that three main psychological processes are at work when people are thinking morally about animals: attribution, emotion, and identity (see Figure 17.1). At the cognitive level, we focus on attributions of intelligence, experience, harmfulness, and categorization. At the level of emotions, we examine both

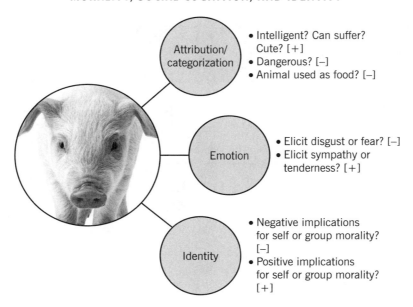

- Intelligent? Can suffer?
  Cute? [+]
- Dangerous? [–]
- Animal used as food? [–]

- Elicit disgust or fear? [–]
- Elicit sympathy or
  tenderness? [+]

- Negative implications
  for self or group morality?
  [–]
- Positive implications
  for self or group morality?
  [+]

Attribution/categorization

Emotion

Identity

FIGURE 17.1. Factors shown to enhance [+] or reduce [–] the perceived moral standing of animals.

the emotions that animals elicit and the emotions we feel about our treatment of animals. Finally, for identity, we examine how our treatment of animals, or prevailing attitudes about the treatment of animals, can challenge our moral identities, resulting in a number of downstream consequences. We then use this model of thinking morally about animals to point to empirical shortcomings and future directions for this field.

Historical Context

Unlike many of the contributions to this volume, our approach to thinking morally about animals is not steeped in a particular theoretical tradition. Rather, we adopt a domain-based approach to the study of morality and animals. By this we mean that the study of animals is an important domain in its own right, and one in which we can see multiple theories of human psychology more generally at work. The notion that we should focus on domains in addition to psychological processes was outlined by Paul Rozin (2006). Rozin argues that psychology has been focused primarily on uncovering domain-general processes and that this has resulted in a relative neglect of understand-

ing specific domains. In this chapter, we focus on such a domain.

Within the domain of animals and morality, we see several important psychological theories of morality at work. In this chapter, we employ to a greater or lesser extent perspectives on mind perception (Waytz, Gray, Epley, & Wegner, 2010) and the social intuitionist model (Haidt, 2001). We also draw on a range of established moral psychological phenomena and effects, including motivated cognition (Dunning, 1999; Kunda, 1990), moral identity processes (Minson & Monin, 2012), moral emotions (especially disgust, guilt, and tenderness), and rationalizations (Mercier, 2011; Piazza et al., 2015), and make the distinction between judgment and decision making. Finally, we cast an even broader net to draw on social psychological classics such as cognitive dissonance theory (Festinger, 1957), the stereotype content model (Fiske, Cuddy, Glick, & Xu, 2002), and the study of prejudice.

Theoretical Stance

Our moral judgment and behavior toward animals draw on three bases: cognition, emotion, and identity. Below we outline how all three can change the way we engage morally with animals.

Cognition

Cognitive processes capture how we think about animals. We focus on how animals are perceived, specifically the types of minds they are believed to possess, and how they are categorized.

When deciding who to care about, minds matter (see Schein & Gray, Chapter 37, this volume; Waytz & Young, Chapter 19, this volume). There are at least two correlated dimensions along which people attribute mind: agency (complex cognition; e.g., intelligence) and experience (emotion; e.g., capacity to feel pain). Humans and animals differ on both dimensions, with animals being seen as lacking primarily agency but also experience, compared with humans (Gray, Gray, & Wegner, 2007). Mind attribution is an important part of deciding which people are worthy of moral concern (Gray, Knobe, Sheskin, Bloom, & Feldman-Barrett, 2011; Loughnan, Haslam, Murnane, et al., 2010). Likewise, minds matter for thinking morally about animals (Piazza, Landy, & Goodwin, 2014; Sytsma & Machery, 2012).

The link between mind attribution to animals and moral concern is simply demonstrated. In a correlational study, Bastian and colleagues (Bastian, Loughnan, Haslam, & Radke, 2012) showed that as mind attribution to animals increased, their perceived edibility decreased. Similarly, vegetarians, whose moral concern for animals at least extends to not eating them, attribute to animals more mental capacities than do omnivores (Bastian, Loughnan, et al., 2012; Bilewicz, Imhoff, & Drogosz, 2011). Finally, in ongoing work, we (Piazza & Loughnan, 2016) have recently found that experimentally manipulating an animal's intelligence serves to decrease its perceived edibility, increase condemnation at its consumption, and increase the amount of guilt people feel about eating the animal, though this does not apply to animals currently being consumed as food in the perceiver's culture (see the section on emotion later in the chapter). Stated otherwise, mind attribution is important both for moral decision making and moral judgments.

Mind attribution to animals is not the only attributional factor influencing judgments of animal moral standing. Recently, Piazza et al. (2014) found that, as with humans, the character of the animal also matters. Animals that are seen as dangerous and harmful, particularly to human beings (e.g., snakes, sharks), suffer declinations in moral standing. Importantly, the harmful character of the animal had an effect on the animal's moral standing independent of the amount of mind (e.g., intelligence) attributed to it.

Concerns about the harmful nature of the animal raise issues pertaining to human welfare. By contrast, mind attribution may affect judgments of moral standing by making animals appear more human, thus exploiting the care we typically reserve for human beings. Anthropomorphizing animals—that is, ascribing to them uniquely human traits, such as social intelligence—generally leads us to care about them more. Indeed, people both report more distress and recommend harsher punishment when led to believe that someone abused an animal similar to a human (a monkey) versus a dissimilar animal (a beetle; see Plous, 1993). Consistent with this finding, making animals appear more human-like by closing the human–animal divide increases concern for their welfare (Bastian, Costello, Loughnan, & Hodson, 2012).

Although the world is populated by a plethora of animal species, lay people tend to organize fauna into a relatively small number of categories or "folk taxa": pets, food, and dangerous animals, for example. These categories are flexible, and the same animal can occupy different categories for different people and can change categories over time. Consider the case of the wolf (*Canine lupus*). Once considered a predator, widespread agriculture and firearms turned it into a pest, and its near extinction turned it into protected wildlife. Another example would be the rabbit (*Leporidae*), which has transformed from game into pest, pet, and petri dish. It has long been known in psychology that categorization shapes judgment and decision making (Barsalou, 1990), and this is no exception for animals and morality. Bratanova, Loughnan, and Bastian (2011) presented American participants with an animal native to Papua New Guinea, the Bennett's tree kangaroo (*Dendrolagus bennettianus*). Capitalizing on participants' lack of knowledge about the animal, half were manipulated to believe the animal was food, and half to believe that it was wildlife. They found that compared with categorization as wildlife, being seen as "food" reduced attributions of moral concern to the animal. This occurred despite participants' not eating the animal, minimizing self-interest concerns. It appears that simply being categorized as a "food animal" is sufficient to diminish an animal's moral standing.

The preceding discussion—in particular, that on categorization—has considered cognition about animals' minds and moral standing as a relatively cool, cognitive process. We can see that viewing an animal as mentally complex increases moral concern, whereas seeing it as food decreases concern. As we outline in the next two sections, however, motivation and emotion play an important role in determining which animals we consider worthy of concern, and when.

Motivational Influences on Animal Trait Perception

Moral judgments and decisions about animals do not take place in a cold, cognitive vacuum but are additionally influenced by people's motivations, particularly motivations to see oneself in a positive light (Piazza et al., 2015). We argue that people attribute and deny mind, humanity, and sometimes moral standing to animals when it is in their interests to do so.

Perhaps the clearest case of people being motivated to alter their perception of animals is when they inflict harm on them, whether directly or indirectly. Eating meat can be one such situation in which people are motivated to view animals as relatively lacking in mind and as possessing lesser moral standing. In a simple study, Loughnan, Haslam, and Bastian (2010) had participants eat either beef or cashew nuts and then report their moral concern for animals in general and cows in particular. Compared with people who ate nuts, people who ate beef reported more constricted moral concern for animals in general and lower moral status afforded to a cow. What might be

driving this effect? We know that people have a tendency to withdraw mind from people who are suffering (Kozak, Marsh, & Wegner, 2006), so perhaps the root lies in emphasizing the suffering caused by meat production. Evidence for this account comes from work showing that having people write about the origins of meat compared with the origins of vegetables causes them to deny animals more mind and feel emotionally better about meat consumption (Bastian, Loughnan, & Haslam, 2012). If it is the case that denying food animals minds makes people feel better, it is little stretch to conclude that they are motivated to view food animals as possessing lesser moral standing.

Just as reducing animals' minds can be beneficial to people, so too can increasing mind attribution. In the sociality, effectance, and elicited agent knowledge (SEEK) model of anthropomorphism, Epley, Waytz, and Cacioppo (2007) lay out a series of conditions that will increase the likelihood of attributing mind to animals. Two of these conditions hinge on human needs: the need to feel socially connected (sociality) and the need to understand the world (efficacy). For instance, we attribute more "uniquely human" traits to pet animals when we are lonely (Epley, Waytz, Akalis, & Cacioppo, 2008), and we attribute more mind to a dog when we need to understand its behavior (Epley et al., 2008). Where these increases in mind attribution transfer into increased moral concern waits to be seen.

Emotion

Animals evoke a range of emotions, from fear to compassion. Which emotions get evoked is primarily a function of the characteristics people attribute to animals and, once evoked, emotions guide our moral judgments and treatment of animals. Fear, disgust, sympathy, and tenderness are emotions in particular that appear to strongly influence the way we treat animals.

Fear, Disgust, and Sympathy

Research by Piazza et al. (2014) explored two attributional dimensions pertinent to the moral standing of animals: harmfulness and mind. Animals perceived as dangerous (e.g., spiders, snakes, wolves) tended to elicit fear and were judged to have lower levels of moral standing. By contrast, animals perceived as highly intelligent and emotional (e.g., dogs, dolphins, elephants) tended to elicit higher levels of sympathy (i.e., concern for their suffering) and were ascribed higher levels of moral standing.

Disgust is an emotion that is directly pertinent to the treatment of animals as a food source. For example, research by Ruby and Heine (2012) found that across cultures the appearance of an animal (whether it was seen as cute or ugly) was a strong predictor of whether an animal was seen as edible or disgusting. Intelligent animals are seen as less edible, on average, than less intelligent animals (Bastian et al., 2012), consistent with the findings by Piazza and Loughnan (2016) that intelligent animals tend to be afforded moral standing. However, intelligent animals are not always afforded moral standing. As suggested by a motivated cognition perspective (e.g., Dunning, 1999; Kunda, 1990), people tend to use intelligence information about animals in a manner that promotes their self-interested ends. Recent studies by the authors (Piazza & Loughnan, 2016) found that, all else equal, people think it is wrong to use intelligent animals as food; however, this is not the case when the animal is conventionally used for meat (see Figure 17.1). In a recent unpublished line of work, we had participants consider one of three animals: a fictitious, alien animal they had no exposure to; a tapir, an exotic animal that Westerners do not eat; and a pig, an animal commonly eaten in Western cultures. All participants received the same information about the intelligence of the animal; however, it was only for the pig that the information about the animal's intelligence was ignored when forming a moral judgment about the animal. Participants in the pig condition thought it was less wrong to use the animal as a food source, and they felt less guilt about doing so, compared with the other animal conditions.

Interestingly, the experience of sympathy toward highly intelligent animals is somewhat discrepant with the data for human targets. Research suggests that highly intelligent human targets are afforded respect, but not sympathy (Fiske, Cuddy, & Glick,

2007). One possible explanation for this disparity is that the relationship between sympathy and intelligence is curvilinear. It may be that human targets are ascribed more baseline intelligence than animal targets, so highly intelligent animals only begin to approach the levels of low intelligent humans (e.g., children). It may be that for sympathy to be evoked the animal must possess intelligence to a degree that approximates the lower end of the spectrum for humans. This hypothesis awaits empirical testing.

Tenderness

Tenderness is an emotion we feel in the presence of entities that possess neotenous, "cute," or baby-like features, for example, large head, protruding forehead, large eyes, chubby cheeks, and small nose and mouth (Sherman & Haidt, 2011). Such entities evoke nurturing responses. For example, human baby faces have been found to elicit care motivations and to activate reward regions of the brain (e.g., nucleus accumbens), particularly for women (Glocker et al., 2009; Sprengelmeyer, et al., 2009). The same goes for cute animals. When people view images of cute, young animals (e.g., puppies and kittens vs. dogs and cats), they exert more behavioral care, operationalized in terms of improved performance on a fine-motor task and reductions in grip strength (Sherman, Haidt, & Coan, 2009).

But does cuteness serve to foster moral attitudes toward animals? Sherman and Haidt (2011) have argued that cuteness fosters social engagement rather than care more specifically. They argue that cute entities become objects of moral concern by engaging positive social attention. Grauerholz (2007) argued that "cute" animal images are sometimes used to strategically advertise meat products in a way that enhances positive reactions from consumers by presenting a relatable image of the animal, thus dissociating animal suffering from the meat product. This raises the question of whether cuteness might motivate or demotivate meat consumption. On the one hand, cuteness might raise perceptions of moral standing, thus demotivating meat consumption. On the other hand, cuteness might make the animal less disgusting, motivating meat consumption.

A recent study by Piazza, McLatchie, Olesen, and Tomaszczuk (2016) found evidence that cuteness tends to increase an animal's moral standing. The authors presented participants with images of baby and adult farm animals (e.g., chicks/chickens, piglets/pigs) and made ratings of the animals in a between-subjects design. Baby animals were rated more cute and elicited tenderness more than adult animals, and they were also attributed greater moral standing, despite being perceived as no more intelligent. Furthermore, cuteness (which highly correlated with feelings of tenderness) and harmfulness independently predicted attributions of moral standing. From this research we see that cuteness is an important factor contributing to the moral standing of animals, orthogonal to harmfulness. However, this study did not test whether cuteness serves to motivate or demotivate meat consumption. Further studies by Piazza and Loughnan (2016) suggest that, at least for women, feeling tenderness for an animal temporarily suppresses appetite for meat. In one study, the authors had participants rate their appetite for a meat dish that was derived from an adult cow or calf, or no information about the animal source was given. Providing an image of the animal along with the meat reduced the meat's appeal, but the effect was largest when the animal was a baby, and reductions in appetite occurred only among female participants.

Moderators of Emotion

There are important moderators of the emotions people experience toward animals. Vegetarians and vegans have been shown to express greater empathy toward animals than omnivores (Preylo & Arikawa, 2008). They also exhibit greater activation of empathy-related brain regions when viewing images of animals suffering (Filippi et al., 2010). Individuals who had owned a pet as a child also exhibit greater empathy toward animals, and this empathy appears to predict meat avoidance practices in adulthood (Rothgerber & Mican, 2014). At the same time, not all individuals who empathize with animals adopt a vegetarian diet. This may be because high-empathy omnivores engage in "look the other way" strategies to avoid feeling sympathy for animals used as food (Rothgerber, 2014). This process may be similar to the way people seek to avoid feeling empathy toward human victims because of the behavioral implications such feelings entail (Shaw, Batson, & Todd, 1994).

Emotion Regulation

Very little is known about how people regulate the emotions they feel toward animals, or the guilt they might experience as a conflicted omnivore. Research on emotion regulation suggests reappraisal is an important process (Gross & Johns, 2003). Rationalization is one form of reappraisal. Rationalization involves generating reasons for one's behavior when it is called into question by others (Haidt, 2001; Mercier, 2011). These reasons do not have to be thought out ahead of time; they can simply be generated on the spot. At least one study has shown rationalization to be an effective strategy for omnivores. Piazza et al. (2015, Study 4) found that omnivores who highly endorsed various "4N" justifications for eating meat (that it is Necessary, Natural, Normal, and Nice to eat meat) tended to experience less guilt about their animal-product consumption than omnivores who were less persuaded by these justifications. Thus rationalization may be an important mechanism for regulating guilt toward animal suffering.

Identity

Much of the research on morality and animals has focused on the animal; how people think and feel about the animal will influence how much they care about it. The preceding discussion of emotion regulation hints at the important additional factor of how people think and feel about *themselves*. People's interactions with animals will shape how they see themselves, allowing them to maintain and enjoy important aspects of their identities. Indeed, people appear to believe that animals can directly contribute to their identity. Eating aggressive animals makes some people think they will become more aggressive, effectively ingesting not only the meat but the mentality of the beast (Rozin & Nemeroff, 1990). More broadly—and less literally—eating animals has implications for our identities, challenging some and bolstering others.

Recent perspectives in moral psychology suggest that the morality of others can sometimes serve as a threat to one's own moral identity (Minson & Monin, 2012; Monin, Sawyer, & Marquez, 2008). The reason is that moral positions have normative force, that is, they are thought to apply to everyone, not just the individuals who profess them. Thus the moral action of one individual (or group of individuals) can be interpreted as a tacit condemnation of those individuals who fail to do likewise.

In the domain of animals, this tacit moral condemnation can be observed most clearly in the reactions of omnivores toward the "moral" motivations of vegetarians and vegans. Morally motivated vegetarians can pose an implicit (and at times explicit) reproach to omnivores. One response to this reproach is to engage in explicit meat-eating justifications (Piazza et al., 2015); another response is to openly derogate ethical vegetarians as self-righteous or misguided—for example, by questioning whether food animals actually suffer as vegetarians claim they do (Rothgerber, 2014).

Is there evidence to support the idea that omnivores feel morally threatened by ethical vegetarians? A study by Minson and Monin (2012) showed that omnivores were more hostile toward vegetarians when they thought that vegetarians perceived their own group as morally superior to meat eaters. More direct evidence comes from a recent study conducted by one of the authors (Piazza & Loughnan, 2016) with a sample of American omnivores and meat abstainers. In this study omnivores rated vegetarians as significantly more self-righteous than meat abstainers, consistent with the idea that vegetarians pose a particular kind of symbolic threat to omnivores—one in which omnivores perceive vegetarians as claiming a moral high ground with regards to their eating habits.

A motivational approach would predict that omnivores become more hostile toward vegetarians insofar as vegetarians are perceived to pose a threat to their moral identity. One way vegetarians might pose such a threat is by growing in numbers. The more prevalent ethical vegetarians become, it would seem, the more valid their moral position becomes, which we would expect to be threatening to omnivores, who at least in the United States currently outnumber vegetarians and vegans 20:1 (Ruby, 2012). Indeed, a recent correlational study by Piazza and colleagues (2016) found exactly the pattern of relationships we might expect if ethical vegetarians pose a moral identity threat to omnivores. Participants rated the prevalence of various groups (among them meat eaters, semivegetarians, strict vegetarians, and vegans), and responded to a multi-item measure of vegan-directed prejudice (e.g., "I would be uncomfortable with a strict vegetarian or vegan teaching my child"). In line with predictions, prejudice toward vegans increased as vegans were perceived to be increasingly prevalent in American society. Conversely, prejudice toward vegans *decreased* as meat eaters were perceived to be increasingly prevalent in society.

In short, seeing others as treating animals more morally than oneself appears to raise concerns about one's moral identity. These concerns with seeing the self as moral can manifest in a range of ways, including derogation of animals and of other people.

Empirical Challenges

One of the central ideas motivating our perspective is that people avoid harming animals or recognizing that they harm animals because doing so would make them feel bad about themselves. Although there is some evidence that denying meat animals minds reduces negative affect (Bastian et al., 2012) and that people imagine harming intelligent animals will make people feel bad (Piazza & Loughnan, 2016), at present the argument remains speculative. Do people feel that their moral self or moral identity is undermined when they are reminded how their behavior harms animals? Alternatively, does reminding people that they contribute to the suffering of animals temporarily undermine their moral self, motivating them to seek out ways of restoring their moral credibility? In short, is our treatment of animals meaningfully tied to our sense of ourselves as moral people? It may be that challenges to the moral self is a point which underlies many of the effects when it comes to thinking morally about animals. To the extent that people feel secure or insecure in their own moral identity, they may think differently about animals. If such an account were true, thinking morally about animals would be inexorably tied to thinking morally about the self.

The study of how people think morally about animals is still relatively young. At present, we feel the effects identified in this domain are somewhat decomposed (see Figure 17.1). We know, for instance, that categorization changes judgments of moral concern and that cuteness increases moral concern. What happens when a cute animal is categorized as food? We know that seeing an animal as more intelligent increases our concern for its well-being, and that seeing an animal as similar to humans increases our concern for its well-being. What happens when an animal looks a lot like a human but is unintelligent or dangerous? What about when it looks, acts, and interacts in a very different way to humans but is highly intelligent? Put simply, it may be that some of these effects more powerfully determine our moral concern than others. To investigate this possibility, rather than seeking new effects, future research could compare and contrast these identified effects, finding the prime movers of our concern for animal welfare. If our ultimate aim were to increase people's concern for animals, it is important to know the major determinants of thinking morally about animals.

Extension and Expansion

We see the study of animals and morality as an important, real-world domain of human morality. There are two potential applications of this work. The first would be to find ways of increasing moral concern for animals. Animal rights organizations are heavily investing in increasing public concern for animals, be they wildlife or farm animals. Understanding how presenting, categorizing, and attributing mind to animals can increase concern and how this interacts with the way people see themselves are important areas of research which can be employed in this domain. To take a concrete example, if eating animals is a threat to moral identity,

animal rights organizations may look to find ways of affirming the identity benefits of adopting a reduced- or no-meat diet. The second application would be the diabolic opposite: identifying ways to decrease moral concern for animals used for profit or whose welfare poses a hurdle to economic interest.

This chapter opened with the observation that animals exist in the gray area between humans and objects, at the margins of our moral concern. Other entities reside here as well: fetuses, people in comas, violent criminals, homeless people (Gray et al., 2007). For some people, these entities are clearly within our scope of moral concern; for other people, they are beyond the boundary of entities we need to care about. Perhaps, most importantly, we have shown how moral concern for animals is a profoundly malleable process; whether a given animal is offered moral standing depends on a number of motivational factors, chief among them whether the animal's suffering has direct implications for the actor's own moral identity. By delving deeply into the specific domain of animals and morality we have shown how a nuanced picture can be painted of human morality, and how this can have practical implications. Similarly, other cases at the margins of moral concern may benefit from this treatment.

Animals are an important part of our moral world. Our attitudes range from loving them like family members to mass slaughter and extinction. We feel that this is a field in which the psychology of morality can explain commonplace moral behavior. To add to Levi-Strauss, animals are not only good to think about, but good to think about morally.

REFERENCES

Amiot, C. E., & Bastian, B. (2015). Toward a psychology of human–animal relations. *Psychological Bulletin, 141,* 6–47.

Barsalou, L. W. (1990). Access and inference in categorization. *Bulletin of the Psychonomic Society, 28,* 268–271.

Bastian, B., Loughnan, S., Haslam, N., & Radke, H. R. M. (2012). Don't mind meat?: The denial of mind to animals used for human consumption. *Personality and Social Psychology Bulletin, 38,* 247–256.

Bilewicz, M., Imhoff, R., & Drogosz, M. (2011).

The humanity of what we eat: Conceptions of human uniqueness among vegetarians and omnivores. *European Journal of Social Psychology, 41*, 201–209.

Bratanova, B., Loughnan, S., & Bastian, B. (2011). The effect of categorization as food on the perceived moral standing of animals. *Appetite, 57*, 193–196.

Dunning, D. (1999). A newer look: Motivated social cognition and the schematic representation of social concepts. *Psychological Inquiry, 10*, 1–11.

Epley, N., Waytz, A., Akalis, S., & Cacioppo, J. T. (2008). When we need a human: Motivational determinants of anthropomorphism. *Social Cognition, 26*(2), 143–155.

Epley, N., Waytz, A., & Cacioppo, J. T. (2007). On seeing human: A three-factor theory of anthropomorphism. *Psychological Review, 114*, 864–886.

Festinger, L. A. (1957). *A theory of cognitive dissonance*. Stanford, CA: Stanford University Press.

Filippi, M., Riccitelli, G., Falini, A., Di Salle, F., Vuilleumier, P., Comi, G., & Rocca, M. A. (2010). The brain functional networks associates to human and animal suffering differ among omnivores, vegetarians and vegans. *PLOS ONE, 5*(5), e10847.

Fiske, S. T., Cuddy, A. J. C., & Glick, P. (2007). Universal dimensions of social cognition: Warmth and competence. *Trends in Cognitive Sciences, 11*, 77–83.

Fiske, S. T., Cuddy, A., Glick, P., & Xu, J. (2002). A model of (often mixed) stereotype content: Competence and warmth respectively follow from perceived status and competition. *Journal of Personality and Social Psychology, 82*, 878–902

Glocker, M. L., Langleben, D. D., Ruparel, K., Loughead, J. W., Gur, R. C., & Sachser, N. (2009). Baby schema in infant faces induces cuteness perception and motivation for caretaking in adults. *Ethology, 115*(3), 257–263.

Grauerholz, L. (2007). Cute enough to eat: The transformation of animals into meat for human consumption in commercialized images. *Humanity and Society, 31*, 334–354.

Gray, H., Gray, K., & Wegner, D. (2007). Dimensions of mind perception. *Science, 619*, 315.

Gray, K., Knobe, J., Sheskin, M., Bloom, P., & Feldman-Barrett, L. F. (2011). More than a body: Mind perception and the nature of objectification. *Journal of Personality and Social Psychology, 101*, 1207–1220.

Gross, J. J., & John, O. P. (2003). Individual differences in two emotion regulation processes: Implications for affect, relationships, and well-being. *Journal of Personality and Social Psychology, 85*(2), 348–362.

Haidt, J. (2001). The emotional dog and its rational tail: A social intuitionist approach to moral judgment. *Psychological Review, 108*, 814–834.

Haslam, N., Kashima, Y., Loughnan, S., Shi, J., & Suitner, C. (2008). Subhuman, inhuman, and superhuman: Contrasting humans with nonhumans in three cultures. *Social Cognition, 26*(2), 248–258.

Kozak, M., Marsh, A., & Wegner, D. (2006). What do I think you're doing?: Action identification and mind attribution. *Journal of Personality and Social Psychology, 90*, 543–555.

Kunda, Z. (1990). The case for motivated reasoning. *Psychological Bulletin, 108*, 480–498.

Levi-Strauss, C. (1962). *The savage mind*. Paris: Librairie Plon.

Loughnan, S., Haslam, N., & Bastian, B. (2010). The role of meat consumption in the denial of moral status and mind to meat animals. *Appetite, 55*, 156–159.

Loughnan, S., Haslam, N., Murnane, T., Vaes, J., Reynolds, C., & Suitner, C. (2010). Objectification leads to depersonalization: The denial of mind and moral concern to objectified others. *European Journal of Social Psychology, 40*, 709–717.

Mercier, H. (2011). What good is moral reasoning? *Mind and Society, 10*(2), 131–148.

Minson, J. A., & Monin, B. (2012). Do-gooder derogation: Disparaging morally motivated minorities to defuse anticipated reproach. *Social Psychological and Personality Science, 3*(2), 200–207.

Monin, B., Sawyer, P. J., & Marquez, M. J. (2008). The rejection of moral rebels: Resenting those who do the right thing. *Journal of Personality and Social Psychology, 95*(1), 76–93.

Piazza, J., Landy, J. F., & Goodwin, G. P. (2014). Cruel nature: Harmfulness as an important, overlooked dimension in judgments of moral standing. *Cognition, 131*, 108–124.

Piazza, J., & Loughnan., S. (2016). When meat gets personal, animals' minds matter less: Motivated use of intelligence information in judgments of moral standing. *Social Psychological and Personality Science, 7*, 867–874.

Piazza, J., McLatchie, N., Olesen, C., & Tomaszczuk, M. (2016). [*Cuteness promotes moral standing and reduces appetite for meat among women*]. Unpublished raw data.

Piazza, J., Ruby, M. B., Loughnan, S., Luong, M., Kulik, J., Watkins, H. M., & Seigerman, M. (2015). Rationalizing meat consumption: The 4Ns. *Appetite, 91*, 114–128.

Plous, S. (1993). Psychological mechanisms in the human use of animals. *Journal of Social Issues, 49*, 11–52.

Preylo, B. D., & Arikawa, H. (2008). Comparison of vegetarians and non-vegetarians on pet attitude and empathy. *Anthrozoös, 21*(4), 387–395.

Rothgerber, H. (2014). Efforts to overcome vegetarian-induced dissonance among meat eaters. *Appetite, 79*, 32–41.

Rothgerber, H., & Mican, F. (2014). Childhood pet ownership, attachment to pets, and subsequent meat avoidance: The mediating role of empathy toward animals. *Appetite, 79*, 11–17.

Rozin, P. (2006). Domain denigration and process preference in academic psychology. *Perspectives on Psychological Science, 1*, 365–376.

Rozin, P., & Nemeroff, C. J. (1990). The laws of sympathetic magic: A psychological analysis of similarity and contagion. In J. Stigler, R. A. Shweder, & G. Herdt (Eds.), *Cultural psychology: Essays on comparative human development* (pp. 205–232). Cambridge, UK: Cambridge University Press.

Ruby, M. B. (2012). Vegetarianism: A blossoming field of study. *Appetite, 58*, 141–150.

Ruby, M. B., & Heine, S. (2012). Too close to home: Factors predicting meat avoidance. *Appetite, 59*, 47–52.

Shaw, L. L., Batson, C. D., & Todd, R. M. (1994). Empathy avoidance: Forestalling feeling for another in order to escape the motivational consequences. *Journal of Personality and Social Psychology, 67*(5), 879–887.

Sherman, G. D., & Haidt, J. (2011). Cuteness and disgust: The humanizing and dehumanizing effects of emotion. *Emotion Review, 3*(3), 1–7.

Sherman, G. D., Haidt, J., & Coan, J. A. (2009). Viewing cute images increases behavioral carefulness. *Emotion, 9*(2), 282–286.

Sprengelmeyer, R., Perrett, D. I., Fagan, E. C., Cornwell, R. E., Lobmaier, J. S., Sprengelmeyer, A., . . . Young, A. W. (2009). The cutest little baby face: A hormonal link to sensitivity to cuteness in infant faces. *Psychological Science, 20*(2), 149–154.

Sytsma, J., & Machery, E. (2012). Two sources of moral standing. *Review of Philosophy and Psychology, 3*, 303–324.

Waytz, A., Gray, K., Epley, N., & Wegner, D. M. (2010). Causes and consequences of mind perception. *Trends in Cognitive Sciences, 14*, 383–388.

PART IV
MORALITY AND INTERGROUP CONFLICT

QUESTIONS ANSWERED IN PART IV

CHAPTER 18 Why did moral judgment evolve?

CHAPTER 19 Do people deploy the same moral cognition
across social contexts, or are there critical cleavages within moral cognition?

CHAPTER 20 If humans are innately good, cooperative, fair, and averse
to harming one another, why does widespread intergroup violence continue
to afflict society?

CHAPTER 21 If some stereotypes seem to be universal,
are they necessarily immoral?

CHAPTER 18

Morality Is for Choosing Sides

Peter DeScioli
Robert Kurzban

Why did moral judgment evolve?

To help people choose sides when conflicts erupt within groups with complex coalitions and power hierarchies.

Theories of morality have largely tried to explain the brighter side of behavior, answering questions about why people behave in ways that are kind, generous, and good. Our proposal focuses not on explaining moral behavior but, rather, on explaining moral judgment. Consider someone reading a news story about a man who pays a woman to have sex with him. Many people would judge—in an intuitive way (Haidt, 2012)—that both the man's and woman's actions are morally wrong. Our interest lies in the explanation for these and similar judgments.

Theories that attempt to explain moral behavior often point to altruism or benefits (de Waal, 1996; Krebs, 2005; Ridley, 1996; Wright, 1994). The theory of reciprocal altruism (Trivers, 1971), for instance, explains why people enter into voluntary exchanges with one another: to reap the benefits of trade. Such theoretical moves are considerably less straightforward for explaining moral judgment. For example, condemning the exchange of sex for money does not transparently confer benefits to the condemner.

What, then, might be the benefits gained through moral judgments? Consider a situation in which a person accuses someone of witchcraft, such as in Arthur Miller's *The Crucible*. Specifically, suppose that a young, low-status woman accuses an older, more prominent woman of witchcraft. Other members of the community can respond in a few different ways.

One obvious move for a self-interested observer is to curry favor with the higher-status woman. Choosing sides based on status often occurs in very hierarchical groups such as the military (Fiske, 1992). It is also observed in nonhuman animals: For instance, hyenas join fights and support the higher-status and more formidable fighter (Holekamp, Sakai, & Lundrigan, 2007). This strategy has a downside: It empowers high-status individuals to win all of their conflicts and hence gives them an incentive to exploit other people; they essentially become dictators (Boehm, 1999). Even so, individuals can benefit by siding with dictators because they avoid making powerful enemies. However, humans often do the opposite, siding with the lower-status accuser, as in the hypothetical (and actual) witchcraft case. When might siding with the lower-status accuser be an advantage?

A second strategy for choosing sides is based on relationships: Support closer family or friends, even if they are lower status. Individuals can gain by supporting allies if those allies in turn support them in the future. But alliances have a downside too: If each disputant has a cohort of close friends, then the dispute will expand to include more people on each side and could be even more costly to both the original disputants and their supporters. Research shows that alliances can be extremely damaging at every scale of conflict, from personal to international disputes (Snyder, 1984, 1997; Cooney, 1998, 2003).

Although humans often support their friends and family in conflicts, they do not always do so. This was the case in *The Crucible* and in numerous real-world witchcraft accusations. Many societies judge black magic to be so morally wrong that it gives cause to abandon one's closest friends and even to seek their death. Executions for witchcraft continue in modern times. In India, for instance, the National Crime Records Bureau documented 2,097 murders of accused witches between 2000 and 2012, despite new laws prohibiting witch hunts (Kapoor, 2015). Around the world, similarly fatal judgments regularly occur for premarital sex, homosexuality, blasphemy, and other harmless offenses that are punishable by death in some societies (Appiah, 2010; Levy, 1993; Sarhan & Burke, 2009; United Nations Commission on Human Rights, 2000). How could it be advantageous to turn against someone, even family and friends, merely because they have (allegedly) done something deemed morally wrong by the community?

We have proposed (DeScioli & Kurzban, 2013) that the benefit of siding with moralistic accusers occurs when *other third parties to the conflict do so as well*. Moral judgment functions as a side-taking strategy and provides an alternative strategy to choosing sides based on status or relationships. Moral side-takers choose sides based on actions. They oppose the disputant who has taken the more morally wrong action—whether prostitution, witchcraft, homicide, or blasphemy—as established by previous moral debates in the community.

The moral side-taking strategy avoids two key problems with choosing sides based on status and alliances. First, observers do not empower dictators because they do not always side with the same people. Second, they do not create escalating and expanding alliances because observers all choose the same side, provided they use the same moral rules. Moral judgment allows observers to *dynamically coordinate* their side-taking choices in the sense that they all take the same side, but they can also dynamically change whom they support based on the actions each party has taken. Notice that moral side-taking is effective at coordination only when everyone agrees, or at least acknowledges, what counts as a morally wrong action.

Hence, moral judgment adds to the human repertoire of strategies for managing other people's conflicts. It does not entirely displace bandwagon or alliance strategies because choosing sides is a coordination game, and coordination games have multiple equilibria (Schelling, 1960). But morality does explain why people sometimes oppose powerful people and close friends—because morality is designed for exactly this purpose, so as to avoid the costs of those strategies.

The side-taking theory explains why moral condemnation can be so destructive. Moral condemnation causes great harm to alleged wrongdoers for harmless or beneficial behaviors, including witchcraft, premarital sex, homosexuality, interest-bearing loans, and scientific research. Popular theories of morality based on cooperation (de Waal, 1996; Krebs, 2005; Ridley, 1996; Wright, 1994) predict that moral judgment will generally maximize welfare, but instead many humans seek prison or death for harmless offenses. In contrast, the side-taking theory is consistent with this destructive behavior because moral judgment functions not to promote welfare but to synchronize side-taking, even if doing so harms many others.

This view of moral judgment explains another important moral phenomenon: people's decisions to comply with moral rules even when breaking the rules benefits them. In a social world in which the community gangs up against wrongdoers, it is costly to engage in prohibited actions. The side-taking hypothesis therefore simultaneously accounts for condemnation as well as *conscience*, psychological mechanisms designed to inhibit actions deemed wrong by the local community.

The side-taking theory explains why people's moralistic punishments are aimed at retribution rather than deterrence, as documented by moral psychology (Carlsmith, Darley, & Robinson, 2002). Theories based on cooperation straightforwardly predict that moralistic punishment will aim at deterring harmful behavior. Instead, people seek retribution for wrongdoers independent of the potential for punishment to deter future violations. The side-taking account holds that an observer's retributive motives are designed to direct their aggression toward the weaker side of a dispute in order to convincingly join the stronger side, where the stronger side in this case means the side with the moral high ground and hence the majority of supporters. Moralistic punishment is retributive because it is designed for side-taking rather than deterring harm.

The side-taking theory also explains why moral judgment includes an ideal of impartiality. Although people's judgments are, in fact, often biased and partial, people at the same time advocate an ideal of impartiality, especially for their opponent's judgments. The side-taking hypothesis holds that the ideal of impartiality functions to decouple moral side-taking from alliances, ultimately to avoid the costs of escalating alliances in disputes.

Finally, this theory illuminates variation in moral rules across individuals and groups. If the dynamic coordination view is correct, then many different moral rules could serve the function of synchronizing side-taking, as long as the local community agrees on the rules. Different societies have different types of conflicts, and people mint new moral rules to cover them. Further, individuals can differ in how they are personally affected by particular rules. For instance, people who pursue short-term mating are worse off when promiscuity is moralized and punished (Kurzban, Dukes, & Weeden, 2010; Weeden, 2003). Other people who pursue long-term mating might benefit from moralizing promiscuity in the interest of guarding their mates. These differences in incentives explain why people differ and disagree about moral rules (DeScioli, Massenkoff, Shaw, Petersen, & Kurzban, 2014; Kurzban et al., 2010; Robinson & Kurzban, 2007).

Historical Context

The historical context for the side-taking theory includes two parallel but mostly separate research strands: moral psychology and evolutionary theories of morality.

Research in moral psychology has focused on proximate psychological questions. Studies typically examine people's moral judgments about someone's actions (or inactions) in controlled vignettes. Researchers tend to examine issues such as selfish motives versus the greater good, compliance with moral rules when anonymous, intentional versus accidental violations, taboo trade-offs between wrongful actions and overall welfare, and the desire to punish wrongdoers (reviewed in Haidt, 2012).

This research tradition in moral psychology has been largely silent about the evolutionary functions that explain why humans make moral judgments at all. Many researchers either do not address the evolved functions of moral judgment or refer to generic and vague functions, such as the folk wisdom that morality holds society together.

In parallel, evolutionary scholars have viewed morality through the lens of altruism. Starting with Darwin (1871), this was primarily a theoretical problem, asking how natural selection could favor altruistic behavior. Researchers developed models to show how cooperation can evolve, including the conditions and abilities it requires. This work yielded an impressive array of theories, including kin selection, reciprocity, partner choice, and costly signaling. Evolutionary researchers tested these models in thousands of empirical studies, often on nonhuman animals, and many models have extremely impressive empirical support.

However, very little work in the evolutionary tradition measures, or even engages with, moral judgment. Researchers with an evolutionary perspective have largely assumed that cooperation and morality are the same thing (e.g., de Waal, 1996; Krebs,

2005; Ridley, 1996; Wright, 1994). Hence there is a stark divide between moral psychology, which has proceeded with relatively little theory, and evolutionary accounts of morality, largely uninformed by empirical findings from moral psychology.

Haidt (2007, 2012) began to fuse these two research traditions. He combined moral psychology, cross-cultural research, and evolutionary theories to create a set of fundamental moral foundations, each grounded by different evolutionary models—kin selection, reciprocity, group cooperation, dominance hierarchies, and pathogen avoidance. The result was an impressive overarching theory that had strong appeal both for moral psychologists and for evolutionary researchers.

Haidt's moral foundations theory is an impressive attempt to reconcile moral psychology with evolution. However, the account misses distinctive elements of human morality. The evolutionary ideas that animate moral foundations theory apply to many different animal species, but moral judgment is an extreme and unusual—possibly unique—human trait, analogous to an elephant's trunk. If researchers applied only broad theories about animal noses to understand an elephant's trunk, they would be missing the trunk's unique grasping and communication abilities.

The theories underlying the moral foundations explain why people show behaviors such as parental care, trade, and dominance. But they do not explain why people make *moral judgments* about these behaviors. To return to the opening example, reciprocity theory does not explain why people morally judge the act of exchanging sex for money, especially because prostitution is an exchange. Similarly, none of the foundations explain why moral judgment focuses particularly on actions and differs in this respect from people's decisions about welfare, precautions, economics, and conventions. Traditional evolutionary models predict consequentialist rather than deontological mechanisms (DeScioli & Kurzban, 2009a). Last, traditional evolutionary models do not explain why people disagree about morality and why they debate the moral rules in their community.

The side-taking theory develops additional game-theoretic tools to understand what is distinctive about human moral judgment. Rather than using previous evolutionary models, it develops a new model based on side-taking games to explain the unique human behaviors revealed by moral psychology. It addresses why humans assign moral values to actions, announce moral judgments to other individuals, debate moral rules, and show aggression toward wrongdoers. It provides an explanation for why moral judgment is deontological rather than consequentialist, why punishment is aimed at retribution rather than deterrence, why judgments are held to an ideal of impartiality, and why moral rules vary over time and across cultures. We propose that these moral phenomena result from an evolved strategy for choosing sides in disputes. As such, moral judgment is part of a larger repertoire of adaptations for managing one's own and others' conflicts, including the cognitive abilities to assess an opponent's fighting power, recognize property conventions, and form alliances (DeScioli & Karpoff, 2015; DeScioli, Karpoff, & De Freitas, 2017; DeScioli & Kurzban, 2009b; DeScioli, Rosa, & Gutchess, 2015; DeScioli & Wilson, 2011).

Theoretical Stance

The side-taking theory differs from other theories in how it treats some debates in the literature and, more important, in the functions it proposes for moral mechanisms.

First, on the perennial issue of whether morality is universal or culturally relative, some scholars assume that an evolutionary basis for morality implies that humans will have a small set of universal moral rules and, further, that cultural variation undermines evolutionary accounts (e.g., Prinz, 2007). The side-taking theory, in contrast, holds that humans possess the evolved ability to create and learn new moral rules so that they can be tailored to new types of conflict. As a result, moral cognition is, in itself, universal, while at the same time moral rules differ across groups and within groups over time. Some rules are more stable than others because they tend to be supported by majorities, such as rules against lying, stealing, and killing, whereas other rules are more variable because they receive mixed support, such as rules about promiscuity and drug use.

Second, there is a related issue about whether morality is innate or learned. We take the position that learning cannot occur without innate mechanisms specialized for learning in that domain (Pinker, 1989), so the usual dichotomy is misleading. The side-taking theory holds that moral cognition includes mechanisms for learning the active moral rules in the social environment, including different rules for different subgroups and types of interactions. It further holds that people do not only passively internalize the group's rules but rather, they actively advocate for self-serving rules and readily violate rules when they can get away with it.

Third, there is a debate about whether moral judgment is intuitive or deliberative. The side-taking theory holds that moral judgment is largely unconscious, like many complex cognitive processes. However, a critical part of its function is to persuade other people to take the same side. For this purpose, people have the ability to formulate their moral judgments into language so they can be announced to others. Moreover, people can simulate moral debates in their private thoughts in order to build more convincing moral arguments. These communicative elements explain why moral judgment has a deliberative component.

Fourth, there is a question about whether moral judgment is a single process or multiple processes (DeScioli & Kurzban, 2009a; DeScioli, Asao, & Kurzban, 2012). We first note that every major cognitive ability includes a large number of processes, just as any software application does. The real question is whether moral judgment's many processes are unified by an overarching function, just as word processing or e-mail applications have overarching functions. The side-taking theory holds that moral judgment is indeed unified in this sense because it is structured by the primary function of choosing sides in disputes. In order to perform this function, moral cognition interacts with a wide array of mechanisms specialized for different areas of social life, including mechanisms for processing kin relations, reciprocity, property, hierarchy, and coalitions. This is, again, analogous to the complex interactions of apps for e-mail, photos, and social networks on modern phones. Nevertheless, moral cognition is a distinct and unified program organized around the problem of choosing sides.

Last, the side-taking theory differs in the functions it proposes for moral cognition. Broadly, the primary function of moral judgment is not to guide one's own behavior (conscience) but to judge other people's behavior (condemnation). The conscience component of moral judgment is essentially defensive. People morally evaluate their own potential actions in order to avoid other people's condemnation. Because conscience functions to simulate and avoid condemnation, the structure of moral judgment is best understood from the condemner's perspective. Condemners face the problem of choosing sides and doing so in a landscape of prior loyalties and status hierarchies. The side-taking theory uses this adaptive problem to understand how moral judgment works, differing from cooperation theories that view morality as designed to motivate good behavior.

Evidence

There is, of course, a tremendous amount of evidence about how moral judgments operate. We focus on a few patterns of evidence that we think are crucial for inferring the functions of moral judgment. First and foremost, we think any theory of morality must explain why moral judgment focuses on the actions people choose rather than only on the consequences they intend.

In moral philosophy, *consequentialism* is the idea that the morality of an act depends *only* on the consequences of the act (Sinnott-Armstrong, 2006). In contrast, deontological theories are *nonconsequentialist* because they also consider the category of the action, such as lying or stealing, independent of the intended consequences. This allows deontological philosophers such as

Kant to conclude, for example, that lying is morally wrong even if it can save lives (Kant, 1785/1993).

Many experiments in moral psychology show deontological patterns in people's moral judgments. A well-known example is the finding that most people think it is immoral to push one person off of a footbridge in order to save five people from being killed by a runaway trolley. In this case, people judge the action of killing to be morally wrong, even if leads to better consequences (fewer deaths). In an interesting contrast, however, most people think it is permissible to switch the trolley to a side track, where it will kill one person, to save the five people on the main track. These results, and many others like them (Baron, 1994; Baron & Spranca, 1997; De Freitas, DeScioli, Nemirow, Massenkoff, & Pinker, in press; DeScioli, Bruening, & Kurzban, 2011; DeScioli, Christner, & Kurzban, 2011; Kurzban et al., 2012; Mikhail, 2007; Tetlock, 2003; Waldmann & Dieterich, 2007), illustrate that people's evaluations of the wrongness of actions depends on the details of the actions themselves, as opposed to the intended outcomes (which are the same in both the footbridge and switch cases).

This basic observation is not predicted by many prominent theories of morality. We take a moment to come at this problem obliquely because it is easy to overlook. Consider a different context—parental care. Kin selection theory explains why some organisms are designed to provide resources to offspring and also explains how parents make trade-offs when allocating resources across multiple offspring (Hamilton, 1964; Trivers, 1974). Now imagine that researchers observed a species of bird in which mothers sometimes eject eggs from the nest. The researchers propose that this ejection behavior maximizes inclusive fitness by optimally allocating resources to higher quality eggs while ejecting lower quality eggs.

Notice first that this is a specific consequentialist function: Mothers maximize a consequence: inclusive fitness. This makes sense because natural selection is a process driven by consequences, and organisms are usually consequentialist—most animals do not shy from killing, lying, stealing, infanticide, siblicide, or cannibalism when they can

maximize fitness by doing so (e.g., Mock, 2004).

The allocation hypothesis for ejection makes specific predictions tied to its proposed function. A mother bird's ejection behavior should be sensitive to factors that affect costs and benefits, such as the number of other eggs, the scarcity of food in the environment, the risk of predation, or the age and reproductive potential of the mother.

What if, instead, researchers observed that a mother's ejections depended primarily on the egg's color, independent of its quality or the number of other eggs? This observation would constitute an anomaly left unexplained by the theory. If it was found repeatedly, over and over, that the color of the eggs overrides the cost–benefit calculus of kin selection, then the parental allocation hypothesis would be called into question.

Recognizing the theory's failure, researchers might look further and find that this bird species is parasitized by cuckoo eggs that tend to differ in color (Brooke & Davies, 1988). Suppose it turns out that the mother's ejection behavior is not designed to optimally distribute resources among her offspring but rather to remove cuckoo parasites. In this case, the theory's empirical failure would allow researchers to discover an altogether different type of explanation.

Now consider a theory of morality that proposes that moral judgments are designed to improve the overall welfare of families, friends, or groups (de Waal, 1996; Krebs, 2005; Ridley, 1996; Wright, 1994). Such theories predict that people should condemn and desire to punish acts *depending on the welfare consequences*. In particular, people should condemn acts that lead to aggregate fitness losses and not condemn acts that lead to fitness gains. The *way* in which these gains and losses are realized—analogous to the color of the eggs—should be irrelevant. Evidence that people's moral judgments closely track the way gains are produced, the particular actions taken, the means by which goals are sought, is evidence against the welfare-improvement theory. Even worse for the theory is the condemnation of actions that produce obvious and large welfare gains. If moral judgment were for improving welfare, pushing the man off of the footbridge should be praiseworthy, not blameworthy.

Arguably still worse for altruism theories are moral rules that guarantee welfare losses. Across cultures, moral rules prohibit any number of victimless, mutually profitable transactions. Historically, an obvious example is the prohibition against charging interest, which prevents mutually profitable loans. In India, the prohibition against killing cows has long caused substantial harms (Suri, 2015). Any number of similar rules continue to undermine potential welfare gains.

We suggest that the tremendous array of data showing that people's judgments are deontological, along with the ubiquity of welfare-destroying moral rules, all constitute serious evidence against welfare-based theories of morality.

The side-taking hypothesis does not run afoul of these problems. This theory requires that a rule is known and that its violation can be recognized by observers; because rules are for *coordinated side-taking* rather than *welfare-enhancement,* they can include a wide range of contents, including welfare-destroying contents. In short, deontological judgment is a set of observations that is, we think, fatal for welfare theories but consistent with the side-taking theory.

There are several other areas of active research that provide evidence relevant to the side-taking hypothesis. First, research has found that people's tendency to moralize an issue depends on their power and alliances (Jensen & Petersen, 2011; Petersen, 2013). This evidence supports the idea that moral judgement is a strategy that people selectively deploy depending on whether they are most advantaged when others choose sides according to moral judgment, power, or alliances. Second, the side-taking theory points to *impartiality* as a core feature of moral judgment because it is designed as an alternative to partial alliances. Recent work on fairness judgments points to a similar role for impartiality in suppressing alliances in the context of allocating resources (Shaw, 2013). Third, the side-taking hypothesis emphasizes variability in moral rules and also people's debates and arguments about which moral rules will structure side-taking in their community. Consistent with this idea, research shows that people actively advocate for the moral rules that most advantage them over other people (Aarøe & Petersen, 2013; DeScioli et al., 2014; Kurzban et al., 2010; Petersen, Aarøe, Jensen, & Curry, 2014; Tybur, Lieberman, Kurzban, & DeScioli, 2013).

Extension and Expansion

One area for expansion is investigating how people decide whether to enter conflicts and which side-taking strategy to use if they do so. The dynamic coordination hypothesis proposes that morality is designed around the problem of taking sides in disputes, but it does not require that people always use moral judgment to choose sides. In some situations, one might choose to side with, for example, one's close relative or ally or with the higher-status individual. The best strategy depends on the details of the situation. We predict that people will use moral judgment to choose sides as a function of features of the situation, such as the magnitude of the moral violation, the relative status of the individuals involved, the number of observers to the actions, and other elements that affect an individual's costs and benefits in the side-taking game.

The side-taking proposal also raises the question of why observers do not always sit out of disputes to avoid any fighting costs to themselves. Indeed, if there were no social costs to sitting out, then the dynamic coordination hypothesis would be contradicted, because players would not have an incentive to choose sides in the first place. However, we suspect that sitting out is often costly and damages preexisting relationships, especially when conflicts include one's friends and allies. One goal for future research is to measure the damage to relationships caused by sitting out of conflicts when one's friends and allies are involved. Insofar as one of the functions of friendship is to cultivate allies when disputes arise (DeScioli, Kurzban, Koch, & Liben-Nowell, 2011; DeScioli & Kurzban, 2009b; DeScioli & Kurzban, 2011), we suspect that failing to come to a friend's aid in conflicts will indeed damage these relationships, possibly to the same degree as siding against one's friend. If so, then when an observer is confronted by a dispute between two of their friends, sitting out might, in some cases, be the worst option because it damages both relationships. Further, siding against a friend who is morally wrong (e.g., someone who lied or cheated) might not damage that relationship as much as when the friend is in the right, because at least the friend could still count on the observer's support when they are not in the wrong in the future. Additional work can examine how observers manage trade-offs between coordinating with other observers and minimizing damage to their own relationships with each side of the dispute.

REFERENCES

Aarøe, L., & Petersen, M. B. (2013). Hunger games: Fluctuations in blood glucose levels influence support for social welfare. *Psychological Science, 24,* 2550–2556.

Appiah, K. A. (2010). *The honor code: How moral revolutions happen.* New York: Norton.

Baron, J. (1994). Nonconsequentialist decisions. *Behavioral and Brain Sciences, 17,* 1–10.

Baron, J., & Spranca, M. (1997). Protected values. *Organizational Behavior and Human Decision Processes, 70,* 1–16.

Boehm, C. (1999). *Hierarchy in the forest.* Cambridge, MA: Harvard University Press.

Brooke, M. de L., & Davies, N. B. (1988). Egg mimicry by cuckoos *Cuculus canorus* in relation to discrimination by hosts. *Nature, 335,* 630–632.

Carlsmith, K. M., Darley, J. M., & Robinson, P. H. (2002). Why do we punish?: Deterrence and just deserts as motives for punishment. *Journal of Personality and Social Psychology, 83,* 284–299.

Cooney, M. (1998). *Warriors and peacemakers: How third parties shape violence.* New York: New York University Press.

Cooney, M. (2003). The privatization of violence. *Criminology, 41,* 1377–1406.

Darwin, C. (1871). *Descent of man, and selection in relation to sex.* New York: Appleton.

De Freitas, J., DeScioli, P., Nemirow, J., Massenkoff, M., & Pinker, S. (in press). Kill or die: Moral judgment alters linguistic coding of causality. *Journal of Experimental Psychology: Learning, Memory, and Cognition.*

de Waal, F. B. M. (1996). *Good natured: The origins of right and wrong in humans and other animals.* Cambridge, MA: Harvard University Press.

DeScioli, P., Asao, K., & Kurzban. R. (2012). Omissions and byproducts across moral domains. *PLOS ONE, 7,* e46963.

DeScioli, P., Bruening, R., & Kurzban. R. (2011). The omission effect in moral cognition: Toward a functional explanation. *Evolution and Human Behavior, 32,* 204–215.

DeScioli, P., Christner, J., & Kurzban, R. (2011). The omission strategy. *Psychological Science, 22,* 442–446.

DeScioli, P., & Karpoff, R. (2015). People's judgments about classic property law cases. *Human Nature, 26,* 184–209.

DeScioli, P., Karpoff, R., & De Freitas, J. (2017). Ownership dilemmas: The case of finders versus landowners. *Cognitive Science, 41,* 502–522.

DeScioli, P., & Kurzban, R. (2009a). Mysteries of morality. *Cognition, 112,* 281–299.

DeScioli, P., & Kurzban, R. (2009b). The alliance hypothesis for human friendship. *PLOS ONE, 4,* e5802.

DeScioli, P., & Kurzban, R. (2011). The company you keep: Friendship decisions from a functional perspective. In J. I. Krueger (Ed.), *Social judgment and decision making* (pp. 209–225). New York: Psychology Press.

DeScioli, P., & Kurzban, R. (2013). A solution to the mysteries of morality. *Psychological Bulletin, 139,* 477–496.

DeScioli, P., Kurzban, R., Koch, E. N., & Liben-Nowell, D. (2011). Best friends: Alliances, friend ranking, and the MySpace social network. *Perspectives on Psychological Science, 6,* 6–8.

DeScioli, P., Massenkoff, M., Shaw, A., Petersen, M. B., & Kurzban, R. (2014). Equity or equality?: Moral judgments follow the money. *Proceedings of the Royal Society B: Biological Sciences, 281,* 2014–2112.

DeScioli, P., Rosa, N. M., & Gutchess, A. H. (2015). A memory advantage for property. *Evolutionary Psychology, 13,* 411–423.

DeScioli, P., & Wilson, B. (2011). The territorial foundations of human property. *Evolution and Human Behavior, 32,* 297–304.

Fiske, A. P. (1992). The four elementary forms of sociality: Framework for a unified theory of social relations. *Psychological Review, 99,* 689–723.

Haidt, J. (2007). The new synthesis in moral psychology. *Science, 316,* 998–1002.

Haidt, J. (2012). *The righteous mind.* New York: Vintage Books.

Hamilton, W. (1964). The genetic evolution of social behaviour. *Journal of Theoretical Biology, 7,* 1–52.

Holekamp, K. E., Sakai, S. T., & Lundrigan, B. L. (2007). Social intelligence in the spotted hyena (*Crocuta crocuta*). *Philosophical Transactions of the Royal Society B: Biological Sciences, 362,* 523–538.

Jensen, N. H., & Petersen, M. B. (2011). To defer

or to stand up: How offender formidability affects moral outrage. *Evolutionary Psychology, 9*, 118–136.

Kant, I. (1993). *Grounding for the metaphysics of morals* (J. W. Ellington, Trans.). Indianapolis, IN: Hackett. (Original work published 1785)

Kapoor, M. (2015, March 19). Witch hunting on the rise across several Indian states. *India Times*. Retrieved from *www.indiatimes.com/news/india/witch-hunting-on-the-rise-across-several-indian-states-231133.html*.

Krebs, D. (2005). The evolution of morality. In D. M. Buss (Ed.), *The handbook of evolutionary psychology* (pp. 747–771). Hoboken, NJ: Wiley.

Kurzban, R., DeScioli, P., & Fein, D. (2012). Hamilton vs. Kant: Pitting adaptations for altruism against adaptations for moral judgment. *Evolution and Human Behavior, 33*, 323–333.

Kurzban, R., Dukes, A., & Weeden, J. (2010). Sex, drugs and moral goals: Reproductive strategies and views about recreational drugs. *Proceedings of the Royal Society B: Biological Sciences, 277*, 3501–3508.

Levy, L. W. (1993). *Blasphemy: Verbal offense against the sacred, from Moses to Salman Rushdie*. New York: Knopf.

Mikhail, J. (2007). Universal moral grammar: Theory, evidence and the future. *Trends in Cognitive Sciences, 11*, 143–152.

Mock, D. W. (2004). *More than kin and less than kind: The evolution of family conflict*. Cambridge, MA: Oxford University Press

Petersen, M. B. (2013). Moralization as protection against exploitation: Do individuals without allies moralize more? *Evolution and Human Behavior, 34*, 78–85.

Petersen, M. B., Aarøe, L., Jensen, N. H., & Curry, O. (2014). Social welfare and the psychology of food sharing: Short-term hunger increases support for social welfare. *Political Psychology, 35*, 757–773.

Pinker, S. (1989). *Learnability and cognition: The acquisition of argument structure*. Cambridge, MA: MIT Press.

Prinz, J. J. (2007). Is morality innate? In W. Sinnott-Armstrong (Ed.), *Moral psychology: Vol. 1. Evolution of morals* (pp. 367–406). Cambridge, MA: MIT Press.

Ridley, M. (1996). *The origins of virtue*. London: Penguin Books.

Robinson, P. H., & Kurzban, R. (2007). Concordance and conflict in intuitions of justice. *Minnesota Law Review, 91*, 1829–1907.

Sarhan, A., & Burke, J. (2009, September 13). How Islamist gangs use Internet to track, torture and kill Iraqi gays. *The Guardian*. Retrieved from *www.guardian.co.uk/world/2009/sep/13/iraq-gays-murdered-militias*.

Schelling, T. C. (1960). *The strategy of conflict*. Cambridge, MA: Harvard University Press.

Shaw, A. (2013). Beyond "to share or not to share": The impartiality account of fairness. *Current Directions in Psychological Science, 22*, 413–417.

Sinnott-Armstrong, W. (2006). Consequentialism. In E. N. Zalta (Principal Ed.) & U. Nodelman (Senior Ed.), *Stanford encyclopedia of philosophy*. Stanford, CA: Stanford University. Available at *http://plato.stanford.edu*.

Snyder, G. H. (1984). The security dilemma in alliance politics. *World Politics, 36*, 461–495.

Snyder, G. H. (1997). *Alliance politics*. Ithaca, NY: Cornell University Press.

Suri, M. (2015, April 17). A ban on beef in India is not the answer. *New York Times*. Available at *http://nyti.ms/1yB4ORa*.

Tetlock, P. E. (2003). Thinking the unthinkable: Sacred values and taboo cognitions. *Trends in Cognitive Science, 7*, 320–324.

Trivers, R. L. (1971). The evolution of reciprocal altruism. *Quarterly Review of Biology, 46*, 35–57.

Trivers, R. L. (1974). Parent–offspring conflict. *American Zoologist, 14*, 249–264.

Tybur, J. M., Lieberman, D., Kurzban, R., & DeScioli, P. (2013). Disgust: Evolved function and structure. *Psychological Review, 120*, 65–84.

United Nations Commission on Human Rights. (2000). *Civil and political rights, including questions of disappearances and summary executions*. New York: Author.

Waldmann, M. R., & Dieterich, J. (2007). Throwing a bomb on a person versus throwing a person on a bomb: Intervention myopia in moral intuitions. *Psychological Science, 18*, 247–253.

Weeden, J. (2003). *Genetic interests, life histories, and attitudes towards abortion*. Unpublished doctoral dissertation, University of Pennsylvania, Philadelphia, PA.

Wright, R. (1994). *The moral animal*. New York: Pantheon.

CHAPTER 19

Morality for Us versus Them

Adam Waytz
Liane Young

Do people deploy the same moral cognition across social contexts, or are there critical cleavages within moral cognition?

We propose that conceptualizing moral cognition for close others as fundamentally different from moral cognition for distant others can help explain systematic differences in how people deploy social cognition (e.g., theory of mind), as well as how people apply moral foundations across different motivational contexts.

Moral cognition—which encompasses our ability to determine whether an action is right or wrong—allows us to navigate the social world. Critically, we identify actions as right or wrong *in order to* identify agents as friendly or hostile and to decide how to act and react ourselves. In turn, our social cognition—our ability to make sense of others and ourselves—supports our capacity for moral thinking and doing. That is, our assessments of others as moral actors depend on our assessments of others' mental states, including their beliefs, intentions, and motivations. Attributing minds to others and reasoning about the contents of those minds are crucial components of both moral judgment and social interaction (Gray & Wegner, 2009; Gray, Young, & Waytz, 2012; Waytz, Gray, Epley, & Wegner, 2010). When determining whether an individual is friend or foe, it is insufficient to evaluate agents on the basis of their external, observable ac-

tions; moral judgment depends on an assessment of internal mental states. For example, innocent intentions in the case of accidents (e.g., putting poison in a colleague's coffee while believing it to be sugar, inadvertently causing the colleague's death) decrease blame, whereas malicious intentions even in the absence of actual harm (e.g., putting sugar in a colleague's coffee while believing it to be poison, enhancing the colleague's enjoyment of the coffee) increase blame (for reviews, see Young & Dungan 2012; Young & Tsoi, 2013). Recent work reveals that mental state information informs moral judgments of not only individuals but also entire groups of people (e.g., corporations, unions, countries; Waytz & Young 2012; Waytz & Young 2014), animals (e.g., Gray, Gray, & Wegner, 2007; Piazza, Landy, & Goodwin, 2014; Waytz, Cacioppo, & Epley, 2010), and technology (Waytz, Heafner, & Epley, 2014).

In this chapter, we propose that systematic differences in how people deploy social cognition, in particular mental state reasoning (theory of mind; ToM), as well as how people apply moral foundations across different contexts, reflect critical cleavages within moral cognition. Specifically, we propose that moral cognition as applied to individuals we identify as members of our inner social circle, "us," is fundamentally different from moral cognition as applied to individuals we identify as outside of our social circle, "them."

In this chapter, we survey evidence suggesting that people focus on different aspects of mental states, as well as different moral foundations, depending on their relationship with the moral target. In particular, we suggest that people make the following distinctions when judging close versus distant others. By "close" others, we mean people who are socially close or people with whom we desire social closeness—those who we feel belong to our ingroups, are similar to us, and are likeable. By "distant" others, we mean people who are socially distant or people with whom we prefer social distance—those who we feel belong to our outgroups, are dissimilar to us, and are unlikeable. First, we propose that when considering close versus distant others, people focus on different moral characteristics, preferentially seeking information about and attending to others' experience-based mental states (e.g., emotions, feelings) versus agency-based mental states (e.g., intentions, plans, goals, beliefs), assigning greater moral patiency (i.e., the degree to which an individual deserves moral treatment) versus moral agency (i.e., the degree to which an individual is morally responsible for his or her actions), and attributing love-oriented motivations versus hate-oriented motivations for actions. Second, we propose that people assign different weight to different moral foundations, focusing more on considerations of loyalty and purity for close others and more on considerations of fairness and harm for distant others.

Moral Characteristics

Effective social interaction requires considering others' minds; however, which aspects of another person's mind we consider varies significantly from moment to moment. When approaching a potential romantic partner, we wonder, "Does this person find me attractive?" When interacting with a fussy child, we wonder, "What does this person need?" When asking the boss for a raise, we wonder, "Is this person in a good mood?" We propose that, more broadly, the aspects of mind we consider differ systematically depending on whether we are interacting with close or distant others, targets that typically activate different motivations.

In one set of studies examining people's reasoning about outgroup actions, we found that different motivations elicit selective attention to distinct kinds of mental states (Waytz & Young, 2014). In these studies, we experimentally manipulated American participants' motivational aims: to predict the actions of an outgroup country (effectance motivation) or to affiliate with the outgroup country (affiliation motivation). We asked people first to write short essays about either how they might accurately predict what the country might do in the future (effectance) or how they might establish an allegiance with the country (affiliation) and then to evaluate various characteristics of that country. These judgments included evaluating the importance of attending to the country's *agentive mental states* (i.e., capacities for planning, intending) and *experiential mental states* (i.e., capacities for emotion, feeling; Gray et al., 2007) and also whether or not the country possessed these mental states. Across studies, participants induced to experience effectance motivation allocated greater attention to *agentive mental states* relative to *experiential mental states* compared with participants induced to experience affiliation motivation. In addition, we found that people attributed greater trustworthiness and warmth-based traits when they were motivated by affiliation versus by effectance.

People's preferential perception of close others in terms of experience and prosocial motivations and their preferential perception of distant others in terms of agency and antisocial motivations is also broadly consistent with the hypothesis that people represent close versus distant others as different moral archetypes as well. Together with moral typecasting theory (Gray & Wegner, 2009), this research suggests that people should represent distant others more as moral agents (capable of doing good or evil) and close others more as moral patients (capable of having good and evil done to them). Based on this distinction, people should focus more on judgments of moral rights when evaluating close others and more on judgments of moral responsibility when evaluating distant others. Study 4 of our research described above provides partial support for this hypothesis (Waytz & Young, 2014). We found that people assigned greater *moral responsibility* to an outgroup country in the effectance condition but also marginally greater *moral rights* to the outgroup country in the affiliation condition.

Additional suggestive evidence of this distinction between perceiving close others as moral patients and distant others as moral agents comes from Study 7 of Gray and Wegner's (2009) work on moral typecasting. In this study, they demonstrate that people treat both good agents (e.g., the Dalai Lama) and bad agents (e.g., Ted Bundy) more like moral agents than moral patients (e.g., an orphan), inflicting more pain and less pleasure on these targets based on the belief that agents in general are able to tolerate adverse experiences. However, in this study people nevertheless treated good agents, compared with bad agents, more like moral patients, suggesting that people might afford patiency to targets with whom they might desire social closeness (relative to targets they might want to avoid).

Yet another study examined this moral distinction between close and distant others by asking American participants to listen to ostensible American or Afghan soldiers speak about atrocities they committed during war and justifications for these atrocities (Coman, Stone, Castano, & Hirst, 2014). When prompted to recall information from these narratives, participants recalled fewer of the atrocities committed by and more of the justifications for American soldiers compared with Afghan soldiers. In other words, people recalled outgroup members more as moral agents who inflicted harm on others (e.g., tortured enemy soldiers) and ingroup members more as moral patients, forced to commit atrocities to avoid further attack. Of course, this pattern, along with the one described above (Gray & Wegner, 2009), is consistent with generic ingroup bias, the desire to see ingroup members as more moral and to treat ingroup members better. Thus more targeted research is needed to test the hypothesis that people perceive close others as moral patients and distant others as moral agents.

The findings described above suggest that reasoning about the particular mental states essential for moral cognition is determined both by the features of the target and by the *motivations* of the judge. When interacting with distant others, the motivation for predicting and anticipating their actions, avoiding them, or blaming them for wrongdoing leads people to attend to the plans, intentions, and goals of others. When interacting with close others, the motivation for affiliation and moral justification can lead people to attend to these mental states as well but also appears to increase people's desire to understand others' emotions and feelings, which are critical components of empathy (Batson, 2011; Zaki & Ochsner, 2012). Thus the different motivations that are typically activated toward socially close and socially distant others drive different applications of moral cognition to these targets.

A recent functional magnetic resonance imaging (fMRI) experiment we conducted also supports the idea that people attend to different aspects of mental states when they are motivated by cooperation versus competition (Tsoi, Dungan, Waytz, & Young, 2016). Participants played a game (modeled after "rock, paper, scissors") involving a series of dyadic interactions requiring participants to think about what their partners are thinking. Interactions were either competitive and zero sum—for example, if the participant guesses "paper" and his or her partner guesses "rock," the participant *alone* wins a monetary reward—or cooperative—for example, if the participant and his or her partner both guess "paper," both parties earn a reward *jointly*. We found that, although brain regions for mental state reasoning were recruited similarly robustly for both competitive and cooperative trials, these regions discriminated between competition and cooperation in their spatial patterns of activity. The results suggest that these regions encode information that separates competition from cooperation—

perhaps the difference between agency-based and experience-based mental states, alongside the consideration of an individual as a moral agent versus a moral patient, as consistent with the behavioral research presented above.

In another line of work, we have examined how people attribute a distinct type of mental state—motivation—to close and distant others in the context of moral conflict over political and religious issues. In particular, we examined real-world conflict groups, American Democrats and Republicans, as well as Israelis and Palestinians in the Middle East (Waytz, Young, & Ginges, 2014), and assessed how people attribute different motivations to their ingroups and outgroups. In these experiments, we tested whether people deliver different assessments of the mental states, namely, the motivations underlying conflict for groups with whom they typically compete (i.e., outgroups) versus cooperate (i.e., ingroups). In political and ethnoreligious intergroup conflict, adversaries attributed their own group's aggression to ingroup love more than outgroup hate and their outgroup's aggression to outgroup hate more than ingroup love. For example, Israelis reported that Israelis support bombing of Gaza because of their love of Israelis, not hatred of Palestinians; and Palestinians attributed Israeli aggression to outgroup hate (toward Palestinians) and Palestinian violence to ingroup love (toward Palestinians). Similarly, both Democrats and Republicans attributed political conflict initiated by the opposing party to outgroup hate, but they attributed conflict initiated by their own party to ingroup love. Critically, this biased pattern of attribution also increased moral attitudes and behaviors associated with conflict intractability, including unwillingness to negotiate and unwillingness to vote for compromise solutions. Again, these findings suggest that people place different emphases on different mental states when reasoning about the morality of close and distant others.

Moral Foundations

Beyond focusing on different mental and moral characteristics when interacting with close versus distant others, people also appear to rely on entirely different psychological foundations for what constitutes right and wrong. Moral foundations theory (MFT; Graham et al., 2013; Haidt & Joseph, 2004; Haidt & Graham, 2007) suggests that these foundations fall into two types—binding foundations (ingroup loyalty, respect for authority, and purity/sanctity), which emphasize values that bind and build social groups, and individualizing foundations (care–harm, justice–cheating), which emphasize the rights of individuals, regardless of group membership. These domains appear to be defined by their descriptive content (e.g., shooting a person belongs to the harm domain; taking more than one's share belongs to the fairness domain). Meanwhile, other researchers highlight the key role of the relational context of an action (e.g., taking a car from a stranger is considered stealing, while taking a car from a sibling may constitute borrowing; Carnes, Lickel, & Janoff-Bulman, 2015; Fiske & Tetlock, 1997; Kurzban, DeScioli, & Fein, 2012; Rai & Fiske, 2011). Applying this context-driven account to the use of moral foundations, we suggest that moral foundations are differently deployed depending on the identities of the parties involved and, importantly, their relationship. Recent work indicates that when people consider socially close versus distant others, they focus more on binding foundations relative to individualizing foundations. In particular, people seem to focus on considerations of purity versus harm and loyalty versus fairness; in addition, individual differences in endorsement of binding versus individualizing values track with treatment of ingroup relative to outgroup members, as reviewed below.

First, recent research examines the relevance of harm and purity norms for different relational contexts. People judge purity violations committed within their own group and harm violations outside their group more harshly (Dungan, Chakroff, & Young, 2017). In one study, moral condemnation increased as the target of a purity violation became more self-relevant, whereas the opposite pattern was true for harm. Another study extended this distinction to the level of groups. People who strongly identified with their ingroup delivered particularly harsh moral judgments of purity violations (but not harms) compared with people who weakly identified with their ingroup. When it comes to purity violations, people may be especially harsh on the people closest to them—those who have the greatest potential to affect them either indirectly by association or directly via physical or moral contamination. Indeed, in a third study, across a wide array of violations varying in severity, people judged that it is more morally wrong to defile (vs. harm) oneself, but it is more morally wrong to harm (vs. defile) another person. Concerns about oneself may track with concerns about one's group (ingroup). Keeping oneself pure may be advantageous only insofar as others in close proximity also maintain their purity; thus concerns about contagion or contamination may apply more to ingroup members. As such, condemnation of another person's impurity may still stem from concerns about one's own purity.

Additional evidence supports the account that concerns about purity are more salient when one is considering oneself, whereas concerns about harm are more salient when one is considering others (Chakroff, Dungan, & Young, 2013; Rottman, Kelemen, & Young, 2014). This body of research also shows that mental state reasoning is deployed for moral judgments of harmful acts to a significantly greater extent than for moral judgments of impure acts (Chakroff, Dungan, & Young, 2013; Russell & Giner-Sorolla, 2011; Young & Saxe, 2011).

Second, other moral concerns such as loyalty as opposed to justice or fairness may also apply more to the ingroup. Pilot data indicate that people prefer loyal friends and family but value justice and fairness across group boundaries (Dungan, Waytz, & Young, 2017). Indeed, recent work on whistle-blowing decisions directly reveals the tension between norms concerning loyalty (to friends and family who support oneself) and norms concerning justice and fairness for all (Waytz, Dungan, & Young, 2013). In several experiments, we primed participants with specific moral values—fairness versus loyalty. Participants were instructed to write an essay about either the value of fairness over loyalty or the value of loyalty over fairness. Participants who had written pro-fairness essays were more likely to blow the whistle on unethical actions committed by other members of their communities. Par-

ticipants who had written pro-loyalty essays were more likely to keep their mouths shut in solidarity. However, regardless of condition, participants were less likely to blow the whistle on friends and family than on strangers and acquaintances, suggesting that the foundation of loyalty is far more relevant for close others.

Another line of work shows that people describe immoral behavior committed by one's ingroup more in terms of binding foundations and describe immoral behavior committed by one's outgroup in terms of individualizing foundations (Leidner & Castano, 2012). When Americans were asked to describe American soldiers or Australian soldiers (an outgroup) engaging in wartime atrocities toward Iraqis, they described these atrocities more in terms of loyalty and authority for American soldiers and more in terms of harm and fairness for Australian soldiers.

Finally, convergent evidence indicates that individual differences in endorsement of binding values—loyalty, purity, and authority—track with the treatment of ingroup versus outgroup members (Smith, Aquino, Koleva, & Graham, 2014). In particular, people who strongly endorsed binding values were also more likely to support torturing outgroup members posing a critical threat to ingroup members and to preserve scarce resources for ingroup members, thereby withholding them from outgroup members; this pattern, though, was unique to individuals reporting a weak moral identity or moral self-concept.

Conclusion

Gray and Wegner (2009, p. 506) note, "It is difficult to be moral or immoral alone in a room." After all, the primary function of morality is to make sense of and interact with the social beings around us. Identifying an action as right or wrong matters only insofar as we are able to interpret others' behavior as hostile or benevolent and to decide how to respond. The many components of moral cognition all operate in the service of social navigation: Assessments of moral traits and mental states support evaluations of others' behavior, including judgments of their moral worth and blameworthiness; moral foundations guide intuitive ethics. Yet assessments of moral and mental traits and applications of moral foundations, as well as consequent judgments and behaviors, depend crucially on the social and motivational context.

Furthermore, as Rai and Fiske (2011) propose, people might consider the same individual using different relational models in different situations and therefore apply different moral motives (e.g., two individuals might invoke the communal sharing model when exchanging jazz records but the market pricing model when one sells the other one a bicycle). By the same token, the same interaction partner might occupy close or distant status depending on context. For example, a salesperson might consider a sales colleague to be an ally when considering how to best a competing organization, but not when their mutual organization offers a Rolex watch for its salesperson-of-the-month award. Given the flexibility of relationship status, we predict that, over the course of a relationship, people might rely differentially on different moral characteristics and moral foundations, as established here.

This prediction also helps explain why when affiliative relationships turn acrimonious, they become difficult to repair (Keysar, Converse, Wang, & Epley, 2008; Kramer, 1999; Lount, Zhong, Sivanathan, & Murnighan, 2008; Waytz et al., 2014): because morality has shifted. When an ally turns even momentarily into an enemy, people shift their focus from concerns about the other side's moral rights (patiency) and moral norms concerning social cohesiveness to a focus on concerns about the other side's moral responsibility and norms concerning individual morality. This shift in moral focus might then contribute to a cycle of blame and a desire for punishment for the ostensible offender. Perhaps more optimistically, in the rarer cases of enemies becoming allies, morality should shift in a positive direction to reinforce conciliation. For example, when formerly warring countries establish a peace treaty, the focus of these parties should shift to moral rights and establishing social cohesion rather than finger-pointing over past wrongs. We welcome future research to test these hypotheses and to elucidate key differences in moral cognition for "us" versus "them."

REFERENCES

Batson, C. D. (2011). *Altruism in humans*. Oxford, UK: Oxford University Press.

Carnes, N. C., Lickel, B., & Janoff-Bulman, R. (2015). Shared perceptions: Morality is embedded in social contexts. *Personality and Social Psychology Bulletin, 41*(3), 351–362.

Chakroff, A., Dungan, J., & Young, L. (2013). Harming ourselves and defiling others: What determines a moral domain? *PLOS ONE, 8*(9), e74434.

Coman, A., Stone, C. B., Castano, E., & Hirst, W. (2014). Justifying atrocities: The effect of moral-disengagement strategies on socially shared retrieval-induced forgetting. *Psychological Science, 25*(6), 1281–1285.

Dungan, J., Chakroff, A., & Young, L. (2017). The relevance of moral norms in distinct relational contexts: Purity versus harm norms regulate self-directed actions. *PLOS ONE 12*(3), e0173405.

Dungan, J., Waytz, A., & Young, L. (2017). *Loyalty and fairness within and across group boundaries*. Manuscript in preparation.

Fiske, A. P., & Tetlock, P. E. (1997). Taboo trade-offs: Reactions to transactions that transgress the spheres of justice. *Political Psychology, 18*(2), 255–297.

Graham, J., Haidt, J., Koleva, S., Motyl, M., Iyer, R., Wojcik, S., & Ditto, P. H. (2013). Moral foundations theory: The pragmatic validity of moral pluralism. *Advances in Experimental Social Psychology, 47,* 55–130.

Gray, H. M., Gray, K., & Wegner, D. M. (2007). Dimensions of mind perception. *Science, 315*(5812), 619–619.

Gray, K., & Wegner, D. M. (2009). Moral typecasting: Divergent perceptions of moral agents and moral patients. *Journal of Personality and Social Psychology, 96*(3), 505–520.

Gray, K., Young, L., & Waytz, A. (2012). Mind perception is the essence of morality. *Psychological Inquiry, 23*(2), 101–124.

Haidt, J., & Graham, J. (2007). When morality opposes justice: Conservatives have moral intuitions that liberals may not recognize. *Social Justice Research, 20*(1), 98–116.

Haidt, J., & Joseph, C. (2004). Intuitive ethics: How innately prepared intuitions generate culturally variable virtues. *Daedalus, 133*(4), 55–66.

Keysar, B., Converse, B. A., Wang, J., & Epley, N. (2008). Reciprocity is not give and take: Asymmetric reciprocity to positive and negative acts. *Psychological Science, 19*(12), 1280–1286.

Kramer, R. M. (1999). Trust and distrust in organizations: Emerging perspectives, enduring questions. *Annual Review of Psychology, 50*(1), 569–598.

Kurzban, R., DeScioli, P., & Fein, D. (2012). Hamilton vs. Kant: Pitting adaptations for altruism against adaptations for moral judgment. *Evolution and Human Behavior, 33,* 323–333.

Leidner, B., & Castano, E. (2012). Morality shifting in the context of intergroup violence. *European Journal of Social Psychology, 42*(1), 82–91.

Lount, R. B., Zhong, C., Sivanathan, N., & Murnighan, J. K. (2008). Getting off on the wrong foot: Restoring trust and the timing of a breach. *Personality and Social Psychology Bulletin, 34,* 1601–1612.

Piazza, J., Landy, J. F., & Goodwin, G. P. (2014). Cruel nature: Harmfulness as an important, overlooked dimension in judgments of moral standing. *Cognition, 131*(1), 108–124.

Rai, T. S., & Fiske, A. P. (2011). Moral psychology is relationship regulation: Moral motives for unity, hierarchy, equality, and proportionality. *Psychological Review, 118*(1), 57–75.

Rottman, J., Kelemen, D., & Young, L. (2014). Tainting the soul: Purity concerns predict moral judgments of suicide. *Cognition, 130*(2), 217–226.

Russell, P. S., & Giner-Sorolla, R. (2011). Moral anger, but not moral disgust, responds to intentionality. *Emotion, 11*(2), 233–240.

Smith, I., Aquino, K., Koleva, S., & Graham, J. (2014). The moral ties that bind . . . even to out-groups: The interactive effect of moral identity and the binding moral foundations. *Psychological Science, 25,* 1554–1562.

Tsoi, L., Dungan, J., Waytz, A., & Young, L. (2016). Distinct neural patterns of social cognition for cooperation versus competition. *NeuroImage, 137,* 86–96.

Waytz, A., Cacioppo, J., & Epley, N. (2010). Who sees human?: The stability and importance of individual differences in anthropomorphism. *Perspectives on Psychological Science, 5*(3), 219–232.

Waytz, A., Dungan, J., & Young, L. (2013). The whistleblower's dilemma and the fairness–loyalty tradeoff. *Journal of Experimental Social Psychology, 49,* 1027–1033.

Waytz, A., Gray, K., Epley, N., & Wegner, D. M. (2010). Causes and consequences of mind perception. *Trends in Cognitive Sciences, 14*(8), 383–388.

Waytz, A., Heafner, J., & Epley, N. (2014). The mind in the machine: Anthropomorphism increases trust in an autonomous vehicle. *Journal of Experimental Social Psychology, 52,* 113–117.

Waytz, L., & Young, L. (2012). The group-member mind tradeoff: Attributing mind to groups versus group members. *Psychological Science, 23,* 77–85.

Waytz, A., & Young, L. (2014). Two motivations for two dimensions of mind. *Journal of Experimental Social Psychology, 55,* 278–283.

Waytz, A., Young, L., & Ginges, J. (2014). A motive attribution asymmetry for love versus hate drives intractable conflict. *Proceedings of the National Academy of Sciences of the USA, 111*(44), 15687–15692.

Young, L., & Dungan, J. (2012). Where in the brain is morality?: Everywhere and maybe nowhere. *Social Neuroscience, 7,* 1–10.

Young, L., & Saxe, R. (2011). When ignorance is no excuse: Different roles for intent across moral domains. *Cognition, 120,* 202–214.

Young, L., & Tsoi, L. (2013). When mental states matter, when they don't, and what that means for morality. *Social and Personality Psychology Compass, 7*(8), 585–604.

Zaki, J., & Ochsner, K. N. (2012) The neuroscience of empathy: Progress, pitfalls and promise. *Nature Neuroscience, 15,* 675–680.

CHAPTER 20

Pleasure in Response to Outgroup Pain as a Motivator of Intergroup Aggression

Mina Cikara

> **If humans are innately good, cooperative, fair, and averse to harming one another, why does widespread intergroup violence continue to afflict society?**
>
> Several factors contribute to fomenting aggression between groups; here I focus on the role of pleasure in response to outgroup pain.

Humans reliably divide their social world into *us* and *them*. This fundamental tendency is the source of humanity's greatest triumphs but also of its greatest tragedies. Banding together allows people to satisfy their own material and psychological needs (Allport, 1954) and to develop norms and practices that bolster our most cherished social institutions (e.g., Keltner, 2009; Tomasello, 2009). However, group living also results in violence and conflict between groups (Cohen & Insko, 2008). According to one statistic, more than 200 million people have been killed in acts of genocide, war, and other forms of group conflict in the last 100 years (Woolf & Hulsizer, 2004).

It is difficult to reconcile these statistics on intergroup violence with the well-documented moral prohibitions against harm that guide most people's behavior most of the time. In lab studies, people are willing to pay more to prevent harm to others relative to themselves (Crockett, Kurth-Nelson, Siegel, Dayan, & Dolan, 2014); they even exhibit physiological aversion responses when the harm they are causing is not real (e.g., shooting a person with a fake gun; Cushman, Gray, Gaffey, & Mendes, 2012). These results are not unique to the lab setting or to harming innocent strangers. Analysis of combat activity during the U.S. Civil War and World War I reveal that soldiers would shoot over the heads of enemy combatants. Thus harm aversion exerts its effects even in large-scale group conflict (Grossman, 1996). So how *do* people eventually overcome their aversion to doing harm in order to participate in intergroup aggression? Several factors are critical for fomenting intergroup violence, including moral disengagement, moral justification, and dissonance reduction (for an excellent review and theoretical integration, see Littman & Paluck, 2014; see also Waytz & Young, Chapter 19, this volume). Here I focus on another complementary mechanism: pleasure in response to outgroup pain.

Key Terms: Empathy, Schadenfreude, and Harm

Empathy refers to the collection of affective and cognitive processes that allow people to recognize emotional experiences in others, experience matched sensations and emotions, and move to alleviate those others' suffering (Batson, 2009). However, people do not empathize with all others all of the time (nor would it be adaptive if they did). Though it is not often conceptualized as an intergroup emotion, empathy is reliably moderated by group membership; people feel less empathy for outgroup relative to ingroup members. We refer to this difference as the *intergroup empathy bias* (Bruneau, Cikara, & Saxe, 2017; Cikara, Bruneau, & Saxe, 2011; Cikara, Bruneau, Van Bavel, & Saxe, 2014). People self-report this bias and exhibit decreased (and sometimes absent) physiological responses associated with empathy when witnessing outgroup relative to ingroup members in physical or emotional pain (see Cikara & Van Bavel, 2014, for a recent review). This bias matters because the absence of empathy implies a reduction in motivation to help those in pain (Zaki & Cikara, 2015).

What is left in the absence of empathy? Apathy: indifference toward outgroup suffering. However, it is important to note that, although apathy may engender neglect, it should not promote active harm. An alternative to apathy is the opposite of empathy: pleasure in response to others' misfortunes—*Schadenfreude*—or displeasure in response to others' triumphs—*Glückschmerz*. In contrast to apathy, pleasure and pain are feasible motivators of overt intergroup aggression.

Feeling pleasure in response to outgroup misfortune is arguably a natural if not adaptive response in zero-sum environments: Negative outcomes for "them" indicate positive outcomes for "us," and are therefore pleasurable. However, experiencing Schadenfreude as a passive observer of outgroup members' pain is very different from being responsible for *causing* outgroup members' pain. Here I propose that intergroup Schadenfreude is a natural response that supports the learning of an otherwise repugnant behavior: actively doing harm to others. If observing outgroup members' pain is consistently accompanied by feeling pleasure, people may learn over time to endorse and *do* harm to individual outgroup targets.

Relevant Debates

Ingroup Love versus Outgroup Hate as Motivators of Intergroup Aggression

Social categorization is fundamental for group living. It guides decisions about whom to approach or avoid and allows us to generalize our existing knowledge about social groups to novel targets (Bruner, 1957). Social categorization also requires that people categorize themselves (Tajfel & Turner, 1979). Shifting from an individual ("I" or "me") to a collective ("we" or "us") self-concept is called *social identification* (Ellemers, 2012). Greater identification engenders greater ingroup favoritism, which in turn reinforces the boundaries between "us" and "them" (Tajfel & Turner, 1986; for a review, see Hewstone, Rubin, & Willis, 2002). Indeed, in the absence of conflict, ingroup love is a better predictor of inequitable resource allocation and intergroup bias that than outgroup hate is (Brewer, 1999). Ingroup love, however, is not sufficient to ignite intergroup conflict. This is why most outgroups elicit indifference rather than aggression.

Instead, intergroup aggression is driven by competition over resources and incompatibility between groups' goals: Consider, for example, the violence against Jews in prewar Europe or brawling among rival sports fans (Campbell, 1965; Fiske & Ruscher, 1993; Sherif, Harvey, White, Hood, & Sherif, 1961; Sidanius & Pratto, 1999). Competition transforms indifference into emotions such as fear, hatred, and disgust (Chang, Krosch, & Cikara, 2016; Cuddy, Fiske, & Glick, 2007; Mackie & Hamilton, 1993). These emotions are then used to justify overt discrimination against outgroups and their members (Brewer, 2001). Outgroups are dehumanized or, worse yet, demonized, which places them beyond the boundary of justice that applies to the ingroup (Bar-Tal, 1989; Opotow, 2005; Staub, 1989).

The stereotype content model makes specific predictions about which social groups elicit apathy versus disgust versus threat (Fiske, Cuddy, Glick, & Xu, 2002; Fiske, Chapter 21, this volume). People harbor disgust for groups that are stereotyped as competitive (or exploitative) and low status (e.g., drug addicts, welfare recipients), whereas people are threatened by groups that are stereotyped as competitive but high status (e.g., wealthy professionals, model minorities). We have run several experiments to see whether "ingroup love" was sufficient to explain moral exclusion and to harm outgroups (in which case, all outgroups should be treated equivalently) or whether our results were better explained by outgroup hate (which should specifically target competitive outgroups). In one experiment, we used the famous trolley dilemma to investigate whether stereotypes motivated people to value some social groups' lives over others (Cikara, Farnsworth, Harris, & Fiske, 2010). On each trial we assigned different stereotyped targets' photos to the "sacrificed" and "saved" roles; we asked participants to indicate how morally acceptable it was for a third party named Joe to push one target (e.g., a drug addict) off a bridge to save five others (e.g., five students). Not surprisingly, participants reported that it was most acceptable to save cooperative, high-status groups (e.g., Americans and students). More important, participants did not value different kinds of outgroup members' lives equivalently. It was most morally acceptable to sacrifice, and least acceptable to save, competitive, low-status (i.e., disgust) targets. Specifically, 84% of our respondents said it was acceptable for Joe to push competitive, low-status targets off a bridge to save five cooperative, high-status targets. This finding is remarkable when juxtaposed with the finding that 88% of people say this same act is *unacceptable* when the targets remain unidentified (Hauser, Cushman, Young, Jin, & Mikhail, 2007).

Critically, we have found that participants' endorsement of harm shifts to threatening outgroups when the harm is not fatal. In one experiment, we asked participants to imagine that they had to decide whether to assign one person to receive painful electric shocks in order to spare another four people. On each trial, we assigned different stereotyped targets' photos to the "scapegoat"

role. This time, participants said it was most acceptable to harm competitive, *high-status* targets (e.g., wealthy women, businessmen; Cikara & Fiske, 2011). Thus it appears that ingroup love is not specific enough to predict which social groups will be targeted for aggression. Instead, the specific outgroups and their associated stereotypes matter.

Banality of Evil or Virtuous Violence?

Participation in intergroup violence requires that people behave in ways that they would otherwise find aversive. The first several decades of social psychology were largely dedicated to understanding the circumstances that enable people to engage in antisocial behavior. For example, we know that harmful behavior is more likely to arise when individuals' sense of personal responsibility is mitigated by obedience to authority (Milgram, 1965), anonymity (Diener, 1979; Festinger, Pepitone, & Newcomb, 1952), or diffusion/displacement of responsibility (Bandura, 1999) and when the salience of individuals' own moral standards is low (Prentice-Dunn & Rogers, 1989). Although they are relevant, none of these explanations is unique to intergroup contexts. Even in the absence of an outgroup, these circumstances could lead individuals in crowds to engage in immoral behavior (e.g., out of individual self-interest). More important, these explanations largely adhere to the "banality of evil" perspective (Arendt, 1976). By these accounts, people are not actively choosing to act immorally so much as they are reflexively responding to the pressures exerted by the situation.

An important alternative is the way that perpetrators of intergroup harm explicitly reframe and/or justify their behavior as serving a greater good (Pinter & Wildschut, 2012). For example, participants rate torture as more acceptable when their own country rather than other countries engages in it (Tarrant, Branscombe, Warner, & Weston, 2012). High identification and coordinated behavior with the ingroup are critical conditions for acting on behalf of a group in general and for intergroup aggression in particular (Reicher, Haslam, & Rath, 2008; Cikara & Paluck, 2013). As collective identities become "fused" with one's individual identity, people may act as representatives of the group rather than as individual agents (Ellemers, 2012), allowing group goals to supplant individual goals. If the ingroup's goals require harming the outgroup, people who are highly identified with the group may deliberately choose to endorse or do harm because they believe it is the right thing to do (Fiske & Rai, 2015; Reicher et al., 2008; Rai, Chapter 24, this volume). Said another way, our moral codes may promote fairness and prohibition against harm in interpersonal contexts, but we bring different rules and expectations to bear on competitive intergroup interactions (Cohen, Montoya, & Insko, 2006; Rhodes & Chalik, 2013). This is an important perspective because intergroup Schadenfreude may be one important cue people use to rationalize the acceptability of harming outgroup members. A complete account of intergroup aggression would have to integrate the contributions of lower-level affective signals (absence of negative and/or presence of positive affect), as well as higher-order cognitions reflecting on those signals.

Intergroup Schadenfreude as a Motivator of Intergroup Aggression

Though several conditions predict Schadenfreude (see Smith, Powell, Combs, & Schurtz, 2009, and Van Dijk, Ouwerkerk, Smith, & Cikara, 2015, for reviews), I focus on the effect of intergroup competition here (Cikara & Fiske, 2013). In order for Schadenfreude to qualify as an intergroup emotion, people must feel it *on behalf of their group*. However, people only appraise events from an intergroup perspective when they are highly identified with the ingroup (Mackie, Devos, & Smith, 2000); therefore, Schadenfreude should correlate with group identification. Consistent with this prediction, college basketball fans' identification with their team predicted greater Schadenfreude in response to a rival player's injury (Hoogland et al., 2014). In another study, hardcore soccer fans smiled more intensely when they watched a rival soccer team miss a penalty kick relative to when they watched their favored team make a goal (Boecker, Likowski, Pauli, & Weyers, 2015). In both

of these examples, rivals' misfortunes are cause for pleasure only because fans identified strongly with their favored team. Of course, both of these studies focus on (1) groups with a history of rivalry and (2) Schadenfreude in response to events that are related to the basis for that rivalry (e.g., asking sports fans how they feel about sports-related outcomes). How much information is necessary to evoke intergroup Schadenfreude? Is a history of rivalry required? Does Schadenfreude extend to events that are irrelevant to the intergroup competition? One way to address these questions is to examine the minimal conditions under which participants exhibit intergroup Schadenfreude.

In a series of recent experiments, we found that participants exhibited greater Schadenfreude (and Glückschmerz) toward competitive outgroups relative to ingroup members only minutes after being assigned to novel groups in competition for $1 (Cikara et al., 2014).

In the first experiment, we assigned participants to novel groups—the Eagles or the Rattlers—purportedly based on their personalities (in reality, we randomly assigned them to teams). We also manipulated whether groups were competitive, cooperative, or independently working toward winning a $1 bonus. We told participants that we would award bonuses depending on participants' and their teams' performance in an upcoming problem-solving challenge. In the competitive condition, in which only one team could win the bonus, participants reported greater Schadenfreude toward outgroup relative to ingroup members, even though the misfortunes were irrelevant to the upcoming competition (e.g., "Brendan accidentally walked into a glass door"). Intergroup Schadenfreude was attenuated when groups worked independently for the bonus and eliminated when groups were told they were going to work together to earn the bonus. We included unaffiliated targets as a baseline in a second experiment, including only the competitive condition. We found that participants responded to unaffiliated targets (people who did not fit the profile of either an Eagle or a Rattler) the same way they responded to ingroup targets. These results indicate that, rather than uniquely shielding the ingroup from Schadenfreude, people reserve Schadenfreude only for competitive outgroups (Cikara et al., 2014). It is worth noting that using novel groups has the added benefit of controlling for preexisting negative attitudes, resentment regarding the outgroup's past successes (Hareli & Weiner, 2002), and perceptions that past success was ill gotten (Feather and Sherman, 2002).

These effects also emerge in more subtle social contexts. For example, we have found that people smile more when targets who are merely stereotyped as competitive (e.g., an investment banker) experience bad events (relative to good events; Cikara & Fiske, 2012). Together, these results indicate that a target can evoke these malicious emotional responses in the absence of any personal history or direct contact with the perceiver, due only to their group membership and its associated stereotypes.

Thus, Schadenfreude appears to be a prepared or "natural" response in contexts that are or are perceived as zero-sum. If a threatening outgroup is unhappy, "we" are pleased; no learning is required. Remember, however, that experiencing pleasure in response to the observation of outgroup harm is very different from becoming the first-person agent of harm. Given that group survival may require some members to harm outgroups on behalf of the ingroup, one intriguing possibility is that Schadenfreude motivates participation in intergroup aggression by *teaching* people to overcome the aversion to harming outgroup members.

Insights from Cognitive Neuroscience

Many regions of the brain are implicated in encoding and representing reward, but the ventral striatum (VS) is associated specifically with reinforcement learning. By many accounts, this region supports learning stimulus-value associations and acquiring predictive value representation in the service of guiding behavior (O'Doherty, 2004). In other words, this region supports learning from our experience so we can repeat behaviors that yield rewards. There are now several functional magnetic resonance imaging (fMRI) studies investigating Schadenfreude, all of which find that greater VS engagement is correlated with greater Schadenfreude (e.g., Singer et al., 2006; Takahashi et al.,

2009). This Schadenfreude–VS association generalizes to intergroup contexts. For example, baseball fans of either the Boston Red Sox or New York Yankees, watched their favored team compete with other teams while lying in the fMRI scanner. Fans of both teams reported pleasure and exhibited greater activity in the VS when watching their own team do well and when watching the rival team fail (even when rival failed against a third, lower ranked team, the Baltimore Orioles; Cikara, Botvinick, & Fiske, 2011). These findings extend to contexts in which victims are merely associated with the rival team. Soccer fans exhibited VS activity when watching a rival team's *fan* receive a painful electric shock (Hein, Silani, Preuschoff, Batson, & Singer, 2010). Note that in neither case are participants in direct competition. Instead, outgroup failure and pain take on a positive value by virtue of participants' affiliation with their favored team.

These studies provide only correlational evidence, but they suggest an intriguing possibility: that the capacity for intergroup aggression may have developed, in part, by appropriating basic reinforcement-learning processes and associated neural circuitry in order to overcome harm aversion. Again, these results are correlational, but greater VS response to a rival's suffering in the context of the baseball and soccer studies described above predicted an increased desire to harm rival team fans (Cikara et al., 2011) and a decreased willingness to relieve a rival fan's pain (by accepting a proportion of the pain for oneself; Hein et al., 2010). These data implicate both the VS's valuation function—evaluating outgroup harm as positive—but also its motivation function—learning to select behaviors that harm the outgroup and associated individuals. They also support the prediction that the pleasure–harm association generalizes to individuals merely associated with the teams under consideration.

Implications and Future Directions

It is critical to understand failures of empathy and Schadenfreude as they unfold between groups (as opposed to individuals) because intergroup contexts significantly increase opportunities for violence. First, harm can be justified as being morally necessary in the absence of any personal grievance (e.g., in defense of the ingroup and its values; Fiske & Rai, 2015; Reicher et al., 2008). Second, the pleasure–pain association generalizes to entire groups; individuals who have done nothing to provoke violence become targets by virtue of their affiliation with a competitive, threatening outgroup.

One outstanding question is whether increased willingness to harm outgroup members predicts increased identification with the ingroup. For example, Littman (2015) finds that ex-combatants in Uganda and Liberia who were abducted by the Lord's Resistance Army (LRA) as youths and forced to harm loved ones on its behalf are more highly identified with the LRA than abducted youths who were not forced to harm loved ones. One possibility is that the pleasure of doing outgroup harm may further reinforce group identification, creating a self-perpetuating cycle of collective violence (Littman & Paluck, 2014). This is a somewhat provocative prediction, because it runs counter to the prediction made by cognitive dissonance theory. On an overjustification account (Deci, Koestner, & Ryan, 1999), *decreased* Schadenfreude and *increased* harm aversion would predict greater identification with the outgroup, because participants have to overcome greater psychological barriers in order to do harm. Alternatively, the presence of positive affect in response to doing harm could also be a source of dissonance. We are presently running studies to adjudicate among these hypotheses.

Finally, it would be irresponsible to refrain from reiterating that participation in intergroup aggression is a multiply determined phenomenon with many causes and consequences. Intergroup competition, group identification, and moral justifications are all motivators of intergroup aggression (at least in humans). However, linking outgroup aggression to reinforcement learning expands the reach of our research not only to other areas of scientific inquiry (e.g., behavioral neuroscience, cognitive neuroscience, economics, biology) and other model organisms (e.g., rodent and primate models), but also to political and educational institutions with the power to make and implement policy. Ultimately, a better understanding of *all* the mechanisms promoting intergroup aggression will inform best practices for defusing it.

NOTE

This chapter is based on an article I wrote for *Current Opinion in Behavioral Sciences* (Cikara, 2015).

REFERENCES

Allport, G. W. (1954). *The nature of prejudice.* Reading, MA: Addison Wesley.

Arendt, H. (1976). *Eichmann in Jerusalem: A report on the banality of evil.* London: Penguin.

Bandura, A. (1999). Moral disengagement in the perpetration of inhumanities. *Personality and Social Psychology Review, 3,* 193–209.

Bar-Tal, D. (1989). Delegitimization: The extreme case of stereotyping and prejudice. In D. Bar-Tal, C. Graumann, A. Kruglanski, & W. Stroebe (Eds.), *Stereotyping and prejudice: Changing conceptions* (pp. 169–182). New York: Springer-Verlag.

Batson, C. D. (2009). These things called empathy: Eight related but distinct phenomena. In J. Decety & W. J. Ickes (Eds.), *The social neuroscience of empathy* (pp. 3–15). Cambridge, MA: MIT Press.

Boecker, L., Likowski, K. U., Pauli, P., & Weyers, P. (2015). The face of schadenfreude: Differentiation of joy and schadenfreude by electromyography. *Cognition and Emotion, 29*(6), 1117–1125.

Brewer, M. B. (1999). The psychology of prejudice: Ingroup love and out-group hate? *Journal of Social Issues, 55*(3), 429–444.

Brewer, M. B. (2001). In-group identification and intergroup conflict: When does in-group love become out-group hate? In R. D. Ashmore, L. Jussim, & D. Wilder (Eds.), *Social identity, inter-group conflict, and conflict reduction* (pp. 17–41). New York: Oxford University Press.

Bruneau, E. G., Cikara, M., & Saxe, R. (2017). Parochial empathy predicts the reduced altruism and the endorsement of passive harm. *Social Psychological and Personality Science.*

Bruner, J. S. (1957). On perceptual readiness. *Psychological Review, 64*(2), 123–152.

Campbell, D. T. (1965). Ethnocentric and other altruistic motives. In D. Levine (Ed.), *Nebraska symposium on motivation* (Vol. 13, pp. 283–311). Lincoln: University of Nebraska Press.

Chang, L. W., Krosch, A. R., & Cikara, M.

(2016). Effects of intergroup threat on mind, brain, and behavior. *Current Opinion in Psychology, 11,* 69–73.

Cikara, M. (2015). Intergroup Schadenfreude: Motivating participation in collective violence. *Current Opinion in Behavioral Sciences, 3,* 12–17.

Cikara, M., Botvinick, M. M., & Fiske, S. T. (2011). Us versus them: Social identity shapes neural responses to intergroup competition and harm. *Psychological Science, 22,* 306–313.

Cikara, M., Bruneau, E. G., & Saxe, R. (2011). Us and them: Intergroup failures of empathy. *Current Directions in Psychological Science, 20,* 149–153.

Cikara, M., Bruneau, E. G., Van Bavel, J. J., & Saxe, R. (2014). Their pain gives us pleasure: How intergroup dynamics shape empathic failures and counter-empathic responses. *Journal of Experimental Social Psychology, 55,* 110–125.

Cikara, M., Farnsworth, R. A., Harris, L. T., & Fiske, S. T. (2010). On the wrong side of the trolley track: Neural correlates of relative social valuation. *Social Cognitive and Affective Neuroscience, 5*(4), 404–413.

Cikara, M., & Fiske, S. T. (2011). Bounded empathy: Neural responses to out-group targets' (mis)fortunes. *Journal of Cognitive Neuroscience, 23,* 3791–3803.

Cikara, M., & Fiske, S. T. (2012). Stereotypes and Schadenfreude: Affective and physiological markers of pleasure at others' misfortunes. *Social Psychological and Personality Science, 3,* 63–71.

Cikara, M., & Fiske, S. T. (2013). Their pain, our pleasure: Stereotype content and Schadenfreude. *Annals of the New York Academy of Sciences, 1299,* 52–59.

Cikara, M., & Paluck, E. L. (2013). When going along gets you nowhere and the upside of conflict behaviors. *Social and Personality Psychology Compass, 7*(8), 559–571.

Cikara, M., & Van Bavel, J. J. (2014). The neuroscience of intergroup relations: An integrative review. *Perspectives on Psychological Science, 9,* 245–274.

Cohen, T. R., & Insko, C. A. (2008). War and peace: Possible approaches to reducing intergroup conflict. *Perspectives on Psychological Science, 3*(2), 87–93.

Cohen, T. R., Montoya, R. M., & Insko, C. A. (2006). Group morality and intergroup relations: Cross-cultural and experimental evidence. *Personality and Social Psychology Bulletin, 32,* 1559–1572.

Crockett, M. J., Kurth-Nelson, Z., Siegel, J. Z., Dayan, P., & Dolan, R. J. (2014). Harm to others outweighs harm to self in moral decision making. *Proceedings of the National Academy of Sciences of the USA, 111,* 17320–17325.

Cuddy, A. J. C., Fiske, S. T., & Glick, P. (2007). The BIAS map: Behaviors from intergroup affect and stereotypes. *Journal of Personality and Social Psychology, 92,* 631–648.

Cushman, F., Gray, K., Gaffey, A., & Mendes, W. B. (2012). Simulating murder: The aversion to harmful action. *Emotion, 12,* 2–7.

Deci, E. L., Koestner, R., & Ryan, R. M. (1999). A meta-analytic review of experiments examining the effects of extrinsic rewards on intrinsic motivation. *Psychological Bulletin, 125*(6), 627.

Diener, E. (1979). Deindividuation, self-awareness and disinhibition. *Journal of Personality and Social Psychology, 37,* 1160–1171.

Ellemers, N. (2012). The group self. *Science, 336*(6083), 848–852.

Feather, N. T., & Sherman, R. (2002). Envy, resentment, schadenfreude, and sympathy: Reactions to deserved and undeserved achievement and subsequent failure. *Personality and Social Psychology Bulletin, 28*(7), 953–961.

Festinger, L., Pepitone, A., & Newcomb, T. (1952). Some consequences of deindividuation in a group. *Journal of Abnormal and Social Psychology, 47,* 382–389.

Fiske, A. P., & Rai, T. S. (2015). *Virtuous violence: Hurting and killing to create, sustain, end and honor social relationships.* Cambridge, UK: Cambridge University Press.

Fiske, S. T., Cuddy, A. J. C., Glick, P., & Xu, J. (2002). A model of (often mixed) stereotype content: Competence and warmth respectively follow from perceived status and competition. *Journal of Personality and Social Psychology, 82,* 878–902.

Fiske, S. T., & Ruscher, J. B. (1993). Negative interdependence and prejudice: Whence the affect? In D. M. Mackie & D. L. Hamilton (Eds.), *Affect, cognition, and stereotyping: Interactive processes in group perception* (pp. 239–268). San Diego, CA: Academic Press.

Grossman, D. (1996). *On killing: The psychological cost of learning to kill in war and society.* New York: Back Bay Books.

Hareli, S., & Weiner, B. (2002). Dislike and envy as antecedents of pleasure at another's misfortune. *Motivation and Emotion, 26*(4), 257–277.

Hauser, M., Cushman, F., Young, L., Jin, R. K.-X., & Mikhail, J. (2007). A dissociation between moral judgments and justifications. *Mind and Language, 22*(1), 1–21.

Hein, G., Silani, G., Preuschoff, K., Batson, C. D., & Singer, T. (2010). Neural responses to in-group and out-group members' suffering predict individual differences in costly help-ing. *Neuron, 68,* 149–160.

Hewstone, M., Rubin, M., & Willis, H. (2002). Intergroup bias. *Annual Review of Psychology, 53*(1), 575–604.

Hoogland, C. E., Schurtz, D. R., Cooper, C. M., Combs, D. J., Brown, E. G., & Smith, R. H. (2014). The joy of pain and the pain of joy: In-group identification predicts schadenfreude and gluckschmerz following rival groups' fortunes. *Motivation and Emotion, 39,* 260–281.

Keltner, D. (2009). *Born to be good: The science of a meaningful life.* New York: Norton.

Littman, R. (2015). *Perpetrating violence increases identification with violent groups: Survey evidence from former combatants.* Manuscript in under review.

Littman, R., & Paluck, E. L. (2014). The cycle of violence: Understanding individual participation in collective violence. *Advances in Political Psychology, 36,* 79–99.

Mackie, D. M., Devos, T., & Smith, E. R. (2000). Intergroup emotions: Explaining offensive action tendencies in an intergroup context. *Journal of Personality and Social Psychology, 79*(4), 602–616.

Mackie, D. M., & Hamilton, D. (1993). *Affect, cognition, and stereotyping.* San Diego, CA: Academic Press.

Milgram, S. (1965). Some conditions of obedience and disobedience to authority. *Human Relations, 18,* 57–76.

O'Doherty, J. P. (2004). Reward representations and reward-related learning in the human brain: Insights from neuroimaging. *Current Opinion in Neurobiology, 14*(6), 769–776.

Opotow, S. (2005). Hate, conflict, and moral exclusion. In R. J. Sternberg (Ed.), *The psychology of hate* (pp. 121–153). Washington, DC: American Psychological Association.

Pinter, B., & Wildschut, T. (2012). Self-interest masquerading as ingroup beneficence: An altruistic rationalization explanation of the interindividual–intergroup discontinuity effect. *Small Group Research, 43,* 105–123.

Prentice-Dunn, S., & Rogers, R. W. (1989). Deindividuation and the self-regulation of behavior. In P. B. Paulus (Ed.), *The psychology of group influence* (2nd ed., pp. 86–109). Hillsdale, NJ: Erlbaum.

Reicher, S., Haslam, S. A., & Rath, R. (2008). Making a virtue of evil: A five-step social identity model of the development of collective hate. *Social and Personality Psychology Compass, 2,* 1313–1344.

Rhodes, M., & Chalik, L. (2013). Social categories as markers of intrinsic interpersonal obligations. *Psychological Science, 24*(6), 999–1006.

Sherif, M., Harvey, O. J., White, B. J., Hood, W. R., & Sherif, C. W. (1961). *Intergroup cooperation and competition: The Robbers Cave experiment.* Norman, OK: University Book Exchange.

Sidanius, J., & Pratto, F. (1999). *Social dominance: An intergroup theory of social hierarchy and oppression.* New York: Cambridge University Press.

Singer, T., Seymour, B., O'Doherty, J. P., Stephan, K. E., Dolan, R. J., & Frith, C. D. (2006). Empathic neural responses are modulated by the perceived fairness of others. *Nature, 439,* 466–469.

Smith, R. H., Powell, C. A. J., Combs, D. J. Y., & Schurtz, R. D. (2009). Exploring the when and why of *Schadenfreude. Social and Personality Psychology Compass, 3,* 530–546.

Staub, E. (1989). *The roots of evil: The origins of genocide and other group violence.* New York: Cambridge University Press.

Tajfel, H., & Turner, J. (1979). An integrative theory of intergroup conflict. In W. G. Austin & S. Worschel (Eds.), *The social psychology of intergroup relations* (pp. 33–47). Pacific Grove, CA: Brooks/Cole.

Tajfel, H., & Turner, J. C. (1986). The social identity theory of inter group behavior. In S. Worchel & W. G. Austin (Eds.), *Psychology of intergroup relations* (pp. 7–24). Chicago: Nelson.

Takahashi, H., Kato, M., Matsuura, M., Mobbs, D., Suhara, T., & Okubo, Y. (2009). When your gain is my pain and your pain is my gain: Neural correlates of envy and Schadenfreude. *Science, 323,* 937–939.

Tarrant, M., Branscombe, N. R., Warner, R. H., & Weston, D. (2012). Social identity and perceptions of torture: It's moral when we do it. *Journal of Experimental Social Psychology, 48*(2), 513–518.

Tomasello, M. (2009). *Why we cooperate.* Cambridge, MA: MIT Press.

Van Dijk, W. W., Ouwerkerk, J. W., Smith, R. H., & Cikara, M. (2015). The role of self-evaluation and envy in Schadenfreude. *European Review of Social Psychology, 26,* 247–282.

Woolf, L. M., & Hulsizer, M. R. (2004). Hate groups for dummies: How to build a successful hate group. *Humanity and Society, 28*(1), 40–62.

Zaki, J., & Cikara, M. (2015). Addressing empathic failures. *Current Directions in Psychological Science, 24,* 471–476.

CHAPTER 21

How Can Universal Stereotypes Be Immoral?

Susan T. Fiske

> **If some stereotypes seem to be universal, are they necessarily immoral?**
>
> People around the world are disgusted by homeless people, envy rich people, and pity older people, not because they deserve it, but because of people's universal preoccupations with status and trust.

A Puzzle

Our Issue

Some stereotypes seem to be universal, but not because they are true. People around the world share some prejudices that are arguably arbitrary (Cuddy et al., 2009; Durante et al., 2013; Fiske & Durante, 2016). Here's an example: Many societies keep reinventing moral disgust at people who simply lack an address. Americans report that our society finds homeless people disgusting. Belgians, English, Irish, Italians, Japanese, and Portuguese share disgust toward homeless people. Also, Americans, Australians, Belgians, Italians, and Spanish report disgust about immigrants. The Irish are disgusted by roaming travelers. Greeks, Portuguese, Spanish, and Swiss think Roma (gypsies) are disgusting. Australians and Lebanese likewise view refugees with disgust, as do the Swiss with asylum seekers. Malaysians, Pakistanis, and Spanish are disgusted by beggars, and South Africans by illegal squatters. Egyptians report disgust toward Bedouins. Why do societies commonly feel disgusted by their itinerant vagrants? Disgust is a moral emotion that expresses avoiding contamination, and we have some ideas about why this happens.

On the opposite note, why do people usually resent the rich? Envy, not disgust, is the theme in attitudes toward the rich or upper class, among Americans, Australians, Belgians, Bolivians, Canadians, Chileans, Costa Ricans, Egyptians, English, Greeks, Israelis, Lebanese, Mexicans, New Zealanders, Peruvians, Spanish, Swiss, Turks, and Ugandans. Envy is a volatile emotion that condemns the target for having ill-gotten gains that should be taken away.

A third case example: Why do we pity the old? Americans, Australians, Bolivians, Canadians, Costa Ricans, English, Greeks, Indians, Israelis, Italians, Malaysians, Mexicans, Portuguese, South Africans, Spanish, Swiss, and Ugandans all describe the elderly as pitiable. And contrary to conventional wisdom, Eastern populations even are more negative than Western ones (North & Fiske, 2015). Pity is in effect a moral emotion that promises sympathy, but only as long as its targets know their place.

Our Constructs: How We Think about This Puzzle

This pattern is disturbing, raising questions of good and evil. All three patterns are evil in the sense of denying others their full humanity. The answer I present here offers two primary dimensions for making sense of other people, and these three exemplars fit three different combinations of the two basic dimensions. One dimension, warmth (trustworthiness), interprets the others' intent for good or ill. The second dimension (competence) interprets their capacity to act on those intentions (Fiske, 2015; Fiske, Cuddy, Glick, & Xu, 2002).

In this model, homeless people appear as the most extremely negative outgroup, allegedly low on both warmth and competence. They are dehumanized in that people have difficulty imaging what's going on inside their minds and what they do on a typical day. The brain's theory-of-mind network responds to them less as people (less medial prefrontal cortex) and more as disgusting objects (insula; Harris & Fiske, 2006).

What's more, people's reaction to them as disgusting is a moral reaction, both blaming them for their incompetence and for their exploitative intent (not playing by the rules). Other groups that have no fixed address also disgust people because they seem to have no redeeming qualities, and perhaps observers want to avoid contamination by their stigma. Also, someone who lacks an address is less accountable to and invested in society, so how can they be trusted or respected?

Rich people, one contrasting case, do demand respect for their apparent competence because of their prestige, but they seem untrustworthy because they do not apparently have others' interests at heart. People's ambivalence creates envy and going along to get along, because the rich control resources, but the rich also provoke attack when the chips are down (Cuddy, Fiske, & Glick, 2007). People are pleased when bad events happen to them, reactions expressed by both self-report and electromyography of the smile muscles (*zygomaticus major;* Cikara & Fiske, 2012).

This Schadenfreude toward the rich is arguably dehumanizing because only the envied are its targets among outgroups. People are glad when the high and mighty fall a notch, and people do not delight in their good fortune, unlike all other groups, even the disgusting homeless. Dehumanization of the rich portrays them as unfeeling automatons (Haslam, 2006), so people judge them as lacking in typical human nature, a moral judgment. Observers deny their full human experience.

Finally, older people occupy the opposite quadrant, judged as well intentioned but incompetent. Pity is a moral evaluation of someone with undeserved bad outcomes (Weiner, Perry, & Magnusson, 1988). Elders lose that pity and sympathy if they reveal selfish intent: resisting orderly succession (not retiring), consuming shared resources (using up social security), or invading generational identities (adopting youth culture; North & Fiske, 2013). Pity is a moral emotion (they may deserve better, but only if they adhere to cooperative prescriptions). But pity is also dehumanizing because it disallows their human freedom and disrespects their human abilities.

Thus, arguably, three distinct, salient, and nearly universal stereotypes express moral judgments and accompanying moral emotions that enable dehumanization, which itself seems morally problematic. The morality and moralizing of prejudices touch several raw nerves in society, now and in the past.

Context: Some Debates

Psychological scientists used to treat all stereotypes as alike, interchangeable for research purposes (Fiske, 1998). From the 1940s to the 1960s, prejudiced people allegedly had personality defects that generated broad-based ethnocentrism. In the 1980s and 1990s, exciting advances revealed many general and normal processes of stereotyping—for example, that stereotypes are more automatic, uncontrollable, and widespread than lay people think. This era brought the

Implicit Association Test (Greenwald & Banaji, 1995), revealing spontaneous negative associations to outgroups, an insight now part of popular and professional culture. This era also showed the fundamental categorization of people into ingroup and outgroup (Turner & Tajfel, 1979), predicting ingroup favoritism and perceived outgroup homogeneity. Many other insights followed from understanding basic social cognitive processes of attention, inference, and memory. What these paradigm shifts meant was that prejudice is not the product of sick minds but of normal cognition. Nevertheless, the focus on process treated all stereotypes as similar (simply negative).

The stereotype content model (SCM) offered an alternative perspective, on the premise that distinct historical and cultural contexts lead to distinct biases (Fiske, 1998). For example, when Chinese laborers built American railroads in the mid-19th century, they were viewed in animalistic terms. Since their expulsion, Chinese immigrants today are seen as automatons: scientifically talented and technically savvy. The stereotype content depends on who happens to arrive and what jobs they happen to have, but observers apply their context-driven stereotypes to an entire ethnicity. Stereotypes are accidents of history, so they are not all alike, as groups' immigration histories differ, for example.

A contrasting perspective is that stereotypes reflect reality—accurate perceptions of group differences. Scientific debates on this point predate Gordon Allport (1954), whose brilliant analysis pointed out that we have no criteria for so-called accuracy. If two groups show mean differences, they always show overlapping distributions, and the majority of individuals are not well represented by the mean. An expected value may operate in statistics but not in social life, where differences are small and wrong assumptions costly. Moreover, a single statement that a group has a certain characteristic raises the questions: How much? What proportion? Compared to whom? In whose judgment?

The SCM offers an alternative to stereotype accuracy, explaining the cultural origins of stereotypes in the historical moment's intergroup relations. Principles of social structure, therefore, predict stereotype content. Although specific intergroup contexts may change, the context-to-stereotype principles appear systematic. So they have parsimony on their side, in contrast to ad hoc interpretations of the accuracy of each specific group stereotype. But they also provide a more nuanced account than mere negativity.

According to the SCM, intergroup interdependence predicts the warmth dimension. Cooperating groups seem friendly and trustworthy; competing groups seem exploitative and untrustworthy. Observers extrapolate from a particular intergroup structure of interdependence to characteristics of the entire outgroup. In assessing interdependence, both economic and value cooperation/competition matter here (Kervyn, Fiske, & Yzerbyt, 2015). Observers in effect mimic the sentry's call—"Who goes there, friend or foe?"—where the foe might have hostile intent to compete over tangible resources or shared values. Only those people who share resources and values are warm.

Upon deciding the warmth dimension, one needs to know the others' ability to enact their benign or ill intent. The competence judgment follows from the others' prestige: High-status groups are presumed competent, and low-status ones incompetent. Despite the plausible role of circumstances, people perceive groups to get what they deserve on the basis of who they are. To the extent that context determines societal rank, this perception ignores arbitrary causes of rank and perceived competence.

Stereotypes are historical accidents, not enduring truths. But the principles underlying them have some apparently universal elements.

Theoretical Stance

The SCM argues for universal human preoccupations with status and trust. Regarding status, all human organizations develop hierarchies, either overt or subtle (Gruenfeld & Tiedens, 2010). Primates do it; dogs, birds, and bees do it (Fiske, 2010). Social comparison structures our sociality, creating scorn downward and envy upward (Fiske, 2011). Status organizes interactions, giving priority to those on top. In stable hierarchies, the high-status individuals can relax and neglect their subordinates, whereas the low-status persons must stay vigilant and stand aside. Unstable hierarchies cost the high-status more, as they must constantly defend their position. In either case, status differences get reified by attributing competence to the high-status and incompetence to the low, justifying their respective ranks. Little account is taken of circumstances, opportunities, and challenges.

Regarding the other dimension, trust, interdependence predicts warmth. Again, human interdependence is universal; no one survives and thrives—let alone reproduces—alone. Patterns of interdependence prominently include cooperation, with shared goals wherein each needs the other to gain the desired outcome, and competition, with mutually exclusive goals that each gains only at the other's expense (Kelley & Thibaut, 1978; Rusbult & Van Lange, 2003). Again, the SCM predicts that societal structures get reified and justified, with cooperative groups seen as intrinsically trustworthy and friendly, competitive groups seen as intrinsically otherwise. Circumstances again are ignored.

What's the alternative? In theory, people could take more account of groups' situations that enable status or force interdependence of different kinds. Instead, the SCM posits a kind of group-level correspondence bias (Gilbert & Malone, 1995; Jones, 1979), in that a group's structural position and consequent behavior is interpreted to reflect their dispositions. For example, if Latino immigrants enter the United States to fill low-wage jobs, one interpretation is that they are the dregs of their society, taking away American jobs, so they are inherently incompetent and untrustworthy. An alternative interpretation is that they have to work so hard to get here that they are selected for effortful ingenuity, and, upon arrival, they take jobs no one else wants, so they grow the economy. A structural interpretation is that Mexico's birthrates and economy created conditions that gave young men incentive to migrate (and now that their birthrates have fallen and their economy has improved, net migration is zero; Massey, Durand, & Pren, 2014). The moral judgment follows from dispositionally interpreting their structural place in society.

Another theoretical contrast would hold that some stereotypes could arguably be quasi-biological (especially gender, age, race,

perhaps class), so social structure would have no causal role in stereotype content. This biological stance might seem to explain some of the SCM groups.

Among our three opening puzzles, older people seeming incompetent but warm might be the best case for this biological perspective. Yet it would be a blunt approach, because the evidence on both dimensions is mixed. For example, although fluid intelligence (speed) declines with age, crystallized intelligence (knowledge) grows (Salthouse, 2012). And older people indeed experience more positive affect with age (Charles & Carstensen, 2010), making them warmer, but their health is worse, giving them cause for complaint. The biological reality approach is also tenuous because older people did not always live so long as they do now to show these biologically driven patterns. Besides, the negative overall elder stereotype is more prevalent in countries with aging populations to manage (North & Fiske, 2015), which is more consistent with circumstances than sheer biology.

The biological approach has a harder time explaining social-class stereotypes (e.g., for rich people), unless they are genetically selected by social Darwinism favoring cold competence as a key to success. One might, in parallel, explain homelessness as the purview of biologically incompetent, antisocial individuals. The near-universal cultural patterns for these groups' stereotypes might make this argument seem more plausible. But homelessness is in fact most often temporary, so how can a group be biologically predisposed to be vagrant one month and the next month not, under other circumstances? Moreover, how would one explain cultural idiosyncrasies regarding other groups—for example, unemployed people as disgusting versus pitiable, depending on social welfare systems? Ambivalent sexist stereotypes of women depend also on social systems (Eagly & Steffen, 1984; Glick et al., 2000). So a purely biological account of group images reflecting reality is problematic for several reasons, even beyond Allport's (1954) objections about criteria, noted earlier.

A variant on this position is that prejudices evolve for functional reasons, dating back to ancestral adaptations. This argument works better for gender and age than race (Cosmides, Tooby, & Kurzban, 2003), and arguably not at all for other, more recent in-group–outgroup distinctions, such as modern occupations (e.g., investment bankers).

More compatible social evolutionary perspectives argue that group stereotypes pattern themselves after specific types of threat to the ingroup (e.g., contamination, betrayal, attack; Cottrell & Neuberg, 2005). Or that stereotypes are functional reactions to intergroup relations that vary on relative power, relative status, and goal compatibility (Alexander, Brewer, & Hermann, 1999), dimensions related to the SCM but more differentiated (Fiske, Xu, Cuddy, & Glick, 1999; Fiske et al., 2002). The SCM locates itself away from accuracy claims and toward more structural, functional approaches.

Evidence for the SCM and for Our Three Cases

Our Evidence

We suggest that societies reinvent similar stereotypes—particularly for homeless, rich, or elders—because of similar structures that cut across cultures. Status predicts competence stereotypes, and interdependence predicts warmth stereotypes. The evidence supports each in turn.

As basic as it is to social life, status triggers stereotypes of competence to an astonishing degree around the world. Belief in meritocracy is not just an American dream that people get what they deserve. People everywhere assume that high-status people are competent (across 36 samples, average r = .90, range = .74–.99, all p's < .001; Durante et al., 2013). The correlations are in the range of reliabilities, but not because SCM studies ask the same question twice. The status measure asks about the demographic variables of economic success and job prestige, whereas the competence measure attributes a psychological trait of capability. From a moral standpoint, the assumption that people deserve their status makes a dispositional explanation for both success and failure. The rich get credit, and the poor get blame, without regard to circumstance.

Likewise, interdependence structures also define social life, triggering stereotypes of warmth (friendly, sincere). Beliefs that cooperators are nice and trustworthy, whereas competitors are mean, are robust. Consis-tent but small correlations have averaged r = −.32 (Durante et al., 2013). Improving both the warmth and competition measures substantially increases their correlation (Kervyn et al., 2015). The most reliable correlation occurs (1) when competition measures include both economic and values (tangible and symbolic resources), and (2) warmth measures include both sociability/friendliness and trustworthiness/morality. Judging competitors as less moral—insincere and untrustworthy—is part of the structure–stereotype link.

The downstream consequences of the structure-driven stereotypes are emotional prejudices. In our examples, the low-warmth–low-competence combination, exemplified by homeless people, reliably elicits disgust (Fiske et al., 2002). Other members of this quadrant, besides people without an address (immigrants, refugees, travelers, Roma, Bedouins), include drug addicts. Groups in the cold-but-competent quadrant include not only the resented rich but also business people in general and entrepreneurial ethnic groups (often Jews and Asians), all prompting envy. Warm-but-incompetent groups, besides older people, include the disabled and children, all receiving pity.

Falsification

Although the SCM has been supported around the world and across the last century of measuring stereotypes (Fiske, 2015), critics challenge the warmth dimension (every laboratory gets the competence dimension). First, some suggest that morality, not warmth, is the key term. The original theory and evidence proposed by Abele and Wojciszke (2007) use this term (or *communion*). We have been inclined to lump together as warmth both trustworthiness and sociability, which typically correlate, except for a con artist who uses friendliness as a means for untrustworthy goals. Admittedly, sociability and morality can be separately predictive, especially in perceiving the ingroup (Brambilla & Leach, 2014; Goodwin, Piazza, & Rozin, 2014). The relevant dimensions depend on level of analysis: Though they are separable, friendliness correlates with morality; competence correlates with assertiveness (Abele, Hauke, Peters, Louvet, Szymkow, & Duan, 2016). As lumpers, not splitters, we prefer the overall level of analysis, and we see the SCM as surviving this challenge but with the noted amendments.

Another challenge views the warmth dimension as emerging only from theory, not spontaneous usage (Koch, Imhoff, Dotsch, Unkelbach, & Alves, 2016). Concerned with whether we were inventing these two dimensions and demonstrating only existence proof (people *can* array groups by warmth and competence, but do not necessarily *do* so), we conducted a multidimensional scaling (MDS) study that was more consistent with generating warmth and competence dimensions than not (Kervyn & Fiske, 2016; see also Yzerbyt, 2016). The older Rosenberg, Nelson, and Vivekananthan (1968) MDS generates social good–bad × task good–bad, which are cognate with the SCM warmth × competence. Moreover, also consistent with the SCM studies, Durante, Volpato, and Fiske (2010) independently generated these dimensions from content-analyzing fascist descriptions of social groups. Reanalysis of the Katz and Braly (1933) adjectives fits the same space for historically relevant groups (Bergsieker, Leslie, Constantine, & Fiske, 2012). All these studies speak to support for the SCM dimensions by using other methods of generating them.

Finally, one might argue that the SCM is a WEIRD invention (Henrich, Heine, & Norenzayan, 2010). Indeed, the SCM basic premises do show cultural variation (Fiske & Durante, 2016). The basic hypothesis is that a society's groups will array in a two-dimensional warmth-by-competence space, producing a warmth–competence correlation of approximately zero. Most cultures do produce this pattern, but cultures like the United States, with higher income inequality, show the pattern most clearly. Nations with lower income inequality do not differentiate the mixed (high–low, low–high) combinations as clearly. In fact, the warmth–competence correlation is predicted by national income inequality (Durante et al., 2013). This fits the idea that the mixed quadrants help justify status inequality, describing the deserving and undeserving poor, the deserving and undeserving rich. Lower income inequality tends to produce a larger set of ingroups, all eligible for the social safety net, and then some extreme outgroups (e.g., refugees), low on both dimensions and beyond the pale.

Other cultural variants suggest that East Asian countries, with a more active modesty norm, do not promote societal reference groups (citizens, middle class) to the high–high quadrant, as Westerners do (Cuddy et al., 2009). They assign those ingroups a more neutral location. But because their outgroups land in the usual locations, the SCM seems supported.

Needed Data

Some anomalous SCM data come from high-conflict societies. In Ireland, Israel, and some Arab countries, the warmth–competence correlation is high, but not because of income equality. Data show that conflict simplifies the SCM space to *us* (all good) versus *them* (all bad; Durante, Fiske, Gelfand, et al., 2017).

Besides examining cultural and historical generality, SCM needs exploration at earlier ages. When do children distinguish interdependence/warmth and status/competence? Arguably, infants recognize good and ill intent, as well as status/competence. And school-age children, as well as street children, have generated SCM-compatible data in the Dominican Republic (Anselin, 2004). But more data would be better.

People's perceptions of animal species (pets, predators, vermin, livestock) follow the SCM space (Sevillano & Fiske, 2015), but perhaps other species see conspecifics in similar terms. Some attempts to explore the warmth and competence dimensions ask the question, Do dogs do it? Dogs clearly make social comparisons up and down (Range, Horn, Viranyi, & Huber, 2009), a feature of human status hierarchies that predicts perceived competence.

Corporations get sorted into SCM space by their apparent worthy or unworthy intents and their apparent competence (Kervyn, Fiske, & Malone, 2012). Perhaps other entities—software? cars?—also vary accordingly. The key is the entity displaying intent and capability.

Extension and Expansion: Beyond the SCM

In prejudice, one size does not fit all. Stereotyping is not just hating a group (though many of the most deadly biases are precisely that). Rather, some systematic and apparently universal principles apply, with variations. From a moral perspective, the apparently main dimensions represent moral judgments that an outgroup has evil intent (low warmth) or lacks drive (low competence). In either case, they become less deserving, less fully human.

The tendency to explain group positions in terms of stereotypes reifies, essentializes, and justifies group differences that may at least as much result from circumstance. As such, stereotyping allows societies to ignore these inequalities, or even to support them, immoral responses in themselves.

REFERENCES

Abele, A. E., Hauke, N., Peters, K., Louvet, E., Szymkow, A., & Duan, Y. (2016). Facets of the fundamental content dimensions: Agency with competence and assertiveness—Communion with warmth, and morality. *Frontiers in Psychology.* Available at *www.ncbi.nlm.nih. gov/pmc/articles/PMC5118442.*

Abele, A. E., & Wojciszke, B. (2007). Agency and communion from the perspective of self versus others. *Journal of Personality and Social Psychology, 93*(5), 751–763.

Alexander, M. G., Brewer, M. B., & Hermann, R. K. (1999). Images and affect: A functional analysis of out-group stereotypes. *Journal of Personality and Social Psychology, 77*(1), 78–93.

Allport, G. W. (1954). *The nature of prejudice.* Reading, MA: Addison Wesley.

Anselin, I. (2004). *Assessing Dominican children's views of societal groups: Using the stereotype content model.* Unpublished senior thesis, Princeton University, Princeton, NJ.

Bergsieker, H. B., Leslie, L. M., Constantine, V. S., & Fiske, S. T. (2012). Stereotyping by omission: Eliminate the negative, accentuate the positive. *Journal of Personality and Social Psychology, 102*(6), 1214–1238.

Brambilla, M., & Leach, C. W. (2014). On the importance of being moral: The distinctive role of morality in social judgment. *Social Cognition, 32*(4), 397–408.

Charles, S. T., & Carstensen, L. L. (2010). Social and emotional aging. *Annual Review of Psychology, 61,* 383–409.

Cikara, M., & Fiske, S. T. (2012). Stereotypes and Schadenfreude: Behavioral and physiological markers of pleasure at others' misfortunes. *Social Psychological and Personality Science, 3,* 63–71.

Cosmides, L., Tooby, J., & Kurzban, R. (2003). Perceptions of race. *Trends in Cognitive Sciences, 7*(4), 173–179.

Cottrell, C. A., & Neuberg, S. L. (2005). Different emotional reactions to different groups: A sociofunctional threat-based approach to "prejudice." *Journal of Personality and Social Psychology, 88*(5), 770–789.

Cuddy, A. J. C., Fiske, S. T., & Glick, P. (2007). The BIAS map: Behaviors from intergroup affect and stereotypes. *Journal of Personality and Social Psychology, 92,* 631–648.

Cuddy, A. J. C., Fiske, S. T., Kwan, V. S. Y., Glick, P., Demoulin, S., Leyens, J.-P., . . . Ziegler, R. (2009). Stereotype content model across cultures: Towards universal similarities and some differences. *British Journal of Social Psychology, 48,* 1–33.

Durante, F., Fiske, S. T., Gelfand, M., Crippa, F., Suttora, C., Stillwell, A., . . . Teymoori, A. (2017). Ambivalent stereotypes link to peace, conflict, and inequality across 38 nations. *Proceedings of the National Academy of Sciences of the USA.*

Durante, F., Fiske, S. T., Kervyn, N., Cuddy, A. J. C., Akande, A., Adetoun, B. E., . . . Storari, C. C. (2013). Nations' income inequality predicts ambivalence in stereotype content: How societies mind the gap. *British Journal of Social Psychology, 52,* 726–746.

Durante, F., Volpato, C., & Fiske, S. T. (2010). Using the stereotype content model to examine group depictions in fascism: An archival approach. *European Journal of Social Psychology, 40,* 465–483.

Eagly, A. H., & Steffen, V. J. (1984). Gender stereotypes stem from the distribution of women and men into social roles. *Journal of Personality and Social Psychology, 46*(4), 735–754.

Fiske, S. T. (1998). Stereotyping, prejudice, and discrimination. In D. T. Gilbert, S. T. Fiske, & G. Lindzey (Eds.), *Handbook of social psychology* (4th ed., Vol. 2, pp. 357–411). New York: McGraw-Hill.

Fiske, S. T. (2010). Interpersonal stratification: Status, power, and subordination. In S. T. Fiske, D. T. Gilbert, & G. Lindzey (Eds.), *Handbook of social psychology* (5th ed., pp. 941–982). New York: Wiley.

Fiske, S. T. (2011). *Envy up, scorn down: How status divides us.* New York: Russell Sage Foundation.

Fiske, S. T. (2015). Intergroup biases: A focus on stereotype content. *Current Opinion in Behavioral Sciences, 3,* 45–50.

Fiske, S. T., Cuddy, A. J., Glick, P., & Xu, J. (2002). A model of (often mixed) stereotype content: Competence and warmth respectively follow from perceived status and competition.

Journal of Personality and Social Psychology, 82, 878–902.

Fiske, S. T., & Durante, F. (2016). Stereotype content across cultures: Variations on a few themes. In M. J. Gelfand, C.-Y. Chiu, & Y.-Y. Hong (Eds.), *Advances in culture and psychology* (Vol. 6, pp. 209–258). New York: Oxford University Press.

Fiske, S. T., Xu, J., Cuddy, A. C., & Glick, P. (1999). (Dis)respecting versus (dis)liking: Status and interdependence predict ambivalent stereotypes of competence and warmth. *Journal of Social Issues, 55,* 473–491.

Gilbert, D. T., & Malone, P. S. (1995). The correspondence bias. *Psychological Bulletin, 117,* 21–38.

Glick, P., Fiske, S. T., Mladinic, A., Saiz, J. L., Abrams, D., Masser, B., . . . López, W. (2000). Beyond prejudice as simple antipathy: Hostile and benevolent sexism across cultures. *Journal of Personality and Social Psychology, 79,* 763–775.

Goodwin, G. P., Piazza, J., & Rozin, P. (2014). Moral character predominates in person perception and evaluation. *Journal of Personality and Social Psychology, 106*(1), 148–168.

Greenwald, A. G., & Banaji, M. R. (1995). Implicit social cognition: Attitudes, self-esteem, and stereotypes. *Psychological Review, 102*(1), 4–27.

Gruenfeld, D. H., & Tiedens, L. Z. (2010). Organizational preferences and their consequences. In S. T. Fiske, D. T. Gilbert, & G. Lindzey (Eds.), *Handbook of social psychology* (5th ed., pp. 1252–1287). New York: Wiley.

Harris, L. T., & Fiske, S. T. (2006). Dehumanizing the lowest of the low: Neuro-imaging responses to extreme outgroups. *Psychological Science, 17,* 847–853.

Haslam, N. (2006). Dehumanization: An integrative review. *Personality and Social Psychology Review, 10*(3), 252–264.

Henrich, J., Heine, S. J., & Norenzayan, A. (2010). The weirdest people in the world? *Behavioral and Brain Sciences, 33*(2–3), 61–83.

Jones, E. E. (1979). The rocky road from acts to dispositions. *American Psychologist, 34,* 107–117.

Katz, D., & Braly, K. (1933). Racial stereotypes of one hundred college students. *Journal of Abnormal and Social Psychology, 28*(3), 280–290.

Kelley, H. H., & Thibaut, J. W. (1978). *Interpersonal relations: A theory of interdependence.* New York: Wiley.

Kervyn, N., & Fiske, S. T. (2016). *SCM in MDS I.* Université Catholic de Louvain-la-neuve, Belgium. Unpublished manuscript.

Kervyn, N., Fiske, S. T., & Malone, C. (2012). Brands as intentional agents framework: How perceived intentions and ability can map brand perception. *Journal of Consumer Psychology, 22,* 166–176.

Kervyn, N., Fiske, S. T., & Yzerbyt, Y. (2015). Foretelling the primary dimension of social cognition: Symbolic and realistic threats together predict warmth in the stereotype content model. *Social Psychology, 46,* 36–45.

Koch, A., Imhoff, R., Dotsch, R., Unkelbach, C., & Alves, H. (2016). The ABC of stereotypes about groups: Agency/socio-economic success, conservative–progressive beliefs, and communion. *Journal of Personality and Social Psychology, 110*(5), 675–709.

Massey, D. S., Durand, J., & Pren, K. A. (2014). Explaining undocumented migration to the U.S. *International Migration Review, 48*(4), 1028–1061.

North, M. S., & Fiske, S. T. (2013). Act your (old) age: Prescriptive, ageist biases over succession, identity, and consumption. *Personality and Social Psychology Bulletin, 39*(6), 720–734.

North, M. S., & Fiske, S. T. (2015). Modern attitudes toward older adults in the aging world: A cross-cultural meta-analysis. *Psychological Bulletin, 141*(5), 993–1021.

Range, F., Horn, L., Viranyi, Z., & Huber, L. (2009). The absence of reward induces inequity aversion in dogs. *Proceedings of the National Academy of Sciences of the USA, 106*(1), 340–345.

Rosenberg, S., Nelson, C., & Vivekananthan, P. S. (1968). A multidimensional approach to the structure of personality impressions. *Journal of Personality and Social Psychology, 9*(4), 283–294.

Rusbult, C. E., & Van Lange, P. A. M. (2003). Interdependence, interaction, and relationships. *Annual Review of Psychology, 54,* 351–375.

Salthouse, T. (2012). Consequences of age-related cognitive declines. *Annual Review of Psychology, 63,* 201–226.

Sevillano, V., & Fiske, S. T. (2015). Warmth and competence in animals. *Journal of Applied Social Psychology, 46,* 276–293.

Tajfel, H., & Turner, J. C. (1979). An integrative theory of intergroup conflict. In W. G. Austin & S. Worchel (Eds.), *The social psychology of intergroup relations* (pp. 33–47). Monterey, CA: Brooks/Cole.

Weiner, B., Perry, R. P., & Magnusson, J. (1988). An attributional analysis of reactions to stigmas. *Journal of Personality and Social Psychology, 55*(5), 738–748.

Yzerbyt, V. (2016). *SCM MDS II.* Université Catholic de Louvain-la-neuve, Belgium. Unpublished manuscript.

PART V
MORALITY AND CULTURE

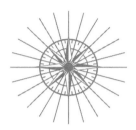

QUESTIONS ANSWERED IN PART V

CHAPTER 22 What are the moral intuitions people have,
and why do they have them?

CHAPTER 23 How does motivation underlie morality?

CHAPTER 24 Are there *any* universally held moral rules that apply
across social–relational contexts?

CHAPTER 25 Why do people care about living up to moral values?

CHAPTER 26 Are moral heroes (e.g., Martin Luther King, Jr.) masterminds
with exceptional moral character, or are they merely symbolic puppets?

CHAPTER 27 Is morality universal?

CHAPTER 28 How does history shape moral values?

CHAPTER 22

Moral Foundations Theory
On the Advantages of Moral Pluralism over Moral Monism

Jesse Graham
Jonathan Haidt
Matt Motyl
Peter Meindl
Carol Iskiwitch
Marlon Mooijman

> **What are the moral intuitions people have, and why do they have them?**
>
> Moral foundations theory approaches this question through the four lenses of nativism, cultural learning, intuitionism, and pluralism.

Moral foundations theory (MFT; Graham et al., 2013; Haidt & Joseph, 2004) was designed to explain both the variety and universality of moral judgments. It makes four central claims about morality.

   1. *There is a first draft of the moral mind.* Nativism is the view that the mind is not a blank slate; it is organized in advance of experience. Evolutionary processes created a first draft of the mind, which is then edited by experience (Marcus, 2004). For example, young Rhesus monkeys who showed no previous fear of snakes (including plastic snakes) watched a video of another monkey reacting fearfully (or not) to a plastic snake. The young Rhesus monkeys learned from a single exposure to the snake-fearing monkey to be afraid of the snake. These monkeys, though, did not learn to be fearful of other stimuli that they may not be "wired" to fear, such as flowers (Mineka & Cook, 1988). These findings suggest that the monkeys may be predisposed to learning some things and not other things. People may similarly be more prone to learning some moral values. For example, young children derive pleasure from fair exchanges and displeasure from unfair exchanges, potentially because fairness promotes more effective interactions between individuals within social groups (Tooby, Cosmides, & Barrett, 2005; Richerson & Boyd, 2005). Therefore, MFT is a nativist theory—it proposes that there

is a first draft of the moral mind that developed in response to evolutionary pressures and is organized prior to experience.

2. *The first draft of the moral mind gets edited during development within a culture.* MFT is also a cultural theory that describes the "editing process" by which the universal first draft of the moral mind becomes a culturally specific and culturally competent adult morality. For example, Hindu cultures emphasize respect for elders and other authorities, as can be seen in the common practice of children bowing to elders and often touching elders' feet. By the time these children reach adulthood, they have gained culturally specific knowledge that may lead them to automatically initiate bowing movements when encountering elders or other revered people. In more individualistic and secular cultures that do not emphasize respect for authority, children are not taught to bow to elders. This might make it easier for them to address authority figures by first name or question their authority later in life. These different social practices in different cultures help explain cultural differences in moral values (e.g., Haidt, Koller, & Dias, 1993). The social practices are not written on a blank slate. It is highly unlikely that there could be a society in which bowing and feet-kissing were done as shows of disrespect or contempt or were aimed primarily at one's subordinates. Primates have an innate toolkit for managing hierarchical relationships, but cultures vary in how they teach their children to apply these tools. You need to know something about this toolkit, this "first draft" of the moral mind, as well as the culture in which a mind develops.

3. *Intuitions come first.* MFT is an intuitionist theory that builds on the social intuitionist model (SIM; Haidt, 2001). Like other types of evaluations, moral judgments happen quickly, often in less than one second of seeing an action or learning the facts of a case (Haidt, 2001; Zajonc, 1980). These judgments are associative, automatic, relatively effortless, and rapid, and they rely on heuristic processing; they occur by processes that many researchers call "System 1" thinking (Bruner, 1960; Kahneman, 2011; Stanovich & West, 2000). The SIM describes

the many System 1 and System 2 processes that occur when people make moral judgments during social interactions. But the SIM says that automatic, System 1 processes generally occur first and drive System 2 thinking, particularly when a person needs to invent a justification that can be shared with others.

4. *There are many psychological foundations of morality.* Lastly, MFT is a pluralist theory that posits that because there were numerous adaptive social challenges throughout evolutionary history, there are many different moral foundations that emerged in response to those challenges. Most research to date has concentrated on five moral foundations:

a. *Care/harm.* Mammals have an unusually long period of development during which they are dependent upon their caretakers. Therefore, caretakers who were more sensitive to the needs and distress of their children were more likely to have children who survived into adulthood. This sensitivity generalizes beyond our own children and can be activated when we learn of other people's children or even see photos of animal babies that activate our urges to care and protect, sometimes linked to anger toward the perpetrator of the harm.

b. *Fairness/cheating.* All social animals interact with each other, and although there are debates as to whether any nonhuman animals have a sense of "fairness" (see McAuliffe & Santos, Chapter 40, this volume), there is little debate that the sense of fairness can be found across human cultures (Fiske, 1991), that it emerges well before the age of 5 and possibly before the age of 1 (Hamlin, Wynn, & Bloom, 2007; LoBue, Chiong, Nishida, DeLoache, & Haidt, 2011; see also the chapters in Section IX, this volume), and that it is related to the evolutionary process that Trivers (1971) described in his famous article on reciprocal altruism. People monitor the behavior and reputations of others; those linked to cheating become less attractive as partners for future interactions.

c. *Loyalty/betrayal.* There are finite resources, and coalitions compete for these resources. The coalitions that are most co-hesive tend to prevail over less cohesive rival coalitions, as Darwin noted in *The Descent of Man* (1871) while wrestling with the question of the origins of morality. The in-tuitions generated by this foundation gen-eralize to brand loyalty, political partisan-ship, and sports fandom today. When people show signs of being disloyal, they are labeled as traitors and may be ostracized from their groups or even put to death (e.g., treason is an offense punishable by death in the United States). When people are loyal group mem-bers, they are extolled as virtuous (e.g., as patriots).

    d. *Authority/subversion.* Primates evolved for life in hierarchies. Nonhuman alpha males are generally more like bullies than like leaders. Human alphas can go ei-ther way, but there can be little doubt that the psychology of authority is essential for understanding human political behavior (Boehm, 1999; De Waal, 1996). Groups and companies that have clear lines of authority, in which the authority is respected and seen as legitimate, generally function better than leaderless or normless groups or groups with autocratic and domineering leadership (Pfef-fer, 1998; Sherif, 1961). People who do not respect authorities or traditions are often os-tracized or punished for insubordination.

    e. *Purity/degradation.*[1] Pathogens and parasites threaten survival, and or-ganisms that avoid contact with these con-taminants are more likely to survive than their counterparts. The adaptive pressure to make accurate judgments about disease risk is especially strong for a group-living species whose diet includes scavenging, as seems to have been the case for early hu-mans. The uniquely human emotion of dis-gust seems well tuned as a "guardian of the mouth" for a highly social and omnivorous species (Rozin, Haidt, & McCauley, 2008) Research on the "behavioral immune sys-tem" (Schaller & Park, 2011) shows that contamination concerns can be generalized to social practices, including being fearful of dissimilar others (e.g., immigrants) and a rejection of people who do not live in ac-cordance with the group's sacred practices (e.g., LGBTQIA individuals in the eyes of many Christians).

Although most research has focused on these five moral foundations, there likely are many other moral foundations; example candidate foundations under investigation are liberty/oppression (Haidt, 2012; Iyer, Koleva, Graham, Ditto, & Haidt, 2012), eq-uity/undeservingness (Meindl, Iyer, & Gra-ham, 2017), and honesty/lying (Graham, Meindl, Koleva, Iyer, & Johnson, 2015; Hofmann, Wisneski, Brandt, & Skitka, 2014; Iyer, 2010).

Historical Context

MFT arose from three streams of research: the cultural anthropology of morality, evo-lutionary psychology, and the "automaticity revolution" within social psychology. Below we highlight some key findings in each area that contributed to the development of MFT.

    Until recently, most prominent theories in moral psychology conceived of the moral do-main as a set of norms and regulations about how individuals should treat other individu-als; theorists generally focused on concepts of harm, rights, and justice (e.g., Kohlberg, 1969; Turiel, 1983), or care and compassion (Gilligan, 1982; Hoffman, 1982). However, Shweder (2008; Shweder, Much, Mahapa-tra, & Park, 1997) proposed that this con-ception of morality reflected the distinctly individualistic conception of the self held widely in secular Western contexts. Based on his fieldwork in India, Shweder proposed that moral psychology had failed to address much of the moral domain that would re-sult from a more global survey of societies. People in all cultures may have moral and regulatory concepts related to harm, rights, and justice (which he called the "ethic of autonomy"), but in many cultures one can also find a concept of self as an office holder in a social system, related to a set of moral and regulatory concepts such as loyalty and duty (which he called the "ethic of com-munity"). One can also find conceptions of the self as a vessel for, or bearer of, a divine soul or spark, with moral and regulatory no-tions that preserve one's purity and sanctity (which he called the "ethic of divinity").

    Shweder's pluralistic conception of the moral domain mapped well onto the mul-tiple findings and theories coming out of work on the evolution of moral behavior. Evolutionary psychologists have long held that innate mental structures, shaped over evolutionary time, predispose humans to certain behaviors, emotional reactions, and forms of learning. Bowlby's (1969) attachment theory was an explicitly evolutionary theory that rejected the unconstrained learning theories of Freudians and behaviorists. Trivers's (1971) classic paper on reciprocal altruism explained how a set of moral–emotional responses to cheaters and cooperators could have evolved as the psychological foundations of judgments of fairness. But how many of these evolved mechanisms are there, and which ones are the most important ones for understanding human morality?

To begin answering those questions, one must consider how moral judgments occur at the cognitive level. It has long been established that there exist two general forms of cognition, often called System 1 (fast, effortless, and intuition-based) and System 2 (slower, more effortful, involving conscious deliberate reasoning; see Bruner & Austin, 1986; Metcalfe & Mischel, 1999; see review in Kahneman, 2011). Whereas Kohlberg's (1969) moral psychology focused on System 2 processes, the "automaticity revolution" of the 1990s shifted the focus of the field toward System 1. Bargh and Chartrand (1999), noting the remarkable accuracy of social judgments based on "thin slices" of behavior (Ambady & Rosenthal, 1992), questioned whether conscious thinking generally precedes judgments or merely follows afterward. They wrote: "So it may be, especially for evaluations and judgments of novel people and objects, that what we think we are doing while consciously deliberating in actuality has no effect on the outcome of the judgment, as it has already been made through relatively immediate, automatic means" (Bargh & Chartrand, 1999, p. 475).

Drawing on this work, Haidt (2001) formulated the SIM, which proposed that moral evaluations generally occur rapidly and derive from System 1 intuitive processing. System 2 plays many roles in moral judgment, but by its very nature it tends to engage only after an initial System 1 evaluation is made, and it tends to be employed as people engage in (or prepare to engage in) discussion with each other. Moral Foundations Theory was created to go beyond the SIM: Granting that "intuitions come first," what exactly are these intuitions, where do they come from, how do they develop, and why does morality vary across cultures?

In an effort to determine the best candidates for the foundations of moral thinking, Haidt and Joseph (2004) surveyed anthropological and evolutionary approaches to moral judgment. They searched for the concerns, perceptions, and emotional responses that occur in the accounts of multiple anthropologists (e.g., reciprocity as described by Malinowski, 1922/2002) and that also fit into existing evolutionary frameworks (e.g., Trivers's reciprocal altruism).

Haidt and Joseph (2004) drew from Shweder's theory of moral discourse, Fiske's (1991) models of interpersonal relationships, Schwartz and Bilsky's (1990) theory of values, and evolutionary models such as De Waal's (1996) "building blocks" of morality in other primates. They identified five best candidates—five clear and direct bridges between the anthropological and evolutionary literatures. These five became the original five foundations of MFT, although, as we have said, we believe there are others. (For a review of the history of MFT and the evolutionary basis of each foundation, see Graham et al., 2013, and Haidt, 2012, Chapters 6–8.)

Theoretical Stance

MFT has been critiqued from the standpoint of multiple other theories in moral psychology. Some of these critiques have focused on MFT's central claim of nativism (e.g., Suhler & Churchland, 2011). Others have critiqued our embrace of intuitionism (e.g., Narvaez, 2008). But in the last few years, most critiques have centered on MFT's tenet of moral pluralism, with critics proposing alternative forms of pluralism or decomposing specific foundations. For instance, the model of moral motives (Janoff-Bulman & Carnes, 2013, and Chapter 23, this volume) proposes that—in addition to the five moral foundations—there also exist group-focused social justice concerns not covered by care and fairness. And relationship regulation theory (Rai & Fiske, 2011; Rai, Chapter 24, this volume) argues that you need to examine the social relations in a given context in order to understand the dominant moral motivations at play (unity, hierarchy, equality, or proportionality). Others have argued that individual moral foundations as proposed by MFT can be multidimensional, with fairness being perceived as equality or equity (Meindl et al., 2017) or purity containing multiple components (Pizarro, 2016). These critiques and resulting debates have been fruitful in refining and reconciling different pluralist approaches to morality (see also Graham et al., 2013, Section 4.3).

Perhaps the most active debate these days, however, is not between different *forms* of moral pluralism but between moral pluralism and moral *monism*. By moral monism we mean theories stating that all morality can be boiled down to one thing, whether that one thing be reasoning about justice (Kohlberg, 1969), intuitive moral grammar (Mikhail, 2007), mutualistic fairness intuitions (Baumard, André, & Sperber, 2013), or perceptions of harm within a dyad (Gray, Schein, & Ward, 2014). MFT was created to capture the richness of moral diversity and move moral psychology beyond monist moral accounts. Yet the pluralistic nature of morality remains a topic of scientific debate. For instance, Gray and colleagues (Gray & Keeney, 2015; Schein & Gray, 2015a, 2015b, Chapter 37, this volume) have proposed dyadic morality theory (DMT), arguing that the seeming plurality in moral attitudes and beliefs can be fully explained by perceptions of harm. All moral judgments, in this view, are produced by a single process of linking stimuli to the cognitive template of an intentional agent causing harm to a vulnerable patient: "a dyadic template suggests not only that perceived suffering is tied to immorality, but that all morality is understood through the lens of harm" (Gray, Young, & Waytz, 2012, p. 108). They apply this framework to political psychology, asserting that "moral disagreements can be understood with one simple question: 'what do liberals and conservatives see as harmful?'" (Schein & Gray, 2015b). We agree that if you had to pick one foundation as the most important single one, in terms of both importance and prototypicality, Care/harm is probably the

best candidate. Evidence has been shown for the centrality, ubiquity, and prototypicality of harm in (negative) moral judgments (Gray et al., 2014; Schein & Gray, 2015a), and this is quite compatible with MFT (especially in WEIRD societies; see Haidt et al., 1993). However, no evidence has been found for DMT's more novel claim that all moral judgments work essentially the same at a cognitive level and that all morality boils down to harm perception (for more on the gulf between DMT's claims and the evidence, see Haidt, Graham, & Ditto, 2015).

In addition, Gray and colleagues contrast this shape-shifting version of their own theory with a straw-man version of MFT as a theory of five Fodorian modules that are completely separate, nonoverlapping, domain-specific, and fully encapsulated processing systems (see also Valdesolo, Chapter 10, this volume). But, in fact, MFT employs the more flexible and overlapping notion of modularity developed by anthropologists Sperber and Hirschfeld (2004). As explained in the main statement on MFT's modularity, the foundations are *developmental constructs*—they refer to what is innately given as part of the "first draft" of the evolved human mind, which then gets elaborated in culturally specific ways:

> Each of these five [sets of concerns] is a good candidate for a Sperber-style learning module. However, readers who do not like modularity theories can think of each one as an evolutionary preparedness (Seligman, 1971) to link certain patterns of social appraisal to specific emotional and motivational reactions. All we insist upon is that the moral mind is partially structured in advance of experience so that five (or more) classes of social concerns are likely to become moralized during development (Haidt & Joseph, 2007, p. 381).

Dyadic morality proponents have recently sacrificed much of their parsimony by offering "harm pluralism" (see Schein & Gray, Chapter 37, this volume). The theory was extremely parsimonious in its original form, wherein all morality boils down to a specific harm: "harm involves the perception of two interacting minds, one mind (an agent) intentionally causing suffering to another mind (a patient)" (Schein & Gray, 2015a). But now, with "harm pluralism," it is unclear whether a single template-matching process is still being argued for or whether multiple different cognitive templates of harm (physical–emotional harm, cheating harm, group harm, disrespect harm, soul harm, etc.) are proposed. When harm is stretched and diluted so much that it means any kind of moral badness, then DMT becomes little more than the claim that moral judgments are intrinsically about dyads without providing any framework for understanding plurality in moral judgments (e.g., if group harm, disrespect harm, and soul harm are the harms that liberals and conservatives perceive differentially, then how does DMT help explain why they do so?). Is DMT offering a semi-blank-slate theory in which the dyadic template is innate, but all knowledge of kinds of harm is learned, and *anything* could be taught to kids to be harmful? Or is DMT saying (as MFT does) that there is something about evolved bodily processes that seems to attract moralization in surprisingly similar forms around the world? Does DMT say that the cultural similarities are a coincidence, or do they posit some form of innate preparedness to learn about harmfulness, cheating, betrayal, disrespect, and degradation? If the latter, DMT has lost its claim to parsimony, and it's no longer clear what, if anything, the theory proposes that is really in contrast with MFT.

Dyadic morality could be usefully integrated with MFT if one examines harm as more central than other foundations without reducing these foundations to just less prototypical forms of harm. The empirical evidence in favor of this kind of moral pluralism is by now very extensive, whereas the evidence in support of monism is limited and contested (Graham, 2015; Haidt, Graham, & Ditto, 2015). We summarize these two bodies of evidence in the next section.

Evidence for MFT's Pluralism over Moral Monism

MFT rests on four falsifiable claims about human morality: nativism, cultural learning, intuitionism, and pluralism. As we noted previously, "if any of these claims is disproved, or is generally abandoned by psychologists, then MFT would need to be abandoned, too" (Graham et al., 2013). Here we examine evidence for one of the most contentious of these claims: pluralism. How do we know there are really multiple moral foundations and that they don't all boil down to one thing, such as justice (Kohlberg, 1969) or perceptions of dyadic harm (Gray et al., 2014)? Studies showing differences between harm and impurity judgments have been critiqued recently by the monist argument that impurity is just a weird and less severe form of harm and that impurity is no more than "(perceived) harm involving sex" (Gray & Keeney, 2015; see also Graham, 2015, on the absence of any evidence that harm/impurity differences are solely attributable to weirdness and severity). So as a test case we examine the evidence for pluralist conceptions of (im)purity concerns, contra monist approaches that would see them as essentially reducible to harm (e.g., Gray et al., 2014).

First, Purity/degradation judgments predict important thoughts and behaviors over and above Care/harm judgments. For instance, purity concerns uniquely predict (beyond other foundations and demographics such as political ideology) culture-war attitudes about gay marriage, euthanasia, abortion, and pornography (Koleva, Graham, Haidt, Iyer, & Ditto, 2012). Purity also predicts opposition to stem cell research (Clifford & Jerit, 2013), environmental attitudes (Rottman, Kelemen, & Young, 2015), lawsuits (Buccafusco & Fagundes, 2015), and social distancing in real-world social networks (Dehghani et al., 2016). Moral concerns about impurity uniquely predict moral judgments of suicide, far more than do judgments about harm (Rottman, Kelemen, & Young, 2014a, 2014b). In line with multiple demonstrations of basic discriminant validity between the foundations (Graham et al., 2011), several recent studies showed that purity judgments are a stronger predictor of disgust sensitivity than are judgments related to any other foundation (Wagemans, Brandt, & Zeelenberg, 2017). Finally, even responses to sacrificial dilemmas (which require harming one person to avoid harming several others) are predicted by multiple foundations, not just care/harm:

Inconsistent with Moral Dyad Theory, our results did not support the prediction that Harm concerns would be the unequivocally most important predictor of sacrifice endorsement. Consistent with Moral Foundations Theory, however, multiple moral values are predictive of sacrifice judgments: Harm and Purity negatively predict, and Ingroup positively predicts, endorsement of harmful action in service of saving lives, with Harm and Purity explaining similar amounts of unique variance. The present study demonstrates the utility of pluralistic accounts of morality, even in moral situations in which harm is central. (Crone & Laham, 2015)

Second, impurity judgments can actively *do* things that harm judgments cannot. Framing environmental issues in terms of purity (vs. harm) experimentally increased moderate and conservative support for environmental initiatives up to liberal levels (Feinberg & Willer, 2013). Purity framing also reduced polarization on the Affordable Care Act (Feinberg & Willer, 2015) and increased conservatives' liberal attitudes more generally (Day, Fiske, Downing, & Trail, 2014). Group-based discrimination in moral judgment has been shown to be specific to the domain of moral purity: Purity information can experimentally increase both praise and condemnation of others (Masicampo, Barth, & Ambady, 2014). Similarly, exposure to purity similarity information can experimentally reduce social distancing, more so than similarity information related to any other moral concerns (Dehghani et al., 2016). And studies of the processes of moralization through "moral shock" (e.g., increasing moral convictions about abortion following graphic pictures of aborted fetuses) showed that such moralization is mediated by disgust and not by anger or harm appraisals, disconfirming dyadic morality on its own terms (Wisneski & Skitka, 2016).

Third, there is growing evidence that moral judgments about harm versus impurity operate in different ways at a cognitive level. These different kinds of judgments have been associated with different facial micro-expressions (Cannon, Schnall, & White, 2011) and neural systems (Parkinson et al., 2011; Wasserman, Chakroff, Saxe, & Young, 2017). Unique developmental pathways for purity

judgments have been proposed, involving both feelings and normative information in concert (Rottman & Kelemen, 2012). Impurity and harm judgments respond in opposite ways to experimental manipulations of abstract–concrete mindsets (Napier & Luguri, 2013) and approach–avoidance motivations (Cornwell & Higgins, 2013); further, priming parental status increases severity of purity judgments, but not harm judgments (Eibach, Libby, & Ehrlinger, 2009). Purity concerns have been shown to function to protect the self, while harm concerns function to protect others (Chakroff, Dungan, & Young, 2013). A study of the "symbolic purity of mind" concluded that religious people felt intuitive disgust at their own heretical thoughts, a disgust that was "meaningfully distinct from anger as a moral emotion" (Ritter, Preston, Salomon, & Relihan-Johnson, 2015). Intention has been shown to matter less for impurity than for harm judgments (Young & Saxe, 2011), and this is supported by the finding that accidental versus intentional harms produce differential activation in the right temperoparietal junction, while accidental versus intentional purity violations show no such distinction (Chakroff et al., 2015). Compared to harm judgments, impurity judgments involve less condemnation of the act itself but more condemnation of the actor (Uhlmann & Zhu, 2013); this "harmful situations, impure people" attribution asymmetry for purity versus harm judgments has also been found while controlling for severity and weirdness (Chakroff & Young, 2015).

Even in their attempt to explain away all these harm/impurity differences as merely attributable to weirdness and severity, Gray and Keeney (2015) were forced to conclude: "as in Study 2, this suggests that severity and weirdness likely do not account for all differences between harm and impurity scenarios." Although more evidence exists for some foundation distinctions than others—for example, not much work has been done differentiating loyalty from authority judgments—the evidence on care vs. purity (and on individualizing vs. binding foundations more generally) clearly supports some form of moral pluralism and calls into question monist theories of moral judgment.

Extension and Expansion

The ongoing debates and plurality of approaches in this *Atlas* volume demonstrate that this is the golden age of the science of morality (see also Graham & Valdesolo, in press). In its first decade, MFT has substantially expanded the range of moral concerns under investigation in moral psychology by encouraging researchers to look beyond individual harm and fairness. In the next decade, we expect that MFT will continue to develop, both theoretically and methodologically. Following the idea of method–theory codevelopment (Graham et al., 2013), new constructs (e.g., liberty/oppression concerns) are explored as new methods and measures are developed, such as the recently validated moral foundations vignettes (Clifford et al., 2015) and current efforts to update and improve the Moral Foundations Questionnaire (Graham et al., 2011). MFT is also likely to be applied to increasingly more fields outside of psychology, such as information technology (Dehghani, Sagae, Sachdeva, & Gratch, 2014), law (Silver & Silver, 2017), sociology (Vaisey & Miles, 2014), organizational behavior (Fehr, Yam, & Dang, 2015), sustainability science (Watkins, Aitken, & Mather, 2016), ethics education (Andersen, Zuber, & Hill, 2015), media studies (Tamborini, 2011), and agricultural ethics (Mäkiniemi, Pirttilä-Backman, & Pieri, 2014).

Finally, we expect that MFT will continue to be useful for understanding political differences and debates. Richard Shweder and other anthropologists have long been arguing that the moral domain is far broader than what was being studied by researchers coming from a secular Western perspective—what we would now call a WEIRD perspective (Henrich, Heine, & Norenzayan, 2010). MFT was created to further develop this insight by offering a list of specific foundations. MFT was not created to study political differences, but it was immediately put to that use as political polarization continued to rise in the United States and left and right came to seem increasingly like separate cultures (Haidt & Graham, 2007). MFT has often been used as the basis for advice given to left-leaning parties to help them see what they often failed to see about conservative morality: Conservatives care far more about moral issues related to loyalty (e.g., patriotism and nationalism), authority (e.g., law and order, respect for parents and the police), and purity (e.g., religious and traditional restrictions on sexuality and drug use; perceptions of moral decay more generally).

America and Europe are now being convulsed by political movements whose morality is quite explicitly based on the loyalty, authority, and purity foundations. These movements embrace the label *nationalism;* some of them even embrace a "blood and soil" version of nationalism that is often linked to theories of racial supremacy (Graham & Haidt, 2012). In every Western country with a populist rebellion, people are angry at the "globalist" or "cosmopolitan" elite and its morality, which seems (to the nationalists) to be based primarily on the care foundation.

The year 2016 will long be remembered as the year that the educated elite in many Western countries realized that they do not understand the morality of many of their fellow citizens. MFT offers them a way to do so; monist theories do not. MFT has offended intellectuals on the left, who claim that it legitimizes right-wing moralities by dignifying them as real human moralities, rather than condemning them as pathologies or self-soothing mechanisms. But MFT is not a normative theory of the moral concerns people *should* have; it is a descriptive theory of the moral concerns people *do* have (Graham, 2014). The simple fact is that every human community, from street gangs to corporations to academic fields such as social psychology, develops a moral order, a moral "matrix," within which their moral lives take place and their political views are formed.

Moral psychology is hard because—like anthropology—it requires researchers to step outside their matrix and study other matrices without bias. In the process, they often learn a great deal about their home culture. The coming years would be a very good time for social scientists to commit themselves to understanding moralities that are not their own and that they may even find personally offensive. MFT can help.

NOTE

1. In Graham et al. (2013) we used the label *sanctity/degradation* for this foundation; here we revert to the more widely used *purity/degradation*.

REFERENCES

Ambady, N., & Rosenthal, R. (1992). Thin slices of expressive behavior as predictors of interpersonal consequences: A meta-analysis. *Psychological Bulletin, 111,* 256–274.

Andersen, M. L., Zuber, J. M., & Hill, B. D. (2015). Moral foundations theory: An exploratory study with accounting and other business students. *Journal of Business Ethics, 132,* 525–538.

Bargh, J. A., & Chartrand, T. L. (1999). The unbearable automaticity of being. *American Psychologist, 54,* 462–479.

Baumard, N., André, J. B., & Sperber, D. (2013). A mutualistic approach to morality: The evolution of fairness by partner choice. *Behavioral and Brain Sciences, 36*(1), 59–78.

Boehm, C. (1999). *Hierarchy in the forest: The evolution of egalitarian behavior.* Cambridge, MA: Harvard University Press.

Bowlby, J. (1969). *Attachment and loss: Vol. 1. Attachment.* New York: Basic Books.

Bruner, J. S. (1960). *The process of education.* Cambridge, MA: Harvard University Press.

Bruner, J. S., & Austin, G. A. (1986). *A study of thinking.* Piscataway, NJ: Transaction.

Buccafusco, C. J., & Fagundes, D. (2015). The moral psychology of copyright infringement. *Minnesota Law Review, 100.* Available at *http://papers.ssrn.com/sol3/cf_dev/AbsByAuth.cfm?per_id =429612.*

Cannon, P. R., Schnall, S., & White, M. (2011). Transgressions and expressions: Affective facial muscle activity predicts moral judgments. *Social Psychological and Personality Science, 2*(3), 325–331.

Chakroff, A., Dungan, J., Koster-Hale, J., Brown, A., Saxe, R., & Young, L. (2015). When minds matter for moral judgment: Intent information is neurally encoded for harmful but not impure acts. *Social Cognitive and Affective Neuroscience, 11,* 476–184.

Chakroff, A., Dungan, J., & Young, L. (2013). Harming ourselves and defiling others: What determines a moral domain? *PLOS ONE, 8*(9), e74434.

Chakroff, A., & Young, L. (2015). Harmful situations, impure people: An attribution asymmetry across moral domains. *Cognition, 136,* 30–37.

Clifford, S., Iyengar, V., Cabeza, R., & Sinnott-Armstrong, W. (2015). Moral foundations vignettes: A standardized stimulus database of scenarios based on moral foundations theory. *Behavior Research Methods, 47,* 1178–1198.

Clifford, S., & Jerit, J. (2013). How words do the work of politics: Moral foundations theory and the debate over stem cell research. *Journal of Politics, 75*(3), 659–671.

Cornwell, J. F., & Higgins, E. T. (2013). Morality and its relation to political ideology: The role of promotion and prevention concerns. *Personality and Social Psychology Bulletin, 39,* 1164–1172.

Crone, D. L., & Laham, S. M. (2015). Multiple moral foundations predict responses to sacrificial dilemmas. *Personality and Individual Differences, 85,* 60–65.

Darwin, C. (1871). The descent of man (2 vols.). *London, 81,* 130–131.

Day, M. V., Fiske, S. T., Downing, E. L., & Trail, T. E. (2014). Shifting liberal and conservative attitudes using moral foundations theory. *Personality and Social Psychology Bulletin, 40*(12), 1559–1573.

De Waal, F. B. M. (1996). *Good natured: The origins of right and wrong in humans and other animals.* Cambridge, MA: Harvard University Press.

Dehghani, M., Johnson, K. M., Hoover, J., Sagi, E., Garten, J., Parmar, N. J., . . . Graham, J. (2016). Purity homophily in social networks. *Journal of Experimental Psychology: General, 145*(3), 366–375.

Dehghani, M., Sagae, K., Sachdeva, S., & Gratch, J. (2014). Analyzing political rhetoric in conservative and liberal weblogs related to the construction of the "Ground Zero Mosque." *Journal of Information Technology and Politics, 11,* 1–14.

Eibach, R. P., Libby, L. K., & Ehrlinger, J. (2009). Priming family values: How being a parent affects moral evaluations of harmless but offensive acts. *Journal of Experimental Social Psychology, 45*(5), 1160–1163.

Fehr, R., Yam, K. C. S., & Dang, C. (2015). Moralized leadership: The construction and consequences of ethical leader perceptions. *Academy of Management Review, 40,* 182–209.

Feinberg, M., & Willer, R. (2013). The moral roots of environmental attitudes. *Psychological Science, 24*(1), 56–62.

Feinberg, M., & Willer, R. (2015). From gulf to bridge: When Do moral arguments facilitate political influence? *Personality and Social Psychology Bulletin, 41*(12), 1665–1681.

Fiske, A. P. (1991). *Structures of social life: The*

four elementary forms of human relations. New York: Free Press.

Gilligan, C. (1982). *In a different voice: Psychological theory and women's development.* Cambridge, MA: Harvard University Press.

Graham, J. (2014). Descriptive vs. normative psychology. Retrieved March 1, 2017, from *www.yourmorals.org/blog/2014/12/descriptive-vs-normative-moral-psychology.*

Graham, J. (2015). Explaining away differences in moral judgment: Comment on Gray and Keeney. *Social Psychological and Personality Science, 6,* 869–873.

Graham, J., & Haidt, J. (2012). Sacred values and evil adversaries: A moral foundations approach. In P. Shaver & M. Mikulincer (Eds.), *The social psychology of morality: Exploring the causes of good and evil* (pp. 11–31). New York: APA Books.

Graham, J., Haidt, J., Koleva, S., Motyl, M., Iyer, R., Wojcik, S. P., & Ditto, P. H. (2013). Moral foundations theory: The pragmatic validity of moral pluralism. *Advances in Experimental Social Psychology, 47,* 55–130.

Graham, J., Haidt, J., & Nosek, B. A. (2009). Liberals and conservatives rely on different sets of moral foundations. *Journal of Personality and Social Psychology, 96,* 1029–1046.

Graham, J., Meindl, P., Koleva, S., Iyer, R., & Johnson, K. M. (2015). When values and behavior conflict: Moral pluralism and intrapersonal moral hypocrisy. *Social and Personality Psychology Compass, 9,* 158–170.

Graham, J., Nosek, B. A., Haidt, J., Iyer, R., Koleva, S., & Ditto, P. H. (2011). Mapping the moral domain. *Journal of Personality and Social Psychology, 101,* 366–385.

Graham, J., & Valdesolo, P. (in press). Morality. In K. Deaux & M. Snyder (Eds.), *The Oxford handbook of personality and social psychology.* Oxford, UK: Oxford University Press.

Gray, K., & Keeney, J. (2015). Impure, or just weird?: Scenario sampling bias raises questions about the foundation of morality. *Social Psychology and Personality Science, 6,* 859–868.

Gray, K., Schein, C., & Ward, A. F. (2014). The myth of harmless wrongs in moral cognition: Automatic dyadic completion from sin to suffering. *Journal of Experimental Psychology: General, 143*(4), 1600–1615.

Gray, K., Young, L., & Waytz, A. (2012) Mind perception is the essence of morality. *Psychological Inquiry, 23,* 101–124.

Haidt, J. (2001). The emotional dog and its rational tail: A social intuitionist approach to moral judgment. *Psychological Review, 108,* 814–834.

Haidt, J. (2012). *The righteous mind: Why good people are divided by politics and religion.* New York: Pantheon.

Haidt, J., & Graham, J. (2007). When morality opposes justice: Conservatives have moral intuitions that liberals may not recognize. *Social Justice Research, 20,* 98–116.

Haidt, J., Graham, J., & Ditto, P. H. (2015). Dyadic morality is the Volkswagen of moral psychology. Retrieved March 1, 2017, from *www.spsp.org/blog/volkswagen-of-morality.*

Haidt, J., & Joseph, C. (2004). Intuitive ethics: How innately prepared intuitions generate culturally variable virtues. *Daedalus, 133,* 55–66.

Haidt, J., & Joseph, C. (2007). The moral mind: How five sets of innate intuitions guide the development of many culture-specific virtues, and perhaps even modules. *The Innate Mind, 3,* 367–391.

Haidt, J., Koller, S., & Dias, M. (1993). Affect, culture, and morality, or is it wrong to eat your dog? *Journal of Personality and Social Psychology, 65,* 613–628.

Hamlin, K., Wynn, K., & Bloom, P. (2007). Social evaluation by preverbal infants. *Nature, 450,* 557–559.

Henrich, J., Heine, S. J., & Norenzayan, A. (2010). The weirdest people in the world? *Behavioral and Brain Sciences, 33,* 61–83.

Hoffman, M. L. (1982). Development of prosocial motivation: Empathy and guilt. In N. Eisenberg (Ed.), *The development of prosocial behavior* (pp. 218–231). New York: Academic Press.

Hofmann, W., Wisneski, D. C., Brandt, M. J., & Skitka, L. J. (2014). Morality in everyday life. *Science, 345*(6202), 1340–1343.

Iyer, R. (2010). The case for honesty as a moral foundation. Retrieved June 26, 2012, from *www.polipsych.com/2010/12/07/the-case-for-honesty-as-a-moral-foundation.*

Iyer, R., Koleva, S. P., Graham, J., Ditto, P. H., & Haidt, J. (2012). Understanding Libertarian morality: The psychological roots of an individualist ideology. *PLOS ONE, 7*(8), e42366.

Janoff-Bulman, R., & Carnes, N. C. (2013). Surveying the moral landscape: Moral motives and group-based moralities. *Personality and Social Psychology Review, 17*(3), 219–236.

Kahneman, D. (2011). *Thinking, fast and slow.* New York: Farrar, Strauss, & Giroux.

Kohlberg, L. (1969). Stage and sequence: The cognitive-developmental approach to socialization. In D. A. Goslin (Ed.), *Handbook of socialization theory and research* (pp. 347–480). Chicago: Rand McNally.

Koleva, S., Graham, J., Haidt, J., Iyer, R., & Ditto, P. H. (2012). Tracing the threads: How five moral concerns (especially purity) help explain culture war attitudes. *Journal of Research in Personality, 46*, 184–194.

LoBue, V., Chiong, C., Nishida, T., DeLoache, J., & Haidt, J. (2011). When getting something good is bad: Even 3-year-olds react to inequality. *Social Development, 20*(1), 154–170.

Mäkiniemi, J. P., Pirttilä-Backman, A. M., & Pieri, M. (2013). The endorsement of the moral foundations in food-related moral thinking in three European countries. *Journal of Agricultural and Environmental Ethics, 26*, 771–786.

Malinowski, B. (1922/2002). *Argonauts of the Western Pacific: An account of native enterprise and adventure in the archipelagoes of Melanesian New Guinea*. New York: Routledge.

Marcus, G. (2004). *The birth of the mind*. New York: Basic Books.

Masicampo, E. J., Barth, M., & Ambady, N. (2014). Group-based discrimination in judgments of moral purity-related behaviors: Experimental and archival evidence. *Journal of Experimental Psychology: General, 143*(6), 2135–2152.

Meindl, P., Iyer, R., & Graham, J. (2017). *A pleasure/power principle of justice: Distributive justice beliefs are guided by societal concerns for pleasure and power*. Manuscript submitted for publication.

Metcalfe, J., & Mischel, W. (1999). A hot/cool-system analysis of delay of gratification: Dynamics of willpower. *Psychological Review, 106*(1), 3.

Mikhail, J. (2007). Universal moral grammar: Theory, evidence and the future. *Trends in Cognitive Sciences, 11*(4), 143–152.

Mineka, S., & Cook, M. (1988). Social learning and the acquisition of snake fear in monkeys. In T. R. Zentall & J. B. G. Galef (Eds.), *Social learning: Psychological and biological perspectives* (pp. 51–74). Hillsdale, NJ: Erlbaum.

Napier, J. L., & Luguri, J. B. (2013). Moral mind-sets: Abstract thinking increases a preference for "individualizing" over "binding" moral foundations. *Social Psychological and Personality Science, 4*, 754–759.

Narvaez, D. (2008). The social-intuitionist model: Some counter-intuitions. In W. A. Sinnott-Armstrong (Ed.), *Moral psychology: Vol. 2. The cognitive science of morality: Intuition and diversity* (pp. 233–240). Cambridge, MA: MIT Press.

Parkinson, C., Sinnott-Armstrong, W., Koralus, P. E., Mendelovici, A., McGeer, V., & Wheatley, T. (2011). Is morality unified?: Evidence that distinct neural systems underlie moral judgments of harm, dishonesty, and disgust. *Journal of Cognitive Neuroscience, 23*(10), 3162–3180.

Pfeffer, J. (1998). *The human equation: Building profits by putting people first*. Cambridge, MA: Harvard Business Press.

Pizarro, D. (2016). *Disgust and the domain of moral purity*. Paper presented at the annual convention of the Society for Personality and Social Psychology, San Diego, CA.

Rai, T. S., & Fiske, A. P. (2011). Moral psychology is relationship regulation: Moral motives for unity, hierarchy, equality, and proportionality. *Psychological Review, 118*, 57–75.

Richerson, P. J., & Boyd, R. (2005). *Not by genes alone: How culture transformed human evolution*. Chicago: University of Chicago Press.

Ritter, R. S., Preston, J. L., Salomon, E., & Relihan-Johnson, D. (2015). Imagine no religion: Heretical disgust, anger and the symbolic purity of mind. *Cognition and Emotion, 30*, 778–796.

Rottman, J., & Kelemen, D. (2012). Aliens behaving badly: Children's acquisition of novel purity-based morals. *Cognition, 124*, 356–360.

Rottman, J., Kelemen, D., & Young, L. (2014a). Tainting the soul: Purity concerns predict moral judgments of suicide. *Cognition, 130*, 217–226.

Rottman, J., Kelemen, D., & Young, L. (2014b). Purity matters more than harm in moral judgments of suicide: Response to Gray (2014). *Cognition, 133*(1), 332–334.

Rottman, J., Kelemen, D., & Young, L. (2015). Hindering harm and preserving purity: How can moral psychology save the planet? *Philosophy Compass, 10*(2), 134–144.

Rozin, P., Haidt, J., & McCauley, C. R. (2008). Disgust. In M. Lewis, J. M. Haviland-Jones & L. F. Barrett (Eds.), *Handbook of emotions* (3rd ed., pp. 757–776). New York: Guilford Press.

Schaller, M., & Park, J. H. (2011). The behavioral immune system (and why it matters). *Current Directions in Psychological Science, 20*, 99–103.

Schein, C., & Gray, K. (2015a). The unifying moral dyad: Liberals and conservatives share the same harm-based moral template. *Personality and Social Psychology Bulletin, 41*(8), 1147–1163.

Schein, C., & Gray, K. (2015b). Making sense of moral disagreement: Liberals, conservatives, and the harm-based template they share. Retrieved March 1, 2017, from *www.spsp.org/blog/making-sense-of-moral*.

Schwartz, S. H., & Bilsky, W. (1990). Toward a theory of the universal content and structure of values: Extensions and cross-cultural replications. *Journal of Personality and Social Psychology, 58*(5), 878–891.

Seligman, M. E. (1971). Phobias and preparedness. *Behavior Therapy, 2*(3), 307–320.

Sherif, M., Harvey, O. J., White, B. J., Hood, W., & Sherif, C. (1961/1954). *Intergroup conflict and cooperation: The Robbers Cave experiment*. Norman: University of Oklahoma Institute of Group Relations.

Shweder, R. A. (2008). The cultural psychology of suffering: The many meanings of health in Orissa, India (and elsewhere). *Ethos, 36,* 60–77.

Shweder, R., Much, N., Mahapatra, M., & Park, L. (1997). The "big three" of morality (autonomy, community, divinity) and the "big three" explanations of suffering. *Morality and Health, 119,* 119–169.

Silver, J. R., & Silver, E. (2017). Why are conservatives more punitive than liberals?: A moral foundations approach. *Law and Human Behavior, 41*(3), 258.

Sperber, D., & Hirschfeld, L. A. (2004). The cognitive foundations of cultural stability and diversity. *Trends in Cognitive Sciences, 8*(1), 40–46.

Stanovich, K. E., & West, R. F. (2000). Individual difference in reasoning: Implications for the rationality debate? *Behavioral and Brain Sciences, 23,* 645–726.

Suhler, C. L., & Churchland, P. (2011). Can innate, modular "foundations" explain morality?: Challenges for Haidt's moral foundations theory. *Journal of Cognitive Neuroscience, 23*(9), 2103–2116.

Tamborini, R. (2011). Moral intuition and media entertainment. *Journal of Media Psychology, 23,* 39–45.

Tooby, J., Cosmides, L., & Barrett, H. C. (2005). Resolving the debate on innate ideas: Learnability constraints and the evolved interpenetration of motivational and conceptual functions. In P. Carruthers, S. Laurence, & S. Stich (Eds.), *The innate mind: Structure and contents* (pp. 305–337). New York: Oxford University Press.

Trivers, R. L. (1971). The evolution of reciprocal altruism. *Quarterly Review of Biology, 46,* 35–57.

Turiel, E. (1983). *The development of social knowledge: Morality and convention*. Cambridge, UK: Cambridge University Press.

Uhlmann, E. L., & Zhu, L. (2013). Acts, persons, and intuitions: Person-centered cues and gut reactions to harmless transgressions. *Social Psychological and Personality Science, 5,* 279–285.

Vaisey, S., & Miles, A. (2014). Tools from moral psychology for measuring personal moral culture. *Theory and Society, 43,* 311–332.

Wagemans, F. M. A., Brandt, M. J., & Zeelenberg, M. (2017). Disgust sensitivity is primarily associated with purity-based moral judgments. Retrieved from *https://osf.io/preprints/psyarxiv/tvs2b*.

Wasserman, E. A., Chakroff, A., Saxe, R., & Young, L. (2017). Illuminating the conceptual structure of the space of moral violations with searchlight representational similarity analysis. *NeuroImage, 159*(1), 371–387.

Watkins, L., Aitken, R., & Mather, D. (2016). Conscientious consumers: A relationship between moral foundations, political orientation and sustainable consumption. *Journal of Cleaner Production, 134,* 137–146.

Wisneski, D. C., & Skitka, L. J. (2016). Moralization through moral shock: Exploring emotional antecedents to moral conviction. *Personality and Social Psychology Bulletin, 43,* 139–150.

Young, L., & Saxe, R. (2011). When ignorance is no excuse: Different roles for intent across moral domains. *Cognition, 120,* 202–214.

Zajonc, R. B. (1980). Feeling and thinking: Preferences need no inferences. *American Psychologist, 35,* 151–175.

CHAPTER 23

The Model of Moral Motives

A Map of the Moral Domain

Ronnie Janoff-Bulman
Nate C. Carnes

How does motivation underlie morality?

The two innate motivations of approach and avoidance interact with three contexts—intrapersonal, interpersonal, and collective—to yield six specific and culturally invariant motives.

Motivation is fundamental to morality, which involves both an understanding of right and wrong—of what we should or should not do—and the activation or inhibition of these behaviors. The model of moral motives (MMM; Janoff-Bulman & Carnes, 2013a, 2013b) has its roots in the most basic motivational processes recognized in psychology: approach and avoidance. The MMM crosses approach and avoidance processes with distinct levels of analysis reflecting the focus of one's moral behavior: oneself (intrapersonal), another person (interpersonal), or the group (collective). As evident in Figure 23.1, this produces six cells with unique moral motives, each reflecting how to be moral in that context.

The rows of the MMM reflect the two basic motivational processes, which functionally have divergent outcomes. Avoidance processes, which we refer to as *proscriptive* in the moral domain (Janoff-Bulman, Sheikh, & Hepp, 2009), serve to *protect*

the individual, other person, or group; here the enemy is temptation—that is, acting on "bad" desires. In contrast, approach processes, referred to as *prescriptive* in the moral domain, serve to *provide* for the well-being of the individual, other person, or group. Here behaviors must be activated, and motivationally the enemy is apathy—that is, failing to act. From the broadest perspective, proscriptive morality is about not harming, and prescriptive morality is about helping; these are not simply opposite sides of the same coin, because not harming is *not* the same as helping.

Helping and not harming also manifest quite differently depending on the target of one's behavior. Thus regarding intrapersonal behavior, *moderation* is a proscriptive morality involving self-restraint, whereas *industriousness* is a prescriptive moral behavior involving behavioral activation. One might ask how behaviors involving solely the self could qualify as moral. Here it is impor-

	Self (Intrapersonal)	Other (Interpersonal)	Group (Collective)
Protect (Proscriptive regulation)	Moderation	Not Harming	Social Order
Provide (Prescriptive regulation)	Industriousness	Helping/Fairness	Social Justice

FIGURE 23.1. The model of moral motives.

tant to note that all of morality is fundamentally about facilitating social life so that we can reap its benefits; that is, from a distal perspective, it is functionally about making the ingroup better off. From a proximal perspective, moderation protects the individual, but by minimizing overindulgence it also serves to preserve the group's resources. Similarly, industriousness benefits the hardworking individual, but by developing individual competencies it ultimately provides advantages to the group.

The most common, salient forms of morality are at play when the target is another person, or individuated others. Here prescriptive morality includes both *helping* and *fairness*, while proscriptive morality involves *not harming*; prescriptive morality provides for another, whereas proscriptive morality protects the other. The *not harming* cell of our model resembles the dyadic template of morality (Gray, Young, & Waytz, 2012), which involves a perpetrator who harms a patient/victim; however, we would argue for another basic template of morality resembling the *helping* cell of our model that involves a helper who provides aid to a patient/recipient. This prescriptive interpersonal cell of the MMM also includes *fairness*, which involves providing another with his or her due. It is interesting to recognize that the fundamentally human penchant for reciprocity incorporates rudimentary elements of both helping and fairness; returning favors or resources involves not just providing help to another but help that is proportional to the inputs received from the other.

The final two cells of the MMM are those that refer to the group or collective as the target of morality. Here, proscriptive morality is *social order*, and prescriptive morality

is *social justice*. *Social order* serves to protect the group from both internal and external threats, whether these involve physical harm or psychological threats to group identity. Social order involves a strong emphasis on conformity and loyalty in the interests of preserving group solidarity and security. The prescriptive focus on providing is evident in *social justice*, which emphasizes sharing, equality, and communal responsibility. Social order involves inhibiting self-interest and self-expression in the service of the larger group's success, whereas social justice involves activating prosocial behaviors that serve to increase the overall welfare of the group. Both social order and social justice are binding moralities, and their respective binding strategies are discussed at greater length below. Most generally, however, social order binds into relatively homogeneous, impermeable groups based on shared identities, whereas social justice binds people into more inclusive, interdependent groups based on shared goals (Janoff-Bulman, 2009; Janoff-Bulman & Carnes, 2013a; also see Brewer, Hong, & Li, 2004, on two forms of group entitativity).

Our model explains these two innate processes that are generic from a psychological perspective and culturally uniform in their social function, with a special focus on how these processes manifest in different social contexts. However, it is important to clarify that our model does not try to explain the many ways in which cultures elaborate on these basic processes. Learned cultural innovations, including everything from rituals and tradition, gossip and reputation, the rule of law, religion, governmental institutions, penal systems, leadership, and various forms of tribalism, are woven into moral behavior in different ways from culture to culture (see Richerson & Boyd, 2005, for a comprehensive review of culture and evolution). These cultural elaborations on the two basic processes of moral behavior lead to unique societies that emphasize differing moral motives with differing levels of effectiveness.

Historical Context

The MMM is essentially a map of the moral domain, considered at different levels of analysis (intrapersonal, interpersonal, and collective) and reflecting an explicit acknowledgment that morality can involve distinct motivational processes—both inhibition and activation. A dual system of self-regulation, which has alternatively been framed as activation–inhibition, approach–avoidance, and appetitive–aversive motivation—has a long history in psychology and has been recognized as central to our understanding of behavior across diverse psychological domains (for reviews, see, e.g., Carver & Scheier, 2008; Gable, Reiss, & Elliot, 2003). Interestingly, for years work that was done on prosocial behavior, particularly in child development (e.g., Eisenberg & Miller, 1987) and social psychology (e.g., Batson, 1994), was regarded as a literature distinct and separate from morality research. A different line of research on ego depletion and self-control (e.g., Muraven & Baumeister, 2000) also has not been well integrated into the morality literature. These two strands of research reflect distinct regulatory systems—activation and inhibition, or prescriptive and proscriptive—that both play an important role in morality and are integrated into a single model in the MMM.

Apart from the influence of work on motivation in psychology, the strongest influence in the development of our model has been the groundbreaking work of Haidt, Graham, and colleagues (Haidt, 2007, 2008, 2012; Haidt & Graham, 2007; Haidt & Joseph, 2004) on moral foundations theory (MFT). The MFT's five foundations include two that are "individualizing" (i.e., care/harm, fairness/reciprocity) and three that are "binding" (i.e., ingroup/loyalty, authority/respect, and purity/sanctity). This first attempt to map moral principles, coupled with the subsequent development of the Moral Foundations Questionnaire (Graham et al., 2011), has not only served to catalyze an entire field of morality research but has also led to the virtual reification of MFT and its particular foundations.

The development of MFT represented a bottom-up approach to mapping morality (see Haidt & Joseph, 2004). Our own attempt to map the moral domain reflected a top-down approach and, in particular, our desire to provide a systematic, theoretical underpinning for distinct moral principles; the dual regulatory perspective represented in motivational research crossed with the well-worn social psychological categories of the self, the other, and the group (or, alternatively, the intrapersonal, interpersonal, and collective) provided a map that became the MMM. In filling in the six cells of the model, however, we became increasing aware of differences between the MMM and MFT, and particularly of possible omissions from MFT.

Theoretical Stance

In our own mapping of the moral domain, we assumed there would be considerable overlap between the MMM and MFT. In the end, as we explain below, it appears that the five foundations of MFT fall into only three cells of our model—the two interpersonal cells and the proscriptive group cell (social order). MFT's harm/care and fairness/reciprocity foundations fall entirely in the interpersonal column of the MMM, with harm/care straddling both the not harming (proscriptive) and helping/fairness (prescriptive) cell, and fairness/reciprocity fitting squarely in the latter cell. More important, MFT's three binding moralities are encompassed by social order; they are all essentially cultural mechanisms that serve the moral motive of social order. From our perspective, the crucial omission from MFT is the prescriptive group cell (i.e., social justice), and the bulk of our following discussion focuses on the two group-based moralities in the MMM. A few words about the other MFT omissions, however, seem warranted, and here we are referring to the intrapersonal moral motives—moderation and industriousness.

Interestingly, the virtue of moderation has been recognized in the major philosophies of the East and West through the ages. More specifically, protecting against excess via temperance is a core virtue in in Confucianism, Taoism, Buddhism, Hinduism, Athenian philosophy (e.g., Aristotle, Plato), Islam, Judaism, and Christianity (see Dahlsgaard, Peterson, & Seligman, 2005, on "universal virtues"). Thus, in the *Analects,* Confucius advocates self-control and the need to avoid extravagance, and in *Fusul Al-Madami,* Alfarabi emphasizes the importance of moderation. Also, in recent research on the attributes of highly moral people, self-discipline is recognized as a key virtue (Walker & Pitts, 1998). Although the proximal focus is the self, moderation serves to protect the larger community by minimizing wastefulness and safeguarding the group's resources. Similarly, industriousness, which benefits the self, also has implications for the group; hard work, persistence, and conscientiousness ultimately serve to advance the community's knowledge, skills, and resources. Industriousness is often associated with the Protestant ethic, and two valued attributes of highly moral people are hard work and conscientiousness (Walker & Pitts, 1998). Interestingly, in two totally separate attempts to code open-ended responses about morality, a work ethic category had to be added to the five moral foundations categories (Graham, Meindl, Koleva, Iyer, & Johnson, 2015; Hofmann, Wisneski, Brandt, & Skitka, 2014)

The foci of MFT are other people and the group, and it is therefore not surprising that the self-focused moralities are not included in the model. Similarly, the model of morality proposed by Rai and Fiske (2011) also omit these intrapersonal virtues, because they explicitly focus on the relationships between two or more people. Rai and Fiske (2011) identify four moral principles, each of which follows from a particular kind of social relationship. That is, *unity, hierarchy, equality,* and *proportionality* follow respectively from *communal sharing, authority ranking, equality matching,* and *market pricing.* Interestingly, despite their common omission from models of morality focused on others, moderation and industriousness are nevertheless moralities that we believe should be included in a comprehensive map of the moral domain, not only because they are commonly recognized as descriptive of highly moral people, but because they have important moral implications beyond the self and for the larger collective.

Of greater concern than the omission of these intrapersonal moralities, however, is the absence of an important group-based morality, not only because this could not be accounted for by a difference in focus but also because of the role of binding moralities in past discussions of political ideology. More specifically, Haidt and his colleagues (Graham, Haidt, & Nosek, 2009; Graham et al., 2011; Haidt & Graham, 2007) argue that liberals value the individualizing foundations (harm and fairness) more than conservatives, and conservatives value the binding foundations (loyalty, authority, and purity) more than liberals. They claim, in addition, that liberals rely on (only) two moral foundations, whereas conservatives rely on all five foundations, and they conclude that conservatives understand liberals better than liberals understand conservatives (Graham et al., 2009; Haidt, 2007, 2012). In fact, in Haidt's (2012) book, the title of the chapter on morality and political ideology is "The Conservative Advantage."

The provocative implication of these claims is that liberals do not have a binding morality—that is, they are not group-oriented and lack group-based moral concerns. Yet MFT, we believe, omits a crucial group-based morality that is heartily embraced by liberals, and thus the conclusions of Haidt and colleagues likely reflect the limitations of their own model rather than of a liberal ideology. We argue that there is a group-focused prescriptive morality and claim that it is based in a social justice orientation derived from a sense of shared communal responsibility.

Social order and *social justice* are the two collective cells of the MMM. Both are binding moralities, but their binding functions reflect different strategies for dealing with challenges and threats to the group. Most simply, we argue that social justice advances cooperation, whereas social order promotes coordination. The distinction between coordination and cooperation is evident in economic game taxonomies (e.g., DeScioli & Kurzban, 2007). Importantly, however, Thomas, DeScioli, Haque, and Pinker (2014) make the point that cooperation is fundamentally a motivational problem, whereas coordination is basically an epistemological problem. The central challenge of cooperation is that a social actor pays a cost in order to confer a collective benefit, but the social actor should only do this if others cooperate as well. In contrast, the central challenge of coordination is that social actors match the actions of others, but to do this, social actors require common knowledge about what actions to perform (Thomas et al., 2014).

Past work on "solving" cooperation has focused primarily on reciprocity and sanctions (for a review, see Rand & Nowak, 2013) or on individual differences and the features of the situation in determining the decision to cooperate (for a review, see Parks, Joireman, & Van Lange, 2013). Interdependence is a theme that unites much of this literature; cooperation is increased to the extent that social actors' outcomes are more interdependent because of repeated interactions, social preferences, or social identification. Interdependence helps solve the motivational problem inherent to cooperation. We assert that social justice promotes cooperation by emphasizing common goals, binding people interdependently, and relying on approach-based regulation focused on shared benefits.

In contrast, past work on "solving" coordination has focused on different correlating devices such as rules and norms (Van Huyck, Gillette, & Battalio, 1992), leadership (Cartwright, Gillet, & Van Vugt, 2013), and hierarchy (Cooper, DeJong, Forsythe, & Ross, 1994). These correlating devices help solve the epistemological problem inherent to coordination. Recent cross-cultural work on tight versus loose societies (Gelfand, 2012; Gelfand, et al., 2011) found that tight societies are characterized by strict punishment for norm violations, low tolerance for deviant behaviors, and strong norm adherence—clearly features of a social order group morality. This cross-cultural work also found that tight societies generally have a history of severe challenges (e.g., ecological and historical threats) that may have encouraged these societies to develop strong norms for and sanctions on nonconformity, thus enabling them to coordinate social behavior for survival (Gelfand, 2012). We argue that social order advances coordination through its emphasis on organization and strict norm adherence, including conformity and obedience, and its reliance on avoidance-based regulation focused on punishment for deviant behavior (see, e.g., Blanton & Christie, 2003).

Evidence

The importance of distinguishing between the two group-based moralities becomes apparent as we explore the empirical evidence for both social order and social justice, their association with political ideology, and the extent to which the MFT binding moralities are subsumed by social order and not social justice. Evidence will also be presented that supports important distinctions between fairness and social justice.

First, by way of background, it seems worth mentioning that early empirical work on prescriptive versus proscriptive morality found support for important differences between these two regulatory orientations. In a series of seven studies, Janoff-Bulman and colleagues (2009) found that proscriptive morality is focused on transgressions, is mandatory and strict, is typically represented in concrete, specific language, and involves blameworthiness. In contrast, prescriptive morality is focused on "good deeds," is more discretionary, is represented in more abstract language, and involves credit-worthiness rather than blame. Overall, proscriptive moral regulation is condemnatory, whereas prescriptive moral regulation is commendatory (Janoff-Bulman et al., 2009).

In crossing the two regulatory systems with self, other, and group, the six cells of the model are believed to reflect distinct moral orientations. Using 30 items developed to assess the six cells of the MMM, a confirmatory factor analysis provided support for the six cells of the model. More specifically, the 30 items in the MMM scale emerged as six latent constructs corresponding to the moral motives hypothesized in the MMM (Janoff-Bulman & Carnes, 2016). In addition, in this study political orientation was associated with the group-based moral motives, social order and social justice, but not the self-focused or other-focused motives. As expected, social order was positively associated with political conservatism, whereas social justice was positively associated with political liberalism. These relationships between political ideology and the group-based moral motives were replicated in a second study, which again found that liberals endorse social justice and conservatives endorse social order. One group did not support a group-based, binding morality, but it was not liberals, as suggested by Haidt and colleagues, but instead was libertarians (Janoff-Bulman & Carnes, 2016). Libertarians endorse individualizing moralities but eschew a morality based on collective concerns (also see Iyer, Koleva, Graham, Ditto, & Haidt, 2012).

The same associations between political liberalism–conservatism and social justice–social order were found in a different set of studies conducted to explore the role of context in understanding the use of moral principles. In this research, we found that to a considerable extent, morality is embedded in social contexts (Carnes, Lickel, & Janoff-Bulman, 2015). This research examined the contextual bases of the MFT moral foundations supplemented with the MMM social order and social justice motives. There was a high degree of consensus regarding the operative moral principles in different types of groups, with each group type characterized by a distinct pattern of moral principles. For example, loyalty was regarded as particularly important in intimacy groups, and fairness was perceived as playing an important role in task groups. These contextual effects were quite strong; but political ideology did continue to play a role in the between-subjects investigation (Study 2). Political ideology was not associated with any of the MFT individualizing foundations, but it was associated with the MFT binding foundations, as well as social order and social justice. Once again liberalism was positively associated with social justice. Of particular importance was the finding that the three MFT binding foundations—loyalty, authority, and purity—had the same relationship with political ideology as social order, but not social justice; that is, all were positively associated with political conservatism (Carnes et al., 2015). These findings lend support to our contention that the binding foundations of MFT all represent one type of group-based morality—a proscriptive social order morality.

It is also worth pointing out that the MFT fairness foundation and the MMM social justice motive had very different relationships with political ideology. Again, fairness was not associated with political ideology, whereas social justice was positively associated with political liberalism (Carnes et al., 2015). Fairness is not the same as social justice. In a recent series of studies, we focused on the distinct features of each and explored their use in everyday language, instances when they conflict, their associations with each other and with politics, and the impact of concrete–abstract construals (see Bharadwaj & Janoff-Bulman, 2016). We found strong support for treating fairness and social justice as unique, independent constructs. Fairness is individualizing and based in proportionality of inputs and outputs, whereas social justice is based in shared group membership and is concerned with distributions across the group. Fairness relies on personal identities, whereas social justice relies on social identities; and the two principles are uncorrelated. In addition, fairness is relatively universal and not associated with political ideology, whereas social justice is associated with political liberalism and with more abstract thinking (Bharadwaj & Janoff-Bulman, 2016). Social justice is simply not the same as fairness and should not be regarded as subsumed by the fairness foundation in MFT; it is a distinct group-based morality.

Having posited two distinct, overriding group-based moralities, we have become interested in the functional roles of social order and social justice. Both are binding moralities, but they rely on different strategies to bind the group in response to collective threats and challenges. Social order emphasizes conformity and strict norm adherence in the service of coordination, whereas social justice emphasizes interdependence and collaboration in the service of cooperation. Based on these differences, trust of others is likely to differ. More specifically, cooperation is a viable path to problem solving when trust is present; when it is absent, rule-based coordination is likely to be a more effective route to group problem solving. We therefore expected social justice to be positively associated with generalized trust of others and social order to be negatively associated with generalized distrust. We found support for these different relationships in a recent set of studies (Carnes & Janoff-Bulman, 2017), in which trust and distrust emerged as distinct constructs. Most interesting was the finding that societal threat actually strengthened the relationship between social justice and trust.

Extension and Expansion

As distinct group-based moralities, social order and social justice represent different ways of dealing with societal threats and challenges in the service of group survival and well-being. Each may have its own strengths; social order may be particularly effective in responding quickly to severe threats, whereas social justice may be particularly effective when seeking cooperation concerning common goals such as resource allocation. In the study of morality, it seems important to keep in mind that morality is a system of shared standards and rules that play a functional role in facilitating group living and providing social actors with solutions to problems associated with group life. Thus one important direction we are currently investigating involves understanding the specific social problems—such as cooperation and coordination—that morality "solves" and exactly how different moral motives actually "solve" these problems of group living.

The functional role of morality applies to all moral foundations and moral motives—they are in the service of group living. Given that the two group-based moralities of the MMM are the domain of political differences, it seems particularly important to better understand the functional underpinnings of social order and social justice. Despite the disdain with which each side of the political spectrum typically views the other, it is possible that societies in which both types of group-based moralities are well represented are those that can most successfully respond to diverse challenges and threats to the group (see Janoff-Bulman & Carnes, 2016). Thus one important implication of our perspective is that there are strong social regulatory reasons for emphasizing toler-

ance and compromise in political discourse and the broader political arena. At the very least, recognizing the functions of distinct moralities may provide a basis for developing respect for opposing views, even in the context of disagreement.

ACKNOWLEDGMENTS

This research was supported by National Science Foundation Grant Nos. BCS-1053139 (to Ronnie Janoff-Bulman) and DGE-0907995 (to Nate C. Carnes).

REFERENCES

Batson, C. D. (1994). Why act for the public good?: Four answers. *Personality and Social Psychology Bulletin, 20,* 603–610.

Bharadwaj, P., & Janoff-Bulman, R. (2016). *Fairness and social justice: Distinct moralities.* Unpublished manuscript, University of Massachusetts, Amherst, MA.

Blanton, H., & Christie, C. (2003). Deviance regulation: A theory of identity and action. *Review of General Psychology, 7,* 115–149.

Brewer, M. B., Hong, Y., & Li, Q. (2004). Dynamic entitativity: Perceiving groups as actors. In V. Yzerbyt, C. M. Judd, & O. Corneille (Eds.), *The psychology of group perception: Contributions to the study of homogeneity, entitativity and essentialism* (pp. 25–38). Philadelphia: Psychology Press.

Carnes, N. C., & Janoff-Bulman, R. (2017). *Group morality and the function of trust and distrust.* Manuscript submitted for publication.

Carnes, N. C., Lickel, B., & Janoff-Bulman, R. (2015). Shared perceptions: Morality is embedded in social contexts. *Personality and Social Psychology Bulletin, 41,* 351–362.

Cartwright, E., Gillet, J., & Van Vugt, M. (2013). Leadership by example in the weak-link game. *Economic Inquiry, 51,* 2028–2043.

Carver, C. S., & Scheier, M. F. (2008). Feedback processes in the simultaneous regulation of affect and action. In J. Y. Shah & W. L. Gardner (Eds.), *Handbook of motivation science* (pp. 308–324). New York: Guilford Press.

Cooper, R., DeJong, D. V., Forsythe, R., & Ross, T. W. (1994). Alternative institutions for resolving coordination problems: Experimental evidence on forward induction and preplay communication. In J. W. Friedman (Ed.), *Problems of coordination in economic activity* (pp. 129–146). New York: Springer.

Dahlsgaard, K., Peterson, C., & Seligman, M.

E. P. (2005). Shared virtue: The convergence of valued human strengths across culture and history. *Review of General Psychology, 9,* 203–213.

DeScioli, P., & Kurzban, R. (2007). The games people play. In S. Gangestad & J. Simpson (Eds.), *Evolution of mind: Fundamental questions and controversies* (pp. 130–136). New York: Guilford Press.

Eisenberg, N., & Miller, P. A. (1987). The relation of empathy to prosocial and related behaviors. *Psychological Bulletin, 101,* 91–119.

Gable, S. L., Reis, H. T., & Elliot, A. J. (2003). Evidence for bivariate systems: An empirical test of appetition and aversion across domains. *Journal of Research in Personality, 37,* 349–372.

Gelfand, M. J. (2012). Culture's constraints: International differences in the strength of social norms. *Current Directions in Psychological Science, 21*(6), 420–424.

Gelfand, M. J., Raver, J. L., Nishii, L., Leslie, L. M., Lun, J., Lim, B. C., . . . Yamaguchi, S. (2011). Differences between tight and loose cultures: A 33-nation study. *Science, 332,* 1100–1104.

Graham, J., Haidt, J., & Nosek, B. (2009). Liberals and conservatives use different sets of moral foundations. *Journal of Personality and Social Psychology, 96,* 1029–1046.

Graham, J., Meindl, P., Koleva, S., Iyer, R., & Johnson, K. M. (2015). When values and behavior conflict: Moral pluralism and intrapersonal hypocrisy. *Social and Personality Psychology Compass, 9,* 158–170.

Graham, J., Nosek, B. A., Haidt, J., Iyer, R., Koleva, S., & Ditto, P. H. (2011). Mapping the moral domain. *Journal of Personality and Social Psychology, 101,* 366–385.

Gray, K., Young, L., & Waytz, A., (2012). The moral dyad: A fundamental template unifying moral judgment. *Psychological Inquiry, 23,* 206–215.

Haidt, J. (2007). The new synthesis in moral psychology. *Science, 316,* 998–1002.

Haidt, J. (2008). Morality. *Perspectives on Psychological Science, 3,* 65–72.

Haidt, J. (2012). *The righteous mind: Why good people are divided by politics and religion.* New York: Pantheon Books.

Haidt, J., & Graham, J. (2007). When morality opposes justice: Conservatives have moral intuitions that liberals may not recognize. *Social Justice Research, 20,* 98–116.

Haidt, J., & Joseph, C. (2004, Fall). Intuitive ethics: How innately prepared intuitions generate culturally variable virtues. *Daedalus,* pp. 55–66.

Hofmann, W., Wisneski, D. C., Brandt, M. J., & Skitka, L. J. (2014). Morality in everyday life. *Science, 345,* 1340–1343.

Iyer, R., Koleva, S., Graham, J., Ditto, P. H., & Haidt, J. (2012). Understanding libertarian morality: The psychological dispositions of self-identified libertarians. *PLOS ONE, 7,* e42366.

Janoff-Bulman, R. (2009). To provide or protect: Motivational bases of political liberalism and conservatism. *Psychological Inquiry, 20,* 120–128.

Janoff-Bulman, R., & Carnes, N. C. (2013a). Surveying the moral landscape: Moral motives and group-based moralities. *Personality and Social Psychology Review, 17,* 242–247.

Janoff-Bulman, R., & Carnes, N. C. (2013b). Moral context matters: A reply to Graham. *Personality and Social Psychology Review, 17,* 242–247.

Janoff-Bulman, R., & Carnes, N. C. (2016). Social justice and social order: Binding moralities across the political spectrum. *PLOS ONE, 11,* e0152479.

Janoff-Bulman, R., Sheikh, S., & Hepp, S. (2009). Proscriptive versus prescriptive morality: Two faces of moral regulation. *Journal of Personality and Social Psychology, 96,* 521–537.

Muraven, M. R., & Baumeister, R. F. (2000). Self-regulation and depletion of limited resources: Does self-control resemble a muscle? *Psychological Bulletin, 126,* 247–259.

Parks, C. D., Joireman, J., & Van Lange, P. A. (2013). Cooperation, trust, and antagonism: How public goods are promoted. *Psychological Science in the Public Interest, 14*(3), 119–165.

Rai, T. S., & Fiske, A. P. (2011). Moral psychology is relationship regulation: Moral motives for unity, hierarchy, equality, and proportionality. *Psychological Review, 118,* 57–75.

Rand, D. G., & Nowak, M. A. (2013). Human cooperation. *Trends in Cognitive Science, 17,* 413–425.

Richerson, P. J., & Boyd, R. (2005). *Not by genes alone: How culture transformed human evolution.* Chicago: University of Chicago Press.

Thomas, K. A., DeScioli, P., Haque, O. S., & Pinker, S. (2014). The psychology of coordination and common knowledge. *Journal of Personality and Social Psychology, 107,* 657–676.

Van Huyck, J. B., Gillette, A. B., & Battalio, R. C. (1992). Credible assignments in coordination games. *Games and Economic Behavior, 4,* 606–626.

Walker, L. J., & Pitts, R. C. (1998). Naturalistic conceptions of moral maturity. *Developmental Psychology, 34,* 403–419.

CHAPTER 24

Relationship Regulation Theory

Tage S. Rai

Are there *any* universally held moral rules that apply across social–relational contexts?

No; instead, there are universal social–relational contexts that entail competing moral rules, and moral conflicts arise when people use different social–relational models to navigate the same situation.

Ethics change across different social relationships. Our expectations about acceptable behavior among friends, for example, are considerably different from those same expectations among coworkers or strangers. In conjunction with anthropologist Alan Fiske, I developed relationship regulation theory (RRT; Rai & Fiske, 2011) to explain how our sense of right and wrong changes when we are interacting in different relationships, including those with superiors, subordinates, coworkers, and business partners, as well as friends, close loved ones, and strangers. And, relatedly, why individuals, social groups, and cultures disagree about what is morally right and why these disagreements are so intractable.

Change and disagreement are difficult topics to study in moral psychology, because many moral psychologists have predefined the term *moral* to be restricted to reasoning or intuitions regarding right and wrong action that are independent of the social–relational contexts in which they occur. From this perspective, judgments can only be "moral" if they are true at all times in all places, and so moral psychologists have been focused on trying to identify such universal truths. Consequently, studies of moral psychology are often expressly nonrelational, removing any possible influence of knowledge of established social norms, social relationships with and among the actors involved, and consequences for future social interactions in order to isolate how moral judgments occur under "ideal" conditions (Mikhail, 2007). In this framework, variation in moral judgment across social relationships and contexts, such as when people administer electric shocks to another person when ordered by an authority figure (Milgram, 1963) or when people exhibit preferential treatment toward their ingroups (Tajfel, Billig, Bundy, & Flament, 1971), can only be *explained away* as non-moral social biases that compromise correct moral performance. Change is error. Disagreement is the result of error. The idea is that if everyone simply agreed about the actions that took place independent of the context in which they took place, there would be no moral disagreement.

RRT is aimed toward reconceptualizing our moral psychology as *embedded* in social–relational cognition and unpacking the ways in which different social–relational contexts entail correspondingly unique moral motives and beliefs that can and do conflict. According to this perspective, the fundamental bases to our moral psychology are not asocial; instead, they are grounded in the cognition we use to regulate our social relationships, and fundamentally different ways of relating entail fundamentally different moral obligations and transgressions. From this perspective, any action, including intentional violence and unequal treatment, may be perceived as moral or immoral depending on the moral motive employed and how the relevant social relationship is construed. Moral disagreement arises from competing moral motives that

are activated when people employ different social–relational schemas to navigate otherwise identical situations.

What this means is that, in order to understand the bases of our moral psychology, we must begin with the basic kinds of social relations people engage in across cultures. To do so, RRT draws on relational models theory (Fiske, 1992), which develops a taxonomy of four models of social relations that capture the breadth of social life across cultures. RRT extends this work to identify four fundamental and distinct moral motives that drive behavior in these four models for social relations (see Table 24.1).

When people are relating by *market pricing*, they use ratios and rates to make all goods fungible so that they can be traded off against one another; when people are relating using market perspectives, they are motivated by a sense of *proportionality* to make moral judgments based on a utilitarian calculation of costs and benefits, even if it means killing others to achieve a greater good. In the context of fairness, people motivated by proportionality believe that goods should be distributed based on merit and that there should be proportionate representation in decision making.

When people are relating by *equality matching,* all actors in a relationship are

TABLE 24.1. Moral Motives in RRT

Moral motive	Social–relational model	Violence	Distributive justice	Procedural justice
Unity	Communal sharing	To protect ingroup, outsiders or contaminated insiders may be harmed	Free sharing/need-based	Consensus-based
Hierarchy	Authority ranking	Leaders may harm subordinates, subordinates must harm under orders, violence may sometimes be used to contest rank	Rank-based	Superiors decide
Equality	Equality matching	Must respond with violence in kind	Equal division	Equal representation
Proportionality	Market pricing	Violence can be traded off against other goods and used to sacrifice others for the greater good	Merit-based	Proportionate representation

perceived as distinct but equal; when people are relating equally, they are motivated by a sense of *equality* to match exchanges exactly, feeling strong obligations to treat everyone the same and to reciprocate any violence in kind. In the context of fairness, people motivated by equality believe that goods should be distributed equally no matter what and that there should be equal representation in decision making.

When people are relating by *authority ranking,* social interactions are characterized by the salience of hierarchical rank between superiors and subordinates; when people are relating hierarchically they are motivated by a sense of *hierarchy* in which subordinates must respect, defer to, and obey superiors, even if the superior's commands require them to engage in violence; superiors are morally entitled to command subordinates but are also obligated to lead, guide, direct, and protect them. In the context of fairness, people motivated by hierarchy believe that leaders should get preferential treatment and access to goods and should make decisions for subordinates.

When people are relating by *communal sharing,* there is a strong sense of oneness and shared essence among everyone in the relationship; when people are relating communally they are motivated by a sense of *unity* to protect their ingroups from any threat to the group's solidarity, even if it requires violence. In the context of fairness, people motivated by unity believe that goods should be shared freely without tracking and distributed based on need, and that all decisions should be made by consensus.

Thus, according to RRT, moral psychology is composed of *motives to make actual relationships correspond with culturally implemented ideals of the four social relational models.* Moral judgment refers to evaluations of the actor's effectiveness at this process based on his or her traits and behaviors. In this framework, moral judgments are not based on the content of actions at all (e.g., did the action cause harm, were people treated unequally), but instead are based on the moral motives people are using in correspondence with the social–relational models they are aiming to satisfy. These moral motives and corresponding social–relational

models capture the breadth of human moral life, but cultures and individuals vary in how they implement them across situations. This differential use of moral motives due to different social–relational models leads to vastly different beliefs about the acceptability of violence, the fair distribution of resources, and decision making in procedural justice.

Throughout the chapter, I focus on the centrality of harm in theories of moral psychology as a way to flesh out these ideas and make three key contributions of RRT concrete.

1. Virtually every major contemporary theory of moral psychology argues that a (or the) core foundation of our moral psychology is a universal prohibition against intentional harm to others. By arguing that any action, including the infliction of intentional harm, can be moral or immoral depending on its social–relational context and that most violence is actually motivated by moral thoughts and sentiments, RRT makes a clear competing prediction to these other theories, as well as all major theories of violence.
2. Whether and what kind of action, including different forms of violence, is deemed morally acceptable and even morally required changes depending on the moral motive being employed.
3. Moral disagreements, including those over the acceptability of violence, result from people viewing identical actions through different social–relational models that entail competing moral motives.

Historical Context

The Age of Enlightenment was characterized by skepticism of tradition and authority as sources of knowledge and faith in the ability of reason and logic to explain several aspects of human life, including morality (Kramnick, 1995). As MacIntyre (1981/2007) has noted, Enlightenment thinkers developed a *rationalist* conception of morality as grounded in abstract, impartial, universal, logical principles that had the potential to be reasoned toward a priori of experience through conscious reasoning. The rationalist conception of morality is a *prescriptive* claim about how we ought to judge and behave. Contemporary debates in moral psychology, a field aimed toward *descriptive* analysis, has largely been characterized by arguments over the extent to which the rationalist conception of morality is an accurate reflection of how people actually make moral judgments.

These arguments focus on two broad sets of questions. Some questions examine how people *process* moral judgment, whereas other questions examine the *content* of moral judgment. Questions related to "process" are concerned with the mental algorithms people use to connect inputs to the output that takes the form of a moral judgment (e.g., conscious reasoning vs. automatic intuition; domain-general vs. domain-specific process). Questions related to content, which is the focus of this chapter, examine what the "inputs" that the mental algorithms work from actually are. In other words, what are the bases or criteria upon which moral judgments are made? If our moral psychology is a system, what problem(s) is it trying to solve?

Theoretical Stance

Like the three moral codes (Shweder, Much, Mahapatra, & Park, 1997) and moral foundations theory (MFT; Haidt & Joseph, 2004; Graham et al., 2012), RRT seeks to broaden our conception of morality to capture the psychology of people outside of modern, Western, liberal contexts to include the moral experiences of those across cultures and history. Where RRT differs from these theories is that by stating that moral psychology functions to regulate social relationships, it is aiming to establish a scientific definition of *moral*, not a folk taxonomy of it. Therefore, RRT cannot capture every aspect of behavior in every folk concept of morality. For example, individual choice, particularly as it relates to the concept of "negative liberty" (Berlin, 1969), is amoral in RRT. Freedom in this sense refers to "freedom from relationships." It draws a line beyond which relationships should not be regulated. There is no morality, in the technical scientific sense specified by RRT, in this space. Whereas MFT can be added to in order to include beliefs that are part of a folk definition of morality but not our scientific definition, RRT cannot.

In some cases, RRT is complementary. For example, whereas MFT argues that people care about fairness, RRT can predict that what people believe to be fair will vary depending on the moral motive people are using. So if people are motivated by unity, they will believe that goods should be distributed freely and based on need within the communal group; if they are motivated by hierarchy, they will believe that goods should be distributed to those highest in rank; if they are motivated by equality, they will believe goods should be distributed equally; and if they are motivated by proportionality, they will believe goods should be distributed based on merit. In other cases, RRT is competing. So whereas MFT argues for a unique moral foundation of purity, RRT argues that purity is tied to communal and authority-based relations. Thus, RRT predicts that when people are morally offended at eating the dead family dog, it is because it is the *family* dog, and that moral disgust at eating dogs in general will be more common in cultures in which dogs are seen as part of the family. In many cases, acts that are perceived as morally wrong in isolation, such as engaging in a sexual act with a McChicken sandwich (Hathaway, 2015), may be seen by ingroup members as morally appropriate and even required if the purpose of the act is to facilitate group identity, bonding, and belonging, as is often the case in fraternities, on sports teams, and in the military (Fiske & Rai, 2014; Carnes, Lickel, & Janoff-Bulman, 2015).

In regard to harm, domain theory (Turiel, 1983), universal moral grammar (Mikhail, 2007), and the harm hypothesis (Gray et al., 2012) argue that a prohibition against intentional harm is a (the) core feature of our moral psychology and that people are violent when their moral sense has failed them somehow. Shweder et al. (1997) and Haidt and colleagues (Haidt & Joseph, 2004; Graham, Haidt, & Nosek, 2009) agree that our moral psychology includes a prohibition against intentional harm but have argued that there are moral judgments that do not involve aversion to harm (or inequality) and in some cases can compete with aversion to harm to ultimately bring harm about. In contrast to all of these approaches, RRT argues that a prohibition against intentional harm is not a foundation of morality at all (no action is). In our framework, whether harm is seen as good or ill depends on its social–relational context, and when intentional harm does occur, it does not reflect a breakdown in our moral psychology. Rather, in most cases, intentionally harming oneself or another person is motivated by moral thoughts and sentiments on the part of the perpetrator to regulate relationships with the victims or third parties. We harm when we feel it is righteous to defend our ingroups, to rectify transgressions, to contest positions in a social hierarchy, to initiate others into new relationships, and more.

If RRT generates a clear competing prediction to all other theories of moral psychology, it also goes against most major theories of violence. Frustration–aggression theories view violence as a breakdown in correct moral functioning, in which a person knows that what he or she is doing is wrong but does it anyway because his or her self-regulatory systems have failed somehow (Dollard, Miller, Doob, Mowrer, & Sears, 1939; DeWall, Baumeister, Stillman, & Gailliot, 2007). Similarly, theories of violence that rest on notions of moral disengagement or dehumanization assume that violence is a mistake that occurs when perpetrators fail to perceive their victims as fellow human beings worthy of moral concern (Bandura, 1999). According to RRT, violence is not a mistake; instead, it is often the result of moral performance. Rational choice and instrumental models of violence, which assume that violence is simply a behavioral strategy that may be pursued if its benefits outweigh its costs relative to nonviolent strategies based on a relevant set of utilities (Felson & Tedeschi, 1993), are theoretically compatible with RRT's view of violence as morally motivated. But where RRT can add to the rational–instrumental account is by providing insight into what the principal relevant utilities are; namely, moral thoughts and sentiments.

Evidence

The primary prediction of RRT is that what is moral or immoral is defined by social–relational context rather than the pure content of action. For example, there is a universal taboo against incest, but what makes incest immoral is the relationship between the partners, not anything about the sex per se, and the relations that count as "incest" vary across cultures and history. If anyone can find an action that is seen as universally moral or immoral regardless of its social–relational context, that would falsify the theory. An answer such as "murder" would not qualify as a testable claim because the term is predefined as immoral by its culture. In contrast, an answer such as "intentional killing" is a testable claim.

The more interesting question is generativity: What can the theory do? What new predictions does it provide? To the extent that moral motives vary across social relations in the patterns described by RRT and the fairness and violence judgments encompassed by each motive cluster together, the theory is generative. RRT has been instrumental in explaining moral judgment and disagreement in domains including war and conflict, consumer behavior, and organizational behavior. For example, in the context of consumer behavior, McGraw, Schwartz, and Tetlock (2012) have shown how profit-seeking, which is perceived as fair when motivated by proportionality in markets, is perceived as unfair by consumers when applied by businesses in communal contexts, such as churches. In the context of organizational behavior, Giessner and Van Quaquebeke (2010) have argued that many conflicts between superiors and subordinates in organizations are due to the two sides perceiving different moral motives to be guiding their working relationship. In my own research, I have been investigating how priming the schema for a given social relation (e.g., communal) leads to greater support for fairness and violence judgments tied to its corresponding moral motive (e.g., unity-based support for need-based distribution and violence toward outgroups).

In regard to harm, Alan Fiske and I analyzed violent practices across cultures and history in our book *Virtuous Violence: Hurting and Killing to Create, Sustain, End, and Honor Social Relationships* (2014). These practices included war, torture, genocide, honor killing, animal and human sacrifice, homicide, suicide, intimate partner violence, rape, corporal punishment, execution, trial by combat, police brutality, hazing, castration, dueling, feuding, contact sports, the violence immortalized by gods and heroes, and more. What we found is that across practices, across cultures, and throughout historical periods, the primary motivations underlying acts of violence are inherently moral. By *moral*, I mean that people are violent because they feel their violence is justified, obligatory, and praiseworthy. They know they are harming fully human beings, and they believe they *should* do it. Violence does not result from a psychopathic lack of morality; it emerges out of the exercise of moral rights and obligations by perpetrators and their social groups.

People everywhere kill in self-defense, to protect the people they love or to get closer to them, to punish a transgression or to make reparations, as retaliation for a previous attack, to establish a strong reputation in order to prevent future attacks, and in obedience to God and other authorities. In almost every case, we have found that the violent act is perceived as obligatory, just, and even praiseworthy by the perpetrators, many local observers, and, in some cases, the victims themselves. Across practices, we find that the purpose of violence is to regulate important social relationships, either to the victim or to third parties that deeply matter to the perpetrator. And in all cases, perpetrators are using violence to create, conduct, sustain, enhance, transform, honor, protect, redress, repair, end, and mourn valued relationships. Of course, there are many different sorts of relationships, and so violence to serve any of those purposes will be unique in different relationships.

Proportionality when market pricing is central to all modern war planning. As Harry Truman put it when describing his decision to drop the atomic bomb on Hiroshima and Nagasaki in World War II, "a quarter of a million of the flower of our young manhood was worth a couple of Japanese cities" (Alperovitz, 1996, p. 516). This kind of proportional thinking, in which the goal is to achieve the greatest good for the greatest number and violence is acceptable if the benefits outweigh the costs, is the stated justification for torture, the use of kill ratios in military decision making, and the willingness to incur collateral damage that results in the deaths of innocent civilians. Nor must the trade-offs only be in human lives. Decisions regarding military spending budgets are predicated on the necessity of assigning a monetary worth to a soldier's life—both the ones we wish to protect and the ones we wish to kill.

Equality underlies the eye-for-an-eye, tooth-for-a-tooth violence that characterizes everyday confrontations in which someone feels entitled to retaliate or "hit back" after they have first been hit. In some cases, equality-motivated violence may be directed toward anyone in the perpetrator's relevant social group, and these acts are seen as morally justified on the part of perpetrators and observers. Blood feuds between gangs and clans persist precisely because victims of an attack feel that they can attack anyone in the perpetrator's group. For example, following an attack by the Abdel-Halim clan on the El-Hanashat clan in Egypt that resulted in twenty-two fatalities in 2002, a surviving El-Hanashat stated "no matter what sacrifices it takes, we are determined to kill as many of them [Abdel-Halims] as were murdered" (Halawi, 2002). In the extreme, victims may attack members of the perpetrators' group who had absolutely nothing to do with the original attack. This is the inherent logic behind terrorist attacks that target civilians. Most recently, victims of ISIS have been forced to don orange jumpsuits during their beheadings and burnings to symbolize that their deaths are retribution for the prisoners being held at Guantanamo Bay (Lamothe, 2014).

The hierarchy-based morality that people use when authority ranking motivates the violent punishment of children by parents, enlisted men by officers, citizens by police and other authorities, and humans by gods. As one policeman put it after fighting erupted between protesters and police in Berkeley, California, "if the parents of these cocksuckers had beat 'em when they were young, we wouldn't have to now. . . . There's a whole bunch of these assholes who've learned some respect for law and order tonight" (Stark, 1972, p. 61). In addition to punishment, rank-motivated violence often creates, negotiates, or reasserts a hierarchical relationship. Men in honor cultures, mafias, and gangs, medieval knights, and youths in all cultures have fought to establish their rank in what they perceived as legitimately contestable hierarchies. Honor, valor, and admiration accrue to those who are victorious, whereas those who do not fight are shamed and excluded. As one bar fighter describes how backing down from a fight would feel, "I'd feel guilty. I'd feel weak. I'd feel like I let myself down. I'd feel like I let anybody else that was involved down" (Copes, Hochstetler, & Forsyth, 2013, p. 12).

It may be difficult to imagine how violence that elevates a person's status and provides him or her with selfish benefits could possibly be morally motivated because we have a tendency to associate morality with selflessness and altruism. But morality has always been selfish. For thousands of years many people have been committed to kindness and peace because they fear God's wrath and want to go to heaven and not to hell. Anytime someone does what is right in order to avoid being shamed, to alleviate their guilt, or to restore their honor in the eyes of their community, their act is selfish, but nonetheless moral. And if we acknowledge that violence that restores honor can be morally motivated, then by extension, violence that *enhances* honor, status, and esteem in the eyes of one's community has the potential to be morally motivated as well.

People relating communally are motivated by unity to engage in violence out of loyalty to each other. They will fight because their fellow group members are fighting, and if one of them is attacked, they will feel like they have all been attacked and will collectively avenge their compatriot. Acts of genocide occur when communal groups are morally motivated to maintain their ingroup unity against what is believed to be the contamination of an outgroup. In contrast, honor killings are intended to cleanse a family of contamination from one of their own, allowing them to reestablish their communal relationship with the larger community that has shunned them. While violence is often driven by communal unity, it is also used to *create* communal unity within relationships; this kind of violence is endemic to brutal initiation rites and hazing, both of which remove an individual from a previous life and integrate him or her into a new one. As one mother described her reasons for initiating her daughter into womanhood through the practice of female circumcision:

> I thought of their future. The woman who is circumcised behaves in a way that forces people around her to respect her. . . . Pharaonic circumcision ensures the woman's strong place in the family. She is very trustworthy because she does not allow men to take advantage of her. She is her own person, even for the man she is married to. This is a source of respect and I think it is more important than how painful it is. The wound heals, but the relationships remain strong." (Abusharaf, 2001, 131–132)

In this example, the mother wants what is best for her daughter and is working to raise a woman who holds the values that are deemed morally correct in her culture. The "perpetrator" loves the "victim" dearly, and any explanation that attempts to account for her violence in terms of "disengagement" or "dehumanization" fails to capture the love, care, and compassion that actually motivate the act.

Together, these models for social relations and their moral motives capture the different ways in which perpetrators are driven to hurt and kill. Many of the acts are ones that modern liberal Americans would deem hideous, repugnant, immoral, and evil. But no matter how heinous these actions may seem to us, the fact is that perpetrators' actions are motivated by moral thoughts and sentiments which are often shared by their social groups.

This claim could be falsified in a few ways. First, if the majority of violence was committed by people who lack the capacity for moral emotions, that would invalidate our theory. Although it is true that psychopaths commit more than their fair share of violence given the less than 1% base rate of psychopathy in the population (Coid, Yang, Ullrich, Roberts, & Hare, 2009), they still only account for a fraction of violent crime—typically less than 10% (Coid,

Yang, Ullrich, Roberts, Moran, et al., 2009). Second, if most violence reflected crimes of convenience against random strangers, such as when an addict attacks someone because he or she needs money for drugs, that would work against our account of violence as morally motivated. But in spite of our fears, these crimes are statistically rare; strangers commit only a small fraction of murders (U.S. Department of Justice Federal Bureau of Investigation, 2010). Still, some critics might argue that when perpetrators claim their actions were morally motivated, these statements only reflect post hoc rationales meant to mitigate blame. But if perpetrators really wanted to mitigate blame to avoid punishment from the law, they would claim that the crime did not happen or that they were not in their right minds and that they regretted it deeply. Instead, perpetrators often brag about their violent actions, and their local social groups often express explicit support for the violence, citing that the victims deserved what they got (Kubrin & Weitzer, 2003). Even when perpetrators' statements are post hoc justifications meant to excuse, they are still important, because they reveal the moral standards of those being appealed to. Thus the leaders of ISIS may actually be cladding their victims in orange jumpsuits and claiming that the beheadings are retaliatory for nonmoral, instrumental propaganda purposes, rather than out of genuine moral motives, but the strategy can only be effective if their stated reasons resonate with moral opinions held by their followers and others in the region.

Experimentally, we are beginning to test RRT's generative predictions regarding violence in a number of interesting ways. For example, using political attitude surveys and behavioral experiments, we have shown that dehumanization of victims only increases violence motivated by instrumental reasons or personal gain. Dehumanization does not increase violence motivated by moral reasons, such as revenge, because morally motivated perpetrators wish to harm complete human beings (Rai, Valdesolo, & Graham, 2017). In another set of experiments, I have found that adding an extrinsic material incentive to commit violence can "crowd out" intrinsic moral motives to commit violence, leading to a reduced likelihood of violence in

the same way that compensating people for doing their civic duty of donating blood can reduce the likelihood of donation (Frey & Oberholzer-Gee, 1997). Finally, using first-person narratives of violent experiences, I am finding that for violence that people do not want to engage in but feel that they are morally obligated to, greater self-control leads to more, not less, violence.

Extension and Expansion

Some definitions slow progress. In moral psychology, a set of ideas drawn from post-Enlightenment Western prescriptive philosophy has clouded our ability to understand the bases of moral judgment. To honestly investigate moral psychology, we must completely separate our own prescriptive ethics from our theory building. RRT is my attempt to do that. It argues that there is a universal structure to our moral psychology, but that it is implemented differently across social relations in ways that lead to extreme moral diversity across cultures and history.

The most important implication of this work is to show that moral disagreements reflect genuinely different social–relational perspectives and motives rather than the actions of "evil" people or errors and biases in judgment on the part of those we disagree with. It shows that, when people are violent, it is because they believe it is right, and therefore focusing on increasing the material consequences of violence, providing body cameras to record behavior, improving self-control, or improving mental health care may not be as effective as community-based interventions that work to shift moral attitudes and make clear to potential perpetrators that their violence hurts social relationships important to them.

Long term, we know that people engage in various kinds of social relationships across cultures and organizations, and my research has found that these social relationships imply very different rules and expectations about fairness and the acceptability of violence. However, the question of why there are these different types of relationships and social structures and under what conditions one is likely to predominate over another is still to be explored. For example, why do people freely share hunting and fishing territories more often than gardens, share water more than food, or share more in areas with fewer organized social structures? When do people rely on simple moral rules such as "do no harm" versus relying on more complex moral rules such as "calculate all utilities on a common metric to determine the optimal choice"? My collaborators and I have already started to investigate these questions through analytic modeling approaches, in which we have identified factors such as the interdependence among individuals, the returns on resources, and the costs of social interaction as critical components to the emergence of different social structures (Nettle, Panchanathan, Rai, & Fiske, 2011). The next step is to experimentally manipulate these factors and examine whether they lead to the emergence of different kinds of social relations and the downstream moral motives they entail. This line of research will ultimately develop a more complete theory of social relations than any that currently exist.

REFERENCES

Abusharaf, R. M. (2001). Virtuous cuts: Female genital circumcision in an African ontology. *Differences, 12,* 112–140.

Alperovitz, G. (1996). *The decision to use the atomic bomb.* New York: Vintage.

Bandura, A. (1999). Moral disengagement in the perpetration of inhumanities. *Personality and Social Psychology Review, 3,* 193–209.

Berlin, I. (1969). *Four essays on liberty* (Vol. 5). Oxford, UK: Oxford University Press.

Carnes, N. C., Lickel, B., & Janoff-Bulman, R. (2015). Shared perceptions: Morality is embedded in social contexts. *Personality and Social Psychology Bulletin, 41,* 351–362.

Coid, J., Yang, M., Ullrich, S., Roberts, A., & Hare, R. D. (2009). Prevalence and correlates of psychopathic traits in the household population of Great Britain. *International Journal of Law and Psychiatry, 32,* 65–73.

Coid, J., Yang, M., Ullrich, S., Roberts, A., Moran, P., Bebbington, P., . . . Hare, R. (2009b). Psychopathy among prisoners in England and Wales. *International Journal of Law and Psychiatry, 32,* 134–141.

Copes, H., Hochstetler, A., & Forsyth, C. J. (2013). Peaceful warriors: Codes for violence among adult male bar fighters. *Criminology, 51,* 761–794.

DeWall, C. N., Baumeister, R. F., Stillman, T. F., & Gailliot, M. T. (2007). Violence restrained: Effects of self-regulation and its depletion on aggression. *Journal of Experimental Social Psychology, 43,* 62–76.

Dollard, J., Miller, N. E., Doob, L. W., Mowrer, O. H., & Sears, R. R. (1939). *Frustration and aggression.* New Haven, CT: Yale University Press.

Felson, R. B., & Tedeschi, J. T. (1993). *Aggression and violence: Social interactionist perspectives.* Washington, DC: American Psychological Association.

Fiske, A. P. (1992). The four elementary forms of sociality: Framework for a unified theory of social relations. *Psychological Review, 99,* 689–723.

Fiske, A. P., & Rai, T. S. (2014). *Virtuous violence: Hurting and killing to create, sustain, end, and honor social relationships.* Cambridge, UK: Cambridge University Press.

Frey, B. S., & Oberholzer-Gee, F. (1997). The cost of price incentives: An empirical analysis of motivation crowding-out. *American Economic Review, 87,* 746–755.

Giessner, S., & Van Quaquebeke, N. (2010). Using a relational models perspective to understand normatively appropriate conduct in ethical leadership. *Journal of Business Ethics, 95,* 43–55.

Graham, J., Haidt, J., Koleva, S., Motyl, M., Iyer, R., Wojcik, S. P., & Ditto, P. H. (2012). Moral foundations theory: The pragmatic validity of moral pluralism. *Advances in Experimental Social Psychology, 47,* 55–130.

Graham, J., Haidt, J., & Nosek, B. A. (2009). Liberals and conservatives rely on different sets of moral foundations. *Journal of Personality and Social Psychology, 96,* 1029–1046.

Gray, K., Young, L., & Waytz, A. (2012). Mind perception is the essence of morality. *Psychological Inquiry, 23,* 101–124.

Haidt, J., & Joseph, C. (2004). Intuitive ethics: How innately prepared intuitions generate culturally variable virtues. *Daedalus, 133,* 55–66.

Halawi, J. (2002, August 15). "Honour" drenched in blood. *Al-Ahram Weekly.* Available at *www.masress.com/en/ahramweekly/22698.*

Hathaway, J. (2015, June 3). Junior varsity baseball team allegedly made love to McChicken sandwich. *Gawker.* Retrieved from *http://gawker.com/junior-varsity-baseball-team-allegedly-made-love-to-mcc-1708834430.*

Kramnick, I. (Ed.). (1995). *The portable Enlightenment reader.* New York: Penguin Books.

Kubrin, C. E., & Weitzer, R. (2003). Retaliatory homicide: Concentrated disadvantage and neighborhood culture. *Social Problems, 50,* 157–180.

Lamothe, D. (2014, August 28). Once again, militants use Guantanamo-inspired orange suit in an execution. *Washington Post.* Retrieved from *www.washingtonpost.com/news/checkpoint/wp/2014/08/28/once-again-militants-use-guantanamos-orange-jumpsuit-in-an-execution.*

MacIntyre, A. (2007). *After virtue* (3rd ed.). Notre Dame, IN: University of Notre Dame Press. (Original work published 1981)

McGraw, A. P., Schwartz, J. A., & Tetlock, P. E. (2012). From the commercial to the communal: Reframing taboo trade-offs in religious and pharmaceutical marketing. *Journal of Consumer Research, 39,* 157–173.

Mikhail, J. (2007). Universal moral grammar: Theory, evidence and the future. *Trends in Cognitive Sciences, 11*(4), 143–152.

Milgram, S. (1963). Behavioral study of obedience. *Journal of Abnormal and Social Psychology, 67*(4), 371–378.

Nettle, D., Panchanathan, K., Rai, T. S., & Fiske, A. P. (2011). The evolution of giving, sharing, and lotteries. *Current Anthropology, 52*(5), 747–756.

Rai, T. S., & Fiske, A. P. (2011). Moral psychology is relationship regulation: Moral motives for unity, hierarchy, equality, and proportionality. *Psychological Review, 118,* 57–75.

Rai, T. S., Valdesolo, P., & Graham, J. (2017). Dehumanization increases instrumental violence, but not moral violence. *Proceedings of the National Academy of Sciences, 114,* 8511–8516.

Shweder, R. A., Much, N. C., Mahapatra, M., & Park, L. (1997). The "big three" of morality (autonomy, community, and divinity), and the "big three" explanations of suffering. In A. Brandt & P. Rozin (Eds.), *Morality and health* (pp. 119–169). New York: Routledge.

Stark, R. (1972). *Police riots: Collective violence and law enforcement.* Belmont, CA: Wadsworth.

Tajfel, H., Billig, M. G., Bundy, R. P., & Flament, C. (1971). Social categorization and intergroup behaviour. *European Journal of Social Psychology, 1,* 149–178.

Turiel, E. (1983). *The development of social knowledge: Morality and convention.* Cambridge, UK: Cambridge University Press.

U.S. Department of Justice Federal Bureau of Investigation. (2010). Crime in the United States, 2009: Expanded homicide data. Retrieved from *www2.fbi.gov/ucr/cius2009/offenses/expanded_information/homicide.html.*

CHAPTER 25

A Stairway to Heaven
A Terror Management Theory Perspective on Morality

Andrea M. Yetzer
Tom Pyszczynski
Jeff Greenberg

> **Why do people care about living up to moral values?**
>
> From a terror management perspective, they care because doing so enables them to view themselves as enduring, significant contributors to a meaningful world who will continue to exist after death, either literally by qualifying for an afterlife, or symbolically, by contributing to something greater than themselves that will last forever.

Although the question of whether gods and religion are necessary for morality has been debated for centuries, the relationship between religion and morality has received surprisingly little attention in recent psychological discussions of morality. On the one hand, many religious traditions view morality as emanating from God and moral behavior as functioning to please him. On the other, most contemporary social psychological theories of religion view belief in gods and religion as by-products of human cognitive proclivities that evolved to serve other functions, and some argue that, in and of itself, religion serves no adaptive function and often promotes harmful and immoral behavior (e.g., Dawkins, 2006). This chapter is focused on what terror manage-

ment theory (TMT; Solomon, Greenberg, & Pyszczynski, 1991, 2015) brings to the discussion of morality and religion by focusing on the interplay of evolved tendencies found in other species with the fruits of the sophisticated intellect uniquely characteristic of humankind and the existential problems to which these abilities gave rise. TMT posits that dawning awareness of the inevitability of death inspired monumental changes in the nature and function of morality for our species.

The current zeitgeist in moral psychology reflects two rather distinct conceptions of what drives moral thought and action. The moral reasoning perspective (e.g., Kohlberg, 1969; Piaget, 1932/1965), which dominated psychology for much of the 20th century, emphasizes relatively rational moral thinking that occurs with varying levels of sophistication, guided by the moral teachings and traditions of one's culture. The more recent moral intuitionist perspective (e.g., Graham et al., 2013; Haidt & Joseph, 2004; Shweder, Much, Mahapatra, & Park, 1997) emphasizes intuitive moral emotions that evolved because they facilitate group living and social harmony and were adapted by cultures over the course of human history to meet their own particular needs. Although these perspectives emphasize different aspects of morality, most psychologists agree that moral thought and behavior involve both rational and intuitive processes.

TMT posits that moral values are part of the cultural worldviews that protect people from anxiety triggered by their awareness of the certainty of death and that these worldviews set forth the standards from which moral behavior is both enacted and evaluated. Further, because individuals are socialized into their culture's worldview, beginning shortly after birth and continuing through the remainder of their lives, morality is manifested in culturally and individually variable ways. Although variable in composition, the formation of cultural worldviews and their standards for moral behavior and moral judgment operate through a universal human process designed to maintain a sense of meaning and safety that provides protection against anxiety and the hope of transcending death. The purpose of this chapter is to use TMT to shed light on the nature and function of moral thought and behavior.

The Biological Roots of Morality

People have long believed that morality is a uniquely human characteristic, perhaps reflecting the special affection the deity feels for our species. Earlier generations of moral psychologists posited that morality requires cognitive capacities unique to our species and that only relatively few people possess enough of these capacities to reason at the highest moral level. However, more recent theorizing views morality as rooted in social proclivities that humankind shares with many other species. De Waal (1996) sug-

gested that the seeds of morality emerged as evolutionary adaptations that promoted order and social harmony among animals living in groups, which facilitated the survival and reproduction necessary for gene perpetuation. Indeed, behaviors that reflect caring for others, sharing, group protection, deference to leaders, and disgust have been documented in a variety of species, including chimpanzees, gorillas, wolves, and even bats (Bekoff & Pierce, 2009). This idea of deep evolutionary roots of morality fits well with Shweder et al.'s, (1997) observation that, despite cultural variations in expression, human cultures exhibit a limited set of moral proclivities that encompasses most of what is relevant to moral concerns. These ideas were integrated by Haidt and colleagues (Haidt & Joseph, 2004, 2007) into moral foundations theory (MFT), which posits that human morality is rooted in a set of deeply rooted moral intuitions that evolved to facilitate group living and that were later institutionalized in specific ways by different cultures, leading to a set of five or six universal moral foundations. From the perspective of MFT, although all human beings share these universal moral intuitions, people differ in terms of which are emphasized and how they are implemented.

TMT sheds light on the forces that changed moral functioning as our species evolved into modern humans. It also sheds light on long-standing disputes about the nature of morality. In particular, it addresses the relationship between gods, religion, and morality. As cultures developed and their moral prescriptions evolved, they formed narratives to explain why particular things were moral or immoral, with religion and gods emerging to legitimize and institutionalize these narratives. TMT fits well with theories that view morality as an evolutionary adaptation that humankind shares with other group-living species, but posits that the emergence of increasingly sophisticated intellectual abilities led to a seismic realization of the inevitability of death, which changed the way morality functions in our species. Our ancestors coped with the terror that their dawning awareness of death produced by generating cultural worldviews that gave meaning to life and enduring value and significance to themselves. These worldviews transformed the primitive moral intuitions of their prehuman ancestors into linguistically elaborated moral values that provided a stairway to heaven through which they could attain literal immortality and extended the impact of reputational concerns into the hope for the symbolic immortality that comes with being remembered as a good person after one has died. Indeed, awareness of death transformed the relationship of individuals to groups, in that groups are something larger and more enduring than oneself that continues to exist after one has gone.

Terror Management Theory

TMT was most directly inspired by the work of Ernest Becker (1971, 1973, 1975), a cultural anthropologist who attempted to integrate ideas from the social sciences and humanities to shed light on what he believed were the essential aspects of human nature, drawing on the ideas of Otto Rank, William James, George Herbert Mead, Friedrich Nietzsche, Sigmund Freud, and many others. TMT infuses Becker's insights into contemporary thinking in experimental social, cognitive, developmental, and personality psychology to provide an integrative framework for thinking about the role of evolution and culture in contemporary psychological functioning. TMT focuses on what self-esteem is, why it's so desperately needed, and the role that awareness of the inevitability of death plays in diverse aspects of life, especially those that bear no obvious relation to the problem of mortality.

TMT (Solomon et al., 1991, 2015) begins with a consideration of how human beings are both similar to and different from other animals. Like all other species, humans are powerfully motivated to continue living and reproduce; in one way or another, all bodily and motivational systems function to facilitate survival and reproduction, which makes it possible to pass genes on to future generations. However, our species evolved unique cognitive capacities for the use of symbols, autonoetic thought, and self-awareness that provided increased flexibility in behavior that enabled us to survive and prosper in diverse and changing environments. This oth-

erwise adaptive sophisticated intellect led to awareness of the inevitability of death—the basic, undeniable fact that life will cease someday and that death may come at any time or for many reasons. This awareness gives rise to the potential for overwhelming terror, because it runs counter to the multiple biological, physiological, and psychological systems geared toward survival. If left unbridled, this potential for terror would drastically hinder our species' capacity for adaptive functioning and be extremely unpleasant for individual human beings.

TMT posits that our ancestors used the same cognitive capacities that made them aware of death to manage their terror by shaping ways of construing reality to defuse the threat. The problem with death is that it can be forestalled for only so long—awareness of this inevitability is the essence of the human existential dilemma. Because nothing can be done to change this ultimate truth, our ancestors molded their understanding of reality to cope with the problem of inevitable death. Given how little was known about the workings of the world, death-denying ideas easily won out over less optimistic ones. Ideas about life and death that helped deny this unfortunate truth were especially appealing, likely to be spread, and eventually constituted *cultural worldviews* that provided order, meaning, and permanence to people's conceptions of the world and their lives within it. Thus the potential for terror that resulted from awareness of the inevitability of death influenced the nature of the ideas that became accepted as worldly and other-worldly wisdom.

Inventing cultural worldviews that imbue life with cosmic meaning in which human beings played a significant role that does not end with physical death was the centerpiece of our ancestors' solution to their existential dilemma. A sense of personal significance, *self-esteem*, was attained by viewing oneself as living up to the standards of value prescribed by one's worldview. Thus self-esteem is a cultural creation that requires exemplifying what is valued by one's culture. Being a valued member of a meaningful and enduring universe makes it possible to transcend death.

TMT posits that our ancestors used their ingenuity to invent a world of ideas in which death is defeated and that this humanly created spiritual dimension continues to manage existential terror to this day. These cultural innovations drastically changed the way our species lives, from animals coping with the demands of external reality to symbolic beings who live in a world of beliefs and values (i.e., cultural worldviews) designed to elevate them above the rest of nature. This explains why the mental and spiritual dimensions of existence are generally valued above the physical ones and why people prefer to think of themselves as distinct from and superior to other animals (for a recent review of research on people's denial of their animal nature, see Goldenberg, 2012). Because bodies undeniably die and decay, we humans must be more than bodies; thus we construe ourselves as spiritual and moral beings for whom physical existence is a mere step toward a more perfect form of existence that is eternal and unlimited.

TMT posits that people protect themselves from death-related fear with a cultural anxiety buffer that consists of three components: cultural worldviews that explain the nature of reality; self-esteem that enables people to view themselves as beings of primary value; and close personal attachment relationships that validate one's cultural worldview and self-esteem. Cultural worldviews are comprised of personally held values, morals, and beliefs about the world that establish order, meaning, and permanence to life. Cultural worldviews provide the standards that moral behavior should reflect, and against which moral judgments are made. Whether it is moral to eat dogs, to masturbate, to wear revealing clothing, to drink alcohol, or to have multiple spouses varies from culture to culture. Living up to these cultural standards through carefully conducted behavior provides the sense of self-esteem that gives one hope of literal and symbolic immortality.

Typically linked to the culture's religious beliefs, literal immortality is the belief that life extends beyond the physical world into some form of afterlife, such as heaven, reincarnation, or nirvana. Symbolic immortality, on the other hand, is the hope of transcending physical death by living on in the hearts and minds of the living, or by leaving tangible artifacts of one's existence in the physical world. Said differently, culture affords human beings opportunities to be part of something greater than themselves through various group memberships, such as family, political, ethnic, national, or even sports team affiliations. Individual contributions such as works of art, literature, or science, contributing to the welfare of one's group, and having children are all means to live on through these groups, as well as through the history and continued development of the world we leave behind when we die. Despite their differences, the hope of both literal and symbolic immortality requires living up to the moral standards of one's cultural worldview—which enables one to view oneself as a valuable participant in a meaningful reality. This is the essence of self-esteem.

All worldviews are individualized interpretations of cultural constructions that provide meaning and safety; thus they differ across individuals due to variations in information and experience that begin with socialization and continue over the course of life. TMT suggests that one's cultural worldview begins developing shortly after birth, beginning with the reliance on our initial attachment figures (for a review, see Mikulincer, Florian, & Hirschberger, 2004), and then matures over the course of one's psychological development as we learn about the world through parents, peers, teachers, religious and political leaders, and others, eventually emerging as one's own individualized worldview. What initially emerges from reliance on primary attachment figures to quell innate emotional reactions to things that threaten one's continued existence gradually transitions to a desire for approval from one's parents and significant others, and then to a more general desire to be a good and valuable person in the eyes of both other members of one's culture and, in most cases, one's God. Thus we are socialized to strive for self-esteem by living up to the moral standards of the worldview that we come to accept as reality. When we do, we feel that we are enduringly significant symbolic beings, valued and protected, and worthy of living on literally or symbolically beyond our physical deaths.

The development of one's worldview and one's sense of value within it reflects the old adage, "it takes a village." Our worldview and sense of value within it are living entities that require social consensus and constant validation to maintain one's faith that the world really is as we believe it to be, and that we really are the valued persons we believe ourselves to be. Because the beliefs and values of our worldviews are human creations that do not typically reflect observable objective experience and often actually run counter to observable reality, our faith in them requires that our communities share our beliefs and values and agree that we are indeed living up to them. Without such certainty, our worldviews and self-esteem are unable to effectively protect us from anxiety.

As Skitka and colleagues (Skitka, Bauman, & Sargis, 2005) have shown, moral beliefs and behavior are the most important determinant of people's evaluations of both self and others. This probably reflects the critical role that moral intuitions played in regulating the behavior of our prehuman ancestors, which likely continued to be of paramount importance throughout human history. Social animals require ways of regulating their behavior to facilitate cooperation, minimize conflict, and promote the interests of one's own group over others. It seems likely that, in addition to communicating ways to adapt to the physical environment, emerging human linguistic capacities were also used to help regulate interpersonal behavior; moral injunctions and imperatives were likely to be more effective if they could be communicated with others. But when human intelligence reached the point at which awareness of the inevitability of death emerged, it set in motion changes in human functioning in general and morality in particular that forever altered the nature of our species and the moral principles that regulate our behavior. Human beings became *cultural animals* (Greenberg, Pyszczynski, & Solomon, 1986). Although many species show signs of fear in response to threats to continued existence, we humans are unique in our awareness that death is our inevitable fate. Although fear in response to threats that can be avoided or escaped is adaptive because it motivates behavior to escape the threatening situation, fear in response to a future event for which there is no solution is not. Because there is nothing that can be

done to reverse the reality of human mortality, our ancestors adapted their understanding of the world to create an imagined reality in which death could be transcended. This usually entailed construing themselves as spiritual beings with souls who would continue to exist after death.

As others have suggested (e.g., Atran, 2002; Boyer, 2001), early humans probably attributed mind and intent to inanimate aspects of nature, which led them to imagine an invisible dimension that controlled the natural world. With dawning awareness of death, they used the concept of an immortal soul as a way of distancing themselves from their mortal nature. Over time, they gradually made the spirits more powerful, transforming them into deities who controlled life, death, and admission to the afterlife. These imaginary beings were imbued with human characteristics that were probably inspired by experience with powerful humans, such as their own parents, tribal leaders, and kings, leading to conceptions of gods who are demanding, egotistic, and sometimes cruel on the one hand, but compassionate and caring on the other. As Feuerbach (1841/1989) famously put it, "Man created God in his own image." For a more thorough presentation of the TMT analysis of the emergence of specific characteristics of gods and religion, see Pyszczynski, Solomon, and Greenberg (2015; Pyszczynski, 2016). Of course we acknowledge that, like all theories of early human history, our analysis is speculative and likely to be difficult to assess empirically. But the functional aspects of this analysis are consistent with experimental findings regarding contemporary human functioning.

From the perspective of TMT, moral behavior and moral judgment are central components of this anxiety buffering system. Because being certain of the validity of our worldviews is needed to protect us from death anxiety, we like those who endorse our views and dislike those who challenge or violate them. If confidence in our cultural worldview and self-esteem is our main line of defense against existential terror, and we attain this confidence through the consensual validation provided by others, then those with different worldviews and who do not value us highly must clearly be wrong and be judged accordingly. Those who violate the moral dictates of our culture challenge their validity. A person who fails to abide by moral principles is implicitly suggesting that these principles do not always apply; because these principles are essential for our victory over death, moral transgressors must be punished accordingly. And because our own immortality, both literal and symbolic, depends on being a valued participant in the meaningful reality provided by our culture, we are compelled to live up to the moral prescriptions that we have accepted as a fabric our reality. Thus, because of the important terror management function morality serves, we are highly motivated to uphold morality in ourselves and others.

A large body of research consisting of over 500 studies conducted in more than 30 countries worldwide has provided converging support for the fundamental propositions of TMT. This research has shown that (1) bolstering worldviews, self-esteem, or attachments reduce self-reported anxiety, physiological arousal, and anxiety-related behavior in threatening situation; (2) reminders of death increase striving to maintain one's worldview, self-esteem and close relationships; (3) threats to worldviews, self-esteem, attachments increase death-thought accessibility (DTA); (4) boosts to any of these components reduce the effect of death reminders on DTA, worldview defense, self-esteem striving, or attachment seeking; and (5) evidence for the existence of an afterlife reduce the effects of mortality salience (MS) on worldview defense and self-esteem striving. For more thorough reviews, see Burke, Martens, and Faucher (2010), Greenberg, Vail, and Pyszczynski (2014), or Pyszczynski et al. (2015).

TMT Contributions to Understanding Human Morality

Most contemporary theories of morality emphasize the role that morality plays in facilitating cooperation and minimizing conflict within groups and success in competition with other groups (e.g., Graham et al., 2013; Haidt & Joseph, 2004; Norenzayan et al., 2016). While not disputing this important social function of morality, TMT suggests that dawning awareness of the inevitability of death among early modern humans fundamentally transformed the nature of morality by adding an important new function: feeling protected from and transcendent of death by conceiving self as a valued contributor to a meaningful world rather than a vulnerable, purely material animal fated only to obliteration upon death. As moral beings, we can live on either literally through an enduring soul, symbolically through being revered and remembered contributors to the world, and most often, in both ways. Through morality, we learned whether we were pleasing the gods and also serving our ancestors and descendants and our tribes and nations. In this way, doing the right thing became much more than just getting along with those with whom we interacted in our daily lives; it became a way to warrant an eternal place in the world. Consequently, people could now justify behavior that deviated from the wishes of powerful others; people could view behavior that offended local authorities as serving more important purposes.

This in no ways implies that morality lost its function of maintaining harmony within groups. Indeed, social moral conventions probably served as important inspiration for the character and preferences of the spirit world that our ancestors created. Because moral behavior was so highly valued by one's group, people assumed that the gods shared these preferences. Indeed, ideas about what pleased the all-knowing gods may have originated in the preferences of powerful humans, such as parents, tribal leaders, and kings. This could help explain the demanding, jealous, egotistic, and vindictive nature of the gods that our ancestors created, a tendency that led to inspiring musings from comedians such as George Carlin and Louis C. K.: "Religion has actually convinced people . . . that there's an invisible man who lives in the sky who watches everything you do, every minute of every day. And who has a special list of ten things he does not want you to do. And if you do any of these ten things, he has a special place, full of fire and smoke and burning torture and anguish, where he will send you to remain and suffer and burn and choke and scream and cry, forever and ever, till the end of time. But he loves you!" (Carlin, 2002, p. 28)

Indeed, this new function for morality in the context of an invisible dimension of spirits and deities brought with it a new function for other people—that of validating the existence of these death-defeating entities that cannot be directly observed. As Festinger (1957) pointed out, people are especially dependent on the views of others when it comes to domains in which there are no clear physical referents. Since gods, spirits, and other-worldly dimensions cannot be observed, people are especially dependent on others who share their beliefs in such things to give them confidence in their existence. We agree with many that religions function, in part, to promote group solidarity by bringing people together into a world of fictive kinship. However, TMT views awareness of death as the catalyst for the development and elaboration of spiritual worlds in which moral goodness is rewarded. These belief systems required people to come together to provide the social validation that belief in such invisible entities requires. For a discussion of how the pursuit of death-denying spiritual beliefs may have led to the emergence of both architecture and agriculture as a way of feeding the large number of workers that were needed to build ancient temples at Göbekli Tepe and Catahouluk, which precede any known signs of agriculture by at least 1,000 years, see Solomon et al. (2015) and Schmidt (2010).

We view the TMT perspective as complementary to other contemporary theories of human morality. Whereas TMT adds an existential dimension to the social adaptationist underpinnings of MFT, MFT points to the role of intuitions that evolved in our prehuman ancestors as providing inspiration for the preferences they attributed to the gods they invented to help them cope with the terror that resulted from realization of their mortal nature. The idea that cultures built on evolved preverbal intuitions helps explain the specific content of worldviews, for example, why concerns about caring, fairness, authority, group loyalty, and purity are so ubiquitous in human cultures. Human verbal capacities made it possible to embed these intuitions in death-denying narrative stories that explained their origins, justified their existence, and added a new incentive for following them—the hope of immortality. Thus moral values are an integral part of culturally shared conceptions of reality that set standards for behavior through which individuals evaluate themselves and others; people gain anxiety-buffering self-esteem to the extent their behavior is seen as measuring up to the culture's moral standards (Skitka et al., 2005).

Empirical Evidence for Death Awareness in Moral Behavior and Judgment

The literature supporting the fundamental propositions of TMT is considerable, but several studies illustrate that thoughts of death inspire reactions in accordance with rudiments of morality, including responses to perpetrators and victims of moral transgressions, and increased adherence to the moral foundations posited by MFT. The very first TMT study demonstrated that reminders of death influence moral judgments, leading judges to set higher bond for a woman arrested for prostitution (Rosenblatt, Greenberg, Solomon, Pyszczynski, & Lyon, 1989), which can be construed as a violation of the sanctity/degradation foundation. In a similar vein, a study by Landau and colleagues (2006) demonstrated that death reminders led to an increase in negative evaluations of sexually provocative women. Florian and Mikulincer (1997) found that MS led to more severe ratings of diverse moral transgressions (e.g., someone who steals money from a designated education fund), as well as harsher punishment recommendations for transgressors. From an MFT perspective, Florian and Mikulincer's transgressor violated morals associated with care/harm and fairness.

Indeed, there is a large body of evidence supporting the role of fear of death in each of the moral foundations posited by MFT (for a review, see Kesebir & Pyszczynski, 2011). When care-related values are salient, MS increases prosocial behavior (e.g., Jonas, Sullivan, & Greenberg, 2013). Regarding the fairness/cheating foundation, research has found that death-related cognitions are more accessible when learning about innocent victims who have been severely injured than victims whose condition was due to their own actions (Hirschberger,

2006); conversely, derogation of the victim of a random tragedy increased when death is salient (Landau, Greenberg, & Solomon, 2004). Additionally, as justice is central to the fairness foundation, research has shown that MS increases the appeal of justice-based arguments for military action and support for violence, even if the benefits of using such force is low (Hirschberger et al., 2016). With regard to the sanctity/degradation foundation, many studies have shown death reminders increase disgust responses (for a review, see Goldenberg, 2012)—the characteristic emotion related to this foundation. For example, research has found increases in emotional reactions to disgust primes following MS, as well as increases in DTA when primed with disgusting pictures (Cox, Goldenberg, Pyszczynski, & Weise, 2007; see also Goldenberg et al., 2001).

In terms of loyalty/betrayal, Castano and Dechesne (2005) reviewed a large body of evidence showing that MS increases ingroup favoritism, outgroup hostility, perceptions of group entitativity, and stereotyping. Interestingly, research has shown that thoughts of death highlight differences between liberals and conservatives in their reliance on particular moral foundations (Bassett, van Tongeren, Green, Sonntag, & Kilpatrick, 2014; see also Graham, Haidt, & Nosek, 2009), thus illustrating death concerns play a role in ingroup members consensually validating moral values that are part of their shared worldview. Related to the authority/subversion foundation, death reminders have been found to inspire more deference to authority. Cohen, Solomon, Maxfield, Pyszczynski, and Greenberg (2004) found that following MS, support for leaders who proclaimed the unique value of the ingroup increased. Additional research has shown that MS increased support for a local political candidate who promoted a sense of symbolic immortality in the community (Shepherd, Kay, Landau, & Keefer, 2011)—further demonstrating how shared conceptions of reality play a vital role in death transcendence.

TMT suggests that moral behavior and moral judgment serve terror management functions through the promise of symbolic or literal immortality to moral conformists and derogation or punishment of moral transgressors. As previously discussed, lit-eral immortality is connected with religious beliefs as they provide a path for living beyond physical death and symbolic immortality is tied to identification with the culture and valued contributions to it. Indeed, research has found that death reminders increase belief in an afterlife (e.g., Batson & Stocks, 2004; Osarchuk & Tatz, 1973); other research has shown increases in DTA following challenges to one's religious beliefs (Schimel, Hayes, Williams, & Jahrig, 2007). Similarly, MS increases nationalism, defense of one's culture, and striving to live up to the values of one's culture (e.g., Jonas et al., 2008). Furthermore, disrespectfully handling a religious object or a culturally valued object (a flag) led to greater distress following MS (Greenberg, Simon, Porteus, Pyszczynski, & Solomon, 1995), as well as increased support for violence against other nations among American religious fundamentalists and American conservatives (Pyszczynski, Greenberg, Solomon, & Maxfield, 2006; Rothschild, Abdollahi, & Pyszczynski, 2009). Yet in Rothschild et al. (2009), the effects of MS on support for political violence were reversed when participants were primed with compassionate values linked to Jesus in the New Testament. These findings were replicated in a follow-up study with Iranian religious fundamentalists, with Koran-connected compassionate value primes leading to decreases in support for military action against the United States.

Future Directions for TMT

So where does the TMT analysis of morality go from here? As noted above, a substantial body of research has already documented the role of death concerns in diverse aspects of morality. However, the analysis presented here raises some intriguing new questions. If awareness of death created a new function for humankind's moral (and immoral) behavior, this should affect the way moral concerns impinge on thought and action. Death concerns would be expected to increase the impact of religious and afterlife concerns for behavior, and thoughts of God and the afterlife would be expected to influence the specific moral concerns that influence behavior. Similarly, death concerns should shift people's moral attitudes and actions toward establishing a positive legacy for future generations, something recent research is beginning to find (e.g., Maxfield et al., 2014). In general, we would expect that sanctity/degradation concerns specified by MFT would take on extra importance under such circumstances. This also raises questions about how sanctity/degradation and ties with immortality granting belief systems are incorporated into various specific moral concerns: Does the meaning of concerns about caring, fairness, authority, loyalty, and cleanliness change when these values are linked to God, an afterlife, and contributing to one's legacy and future generations? No doubt there is substantial cultural variability in how these connections play out, both within broad cultural groups and within specific subcultural groups. There are also likely important individual differences in the way specific members of these cultural groups respond to the competing demands placed on them by the moral teachings of their cultures. Important questions also arise regarding how religious–cultural precepts affect the behavior of nonbelievers and people alienated from the mainstream secular culture. How do those who have rejected religious and cultural beliefs after being socialized into them as children differ from those who have sustained the beliefs they were raised to accept?

Another potentially fruitful direction for future research may lie in applying these ideas to better understand the psychological processes set in motion by traumatic life events. Anxiety buffer disruption theory (ABDT; Pyszczynski & Kesebir, 2011) suggests that traumatic experiences produce their devastating consequences by leading to a breakdown in the normal functioning of the anxiety buffering system. This leaves the affected individuals unable to effectively manage their fears, essentially naked in the face of a devastating confrontation with death. Recent theories of trauma emphasize the role of moral injury in adverse psychological outcomes, such as posttraumatic stress disorder (PTSD) symptoms (e.g., Litz et al., 2009). Briefly, moral injury results from the experience of perpetrating (e.g., killing another human being), indirectly experiencing (e.g., handling human remains), or bearing witness to (e.g., witnessing the rape of friend) an atrocious event that violates one's deeply held moral values or expectations. Traumatic experiences such as these can disrupt the capacity of one's worldview and self-esteem to provide protection against anxiety, perhaps leading to PTSD symptoms in some cases, or a collapse of moral self-regulation, the experience of depression or even antisocial behavior in others. Better understanding of the role of morality in managing death-related anxiety and traumatic sequelae could thus shed light on many of the important problems our society is currently facing.

REFERENCES

Atran, S. (2002). *In gods we trust: The evolutionary landscape of religion.* New York: Oxford University Press.

Bassett, J. F., Van Tongeren, D. R., Green, J. D., Sonntag, M. E., & Kilpatrick, H. (2014). The interactive effects of mortality salience and political orientation on moral judgments. *British Journal of Social Psychology, 54*(2), 306–323.

Batson, C. D., & Stocks, E. L. (2004). Religion: Its core psychological function. In J. Greenberg, S. L. Koole, & T. Pyszczynski (Eds.), *Handbook of experimental existential psychology* (pp. 141–155). New York: Guilford Press.

Becker, E. (1971). *The birth and death of meaning: An interdisciplinary perspective on the problem of man* (2nd ed.). New York: Free Press.

Becker, E. (1973). *The denial of death.* New York: Free Press.

Becker, E. (1975). *Escape from evil.* New York: Free Press.

Bekoff, M., & Pierce, J. (2009). *Wild justice: The moral lives of animals.* Chicago: University of Chicago Press.

Boyer, P. (2001). *Religion explained: The evolutionary origins of religious thought.* New York: Basic Books.

Burke, B. L., Martens, A., & Faucher, E. H. (2010). Two decades of terror management theory: A meta-analysis of mortality salience research. *Personality and Social Psychology Review, 14*, 155–195.

Carlin, G. (2001). *Napalm and Silly Putty.* New York: Hyperion Books.

Castano, E., & Dechesne, M. (2005). On defeating death: Group reification and social identification as immortality strategies. *European Review of Social Psychology, 16*, 221–255.

Cohen, F., Solomon, S., Maxfield, M., Pyszc-zynski, T., & Greenberg, J. (2004). Fatal attraction: The effects of mortality salience on evaluations of charismatic, task-oriented, and relationship-oriented leaders. *Psychological Science, 15*, 846–851.

Cox, C. R., Goldenberg, J. L., Pyszczynski, T., & Weise, D. (2007). Disgust, creatureliness and the accessibility of death-related thoughts. *European Journal of Social Psychology, 37*, 494–507.

Dawkins, R. (2006). *The God delusion*. Boston: Houghton Mifflin.

De Waal, F. B. (1996). *Good natured: The origins of right and wrong in humans and other animals*. Cambridge, MA: Harvard University Press.

Festinger, L. (1957). *A theory of cognitive dissonance*. Evanston, IL: Row Peterson.

Feuerbach, L. A. (1989). *The essence of Christianity* (G. Eliot, Trans.). New York: Prometheus Books. (Original work published 1941)

Florian, V., & Mikulincer, M. (1997). Fear of death and the judgment of social transgressions: A multidimensional test of terror management theory. *Journal of Personality and Social Psychology, 73*, 369–380.

Goldenberg, J. L. (2012). A body of terror: Denial of death and the creaturely body. In P. R. Shaver & M. Mikulincer (Eds.), *Meaning, mortality, and choice: The social psychology of existential concerns* (pp. 93–110). Washington, DC: American Psychological Association.

Goldenberg, J. L., Pyszczynski, T., Greenberg, J., Solomon, S., Kluck, B., & Cornwell, R. (2001). I am not an animal: Mortality salience, disgust, and the denial of human creatureliness. *Journal of Experimental Psychology: General, 130*, 427–435.

Graham, J., Haidt, J., Koleva, S., Motyl, M., Iyer, R., Wojcik, S., & Ditto, P. H. (2013). Moral foundations theory: The pragmatic validity of moral pluralism. In P. Devine & A. Plant (Eds.), *Advances in experimental social psychology* (Vol. 47, pp. 55–130). San Diego, CA: Academic Press.

Graham, J., Haidt, J., & Nosek, B. A. (2009). Liberals and conservatives rely on different sets of moral foundations. *Journal of Personality and Social Psychology, 96*, 1029–1046.

Greenberg, J., Pyszczynski, T., & Solomon, S. (1986). The causes and consequences of a need for self-esteem: A terror management theory. *Public Self and Private Self, 189*, 189–212.

Greenberg, J., Simon, L., Porteus, J., Pyszczynski, T., & Solomon, S. (1995). Evidence of a terror management function of cultural icons: The effects of mortality salience on the inappropriate use of cherished cultural symbols. *Personality and Social Psychology Bulletin, 21*, 1221–1228.

Greenberg, J., Vail, K., & Pyszczynski, T. (2014). Terror management theory and research: How the desire for death transcendence drives our strivings for meaning and significance. *Advances in Motivation Science, 1*, 85–134.

Haidt, J., & Joseph, C. (2004) Intuitive ethics: How innately prepared intuitions generate culturally variable virtues. *Daedalus, 133*, 55–66.

Haidt, J., & Joseph, C. (2007). The moral mind: How five sets of innate intuitions guide the development of many culture-specific virtues, and perhaps even modules. In P. Carruthers, S. Laurence, & S. Stich (Eds.), *The innate mind* (Vol. 3, pp. 367–391). New York: Oxford University Press.

Hirschberger, G. (2006). Terror management and attributions of blame to innocent victims: Reconciling compassionate and defensive responses. *Journal of Personality and Social Psychology, 91*, 832–844.

Hirschberger, G., Pyszczynski, T., Ein-Dor, T., Shani Sherman, T., Kadah, E., Kesebir, P., & Park, Y. C. (2016). Fear of death amplifies retributive justice motivations and encourages political violence. *Peace and Conflict: Journal of Peace Psychology, 22*, 67–74.

Jonas, E., Martens, A., Niesta, D., Fritsche, I., Sullivan, D., & Greenberg, J. (2008). Focus theory of normative conduct and terror management theory: The interactive impact of mortality salience and norm salience on social judgment. *Journal of Personality and Social Psychology, 95*, 1239–1251.

Jonas, E., Sullivan, D., & Greenberg, J. (2013). Generosity, greed, norms, and death: Differential effects of mortality salience on charitable behavior. *Journal of Economic Psychology, 35*, 47–57.

Kesebir, P., & Pyszczynski, T. (2011). A moral–existential account of the psychological factors fostering intergroup conflict. *Social and Personality Psychology Compass, 5*, 878–890.

Kohlberg, L. (1969). Stage and sequence: The cognitive-developmental approach to socialization. In D. A. Goslin (Ed.), *Handbook of socialization theory and research* (pp. 347–480). Chicago: Rand McNally.

Landau, M. J., Goldenberg, J. L., Greenberg, J., Gillath, O., Solomon, S., Cox, C., . . . Pyszczynski, T. (2006). The siren's call: Terror management and the threat of men's sexual attraction to women. *Journal of Personality and Social Psychology, 90*, 129–146.

Landau, M. J., Greenberg, J., & Solomon, S. (2004). The motivational underpinnings of religion. *Behavioral and Brain Sciences, 27*, 743–744.

Litz, B. T., Stein, N., Delaney, E., Lebowitz, L., Nash, W. P., Silva, C., & Maguen, S. (2009). Moral injury and moral repair in war veterans: A preliminary model and intervention strategy. *Clinical Psychology Review, 29,* 695–706.

Maxfield, M., Greenberg, J., Pyszczynski, T., Weise, D., Kosloff, S., Soenke, M., . . . Blatter, J. (2014). Increases in generative concern among older adults following reminders of mortality. *International Journal of Aging and Human Development, 79,* 1–21.

Mikulincer, M., Florian, V., & Hirschberger, G. (2004). The terror of death and the quest for love: An existential perspective on close relationships. In J. Greenberg, S. L. Koole, & T. Pyszczynski (Eds.), *Handbook of experimental existential psychology* (pp. 287–304). New York: Guilford Press.

Norenzayan, A., Shariff, A. F., Gervais, W. M., Willard, A. K., McNamara, R. A., Slingerland, E., & Henrich, J. (2016). The cultural evolution of prosocial religions. *Behavioral and Brain Sciences, 39,* 1–86.

Osarchuk, M., & Tatz, S. J. (1973). Effect of induced fear of death on belief in afterlife. *Journal of Personality and Social Psychology, 27,* 256–260.

Piaget, J. (1965). *The moral judgement of the child* (M. Gabain, Trans.). New York: Free Press. (Original work published 1932)

Pyszczynski, T. (2016). God save us: A terror management perspective on morality. In J. P. Forgas, L. Jussim, & P. A. M. von Lange (Eds.), *The social psychology of morality: The Sydney Symposium of Social Psychology* (Vol. 18, pp. 21–39). New York: Routledge.

Pyszczynski, T., Abdollahi, A., Solomon, S., Greenberg, J., Cohen, F., & Weise, D. (2006). Mortality salience, martyrdom, and military might: The Great Satan versus the Axis of Evil. *Personality and Social Psychology Bulletin, 32,* 525–537.

Pyszczynski, T., Greenberg, J., Solomon, S., & Maxfield, M. (2006). On the unique psychological import of the human awareness of mortality: Theme and variations. *Psychological Inquiry, 17,* 328–356.

Pyszczynski, T., & Kesebir, P. (2011). Anxiety buffer disruption theory: A terror management account of posttraumatic stress disorder. *Anxiety, Stress, and Coping, 24,* 3–26.

Pyszczynski, T., Solomon, S., & Greenberg, J. (2015). Thirty years of terror management theory: From genesis to revelation. In M. Zanna & J. Olson (Eds.), *Advances in experimental social psychology* (Vol. 52, pp. 1–70). Waltham, MA: Academic Press.

Rosenblatt, A., Greenberg, J., Solomon, S., Pyszczynski, T., & Lyon, D. (1989). Evidence for terror management theory: I. The effects of mortality salience on reactions to those who violate or uphold cultural values. *Journal of Personality and Social Psychology, 57,* 681–690.

Rothschild, Z., Abdollahi, A., & Pyszczynski, T. (2009). Does peace have a prayer?: The effect of mortality salience, compassionate values and religious fundamentalism on hostility toward out-groups. *Journal of Experimental Social Psychology, 45,* 816–827.

Schimel, J., Hayes, J., Williams, T. J., & Jahrig, J. (2007). Is death really the worm at the core?: Converging evidence that worldview threat increases death-thought accessibility. *Journal of Personality and Social Psychology, 92,* 789–803.

Shepherd, S., Kay, A. C., Landau, M. J., & Keefer, L. A. (2011). Evidence for the specificity of control motivations in worldview defense: Distinguishing compensatory control from uncertainty management and terror management processes. *Journal of Experimental Social Psychology, 47,* 949–958.

Schmidt, K. (2010). Göbekli Tepe—the Stone Age Sanctuaries: New results of ongoing excavations with a special focus on sculptures and high reliefs. *Documenta Praehistorica, 37,* 239–256.

Shweder, R. A., Much, N. C., Mahapatra, M. & Park, L. (1997). The "big three" of morality (autonomy, community, divinity) and the "big three" explanations of suffering. In A. M. Brandt & P. Rozin (Eds.), *Morality and health* (pp. 119–169). New York: Routledge.

Skitka, L. J., Bauman, C. W., & Sargis, E. G. (2005). Moral conviction: Another contributor to attitude strength or something more? *Journal of Personality and Social Psychology, 88,* 895–917.

Solomon, S., Greenberg, J., & Pyszczynski, T. (1991). A terror management theory of social behavior: The psychological functions of self-esteem and cultural worldviews. *Advances in Experimental Social Psychology, 24,* 93–159.

Solomon, S., Greenberg, J., & Pyszczynski, T. (2015). *The worm at the core: The role of death in life.* New York: Random House.

CHAPTER 26

Moral Heroes Are Puppets

Jeremy A. Frimer

Are moral heroes (e.g., Martin Luther King, Jr.) masterminds with exceptional moral character, or are they merely symbolic puppets?

Exploiting attribution biases in observers, I suggest that followers manufacture moral heroes out of ordinary persons by encouraging charismatic speeches and propagating heroic images.

As the United States invaded Iraq and tortured prisoners in Guantanamo Bay, progressive-minded Americans prayed for a champion, a moral hero to save the country's collective soul. A young, charismatic senator from Illinois emerged. With little in the way of executive experience and yet much in the way of oratory prowess, Barack Obama shared a message of change, hope, and compassion that intoxicated and mobilized the political Left. Pundits likened him to John F. Kennedy and Martin Luther King, Jr., two of the great American moral heroes of the 20th century (Burns, 2008). Obama won the presidency in 2008 and then a Nobel Peace Prize 9 months later. The savior had arrived.

Many people quickly praised Obama's moral greatness. Illustratively, the closing date for nominations for the Nobel Peace Prize that Obama went on to win was just *12 days* into his presidency. Many world leaders congratulated Obama on his award. However, not everyone did. One sober critic and former Nobel Peace Prize Laureate, Lech Walesa, noted the baselessness of the award, asking, "So soon? Too early. He has no contribution so far" (Chazan & Macdonald, 2009).

Walesa's words were prescient. Soon came Obama's fall—from deity to banality. By most metrics, Obama was, quite simply, an average president. Seven years into his presidency, Obama's public approval ratings sat at approximately 45%, which are remarkably unremarkable for U.S. presidents at that point in their tenure ("Presidential Approval Ratings—Barack Obama," 2015). Experts rank Obama 18th among the 43 presidents, just behind George H. W. Bush (Rottinghaus & Vaughn, 2015). Is it possible that the public, pundits, and even the Nobel Committee mistook a mediocre man for a moral mastermind? If so, how did so many people form an inflated impression of Obama?

This chapter presents the view that Obama's story is representative and illustrative of the ascendance of ordinary persons to moral heroism and the basic social cognitive processes underlying these transformations. In the eyes of followers, oratory and visual campaigns can transform an otherwise ordinary person into a moral hero. This view challenges a common notion, both in the population and among some researchers, that moral leaders are innately great persons—intelligent, skillful, wise, and altruistic at heart (Kinsella, Ritchie, & Igou, 2015). I present the view that this romanticized notion of moral heroes is overblown and that much of moral heroism is a social construction. Moral heroes, like Obama, may be charismatic orators who communicate the right message with the right look for their time and place (Bligh & Kohles, 2009). The perception of moral heroism may only be skin deep, not extending beyond these superficial characteristics. Simply put, the moral hero may be less like a mastermind and more like a puppet.

Historical Context

For centuries, scholars have debated just how much individual brilliance is responsible for the influence that leaders seem to have. The original "great man" theory of leadership proposed that a small number of exceptional individuals (e.g., Napoleon, Martin Luther King, Jr.) is responsible for most of the important changes in history. According to the great man theory, these individuals had that "special something," which may have included intelligence, altruism, skill, and charisma; these personal qualities allowed the hero to change the course of history (Carlyle, 1840; Woods, 1913). Contra this dispositional account were theories that attributed the apparent greatness of these figures to their historical context and to a bidirectional relationship with their followers (James, 1880; Spencer, 1896; Weber, 1947).

The debate surfaced in more generalized form in social and personality psychology when Walter Mischel (1968) critiqued personality psychology. Mischel suggested that everyday intuitions about personality are wrong—behavior is far more a product of situational pressures than it is of enduring dispositions. Personality psychologists (e.g., Bem & Allen, 1974; Funder & Ozer 1983) counterargued, leading to a standoff.

All-encompassing generalizations about whether dispositions or situations are responsible for behavior are now rare. Current theories tend to be interactionist in nature—behavior is primarily the result of the dynamic interplay between individuals and situational forces (e.g., Fleeson, 2004). That is, moral heroism is likely the product of the right person (disposition) being in the right place and time (situation). Precisely which dispositional characteristics, external forces, and causal processes between them underlie moral heroism remains a point a departure among scholars.

Theoretical Stance

Rooted in trait theory (Allport, 1937; Cattell, 1950; Murray 1938; see Ozer & Benet-Martinez, 2006, for a review) and heavier on the dispositional side is what I will informally call the "mastermind theory"—that moral heroes have a strong moral character, which includes compelling moral reasoning (Kohlberg, 1984) and a heartwarming life story (McAdams & Guo, 2015; Colby & Damon, 1992). Personal development or talent is a necessary prerequisite for becoming a moral hero.

I will call the alternative view, which is consistent with the social identity approach (Tajfel & Turner, 1979), the "puppet theory." The puppet theory suggests that groups manufacture moral heroes out of otherwise ordinary persons to symbolize the cause and unite followers. The Monty Python film, *Life of Brian,* satirized the life of Jesus Christ and captured the essence of the puppet theory. Brian was a Jewish rebel; while running from Roman soldiers, he stumbled into a line of mystics and prophets. To avoid being detected, Brian mumbled nonsensical blessings, which had the unintended effect of drawing a devoted following. Brian became a living deity, ending with his crucifixion.

In the puppet theory, dispositional prerequisites for moral heroism are only skin deep, limited to impression management functions such as oratory skills and physical appearance. Followers play an often unrecognized and important role in the lives of moral heroes. The puppet theory is also consistent with evolutionary accounts positing that maintaining hierarchy (A. P. Fiske, 1992) and sacralizing mundane objects or people (Atran & Norenzayan, 2004; Tetlock, 2003) binds followers into cooperative groups, which tend to out-compete discordant groups and lone individuals for scant resources. The puppet theory suggests that followers romanticize and elevate a person to the status of moral hero because doing so confers upon group members an adaptive advantage.

Sacralizing an object, a practice, or a person binds people together, but it may achieve this end by suppressing rational thought processes (Haidt, 2012). Communication surrounding moral heroes exploits the uncritical thinking of starstruck followers, deceiving them into becoming loyal group members. Observers effectively apply the "duck test" when encountering potential moral heroes—if it looks like a duck, and quacks like a duck, and walks like a duck, then it is probably a duck. Analogously, if someone talks like a moral hero and looks like a moral hero, then he or she must be a moral hero. The duck test may be especially likely to fail in the detection of moral heroes because of the incentive structure built into impression formation. To maximize both social and material rewards, people do best when they *appear* moral to others while *behaving* selfishly in private (Batson, 2008; Frimer, Schaefer, & Oakes, 2014; Shariff & Norenzayan, 2007; von Hippel & Trivers, 2011). The costs associated with sending such an elaborate signal of their moral virtue (Lyons, 2005) may be worth it to the hero: heroes tend to have lots of children (Rusch, Leunissen, & van Vugt, 2015).

The perception of moral heroism may also benefit followers by serving a symbolic and motivational function (Allison & Goethals, 2010; Pfeffer, 1981). Moral heroes tend to emerge during times of crisis (Bligh, Kohles, & Meindl, 2004; Haslam et al., 2001; Pillai & Meindl, 1998; Weber, 1947). Even though followers may hold erroneously romanticized impressions of their leaders, these impressions may optimize the performance of followers (de Luque, Washburn, Waldman, & House 2008).

Evidence

Next, I describe evidence that supports the puppet theory, in form of two modes by which followers prop up moral heroes.

The Hero's Speech

First, I suggest that followers prop up moral heroes by encouraging them to make emotionally stirring, charismatic, prosocial speeches. These speeches may cause audiences to form an impression that the speaker is a moral hero. To experience this phenomenon, recall Obama's speech at the 2004 Democratic National Convention (DNC) that launched him on the world stage:

> If there's a child on the south side of Chicago who can't read, that matters to me, even if it's not my child. If there's a senior citizen somewhere who can't pay for her prescription and has to choose between medicine and the rent, that makes my life poorer, even if it's not my grandmother. If there's an Arab American family being rounded up without benefit of an attorney or due process, that threatens my civil liberties.

Obama and moral heroes tell tear-jerking, morally elevating stories that may seem unique. However, these speeches conform to a pattern. The hero's story begins with a childhood mentor who leads the young hero to witness the suffering of others. Through this experience, the budding moral hero develops a clear moral purpose and decides to repair the problems through some altruistic goal pursuit (McAdams & Guo, 2015; McNamee & Wesolik, 2014; Walker & Frimer, 2007).

These stirring remarks tick all the boxes in the charismatic speech checklist, which include: a shared history and identity; praise for followers' agency; similarities between followers and the leader; shared moral values, long term goals, faith, and hope. And they avoid pitfalls such as discussing individuals' self-interest, instrumental thinking, and short-term goals (Shamir, Arthur,

& House, 1994). Communicating a message that resonates with a group's core values and oratory skills are critical components of a charismatic speech (Awamleh & Gardner, 1999; Frimer, Biesanz, Walker, & MacKinlay, 2013).

Evidence is accumulating that these speeches are effective at convincing audiences of the speaker's greatness but reveal *surprisingly little* about the speaker's character. Independent of their behavior as leaders, politicians gain approval from the population simply by communicating in a prosocial manner. A recent study found that prosocial language during floor debates in the U.S. Congress predicts public approval 6 months later (Frimer, Aquino, Gebauer, Zhu, & Oakes, 2015). In fact, prosocial language is the best single explanation for why Americans approve or disapprove of their government—surpassing other explanations such as Congressional productivity and conflict, the economy, and world events.

In laboratory studies, delivering a prosocial speech changes how an audience perceives the speaker, creating expectations that the prosocial speaker will behave generously toward a stranger. However, people who deliver prosocial speeches turn out to be *no more likely* to behave generously toward a stranger than people who use less flowery language (Frimer, Zhu, & Decter-Frain, 2016). Ordinary people are surprisingly flexible with their words, able to ramp up the prosocial language when they like (Frimer et al., 2015). Talk seems to be a deceptively poor harbinger of action and personal virtue.

Underlying this misattribution is a generic psychological process. Prosocial speeches may build false impressions because of the correspondence bias, whereby audiences make dispositional inferences from small verbal displays, even when the audience is aware of the situational forces that led to the speech (Jones & Harris, 1967). Audiences default to making dispositional inferences because the speaker is in plain view (perceptually salient), whereas the forces that coaxed the speaker into saying what he or she did are invisible (Gilbert & Malone, 1995). The present findings suggest that speeches serve a distinctly *social* function—to persuade others (S. T. Fiske, 1992). Future research should investigate whether people can intentionally manipulate an audience's perceptions of them and rally cause-promoting behavior merely by delivering a charismatic speech.

The Hero Pose

Portraiture is a second mode by which followers manufacture moral heroes. Once again, the story of Barack Obama is illustrative. As Obama ran for the presidency in 2008, an image symbolizing his message and his campaign went viral. Above the words *hope, change,* or *progress* was a stylized blue-and-red portrait of Obama, gazing pensively upwards and to his left (the viewer's right).

This gaze turns out to be the quintessential posture of the moral hero. Images of other moral heroes, such as Martin Luther King, Jr., Mother Teresa, and Nelson Mandela, also depict them with this posture more often than one would expect merely by chance and more often than images of such celebrities as Elvis Presley, Brad Pitt, and Marilyn Monroe do (Frimer & Sinclair, 2016). This curious tendency for images to depict heroes gazing up and to the viewer's right may be the result of their ideologically minded followers selecting and propagating these specific images to promote the common cause. When tasked with selecting a single image of a leader to go on a poster to represent the social cause, people tend to select the up-and-right posture (Frimer & Sinclair, 2016).

What do these followers perceive in these up-and-right poses that make the depicted individual seem so heroic? One possibility is that these poses make the subject seem calm and rational. The left cerebral hemisphere, which is more responsible for voluntary emotional displays, controls the muscles on the left side of the face (Rinn, 1984). Stemming from this basic left–right asymmetry in neurological functioning, the right side of the face may be less emotionally expressive than the left (e.g., Sackeim, Gur, & Saucy, 1978). Perhaps followers select up-and-right posed images of their leaders to portray the subject as rational and calm, and thus ready to make good decisions as a leader.

At a semantic level, the hero's gaze (up and to the viewer's right) may also activate a system of conceptual metaphors that link intrinsically meaningless directions to personal virtue (Lakoff & Johnson, 1980). The horizontal dimension is steeped in metaphor, with the right being superior to the left. This evident in terms such as *righteous,* the term *right,* meaning "correct," and the Latin word *sinister,* meaning "left." Moreover, the vertical dimension also carries evaluative tones, with up being better than down. This is evident in such terms as *uplifting, reach for the skies,* and *heaven above* (Haidt & Algoe, 2004). The term *upright* neatly summarizes the metaphorically superior direction. Resultantly, looking upward and looking rightward (in the viewer's reference) makes a person look warm, competent, proud, and optimistic (but not more attractive; Frimer & Sinclair, 2016).

The hero gaze may also communicate a sense of agency—that the moral hero has the capacity to make things happen. People conceive of agents as being on the left. When asked to draw an event in which a circle pushes a square, people tend to draw the circle (the agent) to the left of the square (the patient; Chatterjee, Southwood, & Basilico, 1999). By depicting the hero facing toward the viewer's right, the viewer may perceive the hero as agentic. Future research should investigate the underlying perceptual mechanisms responsible for the hero pose and test whether seeing the hero pose can mobilize cause-promoting behavior from followers.

Extension and Expansion

What evidence would falsify the puppet theory? A finding that budding moral heroes have character strengths that are unrelated to impression management, such as unobtrusive measures of altruism, honesty, and empathy, would constitute falsifying evidence.

An expansion of the theory is to investigate other mechanisms by which groups create the perception of moral heroism. One promising avenue is the giving of awards (e.g., the Nobel Peace Prize, the Carnegie Medal). A second expansion is to work out how critical followers select and prop up moral heroes. In the case of Obama, these active followers may have been people such as Jack Corrigan

and Mary Beth Cahill, who selected Obama to give the 2004 DNC speech, and Shepard Fairey, the artist behind the stylized red-and-blue portrait of an inspirationally gazing Obama. How the larger group also plays a causal role also remains unclear. A final extension is to devise and test procedures for minimizing the persuasive effects endemic in moral heroism, to facilitate leadership selection based on substantive action (e.g., track record) and less so on baseless persuasive tactics.

When asked to name famous moral heroes of recent years, Americans list Martin Luther King, Jr., Nelson Mandela, Mohandas Gandhi, and John F. Kennedy—but rarely Obama (Frimer & Sinclair, 2016). What did the former individuals do that Obama did not? Perhaps Obama did something that that the others did not, which caused his fall from grace. Whereas the classic moral heroes died by an assassin's bullet or were incarcerated, Obama actually had to show his character—he took office.

REFERENCES

Allison, S. T., & Goethals, G. R. (2010) *Heroes: What they do and why we need them.* New York: Oxford University Press

Allport, G. W. (1937). *Personality: A psychological interpretation.* Oxford, UK: Holt.

Atran, S., & Norenzayan, A. (2004). Religion's evolutionary landscape: Counterintuition, commitment, compassion, communion. *Behavioral and Brain Sciences, 27,* 713–770.

Awamleh, R., & Gardner, W. L. (1999). Perceptions of leader charisma and effectiveness: The effects of vision content, delivery, and organizational performance. *Leadership Quarterly, 10,* 345–373.

Batson, C. D. (2008). Moral masquerades: Experimental exploration of the nature of moral motivation. *Phenomenology and the Cognitive Sciences, 7,* 51–66.

Bem, D. J., & Allen, A. (1974). On predicting some of the people some of the time: The search for cross-situational consistencies in behavior. *Psychological Review, 81,* 506–520.

Bligh, M. C., & Kohles, J. C. (2009). The enduring allure of charisma: How Barack Obama won the historic 2008 presidential election. *Leadership Quarterly, 20,* 483–492.

Bligh, M. C., Kohles, J. C., & Meindl, J. R. (2004). Charisma under crisis: Presidential leadership, rhetoric, and media responses before and after the September 11th terrorist attacks. *Leadership Quarterly, 15,* 211–239.

Burns, P. J. (2008, December 7). Kennedy, King, and now Obama. *Huffington Post.* Available at *www.huffingtonpost.com/peter-j-burns/kennedy-king-and-now-obam_b_141914.html.*

Carlyle, T. (1840). *On heroes, hero-worship and the heroic in history.* London: Chapman & Hall.

Cattell, R. B. (1950). *Personality: A systematic theoretical and factual study.* New York: McGraw-Hill.

Chatterjee, A., Southwood, M. H., & Basilico, D. (1999). Verbs, events and spatial representations. *Neuropsychologia, 37*(4), 395–402.

Chazan, G., & Macdonald, A. (2009, October 11). Nobel committee's decision courts controversy. *Wall Street Journal.* Retrieved from *www.wsj.com/articles/SB125509603349176083.*

Colby, A., & Damon, W. (1992). *Some do care: Contemporary lives of moral commitment.* New York: Free Press.

de Luque, M. S., Washburn, N. T., Waldman, D. A., & House, R. J. (2008). Unrequited profit: How stakeholder and economic values relate to subordinates' perceptions of leadership and firm performance. *Administrative Science Quarterly, 53,* 626–654.

Fiske, A. P. (1992). The four elementary forms of sociality: Framework for a unified theory of social relations. *Psychological Review, 99,* 689–723.

Fiske, S. T. (1992). Thinking is for doing: Portraits of social cognition from Daguerreotype to laserphoto. *Journal of Personality and Social Psychology, 63,* 877–889.

Fleeson, W. (2004). Moving personality beyond the person–situation debate: The challenge and the opportunity of within-person variability. *Current Directions in Psychological Science, 13,* 83–87.

Frimer, J. A., Aquino, K., Gebauer, J. E., Zhu, L., & Oakes, H. (2015). A decline in prosocial language helps explain public disapproval of the U.S. Congress. *Proceedings of the National Academy of Sciences of the USA, 112,* 6591–6594.

Frimer, J. A., Biesanz, J. C., Walker, L. J., & MacKinlay, C. W. (2013). Liberals and conservatives rely on common moral foundations when making moral judgments about influential people. *Journal of Personality and Social Psychology, 104,* 1040–1059.

Frimer, J. A., Schaefer, N. K., & Oakes, H. (2014). Moral actor, selfish agent. *Journal of Personality and Social Psychology, 106,* 790–802.

Frimer, J. A., & Sinclair, L. (2016). Moral heroes

look up and to the viewer's right. *Personality and Social Psychology Bulletin, 42,* 400–410.

Frimer, J. A., Zhu, L., & Decter-Frain, A. (2016). *Do givers leak their social motives through what they talk about?: Maybe not.* Manuscript submitted for publication.

Funder, D. C., & Ozer, D. J. (1983). Behavior as a function of the situation. *Journal of Personality and Social Psychology, 44,* 107–112.

Gilbert, D. T., & Malone, P. S. (1995). The correspondence bias. *Psychological Bulletin, 117,* 21–38.

Haidt, J. (2012). *The righteous mind: Why good people are divided by politics and religion.* New York: Random House.

Haidt, J., & Algoe, S. (2004). Moral amplification and the emotions that attach us to saints and demons. In J. Greenberg, S. L. Koole, & T. Pyszczynski (Eds.), *Handbook of experimental existential psychology* (pp. 322–335). New York: Guilford Press.

Haslam, S. A., Platow, M. J., Turner, J. C., Reynolds, K. J., McGarty, C., Oakes, P. J., . . . Veenstra, K. (2001). Social identity and the romance of leadership: The importance of being seen to be "doing it for us." *Group Processes and Intergroup Relations, 4,* 191–205.

James, W. (1880). Great men, great thoughts and the environment. *Atlantic Monthly, 46,* 441–459.

Jones, E. E., & Harris, V. A. (1967). The attribution of attitudes. *Journal of Experimental Social Psychology, 3,* 1–24.

Kinsella, E. L., Ritchie, T. D., & Igou, E. R. (2015). Zeroing in on heroes: A prototype analysis of hero features. *Journal of Personality and Social Psychology, 108,* 114–127.

Kohlberg, L. (1984). *Essays on moral development: Vol. 2. The psychology of moral development.* San Francisco: Harper & Row.

Lakoff, G., & Johnson, M. (1980). The metaphorical structure of the human conceptual system. *Cognitive Science, 4,* 195–208.

Lyons, M. T. (2005). Who are the heroes?: Characteristics of people who rescue others. *Journal of Cultural and Evolutionary Psychology, 3,* 245–254.

McAdams, D. P., & Guo, J. (2015). Narrating the generative life. *Psychological Science, 26,* 475–483.

McNamee, S., & Wesolik, F. (2014). Heroic behavior of Carnegie Medal heroes: Parental influence and expectations. *Peace and Conflict: Journal of Peace Psychology, 20,* 171–173.

Mischel, W. (1968). *Personality and assessment.* London: Wiley,

Murray, H. A. (1938). *Explorations in personality.* New York: Oxford University Press

Ozer, D. J., & Benet-Martínez, V. (2006). Personality and the prediction of consequential outcomes. *Annual Review of Psychology, 57,* 401–421.

Pfeffer, J. (1981). Management as symbolic action: The creation and maintenance of organizational paradigms. In L. L. Cummings & B. M. Staw (Eds.), *Research in organizational behavior* (Vol. 3, pp. 1–52). Greenwich, CT: JAI Press.

Pillai, R., & Meindl, J. R. (1998). Context and charisma: A "meso" level examination of the relationship of organic structure, collectivism, and crisis to charismatic leadership. *Journal of Management, 24,* 643–671.

Presidential approval ratings—Barack Obama. (2015). Retrieved from *www.gallup.com/poll/116479/barack-obama-presidential-job-approval.aspx.*

Rinn, W. E. (1984). The neuropsychology of facial expression: A review of the neurological and psychological mechanisms for producing facial expressions. *Psychological Bulletin, 95,* 52–77.

Rottinghaus, B., & Vaughn, J. (2015, February 16). New rankings of U.S. presidents put Lincoln at no. 1, Obama at 18; Kennedy judged the most overrated. *Washington Post.* Retrieved from *www.washingtonpost.com/news/monkey-cage/wp/2015/02/16/new-ranking-of-u-s-presidents-puts-lincoln-1-obama-18-kennedy-judged-most-overrated/?utm_term=.5e599c4ec05f.*

Rusch, H., Leunissen, J. M., & van Vugt, M. (2015). Historical and experimental evidence of sexual selection for war heroism. *Evolution and Human Behavior, 36,* 367–373.

Sackeim, H. A., Gur, R. C., & Saucy, M. C. (1978). Emotions are expressed more intensely on the left side of the face. *Science, 202,* 434–436.

Shamir, B., Arthur, M. B., & House, R. J. (1994). The rhetoric of charismatic leadership: A theoretical extension, a case study, and implications for research. *Leadership Quarterly, 5,* 25–42.

Shariff, A. F., & Norenzayan, A. (2007). God is watching you: Priming God concepts increases prosocial behavior in an anonymous economic game. *Psychological Science, 18,* 803–809.

Spencer, H. (1896). *The study of sociology.* New York: Appleton.

Tajfel, H., & Turner, J. C. (1979). An integrative theory of intergroup conflict. In W. G. Austin & S. Worchel (Eds.), *The social psychology of intergroup relations* (pp. 33–47). Monterey, CA: Brooks/Cole.

Tetlock, P. E. (2003). Thinking the unthinkable: Sacred values and taboo cognitions. *Trends in Cognitive Sciences, 7,* 320–324.

von Hippel, W., & Trivers, R. (2011). The evolution and psychology of self-deception. *Behavioral and Brain Sciences, 34,* 1–16.

Walker, L. J., & Frimer, J. A. (2007). Moral personality of brave and caring exemplars. *Journal of Personality and Social Psychology, 93,* 845–860.

Weber, M. (1947). *The theory of social and economic organization.* New York: Free Press.

Woods, F. A. (1913). *The influence of monarchs: Steps in a new science of history.* New York: Macmillan.

CHAPTER 27

Morality

A Historical Invention

Edouard Machery

> **Is morality universal?**
>
> According to the *historicist view of morality* presented in this chapter, morality is a learned, culturally specific phenomenon; the distinction between moral judgment and other normative judgments is not a product of evolution, but it is rather a historical invention that reuses a motley of evolved processes and must be relearned by children generation after generation.

Morality is often taken to be a fundamental building block of cognition on a par with folk psychology, the intuitive theory of agents, and folk biology, all of which are universal and the products of evolution. This *fundamentalist view* dominates theorizing about morality at the intersection of anthropology and evolutionary biology, and it has been extremely influential in moral psychology and social cognitive neuroscience. An important consequence of the fundamentalist view of morality is the claim that people across cultures and times intuitively distinguish two types of norms (i.e., attitudes about what one ought to do or not to do, about what is permissible or impermissible, or about whether an action, a person, or a character trait is bad or good, right or wrong): moral norms and nonmoral norms. There is no doubt that Westerners

draw this distinction: Although they may be unable to define what makes a norm moral or an action morally wrong (in contrast to just wrong), Westerners have no difficulty classifying an assertion such as "Thou shall not kill" as expressing a moral norm and assertions such as "Look left before crossing the street" and "Men should wear a tie at work" as expressing nonmoral norms. But is this distinction innate and universal, or is it rather learned and culturally specific?

The *historicist view* proposes that morality is culturally specific—morality is only found in some cultures—and instead of being a product of evolution, it is a product of particular, still ill-understood, historical circumstances. Developmentally, children learn to single out a subset of norms and values, which comes to constitute the moral domain. These norms acquire a distinctive motivational, emotional, and cognitive role. From a cognitive point of view, morality depends on a subset of the cognitive processes, emotions, and motivational structures involved in social cognition. One can thus draw an analogy between morality and the capacity to play chess: Chess playing relies on evolved, universal cognitive processes (visual recognition, spatial memory, etc.), but it is not a product of evolution; it is the outcome of particular historical and cultural conditions, and people must learn to play chess.

Social behavior depends on a complex set of evolved processes, many of which are homologous to processes found in other species, and some of which are only found among human beings. These social processes involved emotions (e.g., anger), emotional processes (e.g., empathy), and motivational structures (e.g., a motivation to help people in need). Of central importance for human social behavior is normative cognition, a universal, evolved building block of human cognition. Normative cognition involves the capacity to make normative judgments; a memory store for norms one is committed to; a learning system for norms; a set of motivational structures, including a motivation to comply with the norms one endorses and a motivation to punish norm violators; and emotions (e.g., outrage or disgust elicited by norm violation, admiration or even awe at normative behaviors, guilt and shame elicited by one's own norm violations). Some components of normative cognition may be specific to the domain of norms, others may be domain-general: Among the latter, outrage elicited by norm violation is, for instance, just a form of anger, and the memory store for norms is probably not a dedicated, dissociable memory store. Normative cognition is universal, develops early and reliably, and may well be specific to human beings.

In some cultures, morality builds up on normative cognition and on other components of social cognition. Relying probably on the cues provided by their social environment (parents and peers), children single out a subset of norms among the norms that are prevalent in their environment and learn to treat these norms in a distinctive manner. These norms come to constitute the moral domain. The distinctive cognitive, motiva-

tional, and emotional role of these norms draws on universal, evolved components of social and normative cognition.

Historical Context

The historicist view of morality was in part developed in reaction to an ever-growing literature at the intersection of evolutionary biology, anthropology, psychology, and philosophy (e.g., Singer, 1981, 2000; Boehm, 1982, 1999; Alexander, 1987; Ruse, 1986; Dennett, 1995; Kitcher, 1998; Wilson, 2002; Joyce, 2006; Street, 2006). Contributors to this literature set themselves the task of explaining morality in evolutionary terms—their goal is then to provide plausible, albeit admittedly speculative, scenarios that would explain why natural selection would have favored morality—or to determine the philosophical significance of the evolution of morality. A pervasive problem in this literature is that the notion of morality typically remains unexplained (Machery & Stich, 2013; Stich, Chapter 55, this volume). Sometimes evolutionary-minded scientists use "morality" to refer, more or less explicitly, to phenomena *distinct from morality,* such as psychological altruism, behavioral altruism (Alexander, 1987), or fairness (Baumard, André, & Sperber, 2013). Other times, it remains entirely unclear what this trait is—morality—that is to be explained in evolutionary terms.

The second impulse for the development of the historicist view of morality comes from the cultural and demographic research on morality associated with Richard Shweder, Jonathan Haidt, and Paul Rozin on the one hand (e.g., Rozin, Lowery, Imada, & Haidt, 1999) and with Jonathan Haidt and Jesse Graham on the other hand (e.g., Haidt & Joseph, 2004; Graham et al., 2013; Haidt, 2012). This body of research—in particular, Rozin et al.'s CAD model or Graham and Haidt's moral foundations theory—purports to show that the domain of morality—roughly, what counts as a moral norm, motivation, or value—varies across demographic groups in a predictable manner. For instance, American conservatives are said to moralize a broader set of values than liberals, including values related to loyalty to one's group (e.g., patriotism) and authority (e.g., Graham, Haidt, & Nosek, 2009). That people value different things across demographic groups (e.g., across cultures) or that there are different norms across groups is not really surprising, although the extent of this variation may be unexpected. What *is* surprising is the claim that the *moral domain* varies as a function of demographic variables. However, establishing that claim requires a distinction between moral values and nonmoral values or between moral norms and nonmoral norms, and psychologists and anthropologists committed to the cultural and demographic research on morality have often been silent about how to draw this distinction. Some definitions identify morality with the whole normative domain, others are stipulative and, thus, arbitrary.

To determine whether morality is a trait that evolved and to determine whether the moral domain genuinely varies across cultures and demographic groups requires *delineating the moral domain*: identifying what distinguishes moral norms from other norms (such as etiquette norms, coordination norms, and prudential norms) and moral values from other values (Machery, 2012). Attempting to delineate the moral domain raises at least three distinct clusters of empirical questions:

1. Do moral norms differ from other kinds of norms, and in what ways? Do people treat them differently, and how?
2. Is this distinction universal and ancient?
3. Where does this distinction come from? Is it an adaptation? If so, what is its function and what is its phylogeny? Or, rather, is it a cultural invention?

The historicist view of morality grew out of the failures of previous attempts to answer these questions and out of new research aimed at delineating the moral domain.

Theoretical Stance

The historicist view stands in sharp contrast with previous attempts to delineate the moral domain. According to Turiel and colleagues' moral domain theory (e.g., Turiel, 1983), from a very early age on (2 1/2 years in some studies), people distinguish two kinds of wrong action. Those actions (e.g., hitting another child) that are judged worse are also judged to be authority-independent (they would still be wrong if the relevant authority allowed people to act this way) and to be wrong everywhere; finally, people justify their opinion that these actions are wrong by appealing to considerations of harm, justice, or rights. Turiel and colleagues call the norms prohibiting these actions "moral norms." By contrast, those actions (e.g., leaving the classroom without asking permission) that are judged to be less wrong are judged to be authority-dependent (they would not be wrong if the relevant authority allowed people to act this way) and to be wrong only locally; finally, people justify their opinion that these actions are wrong by appealing to authority and convention. Turiel and colleagues call the norms prohibiting these actions "conventional norms." On the basis of their substantial empirical research, they argue that the distinction between moral and conventional norms is a universal and, plausibly, ancient feature of the human mind.

Turiel and colleagues' moral domain theory has been widely endorsed (e.g., Blair, 1995; Nichols, 2004), but recent findings suggest that the separation of wrong actions into two kinds is an artifact of the restricted class of actions used by Turiel and colleagues to distinguish moral and conventional norms. When a larger class of actions is used, the different features that are meant to characterize moral and nonmoral norms (wrongness, authority-dependence, universality, justification type) come apart, and the conjunction of these properties fail to distinguish moral from nonmoral norms (Shweder, Mahapatra, & Miller, 1987; Haidt, Koller, & Dias, 1993; Kelly, Stich, Haley, Eng, & Fessler, 2007).

More recently, Nichols (2004) has argued that the distinction between moral and nonmoral norms is to be drawn in terms of emotions. Nichols distinguishes two types of norms: affect-backed norms and norms that are not backed by affect. The former prohibit actions that independently elicit an emotional reaction. "Thou shall not kill" expresses an affect-backed norm because it prohibits an action—that is, murder—that elicits a negative emotional reaction. "Wear a tie at work" does not express an affect-backed norm because the sight of people who do not wear a tie at work does not elicit any emotional reaction.

Nichols's (2004) proposal for delineating the moral domain—sentimental rules theory—is undermined by the following dilemma. Either being an affect-backed norm is sufficient for being moral, or it is not. It cannot be sufficient because, as Nichols (2002) shows, there are affect-backed norms—namely, etiquette norms forbidding disgusting actions—that are not moral. On the other hand, if being an affect-backed norm is not sufficient for being moral, Nichols seems unable to explain the phenomenon of moralization, which happens when an action or a trait previously judged morally neutral (e.g., smoking or obesity) becomes morally wrong because it starts eliciting a negative emotion (e.g., Rozin, Markwith, & Stoess, 1997; Rozin, 1999).

Finally, Gray, Young, and Waytz (2012) have recently proposed that norms against inflicting pain constitute the essence of the moral domain (for another recent proposal, see Sousa, Holbrook, & Piazza, 2009). However, this proposal does not do justice to moral norms against victimless actions, such as incest prohibition and other taboos. Any account that ignores this kind of norms or that relegates them to the periphery of the moral domain is unsatisfying (but see Gray, Schein, & Ward, 2014, for discussion).

Evidence

Norms that Westerners recognize as moral form a distinct psychological kind (Skitka, Bauman, & Sargis, 2005; Skitka, Bauman, & Mullen, 2008; Skitka, 2010). Although recognizing a norm as moral correlates with attitude strength, for Westerners moral norms are not simply strongly endorsed norms (i.e., norms Westerners are certain of), norms about subjectively important issues, or norms that are connected to their self-concept. Variance in whether norms are viewed as moral contributes to explaining a large range of phenomena among Westerners: motivation to act politically to promote one's policy views, difficulty in resolving conflict, intolerance of disagreement, willingness to use violence, willingness to flout the law, and immunity to the influence of group majority opinion (see Skitka, 2010, for a review). Using Asch's paradigm (1951, 1955), Lisciandra, Postma-Nilsenová, and Colombo (2013) have also shown that Western participants' opinions are less likely to be influenced by group opinion when it bears on a moral issue. Wright, Cullum, and Schwab (2008) examined how people split a windfall profit between themselves and other participants who disagree with them about a particular issue and found that people split less fairly when they view the topic of disagreement as moral.

This body of evidence suggests that Westerners' distinction between moral and nonmoral norms is more than just verbal: Rather, it marks distinct psychological constructs. But do other cultures draw a similar distinction? And does it have the same psychological significance?

The first body of evidence to support the claim that the domain of morality is culturally specific and the product of particular historical circumstances comes from linguistics. In line with the proposal that normative cognition is a fundamental building block of cognition, deontic modals—that is, words translating *ought*—and translations of the normative predicates *good* and *bad* are apparently found in every language (Wierzbicka, 2001, 167–169; Wierzbicka, 2007). By contrast, expressions related to the moral domain in the United States are not found in all languages. Whereas judgments about whether something is "right" and "wrong" in the United States are tightly connected to whether the action belongs to the moral domain (Skitka, 2010), translations of *right* and *wrong* are not found in every language. Furthermore, many languages do not have a translation of *moral* and thus do not lexicalize the distinction between moral and nonmoral norms (Wierzbicka, 2007, p. 68). If the moral domain were a fundamental feature of human cognition, we would expect the distinction between moral and nonmoral norms to be lexicalized in every language, as are deontic modals and the distinction between *good* and *bad*.

The second body of evidence comes from an ongoing research program meant to determine how people divide the norms they endorse into different kinds (see Machery, 2012, for a description). In line with the psychological evidence reviewed above, unpublished preliminary results suggest that Americans draw a sharp distinction between moral and nonmoral norms and also distinguish different kinds of moral and nonmoral norms. In contrast, Indian participants do not seem to draw the distinction between moral and nonmoral norms, suggesting that the moral domain may not be a universal.

Much additional evidence needs to be collected to support the historicist view of morality. Anthropological and cross-cultural information remains insufficient to be fully confident that the distinction between moral and nonmoral norms is only culturally and historically local.

The historical details remain entirely unknown: What historical circumstances resulted in the singling out of a distinct set of norms and the creation of the moral domain? Can the moral domain be traced back to ancient Greece or to Judaism and Christianity? Or perhaps it is a more recent historical development, possibly connected to the rise of an individual-centered social life. It may also have emerged in response to the weakening of traditional justifications for norms such as religion—people are motivated to comply with their norms because these norms have been given to them by their god or gods— and tradition—people are motivated to comply with their norms because their ancestors have always complied with them. The weakening of religion and tradition in Western cultures (and possibly in other cultures) may have led to the emergence of an alternative way of thinking about norms and of being motivated by them.

It is also important to understand the factors that lead to the carving of a moral domain within the domain of norms. Is having a monotheistic, personal god a factor related to the emergence of a moral domain? The existence of a capitalist market? Or something else? Answering these questions will be easier if morality emerged in several cultures rather than in a single culture (Levine et al., 2016).

Extension and Expansion

The historicist view of morality has important consequences for moral philosophy. Over the last 30 years, philosophers have appealed to the alleged evolution of morality to either "debunk" morality—that is, to support the view that we are not justified in holding our moral beliefs—or to defend morality (for the former, see, e.g., Ruse, 1986; Joyce, 2006; Street, 2006; for the latter, see, e.g., Rottschaefer, 1998). These arguments turn out to be futile if morality did not evolve (Machery & Mallon, 2010). There is naturally a sense in which morality evolved: Just like any other human trait— for example, chess, driving, or scientific cognition—it rests on evolved psychological capacities and processes. Exactly as chess relies on spatial memory and means–end reasoning—psychological capacities with a deep phylogeny—morality relies on evolved capacities, including human normative cognition. However, if the claim that morality evolved means nothing more than this, it fails to have the striking implications moral philosophers have typically had in mind.

Morality exerts a strong, distinct pull on Westerners (Wright et al., 2008; Skitka, 2010): They care distinctively about the moral norms tagged as moral, and they are particularly upset when moral norms happen to be violated. It's no accident that, in the film *An Inconvenient Truth,* Al Gore described acting against climate change in moral terms, or that American Conservative Christians called their movement "the Moral Majority." Morality also motivates Westerners, often leading them to condemn ways of life different from their own. Moralizers want the moral order to prevail around them—think of American Conservative Christians describing same-sex marriage as a moral abomination—as well as far from them! They go around lecturing people, at home and around the world, about how they should live. And not only do they lecture people, moralizers are also sometimes ready to use violence to impose their moral order.

The historicist view of morality highlights the historical and parochial nature of morality: If it is correct, it could have been the case that Westerners did not form a moral domain at all, and many cultures have not formed such a domain. The contingent and parochial nature of morality should at the very least lead us to subject the motivational pull of morality and the emotions it elicits to severe scrutiny: Westerners' moral emotions and their moral motivation may not be justified. The historicist view of morality has thus the potential to undermine the intolerance that moralizing often breeds.

REFERENCES

Alexander R. D. (1987). *The biology of moral systems*. Hawthorne, NY: Aldine de Gruyter.

Asch, S. (1951). Effects of group pressure on the modification and distortion of judgments. In H. Guetzkow (Ed.), *Groups, leadership and men* (pp. 177–190). Pittsburgh, PA: Carnegie Press.

Asch, S. (1955). Opinions and social pressure. *Scientific American, 193*, 33–35.

Baumard, N., André, J. B., & Sperber, D. (2013). A mutualistic approach to morality: The evolution of fairness by partner choice. *Behavioral and Brain Sciences, 36*, 59–78.

Blair, R. J. R. (1995). A cognitive developmental approach to morality: Investigating the psychopath. *Cognition, 57*, 1–29.

Boehm, C. (1982). The evolutionary development of morality as an effect of dominance behavior and conflict interference. *Journal of Social and Biological Structures, 5*, 413–421.

Boehm, C. (1999). *Hierarchy in the forest: The evolution of egalitarian behavior*. Cambridge, MA: Harvard University Press.

Dennett, D. C. (1995). *Darwin's dangerous idea: Evolution and the meanings of life*. New York: Simon & Schuster.

Graham, J., Haidt, J., Koleva, S., Motyl, M., Iyer, R., Wojcik, S. P., & Ditto, P. H. (2013). Moral foundations theory: The pragmatic validity of moral pluralism. *Advances in Experimental Social Psychology, 47*, 55–130.

Graham, J., Haidt, J., & Nosek, B. A. (2009). Liberals and conservatives rely on different sets of moral foundations. *Journal of Personality and Social Psychology, 96*, 1029.

Gray, K., Schein, C., & Ward, A. F. (2014). The myth of harmless wrongs in moral cognition: Automatic dyadic completion from sin to suffering. *Journal of Experimental Psychology: General, 143*, 1600–1615.

Gray, K., Young, L., & Waytz, A. (2012). Mind perception is the essence of morality. *Psychological Inquiry, 23*, 101–124.

Haidt, J. (2012). *The righteous mind: Why good people are divided by politics and religion*. New York: Vintage.

Haidt, J., & Joseph, C. (2004). Intuitive ethics: How innately prepared intuitions generate culturally variable virtues. *Daedalus, 133*, 55–66.

Haidt, J., Koller, S., & Dias, M. (1993). Affect, culture, and morality, or is it wrong to eat your dog? *Journal of Personality and Social Psychology, 65*, 613–628.

Joyce, R. A. (2006). *The evolution of morality*. Cambridge, MA: MIT Press.

Kelly, D., Stich, S. P., Haley, K. J., Eng, S. J., & Fessler, D. M. T. (2007). Harm, affect, and the moral/conventional distinction. *Mind and Language, 22*, 117–131.

Kitcher, P. (1998). Psychological altruism, evolutionary origins, and moral rules. *Philosophical Studies, 98*, 283–316.

Levine, S., Rottman, J., Taylor, D., O'Neill, E., Stich, S. P., & Machery, E. (2016, June). *The moral domain across religions*. Paper presented at the annual meeting of the Society for Philosophy and Psychology, Duke University, Durham, NC.

Lisciandra, C., Postma-Nilsenová, M., & Colombo, M. (2013). Conformorality: A study on group conditioning of normative judgment. *Review of Philosophy and Psychology, 4*, 751–764.

Machery, E. (2012). Delineating the moral domain. In *The Baltic International Yearbook of Cognition, Logic and Communication: Vol. 7. Morality and the cognitive sciences*. Available at *http://dx.doi.org/10.4148/biyclc.v7i0.1777*.

Machery, E., & Mallon, R. (2010). Evolution of morality. In J. M. Doris & the Moral Psychology Research Group (Eds.), *The moral psychology handbook* (pp. 3–46). Oxford, UK: Oxford University Press.

Machery, E., & Stich, S. P. (2013). You can't have it both ways. *Behavioral and Brain Sciences, 36*, 95.

Nichols, S. (2002). Norms with feeling: Towards a psychological account of moral judgment. *Cognition, 84*, 221–236.

Nichols, S. (2004). *Sentimental rules: On the natural foundations of moral judgment*. New York: Oxford University Press.

Rottschaefer, W. A. (1998). *The biology and psychology of moral agency*. New York: Cambridge University Press.

Rozin, P. (1999). The process of moralization. *Psychological Science, 10*, 218–221.

Rozin, P., Lowery, L., Imada, S., & Haidt, J. (1999). The CAD triad hypothesis: A mapping between three moral emotions (contempt, anger, disgust) and three moral codes (community, autonomy, divinity). *Journal of Personality and Social Psychology, 76*, 574–586.

Rozin, P., Markwith, M., & Stoess, C. (1997). Moralization and becoming a vegetarian: The transformation of preferences into values and the recruitment of disgust. *Psychological Science, 8*, 67–73.

Ruse, M. (1986). *Taking Darwin seriously*. Oxford, UK: Blackwell.

Shweder, R. A., Mahapatra, M., & Miller, J. (1987). Culture and moral development. In J. Kagan & S. Lamb (Eds.), *The emergence of morality in young children* (pp. 1–82). Chicago: University of Chicago Press.

Singer, P. (1981). *The expanding circle: Ethics and sociobiology*. Oxford, UK: Oxford University Press.

Singer, P. (2000). *A Darwinian left: Politics, evolution, and cooperation*. New Haven, CT: Yale University Press.

Skitka, L. J. (2010). The psychology of moral conviction. *Social and Personality Psychology Compass, 4*, 2672–2681.

Skitka, L. J., Bauman, C. W., & Mullen, E. (2008). Morality and justice: An expanded theoretical perspective and review. In K. A. Hedgvedt & J. Clay-Warner (Eds.), *Advances in group processes* (Vol. 25, pp. 1–27). Bingley, UK: Emerald Group.

Skitka, L. J., Bauman, C. W., & Sargis, E. G. (2005). Moral conviction: Another contributor to attitude strength or something more? *Journal of Personality and Social Psychology, 88*, 895–917.

Sousa, P., Holbrook, C., & Piazza, J. (2009). The morality of harm. *Cognition, 113*, 80–92.

Street, S. (2006). A Darwinian dilemma for realist theories of value. *Philosophical Studies, 127*, 109–166.

Turiel, E. (1983). *The development of social knowledge*. Cambridge, UK: Cambridge University Press.

Wierzbicka, A. (2001). *What did Jesus mean?: Explaining the Sermon on the Mount and the Parables in simple and universal human concepts*. New York: Oxford University Press.

Wierzbicka, A. (2007). Moral sense. *Journal of Social, Evolutionary, and Cultural Psychology, 1*, 66–85.

Wilson, D. S. (2002). *Darwin's cathedral: Evolution, religion and the nature of society*. Chicago: University of Chicago Press.

Wright, J. C., Cullum, J., & Schwab, N. (2008). The cognitive and affective dimensions of moral conviction: Implications for attitudinal and behavioral measures of interpersonal tolerance. *Personality and Social Psychology Bulletin, 34*, 1461–1476.

CHAPTER 28

The History of Moral Norms

Jesse J. Prinz

> **How does history shape moral values?**
>
> There are several different theoretical perspectives on moral change, and each has led to lines of evidence that shed light on the nature of morality.

The cognitive sciences tend to focus on synchronic methods: studying mental life here and now in living populations. Occasionally, work is also done exploring evolutionary accounts, which is an especially popular approach when it comes to studying morals. Far less frequent is work on the history of morals. This is, in part, because history is difficult to study using psychological methods. This neglect is unfortunate, however, because changes over historical time can deepen our understanding of moral psychology. Like evolutionary approaches, historical approaches help us understand both the mechanisms of morality and their function. But historical approaches also shed light on moral learning, sociocultural contributors to moral norms, transformations over time, and moral conflict. In this chapter, I consider relevant work in philosophy and cultural history, as well as research in the social sciences: anthropology, behavioral economics, political science, sociology, and psychology. Working together, these fields can deepen our understanding of how morality works.

Historical Context

The idea that history matters when trying to understand morality has long been recognized in philosophical ethics. I illustrate with several examples

In the *Leviathan* (1968), Thomas Hobbes argues that human beings are naturally disposed to exist in a state of war of all against all, and that we erect powerful governments (monarchies) to impose law and order. Thus Hobbes combines psychological egoism—the view that we are motivated by self-interest—with a social contract theory; by giving authority to a sovereign, we best protect ourselves. On this view, obedience to authority is not a natural instinct but the result of a historical process.

David Hume presents an opposing view in his *Treatise Concerning Human Nature* (1978). He believes that we are naturally benevolent rather than purely selfish but that our benevolence is applied most readily to our near and dear. Thus natural benevolence is not enough to ensure that we will respect the property of strangers. To ensure safety and security, we must cultivate moral regard for unrelated others. Hume believes that moral rules are grounded in sentiments of approval and disapproval. Therefore, security demands that we all come to disapprove of injustice in the case of unrelated third parties. We do this by adopting a general point of view, which assesses the merit of an action not from our own perspective but from a more generic point of view. Crucially, this is not a natural instinct but must be socially conditioned. Thus Hume calls justice an "artificial virtue."

A different historical approach is advocated by Karl Marx in *Capital* (1982) and other writings. According to the standard synthesis (see, e.g., Laibman, 1984), Marx sees the history of society progressing through a series of stages: primitive communism, slave society, feudalism, capitalism, socialism, and stateless, global communism. Each stage transition is driven by changes in material conditions. For example, primitive communism leads to resource surpluses as subsistence technologies improve, and that leads to stratification and slavery. For present purposes, the crucial thing to note is that Marx sees values (which he often discusses under the rubric of "ideology") as shifting over historical time. For example, we transition from egalitarian to hierarchical as we move from primitive communism to slave-based economies and feudalism.

Hobbes, Hume, and Marx each deliver vindicating narratives: Morality makes progress over history. A very different view is promulgated by Friedrich Nietzsche in *On the Genealogy of Morality* (1994). Nietzsche focuses on what he calls Christian values, including ascetic ideals (poverty, modesty, chastity, restraint, etc.) and the idea that punishment is matter of holding people responsible. He argues that Christian morality derives from the resentment that early Christians had toward their Roman oppressors. Romans valued indulgence and excess, and they punished people because they experienced joy in venting power. When Christians gained control, they turned the Roman virtues into vices out of spite.

Each of these historical approaches posits factors that drive moral change, and each makes different claims about the underlying psychology. The examples illustrate how historical analyses can shed light on motivations underlying morality and moral change. Empirical methods can contribute to adjudicating historical hypotheses and their psychological commitments.

Theoretical Stance

Broad theoretical perspectives can be culled from these philosophical traditions, and each remains operative in contemporary research.

Hobbes sees the emergence of morality as a rational solution to a coordination problem. We have to figure out how to get along with others. We want to maximize our own lot but realize that others want the same, and the result is a bad outcome for all. This prefigures game-theoretical approaches to morality, according to which sanctions can promote cooperation despite a constant incentive to defect (Kavka, 1986). Game-theoretical approaches are sometimes presented as models of historical change (Richerson & Boyd, 1998), and they have also been used to model evolutionary processes (Axelrod, 1984). Traditionally, game theory assumes rational choice: Each agent will aim to maximize individual utility. This assumption has not held up well empirically. Rational-choice models are vulnerable to free-rider problems (it predicts people will defect whenever they can personally profit), and they fail to appreciate the power of social norms (e.g., we reject unfair offers in economic games even if we stand to gain). Therefore game-theoretical models now include incentive structures based on norms. Such models are still Hobbesian, as they imply that norms are the means by which we increase cooperation and overcome conflict. This basic idea is also integral to a broader family of models that aim to explain the why people work together and form cohesive societies. I use the term *conflict and coordination* to subsume these theoretical approaches.

Hume's account draws attention to the role of emotions in morality. This is a popular approach in contemporary moral psychology (e.g., Haidt, 2001), and some attention has been paid to the role of emotions in moral change (e.g., Rozin, Markwith, &

Stoess, 1997; Nichols, 2002). Emotions have also been investigated by political scientists, historians, and sociologists. Elias's (2000) classic study of the "civilizing process" explores the way shame and embarrassment have been marshaled since the Middle Ages to regulate public displays of natural bodily functions, such as spitting, nose blowing, excretion, and sex. According to the theoretical model suggested by this tradition, there are certain sentiments that we have naturally, and these will be effective in promoting moral reform and predictive of which values endure over time. Hume also predicts that sympathy can play a role in broadening moral concern for others.

The Marxian approach has more recent adherents as well. It is a major inspiration behind materialist anthropology, which emphasizes the impact of technological change on social arrangements and values (Harris, 1989). Within history, too, there are efforts to explain transformations with reference to changes in economic factors (e.g., Williams, 1944). Likewise, some sociologists emphasize structure over culture in explaining the endurance and endorsement of unequal resource distributions (e.g., Kluegel & Smith, 1986). There is also work in political science looking at the impact of industrialization on values (Inglehart, 1997).

Nietzsche's genealogical approach is less frequently invoked in contemporary social science, though it has been championed by influential social theorists, most notably Foucault (1977), who picks up on the idea that progress is often illusion. He describes the transition from judicial torture to the penitentiary as a new system of domination that uses discipline and surveillance rather than public spectacle and pain. Another theoretical insight that emerges from Nietzsche is the importance of power struggles in shaping moral change. Such conflicts lead to the construction of new concepts and new binaries, such as the Christian contrast between good and evil. Some historians of ideas advance theses of this kind. For example, Pearce (1988) explores the contrast between savagism and civilization that was used to justify westward expansion in American and genocide of its indigenous populations. Nietzsche also observes that we tend to mistake contingent values for enduring truths.

This aligns with the empirical finding that different historical trajectories lead to deeply entrenched ideologies that are grounded in grand narratives and mistaken for absolute truths (Freeden, 1996). Research on ideology in political science relates to psychological work on polarization and group conflict (Abramowitz & Saunders, 2008).

These theoretical orientations are, to some extent, competing, but they can also be combined. For example, some game-theoretical models make reference to rational choice, emotions, and material conditions (e.g., Gintis, Fehr, Bowles, & Boyd, 2005). In some cases, the same historical transformation has been explained in several different ways. This has given rise to theoretical debates, as I discuss in the case of slavery and abolition. There are also mixed accounts that recognize multiple factors in moral change (e.g., Blackburn, 1988, appeals to economic factors, power struggles, and philanthropic sentiments to explain the end of slavery).

Evidence

Theoretical accounts of moral change are often supported by empirical work of various kinds, ranging from historical case studies to population surveys, modeling with economic games, and laboratory experiments. Here, some examples are used to illustrate the diversity of methods, time scales, and explanations that have been offered. The theoretical orientations introduced above are used to frame this survey, bearing in mind that many researchers' theoretical commitments are merely implicit or open to explanatory pluralism. The study of historical change is too vast and varied to allow for a systematic analysis, so the divisions used here bring some order to an otherwise unwieldy field of inquiry.

Moral Diversity and Transformation

Before reviewing evidence concerning the nature of moral change, it will help to point out that values do in fact vary and transform. If moral values were the same everywhere and constant, it would be difficult to motivate historical inquiry. Moral diversity and transformation are easy to establish by looking at the contemporary world and changes over the last century.

There are many subcultures that continue to promote traditional moral practices that are now highly regulated by most nations. Consider honor killing, which claims an estimated 5,000 lives each year, though the actual figure may be much higher due to underreporting (United Nations Population Fund, 2000). Methods including beating, stabbing, decapitation, and stoning. The victims are overwhelmingly young women, and the perpetrators are overwhelmingly male relatives, especially fathers and brothers. In many cases, the victim is killed for marrying someone who is not approved of by her family, and in some cases the victim is killed for having been the victim of a sexual assault. Another example is child marriage. Most nations place an 18-year minimum on marriage without special permission, yet some 15 million girls get married below that age each year. Well over 200 million married women today said their vows before their 15th birthdays (Save the Children, 2016).

In the West, where honor killing and child marriage are less common, we are shocked by such statistics, though we must bear in mind that much of our behavior would shock members of more traditional societies. Indeed, behaviors that are commonplace in Western societies include many that would be regarded as warranting honor killing within those subcultures that carry out this practice.

We must also acknowledge that there is a tremendous amount of moral diversity within Western culture. This is nowhere more apparent than in partisan politics. Political divisions are often moral divisions, and individuals raised in the same nation divide on many moral matters, including capital punishment, abortion, and lesbian, gay, bisexual, and transgender (LGBT) rights. All of these debates have changed over time, with legal reforms reflecting dramatic alternations in moral outlook.

It is easy to find other moral issues that have undergone significant change over the last century or so, sometimes at an international scale. One curious example is dueling, which became a common practice among the European upper classes between the Renaissance and the early 20th century (Hopton, 2007). It emerged out of medieval trials by combat and dissipated after World War I. There were occasional revivals between the wars, in South America and Nazi Germany, for example, but the practice died out thereafter. The change coincided with a decline in the military aristocracy and with a general decline in honor culture in the West (though see Appiah, 2010, for an argument that dueling simply lost its honorable veneer).

Another moral change that took place in recent history is women's suffrage. Though denial of women's suffrage was sometimes presented as a prudential issue based on pseudoscientific beliefs about gender differences, voting became widely regarded as a moral matter, expressed in the language of rights. A century ago, few women could vote in national elections. In 1900, only 1% of the world's nations allowed women to vote, as compared with the 19% in which men could vote; by 1950, the number exceeded 40% for women and 50% for men; and, by the 1990s, 96% of the world's nations held elections, and suffrage was granted to both women and men in all of them (Ramirez, Soysal, & Shanahan, 1997). Since then, the few outlier nations—Oman, Qatar, Saudi Arabia, and United Arab Emirates—have held elections, at least municipally, and women were able to vote. This trend shows a fivefold increase in democratic practices overall, but the change for women has been far more dramatic: in 1892, no country gave women the right to vote in national elections, and now women can vote everywhere. Institutionalized discrimination against women remains widespread, but there has been a revolutionary change in values and policies with respect to suffrage.

To give one final example, consider changing attitudes toward overt imperialism. The 19th century saw a consolidation of power in Europe as nation states took form in the wake of the Napoleonic wars. Meanwhile, the United States became the biggest economy in the world. This set the stage for an age of empire, in which Western powers—and subsequently Asian powers—actively sought to expand territorial boundaries, conquering as much as they could, including much of the African continent. People in the conquering nations spoke proudly of empire building, and moral arguments were advanced to justify conquest. By the end of the 20th century, attitudes had changed. Imperialism continues, of course, but through cultural influence, coercive trade agreements, international policing, puppet governments, and provisional occupations. "Empire" has become a bad word (Cox, 2004). Now, overt territorial expansion is demonized (Kuwait, Crimea), and foreign invasion must be presented as defense or liberation.

Conflict and Coordination

The foregoing examples confirm that values change historically, but theoretical accounts are needed to explain such changes, and empirical evidence is needed to support theories. One class of theories explores conflicts (e.g., crime, war, competition) and forms of social coordination that emerge in their wake (e.g., cooperation and coercive control). Some authors construct mathematical models and compare their models with actual historical trends. For example, Gartzke and Rohner (2010) attempt to explain the expansion and dissolution of empires using such variables as military technology, military costs, need for resources, available labor, market freedom, and threat of insurrection. They claim that historical facts about the rise and fall of empires relate to such variables; territorial expansion helps economies grow, but then leads to diminishing returns and decolonization.

A different model is advanced by Turchin (2006), who focuses on "metaethnic frontiers"—places where competition between groups is particularly intense. This leads to war, according to Turchin, and war leads to increased intersocietal cooperation, planting the seeds for empire. Instability comes when gaps increase between ruling elites and the masses. Turchin applies his theories to numerous historical cases: Romans, Normans, Carolingians, Mongols, Muscovites, and Americans, among others. In other work, he uses mathematical models to capture sweeping historical changes (Turchin, 2003). The approach is reductionist, which makes traditional historians squeamish, but Turchin makes efforts to accommodate unexpected one-off events such as the Black Death.

Other researchers have tried to model a social change that occurred long before the emergence of empires: the transition from small bands of individuals to larger scale societies with hundreds of members. From the perspective of traditional evolutionary theory, large-scale societies are a puzzle. With small groups, cooperation is promoted by kin selection (helping close relatives; Hamilton, 1964) and reciprocal altruism (helping those who help us; Trivers, 1971). Both increase prospects for our genes. With larger groups, we must cooperate with unrelated strangers, including some who may never have an opportunity to reciprocate. There are two effective ways to promote such behavior: indirect reciprocity (cases in which benefits conferred on one person spread to others, benefiting the group as a whole), and altruistic punishment (punishing anyone who defects, even at some personal cost, regardless of whether or not you are the victim of the defection). Biological evolution has a hard time accounting for either, as they require that individuals incur costs without direct benefit, but cultural group selection has been postulated as a possible explanation (Mesoudi & Jensen, 2012). For example, Henrich and Boyd (2001) propose a model in which a weak tendency toward social conformity, coupled with a small amount of punishment behavior, leads to a spread of altruistic punishment; groups in which this happens then outperform other groups, leading to the stabilization of punishment norms. Empirical tests using economic games have confirmed that altruistic punishment occurs and increases cooperation (Fehr & Gächter, 2002); altruistic punishment increases in contexts of group competition (Rebers & Koopmans, 2012); and it is also more prevalent in large societies (Marlowe et al., 2008).

It must be noted that many researchers working within the Hobbesian conflict and coordination cohesion tradition tell progress narratives: they claim that we are getting more peaceful over time. An extreme case of this is Pinker (2011), who charts reductions in crime, homicide, and war fatalities, and he argues that the Leviathan (i.e., a stronger state) plays a significant role in this change. But optimism is not shared by all. Critics argue that Pinker overestimates violence in small-scale societies (Ferguson, 2013), misses upward trends in crime (Walby, Towers, & Francis, 2016), and underestimates 20th-century war fatalities (Kolbert, 2011). Turchin (2006) cautions that periods of peace are often temporary (the Pax Romana lasted just over 200 years).

Emotions

Emotions are another factor implicated in the history of values. For David Hume, values are constituted by our emotional attitudes, so changing values requires emotional change. There has been much research on morally relevant emotions, including research on how these wax and wane over time (Frevert, 2011). Other historical investigations explore the changing role of love in marriage norms (Reddy, 2010), the emergence of sympathy (Gaston, 2010), the role of anger in activism (Lamb-Books, 2016), and political uses of fear (Bourke, 2006). Other studies look at the role of emotions in the psychological process of moralization.

One example is Rozin et al.'s (1997) work on moral vegetarianism. As compared with people who become vegetarian for health reasons, moral vegetarians show higher levels of disgust toward eating meat, and they endorse more reasons for avoiding meat. Rozin et al. interpret these findings as showing emotional mediation of the moral value attention must be paid to. Rozin and Singh (1999) also look at the role of emotion in the moralization of smoking. They find that moral attitudes toward cigarettes correlate with disgust and increase across three generations.

In another study involving disgust, Nichols (2002) examines the history of etiquette norms. The Renaissance philosopher Desiderius Erasmus (1530/1985) wrote a highly influential etiquette manual, which contains rules that vary in their current standing; some still ring true ("Turn away when spitting") and others have lost their relevance ("If given a napkin, put it over either the left shoulder or the left forearm"). Using this manual, Nichols had coders rate items on two dimensions: Does the norm continue to hold? And does the behavior it describes elicit core disgust? "Core disgust" is disgust elicited by bodily products and fluids. Nichols found that preservation over historical time was positively related to core disgust, suggesting that emotions play a role in the cultural transmission of norms.

Other examples can be found in the annals of cultural history. Consider foot binding, which was practiced in China for a millennium (Ping, 2000). The origins of foot binding are something of a mystery, but its disappearance is well documented, as it happened over the course of a few decades in the early 20th century. One study, based on a 1929 survey in Tinghsien, reports that bound feet were found in 99.2% of women over 40, in about 60% of women ages 20–24, in under 20% of women between 15 and 19, and in none of the girls under 10, which is over the age when the procedure was traditionally initiated (Gamble, 1943). This pattern shows a strikingly fast cultural change, going from near universality among women to total elimination, with some major drops in 5-year periods. This was a period of economic and political change in China, which witnessed a rapid increase in foreign contact. Some efforts to eliminate foot binding were spearheaded by foreigners, but there were also local movements. In the present context, attention must be paid to the methods used to change values. At the turn of the 20th century, a British woman named Alicia Little founded the *T'ien tsu hui* (Natural Foot Society), which aimed to convince Chinese women that bound feet are unnatural and hence repellant. Efforts to vilify bound feet as unnatural can also be found among Chinese reformers, dating as far back as the 18th century. Drucker (1981) catalogues arguments from the critic Li Juchen, which include the charge that binding feet tampers with the natural order, violates human nature, degrades the upper classes, makes women move unsteadily, and causes illness. Notice that each of these arguments could instill disgust.

Efforts to enact moral change by recruiting emotions are not limited to disgust. A wider range can be found in the work of historians who study the antislavery movements. Slavery is now regarded as perhaps the greatest of all evils. Yet it was practiced from ancient times to the present day. With the colonization of the Americas, it grew in scale and acquired a racial pretext. By the turn of 19th century, slavery was a central component of the most profitable industries in Brazil, the United States, and the Caribbean. By the end of the century, the institution had been outlawed in all of these places, and popular opinion had shifted. There are many theories of how this happened, and many factors that may have contributed, but there is no doubt that emotions played an important role in the rhetoric of those who fought for abolition.

One factor in public discourse about slavery was fear. Slavery is an extreme form of violence against persons and human dignity; it requires brutality to enforce. The inevitable result is insurrection. According to one count, there were 250 slave revolts in America and countless more plots, outbreaks, and reprisals (Aptheker, 1943, p. 162). There were also many thousands of escapes. African captives mutinied on slave ships, as well, on as many as 10% of the voyages across the Atlantic (Richardson, 2001). This pattern was repeated wherever there were slaves, with major revolts in Brazil and throughout the Caribbean: Barbados, Curaçao, Dominica, Grenada, Guyana, Jamaica, Puerto Rico, and throughout the Virgin Islands and West Indies. The most successful revolt was carried out in Haiti—then the French island of Saint Domingue. Slaves managed to oust French colonists and gain independence. They also managed to defeat the French army and expel forces from England and Spain. All these insurrections caused tremendous fear in whites. They were used to justify even more oppressive treatment of slaves (Horne, 2015), but they also played a role in abolition. Thomas Jefferson was very anxious about slave revolts, and he enacted embargos against Haiti after the revolution there to prevent knowledge of their success from spreading (Matthewson, 1995). Soon after, he encouraged Congress to ban the international slave trade, reducing the chance that rebellious Africans and those who knew about Caribbean uprisings would enter U.S. soil. Leading abolitionists expressed fear as well. William Lloyd Garrison used fear of insurrection to argue for immediate abolition in the United States rather than gradualism (Abzug, 1970), and Thomas Fowell Buxton invoked fear to lobby effectively for abolition in the British parliament (Matthews, 2006).

Other emotions were recruited as well. Opponents of slavery described the institution as a grave sin, which may have elicited shame and guilt, and they also called on white people to sympathize with slaves. The famous emblem of the antislavery movements shows a slave in chains emblazoned with the words "Am I not a man and a brother?" Much has been written about such appeals to sympathy, which were inspired by British moralists such as Adam Smith (Carey, 2005). Also prevalent were appeals to anger and righteous indignation. Woods (2015) illustrates the trend in the discourse of the English abolitionists Thomas Clarkson and William Wilberforce. One might also suppose that anger and indignation played a role in motivating slave uprisings. Curiously, such terms appear infrequently in slave narratives, and anger is most often attributed to slave masters and mistresses in these texts (Andrews & Gates, 2000). In a classic study of the Haitian Revolution, James (1938) notes that the slaves were less vengeful than their masters. Perhaps emotions such as determination and hope animated the slaves who fought oppression, and those efforts helped to awaken white anxiety and conscience.

Material Factors

Emotions help to explain the psychological mechanisms behind moral change, but some authors seek to explain large-scale societal factors as well. Those who follow in the materialist tradition popularized by Marx tend to focus on economic variables.

For example, Williams (1944) offers a classic explanation of British abolitionism that draws attention to changing profit margins. At first, slavery in the New World was a boon to the British economy, and it helped finance industrialization, but then, as sugar prices fell, slave industries were losing value, and Britain shifted toward a wage-based industrial economy. This account has been a challenge to those who think that humanitarian motives drove abolition (Drescher, 1977), but evidence suggests that economic changes may have played a role (e.g., Ryden, 2001). Economic arguments have often been given to explain why slavery was abolished in the American North and also why it persisted so long (McManus, 1973). There are also economic accounts, based on demographic data, of the shift from European indentured servitude to African chattel slavery in early British America (Menard, 1980).

Economic models have been used to examine many other moral attitudes. The contrast between farming and herding economies has been used to explain differences in attitudes toward violence in African societies (Edgerton, 1971) and in North America (Cohen & Nisbett, 1994). Talhelm et al. (2014) credit rice farming with collectivism, as compared with individualism. Morris (2015) argues that the transition from farming to fossil fuels ushered in democracy and gender equality. Harris (1989) sketches materialistic explanations of many moralized practices: incest, cannibalism, male dominance, and others.

There are also economic accounts of changes in marriage norms. Scheidel (2009) argues that the transition from polygamy to monogamy resulted from a reduction in male income inequality after the fall of the Greek palace system. Coontz (2004) credits industrialization with the rise of marriages based on love. Werner (1979) argues that tolerance for gay relationships increases with the cost of child rearing. Eagly and Wood (1999) examine the relationship between increasing gender equality in relationships and the economic empowerment of women.

Some critics worry that materialist explanations are overly deterministic, but analyses such as these do provide evidence for correlations between values and economic variables, indicating some impact in certain cases.

Power

Another approach to moral change focuses on power arrangements. These can be linked to economic variables, but there is also evidence that values can be affected by contingent historical factors in which different groups struggle for control. Such conflicts can give rise to illusory beliefs about progress. This explanatory framework has been less intensively studied by social scientists, but possible examples can be identified.

Consider the Cold War. Capitalism and communism are economic systems, but the contingencies of revolution and conquest determined which countries ended up on either side of this divide. Citizens in both camps were then socialized to believe in their own moral superiority. Another example is mass incarceration. There are now more African Americans in jail or on probation or parole than were enslaved in 1850 (Alexander, 2010). These numbers reflect policies that have a moral character—especially drug laws—but their net effect is the preservation of a racially based power imbalance.

Western democracy has also been subjected to a power-theoretical analysis. Many people believe that Western systems of government are fair because they are democratic, but defenders of the "elite theory" argue that power is hoarded by members of a ruling class (Higley & Burton, 2006). Consistent with this, Gilens and Page (2014) collected opinions about nearly 2,000 U.S. policies and found widespread endorsements among economic elites and business interests; in contrast, the preferences of average citizens showed no relationship to public policy. They conclude that the United States is an oligarchy.

Extension and Expansion

The foregoing examples illustrate the diversity of research programs that aim to identify and explain changes in values. These operate at different levels of analysis, cover many time scales, and deploy a wide range of methods, including social history, demography, national polling, game-theoretical modeling, and laboratory experiments. There are also different theoretical approaches, as emphasized here. These are often presented as competitors; for example, economic factors are sometimes contrasted with changes in cultural ideals; emotion is contrasted with utility maximization; contingent power struggles are contrasted with law-like changes. But mixed models are easy to imagine, with causal arrows in all directions.

From the perspective of moral psychology, the phenomenon of historical change has several lessons to offer. It reminds us that values can shift and are not completely determined by biology. It can shed light on the mechanisms of moral learning, including emotions. It can also expose factors that lead harmful values to become entrenched, such as ingroup bias and profit motives. Historical analyses can also be informed by psychological research, leading to richer explanations of societal change. The cognitive sciences have tended to neglect historical approaches, and historians often neglect psychology, but there is much to learn from their intersection.

REFERENCES

Abramowitz, A. I., & Saunders, K. L. (2008). Is polarization a myth? *Journal of Politics, 70,* 542–555.

Abzug, R. H. (1970). The influence of Garrisonian abolitionists' fears of slave violence on the antislavery argument, 1829–40. *Journal of Negro History, 55,* 15–26.

Alexander, M. (2010). *The new Jim Crow: Mass incarceration in the age of colorblindness.* New York: New Press.

Andrews, W. L., & Gates, H. L. (Eds.). (2000). *Slave narratives.* New York: Penguin.

Appiah, K. A. (2010). *The honor code: How moral revolutions happen.* New York: Norton.

Aptheker, H. (1943). *American Negro slave revolts.* New York: Columbia University Press.

Axelrod, R. (1984). *The evolution of cooperation.* New York: Basic Books.

Blackburn, R. (1988). *The overthrow of colonial slavery, 1776–1848.* New York: Verso.

Bourke, E. (2006). *Fear: A cultural history.* Emeryville, CA: Counterpoint.

Carey, B. (2005). *British abolitionism and the rhetoric of sensibility: Writing, sentiment, and slavery, 1760–1807.* London: Palgrave.

Cohen, D., & Nisbett, R. E. (1994). Self-protection and the culture of honor: Explaining Southern violence. *Personality and Social Psychology Bulletin, 20,* 551–567.

Coontz, S. (2004). The world historical transformation of marriage. *Journal of Marriage and Family, 66,* 974–979.

Cox, M. (2004). Empire, imperialism and the Bush doctrine. *Review of International Studies, 30,* 585–608.

Drescher, S. (1977). *Econocide: British slavery in the era of abolition.* Chapel Hill, NC: University of North Carolina Press.

Drucker, A. R. (1981). The influence of Western women on the anti-footbinding movement, 1840–1911. *Historical Reflections, 8,* 179–199.

Eagly, A. H., & Wood, W. (1999). The origins of sex differences in human behavior: Evolved dispositions versus social roles. *American Psychologist, 54,* 408–423.

Edgerton, R. B. (1971). *The individual in cultural adaptation: A study of four East African peoples.* Berkeley: University of California Press.

Elias, N. (2000). *The civilizing process* (E. Jephcott, Trans.). Malden, MA: Blackwell. (Original work published 1939)

Erasmus, D. (1985). *On good manners for boys.* In J. Sowards (Ed.), *Collected works of Erasmus* (Vol. 25, pp. 269–290). Toronto, Ontario, Canada: University of Toronto Press. (Original work published 1530)

Fehr, E., & Gächter, S. (2002). Altruistic punishment in humans. *Nature, 415,* 137–140.

Ferguson, B. (2013). Pinker's list: Exaggerating prehistoric war mortality. In D. Fry (Ed.), *War, peace and human nature* (pp. 112–131). Oxford, UK: Oxford University Press.

Foucault, M. (1977). *Discipline and punish: The birth of the prison* (A. M. Sheridan-Smith, Trans.). New York: Vintage.

Freeden, M. (1996). *Ideologies and political theory: A conceptual approach.* Oxford, UK: Oxford University Press.

Frevert, U. (2011). *Emotions in history: Lost and found.* Budapest, Hungary: Central European University Press.

Gamble, S. D. (1943). The disappearance of footbinding in Tinghsien. *American Journal of Sociology, 49,* 181–183.

Gartzke, E., & Rohner, D. (2010). The political economy of imperialism, decolonization and development. *British Journal of Political Science, 41,* 525–556.

Gaston, S. (2010). The impossibility of sympathy. *Eighteenth Century, 51,* 129–152.

Gilens, M., & Page, B. (2014). Testing theories of American politics: Elites, interest groups, and average citizens. *Perspectives on Politics, 12,* 564–581.

Gintis, H., Fehr, E., Bowles, S., & Boyd, R. (2005). *Moral sentiments and material interests: The foundations of cooperation in economic life.* Cambridge, MA: MIT Press.

Haidt, J. (2001). The emotional dog and its rational tail: A social intuitionist approach to moral judgment. *Psychological Review, 108,* 814–834.

Hamilton, W. D. (1964). The genetical evolution of social behavior. *Journal of Theoretical Biology, 7,* 1–52.

Harris, M. (1989). *Our kind.* New York: Harper Collins.

Henrich, J., & Boyd, R. (2001). Why people punish defectors: Weak conformist transmission can stabilize costly enforcement of norms in cooperative dilemmas. *Journal of Theoretical Biology, 208,* 79–89.

Higley, J., & Burton, M. (2006). *Elite foundations of liberal democracy.* Lanham, MD: Rowman & Littlefield.

Hobbes, T. (1968). *Leviathan* (C. B. MacPherson, Ed.). New York: Penguin. (Original work published 1651)

Hopton, R. (2007). *Pistols at dawn: A history of dueling.* London: Piatkus Books.

Horne, G. (2015). *Confronting black Jacobins: The U.S., the Haitian Revolution, and the origins of the Dominican Republic.* New York: New York University Press.

Hume, D. (1978). *A treatise of human nature* (P. H. Nidditch, Ed.). Oxford, UK: Oxford University Press. (Original work published 1739)

Inglehart, R. (1997). *Modernization and postmodernization: Cultural, economic, and political change in 43 societies.* Princeton, NJ: Princeton University Press.

James, C. L. R. (1938). *The Black Jacobins: Toussaint L'Ouverture and the San Domingo Revolution.* New York: Vintage Books.

Kavka, G. (1986). *Hobbesean moral and political theory.* Princeton, NJ: Princeton University Press.

Kluegel, J. R., & Smith, E. R. (1986). *Beliefs about inequality.* New York: Walter de Gruyter.

Kolbert, E. (2011). Peace in our time. *New Yorker, 87*(30), 75–78.

Laibman, D. (1984). Modes of production and theories of transition. *Science and Society, 48,* 257–294.

Lamb-Books, B. (2016). *Angry abolitionists and the rhetoric of slavery: Moral emotions in social movements.* New York: Palgrave.

Marlowe, F., Berbesque, J. C., Barr, A., Barrett, C., Bolyanatz, A., Cardenas, J. C., . . . Tracer, D. (2008). More "altruistic" punishment in larger societies. *Proceedings of the National Academy of Sciences of the USA, 275,* 587–590.

Marx, K. (1982), Capital: A critique of political economy (B. Fowkes, Trans.). New York: Penguin Books. (Original work published 1867)

Matthews, G. (2006). *Caribbean slave revolts and the British abolitionist movement.* Baton Rouge: Louisiana State University Press.

Matthewson, T. (1995). Jefferson and Haiti. *Journal of Southern History, 61,* 209–248.

McManus, E. J. (1973). *Black bondage in the North.* Syracuse, NY: Syracuse University Press.

Menard, R. R. (1980). The tobacco industry in the Chesapeake colonies, 1617–1730: An interpretation. *Research in Economic History, 5,* 109–177.

Mesoudi, A., & Jensen, K. (2012). Culture and the evolution of human sociality. In J. Vonk & T. Shackelford (Eds.), *The Oxford handbook of comparative evolutionary psychology* (pp. 419–433). Oxford, UK: Oxford University Press.

Morris, I. (2015). *Foragers, farmers, and fossil fuels: How human values evolve.* Princeton, NJ: Princeton University Press.

Nichols, S. (2002). On the genealogy of norms: A case for the role of emotion in cultural evolution. *Philosophy of Science, 69,* 234–255.

Nietzsche, F. (1994). *On the genealogy of morality* (C. Diethe, Trans.). Cambridge, UK: Cambridge University Press. (Original work published 1887)

Pearce, R. H. (1988). *Savagism and civilization: A study of the Indian and the American mind.* Berkeley: University of California Press.

Ping, W. (2000). *Aching for beauty: Footbinding in China.* Minneapolis: University of Minnesota Press.

Pinker, S. (2011). *The better angels of our nature: Why violence has declined.* New York: Viking.

Ramirez, F. O., Soysal, Y., & Shanahan, S. (1997). The changing logic of political citizenship: Cross-national acquisition of women's suffrage rights, 1890 to 1990. *American Sociological Review, 62,* 735–745.

Rebers, S., & Koopmans, R. (2012) Altruistic punishment and between-group competition. *Human Nature, 23,* 173–190.

Reddy, W. (2010). The rule of love: The history of Western romantic love in comparative perspective. In L. Passerini, L. Ellena, & A. C. T. Goeppert (Eds.), *New dangerous liaisons: Discourses on Europe and love in the twentieth century* (pp. 33–57). New York: Berghahn Books.

Richardson, D. (2001). Shipboard revolts, African authority and the Atlantic slave trade. *William and Mary Quarterly, 58,* 69–92.

Richerson, P., & Boyd, R. (1998). The evolution of ultrasociality. In I. Eibl-Eibesfeldt & F. K. Salter (Eds.), *Indoctrinability, ideology and warfare.* New York: Berghahn Books.

Rozin, P., Markwith, M., & Stoess, C. (1997). Moralization: Becoming a vegetarian, the conversion of preferences into values and the recruitment of disgust. *Psychological Science, 8,* 67–73.

Rozin, P., & Singh, L. (1999). The moralization of cigarette smoking in America. *Journal of Consumer Behavior, 8,* 321–337.

Ryden, D. (2001). Does decline make sense?: The West Indian economy and the abolition of the slave trade. *Journal of Interdisciplinary History, 31,* 347–374.

Save the Children. (2016). *Every last girl: Free*

to live, free to learn, free from harm. London: Author.

Scheidel, W. (2009). A peculiar institution?: Greco-Roman monogamy in global context. *History of the Family, 14,* 280–291.

Talhelm, T., Zhang, X., Oishi, S., Shimin, C., Duan, D., Lan, X., & Kitayama, S. (2014). Large-scale psychological differences within China explained by rice versus wheat agriculture. *Science, 344,* 603–608.

Trivers, R. L. (1971). The evolution of reciprocal altruism. *Quarterly Review of Biology, 46,* 34–57.

Turchin, P. (2003). *Historical dynamics: Why states rise and fall.* Princeton, NJ: Princeton University Press.

Turchin, P. (2006). *War and peace and war: The life cycles of imperial nations.* New York: Pi Press.

United Nations Population Fund. (2000). State of world population 2000: Lives together, worlds apart: Men and women in a time of change. Available at *www.unfpa.org/swp/2000/english/index.html.*

Walby, S., Towers, J., & Francis, B. (2016). Is violent crime increasing or decreasing?: A new methodology to measure repeat attacks making visible the significance of gender and domestic relations. *British Journal of Criminology, 56,* 1203–1234.

Werner, D. (1979). A cross-cultural perspective on theory and research on male homosexuality. *Journal of Homosexuality, 4,* 345–362.

Williams, E. (1944). *Capitalism and slavery.* Chapel Hill, NC: University of North Carolina Press.

Woods, M. E. (2015). A theory of moral outrage: Indignation and eighteenth-century British abolitionism. *Slavery and Abolition, 36,* 662–683.

PART VI
MORALITY AND THE BODY

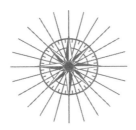

QUESTIONS ANSWERED IN PART VI

CHAPTER 29 How is morality revealed in the body?

CHAPTER 30 What is the nature of moral psychological processing?

The Moralization of the Body
Protecting and Expanding the Boundaries of the Self

Gabriela Pavarini
Simone Schnall

> **How is morality revealed in the body?**
>
> Protecting the body coincides with a desire to keep resources for the self, whereas breaking these boundaries (e.g., through physical touch) coincides with a desire to share with others.

Visible and mobile, my body is a thing among things; it is one of them. It is caught in the fabric of the world, and its cohesion is that of a thing. But, because it moves itself and sees, it holds things in a circle around itself.
—MERLEAU-PONTY (1964, p. 163)

Human minds reside in fleshy, physical bodies. Concrete and clearly delineated, the body separates internal, private experience from external objects and people. It is the space where awareness simultaneously arises from internally generated streams (e.g., heart rate) and external pathways or the "circle around itself" (e.g., vision, smell). Our senses convey that other beings are exterior to oneself and that our boundaries separate the self from others. Processes such as physical closeness, touch, or synchronicity may blur those boundaries and induce feelings of being together and united as "one" (Gallace & Spence, 2010; Paladino, Mazzurega, Pavani, & Schubert, 2010). Exposure to cues of contamination and injury, on the other hand, may induce a strong sense of repulsion and a desire to protect the psychological and physical boundaries of the self. Individuals therefore experience an ongoing process of subjectively redefining their physical and psychological boundaries, whereby other people are either kept separate, rejected, and condemned or brought closer, incorporated, and united with the self. Human morality unfolds in this dynamic process of protecting and expanding the boundaries of the self.

At its essence, morality can be viewed as concerning resource allocation. "Being moral" normally refers to the willingness to allocate personal resources to others. This includes helping others achieve their goals, comforting them, and sharing valuable goods such as food and information (Eisenberg, Fabes, & Spinrad, 2006; Tomasello & Vaish, 2013; Warneken & Tomasello, 2009). Therefore, a substantial part of our everyday morality involves decisions on whether to keep our psychological, physical, and material resources to ourselves or, instead, give them away. For social life to be sustainable, human groups develop a shared understanding of who possesses what and the extent to which these resources are distributed and shared. In the present chapter we demonstrate how the negotiation of psychological and material resources with others is grounded in processes of the physical body, such as those that support disease avoidance. In what follows, we discuss the historical roots of our approach, its theoretical standpoint, and the accruing empirical evidence in support of it.

Historical Context and Theoretical Stance

Broadly speaking, our approach is based on views of cognition as grounded or embodied in several different ways, including simulations, situated action, and bodily states (e.g., emotions). This view opposes traditional theories of cognition that assume that knowledge is stored in amodal, semantic memory systems separate from systems that support perception, action, and introspection. The embodied approach emerged from efforts in several different disciplines, such as cognitive linguistics (Lakoff & Johnson, 1980, 1999), anthropology (Hutchins, 1995), neuroscience (Damasio, 1994), philosophy (Prinz, 2002) and psychology (Barsalou & Wiemer-Hastings, 2005; Schwarz, 2000; Smith & Semin, 2004). Across disciplines, this novel approach has received consistent empirical support (see Landau, Meier, & Keefer, 2010; Meier, Schnall, Schwarz, & Bargh, 2012; Niedenthal, Barsalou, Winkielman, Krauth-Gruber, & Ric, 2005, for reviews).

In the moral domain, the social intuitionist model (Haidt, 2001; also see Nichols, 2004; Prinz, 2007, for similar approaches) suggests that, just like other types of judgments, moral judgments are guided by feelings and intuitions. This view contrasts with purely rationalist approaches to morality (Kohlberg, Levine, & Hewer, 1983; Nucci & Turiel, 1978) and is inspired by philosophical traditions suggesting a central role for emotions in human morals (e.g., Hume, 1777/1960). Several studies have shown that morally relevant actions trigger strong feel-

ings such as disgust, anger, or happiness and that these feelings guide how morally right or wrong individuals judge these actions to be (Cannon, Schnall, & White, 2011; Rozin, Lowery, Imada, & Haidt, 1999; Schnall, Haidt, Clore, & Jordan, 2008; for a review, see Schnall, 2017).

Beyond emotions, other physical properties of the body also map onto abstract moral concepts. As one example, moral impurity is mapped onto physical impurity, such that engaging in morally reprehensible acts induces a desire to physically cleanse one's body (Zhong & Liljenquist, 2006), and feelings of physical disgust are indicative of moral condemnation (Schnall, Haidt, et al., 2008). Physical closeness is mapped onto subjective closeness and the sharing of moral essences with others. Touching a saintly, virtuous person makes one feel morally upright, whereas approaching an immoral other makes one feel sinful (Nemeroff & Rozin, 1994; Newman, Diesendruck, & Bloom, 2011).

Embodied morality assumes, therefore, that the body is a source domain for complex ethical concepts. In this chapter, we advance the idea that fundamental elements of human morality unfold in the process of protecting and expanding physical boundaries of the self. There is extensive evidence that humans strive to protect their bodily container, keeping a distance from potential contaminants and other threats to body integrity. As we aim to demonstrate, this process of safeguarding one's physical bodily boundaries is intrinsically linked to the process of keeping one's material and psychological resources to oneself (i.e., an unwillingness to connect and share with others). On the flip side, greater willingness to break those boundaries (e.g., through physical touch) coincides with a subjective sense of closeness and a desire to share one's own resources with others.

Evidence

Morality as the Protection of One's Boundaries

Humans have a fundamental tendency to protect their bodies against illness, disease, and contamination. Beyond physiological immune responses, human beings are also equipped with a sophisticated set of psychological mechanisms, the *behavioral immune system* (Murray & Schaller, 2016; Schaller & Park, 2011). This system serves as a first line of defense against pathogens. For example, newborn babies spontaneously wrinkle their noses and turn down the corners of their mouths when given a bitter solution, in an involuntary attempt to prevent toxins and pathogens from entering their bodies (Rosenstein & Oster, 1988). Individuals are highly sensitive to morphological and olfactory cues that connote the presence of pathogens and promptly react when exposed to potentially harmful substances, such as a stranger's pus-oozing sore or maggots crawling inside one's meal (Curtis, Aunger, & Rabie, 2004; Curtis, de Barra, & Aunger, 2011; Curtis & Biran, 2001; Rozin, Lowery, & Ebert, 1994; Schaller, Miller, Gervais, Yager, & Chen, 2010). Even subtle cues of potential pathogen infection trigger a chain of reactions that include a sense of disgust and revulsion and avoidant behavioral tendencies.

Because many diseases are transmitted as a result of interpersonal encounters, the perceived threat of infection may reduce people's inclination for social interaction. Indeed, a study found that levels of extraversion were lower among populations with high prevalence of infectious diseases (Schaller & Murray, 2008). At the individual level, participants who were chronically worried about germ contamination or primed with pathogen salience also reported being less extroverted (Duncan, Schaller, & Park, 2009; Mortensen, Becker, Ackerman, Neuberg, & Kenrick, 2010, but see Kupfer & Tybur, 2017). Critically, the salience of potential contaminants also predicts discriminatory behavior against people who appear likely to transmit new pathogens or whose appearance is somewhat atypical. When the threat posed by infectious pathogens is made salient, participants report greater prejudice against people who are obese or have physical disabilities (Park, Faulkner, & Schaller, 2003; Park, Schaller, & Crandall, 2007) and toward outgroup members (Faulkner, Schaller, Park, & Duncan, 2004; Navarrete, Fessler, & Eng, 2007). These findings suggest that psychological mechanisms that

evolved to protect one's physical body predict morally relevant cognition and behavior.

Possibly driven by the same mechanism, actions that potentially harm or physically contaminate one's body in the absence of any obvious interpersonal connotation are moralized. Those include, among others, lack of hygiene, excessive food ingestion (Sheikh, Botindari, & White, 2013), smoking (Rozin & Singh, 1999), and suicide (Rottman, Kelemen, & Young, 2014b). All these actions are often referred to as "wrong" and "immoral." Indeed, suicide is still considered a crime in many places throughout the world (Stephan, 2016). In the same vein, individuals strongly condemn actions that trigger a sense of repulsion, such as cannibalism, incest, and bestiality, even when the act is private and arguably harmless to others (Haidt, Bjorklund, & Murphy, 2000; Haidt, Koller, & Dias, 1993; Haidt & Hersh, 2001). Finally, the same cognitive-enhancing drug was judged as more morally reprehensible when administered through an injection, cuing potential bodily harm to the individual, than if taken as a pill (Scheske & Schnall, 2012). All these examples illustrate how the strong avoidant tendency triggered by slight cues of bodily threat may take the form of abstract moral values and raise a condemnatory eyebrow.

These examples also suggest that morality goes beyond concerns about harm and fairness. Even though people's justifications of moral judgments may include appeals to harm, they are often not the true causes of those judgments. Feelings of disgust toward taboo-breaking actions or bodily norm violations are predicted neither by harm to others (Giner-Sorolla, Bosson, Caswell, & Hettinger, 2012; Gutierrez & Giner-Sorolla, 2007) nor by intentionality (Astuti & Bloch, 2015; Russell & Giner-Sorolla, 2011b; Young & Tsoi, 2013). Moreover, judgments of impure, disgusting acts are very distinct from other moral judgments: They are less elaborately justified (Russell & Giner-Sorolla, 2011c) and more resistant to contradicting evidence (Russell & Giner-Sorolla, 2011a), and they involve a unique set of neural systems (Borg, Lieberman, & Kiehl, 2008; Parkinson et al., 2011).

In light of the above evidence, we argue that the condemnation of impurity is a reflection of people's high sensitivity and fundamental aversion to cues of illness and contamination (see Chakroff, Dungan, & Young, 2013; Inbar & Pizarro, 2014; Tybur, Lieberman, Kurzban, & DeScioli, 2013, for similar views). Although moral actions in the purity domain do not cause direct or intentional harm to others, individuals who engage in actions that potentially risk the safety and integrity of their own bodies are arguably more likely to carry and transmit pathogens. In other words, even though so-called impure actions do not cause any direct interpersonal harm, affiliating with perpetrators of these actions may in some cases represent a risk to the purity of one's own body in the long run. In this context, feelings of disgust and the condemnation of those actions effectively keep "impure others" away, protecting the self from potential physical contamination.

Disgust is such a powerful response that even completely neutral actions become moralized when coupled with it. In one study, for example, 7-year-olds rated unusual, morally neutral actions (e.g., covering one's head with sticks) as morally wrong when the action had been described as disgusting (and coupled with a disgusting smell) or unnatural, but not when described as "boring" (Rottman & Kelemen, 2012). These results indicate that children acquire moral beliefs about neutral actions associated with repulsion and disgust in an easy and effortless manner. Such moralizing effects of disgust on neutral actions have also been shown in samples of adults (Chapman & Anderson, 2014; Horberg, Oveis, Keltner, & Cohen, 2009; Wheatley & Haidt, 2005), which points to people's general reliance on feelings of disgust guiding their social judgments.

Last but not least, we find it important to note that there are multiple layers of cultural meaning associated with moral impurity. Beyond individual concerns related to the protection of one's physical body, there are several societal (e.g., religious) factors underlying judgments of "impure actions" such as incest and suicide. These factors are not discussed in this present chapter, but we point out that concerns surrounding bodily harm and contamination are not the only factor responsible for the moralization of im-

purity. The specific ways in which different cultures elaborate purity concerns are complex, diverse, and intertwined with several other factors, including specific dynamics of power and status maintenance in a particular society. Nevertheless, the fact that virtually every culture across history places purity-related practices in the sphere of morality hints at some evolutionary basis for those concerns (see Haidt & Joseph, 2007).

Physical disgust may have been not only co-opted to promote harsh judgments of actions that connote impurity but also to moral violations in general. Already at the age of 6, children consistently call moral violations "disgusting," and more so than merely negative events (Danovitch & Bloom, 2009). They also consider severe violations (e.g., "stealing money from a little kid") more disgusting than less severe ones (e.g., "stealing a candy from the supermarket"; Stevenson, Oaten, Case, Repacholi, & Wagland, 2010). Interestingly, one study found that parents' physical disgust in reaction to items such as ice cream with ketchup predicted children's reactions to sociomoral elicitors outside the purity domain, suggesting that parental physical disgust shapes children's rejection of transgressors in general (Stevenson et al., 2010).

Adults as well as children identify moral violations as "disgusting" and display spontaneous expressions of physical distaste in reaction to unfair actions (Cannon et al., 2011; Chapman, Kim, Susskind, & Anderson, 2009). Similarly, individuals highly sensitive to disgust judge moral transgressions to be more wrong than those who are less disgust sensitive (Chapman & Anderson, 2014; Horberg et al., 2009). Finally, a series of studies suggested that extraneous feelings of disgust induced by hypnosis (Wheatley & Haidt, 2005), noxious smells, dirty spaces, disgusting video clips (Schnall, Haidt, et al., 2008), disgusting noises (Seidel & Prinz, 2013), or bitter drinks (Eskine, Kacinik, & Prinz, 2011) rendered harsher moral judgments in several moral domains, particularly for participants highly sensitive to bodily cues.

Why does the effect of disgust extend to moral judgments beyond purity, given that these transgressions are unrelated to physical infection? As suggested elsewhere

(Schnall, 2017), it is possible that the state of physical disgust leads to a general mindset of resource scarcity and increased attempts to maximize personal resources. Individuals may wish to keep a distance from "impure" others but may also want to make sure they do not affiliate with self-interested partners who may exhaust their resources. Therefore, it makes sense that they would react more strongly to cues indicating that others are selfish, unfair, dishonest, or uncooperative, given that those people would likely deplete them of their resources. These strong reactions lead them to judge their transgressions more harshly and prevent them from establishing potentially costly partnerships.

If this suggestion were true, one would expect that participants experiencing disgust would not only avoid contact with selfish others but also act selfishly themselves, in order to maximize their own resources. Indeed, a recent series of studies observed that participants who had been primed with disgust by watching a video clip or handling products such as antidiarrheic medicine were more likely to cheat on a game than those in the neutral condition (Winterich, Mittal, & Morales, 2014). Equally, a related study found that participants who had been primed with facial expressions of disgust were more likely to cheat on a dice-rolling task, particularly if they were highly sensitive to disgust (Lim, Ho, & Mullette-Gillman, 2015). In sum, the feeling that protects the physical boundaries of the self facilitates immoral action in order to protect one's material resources.

The present suggestion poses an interesting paradox in the context of economic games such as the Ultimatum Game. In this game, participants are asked to decide whether to accept or reject another participant's monetary offers, which are either fair or unfair splits of a total amount (e.g., $5 each vs. $9 for one participant and $1 for the other). If the participant rejects the offer, neither party receives any funds. Unfair splits are normally rejected in an attempt to express one's disapproval of the other person's unfair behavior. Based on previous evidence, one may predict that disgusted participants would be particularly disapproving of the other player's unfair behavior and averse

to establishing potential alliances with this player. On the other hand, they would also wish to *accept* the offer, as this would maximize their own material resources because a low offer is better than nothing at all.

A careful analysis of the literature supports these predictions. When the person who made the unfair offer was salient—for example, if participants could see the other player behind an opaque wall—participants feeling disgusted were less likely to accept the other player's offer than those who were not experiencing disgust (Harlé & Sanfey, 2010; Moretti & di Pellegrino, 2010). Their rejection was probably an attempt to avoid establishing any cooperative alliances with a self-interested party. On the other hand, when the unfair offer was made by an anonymous proposer, participants tested in a smelly room were in fact *more* likely to accept the offer in comparison with those who made the decision in a neutrally scented environment (Bonini et al., 2011). Hence disgusted individuals act in ways that maximize their personal resources but also minimize potential physical connections with self-interested parties.

In sum, this section provides evidence supporting the idea that the psychological system that sets the boundaries of the physical body also sets boundaries of the moral domain. First, perceived threat of physical infection reduces people's inclination for social interaction (Schaller & Murray, 2008) and triggers strong avoidant tendencies that may take the form of abstract moral values such as one's views on immigration laws (Faulkner et al., 2004). Second, actions that potentially harm or physically contaminate one's body in the absence of any obvious interpersonal harm, such as excessive food ingestion and suicide, often become moralized (Rottman, Kelemen, & Young, 2014a; Sheikh et al., 2013). Indeed, even completely neutral actions are judged as "wrong" when coupled with disgust (Rottman & Kelemen, 2012). Lastly, the effects of disgust on moral behavior and moral judgments extend beyond the domain of purity (Chapman & Anderson, 2014), which suggests that physical disgust may lead to a general mindset of scarcity. This mindset may in turn lead to increased attempts to maximize personal resources, a hypothesis that is consistent with current empirical evidence (e.g., Winterich et al., 2014).

Morality as the Expansion of One's Boundaries

One of the most effective ways of protecting one's body against physical and biological contamination is physical cleanliness. Washing the self physically removes potential pathogens from one's skin, enhancing both individual and group fitness (Curtis et al., 2011; Curtis, 2003). Perhaps due to its crucial importance to group survival, actions that promote the physical purity of one's body are moralized. In the same way that actions that potentially harm one's body, such as cannibalism or lack of hygiene, are referred to as "morally wrong," actions that physically clean one's body or protect it against contamination are called "virtuous." These actions include bathing, abstaining from sexual activity, and hand washing, which are at the core of several prescriptive faiths (Durkheim, 1912; Haidt & Graham, 2006; Haidt & Joseph, 2007).

Whereas other people's "impure" actions invoke a sense of moral disgust and outrage, actions that promote the purity of their bodies trigger flashes of positive affect. For example, participants asked to imagine positive behavior in the purity domain, such as keeping one's house clean and tidy and resisting temptations to unhealthy foods, showed relaxation of the inside brow (i.e., the corrugator supercilii muscle), suggesting decreased negative affect, and muscle relaxation directly predicted the extent to which they approved of those behaviors (Cannon et al., 2011).

In a parallel to the moralization of impure acts, positive actions in the purity domain are very distinct from other types of virtue, including kindness, loyalty, respect, and fairness (Graham et al., 2009; Haidt & Joseph, 2007). These actions differ in the fundamental sense that they do not bear direct, intentional consequences to other people's well-being. From a broader perspective, however, if pathogens are spread by physical contact, safeguarding one's own body from contaminants protects other people's bodies from getting physically contaminated, especially when individuals are expected to interact closely.

When bodies are clean, cooperative alliances become more likely. An accruing line of evidence suggests that cleanliness facilitates approach and is used as information about other people's moral character. A field experiment, for instance, found that the neater, cleaner, and better dressed criminal defendants were in court, the more lenient was the punishment applied to them (Stewart, 1985). Similarly, unconscious activation of cleanliness concepts in an experimental context led to more lenient judgments of other people's transgressions (Huang, 2014; Schnall, Benton, & Harvey, 2008). Furthermore, studies in the domain of interpersonal relationships indicate that nonsmokers are rated as more trustworthy than smokers (Seiter, Weger, Merrill, McKenna, & Sanders, 2010). Keeping clean and groomed is also a tactic to attract romantic partners (Aunger et al., 2010; Buss, 1988). All in all, these findings suggest that actions that actively protect the body against pathogens or disease inspire positive social judgments and partnership.

Whereas disgust leads to attempts to maximize personal resources, a sense of cleanliness motivates prosocial behavior. In a field study, passengers in a clean-scented train compartment were less likely to leave garbage (e.g., used cups) on the seats and on the floor (de Lange, Debets, Ruitenburg, & Holland, 2012). Similar effects apply to prosocial behaviors beyond the purity domain. Critically, participants who completed an experiment in a clean-scented or orderly room were more likely to reciprocate trust and to donate to charity relative to participants in a neutrally scented or disorderly room (Liljenquist, Zhong, & Galinsky, 2010; Vohs, Redden, & Rahinel, 2013). In other words, disgust signals resource scarcity, whereas reminders of cleanliness signal that the environment is safe to give personal resources away and establish new cooperative alliances.

Given that physical cleanliness is linked to virtue, it is not surprising that individuals physically wash themselves in attempts to regain moral self-worth and other people's approval after a moral transgression. Indeed, in a seminal study, people who had recalled past unethical deeds (vs. neutral events) found cleansing products and antiseptic wipes especially appealing (Zhong & Liljenquist, 2006), a finding referred to as the "Macbeth effect." This tendency to physically wash away one's sins has been replicated in several different contexts (de Zavala, Waldzus, & Cypryanska, 2014; Denke, Rotte, Heinze, & Schaefer, 2014; Gollwitzer & Melzer, 2012; Lee & Schwarz, 2010; for a review, see West & Zhong, 2015).

In the same vein, participants who had their moral standing called into question by either an unethical recall or exposure to another person's superior moral standing did not feel as threatened or regretful when this was associated with a physical cleansing intervention (Cramwinckel, van Dijk, Scheepers, & van den Bos, 2013; Lee, Tang, Wan, Mai, & Liu, 2015; Reuven, Liberman, & Dar, 2014; Xu, Bègue, & Bushman, 2014). Physically cleansing the surface of one's body thus alleviates the distressing consequences of unethical behavior, such as feelings of guilt, as well as threats to one's moral self-image. Given that people intuitively make more positive judgments of those who look "clean" and less likely to transmit pathogens, this physical cleansing intervention possibly helps in regaining others' approval. In other words, it prepares the individual to reengage with others in a physical and moral sense.

When individuals engage with others in a positive fashion, this connection is often translated into physical proximity, making individuals more vulnerable to transmitted pathogens. It makes sense, therefore, that humans would be selective of whom they approach and whom they allow to approach. Of special importance to this chapter, these decisions to either physically avoid or approach others seem to be related to judgments of moral character. Social grooming, for example, which involves direct contact with skin flakes and debris of others, is more frequent among psychologically close individuals who also share material resources such as food (Dunbar, 2010; Roubová, Konečná, Šmilauer, & Wallner, 2015; see also Schnall, 2011).

Whereas watching others being selfish invokes repulsion and a desire to physically distance oneself from the target, witnessing someone giving away their resources to others triggers strong approach tendencies. Feelings of gratitude induced by being the recipient of someone else's intentionally directed benefit create a desire to physically approach the person who provided the benefit (Hertenstein, Keltner, App, Bulleit, & Jaskolka, 2006; McCullough, Kilpatrick, Emmons, & Larson, 2001). Witnessing uncommon expressions of selflessness directed to third parties renders similar effects. Critically, breastfeeding mothers who had watched a moving video clip about a selfless character were more likely to hug and nurse their babies compared with mothers who had watched a comedy (Silvers & Haidt, 2008). These examples suggest that witnessing other people's expressions of virtue toward the self or others motivate individuals to physically connect their bodies to other people's bodies.

Tactile contact, in turn, redefines psychological boundaries and shapes sociomoral relationships. Several studies have shown, for example, that even light and brief tactile contacts (e.g., a pat on the back) between adults increases compliance and helping behavior, such as giving back a dime left in a phone booth (Brockner, Pressman, Cabitt, & Moran, 1982; Guéguen, 2004; Hornik, 1987; Hornik & Ellis, 1988; Willis & Hamm, 1980). This suggests that physically uniting the surfaces of one's body to another's leads to a greater willingness to share material resources with others. A soft touch on the back can also shift people's social judgments. Participants who were touched on the back by the clerks while checking out books at the library attributed more positive traits (e.g., "helpful") to the library personnel than they did when no contact had occurred (Fisher, Rytting, & Heslin, 1976). Similar effects of touch on person perception have been observed in several other contexts (Erceau & Guéguen, 2007; Hornik, 1992; Steward & Lupfer, 1987), including interpersonal attraction and courtship (Guéguen, 2007, 2010).

Touch is our first sense to develop, and the skin is arguably our most basic means of contact with the external world (Field, 2014). Babies depend on long and sustained bodily contact with the mother for survival, including locomotion, regulation of body temperature, and nursing. It is thus unsurprising that touch develops as a crucial signal of trust and security and prepares individuals to establish cooperative alliances.

Beyond touch, actually incorporating other people's bodily substances into one's own bodily envelope is a strong cue for subjective intimacy (Fiske, 2004). For instance, adult pairs eating together are perceived as more intimate, close, and attracted to each other when the context involves feeding and potential transfer of germs compared to when such contact is absent (Alley, 2012; Miller, Rozin, & Fiske, 1998). At a group level, exchanges of food and communal feasts signal alliance, solidarity, and group membership (Johnson, White, Boyd, & Cohen, 2011; Rozin, 1990). Sharing personal objects, such as pieces of clothing and toothbrushes (Brooks, Dai, & Schweitzer, 2014; Curtis et al., 2004; Gentina, 2014; Miller et al., 1998), also constitutes bonds of trust between non-kin. In accordance with an embodied cognitive approach, these examples suggest that physical processes relevant to the purity of the body create an ontological scaffold for the development of morally relevant behavior and judgments.

In sum, this section provides evidence that psychological systems designed to keep one's body clean and regulating physical proximity to others also define boundaries in the moral domain. First, physical cleanliness is used as a cue to judge who is a friend and who is a foe (e.g., Stewart, 1985) and affects our own sense of moral worth (Cramwinckel et al., 2013; Lee et al., 2015). Second, acts that actively promote physical purity are often moralized and have the abstract status of virtue conferred upon them (Haidt & Graham, 2006; Haidt & Joseph, 2007). Third, the process of sharing material and psychological resources with others is connected to the blur of physical bodily boundaries, for example, through touch or the sharing of bodily substances (Alley, 2012; Hertenstein et al., 2006). Therefore, processes of the physical body related to cleanliness and proximity to others are directly relevant to social judgments and morally relevant behavior.

Extension and Expansion

There are several provocative implications of this embodied morality approach. We present evidence that practices that promote or potentially taint the physical purity of the body are given the abstract status of "moral" or "immoral," including excessive food ingestion, suicide, and incest. The moralization of such acts means that implicit processes that arise from a highly sensitive behavioral system of defense against body injury and contamination are implicated in real-life moral decisions. Similar processes probably ground moral opinions about many other contemporary human practices that relate to the body, including prostitution, organ trading, abortion, surrogacy, and many others. When actual interpersonal harm is absent, are feelings of disgust and aversion valid bases for the legal regulation of these actions? How are these intuitive processes functionally connected to conscious deliberation and analysis?

We further present evidence that the extent to which one's own body is clean or dirty, physically strong or vulnerable, predicts how one interacts with and evaluates others. It predicts not only whether individuals behave in a sociable and extroverted fashion but also their attitudes toward obese people, homosexuals, people with disabilities, immigrants, and many other groups. These findings elegantly demonstrate that moral judgments are rooted in people's bodies and that the rationale behind these judgments is not always available to conscious consideration. Critically, they weaken the certainty we strive for in making relevant moral decisions and point to the importance of acknowledging and understanding the influence of such implicit processes in moral decisions that affect the lives of many.

Human morality concerns abstract ideas about what is wrong and evil, right and commendable. It is also about regulating our personal relationships with others (Rai & Fiske, 2011), and distinguishing friends from foes (Hamlin, 2014). Finally, it is about making decisions on what personal resources to give away, when, and to whom (Eisenberg et al., 2006; Tomasello & Vaish, 2013; Warneken & Tomasello, 2009). This moral system sustains the formation of successful alliances and the cooperation required for sustainable group living. Nonetheless, one must not forget that humans navigate the social sphere in concrete, material bodies and that moral decisions often result in approaching or avoiding others in a physical sense. It is, therefore, hardly surprising that a complex system dedicated to regulating the physical boundaries and purity of the body implicitly unfolds while we make abstract decisions about other people and the consequences of their actions. As Merleau-Ponty (1962, p. 146) pointed out, "the body is our general medium for having a world," and, as demonstrated, it is through the body that we make judgments and act in the moral world we share with others.

REFERENCES

Alley, T. R. (2012). Contaminated and uncontaminated feeding influence perceived intimacy in mixed-sex dyads. *Appetite, 58,* 1041–1045.

Astuti, R., & Bloch, M. (2015). The causal cognition of wrong doing: Incest, intentionality, and morality. *Frontiers in Psychology, 6.*

Aunger, R., Schmidt, W.-P., Ranpura, A., Coombes, Y., Maina, P. M., Matiko, C. N., & Curtis, V. (2010). Three kinds of psychological determinants for hand-washing behaviour in Kenya. *Social Science and Medicine, 70,* 383–391.

Barsalou, L. W., & Wiemer-Hastings, K. (2005). Situating abstract concepts. In D. Pecher & R. Zwaan (Eds.), *Grounding cognition: The role of perception and action in memory, language, and thought* (pp. 129–163). New York: Cambridge University Press.

Bonini, N., Hadjichristidis, C., Mazzocco, K., Demattè, M. L., Zampini, M., Sbarbati, A., & Magon, S. (2011). Pecunia olet: The role of incidental disgust in the ultimatum game. *Emotion, 11,* 965–969.

Borg, J. S., Lieberman, D., & Kiehl, K. A. (2008). Infection, incest, and iniquity: Investigating the neural correlates of disgust and morality. *Journal of Cognitive Neuroscience, 20,* 1529–1546.

Brockner, J., Pressman, B., Cabitt, J., & Moran, P. (1982). Nonverbal intimacy, sex, and compliance: A field study. *Journal of Nonverbal Behavior, 6,* 253–258.

Brooks, A. W., Dai, H., & Schweitzer, M. E. (2014). I'm sorry about the rain!: Superfluous apologies demonstrate empathic concern and increase trust. *Social Psychological and Personality Science, 5,* 467–474.

Buss, D. M. (1988). The evolution of human intrasexual competition: Tactics of mate attraction. *Journal of Personality and Social Psychology, 54,* 616–628.

Cannon, P. R., Schnall, S., & White, M. (2011). Transgressions and expressions: Affective facial muscle activity predicts moral judgments. *Social Psychological and Personality Science, 2,* 325–331.

Chakroff, A., Dungan, J., & Young, L. (2013). Harming ourselves and defiling others: What determines a moral domain? *PLOS ONE, 8,* e74434.

Chapman, H. A., & Anderson, A. K. (2014). Trait physical disgust is related to moral judgments outside of the purity domain. *Emotion, 14,* 341–348.

Chapman, H. A., Kim, D. A., Susskind, J. M., & Anderson, A. K. (2009). In bad taste: Evidence for the oral origins of moral disgust. *Science, 323,* 1222–1226.

Cramwinckel, F. M., van Dijk, E., Scheepers, D., & van den Bos, K. (2013). The threat of moral refusers for one's self-concept and the protective function of physical cleansing. *Journal of Experimental Social Psychology, 49,* 1049–1058.

Curtis, V. (2003). Talking dirty: How to save a million lives. *International Journal of Environmental Health Research, 13,* S73–S79.

Curtis, V., Aunger, R., & Rabie, T. (2004). Evidence that disgust evolved to protect from risk of disease. *Proceedings: Biological Sciences (Biology Letters), 277,* 131–133.

Curtis, V., & Biran, A. (2001). Dirt, disgust, and disease: Is hygiene in our genes? *Perspectives in Biology and Medicine, 44,* 17–31.

Curtis, V., de Barra, M., & Aunger, R. (2011). Disgust as an adaptive system for disease avoidance behaviour. *Philosophical Transactions of the Royal Society of London: Series B. Biological Sciences, 366,* 389–401.

Damasio, A. R. (1994). *Descartes' error: Emotion, rationality and the human brain.* New York: Putnam.

Danovitch, J., & Bloom, P. (2009). Children's extension of disgust to physical and moral events. *Emotion, 9,* 107–112.

de Lange, M. A., Debets, L. W., Ruitenburg, K., & Holland, R. W. (2012). Making less of a mess: Scent exposure as a tool for behavioral change. *Social Influence, 7,* 90–97.

de Zavala, A., Waldzus, S., & Cypryanska, M. (2014). Prejudice towards gay men and a need for physical cleansing. *Journal of Experimental Social Psychology, 54,* 1–10.

Denke, C., Rotte, M., Heinze, H.-J., & Schaefer, M. (2014). Lying and the subsequent desire for toothpaste: Activity in the somatosensory cortex predicts embodiment of the moral-purity metaphor. *Cerebral Cortex, 26,* 477–484.

Dunbar, R. I. M. (2010). The social role of touch in humans and primates: Behavioural function and neurobiological mechanisms. *Neuroscience and Biobehavioral Reviews, 34,* 260–268.

Duncan, L. A., Schaller, M., & Park, J. H. (2009). Perceived vulnerability to disease: Development and validation of a 15-item self-report instrument. *Personality and Individual Differences, 47,* 541–546.

Durkheim, E. (1912). *The elementary forms of religious life.* New York: Free Press.

Eisenberg, N., Fabes, R. A., & Spinrad, T. (2006). Prosocial development. In N. Eisenberg (Ed.), *Handbook of child psychology: Social, emotional, and personality development* (pp. 646–718). Hoboken, NJ: Wiley.

Erceau, D., & Guéguen, N. (2007). Tactile contact and evaluation of the toucher. *Journal of Social Psychology, 147,* 441–444.

Eskine, K. J., Kacinik, N. A., & Prinz, J. (2011). A bad taste in the mouth: Gustatory disgust influences moral judgment. *Psychological Science, 22,* 295–299.

Faulkner, J., Schaller, M., Park, J. H., & Duncan, L. A. (2004). Evolved disease-avoidance mechanisms and contemporary xenophobic attitudes. *Group Processes and Intergroup Relations, 7,* 333–353.

Field, T. (2014). *Touch.* Cambridge, MA: MIT Press.

Fisher, J. D., Rytting, M., & Heslin, R. (1976). Hands touching hands: Affective and evaluative effects of an interpersonal touch. *Sociometry, 39,* 416–421.

Fiske, A. P. (2004). Four modes of constituting relationships: Consubstantial assimilation; space, magnitude, time, and force; concrete procedures; abstract symbolism. In N. Haslam (Ed.), *Relational models theory: A contemporary overview* (pp. 61–146). Mahwah, NJ: Erlbaum.

Gallace, A., & Spence, C. (2010). The science of interpersonal touch: An overview. *Neuroscience and Biobehavioral Reviews, 34,* 246–259.

Gentina, E. (2014). Understanding the effects of adolescent girls' social positions within peer groups on exchange practices. *Journal of Consumer Behaviour, 13,* 73–80.

Giner-Sorolla, R., Bosson, J. K., Caswell, T. A., & Hettinger, V. E. (2012). Emotions in sexual morality: Testing the separate elicitors of anger and disgust. *Cognition and Emotion, 26,* 1208–1222.

Gollwitzer, M., & Melzer, A. (2012). Macbeth and the joystick: Evidence for moral cleansing after playing a violent video game. *Journal of Experimental Social Psychology, 48,* 1356–1360.

Graham, J., Haidt, J., & Nosek, B. (2009). Liberals and conservatives use different sets of moral fondations. *Journal of Personality and Social Psychology, 96,* 1029–1046.

Guéguen, N. (2004). Nonverbal encouragement of participation in a course: The effect of touching. *Social Psychology of Education, 7,* 89–98.

Guéguen, N. (2007). Courtship compliance: The effect of touch on women's behavior. *Social Influence, 2,* 81–97.

Guéguen, N. (2010). The effect of a woman's incidental tactile contact on men's later behavior. *Social Behavior and Personality: An International Journal, 38,* 257–266.

Gutierrez, R., & Giner-Sorolla, R. (2007). Anger, disgust, and presumption of harm as reactions to taboo-breaking behaviors. *Emotion, 7,* 853–868.

Haidt, J. (2001). The emotional dog and its rational tail: A social intuitionist approach to moral judgment. *Psychological Review, 108,* 814–834.

Haidt, J., Bjorklund, F., & Murphy, S. (2000). *Moral dumbfounding: When intuition finds no reason.* Unpublished manuscript.

Haidt, J., & Graham, J. (2006). Planet of the Durkheimians, where community, authority, and sacredness are foundations of morality. In J. Jost, A. C. Kay, & H. Thorisdotti (Eds.), *Social and psychological bases of ideology and system justification* (pp. 371–401). New York: Oxford University Press.

Haidt, J., & Hersh, M. A. (2001). Sexual morality: The cultures and emotions of conservatives and liberals. *Journal of Applied Social Psychology, 31,* 191–221.

Haidt, J., & Joseph, C. (2007). The moral mind: How 5 sets of innate intuitions guide the development of many culture-specific virtues, and perhaps even modules. In P. Carruthers, S. Laurence, & S. Stich (Eds.), *The innate mind* (pp. 367–391). New York: Oxford University Press.

Haidt, J., Koller, S. H., & Dias, M. G. (1993). Affect, culture, and morality, or is it wrong to eat your dog? *Journal of Personality and Social Psychology, 65,* 613–628.

Hamlin, J. K. (2014). The origins of human morality: Complex socio-moral evaluations by preverbal infants. In J. Decety & Y. Christen (Eds.), *New frontiers in social neuroscience* (pp. 165–188). New York: Springer.

Harlé, K. M., & Sanfey, A. G. (2010). Effects of approach and withdrawal motivation on interactive economic decisions. *Cognition and Emotion, 24,* 1456–1465.

Hertenstein, M. J., Keltner, D., App, B., Bulleit, B. A., & Jaskolka, A. R. (2006). Touch communicates distinct emotions. *Emotion, 6,* 528–533.

Horberg, E. J., Oveis, C., Keltner, D., & Cohen,

A. B. (2009). Disgust and the moralization of purity. *Journal of Personality and Social Psychology, 97*, 963–976.

Hornik, J. (1987). The effect of touch and gaze upon compliance and interest of interviewees. *Journal of Social Psychology, 127*, 681–683.

Hornik, J. (1992). Tactile stimulation and consumer response. *Journal of Consumer Research, 19*, 449–458.

Hornik, J., & Ellis, S. (1988). Strategies to secure compliance for a mall intercept interview. *Public Opinion Quarterly, 52*, 539–551.

Huang, J. L. (2014). Does cleanliness influence moral judgments?: Response effort moderates the effect of cleanliness priming on moral judgments. *Frontiers in Psychology, 5*, 1276.

Hume, D. (1960). *An enquiry concerning the principles of morals*. La Salle, IL: Open Court. (Original work published 1777).

Hutchins, E. (1995). *Cognition in the wild*. Cambridge, MA: MIT Press.

Inbar, Y., & Pizarro, D. A. (2014). Pollution and purity in moral and political judgment. In J. Wright & H. Sarkissian (Eds.), *Advances in experimental moral psychology* (pp. 112–129). London: Bloosmbury Academic.

Johnson, K. A., White, A. E., Boyd, B. M., & Cohen, A. B. (2011). Matzah, meat, milk, and mana: Psychological influences on religio-cultural food practices. *Journal of Cross-Cultural Psychology, 42*, 1421–1436.

Kohlberg, L., Levine, C., & Hewer, A. (1983). *Moral stages: A current formulation and a response to critics*. Basel, Switzerland: Karger.

Kupfer, T. R., & Tybur, J. M. (2017). Pathogen disgust and interpersonal personality. *Personality and Individual Differences, 116*, 379–384.

Lakoff, G., & Johnson, M. (1980). *Metaphors we live by*. Chicago: Chicago University Press.

Lakoff, G., & Johnson, M. (1999). *Philosophy in the flesh: The embodied mind and its challenge to Western thought*. New York: Basic Books.

Landau, M. J., Meier, B. P., & Keefer, L. A. (2010). A metaphor-enriched social cognition. *Psychological Bulletin, 136*, 1045–1067.

Lee, S. W. S., & Schwarz, N. (2010). Dirty hands and dirty mouths: Embodiment of the moral-purity metaphor is specific to the motor modality involved in moral transgression. *Psychological Science, 21*, 1423–1425.

Lee, S. W. S., Tang, H., Wan, J., Mai, X., & Liu, C. (2015). A cultural look at moral purity: Wiping the face clean. *Frontiers in Psychology, 6*.

Liljenquist, K., Zhong, C.-B., & Galinsky, A. D. (2010). The smell of virtue: Clean scents promote reciprocity and charity. *Psychological Science, 21*, 381–383.

Lim, J., Ho, P. M., & Mullette-Gillman, O. A. (2015). Modulation of incentivized dishonesty by disgust facial expressions. *Frontiers in Neuroscience, 9*, 250.

McCullough, M. E., Kilpatrick, S. D., Emmons, R. A., & Larson, D. B. (2001). Is gratitude a moral affect? *Psychological Bulletin, 127*, 249–266.

Meier, B. P., Schnall, S., Schwarz, N., & Bargh, J. A. (2012). Embodiment in social psychology. *Topics in Cognitive Science, 4*, 705–716.

Merleau-Ponty, M. (1962). *Phenomenology of perception*. London: Routledge.

Merleau-Ponty, M. (1964). *The primacy of perception: and other essays on phenomenological psychology, the philosophy of art, history and politics*. Evanston, IL: Northwestern University Press.

Miller, L., Rozin, P., & Fiske, A. P. (1998). Food sharing and feeding another person suggest intimacy: Two studies of American college students. *European Journal of Social Psychology, 28*, 423–436.

Moretti, L., & di Pellegrino, G. (2010). Disgust selectively modulates reciprocal fairness in economic interactions. *Emotion, 10*, 169–180.

Mortensen, C. R., Becker, D. V., Ackerman, J. M., Neuberg, S. L., & Kenrick, D. T. (2010). Infection breeds reticence: The effects of disease salience on self-perceptions of personality and behavioral avoidance tendencies. *Psychological Science, 21*, 440–447.

Murray, D. R., & Schaller, M. (2016). The behavioral immune system: Implications for social cognition, social interaction, and social influence. *Advances in Experimental Social Psychology, 53*, 75–129.

Navarrete, C. D., Fessler, D. M. T., & Eng, S. J. (2007). Elevated ethnocentrism in the first trimester of pregnancy. *Evolution and Human Behavior, 28*, 60–65.

Nemeroff, C., & Rozin, P. (1994). The contagion concept in adult thinking in the United States: Transmission of germs and of interpersonal influence. *Ethos, 22*, 158–186.

Newman, G. E., Diesendruck, G., & Bloom, P. (2011). Celebrity contagion and the value of objects. *Journal of Consumer Research, 38*, 215–228.

Nichols, S. (2004). *Sentimental rules: On the natural foundations of moral judgment*. New York: Oxford University Press.

Niedenthal, P. M., Barsalou, L. W., Winkielman, P., Krauth-Gruber, S., & Ric, F. (2005). Embodiment in attitudes, social perception, and emotion. *Personality and Social Psychology Review, 9*, 184–211.

Nucci, L. P., & Turiel, E. (1978). Social interactions and the development of social concepts in preschool children. *Child Development, 49*, 400–407.

Paladino, M.-P., Mazzurega, M., Pavani, F., & Schubert, T. W. (2010). Synchronous multisensory stimulation blurs self–other boundaries. *Psychological Science, 21,* 1202–1207.

Park, J. H., Faulkner, J., & Schaller, M. (2003). Evolved disease-avoidance processes and contemporary anti-social behavior: Prejudicial attitudes and avoidance of people with physical disabilities. *Journal of Nonverbal Behavior, 27,* 65–87.

Park, J. H., Schaller, M., & Crandall, C. S. (2007). Pathogen-avoidance mechanisms and the stigmatization of obese people. *Evolution and Human Behavior, 28,* 410–414.

Parkinson, C., Sinnott-Armstrong, W., Koralus, P. E., Mendelovici, A., McGeer, V., & Wheatley, T. (2011). Is morality unified?: Evidence that distinct neural systems underlie moral judgments of harm, dishonesty, and disgust. *Journal of Cognitive Neuroscience, 23,* 3162–3180.

Prinz, J. (2002). *Furnishing the mind.* Cambridge, MA: MIT Press.

Prinz, J. (2007). *The emotional construction of morals.* New York: Oxford University Press.

Rai, T. S., & Fiske, A. P. (2011). Moral psychology is relationship regulation: Moral motives for unity, hierarchy, equality, and proportionality. *Psychological Review, 118,* 57–75.

Reuven, O., Liberman, N., & Dar, R. (2014). The effect of physical cleaning on threatened morality in individuals with obsessive–compulsive disorder. *Clinical Psychological Science, 2,* 224–229.

Rosenstein, D., & Oster, H. (1988). Differential facial responses to four basic tastes in newborns. *Child Development, 59,* 1555–1568.

Rottman, J., & Kelemen, D. (2012). Aliens behaving badly: Children's acquisition of novel purity-based morals. *Cognition, 124,* 356–360.

Rottman, J., Kelemen, D., & Young, L. (2014a). Purity matters more than harm in moral judgments of suicide: Response to Gray (2014). *Cognition, 133,* 332–334.

Rottman, J., Kelemen, D., & Young, L. (2014b). Tainting the soul: Purity concerns predict moral judgments of suicide. *Cognition, 130,* 217–226.

Roubová, V., Konečná, M., Šmilauer, P., & Wallner, B. (2015). Whom to groom and for what?: Patterns of grooming in female Barbary macaques (Macaca sylvanus). *PLOS ONE, 10,* e0117298.

Rozin, P. (1990). Social and moral aspects of food and eating. In I. Rock (Ed.), *The legacy of Solomon Asch: Essays in cognition and social psychology* (pp. 97–110). New York: Psychology Press.

Rozin, P., Lowery, L., & Ebert, R. (1994). Varieties of disgust faces and the structure of disgust. *Journal of Personality and Social Psychology, 66,* 870–881.

Rozin, P., Lowery, L., Imada, S., & Haidt, J. (1999). The CAD triad hypothesis: A mapping between three moral emotions (contempt, anger, disgust) and three moral codes (community, autonomy, divinity). *Journal of Personality and Social Psychology, 76,* 574–586.

Rozin, P., & Singh, L. (1999). The moralization of cigarette smoking in the United States. *Journal of Consumer Psychology, 8,* 321–337.

Russell, P. S., & Giner-Sorolla, R. (2011a). Moral anger is more flexible than moral disgust. *Social Psychological and Personality Science, 2,* 360–364.

Russell, P. S., & Giner-Sorolla, R. (2011b). Moral anger, but not moral disgust, responds to intentionality. *Emotion, 11,* 233–240.

Russell, P. S., & Giner-Sorolla, R. (2011c). Social justifications for moral emotions: When reasons for disgust are less elaborated than for anger. *Emotion, 11,* 637–646.

Schaller, M., Miller, G. E., Gervais, W. M., Yager, S., & Chen, E. (2010). Mere visual perception of other people's disease symptoms facilitates a more aggressive immune response. *Psychological Science, 21,* 649–652.

Schaller, M., & Murray, D. R. (2008). Pathogens, personality, and culture: Disease prevalence predicts worldwide variability in sociosexuality, extraversion, and openness to experience. *Journal of Personality and Social Psychology, 95,* 212–221.

Schaller, M., & Park, J. H. (2011). The behavioral immune system (and why it matters). *Current Directions in Psychological Science, 20,* 99–103.

Scheske, C., & Schnall, S. (2012). The ethics of "smart drugs": Moral judgments about healthy people's use of cognitive-enhancing drugs. *Basic and Applied Social Psychology, 34,* 508–515.

Schnall, S. (2011). Clean, proper and tidy are more than the absence of dirty, disgusting and wrong. *Emotion Review, 3,* 264–266.

Schnall, S. (2017). Disgust as embodied loss aversion. *European Review of Social Psychology, 28,* 50–94.

Schnall, S., Benton, J., & Harvey, S. (2008). With a clean conscience: Cleanliness reduces the severity of moral judgments. *Psychological Science, 19,* 1219–1222.

Schnall, S., Haidt, J., Clore, G. L., & Jordan, A. H. (2008). Disgust as embodied moral judgment. *Personality and Social Psychology Bulletin, 34,* 1096–1109.

Schwarz, N. (2000). Emotion, cognition, and

decision making. *Cognition and Emotion, 14,* 433–440.

Seidel, A., & Prinz, J. (2013). Sound morality: Irritating and icky noises amplify judgments in divergent moral domains. *Cognition, 127,* 1–5.

Seiter, J. S., Weger, H., Merrill, M. L., McKenna, M. R., & Sanders, M. L. (2010). Nonsmokers' perceptions of cigarette smokers' credibility, likeability, attractiveness, considerateness, cleanliness, and healthiness. *Communication Research Reports, 27,* 143–158.

Sheikh, S., Botindari, L., & White, E. (2013). Embodied metaphors and emotions in the moralization of restrained eating practices. *Journal of Experimental Social Psychology, 49,* 509–513.

Silvers, J. A., & Haidt, J. (2008). Moral elevation can induce nursing. *Emotion, 8,* 291–295.

Smith, E. R., & Semin, G. R. (2004). Socially situated cognition: Cognition in its social context. *Advances in Experimental Social Psychology, 36,* 53–117.

Stephan, S. (2016). *Rational suicide, irrational laws: Examining current approaches to suicide in policy and law.* New York: Oxford University Press.

Stevenson, R. J., Oaten, M. J., Case, T. I., Repacholi, B. M., & Wagland, P. (2010). Children's response to adult disgust elicitors: Development and acquisition. *Developmental Psychology, 46,* 165–177.

Steward, A. L., & Lupfer, M. (1987). Touching as teaching: The effect of touch on students' perceptions and performance. *Journal of Applied Social Psychology, 17,* 800–809.

Stewart, J. E. (1985). Appearance and punishment: The attraction-leniency effect in the courtroom. *Journal of Social Psychology, 125,* 373–378.

Tomasello, M., & Vaish, A. (2013). Origins of human cooperation and morality. *Annual Review of Psychology, 64,* 231–255.

Tybur, J. M., Lieberman, D., Kurzban, R., & DeScioli, P. (2013). Disgust: Evolved function and structure. *Psychological Review, 120,* 65–84.

Vohs, K. D., Redden, J. P., & Rahinel, R. (2013). Physical order produces healthy choices, generosity, and conventionality, whereas disorder produces creativity. *Psychological Science, 24,* 1860–1867.

Warneken, F., & Tomasello, M. (2009). Varieties of altruism in children and chimpanzees. *Trends in Cognitive Sciences, 13,* 397–402.

West, C., & Zhong, C.-B. (2015). Moral cleansing. *Current Opinions in Psychology, 6,* 221–225.

Wheatley, T., & Haidt, J. (2005). Hypnotic disgust makes moral judgments more severe. *Psychological Science, 16,* 780–784.

Willis, F. N., & Hamm, H. K. (1980). The use of interpersonal touch in securing compliance. *Journal of Nonverbal Behavior, 5,* 49–55.

Winterich, K. P., Mittal, V., & Morales, A. C. (2014). Protect thyself: How affective self-protection increases self-interested, unethical behavior. *Organizational Behavior and Human Decision Processes, 125,* 151–161.

Xu, H., Bègue, L., & Bushman, B. J. (2014). Washing the guilt away: Effects of personal versus vicarious cleansing on guilty feelings and prosocial behavior. *Frontiers in Human Neuroscience, 8,* 97.

Young, L., & Tsoi, L. (2013). When mental states matter, when they don't, and what that means for morality. *Social and Personality Psychology Compass, 7,* 585–604.

Zhong, C.-B., & Liljenquist, K. (2006). Washing away your sins: Threatened morality and physical cleansing. *Science, 313,* 1451–1452.

CHAPTER 30

Grounded Morality

Simon M. Laham
Justin J. Kelly

What is the nature of moral psychological processing?

Grounded approaches suggest that a full understanding of moral phenomena must consider the way that mental representations and psychological processes are shaped by the physical bodies and environments in which they operate.

Moral phenomena, from moral concepts to psychological processes (such as moral perception or categorization) to moral judgments, decisions, and behaviors can only be fully understood by taking a *grounded approach to moral psychology*. Grounded approaches can be thought of as broad frameworks that take seriously the fact that psychological concepts, processes, and outputs are (at least partially) shaped by the way our physical bodies interact with the world. In contrast to classical accounts of cognition as computation over amodal representations, grounded accounts conceive of cognition as multimodal simulation and emphasize the role of bodily states and the body–environment nexus in thinking and feeling (see Barsalou, 2008, for a review).

The term *grounded cognition* (sometimes *embodied cognition*) is ambiguous (Goldman & de Vignemont, 2009; Wilson, 2002); we focus here on three senses of the term. First, we hold that moral concepts (such as justice and goodness) are *metaphorically*

structured; second, that moral psychological processes (such as moral perception and judgment) are at least partially informed by *afferent feedback from the body*; and, third, that moral phenomena are best studied and conceptualized with reference to the temporal, spatial, and social contexts in which they are *embedded* or *situated*. Thus moral cognition is best conceived of as being metaphorically structured, embodied, and embedded.

The implications of such assumptions are manifold and require new conceptual, theoretical, and empirical approaches to the study of moral psychology. Although such considerations are unlikely to be *sufficient* for a comprehensive account of the psychology of morality, they are certainly *necessary*.

Historical Context

Grounded approaches are usually best understood in contrast to standard or classical accounts of cognition. The central assumption of *classical accounts* is that thinking is information processing—computations performed over amodal mental representations. Such representations are abstract, often quasi-linguistic symbols that bear no intrinsic relationships to the physical or functional features of their referents. This view of cognition came to prominence with the cognitive revolution, during which the computer metaphor of mind and functionalism justified a psychology in which the software of the mind was deemed largely independent of the hardware of the body (see Gardner, 1985, for a historical account of the cognitive revolution).

In stark contrast to classical accounts, grounded approaches seek to put the mind and body back together (see Barsalou, 2008; Glenberg, 2010; Niedenthal, Barsalou, Winkielman, Krauth-Gruber, & Ric, 2005, for reviews). One common feature of grounded approaches (of which there are a variety) is that they conceive of thought as involving modal representations. These are representations utilized by specific modal systems (e.g., perceptual, motor, introspective) and are thought to retain something of the physical and functional features of their referents (see Goldman & de Vignemont, 2009). On this account, concepts (even abstract concepts) are *multimodal* (not amodal) representations, and thinking is simulation—offline reenactment of sensory and motor experience.

Such approaches have garnered increased attention in psychology of late, but they are not all that new in the history of thought. Grounded accounts of the mind have deep historical roots in the Western philosophical tradition. The views of the ancients were distinctly grounded, holding knowledge to be represented modally and via imagery (see Barsalou, 1999). The British empiricists, too, endorsed philosophies of mind similar to contemporary theories of grounded cognition (see Boroditsky & Prinz, 2008). Even within psychology, early conceptions of mental constructs had a distinctly grounded flavor. Galton (1884), for example, defined attitudes in terms of body posture, and Darwin (1872/1904) similarly featured posture and other motor responses in his definition of the construct. Early accounts of attitudes

in social psychology also had a distinctly embodied flavor, emphasizing the role of action in attitude acquisition and processing (Allport, 1935).

In contemporary cognitive science, a wide variety of theories fall under the umbrella of *grounded cognition*. Some emphasize metaphors as the building blocks of abstract concepts (e.g., Lakoff & Johnson, 1980), others posit simulation and reenactment as constitutive of thought (e.g., Barsalou, 1999), and yet others stress the situated, contextual constraints on cognitive processes (e.g., Smith & Semin, 2007). Although such varied accounts share some features, they differ on others (see Wilson, 2002, for a review). As such, there is no single theory of grounded cognition. Rather, these varied efforts are best thought of as specific theoretical instantiations of a general framework that holds that the functions performed by the brain can only fully be understood if we appreciate the facts that (1) bodies house brains and (2) bodies interact with particular social–spatial–temporal environments. In what follows, we argue that moral psychology would benefit from appreciating these facts.

Theoretical Stance

In light of these basic properties of grounded approaches, the three senses of *grounded* we note above are worth explicating here, with particular reference to moral psychology. These concepts are introduced here but are not fully explored until the following section.

Certain theories of grounded cognition suggest that abstract concepts, including moral concepts such as goodness, justice, and divinity, which do not have any obvious sensory or motor features, can nevertheless be accommodated within a multimodal representational system because they are *metaphorically grounded* in the concrete world of sense and action (see Landau, Meier, & Keefer, 2010, for a review). Conceptual metaphor theory (Lakoff & Johnson, 1980), for example, states that abstract concepts are understood via analogical extensions of sensory and motor experience. Our experience with the everyday physical world—the world of spatial relations, temperature, weight, direction, size—forms the basis of our understanding of more abstract, non-physical elements of our moral worlds. Properties of these physical source domains (and relations among such properties) are extended to abstract target domains. *Divinity*, for example, is spatially *up* (Meier, Hauser, Robinson, Friesen, & Schjeldahl, 2007), as is *moral* (Meier, Sellbom, & Wygant, 2007), whereas *bad* and *immoral* are *down* (Meier & Robinson, 2004). Importantly, on many grounded cognition accounts, thinking about goodness and badness involves (among other things) the reenactment of the sensory and motor experiences involved with spatial verticality. Abstract concepts are thus grounded in our sensory and motor experiences of the world.

A related implication of some grounded approaches is that moral cognition—which involves reenactment of sensory–motor experiences related to the source domains of abstract moral concepts—will be influenced by afferent feedback from the body. To the extent that modality-specific motor representations partly constitute moral concepts, engaging in certain actions (or covertly simulating them) is likely to play a causal role in moral thought. If *goodness* is partly constituted by motor representations of *up*, then engaging in physical, upward movements, for example, should potentiate the goodness concept. Moral cognition is thus *embodied* to the extent that body-related mental representations (pertaining to morphology, posture, and action) are causally implicated in cognitive processing. Action (and action representation) is not simply an output of a cognitive process but a causal component of the process itself.

Research on embodied attitudes is illustrative of this point. Work on the affective compatibility effect shows that behavioral responses to valenced stimuli are facilitated when there is a match between the valence of a stimulus and the valence of the response (see Laham, Kashima, Dix, & Wheeler, 2015, for a review). Arm flexion, for example (when framed as approach), is facilitated in response to positive stimuli, and arm extension (when framed as avoidance) is facilitated in response to negative stimuli. According to grounded cognition accounts, the mental representation of a favored attitude object is partly constituted by motor representations of actions typically performed on the object (e.g., pulling toward the self). Thus, activating a representation of the object involves the motor representation of pulling, which facilitates the overt pulling response. In a similar way, to the extent that *moral* attitude objects are processed using multimodal representations partly constituted by motor representations, the performance of certain actions during moral stimulus processing may influence moral cognition and moral judgment.

On the third sense of *grounded* that we are using here, moral cognition is *embedded* (or situated) to the extent that it depends upon the social–physical environment in which it takes place. This is not a new idea for social psychologists (see Meier, Schnall, Schwarz & Bargh, 2012; Smith & Semin, 2007), but the centrality of context seems to have been overlooked in much moral psychological theorizing. Moral thought and its outputs are malleable and sensitive to contextual cues. And although moral psychology is replete with examples of the context sensitivity of moral judgments (see Sinnott-Armstrong, 2008, and below for reviews), most researchers do not treat such effects as integral to their theories but rather as noise that masks more stable moral preferences (cf., Rai & Fiske, 2011).

Taken together, these three senses of *grounded* suggest theorizing in moral psychology that (1) treats abstract moral concepts as metaphorically structured, (at least partially) grounded in concrete source domains; (2) holds that moral cognition is influenced by afferent bodily feedback; and (3) builds the context-sensitivity of moral cognition, judgment, and behavior into the bedrock of theory.

Such theorizing is not prevalent in moral psychology. The majority of extant accounts in the domain either implicitly or explicitly draw on classical cognition or are ambiguous on the nature of the representations and processes implicated in moral phenomena. Haidt's social intuitionist model (Haidt, 2001), for example, posits roles for intuitive and deliberative processes in moral judgment and emphasizes "gut reactions" (which may very well be realized in multimodal representations), but the nature of these representations and processes is not fully explicated. Greene's dual-process model (Greene, Sommerville, Nystrom, Darley, & Cohen, 2001) also gives roles to intuitive, affective, and deliberative processes in moral dilemma resolution but, again, is silent about the nature of the representations over which such processes may operate. Another prominent theory in moral psychology, universal moral grammar (UMG; Mikhail, 2007), is an explicitly computational theory that does not clearly make room for grounded representations or processes.

Theories that take metaphor, embodiment, and embeddedness seriously may have numerous advantages over those that do not. Not only might such theories better accommodate the range of empirical findings outlined herein, but they have numerous *extraempirical virtues*.

First, they are generative. Grounded approaches are productive of a range of hypotheses not readily derivable from classical cognition accounts. It is difficult to see, for example, how afferent bodily feedback effects might be predicted from classical cognition accounts of moral judgment. And although classical accounts may very well be able to accommodate such findings post hoc, it is more difficult to see how they would generate such predictions a priori (see Niedenthal et al., 2005, for a similar point in the domain of social psychology).

Second, grounded approaches may better serve to integrate or unify (moral) psychological sciences (Glenberg, 2010). As Meier et al. (2012) note, grounded approaches use a conceptual vocabulary that enables potential integration of evolutionary and developmental approaches with mechanistic accounts of cognition. Notions of phylogenetic and ontogenetic scaffolding are more easily interpretable within frameworks that readily ground complex, abstract concepts (the province of adult humans) in sensory–motor experience.

Evidence

Research on each of the three different senses of grounded morality—metaphorically structured moral concepts, embodied morality, embedded morality—is at differ-

ent stages of development. Work on moral metaphors has yielded numerous demonstrations of proof of concept (despite some replicability concerns) and now requires theoretical development and integration. Work on embodied morality, however, has yet to sufficiently demonstrate the existence of key effects. Research on the context specificity of moral judgment and behavior abounds, but such effects have yet to be integrated into theories stressing embeddedness as a theoretically central notion.

Metaphors and Morality

The majority of work demonstrating that abstract moral concepts are metaphorically grounded in nonmoral source domains uses a metaphorical transfer methodology (see Landau et al., 2010, for a review). This involves manipulating psychological states related to the source (or target) domain and observing whether effects are observed in the target (or source) domain that are consistent with the metaphoric relation. This technique has provided support for the following conceptual moral metaphors: *good is up–bad is down* (e.g., Meier & Robinson, 2004); *good is right–bad is left* (for right-handers, the reverse for left-handers; Casasanto, 2009); *moral is bright–immoral is dark* (Meier, Robinson, & Clore, 2004); *morality is cleanliness* (e.g., Lee & Schwarz, 2010); *divinity is up* (Meier et al., 2007); *powerful is up–powerless is down* (e.g., Schubert, 2005), and many others (see Landau et al., 2010, for a review).

This research suggests that at least some concepts involved in moral cognition are (at least partially) metaphorically grounded in concrete source domains. At the moment, however, work on moral metaphors is piecemeal and consists of a host of demonstration studies with little attempt at theoretical integration (a concern echoed in Meier et al., 2012; Landau et al., 2010). What is needed is a mechanistic account of how conceptual metaphors are formed and represented and how they operate in moral judgment and decision making. Such accounts may help to answer important questions about conceptual metaphors of morality: Are all moral concepts metaphorically structured? Are some moral concepts only partially metaphorically structured? More deeply: Are conceptual metaphors a consequence of, constitutive of, or epiphenomenal to moral cognition? What are the limits of metaphorical structuring?

Answering this last question, which involves identifying boundary conditions to metaphorical structuring, may be useful not only in specifying theory but also in making sense of the replicability problem in this area. Certain studies on moral metaphors (e.g., Zhong & Liljenquist's [2006] work on morality and cleanliness) have proved difficult to replicate (see Earp, Everett, Madva, & Hamlin, 2014; Fayard, Bassi, Bernstein, & Roberts, 2009; Johnson, Cheung, & Donnellan, 2014). Having an idea of theoretically specified boundaries to conceptual metaphor may give us an a priori sense of what kinds of metaphors are likely to exist within the moral domain.

Bodies and Morality

Whereas moral metaphor work requires theory development, moral embodiment work requires demonstration studies. To date, there is little research that explicitly links afferent body feedback causally to moral cognition.

There is some correlational evidence, however, suggestive of the role of afferent feedback in the moral domain (Chapman, Kim, Susskind & Anderson, 2009; Cannon, Schnall, & White, 2011; Whitton, Henry, Rendall, & Grisham, 2014). Various studies have monitored facial muscle activity via electromyography (EMG) during the presentation of moral stimuli. Chapman et al. (2009), for example, measured EMG activity during fair and unfair offers in the Ultimatum Game. Activity of the levator labii muscles, responsible for wrinkling up the nose in disgust, was strongly elicited by unfair offers.

Cannon et al. (2011) used EMG to measure facial expressions in response to a variety of moral violations. Electrodes were placed over three sites: levator labii (i.e., facial disgust), zygomaticus (i.e., smiling/positive affect), and corrugator muscles (i.e., frowning/facial anger). The researchers observed increased facial disgust in response to purity and fairness violations, the latter

effect resonating with the findings of Chapman et al. (2009). This activity was correlated with condemnation of purity and fairness violations. Corrugator activity was increased by harm violations and was also associated with moral judgments about harm.

It is not clear from such findings, however, whether facial muscle activity (or mental representations thereof) play a *causal* role in moral cognition (a requirement of many embodied accounts; see Goldman & de Vignemont, 2009); facial muscle activity could be simply epiphenomenal. To explore such a possibility, one must move beyond correlational designs.

One strategy would be to use interference paradigms. Noninvasive interference with facial expressions is commonly done by placing a pen across participants' teeth and lips, which enforces a "neutral" facial expression. This technique, used in the well-known humor studies of Strack, Martin, and Stepper (1988), is now well established (Niedenthal, 2007; Niedenthal, Brauer, Halberstadt, & Innes-Ker, 2001; Oberman, Winkielman, & Ramachandran, 2007) as a means of testing the causal role of facial feedback in emotion processing. By comparing groups that do versus do not have certain facial muscles obstructed, one can test the claim that facial feedback is causally implicated in moral judgment.

The face, of course, is not the only source of peripheral afferent feedback that may play a role in the moral domain. Work on attitudes, for example, has demonstrated the role of flexion and extension arm movements in both the processing of valenced information and attitude acquisition (e.g., Laham et al., 2015). Given that morally relevant stimuli are typically strongly valenced and that moral judgments are essentially attitudes (e.g., X is good; X is wrong), one might predict that flexion and extension arm movements (suitably contextually framed) might (1) differentially influence the processing of moral stimuli and (2) play a role in the acquisition of moral attitudes. Additional work might involve the study of individual differences in morphology and of postural variations in moral cognition. Work on embodied morality is in its early phases, and numerous avenues are open for future demonstration studies.

Contexts and Morality

Moral judgments, like other social judgments, are context dependent (see Sinnott-Armstrong, 2008, for a review). Situational factors such as decision frames (e.g., Laham, 2009), processing fluency (e.g., Laham, Alter, & Goodwin, 2009), and even wording (e.g., Petrinovich & O'Neill, 1996) all influence moral judgments.

Yet, while contextual effects abound in moral psychology, broader theories of morality tend to downplay their theoretical import. Moral foundations theory (MFT; Haidt & Joseph, 2004; Haidt, 2012), for example, posits the existence of five (or six) moral value domains that guide the majority of our moral judgments: care/harm, fairness/cheating, loyalty/betrayal, authority/subversion, sanctity/degradation (and perhaps liberty/oppression). Although this theory recognizes a plurality of values, it does not focus on the flexibility with which such values are applied in judgments.

Moral values and preferences may be less stable than we think. Work on self-persuasion (e.g., Briñol, McCaslin, & Petty, 2012) and audience design (or the *saying is believing effect*; e.g., Higgins & Rholes, 1978), for example, suggests that attitudes are influenced by the social contexts in which they are processed. There is no reason to expect moral preferences to be immune to such effects.

Take relational context: Ample work shows that various aspects of our psychology are attuned to the relational contexts in which we are embedded (Fiske, 1991). Moral judgments, decisions, and behaviors are embedded within particular relationships (Rai & Fiske, 2011), and this fact changes the way that foundational moral values manifest. Rai and Fiske (2011) argue that people pursue different moral motives in different relational contexts—*unity* in communal sharing relationships, *equality* in equality matching relationships, *hierarchy* in authority ranking relationships, and *proportionality* in market pricing relationships. What this means is that moral concerns will be different in different social–relational contexts. In numerous recent studies, Simpson and Laham (2015a, 2015b; also Simpson, Laham, & Fiske, 2016) found that the relational contexts in which moral foundational violations and values are processed influence judgments about such violations and values.

There are many other contextual factors that influence moral judgments. What is needed is a move in theorizing to take these effects seriously, not to view them merely as noise. Moral cognition is situated, or embedded, in social–physical environments. This is not just to say, tritely, that any particular instance of moral cognition takes place in particular social–spatial–temporal milieus but that the particulars of the milieu influence the very nature of moral cognition. Theories of moral cognition need to place context specificity more centrally.

Extension and Expansion

We have explored three senses of *grounded* in this chapter and have considered how research in each of these domains might progress. There are numerous other senses of *grounded* that may also have implications for research in moral cognition, some of which have been explored elsewhere. Prinz (2007), for example, suggests that moral concepts are grounded in emotions—that "the concepts of right and wrong are constituted by a variety of emotions of praise and blame" (Boroditsky & Prinz, 2008, p. 104)—and work on simulation accounts of theory of mind (e.g., Goldman, 2006) have clear implications for the role of multimodal reenactment in the kinds of empathic processes central to moral cognition.

There are two additional ways in which moral cognition may be grounded: It is *time pressured*, and it may involve *offloading* of work onto the environment (Wilson, 2002). Although embeddedness is typically taken to mean merely context specific, there is a deeper sense in which moral cognition is situated or embedded within social–spatial–temporal milieus. Moral perception, categorization, decision making, and so on all take place "online" and in "real time"—each process requires time-constrained responsiveness to the environment, ongoing information collection, and updating. To the extent that laboratory contexts implement "artificial time"—for example, unlimited time to decide whether one will engage a perpetrator—lab results may give a misleading characterization of moral cognition. Although time pressure has been used as a manipulation in moral psychological research (e.g., Suter & Hertwig, 2011), it is typically employed within classical-cognition dual-process accounts and does not often feature centrally in theorizing. More attention could be paid to the time course of moral cognition and the implications of implementing different time constraints within the laboratory.

A more radical notion of embeddedness construes cognition as distributed not only within minds but also across minds and environments (e.g., Clark, 1999; Hutchins, 1995). On such accounts, what does the thinking is the organism–environment system, not the organism itself. Whereas such approaches raise numerous ontological questions, the less radical notion that we offload cognitive work onto the environment is not so problematic (Wilson, 2002). During problem solving, for example, we may engage in epistemic actions, using the environment to do some of our thinking for us (e.g., Kirsh & Maglio, 1994). One intriguing possibility is that we might offload *moral* work onto the environment. Schwartz and Sharpe (2011), for example, claim that the prevalence of ethical rules and guidelines in the workplace may constitute an offloading of moral decision making onto the environment. Moral judgment and decision making becomes less about a reflective weighing of the moral costs and benefits of certain actions and more a mindless adherence to externally represented rules.

Taken together, the implications of the various senses of groundedness explored throughout this chapter are potentially radical. What they suggest is that theories of moral cognition need to incorporate the facts that moral thought and action happen in particular, time-constrained situations and are implemented in a cognitive system using representations that are multimodal and grounded, by metaphoric relation, to concrete base domains. We do not think that grounded approaches will prove sufficient to provide a complete picture of moral cognition—theoretical tools from other frameworks may also be necessary. However, we do not think that a comprehensive account of moral psychology can ignore the notions that moral cognition *is for moral action* and that the body–environment nexus shapes the very nature of moral thought.

REFERENCES

Allport, G. W. (1935). Attitudes. In C. Murchinson (Ed.), *A handbook of social psychology* (pp. 798–844). Worcester, MA: Clark University Press.

Barsalou, L. W. (1999). Perceptual symbol systems. *Behavioral and Brain Sciences, 22,* 577–660.

Barsalou, L. W. (2008). Grounded cognition. *Annual Review of Psychology, 59,* 617–645.

Boroditsky, L., & Prinz, J. (2008). What thoughts are made of. In G. R. Semin & E. R. Smith (Eds.), *Embodied grounding: Social, cognitive, affective and neuroscientific approaches* (pp. 98–115). Cambridge, UK: Cambridge University Press.

Briñol, P., McCaslin, M. J., & Petty, R. E. (2012). Self-generated persuasion: Effects of the target and direction of arguments. *Journal of Personality and Social Psychology, 102,* 925–940.

Cannon, P. R., Schnall, S., & White, M. (2011). Transgressions and expressions: Affective facial muscle activity predicts moral judgments. *Social Psychology and Personality Science, 2*(3), 325–331.

Casasanto, D. (2009). Embodiment of abstract concepts: Good and bad in right- and left-handers. *Journal of Experimental Psychology: General, 138,* 351–367.

Chapman, H. A., Kim, D. A., Susskind, J. M., & Anderson, A. K. (2009). In bad taste: Evidence for the oral origins of moral disgust. *Science, 323,* 1222–1226.

Clark, A. (1999). An embodied cognitive science. *Trends in Cognitive Sciences, 3,* 345–351.

Darwin, C. (1904). *The expression of emotion in man and animals.* London: Murray. (Original work published 1872)

Earp, B. D., Everett, J. A. C., Madva, E. N., & Hamlin, J. K. (2014). Out, damned spot: Can the "Macbeth effect" be replicated? *Basic and Applied Social Psychology, 36,* 91–98.

Fayard, J. V., Bassi, A. K., Bernstein, D. M., & Roberts, B. W. (2009). Is cleanliness next to godliness? Dispelling old wives' tales: Failure to replicate Zhong and Liljenquist (2006). *Journal of Articles in Support of the Null Hypothesis, 6,* 21–30.

Fiske, A. P. (1991). *Structures of social life: The four elementary forms of human relations.* New York: Free Press.

Galton, F. (1884). Measurement of character. *Fortnightly Review, 42,* 179–185.

Gardner, H. (1985). *The mind's new science: A history of the cognitive revolution.* New York: Basic Books.

Glenberg, A. M. (2010). Embodiment as a unifying perspective for psychology. *Wiley Interdisciplinary Reviews: Cognitive Science, 1,* 586–596.

Goldman, A. (2006). *Simulating minds: The philosophy, psychology and neuroscience of mindreading.* Oxford, UK: Oxford University Press.

Goldman, A., & de Vignemont, F. (2009). Is social cognition embodied? *Trends in Cognitive Sciences, 13,* 154–159.

Greene, J. D., Sommerville, R. B., Nystrom, L. E., Darley, J. M., & Cohen, J. D. (2001). An fMRI investigation of emotional engagement in moral judgment. *Science, 293,* 2105–2108.

Haidt, J. (2001). The emotional dog and its rational tail. *Psychological Review, 108,* 814–834.

Haidt, J. (2012). *The righteous mind: Why good people are divided by politics and religion.* New York: Pantheon.

Haidt, J., & Joseph, C. (2004). Intuitive ethics: How innately prepared intuitions generate culturally variable virtues. *Daedalus, 133,* 55–66.

Higgins, E. T., & Rholes, W. S. (1978). "Saying is believing": Effects of message modification on memory and liking for the person perceived. *Journal of Experimental Social Psychology, 14,* 363–378.

Hutchins, E. (1995). *Cognition in the wild.* Cambridge, MA: MIT Press.

Johnson, D. J., Cheung, F., & Donnellan, M. B. (2014). Does cleanliness influence moral judgments?: A direct replication of Schnall, Benton, and Harvey (2008). *Social Psychology, 45*(3), 209–215.

Kirsh, D., & Maglio, P. (1994). On distinguishing epistemic from pragmatic action. *Cognitive Science, 18,* 513–549.

Laham, S. M. (2009). Expanding the moral circle: Inclusion and exclusion mindsets and the circle of moral regard. *Journal of Experimental Social Psychology, 45,* 250–253.

Laham, S. M., Alter, A. L., & Goodwin, G. (2009). Easy on the mind, easy on the wrongdoer: Discrepantly fluent violations are deemed less morally wrong. *Cognition, 112,* 462–466.

Laham, S. M., Kashima, Y., Dix, J., & Wheeler, M. (2015). A meta-analysis of the facilitation of arm flexion and extension movements as a function of stimulus valence. *Cognition and Emotion, 29,* 1069–1090.

Lakoff, G., & Johnson, M. (1980). *Metaphors we live by.* Chicago: University of Chicago Press.

Landau, M. J., Meier, B. P., & Keefer, L. A. (2010). A metaphor-enriched social cognition. *Psychological Bulletin, 136,* 1045–1067.

Lee, S. W., & Schwarz, N. (2010). Dirty hands and dirty mouths: Embodiment of the moral-purity metaphor is specific to the motor modality involved in moral transgression. *Psychological Science, 21,* 1423–1425.

Meier, B. P., Hauser, D. J., Robinson, M. D., Friesen, C. K., & Schjeldahl, K. (2007). What's "up" with God?: Vertical space as a representation of the divine. *Journal of Personality and Social Psychology, 93,* 699–710.

Meier, B. P., & Robinson, M. D. (2004). Why the sunny side is up. *Psychological Science, 15,* 243–247.

Meier, B. P., Robinson, M. D., & Clore, G. L. (2004). Why good guys wear white: Automatic inferences about stimulus valence based on brightness. *Psychological Science, 15,* 82–87.

Meier, B. P., Schnall, S., Schwarz, N., & Bargh, J. A. (2012). Embodiment in social psychology. *Topics in Cognitive Science, 4*(4), 705–716.

Meier, B. P., Sellbom, M., & Wygant, D. B. (2007). Failing to take the moral high ground: Psychopathy and the vertical representation of morality. *Personality and Individual Differences, 43*(4), 757–767.

Mikhail, J. (2007). Universal moral grammar: Theory, evidence and the future. *Trends in Cognitive Sciences, 11,* 143–152.

Niedenthal, P. M. (2007). Embodying emotion. *Science, 316,* 1002–1005.

Niedenthal, P. M., Barsalou, L. W., Winkielman, P., Krauth-Gruber, S., & Ric, F. (2005). Embodiment in attitudes, social perception and emotion. *Personality and Social Psychological Review, 9,* 184–211.

Niedenthal, P. M., Brauer, M., Halberstadt, J. B., & Innes-Ker, A. H. (2001). When did her smile drop?: Facial mimicry and the influences of emotional state on the detection of change in emotional expression. *Cognition and Emotion, 15*(6), 853–864.

Oberman, L. M., Winkielman, P., & Ramachandran, V. S. (2007). Face to face: Blocking facial mimicry can selectively impair recognition of emotional expressions. *Social Neuroscience, 2*(3–4), 167–178.

Petrinovich, L., & O'Neill, P. (1996). Influence of wording and framing effects on moral intuitions. *Ethology and Sociobiology, 17,* 145–171.

Prinz, J. J. (2007). *The emotional construction of morals.* Oxford, UK: Oxford University Press.

Rai, S. T., & Fiske, A. P. (2011). Moral psychology is relationship regulation: Moral motives for unity, hierarchy, equality, and proportionality. *Psychological Review, 118,* 57–75.

Schubert, T. W. (2005). Your highness: Vertical positions as perceptual symbols of power. *Journal of Personality and Social Psychology, 89,* 1–21.

Schwartz, B., & Sharpe, K. (2011). *Practical wisdom.* New York: Riverhead Books.

Simpson, A., & Laham, S. M. (2015a). Different relational models underlie prototypical left and right positions on social issues. *European Journal of Social Psychology, 45,* 204–217.

Simpson, A., & Laham, S. M. (2015b). Individual differences in relational construal are associated with variability in moral judgment. *Personality and Individual Differences, 74,* 49–54.

Simpson, A., Laham, S. M., & Fiske, A. P. (2016). Wrongness in different relationships: Relational context effects on moral judgment. *Journal of Social Psychology, 156,* 594–609.

Sinnott-Armstrong, W. (2008). Framing moral intuitions. In W. Sinnott-Armstrong (Ed.), *Moral psychology: Vol. 2. The cognitive science of morality: Intuition and diversity* (pp. 47–76). Cambridge, MA: MIT Press.

Smith, E. R., & Semin, G. R. (2007). Situated social cognition. *Current Directions in Psychological Science, 16,* 132–135.

Strack, F., Martin, L. L., & Stepper, S. (1988). Inhibiting and facilitating conditions of the human smile: A nonobtrusive test of the facial feedback hypothesis. *Journal of Personality and Social Psychology, 54,* 768–777.

Suter, R. S., & Hertwig, R. (2011). Time and moral judgment. *Cognition, 119,* 454–458.

Whitton, A. E., Henry, J. D., Rendell, P. G., & Grisham, J. R. (2014). Disgust, but not anger provocation, enhances levator labii superioris activity during exposure to moral transgressions. *Biological Psychology, 96,* 48–56.

Wilson, M. (2002). Six views of embodied cognition. *Psychonomic Bulletin and Review, 9,* 625–636.

Zhong, C., & Liljenquist, K. (2006). Washing away your sins: Threatened morality and physical cleansing. *Science, 313,* 1451–1452.

PART VII
MORALITY AND BELIEFS

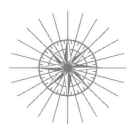

QUESTIONS ANSWERED IN PART VII

CHAPTER 31 How do people answer the question of why good and bad people exist and why good and bad events occur?

CHAPTER 32 To what extent do ordinary individuals regard moral beliefs as capturing objective truths about morality, and how do their views about this predict other attitudes and behaviors?

CHAPTER 33 Is morality intuitive or deliberative?

CHAPTER 34 Does moral psychology need a workable concept of free will?

CHAPTER 35 How do religious and secular institutions make us moral?

CHAPTER 36 Why are intelligent design arguments so moralized?

CHAPTER 31

Moral Vitalism

Brock Bastian

> **How do people answer the question of why good and bad people exist and why good and bad events occur?**
>
> Moral vitalism is a lay belief that good and evil forces exist in the natural world; it provides an answer for why good and bad things happen, shapes how people respond to these events, and may be especially pronounced in capricious contexts.

The role of spiritual beliefs in moral reasoning and judgment have been sorely overlooked. To date, links between morality and spirituality have been drawn by focusing on how a belief in God may shape thinking and behavior (e.g., Shariff & Norenzayan, 2007) but have not sought to penetrate into the nature of spiritual cognition. Other work has focused on issues of sanctity or purity, linking spirituality to concerns over biological contamination (e.g., Haidt & Joseph, 2004), yet how this translates into specific moral beliefs that contribute to purity concerns within the moral domain has not been specified. Moral vitalism captures a mode of thinking that assumes that good and evil are active *forces* that can exert a profound influence on people and events. It is a lay theory that embraces the dual beliefs that forces of good and evil (1) actually exist and (2) may cause moral and immoral events to occur. As such, the theory of moral vitalism aims to understand how spiritual beliefs within the moral domain are structured and

how they influence moral cognition and behavior.

Moral vitalism is understood to be a lay theory that people rely on to understand their worlds. To this extent, a belief that there are forces of good and evil in the natural world is attractive because it provides people with a convenient explanation for why good and bad things happen, as well as what makes people good or bad. People who endorse a belief in moral vitalism agree with statements such as "There are underlying forces of good and evil in this world"; "Either the forces of good or the forces of evil are responsible for most of the events in the world today"; and "The forces of good and evil often motivate human behavior." In this way moral vitalism acts as a heuristic for navigating the complex world of moral judgment and behavior. Like other lay theories, moral vitalism may often be largely implicit and poorly articulated. As such, people may assume that good and evil are actual objective phenomena that are manifested in the world and that possess power, force, and intentionality, yet be unable to specify why or how this is so. This understanding of good and evil may, in turn, shape how people reason about morally relevant events, yet they may lack insight into the influence of these beliefs.

In terms of how moral vitalism may affect moral reasoning, it is argued that this should be especially apparent in how people reason about issues concerning moral contagion and contamination—that is, concerns about the potential influence of nonmaterial good and evil forces being transferred between people. For instance, Bastian et al. (2015) found that moral vitalists tend to be concerned about having direct or indirect contact with immoral others, due to the possibility of contagion or contamination. This effect also extended beyond the physical domain. Moral vitalists were also concerned over their own mental purity and felt susceptible to the forces of evil when entertaining immoral thoughts. To this extent, moral vitalists view immoral essences—the forces of evil—as having the capacity to "infect" and corrupt people's minds and bodies. This need not happen through physical contact but may also occur through mental content alone. As such, moral vitalists entertain a naïve model of spirit possession and are concerned about the possibility of being possessed by the forces of evil: Having immoral thoughts is dangerous because it invites the influence of evil in one's life.

The concept of moral vitalism aims to uncover an important dimension of moral understanding that manifests itself within everyday moral cognition. It aims to take account of the role of spiritual belief within the moral domain by focusing on core underlying assumptions rather than specific tenets of religious or political belief. As such it allows a deeper understanding of how these assumptions may shape moral reasoning and an analysis of these beliefs across a spectrum of religious, nonreligious, and politically diverse populations.

Historical Context

Vitalistic thinking refers to the tendency to attribute force, power, or causality to some nonmaterial "spirit" or "soul-stuff" in order to explain observable events. This type of reasoning is not only evident within many traditional belief systems (Atran et al., 2002; Frazer, 1890/1959), but also within early scientific and psychological theorizing (Jung, 1917/1983; Bechtel & Richardson, 1998), and remains prominent within children's naïve understandings of biology (Inagaki & Hatano, 2004; Morris, Taplin, & Gelman, 2000). For instance, the notion of "life force" often provides a convenient placeholder for understanding how things grow or what makes the body work. Vitalism is a form of reasoning that shares many similarities with psychological essentialism in that it functions to provide causal explanations for observable phenomena and is evident in contexts in which more scientific or mechanistic understandings are lacking.

By introducing the notion of lay theories of underlying spiritual forces into the domain of moral cognition, moral vitalism brings a novel perspective to how we think about current debates within the field of moral psychology. For instance, it suggests that at least some of our moral reasoning is born from our desire to make sense of the world. That is, morality can arise as a function of our need to predict and understand our environment. This diverges from some accounts that view morality as arising from the need to protect persons, groups, or norms (such as moral foundations theory; Haidt & Joseph, 2004). However, it shares some similarities with other accounts that emphasize the role of sense making in the context of harm (such as the notion of dyadic completion; Gray, Young, & Waytz, 2012). Yet it goes beyond such accounts by suggesting that, in efforts to understand their worlds, people often rely on beliefs that have explanatory power. Beyond completing a moral dyad of victim and perpetrator, moral vitalism serves to explain why there are victims and perpetrators in the first place. To this extent, it provides a filler explanation, or a placeholder concept, for why morally relevant events occur.

As a formal theory, moral vitalism reflects a basic form of cognition (belief) that is likely universal and probably arose as an explanation for life-threatening events, such as disease, in contexts in which other (i.e., more scientific) explanations were not available. As such, it is likely to be evident across a range of cultures, and yet it is also likely to be reinforced within particular cultural contexts. For instance, in capricious contexts, moral vitalism may be heightened, as it provides a convenient answer to otherwise incoherent and unpredictable events. As such, it is likely that moral vitalism may become more pronounced in contexts in which intergroup conflict is common or may be relied on to understand especially heinous crimes. When people feel they lack a clear explanation for how or why harmful events arise, moral vitalism may become a default strategy that allows making sense of the world.

Moral vitalism may be reinforced within contexts in which such beliefs have been developed into more elaborate forms of spiritual tradition, such as in contexts where religious belief is especially prominent. In these contexts, people have developed more complex and anthropomorphized understandings of good and evil (such as gods and devils), therefore a reliance on these forces of good and evil for understanding morally relevant events will be especially common.

The construct of moral vitalism sits to the side of a clear-cut debate over intuition versus cognition. The reason is that, as a theory, it is not defined by moral judgment but rather by a belief in the underlying nature of the moral world. To this extent, it throws a new light on many current approaches to understanding morality, suggesting that morality may be as much characterized by a set of beliefs about the nature of the world as it is by the basis on which people make moral judgments. From the perspective of moral vitalism, moral judgment is simply the output of a more basic set of beliefs about the underlying nature of what it means to be right or wrong.

Theoretical Stance

Moral vitalism captures a lay theory or naïve thinking and its influence on the moral domain. As such, it shares some similarities with theories that emphasize intuitionist thinking—such as moral foundations theory (MFT; Graham, Haidt, & Nosek, 2009; Haidt & Joseph, 2004). Still, there are important differences. Whereas MFT focuses on intuitions within the domain of moral judgment—such as "is it wrong?"—moral vitalism focuses on a belief regarding the underlying reality of the moral world. A belief in moral vitalism is not measured by *how* people make moral judgments, but it may provide an explanation for *why* they make such judgements. Moral vitalism is perhaps most closely aligned with the purity dimension of MFT, given a similar emphasis on concerns regarding purity and contagion. In fact, we might expect similar origins of both purity concerns and moral vitalism—specifically, biological disease (Haidt & Joseph, 2004; van Leeuwen, Park, Koenig, & Graham, 2012). From a moral vitalism perspective, one would predict that these beliefs may have formed to explain the capricious effects of disease on human health—deaths were understood to be the direct result of the forces of evil. Indeed, this kind of thinking is not uncommon in the current age, with some blaming God, or a failure to be protected by God, for their ill health (see Gray & Wegner, 2010). As such, moral vitalism may help to explain how concerns over disease were transformed into moral concerns over purity.

Comparing moral vitalism to theories focusing on the attribution of moral character (e.g., Goodwin, 2015) also highlights some important differences and similarities. For instance, moral vitalists see moral action as in part determined by forces that are independent of people. To the extent that moral vitalists also endorse a naïve model of spirit possession (see Bastian et al., 2015), they are also likely to endorse a naïve model of exorcism: People can be not only be lured *by* evil, but they can also be reformed *from* evil. It is likely that for the moral vitalist evil actions are understood to be less the result of intentional action on behalf of the individual than a result of evil forces residing in the world and within people. As such, the moral vitalist is likely to afford moral character a less salient explanatory role. Supportive of this, moral vitalism appears to be relatively distinct from a similar construct focusing on pure good and evil recently published by Webster and Saucier (2013) that focuses on purely good or evil people, as opposed to purely good or evil forces (see Bastian et al., 2015).

Also interesting to consider is the link between moral vitalism and previous work on moral cleansing. The literature on moral cleansing suggests that the link between physical and moral disgust is embodied, and thus people may be motivated to physically cleanse when they are reminded of their own immoral behavior (see Zhong & Liljenquist, 2006). Other work suggests that after an immoral act people may engage in moral behavior in order to regain their sense of moral worth (Sachdeva, Iliev, & Medin, 2009). From a moral vitalism perspective, immoral behavior may be viewed as placing one at risk of being influenced or possessed by the forces of evil, and compensatory actions may be understood as attempts to guard against this possibility. Moral vitalists may be especially likely to engage in these compensatory forms of action. It is also likely, however, that for moral vitalists, compensatory action may be as much symbolic as concrete: It is not only about compensating for actual harm done but also about protecting oneself from the influence of evil. Symbolic actions may thus be more heavily weighted by moral vitalists in achieving compensation.

It is also interesting to consider the connection between moral vitalism and dual-process theories of moral judgment (e.g., Greene, Sommerville, Nystrom, Darley, & Cohen, 2001). Given their reliance on notions of pure good and evil, moral vitalists are likely to see moral judgments as relatively clear-cut and, as such, are more likely to be deontological in their moral reasoning. Moreover, they may be especially likely to see any immoral act, whether justified on utilitarian grounds (such as in the case of the Heinz dilemma) or not, as putting the individual at risk of evil.

Finally, moral vitalism shares some similarities with an understanding of morality as arising from the process of dyadic completion (Gray et al., 2012). Dyadic completion suggests that, in view of a victim, people will seek to attribute blame to someone, even to God. Just so, moral vitalism suggests that a belief in the forces of good and evil is often relied on in contexts where the causes of good and bad actions or outcomes are uncertain or unclear. Yet, although moral vitalism does indicate a form of dyadic thinking (good vs. evil), the belief in such forces does not rely on the existence of a specific immoral act. A belief in moral vitalism is likely to be relatively stable across most contexts. Indeed, given that it plays a central role in how people understand their worlds, even having this belief challenged may represent a significant existential threat. People are likely to endorse this lay theory or not and are unlikely to change their beliefs regarding moral vitalism based on their exposure to a specific immoral deed. Although it is possible that moral vitalism may be heightened (or become more chronically accessible) in contexts characterized by high levels of threat, it is relied on to make sense of apparent harm in general, rather than triggered by specific instances of harm doing.

Evidence

Bastian et al. (2015) provide initial evidence for the construct of moral vitalism in terms of its measurement and also its predictive validity. After establishing a reliable and valid measure of moral vitalism beliefs, Bastian and colleagues examined whether moral vitalists indeed do view the world as containing moral forces that can possess and influence people. Specifically, they provided participants with two vignettes. The first was about John, a decent man, but who, for a $10 bet, signed a piece of paper saying he would sell his soul to the devil and then posted it on the Internet. The second was about Kristen, an adventurous young woman who participated in a séance. In both cases, moral vitalists viewed these actions as dangerous and as increasing the likelihood of the individual in question being possessed by evil, and they believed that the individual's character would change for the worse. From this perspective, by engaging in spiritually risky behavior, they ran the risk of being influenced by evil and therefore were viewed as more likely to have lustful thoughts, to lie, to cheat, and to become aggressive. This study shows that not only do moral vitalists worry about the potential influence of evil, but they also believe that evil can have tangible effects on a person's behavior and that these effects may even extend beyond the immediate context, more broadly shaping the person for the worse. Critically, these associations emerged independent of religiosity, suggesting that moral vitalism is capturing a specific construct within moral cognition that, although associated with religiosity, is not defined by it.

In a follow-up study, Bastian and colleagues (2015) demonstrated that moral vitalists were especially concerned about moral contagion and would be less likely to consume food that had been touched by immoral people. They were told that a chocolate biscuit or an apple was either clean, had been lying on the floor of the supermarket, had been recovered from a thief who had stolen the items, or had been taken from the shopping basket of a known child molester before apprehension by police. Moral vitalists rated how disgusting it would be to eat each item. There was an overall association between moral vitalism and increased disgust; however, this was especially clear in the case of the items that had been in contact with immoral others. Controlling for individual differences in disgust sensitivity, as well as self-rated disgust associated with eating the food when it had been on the floor, moral vitalism remained a unique predictor of disgust associated with eating food items that had been in contact with immoral others (thief or child molester).

These findings support the link between moral vitalism and concerns over moral contagion through secondary contact. If there are forces of evil in the world, then it is possible that this evil could be passed through direct or indirect physical contact. The theory of moral vitalism suggests, however, that the forces of evil may not only be transferred between people but may also be capable of infecting and corrupting people's minds. Just as signing a piece of paper that says you will sell your soul to the devil is believed to lead to possession by the forces of evil, entertaining immoral thoughts may also leave this door open to such influences. Bastian and colleagues tested this possibility by asking people to think about a "sin of the flesh" ("something bodily that you enjoyed doing in the moment but felt guilty about doing or feels 'dirty' to think about"). They were then asked to complete a task in which they were instructed to let their minds wander for a short period of time, noting how many times their thoughts returned to the sin. Next, they were asked to indicate whether they felt that the forces of evil had influenced their thoughts. Moral vitalism predicted the extent to which people thought that evil had been playing a role in producing their immoral thoughts. Participants were then told that they would next read a short informational piece and that they could choose between two different essays. One essay was titled "Strategies to control your thoughts: Five ways to keep unwanted thoughts at bay," and the other essay was titled "Letting your thoughts rule: How to maintain an open and flexible mind." Moral vitalists were more likely to choose the essay on thought control, indicating that they felt threatened by their immoral thoughts and felt the need to find ways of controlling those thoughts.

To date, the evidence suggests that moral vitalism captures a lay theory that uniquely shapes how people reason within the moral domain. Our theory suggests that these beliefs should be related to other work on purity, such as that focused on MFT. A link between moral vitalism and the purity domain of the moral foundations questionnaire would indeed support the proposed role of moral vitalism in motivating concerns over contamination and contagion. Just so, showing that moral vitalists are especially likely to engage in physical cleansing-—type behavior in response to immoral actions would further highlight this link. Furthermore, demonstrating that moral vitalists might be more likely to engage in compensatory actions, such as performing moral deeds in response to reminders of immoral action, would provide support to the notion that moral vitalists are concerned about maintaining their moral integrity, which, in turn, serves to guard against the possibility of moral corruption. Finding that moral vitalism was especially predictive of symbolic responses rather than more concrete responses (in cases of both cleansing and compensatory action) would highlight the specific contribution of these beliefs and the associated motivation to protect oneself from metaphysical forces of evil.

Extension and Expansion

Our work on moral vitalism is only just beginning. A key question in this work is how these beliefs may play into the ways in which people understand ideological differences. We suggest that moral vitalists are likely to struggle with exposure to ideologically diverse environments. The reason is that a person's ideological system reflects basic tenets about what is right or wrong and how one should live one's life. For the moral vitalist, living the right way means that he or she is in touch with the forces of good in the world, and living the wrong way means that he or she is susceptible to the forces of evil. In the case in which disagreements exist over what is right or wrong, the moral vitalist is likely to view those whose worldviews differ in fundamental ways as harbingers of evil. Just so, they are likely to imbue their own ideological commitments with the forces of good. From this starting point, conflicts over "how to live" become disputes about the "good in us" versus the "evil in them," ensuring that both ideological commitments and ideological conflicts are heavily weighted in the moral vitalists' understanding of the world they live in.

In some ways, our approach to linking a belief in moral vitalism to an understanding of ideologically based group differences shares similarities with work on psychological essentialism (Bastian & Haslam, 2006; Haslam, Rothschild, & Ernst, 2000; Prentice & Miller, 2006). Just as biological essentialists come to view social categories as indicative of an underlying causal biological essence, moral vitalists come to view ideological categories as indicative of an underlying causal moral essence. This suggests a number of parallels between moral vitalism and psychological essentialism in understanding the influence of lay theories on social categorization and intergroup dynamics. For instance, just as essentialists seek to maintain their own groups' biological purity (Wagner et al., 2010), moral vitalists are likely to seek to maintain their groups' moral purity.

Of interest, also, is the link between moral vitalism and group commitment. Compared with constructs such as identity fusion (Swann, Jetten, Gómez, Whitehouse, & Bastian, 2012), which predict a willingness to fight and die for the group, it is likely that moral vitalists are more likely to remain committed to their values or beliefs. Although moral vitalism may not be a strong predictor of group-based action, it may be a strong predictor of a willingness to make sacrifices to protect sacred values (e.g., Ginges, Atran, Medin, & Shikaki, 2007).

By developing a focus on specific spiritual beliefs, moral vitalism opens the door to new insights and novel approaches to understanding how people structure their moral worlds. To this extent, moral vitalism serves to build a bridge between work on religious belief and work on moral cognition, providing a template for theory building that integrates with but also challenges current models and themes within the field of moral psychology.

REFERENCES

Atran, S., Medin, D., Ross, N., Lynch, E., Vapnarksy, V., Ek', E., . . . Baran, M. (2002). Folkecology, cultural epidemiology, and the spirit of the commons: A garden experiment in the Maya lowlands, 1991–2001. *Current Anthropology, 43*, 421–450.

Bastian, B., Bain, P., Buhrmester, M. D., Gómez, Á., Vázquez, A., Knight, C. G., & Swann, W. B. J. (2015). Moral vitalism: Seeing good and evil as real, agentic forces. *Personality and Social Psychology Bulletin, 41*(8), 1069–1081.

Bastian, B., & Haslam, N. (2006). Psychological essentialism and stereotype endorsement. *Journal of Experimental Social Psychology, 42*, 228–235.

Bechtel, W., & Richardson, R. C. (1998). Vitalism. In E. Craig (Ed.), *Routledge encyclopedia of philosophy* (pp. 639–643). London: Routledge

Frazer, J. G. (1959). *The golden bough: A study in magic and religion* (T. H. Gaster, Ed.). New York: Macmillan. (Original work published 1890).

Ginges, J., Atran, S., Medin, D., & Shikaki, K. (2007). Sacred bounds on rational resolution of violent political conflict. *Proceedings of the National Academy of Sciences of the USA, 104*(18), 7357–7360.

Goodwin, G. P. (2015). Moral character in person perception. *Current Directions in Psychological Science, 24*(1), 38–44.

Graham, J., Haidt, J., & Nosek, B. (2009). Liberals and conservatives rely on different sets of moral foundations. *Journal of Personality and Social Psychology, 96*, 1029–1046.

Gray, K., & Wegner, D. M. (2010). Blaming God for our pain: Human suffering and the divine mind. *Personality and Social Psychology Review, 14*, 7–16.

Gray, K., Young, L., & Waytz, A. (2012). Mind perception is the essence of morality. *Psychological Inquiry, 23*(2), 101–124.

Greene, J. D., Sommerville, R. B., Nystrom, L. E., Darley, J. M., & Cohen, J. D. (2001). An fMRI investigation of emotional engagement in moral judgment. *Science, 293,* 2105–2108.

Haidt, J., & Joseph, C. (2004). Intuitive ethics: How innately prepared intuitions generate culturally variable virtues. *Daedalus, 133*(4), 55–66.

Haslam, N., Rothschild, L., & Ernst, D. (2000). Essentialist beliefs about social categories. *British Journal of Social Psychology, 39,* 113–127.

Inagaki, K., & Hatano, G. (2004). Vitalistic causality in young children's naive biology. *Trends in Cognitive Science, 8,* 356–362.

Jung, C. G. (1983). Excerpts from *On the psychology of the unconscious: Two essays.* In A. Storr (Ed.), *The essential Jung* (pp. 68–71). Princeton: Princeton University Press. (Original work published 1917)

Morris, S. C., Taplin, J. E., & Gelman, S. A. (2000). Vitalism in naive biological thinking. *Developmental Psychology, 36,* 582–595.

Prentice, D. A., & Miller, D. T. (2006). Essentializing differences between women and men. *Psychological Science, 17,* 129–135.

Sachdeva, S., Iliev, R., & Medin, D. L. (2009). Sinning saints and saintly sinners: The paradox of moral self-regulation. *Psychological Science, 20,* 523–528.

Shariff, A. F., & Norenzayan, A. (2007). God is watching you: Priming God concepts increases prosocial behavior in an anonymous economic game. *Psychological Science, 18,* 803–809.

Swann, W. B., Jr,, Jetten, J., Gómez, A., Whitehouse, H., & Bastian, B. (2012). When group membership gets personal: A theory of identity fusion. *Psychological Review, 119,* 441–456.

van Leeuwen, F., Park, J. H., Koenig, B. L., & Graham, J. (2012). Regional variation in pathogen prevalence predicts endorsement of group-focused moral concerns. *Evolution and Human Behavior, 33,* 429–437.

Wagner, W., Kronberger, N., Nagata, M., Sen, R., Holtz, P., & Palacios, F. F. (2010). Essentialist theory of "hybrids": From animal kinds to ethnic categories and race. *Asian Journal of Social Psychology, 13,* 232–246.

Webster, R. J., & Saucier, D. A. (2013). Angels and demons are among us: Assessing individual differences in belief in pure evil and belief in pure good. *Personality and Social Psychology Bulletin, 39,* 1455–1470.

Zhong, C. B., & Liljenquist, K. (2006). Washing away your sins: Threatened morality and physical cleansing. *Science, 313,* 1451–1452.

CHAPTER 32

The Objectivity of Moral Beliefs

Geoffrey P. Goodwin

To what extent do ordinary individuals regard moral beliefs as capturing objective truths about morality, and how do their views about this predict other attitudes and behaviors?

Ordinary people typically regard moral beliefs about the wrongness of harmful or unjust acts as objectively true and the extent to which they do so predicts both moral intolerance and moral commitment.

Do ordinary individuals regard their moral beliefs as representing objective facts about the world? Or do they instead regard their moral beliefs as expressing mere personal preferences or tastes? Questions about the objectivity of moral beliefs have perplexed philosophers for centuries. Recently, ordinary individuals' "meta-ethical" beliefs about these issues have been investigated. This research informs philosophical analysis and provides psychological insight into the nature of everyday moral cognition. It also reveals novel ways in which meta-ethical beliefs may influence moral tolerance and commitment.

A basic method used to assess the perceived objectivity of people's moral beliefs is to probe their understanding of divergent moral opinions (see e.g., Goodwin & Darley, 2008; Nichols, 2004; Wainryb, Shaw, Langley, Cottam, & Lewis, 2004). For instance, subjects might be presented a situation in which two parties diverge on whether a particular act of theft is morally wrong—

one party thinks the act is wrong, whereas the other thinks it is permissible. The key question is whether subjects think that one party must be mistaken, as with ordinary factual disagreements, or whether they instead allow that neither party need be mistaken, as if the conflict were one of brute preference or taste. The conclusion that at least one party must be mistaken implies that people see the issue in question as objective. The data that emerge from existing studies using this method are robust, but their interpretation is not yet settled. My aim in this chapter is to survey and interpret the literature as it currently stands and to point to new research opportunities.

Terminology

During the 20th century, a variety of moral skepticisms came to populate the philosophical literature. A common feature of these skeptical views is their denial of the claim that ordinary moral beliefs represent objectively true facts about the world.[1] But the way these skeptical views come to this conclusion varies widely. One sort of skeptical view, variously labeled as *expressivism, emotivism,* or more broadly, *noncognitivism,* denies that moral beliefs are candidates for truth in the first place (they are not "truth apt"; see Sinnott-Armstrong, 2006). According to this sort of view, moral beliefs are mere expressions of emotion or attitude and so do not purport to represent any assertion that could be either true or false (e.g., Ayer, 1936; Stevenson, 1944). On these views, an assertion that "stealing is wrong" is simply an expression of disapproval, which can neither be true nor false (in the same way that an expression of applause, or booing, at the end of a musical concert, can be neither true nor false). A closely related view—prescriptivism—is that moral beliefs are essentially normative commands or prescriptions—which also cannot be true or false (Hare, 1952, 1981).

In contrast, moral nihilists take a different skeptical tack. They do not deny that moral claims could, in principle, be true or false. But they deny that any moral claims are, in fact, true because no moral properties exist. A famous articulation of this view is found in Mackie's (1977) "error theory," which claimed that, although moral beliefs could in principle be true, they are in fact *all false.* Related views claim that moral beliefs could, in principle, be true or false, but none in fact have the property of being *true* or *false* (Joyce, 2001). Thus, whereas noncognitivism denies moral truth aptness, nihilism, which is cognitivist, simply denies moral truth (and sometimes falsehood; see Sinnott-Armstrong, 2006, 2011).

A final sort of moral skepticism denies neither moral truth aptness nor moral truth, but argues that moral truth is fundamentally relative to a particular local system of appraisal. Moral *subjectivism* is the idea that moral truth must be assessed relative to an individual appraiser. Moral *relativism* is the idea that moral truth must be assessed relative to a particular culture, society, or group (e.g., Harman, 1975; for clear descriptions of moral relativism, see Gowans, 2015; Shafer-Landau, 2003, 2004). In either case, what is morally true for one person or group

may not be morally true for another person or group, and so the claim that moral beliefs capture something objectively true about the world is denied. A useful analogy for moral relativism is that the claim "January is a winter month" may simultaneously be true in one hemisphere of the world but false in another (see Sarkissian, Park, Tien, Wright, & Knobe, 2011)—according to moral relativism, this dependence on context holds for the truth of moral beliefs as well.

In contrast to each of these skeptical views, moral objectivism posits that some moral assertions represent objective truths independent of any particular system of appraisal. This idea has been philosophically controversial. Yet, many philosophers, even those who deny moral objectivism, have assumed that moral objectivism is the best approximation of ordinary individuals' meta-ethical views and have built this assumption into their theorizing (e.g., Smith, 1994; Mackie, 1977). This widespread assumption is often thought to have the consequence of shifting the burden of proof onto moral skeptics, who must not only argue positively for their own skeptical views, but must also account for, and explain away, the objectivist views of ordinary folk (see e.g., Sayre-McCord, 1986).

However, whereas traditional analytical philosophers have been content to rely on their own assumptions about ordinary individuals' moral cognition, modern empirically minded philosophers have confronted the psychological reality directly. In this way, their investigations intersect with those of moral psychologists, whose interest in moral objectivity is grounded not in the desire to inform philosophical debate, per se, but in the desire to understand ordinary moral cognition.

Relation to Other Psychological Research

Psychological research on moral objectivity is connected with (though distinct from) research on several other aspects of moral cognition, including "moral mandates" (Skitka, Bauman, & Sargis, 2005), "protected" or "sacred" values (Baron & Spranca, 1997; Tetlock, 2003; Tetlock, Kristel, Elson, Green, & Lerner, 2000), and "naïve realism," (Ross & Ward, 1996). Most perti-nently, it connects closely with Elliot Turiel's developmental work investigating children's tendency to treat their moral beliefs as hav-ing warrant independent of immediate au-thority or cultural norms (Turiel, 1978, 1983; Turiel, Hildenbrandt, & Wainryb, 1991). It is worth scrutinizing the relation between these research streams so as to best appreciate how they complement rather than overlap with one another.

Turiel and colleagues' research investi-gated whether moral actions that children regard as wrong, such as one child hitting another, are still judged wrong when a rel-evant authority figure, or an alternative cul-ture, deems them acceptable (or "okay"). Children typically judged that such actions were still wrong even under such modified conditions, essentially stipulating that their wrongness was independent of local author-ity and culture. In contrast, research on moral objectivity presents subjects (usually adults) with a moral disagreement and asks whether such disagreement implies that at least one of the two parties must be mistak-en—thereby implying that the issue at stake is an objective one (Goodwin & Darley, 2008, 2012; Sarkissian et al., 2011). Vari-ants on this procedure have asked subjects whether they think there can be a correct answer regarding the disagreement (Good-win & Darley, 2008, 2012).

Turiel's procedure reveals important as-pects of children's moral thought, but it does not speak directly to questions about moral objectivity. It calls only for what philoso-phers refer to as a "first order" judgment of moral wrongness, whereas the procedures used in research on moral objectivity call for a "second order" judgment of the moral truth, falsehood, correctness, or mistaken-ness of a first-order moral judgment. In say-ing that a particular action is "still wrong," independent of any backing by a relevant authority or cultural norm, children are not necessarily indicating a belief in an objec-tive moral truth. To see this, consider what a noncognitivist (e.g., an emotivist) might say in response to Turiel's probe—under a changed normative regime, they may also in-dicate that the behavior in question is "still wrong," intending to convey only that their expression of disapproval would be unabat-ed, rather than a belief in an objective moral fact. A moral subjectivist might make a simi-lar response. Only moral relativists would be moved to change their response in the face of an altered normative regime. As such, Tu-riel's procedure does not clearly distinguish objectivists from nonobjectivists (nor was it intended to); it assesses the perceived scope or generalizability of meta-ethical beliefs but not their perceived objectivity (see also Goodwin & Darley, 2010).

Theories and Findings Regarding Lay Meta-Ethics

In contrast, current methods of measuring meta-ethical beliefs—which call for subjects to indicate whether a moral disagreement implies that at least one of the disagree-ing parties must be mistaken—distinguish objectivists from nonobjectivists (though these methods are not sensitive enough to distinguish between the rich variety of non-objectivist positions outlined earlier). They differ from prior methods, which measured meta-ethical views at the dispositional level and which failed to distinguish meta-ethical from first-order views (e.g., Forsyth, 1980, 1981; Forsyth & Berger, 1982; see Goodwin & Darley, 2010, for a critique).

One theory of lay meta-ethics is that people are moral objectivists about a ca-nonical set of moral beliefs pertaining to the wrongness of harmful or unjust acts. Early evidence for this view emerged from a pio-neering study by Nichols (2004), in which subjects indicated which of two parties was correct in the wake of a disagreement over a moral transgression. Respondents also had the option of indicating that there is simply no fact of the matter as to who was correct. Results varied from one experi-ment to the next, depending on the nature of the transgression. But, in the most well-powered study, almost three-quarters of the subjects responded as moral objectivists in response to a disagreement over the wrong-ness of hitting another person (Study 3). Using a slightly different method, Wainryb et al. (2004) found evidence that children of ages 5, 7, and 9 tended to approach moral disagreements in an objectivist fashion, indi-cating that there was only one right answer to a moral disagreement (see also Nichols & Folds-Bennett, 2003).

Goodwin and Darley (2008) expanded upon this research by surveying a wider range of moral beliefs and by using a slightly different procedure. Subjects were presented with an ostensible disagreement over a moral issue, in which another person in the experiment had allegedly come to a different conclusion than they themselves had regarding a canonical moral issue (e.g., that robbery or murder is wrong). They were asked to indicate whether the other person (or themselves) was mistaken, or whether instead neither party need be mistaken,[2] and whether there could be a correct answer regarding the issue. Owing to their high intercorrelation, these two variables were combined into a single measure of objectivity. Two further methodological precautions were added. Subjects were asked to indicate why they thought the other person could have come to a different conclusion. These responses were carefully scrutinized to ensure that subjects' assumed reason for the disagreement was not that the other person had made different factual assumptions about the act in question (e.g., regarding its underlying motivation or likely consequences). Any postulated difference of this sort might have led subjects to think that the other person had a different action in mind, implying that the disagreement that had arisen was not genuine. In the rare cases where subjects did make such interpretations, these data were eliminated. How strongly subjects agreed with the first-order moral beliefs was also measured, and this measure of belief extremity was controlled for in the main statistical analyses.

The main upshot of these analyses was that subjects typically indicated highly objectivist responses regarding canonical moral disagreements about harm or injustice (e.g., in response to disagreements over the wrongness of cheating, stealing, or harming another person). That is, subjects typically indicated that the other party was mistaken in the face of the disagreement and that there was indeed a correct answer to the issue in question. Their responses to moral disagreements were more objectivist than their responses to disagreements over social conventional violations (e.g., the "wrongness" of wearing pajamas to a lecture), and

almost as objectivist as their responses regarding basic matters of empirical fact (e.g., whether Boston is north of Los Angeles). These differences were observed while statistically controlling for differences across the categories in terms of how strongly (or extremely) the first-order beliefs were held.

However, as Nichols (2004) had also suggested, Goodwin and Darley (2008) observed considerable variation in the objectivity subjects attributed to different moral beliefs. This issue was explored more fully in Goodwin and Darley (2012), who found that beliefs about the wrongness (or badness) of negative acts were seen as more objective than beliefs about the rightness (or goodness) of positive acts, both when controlling for, and equating for, first-order judgment extremity. Wrongness is seen as a more objective moral property than goodness or rightness. Moral beliefs about the wrongness of harmful or unjust acts were seen as especially objective, but the wrongness of even some purely "symbolic," nonharmful acts, such as discreetly urinating on a memorial, was also regarded as highly objective.

This research, therefore, shows that ordinary individuals appear to be "meta-ethical pluralists," attributing objectivity to some but not all moral beliefs (see Gill, 2008, 2009, for philosophical endorsement of such a pluralist position). Wright, Grandjean, and McWhite (2013) provided further support for meta-ethical pluralism, showing that individuals provide diverging assessments of objectivity even among a set of moral beliefs that they themselves (and not the researchers) had designated as "moral."

Other research on this topic has explored whether individual differences in personality, religiosity, or cognitive style might account for some of the variation in the perceived objectivity of moral beliefs. Grounding morality in a divine being appears to predict greater moral objectivity (Goodwin & Darley, 2008), whereas greater openness to experience predicts lesser moral objectivity (Feltz & Cokely, 2008). Age is also an important predictor. Nichols (2004) found that within a sample of undergraduate subjects, years in college predicted lowered objectivity ratings (Study 2, although this finding was not observed in a later study, Study 3). Beebe and Sackris (2016) similarly found that college-age subjects were less likely than both younger and older subjects to respond as moral objectivists. However, all of the existing evidence on individual differences comes from cross-sectional correlational designs, rather than longitudinal or experimental designs, and most of the existing studies have not robustly controlled for possible third-variable confounds. More research is needed to determine the likely causal pathways more conclusively.

Challenge to the Standard View

Taken as a whole, the research just described appears to indicate that ordinary individuals are moral objectivists about at least a limited class of canonical moral transgressions, notwithstanding their overall metaethical pluralism. However, this conclusion has recently been contested. Sarkissian and colleagues (2011) argued that the possibility of a deeper lay moral relativism had not been explored fully. Although people may indicate that a mistake has been made if two parties from within the same moral culture disagree, this does not mean they would respond similarly if the two parties were from different moral cultures. If subjects no longer provide objectivist responses to disagreements of that sort, it would provide evidence that they are, in fact, moral relativists deep down. To explore this idea, Sarkissian and colleagues examined how people judge disagreements between appraisers from radically different moral cultures. The disagreements concerned canonical moral harms, such as stabbing someone else with a knife or killing someone. In one case, an American student disagreed with a member of the "Mamilons," a remote Amazonian tribe. In an even more exotic case, an American student disagreed with a member of the "Pentars," an alien species that has "a very different sort of psychology from human beings" in that "they are not at all interested in friendship or love" and "their main goal is simply to increase the total number of equilateral pentagons in the universe" (p. 488). Sarkissian et al. (2011) compared responses to these two cases with responses to a case in which two American observers disagreed. The case in which two

individuals from the same culture disagreed elicited objectivist responses on average, just as in previous research. But the two cross-cultural cases elicited less objectivist responses. This was especially pronounced in the alien (Pentar) case, for which responses were located at, or slightly below, the midpoint of a scale assessing agreement with the idea that one of the disagreeing parties "must be wrong."

Two features of Sarkissian and colleagues' (2011) data appear to provide evidence of moral relativism. First, in the cases of cross-cultural disagreement, there is the low *absolute* level of agreement with the item assessing whether one of the disagreeing parties must be mistaken—in the most exotic case (the alien Pentars), responses trended toward the "disagree" end of the scale, thus implying a nonobjectivist position. Second, there is the *relative* difference between all three conditions—the fact that the degree of cultural difference between the disagreeing parties moderated subjects' responses indicates that they were indeed sensitive to the frame of reference according to which moral beliefs are evaluated—thus implying a relativistic stance. The methodology of these studies is extremely clever and represents an important challenge to the standard objectivist interpretation.

Yet, as intriguing as this evidence is, the conclusions Sarkissian et al. (2011) draw may be contested. Sousa, Piazza, and Goodwin (2017) argue that subjects' responses may have been moderated by the degree of cultural distance between the two disagreeing parties, not because they were relativists deep down but, rather, because they assumed that the respective judges were interpreting the described actions in fundamentally different ways. In Sarkissian et al.'s (2011) studies, the actions were described in very sparse terms, leaving room for a variety of interpretations. In one case, there was disagreement over the moral wrongness of the following action: "Dylan buys an expensive new knife and tests its sharpness by randomly stabbing a passerby on the street." In another case, the action was: "Horace finds his youngest child extremely unattractive and therefore kills him." At first glance, these action descriptions may seem relatively straightforward. But they, in fact, contain many potential ambiguities—nothing is said or implied about the reason or motivation for the action (e.g., whether it was selfishly or prosocially motivated—for instance, it might have served to protect the community from an unspecified threat), nor about the moral status or consent of the apparent victim (e.g., whether the victim had done anything to deserve harsh treatment, or whether the act was against the victim's will). This therefore leaves room for the possibility that subjects attributed quite different interpretations of the actions to different observers. Any apparent disagreement between the two observers would therefore dissolve—not because the subjects are truly moral relativists but, rather, because they assumed the disagreeing parties were rendering judgments about fundamentally different actions and were therefore meeting at cross-purposes. In that case, both parties could be judged correct without implying a relativistic stance. Indeed, Sousa et al. (2017) demonstrate that when these actions are described in more precise ways so as to eliminate these critical ambiguities, subjects' responses return to being objectivist.

In a related vein, the fact that the alien Pentars' psychology is so far removed from ordinary human psychology may cause subjects to wonder whether the Pentars are even capable of understanding that some of the actions described may thwart the interests of the victim. If the Pentars were incapable of understanding this, it would again appear that their moral judgments concern a fundamentally different action (i.e., one that did not impinge on the interests of the victim), thus dissolving any ostensible disagreement they might appear to have with an American observer. Here, too, Sousa et al. (2017) showed that when the aliens are described as being capable of *understanding* that the actions did impinge on the interests of the victim, even while other aspects of their psychology are very remote, objectivist rather than relativist responding is the norm. This debate is not yet resolved, but at this stage, it appears that there are still good reasons to favor the view that lay individuals typically hold an objectivist position about canonical moral transgressions, notwithstanding considerable variability across issues and across individuals.

Connection to Behavior

Meta-ethical beliefs have recently been explored in connection with two important practical issues: moral tolerance and moral commitment. A priori, it is not entirely obvious what meta-ethical stance ought to predict greater tolerance. Some philosophers have drawn a link between nonobjectivist positions and an ethic of moral tolerance, assuming that moral relativists (for instance) would be more likely to endorse tolerance and noninterference when it comes to other cultures' questionable moral practices (Gowans, 2015). However, other philosophers have noted that moral objectivists may in fact be more open-minded in relation to other people who disagree with them over moral issues; rather than treating moral disagreements as irresolvable clashes of brute preferences, objectivists believe that there is a true fact of the matter as to who is correct, and so they should be receptive to new information that might legitimately change their view (Snare, 1992). The existing research conducted on this issue has supported only the first view—moral objectivists do appear to be less tolerant of divergent moral opinions than nonobjectivists. Framed more positively, this research shows that moral objectivism predicts greater moral conviction and steadfastness. Goodwin and Darley (2012) found that objectivism predicted greater discomfort with another person who disagreed with subjects' own moral positions concerning the wrongness of various actions, even after controlling for subjects' first-order judgments of how wrong the actions were. Similarly, Wright, McWhite, and Grandjean (2014) found that objectivists were more likely to indicate attitudinal intolerance toward a disagreeing other person (discomfort with that person's beliefs) and were also less inclined to help that person if they were in need (a quasi-behavioral measure). As in other areas of this literature, the evidence for the link between objectivism and intolerance is correlational only and does not yet establish a causal claim.

Moral objectivity may also predict greater commitment to acting morally. This possibility has been explored in two complementary ways. Young and Durwin (2013) postulated that greater moral objectivity leads to greater prosociality. In two experiments, they stopped passersby in the street, priming some of them with moral objectivism (or, in their terminology, "moral realism") by asking: "Do you agree that some things are just morally right or wrong, good or bad, wherever you happen to be from in the world?" and others with nonobjectivism ("antirealism") by asking: "Do you agree that our morals and values are shaped by our culture and upbringing, so that there are no absolute right answers to any moral questions?" When primed with objectivism, subjects were more likely to donate money to a charity of their choice (Study 1) and more inclined to donate higher amounts (Study 2)[3], compared with subjects in the antirealism and control conditions. It therefore appears that greater objectivism may lead to more prosocial behaviors.

Rai and Holyoak (2013) explored a related idea, namely that greater objectivism inclines people not to cheat in a context in which doing so would be personally advantageous and undetectable. Subjects were randomly assigned to one of three conditions. In the objectivism (or, in the researchers' terms, "absolutism") condition, they read a moral argument denouncing the practice of female genital mutilation, which called for strong intervention to end it, and which was laced with reference to objective moral truths. In the relativism condition, subjects read a moral argument advocating tolerance of female genital mutilation based on the inescapable relativity of moral truths. Subjects in the control condition read a neutral passage. Subsequently, all subjects self-reported the outcome of a dice roll that determined their monetary payment for the experiment, and were afforded an opportunity to misreport their score with impunity. The results showed that only subjects in the moral relativism condition were more likely to report higher scores than would be expected by chance. Their scores were also significantly higher than the scores reported by subjects in the other two conditions (which did not differ from one another). A subsequent experiment showed that subjects primed with moral objectivism were less likely to indicate willingness to perform a minor moral infraction (purchasing an item for an incorrectly low listed price) than subjects primed with

moral relativism or control subjects. Across the two experiments, the relative influence of the experimental conditions varied with respect to the control condition—only relativism deviated from control in Study 1, whereas only objectivism deviated from control in Study 2. Rai and Holyoak (2013) speculate that the difference rests in subjects' different initial predispositions toward the acts in question. In Study 1, subjects were initially predisposed *not* to cheat, and so exposure to moral relativism weakened this tendency (exposure to objectivism did not alter the existing tendency). In contrast, in Study 2, subjects were initially predisposed to engage in the infraction, which exposure to moral objectivism blocked, but which exposure to relativism did not affect. It therefore seems from this research that moral objectivism protects against dishonesty.

Overall, this research makes a valuable contribution by exploring ways that meta-ethical beliefs may contribute to real moral behaviors and attitudes. It suggests that moral objectivism may lead to greater moral commitment, prosociality, and conviction—characteristics that may be valuable in many circumstances, though not unerringly. Notably, researchers have also speculated that moral objectivism may fuel repugnant antisocial moral commitments, including those that underlie terrorist acts (Ginges & Atran, 2009, 2011; Ginges, Atran, Medin, & Shikaki, 2007).

Ways to Advance Behavioral Research

However, two important limitations exist with the present experimental investigations of the causal influence of moral objectivism on behavior. In none of the Young and Durwin (2011) or Rai and Holyoak (2013) studies were manipulation checks included, and so there is no direct evidence that the experimental manipulations actually moved subjects' meta-ethical beliefs. Moreover, in both studies, there are significant concerns about experimenter demand. In Young and Durwin's (2013) study, the procedure is highly suggestive. subjects are asked a very pointed question about the fundamental nature of morality, which indicates how the requestor is likely to respond to a refusal to donate money; in the objectivism case ("Do you agree that some things are just morally right or wrong, good or bad, wherever you happen to be from in the world?"), the requestor could be presumed to respond in a more negative and intolerant manner to a refusal to donate. This factor, rather than any change in subjects' meta-ethical beliefs, may account for the results. A similar concern applies to Rai and Holyoak's (2013) studies. By conveying a meta-ethical stance to subjects, the experimenters may have unwittingly conveyed information about how they would likely react (publicly or privately) if the participant were to cheat (Study 1) or to indicate antisocial intentions (Study 2)—namely, less permissively in the objectivism condition and more permissively in the relativism condition. Once again, it is not clear that a change in subjects' meta-ethical beliefs is actually what caused their change in behavior, as opposed to a change in their beliefs about the experimenter's wishes.[4] Future investigations would be well served to address this issue rigorously. One strategy may be to present priming information in such a way that it is clear that the researchers are not endorsing the meta-ethical position in question. It would also be important to measure whether priming information actually changes meta-ethical beliefs, which is not yet known from the existing studies.

Conclusion

Questions about the perceived objectivity of ordinary individuals' moral beliefs have yielded several important discoveries. The present state of research indicates that people typically take objectivist stances toward canonical moral issues concerning the infliction of harm or injustice, at least when considering moral disagreements within their own moral culture. Some symbolic, victimless, moral transgressions are also perceived in an objectivist way. The picture is less clear when it comes to moral disagreements that cut across moral cultures, but there is reason for optimism that this controversy will reach an empirical resolution. Exciting research has begun to explore the behavioral implications of meta-ethical stances, suggesting that moral objectivism may predict greater

moral commitment, conviction, and intolerance. This area of research illustrates how a fundamental philosophical issue—far from being removed from everyday life—in fact plays out in concrete ways in the moral cognition and behavior of ordinary individuals.

ACKNOWLEDGMENTS

I thank Dena Gromet and Jesse Graham for valuable comments on an earlier draft of this chapter.

NOTES

1. In accordance with the focus in the existing empirical literature, here I am focusing only on "metaphysical" moral skepticism, which denies that any moral beliefs can be true. "Epistemological" moral skepticism is distinct, in that it denies or questions whether any moral beliefs can be justified or known (see Sinnott-Armstrong, 2006). The two can come apart because one might deny moral knowledge without denying moral truth (though the reverse is not plausible; for further discussion, see Sinnott-Armstrong, 2006, 2011).

2. Goodwin and Darley (2008, 2012) framed the disagreements as being between the participant him- or herself and another person, though other research has asked subjects to comment on disagreements they are not personally involved in (e.g., Nichols, 2004; Sarkissian et al., 2011). Both methods have relative strengths and weaknesses; the first-person method allows an assessment of beliefs the experimenters know the subjects care about, whereas the third-person method removes potential distortions that might emerge from having one's own, expressed moral beliefs challenged.

3. Study 2 in this investigation did not replicate the finding that subjects primed with objectivism were more likely to donate at all, but it showed that among those who donated, individuals primed with objectivism donated more.

4. This criticism does not depend on subjects being concerned solely about their behavior being detected and brought to their attention by the experimenter. Subjects' behavior may also be influenced simply by their knowing how negatively the experimenter would react privately, or even by their knowing that their behavior goes against the experimenter's wishes (regardless of whether the experimenter would ever find out about it).

REFERENCES

Ayer, A. J. (1936). *Language, truth, and logic.* London: Gollancz.

Baron, J., & Spranca, M. (1997). Protected values. *Organizational Behavior and Human Decision Processes, 70,* 1–16.

Beebe, A., & Sackris, D. (2016). Moral objectivism across the lifespan. *Philosophical Psychology, 29,* 912–929.

Feltz, A., & Cokely, E. T. (2008). The fragmented folk: More evidence of stable individual differences in moral judgments and folk intuitions. In B. C. Love, K. McRae, & V. M. Sloutsky (Eds.), *Proceedings of the 30th annual conference of the Cognitive Science Society* (pp. 1771–1776). Austin, TX: Cognitive Science Society.

Forsyth, D. R. (1980). A taxonomy of ethical ideologies. *Journal of Personality and Social Psychology, 39,* 175–184.

Forsyth, D. R. (1981). Moral judgment: The influence of ethical ideology. *Personality and Social Psychology Bulletin, 7,* 218–223.

Forsyth, D. R., & Berger, R. E. (1982). The effects of ethical ideology on moral behavior. *Journal of Social Psychology, 117,* 53–56.

Gill, M. B. (2008). Metaethical variability, incoherence, and error. In W. Sinnott-Armstrong (Ed.), *Moral psychology: Vol. 2. The cognitive science of morality: Intuition and diversity* (pp. 387–401). Cambridge, MA: MIT Press.

Gill, M. B. (2009). Indeterminacy and variability in meta-ethics. *Philosophical Studies, 145,* 215–234.

Ginges, J., & Atran, S. (2009). What motivates participation in violent political action: Selective incentives or parochial altruism? *Annals of the New York Academy of Sciences, 1167,* 115–123.

Ginges, J., & Atran, S. (2011). War as a moral imperative (not just practical politics by other means). *Proceedings of the Biological Sciences, 278,* 2930–2938.

Ginges, J., Atran, S., Medin, D., & Shikaki, K. (2007). Sacred bounds on rational resolution of violent political conflict. *Proceedings of the National Academy of Sciences of the USA, 104,* 7357–7360.

Goodwin, G. P., & Darley, J. M. (2008). The psychology of meta-ethics: Exploring objectivism. *Cognition, 106,* 1339–1366.

Goodwin, G. P., & Darley, J. M. (2010). The perceived objectivity of ethical beliefs: Psychological findings and implications for public policy. *Review of Philosophy and Psychology, 1,* 1–28.

Goodwin, G. P., & Darley, J. M. (2012). Why are some moral beliefs perceived to be more objective than others? *Journal of Experimental Social Psychology, 48,* 250–256.

Gowans, C. (2015). Moral relativism. In E. N. Zalta (Ed.), *The Stanford encyclopedia of philosophy.* Stanford, CA: Metaphysics Research Lab, Center for the Study of Language and Information, Stanford University. Available at *https://plato.stanford.edu/entries/moral-relativism.*

Hare, R. M. (1952). *The language of morals.* Oxford, UK: Clarendon Press.

Hare, R. M. (1981). *Moral thinking.* Oxford, UK: Clarendon Press.

Harman, G. (1975). Moral relativism defended. *Philosophical Review, 84,* 3–22.

Joyce, R. (2001). *The myth of morality.* Cambridge, UK: Cambridge University Press.

Mackie, J. (1977). *Ethics: Inventing right and wrong.* London: Penguin.

Nichols, S. (2004). After objectivity: An empirical study of moral judgment. *Philosophical Psychology, 17,* 3–26.

Nichols, S., & Folds-Bennett, T. (2003). Are children moral objectivists? Children's judgments about moral and response-dependent properties. *Cognition, 90,* B23–B32.

Rai, T. S., & Holyoak, K. J. (2013). Exposure to moral relativism compromises moral behavior. *Journal of Experimental Social Psychology, 49,* 995–1001.

Ross, L., & Ward, A. (1996). Naive realism in everyday life: Implications for social conflict and misunderstanding. In T. Brown, E. S. Reed, & E. Turiel (Eds.), *Values and knowledge* (pp. 103–135). Hillsdale, NJ: Erlbaum.

Sarkissian, H., Park, J., Tien, D., Wright, J. C., & Knobe, J. (2011). Folk moral relativism. *Mind and Language, 26,* 482–505.

Sayre-McCord, G. (1986). The many moral realisms. *Southern Journal of Philosophy, 24*(Suppl.), 1–22.

Shafer-Landau, R. (2003). *Moral realism: A defense.* Oxford, UK: Oxford University Press.

Shafer-Landau, R. (2004). *Whatever happened to good and evil?* Oxford, UK: Oxford University Press.

Sinnott-Armstrong, W. (2006). *Moral skepticisms.* New York: Oxford University Press.

Sinnott-Armstrong, W. (2011). Moral skepticism. In E. N. Zalta (Ed.), *The Stanford encyclopedia of philosophy.* Stanford, CA: Metaphysics Research Lab, Center for the Study of Language and Information, Stanford University. Retrieved from *http://plato.stanford.edu/archives/fall2011/entries/skepticism-moral.*

Skitka, L. J., Bauman, C. W., & Sargis, E. G. (2005). Moral conviction: Another contributor to attitude strength or something more?

Journal of Personality and Social Psychology, 88, 895–917.

Smith, M. (1994). *The moral problem.* Oxford, UK: Blackwell.

Snare, F. (1992). *The nature of moral thinking.* London: Routledge.

Sousa, P., Piazza, J., & Goodwin, G. P. (2017). *Folk moral objectivism.* Manuscript in preparation.

Stevenson, C. (1944). *Ethics and language.* New Haven, CT: Yale University Press.

Tetlock, P. E. (2003). Thinking the unthinkable: Sacred values and taboo cognitions. *Trends in Cognitive Sciences, 7,* 320–324.

Tetlock, P. E., Kristel, O. V., Elson, B., Green, M., & Lerner, J. (2000). The psychology of the unthinkable: Taboo trade-offs, forbidden base rates, and heretical counterfactuals. *Journal of Personality and Social Psychology, 78,* 853–870.

Turiel, E. (1978). Social regulations and domains of social concepts. In W. Damon (Ed.), *New directions for child development: Vol. 1. Social cognition* (pp. 45–74). New York: Gardner.

Turiel, E. (1983). *The development of social knowledge.* Cambridge, UK: Cambridge University press.

Turiel, E., Hildenbrandt, C., & Wainryb, C. (1991). Judging social issues: Difficulties, inconsistencies, and consistencies. *Monographs of the Society for Research in Child Development, 56,* 1–103.

Wainryb, C., Shaw, L. A., Langley, M., Cottam, K., & Lewis, R. (2004). Children's thinking about diversity of belief in the early school years: Judgments of relativism, tolerance, and disagreeing persons. *Child Development, 75,* 687–703.

Wright, J. C., Grandjean, P., & McWhite, C. (2013). The role of dispositional vs. situational threat-sensitivity in our moral judgments. *Journal of Moral Education, 42,* 383–397.

Wright, J. C., McWhite, C., & Grandjean, P. (2014). The cognitive mechanisms of intolerance: Do our meta-ethical commitments matter? In T. Lombrozo, S. Nichols, & J. Knobe (Eds.), *Oxford studies in experimental philosophy* (Vol. 1, pp. 28–61). New York: Oxford University Press.

Young, L., & Durwin, A. J. (2013). Moral realism as moral motivation: The impact of meta-ethics on everyday decision-making. *Journal of Experimental Social Psychology, 49,* 302–306.

CHAPTER 33

Folk Theories in the Moral Domain

Sara Gottlieb
Tania Lombrozo

Is morality intuitive or deliberative?

This distinction can obscure the role of folk moral theories in moral judgment; judgments may arise "intuitively" yet result from abstract theoretical and philosophical commitments that participate in "deliberative" reasoning.

Context

Physician-assisted suicide was, according to the Gallup Poll, the most controversial social issue in 2010: 46% of the individuals surveyed indicated that it was morally acceptable, and a matching 46% indicated that it was morally wrong (Saad, 2010). It remained controversial in 2012 when Massachusetts voted against the Death with Dignity Act by a narrow 1%. And in 2014, the issue regained momentum in the media with Brittany Maynard, the terminally ill 29-year-old who publicly documented the decision to take her own life.

Individuals support or oppose physician-assisted suicide for a variety of reasons. The American College of Physicians put forth an official stance in a 2001 position paper, stating that although "arguments supporting physician-assisted suicide highlight the duty to relieve patient suffering or stem from a vigorous understanding of the duty

to respect patient autonomy" (Snyder & Sulmasy, p. 211), the Hippocratic Oath requires that physicians follow a tradition of healing and comfort and never intentionally bring about the death of any patient. They wrote, "Just as society can direct that no one has the 'right' to sell himself or herself into slavery, so too can society direct that no one has a 'right' to assistance with suicide" (p. 212).

This example illustrates one process by which moral judgments can be reached: through the explicit consideration and weighing of relevant moral principles, such as respecting patient rights or adhering to natural law concerning time of death. But is this how the respondents to the 2010 Gallup Poll reached their judgments, as well? Traditional and more contemporary accounts of moral judgment offer different responses. According to more traditional accounts, such as those grounded in classic work by Kohlberg (Kohlberg, 1969; Turiel, 1983), moral judgments typically result from a process of explicit moral reasoning—or "deliberation"—akin to that offered by the American College of Physicians. More recent accounts, such as Haidt's (2001) social intuitionist model, however, challenge the idea that moral justifications are causally responsible for their corresponding judgments. Instead, they argue that moral judgment is a fundamentally "intuitive" phenomenon, with a large literature suggesting that moral attitudes on issues related to sanctity of life, which typically divide liberal and conservative voters, are guided by *affect*—most notably disgust (Inbar, Pizarro, & Bloom, 2012; Inbar, Pizarro, Knobe, & Bloom, 2009; Inbar, Pizarro, Iyer, & Haidt, 2012; Inbar, Pizarro, & Bloom, 2012).

These opposing approaches differ critically on the emphasis they place on *deliberative* versus *intuitive* processes, a distinction that has paved the way for widespread "dual-systems" or "dual-process" accounts of moral reasoning (Greene, 2007; Greene, Sommerville, Nystrom, Darley, & Cohen, 2001; Greene, Morelli, Lowenberg, Nystrom, & Cohen, 2008; Greene, Nystrom, Engell, Darley, & Cohen, 2004). In this chapter we argue that, although dual-systems approaches have been useful in many ways, a sharp boundary between intuition and deliberation potentially obscures important phenomena in moral judgment. In particular, we argue that, in many cases, moral judgments can arise "intuitively" yet result from abstract and coherent theoretical commitments that participate in "deliberative" reasoning. One example comes from the case of physician-assisted suicide, which implicitly ties a terminally ill patient's deciding mind to her failing body. For this and other issues that bear on the sanctity of life, moral judgments could depend not only on affect but also on relatively abstract and coherent metaphysical commitments concerning the relationship between the mind and the body—what has typically been referred to as "intuitive dualism" in the psychological literature (Bloom, 2004a; Greene, 2011). We propose that theoretical commitments such as those embodied in intuitive dualism play an important role in moral judgment, but in a manner that cross-cuts the traditional intuition–deliberation divide. This hybrid proposal borrows insights from both traditional

and contemporary accounts of moral judgment from social psychology, but also draws on research from both cognitive and developmental psychology on intuitive theories of the natural world.

To argue for this proposal, we first provide a brief review of evidence that has been used to support the dual-process perspective in moral psychology. We then suggest that the distinction between intuitive and deliberative processing is potentially problematic when it comes to describing the role of more abstract commitments in moral judgment, as in the example of physician-assisted suicide and intuitive dualism. To make sense of such cases, we turn to literature on intuitive theories in other domains and argue for "folk theories" that play a role in shaping moral judgment. We then present evidence for this position, including our own recent work, which documents systematic relationships between people's metaphysical and epistemic commitments, on the one hand, and their intuitive judgments concerning bioethical issues such as physician-assisted suicide, on the other.

Intuition versus Deliberation: A Dual-Process Perspective

Dual-process theories, of which there are many (Evans & Stanovich, 2013), typically differentiate two types of thinking: one intuitive and the other deliberative. Intuition and deliberation typically map onto mental processes underlying decision making and behavior differentiated according to whether they operate automatically or in a controlled manner. This distinction, in turn, can be operationalized either behaviorally—with automatic processes manifesting themselves under cognitive load or time pressure—or by isolating distinct neural correlates (e.g., the ventromedial prefrontal cortex [vmPFC] vs. dorsolateral prefrontal cortex [DLPFC] for automatic vs. controlled processes in the case of deontological vs. utilitarian judgment; Greene et al., 2001; Greene et al., 2004). The distinction between automatic and controlled processes and, correspondingly, between intuitive and deliberative judgments has been particularly influential in moral psychology.

Although there are many flavors of dual-process theories (see Evans & Stanovich, 2013), most agree in linking intuitive versus deliberative processing with the pairs of opposing attributes identified in Table 33.1. Evidence for the distinction between intuitive and deliberative processing accordingly focuses on these attributes, with particular emphasis on the first three.

Initial support for dual-process approaches to the moral domain came from functional neuroimaging studies investigating the extent to which brain processes associated with emotion (e.g., vmPFC, amygdala) are engaged in response to different kinds of moral dilemmas (Greene et al., 2001; Greene et al., 2004). For example, Greene and colleagues presented participants with variants on trolley car problems, such as the hypothetical footbridge case, in which a participant must decide whether it is permissible to push one person in front of a train to prevent the train from hitting five others. Scenarios of this sort create a tension between deontological bases for judgments, which reflect rights and duties, and utilitarian bases for judgment, which require favoring the greater good. Greene et al. (2001) found that "personal" moral dilemmas—those like the footbridge case that involve causing direct harm, often through touch—tended to elicit neural activity associated with emotion. In contrast, Greene et al. (2004) found

evidence for brain processes associated with cognitive control (e.g., DLPFC) in utilitarian moral judgment. These initial findings supported the idea that deontological judgments emerge from "intuition" (with an important role for automatic emotional processing) and utilitarian judgments from more controlled deliberation.

Subsequent work has backed up the association between deontology and more intuitive processing, on the one hand, and between utilitarian judgments and deliberation, on the other (Paxton, Ungar, & Greene, 2012). For example, patients with frontotemporal dementia (characterized by "emotional blunting") are three times more likely than healthy controls to answer in favor of pushing the man off the footbridge for utilitarian benefit (Mendez, Anderson, & Shapira, 2005). At the cellular level, citalopram, a selective serotonin reuptake inhibitor (SSRI), increases the availability of serotonin in the bloodstream, thereby increasing certain emotional responses and deontological moral judgment, whereas antianxiety drugs such as lorazepam can reduce deontological inclinations (Perkins et al., 2013). And, at a behavioral level, utilitarian judgments are more affected by cognitive load (Greene et al., 2008; Trémolière, Neys, & Bonnefon, 2012), associated with longer decision time (Suter & Hertwig, 2011), and associated with reflective, as opposed to intuitive, mindsets (Paxton et al., 2012).

One implication of dual-process approaches is that moral judgments (which reflect a mix of intuition and deliberation) can seriously depart from moral justifications (which fall on the side of deliberation). And, in fact, there is evidence that the two diverge. Haidt (2001), for example, argues for a phenomenon he calls "moral dumbfounding," which refers to an individual's inability to produce moral justifications for moral judgments. As evidence, he presents the case of Mark and Julie—siblings who decide to engage in consensual sex, use protection, and find that it brings them closer together. An overwhelming number of individuals find this wrong, but when probed for reasons why, fail to produce reliable justifications. Haidt (2001) claims that "moral reasoning does not cause moral judgment; rather, moral reasoning is usually a post hoc construction, generated

TABLE 33.1. Attributes of Intuitive and Deliberative Processing

	Intuitive	Deliberative
Process	Automatic	Controlled
Speed of processing	Fast	Slow
Role of affect	Often high	Often low
Level of consciousness	Nonconscious	Conscious
Representation	Contextualized	Abstract
Accuracy	"Good enough"	Often high
Evolutionary origin	Distant	Recent
Type of belief	Implicit	Explicit

after a judgment has been reached" (p. 814). Other empirical work similarly suggests that moral justifications are not responsible for their corresponding moral judgments (Hauser, Cushman, Young, Jin, & Mikhail, 2007) and that even when individuals can provide justifications, they sometimes fail to recognize the full set of factors that influenced their judgments (Cushman, Young, & Hauser, 2006).

Dual-systems approaches can also accommodate cases in which moral judgments and moral justifications systematically cohere—the approach does not reject the possibility that moral justifications can sometimes influence judgments or that justifications will match judgments because they are generated post hoc. A bigger challenge for most dual-systems approaches would come from evidence for representational structures that blur the crucial distinction between "intuitive" and "deliberate" processing. A candidate for such a structure comes from research in cognitive and developmental psychology that aims to characterize people's intuitive theories of the natural world, such as folk psychological, folk biological, and folk physical beliefs. As we detail in the next section, "intuitive" theories don't fit neatly on a single side of the intuitive–deliberative divide.

Drawing an Analogy to Folk Scientific Theories

A broad literature in cognitive and developmental psychology suggests that children hold rich intuitive theories of the world even before they begin formal education (e.g., Carey, 2000; Keil, 2011). In the domain of physics, for example, students hold theories grounded in the belief that forces transfer from one object to another upon contact and must dissipate before those objects cease moving (Clement, 1982; McCloskey, 1983). In the domain of biology, children hold intuitive theories of adaptation grounded in a belief that all members of a species evolve together such that each individual organism will produce offspring that are better adapted than the parent was at birth (Shtulman, 2006; Shtulman & Schulz, 2008). Although these initial theories continue to play a role throughout the lifespan (Shtul-

man & Valcarcel, 2012), novel theories are also acquired through everyday experience (e.g., Kempton, 1986; Vosniadou & Brewer, 1994) and through formal education (e.g., Shtulman & Calabi, 2013). We refer to such theories as "folk theories," both to differentiate them from full-fledged scientific theories and to avoid the implication that such theories are necessarily "intuitive" in the dual-systems sense.

Folk theories are characterized along three dimensions: structural, functional, and dynamic (Gopnik & Wellman, 2012; Gopnik & Meltzoff, 1997). At a structural level, folk theories specify law-like regularities and involve coherent, abstract, and typically causal representations of the world. At a functional level, theories support important judgments and behaviors, including predictions, explanations, counterfactuals, and interventions. And at a dynamic level, folk theories are revised in light of new evidence. These features differentiate folk theories from other kinds of mental representations, such as heuristics, networks of semantic association, or simple schemas.

The characteristic structural, functional, and dynamic properties of folk theories potentially muddy the distinction between intuitive and deliberative. Some characteristics of folk theories put them on the "intuitive" end, and it is not a coincidence that they are sometimes called *intuitive* theories: They often generate judgments quickly and are cognitively opaque in the sense that they operate over representations and processes that are not necessarily explicitly available. They are also often invoked to explain errors. On the other hand, they have some characteristics that align them with deliberation. At a structural level, they tend to involve fairly abstract representations. At a functional level, they support explanations that involve explicit appeal to theoretical content. And at a functional level, they are responsive to evidence and argumentation—learning processes more naturally associated with deliberation. So how do folk theories fit into a dual-systems approach to the moral domain?

Most approaches to moral psychology recognize an important role for folk theories in analyzing or structuring the *input* to moral judgment. For example, moral judgments can depend critically on causal analyses predicated on folk physical assumptions and on analyses of an agent's intentions that depend on folk psychological mechanisms (e.g., Cushman, 2008). (Exceptions to this generalization include approaches that deny the existence of folk theories altogether or that reject the premise that folk scientific analysis "precedes" moral analysis, e.g., Knobe, 2010.) But we wish to suggest something stronger: that folk theories not only structure the input to moral judgment but can also embody theoretical commitments that play a role in explicit moral deliberation and in "educating" moral intuitions. This process can occur in two ways: if the theories themselves contain moral content, or if the theories involve general commitments—such as dualism—that inform and constrain moral judgments. In the next sections, we provide evidence for both of these possibilities.

Evidence for Folk Moral Theories: The Building Blocks

What might intuitive *moral* theories look like? Such theories can be understood as a special type of folk theory specifically within the moral domain. At a structural level, folk moral theories should be abstract and rule-based in nature. At a functional level, folk moral theories should support moral judgments and justification. And at a dynamic level, moral theories should be responsive to new evidence, be it through direct instruction or more implicit learning mechanisms. We review evidence for each of these in turn.

Structurally, there is good evidence that at least some moral "rules" are represented in terms of fairly abstract causal structure (Mikhail, 2011; Waldmann & Dieterich, 2007) and formulated over fairly abstract concepts, even in early childhood (Hamlin, 2013). For example, Waldmann and Dieterich (2007) found that individuals are more willing to accept a utilitarian trade-off that involves harming a few individuals to save a greater number of people if the intervention is targeted at the agent and not the patient. These findings suggest not only that moral "rules" are formulated over abstract causal structure but also that the causal analysis in-

volves morally relevant distinctions, such as that between agent and patient.

Functionally, folk moral theories should at least partially govern more implicit moral judgments, such as judgments concerning which actions (interventions) are morally permissible. This is what Lombrozo (2009) found in a study investigating whether individuals' explicit utilitarian and deontological moral commitments predict "intuitive" moral responses to trolley car problems. Those participants with explicit utilitarian moral preferences were more likely not only to judge action in trolley car scenarios (all of which involved sacrificing one life for five) more permissible but also to offer more consistent judgments when two scenarios were presented side-by-side—a manipulation that's been shown to facilitate the extraction and application of rules (Gentner & Medina, 1998).

Finally, moral theories should have dynamic properties—they should change in response to evidence through a process of theory revision. Haidt (2001) influentially suggested that moral intuitions drive moral reasoning "just as surely as a dog wags its tail" (p. 830). But others have suggested that moral intuitions *are* dynamic and open to revision, in perhaps subtle ways. Pizarro and Bloom (2003) proposed that individuals "educate" moral intuitions either through the mere act of thinking or through selectively exposing themselves to certain experiences in the world. The former mechanism for theory change falls squarely on the side of deliberation: Humans can engage in complex courses of private reflection, activating new and sometimes contradictory intuitions. Over time, deliberation of this kind could "tune" intuitions to conform to the outputs of more deliberative reasoning (see also Railton, 2014).

Individuals can also dynamically alter intuitions in more indirect ways—for instance, by controlling their experiences, thus exerting distal control to shift intuitions. Evidence for this comes from work on implicit racial attitudes and the ease with which automatic judgments can be manipulated by a variety of explicit techniques. For instance, participants exposed to positive African American exemplars, both in the laboratory and in a formal course on racism taught by an African American professor, exhibit reduced implicit biases (Dasgupta & Greenwald, 2001; Rudman, Ashmore, & Gary, 2001), and, in light of this, an individual could set out to systematically alter her environment. Studies of this sort illustrate the porous boundaries between intuitive and deliberative processes; intuitions can be tuned up, in both the presence and the absence of new experiential data from the world, and, although this "learning" process may be initiated by deliberative choice in a distal sense, the learned intuitions could subsequently respond in relatively fast and automatic ways.

Folk Moral Theories as Theories

So far we've provided isolated examples of theory-like structural, functional, and dynamic characteristics within the moral domain. However, such isolated examples are insufficient to support the stronger claim that people possess moral *theories* as such. For this stronger claim, we would want additional evidence that these isolated theory-like elements are integrated into a somewhat coherent whole. For instance, we would want evidence that the consequentialist commitments that predict trolley car judgments in Lombrozo (2009) are relatively abstract (a structural property) and responsive to evidence (a dynamic property) and that they engage with other relevant moral beliefs.

Systematic coherence is often treated as one of the most compelling sources of evidence for folk theories as distinct from other mental representations. For instance, in the domain of biology, Slaughter and Lyons (2003) taught preschool-age children about the functional roles of different organs in the body and found that this influenced their conceptions of death, suggesting a coherent and interconnected set of biological beliefs related to bodily function. With adults, Shtulman (2006) found that students tended to hold relatively coherent "transformational" or "variational" views of natural selection, rather than clusters of unrelated beliefs. Do we have evidence for such coherence in the moral domain?

Little work has focused on questions of coherence directly, but the study of moral vegetarianism provides an instructive example. At a structural level, we know that moral vegetarianism is supported by relatively abstract beliefs that can be explicitly articulated and applied. Beardsworth and Keil (1992), for example, found that moral vegetarians can explicitly identify motivations for their view, citing concerns for animal welfare or a utilitarian concern for environmental sustainability, both of which reflect broad-ranging commitments. At a functional level, we know that these beliefs guide behavior (i.e., food choices) but also explanations, predictions, and other judgments. Vegetarians, for instance, are more likely to conceive of animals as possessing a wider range of mental states—including the ability to experience pain and suffering (Bastian, Loughnan, Haslam, & Radke, 2012).

And, finally, at a dynamic level, there's good reason to believe that beliefs about vegetarianism are susceptible to deliberation and argumentation (e.g., cases of children who become vegetarian independently of their parents, often through discussions with other kids; Hussar & Harris, 2010), but also that explicit commitments to vegetarianism can have long-term effects on an automatic affective response: disgust. Many vegetarians report feeling disgusted at the mere thought of eating meat (Rozin, Markwith, & Stoess, 1997), which would, from an emotivist account, suggest that vegetarians have higher levels of dispositional sensitivity to disgust than nonvegetarians. However, research suggests that disgust does not, at least initially, play a causal role in the decision to become vegetarian: although feelings of disgust toward meat eating increase over the course of being vegetarian, those who report being motivated by moral concerns (as opposed to health concerns) do not report high dispositional levels of disgust sensitivity (Fessler, Arguello, Mekdara, & Macias, 2003), challenging the idea that affective intuitions are the primary *drivers* of moral judgment. This line of research thus suggests that moral vegetarians' disgust reactions to meat eating are a by-product of, as opposed to a cause of, their moral theories. The moral theory has arguably "educated" or "tuned" the individual's affective responses.

The case or moral vegetarianism provides a nice example of how a folk moral theory (in this case about animal rights or welfare) can blur the boundary between intuitive and deliberative processing, with some affective and automatic components, and others that are clearly abstract and explicit. It's important to note, however, that not all representations with moral content will necessarily conform to the structure of a folk theory. In fact, some findings argue against theory-like representations for some moral content. For example, Goodwin and Darley (2008) found that individuals vary in their meta-ethical commitments to moral objectivism, but that judgments also depend strongly on concrete features of specific moral judgments, such as their content and valence (Goodwin & Darley, 2012). In other words, it could be misleading to classify some people as "moral objectivists" and some as "moral relativists," where the label is taken to reflect an abstractly represented commitment with broad and systematic scope. Instead, a given individual will appear to be objectivist in some contexts and relativist in others (see also Sarkissian, Park, Tien, Wright, & Knobe, 2011; Uttich, Tsai, & Lombrozo, 2014), suggesting that judgments result from a more contextualized process or representation. More research is needed to truly test the "theory-like" credentials of meta-ethical commitments concerning objectivism, but the example raises an important point: Even if some moral judgments result from mental representations that we can properly call theories, it doesn't follow that all do. In fact, it's quite likely that moral judgments are supported by a host of representational formats.

Having considered the case of vegetarianism—which involves moral commitments affecting moral judgment—we now move into evidence from our own work that illustrates a role for high-level *philosophical* commitments in moral judgment.

The Case of Intuitive Dualism

Debates over sanctity of life bioethical issues (e.g., abortion, physician-assisted suicide) often hang critically on the question of when a mere bundle of cells comes to have (or lose) a mind or soul. Bloom (2004a, 2006) argues that we are intuitive dualists who separate the physical body from the nonphysical mind; Bloom (2004a) argues that "we do not feel as if we are bodies, we feel as if we occupy them" (p. 191), and that this dualist tendency has implications for moral judgment. Greene (2011) similarly explains that "the debate over abortion is ultimately a metaphysical one. The question is not whether a fertilized egg is alive, but whether it is host to a 'human life,' i.e., a human soul. Without a soul in balance, there is no abortion debate. Likewise for the debates over human stem cell research and euthanasia" (p. 21).

Dualism has historically been associated with metaphysical commitments about the relationship between the mind and the material. For instance, the *Stanford Encyclopedia of Philosophy* (Robinson, 2011) defines dualism as "the theory that the mental and the physical—or mind and body or mind and brain—are, in some sense, radically different kinds of thing." Within psychology, however, the term *intuitive dualism* has been used to cast a much wider net. Scales that have been designed to measure intuitive dualist tendencies (Stanovich, 1989) are not restricted to items that involve the relationship between the mind and the body but also include concepts related to religious beliefs in a soul or afterlife (e.g., "My consciousness will survive the disintegration of my physical body") and more general views about determinism and reduction in science (e.g., "Knowledge of the mind will forever be beyond the understanding of sciences like physics, neurophysiology, and psychology"). Similarly, experimental manipulations of dualist beliefs (Preston, Ritter, & Hepler, 2013) involve vignettes that also vary in determinism, free will, and reductionist explanations for the human mind.

In recent work (Gottlieb & Lombrozo, in preparation), we have created the Dualism+ Scale, designed to measure both narrow metaphysical beliefs related to dualism and related but conceptually distinct beliefs, such as those concerning a soul, determinism, scientific reductionism, and epistemological beliefs about the scope of science in explaining mental life (see Table 33.2). We find that Dualism+ scores are predictive of

TABLE 33.2. The Five Components of the Dualism+ Scale, as Supported by a Factor Analysis, along with a Representative Item from Each

Religious commitments to a soul; afterlife beliefs	"Every person has a soul."
Scope of science in explaining the mind	"Explaining everything that makes us human in strictly scientific terms in some way decreases the value of life."
Free will	"People always have the ability to do otherwise."
Determinism	"People's choices and actions must happen precisely the way they do because of laws of nature and the way things were in the distant past."
Mind–brain identity	"Minds are not the same as brains."

five highly controversial bioethical issues that, as Greene (2006) suggested, hinge critically on philosophical commitments: abortion, physician-assisted suicide, cloning humans, cloning animals, and research using embryonic stem cells. However, the component of the Dualism+ scale that drives this relationship is not about the metaphysics of the mind–brain relationship itself ("mind–brain identity"), but about the scope of science and the affective consequences of providing scientific explanations ("scope of science in explaining the mind"; see also Gottlieb & Lombrozo, in press): We found that participants' scope of science subscore significantly predicted bioethical judgments, even when controlling for individual differences in political orientation, religiosity, disgust sensitivity, and cognitive style (Frederick, 2005).

This finding suggests a causal relationship between commitments concerning the scope of science and bioethical judgments, but it could be that—as with vegetarianism—the relationship is mediated by affective processes. In fact, bioethical attitudes fall into a class of purity-based sociopolitical issues that are affected by individual differences in

disgust sensitivity (Inbar et al., 2009). They are thus canonical examples of moral judgments that are more affective, automatic, and "intuitive" in nature.

Our study also included a measure of disgust sensitivity (Haidt, McCauley, & Rozin, 1994, modified by Olatunji et al., 2007), which revealed that those individuals who are opposed to describing the mind in scientific terms display high levels of disgust sensitivity, even while statistically controlling for political conservatism and religiosity—two factors that have been strongly linked to disgust sensitivity (Inbar et al., 2009; Terrizzi, Shook, & Ventis, 2012). Just as moral vegetarianism can recruit disgust at the thought of eating meat, it could be that beliefs about the scope of science can result in a disgust response to stimuli that implicitly or explicitly violate those commitments, such as physician-assisted suicide. Alternatively, it could be that opposition to scientific descriptions of the mind is itself caused by disgust, which can be elicited by a reminder that the human mind is nothing beyond its physical components (see Rozin, Haidt, & McCauley, 1999, for relevant discussion on animal reminder disgust). Future experimental work—which isolates the direct effect of reductionist descriptions of the mind on state levels of disgust (and vice versa)—will be useful in teasing apart these two pathways.

In sum, our initial findings on the relationship between Dualism+ and views on sanctity of life bioethical issues, such as physician-assisted suicide, suggest a moderate relationship between philosophical commitments and bioethical views. However, the philosophical commitments related to bioethical views concern the scope of science, not the mind–body relationship (narrowly construed). Although further research is certainly required, our findings are consistent with the basic proposal that theory-like commitments—in this case relatively broad and abstract epistemic commitments about science—affect moral judgments, likely in automatic and (in this case) affectively laden ways. Like the example of vegetarianism—and the examples from the preceding section—this points to the possibility of mental representations that take the form of folk theories that interact with moral judgment and that cross-cut the traditional distinction between intuition and deliberation.

Future Directions

We have argued for the reality of folk moral theories—a form of mental representation distinct from those typically acknowledged by dual-systems approaches. Drawing upon work from cognitive development and cognitive psychology, we suggest that folk theories can involve abstract commitments with structural, functional, and dynamic elements that blur the distinction between intuition and deliberation. In particular, folk theories can involve abstract representations that can be explicitly and deliberatively engaged but that can also be applied in relatively automatic and implicit ways.

Many elements of our proposal are not in conflict with traditional dual-process approaches. A dual-process theorist can readily accommodate *both* intuitive and deliberative elements to moral judgment, with corresponding mental representations and processes for each. Moreover, such a perspective can accommodate interaction between systems and change over time. In its weakest form, our evidence is merely a warning that the intuition–deliberation distinction can potentially obscure the nature of moral judgment by discounting the contributions of theory-like elements, some of which are intuitive and some of which are deliberative. But in its stronger form, our position argues for the existence of a complex form of representation—a folk theory—that is not merely a collection of elements from an intuitive system and elements from a deliberative system but, instead, a *coherent* representation that does not find a natural home in either system.

The evidence we've marshaled is suggestive but arguably falls short of establishing this stronger position. In part, the reason for this is that research has not approached moral judgment with the aim of testing the presence and boundaries of folk theories. Thus many questions remain open, and we see the value of our proposal in part as a spur to further research. We conclude by highlighting two directions for such research that we see as especially valuable.

First, one of the most compelling forms of evidence for folk theories—as distinct from other forms of mental representation—comes in the coherence of the mental representation. It's also coherence between intuitive and deliberative elements that arguably poses the greatest challenge to dual-process approaches. But to what extent are folk moral theories coherent? Or, to complicate matters further, in what form are they coherent, and is this form of coherence a true challenge to dual-process approaches?

Second, how do education and affect interact in the dynamic tuning of moral judgment? Our evidence for the role of epistemological commitments in bioethical judgment complements Pizarro and Bloom's (2003) proposal that various forms of distal control can revise and reshape the nature of moral intuitions. This view suggests that individuals who oppose scientifically reductionist descriptions of the mind may actively avoid certain forms of education (such as neuroscientific education) or even purposefully engage in religious dialogue that argues *against* a reductionist picture of human nature. On the other hand, if these same individuals actively engage with neuroscience, they could experience a dampened emotional response due to a shift in underlying moral intuitions that accrues over time. We could test this hypothesis by gathering longitudinal data on how science education influences metaphysical and epistemological commitments, both at intuitive and more explicit levels, and therefore how it affects bioethical judgments. This empirical question is especially relevant in a culture that is becoming increasingly "scientific" and reductionist in nature (Farah & Hook, 2013). Although Bloom (2004b) is skeptical of the extent to which neuroscientific explanations can revise dualist intuitions, conceiving of these commitments as a more general form of folk theory suggests that they may be revised in light of new experiential data.

In sum, we have argued in favor of a unique role for theory-like representations in moral judgment that cross-cut the intuitive–deliberative distinction. And although this view is relatively new to the moral psychology literature, it draws heavily upon the literature on folk theories of the natural world, which can be explicit and law-like in principle but engaged in implicit ways. We suggest that this approach is useful in making sense of intuitions regarding fantastical variants on trolley-car dilemmas and other high-conflict scenarios invoked for moral psychology research. But more important, and certainly more timely, this approach provides insight into the real-world judgments that divide individuals when it comes to matters of life and death, such as in cases of physician-assisted suicide.

REFERENCES

Bastian, B., Loughnan, S., Haslam, N., & Radke, H. R. (2012). Don't mind meat? The denial of mind to animals used for human consumption. *Personality and Social Psychology Bulletin, 38*(2), 247–256.

Beardsworth, A., & Keil, T. (1992). The vegetarian option: Varieties, conversions, motives and careers. *Sociological Review, 40*(2), 253–293.

Bloom, P. (2004a). *Descartes' baby: How the science of child development explains what makes us human.* New York: Basic Books.

Bloom, P. (2004b). Natural-born dualists. *Edge.* Available at *www.edge.org/conversation/paul_bloom-natural-born-dualists.*

Bloom, P. (2006). Seduced by the flickering lights of the brain. *Seed Magazine, 27.* Available at *http://seedmagazine.com/content/article/seduced_by_the_flickering_lights_of_the_brain.*

Carey, S. (2000). Science education as conceptual change. *Journal of Applied Developmental Psychology, 21*(1), 13–19.

Clement, J. (1982). Students' preconceptions in introductory mechanics. *American Journal of Physics, 50*(1), 66–71.

Cushman, F. (2008). Crime and punishment: Distinguishing the roles of causal and intentional analyses in moral judgment. *Cognition, 108*(2), 353–380.

Cushman, F., Young, L., & Hauser, M. (2006). The role of conscious reasoning and intuition in moral judgment: Testing three principles of harm. *Psychological Science, 17*(12), 1082–1089.

Dasgupta, N., & Greenwald, A. G. (2001). On the malleability of automatic attitudes: Combating automatic prejudice with images of admired and disliked individuals. *Journal of Personality and Social Psychology, 81*(5), 800.

Evans, J. S. B., & Stanovich, K. E. (2013). Dual-process theories of higher cognition: Advancing the debate. *Perspectives on Psychological Science, 8*(3), 223–241.

Farah, M. J., & Hook, C. J. (2013). The seductive allure of "seductive allure." *Perspectives on Psychological Science, 8*(1), 88–90.

Fessler, D. M., Arguello, A. P., Mekdara, J. M., & Macias, R. (2003). Disgust sensitivity and meat consumption: A test of an emotivist account of moral vegetarianism. *Appetite, 41*(1), 31–41.

Frederick, S. (2005). Cognitive reflection and decision making. *Journal of Economic Perspectives, 19,* 25–42.

Gentner, D., & Medina, J. (1998). Similarity and the development of rules. *Cognition, 65,* 263–297.

Goodwin, G. P., & Darley, J. M. (2008). The psychology of meta-ethics: Exploring objectivism. *Cognition, 106*(3), 1339–1366.

Goodwin, G. P., & Darley, J. M. (2012). Why are some moral beliefs perceived to be more objective than others? *Journal of Experimental Social Psychology, 48*(1), 250–256.

Gopnik, A., & Meltzoff, A. N. (1997). *Words, thoughts, and theories.* Cambridge, MA: MIT Press.

Gopnik, A., & Wellman, H. M. (2012). Reconstructing constructivism: Causal models, Bayesian learning mechanisms, and the theory theory. *Psychological Bulletin, 138*(6), 1085–1108.

Gottlieb, S. & Lombrozo, T. (in preparation). *Dissociable components of mind-body dualist attitudes predict bioethical judgments.* Manuscript in preparation.

Gottlieb, S., & Lombrozo, T. (in press). Can science explain the human mind? Intuitive judgments about the limits of science. *Psychological Science.*

Greene, J. D. (2007). The secret joke of Kant's soul. In W. Sinnott-Armstrong (Ed.), *Moral psychology* (Vol. 3, pp. 35–80). Cambridge, MA: MIT Press.

Greene, J. D. (2011). Social neuroscience and the soul's last stand. In A. Todorov, S. T. Fiske, & D. A. Prentice (Eds.), *Social neuroscience: Toward understanding the underpinnings of the social mind* (pp. 263–273). New York: Oxford University Press.

Greene, J. D., Morelli, S. A., Lowenberg, K., Nystrom, L. E., & Cohen, J. D. (2008). Cognitive load selectively interferes with utilitarian moral judgment. *Cognition, 107*(3), 1144–1154.

Greene, J. D., Nystrom, L. E., Engell, A. D., Darley, J. M., & Cohen, J. D. (2004). The neural bases of cognitive conflict and control in moral judgment. *Neuron, 44*(2), 389–400.

Greene, J. D., Sommerville, R. B., Nystrom, L. E., Darley, J. M., & Cohen, J. D. (2001). An fMRI investigation of emotional engagement in moral judgment. *Science, 293*(5537), 2105–2108.

Haidt, J. (2001). The emotional dog and its rational tail: A social intuitionist approach to moral judgment. *Psychological Review, 108,* 814–834.

Haidt, J., McCauley, C., & Rozin, P. (1994). Individual differences in sensitivity to disgust: A scale sampling seven domains of disgust elicitors. *Personality and Individual Differences, 16*(5), 701–713.

Hamlin, J. K. (2013). Moral judgment and action in preverbal infants and toddlers: Evidence for an innate moral core. *Current Directions in Psychological Science, 22*(3), 186–193.

Hauser, M., Cushman, F., Young, L., Jin, R., & Mikhail, J. (2007). A dissociation between moral judgments and justifications. *Mind and Language, 22*(1), 1–21.

Hussar, K. M., & Harris, P. L. (2010). Children who choose not to eat meat: A study of early moral decision-making. *Social Development, 19*(3), 627–641.

Inbar, Y., Pizarro, D. A., & Bloom, P. (2012). Disgusting smells cause decreased liking of gay men. *Emotion, 12,* 23–27.

Inbar, Y., Pizarro, D., Iyer, R., & Haidt, J. (2012). Disgust sensitivity, political conservatism, and voting. *Social Psychological and Personality Science, 3*(5), 537–544.

Inbar, Y., Pizarro, D. A., Knobe, J., & Bloom, P. (2009). Disgust sensitivity predicts intuitive disapproval of gays. *Emotion, 9*(3), 435.

Keil, F. C. (2011). Science starts early. *Science, 331*(6020), 1022–1023.

Kempton, W. (1986). Two theories of home heat control. *Cognitive Science, 10*(1), 75–90.

Knobe, J. (2010). Person as scientist, person as moralist. *Behavioral and Brain Sciences, 33*(4), 315–329.

Kohlberg, L. (1969). Stage and sequence: The cognitive-developmental approach to socialization. In D. A. Goslin (Ed.), *Handbook of socialization theory and research* (pp. 151–235). New York: Academic Press.

Lombrozo, T. (2009). The role of moral commitments in moral judgment. *Cognitive Science, 33*(2), 273–286.

McCloskey, M. (1983). Naive theories of motion. Available at *www.researchgate.net/publication/239563618_Naive_theories_of_motion.*

Mendez, M. F., Anderson, E., & Shapira, J. S. (2005). An investigation of moral judgement in frontotemporal dementia. *Cognitive and Behavioral Neurology, 18*(4), 193–197.

Mikhail, J. (2011). *Elements of moral cognition: Rawls' linguistic analogy and the cognitive science of moral and legal judgment.* Cambridge, UK: Cambridge University Press.

Olatunji, B. O., Williams, N. L., Tolin, D. F., Abramowitz, J. S., Sawchuk, C. N., Lohr, J. M., & Elwood, L. S. (2007). The Disgust Scale: Item analysis, factor structure, and suggestions for refinement. *Psychological Assessment, 19*(3), 281–297.

Paxton, J. M., Ungar, L., & Greene, J. D. (2012). Reflection and reasoning in moral judgment. *Cognitive Science, 36*(1), 163–177.

Perkins, A. M., Leonard, A. M., Weaver, K., Dalton, J. A., Mehta, M. A., Kumari, V., . . . Ettinger, U. (2013). A dose of ruthlessness: Interpersonal moral judgment is hardened by the anti-anxiety drug lorazepam. *Journal of Experimental Psychology: General, 142*(3), 612.

Pizarro, D. A., & Bloom, P. (2003). The intelligence of the moral intuitions: A comment on Haidt (2001). *Psychological Review, 110,* 193–196.

Preston, J. L., Ritter, R. S., & Hepler, J. (2013). Neuroscience and the soul: Competing explanations for the human experience. *Cognition, 127*(1), 31–37.

Railton, P. (2014). The affective dog and its rational tale: Intuition and attunement. *Ethics, 124*(4), 813–859.

Robinson, H. (2011). Dualism. In E. N. Zalta (Ed.), *Stanford encyclopedia of philosophy.* Stanford, CA: Metaphysics Research Lab, Center for the Study of Language and Information, Stanford University. Retrieved from *https://plato.stanford.edu/archives/win2011/entries/dualism.*

Rozin, P., Haidt, J., & McCauley, C. R. (1999). Disgust: The body and soul emotion. In T. Dalgleish & M. Power (Eds.), *Handbook of cognition and emotion* (pp. 429–445). Chichester, UK: Wiley.

Rozin, P., Markwith, M., & Stoess, C. (1997). Moralization and becoming a vegetarian: The transformation of preferences into values and the recruitment of disgust. *Psychological Science, 8*(2), 67–73.

Rudman, L. A., Ashmore, R. D., & Gary, M. L. (2001). "Unlearning" automatic biases: The malleability of implicit stereotypes and prejudice. *Journal of Personality and Social Psychology, 81,* 856–868.

Saad, L. (2010). Four moral issues sharply divide Americans. Available at *www.gallup.com/poll/137357/four-moral-issues-sharply-divide-americans.aspx.*

Sarkissian, H., Park, J., Tien, D., Wright, J. C., & Knobe, J. (2011). Folk moral relativism. *Mind and Language, 26*(4), 482–505.

Shtulman, A. (2006). Qualitative differences between naive and scientific theories of evolution. *Cognitive Psychology, 52,* 170–194.

Shtulman, A., & Calabi, P. (2013). Tuition vs. intuition: Effects of instruction on naive theories of evolution. *Merrill–Palmer Quarterly, 59,* 141–167.

Shtulman, A., & Schulz, L. (2008). The relation between essentialist beliefs and evolutionary reasoning. *Cognitive Science, 32,* 1049–1062.

Shtulman, A., & Valcarcel, J. (2012). Scientific knowledge suppresses but does not supplant earlier intuitions. *Cognition, 124,* 209–215.

Slaughter, V., & Lyons, M. (2003). Learning about life and death in early childhood. *Cognitive Psychology, 46*(1), 1–30.

Snyder, L., & Sulmasy, D. P. (2001). Physician-assisted suicide. *Annals of Internal Medicine, 135*(3), 209–216.

Stanovich, K. E. (1989). Implicit philosophies of mind: The dualism scale and its relation to religiosity and belief in extrasensory perception. *Journal of Psychology, 123*(1), 5–23.

Suter, R. S., & Hertwig, R. (2011). Time and moral judgment. *Cognition, 119*(3), 454–458.

Terrizzi, J. A., Jr., Shook, N. J., & Ventis, W. L. (2012). Religious conservatism: An evolutionarily evoked disease-avoidance strategy. *Religion, Brain and Behavior, 2*(2), 105–120.

Trémolière, B., De Neys, W., & Bonnefon, J. F. (2012). Mortality salience and morality: Thinking about death makes people less utilitarian. *Cognition, 124*(3), 379–384.

Turiel, E. (1983). *The development of social knowledge: Morality and convention.* Cambridge, UK: Cambridge University Press.

Uttich, K., Tsai, G., & Lombrozo, T. (2014). Exploring metaethical commitments: Moral objectivity and moral progress. *Advances in Experimental Moral Psychology,* 188–208.

Vosniadou, S., & Brewer, W. F. (1994). Mental models of the day/night cycle. *Cognitive Science, 18*(1), 123–183.

Waldmann, M. R., & Dieterich, J. H. (2007). Throwing a bomb on a person versus throwing a person on a bomb: Intervention myopia in moral intuitions. *Psychological Science, 18*(3), 247–253.

CHAPTER 34

Free Will and Moral Psychology

Roy F. Baumeister

> **Does moral psychology need a workable concept of free will?**
>
> Yes; free will is about being able to act differently in the same situation, which is also the basis of moral judgment and exhortation.

The nature of morality is one of the grand, eternal questions. The question of free will is another. These are highly interrelated questions, even though psychologists have tended to treat them separately. My own intellectual pursuits have led me to moral psychology by way of the question of free will. The purpose of this brief chapter is to elucidate the centrally important and powerful overlap between free will theory and moral psychology.

Free will is a contentious term. Much acrimonious debate about free will persists because people use wildly different definitions, so they are arguing about different things. For example, Montague (2008, p. R584) defined free will as "the idea that we make choices and have thoughts independent of anything remotely resembling a physical process" and "a close cousin to the idea of the soul." He and some others have treated free will as a kind of exemption from causality. No wonder he regarded the notion as unscientific, even antiscientific! Meanwhile, another biologist, Brembs (2010), understood free will as random, unpredictable behavior. He observed that randomly breaking from established patterns can be adaptive for foiling predators—thus grounding free will firmly in the context of biological evolution (the opposite of Montague). Third, elsewhere, a team of philosophers and psychologists came up with a quite different definition as a basis for a research grant competition: Free will is the basis or capacity for free action, which means that the person could act in different ways in the same situation (Haggard, Mele, O'Connor, & Vohs, 2010). It is easy to see why three serious scholars holding those three definitions (and each assuming that the group shares his definition, rather than using three different ones) might disagree vehemently and even doubt each other's wisdom. The definition by Haggard and colleagues (2010) does not assume anything like a soul, for example, so naturally Montague's objections would seem absurdly irrelevant to Haggard and colleagues (2010).

In my experience, people who disagree severely about free will frequently turn out to agree to a great extent about how human behavior actually occurs. The question of freedom is thus just a semantic issue based on definitions. The more interesting questions, to me, are how that kind of behavior actually occurs, rather than whether or in what sense it deserves the title of "free will."

In short, my professional interest is in understanding how human behavior comes about, and so arguments about definitions are peripheral. But one cannot discuss something without defining it, so it is necessary to choose a definition. I follow the one proposed by Haggard et al. (2010), as outlined above—namely, being able to act in different ways in the same situation. My goal is to develop a scientific theory of free will (see Baumeister, 2008; Baumeister & Monroe, 2014). On that basis, the theory is causal (so no exemption from causality). Scientific theories also do not invoke supernatural forces, so souls as causal agents are also excluded. The goal is to understand human agency and choice.

In other words, most scholars agree that human action is brought about by some remarkable capacities. It evolved from the simpler forms of agency that many other animals have, which guide their choices and actions. It adds something extra, such as the ability to incorporate language and complex ideas into the causation of action. That is what people call free will. One can argue endlessly about whether it deserves that definition, but to me the more interesting question is how to explain it.

Morality is an important component of this extra kind of complex ideation that humans incorporate into causing action. They do so pretty much uniquely among mammals. For example, sometimes a wild animal gets loose in suburbia and kills a human being. The authorities capture the animal and sometimes put it to death, sometimes not—but in neither case do they first put it on trial, as they would if it were a morally responsible being. Its fate does not depend, for example, on whether it perpetrated harm as premeditated intention or as impulse.

My point of departure is that moral principles presuppose free will, or something pretty close to it. A moral judgment is essentially a judgment about whether someone should have acted differently. To say that someone should have acted differently is to presuppose that the person could have acted differently. It would be absurd to blame someone for failing to do the impossible. When it is clear that a person could not have acted differently, others tend not to moralize or judge. Indeed, some people try to escape from guilt by arguing that they could not have done otherwise (e.g., Baumeister, Stillwell, & Wotman, 1990). The fact that that argument works is based on the assumption of free will: *If I was not free to act differently, I cannot be blamed.* Blame rests on the basic assumption of free will, namely, that I could have done something else, something better.

I also understand free will as something specific to humankind. Brembs's (2010) emphasis on random behavior was stimulated partly by his and colleagues' research on random behavior in fruit flies, which was covered in the mass media as evidence suggesting that fruit flies enjoyed free will. But most scholars balk at ascribing free will to such simple species, as do I. Even so, scientists should probably resist the philosophical preference for all-or-nothing judgments, such as whether people have free will or not. Agency likely evolved in a series of steps, and freedom is not absolute but on a continuum (like the vast majority of psychological variables and processes!).

Let us consider, therefore, how the human free will evolved out of the agentic capabilities of simpler animals, and what new features were added. Human choice may indeed share many key features, processes, and biological substrates with what simpler animals do. However, it is also qualitatively different in crucial ways. The ability to base behavior on moral reasoning is an important one of these. Early humans discovered moral rules, and their social life selected in favor of people who were able to use those rules to guide their behavior.

Morality was discovered, whereas religion was invented. Most if not all world societies have religions, and they have quite different and incompatible content: If one group's god is the only god, then the other gods worshiped by other groups cannot exist. Most, if not all, societies have morals, too. But unlike religion, these various cultural moral systems are quite similar and compatible with each other. They prescribe and prohibit mostly the same actions, except for a few details that often lack any basis or that are on a continuum on which agreement is desirable and there is no single optimal point, such as sexual morality. (Even with sex, there are plenty of similarities across cultures.)

Moral rules are in a sense bottom-up, despite being discovered. (Indeed, religion tends to be top-down, originating in some particular set of teachings and ostensible revelations. It may be generally true that discovered realities are bottom-up whereas invented ones are top-down.) Moral dilemmas do not all have correct answers, as would presumably happen if all were derived from some overarching system. (Laws, where there is a central adjudicating body, supposedly have correct resolutions: In principle the law does prescribe at least one legally correct way to act in any given situation.) They originate in the requirements of social systems, and these various requirements are not all fully compatible. It is hard to imagine a society whose response to the Judeo-Christian Ten Commandments would be, "Oh, our moral rules are exactly the opposite!" Social systems function best when people refrain from killing, lying, stealing, and the like. Pretty much every society discovers this. When one travels to a new country with a very different culture, one may have to learn the religious beliefs and practices, but usually one can assume that the basic moral rules are the same as back home.

The fact that moral rules are quite similar across cultures supports the view that they were discovered rather than invented. They represent solutions to problems of collective action, and the same solutions are discovered everywhere, not unlike the way that arithmetic was discovered independently by many different cultures who nonetheless found that the same calculations yielded the same answers.

The question with morality is not what the rules are, because most societies largely agree on the rules. The question is why should one obey them. In particular, many moral rules boil down to restraining self-interest in favor of doing what is good for the social group and system—but why should one not pursue self-interest, as nature designed brains to do? Religion has at many times provided a

conveniently useful answer to that, insofar as many religions attribute moral rules to divine commands. (This itself seems to have been a discovered solution, because early human societies had both religion and morality but did not link them; Norenzayan et al., 2014). One should obey the moral rules because a god said so.[1] The question of why one should bother doing what a god says to do somehow does not come up. The top-down nature of religion means that there is a top, namely a god, beyond which one does not seek a higher authority.

MacIntyre's (1981) analysis of the modern moral dilemma emphasizes precisely this point. In medieval Europe, there were three key conceptual foundations: a view of untutored human nature, a view of human perfectability linked to religious salvation, and a set of moral rules that show how the person can move from the one state to the other. Without religion, the salvation component is gone, leaving only the vision of untutored human nature a set of moral rules, but with no real reason to obey them (other than social pressure). MacIntyre said much of recent moral philosophy has groped for a replacement for salvation, to give people such a reason to obey the moral rules. In a sense, modern moral philosophy has struggled to solve an unsolvable problem.

In this analysis, moral principles are not themselves a product of evolution. But the capacity to guide behavior by morality certainly is. An advanced form of agency, of behavior control, is a major part of that. That is, humankind evolved something that some people call free will—and did so at least in part because it enabled people to behave morally.

Animal agency presumably evolved in an amoral context and for amoral reasons. Animals evolved the ability to make choices so as to survive and reproduce better. The origins of the central nervous system are in locomotion and digestion, thus (to oversimplify) to control moving around so as to eat (Ghysen, 2003).

Human free will is mostly a moral instrument, that is, a set of cognitive capabilities related to behavior control that evolved to deal with moral issues so as to maintain a good moral reputation, essential for attracting others. The central themes of human evolution are involved here, as recently elucidated by Tomasello (2014). Cooperation with non-kin is quite rare in other primates, but it is central to human social life. Cooperation creates vulnerability: One works with another, who may be tempted to betray the cooperation for his or her own advantage. Most animals would betray. For example, if two creatures work together to chase prey, and one catches it, that one will consume the prey rather than sharing. This is natural: The animal is hungry and it has captured food, so of course the natural and adaptive next action is to eat it. Advanced self-control is needed to resist that temptation. And why should it? The crucial answer to that question is something only humans seem to understand. If you betray another's trust, then that other will not trust you next time. In a human society in which social information is shared (i.e., gossip), the one you betrayed will tell others, and they will not trust you either. *You will not be able to get others to cooperate with you,* and insofar as survival depends on cooperation, you will be in mortal danger. In a cooperative society, your very survival depends on being able to overcome the natural impulse to betray the cooperative partner. This is key selection factor in the evolution of self-control, which in turn is a major component of what people call free will.

Hence we are descended from the humans who mastered enough self-control to overcome selfish temptations so as to cooperate. More broadly, as Tomasello (2014) elaborates, successful humans had to be concerned about their moral reputation, at least in the sense that they had to base their actions on getting others to perceive them as trustworthy partners for cooperative acts.

My hypothesis is that the need to sustain a good reputation, so as to attract cooperative partners, was the basis for the discovery of morality. Early humans needed guidelines to know what would make them morally attractive to others, not because of religion or idealism or whatever, but as a matter of survival. Reciprocating favors, keeping promises, sharing, and other virtues reflect the discovery that such patterns of behavior will ensure future opportunities for cooperation.

In this view, the origins of what people call free will are neither in random behavior nor in rational choice, but in self-control: One has to inhibit the natural impulse to get all that one can for oneself, so as instead to share resources with others. To do that, one has to use self-control, the "moral muscle" (Baumeister & Exline, 1999), so as to act in ways that others will respect as morally virtuous.

Striking evidence of the interpersonal basis for moral behavior was provided by Engelmann, Herrmann, and Tomasello (2012). They confronted adult chimpanzees and 5-year-old human children with a behavioral dilemma that involved sharing and stealing. Some confronted this alone, while others did so in the presence of conspecifics. The chimpanzees' moral behavior was the same regardless of the presence of other chimps. Human children behaved more morally when others were watching than when alone. Thus, by 5 years of age, human children are concerned about their moral reputation in a way that adult chimps are not.

If free will evolved partly to serve moral purposes, then people would use the concept of free will especially in connection with making moral judgments. Some evidence for this was provided by Clark and colleagues (2014). Their work was based on Nietzsche's (1889/1954) somewhat flippant claim that the concept of free will was invented as a basis for condemning and punishing other people for immoral actions. Clark et al. (2014) showed that people's belief in free will increased when they were exposed to immoral misdeeds by other people. This confirms the observation I made earlier in this essay: Moral judgments essentially assert that the person *should have acted differently.* And that assumes that the person could have done so, which is the essence of the Haggard et al. (2010) definition of free will.

The literature on free will has been greatly swayed, and in my view egregiously misled (see also Mele, 2009), by the classic studies by Libet (1985, 2004). In those studies, participants were told to make a random choice of when to initiate a finger or wrist movement, and to note the exact time on a clock that registered milliseconds. The findings indicated that brain activity commenced prior to when people recorded that they had made the decision.

Libet's findings can be useful and thought-provoking in some contexts, but they have nothing to do with free will. One key reason is that choosing randomly to make a meaningless response is totally divorced from the natural, evolved function of human agency. In fact, the instructions to participants in the study specified that they should not plan when to make the movement—thereby removing the last possible vestige of anything that free will would be useful for.

Free will evolved in part (and a big part) to enable people to make moral choices. Libet's procedures were thoroughly stripped of any moral aspect. I am not surprised that brain activity preceded the recollection of conscious "decision," not that that means all that much. (Indeed, if we assume that all conscious thought is the result of brain processes, then brain activity would always precede a conscious thought.) I hypothesize that conscious thought about moral choices would yield brain patterns quite different from those associated with the decision to make a meaningless finger movement.[2] Neuroscientists interested in morality should start there.

Forgiveness offers another sphere in which to investigate and elucidate the moral aspects of free will. Shariff et al. (2014) showed that people who disbelieved in free will recommended more lenient sentences to hypothetical criminals than believers did. They also condemned people who had transgressed against them personally less, in autobiographical data. These findings seem to suggest that belief in free will reduces forgiveness. If people do not have free will and their behavior is determined, it seems unfair to punish them for their misdeeds to the same extent as if they had freely chosen to misbehave.

However, other evidence suggests that within close relationships, the opposite pattern is found: Belief in free will leads to more forgiveness (for review, see Baumeister & Brewer, 2012). A follow-up analysis on the Shariff et al. (2014) data revealed that belief in free will interacted with relationship closeness to determine blame. The closer the relationship, the more that belief in free will increased forgiveness. Belief in free will led to harsh condemnation mainly when there was no close relationship.

All of this fits perfectly with the idea of free will as a moral agency that evolved for human moral culture. With strangers and hypothetical persons, one's interest is to promote moral behavior so as to maintain the social system's ability to function smoothly and effectively. Morality only works if most of the people respect its rules most of the time, and the more uniformly people conform to moral rules, the better the system works for everyone, because trust and cooperation are facilitated. As Clark et al. (2014) showed, belief in free will is motivated by the wish to uphold the social rules by punishing people who break them.

With a close relationship partner, however, one's interest is in maintaining the relationship. It is therefore more important to forgive the person so that the relationship can continue. Crucially, too, one wants to believe that the partner can change. The purpose of moral condemnation of a partner is not to affirm abstract rules for society in general (as in the stranger judgments), but, rather, it is to convince the partner to change so as to facilitate a good relationship (again, with trust and cooperation).

To conclude: Moral psychology and free will theory have much to offer each other, and indeed neither really works without the other. Moral judgment assumes that the person could act otherwise in that situation (and perhaps should have). Free will evolved to enable people to make moral choices, not random ones. Societies have promoted belief in free will because that belief enables them to function better.

NOTES

1. And perhaps because the god will kick your ass if you disobey his rules.
2. To be sure, there are automatic moral responses, especially in well-socialized humans. Humans are willing to try trusting and cooperation. Conscious thought might come into play when one is offered a cooperative partnership by someone who has betrayed others in the past.

REFERENCES

Baumeister, R. F. (2008). Free will in scientific psychology. *Perspectives on Psychological Science, 3,* 14–19.

Baumeister, R. F., & Brewer, L. E. (2012). Believing versus disbelieving in free will: Correlates and consequences. *Personality and Social Psychology Compass, 6*(10), 736–745.

Baumeister, R. F., & Exline, J. (1999). Virtue, personality, and social relations: Self-control as the moral muscle. *Journal of Personality, 67,* 1165–1194.

Baumeister, R. F., & Monroe, A. E. (2014). Recent research on free will: Conceptualizations, beliefs, and processes. *Advances in Experimental Social Psychology, 50,* 1–52.

Brembs, B. (2010). Towards a scientific concept of free will as a biological trait: Spontaneous actions and decision-making in invertebrates. *Proceedings of the Royal Society B: Biological Sciences.* Available at *http://rspb.royalsocietypublishing.org/content/early/2010/12/14/rspb.2010.2325.*

Clark, C. J., Luguri, J. B., Ditto, P. H., Knobe, J., Shariff, A. F., & Baumeister, R. F. (2014). Free to punish: A motivated account of free will belief. *Journal of Personality and Social Psychology, 106,* 501–513.

Engelmann, J. M., Herrmann, E., & Tomasello, M. (2012). Five-year-olds, but not chimpanzees, attempt to manage their reputations. *PLOS ONE, 7,* 1–7.

Ghysen, A. (2003). The origin and evolution of the nervous system. *International Journal of Developmental Biology, 47,* 555–562.

Haggard, P., Mele, A., O'Connor, T., & Vohs, K. (2010). Lexicon of key terms. Available at *www.freewillandscience.com/wp/?page_id=63.*

Libet, B. (1985). Unconscious cerebral initiative and the role of conscious will in voluntary action. *Behavior and Brain Sciences, 8,* 529–566.

Libet, B. (2004). *Mind time: The temporal factor in consciousness.* Cambridge, MA: Harvard University Press.

MacIntyre, A. (1981). *After virtue.* Notre Dame, IN: Notre Dame University Press.

Mele, A. R. (2009). *Effective intentions: The power of conscious will.* New York: Oxford University Press.

Montague, R. P. (2008). Free will. *Current Biology, 18,* R584–R585.

Nietzsche, F. (1954). *Twilight of the idols* (W. Kaufmann, Trans.). New York: Penguin Books. (Original work published 1889)

Norenzayan, A., Shariff, A. F., Gervais, W. M., Willard, A. K., McNamara, R. A., Slingerland, E., & Henrich, J. (2014). The cultural evolution of prosocial religions. *Behavioral and Brain Sciences.* Available at *www2.psych.ubc.ca/~ara/Manuscripts/2016%20Norenzayan%20cultural%20evolution.pdf.*

Shariff, A. F., Greene, J. D., Karremans, J. C., Luguri, J., Clark, C. J., Schooler, J. W., . . . Vohs, K. D. (2014). Free will and punishment: A mechanistic view of human nature reduces retribution. *Psychological Science, 25,* 1563–1570.

Tomasello, M. (2014). *The natural history of human thinking.* Cambridge, MA: Harvard University Press.

CHAPTER 35

The Geographies of Religious and Nonreligious Morality

Brett Mercier
Azim Shariff

> **How do religious and secular institutions make us moral?**
>
> To encourage us to put group interest ahead of self-interest, religious and secular institutions use related but distinct mechanisms which activate our evolved sensitivity to reputational concerns.

Our Growing Moral Habitat

For the first 95% of its existence, *Homo sapiens*' moral habitat comfortably fit in a small island. Our species shared some of this territory with other animals that, over time, had evolved to cooperate with each other under a constrained set of circumstances. Human and nonhuman animals largely overlapped in their reliance on kin selection and direct reciprocity. As our species' cognitive and linguistic faculties developed, we expanded our moral territory to include new lands containing reputation-based indirect reciprocity. But for hundreds of thousands of years, our ancestors did not venture much beyond this moral island.

The beginning of the Neolithic epoch kicked off a great age of moral exploration. As the last ice age receded, the air became more highly oxygenated (Jaccard, Galbraith, Froelicher, & Gruber, 2014), and a previously variable climate stabilized (Sowers &

Bender, 1995), laying the groundwork for an agricultural revolution. Facing already increasing population sizes and declining game availability (Barker, 2009), nomadic bands of hunter–gatherers began to settle into communities and multiply further. The larger group sizes, division of labor, and the expanded possibilities for accumulating static and unequal wealth all represented a dramatic shift in human lifestyles. The traditional, evolved mechanisms of kin selection and reciprocity could not on their own support these new circumstances and larger population (Henrich, 2004). Thus the simple resources of the moral habitat that humans had hitherto enjoyed for generations became strained, and our species struck out to find new moral territories.

Many brave moral explorers found themselves seduced by the fabled lost continent of genetic group selection. Theoretically, genetic group selection relies on certain evolutionary conditions—including intense group competition with very limited genetic mixing between those groups—that were absent during the critical period of human history. But other explorers were more successful, forging out west toward a vast supercontinental cluster called Culture. There they found two vast continents of moral territories, each relying on different sets of institutions. Following North (1990), we define institutions as rules or norms that attempt to govern human actions and the means by which these rules are enforced. On one continent, *Religionia,* the institutions promoting ethical behavior were built on beliefs, teaching, and rituals rooted in supernatural assumptions. The other continent—*Secularia*—was characterized by nonsupernatural secular institutions. This chapter explores and compares the geography of these two moral continents.

Religionia

In retrospect, Religionia seems like an obvious place where morality was to be found. In fact, many—including Voltaire (1727/1977), Dostoyevsky (1880/2014) and even George Washington (Spalding & Garrity, 1996)—have argued that religion represents a central and indispensable core of morality. Today, this belief is still common. For the (slight) majority of Americans, one of the common and core features of religions—the belief in God—is a necessary precondition for being a moral person (Pew Research Center, 2014). This number is even higher in other parts of the world, reaching 99% in such places as Indonesia and Ghana. Though some countries, such as those in Western Europe, see much smaller proportions, global intuitions about the connection between religion and morality are strong. But a scientifically informed understanding about what and whether religion offered to our moral habitat has only come relatively recently.

Modern researchers have done much to map the geography of Religionia. Surveys in a number of different countries have found that the more religious an individual is, the more he or she reports engaging in prosocial behaviors (Koenig, McGue, Krueger, & Bouchard, 2007; Monsma, 2007; Smidt, 1999). Religious people are more likely to say they volunteer (Campbell & Yonish, 2003), participate in social change organizations (Guo, Webb, Abzug, & Peck, 2013), donate blood (Brooks, 2003), and give money to religious charities, to nonreligious charities (Brooks, 2006; Wuthnow, 1999), and to friends and family who are in need (Brooks, 2003). Controlling for relevant factors such as age and income, religiosity is related to lower levels of self-reported criminal behavior such as theft, property crimes, and drug use (Baier & Wright, 2001; Evans, Cullen, Dunaway, & Burton, 1995). Although this research suggests that religious institutions contribute to prosocial behavior, it is based only on individuals' self-reports of their own behavior. To overcome this limitation, researchers have measured prosocial behavior in laboratory experiments, such as economic games or artificially created opportunities for helping. Unlike on self-report measures, a meta-analysis of these studies revealed no relationship between religion and prosocial behavior (Kramer, Kelly, & Shariff, 2017).

Why not? One possibility is that religious individuals overreport their level of prosociality to present themselves in a positive way. Consistent with this explanation, research has shown that religious individuals are more likely to respond to questions in socially desirable ways (Sedikides & Gebauer, 2010). However, the discrepancy between the findings for self-report and behavioral measures of prosociality may also be partially explained by situational factors. That is, religion may momentarily affect prosocial behavior in ways that are not captured in the laboratory studies that use religion merely as an individual-difference variable. In other words, the effect of religion on prosocial behavior may be explained by certain features of the religious *situation* rather than religious disposition. Instead of simply relying on dispositional religiosity to encourage people toward prosocial behavior across all situations, one may better capture religion's prosocial effect by simulating the "religious situation" in the lab. In support of this, a meta-analysis found that reminders of religious concepts, such as unscrambling words related to religious concepts (Shariff & Norenzayan, 2007), reading Bible verses (Carpenter & Marshall, 2009), or hearing the Muslim prayer call (Aveyard, 2014; Duhaime, 2014), reliably make the religious—but not the nonreligious—behave more prosocially (Shariff, Willard, Andersen, & Norenzayan, 2015). This increased prosociality in response to religious situations has been demonstrated in a variety of different domains, including increasing donations to charity (Malhotra, 2010), generosity (Shariff & Norenzayan, 2007), and honesty (Randolph-Seng & Nielsen, 2007) and decreasing hypocrisy (Carpenter & Marshall, 2009), cheating (Aveyard, 2014), and porn consumption (Edelman, 2009).

The connection between religion and morality, although tenuous in the infancy of religion, has grown stronger through the process of cultural evolution sifting through the varieties of religious experience that emerged throughout the world. Through the differential survival and transmission of certain beliefs, teachings, and rituals, "winners" that proved mentally sticky and socially useful have persisted. Those ideas that failed to catch on, be it through being overly counterintuitive (such as the Order of the Solar Temple, which mixed Christianity, UFOs, New Age philosophy, and Freemason rituals) or socially detrimental (such as universal celibacy among the Shakers), were diminished or extinguished altogether.

Thus the initial shores of Religionia offered little in terms of habitable moral territory, but nonetheless held a promise of better lands. Anthropologists and archaeologists have found that early religions and those still practiced by small bands of foragers tend to be nonmoralistic, with relatively small gods with weak abilities (Boehm, 2008; Peoples, Duda, & Marlowe, 2016; Roes & Raymond, 2003; Stark, 2001; Swanson, 1960). As the explorers pushed further inland, they discovered more bountiful resources. The emergence of specific religious beliefs—first, afterlife beliefs and later morally punitive supernatural and monitoring agents (i.e. "high gods")—proved particularly powerful in galvanizing cooperation and rule following. The effectiveness of supernatural watching and punishment relied on a number of existing human adaptations, including a hypersensitivity to detecting agency (Barrett & Johnson, 2003) and a bias toward seeing the world in terms of design and purpose (Kele-men, 2004) which left humans prone to belief in supernatural watchers. The extreme sensitivity to reputational concerns (itself the evolutionary product of a reciprocity-based morality) made it easy for humans to begin acting as though these supernatural watchers could see if they were being naughty or nice.

Several converging lines of evidence have isolated that it is the monitoring and punitive aspect agents that serves as the active ingredient in encouraging normative behavior.

As group sizes increase, and the need for cultural crutches for cooperation intensify, the gods grow larger and more moralistic (Roes & Raymond, 2003; Watts et al., 2015). Situations that further exacerbate the need for cooperation—such as resource scarcity—are also associated with the presence of more powerful monitoring deities (Botero et al., 2014). For example, even after controlling for relevant variables, the belief in Hell—but not in Heaven—predicts lower crime rates and, in developing countries, stronger economic growth (Shariff & Rhemtulla, 2012; Barro & McCleary, 2003). In a multisite, cross-cultural study, Purzycki et al. (2016) measured how adherents to a variety of different religions living in several different countries behaved in an anonymous resource allocation task. Controlling for a variety of different factors, such as economic differences between countries, people who reported greater belief in gods that are moralistic, knowledgeable, and punitive were more fair and honest in their allocations to others.

Lab studies have found similar conclusions. For example, students who believed in a punitive God were less likely to cheat on an academic task, and those who believed in a forgiving God were more likely to cheat (Shariff & Norenzayan, 2011). Recently, it has been shown that priming the punitive aspects of God increases prosocial intentions, but God concepts stripped of their punitive elements have a much more circumscribed effect (Yilmaz & Bahçekapili, 2015). Meanwhile, limited research suggests that not only might the supernatural "carrot" fail to evoke prosocial behavior, but it may actually compromise such behavior. Religious participants asked to reflect on God's forgiving nature were more likely to cheat and steal than those in control conditions (DeBono, Shariff, Poole, & Muraven, 2017).

Part of what made the belief in punitive supernatural agents a particularly fruitful area in our moral habitat was its linkages to other aspects that made up the cultural "packages" that we call religions. For example, tying these agent beliefs to morally dependent afterlife beliefs, to sets of rituals that deepened faith and communicate shared beliefs, to sacred values that made violations a threat to meaning and identity, all enhanced the power that the beliefs in punitive gods would have had on its own. Indeed, the religions of Religionia grew more effective by connecting vast areas of different territory, making those areas more than the sum of their parts (see Shariff & Mercier, 2016, for a more in-depth discussion of this point).

Secularia

But Religionia was not the only new moral territory discovered by the intrepid human explorers. Further north, humans found land that allowed them to layer their small-scale moralities with secular institutions. Like those claiming that religion is necessary for morality, many have argued that secular institutions are necessary to enforce cooperation—perhaps none so notably as the political philosopher Thomas Hobbes. Hobbes (1651–1974) observed that people's interests often conflict with those of others, and, if not deterred by some outside force, people tend to resolve these conflicts though violence. To prevent these conflicts from creating a state of perpetual violence, he argued that people should enter into a social contract by which they cede their rights to a powerful sovereign authority in exchange for protection. This authority could punish those who use violence, reducing the incentive to use it as a means of resolving conflicts. And for Hobbes, this sovereign authority had to be secular, so it could apply to all members of society, not just the members of a particular religion.

Although he lacked the empirical evidence available to modern scholars, Hobbes's intuitions about violence turned out to be accurate. Periods of history in which there were no forms of government to regulate behavior appear to have been as violent and chaotic as Hobbes predicted they would be. Forensic analysis of the remains of people living in societies without organized forms of government or religion, such as ancient hunter–gatherers (Mithen, 1999), have indicated that even the most peaceful of these societies were much more violent than modern industrialized societies (McCall & Shields, 2008; See Figure 35.1).

However, as with Religionia, the coastal territory discovered by early explorers of Secularia was of limited value, and it took the explorers a long time to reach the resource-rich territory that is occupied by modern states.

In early groups of hunter–gatherers, conflict resolution was generally left to the parties involved. The human tendency for revenge, particularly the desire to seek lethal retaliation in response to the death of a relative, led these groups to have high rates of killing and blood feuds between genetically related groups (Boehm, 1984). In these largely egalitarian groups, the earliest forms of third-party mediation consisted of other members' attempts to resolve a conflict, such as by distracting the participants or, in serious cases, encouraging one of the parties to leave the group (Boehm, 2012). After the agricultural revolution made this type of mobility impractical, groups began to give their leaders increasing authority to mediate disputes, which reduced revenge-based feuding (Ericksen & Horton, 1992). This increase in authority, which became hereditary, combined with the development of social stratification facilitated by the greater potential for material wealth, laid the foundation for the development of early state societies (Johnson & Earle, 2000). As these state societies began to grow in size, they eventually developed military forces paid for with taxation, giving them a much greater ability to enforce and monitor mediation decisions (Boehm, 2012).

To determine how effective these state societies were at preventing violence, we can compare contemporaneous societies that were at different points of state develop-

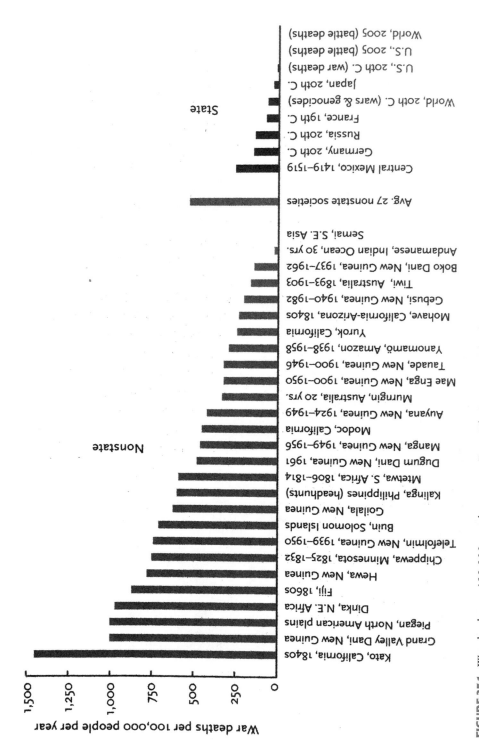

FIGURE 35.1. War deaths per year. From *The Better Angels of Our Nature: Why Violence Has Declined*, by Steven Pinker. Copyright © 2011 by Steven Pinker. Used by permission of Viking Books, an imprint of Penguin Publishing group, a division of Penguin Random House LLC. All rights reserved. Any third party use of this material, outside of this publication, is prohibited. Interested parties must apply directly to Penguin Random House LLC for permission. Sources: Nonstate: Hewa and Goila from Gat, 2006; others from Keeley, 1996. Central Mexico, Germany, Russia, France, Japan: Keeley, 1996. United States in the 20th Century: Leland and Oboroceanu, 2010. World in 20th century: White, 2011; World in 2005: Human Security Report Project, 2008. Reproduced by permission of Penguin Books Ltd.

342

ment. Doing so indicates that, for a given moment in history, those societies that had established state governments had significantly lower rates of violence (Steckel & Rose, 2002). Likewise, when ungoverned areas come under state control, they typically experience significant reductions in crime and violence (Wiessner, 2010).

Although it took until the 16th century for Hobbes to write about the social contract, the earliest formal social contracts can be traced back to the development of citizenship in ancient Greece. Citizenship can be loosely defined as a contract between an individual and society in which the individual provides services, such as taxes, military service, or civic duties in exchange for entitlement to specific rights and protections from a government (Isin & Turner, 2007). In its earliest forms, such as in ancient Athens, these protections basically consisted of a government-provided military force tasked with maintaining order, whereas things like investigating crimes were left up to individual members of society (Hunter, 1994). The modern idea of a stand-alone government-sponsored police force designed to protect and serve individual citizens did not emerge until the early 19th century, with the creation of the Metropolitan Police Service in London (Monkkonen, 1992). The success of this force led it to be emulated throughout the world (Emsley, 2014).

Third-party mediation in secular institutions—which includes the surveillance, apprehension, judgment, and punishment of codified normative transgressions—continues to be an important aspect in promoting cooperation today. Studies have shown that increases in the number of police in a society decreases the amount of crime (Levitt, 2002; Skogan & Frydl, 2004), as do increases in other methods of surveillance: cameras that reduce auto theft and shootings (Caplan, Kennedy, & Petrossian, 2011; Ratcliffe, Taniguchi, & Taylor, 2009), photo radar that decreases rates of speeding (Bloch, 1998; Chen, Wilson, Meckle, & Cooper, 2000), and random breath tests and increased surveillance that reduce rates of drinking and driving (Homel, Carseldine, & Kearns, 1988; Ross, 1984). Overall, as the perceived certainty and magnitude of third-party punishment for breaking laws increases, so does the compliance with those laws (Cusson, 1993; Nagin & Paternoster, 1991; Paternoster, 1987).

As with religious institutions, the challenges posed by large groups and limited resources led societies to develop secular institutions, such as property rights, to deter "free riding." One problem groups face as they increase in size is referred to as the "tragedy of the commons" (Hardin, 1968). When a finite resource is shared or "common" to a group of people, each individual benefits from using the resource. However, the cost of depleting of the resource is shared across the entire community, meaning each individual's gain from using the resource exceeds his or her depletion cost, and everyone has an incentive to use the resource until it is depleted. Although reputational concerns can prevent this exploitation in small groups (Milinski, Semmann, & Krambeck, 2002), it is unlikely to do so in large groups, where peoples' reputations are unknown or cannot be remembered.

Although ownership among early hunter–gatherers was restricted to things that could be easily transported, such as tools and weapons, the development of agriculture provided a means of signaling unambiguous possession of land, facilitating the extension of ownership to territory (Krier, 2009). Individual ownership of land worked as a deterrent to the free riding that occurs in communal agriculture, in which individuals have an incentive to reap more than their fair share of a combined harvest. One solution to Hardin's (1968) tragedy of the commons is to carve the commons up and give people dominion over a slice. Thus the concept of property, defined as a claim of possession enforced by the state, gained traction (Pipes, 2007). In addition to deterring free riding and the overuse of resources, enforcement of property rights encourages exchange and investment (Demsetz, 1967; North, 1990), making enforcement of property rights one of the most important determinants of economic growth (Knack & Keefer, 1995). Indeed, Ferguson (2011) argues that well-enforced and widespread property rights played a central role in the rise of the United States as an economic superpower, whereas

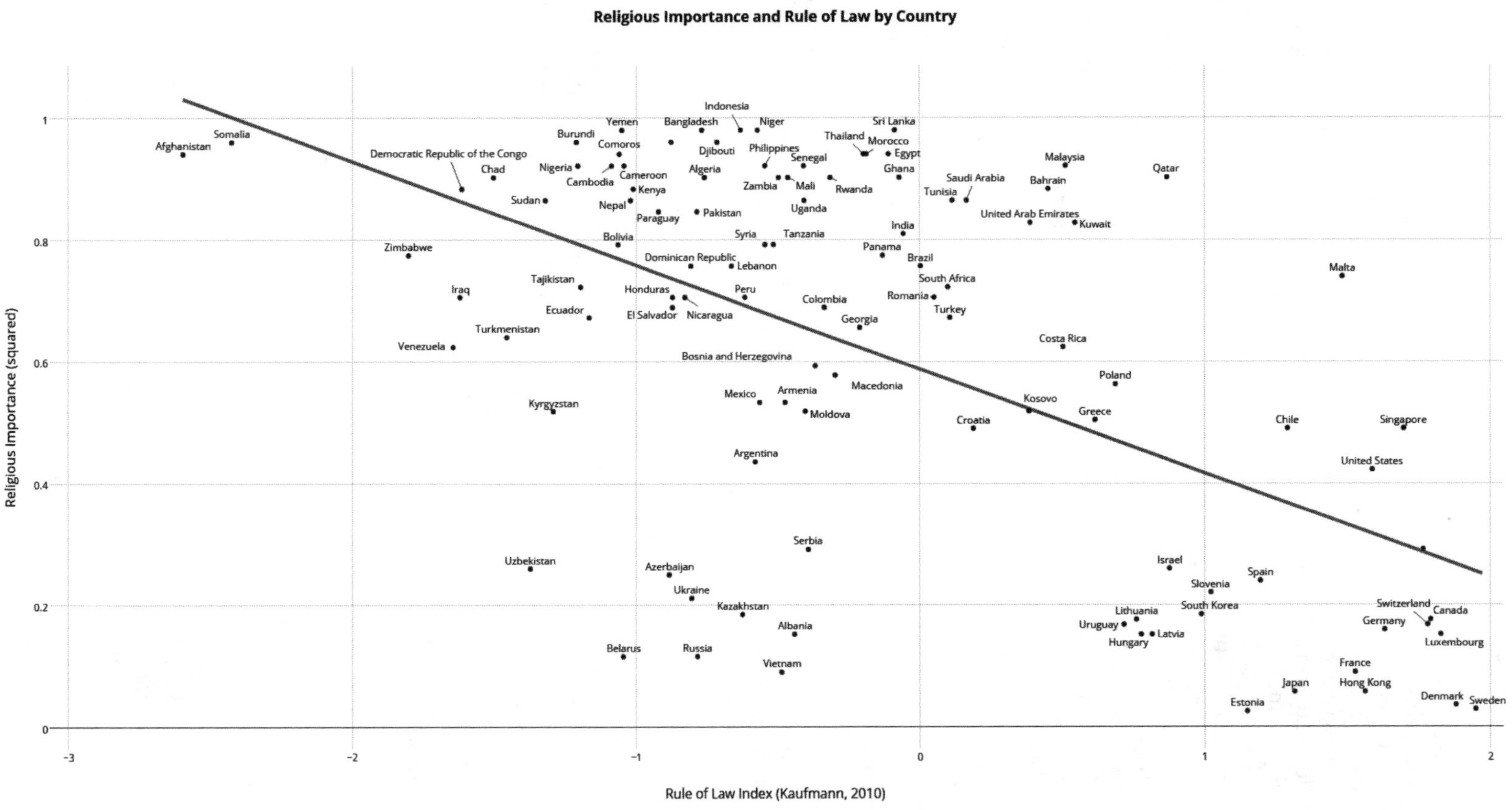

FIGURE 35.2. Religious importance (World Values Survey, 2014) and the rule of law index (Kaufmann, Kraay, & Mastruzzi, 2011) by country.

similar societies without widespread property rights, such as nations in South America, struggled.

However, not all common resources can be divided into pieces. When common pool resources were difficult or impossible to privatize, many societies developed institutions that restricted the use of these resources to prevent depletion (Ostrom, 1990). These types of institutions have successfully regulated the use of a diverse range of common resources, including common pasture for farm animals (Netting, 1981), forestry land (McKean, 1992), and access to water (Saleth & Dinar, 2004). In contrast, there are a number of cases in which failure to establish an institution to regulate a common resource led to depletion: Beaver stocks during the fur trade (Berkes, 1999) and whale stocks during the nineteenth century (Davis, Gallman, & Gleiter, 2007) are just two examples.

Finally, an important step in the evolution of secular institutions was the development of "the rule of law," under which all individuals in a society—including the lawmakers and leaders—are subject to the same, stable code of laws (in contrast to systems in which certain authorities are exempt from the law, such as a dictatorship). By preventing rulers from abusing their power, the rule of law has been shown to increase human rights protections (Cross, 1999) and to lower levels of government corruption (Kimbro, 2002).

The rule of law is also valuable because it signals that the rules are predictable, consistent, and fairly applied, and thus worth following (North, 1990). Research has found that for individuals who have had contact with the legal system, judgments about the fairness of the decision process and about the motives of authorities were the best predictors of people's willingness to accept the decision made, regardless of the type of contact or the legal authority involved (Tyler & Huo, 2002). Other research on mediation has found that the more people perceive mediation processes to be fair, the more likely they are to comply with the outcome of mediation (Pruitt, Peirce, McGillicuddy, Welton, & Castrianno, 1993). Overall, the extent to which people perceive that laws are being fairly applied to everyone is the best predictor of compliance with those laws (Tyler, 2003).

Comparing the Continents

We should not belabor the metaphor of separate continents too much. In truth, there is much trade on the isthmus between the continents; many societies experienced much overlap and interaction between these two different moral institutions. A good example is the monogamous marriage norm. This was a moral norm (aimed particularly at those powerful men who had the option of violating it) that spread because of Christianity but succeeded because it offered societies a way to reduce violent competition between males within the group (Henrich, Boyd & Richerson, 2012). Though the origins of the norm were rooted in religious institutions, the norm became legally codified by secular governments to the point where a religion without it—Mormonism—was forced by the local secular institutions to adopt it.

That all said, secular and religious moralities have often operated in a hydraulic fashion: More of one meant less of the other. Countries that have a higher quality of secular institutions (as measured by level of economic development) tend to have citizens who are less religious (McCleary & Barro, 2006). Similarly, the stronger the rule of law is in a country, the smaller is the share of individuals saying that religion is an important part of their life (Berggren & Bjørnskov, 2013; See Figure 35.2).

This hydraulic relationship occurs with institutions promoting financial security as well; the better a country's social safety net, the less religious individuals in that country tend to be (Inglehart & Norris, 2004). When trust in the government is threatened, such as during periods of political instability, commitment to religion increases, and when belief in God's control over the world is threatened, people desire a more controlling government (Kay, Shepherd, Blatz, Chua, & Galinsky, 2010).

There are also a number of key differences separating the two continents. When rules are perceived to be established and enforced by divine commandment, they tend to be seen as more sacred and inviolable than rules based on nonreligious roots (Piazza & Landy, 2013). For example, nonreligious people are more willing than the religious to violate a moral rule when doing so leads to a positive outcome, such as killing one person to save several others (Szekely, Opre, & Miu, 2015). When asked why moral violations are wrong, religious people are more likely to endorse rule-based explanations (e.g. "Infidelity is wrong"), while the nonreligious are more likely to endorse *consequence*-based explanations (e.g. "Infidelity could hurt one's partner if they find out"; Piazza, 2012). Similarly, feelings of compassion tend to have a stronger influence on the moral decisions of the nonreligious than the religious (Saslow et al., 2013). Thus, whereas the religious tend to make "deontological" moral decisions based on whether or not a given action violates a moral rule, the nonreligious are more likely to make "utilitarian" decisions based on a consideration of the consequences of particular actions.

Religious rules also are more likely to be considered "sacred values" (Sheikh, Ginges, Coman, & Atran, 2012), meaning they are believed to possess "transcendental significance that precludes comparisons, trade-offs, or indeed any mingling with secular values" (Tetlock, Kristel, Elson, Green, & Lerner, 2000, p. 853). Individuals who hold sacred values consider it wrong to even consider trading sacred values for material incentives, and offers to do so often backfire by increasing commitment to a sacred value (Tetlock et al., 2000). For example, one study presented individuals involved in the Israeli–Palestinian conflict with a potential peace deal involving the exchange of sacred values (e.g., land for peace). Although individuals generally did not support the deal, adding an additional financial incentive (in the form of $1 billion in reparations) increased moral outrage and support for violent opposition to the deal (Ginges, Atran, Medin, & Shikaki, 2007). Other research has demonstrated that Palestinians who view issues in the Israeli–Palestinian conflict as sacred were more resistant to social influence on these issues and were less likely to consider opportunities to exit the conflict (Sheikh, Ginges, & Atran, 2013). Similarly, among Jewish residents of the West Bank, support for violent action against Palestinians is unrelated to the perceived effectiveness of that action (Ginges & Atran, 2011). This type of resolve, which is immune to social influ-

ence and insensitive to outcomes, can be a valuable resource in intergroup conflict. In a historical analysis of asymmetric conflicts, Mack (1975) argues that resolve is an important factor that has often allowed a weaker power to defeat an otherwise much stronger adversary. In line with this finding, researchers have argued that sacred values have given groups such as the Islamic State the resolve to overcome numerous opponents with orders of magnitude more military personnel and weaponry (Atran, Sheikh, & Gomez, 2014).

Viewing rules as the sacred result of divine commands can also be a powerful motivation to adhere to them. In support of this idea, people who view rules in a deontological way are less likely to violate these rules (Xu & Ma, 2015). Other research has found that priming people to think about morality as objective increases donations to charity (Young & Durwin, 2013), whereas priming people to think about morality as subjective increases cheating (Rai & Holyoak, 2013).

Although sacred values can be valuable in intergroup conflicts, they can also present a significant barrier to conflict resolution. As the intractability of the Jewish–Palestine conflict can attest, when two different groups hold conflicting, nonnegotiable sacred values, disagreements can be very difficult to resolve.

Religious and secular institutions also differ in the scope of their application. As discussed earlier, religious situations only make the religious more prosocial, suggesting that Hobbes was correct in his criticism that religious institutions would not apply to everyone. Currently there are estimated 750 million nonbelievers worldwide (Zuckerman, 2007) and the proportion of nonbelievers in almost all industrialized nations has been steadily increasing over the last century (Voas, 2008). This nonuniversal application of religious institutions represents a significant limitation to their ability to enforce cooperation.

Secular institutions, on the other hand, cannot be ignored through disbelief. When governments pass laws, they apply to all members of society, even those who disagree with them. In a demonstration of this, one study found that, although religious primes only made the religious more prosocial, secular primes increased prosociality among both the religious and the nonreligious (Shariff & Norenzayan, 2007).

The universal applicability of secular institutions also comes at a significant cost. For example, the United States alone spends an estimated $100 billion per year on law enforcement (Ashton, Petteruti, & Walsh, 2012). While relying on supernatural enforcement is not entirely cost-free—the necessary demonstrations of commitment to religions are often quite costly—having one's transgressions deterred by an invisible omniscient agent can be substantially cheaper than the secular alternative.

Charting the Course Forward

Compelling research has recently shown how religiosity's long-known salutary effects on health and happiness are moderated by country-level features. In places where life is difficult, religion is positively associated with both happiness and longevity. But in places where life is easier and where religion is less of a social norm, the effect is flat. Though the data do not yet exist, something similar may exist for the relationship between religion and morality. Religion may serve a critical function for encouraging norm-following in less developed parts of the world. In places where secular institutions have been sufficiently built, they may do sufficient moral work as to render the religion morally unnecessary. In a way, this would complete the life cycle arc of Religionia. Religious institutions began by providing groups with valuable advantages at a time when secular institutions were unable to do so, facilitating the development of large-scale societies. However, as these societies develop secular institutions capable of effectively enforcing cooperation without religion, religion—especially the parts of religion like supernatural punishment that may exist for the primary purpose of enforcing cooperation—may become less prevalent. Whether the next step in our species' moral journey is to vacate Religionia entirely, to settle in the more fertile lands up North, remains a matter of open, heated, and consequential debate.

REFERENCES

Ashton, P., Petteruti, A., & Walsh, N. (2012). *Rethinking the blues: How we police in the U.S. and at what cost.* Washington, DC: Justice Policy Institute.

Atran, S., Sheikh, H., & Gomez, A. (2014). Devoted actors sacrifice for close comrades and sacred cause. *Proceedings of the National Academy of Sciences of the USA, 111*(50), 17702–17703.

Aveyard, M. E. (2014). A call to honesty: Extending religious priming of moral behavior to Middle Eastern Muslims. *PLOS ONE, 9*(7), e99447.

Baier, C. J., & Wright, B. R. (2001). "If you love me, keep my commandments": A meta-analysis of the effect of religion on crime. *Journal of Research in Crime and Delinquency, 38*(1), 3–21.

Barker, G. (2009). *The agricultural revolution in prehistory: Why did foragers become farmers?* New York: Oxford University Press.

Barrett, J. L., & Johnson, A. H. (2003). The role of control in attributing intentional agency to inanimate objects. *Journal of Cognition and Culture, 3*(3), 208–217.

Barro, R. J., & McCleary, R. (2003). *Religion and economic growth* (Working Paper No. 9682). Cambridge, MA: National Bureau of Economic Research. Available at *www.nber.org/papers/w9682.pdf.*

Berggren, N., & Bjørnskov, C. (2013). Does religiosity promote property rights and the rule of law? *Journal of Institutional Economics, 9*(02), 161–185.

Berkes, F. (1999). *Sacred ecology: Traditional ecological knowledge and resource management.* Philadelphia: Taylor & Francis.

Bloch, S. (1998). Comparative study of speed reduction effects of photo-radar and speed display boards. *Transportation Research Record: Journal of the Transportation Research Board, 1640,* 27–36.

Boehm, C. (1984). *Blood revenge: The enactment and management of conflict in Montenegro and other tribal societies.* Lawrence: University Press of Kansas.

Boehm, C. (2008). Purposive social selection and the evolution of human altruism. *Cross-Cultural Research, 42*(4), 319–352.

Boehm, C. (2012). Ancestral hierarchy and conflict. *Science, 336*(6083), 844–847.

Botero, C. A., Gardner, B., Kirby, K. R., Bulbulia, J., Gavin, M. C., & Gray, R. D. (2014). The ecology of religious beliefs. *Proceedings of the National Academy of Sciences of the USA, 111*(47), 16784–16789.

Brooks, A. C. (2003). Religious faith and charitable giving. *Policy Review, 121.* Available at *www.hoover.org/research/religious-faith-and-charitable-giving.*

Brooks, A. C. (2006). *Who really cares: The surprising truth about compassionate conservatism—America's charity divide—who gives, who doesn't, and why it matters.* New York: Basic Books.

Campbell, D. E., & Yonish, S. J. (2003). Religion and volunteering in America. In C. Smidt (Ed.), *Religion as social capital: Producing the common good* (pp. 87–106). Waco, TX: Baylor University Press.

Caplan, J. M., Kennedy, L. W., & Petrossian, G. (2011). Police-monitored CCTV cameras in Newark, NJ: A quasi-experimental test of crime deterrence. *Journal of Experimental Criminology, 7*(3), 255–274.

Carpenter, T. P., & Marshall, M. A. (2009). An examination of religious priming and intrinsic religious motivation in the moral hypocrisy paradigm. *Journal for the Scientific Study of Religion, 48*(2), 386–393.

Chen, G., Wilson, J., Meckle, W., & Cooper, P. (2000). Evaluation of photo radar program in British Columbia. *Accident Analysis and Prevention, 32*(4), 517–526.

Cross, F. B. (1999). The relevance of law in human rights protection. *International Review of Law and Economics, 19*(1), 87–98.

Cusson, M. (1993). Situational deterrence: Fear during the criminal event. *Crime Prevention Studies, 1,* 55–68.

Davis, L. E., Gallman, R. E., & Gleiter, K. (2007). *In pursuit of Leviathan: Technology, institutions, productivity, and profits in American whaling, 1816–1906.* Chicago: University of Chicago Press.

DeBono, A., Shariff, A., Poole, S., & Muraven, M. (in press). Forgive us our trespasses: Priming a forgiving (but not a punishing) God increases unethical behavior. *Psychology of Religion and Spirituality.*

Demsetz, H. (1967). Toward a theory of property rights. *American Economic Review, 57,* 347–358.

Dostoyevsky, F. (2014). *The brothers Karamazov* (C. Garnett, Trans.). New York: Lowell Press. (Original work published 1880)

Duhaime, E. (2014). *Did religion facilitate the evolution of large-scale cooperative societies?* Unpublished master's thesis, University of Cambridge, Cambridge, UK.

Edelman, B. (2009). Markets: Red light states: Who buys online adult entertainment? *Journal of Economic Perspectives, 23*(1), 209–220.

Emsley, C. (2014). *The English police: A political and social history.* New York: Routledge.

Ericksen, K. P., & Horton, H. (1992). "Blood feuds": Cross-cultural variations in kin group vengeance. *Cross-Cultural Research, 26*(1–4), 57–85.

Evans, T. D., Cullen, F. T., Dunaway, R. G., & Burton, V. S. (1995). Religion and crime reexamined: The impact of religion, secular controls, and social ecology on adult criminality. *Criminology, 33*(2), 195–224.

Ferguson, N. (2011). *Civilization: The West and the rest.* New York: Penguin Group.

Gat, A. (2006). *War in human civilization.* New York: Oxford University Press.

Ginges, J., & Atran, S. (2011). War as a moral imperative (not just practical politics by other means). *Proceedings of the Royal Society of London: B. Biological Sciences, 278*(1720), 2930–2938.

Ginges, J., Atran, S., Medin, D., & Shikaki, K. (2007). Sacred bounds on rational resolution of violent political conflict. *Proceedings of the National Academy of Sciences of the USA, 104*(18), 7357–7360.

Guo, C., Webb, N. J., Abzug, R., & Peck, L. R. (2013). Religious affiliation, religious attendance, and participation in social change organizations. *Nonprofit and Voluntary Sector Quarterly, 42*(1), 34–58.

Hardin, G. (1968). The tragedy of the commons. *Science, 162,* 1243–1248

Henrich, J. (2004). Cultural group selection, coevolutionary processes and large-scale cooperation. *Journal of Economic Behavior and Organization, 53*(1), 3–35.

Henrich, J., Boyd, R., & Richerson, P. J. (2012). The puzzle of monogamous marriage. *Philosophical Transactions of the Royal Society: B. Biological Sciences, 367*(1589), 657–669.

Hobbes, T. (1974). *Leviathan.* New York: Penguin. (Original work published 1651)

Homel, R., Carseldine, D., & Kearns, I. (1988). Drink-driving countermeasures in Australia. *Alcohol, Drugs, and Driving, 4*(2), 113–144.

Human Security Report Project. (2008). *Miniatlas of human security.* Washington, DC: World Bank.

Hunter, V. J. (1994). *Policing Athens: Social control in the Attic lawsuits, 420–320 B.C.* Princeton, NJ: Princeton University Press.

Inglehart, R., & Norris, P. (2004). *Sacred and secular: Religion and politics worldwide.* Cambridge, UK: Cambridge University Press.

Isin, E. F., & Turner, B. S. (2007). Investigating citizenship: An agenda for citizenship studies. *Citizenship Studies, 11*(1), 5–17.

Jaccard, S. L., Galbraith, E. D., Froelicher, T. L., & Gruber, N. (2014). Ocean (de)oxygenation across the last deglaciation. *Oceanography, 27*(2), 26–35.

Johnson, A. W., & Earle, T. K. (2000). *The*

evolution of human societies: From foraging group to agrarian state. Stanford, CA: Stanford University Press.

Kaufmann, D., Kraay, A., & Mastruzzi, M. (2011). The worldwide governance indicators: Methodology and analytical issues. *Hague Journal on the Rule of Law, 3*(2), 220–246.

Kay, A. C., Shepherd, S., Blatz, C. W., Chua, S. N., & Galinsky, A. D. (2010). For God (or) country: The hydraulic relation between government instability and belief in religious sources of control. *Journal of Personality and Social Psychology, 99*(5), 725–739.

Keeley, L. H. (1996). *War before civilization: The myth of the peaceful savage.* New York: Oxford University Press.

Kelemen, D. (2004). Are children "intuitive theists"? Reasoning about purpose and design in nature. *Psychological Science, 15*(5), 295–301.

Kimbro, M. B. (2002). A cross-country empirical investigation of corruption and its relationship to economic, cultural, and monitoring institutions: An examination of the role of accounting and financial statements quality. *Journal of Accounting, Auditing and Finance, 17*(4), 325–350.

Knack, S., & Keefer, P. (1995). Institutions and economic performance: Cross-country tests using alternative institutional measures. *Economics and Politics, 7*(3), 207–227.

Koenig, L. B., McGue, M., Krueger, R. F., & Bouchard, T. J. (2007). Religiousness, antisocial behavior, and altruism: Genetic and environmental mediation. *Journal of Personality, 75*(2), 265–290.

Kramer, S. R., Kelly, J., & Shariff, A. F. (2017). *Religious prosociality: A meta-analysis.* Manuscript in preparation.

Krier, J. E. (2009). Evolutionary theory and the origin of property rights. *Cornell Law Review, 95*, 139–160.

Leland, A., & Oboroceanu, M. J. (2010). *American war and military operations casualties: Lists and statistics.* Washington, DC: Congressional Research Service. Retrieved from: *http://fpc.state.gov/documents/organization/139347.pdf.*

Levitt, S. D. (2002). Using electoral cycles in police hiring to estimate the effects of police on crime: Reply. *American Economic Review, 92*(4), 1244–1250.

Mack, A. (1975). Why big nations lose small wars: The politics of asymmetric conflict. *World Politics, 27*(2), 175–200.

Malhotra, D. (2010). (When) are religious people nicer?: Religious salience and the "Sunday effect" on pro-social behavior. *Judgment and Decision Making, 5*, 138–143.

McCall, G. S., & Shields, N. (2008). Examining the evidence from small-scale societies and early prehistory and implications for modern theories of aggression and violence. *Aggression and Violent Behavior, 13*(1), 1–9.

McCleary, R. M., & Barro, R. J. (2006). Religion and economy. *Journal of Economic Perspectives, 20*(2), 49–72.

McKean, M. A. (1992). Success on the commons: A comparative examination of institutions for common property resource management. *Journal of Theoretical Politics, 4*(3), 247–281.

Milinski, M., Semmann, D., & Krambeck, H. J. (2002). Reputation helps solve the "tragedy of the commons." *Nature, 415*(6870), 424–426.

Mithen, S. (1999). Symbolism and the supernatural. In R. Dunbar, C. Knight, & C. Power (Eds.), *The evolution of culture: A historical and scientific overview* (pp. 147–171). New Brunswick, NJ: Rutgers University Press.

Monkkonen, E. H. (1992). History of urban police. *Crime and Justice, 15*, 547–580.

Monsma, S. V. (2007). Religion and philanthropic giving and volunteering: Building blocks for civic responsibility. *Interdisciplinary Journal of Research on Religion, 3*, 2–28.

Nagin, D. S., & Paternoster, R. (1991). Preventive effects of the perceived risk of arrest: Testing an expanded conception of deterrence. *Criminology, 29*, 561–587.

Netting, R. M. (1981). *Balancing on an Alp: Ecological change and continuity in a Swiss mountain community.* Cambridge, UK: Cambridge University Press

North, D. C. (1990). *Institutions, institutional change and economic performance.* Cambridge, UK: Cambridge University Press.

Ostrom, E. (1990). *Governing the commons.* Cambridge, UK: Cambridge University Press.

Paternoster, R. (1987). The deterrent effect of the perceived certainty and severity of punishment: A review of the evidence and issues. *Justice Quarterly, 4*(2), 173–217.

Peoples, H. C., Duda, P., & Marlowe, F. W. (2016). Hunter-gatherers and the origins of religion. *Human Nature, 27*, 261–282.

Pew Research Center. (2014). Worldwide, many see belief in God as essential to morality. Retrieved from *www.pewglobal. org/2014/03/13/worldwide-many-see-belief-in-god-as-essential-to-morality.*

Piazza, J. (2012). "If you love me keep my commandments": Religiosity increases preference for rule-based moral arguments. *International Journal for the Psychology of Religion, 22*(4), 285–302.

Piazza, J., & Landy, J. F. (2013). "Lean not on your own understanding": Belief that morality is founded on divine authority and non-utilitarian moral thinking. *Judgment and Decision Making, 8*(6), 639–661.

Pinker, S. (2011). *The better angels of our nature: The decline of violence in history and its causes.* London, UK: Penguin.

Pipes, R. (2007). *Property and freedom.* New York: Vintage.

Pruitt, D. G., Peirce, R. S., McGillicuddy, N. B., Welton, G. L., & Castrianno, L. M. (1993). Long-term success in mediation. *Law and Human Behavior, 17*(3), 313–330.

Purzycki, B. G., Apicella, C., Atkinson, Q. D., Cohen, E., McNamara, R. A., Willard, A. K., . . . Henrich, J. (2016). Moralistic gods, supernatural punishment and the expansion of human sociality. *Nature, 530,* 327–330.

Rai, T. S., & Holyoak, K. J. (2013). Exposure to moral relativism compromises moral behavior. *Journal of Experimental Social Psychology, 49*(6), 995–1001.

Randolph-Seng, B., & Nielsen, M. E. (2007). Honesty: One effect of primed religious representations. *International Journal for the Psychology of Religion, 17*(4), 303–315.

Ratcliffe, J. H., Taniguchi, T., & Taylor, R. B. (2009). The crime reduction effects of public CCTV cameras: A multi-method spatial approach. *Justice Quarterly, 26*(4), 746–770.

Roes, F. L., & Raymond, M. (2003). Belief in moralizing gods. *Evolution and Human Behavior, 24*(2), 126–135.

Ross, H. L. (1984). Social control through deterrence: Drinking-and-driving laws. *Annual Review of Sociology, 10*(1), 21–35.

Saleth, R. M., & Dinar, A. (2004). *The institutional economics of water: A cross-country analysis of institutions and performance.* Cheltenham, UK: Edward Elgar.

Saslow, L. R., Willer, R., Feinberg, M., Piff, P. K., Clark, K., Keltner, D., & Saturn, S. R. (2013). My brother's keeper?: Compassion predicts generosity more among less religious individuals. *Social Psychological and Personality Science, 4*(1), 31–38.

Sedikides, C., & Gebauer, J. E. (2010). Religiosity as self-enhancement: A meta-analysis of the relation between socially desirable responding and religiosity. *Personality and Social Psychology Review, 14,* 17–36.

Shariff, A. F., & Mercier, B. (2016). The evolution of religion and morality. In J. R. Liddle & T. K. Shackelford (Eds.), *The Oxford handbook of evolutionary psychology and religion.* New York: Oxford University Press.

Shariff, A. F., & Norenzayan, A. (2007). God is watching you: Priming God concepts increases prosocial behavior in an anonymous economic game. *Psychological Science, 18*(9), 803–809.

Shariff, A. F., & Norenzayan, A. (2011). Mean gods make good people: Different views of God predict cheating behavior. *International Journal for the Psychology of Religion, 21*(2), 85–96.

Shariff, A. F., & Rhemtulla, M. (2012). Divergent effects of beliefs in heaven and hell on national crime rates. *PLOS ONE, 7*(6), e39048.

Shariff, A. F., Willard, A. K., Andersen, T., & Norenzayan, A. (2015). Religious priming: A meta-analysis with a focus on prosociality. *Personality and Social Psychology Review, 20,* 27–48.

Sheikh, H., Ginges, J., & Atran, S. (2013). Sacred values in the Israeli–Palestinian conflict: Resistance to social influence, temporal discounting, and exit strategies. *Annals of the New York Academy of Sciences, 1299*(1), 11–24.

Sheikh, H., Ginges, J., Coman, A., & Atran, S. (2012). Religion, group threat and sacred values. *Judgment and Decision Making, 7*(2), 110–118.

Skogan, W., & Frydl, K. (Eds.). (2004). *Fairness and effectiveness in policing: The evidence.* Washington, DC: National Academies Press.

Smidt, C. (1999). Religion and civic engagement: A comparative analysis. *Annals of the American Academy of Political and Social Science, 565*(1), 176–192.

Sowers, T., & Bender, M. (1995). Climate records covering the last deglaciation. *Science, 269*(5221), 210.

Spalding, M., & Garrity, P. J. (1996). *A sacred union of citizens: George Washington's Farewell Address and the American character.* Lanham, MD: Rowman & Littlefield.

Stark, R. (2001) Gods, rituals, and the moral order. *Journal for the Scientific Study of Religion, 40,* 619–636.

Steckel, R. H., & Rose, J. C. (2002). *The backbone of history: Health and nutrition in the Western hemisphere.* Cambridge, UK: Cambridge University Press.

Swanson, G. E. (1960). *The birth of the gods: The origin of primitive beliefs.* Ann Arbor: University of Michigan Press.

Szekely, R. D., Opre, A., & Miu, A. C. (2015). Religiosity enhances emotion and deontological choice in moral dilemmas. *Personality and Individual Differences, 79,* 104–109.

Tetlock, P. E., Kristel, O. V., Elson, S. B., Green, M. C., & Lerner, J. S. (2000). The psychology of the unthinkable: Taboo trade-offs, forbidden base rates, and heretical counterfactuals. *Journal of Personality and Social Psychology, 78*(5), 853–870.

Tyler, T. R. (2003). Procedural justice, legitimacy, and the effective rule of law. *Crime and Justice, 30,* 283–357.

Tyler, T. R., & Huo, Y. (2002). *Trust in the law: Encouraging public cooperation with the police and courts.* New York: Russell Sage Foundation.

Voas, D. (2008). The continuing secular transition. In D. Pollack & D. V. A. Olson (Eds.), *The role of religion in modern societies* (pp. 25–49). New York: Taylor & Francis.

Voltaire. (1977). *The portable Voltaire* (B. R. Redman, Trans.). New York: Penguin Books. (Original work published 1727)

Watts, J., Greenhill, S. J., Atkinson, Q. D., Currie, T. E., Bulbulia, J., & Gray, R. D. (2015). Broad supernatural punishment but not moralizing high gods precede the evolution of political complexity in Austronesia. *Proceedings of the Royal Society of London B, 282*(1804), 2014–2556.

White, M. (2011). *The great big book of horrible things. The definitive chronicle of history's 100 worst atrocities.* New York: Norton.

Wiessner, P. F. (2010). *Youths, elders, and the wages of war in Enga province, Papua New Guinea.* Canberra: Australian National University.

World Values Survey Association. (2014). World Values Survey, Wave 6, 2010–2014 [Data file]. Available at *www.worldvaluessurvey.org/WVSDocumentationWV6.jsp.*

Wuthnow, R. (1999). Mobilizing civic engagement: The changing impact of religious involvement. In T. Skocpol & M. P. Fiorina (Eds.), *Civic engagement in American democracy* (pp. 331–363). Washington, DC: Brookings Institution Press.

Xu, Z. X., & Ma, H. K. (2015). How can a deontological decision lead to moral behavior?: The moderating role of moral identity. *Journal of Business Ethics, 137,* 537–549.

Yilmaz, O., & Bahçekapili, H. G. (2015). Without God, everything is permitted?: The reciprocal influence of religious and meta-ethical beliefs. *Journal of Experimental Social Psychology, 58,* 95–100.

Young, L., & Durwin, A. J. (2013). Moral realism as moral motivation: The impact of meta-ethics on everyday decision-making. *Journal of Experimental Social Psychology, 49*(2), 302–306.

Zuckerman, P. (2007). Atheism: Contemporary numbers and patterns. In M. Martin (Ed.), *The Cambridge companion to atheism* (pp. 47–66). Cambridge, UK: Cambridge University Press.

CHAPTER 36

The Egocentric Teleological Bias

How Self-Serving Morality Shapes Perceptions of Intelligent Design

Jesse L. Preston

Why are intelligent design arguments so moralized?

Egocentric biases foster a false perception of "suspicious serendipity" and so create illusions of intelligent design with self-serving moral judgments.

The *argument from design* is one of the most common proofs offered for the existence of God. Essentially, the argument comes down to an observation of complexity and order in the world, in life, and in our universe and an inference that this is far too much order and complexity to have come about by random chance. Rather, such perfect orchestration implies some invisible hand conducting the orchestra—that is, God. Intelligent design arguments are also highly moralized, in part because of the obvious connection to religious belief. But also, they hinge on an implicit perception of a *moral purpose* in that design. Here I argue that egocentric biases (centered on the self, humans, earth, and life) are key to creating illusions of intelligent design, by creating a strong sense of "suspicious serendipity": simultaneously enhancing the perceived unlikeliness and benefit of one's own personal outcomes.

Intelligent Design: A Brief History

One favorite example of the design argument is the amazing human eye. Socrates suggested the correspondence between parts of the human body (e.g., the eyelids protecting the eyeballs) was a clear sign of "clever planning." The naturalist William Paley (1802) compared the complexity of the human eye to finding a watch on the beach: "Suppose I had found a watch upon the ground, and it should be inquired how the watch happened to be in that place . . . the inference, we think is inevitable: the watch must have had a maker, and been designed for a purpose." Just as the intricate functions of a pocket watch implies there was a watchmaker responsible for its design, Paley argued, so does the fitness of species to the demands of their environment imply design by God. Design arguments are a specific instance of teleological reasoning (Kelemen,

1999), a tendency to see any kind of functional outcome as being created for that purpose—whether they were designed or not. For example, young children might accurately perceive that a chair is "for sitting" but also that a large rock might be "for sitting" as well (Kelemen, 1999; Keleman & DiYanni, 2005). The tendency toward teleological thinking has implications for intuitive interpretations of evolution as guided by God (rather than natural selection). By seeing the fit between various species and their environment (the long neck of a giraffe, the thick fur of a polar bear), it easy to infer intention and design. Modern versions of the argument (e.g., "intelligent design theory"; Dembski, 2004) also point to the apparent irreducible biological complexity of the eye and other organic structure (Behe, 1996), and a universe that seems to be fine-tuned for life (Barrow & Tipler, 1988; White, 2000).

There is something genuinely compelling to the argument: How else could a thing so complex and useful (whether a pocket watch, an eye, or a universe) come about by accident? Ultimately the design argument does not hinge on the specific details and data, but how much an outcome *seems* to be designed. The experience itself is the argument. People are skilled at drawing causal connections under uncertainty (Tversky & Kahneman, 1980; Weiner, 1985), and the kinds of causes people tend to infer match the outcome (White, 2009)—that is, big events cause big effects and good reasons for good outcomes (LeBoeuf & Norton, 2012). Design inferences are a special kind of explanation that is reserved for those effects that seem most designed, in particular those that seem very unlikely to occur by chance (e.g., arise from multiple conjunctive events and patterns of "nonrandom" action such as longer streaks in the "hot-hand" effect; Caruso, Waytz, & Epley, 2010), and whose outcomes seem to satisfy some goal (Luo, & Baillargeon, 2005): In other words, a *small chance* combined with a *big splash*. Design inferences are especially likely when the outcome that is particularly favorable, or seems to satisfy a goal. And so there is an important moral component to the design inference, that we see design where there is something helpful. When combined, a small

chance and a big splash create a kind of *suspicious serendipity*—a positive outcome that seems too good to be true. Teleological reasoning solves the problem of unexplained patterns by attributing it to goal-directed behavior.

However, converging lines of research in psychology suggest that apparent design may sometimes be illusory (Lombrozo, Shtulman, & Weisberg, 2006). We perceive order and patterns in events, sometimes where they do not exist (such as optical illusions). People have poor understanding of what true randomness really looks like (Gilovich, 1991; Wagenaar, 1972), and so may make inferences of order where there is really just a more aesthetic version of disorder. Egocentric biases are partly responsible for creating illusions of design, by simultaneously enhancing the perceived unlikeliness and benefit of one's own personal outcomes. First, egocentrism blinds us to alternate realities, the other ways that things could be than the particular arrangement we presently enjoy. This also includes an ignorance of other ways that events and outcomes could arrange themselves to be "fine-tuned." Second, egocentrism increases the sense of relevance for personal outcomes relative to other events—it is about all about me. Events seem to revolve around the self, and events which favor oneself seem much more significant and of greater impact overall than those that affect other people. Egocentric biases thereby *create suspicious serendipity* by creating systematic illusions of order centered on one's own experience.

Important here, egocentric biases are not just centered on the individual self, but may be observed at radiating levels around the self, for example, anthropocentrism, geocentricism, and biocentrism (see Table 36.1). For example, an *anthropocentric* perspective places humans at the top of the animal kingdom, separate from lower beasts and closer to images of God. Here I describe how each of these different levels of egocentrism is associated with a corresponding illusion of design, by making the outcome seem more "special" and therefore deserving of an intentional cause. I discuss each of these levels of egocentrism, the illusions of intelligent design associated with each bias, and the moral implications of each of these biases.

TABLE 36.1. Egocentric Biases and Their Corresponding Illusions of Design

Bias	Design illusion	Moral implications
Egocentrism	Personal life events are "meant to be."	System justification
	Consciousness as the soul	Victim blaming
Anthropocentrism	Humans are created in God's image.	Dehumanization
Geocentricism	Classic: Earth as the center of the Universe.	Environmental apathy
	Neo-geocentricism: Earth as a special habitat for life	
Biocentrism	Anthropic principle (fine-tuned universe)	Life is sacred.

Egocentrism

Each of us is located in a particular self, and it is from this self that one sees and acts on the world. Egocentrism refers to the difficulty we all experience in stepping outside our own perspective to consider others' points of view, or to view our own position more objectively (Piaget, 2013; Zuckerman, Kernis, Guarnera, Murphy, & Rappoport, 1983). For example, young children are notoriously egocentric and fail to understand that others' beliefs or perspectives might differ from their own (Piaget, 2013). Being able to overcome the egocentric perspective is a developmental hallmark of cognitive maturity. But in some ways the egocentric perspective is an inescapable bias, because we are all tethered to our own minds and personal point of view on the world. Consciousness is itself inherently egocentric, and the phenomenal experience of mind as a point of view enhances mind–body dualism and the belief in a personal "soul" (Preston, Gray, & Wegner, 2006). Though we mostly grow out of the childish forms of egocentrism, we are still biased toward our own perspective; we just become better able to adjust for it in adulthood (Epley, Morewedge, & Keysar, 2004).

One side effect of being stuck in our own point of view is that we tend to interpret our own life events as more special than others, particularly the coincidences and chance occurrences that become life-altering events. For example, people higher in trait egocentrism are also higher on judgments of psychic causes for coincidence (Moore, Thalbourne, & Storm, 2010). But in general, people tend to think of their own coincidences as more surprising than others' coincidences (Falk,

1989), and the belief in "synchronicity" supports the intuition that coincidences are meaningful and must be intended for some reason (Jung, 2010). For example, a chance meeting of two strangers on a train could lead to a conversation, a date, a marriage, and later a family. For these two people, it may be tempting to perceive their chance meeting as fate, as the odds against meeting each other seem so infinitesimal. But if they had not met, it is also likely they might find a different romance and destiny elsewhere. Any one given meeting and romance may be itself very unlikely, but the general prospects of love and romance are very high. Likewise, consider a person who has just won the lottery. From his or her point of view, this is a highly unlikely event (and indeed it is) and also very favorable. It is not uncommon for lottery winners to thank God and praise His generosity and wisdom in providing such a blessed windfall. But a person reading the online article about the lottery winner may be more cynical. After all, although the odds of any one person winning a lottery are low, the odds of *someone* winning are very high. Winning a lottery is really only remarkable to the winner.

To the recipient, an unexpected good outcome serves a function, and so seems to fulfill a purpose. Indeed, when people underestimate the how their own actions facilitate pleasant outcomes, they can attribute the outcome to some benevolent external agent (Gilbert, Brown, Pinel, & Wilson, 2000). People also believe more strongly in personal miracles than miracles for others (Proudfoot & Shaver, 1975; Spilka, Shaver, & Kirkpatrick, 1985), and events seem more "miraculous" when one is personally affected by the outcome (Ransom & Alicke, 2012).

Moral Consequences

For the most part, belief in synchronicity and things as "meant to be" may be a harmless and pleasant illusion. But this is because, for the most part, the unexpected events we experience in our lives are relatively harmless and pleasant. It's nice to think that the good things that happen to us happen for a reason (Taylor & Brown, 1988). But not all things that happen are nice, and the flip side of belief in personal miracles and fate is the belief in a just world (Lerner & Miller, 1978). If we believe in fate and divine justice, how are we to make sense to chaos and tragedy? When tragedy strikes us personally, we may also see it as caused by God (Gray & Wegner, 2010), perhaps to teach us some important life lesson (Bering, 2002). But tragedies observed from a distance can reinforce system justification (Jost, Banaji, & Nosek, 2004) and victim blaming (Lerner & Simmons, 1966), a general lack of sympathy for the strife experienced by others.

Anthropocentrism

Recently the Working Group of the Anthropocene argued that we have entered the Anthropocene age—where the Earth is dominated by human activity (Kolbert, 2011). But through our short history as a species, we humans have long granted ourselves a special status among species. The dominance of humans over other animals has long been interpreted as a position of privilege among life forms, that we are not just fitter, but *better*. Humans are unique in that they are often depicted as the image of God. The strongest challenge to this anthropocentric bias is still Charles Darwin's *On the Origin of Species* (1859). It was here that Darwin described a way that a natural random process can systematically bring about order and function: *natural selection*. Natural selection was a threat to the design argument not just because it offered an alternative hypothesis to creationism, but because it directly challenged the notion that apparent design implies a designer. Natural selection directly challenged anthropocentric biases because it implied humans are not a privileged species, just currently an advantaged

one. The original form was cautious, making the point only on the last page. It was this particular point that aroused the most offense. For all our pretenses of superiority—the civility, mind, morality—we are not as high and mighty as we thought.

Despite widespread (though not universal) acceptance of evolution by natural selection, there is still an implicit separation between humans and other species—we see species most similar to ourselves as possessing greater intelligence (Morewedge, Preston, & Wegner, 2007) and diminish the experiences of species different from us. Animals that look like us—even robots—seem more intelligent (Broadbent et al., 2013). The pervasiveness of the bias is revealed by the fact that when people attempt to include other animals, they tend to do so by adopting an anthropocentric stance—that animals are like people (Tyler, 2003). In trying to identify what makes us special, some scientists have pointed to our larger frontal lobes that make us smart, opposable thumbs that allow us to use tools, use of grammar and language to communicate, and ability to transmit knowledge through culture. For better or for worse, those traits have brought humans to where we are now able to effectively dominate the planet and all its species with a world population of over 7 billion. But this is constantly being challenged by ideas that other species have intelligences that we have been unaware of or cannot comprehend—for example, dolphins, chimpanzees, bees, and ants may each have cognition and means of communication that we cannot fathom (Beck, 2013). Sure, a dolphin may not score well on the SATs, but there is no way of knowing what intelligence tests of other species we would fail.

Moral Consequences

Humans are seen as a privileged and special species, the favorite of all of God's creation. Humans are seen as so remarkable, that we must be imperfect versions of the gods—or rather that gods are perfected humans. This closeness to the divine is not just in appearance, but humans are perceived to have greater have free will, complex emotions, mind, consciousness, and a soul—Godly traits that we do not necessarily share with our animal friends. Dehumanization (Haslam, 2006) takes away these traits away from others, which grants a "full" human the moral right to treat those without these features harshly. This has implications for our treatment of other animals, as well as our treatment of other humans that we deny full "human" capacity.

Geocentricism

For millennia, humans had been tracking the motion of stars and planets in the night sky, but assumed that that we (or the Earth) stood at the epicenter for this great celestial circumambulation. It was not until 1543 when Copernicus introduced the heliocentric model with the publication of *On the Revolutions of the Heavenly Spheres* that this idea was properly challenged. The problem of geocentricism sparked one of the most explosive and infamous conflicts between science and religion to date. Interestingly, at the time there was no explicit biblical doctrine of an Earth-centered universe, but a few scant references to the world *not moving* (Psalm 96:10; Psalm 93:1). But the idea of a universe centered on Earth fit well with the idea of a designer Earth made by God as the home of His favorite creation: humankind. In spite of the importance of Copernicus's work, it was only published after his death, for fear of Church response.

The change from geocentric to heliocentric model was a scientific revolution—shedding off the outdated ideas for new exciting ones—but also a revolution in our own perspective taking in science. It marks the moment that science became "grown up." In addition to being the paradigm of paradigm shifts, geocentricism is also an apt analogy for egocentric biases in general—it represents the ignorant perspective that one is the center of the universe, and that everything revolves around you. In fact, from our point of view on Earth, that is exactly what it looks like- all other heavenly bodies appear to move in predictable patterns around us. Without the aid of science and technology, we lack the perspective to see our own movement in space relative to these other objects. And so from a naïve point of view it appears as though Earth is the middle of

it all. Still, like any great illusion, geocentricism persists despite the fact that we know it's not true—we still define our days by sunset and sunrise, not earthset and earthrise.

While this classic form of geocentricism is now almost universally rejected, there is still a pervasive form of neo-geocentricism emphasizing the specialness of planet Earth. Earth is located in the "Goldilocks zone" relative to the sun, seen as producing temperatures "just right" for life (Rampino & Caldeira, 1994). Earth also has some other key features that make life as we know it possible—an ozone layer and magnetic field to counter radiation, an oxygen-rich atmosphere, plenty of water, and daily orbit to regulate temperature. Thus, despite its unremarkable address in the universe, the Earth retains its remarkable status as a unique habitat for life.

Today, the search for other Earth-like planets poses one challenge to the idea that Earth is special. At present, a small handful of such planets have been found that may be able to support life as we know it. But the idea that Earth is special is also biased by the notion that we expect life to be "life-as-we-know-it"—that is, life elsewhere exists in relatively the same conditions as life on Earth. Carl Sagan (1973) noted, for example, that we have a "carbon chauvinism" when it comes to looking for extraterrestrial life, because we assume that life on other planets ought to be made of the same stuff as we are. Likewise, the search for life may be biased by temperature chauvinism, oxygen chauvinism, and other egocentric limitations of imagination of other possible forms of life.

Moral Consequences

One moral consequence of neo-geocentricism is the idea that nature itself somehow strives to maintain an equilibrium suited for sustaining life. The specialness of Earth as a home for life contributes to the concept of Earth as "mother nature" or "Gaia," an intentional life-giving entity. In studies of teleological reasoning, sentences with explicit Gaia or Earth-preservation content are more likely to be endorsed, even without time pressure (Kelemen & Rosset, 2009). The consequence of the geocentric belief in the specialness of Earth is that, ironically, people may underestimate human impact on the Earth and our capacity for irreparable harm to the delicate balance it holds for life. If Mother Nature is perceived to restore balance and act to protect her own well-being, then she has the ability to "take care of herself." This kind of reasoning is a common theme among liberal climate change deniers, that it is somehow absurd to think that we humans could destroy the mighty power of our Mother Nature.

Biocentrism

The final level of egocentrism I discuss is *biocentrism*—the egocentric emphasis on *life* over all other forms. However, this level of egocentrism may also be universe-centrism, as it relates to a belief in our own universe is particularly special and designed. These both relate to the *anthropic principle* (Barrow & Tipler, 1988)—which highlights that in order to be able to develop sentient life forms (like ourselves), our universe needs to have the specific set of parameters and laws it does, and any deviation from those parameters would mean render the evolution of life impossible

There are different versions of the anthropic principle—the *strong* anthropic principle implies a designer—that the universe was somehow compelled to create life (Barrow & Tipler, 1988), but the *weak* anthropic principle version merely points out the egocentric nature of the problem: The ostensible "fine-tuning" is due to the fact that our own observation self-selects us into a universe where life must be allowed to exist (Carter, 1974/2011; the *anthropic bias,* Bostrom, 2002). As it happens, there exists a universe that can support life, but if there were not we would not know any better. We therefore should not be surprised that the universe falls within the narrow range of natural laws that allow conscious life to exist; otherwise, we would not be here to make that observation.

Arguments against the strong anthropic principle usually come in the form of normalizing the apparent improbability of our life-supporting universe. One way to change the probability is the multiverse theory, that

posits that ours is just one of innumerable (possibly infinite) universes, each of which may have its own laws of physics. Given an infinite number of universes with an infinite array of physical properties, the odds of finding one life-supporting universe skyrocket from virtually impossible to virtually inevitable. From this point of view, no one universe is any less likely than the others; it had to turn out some way. Our universe happens to be one of the lucky universes fit to support life as we know it. But, from our egocentric point of view it seems more than mere luck. We are holding the winning lotto ticket of universes, but like all lottery winners it seems just too unlikely and special to be anything less than a gift from God. And, like the proverbial lottery winner, this reasoning falls prey to the *retrospective gambler's fallacy* (Oppenheimer & Monin, 2009), where rare/extraordinary events are presumed to occur as part of a longer sequence of occurrences. For example, people estimate that a gambler who just rolled three 6's in dice has been playing for longer than a gambler who rolled 2, 4, and 5. People do understand that streaks and rare events do happen occasionally. So when confronted with a rare event, we seek to normalize it by placing it in a series of more mundane events. In the case of the fine-tuned universe argument: Just because our universe appears to be particularly unlikely does not mean we know anything about the likelihood that other universes exist (Hacking, 1987). However, we may perceive the other universes to occur with high frequency to make sense of our "special" universe occurring even once.

One way to increase the odds of life even further, Lee Smolin (2007) has proposed a theory of "fecund universes" that life-supporting universes are more likely to occur than not. The theory supposes that black holes provide a way for universes to reproduce by recycling material from one universe into a new one. Black holes draw in matter and produce baby universes on the other side, with the same laws of physics as its parent universe. As it turns out, many of the same "fine-tuned" laws of physics that create the cosmic conditions for a life-supporting universe (e.g., rate of expansion, gravitational constant) also create the cosmic conditions necessary to produce black holes. So, while universes that cannot support life also tend to be unhealthy universes that die young, healthy life-supporting universe are more also likely to have black holes, and so are better able to reproduce. Thus, universes that are able to sustain life have a tidy means of cosmological natural selection. This would mean more life-supporting universes than not, increasing the chances of finding oneself in such a universe considerably (Smolin, 2007).

Moral Consequences

Opponents of the idea of a fine-tuned universe aim to deflate the argument from design by changing the apparent probability. If odds are high, then it does not need the directed hand of an intentional being. But another approach is to question whether a life-supporting universe is actually special enough product to warrant a design explanation. This is a tricky assumption to overcome because the idea life is special seems so obviously true. But I suggest this is just one more form of egocentrism: We think life is special because we are things that are alive and isn't that nice for us. The natural corollary of the belief that life is special is that life is "sacred" in principle and needs to be protected. Though I argue it is certainly a bias, it is perhaps the most fundamental of all moral principles we hold, that guides all kinds of moral judgments covering issues from war, abortion, euthanasia, and murder.

Conclusion

Just as the gravity of massive objects bends the appearance of light toward the mass, the egocentric point of view distorts perception around the self. Egocentric biases can create pervasive illusions of design by creating a sense of *suspicious serendipity*: one's own favorable outcomes seem more favorable, and less likely. And so it seems like the life, the world, and the universe was made for us, because it suits us just so perfectly.

REFERENCES

Adams, D. (1988). *The salmon of doubt*. New York: Random House.

Barrow, J. D., & Tipler, F. J. (1986). *The anthropic cosmological principle*. New York: Oxford University Press.

Beck, J. (2013). Why we can't say what animals think. *Philosophical Psychology, 26*(4), 520–546.

Behe, M. J. (1996). *Darwin's black box: The biochemical challenge to evolution*. New York: Touchstone Books.

Bering, J. M. (2002). The existential theory of mind. *Review of General Psychology, 6*, 3–24.

Bostrom, N. (2002). *Anthropic bias: Observation selection effects in science and philosophy*. New York: Routledge.

Broadbent, E., Kumar, V., Li, X., Sollers, J., III, Stafford, R. Q., MacDonald, B. A., & Wegner, D. M. (2013). Robots with display screens: A robot with a more humanlike face display is perceived to have more mind and a better personality. *PLOS ONE, 8*(8), e72589.

Carter, B. (2011). Large number coincidences and the anthropic principle in cosmology. *General Relativity and Gravitation, 43*(11), 3225–3233. (Original work published 1974)

Caruso, E. M., Waytz, A., & Epley, N. (2010). The intentional mind and the hot hand: Perceiving intentions makes streaks seem likely to continue. *Cognition, 116*, 149–153.

Darwin, C. (1859). *On the origin of species*. London: John Murray.

Dembski, W. A. (2004). *The design revolution*. Nottingham, UK: Intervarsity Press.

Epley, N., Morewedge, C., & Keysar, B. (2004). Perspective taking in children and adults: Equivalent egocentrism but differential correction. *Journal of Experimental Social Psychology, 40*, 760–768.

Falk, R. (1989). Judgment of coincidences: Mine versus yours. *American Journal of Psychology, 102*, 477–493.

Gilbert, D. T., Brown, R. P., Pinel, E. C., & Wilson, T. D. (2000). The illusion of external agency. *Journal of Personality and Social Psychology, 79*, 690–700.

Gilovich, T. (1991). *How we know what isn't so: The fallibility of human reason in everyday life*. New York: Free Press.

Gray, K., & Wegner, D. M. (2010). Blaming God for our pain: Human suffering and the divine mind. *Personality and Social Psychology Review, 14*, 7–16.

Hacking, I. (1987). The inverse gambler's fallacy: The argument from design: The anthropic principle applied to Wheeler universes. *Mind, 96*, 331–340.

Haslam, N. (2006). Dehumanization: An integrative review. *Personality and Social Psychology Review, 10*(3), 252–264.

Jost, J. T., Banaji, M. R., & Nosek, B. A. (2004). A decade of system justification theory: Accumulated evidence of conscious and unconscious bolstering of the status quo. *Political Psychology, 25*(6), 881–919.

Jung, C. G. (2010). Synchronicity: An acausal connecting principle. In G. Adler & R. F. C. Hull (Trans.), *Collected works of C. G. Jung: Vol. 8. Structure and dynamics of the psyche.* Princeton, NJ: Princeton University Press.

Kelemen, D. (1999). Why are rocks pointy?: Children's preference for teleological explanations of the natural world. *Developmental Psychology, 35,* 1440–1452.

Kelemen, D., & DiYanni, C. (2005). Intuitions about origins: Purpose and intelligent design in children's reasoning about nature. *Journal of Cognition and Development, 6,* 3–31.

Kelemen, D., & Rosset, E. (2009). The human function compunction: Teleological explanation in adults. *Cognition, 111*(1), 138–143.

Kolbert, E. (2011). Enter the Anthropocene: Age of man. *National Geographic, 219*(3), 60.

LeBoeuf, R. A., & Norton, M. I. (2012). Consequence–cause matching: Looking to the consequences of events to infer their causes. *Journal of Consumer Research, 39,* 128–141.

Lerner, M. J., & Miller, D. T. (1978). Just world research and the attribution process: Looking back and ahead. *Psychological Bulletin, 85,* 1030–1051.

Lerner, M. J., & Simmons, C. H. (1966). Observer's reaction to the "innocent victim": Compassion or rejection? *Journal of Personality and Social Psychology, 4*(2), 203–210.

Lombrozo, T., Shtulman, A., & Weisberg, M. (2006). The intelligent design controversy: Lessons from psychology and education. *Trends in Cognitive Sciences, 10,* 56–57.

Luo, Y., & Baillargeon, R. (2005). Can a self-propelled box have a goal?: Psychological reasoning in 5-month-old infants. *Psychological Science, 16,* 601–608.

Moore, T., Thalbourne, M. A., & Storm, L. (2010). A study on coincidences. *Australian Journal of Parapsychology, 10*(2), 154.

Morewedge, C. K., Preston, J., & Wegner, D. M. (2007). Timescale bias in the attribution of mind. *Journal of Personality and Social Psychology, 93,* 1–11.

Oppenheimer, D. M., & Monin, B. (2009). The retrospective gambler's fallacy: Unlikely events, constructing the past, and multiple universes. *Judgment and Decision Making, 4*(5), 326–334.

Paley, W. (1802). *Natural theology: Or, evidences of the existence and attributes of the deity.* London: J. Faulder.

Piaget, J. (2013). *The construction of reality in the child.* New York: Basic Books.

Preston, J., Gray, K., & Wegner, D. M. (2006). The Godfather of soul. *Behavioral and Brain Sciences, 29*(05), 482–483.

Proudfoot, W., & Shaver, P. (1975). Attribution theory and the psychology of religion. *Journal for the Scientific Study of Religion, 24,* 317–330.

Rampino, M. R., & Caldeira, K. (1994). The Goldilocks problem: Climatic evolution and long-term habitability of terrestrial planets. *Annual Review of Astronomy and Astrophysics, 32*(1), 83–114.

Ransom, M. R., & Alicke, M. D. (2012). It's a miracle: Separating the miraculous from the mundane. *Archive for the Psychology of Religion, 34*(2), 243–275.

Sagan, C. (1973). *Carl Sagan's cosmic connection: An extraterrestrial perspective.* Cambridge, UK: Cambridge University Press.

Smolin, L. (2007). Scientific alternatives to the anthropic principle. In B. Carr (Ed.), *Universe or multiverse?* (pp. 323–366). Cambridge, UK: Cambridge University Press.

Spilka, B., Shaver, P., & Kirkpatrick, L. A. (1985). A general attribution theory for the psychology of religion. *Journal for the Scientific Study of Religion, 24,* 1–20.

Taylor, S. E., & Brown, J. D. (1988). Illusion and well-being: A social psychological perspective on mental health. *Psychological Bulletin, 103,* 193–210.

Tversky, A., & Kahneman, D. (1980). Causal schemas in judgments under uncertainty. In M. Fishbein (Ed.), *Progress in social psychology* (pp. 49–72). Hillsdale, NJ: Erlbaum.

Tyler, T. (2003). If horses had hands . . . . *Society and Animals, 11*(3), 267–281.

Wagenaar, W. A. (1972). Generation of random sequences by human subjects: A critical survey of literature. *Psychological Bulletin, 77,* 65–72.

Weiner, B. (1985). "Spontaneous" causal thinking. *Psychological Bulletin, 97,* 74–84.

White, P. A. (2009). Property transmission: An explanatory account of the role of similarity information in causal inference. *Psychological Bulletin, 135,* 774–793.

White, R. (2000). Fine-tuning and multiple universes. *Noûs, 34,* 260–276.

Zuckerman, M., Kernis, M. H., Guarnera, S. M., Murphy, J. F. & Rappoport, L. (1983). The egocentric bias: Seeing oneself as cause and target of others' behavior. *Journal of Personality, 51,* 621–630.

PART VIII
DYNAMIC MORAL JUDGMENT

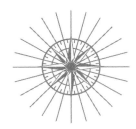

QUESTIONS ANSWERED IN PART VIII

CHAPTER 37 What explains whether acts—from masturbation and homosexuality to smoking and meat eating—are seen as personal preferences or as moral wrongs?

CHAPTER 38 How do people deal with a morally complex and contradictory world?

CHAPTER 39 What is blame, and why do people blame so liberally even when there are compelling reasons to mitigate it?

CHAPTER 37

Moralization

How Acts Become Wrong

Chelsea Schein
Kurt Gray

What explains whether acts—from masturbation and homosexuality to smoking and meat eating—are seen as personal preferences or as moral wrongs?

According to the theory of dyadic morality, the answer is perceived harm.

What Makes an Act Wrong?

Morality evolves. Nowhere is this evolution more apparent than in the shifting norms regarding the morality of masturbation (Laqueur, 2003). In the ancient world, masturbation was not only tolerated but celebrated as a way to increase fertility. Ancient Egyptians even told tales of the God Atum who allegedly created the world through masturbation. While Judeo-Christian societies never quite celebrated masturbation, the Bible and early Judeo-Christian scholars were largely silent on the topic. Autoeroticism remained in the moral background until the Enlightenment, when there was widespread moral panic concerning the ills of masturbation. Why is self-pleasure celebrated at one time but seen as a serious sin at another? The answer may lie with perceptions of harm.

The Question of Moralization

The history of masturbation might seem frivolous, but understanding the basis of moralization—the movement of a previously neutral act into the moral sphere (Rozin, 1999)—and demoralization—the movement of an act out of the moral sphere—is of utmost importance. Given morality's connection to the law, understanding moralization is central to questions of moral rights, freedom and imprisonment, and even life and death. Indeed, the moralization of consensual sexual acts continues to have grave consequences—being gay is punishable by death in 12 countries and illegal in 66 others (Cameron & Berkowitz, 2015).

The theory of dyadic morality (TDM) proposes that changes in moral judgment over time are driven by changes in perceived

363

harm. In the context of masturbation, such harm may seem preposterous, but, as we explore, what matters for morality is *perceptions* of harm.

With masturbation, perceptions of harm were induced through a 1720 pamphlet titled "Onania, or, The Heinous Sin of Self Pollution, and all its Frightful Consequences," which contained pseudoscientific claims about the dangers of masturbation. These apparent dangers ignited a moral panic in the United States and Europe that lasted for two centuries, which in turn inspired even more perceptions of harm. One well-regarded doctor claimed that, "neither the plague, nor war, nor small-pox, nor similar diseases, have produced results so disastrous to humanity as the pernicious habit of Onanism" (Dr. Adam Clarke, quoted in Kellogg, 1890, p. 233). In fact, the moral panic surrounding masturbation only really began to quell with the normalization of sex by pioneers such as Alfred Kinsey—that is, when it was seen as more harmless.

Inspired by historical examples, this chapter proposes that perceptions of harm are key in understanding why certain acts enter the moral sphere. We start first with a brief overview of the TDM and address how it sheds light on moralization. We then explore the broader historical context and contrast dyadic morality's predictions with those of other theories. Next, we review the evidence on moralization and highlight where more empirical research is needed. Finally, we explore implications for a divided political world.

The Theory of Dyadic Morality

The TDM is an evolutionary inspired and culturally pluralistic theory of moral cognition (Schein & Gray, 2017). It proposes that moral cognition revolves around a unifying cognitive template, called the moral dyad, which consists of *an intentional agent causing damage to a vulnerable patient*. This template is built on perceptions of two interacting minds, a "thinking doer" capable of intending (the moral agent) and a "vulnerable feeler" capable of suffering (the moral patient; Wegner & Gray, 2016).

Dyadic morality suggests that negative norm violations (Monroe, Guglielmo, & Malle, 2012; Nichols, 2002; Sripada & Stich, 2007) are judged as immoral to the extent that they exemplify the dyadic template. In other words, acts are wrong to the extent that they involve *harm*—a very specific, dyadic kind of harm. Consistent with this idea, more harmful acts are judged as more immoral, and both greater suffering and greater intentionality lead to more moral condemnation (Hart & Honoré, 1985). Murder is more immoral than attempted killing, and a calculated, planned slaughter is more immoral than a lover's rage-induced homicide (for reviews, see Gray, Waytz, & Young, 2012; Gray, Young, & Waytz, 2012; Schein & Gray, 2017).

Importantly, the harm of dyadic morality is not the objective, reasoned, historically debated, rationalist harm historically debated by psychologists (Haidt, 2001; Kohlberg, 1969). Instead, harm is subjective, emotional, and intuitive—it is a matter of *perception*. The subjectivity of perceived harm means that some can see masturbation (or homosexuality) as "clearly" harmful—for example, causing damage to children—whereas others can see these acts as "clearly" harmless. Whether an act seems harmful drives whether it is viewed as a personal preference or a grave sin.

At the heart of dyadic morality are the two complementary processes of *dyadic comparison* and *dyadic completion*. Dyadic comparison can be summed up as *what seems harmful is immoral* (Schein & Gray, 2015). Dyadic morality predicts that acts are compared with a cognitive template of harm, with closer matches resulting in more robust moral judgment. That is, acts are judged as immoral to the extent that they seem harmful (Schein & Gray, 2015). If we told you that act X involves a man intentionally causing harm to a little girl, you would think it immoral because it seems to involve harm.

On the flip side, dyadic completion predicts that *what is immoral seems harmful* (Gray, Schein, & Ward, 2014). Once judgments of immorality have been made, perceptions align to make acts consistent with the dyadic template—that is, to more clearly involve an intentional agent causing damage to a suffering patient (Clark, Chen, & Ditto, 2015; DeScioli, Gilbert, & Kurzban, 2012; Gray et al., 2014; Liu & Ditto, 2013). If we were to tell you that an act X was extremely immoral, you would automatically assume that the act is harmful and produces victims (Liu & Ditto, 2013).

Moralization Is Driven by the Dyadic Loop

Combined, dyadic comparison and dyadic completion form the *dyadic loop* (Schein & Gray, 2014, 2016), a dynamic feedback cycle that mutually amplifies perceptions of harm (i.e., *harmification*) and immorality (i.e., *moralization*). (See Figure 37.1.) In the dyadic loop, initial perceptions of harm activate perceptions of immorality, which in turn activate more perceptions of harm, which lead to increased perceptions of immorality, which lead to increased perceptions of harm, and so on.

It is the dyadic loop that drives moralization. Acts that are initially ambiguously immoral or harmful get drawn into the gravitational pull of the dyadic loop, which drives complementary perceptions of harm and immorality. Typically this process is initiated by the perception of suffering patients, who are often children (Schein, Goranson, & Gray, 2015). Consider smoking: Where

once it was a lifestyle choice, the recognition that children suffer from secondhand smoke pulled smoking into the dyadic loop (Rozin, 1999)—and made it seem immoral. The perceived suffering of children is evident in moral debates against homosexuality, masturbation, pornography, and smoking (Comer, 2012; Laqueur, 2004; Pierce, 2001).

Of course, suffering alone is not typically immoral, which is why moralization involves the perception of intentional agents who perpetrate that suffering. The moralization of smoking received a large push when people realized that tobacco companies were intentionally hiding the dangers of cigarettes. This same perceived malice is partially behind moral opposition to genetically modified organisms (GMOs), as people see large corporations as intentionally doing harm to reap a profit (Bollinger, 2014). Perceptions of malicious agency can then lead to additional perceptions of suffering, and then to even harsher moral judgments in an ongoing "creep" of perceived harm (Haslam, 2016) and immorality (Schein & Gray, 2016). More succinctly, we can say that *harmification leads to moralization; moralization in turn leads to more harmification.*

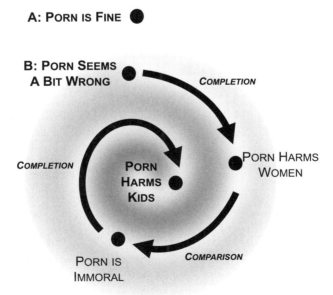

FIGURE 37.1. The dyadic loop is a dynamic feedback cycle in which the processes of dyadic comparison and dyadic completion mutually reinforce each other, leading to moralization and "harmification"— and therefore to political polarization. Reprinted with permission from Gray and Schein (2017).

Demoralization

Dyadic morality predicts that harm is also central to demoralization, such that reduced perceptions of harm should reduce moral condemnation—an idea borne out in historical trends. Once Kinsey and other sex-positive scholars revealed masturbation to be harmless—and even healthy—it began to leave the moral domain, at least for most liberals (Day, 2013). The same is becoming true of gay marriage, as research reveals that children raised by gay parents are no worse off than those of straight parents (Patterson, 2006). Vaping also seems more morally acceptable than smoking, in large part because it is unclear whether it causes harm (Palazzolo, 2013).

Of course, because harm is subjective and intuitive, its perception can persist in the face of even "objective" evidence otherwise. In the case of gay marriage, even opponents who were aware of the social science data about children raised by gay parents nevertheless saw irreparable harm to children from changing the definition of marriage (*Obergefell v. Hodges*, 2015).

Although dyadic morality suggests that demoralization occurs through deharmification, the dyadic loop has a kind of cognitive gravity (i.e., it is an attractor state; Schein & Gray, 2014; Spivey & Dale, 2004), which suggests that it is easier for acts to become moralized than demoralized (Schein & Gray, 2016). This explains why people raised in a strict religious household may still get an implicit twinge of immorality (and harm) when contemplating masturbation, even if they rationally think it a matter of personal preference.

Historical Context

The importance of harm in moralization is rooted in classic moral philosophy and moral psychology (Bentham, 1879; Mill, 1861). Informed by the classic moral philosophies of Kant and Mill, early developmental models of morality focused upon justice and harm (Kohlberg, 1969; Piaget, 1932), and their studies found that young children differentiate violations of social convention (e.g., not raising one's hand in class) from moral violations (e.g., hitting another child) based on the presence of harm (Smetana, 1985; Turiel, Killen, & Helwig, 1987).

However, anthropological research seemed to challenge this centrality of harm (Shweder, Mahapatra, & Miller, 1987). Although both Indians and Americans morally condemned canonically harmful acts such as stealing and killing, some Brahmin Indians also condemned acts that lacked clear objective harm, such as an eldest son eating chicken after his father's death. If morality is about harm, how can people condemn these objectively harmless acts?

Inspired by this anthropological research, moral foundations theory (MFT; Haidt, 2012) argued that morality is grounded in a set of innate yet culturally shaped moral "foundations," of which harm is only one. One can think of moral foundations as cognitive modules, which are like "little switches in the brains of all animals" which are "triggered" by specific moral "inputs" (Haidt, 2012, p. 123). According to MFT, the Indians in Shweder's study condemned the eldest son's chicken eating because it activated a distinct "purity module." Although there is very little evidence for these distinct moral "foundations" (Gray & Keeney, 2015; Schein & Gray, 2017), MFT nicely highlights cultural pluralism and the moral condemnation of acts which seem—at least to Western eyes—rather harmless.

Although dyadic morality acknowledges that people morally condemn diverse acts, it denies that they are truly harmless, because harm is a matter of intuitive perception. Take the example of consensual incest, a canonical "harmless wrong" in moral psychology (Haidt, 2001). Although this act may be designed to be "objectively" harmless, participants still see harm in this act, as well as others (Royzman, Kim, & Leeman, 2015). Importantly, these perceptions occur within milliseconds (Gray et al., 2014) and exquisitely predict subsequent moral judgments (Schein & Gray, 2015).

Some have argued that TDM denies pluralism, but, arguably, dyadic morality advocates for even more pluralism than MFT, as it suggests that both morality and harm are sensitive to cultural construction (Wegner & Gray, 2016). Philosophers (Rachels, 1986) and psychologists (Asch, 1952; Turiel,

Hildebrandt, Wainryb, & Saltzstein, 1991) have long recognized that understanding moral judgments requires taking into consideration the "situational meaning" (Asch, 1952) or "informational assumptions" (Turiel et al., 1991) within a given culture.

Consider again the case of Brahmin Indians condemning postfuneral chicken eating. This culture also believes that when the son eats meat, it will pollute his dead father's soul, condemning him to eternal suffering (Shweder, 2012). Thus this celebrated example does not reveal the importance of harmless wrongs, but instead the importance of *perceptions* of harm—and the link from harm to immorality. TDM further suggests that focusing on the perceptual nature of harm is imperative for understanding moralization.

Theoretical Stance

That harm can drive moral condemnation is uncontroversial, as research has long illustrated that perceptions of interpersonal harm differentiate violations of conventional norms from moral wrongs in both children (Smetana, 1985; Turiel et al., 1987) and adults (Huebner, Lee, & Hauser, 2010). However, dyadic morality argues that perceived harm is the best—and most proximal—predictor of moralization, even for ostensibly "harmless" violations.

Of course, there might be other pathways that contribute to moralization. For example, an act can simply be labeled as immoral through testimony of a parent or persuasive demagogue (Sripada & Stich, 2007; Harris & Koenig, 2006). However, TDM suggests that even when this top-down labeling occurs, harm is indelibly activated (DeScioli et al., 2012; Clark et al., 2015; Gray et al., 2014), which is important for making this moral judgment intuitive.

Although all moral psychologists likely agree that harm can cause and reinforce moral judgments, there are still questions about whether harm causes the moral condemnation of "purity" violations, such as eating odd food, cursing God, or even having sex with a dead chicken (Haidt, 2001). According to MFT, issues such as gay marriage (Inbar, Pizarro, & Bloom, 2012), smoking

(Rozin, 1999), and genetically modified foods (Scott, Inbar, & Rozin, 2016; though see Gray & Schein, 2016) are labeled as immoral to the extent that they activate feelings of disgust. The "disgust as moralizer" account is intuitive, as many popular arguments against gay marriage appeal to the violation of natural order (e.g. "God created Adam and Eve not Adam and Steve") or visceral disgust (Nussbaum, 2010). However, recent evidence suggests that harm is a more important moralizer than disgust.

Evidence

At first glance, there seems to be clear evidence in favor of the disgust-as-moralizer account. Studies reveal that disgust amplifies moral condemnation of ostensibly harmless acts such as gay marriage and eating a dead dog (Inbar et al., 2012; Wheatley & Haidt, 2005; Schnall, Haidt, Clore, & Jordan, 2008); however, these results suffer from multiple problems.

First, they may not be replicable: A recent meta-analysis (Landy & Goodwin, 2015) and a large-sample, independent replication attempt (Johnson et al., 2016) both failed to replicate the causal impact of incidental disgust on moral judgment. Second, these results hint only that disgust can amplify moral condemnation (shifting an act from somewhat immoral to very immoral), rather than actually causing *moralization* (transforming an act from nonmoral to moral; Pizarro, Inbar, & Helion, 2011). Third, dyadic morality suggests that these acts are not harmless at all, because harm is a matter of perception. Fourth, these studies use a very small subset of acts and do not compare immoral disgusting acts (selling children tainted blood) to nonmoral disgusting acts (vomiting on yourself).

Dyadic morality suggests that harm—not disgust—is the key driver of moralization, a prediction supported by our recent research. In one study, we asked participants to rate the immorality, harmfulness, and disgustingness of 24 different disgusting actions (adapted from Tybur, Lieberman, & Griskevicius, 2009) including sexually disgusting acts (e.g., performing oral sex), pathogen-related disgusting acts (e.g., seeing a cockroach run across the floor), and moral violations (e.g., deceiving a friend). We found that perceptions of harm best differentiated the disgusting immoral violations from the merely disgusting acts (Schein, Ritter, & Gray, 2016). In two other studies, we asked participants to rate the immorality of gay marriage and sacrilegious thoughts. Although feelings of disgust did predict ratings of immorality, these ratings were fully mediated by perceptions of harm (Schein et al., 2016). In other words, disgusting acts are moralized to the extent that they seem harmful, consistent with dyadic morality

Careful thought suggests that disgust alone cannot be the source of moralization, as there are many acts that evoke disgust that are not immoral, such as cleaning up your child's diarrhea. What distinguishes the merely gross from the morally wrong are perceptions of harm, an idea supported by research on perceptions of GMOs (Scott et al., 2016). In this study, which contained a representative sample of Americans, participants were opposed to GMOs to the extent that they saw them as harmful—even those participants who believed that their moral judgments were unrelated to harm (Gray & Schein, 2016).

One of the cleanest examinations of moralization investigates the impact of testimony upon the moral judgments of 7-year-olds exposed to novel and ostensibly harmless acts, such as aliens on a different planet "covering their heads with sticks" or "sprinkling blue water into a big puddle" (Rottman, Young, & Kelemen, 2017). Researchers manipulated either the presence of disgust feelings (via fart spray) or the presence of testimony of anger or disgust (e.g., "that act is disgusting"). Although researchers found no effect of incidental disgust upon moral judgments, they did find an effect of testimony. When children were told that an act was bad—through either anger and disgust—they rated it as more immoral. Importantly, there was no difference between anger and disgust testimonies.

Even more importantly, both kinds of testimony engendered substantial perceptions of harm—and the extent to which children linked acts to harm was the best predictor of moralization, consistent with TDM. A follow-up study revealed that giving children testimony about an act's harmfulness was the most powerful route to moralization (Rottman et al., 2017). When children were told that an ostensibly harmless act nevertheless hurt others, they robustly judged that act as immoral—even 3 months later. These results reveal that although moral information can be learned directly through testimony, it persists intuitively through perceptions of harm.

Extensions and Implications

From changing norms on masturbation and homosexuality to the increased condemnation of smoking, there are ample historical examples of acts shifting from personal preferences to moral concerns and back again. Using history as inspiration, we suggest that moral psychology should empirically test predictors of shifting moral attitudes; dyadic morality predicts that an association with harm should be a highly effective way for an act to enter the moral sphere.

Studying changes in morality over time can also provide an insight into moral polarization. Differing initial assumptions about the harmfulness of a given act can activate differing perceptions of immorality, which the dyadic loop can entrench via complementary perceptions of harm and immorality—and lead to intense disagreement across politics or religion. Importantly, although perceptions of harm can cause polarization, they may also provide the seeds of potential reconciliation.

In the midst of bitter political discourse, it is tempting to conclude that liberals and conservatives have fundamentally different moral minds. However, dyadic morality suggests that there is not an insurmountable moral chasm across politics. Instead, our research reveals that for both liberals and conservatives, perceptions of harm serves as a common currency, or *lingua franca*, for morality (Schein & Gray, 2015).

Given that harm can serve as a common language, focusing on the relative harms and merits of a particular act provides one model for productive moral dialogue (Greene, 2013). The Theory of Dyadic Morality may therefore help to remind us that our moral opponents are not monsters, but instead are good people who just see harm differently.

REFERENCES

Asch, S. E. (1952). *Social psychology*. Englewood Cliffs, NJ: Prentice-Hall.

Bentham, J. (1879). *An introduction to the principles of morals and legislation*. Oxford, UK: Clarendon Press.

Bollinger, T. (2014). Exposed: GMOs and Franken-Foods: How your daily diet could cause cancer. Retrieved from *www.thetruthaboutcancer.com*.

Cameron, D., & Berkowitz, B. (2015, June 26). The state of gay rights around the world. Retrieved from *www.washingtonpost.com/graphics/world/gay-rights*.

Clark, C. J., Chen, E. E., & Ditto, P. H. (2015). Moral coherence processes: Constructing culpability and consequences. *Current Opinion in Psychology, 6*, 123–128.

Comer, M. (2012, April 24). Anti-gay N.C. pastor: Amendment One defeat will cause "nuclear holocaust" [Blog post]. Retrieved February 13, 2013, from *http://interstateq.com/archives/5216*.

Day, N. (2013, June 21). How to address the masturbating child. *The Atlantic*. Retrieved from *www.theatlantic.com/health/archive/2013/06/how-to-address-the-masturbating-child/277026*.

DeScioli, P., Gilbert, S., & Kurzban, R. (2012). Indelible victims and persistent punishers in moral cognition. *Psychological Inquiry, 23*(2), 143–149.

Gray, K., & Keeney, J. E. (2015). Disconfirming moral foundations theory on its own terms: Reply to Graham (2015). *Social Psychological and Personality Science, 6*, 874–877.

Gray, K., & Schein, C. (2016). No absolutism here: Harm predicts moral judgment 30× better than disgust—Commentary on Scott, Inbar, & Rozin (2015). *Perspectives on Psychological Science, 11*(3), 325–329.

Gray, K., Schein, C., & Ward, A. F. (2014). The myth of harmless wrongs in moral cognition: Automatic dyadic completion from sin to suffering. *Journal of Experimental Psychology: General, 143*(4), 1600–1615.

Gray, K., Waytz, A., & Young, L. (2012). The moral dyad: A fundamental template unifying moral judgment. *Psychological Inquiry, 23*, 206–215.

Gray, K., Young, L., & Waytz, A. (2012). Mind perception is the essence of morality. *Psychological Inquiry, 23*, 101–124.

Greene, J. D. (2013). *Moral tribes: Emotion, reason, and the gap between us and them*. New York: Penguin.

Haidt, J. (2001). The emotional dog and its rational tail: A social intuitionist approach to moral judgment. *Psychological Review, 108*(4), 814–834.

Haidt, J. (2012). *The righteous mind: Why good people are divided by politics and religion*. New York: Pantheon Books.

Harris, P. L., & Koenig, M. A. (2006). Trust in testimony: How children learn about science and religion. *Child Development, 77*(3), 505–524.

Hart, H. L. A., & Honoré, T. (1985). *Causation in the law* (2nd ed.). New York: Oxford University Press.

Haslam, N. (2016). Concept creep: Psychology's expanding concepts of harm and pathology. *Psychological Inquiry, 27*(1), 1–17.

Huebner, B., Lee, J. J., & Hauser, M. D. (2010). The moral–conventional distinction in mature moral competence. *Journal of Cognition and Culture, 10*(1), 1–26.

Inbar, Y., Pizarro, D., & Bloom, P. (2012). Disgusting smells cause decreased liking of gay men. *Emotion, 12*(1), 23–27.

Johnson, D. J., Wortman, J., Cheung, F., Hein, M., Lucas, R. E., Donnellan, M. B., . . . Narr, R. K. (2016). The effects of disgust on moral judgments: Testing moderators. *Social Psychological and Personality Science, 7*, 640–647.

Kellogg, J. H. (1890). *Plain facts for old and young: Embracing the natural history and hygiene of organic life*. Burlington, IA: Segner.

Kohlberg, L. (1969). Stage and sequence: The cognitive-developmental approach to socialization. In T. Mischel (Ed.), *Cognitive development and epistemology* (pp. 151–235). New York: Academic Press.

Landy, J. F., & Goodwin, G. P. (2015). Does incidental disgust amplify moral judgment?: A meta-analytic review of experimental evidence. *Perspectives on Psychological Science, 10*(4), 518–536.

Laqueur, T. W. (2003). *Solitary sex?: A cultural history of masturbation*. New York: Zone Books.

Liu, B., & Ditto, P. H. (2013). What dilemma?: Moral evaluation shapes factual belief. *Social Psychological and Personality Science, 4*(3), 316–323.

Mill, J. S. (1861). *Utilitarianism*. New York: Oxford University Press.

Monroe, A. E., Guglielmo, S., & Malle, B. F. (2012). Morality goes beyond mind perception. *Psychological Inquiry, 23*(2), 179–184.

Nichols, S. (2002). Norms with feeling: Towards a psychological account of moral judgment. *Cognition, 84*(2), 221–236.

Nussbaum, M. C. (2010). *From disgust to humanity: Sexual orientation and constitutional law*. New York: Oxford University Press.

Obergefell v. Hodges, 135 S. Ct. 2071 (2015).

Retrieved from *www.supremecourt.gov/opinions/14pdf/14-556_3204.pdf*.

Palazzolo, D. L. (2013). Electronic cigarettes and vaping: A new challenge in clinical medicine and public health: A literature review. *Frontiers in Public Health, 1,* 56. Available at *www.ncbi.nlm.nih.gov/pmc/articles/PMC3859972*.

Patterson, C. J. (2006). Children of lesbian and gay parents. *Current Directions in Psychological Science, 15*(5), 241–244.

Piaget, J. (1932). *The moral judgment of the child.* New York: Harcourt Brace.

Pierce, J. (2001, May 4). Opponents of pornography contend it's not "harmless" or victimless. Retrieved October 16, 2015, from *www.bpnews.net/10832/opponents-of-pornography-contend-its-not-harmless-or-victimless*.

Pizarro, D., Inbar, Y., & Helion, C. (2011). On disgust and moral judgment. *Emotion Review, 3*(3), 267–268.

Rachels, J. (1986). *The elements of moral philosophy.* Philadelphia: Temple University Press.

Rottman, J., Young, L., & Kelemen, D. (2017). The impact of testimony on children's moralization of novel actions. *Emotion, 17*(5), 811–827.

Royzman, E., Kim, K., & Leeman, R. F. (2015). The curious tale of Julie and Mark: Unraveling the moral dumbfounding effect. *Judgment and Decision Making, 10*(4), 296–313.

Rozin, P. (1999). The process of moralization. *Psychological Science, 10*(3), 218–221.

Schein, C., Goranson, A., & Gray, K. (2015). The uncensored truth about morality. *Psychologist, 28*(12), 982–985.

Schein, C., & Gray, K. (2014). The prototype model of blame: Freeing moral cognition from linearity and little boxes. *Psychological Inquiry, 25*(2), 236–240.

Schein, C., & Gray, K. (2015). The unifying moral dyad: Liberals and conservatives share the same harm-based moral template. *Personality and Social Psychology Bulletin, 41*(8), 1147–1163.

Schein, C., & Gray, K. (2016). Moralization and harmification: The dyadic loop explains how the innocuous becomes harmful and wrong. *Psychological Inquiry, 27*(1), 62–65.

Schein, C., & Gray, K. (2017). The theory of dyadic morality: Reinventing moral judgment by redefining harm. *Personality and Social Psychology Review.* [Epub ahead of print] Available at *www.researchgate.net/publication/316926091_The_Theory_of_Dyadic_Morality_Reinventing_Moral_Judgment_by_Redefining_Harm*.

Schein, C., Ritter, R., & Gray, K. (2016). Harm mediates the disgust–immorality link. *Emotion, 16,* 862–876.

Schnall, S., Haidt, J., Clore, G. L., & Jordan, A. H. (2008). Disgust as embodied moral judgment. *Personality and Social Psychology Bulletin, 34*(8), 1096–1109.

Scott, S., Inbar, Y., & Rozin, P. (2016). Evidence for absolute moral opposition to genetically modified food in the United States. *Perspectives on Psychological Science, 11,* 315–324.

Shweder, R. A. (2012). Relativism and universalism. In D. Fassin (Ed.), *A companion to moral anthropology* (pp. 85–102). Hoboken, NJ: Wiley.

Shweder, R. A., Mahapatra, M., & Miller, J. (1987). Culture and moral development. In J. Kagan & S. Lamb (Eds.), *The emergence of morality in young children* (pp. 1–83). Chicago: University of Chicago Press.

Smetana, J. G. (1985). Preschool children's conceptions of transgressions: Effects of varying moral and conventional domain-related attributes. *Developmental Psychology, 21*(1), 18–29.

Spivey, M. J., & Dale, R. (2004). On the continuity of mind: Toward a dynamical account of cognition. In B. Ross (Ed.), *Psychology of learning and motivation* (Vol. 45, pp. 87–142). Cambridge, MA: Academic Press.

Sripada, C. S., & Stich, S. (2007). A framework for the psychology of norms. In P. Carruthers, S. Laurence, & S. Stich (Eds.), *The innate mind: Vol. 2. Culture and cognition* (pp. 280–301). New York: Oxford University Press.

Turiel, E., Hildebrandt, C., Wainryb, C., & Saltzstein, H. D. (1991). Judging social issues: Difficulties, inconsistencies, and consistencies. *Monographs of the Society for Research in Child Development, 56*(2), 1–116.

Turiel, E., Killen, M., & Helwig, C. C. (1987). Morality: Its structure, functions, and vagaries. In J. Kagan & S. Lamb (Eds.), *The emergence of morality in young children* (pp. 155–243). Chicago: University of Chicago Press.

Tybur, J. M., Lieberman, D., & Griskevicius, V. (2009). Microbes, mating, and morality: Individual differences in three functional domains of disgust. *Journal of Personality and Social Psychology, 97*(1), 103–122.

Wegner, D. M., & Gray, K. (2016). *The mind club: Who thinks, what feels, and why it matters.* New York: Viking.

Wheatley, T., & Haidt, J. (2005). Hypnotic disgust makes moral judgments more severe. *Psychological Science, 16*(10), 780–784.

CHAPTER 38

Moral Coherence Processes and Denial of Moral Complexity

Brittany S. Liu
Sean P. Wojcik
Peter H. Ditto

> **How do people deal with a morally complex and contradictory world?**
>
> Moral judgment is an intuitive phenomenon, best understood as a process of implicit meaning making that often results in the denial of moral complexity and the shaping of descriptive beliefs to be consistent with prescriptive intuitions.

In May 2015, legislators in Nebraska made headlines when they overrode their governor's veto of a bill to ban the death penalty, making capital punishment illegal in the state. Advocates for the ban argued that the death penalty is neither moral nor effective, "It's not pro-life, it's not limited government, and doesn't deter crime" ("Killing it," 2015). Nebraska Governor Pete Ricketts, on the other hand, argued that, in fact, capital punishment was both: "as a Catholic, I'm confident that [capital punishment] aligns with Catholic catechism and that this aligns with public safety" (Bellware, 2015).

What we find fascinating about debates like this is that the two opposing camps both believe they hit the rhetorical jackpot. Not only do both sides believe that their view of the death penalty has the moral high ground, but both also believe the evidence shows that their position would be most ef-

fective in improving the public good. Rather than recognizing the inherent moral trade-offs that have made capital punishment a divisive political issue for decades in the United States, both sides in Nebraska's recent flare-up believe they are in a win–win situation, with both morality and the facts clearly on their side.

Scholars have long recognized individuals' tendency to mold seemingly contradictory information about their social world into a coherent whole (Cooper, 2007). Moral judgment, we suggest, is no different, and in this chapter we explore how a desire for moral coherence can lead to the denial of moral complexity and encourage people to shape their descriptive understanding of the world to fit their prescriptive understanding of it. Moreover, we argue that people's tendency to conflate moral and practical good plays a crucial role in exacerbating political conflict by leading individuals and groups with differing moral values to hold differing factual beliefs as well.

Historical Context

Leon Festinger's (1957) seminal volume on cognitive dissonance theory reflected a deeper Zeitgeist in psychology, recognizing that humans are fundamentally motivated to simplify and organize their social worlds (Abelson, 1968). Over the years, new theories have challenged, amended, or extended specific aspects of Festinger's original treatment (e.g., Bem, 1972; Harmon-Jones, Amodio, Harmon-Jones, 2009; Simon, Snow, & Read, 2004; Steele, 1988), but all embrace the core notion that individuals strive to construct an internally consistent world in which beliefs and feelings about oneself and others fit together coherently.

The desire for cognitive consistency can motivate rational, evidence-based reasoning, such as when individuals adjust a general belief based on incoming factual information relevant to that belief. But the popularity of cognitive consistency theories has flowed primarily from their prediction of motivated or "backward" forms of reasoning in which normative decision processes are, in effect, reverse engineered to produce the coherent pattern of beliefs that people desire. Cognitive dissonance theory, for example, rose in prominence above its many theoretical competitors largely because of a series of ingenious experiments demonstrating how the normative process of attitudes guiding behavior could be reversed, producing counterintuitive effects in which behavior seemed to guide attitudes instead (e.g., Aronson & Mills, 1959; Festinger & Carlsmith, 1959).

Research on explanatory coherence processes explicitly incorporates this notion of multidirectional influence into theories of cognitive consistency (Read, Vanman, & Miller, 1997; Thagard, 2004). Drawing inspiration from work on neural networks and parallel constraint satisfaction processes (Simon, Pham, Le, & Holyoak, 2001), coherence-based models adopt a dynamic view of consistency seeking in which beliefs, feelings, goals, and actions mutually influence each other and are adjusted iteratively toward a point of maximal internal consistency or "coherence." That is, a coherence perspective depicts people as striving to organize and integrate available information in a way that includes both "rational" bottom-up influences (e.g., adjusting conclusions to fit facts) and less rational top-down ones (e.g., adjusting facts to fit conclusions). Coherence was originally conceived of in terms of the logical consistency between belief elements, but later work has conceptualized coherence more broadly, recognizing that people do not merely favor beliefs that fit together logically but are consistent at an affective or evaluative level as well (Simon, Stenstrom, & Read, 2015; Thagard, 2006).

Importantly, the idea that individuals adjust beliefs to maintain a coherent and comforting view of the world has not been lost on researchers interested in moral reasoning. Struck by people's inclination to blame victims of misfortune for their own fate, Melvin Lerner (Lerner & Simmons, 1966; Lerner, 1980) traced this tendency to a core desire to live in a just world—a world where people get what they deserve and deserve what they get. Unfortunately, maintaining belief in a world of just deserts often requires people to adjust attributions of blame and responsibility such that victims seem to deserve the misfortunes that befall them (Bieneck & Krahé, 2011; Kleinke & Meyer, 1990; Lerner & Miller, 1978).

At a broader level, the social intuitionist view of moral judgment posits a similar tendency to recruit beliefs that support moral feelings (Haidt, 2001, 2012). Building on the philosophy of Hume (1740/1985) and the psychology of Zajonc (1980), the intuitionist view of moral judgment argues that moral evaluation is not the principled affair envisioned in the theories of Kohlberg (1969) and Turiel (1983). Rather, moral evaluations most typically result from "gut" reactions that people support post hoc by recruiting principles consistent with their moral intuitions in order to explain and justify them to others (Haidt, Koller, & Dias, 1993).

Theoretical Stance

Our conceptualization of moral coherence processes builds on this prior work and can be described in three key assertions.

Moral Judgments Are Subject to Coherence Pressures

There is little reason to assume that moral and nonmoral judgments involve fundamentally different psychological processes. In particular, there is good reason to expect moral judgment to be highly susceptible to the motivated reasoning processes that have been well documented across a wide variety of social judgments (Ditto, Pizarro, & Tannenbaum, 2009; Kunda, 1990). Moral judgments are inherently evaluative; they are judgments about whether acts (and the people who engage in them) are good (morally) or bad (morally). Moral reasoning is never value-neutral; moral judgment *is* moral evaluation. Moreover, moral evaluation is a particularly important kind of evaluation for both individuals and social groups. Likely due to the crucial role of moral evaluation in promoting cooperative group behavior (Fehr & Gächter, 2002; Haidt, 2012; Henrich et al., 2006), few topics inflame passions like questions of right and wrong, and few things drive our impressions of others more than their moral virtues and moral failings. In short, morality is something that people think about often and care about deeply (Hofmann, Wisneski, Brandt, & Skitka, 2014; Skitka, Bauman, & Sargis, 2005), and so it should be little surprise that moral judgments are fertile ground for motivated, coherence-based reasoning.

Incoherence Is a Frequent Feature of Moral Evaluation

A coherent moral view is one in which the moral quality of actors and their acts matches the moral quality of the outcomes they produce. But the potential for moral incoherence is high because of two complexities in the relation between the morality of actors/acts and the morality of outcomes.

Complexity 1: Moral Stands

The acts people perceive as most moral are not always the acts that produce the best consequences. Classic moral dilemmas, for example, typically pit consequentialist intuitions, in which the act that produces the best consequences seems most moral, against deontological ones, in which acts are judged as moral or immoral in and of themselves, independent of their consequences. Consider the footbridge variation of the famous trolley dilemma. Most people faced with this dilemma respond that pushing a large man in front of an oncoming train is immoral, even when sacrificing this one life would save the lives of many others (Thomson, 1985). This notion that certain acts (and objects) are "sacred" or "protected" from normal cost–benefit calculations is seen by many as an essential aspect of moral thinking (Atran, Axelrod, & Davis, 2007; Baron & Spranca, 1997; Bartels & Medin, 2007; Tetlock, 2003), and it forms the basis for the kinds of principled moral stands that people typically see as both admirable and inspirational, even when the outcomes they produce are less than ideal.

Complexity 2: Moral Culpability

Despite our preference for a morally just world in which only bad acts result in bad outcomes and bad things only happen to bad people, morally bad outcomes do not necessarily imply either a morally culpable actor or a morally deserving victim. An act is only itself morally bad if the consequences are something the actor intended, caused, and controlled (Malle & Knobe, 1997; Shaver, 1985). If a driver's brakes fail, causing the death of an innocent pedestrian, the outcome is tragic, but no moral shadow is cast upon the driver as long as the brake malfunction is judged to be "accidental" (i.e., the driver did not intend, cause, or have control over the mechanical failure). Similarly, being struck by a runaway car should rationally have no implications for the deceased pedestrian's moral status.

Coherence Pressures Shape Factual Beliefs to Support Moral Intuitions

How, then, do people respond to what is often a morally incoherent world? Over a half century of psychological research suggests that mental conflict of this kind is unstable and tends to initiate cognitive processes that resolve or minimize feelings of inconsistency (Abelson, 1968; Festinger, 1957; Read et al., 1997). Interestingly, however, the notion that people strive to resolve feelings of moral conflict, just as they strive to reduce other forms of cognitive inconsistency, is not well recognized in contemporary research on moral judgment. For example, in research involving moral dilemmas such as the footbridge problem, individuals are faced with a no-win choice between endorsing a morally distasteful act (e.g., killing an innocent man) and rejecting that act and with it the compelling logic of a favorable cost–benefit analysis (e.g., one casualty is better than five). The clear (if implicit) assumption in this research tradition is that individuals struggle their way to either a deontological or a consequentialist conclusion, and then simply live with the unavoidable downside of their either–or decision (cf., Greene et al., 2004).

A coherence perspective, however, predicts instead that people should struggle to *resolve* the conflict between deontological and consequentialist intuitions (Ditto & Liu, 2011). Because the implicit nature of moral intuitions makes them difficult to change, coherence pressures should operate primarily to bring beliefs about the costs and benefits of a given action in line with an individual's gut moral reactions. Thus, an individual experiencing strong moral distaste toward pushing an innocent man to his death might inflate the moral costs of that action (e.g., vividly imagine the pain and suffering the act would inflict on the individual and his loved ones) and minimize the moral benefits (e.g., reconsider the likelihood that a single man is actually large enough to stop the train from killing the others on the tracks). This type of "motivated consequentialism" (Liu & Ditto, 2013) would incline people toward coherent, conflict-free moral beliefs in which the act that feels right morally is also the act that produces the most favorable practical consequences.

A similar process should operate in judgments of moral culpability. If an individual's behavior results in consequences perceived as immoral (e.g., harm to other persons, animals, the environment), a coherence perspective predicts that observers will be most comfortable if they can blame that individual for those bad consequences (i.e., the bad consequences did not occur randomly but were caused by a malevolent actor or a deserving target). Because moral blame requires that actors be held responsible for their behavior, coherence pressures should operate to adjust descriptive beliefs about

the actor's intentions, desires, and level of control in a way that supports an attribution of blame. Similarly, if an individual is the victim of bad consequences, there should be some desire to see that victim as deserving of those consequences.

Overall, a desire for coherent patterns of moral beliefs works to dampen down moral complexity and promote a morally consilient worldview in which the morality of actors and acts matches the consequences they produce. Coherence processes often produce normatively appropriate judgments, such as evaluating acts as more moral to the extent that they produce morally beneficial outcomes or attributing greater moral blame to actors who intend and desire morally bad outcomes. But they can also motivate backward forms of reasoning in which descriptive beliefs about the positivity or negativity of outcomes, or about an individual's degree of intention or control over his or her behavior, are altered in ways that support moral intuitions and motivations.

Evidence

Our own research on moral coherence processes has focused primarily on people's tendency to coordinate beliefs about the morality of acts with beliefs about the consequences of those acts. An extensive literature on motivated judgments of culpability and control in moral evaluation, however, also supports the moral coherence perspective. In the following sections, we first review evidence for moral coherence processes in these two domains before identifying several other moral judgment phenomena that can be subsumed under the moral coherence banner.

Coherence and Consequences

In our initial studies of moral coherence, we sought to directly examine whether people tend to deny morally complex views of acts and their consequences and instead construct a reality in which moral and factual beliefs fit together. In one study (Liu & Ditto, 2013), we surveyed over 1,500 participants concerning their moral beliefs about four controversial issues (capital punishment, embryonic stem cell research, enhanced interrogation, and condom education for high school students). We first asked for evaluations of the "inherent" (i.e., deontological) morality of relevant policies; that is, to what extent an act is morally bad or good independent of its consequences (e.g., the death penalty is morally wrong *even if it prevents violent crime*). We then asked a series of questions assessing factual beliefs about the costs and benefits surrounding these issues (e.g., the deterrent efficacy of capital punishment, the likelihood of wrongful convictions). Judgments across all four issues showed an identical pattern. Although moral feelings about the issues varied substantially across people, individual participants seldom experienced these controversial issues as inherently dilemmic. Rather, a strong and consistent relation was found for judgments about each issue, such that the more an act was seen as inherently immoral, the more participants expected it to produce few benefits and substantial costs.

Other data support the robustness of this pattern. We have found the identical pattern of morality-consequences coordination in judgments about global warming, marijuana use, vegetarianism, casual sex, and same-sex marriage. With same-sex marriage, for example, the more participants believed it was inherently morally right, the more they believed that legalizing same-sex marriage would confer economic benefits and the more they disagreed that it would open legal avenues for other nontraditional marriages, such as polygamy. The same pattern also holds when individuals judge artificial moral scenarios, such as the footbridge dilemma. Compared with people who believed that pushing the large man onto the tracks was morally acceptable, people who found it inherently immoral to sacrifice one life to save others also believed that sacrificing the man would result in a lower probability of success at stopping the trolley and that the man's pain would be more severe (Liu & Ditto, 2013). What is notable about all of these findings is how few people acknowledge a complicated moral world in which morally good acts can have negative trade-offs. Instead, most of us seem to experience a simpler, more coherent moral world in which the acts we see as most moral are also the acts we believe yield the best outcomes.

One might argue that the findings above simply reflect people as good consequential-ists, that those who see the death penalty as morally wrong believe it is wrong *because* they believe it has few benefits and many costs. In order to directly test the key moral coherence proposition that moral intuitions actually shape factual beliefs, we devised an experimental design in which moral intuitions were manipulated and their effect on cost–benefit beliefs examined (Liu & Ditto, 2013). We measured participants' moral and factual beliefs about capital punishment before and after they read an essay advocating either for the inherent morality or inherent immorality of capital punishment. Importantly, the essays contained only purely deontological arguments for or against the death penalty, with neither essay including any mention of capital punishment's potential costs or benefits. The essays successfully changed moral evaluations of capital punishment; those reading the anti-capital punishment essay came to see the death penalty as more immoral, and those reading the pro–capital punishment essay came to see the death penalty as more moral. More crucially, the essays also changed participants' beliefs about the effectiveness of the death penalty, even though no information about effectiveness was included in the essays. As predicted, participants tipped toward seeing capital punishment as inherently immoral also moved toward believing that it had greater costs (e.g., innocents were more likely to be executed) and fewer benefits (e.g., it was unlikely to prevent crime), whereas those encouraged to see capital punishment as inherently moral moved toward believing it had greater benefits and fewer costs. This effect is not limited to capital punishment. Ames and Lee (2015) found that people's moral intuitions about enhanced interrogations shaped their interpretations of facts. Participants read a scenario in which a terrorist plot was foiled thanks to coerced and noncoerced information from an interrogation. Participants who believed enhanced interrogations are morally acceptable also thought the coerced information was more valuable than noncoerced information.

In sum, these studies demonstrate across a wide variety of real and artificial moral dilemmas that people perceive a strong connection between moral goodness and practical effectiveness and that, consistent with the logic of moral coherence, people alter their factual beliefs about the costs and benefits of actions to fit their moral evaluation of those actions.

Coherence and Culpability

Moral evaluations also involve descriptive beliefs about the extent to which actions are intended, caused, and controlled by the actor. The normative principle that people should receive blame only for behavior that they intend, cause, and control is well represented in both the legal system and the judgments of everyday people (Aspinwall, Brown, & Tabery, 2012; Shariff et al., 2014). But a wealth of research demonstrates that people engage in the reverse inference process as well: When motivated to blame and punish others, people construct morally culpable agents by adjusting their descriptive beliefs about intention, causation, and control.

Infants as young as 6 months old attribute more agency for bad outcomes than for good ones (Hamlin & Baron, 2014), and a similar asymmetry has been found repeatedly in studies on adults' attributions of intention. Research on the "side-effect effect," for example, demonstrates that incidental effects of identical actions are perceived as more intended when those side effects are morally bad (e.g., harmful to the environment) than when they are morally good (e.g., helpful to the environment; Knobe, 2003; Knobe & Burra, 2006; Leslie, Knobe, & Cohen, 2006; Pettit & Knobe, 2009).

People who perform morally harmful actions are also perceived as having more control over and being more causally responsible for outcomes compared with those who perform morally ambiguous or positive actions (Alicke, 2000; Cushman, Knobe, & Sinnott-Armstrong, 2008; Phillips & Knobe, 2009). In one clever demonstration of this effect, a young man involved in a traffic accident was seen as more causally responsible for the accident when he was rushing home to hide a vial of cocaine from his parents than when he was rushing home to hide their anniversary present (Alicke, 1992).

Importantly, the desire to assign responsibility for immoral actions can extend to the human capacity for moral responsibility in general. Clark et al. (2014) found that exposure to the immoral actions of others led people to increase not only their belief that those specific actions were freely chosen but also their belief that all of humankind is capable of free action. In one example, students who believed a fellow classmate had cheated on an exam reported higher belief on a measure of free will belief than students not informed of a cheating incident. Even when people are told to assume a completely deterministic universe, they will absolve an individual of moral responsibility for morally neutral acts but insist that a person committing a morally heinous act (e.g., murdering his family) is still morally responsible for that action (Nichols & Knobe, 2007).

In sum, research on judgments of culpability provides strong support for the operation of coherence processes in moral judgment. In a coherent world, morally bad outcomes only result from morally bad acts, and people adjust their beliefs about blame, responsibility, and control to fit this pattern.

Additional Evidence Consistent with Moral Coherence

In this section we briefly review several other lines of research in moral psychology that are consistent with a moral coherence perspective.

Outcome Bias

Highly related to research on moral culpability is a separate literature on outcome bias in moral judgment (Allison, Mackie, & Messick, 1996; Baron & Hershey, 1988; Gino, Shu, & Bazerman, 2010; Mazzocco, Alicke, & Davis, 2004; Walster, 1966). People's tendency to use the consequences of acts to judge their morality is both a feature of moral reasoning—it is the foundational normative principle underlying a consequentialist moral ethic—and a bug—in that it leads to irrational patterns of judgment such as identical acts being evaluated differently depending on the severity of their consequences. Walster (1966), for example, gave participants identical descriptions of a driver whose parked car accidentally rolled backward down a hill, but manipulated the severity of the consequences. The driver was judged more harshly (more careless and more responsible) when the very same action fortuitously had minor consequences (it hit a tree stump and dented the fender) than when the consequences were more serious (it rolled into a store, injuring two people). This pattern is robust (Mazzocco et al., 2004) and nicely demonstrates the kind of multidirectional influence captured by the coherence perspective. In our original work on motivated cost–benefit analyses (Liu & Ditto, 2013), people infer the severity of consequences from moral evaluations of the action. The outcome bias shows the opposite pattern of influence (the morality of an action is inferred from the severity of its consequences).

Dyadic Completion

The dyadic view of morality championed by Gray and colleagues (Gray, Waytz, & Young, 2012; Gray & Wegner, 2009) posits a process of post hoc belief construction that is very similar to our broader view of moral coherence. Gray argues for a fundamental dyadic template underlying all moral judgments in which one individual (the agent) acts in a way that intentionally harms or helps a second individual (the patient). If either component of this dyadic template is not readily available (i.e., there is no obvious agent or patient), people construct them through a process Gray calls dyadic completion. That is, exposure to harmed patients (e.g., victims of a natural disaster) motivates the construction of a culpable agent (e.g., God; Gray & Wegner, 2010), and exposure to agents or acts perceived as morally offensive (e.g., masturbation) motivates the construction of patients who have been harmed (e.g., the masturbator him- or herself; Gray, Schein, & Ward, 2014).

Intentional Harm

Several studies have shown that people perceive intentional acts as having more extreme consequences than unintentional acts (Ames & Fiske, 2013; Gray, 2012), a pattern consistent with a moral coherence perspective (the worse the actor is judged morally, the worse the consequences of his or her actions should be). People give higher dollar estimates for intentional damages than unintentional ones (Ames & Fiske, 2013),

and participants told that a man left a restaurant without paying his bill on purpose remembered the total bill being higher than did participants who were told the man did it by accident (Pizarro, Laney, Morris, & Loftus, 2006). Similarly, Gray (2012) found that shocks hurt less, massages seem more pleasurable, and candy tastes sweeter when the shocking, massaging, and candy giving is said to be well rather than ill intentioned.

Biased Assimilation

A long line of research documents people's tendency to derogate factual information that conflicts with their moral values (e.g., Ames & Lee, 2015; Lord & Taylor, 2009). People treat scientific evidence that supports morally distasteful policies as less valid than identical evidence that supports more morally acceptable policies (e.g., Lord, Ross, & Lepper, 1979) and downplay the seriousness of issues (e.g., climate change) surrounding policies that clash with moral world views (e.g., government regulation of emission levels; Campbell & Kay, 2014; Kahan, Braman, Slovic, Gastil, & Cohen, 2007; Kahan, Jenkins-Smith, & Braman, 2011). When people cannot defend their moral beliefs by dismissing research or downplaying the severity of problems, they often resort to framing their beliefs as not amenable to scientific study (Friesen, Campbell, & Kay, 2015; Munro, 2010). These strategies allow an individual to maintain a coherent moral worldview in which one's moral beliefs are supported (or at least not contradicted) by scientific evidence.

Additional Evidence Needed to Support Moral Coherence

Although a wealth of research in moral psychology is subsumable under the label of moral coherence, less research has been done to test its predictions directly and specifically. In particular, additional experimental research would help to better understand the causal relation between moral intuitions and cost–benefit beliefs. Ideally, this work would examine the relation across multiple moral issues and various methods of manipulating moral intuitions and motivations. Research on moral coherence could also build on research examining coherence processes in other domains (e.g., evaluations of legal evidence), which has sometimes used experimental designs in which judgments are assessed at multiple time points to track iterative changes in belief elements over time (e.g., Simon et al., 2001; Simon et al., 2015), a key prediction of coherence-based models.

Another important focus for future research should be identifying important moderators and boundary conditions of moral coherence processes. Liu and Ditto (2013), for example, identified three consistent moderators of the relation between moral evaluation and factual beliefs. Greater moral conviction about an issue, greater self-perceived knowledge about the issue, and greater political conservatism were all found to be associated with a "tighter" coordination between moral and factual beliefs. Identifying moderators is helpful both practically (to understand the ecological conditions under which one would expect research findings to apply and not apply) and theoretically (moderators often provide hints about the nature of underlying psychological processes).

Finally, moral coherence makes a number of interesting predictions that can be explored about everyday phenomena in which prescriptive and descriptive judgments might become intertwined. Do people judge the attractiveness of moral villains and moral exemplars differently? How about the objective humor of a morally distasteful versus morally neutral joke? Will people evaluate products from morally admirable companies as more effective (or of better quality generally) than identical products from companies seen in a more negative moral light?

Conclusion

Morality is about hard choices. Moral decisions often involve situations in which something bad must be done to produce something good, and they frequently confront individuals with dilemmas about doing the "right" thing, when doing the "wrong" thing would be easier or even produce a better outcome. The moral coherence processes we have described explain how people make difficult moral choices easier by rejecting this complexity in favor of a simpler, more coherent world in which the morality of actors, acts, and outcomes align.

Moral coherence processes have both theoretical and practical implications. Theoretically, moral coherence challenges the field's prevailing hydraulic view of consequentialist and deontological judgment (Ditto & Liu, 2011; Liu & Ditto, 2013). Like the intuitionist view of moral judgment from which it derives, our moral coherence view suggests that, rather than reasoning their way to moral conclusions using either deontological or consequentialist logic, people's moral justifications are guided by visceral reactions about rightness or wrongness (Haidt, 2001). As such, rather than choosing *either* a deontological or consequentialist path to a moral evaluation—the view endorsed either implicitly or explicitly by virtually all contemporary research in moral psychology—a moral coherence view suggests that people should be inclined to embrace any justification that coheres with and supports their moral intuitions, whether that justification is a broad deontological principle, information about consequences, or both. As Baron and Spranca (1997) cleverly noted, "people want to have their non-utilitarian cake and eat it too." Our data confirm that people seldom advocate a solely deontological position but, rather, support their seemingly principled views with motivated consequentialist crutches.

At the practical level, the desire for moral coherence can perturb how people ascribe moral culpability. One unfortunate example is a common tendency to see victims of rape, poverty, and other misfortunes as partly responsible for their own circumstances (Lerner, 1980; Ryan, 1971). But moral coherence can affect judgments about perpetrators as well. A wealth of research now shows that the more morally repugnant an act, the more intention and control is attributed to the perpetrator (Alicke, 2000; Clark et al., 2014). This may help explain why decisions about whether to try young defendants as adults often seem more a function of the abhorrence of the crime than of factors related to their ability to comprehend and control their actions (Ghetti & Redlich, 2001).

Finally, moral coherence processes also help make sense of the immense challenges facing fruitful bipartisan cooperation in the corrosive, hyperpartisan atmosphere of contemporary American politics. Liberals and conservatives have well-documented differences in their moral sensibilities that present challenges to political compromise (e.g., Graham et al., 2013), but it often seems as though liberals and conservatives have different factual realities as well. Whether it is the existence of anthropogenic climate change, or whether capital punishment deters future crime, liberals and conservatives often bring to the discussion their own quite different sets of facts. Our desire for a morally coherent world can lead to a false alignment of prescriptive and descriptive beliefs that can exacerbate conflict in morally diverse societies. It is difficult enough to resolve differences of moral opinion, but when differing moral beliefs affect the interpretation of science, evidence, and facts, bridging moral divides becomes exponentially more challenging.

REFERENCES

Abelson, R. P. (1968). Psychological implication. In R. P. Abelson, E. Aronson, W. J. McGuire, T. M. Newcomb, M. J. Rosenberg, & P. H. Tannenbaum (Eds.), *Theories of cognitive consistency: A sourcebook* (pp. 112–139). Chicago: Rand McNally.

Alicke, M. D. (1992). Culpable causation. *Journal of Personality and Social Psychology, 63,* 368–378.

Alicke, M. D. (2000). Culpable control and the psychology of blame. *Psychological Bulletin, 126,* 556–574.

Allison, S. T., Mackie, D. M., & Messick, D. M. (1996). Outcome biases in social perception: Implications for dispositional inference, attitude change, stereotyping, and social behavior. *Advances in Experimental Social Psychology, 28,* 53–94.

Ames, D. L., & Fiske, S. T. (2013). Intentional harms are worse, even when they're not. *Psychological Science, 24,* 1755–1762.

Ames, D. R., & Lee, A. J. (2015). Tortured beliefs: How and when prior support for torture skews the perceived value of coerced information. *Journal of Experimental Social Psychology, 60,* 86–92.

Aronson, E., & Mills, J. (1959). The effect of severity of initiation on liking for a group. *Journal of Abnormal and Social Psychology, 59,* 177–181.

Aspinwall, L. G., Brown, T. R., & Tabery, J. (2012). The double-edged sword: Does biomechanism increase or decrease judges' sentencing of psychopaths? *Science, 337*(6096), 846–849.

Atran, S., Axelrod, R., & Davis, R. (2007). Sacred barriers to conflict resolution. *Science, 317,* 1039–1040.

Baron, J., & Hershey, J. C. (1988). Outcome bias in decision evaluation. *Journal of Personality and Social Psychology, 54*(4), 569–579.

Baron, J., & Spranca, M. (1997). Protected values. *Organizational Behavior and Human Decision Processes, 70,* 1–16.

Bartels, D. M., & Medin, D. L. (2007). Are morally-motivated decision makers insensitive to the consequences of their choices? *Psychological Science, 18,* 24–28.

Bellware, K. (2015, May 26). Nebraska Gov. Pete Ricketts vetoes bill that would repeal the death penalty. *Huffington Post.* Retrieved from *www.huffingtonpost.com/2015/05/26/nebraska-death-penalty-veto_n_7445592.html.*

Bem, D. J. (1972). Self-perception theory. In L. Berkowitz (Ed.), *Advances in experimental social psychology* (Vol. 6, pp. 1–62). New York: Academic Press.

Bieneck, S., & Krahé, B. (2011). Blaming the victim and exonerating the perpetrator in cases of rape and robbery: Is there a double standard? *Journal of Interpersonal Violence, 26,* 1785–1797.

Campbell, T. H., & Kay, A. C. (2014). Solution aversion: On the relation between ideology and motivated disbelief. *Journal of Personality and Social Psychology, 107*(5), 809–824.

Clark, C. J., Luguri, J. B., Ditto, P. H., Knobe, J., Shariff, A. F., & Baumeister, R. F. (2014). Free to punish: A motivated account of free will belief. *Journal of Personality and Social Psychology, 106,* 501–513.

Cooper, J. (2007). *Cognitive dissonance: Fifty years of a classic theory.* Thousand Oaks, CA: SAGE.

Cushman, F., Knobe, J., & Sinnott-Armstrong, W. (2008). Moral appraisals affect doing/allowing judgments. *Cognition, 108*(1), 281–289.

Ditto, P. H., & Liu, B. (2011). Deontological dissonance and the consequentialist crutch. In M. Mikulincer & P. Shaver (Eds.), *The social psychology of morality: Exploring the causes of good and evil* (pp. 51–70). Washington, DC: American Psychological Association.

Ditto, P. H., Pizarro, D. A., & Tannenbaum, D. (2009). Motivated moral reasoning. In D. M. Bartels, C. W. Bauman, L. J. Skitka, & D. L. Medin (Eds.), *The psychology of learning and motivation* (Vol. 50, pp. 307–338). Burlington, MA: Academic Press.

Fehr, E., & Gächter, S. (2002). Altruistic punishment in humans. *Nature, 415*(6868), 137–140.

Festinger, L. (1957). *A theory of cognitive dissonance.* Stanford, CA: Stanford University Press.

Festinger, L., & Carlsmith, J. M. (1959). Cognitive consequences of forced compliance. *Journal of Abnormal and Social Psychology, 58*(2), 203–210.

Friesen, J. P., Campbell, T. H., & Kay, A. C. (2015). The psychological advantage of unfalsifiability: The appeal of untestable religious and political ideologies. *Journal of Personality and Social Psychology, 108,* 515–529.

Ghetti, S., & Redlich, A. D. (2001). Reactions to youth crime: Perceptions of accountability and competency. *Behavioral Sciences and the Law, 19,* 33–53.

Gino, F., Shu, L. L., & Bazerman, M. H. (2010). Nameless + harmless = blameless: When seemingly irrelevant factors influence judgment of (un)ethical behavior. *Organizational Behavior and Human Decision Processes, 111,* 102–115.

Graham, J., Haidt, J., Koleva, S., Motyl, M., Iyer, R., Wojcik, S. P., & Ditto, P. H. (2013). Moral foundations theory: The pragmatic validity of moral pluralism. *Advances in Experimental Social Psychology, 47,* 55–130.

Gray, K. (2012). The power of good intentions: Perceived benevolence soothes pain, increases pleasure, and improves taste. *Social Psychological and Personality Science, 3,* 639–645.

Gray, K., Schein, C., & Ward, A. F. (2014). The myth of harmless wrongs in moral cognition: Automatic dyadic completion from sin to suffering. *Journal of Experimental Psychology: General, 143,* 1600–1615.

Gray, K., Waytz, A., & Young, L. (2012). The moral dyad: A fundamental template unifying moral judgment. *Psychological Inquiry, 23,* 206–215.

Gray, K., & Wegner, D. M. (2009). Moral typecasting: Divergent perceptions of moral agents and moral patients. *Journal of Personality and Social Psychology, 96,* 505–520.

Gray, K., & Wegner, D. M. (2010). Blaming God for our pain: Human suffering and the divine mind. *Personality and Social Psychology Review, 14,* 7–16.

Greene, J. D., Nystrom, L. E., Engell, A. D., Darley, J. D., & Cohen, J. D. (2004). The neural bases of cognitive conflict and control in moral judgment. *Neuron, 44,* 389–400.

Haidt, J. (2001). The emotional dog and its rational tail: A social intuitionist approach to moral judgment. *Psychological Review, 108,* 814–834.

Haidt, J. (2012). *The righteous mind: Why good people are divided by politics and religion.* New York: Pantheon.

Haidt, J., Koller, S. H., & Dias, M. G. (1993). Affect, culture, and morality, or is it wrong to eat your dog? *Journal of Personality and Social Psychology, 65,* 613–628.

Hamlin, J. K., & Baron, A. S. (2014). Agency attribution in infancy: Evidence for a negativity bias. *PLOS ONE, 9*(5), e96112.

Harmon-Jones, E., Amodio, D. M., & Harmon-Jones, C. (2009). Action-based model of dissonance: A review, integration, and expansion of conceptions of cognitive conflict. *Advances in Experimental Social Psychology, 41,* 119–166.

Henrich, J., McElreath, R., Barr, A., Ensminger, J., Barrett, C., Bolyanatz, A., . . . Ziker, J. (2006). Costly punishment across human societies. *Science, 312,* 1767–1770.

Hofmann, W., Wisneski, D. C., Brandt, M. J., & Skitka, L. J. (2014). Morality in everyday life. *Science, 345*(6202), 1340–1343.

Hume, D. (1985). *A treatise of human nature.* London: Penguin. (Original work published 1740)

Kahan, D. M., Braman, D., Slovic, P., Gastil, J., & Cohen, G. L. (2007). *The second national risk and culture study: Making sense of—and making progress in—the American culture war of fact.* Harvard Law School Program on Risk Regulation (Research Paper No. 08–26). Available at *https://papers.ssrn.com/sol3/papers.cfm?abstract_id=1017189.*

Kahan, D. M., Jenkins-Smith, H., & Braman, D. (2011). Cultural cognition of scientific consensus. *Journal of Risk Research, 14,* 147–174.

Killing it: Nebraska's ban is another sign of the decline in support for the death penalty. (2015, May 30). *The Economist.* Retrieved from *www.economist.com/news/united-states/21652277-nebraskas-ban-another-sign-decline-support-death-penalty-killing-it.*

Kleinke, C., & Meyer, C. (1990). Evaluation of rape victims by men and women with high and low beliefs in a just world. *Psychology of Women Quarterly, 4,* 343–353.

Knobe, J. (2003). Intentional action and side-effects in ordinary language. *Analysis, 63,* 190–193.

Knobe, J., & Burra, A. (2006). The folk concepts of intention and intentional action: A cross-cultural study. *Journal of Cognition and Culture, 6*(1), 113–132.

Kohlberg, L. (1969). Stage and sequence: The cognitive-developmental approach to socialization. In D. A. Goslin (Ed.), *Handbook of socialization theory and research* (pp. 347–489). Chicago: Rand McNally.

Kunda, Z. (1990). The case for motivated reasoning. *Psychological Bulletin, 108,* 480–498.

Lerner, M. (1980). *The belief in a just world: A fundamental delusion.* New York: Plenum Press.

Lerner, M., & Miller, D. (1978). Just world research and the attribution process: Looking back and ahead. *Psychological Bulletin, 85,* 1030–1051.

Lerner, M. J., & Simmons, C. H. (1966). Observer's reaction to the "innocent victim": Compassion or rejection? *Journal of Personality and Social Psychology, 4,* 203–210.

Leslie, A. M., Knobe, J., & Cohen, A. (2006). Acting intentionally and the side-effect effect: Theory of mind and moral judgment. *Psychological Science, 17,* 421–427.

Liu, B. S., & Ditto, P. H. (2013). What dilemma?: Moral evaluation shapes factual beliefs. *Social Psychological and Personality Science, 4,* 316–323.

Lord, C. G., Ross, L., & Lepper, M. R. (1979). Biased assimilation and attitude polarization: The effects of prior theories on subsequently considered evidence. *Journal of Personality and Social Psychology, 37,* 2098–2109.

Lord, C. G., & Taylor, C. A. (2009). Biased assimilation: Effects of assumptions and expectations on the interpretation of new evidence. *Social and Personality Psychology Compass, 3*(5), 827–841.

Malle, B. F., & Knobe, J. (1997). The folk concept of intentionality. *Journal of Experimental Social Psychology, 33*(2), 101–121.

Mazzocco, P. J., Alicke, M. D., & Davis, T. L. (2004). On the robustness of outcome bias: No constraint by prior culpability. *Basic and Applied Social Psychology, 26,* 131–146.

Munro, G. D. (2010). The scientific impotence excuse: Discounting belief-threatening scientific abstracts. *Journal of Applied Social Psychology, 40,* 579–600.

Nichols, S., & Knobe, J. (2007). Moral responsibility and determinism: The cognitive science of folk intuitions. *Nous, 41,* 663–685.

Pettit, D., & Knobe, J. (2009). The pervasive impact of moral judgment. *Mind and Language, 24*(5), 586–604.

Phillips, J., & Knobe, J. (2009). Moral judgments and intuitions about freedom. *Psychological Inquiry, 20,* 30–36.

Pizarro, D. A., Laney, C., Morris, E. K., & Loftus, E. F. (2006). Ripple effects in memory: Judgments of moral blame can distort memory for events. *Memory and Cognition, 34,* 550–555.

Read, S. J., Vanman, E. J., & Miller, L. C. (1997). Connectionism, parallel constraint satisfaction processes, and gestalt principles: (Re)introducing cognitive dynamics to social psychology. *Personality and Social Psychology Review, 1,* 26–53.

Ryan, W. (1971). *Blaming the victim.* New York: Pantheon.

Shariff, A. F., Greene, J. D., Karremans, J. C., Luguri, J. B., Clark, C. J., Schooler, J. W., . . . Vohs, K. D. (2014). Free will and punishment: A mechanistic view of human nature reduces retribution. *Psychological Science, 25,* 1563–1570.

Shaver, K. G. (1985). *The attribution of blame: Causality, responsibility, and blameworthiness.* New York: Springer-Verlag.

Simon, D., Pham, L. B., Le, Q. A., & Holyoak, K. J. (2001). The emergence of coherence over the course of decision making. *Journal of Experimental Psychology: Learning, Memory, and Cognition, 27,* 1250–1260.

Simon, D., Snow, C. J., & Read, S. J. (2004). The redux of cognitive consistency theories: Evidence judgments by constraint satisfaction. *Journal of Personality and Social Psychology, 86,* 814–837.

Simon, D., Stenstrom, D. M., & Read, S. J. (2015). The coherence effect: Blending cold and hot cognitions. *Journal of Personality and Social Psychology, 109,* 369–394.

Skitka, L. J., Bauman, C. W., & Sargis, E. G. (2005). Moral conviction: Another contributor to attitude strength or something more? *Journal of Personality and Social Psychology, 8,* 895–917.

Steele, C. M. (1988). The psychology of self-affirmation: Sustaining the integrity of the self. *Advances in Experimental Social Psychology, 21,* 261–302.

Tetlock, P. E. (2003). Thinking about the unthinkable: Coping with secular encroachments on sacred values. *Trends in Cognitive Science, 7,* 320–324.

Thagard, P. (2004). *Coherence in thought and action.* Boston: MIT Press.

Thagard, P. (2006). *Hot thought: Mechanisms and applications of emotional cognition.* Cambridge, MA: MIT Press.

Thomson, J. J. (1985). The trolley problem. *Yale Law Journal, 94,* 1395–1415.

Turiel, E. (1983). *The development of social knowledge: Morality and convention.* Cambridge, MA: Cambridge University Press.

Walster, E. (1966). Assignment of responsibility for an accident. *Journal of Personality and Social Psychology, 3,* 73–79.

Zajonc, R. B. (1980). Feeling and thinking: Preferences need no inferences. *American Psychologist, 35,* 151–175.

CHAPTER 39

What Is Blame and Why Do We Love It?

Mark D. Alicke
Ross Rogers
Sarah Taylor

What is blame, and why do people blame so liberally even when there are compelling reasons to mitigate it?

Blame is an automatic species of moral judgment in which evidential criteria are revised to support an initial blame hypothesis—this "blame validation" mode can overwhelm tendencies toward mitigation and forgiveness.

Near the end of Anthony Burgess's (1962) novel *A Clockwork Orange,* Alex, the hyperviolent 15-year-old hero, is "cured" of his sickness by behavioral psychologists using classical conditioning. To demonstrate the effectiveness of the treatment, a beautiful, scantily clad woman is paraded before him, and just as his predilections for rape and murder surface, he becomes physically ill and unable to act on his instincts. For the scientists, this is further proof that Alex was a blameless victim of society—one whose behavior could be rectified with an admixture of progressive social reform and behavior modification.

Burgess's picture of a dystopian future satirizes the liberal view of criminality as an accidental by-product of misguided parenting and ineffective social institutions. In Burgess's prospective world, blame, punishment, and incarceration are banished; instead, much as in B. F. Skinner's *Walden Two* (Skinner & Hayes, 1976), society is perfected to the point where harmful and offensive behaviors virtually disappear, making blame irrelevant.

Before considering whether we could or should eliminate blame (the answer is *no!*—but more about that later), it is necessary first to address the more fundamental question of what blame is, a question that neither we nor anyone else has yet answered very clearly. The reason that blame is difficult to define is that it is both a hypothesis that is subject to updating as new data are received and a relatively quick summary judgment. Blame can be as reflexive as in the classic Harry Nilsson (1972) tearjerker: "You're breaking my heart, you're tearing it apart, so fuck you" or as lengthy a process as in an eight-month jury trial that requires sifting through mountains of contradictory evidence.

It is also important to clarify whether blame refers to an offense that is known to have occurred or to one that is still in question. Most theories of blame, including the culpable control model of blame (CCM; Alicke, 2000), focus on the former question, as issues related to establishing whether an offense actually occurred fall more naturally under the auspices of responsibility attribution. Accordingly, in the following discussion, we assume a potentially blameworthy behavior or behavior pattern and consider first the process of ascribing blame and then whether and when blame is an effective means of social control.

Blame's Evolutionary Heritage

Evolutionary perspectives on social behavior assume that moral judgment originates in the need to monitor and punish group members who threaten the group's interests by violating established norms. As the anthropologist Christopher Boehm argues: "when band members started to form consensual moral opinions and punished deviant behaviors and rewarded prosocial ones a new element was added to human evolution" (2012, p. 83). The element that Boehm refers to is social selection of characteristics, especially altruism, that advance the individual's and, by proxy, the group's survival prospects. Moral behavior, therefore, involves compliance with implicit or explicit behavioral guidelines, and moral judgment is the assessment of whether a group member has met or violated these prescriptions.

From the social selection perspective, people are blameworthy when they defect from group standards in a way that threatens or could threaten the group's well-being. The act of blaming, however, transcends blameworthiness. Blame registers to oneself, and/ or signals to others, that the actions and character of a group member are potentially detrimental to the general welfare. Blame is not simply a judgment, therefore, but also a form of direct or indirect social control.

Blame presupposes a character flaw or limitation. Without this, observers, after an initial evaluative reaction, would presumably rescind their judgment and recognize that whatever happened was an excusable blip that can be attributed to unusual or uncontrollable circumstances. Blame that perseveres, therefore, impugns the character of the harm doer. Although forgiveness may occur over time, blame places a permanent stain—even if only a smudge—on impressions of the blamed individual's trustworthiness and reliability.

One might legitimately wonder why, if blame derives from social selection pressures, it is so much more intense on the part of the individual who is directly harmed than it is for observers. The simple answer is that individual selection pressures supersede group considerations. Although the prosperity of the group facilitates individual survival, it still takes a back seat to the needs of self and kin. Nevertheless, third-party punishment, which entails punishing others at cost to oneself, is a routine, and probably unique, facet of human social control (Kahneman, Knetsch, & Thaler, 1986; Turillo, Folger, Lavelle, Umphress, & Gee, 2002), and blame is the judgment that legitimizes its application.

Explanations that reference historical survival needs run the risk of deemphasizing aspects of human cognition and culture that transform the nature of mechanisms that originated to solve specific adaptive problems. Although it makes good sense to trace blame's origins to needs for social control, and although such needs elucidate many facets of blame, blame varies across times and cultures in ways that require additional explanation. Furthermore, human capacities of memory, language, and imagination alter not only the nature of blame, retribution, and forgiveness but also the ways in which these actions and emotions are manifested in social situations and the circumstances that hinder or facilitate them. Human blood feuds, for example, fueled by enhanced memory and imagery processes, have extended for generations (Baumeister, 1999). No other species is capable of carrying on vendettas against families, clans, nations, or religious groups in this way. Most important for present purposes is the fact that blame, as a derivative of moral judgment, is uniquely human and can be applied to harmless offenses based on ideological grounds, visceral reactions, and complex emotions such as feelings of envy or relative deprivation. Thus, whereas blame originated in moral judgment, it is applied to perceived offenses (such as breaking a heart in the Harry Nilsson song) that lie outside the bounds of what are normally considered moral issues.

Spontaneous Evaluations and Reactive Attitudes: Hypotheses about Blame

P. F. Strawson's relatively short paper titled "Freedom and Resentment" is probably the most influential philosophical paper on blame (1962). Strawson introduced the phrase "reactive attitudes" to refer to sentiments such as gratitude, resentment, and indignation that occur spontaneously in response to praiseworthy or censorious actions. Strawson follows a long philosophical tradition, represented most prominently in the moral philosophy of David Hume, in emphasizing the emotional component in moral judgment and blame. For Hume, the emotional component was nearly sovereign: "The mind of man is so formed by nature, that, upon the appearance of certain characters, dispositions, and actions it immediately feels the sentiment of approbation or blame; nor are there any emotions more essential to its frame or constitution" (1748/2007, p. 74).

Inclining toward Blame

Using a terminology adapted to social-psychological research on automatic attitude activation (Fazio, 1989), we refer to Strawson's reactive attitudes as spontaneous evaluations (Alicke, 2000). As described in the CCM, spontaneous evaluations are attitudinal reactions that do not necessarily entail emotions; rather, they are positive or negative evaluations of the actors involved in the event, their characters and values, their actions, and the consequences of those actions. Although emotions are not a necessary component of spontaneous evaluations, they typically accompany them and modulate the strength of the reaction. Or, as one philosopher has stated it, emotions are not

criterial for blame but are a canonical feature of it (McGeer, 2013).

In a recent book that explores the evolutionary heritage and neurobiology of punishment, Hoffman (2014) argues that blame occurs the moment we think that a person has committed a wrong and that mitigation will occur much later. This is the bedrock assumption of the CCM; in contrast to blame models that precede (Shaver, 1985) and succeed (Malle, Guglielmo, & Monroe, 2014) it, the CCM assumes that blame occurs naturally and automatically and that mitigation is the more difficult and complicated task. A more precise way to depict the processes of blame and mitigation or exoneration, however, is to say that blame is a hypothesis that occurs immediately upon witnessing a harmful or offensive action and that it is subject to modification (i.e., mitigation or exoneration) upon further consideration and evidence. In some instances, strong prior understanding of social situations negate blame almost immediately. People generally know what accidents look like, for example, and after an immediate anger response at being thwacked in the face by a branch that the hiker in front of us let go, we immediately recognize that he didn't realize we were so close behind and hold no grudge.

More generally, it is in humans' and other animals' interest to be able quickly to distinguish intentional from unintentional harms: Obviously, zebras who know that lions want to eat them have an advantage over peace-and-love zebras who think that all animals are God's children. Conversely, fleeing from or shunning others who intend to help us is also a costly strategy.

Akin to Pascal's famous wager about God, it makes sense to err on the side of intentionality and blame. Of the two mistakes in Pascal's fourfold table (assuming that God exists when he doesn't; assuming that God doesn't exist when he does), the latter is presumably more harmful, assuming the vengeful (and somewhat neurotic) deity of the Old Testament who demands recognition and allegiance. (Of course, if God doesn't give a fig whether you believe in him or not, then the former mistake means that you will spend a lifetime passing up enticing opportunities in his name, which seems like a worse mistake—but this is a different question for a different paper.) In this same vein, assuming harmful intentions is a safer policy than assuming benevolence, although there is, of course, a price to be paid for unsubstantiated accusations, grudges, and, even worse, unfounded retaliation. As Pinker states the case: "good and evil are asymmetrical: there are more ways to harm people than to help them, and harmful acts can hurt them to a greater degree than virtuous acts can make them better off" (2003, p. 10).

Elements of Perceived Control

Still, the assumption that people are predisposed to blame obviously does not claim that they fail completely to consider evidence about intentionality, causation, and mitigating and extenuating circumstances in evaluating behavior. The CCM assumes that the relationship between the spontaneous evaluations that incline toward blame and rational and deliberate evaluation of the evidence is a compensatory one: In the absence of valenced reactions to the event, the state of the evidence drives the ultimate blame judgment. When spontaneous negative evaluations are strong, however, and are ignited by heightened emotions, evidence will be skewed in a manner that supports the initial blame hypothesis—what Alicke, Rose, and Bloom (2011) have called a "blame validation" mode of information processing, akin to confirmatory hypothesis testing.

Although the assumptions about the primacy of evaluation and blame validation processing have received most of the attention in our empirical work, the CCM was designed also to provide a view of evidence evaluation grounded in perceptions of personal control. Blame, like morality more generally, is predicated on the assumption that people can exercise control over their needs and desires. Only a lunatic (and there are some out there) would blame their cat for returning pregnant after a night on the prowl, but many teen-age daughters would be deprived of the same leniency: The cat cannot consciously monitor and override her desires, but the daughter presumably can. Suppose, however, that the daughter, a 15-year-old wealthy white debutante, remonstrates with her parents that the father

is a black Olympic athlete with an IQ of 175 and a family history of perfect physical and mental health and that she is going to have triplets. Having scored this incredible coup in the human gene pool, do we expect the family to commence with the party announcements? Maybe, but maybe not. Not only do humans establish moral rules and social norms that seem irrelevant or contradictory to inclusive fitness concerns, but they expect people to stick to them.

According to the CCM, three elements of control are most important in assessing blame: behavior control, causal control, and outcome control. Behavior control—also termed "intention of action"—is thwarted by reflexes, accidents, and lack of access to information and norms. We would not blame an epileptic who caused property damage while having a grand mal seizure, nor would we blame a foreign tourist who insulted his host because someone misinformed him about local norms as a practical joke. Each of these actions is unintentional in the sense that the behavior sequence was not initiated purposively or knowingly.

Causal control judgments are complicated by the fact that many causal conditions, including necessity and sufficiency, proximity in space in time to the outcome, and abnormal or counterfactual conditions, among others, are potentially relevant for blame. Causal control is reduced or negated by intervening circumstances and by other competing causes that reduce the actor's unique impact on the outcome.

Outcome control refers to whether the event's consequences occurred in the manner that the actor desired and/or foresaw. The absence of behavior control also indicates the absence of outcome control: People cannot be said to have controlled the outcomes of actions that occurred accidentally, even if they desired them. There are, however, many ways in which intentional behaviors can lead to outcomes that were unforeseen, undesired, or both, and also ways in which intended outcomes can be thwarted (i.e., failed attempts). Perhaps the most interesting cases that have been studied are those in which people achieve desired outcomes in unforeseen ways (e.g., Pizarro, Uhlmann, & Bloom, 2003). We have shown in a recent study, for example, that a pilot who is forced at gunpoint to fly a plane to Cuba is seen to have had more control, and to be more blameworthy, if the hijacking fortuitously allows him to reunite with a girlfriend than if this outcome does not occur, even though his behavioral freedom was equally compromised in both conditions (Rogers et al., in preparation).

In Anglo-American law and most rational perspectives on moral decision making, something very close to behavior, causal, and outcome control (without these labels) are the decision criteria that are prescribed for determining blame. A major assumption of the CCM is that reactions to unfavorable personalities, actions, and outcomes lead observers to alter their perceptions of these decision criteria. In other words, observers' distaste for elements of the action sequence and/or the people involved leads them to evaluate these criteria in a way that justifies the blame attribution they favor (see Alicke, 2000).

Many empirical studies now strongly support the primacy of evaluative reactions in determining blame and its criteria (such as intent and causation). Among these findings from our own lab are the following.

- A person who is driving over the speed limit to hide a vial of cocaine is viewed as a more significant cause of an accident than one who is driving at the same speed in the same circumstances to hide an anniversary present (Alicke, 1992, Study 1).
- People are seen as more causal for later events in an extended causal chain when their initial motives are negative versus positive (Alicke, 1992, Study 4).
- A homeowner who shoots an intruder is blamed more when the intruder turns out to be his daughter's boyfriend than when he is a dangerous criminal (Alicke & Davis, 1989); and judgments about the homeowner's causal influence on the victim's death are mediated by blame attributions, but blame is not mediated by causation (Alicke et al., 2011).
- Individuals whose capacities are diminished (e.g., psychosis, anxiety disorder) are blamed more when these incapacities lead to harm if these individuals contributed to the development of the incapacity (e.g., by experimenting with drugs)

than if their incapacities developed due to circumstances outside of their control (Alicke & Davis, 1990).
- The mutability of an outcome influences blame only if a decision maker was culpable in the events leading up to the harmful outcome (Alicke, Davis, Buckingham, & Zell, 2008).
- Socially unattractive actors are blamed more for harmful outcomes than socially attractive actors, but this effect is reduced if extenuating circumstances are presented before participants learn about the facts that establish the person's dislikable character than if they learn about these circumstances after the unfavorable dispositional information has had time to fester (Alicke & Zell, 2009).
- Participants who learn of negative outcomes and first assess a defendant's legal responsibility for a negligent homicide charge see the facts of the case as more indicative of guilt than do participants who do not assess legal responsibility until after they evaluate the facts, suggesting that the former participants justify or validate their blame attributions by altering their perception of the facts (Alicke, Davis, & Pezzo, 1994).
- People who do good, counternormative things are blamed less for harmful outcomes than are those who do bad, normative things, showing that evaluative "goodness–badness" matters more in causal citation than normativity (Alicke et al., 2011, Study 2).

To date, research designed to test assumptions of the CCM have concentrated largely on judgments of causation, as causal judgment was the central concern of the attributional theories from which interest in blame and responsibility first arose among social psychologists. In recent studies, we have been extending our research to the other main blame criterion—intent. Interest in this topic has exploded among psychologists and philosophers, much of the research being directed at Joshua Knobe's "side effect" problem (Knobe & Fraser, 2008). Side effects, or peripheral consequences, are outcomes that decision makers realize will probably occur if they pursue their focal goal but either don't care about or are willing to accept to achieve their primary goal. From the CCM perspective, the "Knobe effect," the finding that people ascribe more intentionality for negative than for positive side effects, is due to participants having more negative reactions to a decision maker who expresses a lack of concern for harmful consequences (Alicke, 2008).

In our present research, we have been interested in what is probably the more common peripheral effect problem, that is, one in which the peripheral consequence is unforeseen. In a recent study, for example, we described a journalist—Joan—who desired either to help or impede her friend's chances of getting hired for a high-status job. In both cases, prior to her friend's interview, Joan secretly slipped a sedative in her drink. In the *good*-Joan case, the sedative was intended to increase her friend's chances (it was known that the interviewer preferred calm employees), whereas in the *bad*-Joan case, the sedative was intended to undermine her friend's chances (it was known that the interviewer preferred more hyper, energetic employees). In both instances, however, Joan's friend had an unforeseen allergic reaction to the sedative and became very ill. Despite neither character having knowledge of her allergy, bad Joan's unrelated motive—to prevent her friend from getting the job—led to heightened ascriptions of intent and blame for her friend's illness.

One important unresolved issue in studies designed to test CCM assumptions concerns the conditions under which changes in the decision criteria mediate blame effects or when they simply represent post hoc justifications of blame attributions that have already been made. So far, we have been unable to find a consistent pattern: Sometimes judgments of causation or intention mediate blame, sometimes they do not. Both of these paths pose problems for the administration of justice in everyday social life and in the law, although the latter seems more pernicious. If people react unfavorably based on their emotions or personal biases and later, after considering the data regarding behavioral, causal, and outcome control, alter either their perceptions of the evidence or their threshold for how much evidence is needed to blame, there is at least the possibility that the facts might override

their desire to blame. If, however, they simply alter their judgments about causation, intent, foresight, mitigation, and so on only when they are explicitly asked about these criteria, it suggests that their blame attributions are largely emotion-driven and relatively independent of the state of the evidence.

Is It Bad to Blame? Should We Stop?

Western cultural institutions—Christianity and the mental health community being the most prominent—advocate forgiveness and almost uniformly condemn blame. Self-help books on blame endorse these views with titles such as: "Ending the Blame Game"; "Beyond Blame: Freeing Yourself from the Most Toxic Form of Emotional Bullsh*t"; "Stop Blaming, Start Loving!"; and "Beyond Blame: A New Way of Resolving Conflicts in Relationships." Clearly, there is little benefit to holding on to useless grudges or exacting ill-advised retribution.

Nevertheless, when cultural prescriptions clash with our fundamental human nature, there are always questions about both the soundness of these prescriptions and their feasibility. Religious views that discourage sex outside of marriage, for example, have probably had at least a modest civilizing function throughout Western history, especially in promoting stable family arrangements, but have also made people feel guilty about a behavior that is as natural as eating and drinking, with especially punitive consequences for women. And, of course, even with images of hellfire and damnation lurking in the background, even the most pious seem to circumvent these religious prescriptions quite adeptly.

Blame instincts are less entertaining than sexual ones, but they are probably as natural and immediate. Cultural perspectives on blame and forgiveness generally deemphasize the benefits of the former and the liabilities of the latter. Philosophers, by contrast, have noted that refraining from blame indicates a failure to take morality seriously (Coates & Tognazzini, 2013). Furthermore, blame is an assertion of individual rights, an injured party's way of saying that she or he is someone who will not be taken advantage of. Conversely, failure to blame can reflect an unwillingness to take a stand on important moral matters. What would it mean, for example, to cringe upon hearing a person utter racial epithets but to decide that you just can't blame him for it? To put it succinctly, "to foreswear blame is to fail to value what we ought to value" (Franklin, 2013).

In his book on the evolution of forgiveness, McCullough (2008) notes that national surveys have revealed forgiveness to be the fourth most valued personal quality, which is perhaps unsurprising given its widespread endorsement. The New Testament is filled with homilies about forgiveness, such as in Matthew 18:22–23: "Then Peter came and said to Him, 'Lord, how often shall my brother sin against me and I forgive him? Up to seven times?' Jesus said to him, 'I do not say to you up to seven times, but up to seventy times seven.'" But as Bertrand Russell (1957) noted in comparing the morality of Jesus unfavorably to that of Socrates, Jesus was quite capable of vindictive fury, as in Matthew 13:41, "The Son of Man shall send forth his angels, and they shall gather out of His kingdom all things that offend, and them which do iniquity, and shall cast them into a furnace of fire; there shall be wailing and gnashing of teeth." So while the New Testament may be the most influential endorsement of forgiveness in Western cultures, it is by no means a universal one.

Psychologists, beginning at least as far back as Karen Horney (1937), have also highlighted the evils of blame and trumpeted the virtues of forgiveness. McCullough (2008) notes that vindictiveness underlies many of the personality disorders in the *Diagnostic and Statistical Manual of Mental Disorders, Fifth Edition* (DSM-5). One of the reasons for this, however, is that personality disorders in the DSM are almost all externalizing disorders that involve harm to others—such as narcissism, passive–aggressiveness, and psychopathy. From a cognitive-behavioral perspective, self-blame and low self-esteem are the primary causes of depression, which is the most common of all psychological problems. In many circumstances, self-blame is a natural consequence of failing to blame others who deserve it.

There is good reason to believe that future developments in the biological and social sciences will bring into sharper relief the genetic and environmental determinants of behavior and, even more importantly, augment our ability to predict the outcome of their interaction in specific situations. Harking back to the *A Clockwork Orange* example with which we began, the moral question about Alex is whether he is a victim of his nature and environment or whether he has freely chosen to be a violent criminal. As science moves closer to identifying the influences that contribute to violent and aggressive behavior and, indeed, to any harmful or offensive actions, will people stop blaming those who exhibit them?

This question relates to the familiar philosophical debate between compatibilist and incompatibilist positions on responsibility: If behavior is completely determined, can anyone be held morally responsible for their actions? In the simplest case, compatibilists say yes, incompatibilists say no. Nonphilosophers seem unimpressed by this issue. Apparently, the vast majority of people believe in free will in the diverse cultures in which it has been assessed, including the United States, Hong Kong, India, and Colombia (Sarkissian, Chatterjee, DeBrigard, Knobe, Nichols, & Sirker, 2010). Furthermore, and most important, even when people believe that an action is fully causally determined, they continue to ascribe moral responsibility (Nahmias, Morris, Nadelhoffer, & Turner, 2006). From the CCM perspective, these findings demonstrate that the strong need to blame supersedes abstract philosophical considerations, an assumption that has recently been supported in an impressive series of studies on free will and moral responsibility by Clark and colleagues (2014).

Conclusions

In this chapter we reviewed the psychological functions that blame subserves and the process by which it occurs. We argued that even when complex reasoning processes are engaged to make ultimate decisions about blameworthiness, they are likely to be heavily influenced by initial blame hypotheses, especially when these are driven by strong reactions of disapprobation for the actors involved, their behavior, or for the consequences that ensue. Psychologists have tended to view individual blame instances as rational problems to be solved, problems that involve grappling with information about desires, motives, beliefs, causal paths, and the connection among all these with the chain of consequences that behavior sets into motion. We are on board with all this but emphasize that from a functional, evolutionary perspective, blame reflects the standards of conduct by which the group lives and contributes to maintaining order and solidarity. Those who violate the rules and are detected are unlikely to find solace in the fact that genetic and environmental influences contributed to their behavior and may even have fully determined it. When you screw up, *you,* not your genes or your environment, will be blamed and called to account. And for those whose moral functioning is on a par with Alex's in *A Clockwork Orange,* the world's best defense attorney accompanied by a stellar crew of philosophers, psychologists, sociologists, and neuroscientists is unlikely to sway the average juror with impeccable arguments for incompatibilism.

REFERENCES

Alicke, M. D. (1992). Culpable causation. *Journal of Personality and Social Psychology, 63,* 368–378.

Alicke, M. D. (2000). Culpable control and the psychology of blame. *Psychological Bulletin, 126*(4), 556–574.

Alicke, M. D. (2008). Blaming badly. *Journal of Cognition and Culture, 8,* 179–186.

Alicke, M. D., & Davis, T. L. (1989). The role of *a posteriori* victim information in judgments of blame and sanction. *Journal of Experimental Social Psychology, 25,* 362–377.

Alicke, M. D., & Davis, T. L. (1990). Capacity responsibility in social evaluation. *Personality and Social Psychology Bulletin, 16,* 465–474.

Alicke, M. D., Davis, T. L., Buckingham, J. T., & Zell, E. (2008). Culpable control and counterfactual reasoning in the psychology of blame. *Personality and Social Psychology Bulletin, 34,* 1371–1381.

Alicke, M. D., Davis, T. L., & Pezzo, M. V. (1994). *A posteriori* adjustment of *a priori* decision criteria. *Social Cognition, 12,* 281–308.

Alicke, M. D., & Rose, D. (2012). Causal deviance. *Personality and Social Psychology Compass, 6,* 723–725.

Alicke, M. D., Rose, D., & Bloom, D. (2011). Causation, norm violation, and culpable control. *Journal of Philosophy, 108,* 670–696.

Alicke, M. D., & Zell, E. (2009). Social attractiveness and blame. *Journal of Applied Social Psychology, 39,* 2089–2105.

American Psychiatric Association. (2013). *Diagnostic and statistical manual of mental disorders: DSM-5.* Arlington, VA: Author.

Baumeister, R. F. (1999). *Evil: Inside human violence and cruelty.* New York: Freeman.

Boehm, C. (2012). *Moral origins: The evolution of virtue, altruism, and shame.* New York: Basic Books.

Burgess, A. (1962). *A clockwork orange.* New York: Norton.

Clark, C. J., Luguri, J. B., Ditto, P. H., Knobe, J., Shariff, A. F., & Baumeister, R. F. (2014). Free to punish: A motivated account of free will belief. *Journal of Personality and Social Psychology, 106,* 501–513.

Coates, D. J., & Tognazzini, N. A. (Eds.). (2013). *Blame: Its nature and norms.* New York: Oxford University Press.

Fazio, R. H. (1989). On the power and functionality of attitudes: The role of attitude accessibility. In A. R. Pratkanis, S. J. Breckler, & A. G. Greenwald (Eds.), *Attitude structure and function* (pp. 153–179). Hillsdale, NJ: Erlbaum

Franklin, F. E. (2013). Valuing blame. In D. J. Coates & N. A. Tognazzini (Eds.), *Blame: Its nature and norms* (pp. 207–223). New York: Oxford University Press.

Hoffman, M. B. (2014). *The punisher's brain: The evolution of judge and jury.* New York: Cambridge University Press.

Horney, K. (1937). *The neurotic personality of our time.* New York: Norton.

Hume, D. (1978). *A treatise of human nature.* Oxford, UK: Oxford University Press. (Original work published 1739)

Hume, D. (2007). *An enquiry concerning human understanding.* Oxford, UK: Oxford University Press. (Original work published 1748).

Kahneman, D., Knetsch, J. L., & Thaler, R. H. (1986). Fairness and the assumptions of economics. *Journal of Business, 59,* 285–300.

Knobe, J., & Fraser, B. (2008). Causal judgments and moral judgment: Two experiments. In W. Sinnott-Armstrong (Ed.), *Moral psychology: Vol. 2. The cognitive science of morality* (pp. 441–447). Cambridge, MA: MIT Press.

Malle, B. F., Guglielmo, S., & Monroe, A. E. (2014). A theory of blame. *Psychological Inquiry, 25,* 147–186.

McCullough, M. (2008). *Beyond revenge: The evolution of the forgiveness instinct.* New York: Wiley.

McGeer, V. (2013). Civilizing blame. In D. J. Coates & N. A. Tognazzini (Eds.), *Blame: Its nature and norms* (pp. 162–188). New York: Oxford University Press.

Nahmias, E., Morris, S., Nadelhoffer, T., & Turner, J. (2006). Is incompatibilism intuitive? *Philosophy and Phenomenological Research, 73,* 28–53.

Nilsson, H. (1972). You're breaking my heart. On *Son of Smilsson* [CD]. London: RCA.

Pinker, S. (2003). *The blank slate: The modern denial of human nature.* New York: Penguin.

Pizarro, D. A., Uhlmann, E., & Bloom, P. (2003). Causal deviance and the attribution of moral responsibility. *Journal of Experimental Social Psychology, 39,* 653–660.

Rogers, R., Alicke, M. D., Taylor, S. G., Rose, D., Davis, T. L., & Bloom, D. (in preparation). Near hits, (un)lucky strikes, and ascription of intent and blame.

Russell, B. (1957). *Why I am not a Christian: And other essays on religion and related subjects.* New York: Simon & Schuster.

Sarkissian, H., Chatterjee, A., DeBrigard, F., Knobe, J., Nichols, S., & Sirker, S. (2010). Is belief in free will a cultural universal? *Mind and Language, 25,* 346–358.

Shaver, K. G. (1985). *The attribution of blame: Causality, responsibility, and blameworthiness.* New York: Springer-Verlag.

Skinner, B. F., & Hayes, J. (1976). *Walden two.* New York: Macmillan.

Strawson, P. F. (1962). Freedom and resentment. *Proceedings of the British Academy, 48,* 1–25.

Turillo, C. J., Folger, R., Lavelle, J. J., Umphress, E. E., & Gee, J. O. (2002). Is virtue its own reward?: Self-sacrificial decisions for the sake of fairness. *Organizational Behavior and Human Decision Processes, 89,* 839–865.

PART IX
DEVELOPMENTAL AND EVOLUTIONARY ROOTS OF MORALITY

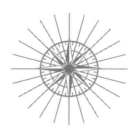

QUESTIONS ANSWERED IN PART IX

CHAPTER 40 Are fairness concerns unique to the human species?

CHAPTER 41 How does the capacity to make moral evaluations develop?

CHAPTER 42 What are the origins of human altruism?

CHAPTER 43 How and when do fairness concerns emerge
over the course of development?

CHAPTER 44 What is the most essential innate psychological mechanism
underlying morality?

CHAPTER 45 What are the rules and patterns guiding the rapid, automatic,
and unconscious processes of moral judgment?

CHAPTER 46 What is the best comprehensive theory
for understanding moral development?

CHAPTER 40

Do Animals Have a Sense of Fairness?

Katherine McAuliffe
Laurie R. Santos

> **Are fairness concerns unique to the human species?**
>
> Recent work on inequity aversion in nonhuman animals demonstrates that other species react to unfairness—at least in some situations; but these new studies also hint that animal fairness concerns may differ in important ways from those of humans.

The Origins of Human Fairness Concerns

One hallmark of human morality is our strong sense of fairness. People sacrifice absolute rewards to ensure that rewards are distributed fairly. Indeed, a large body of work in behavioral economics demonstrates that people are *inequity averse*—we tend to avoid outcomes that lead to unfair distributions of resources (Fehr & Schmidt, 1999). The degree of human inequity aversion sometimes leads our species to seemingly irrational choices: In some cases, people would rather receive nothing than accept an unfair division of resources (Güth, Schmittberger, & Schwarze, 1982; Yamagishi et al., 2009) and are willing to incur costs to ensure that others are treated fairly in third-party situations as well (e.g., Fehr & Fischbacher, 2004). Finally, and perhaps most surprisingly, our species is averse to situations involving inequity even in cases in which we ourselves benefit from the unequal distributions. Adult humans react negatively to cases of *disadvantageous inequity*—in which the individual in question has less of a reward than someone else—as well as cases of *advantageous inequity,* in which the individual in question has more of a reward than another person (Dawes, Fowler, Johnson, McElreath, & Smirnov, 2007; Fehr & Schmidt, 1999; Loewenstein, Thompson, & Bazerman, 1989).

Recent research in developmental psychology has shown that an aversion to inequality may emerge without extensive experience or explicit instruction (for a review, see Blake, McAuliffe, & Warneken, 2014; Sommerville & Ziv, Chapter 43, this volume). By 15 months of age, infants expect other agents to distribute resources equally among other individuals (Geraci & Surian, 2011; Schmidt & Sommerville, 2011; Sloane, Baillargeon, & Premack, 2012). By 4 years of age, children—like their adult counterparts—would rather receive nothing than accept a disadvantageously unfair division of rewards (Blake & McAuliffe, 2011;

McAuliffe, Blake, & Warneken, 2014; Shaw & Olson, 2012). Finally, recent cross-cultural work suggests that fairness concerns appear across human societies, although what constitutes a fair offer varies considerably across cultures (Henrich et al., 2005). The potency, early emergence, and universality of human fairness raises an important question about its origins in the human lineage: Are concepts of what is and is not fair unique to our species, or can we see their roots in other species?

Here, we explore whether our own aversion to unfairness is unique to humans. To examine this issue, we review recent work examining whether nonhuman animals react negatively to unfair outcomes. Studying animals' reactions to unfair reward distributions not only allows us to answer the question of whether fairness is unique to humans but also helps us begin to understand the selective forces that have shaped the human sense of fairness. In this chapter, we first examine the history of work on animal fairness concerns, reviewing over a decade's worth of work on inequity aversion in a number of animal species. We then discuss a framework for making sense of these results. Specifically, we explore whether these findings truly demonstrate human-like inequity aversion. We argue that, although other species react to cases of inequity, other species' responses to apparent unfairness may be supported by mechanisms that are very different from those in humans.

Historical Context: Previous Studies of Inequity Aversion in Animals

The past decade has seen a surge of work testing fairness concerns in nonhuman species (see review in Bräuer & Hanus, 2012; Brosnan, 2006). Specifically, these studies have asked whether any nonhuman animals (hereafter *animals*) show an aversion to unequal payoff distributions. To date, the vast majority of work on inequity aversion in animals has focused on disadvantageously inequitable payoff distributions, as it is likely that this is the kind of unequal situation that animals may find most aversive. In a landmark paper, Brosnan and de Waal (2003) first tested whether animals ex-

hibit fairness concerns. In their now-famous test of inequity aversion, they allowed two brown capuchin monkeys (*Cebus apella*) to trade tokens with a human experimenter for food rewards. The subject monkey always received a low-quality reward (a piece of cucumber) for her reward, but the experimenters varied the reward given to the second partner monkey. In one condition—the *equity condition*—both monkeys received a cucumber as a reward. In the second condition, however—the *inequity condition*—the subject monkey received a cucumber while her partner received a more desirable grape. Brosnan and de Waal (2003) then tested how the subject monkey reacted to these different reward distributions. They found that subject monkeys were less inclined to trade and more likely to reject the cucumber reward in the inequity condition compared with the equity condition. Brosnan and de Waal interpreted these patterns of performance as evidence that capuchin monkeys show sensitivity to unfair pay for equal work and thus that capuchins are averse to reward inequity.

A number of studies have now built on Brosnan and de Waal's (2003) initial test of inequity aversion by investigating inequity aversion in both capuchins and other animals. Although some of these studies have observed inequity aversion effects in capuchins (van Wolkenten, Brosnan, & de Waal, 2007) and other primate species (Brosnan, Schiff, & de Waal, 2005; Hopper, Schapiro, Lambeth, & Brosnan, 2011; Massen, van den Berg, Spruijt, & Sterck, 2012), other studies have failed to find similar levels of inequity aversion, both in capuchins (McAuliffe et al., 2015; Roma, Silberberg, Ruggiero, & Suomi, 2006; Silberberg, Roma, Ruggiero, & Suomi, 2006) and in other primates (Bräuer, Call, & Tomasello, 2006, 2009; McAuliffe, Shelton, & Stone, 2014; Neiworth, Johnson, Whillock, Greenberg, & Brown, 2009). Some of these follow-up studies have offered alternative explanations for the rejections of inequity observed in the original Brosnan and de Waal (2003) task. For instance, a conceptual replication by Roma and colleagues (2006) observed that capuchins were insensitive to what their partners received in an inequity task and instead showed an aversion to cases in which their own food switched from high to low quality. Specifically, they showed that subjects would reject cucumbers if they had received grapes in previous sessions. Based on this finding, Roma and colleagues argued that rejections purported to be due to inequity aversion could instead be due to frustration at having received better rewards in the past. Note that a similar frustration account could also explain Brosnan and de Waal's (2003) inequity aversion results, because monkeys participated as both subjects and partners and thus moved from sessions in which they were receiving grapes to sessions in which they were receiving cucumbers. In a similar vein, Dubreuil, Gentile, and Visalberghi (2006) showed that capuchin monkeys' rejections were not dependent on their partners' rewards but rather on the presence of more preferred, but inaccessible, rewards. Finally, McAuliffe and colleagues (2015) found that capuchins' rejections of both high- and low-quality rewards were very rare overall and were not specific to the conditions in which subjects received unequal rewards for performing the same task.

Although it is hard to perfectly explain the inconsistencies seen in animals' performance on inequity aversion tasks, the crux of the inconsistencies across studies lies in the extent to which inequity aversion occurs specifically in *social* situations. For example, in their original study, Brosnan and de Waal (2003) tested how monkeys would react in a nonsocial version of their original inequity scenario. In this *nonsocial control* condition, the subject monkey received a cucumber for trading his token, but every time he did so a grape was placed into an adjacent empty enclosure. Interestingly, Brosnan and de Waal (2003) found that subject monkeys do show reluctance to trade in this nonsocial condition but report that effects in this condition are still somewhat smaller and less robust over time than the reluctance to trade observed in the inequity condition (see also later analysis in Brosnan & de Waal, 2004). Other investigators, however, have failed to find such a robust difference between social and nonsocial conditions. For example, as discussed above, Dubreuil and colleagues (2006) did not find a difference in the rate of capuchins' rejection of a small reward between a condition in which a second monkey received a higher reward and a control

condition in which the higher reward was merely out of the subjects' reach.

Theoretical Stance: How Social Are Animal Inequity Responses?

Social and Nonsocial Hypotheses for the Evolution of Inequity Aversion

As the above results suggest, there is still some controversy concerning whether primates' reactions to unfair payoff distributions are specifically social phenomena. This issue is important for two reasons. First, human adults and children find inequity more aversive in social compared with nonsocial settings (McAuliffe, Blake, Kim, Wrangham, & Warneken, 2013; Ostojić & Clayton, 2013); if nonhuman animals truly show human-like inequity aversion, we should expect a similar pattern in animals as well as some nonhuman species. Second, the extent to which nonhuman animals show inequity aversion in nonsocial settings bears directly on the two main classes of theoretical explanations that have been proposed to explain why inequity aversion evolved (McAuliffe et al., 2013). In the next section, we review these two different theoretical accounts, examining how each account fits with the available empirical evidence.

The first class of explanations for the evolution of inequity aversion posits that inequity aversion evolved specifically for social situations—it evolved as a means of regulating payoffs from collective action (*social hypothesis*; Brosnan, 2006, 2011). Under this view, inequity aversion evolved to solve the fundamental problem of cooperation—preventing free riders from benefiting from the contributions of others. Under this view, animals might develop negative responses to situations in which conspecifics take more than their fair share (i.e., inequity aversion) of the spoils of collective action, which could then help to solve this free-riding problem.

A second class of theoretical accounts—which we will collectively refer to here as the *nonsocial hypothesis*—explains inequity aversion as a more domain-general phenomenon. Under this account, inequity aversion has nonsocial roots and evolved as part of a more general response for tracking reward distributions (Chen & Santos, 2006). Under this view, the tendency to exhibit aversive responses to receiving a bad deal when better deals are available is beneficial in that it motivates individuals to increase their foraging effort to extract the best possible resources from their environment. Consider, for example, a foraging individual who comes upon a patch of food. Before beginning to forage in this patch, however, the individual sees a better patch of food off in the distance. In this scenario, it would behoove the forager to "reject" its current patch in favor of the more desirable patch. As such, successful animal foragers may have developed psychological mechanisms (e.g., a feeling of "frustration") when they receive rewards that are less than other expected or available rewards. Indeed, numerous findings in comparative cognition suggest that animals experience frustration when they receive a reward that was smaller than the one they expected (e.g., Freidin, Cuello, & Kacelnik, 2009; Santos, Sulkowski, Spaepen, & Hauser, 2002; Tinklepaugh, 1928). Note, however, that such "frustration" responses would have nothing to do with a response to inequity per se but would rather be born of a drive to optimize resource extraction from a given environment.

While the social and the nonsocial hypotheses of inequity aversion differ in their explanations for the emergence of inequity aversion, it is worth noting that the two hypotheses are not entirely mutually exclusive. Indeed, a phenomenon as complex as inequity aversion almost surely involves at least some domain-general mechanisms that are commonly deployed in social interactions. Nevertheless, these two classes of explanations make importantly different predictions about the taxonomic distribution and robustness of inequity aversion. First, if inequity aversion evolved as a means of regulating cooperation, as the social hypothesis argues, then we should only observe inequity aversions in cooperative species. If, on the other hand, inequity aversion is an instantiation of a more generalized mechanism for tracking relative payoff distributions, it should be spread broadly across different taxa. Second, if inequity aversion evolved as a means of stabilizing cooperation, as it is theorized to have done in humans, then

animals should care about equity not just in cases in which they are disadvantaged but also in cases in which they are advantaged; that is, in which they have more than their fair share of a common resource. In contrast to the nonsocial hypothesis, the social hypothesis uniquely predicts that animals—like humans—may show aversion to cases of advantageous inequity as well. In the following sections, we review empirical results for inequity aversion across taxa with the aim of gaining insight into whether one hypothesis is more plausible than the other.

Empirical Evidence for the Social and Nonsocial Hypotheses

Some suggestive support for the social hypothesis comes from studies that have directly compared inequity aversion responses in cooperative versus noncooperative primate species. For example, some research teams have tested inequity aversion responses in both capuchin monkeys—a very cooperative species—and squirrel monkeys (*Saimiri sciureus* and *Saimiri boliviensis*), which are considered to be noncooperative (see Brosnan & de Waal, 2003; Talbot, Freeman, Williams, & Brosnan, 2011). This comparison and others like it (see Brosnan, 2011, for a review) have suggested that cooperative primates tend to show more negative responses to inequity than noncooperative species. Although such findings at first glance hint at a compelling link between cooperation and inequity aversion, they should be interpreted with caution for two reasons. First, although many researchers have studied cooperative species (e.g., Brosnan et al., 2005; Brosnan & de Waal, 2003; Massen et al., 2012; Range, Horn, Viranyi, & Huber, 2009; Wascher & Bugnyar, 2013), relatively few studies have examined inequity aversion in noncooperative species. The distribution of positive evidence for inequity aversion could therefore be an artifact of sampling bias. Second, and perhaps more worryingly, several studies have tested inequity aversion in cooperative primate species and have failed to provide evidence for it (Bräuer et al., 2006; McAuliffe et al., 2015; McAuliffe, Shelton, & Stone, 2014; Neiworth et al., 2009).

In a recent attempt to better understand the link between inequity aversion and co-operation, researchers have begun shifting their focus away from testing primates and toward cooperative species found in other taxonomic groups. Studying inequity aversion in nonprimates has yielded more mixed evidence for the social hypothesis. For example, Range and colleagues (Range et al., 2009; Range, Leitner, & Viranyi, 2012) test-ed whether domestic dogs would show ineq-uity aversion in a task modeled after the ca-puchin inequity paradigm described above. Domestic dogs show extensive intra- and interspecies cooperation and are thought to have evolved from a cooperative wolf-like ancestor. Dogs thus provide an ideal nonpri-mate model in which to investigate whether cooperative species are particularly prone to inequity aversion. Range et al. (2009) allowed dogs to perform a command (give paw) in exchange for a treat. They found that dogs were less willing to give a paw for no reward when their partner was getting a re-ward than when neither individual received a reward. These results were interpreted as evidence that dogs show a rudimentary form of inequity aversion, at least in cases in which a partner receives a reward while the subject receives nothing. Although these and other findings from studies of coopera-tive animals have strengthened the theorized link between inequity aversion and coopera-tion in animals, it is important to note that at least two attempts to induce an inequity aversion effect in dogs have been unsuccess-ful (Horowitz, 2012; McAuliffe, under re-view), suggesting that inequity aversion in dogs may be expressed only under specific conditions.

Providing further suggestive evidence against the social hypothesis are findings showing that inequity aversion is absent in at least one cooperative nonprimate species. Raihani, McAuliffe, Brosnan, and Bshary (2012) tested inequity aversion in coop-erative cleaner fish (*Labroides dimidiatus*). These fish cooperate in male–female pairs to clean client fish. During cleaning interac-tions, cleaners feed against their preference for the protective mucus that covers clients and instead eat the ectoparasites that para-sitize client fish. This feeding dilemma can be simulated in the lab by presenting clean-ers with Plexiglass plates (which simulate cli-ent fish) covered in fish flake (less preferred food, akin to ectoparasites) or prawn (pre-ferred food, akin to client mucus). Raihani and colleagues presented pairs of cleaners with a task that was rewarded with access to a Plexiglass plate, one side of which could be accessed by the subject and the other side by a partner. In equity treatments, the subject performed a task that resulted in an equal payoff for subject and partner. In the inequity cases, the subject performed a task that delivered a more desirable reward to the partner than to the subject. Raihani and colleagues showed that subjects' propensity to perform the task was unaffected by their partner's payoff, suggesting that cleaner fish—despite their extensive intra- and in-terspecies cooperation—are not inequity averse. Thus, when work on dogs and fish is considered together, it is clear that, at least so far, work on cooperative nonprimate spe-cies has not borne out the predictions of the social hypothesis.

Whereas the social hypothesis for the evolution of inequity aversion has garnered weak support at best, the nonsocial hypoth-esis has received indirect support from a number of lines of evidence. For instance, as mentioned above, capuchin monkeys show negative responses both when their partners receive a more favorable reward and when a more favorable reward is placed inacces-sibly (Brosnan & de Waal, 2003). In this way, several researchers have argued that nonsocial domain-general psychological mechanisms such as frustration can explain animals' negative responses in situations of inequity (Hopper et al., 2011; Roma et al., 2006; Silberberg et al., 2006). Moreover, the frustration explanation does not preclude the potentially important effects of social in-formation. Indeed, it is entirely possible that individuals may notice potentially better re-wards in situations in which a conspecific has access to those better rewards compared with cases in which those better rewards are simply present (for a similar effect in humans thinking about their own payoffs, see Solnick & Hemenway, 1998). Under this explanation, stronger frustration effects in social contexts would make sense given that social partners are likely to provide reliable information about what resource payoffs are available in a given environment.

In our view, the current weight of evidence for inequity aversion in animals falls slightly in favor of the nonsocial hypothesis. Inequity aversion responses are not clearly present only in cooperative species, nor are responses to inequity specifically social. We therefore argue that current evidence suggests that apparent disadvantageous inequity aversion in animals most likely relies on domain-general mechanisms for estimating the relative value of different resource distributions. Under this view, animals sometimes respond most strongly to disadvantageous inequity in social settings (e.g., Brosnan & de Waal 2003, 2004) because such cases are more attentionally salient. We therefore contend that inequity aversion has nonsocial roots in animals but has been co-opted for use in the social domain.

Note that this domain-general interpretation of animal inequity aversion sheds important light on the potential origins of inequity aversion and fairness concerns in the human lineage. Based on findings from animals, it would seem reasonable to suspect that disadvantageous inequity aversion has a similarly nonsocial history in our own species but that for some reason—perhaps due to the specific demands of collective action in humans—it became closely linked with cooperation.

What Sets Human Fairness Apart from Animal "Fairness"?

Studies of inequity aversion in animals have suggested that disadvantageous inequity aversion may have nonsocial roots in other species and perhaps even our own species, but clearly the human sense of fairness is a richly social concept. What features of human inequity aversion make it so richly social compared with what we see in animals? In our view, at least three features of human inequity aversion set it apart from inequity aversion in other species. First, when human adults reject inequity, they typically do so to affect others' payoffs and, more specifically, to achieve equality (Dawes et al.,

2007; Güth et al., 1982; McAuliffe, Blake, & Warneken, 2014; but see Yamagishi et al., 2009). By contrast, rejections in the standard animal inequity aversion task have no effect on partners' payoffs (see Henrich, 2004) and, as such, do not create equality. Indeed, a recent study with capuchin monkeys designed to better mirror human inequity aversion tasks showed no evidence for inequity aversion in capuchins and also no evidence that capuchins attempted to create more even payoffs (McAuliffe et al., 2015). This finding suggests that animal rejections of inequity differ substantively from those of humans and raise the intriguing question of why animals are rejecting at all. Second, whereas adults and older children show an aversion to both disadvantageous and advantageous inequity, advantageous inequity aversion is very rare if not entirely absent in animals (Brosnan et al., 2005; Brosnan & de Waal, 2014; Horowitz, 2012; McAuliffe et al., 2015; Sheskin, Ashayeri, Skerry, & Santos, 2014). The prevalence of both forms on inequity aversion in humans supports the idea that inequity aversion is a means of achieving equality in humans, whereas in animals it is a means of avoiding bad deals. Finally, humans care so much about avoiding inequity that they will punish unfair resource allocations in both second-party (Güth et al., 1982; Raihani & McAuliffe, 2012b) and third-party (Fehr & Fischbacher, 2004) contexts. By contrast, in animals, there is little evidence that unfairness motivates punishment (Jensen, Call, & Tomasello, 2007; Raihani & McAuliffe, 2012a; Riedl, Jensen, Call, & Tomasello, 2012).

Conclusion: What Have We Learned from Studies of Inequity Aversion in Animals?

Returning to the question posed in this article's title—Do animals have a sense of fairness?—the answer appears to be a tentative, "not really." At the very least, nonhuman animals do not seem to have what one might want to consider a "human-like" sense of fairness. To date, there is little evidence that animals have a preference for equality per se; instead, animals' performance on so-called inequity aversion tasks appears to be more consistent with a desire to avoid poor payoffs relative to the range of available payoffs. By contrast, humans show a strong preference for equality, sacrificing personal gain to achieve equality from both sides of inequity (Blake & McAuliffe, 2011; Dawes et al., 2007).

Given that animals do not seem to have a human-like sense of fairness, what has the huge amount of work on animal inequity aversion taught us about our own human-like sense of fairness? We argue that work on animal inequity aversion has taught us two important lessons. The first is that some elements of our reactions to distributional inequity are likely deeply rooted in our evolutionary past and, by extension, are most likely innate in humans. Second, based on current evidence, it seems reasonable to suspect that the origins of some aspects of the human sense of fairness are built on generic processes that are generally useful in helping animals navigate their ecological and social environments. Work on animals has also helped focus the direction of future work on understanding why humans, more so than other species, have a preference for equality per se. Answering this question will shed important light on what makes human fairness so unique.

REFERENCES

Blake, P. R., & McAuliffe, K. (2011). I had so much it didn't seem fair: Eight-year-olds reject two forms of inequity. *Cognition, 120*(2), 215–224.

Blake, P. R., McAuliffe, K., & Warneken, F. (2014). The developmental origins of fairness: The knowledge–behavior gap. *Trends in Cognitive Sciences, 18*(11), 559–561.

Bräuer, J., Call, J., & Tomasello, M. (2006). Are apes really inequity averse? *Proceedings of the Royal Society: B. Biological Sciences, 273*(1605), 3123–3128.

Bräuer, J., Call, J., & Tomasello, M. (2009). Are apes inequity averse?: New data on the token-exchange paradigm. *American Journal of Primatology, 71*(2), 175–181.

Bräuer, J., & Hanus, D. (2012). Fairness in nonhuman primates? *Social Justice Research, 25*(3), 256–276.

Brosnan, S. F. (2006). Nonhuman species' reactions to inequity and their implications for fairness. *Social Justice Research, 19*(2), 153–185.

Brosnan, S. F. (2011). A hypothesis of the co-evolution of cooperation and responses to inequity. *Frontiers in Neuroscience, 5*. Available at *www.ncbi.nlm.nih.gov/pmc/articles/PMC3077916*.

Brosnan, S. F., & de Waal, F. (2003). Monkeys reject unequal pay. *Nature, 425*(6955), 297–299.

Brosnan, S. F., & de Waal, F. B. (2004). Animal behaviour: Fair refusal by capuchin monkeys. *Nature, 428*(6979), 140.

Brosnan, S. F., & de Waal, F. B. M. (2014). Evolution of responses to (un)fairness. *Science, 346*(6207), 1251776. Available at *http://science.sciencemag.org/content/346/6207/1251776*.

Brosnan, S. F., Schiff, H. C., & de Waal, F. B. M. (2005). Tolerance for inequity may increase with social closeness in chimpanzees. *Proceedings of the Royal Society: B. Biological Sciences, 272*(1560), 253–258.

Chen, M. K., & Santos, L. R. (2006). Some thoughts on the adaptive function of inequity aversion: An alternative to Brosnan's social hypothesis. *Social Justice Research, 19*(2), 201–207.

Dawes, C. T., Fowler, J. H., Johnson, T., McElreath, R., & Smirnov, O. (2007). Egalitarian motives in humans. *Nature, 446*(7137), 794–796.

Dubreuil, D., Gentile, M. S., & Visalberghi, E. (2006). Are capuchin monkeys (*Cebus apella*) inequity averse? *Proceedings of the Royal Society: B. Biological Sciences, 273*(1591), 1223–1228.

Fehr, E., & Fischbacher, U. (2004). Third-party punishment and social norms. *Evolution and Human Behavior, 25*(2), 63–87.

Fehr, E., & Schmidt, K. M. (1999). A theory of fairness, competition, and cooperation. *Quarterly Journal of Economics, 114*(3), 817–868.

Freidin, E., Cuello, M. I., & Kacelnik, A. (2009). Successive negative contrast in a bird: Starlings' behaviour after unpredictable negative changes in food quality. *Animal Behaviour, 77*(4), 857–865.

Geraci, A., & Surian, L. (2011). The developmental roots of fairness: Infants' reactions to equal and unequal distributions of resources. *Developmental Science, 14*(5), 1012–1020.

Güth, W., Schmittberger, R., & Schwarze, B. (1982). An experimental analysis of ultimatum bargaining. *Journal of Economic Behavior and Organization, 3*(4), 367–388.

Henrich, J. (2004). Animal behaviour: Inequity

aversion in capuchins? *Nature, 428*(6979), 139; discussion 140.

Henrich, J., Boyd, R., Bowles, S., Camerer, C., Fehr, E., Gintis, H., . . . Tracer, D. (2005). "Economic man" in cross-cultural perspective: Behavioral experiments in 15 small-scale societies. *Behavioral and Brain Sciences, 28*(6), 795–815; discussion 815–855.

Hopper, L. M., Schapiro, S. J., Lambeth, S. P., & Brosnan, S. F. (2011). Chimpanzees' socially maintained food preferences indicate both conservatism and conformity. *Animal Behaviour, 81*(6), 1195–1202.

Horowitz, A. (2012). Fair is fine, but more is better: Limits to inequity aversion in the domestic dog. *Social Justice Research, 25*(2), 195–212.

Jensen, K., Call, J., & Tomasello, M. (2007). Chimpanzees are rational maximizers in an ultimatum game. *Science, 318*(5847), 107–109.

Loewenstein, G. F., Thompson, L., & Bazerman, M. H. (1989). Social utility and decision making in interpersonal contexts. *Journal of Personality and Social Psychology, 57*(3), 426–441.

Massen, J. J., van den Berg, L. M., Spruijt, B. M., & Sterck, E. H. (2012). Inequity aversion in relation to effort and relationship quality in long-tailed Macaques (*Macaca fascicularis*). *American Journal of Primatology, 74*(2), 145–156.

McAuliffe, K. (under review). *Inequity aversion in dogs (Canis familiaris) and dingoes (Canis dingo): A test of the domestication hypothesis.* Manuscript submitted for publication.

McAuliffe, K., Blake, P. R., Kim, G., Wrangham, R. W., & Warneken, F. (2013). Social influences on inequity aversion in children. *PLOS ONE, 8*(12), e80966.

McAuliffe, K., Blake, P. R., & Warneken, F. (2014). Children reject inequity out of spite. *Biology Letters, 10*(12). Available at *http://rsbl.royalsocietypublishing.org/content/10/12/20140743.*

McAuliffe, K., Chang, L. W., Leimgruber, K. L., Spaulding, R., Blake, P. R., & Santos, L. R. (2015). Capuchin monkeys, *Cebus apella,* show no evidence for inequity aversion in a costly choice task. *Animal Behaviour, 103*(C), 65–74.

McAuliffe, K., Shelton, N., & Stone, L. (2014). Does effort influence inequity aversion in cotton-top tamarins (*Saguinus oedipus*)? *Animal Cognition, 17*(6), 1289–1301.

Neiworth, J. J., Johnson, E. T., Whillock, K., Greenberg, J., & Brown, V. (2009). Is a sense of inequity an ancestral primate trait?: Testing social inequity in cotton top tamarins (*Saguinus oedipus*). *Journal of Comparative Psychology, 123*(1), 10–17.

Ostojić, L., & Clayton, N. S. (2013). Inequity aversion in human adults: Testing behavioural criteria from comparative cognition. *Animal Cognition, 16*(5), 765–772.

Raihani, N. J., & McAuliffe, K. (2012a). Does inequity aversion motivate punishment?: Cleaner fish as a model system. *Social Justice Research, 25*(2), 213–231.

Raihani, N. J., & McAuliffe, K. (2012b). Human punishment is motivated by inequity aversion, not a desire for reciprocity. *Biology Letters, 8*(5), 802–804.

Raihani, N. J., McAuliffe, K., Brosnan, S. F., & Bshary, R. (2012). Are cleaner fish, *Labroides dimidiatus,* inequity averse? *Animal Behaviour, 84*(3), 665–674.

Range, F., Horn, L., Viranyi, Z., & Huber, L. (2009). The absence of reward induces inequity aversion in dogs. *Proceedings of the National Academy of Sciences of the USA, 106*(1), 340–345.

Range, F., Leitner, K., & Viranyi, Z. (2012). The influence of the relationship and motivation on inequity aversion in dogs. *Social Justice Research, 25*(2), 170–194.

Riedl, K., Jensen, K., Call, J., & Tomasello, M. (2012). No third-party punishment in chimpanzees. *Proceedings of the National Academy of Sciences of the USA, 109*(37), 14824–14829.

Roma, P. G., Silberberg, A., Ruggiero, A. M., & Suomi, S. J. (2006). Capuchin monkeys, inequity aversion, and the frustration effect. *Journal of Comparative Psychology, 120*(1), 67–73.

Santos, L. R., Sulkowski, G. M., Spaepen, G. M., & Hauser, M. D. (2002). Object individuation using property/kind information in rhesus macaques (*Macaca mulatta*). *Cognition, 83*(3), 241–264.

Schmidt, M. F. H., & Sommerville, J. A. (2011). Fairness expectations and altruistic sharing in 15-month-old human infants. *PLOS ONE, 6*(10), 1–7.

Shaw, A., & Olson, K. R. (2012). Children discard a resource to avoid inequity. *Journal of Experimental Psychology: General, 141*(2), 382–395.

Sheskin, M., Ashayeri, K., Skerry, A., & Santos, L. R. (2014). Capuchin monkeys (*Cebus apella*) fail to show inequality aversion in a no-cost situation. *Evolution and Human Behavior, 35*(2), 80–88.

Silberberg, A., Roma, P. G., Ruggiero, A. M., & Suomi, S. J. (2006). On inequity aversion in nonhuman primates. *Journal of Comparative Psychology, 120*(1), 76.

Sloane, S., Baillargeon, R., & Premack, D. (2012). Do infants have a sense of fairness? *Psychological Science, 23*(2), 196–204.

Solnick, S. J., & Hemenway, D. (1998). Is more

always better?: A survey on positional concerns. *Journal of Economic Behavior and Organization, 37*(3), 373–383.

Talbot, C. F., Freeman, H. D., Williams, L. E., & Brosnan, S. F. (2011). Squirrel monkeys' response to inequitable outcomes indicates a behavioural convergence within the primates. *Biology Letters, 7*(5), 680–682.

Tinklepaugh, E. (1928). An experimental study of representative factors in monkeys. *Journal of Comparative Psychology, 13,* 207–224.

van Wolkenten, M., Brosnan, S. F., & de Waal, F. B. M. (2007). Inequity responses of monkeys modified by effort. *Proceedings of the National Academy of Sciences of the USA, 104*(47), 18854–18859.

Wascher, C. A., & Bugnyar, T. (2013). Behavioral responses to inequity in reward distribution and working effort in crows and ravens. *PLOS ONE, 8*(2), e56885.

Yamagishi, T., Horita, Y., Takagishi, H., Shinada, M., Tanida, S., & Cook, K. S. (2009). The private rejection of unfair offers and emotional commitment. *Proceedings of the National Academy of Sciences of the USA 106*(28), 11520–11523.

CHAPTER 41

The Infantile Roots
of Sociomoral Evaluations

Julia W. Van de Vondervoort
J. Kiley Hamlin

How does the capacity to make moral evaluations develop?

The development of morality begins with a sociomoral core, which evolved to sustain large-scale cooperation.

The tendency to evaluate certain people and actions as good, right, and deserving of praise and others as bad, wrong, and deserving of punishment is present in nearly all humans. Although the content of people's moral evaluations (e.g., which specific behaviors are considered morally good and bad) often varies between individuals within and across cultures, all typically developing adults agree that some behaviors are right and some are wrong (Brown, 1991). But when and how does this moral sense develop?

Traditional models of human moral development assert that morality is acquired across development (e.g., Kohlberg, 1969; Piaget, 1932; see Killen & Smetana, 2006, 2014, for reviews). In these models, infants and young children are believed to be either *amoral*, completely lacking a moral sense, or *immoral*, possessing a moral sense that opposes that of adults due to selfishness, egocentrism, or cognitive limitations. Chil-

dren develop a mature moral sense over time as they become increasingly other-focused, experienced, socialized, and cognitively skilled. Prominent models have focused on how children actively learn to distinguish moral concerns from conventional or personal (preference) concerns through parents', teachers', and peers' differential reactions to transgressions within each of these domains (Turiel, 1983; Smetana, 2006) and on how parenting techniques are used to transmit standards of acceptable behavior and how children internalize these values (Grusec & Goodnow, 1994).

Rather than viewing infants as either amoral or immoral, we argue that infants possess an innate sociomoral core, which allows them to evaluate third parties for their morally relevant acts. This core is functional very early in life—as soon as infants are capable of processing the goal-directed actions of agents—and does not require learning or specific experiences to become operational.

Consistent with theories of the evolution of cooperation (see Katz, 2000, for a review), we hypothesize that this core developed to sustain the large-scale cooperation found in human societies, allowing individuals to selectively cooperate only with those likely to cooperate in return.

The Evolution of Cooperative Systems

Although the processes underlying the evolution of cooperation are often debated (Axelrod & Hamilton, 1981; Cosmides & Tooby, 1992; Henrich & Henrich, 2007; Hrdy, 2009; Trivers, 1971), the ubiquitous presence of cooperative efforts in human groups (Brown, 1991) presents a puzzle. Specifically, in order to cooperate, one must be willing to incur costs to oneself to contribute to the success of others; these costs may or may not be reciprocated in the future. Given that reciprocation is uncertain, it is not immediately clear why rational individuals would habitually take on certain costs to cooperate.

One solution to this puzzle is that the benefits of belonging to a cooperative group outweigh the costs of individual cooperative acts. That is, cooperative groups are better able to meet each individual's needs (e.g., to procure food, fight enemies, raise children) and can achieve successes that an individual cannot (e.g., hunt larger game, fight stronger enemies, raise more children). Given the potential benefits of living in cooperative groups, cooperators' willingness to work with, share with, and help others is not so puzzling.

Despite the clear benefits of living in cooperative systems, these systems are vulnerable to individuals who "cheat" the system, receiving all the benefits of others' costly acts but not reciprocating those costs in return. Because cheaters pay no costs, they necessarily outperform cooperators who do, and thus cooperators should eventually be eliminated from the population. The persistence of large-scale cooperation in human societies despite this vulnerability to cheaters raises the question: How do cooperators avoid being taken advantage of? One possibility is that, along with tendencies toward cooperating, humans evolved cognitive capacities

for identifying cooperators and cheaters in their environment and selectively cooperating only with those likely to cooperate in return (e.g., Bull & Rice, 1991). Successful cooperators are those who positively evaluate other cooperators, negatively evaluate noncooperators, and connect these evaluations with appropriate approach and avoidance behaviors. By avoiding cheaters and excluding them from the benefits of group living, the risks associated with noncooperators are mitigated.

Although the inclusion of cooperators and the exclusion of noncooperators reduces the likelihood that costly cooperative acts will not be reciprocated, the complexity of evaluating others' behaviors entails that mistakes are possible: Some cheaters will evade detection. In addition, the possibility of exclusion may not always be sufficient to discourage would-be cheaters. In these cases, the punishment of antisocial behavior acts as an additional discouragement that can sustain cooperative systems, both deterring cheating beforehand and responding to it after the fact (Boyd & Richerson, 1992; Henrich et al. 2006; O'Gorman, Henrich, & Van Vugt, 2009). Adults are willing to incur costs to punish others and even find punishing wrongdoers rewarding (Fehr & Gächter, 2002; de Quervain et al., 2004).

In sum, tendencies to evaluate cooperators and noncooperators, to differentially approach or avoid others based on their likeliness to cooperate, and to punish those who exploit the benefits of a cooperative group may have evolved to sustain large cooperative systems. One way to evaluate the validity of this evolutionary claim is to examine the presence or absence of these tendencies in young humans. Specifically, infants lack the experiences typically thought necessary to engage in sociomoral evaluation, including experiences of being helped or harmed in particular situations, extensive observation of others being helped or harmed, and explicit teaching about which actions are right or wrong. By exploring which (if any) evaluative tenancies develop independently of these experiences, researchers can probe the existence of an innate sociomoral core. To be consistent with the evolutionary claims described above, humans' sociomoral core should be present in infancy, remain intact throughout the lifespan, and constrain how experience and maturation in other domains influences moral development. The research reviewed below provides evidence consistent with the existence of such a core.

Do Infants Possess a Sociomoral Core?

If cooperation and morality did indeed co-evolve, then evolution ought to have endowed us with capacities for identifying and responding to those whose actions would destabilize reciprocal cooperative systems. Specifically, these capacities should relate to behaviors that are relevant to cooperation, such as helping and hindering, giving and taking, and fairness and inequity. As predicted by this evolutionary account, infants appear to understand several aspects of cooperative behaviors. By the end of their first year, infants recognize that intentional agents can work together to achieve a common goal (Henderson & Woodward, 2011), that the experience of being helped and hindered will influence an agent's social preferences (Hamlin, Wynn, & Bloom, 2007; Fawcett & Liszkowski, 2012; Kuhlmeier, Wynn, & Bloom, 2003; see also Lee, Yun, Kim, & Song, 2015), and that valence-matched actions are more similar than actions that share only physical characteristics (e.g., helping and caressing vs. hindering and hitting; Premack & Premack, 1997). Within the second year of life, infants expect that individuals will treat others fairly, dividing resources equally between recipients (Geraci & Surian, 2011; Schmidt & Sommerville, 2011), as long as those individuals are equally meritorious (Sloane, Baillargeon, & Premack, 2012). Together, these results suggest that infants can interpret the morally relevant behaviors of others.

Infants Evaluate Helpers and Hinderers

Perhaps the most direct evidence that infants make sociomoral evaluations comes from studies examining infants' evaluations of "Helpers" and "Hinderers." In these studies, infants are shown one of several distinct puppet shows, in which a Protagonist repeatedly struggles to achieve some goal: to climb a steep hill, to open the lid on a box, or to retrieve a dropped ball (Hamlin & Wynn, 2011; Hamlin et al., 2007; Kuhlmeier et al., 2003; see also Buon et al., 2014; Scola, Holvoet, Arciszewski, & Picard, 2015). Following each unsuccessful attempt, infants see either a Helper facilitate the Protagonist's goal (bumps him up the hill, helps him open the box, returns his ball) or a Hinderer block the Protagonist's goal (bumps him down the hill, slams the box closed, steals the ball away).

After watching alternating helping and hindering events, infants are presented with the Helper and the Hinderer by an experimenter who is unaware of the identity of the agents, and infants' preference for one or the other is determined by which one they spend more time looking at and/or by which one they reach for. By 3 months of age, infants look longer at individuals who have pushed a Protagonist up the hill versus those who pushed him down and look longer at those who gave a Protagonist his ball back versus those who stole it away (Hamlin & Wynn, 2011; Hamlin, Wynn, & Bloom, 2010). This very early preference for Helpers over Hinderers seems to be rooted in a negative evaluation of Hinderers rather than a positive evaluation of Helpers: 3-month-olds look longer toward Helpers than Hinderers and toward neutral puppets than Hinderers, but look equally toward neutral puppets and Helpers (Hamlin et al., 2010). By 4–5 months of age, infants have acquired the ability to make visually guided reaches toward objects (McDonnell, 1975) and selectively reach for Helpers over Hinderers in each of the scenarios described above (Hamlin, 2015; Hamlin & Wynn, 2011; Hamlin et al., 2007; but see Salvadori et al., 2015). Furthermore, unlike 3-month-olds, 6-month-olds engage in both positive and negative social evaluations: They select Helpers over neutral puppets and neutral puppets over Hinderers (Hamlin et al., 2007).

One potential concern is that a preference for Helpers over Hinderers may not be a *social* evaluation at all; perhaps infants are responding based on low-level physical differences between the helping and hindering scenarios (e.g., Scarf, Imuta, Colombo, & Hayne, 2012). This concern can be addressed by demonstrations that infants' preference for Helpers over Hinderers only emerges when the helping and hindering acts are directed toward a certain type of target—specifically, a social agent. Consider that kicking a soccer ball is fundamentally different from kicking a person; though the behavior itself is the same in both cases, ball kicking is not likely to be considered morally relevant, whereas person kicking is. To date, several studies have examined whether infants consider the social status of those targeted by "Helpers" and "Hinderers." First, the studies described above included infants who watched nonsocial versions of the helping and hindering events. In these nonsocial scenarios, Helpers and Hinderers directed their actions toward an inanimate object (an eyeless, motionless object or moving mechanical claw) rather than an animate Protagonist. For example, the "Helper" bumps an eyeless shape up the hill, opens the box with a claw, or rolls the ball back to the claw, and the "Hinderer" puppet bumps the shape down the hill, slams the box closed, or takes the ball and runs offstage. If infants only evaluate the physical characteristics of the actions performed or the end results of the helping and hindering events, then infants should continue to prefer the puppet performing helpful actions in these nonsocial scenarios. Instead, infants do not preferentially look toward or reach for either the "Helper" or the "Hinderer" in any nonsocial condition (Hamlin & Wynn, 2011; Hamlin et al., 2007, 2010). In a second demonstration of the selectivity of infants' evaluations to social targets, a recent study directly examined the distinction as described above, whereby kicking a person is evaluatively worse than kicking a soccer ball. Specifically, this study found that 10-month-olds prefer agents who direct positive behaviors (comforting) toward humans and negative actions (pushing) toward inanimate objects rather than agents who direct negative behaviors toward humans and positive actions toward inanimate objects (Buon et al., 2014). That is, infants' evaluations distinguish individuals whose actions are identical based on which actions were directed toward social others.

Together, these results suggest that cooperative and noncooperative behaviors must be directed toward a social being for infants to form positive or negative evaluations. This is consistent with work suggesting that infants do not attribute goals to nonagents (e.g., Hamlin, Newman, & Wynn, 2009; Mahajan & Woodward, 2009; Meltzoff, 1995) and with the conclusion that evaluations of Helpers and Hinderers are based on their social behaviors rather than on the performance of a specific physical act, the causation of a specific physical outcome, or a specific perceptual feature of the stimuli (see Scarf et al., 2012, and responses by Hamlin, Wynn, & Bloom, 2012; Hamlin, 2015). That said, the evidence provided thus far does not speak to whether infants' preferences are in any sense *moral* evaluations: Infants may simply like those whose actions facilitate others' goals and dislike those whose actions block others' goals, perhaps because they believe those who help others are likely to help them. Indeed, a recent study of the neural correlates of infants' processing of Helping and Hindering events suggests that 6-month-olds' detection of prosociality may be supported by the same processes that support social perception more generally, including the encoding of goal-directed grasping, pointing, and gaze direction (Gredebäck et al., 2015), as opposed to anything specifically moral.

To examine whether infants' prosocial preferences are consistent with moral evaluations, it is critical to determine whether they are sensitive to factors that influence moral judgments in older children and adults. These factors include (among many others) issues such as prosocial and antisocial agents' intentions, their epistemic states, and how the targets of their actions have behaved in the past. In what follows, we provide evidence that infants' evaluations are sensitive to each of these factors.

Infants Consider Intent

When evaluating an individual's action as morally acceptable or unacceptable, adults consider what the individual meant to do, whether or not that individual achieved his or her goal (Cushman, 2008; Malle, 1999; Mikhail, 2007; Young, Cushman, Hauser, & Saxe, 2007). Although the outcome of a person's action does influence adults' moral evaluations (i.e., the case of moral luck; Cushman & Greene, 2012), by considering intentions mature evaluators see past failed attempts, accidents, and other situationally driven outcomes to determine whether an individual possesses an intention to help or to harm.

Although studies using explicit verbal measures have reliably demonstrated that young children focus on outcome rather than intention when making social and moral judgments (e.g., Baird & Astington, 2004; Costanzo, Coie, Grumet, & Farnill, 1973; Cushman, Sheketoff, Wharton, & Carey, 2013; Piaget, 1932), it is possible that age-related changes in responses to verbal tasks are confounded with age-related changes in other domains, masking children's appreciation of the role of intentions in moral evaluations. Indeed, previous studies have demonstrated that by 8–10 months of age infants recognize intentions that go unfulfilled, successfully inferring an agent's attempted, but failed, object-directed goal (e.g., Brandone & Wellman, 2009; Brandone, Horwitz, Aslin, & Wellman, 2014; Hamlin, Hallinan, & Woodward, 2008; Hamlin et al., 2009). Given these results, it seems plausible that infants at the same age could incorporate intention understanding into their sociomoral evaluations.

To determine whether infants' evaluations are sensitive to the intentions of third parties' prosocial and antisocial attempts, we showed infants puppet shows featuring successful and unsuccessful Helpers and Hinderers. Specifically, successful Helpers and Hinderers carried out their intentions to help or hinder the Protagonist in his efforts to open a box (as in Hamlin & Wynn, 2011), whereas failed Helpers and Hinderers were unsuccessful, bringing about outcomes that opposed their intentions. Across various combinations of successful and unsuccessful Helpers and Hinderers, 8-month-olds, but not 5-month-olds, reliably preferred characters with positive intentions regardless of the outcomes they brought about. In contrast, 8-month-olds did not prefer characters that brought about better outcomes when everyone's intentions were the same (Hamlin, 2013). These results suggest that, in contrast to a host of findings with preschool-age children, by 8 months of age infants reliably use intention, rather than outcome, to evaluate others' prosocial and antisocial acts. Several open questions remain, including whether

8-month-olds' evaluations are influenced by outcomes in contexts in which intent is less salient (e.g., accidents; see Le & Hamlin, 2013), and whether infants younger than 8 months could successfully focus on intention in a simpler goal scenario than the one utilized in our studies.

Infants Consider Epistemic States

In addition to considering whether an individual facilitated or blocked an agent's goal, and whether this behavior was performed intentionally, adults' moral evaluations include an appraisal of various other mental states. In doing so, sometimes the same physical action is appropriately viewed as nice, mean, or neither, depending on what the actor was thinking while he or she performed it. For example, the act of giving a gift is typically considered prosocial. However, this evaluation can depend on the gift givers' knowledge of both what the gift is (e.g., whether the box contains a new watch or a large spider) and of what the recipient desires (e.g., whether she prefers watches or exotic pets).

Although the results remain controversial (e.g., Heyes, 2014; Perner & Ruffman, 2005), a growing body of research using various methodologies suggests that infants and toddlers are able to take actors' epistemic states, such as knowledge and belief, into account when interpreting their actions (see Baillargeon, Setoh, Sloane, Jin, & Bian, 2014, for review). In our laboratory we have examined whether infants can also incorporate information about an actor's epistemic state into the evaluation of the actor's social behaviors. In this study, 10-month-olds viewed a scene including three characters: a Protagonist who displayed an unfulfilled goal and two others who observed his failed attempts. First, the Protagonist displayed a preference for one of two toys, each of which was accessible through openings in a high wall. After choosing one toy and not the other four times, doors were inserted into the wall, blocking the Protagonist from reaching either toy. The two other puppets, who had observed the Protagonist's toy choices and so arguably "knew" his preference, then raised each of the doors in alternation. One Lifter allowed the Protagonist to reach the toy he had previously chosen, and the other Lifter allowed the Protagonist to reach the toy he had not previously chosen. When given the choice between the two Lifters, 10-month-olds preferred the Lifter that allowed the Protagonist to reach his preferred toy (Hamlin, Ullman, Tenenbaum, Goodman, & Baker, 2013).

In a second condition, in which the Lifter puppets were offstage during the Protagonist's original object choices and so could not have known which toy he preferred, infants did not prefer either Lifter, despite the fact that one Lifter had (unknowingly) allowed the Protagonist to reach his preferred toy and the other had not (Hamlin et al., 2013). In sum, infants differentially evaluated only characters who knew that they were acting to help or hinder the Protagonist; they did not differentially evaluate those who happened to help or hinder the Protagonist without knowing they were doing so. This pattern of results suggests that infants' evaluations are sensitive to cues regarding who will cooperate in the future rather than who caused positive outcomes.

Infants Consider Previous Behavior

The studies reviewed above demonstrate that infants are likely to approach Helpers and avoid Hinderers and that these tendencies are sensitive to a number of factors critical to identifying when someone is behaving prosocially or antisocially, including intention and epistemic states. That said, not all behaviors that are intentionally and knowingly performed to block others' goals necessarily signal that an individual should be avoided in the future. Indeed, some intentional antisocial behaviors signal that someone is a *good* potential cooperative partner; for example, punishment that is directed toward deserving wrongdoers. Indeed, punishment has been theorized to be critical to stabilizing cooperative systems by reducing the benefits of free riding (e.g., Boyd & Richerson, 1992; O'Gorman et al., 2009); successful cooperators must be both motivated to punish wrongdoers and able to positively evaluate those who punish appropriately.

To examine whether infants consider the context in which an action is performed, we showed infants events in which Helpers and Hinderers interacted with previously prosocial or antisocial Protagonists, who, respectively, deserved either reward or punishment. Over several studies, 4.5-, 8-, and 19-month-olds preferred a character who helped a previously prosocial puppet but preferred a character who hindered a previously antisocial puppet (Hamlin, 2014a; Hamlin, Wynn, Bloom, & Mahajan, 2011). Together, these studies suggest that, rather than simply preferring individuals who intentionally perform prosocial, rather than antisocial, behaviors, infants consider the recipient of the actions and can positively evaluate intentional antisocial behaviors that are directed toward antisocial individuals.

Although positive evaluation of those that direct antisocial behavior toward antisocial individuals is consistent with the claim that infants prefer those that punish wrongdoers, it is not the only possible interpretation. Rather than evaluating an antisocial individual as deserving of punishment, infants may be attracted to the Hinderer of an antisocial other because this behavior reflects a shared (negative) attitude toward that antisocial other. A shared attitude toward the antisocial other may suggest a source of mutual liking and affiliation (as illustrated by the common phrase "the enemy of my enemy is my friend"; e.g., Heider, 1958). In support of this affiliative account, infants also prefer those who hinder individuals that do not share the infant's own food preferences (e.g., Hamlin, Mahajan, Liberman, & Wynn, 2013). Whereas adults can simultaneously dislike an individual's "enemy" because of shared social preferences and disagree that the disliked individual deserves punishment, it is an open question whether infants' dislike of an individual is distinct from their desire to see that individual hindered.

What Does a Preference for Helpers Mean?

We have presented evidence that infants make relatively sophisticated evaluations, preferring those who intentionally and knowingly act to help deserving third parties. Although we take this as suggestive that preverbal infants possess a sociomoral core, some researchers have argued that measurements of infants' preferences (via preferential looking or reaching) are ill suited to provide evidence of infants' higher-order cognition. Proponents of this view claim that, although measures of preference can be used to determine infants' ability to discriminate between objects and explore perceptual processes, the use of preferential looking and reaching paradigms to explore higher-level domains, such as morality, ascribes too rich an interpretation to infants' preferences (Haith, 1998). In line with this perspective, the conclusion that infants make sociomoral evaluations has been questioned (e.g., Scarf et al., 2012; Tafreshi, Thompson, & Racine, 2014).

Preferences for Helpers Are Not Based on Perceptual Cues

Specifically, it has been debated whether infants' preference for helpful rather than unhelpful characters is simply a low-level response to the puppet show stimuli. For example, Scarf and colleagues suggested that infants' preference for Helpers over Hinderers in the hill scenario described above could be due to an association between the "Helper" and the Protagonist's *bouncing* after being pushed up the hill (a positive perceptual event; Scarf et al., 2012). However, when the Protagonist's goal is clear, and his eyes are fixed in the direction of travel, 6- to 11-month-olds prefer the Helper over the Hinderer, regardless of whether the Protagonist bounces when he reaches the top of the hill. In contrast, when the Protagonist's goal is unclear, and his eyes are not fixed in the direction of travel, infants show no preference for Helpers over Hinderers, even when the Protagonist bounces at the top of the hill (Hamlin, 2015). These results suggest that a preference for Helpers is not dependent on low-level perceptual cues but rather due to infants' sensitivity to whether an individual's goal is being facilitated or blocked. These results, combined with infants' sensitivities to whether a behavior targets a social agent, whether an action is performed intentionally and with appropriate mental state information, and whether helping or hindering events target previously prosocial or antisocial individuals, suggest that infants' preferences are both evaluative and consistent with a sociomoral core (for further discussion regarding how preferential looking and reaching can be used to explore early competencies in the social and moral domains, see Hamlin, 2014b).

Preferences for Helpers Are Not Only Evident in Looking and Reaching

In addition, the extent to which preferential looking and reaching paradigms are able to distinguish between preferences based on simple discrimination (the traditional use of the paradigm) and preferences based on positive evaluations has been questioned (Tafreshi, et al., 2014). The claim that an innate sociomoral core supports infants' early emerging capacities to identify and selectively approach Helpers necessitates that infants' preferences be based on positive evaluations of cooperative individuals. One way to explore whether infants' preferences are evaluative is to examine the continuity between the evaluations made in infancy and moral judgments and behaviors across the lifespan. To the extent that infants positively evaluate Helpers, there should be continuity between early evaluations and later behaviors both across children (e.g., the same scenarios should inspire similar judgments and behaviors over development) and on an individual level (e.g., infants who were better at distinguishing prosocial from antisocial others in infancy should be better at other aspects of sociomoral development later in life).

To explore the first prediction, we have explored the continuity between infants' preferences following unfulfilled goal scenarios and toddlers' more complex behavioral reactions to the same individuals. Previous work has shown that 19- to 23-month-olds will selectively give "treats" to Helpers over Hinderers and selectively take "treats" from Hinderers versus Helpers in the box and ball scenarios described above (Hamlin et al., 2011). Further, when puppets' toy preferences are known, 20-month-olds are more likely to give preferred toys to Helpers than to Hinderers, and are more likely to withhold toys from Hinderers rather than Helpers (Van de Vondervoort, Aknin, Kushnir, Slevinsky, & Hamlin, in press). We have also explored 3- to 5-year-olds' responses to helping and hindering scenarios previously shown to infants, and found that preschoolers preferred the Helper, judged the Helper to be "nicer" than the Hinderer, selectively allocated punishment to the Hinderer, and were able to justify their punishment allocations (Van de Vondervoort & Hamlin, 2017). Continuity between infants' preferences for Helpers, toddlers' positive behaviors toward Helpers, and children's positive verbal evaluations of Helpers suggests that preferences at each age do in fact reflect positive evaluations.

The second prediction is being explored in an ongoing project that looks at individual differences among infants' preferences for Helpers versus Hinderers. Although the vast majority of infants prefer helpful characters over unhelpful characters across numerous types of scenarios, there is variation in infants' responding. We are currently exploring whether differences in infants' preferences for Helpers or for Hinderers relates to their sociomoral functioning in early childhood. Parents of now preschool-age children who participated in several studies during infancy are being asked to complete assessments used to identify early warning signs for various social developmental disorders, in particular, those involving deficits in understanding, evaluating, and otherwise behaving appropriately in the sociomoral world (Tan, Mikami, & Hamlin, 2017). Evidence that infants who consistently prefer cooperative characters exhibit greater social and moral competency than infants who consistently prefer uncooperative characters would further support the conclusion that infants' preferences are truly evaluative and critical to social developmental functioning.

Preferences for Helpers Might Reflect Moral Evaluation

In addition to concerns regarding the use of preferential looking and reaching paradigms to measure infants' social evaluations, there has also been debate regarding whether infants' preference for helpful actions can be interpreted as a preference for *moral* behavior (Tafreshi et al., 2014). Specifically, the claim that infants possess a sociomoral core necessitates that infants are concerned with an *objective* moral system. That is, infants' preference for Helpers over Hinderers ought to be due to the increased likelihood that Helpers will contribute to the cooperative system rather than a preference for those who infants see as more likely to help them specifically. An expectation that Helpers will treat the infant well is not equivalent to a sense of what is moral, as an infant concerned with morality will prefer those that act morally even when this conflicts with the infant's own self-interest.

To explore whether infants prefer moral characters over those that act to benefit the infant, an ongoing study in our laboratory asks infants to choose between two characters: one that provides an equal number of resources to the baby and a third character and one that provides more resources to the infant than to the third character (Tan, Woo, & Hamlin, 2017). The extent to which infants prefer the fair distributor over the distributor that benefits the infant will speak to the likelihood that infants' preference for Helpers is related to morality per se, rather than a simple ability to identify those likely to help them.

One final caveat is that providing evidence that infants can make some moral evaluations should in no way be taken to undermine the roles of development, maturation, and experience on moral development. It is not our intention to argue that infants are sensitive to all or even many of the wide variety of factors that adults consider when making moral judgments. Rather, we appreciate the role of maturing cognitive abilities (such as executive functioning, problem solving, counterfactual reasoning), interactions with parents and peers, and socialization within the family and wider community in the development of a mature moral system (see Killen & Smetana, 2006, 2014, for reviews). In contrast with these views, however, we argue that infants do not start as entirely amoral or immoral beings. Rather, infants have been endowed with a sociomoral sense that supports early evaluations of cooperative and noncooperative others, and that (at least somewhat) shapes the influence of various other developmental processes on moral development.

Conclusion

In sum, recent developmental research supports the claim that infants possess a sociomoral core. From extremely early in life, infants make morally relevant evaluations that are nuanced, context dependent, and consistent with adults' reasoned moral judgments. This research supports the claim that morality and cooperation coevolved and suggests that morality is a core aspect of human nature. Future research should explore how this innate sociomoral core constrains the influence of experience and other developmental mechanisms across moral development and in what ways infants' evaluations differ from an adult moral sense.

REFERENCES

Axelrod, R., & Hamilton, W. D. (1981). The evolution of cooperation. *Science, 211,* 1390–1396.

Baillargeon, R., Setoh, P., Sloane, S., Jin, K., & Bian, L. (2014). Infant social cognition: Psychological and sociomoral reasoning. In M. S. Gazzaniga & G. R. Mangun (Eds.), *The cognitive neurosciences* (5th ed., pp. 7–14). Cambridge, MA: MIT Press.

Baird, J. A., & Astington, J. W. (2004). The role of mental state understanding in the development of moral cognition and moral action. *New Directions for Child and Adolescent Development, 103,* 37–49.

Boyd, R., & Richerson, P. J. (1992). Punishment allows the evolution of cooperation (or anything else) in sizable groups. *Ethology and Sociobiology, 13*(3), 171–195.

Brandone, A. C., Horwitz, S., Aslin, R. N., & Wellman, H. M. (2014). Infants' goal anticipation during failed and successful reaching actions. *Developmental Science, 17*(1), 23–34.

Brandone, A. C., & Wellman, H. M. (2009). You can't always get what you want: Infants understand failed goal-directed actions. *Psychological Science, 20*(1), 85–91.

Brown, D. E. (1991). *Human universals.* New York: McGraw-Hill.

Bull, J. J., & Rice, W. R. (1991). Distinguishing mechanisms for the evolution of co-operation. *Journal of Theoretical Biology, 149*(1), 63–74.

Buon, M., Jacob, P., Margules, S., Brunet, I., Dutat, M., Cabrol, D., & Dupoux, E. (2014). Friend or foe?: Early social evaluation of human interactions. *PLOS ONE, 9*(2), e88612.

Cosmides, L., & Tooby, J. (1992). Cognitive adaptations for social exchange. In J. Barkow, L. Cosmides, & J. Tooby (Eds.), *The adapted mind: Evolutionary psychology and the generation of culture* (pp. 163–228). New York: Oxford University Press.

Costanzo, P. R., Coie, J. D., Grumet, J. F., & Farnill, D. (1973). A reexamination of the effects of intent and consequence on children's moral judgments. *Child Development, 44*(1), 154–161.

Cushman, F. (2008). Crime and punishment: Distinguishing the roles of causal and intentional analyses in moral judgment. *Cognition, 108,* 353–380.

Cushman, F., & Greene J. D. (2012). Finding faults: How moral dilemmas illuminate cognitive structure. *Social Neuroscience, 7*(3), 269–279.

Cushman, F., Sheketoff, R., Wharton, S., & Carey, S. (2013). The development of intent-based moral judgment. *Cognition, 127*(1), 6–21.

de Quervain, D. J. F., Fischbacher, U., Treyer, V., Schellhammer, M., Schnyder, U., Buck, A., & Fehr, E. (2004). The neural basis of altruistic punishment. *Science, 305*(5688), 1254–1258.

Fawcett, C., & Liszkowski, U. (2012). Infants anticipate others' social preferences. *Infant and Child Development, 21*(3), 239–249.

Fehr, E., & Gächter, S. (2002). Altruistic punishment in humans. *Nature, 415,* 137–140.

Geraci, A., & Surian, L. (2011). The developmental roots of fairness: Infants' reactions to equal and unequal distributions of resources. *Developmental Science, 14*(5), 1012–1020.

Gredebäck, C., Kaduk, K., Bakker, M., Gottwald, J., Ekberg, T., Elsner, C., . . . Kenward, B. (2015). The neuropsychology of infants' pro-social preferences. *Developmental Cognitive Neuroscience, 12,* 106–113.

Grusec, J. E., & Goodnow, J. J. (1994). Impact of parental discipline methods on the child's internalization of values: A reconceptualization of current points of view. *Developmental Psychology, 30*(1), 4–19.

Haith, M. M. (1998). Who put the cog in infant cognition?: Is rich interpretation too costly? *Infant Behavior and Development, 21*(2), 167–179.

Hamlin, J. K. (2013). Failed attempts to help and harm: Intention versus outcome in preverbal infants' social evaluations. *Cognition, 128*(3), 451–474.

Hamlin, J. K. (2014a). Context-dependent social evaluation in 4.5-month-old human infants: The role of domain-general versus domain-specific processes in the development of evaluation. *Frontiers in Psychology, 5,* 614. Available at *www.ncbi.nlm.nih.gov/pmc/articles/PMC4061491*.

Hamlin, J. K. (2014b). The conceptual and empirical case for social evaluation in infancy: Commentary on Tafreshi, Thompson, and Racine. *Human Development, 57,* 250–258.

Hamlin, J. K. (2015). The case for social evaluation in preverbal infants: Gazing toward one's goal drives infants' preferences for Helpers over Hinderers in the hill paradigm. *Frontiers in Psychology, 5,* 1563.

Hamlin, J. K., Hallinan, E. V., & Woodward, A. L. (2008). Do as I do: 7-month-old infants selectively reproduce others' goals. *Developmental Science, 11*(4), 487–494.

Hamlin, J. K., Mahajan, N., Liberman, Z., & Wynn, K. (2013). Not like me = bad: Infants prefer those who harm dissimilar others. *Psychological Science, 24*(4), 589–594.

Hamlin, J. K., Newman, G., & Wynn, K. (2009). 8-month-olds infer unfulfilled goals, despite contrary physical evidence. *Infancy, 14*(5), 579–590.

Hamlin, J. K., Ullman, T., Tenenbaum, J., Goodman, N., & Baker, C. (2013). The mentalistic basis of core social cognition: Experiments in preverbal infants and a computational model. *Developmental Science, 16*(2), 209–226.

Hamlin, J. K., & Wynn, K. (2011). Young infants prefer prosocial to antisocial others. *Cognitive Development, 26*(1), 30–39.

Hamlin, J. K., Wynn, K., & Bloom, P. (2007). Social evaluation by preverbal infants. *Nature, 450*(7169), 557–559.

Hamlin, J. K., Wynn, K., & Bloom, P. (2010). Three-month-olds show a negativity bias in their social evaluations. *Developmental Science, 13*(6), 923–929.

Hamlin, J. K., Wynn, K., & Bloom, P. (2012). Reply to Scarf et al.: Nuanced social evaluation: Association doesn't compute. *Proceedings of the National Academy of Sciences of the USA, 109*(22), E1427.

Hamlin, J. K., Wynn, K., Bloom, P., & Mahajan, N. (2011). How infants and toddlers react to antisocial others. *Proceedings of the National Academy of Sciences of the USA, 108*(5), 19931–19936.

Heider, F. (1958). *The psychology of interpersonal relations.* New York: Wiley.

Henderson, A. M. E., & Woodward, A. L. (2011). "Let's work together": What do infants understand about collaborative goals? *Cognition, 121,* 12–21.

Henrich, J., McElreath, R., Barr, A., Ensminger, J., Barrett, C., Bolyanatz, A., . . . Ziker, J. (2006). Costly punishment across human societies. *Science, 312,* 1767–1770.

Henrich, N., & Henrich, J. (2007). *Why humans cooperate: A cultural and evolutionary explanation.* Oxford, UK: Oxford University Press.

Heyes, C. (2014). False belief in infancy: A fresh look. *Developmental Science, 17*(5), 647–659.

Hrdy, S. B. (2009). *Mothers and others: The evolutionary origins of mutual understanding.* Cambridge, MA: Harvard University Press.

Katz, L. D. (Ed.). (2000). *Evolutionary origins of morality: Cross-disciplinary perspectives.* Bowling Green, OH: Imprint Academic.

Killen, M., & Smetana, J. (Eds.). (2006). *Handbook of moral development.* Mahwah, NJ: Erlbaum.

Killen, M., & Smetana, J. (Eds.). (2014). *Handbook of moral development* (2nd ed.). New York: Psychology Press.

Kohlberg, L. (1969). *Stages in the development of moral thought and action.* New York: Holt, Rinehart, & Winston.

Kuhlmeier, V., Wynn, K., & Bloom, P. (2003). Attribution of dispositional states by 12-month-olds. *Psychological Science, 14*(5), 402–408.

Le, D. T., & Hamlin, J. K. (2013, April). *Ten-month-olds' evaluations of accidental and intentional actions.* Poster presented at the biannual meeting for the Society for Research in Child Development, Seattle, WA.

Lee, Y., Yun, J., Kim, E., & Song, H. (2015). The development of infants' sensitivity to behavioral intentions when inferring others' social preferences. *PLOS ONE, 10*(9), e0135588.

Mahajan, N., & Woodward, A. (2009). Seven-month-old infants selectively reproduce the goals of animate but not inanimate agents. *Infancy, 14*(6), 667–679.

Malle, B. F. (1999). How people explain behavior: A new theoretical framework. *Personality and Social Psychology Review, 3*(1), 23–48.

McDonnell, P. M. (1975). The development of visually guided reaching. *Perception and Psychophysics, 18*(3), 181–185.

Meltzoff, A. N. (1995). Understanding the intentions of others: Re-enactment of intended acts by 18-month-old children. *Developmental Psychology, 31*(5), 838–850.

Mikhail, J. (2007). Universal moral grammar: Theory, evidence and the future. *Trends in Cognitive Sciences, 11*(4), 143–152.

O'Gorman, R., Henrich, J., & Van Vugt, M. (2009). Constraining free riding in public goods games: Designated solitary punishers can sustain human cooperation. *Proceedings of the Royal Society of London: Series B, 276*(1655), 323–329.

Perner, J., & Ruffman, T. (2005). Infants' insight into the mind: How deep? *Science, 308*(5719), 214–216.

Piaget, J. (1932). *The moral judgment of the child*. London: Kegan Paul, Trench, Trubner.

Premack, D., & Premack, A. J. (1997). Infants attribute value ± to the goal-directed actions of self-propelled objects. *Journal of Cognitive Neuroscience, 9*(6), 848–856.

Salvadori, E., Blazsekova, T., Volein, A., Karap, Z., Tatone, D., Mascaro, O., & Csibra, G. (2015). Probing the strength of infants' preference for Helpers over Hinderers: Two replication attempts of Hamlin and Wynn (2011). *PLOS ONE, 10*(11), e0140570.

Scarf, D., Imuta, K., Colombo, M., & Hayne, H. (2012). Social evaluation or simple association?: Simple associations may explain moral reasoning in infants. *PLOS ONE, 7*(8), e42698.

Schmidt, M. F. H., & Sommerville, J. A. (2011). Fairness expectation and altruistic sharing in 15-month-old human infants. *PLOS ONE, 6*(10), e23223.

Scola, C., Holvoet, C., Arciszewski, T., & Picard, D. (2015). Further evidence for infants' preference for prosocial over antisocial behaviors. *Infancy, 20*(6), 684–692.

Sloane, S., Baillargeon, R., & Premack, D. (2012). Do infants have a sense of fairness? *Psychological Science, 23*(2), 196–204.

Smetana, J. G. (2006). Social-cognitive domain theory: Consistencies and variations in children's moral and social judgments. In M. Killen, & J. G. Smetana (Eds.), *Handbook of moral development* (pp. 119–154). Mahwah, NJ: Erlbaum.

Tafreshi, D., Thompson, J. J., & Racine, T. P. (2014). An analysis of the conceptual foundations of the infant preferential looking paradigm. *Human Development, 57*, 222–240.

Tan, E., Mikami, A. Y., & Hamlin, J. K. (2017). *Performance on infant sociomoral evaluation and action studies predicts preschool social and behavioural adjustment in males*. Unpublished manuscript, University of British Columbia, Vancouver, Canada.

Tan, E., Woo, B. M., & Hamlin, J. K. (2017). *Unfair to whom?: Exploration of infants' preferences for fair versus self-benefiting others*. Unpublished manuscript.

Trivers, R. L. (1971). The evolution of reciprocal altruism. *Quarterly Review of Biology, 46*(1), 35–57.

Turiel, E. (1983). *The development of social knowledge: Morality and convention*. Cambridge, UK: Cambridge University Press.

Van de Vondervoort, J. W., Aknin, L. B., Kushnir, T., Slevinsky, J., & Hamlin, J. K. (in press). Selectivity in toddlers' behavioral and emotional reactions to prosocial and antisocial others. *Developmental Psychology*.

Van de Vondervoort, J. W., & Hamlin, J. K. (2017). Preschoolers' social and moral judgments of third party helpers and hinderers align with infants' social evaluations. *Journal of Experimental Child Psychology, 164*, 136–151.

Young, L., Cushman, F., Hauser, M., & Saxe, R. (2007). The neural basis of the interaction between theory of mind and moral judgment. *Proceedings of the National Academy of Sciences of the USA, 104*(20), 8235–8240.

CHAPTER 42

Atlas Hugged
The Foundations of Human Altruism

Felix Warneken

What are the origins of human altruism?

Evidence from young children and chimpanzees suggests that human altruism is based upon psychological processes that have deep roots in development and evolution, with human-unique social practices building upon these basic tendencies.

Notwithstanding Ayn Rand's embrace of self-interested behavior as a virtue, most people think they have some obligation to help others in need; pure egoism is not often celebrated outside such philosophical treatises. But what is the foundation of our more altruistic orientations toward others? One hypothesis is that altruistic behavior in adults emerges because individuals learn social norms about how to act. This proposal would suggest that young children have a fundamentally "Randian" orientation toward their interactions with others but overcome this inherent selfishness by internalizing social standards. An alternative view is that humans actually do possess moral sentiments to act on behalf of others, even independent of such social teachings. That is, this view suggests that human altruism does not depend on external social norms

alone. Here I propose that one powerful way to illuminate the foundations of human nature is to examine the psychology of young children.

If we looked only at the mature behaviors of adults, we would not be able to ascertain the critical factors that give rise to our altruistic (and selfish) behaviors. However, if we assess the earliest forms of social behaviors in children and trace their development, we get a better handle on the factors that are actually foundational and learn how an individual's tendencies and societal factors interact. Therefore, one main goal here is to review recent studies on altruistic behaviors in young children. In addition, I suggest that, to learn something about humans, we also have to look at nonhumans. Specifically, by comparing our behaviors with those of our closest evolutionary relatives—chimpanzees—we can gain insight into the degree to which human society is actually foundational for our altruistic behaviors or if they are rooted in our phylogenetic inheritance.

Here I argue against the hypothesis that regards the internalization of social norms as the condition sine qua non of human altruistic behaviors. In psychology, in several variations, it has been proposed that socialization practices such as norm internalization, social modeling, and rewarding children for appropriate behaviors are at the center of altruism (Bar-Tal, 1982; Chudek & Henrich, 2011; Dahl, 2015; Dovidio, Piliavin, Schroeder, & Penner, 2006). By contrast, I want to advance the hypothesis that the basic altruistic tendencies of humans are grounded in a biological predisposition that can be shaped by socialization and other factors. Thus, although socialization can shape development, the foundation of human altruism has deeper roots.

To evaluate these different hypotheses, I summarize studies on children's helping behaviors. Briefly put, these studies show that humans act altruistically from a very early age, before specific socialization factors such as the internalization of cultural norms could have had a major impact on children's development. Moreover, I present evidence that chimpanzees also act helpfully toward others on occasion—raising the possibility that humans are perhaps not as special in their psychology as one might think.

Evidence

Helping in Children

A good test case for the study of early altruism is helping behaviors. To help someone with a problem, the helper must be able to cognitively represent the goal another person is trying but failing to achieve and have a motivation to act upon that realization. We regard this helping behavior as altruistically motivated if children act to further the other person's goal rather than to gain a concrete benefit for themselves. Recent studies show that children exhibit helping behaviors from early on in life.

A series of studies have probed children's cognitive sophistication in identifying un-

fulfilled goals and finding ways to help. In these experiments, situations are created in which a person needs help and the child has the opportunity to intervene. For example, results show that when 18-month-olds witness someone unsuccessfully reaching for a dropped object, they will get up and pick it up for the other person. Likewise, when an adult is awkwardly bumping into the doors of a cabinet while carrying a stack of books in both hands, the children will hold the door open (Dunfield & Kuhlmeier, 2013; Dunfield, Kuhlmeier, O'Connell, & Kelley, 2011; Warneken & Tomasello, 2006, 2007). Importantly, toddlers help quite flexibly by retrieving out-of-reach objects, opening closed doors, stacking objects, and even correcting an adult's path of action: Rather than using the experimenter's wrong approach to try to squeeze his hand through a tiny hole in order to retrieve an object from a box, children lifted a flap on the side to get to the object. Fourteen-month-olds already help with the simpler tasks of handing over objects (Warneken & Tomasello, 2007), and, by 18 months, children can help in a whole array of situations in which they have to infer the other person's goal and come up with various ways of how to help (Warneken & Tomasello, 2006). Thus young children rapidly develop the ability to help in a variety of ways.

Eighteen-month-olds show even more sophistication by assessing a person's ignorance when helping. When an adult did not see that a toy had moved from one box to another box, children disregarded the box the person was trying to open and fetched the object from the correct location (Buttelmann, Carpenter, & Tomasello, 2009). This type of response may even be subserved by a representation of false beliefs. In another situation, children warned a protagonist before she reached into one of two buckets when the one she falsely believed contained a desired object actually held a yucky object; but they pointed indiscriminately when she was ignorant (Knudsen & Liszkowski, 2012a, 2012b, 2013). Children seemed to infer that when an adult holds a false belief, the adult is likely to take the wrong course of action and has to be warned beforehand. Together, these studies indicate that children actually try to help other people with the intended goals (and not just blindly join into the adult's activity) and are able to infer these goals based upon the other person's state of knowledge.

With increasing age, toddlers become able to make the right inference based upon more subtle cues. Children at 14–18 months typically help only after a salient cue, such as a person reaching for an object or directly asking the child for help (Svetlova, Nichols, & Brownell, 2009; Warneken & Tomasello, 2007). However, 2-year-olds can help even when such behavioral cues are absent altogether. For example, they helped by returning cans to a person who had not noticed that they had rolled off a table and thus did not provide any cues that she needed help (as compared with a control condition in which no help was necessary; Warneken, 2013). Thus children could help even though concurrent cues to elicit helping were absent, demonstrating that they could use situational cues to infer what to do.

Young children thus show some level of cognitive sophistication. They know when and how to help. But what exactly motivates their helping? One potential explanation is that they want to please their parents or other authority figures (rather than caring about the person needing help). However, children help spontaneously in the parents' absence, proving that they do not help just because of obedience to parental authority or the expectation of praise (Warneken, 2013; Warneken & Tomasello, 2013). Moreover, being watched by others versus acting in private does not seem to concern children before around 5 years of age, showing that reputational concerns are not foundational for their altruism, either (Engelmann, Herrmann, & Tomasello, 2012; Leimgruber, Shaw, Santos, & Olson, 2012). Thus children seem to be genuinely motivated by the other person's goal, not by showing off or demonstrating their mastery in handling the situation in front of others. Further evidence comes from a study that used changes in pupil dilation to measure children's arousal during helping scenarios. Two-year-olds remained aroused when they witnessed a person failing to reach an object but were relieved when the person received

help and attained the goal (Hepach, Vaish, & Tomasello, 2012). Importantly, this relief occurred whether they helped or some other bystander helped out, indicating that the relevant feature was that the other person achieved the goal, not the child's own activity of helping.

Another possible explanation is that children help to obtain a tangible reward. However, this doesn't seem to drive children's helping, either: In most studies, no concrete rewards are used, and children still help. Moreover, children who were offered a reward for helping were not more likely to help than children who helped without a reward (Warneken, Hare, Melis, Hanus, & Tomasello, 2007). In fact, material rewards can have detrimental effects, as children who received a toy for helping were subsequently less likely to help spontaneously than children who had never been "paid" (Warneken & Tomasello, 2008). This indicates that external rewards can undermine children's intrinsic motivation for helping.

Finally, this evidence for helping in early ontogeny makes it implausible that helping requires an adult-like moral value system, as preverbal infants are unlikely to be motivated by normative principles. In fact, it is only in middle to late childhood that children begin to reason about social norms as obligatory. During this period of development, children perceive failures to follow such norms as guilt-evoking (Tomasello & Vaish, 2013), develop a moral self (Kochanska, 2002), and hold themselves and others to the same general standards (Blake, McAuliffe, & Warneken, 2014; Smith, Blake, & Harris, 2013). Therefore, returning to the question about the foundation of human altruism, these studies suggest that young children may have a predisposition for altruistic behavior that is not based upon socialization factors alone, such as reputational concerns about social expectations, a long history of being rewarded for helping, or the internalization of a moral value system. These factors that are known to be relevant for adults (and have been proposed to underlie the emergence of altruistic behavior in children) do not appear to be necessary for the basic altruistic helping behaviors of young children.

Before arriving at the conclusion that socialization alone cannot explain early helping behavior, we have to assess an alternative possibility. Although these particular socialization practices are unlikely to be foundational, toddlers still have several months to be socialized into altruism by other means. Indeed, adults may care so much about turning their (allegedly) selfish children into altruists that children may be on a fast track toward altruism. For example, children grow up in a rich social environment in which they witness and engage in various cooperative activities and may be encouraged to repeat socially desirable behaviors. Experiments show that children's positive interactions and affiliative cues prime children to be more helpful later (Barragan & Dweck, 2014; Carpenter, Uebel, & Tomasello, 2013; Cirelli, Einarson, & Trainor, 2014; Cirelli, Wan, & Trainor, 2014; Hamann, Warneken, & Tomasello, 2012; Kirschner & Tomasello, 2010; Over & Carpenter, 2009). Moreover, the activities children participate in at home are correlated with helping in the lab, and parental discourse about other people's needs and emotions is associated with more helping (Brownell, Svetlova, Anderson, Nichols, & Drummond, 2013; Dahl, 2015; Hammond & Carpendale, 2015). However, the importance of these factors in the initial *emergence* of altruism, as opposed to its subsequent refinement, is difficult to assess from human data alone. Studies with chimpanzees can help in this case. Although social transmission of some group-typical behavior may occur in some domains, such as tool use (Whiten, McGuigan, Marshall-Pescini, & Hopper, 2009), there is currently no indication that chimpanzees transmit cultural norms about appropriate social behavior or actively reward their offspring for social behaviors toward others. Thus studies with chimpanzees can inform us about whether these types of socialization factors are actually necessary for helping behaviors to emerge in the first place.

Helping in Chimpanzees

Recent experiments have tested chimpanzees in situations similar to the helping tasks with children described above. These experiments reveal that chimpanzees also possess basic capacities for helping. For example, chimpanzees helped a caregiver pick up dropped objects without a direct request and without receiving a reward (Warneken & Tomasello, 2006). Moreover, chimpanzees helped an unfamiliar human without any prior personal history in a similar context (Warneken et al., 2007). Chimpanzees also help other chimpanzees by handing over out-of-reach objects (Yamamoto, Humle, & Tanaka, 2009; Yamamoto, Humle, & Tanaka, 2012). Chimpanzees do not simply hand over any old object but seem to know how to help. When a conspecific needed a specific tool to retrieve rewards from an apparatus, chimpanzee subjects handed over the appropriate tool from a set of potential options (Yamamoto et al., 2012). Chimpanzees, not unlike 18-month-olds, are also capable of helping others in a variety of different ways, such as opening a door for a conspecific who is trying to access a piece of food in a neighboring room (Melis, Hare, & Tomasello, 2008; Warneken et al., 2007; for bonobos, see Tan & Hare, 2013). Moreover, when a conspecific struggled to pull in a bag with treats because the rope was attached to bars with a hook, chimpanzees unhooked the rope so that the other could pull it in (Melis et al., 2011). Importantly, in all of these studies, chimpanzees performed these acts selectively in experimental conditions in which help was needed, but they rarely performed these acts in matched control conditions in which the behavior would not have been helpful. Hence, chimpanzees can make inferences about the other individual's goal and help across various situations much like human toddlers. Importantly, some of these situations are novel, ruling out that their helping was simply shaped by previous experience.

Concerning apes' motivation to help, evidence suggests that they too are motivated by the other individual's goal, rather than an immediate benefit for themselves. Chimpanzees offered help without receiving concrete rewards (Greenberg, Hamann, Warneken, & Tomasello, 2010; House, Silk, Lambeth, & Schapiro, 2014; Melis et al., 2008; Melis et al., 2011; Warneken & Tomasello, 2006; Yamamoto et al., 2009, 2012), and chimpanzees who were rewarded for helping were no more likely to help than those who never received a reward (Warneken et al., 2007). Taken together, the basic cognitive ability as well as the basic altruistic motivation to help others appears to be present in chimpanzees as well.

Despite these similarities, there are also several notable differences. One difference is in the cues that elicit helping. Whereas children help proactively—assisting in the absence of concurrent cues or solicitation from the recipient (Knudsen & Liszkowski, 2012a, 2012b, 2013; Warneken, 2013)—chimpanzees only seem to help reactively in response to explicit goal cues. For example, chimpanzees are far more likely to help when the recipient is actively trying to pull in a bag with rewards or communicates toward the subject than when the recipient remains passive (Melis et al., 2011). Similarly, chimpanzees rarely offered a tool to a conspecific partner unless the recipient was actively reaching for it (Yamamoto et al., 2009, 2012). More generally, when recipients are not actively engaged in a task (such as trying to open or retrieve something) but are passively waiting, apes exhibit much lower rates of altruistic behavior (House et al., 2014). It is unclear whether this apparent species- difference is best explained by a difference in the cognitive capacity to compute the need for help or whether this reflects a difference in motivation.

Conclusion

Atlas took it upon himself to carry the sky on his shoulders. Human toddlers are not quite able to make a sacrifice of this scale, but they are willing to help others in more down-to-earth ways that are within their physical powers—such as by picking up clothespins. Importantly, these fairly basic helping behaviors already reflect the core features of altruism seen in adults, and they increase in scope and importance over development (Warneken, 2015). Yet, in contrast to Atlas, children perform these tasks voluntarily. However, to more fully understand the emergence of human-like altruism, we have to look beyond humans (and Titans) to also examine our closest evolutionary relatives. In fact, studies that compare children and chimpanzees show that the basic helping tendencies

are not unique to our species: Chimpanzees also are motivated and able to help others. This provides strong evidence that altruistic behavior can emerge in the absence of norm internalization or moral teachings. Although there is no doubt that human altruistic behavior is shaped by socialization practices and adult moral norms as children grow older, these factors appear to build upon a foundation that has deep roots in evolution, reaching back to at least the last common ancestor of humans and chimpanzees.

ACKNOWLEDGMENTS

I thank Alexandra Rosati for helpful comments and Randi Vogt for editing. This work was supported by a National Science Foundation CAREER award.

REFERENCES

Barragan, R. C., & Dweck, C. S. (2014). Rethinking natural altruism: Simple reciprocal interactions trigger children's benevolence. *Proceedings of the National Academy of Sciences of the USA, 111*(48), 17071–17074.

Bar-Tal, D. (1982). Sequential development of helping behavior: A cognitive-learning approach. *Developmental Review, 2,* 101–124.

Blake, P. R., McAuliffe, K., & Warneken, F. (2014). The developmental origins of fairness: The knowledge–behavior gap. *Trends in Cognitive Sciences, 18*(11), 559–561.

Brownell, C. A., Svetlova, M., Anderson, R., Nichols, S. R., & Drummond, J. (2013). Socialization of early prosocial behavior: Parents' talk about emotion is associated with sharing and helping in toddlers. *Infancy, 18*(1), 91–119.

Buttelmann, D., Carpenter, M., & Tomasello, M. (2009). Eighteen-month-old infants show false belief understanding in an active helping paradigm. *Cognition, 112,* 337–342.

Carpenter, M., Uebel, J., & Tomasello, M. (2013). Being mimicked increases prosocial behavior in 18-month-old infants. *Child Development, 84*(5), 1511–1518.

Chudek, M., & Henrich, J. (2011). Culture–gene coevolution, norm-psychology and the emergence of human prosociality. *Trends in Cognitive Sciences, 15*(5), 218–226.

Cirelli, L. K., Einarson, K. M., & Trainor, L. J. (2014). Interpersonal synchrony increases prosocial behavior in infants. *Developmental Science, 17*(6), 1003–1011.

Cirelli, L. K., Wan, S. J., & Trainor, L. J. (2014). Fourteen-month-old infants use interpersonal synchrony as a cue to direct helpfulness. *Philosophical Transactions of the Royal Society of London: B. Biological Sciences, 369*(1658), 20130400.

Dahl, A. (2015). The developing social context of infant helping in two US samples. *Child Development, 86,* 1080–1093.

Dovidio, J. F., Piliavin, J. A., Schroeder, D. A., & Penner, L. A. (2006). *The social psychology of prosocial behavior.* Mahwah, NJ: Erlbaum.

Dunfield, K. A., & Kuhlmeier, V. A. (2013). Classifying prosocial behavior: Children's responses to instrumental need, emotional distress, and material desire. *Child Development, 84*(5), 1766–1776.

Dunfield, K. A., Kuhlmeier, V. A., O'Connell, L., & Kelley, E. (2011). Examining the diversity of prosocial behaviour: Helping, sharing, and comforting in infancy. *Infancy, 16*(3), 227–247.

Engelmann, J. M., Herrmann, E., & Tomasello, M. (2012). Five-year-olds, but not chimpanzees, attempt to manage their reputations. *PLOS ONE, 7*(10), e48433.

Greenberg, J. R., Hamann, K., Warneken, F., & Tomasello, M. (2010). Chimpanzee helping in collaborative and noncollaborative contexts. *Animal Behaviour, 80*(5), 873–880.

Hamann, K., Warneken, F., & Tomasello, M. (2012). Children's developing commitments to joint goals. *Child Development, 83*(1), 137–145.

Hammond, S. I., & Carpendale, J. I. M. (2015). Helping children help: The relation between maternal scaffolding and children's early help. *Social Development, 24,* 367–383.

Hepach, R., Vaish, A., & Tomasello, M. (2012). Young children are intrinsically motivated to see others helped. *Psychological Science, 23*(9), 967–972.

House, B. R., Silk, J. B., Lambeth, S. P., & Schapiro, S. J. (2014). Task design influences prosociality in captive chimpanzees (*Pan troglodytes*). *PLOS ONE, 9*(9), e103422.

Kirschner, S., & Tomasello, M. (2010). Joint music making promotes prosocial behavior in 4-year-old children. *Evolution and Human Behavior, 31*(5), 354–364.

Knudsen, B., & Liszkowski, U. (2012a). 18-month-olds predict specific action mistakes through attribution of false belief, not ignorance, and intervene accordingly. *Infancy, 17*(6), 672–691.

Knudsen, B., & Liszkowski, U. (2012b). Eighteen- and 24-month-old infants correct others in anticipation of action mistakes. *Developmental Science, 15*(1), 113–122.

Knudsen, B., & Liszkowski, U. (2013). One-year-olds warn others about negative action outcomes. *Journal of Cognition and Development, 14*(3), 424–436.

Kochanska, G. (2002). Committed compliance, moral self, and internalization: A mediational model. *Developmental Psychology, 38*(3), 339–351.

Leimgruber, K. L., Shaw, A., Santos, L. R., & Olson, K. R. (2012). Young children are more generous when others are aware of their actions. *PLOS ONE, 7*(10), e48292.

Melis, A. P., Hare, B., & Tomasello, M. (2008). Do chimpanzees reciprocate received favours? *Animal Behaviour, 76*(3), 951–962.

Melis, A. P., Warneken, F., Jensen, K., Schneider, A. C., Call, J., & Tomasello, M. (2011). Chimpanzees help conspecifics obtain food and non-food items. *Proceedings of the Royal Society of London: Series B, 278*(1710), 1405–1413.

Over, H., & Carpenter, M. (2009). Eighteen-month-old infants show increased helping following priming with affiliation. *Psychological Science, 20*(10), 1189–1193.

Smith, C. E., Blake, P. R., & Harris, P. L. (2013). I should but I won't: Why young children endorse norms of fair sharing but do not follow them. *PLOS ONE, 8*(3), e59510.

Svetlova, M., Nichols, S. R., & Brownell, C. A. (2009). Toddlers' prosocial behavior: From instrumental to empathic to altruistic helping. *Child Development, 81*(6), 1814–1827.

Tan, J., & Hare, B. (2013). Bonobos share with strangers. *PLOS ONE, 8*(1), e51922.

Tomasello, M., & Vaish, A. (2013). Origins of human cooperation and morality. *Annual Review of Psychology, 64,* 231–255.

Warneken, F. (2013). Young children proactively remedy unnoticed accidents. *Cognition, 126*(1), 101–108.

Warneken, F. (2015). Precocious prosociality: Why do young children help? *Child Development Perspectives, 9,* 1–6.

Warneken, F., Hare, B., Melis, A. P., Hanus, D., & Tomasello, M. (2007). Spontaneous altruism by chimpanzees and young children. *PLOS Biology, 5*(7), 1414–1420.

Warneken, F., & Tomasello, M. (2006). Altruistic helping in human infants and young chimpanzees. *Science, 311*(5765), 1301–1303.

Warneken, F., & Tomasello, M. (2007). Helping and cooperation at 14 months of age. *Infancy, 11*(3), 271–294.

Warneken, F., & Tomasello, M. (2008). Extrinsic rewards undermine altruistic tendencies in 20-month-olds. *Developmental Psychology, 44*(6), 1785–1788.

Warneken, F., & Tomasello, M. (2013). Parental presence and encouragement do not influence helping in young children. *Infancy, 18*(3), 345–368.

Whiten, A., McGuigan, N., Marshall-Pescini, S., & Hopper, L. M. (2009). Emulation, imitation, over-imitation and the scope of culture for child and chimpanzee. *Philosophical Transactions of the Royal Society, 364,* 2417–2428.

Yamamoto, S., Humle, T., & Tanaka, M. (2009). Chimpanzees help each other upon request. *PLOS ONE, 4*(10), 1–7.

Yamamoto, S., Humle, T., & Tanaka, M. (2012). Chimpanzees' flexible targeted helping based on an understanding of conspecifics' goals. *Proceedings of the National Academy of Sciences of the USA, 109,* 3588–3592.

CHAPTER 43

The Developmental Origins of Infants' Distributive Fairness Concerns

Jessica A. Sommerville
Talee Ziv

How and when do fairness concerns emerge over the course of development?

Stemming from infant experience, an intuitive sense of distributive fairness emerges within the first 2 years of life, and this sense encompasses many aspects of mature moral responses.

Debates concerning the origins of moral sentiments have long occupied the thoughts of scholars and lay people alike. Well before modern-day experimental psychologists sought to devise tasks to mine mature and developing moral minds and brains, philosophers including Plato, Aristotle, Hobbes, Locke, and Rousseau (among others) theorized about the developmental starting points and subsequent unfolding of moral thoughts and behavior. Central to these age-old and contemporary debates are questions regarding the early nature of moral cognition and behavior, as well as how moral cognition and behavior "get off the ground." Answering such questions can also contribute to our understanding of critical issues in the field of moral psychology writ large, such as whether morality is intuitive or deliberate, monolithic or multifaceted, composed of systems that are general purpose or specialized, and culturally uniform or variable.

Of course, morality consists of a variety of subdomains that include not only concerns of welfare and fairness (Turiel, 1983) but also concerns about loyalty, authority, and sanctity (Graham & Haidt, 2010; Haidt, 2007), perhaps extending to concerns of liberty as well (Haidt, 2012). Our own work has primarily focused on emerging concerns about distributive fairness (i.e., concerns about how goods and resources should be distributed) as a means to understanding the nature of early moral cognition and behavior. Our goal has been to identify the earliest emergence of concerns about distributive fairness and their subsequent developmental trajectory, to provide a precise understanding of the nature of infants' early fairness concerns, and

420

to identify the role of experience (if any) in these concerns. Here, we present evidence that infants possess an intuitive sense of distributive fairness that stems from infants' emerging experience in sharing interactions and discuss how this evidence can inform central questions in moral psychology and moral development.

Distributive Fairness as a Case Study for Understanding Early Moral Development

Considerations of fairness are central to human morality, affecting interpersonal interactions, workplace behaviors, and legal judgments alike. Although principles of fairness are regularly applied in processes of decision making and dispute resolution (procedural fairness) or when considering an appropriate punishment for wrongdoings (retributive fairness), most important among adults' fairness concerns is ensuring the just distribution of goods and resources (distributive fairness). Although adults possess many models for deciding how to distribute resources justly, Western adults' concerns about distributive fairness are often governed by the principle of equality (Deutsch, 1975): All other things being equal, resources should be distributed evenly to recipients. For example, in the context of economic games, adults tend to divide resources equally between themselves and an anonymous partner (Fehr & Fischbacher, 2003) and punish individuals who violate the norm of equal distribution, even at a personal cost (Johnson, Dawes, Fowler, McElreath, & Smirnov, 2009). Adults also take into consideration need and merit in allocating resources. Specifically, they allot greater monetary rewards to themselves if they are told that the amount of work they contributed to a dyadic task was larger than their partner's contribution, particularly when the partner is a stranger (Austin, 1980; Leventhal & Michaels, 1969); and, in allocation decisions based on the joint work of a hypothetical dyad, adults advantage individuals who are described as in need of a larger sum of money to achieve a goal, even though both recipients contributed equal work and

regardless of the cause of the disparity in need (Lamm & Schwinger, 1980).

Recent evidence suggests that by at least the preschool years children are aware of norms that govern resource distribution events and endorse and enact those norms. In third-party situations, if the number of resources equals the number of potential recipients, children default to distributing the resources equally and disregard family relationships or previous friendships (Olson & Spelke, 2008). They will even go as far as deciding to dispose of a resource in order to avoid creating an unequal distribution (Shaw & Olson, 2012). Children also exhibit negative emotional reactions when they receive an unequal allocation (LoBue, Nishida, Chiong, DeLoache, & Haidt, 2011). Furthermore, merit-based distributions are evident by 3 years of age, as children will keep a larger number of rewards for themselves if they contributed more work toward attaining those rewards relative to a partner (Kanngiesser & Warneken, 2012; see also Baumard, Mascaro, & Chevallier, 2012, for evidence of preschooler's merit considerations in third-party situations). Slightly later in development, children take material need into account and share more generously with a poor rather than a rich recipient (Paulus, 2014).

A natural question that extends from this work concerns the point at which sensitivity to fairness first arises in the course of development. At one time it would have been anathema to ask whether infants possess moral concepts and concerns at all. Moral cognition and behavior were initially presumed to be ruled by conscious reasoning processes that are constructed gradually over a protracted period of development via active role taking (Kohlberg, 1969). Subsequent theorists instead suggested that by the preschool period children possess different principles for reasoning about moral, conventional, and personal domains, but nevertheless they have relied on children's verbal judgments and justifications to assess moral sensitivity (Turiel, 1983, 1998; Smetana, 2006). To the extent that moral responses require or rely on conscious reasoning processes that are accessible to verbal report, they would naturally be out of reach of infants. Yet more contemporary research suggests that moral judgments arise at least partially from intuitive emotional processes (Greene & Haidt, 2002; Haidt, 2001), raising the possibility that even infants may be capable of moral responses. Thus we asked whether infants might possess a sensitivity to distributive fairness.

Our Approach and Theoretical Stance

Our approach was to first investigate whether infants possess an intuitive sense of fairness in infancy and subsequently to ask questions concerning the nature of this sensitivity. We began our research with some starting predictions. First, we predicted that an intuitive sense of fairness would be present and detectable in infancy. The past several decades have demonstrated that infants possess rich social knowledge about the world and the causal forces that guide others' behavior, including simple mental states such as intentions (Woodward, 2009), more enduring dispositional characteristics (Kuhlmeier, Wynn, & Bloom, 2003), and extending to conventions and norms (Graham, Stock, & Henderson, 2006). Moreover, more recent research suggests that infants may possess moral sensitivity in other domains, such as care/harm (Hamlin, Wynn, & Bloom, 2007; Hamlin & Wynn, 2011).

Second, given the strong role that experience has been found to play in other aspects of infants' social cognitive knowledge, such as their understanding of goals and intentions (Gerson & Woodward, 2014; Sommerville, Woodward, & Needham, 2005; Sommerville, Hildebrand, & Crane, 2008), we hypothesized that experience would influence infants' fairness sensitivity in terms of both developmental onset and individual differences. In particular, we hypothesized that as agents and observers of sharing behavior and resource distributions, gain infants experiences being both the recipients and actors of fair and unfair behavior, which might spur infants' emerging fairness sensitivity, as well as factors that served to constrain or enhance these types of experiences.

Third, we hypothesized that infants' "moral responses" (to events pertaining to distributive fairness and perhaps extending to other moral subdomains) might in fact be constituted from a range of processes, some of which are more general purpose, others of which are specific to the social or moral domain. We also hypothesized that these processes may range from more basic to more sophisticated, and, accordingly, some would be in place fairly early in development, whereas others might have a more delayed developmental onset. Specifically, we designed tasks to (1) ask whether infants can detect violations of distributive fairness, (2) determine whether infants use information about fairness to guide their affiliative responses, (3) measure whether infants view individuals who abide by fairness norms as praiseworthy and those who violate fairness norms as blameworthy, and (4) determine whether infants act to enforce norms of fairness by rewarding fair behavior and punishing unfair behavior. We then systematically tested infants across a range of ages to determine which of these abilities infants' responses encompass and to determine whether performance across tasks follows a common developmental trajectory or distinct developmental trajectories.

Many of these predictions, and the ensuing results from this work, speak directly to hotly contested issues in moral psychology. Because infants are not yet capable of self-reflective or conscious reasoning, evidence that infants possess a sensitivity to distributive fairness would support claims that at least some aspects of morality are undergirded by relatively automatic affective reactions rather than conscious reasoning or deliberation. Gauging the role that experience plays in the development of a sensitivity to distributive fairness (as well as other moral norms) speaks to issues regarding whether morality is primarily innate or primarily guided by socialization or acculturation. Devising tasks to map onto the potential processes underlying moral responses, and then systematically asking whether infants possess such processes and when they emerge in development, allows us to investigate whether such responses are composed of a unitary process or multiple processes, as well as to ask whether such processes are general purpose or specific to moral responding.

As we present in detail below, our claims are that:

1. Infants possess a sense of distributive fairness: specifically, all things being equal, infants expect resources to be distributed equally to recipients.
2. Infants' sense of distributive fairness undergoes developmental change that appears to be experience dependent.
3. There is individual variability in infants' distributive fairness sensitivity that appears to reflect robust individual differences that are tied, at least in part, to infants' everyday experiences and to dispositional attributes that are related to infants' altruistic tendencies.
4. Infants' reactions to distributive fairness violations appear to incorporate constructs that are specifically moral; infants see those who violate distributive fairness norms as blameworthy and those who abide by such norms as praiseworthy.
5. The ability to enact punishment to enforce distributive fairness norms is likely a (relatively) late development.

Below, we discuss the evidence as it pertains to each of these claims, as well as the implications that this evidence has for the questions raised above.

Evidence

Infants Possess a Sense of Distributive Fairness

In our first foray into investigating infants' fairness concerns, we reasoned that one of the most basic components of a mature sense of distributive fairness likely consists of an ability to detect when fairness norms have been either violated or adhered to. To address whether infants hold expectations of equality in the context of third-party resource distribution events, we tested 15-month-old infants on a resource distribution task (Schmidt & Sommerville, 2011). Infants watched distribution events in which an individual distributed crackers or milk to two recipients; on test, infants' visual attention was timed to static outcomes that depicted either equal resource distribution (2:2 crackers, 5:5 ounces of milk) or unequal resource distribution (3:1 crackers, 8:2 ounces of milk). We found that infants showed significantly longer looking to the unequal outcomes over the equal outcomes; follow-up conditions revealed that infants did not differentiate between those same outcomes when devoid of social context, ruling out alternative explanations based on a preference for asymmetry. These results suggest that 15-month-old infants expect equal outcomes in resource distribution events.

To delve deeper into the nature of infants' representations, we next asked whether infants' sensitivity to fairness norms also guides their social preferences: Do infants prefer to interact with fair individuals over unfair individuals? Fifteen-month-old infants watched live distribution displays in which one actor consistently distributed toys equally among two recipients, whereas the other actor consistently favored one recipient over the other (Burns & Sommerville, 2014). On test trials, infants were presented with both actors and given the opportunity to pick who to affiliate with; on some trials, the distributors simultaneously offered identical toys, on other trials the distributors both invited the infant to come play with them on opposing sides of the room. Infants showed a systematic preference for actors who had previously acted fairly over those who acted unfairly, despite the fact that at the moment of choice, both actors behaved identically. These findings provide some initial information that infants evaluate fair and unfair individuals: Infants' affiliative preferences presumably indicate that they view fair individuals more favorably, or at least less unfavorably, than unfair individuals.

Together, these findings and related results (Sloane, Baillargeon, & Premack, 2012; Geraci & Surian, 2011; Meristo & Surian, 2013, 2014) show that infants possess expectations regarding how goods should be distributed and, more specifically, are aware of at least one distributive fairness norm and use it to guide their social preferences, suggesting that by at least 15 months of age infants' sensitivity to distributive fairness shares some key attributes with older children and adults.

Infants' Sense of Distributive Fairness Undergoes Experience-Related Developmental Change

The next question we sought to answer concerned the developmental trajectory of infants' fairness expectations. On the one hand, a sensitivity to fairness could be evolutionarily derived and thus should be observed early and continuously over development, independently of experience. On the other hand, the emergence of fairness expectations or concerns might rely on experience and thus arise in a more piecemeal fashion across development. In support of this latter possibility, research has shown cross-cultural variability in the degree of adherence to fairness norms in both adults and children (Henrich et al., 2005; Schäfer, Haun, & Tomasello, 2015).

We (Ziv & Sommerville, 2016) recently investigated the developmental trajectory of infants' fairness expectations: Infants at 6, 9, 12, and 15 months of age took part in a resource distribution task that was very similar to the task used by Schmidt and Sommerville (2011). Our first goal was to test the hypothesis that infants' fairness expectations would be developmentally emergent, meaning that there would be a period of developmental transition in infants' fairness expectations. Our results confirmed this hypothesis: Whereas both 12- and 15-month-old infants showed enhanced visual attention to the unequal outcomes, 6-month-old infants did not, suggesting a developmental transition between 6 and 12 months of age.

Our second goal was to test the hypothesis that the developmental transition in infants' fairness expectations would be tied to the onset of infants' naturalistic sharing behavior. Sharing interactions may contribute to the development of a sense of fairness since they emphasize equality and reciprocity. In particular, through the turn-taking nature of sharing interactions infants experience as both recipients and agents of fair and unfair outcomes. Through this process, infants can learn about the impact that fair or unfair behavior has on others, perhaps via their emotional reactions, and subsequently link that feedback to their own feelings as recipients of similar behavior. Consistent with this hypothesis at 9 months of age, an age at which

there is considerable variability in naturalistic sharing, infants' detection of fairness norms was related to whether or not they had begun to engage in naturalistic sharing as measured by parental report. Together, these findings suggest that infants' fairness expectations are developmentally acquired and may depend on their experience in sharing interactions.

Individual Differences in Infants' Fairness Expectations

For adults, there are individual variability and cross-cultural differences in how strongly individuals subscribe to and adhere to these equality norms, as well as other fairness norms. These findings suggest that experience may shape the extent to which individuals subscribe to and adhere to fairness norms.

Our research has revealed that beyond the period of developmental transitions in infants' fairness expectations, stable individual differences in infants' fairness concerns likely emerge and consolidate, and that such individual differences are predicted, at least in part, by experiential factors. One factor that appears to predict individual differences in infants' fairness expectations is the presence or absence of a sibling. Infants 12 and 15 months old with siblings show enhanced distributive fairness expectations (as assessed by the violation of expectation [VOE] task) in comparison with infants without siblings (Ziv & Sommerville, 2016). Frequent interactions with siblings might afford infants more opportunities to directly experience fair and unfair outcomes through regular observation and participation in sharing and resource distribution. Indeed, sibling disputes regularly occur in early childhood (Dunn, 1987), often pertaining to issues of rights and possession (Dunn & Mann, 1987), and provide one of the earliest contexts for applying concepts of morality (Smetana, 1997).

Recent work in our lab has also revealed that parental dispositional tendencies are related to infants' fairness expectations at 12–15 months of age. Specifically, parental empathy, as captured by self-report questionnaires such as the Davis Interpersonal Reactivity Index (IRI; Davis, 1983) is correlated with the extent to which infants show enhanced attention to unfair outcomes. Parents who score higher in affective empathy (i.e., empathic concern) and cognitive empathy (i.e., perspective taking) have infants that show greater attention to unfair over fair outcomes. One possible read of these findings is that they may reflect a shared genetic tendency toward prosociality. Another possibility, which we prefer, is that parents who are more empathic may differ in how frequently they introduce events related to fairness to infants (such as sharing interactions) and the nature of these interactions.

Finally, our work suggests that individual differences in infants' sensitivity to fairness at 12–15 months are predicted by how infants choose to share toys with others. Although the vast majority of infants at 12 months and older are capable of sharing toys, according to parental report and lab studies, infants differ in the extent of their underlying altruistic motivation to share. Across several studies, infants were allowed to select one of two toys and then given the opportunity to share one of these toys with a stranger. Infants who generously share a preferred toy more strongly detect violations to distributive fairness than do infants who share nonpreferred toys with strangers (Schmidt & Sommerville, 2011; Sommerville, Schmidt, Yun, & Burns, 2013; Ziv & Sommerville, 2016). These findings may suggest that infants' degree of altruism predicts the extent of infants' awareness of distributive fairness norms. Again, these results may stem from genetically influenced variability in the degree of prosociality different infants possess. Alternately, these relations may capture the fact that parents differ in their tendency to emphasize prosocial or altruistic tendencies in infants that manifest in increased or decreased awareness of distributive fairness norms and altruistic behavior.

Intriguingly, whereas each of these factors predict variability in infants' fairness expectations at 12–15 months of age, they do not predict variability at younger ages (i.e., 9 and 6 months of age). Coupled with prior results, these findings suggest that factors associated with group-level developmental transitions in infants' fairness expectations (such as whether or not an infant has experience sharing or not) are not necessarily the same factors that predict individual differences beyond this period of development transition (such as the presence or absence of siblings, parental empathy, and the way in which infants share toys).

Infants' Reactions to Distributive Fairness Violations Appear to Incorporate Specifically Moral Constructs

The aforementioned findings suggest that infants can detect violations to distributive fairness norms and use them to guide their social behavior. However, from these results alone it is not clear that there is anything specifically "moral" about these responses. Infants' ability to detect violations to fairness norms could come about from a tendency to attend to social events paired with domain-general statistical learning mechanisms (although it is unlikely that this is the case, because there is no reason to believe that more altruistic infants would be better at detecting statistical regularities than less altruistic infants). Similarly, infants' selections of previously fair individuals could be driven not by an appreciation that one actor behaved morally and the other immorally, but by strategic inferences about how the individual might distribute goods to the infant him- or herself.

In adults and older children, moral considerations include notions of right and wrong, as well as praise and blame. To determine whether infants' representations of fair and unfair behavior include these constructs, after showing infants video clips of one individual distributing goods equally to recipients and another individual distributing goods unequally to recipients, infants saw just the faces of the fair and unfair actor on flanking monitors (DesChamps, Eason, & Sommerville, 2016). After an initial trial in which infants' baseline attention to both faces was measured, infants heard either praise ("Good job! She's a good girl") or admonishment ("Bad job! She's a bad girl").

The results indicated that infants as young as 13 months of age systematically shifted their visual attention as a function of the accompanying vocal stimuli. Infants looked significantly longer to the unfair distributor on admonishment trials than at the fair distributor; on the praise trials, infants looked numerically (but not significantly) longer at the fair distributor than the unfair distributor. These findings suggest that by at least 13 months of age infants associate praise with fair behavior and admonishment with unfair behavior and also that there is an asymmetry in the extent of these associations (i.e., they see unfair behavior as more blameworthy than fair behavior is praiseworthy). An open question for future work is whether younger infants also possess this ability.

The Ability to Enact Punishment to Enforce Distributive Norms Is Likely a (Relatively) Late Development

Finally, adults and older children also act in various ways to enforce moral norms. Specifically, they engage in reward and punishment behaviors to encourage moral actions and discourage immoral actions. We were interested in whether infants are similarly motivated to enforce fairness norms. Infants were presented with a touch screen, and we taught them that touching a colored bar on one side of the screen elicited reward, whereas touching a colored bar on the other side of the screen elicited punishment. We operationalized punishment and reward across studies both in terms of verbal reward and punishment and material reward and punishment—the actor either received a cookie or had a cookie taken away from her (Ziv & Sommerville, in preparation). Then infants saw videos of one actor distributing goods equally to recipients and another actor distributing goods unequally to recipients. On test trials, a picture of one of the actor's faces appeared in the middle of the screen, flanked by the two colored bars, and we recorded infants' spontaneous bar presses.

We found that, on trials in which the fair actor's face appeared, infants pressed the reward bar more frequently than the punishment bar. On trials in which the unfair actor's face appeared, infants pressed the colored bars equally. These findings suggested that infants rewarded the fair actor but neither rewarded nor punished the unfair actor. A follow-up control condition revealed that infants did not show this same pattern of responses to positively and negatively valenced stimuli more broadly (liked and disliked foods). These findings suggest that infants uniquely reward fair behaviors and, perhaps, other acts of prosocial behavior (we are currently testing this possibility).

Intriguingly, these results dovetail with those of Jensen and colleagues (Riedl, Jensen, Call, & Tomasello, 2015), who demonstrated that, although 3-year-old children will intervene to correct an injustice (e.g., returning a stolen item to its rightful owner), these same children appear to be reluctant to engage in punishment. Together, these findings suggest that the tendency to act to enforce moral norms via punishment may occur significantly later than an awareness of moral norms and use of these norms to guide behavior, as well as the ability to recognize particular actions as blameworthy and praiseworthy.

Summary and Implications

The findings herein suggest that infants develop an intuitive sense of distributive fairness over the first year of life, between roughly 6 and 12 months of age, that may be facilitated by their experience engaging in sharing interactions. Furthermore, individual differences beyond this period of developmental acquisition exist and are linked to factors that influence infants' everyday experiences. Our findings also suggest that by 13 months of age infants apply notions of praise and blame to those that adhere to rather than violate distributive fairness norms. Interestingly, however, even slightly older infants cannot fully translate these notions into actions to enforce distributive fairness norms.

Our findings impinge on several questions that are central to classic and contemporary debates. First, the fact that even infants possess a basic sense of distributive fairness suggests that moral responses are driven, at least in part, by relatively automatic affective responses given that infants lack self-reflective conscious reasoning abilities. Second, our findings are relevant to the debate regarding whether morality is innate versus learned, although they do not definitively settle this debate. Of course, the term *innate* has been used in many different ways. As Prinz (2008) points out, some definitions of innateness portray traits or abilities as fixed and impervious to change; in other definitions, traits or abilities are innate if they have a highly circumscribed range of potential manifestations; finally, other definitions attribute innateness to traits or abilities with a greater flexibility in their expressions provided that there is a specialized system evolved solely to produce a given trait or ability. Many contemporary authors follow Marcus's (2004) definition in defining innateness as "organized in advance of experience."

Our results, suggesting that (1) there is a developmental onset of awareness of distributive fairness norms and (2) this developmental onset may be a product of experience, raise the possibility that infants' sensitivity to fairness is mostly acquired through acculturation. Moreover, they allow us to rule out some versions of innateness, such as the possibility that infants' sensitivity to fairness is fixed and impervious to change. However, there are some important caveats to this claim. First, our data so far tell us that there is an association between the onset of participation in sharing interactions and infants' awareness of distributive fairness norms, but this does not necessarily mean that infants' sharing experience drives their fairness concerns (as opposed to the other way around or to a third variable accounting for both tendencies). Intervention studies aimed at enhancing the onset of sharing behavior in younger infants are necessary to determine whether there are downstream consequences for infants' awareness of distributive fairness norms; our initial work in this vein suggests that presharing infants can learn to share through regular practice with reciprocal object exchanges (Xu, Saether, & Sommerville, 2016). Another technique for addressing questions related to innate and learned contributions would be to test infants across cultures using similar paradigms to determine whether the starting point of a given moral construct is shared across cultures or varies from the get-go. If the starting point of distributive fairness norms is consistent across cultures, this would suggest a strong innate basis; if distributive fairness norms differ by culture from the start, this would suggest a strong influence of acculturation. Finally, it is important to point out that, regardless of the developmental origins of a sense of fairness,

development in other subdomains may have other sources (such as harm/care; see Hamlin, 2013).

Our results also speak to issues of the number and types of processes that contribute to morality. Our findings suggest that infants' ability to recognize moral transgressors as blameworthy and moral abiders as praiseworthy is likely distinct from their ability to enact reward and punishment, as the former is in place by at least 13 months of age and the latter is still developing at 16 months of age. Thus these findings suggest that more implicit moral reactions are distinct from explicit moral reactions, at least in infancy. An important question for future research is whether the earliest manifestations of infants' sensitivity to distributive fairness are driven by a single process that is specific to morality or by multiple processes, a subset of which may not be specific to morality. In order to make traction on this issue, it will be important to test infants between 9 and 12 months of age (ages at which an awareness of distributive fairness norms is onsetting) on tasks that investigate their tendency to associate praise and blame with fair and unfair behavior, respectively.

Conclusions

In this chapter, we provided evidence that infants possess an intuitive sense of fairness that likely emerges as a result of experience, particularly with interactions that enable infants to observe and participate in exchanges allowing them to be both the agents and recipients of fair and unfair behavior. Together, our results suggest that a sensitivity to distributive fairness both emerges early and is reliant on experience for both its emergence and subsequent nature. Critically, and perhaps on a hopeful note, these findings suggest that concerns about fairness may be relatively malleable and thus can be enhanced perhaps even earlier in development.

These findings pave the way for future directions. In terms of infants' fairness sensitivity most directly, it is important to understand when and whether infants and/or young children develop other models or principles for resource distributions; some existing work suggests that toward the end of the second year of life infants begin to consider merit in their expectations regarding how goods are typically distributed (Sloane et al., 2012), and recent ongoing work from our lab suggests that infants may incorporate information about recipients' social status in their expectations about resource distributions. Another, broader future direction is to determine when infants recognize both commonalities across different moral subdomains and differences between moral violations and other types of violations, such as social conventions or rules. Finally, it will be interesting to learn how and when infants rank or weigh concerns about the welfare of others against concerns that are more self- or group-serving; emerging work from our lab suggests that infants are more tolerant of violations to fairness norms when there is reason to believe that inequality may benefit same-group members (Burns & Sommerville, 2014). Together, the results from this work will continue to inform classic and contemporary debates in moral psychology and development.

REFERENCES

Austin, W. (1980). Friendship and fairness: Effects of type of relationship and task performance on choice of distribution rules. *Personality and Social Psychology Bulletin, 6*(3), 402–408.

Baumard, N., Mascaro, O., & Chevallier, C. (2012). Preschoolers are able to take merit into account when distributing goods. *Developmental Psychology, 48*(2), 492–498.

Burns, M. P., & Sommerville, J. A. (2014). "I pick you": The impact of fairness and race on infants' selection of social partners. *Frontiers in Psychology, 5.* Available at *www.ncbi.nlm.nih.gov/pmc/articles/PMC3921677.*

Davis, M. H. (1983). Measuring individual differences in empathy: Evidence for a multidimensional approach. *Journal of Personality and Social Psychology, 44*(1), 113–126.

DesChamps, T. D., Eason, A. E., & Sommerville, J. A. (2016). Infants associate praise and admonishment with fair and unfair individuals. *Infancy, 21,* 478–504.

Deutsch, M. (1975). Equity, equality, and need: What determines which value will be used as the basis of distributive justice? *Journal of Social Issues, 31*(3), 137–149.

Dunn, J. (1987). The beginnings of moral understanding: Development in the second year. In J. Kagan & S. Lamb (Eds.), *The emergence of morality in young children* (pp. 91–112). Chicago: University of Chicago Press.

Dunn, J., & Munn, P. (1987). Development of justification in disputes with mother and sibling. *Developmental Psychology, 23*(6), 791–798.

Fehr, E., & Fischbacher, U. (2003). The nature of human altruism. *Nature, 425*(6960), 785–791.

Geraci, A., & Surian, L. (2011). The developmental roots of fairness: Infants' reactions to equal and unequal distributions of resources. *Developmental Science, 14*(5), 1012–1020.

Gerson, S. A., & Woodward, A. L. (2014). Learning from their own actions: The unique effect of producing actions on infants' action understanding. *Child Development, 85*(1), 264–277.

Graham, J., & Haidt, J. (2010). Beyond beliefs: Religions bind individuals into moral communities. *Personality and Social Psychology Review, 14*(1), 140–150.

Graham, S. A., Stock, H., & Henderson, A. M. (2006). Nineteen-month-olds' understanding of the conventionality of object labels versus desires. *Infancy, 9*(3), 341–350.

Greene, J., & Haidt, J. (2002). How (and where) does moral judgment work? *Trends in Cognitive Sciences, 6*(12), 517–523.

Haidt, J. (2001). The emotional dog and its rational tail: A social intuitionist approach to moral judgment. *Psychological Review, 108*(4), 814–834.

Haidt, J. (2007). The new synthesis in moral psychology. *Science, 316*(5827), 998–1002.

Haidt, J. (2012). *The righteous mind: Why good people are divided by politics and religion.* New York: Pantheon.

Hamlin, J. K. (2013). Moral judgment and action in preverbal infants and toddlers: Evidence for an innate moral core. *Current Directions in Psychological Science, 22*(3), 186–193.

Hamlin, J. K., & Wynn, K. (2011). Young infants prefer prosocial to antisocial others. *Cognitive Development, 26*(1), 30–39.

Hamlin, J. K., Wynn, K., & Bloom, P. (2007). Social evaluation by preverbal infants. *Nature, 450*(7169), 557–559.

Henrich, J., Boyd, R., Bowles, S., Camerer, C., Fehr, E., Gintis, H., . . . Henrich, N. S. (2005). "Economic man" in cross-cultural perspective: Behavioral experiments in 15 small-scale societies. *Behavioral and Brain Sciences, 28*(6), 795–815.

Johnson, T., Dawes, C. T., Fowler, J. H., McElreath, R., & Smirnov, O. (2009). The role of egalitarian motives in altruistic punishment. *Economics Letters, 102*(3), 192–194.

Kanngiesser, P., & Warneken, F. (2012). Young

children consider merit when sharing resources with others. *PLOS ONE, 7*(8), e43979.

Kohlberg, L. (1969). Stage and sequence: The cognitive-developmental approach to socialization. In D. A. Goslin (Ed.), *Handbook of socialization theory and research* (pp. 347–480). Chicago: Rand McNally.

Kuhlmeier, V., Wynn, K., & Bloom, P. (2003). Attribution of dispositional states by 12-month-olds. *Psychological Science, 14*(5), 402–408.

Lamm, H., & Schwinger, T. (1980). Norms concerning distributive justice: Are needs taken into consideration in allocation decisions? *Social Psychology Quarterly, 43*(4), 425–429.

Leventhal, G. S., & Michaels, J. W. (1969). Extending the equity model: Perception of inputs and allocation of reward as a function of duration and quantity of performance. *Journal of Personality and Social Psychology, 12*(4), 303–309.

LoBue, V., Nishida, T., Chiong, C., DeLoache, J. S., & Haidt, J. (2011). When getting something good is bad: Even three-year-olds react to inequality. *Social Development, 20*(1), 154–170.

Marcus, G. (2004). *The birth of the mind: How a tiny number of genes creates the complexities of human thought*. New York: Basic Books.

Meristo, M., & Surian, L. (2013). Do infants detect indirect reciprocity? *Cognition, 129*(1), 102–113.

Meristo, M., & Surian, L. (2014). Infants distinguish antisocial actions directed towards fair and unfair agents. *PLOS ONE, 9*(10), e110553.

Olson, K. R., & Spelke, E. S. (2008). Foundations of cooperation in young children. *Cognition, 108*(1), 222–231.

Paulus, M. (2014). The early origins of human charity: Developmental changes in preschooler's sharing with poor and wealthy individuals. *Frontiers in Psychology, 5,* 344. Available at *www.ncbi.nlm.nih.gov/pmc/articles/PMC4071819.*

Prinz, J. (2008). Is morality innate? *Moral Psychology, 1,* 367–406.

Riedl, K., Jensen, K., Call, J., & Tomasello, M. (2015). Restorative justice in children. *Current Biology, 25,* 1731–1735.

Schäfer, M., Haun, D. B., & Tomasello, M. (2015). Fair is not fair everywhere. *Psychological Science, 26,* 1252–1260.

Schmidt, M. F., & Sommerville, J. A. (2011). Fairness expectations and altruistic sharing in 15-month-old human infants. *PLOS ONE, 6*(10), e23223.

Shaw, A., & Olson, K. R. (2012). Children discard a resource to avoid inequity. *Journal of Experimental Psychology: General, 141*(2), 382.

Sloane, S., Baillargeon, R., & Premack, D. (2012). Do infants have a sense of fairness? *Psychological Science, 23,* 196–204.

Smetana, J. G. (1997). Parenting and the development of social knowledge reconceptualized: A social domain analysis. In J. E. Grusec & L. Kuczynski (Eds.), *Parenting and children's internalization of values: A handbook of contemporary theory* (pp. 162–192). New York: Wiley.

Smetana, J. G. (2006). Social-cognitive domain theory: Consistencies and variations in children's moral and social judgments. In M. Killen & J. G. Smetana (Eds.), *Handbook of moral development* (pp. 119–153). Mahwah, NJ: Erlbaum.

Sommerville, J. A., Hildebrand, E. A., & Crane, C. C. (2008). Experience matters: The impact of doing versus watching on infants' subsequent perception of tool-use events. *Developmental Psychology, 44*(5), 1249–1256.

Sommerville, J. A., Schmidt, M. F., Yun, J. E., & Burns, M. (2013). The development of fairness expectations and prosocial behavior in the second year of life. *Infancy, 18*(1), 40–66.

Sommerville, J. A., Woodward, A. L., & Needham, A. (2005). Action experience alters 3-month-old infants' perception of others' actions. *Cognition, 96*(1), B1–B11.

Turiel, E. (1983). *The development of social knowledge: Morality and convention*. Cambridge, UK: Cambridge University Press.

Turiel, E. (1998). The development of morality. In W. Damon & R. M. Lerner (Series Eds.) & N. Eisenberg (Vol. Ed.), *Handbook of child psychology: Vol. 3. Social, emotional, and personality development* (pp. 863–932). New York: Wiley.

Woodward, A. L. (2009). Infants' grasp of others' intentions. *Current Directions in Psychological Science, 18*(1), 53–57.

Xu, J., Saether, L. & Sommerville, J. A. (2016). Experience facilitates the emergence of sharing behavior among 7.5-month-old infants. *Developmental Psychology, 52*(11), 1732–1743.

Ziv, T., & Sommerville, J. A. (2016). Developmental differences in infants' fairness expectations from 6 to 15 months of age. *Child Development*. Available at *http://onlinelibrary.wiley.com/doi/10.1111/cdev.12674/abstract.*

Ziv, T., & Sommerville, J. A. (in preparation). *Infants reward individuals who act fairly in third-party resource distributions*. Unpublished manuscript.

CHAPTER 44

Vulnerability-Based Morality

Anton J. M. Dijker

> **What is the most essential innate psychological mechanism underlying morality?**
>
> A hypothetical care mechanism—triggered by perceptions of vulnerability—can explain many aspects of both moral judgment and behavior.

Research on the psychological and philosophical aspects of morality has strongly focused on how people judge the permissibility or moral wrongness of certain acts given their particular consequences. Yet intuitively, certain properties of the persons affected by those acts must also play a significant role in moral judgment. This is especially evident from the strong feelings that are aroused when children, women, or elderly persons are harmed or benefitted. In particular, not only in everyday life (e.g., Cialdini, Brown, Lewis, Luce, & Neuberg, 1997; Dijker, 2001; Eagly & Crowley, 1986) but also in situations of warfare (e.g., Carpenter, 2003; Hoijer, 2004; McKeogh, 2002), people feel a strong moral obligation to help and protect these categories of individuals, and they respond with moral outrage to the harm doers.

Sometimes, the idea that women and children are more deserving of help and protection than men (also referred to as the "women-and-children-first" norm) seems to be contradicted. For example, the history of human warfare shows many instances of victimization of women and children (Davie, 1929). Yet the contradiction may only be apparent as the slaughtering of women and children during warfare can be interpreted as intentional demoralization of the enemy (Davie, 1929).

Children in particular tend to be used in order to inhibit aggression in situations of potential conflict. For example, when heads of state or military leaders visit each other, displays of military strength often are accompanied with the presence of children offering flowers (Eibl-Eibesfeldt, 1989). More generally, humans employ a rich variety of infantile behaviors (e.g., begging, crying, playing) to ensure aggression reduction, tolerance, and prosocial behavior under everyday conditions (cf. Eibl-Eibesfeldt, 1989; Keltner, Young, & Buswell, 1997).

What properties do children, women, and elderly persons have in common that have these moral implications? The goal of this chapter is to show that the central physical property at stake here is vulnerability and that its perception reliably activates a motivational mechanism that is responsible for a wide variety of moral emotions, judgments, and behaviors. Importantly, I will argue that the perception of vulnerability and its associated motivational mechanism also determine moral judgment and behavior in situations in which one is not visually exposed to individuals of flesh and blood, such as in the trolley problem and the Prisoner's Dilemma—two widely employed research paradigms for investigating moral judgment and behavior. But first I outline the hypothetical psychological mechanism responsible for the moral implications of vulnerability perception.

A Theory of Vulnerability-Based Morality

With respect to living things, *vulnerability* refers to the property or disposition of objects to change into a state of damage (i.e., a state of lowered fitness that is inconsistent with genetic "design specifications") when exposed to certain conditions. For those concerned with the fitness and well-being of others, an assessment of vulnerability would be crucial, as information about this property can help perceivers to predict and thus prevent actual harm. After all, especially in ancestral environments, it would have been much better to prevent injury than to try to relieve harm already inflicted and likely resulting in death (Dijker, 2011).

Evolutionary theory predicts the evolution of a behavioral mechanism (best termed a care mechanism; Dijker & Koomen, 2007) that would motivate especially parents to respond adaptively to this fitness-relevant property of their young offspring. Crucial features of such a mechanism would be that it can be quickly and unconditionally activated by simple perceptual cues that are correlated with vulnerability (e.g., certain physical or behavioral features indicating young age or lack of physical strength; cf. Alley, 1983; Berry & McArthur, 1986; Lorenz, 1943) and that its activation causes different moral emotions or adaptive behavioral goals, dependent on the perceived relevance of the current situation for the well-being of the vulnerable object.

For example, if the perceived events simply indicate a desirable state of well-being of the vulnerable object, tenderness may be felt, associated with appraising the object as "cute" and a desire to stay close to it, keeping a watchful eye on its behavior and the environment. If a threat to, or actual decrease in, the object's well-being is perceived that can be attributed to another agent or the self, moral anger or guilt may be felt, respectively, resulting in protective and aggressive tendencies to prevent (further) harm. Perception of a decrease in well-being in the absence of responsible agents may primarily result in pity or sympathy and a desire to comfort and heal the individual (for a detailed explanation of these and other moral emotions in terms of an activated care mechanism and an attributional process, see Dijker, 2014b).

A care mechanism may be present not only in parents but, in different degrees, in all members of a group of cooperative breeders, and especially in humans (Hrdy, 2009). In humans, an exceptionally strong care system may have evolved, easily activated by the slightest evidence of vulnerability and immaturity, even making vulnerability perception more important than kin recognition and its attitudinal consequences (although kinship remains influential; see Park, Schaller, & Van Vugt, 2008). Complementarily, humans may have evolved a rich variety of ways to intentionally signal vulnerability and immaturity in order to trigger a care system in others (e.g., they may behave in an infantile manner), thereby ensuring aggression reduction, diverse prosocial behaviors, and a rich variety of functional moral emotions (Dijker, 2014b). Note that the influence of the care mechanism on social behavior may be less visible when there is strong competition with motivational mechanisms associated with self-preservation, resulting in primarily fearful, aggressive, or stigmatizing responses (Dijker & Koomen, 2007).

How does this theory help explain responses to moral dilemmas in which persons of flesh and blood with visible vulnerability cues are absent? To answer that question, it is important to realize that vulnerability can also be inferred from knowledge or beliefs about the situational causes of harm and suffering. For example, if information about age and gender of the persons affected is absent and an illness or injury can be entirely attributed to strong situational and uncontrollable factors (e.g., another's careless behavior, a natural disaster, or a genetic defect), people tend to feel sympathy for the affected persons, apparently seeing them as "innocent" or "defenseless." In contrast, these same persons tend to arouse anger and less sympathy when their agency and personal responsibility for their condition are emphasized (e.g., Dijker & Koomen, 2003; Weiner, Perry, & Magnusson, 1988). More recently, Gray and Wegner (2009) introduced a conceptual contrast between "moral patients" and "moral agents" to describe a similar process of sympathy and anger arousal. Asking people to take another's perspective seems to arouse sympathy and reduce aggression in a similar way, as this, too, may stimulate attention to situational causes for the person's condition or behavior (Batson et al., 1997).

The traditional attributional description of these relationships is insufficient to explain why we care about strangers lacking in responsibility for their own illness or suffering (Dijker & Koomen, 2003) and why we would want to improve their condition—an essential motivational aspect of sympathy (Wispé, 1991). However, a truly causal explanation for sympathy arousal is possible by assuming that situational attribution makes victims appear more vulnerable and hence helps to activate a care mechanism. The next section examines how a theory of vulnerability-based morality can be used to improve understanding of responses to the trolley problem and the Prisoner's Dilemma.

The Trolley Problem

In one of the most frequently used dilemmas in psychological research on moral decision making—the trolley problem—a runaway trolley is about to run over and kill five people, but a bystander can throw a switch that will turn the trolley on a side track, where it will kill one person. Research participants are asked if it is permissible to throw the switch. Responses to this bystander version are often compared with those to a version in which a person needs to be pushed from a footbridge onto the track in order to stop the

train and save the five other persons. Typically, no background information is supplied about the individuals that can be sacrificed and saved in this way. It is generally found that very few people consider it permissible to personally kill another person to save five others in the footbridge version, whereas many more people find it acceptable to sacrifice an individual in the bystander version (for reviews see, e.g., Christensen & Gomila, 2012; Mikhail, 2007).

Researchers have explained these judgments primarily in terms of degree of intentionality and the causal relationships between the events leading to the harm. For example, it has been shown that the permissibility of sacrificing a person to save five others in the bystander version depends on the opportunity to interpret the sacrifice as a side rather than an intended effect (Mikhail, 2007) and the extent to which the killing would require close physical contact with the victim (e.g., Greene et al., 2009). This focus has led some to argue that moral judgment can be sufficiently explained in terms of an innate "grammar" underlying people's understanding of the causal structure of the trolley problem (Mikhail, 2007).

Researchers often relate the differential responses to the footbridge and bystander versions of the trolley problem to Kant's emphasis on the moral wrongness or goodness of acts in general and Bentham's focus on the role of perceived consequences and utilities of acts (e.g., the mere number of people that can be saved), respectively. Interestingly, the relatively few studies in which background information has been provided about the persons to be saved and sacrificed are more in line with Hume's emphasis on the role of preexisting attitudes toward the objects of moral judgments (e.g., positive attitudes toward one's own children, husband or wife, or a benefactor). For example, it has been demonstrated that people are less willing to sacrifice a brother or sister (Petrinovich, O'Neill, & Jorgensen, 1993) or to save a group of Nazis (Petrinovich et al., 1993), homeless people (Cikara, Farnsworth, Harris, & Fiske, 2010), or foreigners (Swann, Gómez, Dovidio, Hart, & Jetten, 2010). Especially in light of Kant's position, these causal influences are incongruent with universal principles of morality, as they intro-

tools (Dobres, 2001) probably was as important for their invention and development as their functional properties.

It is interesting to note that several other psychological concepts share certain of the above-mentioned elements of a careful mode of thinking. For example, both the concepts of wisdom (e.g., Sternberg, 1998) and mindfulness (e.g., Brown, Ryan, & Creswell, 2007) assume relationships between thought, sympathy, prosocial tendencies, and aesthetic experience. However, these proposals fail to mention a mechanism responsible for linking general aspects of cognition to prosocial tendencies. From the present perspective, the capacity of wise and mindful persons to acquire a thorough and perhaps objective understanding of how people's lives are affected by the environment (Brown et al., 2007; Sternberg, 1998) and how they are thus made vulnerable increases the likelihood of activation of the care mechanism, enabling these persons to frequently feel tenderness and sympathy in their thinking. Complementarily, frequent activation of the care mechanism in wise and mindful persons helps them to look for, and enhance their knowledge about, environmental threats and opportunities that are relevant to vulnerable beings.

Conclusions

This chapter has attempted to show that, although vulnerability is a property of individuals of flesh and blood, such as children, women, and elderly persons, it can also be inferred from frequently used experimental dilemmas in which concrete individuals are absent or invisible, such as in the trolley problem or the Prisoner's Dilemma. As mentioned, the involvement of vulnerability perception in responding to these dilemmas awaits empirical testing.

The present focus on the perception of vulnerability not only provides new insights into the nature of morality but also encourages us to think about mental states, perhaps unique to humans, in which morality, true understanding, and aesthetic experience are fused. However, it seems likely that a vulnerability-based morality that depends on the activation of a care mechanism and also

partly on fearful and aggressive responses to protect vulnerable beings in effective ways (Dijker, 2014b) competes with other types of morality that primarily depend on fear or aggression. For example, a morality of obedience seems to be strongly related to a tendency to fearfully submit to powerful others and to aggress or show contempt to those who are disobedient and violate norms. Furthermore, although a morality of reciprocity can be partly explained by assuming a general tendency to care for vulnerable or needy others, it strongly relies on people's desire to consistently apply a norm of reciprocity (Gouldner, 1960), requiring a relatively stronger role for distrust, anger, desire to punish nonreciprocators, and a morality of justice. An important issue for future research, therefore, would be to examine the relative importance of different types of morality in different persons, situations, and cultures (see also Haidt, 2007).

REFERENCES

Alley, T. R. (1983). Growth-produced changes in body shape and size as determinants of perceived age and adult caregiving. *Child Development, 54,* 241–248.

Bartz, J. A., Zaki, J., Bolger, N., & Ochsner, K. N. (2011). Social effects of oxytocin in humans: Context and person matter. *Trends in Cognitive Sciences, 15,* 301–309.

Batson, C. D., & Ahmad, N. (2001). Empathy-induced altruism in a prisoner's dilemma: II. What if the target of empathy has defected? *European Journal of Social Psychology, 31,* 25–36.

Batson, C. D., Polycarpou, M. P., Harmon-Jones, E., Imhoff, H. J., Mitchener, E. C., Bednar, L. L., . . . Highberger, L. (1997). Empathy and attitudes: Can feeling for a member of a stigmatized group improve feelings toward the group? *Journal of Personality and Social Psychology, 72,* 105–118.

Bechtel, W., & Abrahamsen, A. (2005). Explanation: A mechanistic alternative. *Studies in the History and Philosophy of Biological and Biomedical Sciences, 36,* 421–441.

Berry, D. S., & McArthur, L. Z. (1986). Perceiving character in faces: The impact of age-related craniofacial changes on social perception. *Psychological Bulletin, 100,* 3–18.

Binmore, K. (2007). *Game theory: A very short introduction.* Oxford, UK: Oxford University Press.

Brown, K. W., Ryan, R. M., & Creswell, J. D. (2007). Mindfulness: Theoretical foundations and evidence for its salutary effects. *Psychological Inquiry, 18,* 211–237.

Burke, E. (1759/1990). *A philosophical enquiry into the origin of our ideas of the sublime and beautiful.* Oxford, UK: Oxford University Press.

Carpenter, R. C. (2003). "Women and children first": Gender, norms, and humanitarian evacuation in the Balkans 1991–95. *International Organization, 57,* 661–694.

Christensen, J. F., & Gomila, A. (2012). Moral dilemmas in cognitive neuroscience of moral decision-making: A principled review. *Neuroscience and Biobehavioral Reviews, 36,* 1249–1264.

Cialdini, R. B., Brown, S. L., Lewis, B. P., Luce, C., & Neuberg, S. L. (1997). Reinterpreting the empathy–altruism relationship: When one into one equals oneness. *Journal of Personality and Social Psychology, 73,* 481–494.

Cikara, M., Farnsworth, R. A., Harris, L. T., & Fiske, S. T. (2010). On the wrong side of the trolley track: Neural correlates of relative social valuation. *Social Cognitive and Affective Neuroscience, 5,* 404–413.

Davie, M. R. (1929). *The evolution of war: A study of its role in early societies.* New Haven, CT: Yale University Press.

Dawes, R. M. (1980). Social dilemmas. *Annual Review of Psychology, 31,* 169–193.

Dijker, A. J. M. (2001). The influence of perceived suffering and vulnerability on the experience of pity. *European Journal of Social Psychology, 31,* 659–676.

Dijker, A. J. M. (2010). Perceived vulnerability as a common basis of moral emotions. *British Journal of Social Psychology, 49,* 415–423.

Dijker, A. J. M. (2011). Physical constraints on the evolution of cooperation. *Evolutionary Biology, 38,* 124–143.

Dijker, A. J. M. (2014a). Consciousness: A neural capacity for objectivity, especially pronounced in humans. *Frontiers in Psychology, 5*(223).

Dijker, A. J. M. (2014b). A theory of vulnerability-based morality. *Emotion Review, 6,* 175–183.

Dijker, A. J. M., Deluster, R., Peeters, N., & De Vries, N. K. (2017). Seeing overweight adults as babies: Physical cues and implications for stigmatization. *British Journal of Psychology.* [Epub ahead of print]

Dijker, A. J. M., & Koomen, W. (2003). Extending Weiner's attribution–emotion model of stigmatization of ill persons. *Basic and Applied Social Psychology, 25,* 51–68.

Dijker, A. J. M., & Koomen, W. (2007). *Stigmatization, tolerance, and repair: An integrative psychological analysis of responses to devi-* *ance.* Cambridge, UK: Cambridge University Press.

Dobres, M. A. (2001). Meaning in the making: Agency and the social embodiment of technology and art. In M. B. Schiffer (Ed.), *Anthropological perspectives on technology* (pp. 47–76). Albuquerque: University of New Mexico Press.

Eagly, A. H., & Crowley, M. (1986). Gender and helping behavior: A meta-analytic review of the social psychological literature. *Psychological Bulletin, 100,* 283–308.

Eibl-Eibesfeldt, I. (1989). *Human ethology.* New York: Aldine de Gruyter.

Gouldner, A. W. (1960). The norm of reciprocity: A preliminary statement. *American Sociological Review, 25,* 161–178.

Gray, K., & Wegner, D. M. (2009). Moral typecasting: Divergent perceptions of moral agents and moral patients. *Journal of Personality and Social Psychology, 96,* 505–520.

Greene, J. D., Cushman, F. A., Stewart, L. A., Lowenberg, K., Nystrom, L. E., & Cohen, J. D. (2009). Pushing moral buttons: The interaction between personal force and intention in moral judgment. *Cognition, 111,* 364–371.

Haidt, J. (2007). The new synthesis in moral psychology. *Science, 316,* 998–1002.

Hamilton, W. D. (1964). The genetical evolution of social behaviour: I and II. *Journal of Theoretical Biology, 7,* 1–52.

Hoijer, B. (2004). The discourse of global compassion: The audience and media reporting of human suffering. *Media, Culture, and Society, 26,* 513–531.

Hrdy, S. B. (2009). *Mothers and others: The evolutionary origins of mutual understanding.* Cambridge, MA: Harvard University Press.

Keltner, D., Young, R. C., & Buswell, B. N. (1997). Appeasement in human emotion, social practice, and personality. *Aggressive Behavior, 23,* 359–374.

Kollock, P. (1998). Social dilemmas: The anatomy of cooperation. *Annual Review of Sociology, 24,* 183–214.

Krebs, D. L. (2007). Deciphering the structure of the moral sense: A review of Marc Hauser's *Moral minds: How nature designed our universal sense of right and wrong. Evolution and Human Behavior, 28,* 294–298.

Krupp, D. B., Debruine, L. M., & Barclay, P. (2008). A cue to kinship promotes cooperation for the public good. *Evolution and Human Behavior, 29,* 49–55.

Lorenz, K. (1943). Die angeborenen Formen möglicher Erfahrung [The innate forms of potential experience]. *Zeitschrift fur Tierpsychologie, 5,* 235–409.

McKeogh, C. (2002). *Innocent civilians: The morality of killing in war.* New York: Palgrave.

Mehu, M., Grammer, K., & Dunbar, R. I. M. (2007). Smiles when sharing. *Evolution and Human Behavior, 28*, 415–422.

Mikhail, J. (2007). Universal moral grammar: Theory, evidence and the future. *Trends in Cognitive Sciences, 11*, 143–152.

Moll, J., Zahn, R., de Oliveira-Souza, R., Krueger, F., & Grafman, J. (2005). The neural basis of human moral cognition. *Nature Reviews/Neuroscience, 6*, 799–809.

Nelissen, R. M. A., Dijker, A. J. M., & de Vries, N. K. (2007). How to turn a hawk into a dove and vice versa: Interactions between emotions and goals in a give-some dilemma game. *Journal of Experimental Social Psychology, 43*, 280–286.

Numan, M. (2012). Neural circuits regulating maternal behavior: Implications for understanding the neural basis of social cooperation and competition. In S. L. Brown, R. M. Brown, & L. A. Penner (Eds.), *Moving beyond self-interest: Perspectives from evolutionary biology, neuroscience, and the social sciences* (pp. 89–108). Oxford, UK: Oxford University Press.

Park, J. T., Schaller, M., & Van Vugt, M. (2008). Psychology of human kin recognition: Heuristic cues, erroneous inferences, and their implications. *Review of General Psychology, 12*, 215–235.

Petrinovich, L., O'Neill, P., & Jorgensen, M. (1993). An empirical study of moral intuitions: Toward an evolutionary ethics. *Journal of Personality and Social Psychology, 64*, 467–478.

Rousseau, D. M., Sitkin, S. B., Burt, R. S., & Camerer, C. (1998). Not so different after all: A cross-discipline view of trust. *Academy of Management Review, 23*, 393–404.

Scruton, R. (2011). *Beauty: A very short introduction.* Oxford, UK: Oxford University Press.

Sternberg, R. J. (1998). A balance theory of wisdom. *Review of General Psychology, 2*, 347–365.

Swann, W. B., Gómez, A., Dovidio, J. F., Hart, S., & Jetten, J. (2010). Dying and killing for one's group: Identity fusion moderates responses to intergroup versions of the trolley problem. *Psychological Science, 21*, 1176–1183.

Trivers, R. L. (1971). The evolution of reciprocal altruism. *Quarterly Review of Biology, 46*, 35–57.

Van Lange, P. A. M., Ouwekerk, J. W., & Tazelaar, M. J. A. (2002). How to overcome the detrimental effects of noise in social interaction: The benefits of generosity. *Journal of Personality and Social Psychology, 82*, 768–780.

Weiner, B., Perry, R. P., & Magnusson, J. (1988). An attributional analysis of reactions to stigmas. *Journal of Personality and Social Psychology, 55*(5), 738–748.

Wiggins, D. (2006). *Ethics: Twelve lectures on the philosophy of morality.* London: Penguin Books.

Wispé, L. (1991). *The psychology of sympathy.* New York: Plenum Press.

Young, L., & Dungan, J. (2012). Where in the brain is morality?: Everywhere and maybe nowhere. *Social Neuroscience, 7*, 1–10.

Zebrowitz, L. A., Fellous, J.-M., Mignault, A., & Andreoletti, C. (2003). Trait impressions as overgeneralized responses to adaptively significant facial qualities: Evidence from connectionist modeling. *Personality and Social Psychology Review, 7*, 194–215.

CHAPTER 45

The Attachment Approach
to Moral Judgment

Aner Govrin

What are the rules and patterns guiding the rapid, automatic, and unconscious processes of moral judgment?

The attachment approach suggests that early interactions with caregivers give rise to a dyadic representation of morality—adult acting upon a child—that determines how moral judgments are construed, used, and understood.

When looking at moral situations, one can discern that despite the variety and differences in content of moral situations, people recognize them immediately, intuitively, and effortlessly. Just think of how situations such as medical negligence, the death penalty, rape, theft, and torture methods used against terrorists are crucially different. And yet people easily categorize all of these situations as requiring right–wrong judgments. What cognitive processes unite different moral situations in one category? How are moral situations represented in our minds? How do people recognize moral situations and notice their patterns?

Recent research in moral psychology has produced strong evidence to suggest that moral judgment is intuitive and accomplished by a rapid, automatic, and unconscious psychological process (Damasio, 1994; Greene & Haidt, 2002; Hauser,

2006; Mikhail, 2000; Shweder & Haidt, 1994). There is, however, considerable disagreement and confusion as to what moral intuitions are and how they work.

The attachment approach to moral judgment suggests that the patterns of people's moral decisions actually follow fairly straightforwardly from internally represented principles or rules acquired in infancy. My assumption is that moral judgment is a complex cognitive achievement that may depend on a set of building block systems that appear early on in human ontogeny and phylogeny. This claim comes in the wake of 20 years of infant research showing that the knowledge accumulated during the first year of life is the foundation on which later learning, including language acquisition, numeracy, object categorization, social relations, and other complex cognitive skills, rests (Ensink & Mayes, 2010; Mandler &

McDonough, 1998; Spelke, 2000; Starkey & Cooper, 1980; Wynn, 1990).

Research in the moral domain has shown that infants have an inherent moral foundation—the capacity and preparedness to judge the actions of others, a certain sense of justice, and an intuitive response to meanness. In a number of studies (Hamlin, Wynn, Bloom, & Mahajan, 2011; Hamlin, Wynn, & Bloom, 2007, 2010; Hamlin, 2013a), babies showed a clear preference for an individual who was being helpful as opposed to someone who obstructed another's path in life. Moreover, the studies show that infants preferred a helpful individual to one who stood on the sidelines and the latter to one who was deliberately unhelpful.

However, the experiments tell us very little about the procedures or moral principles that infants learn, how they encode a moral situation, and what representations they compare it with. My supposition is that, in the same way as an infant born with inherent linguistic faculties will only learn to speak if he or she grows up in the presence of people who talk to him or her, infant–caregiver interactions enable us to construe and give meaning to moral situations.

In order to establish the link between early infancy and the acquisition of basic moral faculties, we have to be able to define (1) the appropriate stimulus that is likely to lead to the learning of the actual processes by which moral judgment is exercised and (2) the deep structures that are common to the entire range of moral situations, including the link between those structures and the initial impetus that made moral learning possible.

How Can These Assertions Be Tested?

There is no direct evidence of the way in which infants acquire moral knowledge, just as there is no direct evidence of the way in which infants learn the deep structures of language. Therefore, we must discover what the deep structures of moral situations are and then look into the way in which these are linked to the first year of a child's life.

The aim is to advance the most basic set of assumptions that can still account for various moral judgments and situations. My account is mainly about moral situations that

involve harming others because they represent an essential component of moral judgment. This seems to be true across cultures (Nichols, 2004).

The fundamental unit of moral situations is the dyad. I term this phenomenon the *dyad-superiority effect* of moral situations. Essentially, this means that moral situations are mentally represented as two parties in conflict. Strong evidence exists for the dyadic nature of moral situations. A series of studies by Gray and colleagues (Gray, Waytz, & Young, 2012) showed that the essence of moral judgment is the perception of two complementary minds—a dyad consisting of an intentional moral agent and a suffering moral patient. As the dyad is being perceived by an observer, there are three parties to a basic moral judgment situation: two conflicting parties—the perceived adult (A) and the perceived child (C)— and an observer (O). O makes a judgment on the dyad $A \rightarrow C$.

O: Observer.
A: Perceived adult (wrongdoer).
C: Perceived child (victim).
$\rightarrow$ Behavior, harm done, overall attitude of A toward C.

Given the huge amount of data that exists in relation to any given moral dyad, how do we organize the information for a particular perceived dyad? How do we extract a judgment from the basic features of A, $\rightarrow$, and C?

It is probably the case that, in the process of reaching a moral judgment, the moral dyad that appears in our minds is weighed up against some prior knowledge we have about dyads. My premise is that we can reach a moral judgment only if, in our minds, we hold some reliable form of prior knowledge of the moral situation, a mental representation of what we know about conflicts in our social environment.

Thus I am assuming that we deal with moral situations in the same way that we deal with other concepts. Moral knowledge, just as other human knowledge, is organized around encodings of prototypical cases, rather than via the use and storage of rules and definitions. In the case of moral judgment, we classify the situation as moral and then judge it according to the preexisting representation it most closely resembles (Hahn & Ramscar, 2001).

My assertion is that the various components of a moral situation—such as intentionality, controllability, personal responsibility, and free will—have an additional layer of representational content that has not been noticed by social psychologists. They are secondary features. They represent something more primary, more basic.

The central underlying thesis that I advance is that the most informative features of moral judgments—intent, free will, and controllability—are supported by a more deeply seated feature—our knowledge about infants (or children) and adults. We possess an affective and cognitive mechanism that is highly sensitive to the distinctions between child-like and adult-like traits. As I discuss, these traits are very instructive when it comes to an understanding of others. The same parameters that are crucial to the attribution of responsibility for a wrongdoing (intentionality, controllability, and free will) are pivotal to the distinction between children and adults.

The evaluation of the moral situation is a derivative of our inner schemas of children (dependents) and adults (independents). In our minds, different expectations, feelings, cognitions, and mental images are associated with children and adults. For example, we are emotionally much more responsive to the suffering of children than to that of adults (Dijker, 2001).

Strong emotional reactivity to the suffering of children and infants is not the only thing that distinguishes the way in which we relate to children and adults. Apparently, children and adults are identified by separate schemas that also involve cognitions and attributions. Children are perceived as weak, needy, helpless, lacking control, vulnerable, dependent, and unable to take care of others. These traits have profound implications for our attributions and moral judgments.

I suggest that we represent each of the parties (A and C) in ways that are comparable to our representations of children and adults. All our efforts are geared to construct the reality of the moral situation in terms of an adult–child dyad. Judgments placing the parties on the child–adult spectrum come to mind quickly and effortlessly, seemingly popping out of nowhere, without much conscious awareness of their origins or of the manner of their formation.

The schemas are fixed around defining features of adults and children, such as big–small, weak–strong, vulnerable–resistant, helpless–powerful, dependent–independent, knowingly–unknowingly, responsible–irresponsible. The schemas are broad enough to handle endless variations of these themes. I suggest that when facing a moral situation the mind uses these schemas to select and organize the information that will most effectively aid us in the judgment process.

In generating a nonconscious moral judgment, we perform two mental operations: We impose a dyadic structure of child–adult (or agent–patient; Gray et al., 2012) upon two parties in conflict, and we compare the behavior of A toward C with our prior expectations of what adults should and should not do to children. Acts that violate our expectations are judged as morally wrong. Although the decision as to which party is C or A is highly subjective, the general traits that are associated with children and those associated with adults are constant and universal.

As Figure 45.1 demonstrates, in generating a nonconscious moral judgment, we perform two mental operations:

1. Evaluating the child-like and the adult-like characteristics of each party and deciding, if we are able to, which of the parties matches an adult schema and which a child schema.
2. Evaluating the relationship between the adult-like and child-like parties in terms of (→), where → is the symbol for the harm done, as well as the overall relation of the independent vis-à-vis the dependent in a particular dyad. That is, we do not have schemas only for children and adults. We also possess a schema for the dyadic relation, centered on prior expectations of how adults should treat children.

The evaluation of child-like and adult-like characteristics in a particular moral situation is observer relative. The same individual in a particular dyad might be construed as A by one person and as C by another. In

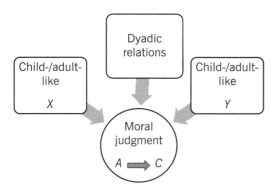

FIGURE 45.1. The attachment model of moral judgment. In generating a nonconscious moral judgment, we perform two mental operations: We impose a dyadic structure of child–adult/agent–patient (Gray et al., 2012) on two parties in conflict, and we compare the behavior of *A* toward *C* with our prior expectations of what adults should and should not do to children. Acts that violate our expectations are judged as morally wrong. Although the decision as to which party is child-like or adult-like is highly subjective, the general traits that are associated with children and those associated with adults are constant and universal.

fact, *construing the parties as C or A is the principal act of moral judgment.* If party *X* matches an adult schema (*A*), and party *Y* matches a child schema (*C*), it means that we think *X* has done harm to *Y* and that we sympathize with *C* and condemn *A*. But this is only true for an observer who perceives *X* as adult-like and *Y* as child-like. So child-like and adult-like schemas are not just cognitive assessments of traits. They incorporate our emotions, judgments, and actions toward the parties.

The general idea is that moral judgment involves computing child-like and adult-like characteristics and comparing the adult-like party's behavior toward the child-like party with our prior expectations. This process is almost like a reflex: It operates quickly and automatically so that, for instance, one cannot help taking into account the child-like face of an adult, the young age of a thief, or the unintended harm of an accidental killing. This is a natural language of relations between dependents and independents that

we all understand without having been consciously instructed in it.

Contrary to what the accounts of sentimentalists or intuitionists may argue (Haidt, 2010; Prinz, 2007), our moral judgments, unlike our aesthetic tastes, are not arbitrary. Even when they lead to contradictory conclusions, they are not entirely flexible. Though it can be said that the construing of moral judgment is "tolerant" and allows diverse cultural and personal projections, it is not the case that each and every projection will be perceived as sensible and/or acceptable. *A dyad will allow certain projections and block others if, and only if, it is construed as A → C.* Moral judgments are therefore constrained by rules that are guided by the knowledge we have as to how dyads should function and work. Our expectations of perceived independents in the presence of dependents impose extrinsic requirements on our moral judgments.

Historical Context

The idea that our moral sense is essentially connected to early ties of dependency between the child and his or her caregiver is not new. It was suggested by John Bowlby's attachment theory and Carol Gilligan's ethics of care (Bowlby, 1944, 1953, 1958, 1980; Gilligan, 1982; Gilligan & Wiggins, 1987). However, the ideas of attachment theory and ethics of care have not been accorded the centrality in moral psychology appropriate to their importance.

Darwin (1874), theorized that social instincts originated in "parental and filial affections" (p. 95). Lakoff and Johnson (1999) write: "Brains tend to optimize on the basis of what they already have, to add only what is necessary. Over the course of evolution, newer parts of the brain have built on, taken input from, and used older parts of the brain" (p. 43). Is it really plausible to suggest that if the infant–caregiver system can be put to work in the service of a parent protecting his or her child, the brain would build a new system to duplicate what it could already do in other social relations?

Dyadic morality (Gray & Wegner, 2008, 2009; Gray et al., 2012) has significantly informed the current theory. Gray and his colleagues suggest that mind perception is the essence of moral judgment. Gray's argument is that a prototypical *immoral act* should include a moral agent who intentionally causes harm and a moral patient who suffers as a result. I see my theory as completing and enriching this perspective, recognizing the deep roots of the agent–patient dyad in the representations of dependents and caregivers.

The attachment approach to moral judgment draws heavily on the theory of schematic representation (Rumelhart & Ortony, 1977) as a simple model for understanding moral judgments. These judgments are based on child and adult schemas. I have chosen schemas because they are often more task-oriented than are exemplars or prototypes and less concerned with recognition and classification. Rather, a schema is a mental framework for organizing important knowledge, creating a meaningful structure of related concepts based on prior experiences. Therefore, schemas seem more appropriate to the moral domain, which involves not merely recognition and classification but also the organization of material in a particular way.

Connectionism

What model of the brain can describe such a hypothesis? Some researchers (Freeman & Ambady, 2011; Harman, Mason, & Sinnott-Armstrong, 2010; Hopfield, 1982; Rumelhart & McClelland, 1986; Thagard, 1989, 2000) argued that a connectionist network model possibly provides us with a way of explaining how people reach judgments about others. Dynamical systems, such as a recurrent connectionist network of the human brain, are powerful in their ability to integrate multiple simultaneous sources of information. In a recurrent connectionist network, there are a number of nodes with connections that can be positive (excitatory) or negative (inhibitory). Positive links connect one set of nodes to other nodes so that, as one of the nodes becomes more excited, its excitation increases the excitation of the other nodes (Freeman & Ambady, 2011). Conversely, as the excitation of one such node lessens or is in receipt of negative levels of excitation, the excitation of the other nodes is lessened. When applied to elements in a moral situation, positive and negative excitation cycles will circulate in the network, and a steady state will be achieved, resulting in a full gestalt of the moral situation as $A \rightarrow C$.

Because a node's activation is a function of all the positive and negative connections to other nodes that are activated in parallel, the final activation of a node (i.e., at the point at which the system stabilizes) can be thought of as the satisfaction of multiple constraints. In a connectionist model, each connection between nodes is a constraint (Freeman & Ambady, 2011). For instance, a node representing the category "baby face" might excite and be excited by another node representing the cognition "wrongdoing was unintentional." When these two nodes are incorporated in a larger recurrent network, the "baby face" node serves as a constraint on the network. That is, for the network to ever achieve stability, activation must flow through that connection and incorporate it into an overall stable pattern that includes all other nodal connections.

Thus nodes in a recurrent network constrain each other in finding the best overall pattern that is consistent with the input. Such a model of a connectionist network can explain how one single component of a dyad influences the other components.

Serious moral dilemmas can also be explained by a connectionist model. These dilemmas require relatively high levels of cognitive processing, because each party is simultaneously associated with "bad" and "good" aspects. Thus each side sort of blocks the conflicting characteristics attributed to each party. The process involves a dynamic competition between victim–perpetrator representations ("they are victims but at the same time perpetrators") that continuously compete. The bombing of civilians in Dresden in World War II, the use of harsh interrogation methods against terrorists, and the bullying of cruel criminals by the police are some of the cases in which moral judgment is effortful and requires a great deal of processing.

For the system to settle into a stable state (e.g., reach a final moral judgment), the parallel and partially active victim-versus-perpetrator category nodes of each party must engage in a dynamic competition, with one gradually gaining activation and the other gradually dying off, as they suppress each other's activation through inhibition.

Note that the model of a holistic dyad representation does not mean that the competing traits of the two parties (actor–patient) must give way to a winner-take-all mechanism. Rather, it would seem more plausible that in serious moral dilemmas there are a multitude of representations also at the level of the dyad and that the competition takes place at that level as well. This is naturally accommodated by a connectionist approach. "Dyad units" represent this domain on various levels of abstraction.

Theoretical Stance

The child–caregiver dyad is perhaps the most undertheorized domain in moral psychology. Though there is an enormous body of literature showing the link between patterns of early attachment and moral behavior (Mikulincer & Florian, 2000; Shaver & Mikulincer, 2012; van IJzendoorn, 1997), the subject of parenthood in infancy remains in the margins, exiled by moral psychology's long-standing cultural bias against it and ignorance of the subject's importance.

In most of the studies, infants were still being perceived apart from their surroundings, as if they possessed an isolated mind that was developing separately from the environment in which they were growing up. For example, Hamlin et al. (2007, 2010) posit that the capacity of infants to evaluate individuals on the basis of their social interactions is unlearned (Hamlin, 2013b).

This lacuna has a long history in moral psychology that stretches from Piaget and Kohlberg to contemporary moral psychology. And yet, infant research conducted outside of moral psychology (Beebe & Lachman, 2002; Emde, 1988; Fonagy & Target, 2007; Mayes, Fonagy, & Target, 2007) shows that out of all the influences around him or her, the one that affects the newborn the most is the maternal care that he or she receives. Despite this consistent finding, theories in moral development have failed to integrate it in any meaningful way.

From another perspective, the attachment approach to moral judgment belongs to a set of theories in psychology that claim that moral judgment takes the form of intuition, accomplished by a rapid, automatic, and unconscious psychological process (Haidt, 2001; Hauser, 2006; Mikhail, 2000; Shweder & Haidt, 1994). But it differs from these theories in many important respects.

First, it posits that moral judgment could arise through the influence of either affect or reason. Emotions and gut feelings are essential parts of moral judgment, but cool reason and consequentialist principles can also influence the dyad construal and add to the computing process. Second, the added value of the attachment approach is that it specifies in detail what exactly goes on "in our heads" when we follow our moral intuitions and the way in which the entire procedure relates to cognitive processes. The intuitions and emotions behind moral judgments are rule based.

By rules, I mean inferential devices for categorization, estimation, paired comparisons, and other judgmental tasks that go beyond the information given. The rule concept denotes an if–then relation of the type *if (cues), then (judgment*; Kruglanski & Gigerenzer, 2011). One of the rules we use in judging moral situations is: If a party is perceived to be child-like (*cues*) then we judge that party as less accountable, less reprehensible, less responsible, less wrathful, and so on.

Third, the important thing is that the rules apply to whole relations, not to specific harmful acts. We do not judge an act as wrongdoing; we judge an entire relationship, a dyad. Wrongdoings are violations of our expectations of independents. Acts are judged as transgressions when an observer evaluates or senses that a dyad went wrong, violated an expected contingency.

One of the main merits of the proposed model is that it has an explanatory power for understanding one of the most haunting questions in moral psychology: Are moral rules absolute and universal, or are they culturally dependent?

Is Morality Universal and Absolute or Culturally Driven?

How can moral knowledge based on dyadic principles claim to be universal when moral systems and values differ so much from one another?

The dyadic principles, it has to be remembered, are not intended to be common to all moral systems. These are principles that are intended to serve as a "toolkit" that a child acquires in order to learn how right–wrong judgments of all kinds are reached. It is the platform on which moral judgments are carried, thought about, and understood. It's somewhat like a car: When we turn on the ignition, the car operates like a car—not a boat—simply because it's built like a car. However, if we don't turn the key, nothing happens. The interactions between infant and caregiver are required in order to feed moral principle acquisition into the system.

However, these infant–caregiver interactions do not determine the content, form, or nature of the specific morality. But they contain all the principles necessary for most moral judgments to be reached in different cultures and among a variety of agents. The cultural and personal differences among agents are encoded as assigning different weight to the various components of the dyad. Hence, the dyadic rules must be rich and specific enough to enable each child to acquire basic moral knowledge but flexible enough to enable him or her to acquire different moral preferences in different cultures.

Evidence

The attachment approach to moral judgment is supported by numerous studies in various disciplines, including moral psychology, infant research, and cognitive neuroscience. Though none of this evidence is unequivocal, when put together, it offers, at the very least, an acceptable level of support for the proposed theory. The theory includes two hypotheses. The first claims that moral principles are determined during the first year of life through parent–child interaction. The second hypothesis deals with the way in which people break moral situations down to their defining components: Who resembles a child, who resembles an adult, and what is the nature of the relations between them?

It has to be noted that the first and second hypotheses are not dependent on one another. In other words, it is conceivable that in the deep structures of moral situations there is a basic identification of the two sides along the dependent–independent axis and an assessment of whether the adult side had behaved in line with our expectations. But this process can be formed in different ways (e.g., through education or cultural influences) and not necessarily in the first year of life. And yet there are many reasons for the belief that the first year of life is critical to the development of moral faculties.

There is a great deal of evidence to support the view that expectations of social relations emerge in the first months of life through infant–caregiver interactions (see Beebe & Stern, 1977; Beebe & Lachmann, 1988; Sander, 1977, 1983, 1985; Stern, 1985, 1998). A principle called ongoing regulations between mother and infant (Beebe & Lachmann, 2002) provides the most basic rule for organizing representations. An infant develops an ability to anticipate when something is likely to happen and an expectation that what he or she does has consequences. In addition, we know that infants have specific capacities that are related to moral judgment: Young infants understand intentional action as goal-directed and rational (Gergely, 2002, 2011; Meltzoff & Moore, 1995; Schwier, Van Maanen, Carpenter, & Tomasello, 2006).

The second hypothesis according to which observers look at both sides for signs of "child" and "adult" is based on indirect evidence. For example, as already noted, the key elements in moral judgment—such as internal and controllable causality and intentionality—are significant because they include a wealth of information about the characteristics of child–adult that the observer is looking for.

Another line of evidence comes from a number of experiments (Berry & Zebrowitz-McArthur, 1985) that indicate that a baby-faced defendant will be considered less likely to have committed an offense intentionally and more likely to have committed it through negligence. Beyond the model's ability to explain a wide range of phenomena, it also gives rise to a number of new and distinctive predictions that future work could directly examine.

The model predicts that any given change in one node of the dyad component (A, C, and →) will lead to changes in all other nodes, as the system works over time to maximally satisfy all of its constraints in parallel. For example, when there are conflicting considerations (such as malice without harm; harm mild but intended; baby face and intended harm; harm planned to affect one individual but intended to save several other potential victims), there is considerable tension between the nodes. This might reduce the system's efficiency and slow down the process, because it will take the system more time to reach a full gestalt of the dyad.

Extension and Expansion

Apart from its contribution to moral psychology, the attachment approach to moral judgment is likely to augment and enrich two other centrally important fields of study: infant and brain research.

From the knowledge acquired by an infant in the first year of life, one can see what the psychologist Susan Carey (2011) termed *core cognition*. Carey argues that explaining the human capacity for conceptual understanding begins with the observation that evolution offers developmental primitives that are much richer than the sensorimotor representations that many assume are the input to all learning. Some of these developmental primitives are embedded in systems of what Carey calls core cognition.

Core cognitions differ from other conceptual representations because they include innate perceptual input analyzers that identify the entities in core domains, a long evolutionary history, continuity throughout development, and iconic (or analog) formats. Core cognition carves the mind into significant subsystems. It is one very distinctive part of the human mind: No other systems of conceptual representations share its suite of characteristics. Thus one could say that if the evolutionary process of natural selection has endowed our minds with input analyzers, then one would think that such processes would be of use to adults, as well as to children.

The theory's big challenge will be to show the way in which the sensorimotor experiences in the first year of life are translated into knowledge about dyadic relations and how they form a set of expectations that is no longer linked to the direct relations between child and caregiver.

In brain research, the challenge will be to prove that moral situations are resolved as a result of "moral computations": Whenever a moral problem arises, the observer computes the "child" and "adult" components of each side of the dyad. The observer then calculates the extent to which the conduct toward the child by the side perceived as the adult deviates from the observer's expectations. Of course, one has to add a subjective component, which is linked to the emotional connection and the way the observer feels toward each party.

The Challenge in the Philosophical Domain

If we unconsciously and intuitively engage in computing each party's child-like and adult-like features and compare the adult-like party's behavior to our former expectations, we are not employing moral principles. Moral principles (such as Kant's categorical imperative or the utilitarian principle) make no reference to particular people, places, or times. Yet moral computation is greatly influenced by these considerations. How, then, do we determine what is right and what is wrong? According to the proposed theory, our only guide to moral right and moral wrong is our innate detection system for child-like and adult-like features and our prior expectations of adults. So, even if there indeed are moral principles, they are not part of the knowledge on which we based our moral judgment.

One way to tackle this problem is to posit that general moral principles such as those suggested by Rawls and Kant enable us to rise above the construal of subjective dyad. Turning the moral mechanism into a universal law enables us, for example, to protect the weak and prevent moral injustices independently of the emotional mechanism that links an individual to a particular party.

In other words, moral principles apply the same parameters to moral judgment as does the dyadic construal. They merely introduce additional cognitions that had not previously been taken into account. Whereas the "natural" psychological mechanism often identifies people as child-like on the basis of resemblance to and membership in that same group, the moral principles compel us to ignore this component and relate to all suffering people as child-like. They might be used as constraints that inhibit personal preference, cultural bias, or any other kind of subjective factors besides the parameters of the general dyadic rules.

In conclusion, given the limited research base, this model—although reflecting available research evidence—primarily serves a heuristic function. I hope, nonetheless, that the model will inspire researchers to gain more empirical data on the mechanisms through which early attachment relations modulate moral judgments.

REFERENCES

Beebe, B., & Lachmann, F. (Eds.). (1988). *Mother–infant mutual influence and precursors of psychic structure.* Hillsdale, NJ: Analytic Press.

Beebe, B., & Lachmann, F. (2002). *Infant research and adult treatment: Co-constructing interactions.* Hillsdale, NJ: Analytic Press.

Beebe, B., & Stern, D. (1977). Engagement–disengagement and early object experiences. In N. Freedman & S. Grand (Ed.), *Communicative structures and psychic structures* (pp. 35–55). New York: Plenum Press.

Berry, D. S., & Zebrowitz-McArthur, L. Z. (1985). Some components and consequences of a babyface. *Journal of Personality and Social Psychology, 48*(2), 312–323.

Bowlby, J. (1944). Forty-four juvenile thieves: Their characters and home-life: II. *International Journal of Psychoanalysis, 25,* 107–128.

Bowlby, J. (1953). *Child care and the growth of love.* London: Penguin Books.

Bowlby, J. (1958). The nature of the child's tie to his mother. *International Journal of Psychoanalysis, 39,* 350–373.

Bowlby, J. (1980). *Attachment and loss.* New York: Basic Books.

Carey, S. (2011). Précis of the origin of concepts. *Behavioral and Brain Sciences, 34*(3), 113–167.

Damasio, A. (1994). *Descartes' error.* Boston: Norton.

Darwin, C. (1874). *The descent of man and selection in relation to sex.* New York: Rand McNally.

Dijker, A. J. (2001). The influence of perceived suffering and vulnerability on the experience of pity. *European Journal of Social Psychology, 31*(6), 659–676.

Emde, R. N. (1988). Reflections on mothering and on reexperiencing the early relationship experience. *Infant Mental Health Journal, 9*(1), 4–9.

Ensink, K., & Mayes, L. C. (2010). The development of mentalisation in children from a theory of mind perspective. *Psychoanalytic Inquiry, 30*(4), 301–337.

Fonagy, P., & Target, M. (2007). The rooting of the mind in the body: New links between attachment theory and psychoanalytic thought. *Journal of the American Psychoanalytic Association, 55*(2), 411–456.

Freeman, J. B., & Ambady, N. (2011). A dynamic interactive theory of person construal. *Psychological Review, 118*(2), 247–279.

Gergely, G. (2002). The development of understanding self and agency. In U. Goswami (Ed.), *Blackwell handbook of childhood cognitive development* (pp. 26–46). Malden, MA: Blackwell.

Gergely, G. (2011). Kinds of agents: The origins of understanding instrumental and communicative agency. In U. Goswami (Ed.), *The Wiley-Blackwell handbook of childhood cognitive development* (2nd ed., pp. 76–105). Hoboken, NJ: Wiley-Blackwell.

Gilligan, C. (1982). *In a different voice: Women's conception of self and morality.* Cambridge, MA: Harvard University Press.

Gilligan, C., & Wiggins, G. (1987). The origins of morality in early childhood relationships. In J. Kagan & S. Lamb (Eds.), *The emergence of morality in young children* (pp. 277–305) Chicago: University of Chicago Press.

Gray, K., Waytz, A., & Young, L. (2012). The moral dyad: A fundamental template unifying moral judgment. *Psychological Inquiry, 23*(2), 206–215.

Gray, K., & Wegner, D. M. (2008). The sting of intentional pain. *Psychological Science, 19*(12), 1260–1262.

Gray, K., & Wegner, D. M. (2009). Moral typecasting: Divergent perceptions of moral agents and moral patients. *Journal of Personality and Social Psychology, 96*(3), 505–520.

Greene, J., & Haidt, J. (2002). How (and where) does moral judgment work? *Trends in Cognitive Sciences, 6*(12), 517–523.

Hahn, U., & Ramscar, M. (Eds.). (2001). *Similarity and categorization.* New York: Oxford University Press.

Haidt, J. (2001). The emotional dog and its rational tail: A social intuitionist approach to moral judgment. *Psychological Review, 108,* 814–834.

Haidt, J. (2010). Moral psychology must not be based on faith and hope: Commentary on Narvaez (2010). *Perspectives on Psychological Science, 5*(2), 182–184.

Hamlin, J. K. (2013a). Failed attempts to help and harm: Intention versus outcome in preverbal infants' social evaluations. *Cognition, 128*(3), 451–474.

Hamlin, J. K. (2013b). Moral judgment and action in preverbal infants and toddlers: Evidence for an innate moral core. *Current Directions in Psychological Science, 22*(3), 186–193.

Hamlin, J. K., Wynn, K., & Bloom, P. (2007). Social evaluation in preverbal infants. *Nature, 450*(7169), 557–559.

Hamlin, J. K., Wynn, K., & Bloom, P. (2010). Three-month-olds show a negativity bias in their social evaluations. *Developmental Science, 13*(6), 923–929.

Hamlin, J. K., Wynn, K., Bloom, P., & Mahajan, N. (2011). How infants and toddlers react to antisocial others. *Proceedings of the National Academy of Sciences of the USA, 108*(50), 19931–19936.

Harman. G., Mason, K., & Sinnott-Armstrong, W. (2010). Moral reasoning. In J. M. Doris (Ed.), *The moral psychology handbook* (pp. 206–245). Oxford, UK: Oxford University Press.

Hauser, M. D. (2006). *Moral minds: How nature designed our universal sense of right and wrong.* London: HarperCollins.

Hauser, M. D. (2007). *Moral minds: The nature of right and wrong.* New York: HarperCollins.

Hopfield, J. J. (1982). Neural networks and physical systems with emergent collective computational abilities. *Proceedings of the National Academy of Sciences of the USA, 79,* 2554–2558.

Kruglanski, A. W., & Gigerenzer, G. (2011). Intuitive and deliberate judgments are based on common principles: Correction to Kruglanski and Gigerenzer. *Psychology Reviews, 118,* 522.

Lakoff, G., & Johnson, M. (1999). *Philosophy in the flesh: The embodied mind and its challenge to Western thought.* New York: Basic Books.

Mandler, J. M., & McDonough, L. (1998). On developing a knowledge base in infancy. *Developmental Psychology, 34*(6), 1274–1288.

Mayes, L., Fonagy, P., & Target, M. (Eds.). (2007). *Developmental science and psychoanalysis: Integration and innovation.* London, UK: Karnac Books.

Meltzoff, A. N., & Moore, M. K. (1995). Infants' understanding of people and things: From body imitation to folk psychology. In J. L. Bermúdez, N. Eilan, & A. Marcel (Eds.), *The body and the self* (pp. 43–69). Cambridge, MA: MIT Press.

Mikhail, J. (2000). Rawls' linguistic analogy: A study of the "generative grammar" model of moral theory described by John Rawls in "A Theory of Justice." Available at *https://papers.ssrn.com/sol3/papers.cfm?abstract_id=766464.*

Mikhail, J. (2011). *Elements of moral cognition: Rawls' linguistic analogy and the cognitive science of moral and legal judgment.* New York: Cambridge University Press.

Mikulincer, M., & Florian, V. (2000). Exploring individual differences in reactions to mortality salience: Does attachment style regulate terror management mechanisms? *Journal of Personality and Social Psychology, 79*(2), 260–273.

Nichols, S. (2004). *Sentimental rules: On the natural foundations of moral judgment.* Oxford, UK: Oxford University Press.

Prinz, J. J. (2007). *The emotional construction of morals.* Oxford, UK: Oxford University Press.

Rumelhart, D. E., & McClelland, J. L. (1986). *Parallel distributed processing: Explorations in the microstructure of cognition: Vol. 1. Foundations.* Cambridge, MA: MIT Press.

Rumelhart, D. E., & Ortony, A. (1977). The representation of knowledge in memory. In R. C. Anderson, R. J. Spiro, & W. E. Montague (Eds.), *Schooling and the acquisition of knowledge* (pp. 99–135). Hillsdale, NJ: Erlbaum.

Sander, L. (1977). The regulation of exchange in the infant–caretaker system and some aspects of the context–content relationship. In M. Lewis & L. Rosenblum (Eds.), *Interaction, conversation, and the development of language* (pp. 133–156). New York: Wiley.

Sander, L. (1983). Polarity paradox and the organizing process in development. In J. D. Call, E. Galenson, & R. Tyson (Eds.), *Frontiers of infant psychiatry* (pp. 315–327). New York: Basic Books.

Sander, L. (1985). Toward a logic of organization in psycho-biological development. In K. Klar & L. Siever (Eds.), *Biological response styles: Clinical implications* (pp. 20–36). Washington DC: American Psychiatric Press.

Schwier, C., Van Maanen, C., Carpenter, M., & Tomasello, M. (2006). Rational imitation in 12-month-old infants. *Infancy, 10*(3), 303–311.

Shaver, P. R., & Mikulincer, M. (2012). An attachment perspective on morality: Strengthening authentic forms of moral decision making. In M. Mikulincer & P. R. Shaver (Eds.), *The social psychology of morality: Exploring the causes of good and evil* (pp. 257–274). Washington, DC: American Psychological Association.

Shweder, R. A., & Haidt, J. (1994). The future

of moral psychology: Truth, intuition, and the pluralist way. In B. Puka (Ed.), *Reaching out: Caring, altruism, and prosocial behavior.* (pp. 336–341) New York: Garland.

Spelke, E. S. (2000). Core knowledge. *American Psychologist, 55*(11), 1233–1243.

Starkey, P., & Cooper, R. G. (1980). Perception of numbers by human infants. *Science, 210*(4473), 1033–1035.

Stern, D. N. (1985). *The interpersonal world of the infant.* New York: Basic Books.

Stern, D. N. (1998). *The interpersonal world of the infant: A view from psychoanalysis and developmental psychology.* London, UK: Karnac.

Thagard, P. (1989). Explanatory coherence. *Behavioral and Brain Sciences, 12*(3), 435–502.

Thagard, P. (2000). *Coherence in thought and action* Cambridge, MA: MIT Press.

van IJzendoorn, M. H. (1997). Attachment, emergent morality, and aggression: Toward a developmental socioemotional model of antisocial behavior. *International Journal of Behavioral Development, 21*(4), 703–727.

Wynn, K. (1990). Children's understanding of counting. *Cognition, 36*(2), 155–193.

CHAPTER 46

Ethogenesis

Evolution, Early Experience, and Moral Becoming

Darcia Narvaez

> **What is the best comprehensive theory for understanding moral development?**
>
> Taking an evolutionary developmental systems standpoint that includes multiple ecological levels and extragenetic inheritances (e.g., developmental niche, self-organization), ethogenesis describes species-typical moral development, which includes relational attunement and communal imagination—orientations and capacities that emerge from the biopsychosocial development of the brain/mind in early life within a species-typical niche.

What is the best comprehensive theory for understanding moral development? Ethogenesis takes an evolutionary developmental systems perspective to describe how moral dispositions are biosocially shaped by experience, especially in early life when basic foundations for biopsychosocial functioning are laid. It describes how development mismatched with the evolved development niche creates a different human nature, one that does not match up with 99% of humanity's history nor displays the characteristics of what Darwin called humanity's "moral sense."

Ethogenesis directs attention to evolved global mindsets that can guide human perception, interpretation, cognition, and behavior. Triune ethics meta-theory (TEM;

Narvaez, 2008, 2014a, 2016) was developed to bring the embodied perspective into moral psychological research (Narvaez, 2010b). TEM is part of the trend toward studying the effects of embodied experience on biopsychosocial functioning. It provides a way to integrate findings across neuroscience, developmental, personality, and clinical psychology. TEM identifies several neurobiologically based moral mindsets and proposes, for example, that self-regulatory capacities are critical for moral functioning. As illustration, when the stress response is activated, blood flows away from the prefrontal cortex, impairing higher order thought processes (Arnsten, 2009); with the mobilization of muscles and survival systems for personal safety, attention is drawn to issues of self-concern. TEM also points out how neurobiological functions critical for moral functioning are significantly shaped by early experience (Schore, 1994, 1996, 1997, 2000, 2001, 2003a, 2003b, 2005, 2013). Notably, the parameters and threshold for the hypothalamic–pituitary–adrenal gland axis are established in early life, so that when early experience is highly stressful, an individual can develop a hyper- or hyporeactive stress response, undermining capacities for social attunement (Lupien, McEwen, Gunnar, & Heim, 2009). The vagus nerve, critically formed by early caregiving, is fundamental to social approach and social closeness (Porges, 2011), capacities necessary for compassionate moral behavior. When basic neurobiological structures are poorly developed, humanity's highest moral capacities are undermined, and self-concern emerges as "normal" and morally justifiable.

The TEM framework for understanding moral development and behavior focuses on three orientations rooted in global brain states identified by MacLean (1990): protectionism, engagement, and imagination. When action is taken from an orientation, trumping other values and actions, it becomes an ethic. The protectionist orientation focuses on self-preservation through general distrust or, more specifically, through social opposition or withdrawal. Protectionist orientations are based in clinical notions of internalizing and externalizing and the power of social stress to direct perception, thought, and action in self-protective ways, guided by primitive survival systems (fight–flight–freeze–faint; Sapolsky, 2004). The individual's social homeostasis is thrown off, and he or she reacts cacostatically, too strongly (aggressively) or too weakly (withdrawing) in a one-up–one-down hierarchical manner. Protectionism can become dispositional if early experience is inadequate or other trauma occurs later in life that impairs neurobiological flexibility.

The engagement orientation draws on notions of emotional presence, relational attunement, and unconditional positive regard (Rogers, 1961), which rely on flexible developmental neurobiological capacities such as vagal tone (Porges, 2011) and socially supportive systems such as the oxytocin system (Carter, 2003). When the evolved developmental niche is provided in childhood, an engagement orientation develops naturally

from experience, learned from experiencing intersubjectivity, emotional presence, reverence, play, and empathy (Emde, Biringen, Clyman, & Oppenheim, 1991; Trevarthen, 2005).

The imagination orientation emerges from executive functions such as planning, foresight, and abstraction (which take decades to fully develop), allowing for an imaginative perspective in social relations beyond face-to-face interaction. The imagination orientation can build on either protectionism or attunement. When imagination builds on relational attunement, as in a species-typical brain, it coordinates cortical and subcortical systems for cooperative and compassionate behavior. When imagination builds on self-protectionism, due to the (misdeveloped) power of survival systems that then hijack cortical systems, it results in an aggressive type (vicious) that seeks control over others or a withdrawing type (detached) in which abstraction capabilities are used without a sense of relational consequence.

Dispositional or Situational?

In any given situation, an orientation can become the mindset that dominates perception and action. For most people, moral mindsets shift frequently, depending on the context— who is present and the task at hand. Moral mindsets can be tonic, slowly aroused, for example, from a physical irritation that goes on too long and surpasses tolerance. Or they can be phasic, suddenly appearing, such as flying off the handle when driving. Sometimes there is a struggle between mindsets, and an oscillation between states can occur. Arpaly (2003) provides two useful examples of how the shifting can occur. The Nazi minister of propaganda, Joseph Goebbels, who organized attacks on Jews during Hitler's regime, occasionally behaved compassionately toward Jews he met, suggesting an engagement mindset. But afterward, because the Jews were members of a group he was trying to help exterminate, he would interpret his kindness as weakness of the will and harden his resolve to not lapse again, increasing his cruelty. In this case, Goebbels appears to have exhibited engagement in the presence of Jews and shifted into vicious imagination outside their presence. The storybook character Huckleberry Finn (Twain, 2001), like Goebbels, also interpreted as weakness of the will his reluctance to remit to the authorities his friend, Jim, a runaway slave. The morals he had been taught included obeying the law. But he could not bring himself to follow the law to turn in runaway slaves. In this case, an engagement mindset trumped rule learning (detached imagination). In these cases you can see mindsets shifting or in conflict, with explicit versus implicit understanding at battle. In the case of Goebbels, the context primed particular states, shifting perception and action, and so he flipped into different mind- and action sets. In the case of Huck, experience and practice changed his perceptions and understanding. Huck's deeper intuitions and tacit knowledge of Jim and his humanity trumped the explicit rules he had been taught.

Moral mindsets can be primed by situation or experience. With attachment priming, caring behavior increases (Mikulincer & Shaver, 2005), whereas with fear priming, self-protectionism ensues (withdrawal, detached or vicious imagination), as seen in terror management theory research (e.g., Mikulincer & Shaver, 2001). A similar withdrawal from engaged relationship is visible in moral disengagement, when emotional detachment and decoupling of relational responsibility lead to lack of caring behavior or worse (Bandura, 1999).

Mindsets can also be deliberately fostered, as in the Rwanda massacre, when radio programs denigrated the Tutsi and later encouraged the massacre against them (Dallaire, 2003). Suspicion and hate can be fostered through education as well, encouraging viciousness toward an outgroup, as before and during the Nazi Germany era toward the Jews (Staub, 1989). On the other hand, compassion training can foster a "broaden and build orientation," with decreased threat vigilance and increased openness (Fredrickson, 2001, 2013; Neff, 2011).

Historical Context: Understanding Moral Developmental Systems and Human Baselines

The humans we see today do not necessarily embody the inherited human moral capacities that need species-typical experiences to develop. Developmental systems theory provides a useful framework for expanding understanding of human heritages and how they develop (Oyama, Griffiths, & Gray, 2001). Organismic adaptation involves resources that are available to subsequent generations—not only genes but culture, ecology, microbiome, and the developmental manifold or system in which an offspring is raised. The latter we call the *evolved developmental niche* (EDN).

The Evolved Development Niche

Like all animals, over the course of evolution humans developed an early-life niche for their offspring that matches up with the maturational schedule of the young. Humans are highly immature at birth, born 9–18 months early compared with other animals (Trevathan, 2011), with the most intense and longest lasting niche for offspring development (over 20 years). Early care evolved to be intense and to follow the EDN, which emerged more than 30 million years ago among social mammals and intensified through human evolution (Konner, 2005, 2010). The EDN for young children includes soothing perinatal experiences, lengthy breastfeeding, responsive caregivers, extensive positive and no negative touch, extensive free play with multiage playmates in nature, and emotional and social support (Konner, 2005; Narvaez, 2013).

Neurobiological and developmental studies show the importance of each of the EDN components in fostering health and social well-being (Narvaez, Panksepp, Schore & Gleason, 2013a, 2013b; Narvaez, Valentino, Fuentes, McKenna & Gray, 2014). An individual's neurobiology is co-constructed by caregivers during early life, when many brain and body systems establish their parameters and thresholds. EDN-consistent care forms biological underpinnings that follow a person the rest of his or her life, barring therapy or other modifying experiences.

In our laboratory, we have examined whether these early experiences influence moral capacities, and they do. For example, preschoolers whose mothers report greater EDN-consistent care show greater empathy, self-control, and conscience (Narvaez, Wang, et al., 2013). A longitudinal sample studying touch found that over the first 3 years of life mothers who used corporal punishment had children who were less self-regulated, less socially engaged, less co-operative, and less socially competent and had more externalizing problems (Narvaez, Wang, Cheng, Gleason, & Lefever, 2015). Mothers providing more positive touch at 4 months had children with greater self-regulation and verbal cognitive intelligence at 36 months, even after controlling for responsive care (Narvaez, Gleason, Wang, Brooks, Lefever, Cheng, & Centers for the Prevention of Child Neglect, 2013). We also find that adult retrospective reports of EDN experience were related to adult attachment, psychopathology, moral capacities (perspective taking, empathy) and moral orientation: Less EDN-consistent childhoods followed a suboptimal pathway to protectionist ethics through psychopathology and low perspective taking or high personal distress, whereas EDN-consistent childhoods formed a chain to secure attachment, low pathology, perspective taking or empathy, and an engagement ethic (Narvaez, Wang & Cheng, 2016).

Darwin's Moral Sense

Is morality innate? Darwin seemed to think so. Darwin (1981) described the moral sense as a set of capacities inherited through the tree of life (from earlier species). The capacities he identified include social pleasure, memory of past behavior, empathy, concern for the opinion of others, and habit control. What we are finding out today from research and social developments is that these capacities are not innate but biosocially constructed. To develop social pleasure and empathy requires experience of each through empathic care and experiences of social enjoyment with caregivers (Emde et al., 1991; Kochanska, 1994, 2002; Kochanska & Aksan, 2004, 2006; Kochanska, Aksan & Koenig, 1995; Kochanska & Coy, 1997; Trevarthen, 2005). Concern for the opinion of others and self-control also require responsive care in childhood (Kochanska, 2002). Memory systems too are influenced by the quality of childhood relationships (Grosjean & Tsai, 2007).

Thus it appears that Darwin's moral sense is not innate. Neither is it learned in the classic sense. Instead, it is deeply embodied in the early "wiring" of the brain, biosocially constructed from embodied social experience. Darwin's moral sense develops under particular conditions, conditions that used to be universal in childhood. How do we know? Because of converging evidence: 99% of human history was spent in small-band hunter–gatherer societies (SBHG; Lee & Daly, 1999); and in these societies, the EDN is provided to children, with slight variation; and members of these societies, from all reports, show the characteristics of Darwin's moral sense. SBHG become a useful baseline to use for human moral development and flourishing (Narvaez, 2013).

Is Morality Innate or Learned?

Some forms of morality are innate and others are co-constructed by social experience, especially in early life when brain systems, their parameters and thresholds, are established. Lower forms of morality (i.e., protectionism) are rooted in more primitive brain functions, the innate survival systems (e.g., fear, anger, panic circuits), with which humans are born. These survival systems are available from birth and can take over a mind when the stress response is activated. If a child is not properly cared for as designed by evolution with the EDN, these primitive survival systems are more likely to dominate personality and morality.

The higher forms of morality (i.e., engagement and communal imagination) are not innate but rely on circuitries that are initially co-constructed in early life when brain systems are highly immature and malleable. These circuits require appropriate early care when systems that facilitate prosociality are in rapid development (e.g., vagus nerve, endocrine systems). The EDN fosters the development of higher forms of moral function, those that are other-regarding, including relational attunement and communal imagination (Narvaez, 2014a). Thereafter, they are maintained by supportive environments, although extreme stress, such as war experience, can lead to a coup by survival systems which take over during stress in social relationships, as in posttraumatic stress disorder. Thus, although humans are born with survival systems that are conditioned up or down from early experience, the higher forms of morality require appropriate evolved care. Early experience sets the foundation for these characteristics. For the vast majority of human genus's existence, a common early childhood was provided to young children. The adult personalities that emerge from this common experience are similar all over the world (Ingold, 1999).

Is Morality Intuitive or Deliberative? One or Two or Many Processes?

Morality involves one's manner of being in the moment, which, of course, involves a shifting combination of intuitive and deliberative processes. Implicit moral processes emerge from social experience throughout life, with foundations established in early life, when all sorts of implicit understandings of the social world are shaped. As Jean Piaget documented thoroughly throughout his studies of cognitive development, implicit understandings and intuitions (schemas) develop first in a domain, guiding behavior; with enough experience and encouragement, explicit understanding emerges and explanations become possible, which he thought were evidence of thorough understanding (Piaget, 1963, 1954). Like any other cognitive development, moral understanding too is initially implicitly held unless it too is encouraged to become explicit (Piaget, 1965).

Specific implicit schemas and deliberate processes are influenced by multiple factors. For example, one's decisions are influenced implicitly by what is chronically accessible (e.g., moral identity; Narvaez, Lapsley, Hagele, & Lasky, 2006), which is influenced by the places where one habitually places one's attention (Murdoch, 1989). It also matters which form of attention is adopted at the time: focused or relational. Focused processing is left-hemisphere directed and narrowly attentive to decontextualized, static pieces of reality (McGilchrist, 2009). An emotionally detached concentrated attention is useful in rare moments when details are needed, but it otherwise misses out on a lot of what is really happening in the moment. In contrast, relational attention, reliant on right-hemisphere capacities (which are underdeveloped when the EDN is missing; Schore, 1994), is alert to the uniqueness of the moment, with a sense of living connection to whatever exists in the moment. A

virtuous person will spend most time in the relational mode, responding to the individuality of the situation, using focused attention relatively rarely.

It is important to understand that automatic processes can be well educated, poorly educated, or uneducated and impulsive. Well-educated automatic moral processes are found in the virtuous person, whose sensibilities, perceptions, interpretations, and explanations are coordinated toward openness and prosociality. Poorly educated automatic processes are developed in "wicked" environments, ones that "train up" the wrong intuitions (Hogarth, 2001). So, for example, a child growing up in a violent home learns intuitions to be distrustful and violent and generalizes these reactions even to contexts that are not in themselves threatening. Or one can have no trained intuitions about something but react according to environmental press or based on what comes to mind (availability heuristic), what has been frequently recalled (accessibility heuristic), or a meme in the culture. With poor executive function from early undercare, one can be morally mindless and dominated by fast but dumb automatic processes, shifting from reaction to reaction. Moral mindfulness, however, combines explicit and implicit capacities for moral agility, based on experience, working at appropriate levels of detail or abstraction as needed.

Deliberate moral processes include following explicit decision trees, reasoning aloud about a case, and deliberating with others about possible joint actions. However, deliberate processes are always influenced by one's history, mood, expertise, reactivity, aims, immediate prior experience, and so forth. A virtuous person is aware of potential biases and takes the time to sort through them, to check reactions with wise others, to reflect on their behavior, and to move toward openness rather than bracing (Bourgeault, 2003).

A well-constructed brain is agile, working at appropriate levels of abstraction, with control or automaticity as needed (Koutstaal, 2013). In a poorly functioning brain, processing can get mired in abstractions, which can lead to depression, or in specifics, which leads to obsession. Or, a brain/mind that relies too much on controlled processes emphasizes rigid rule following, whereas too much reliance on automatic processes can lead to stereotyping. A morally virtuous expert is able to shift attention and processes as needed for particular situations. Deep empathy (built from a species-typical niche) fuels communal imagination and action.

Is Morality Generic or Special?

Moral virtue is a set of capstone capacities that are founded on layers of other capacities (e.g., various forms of physiological or psychological self-regulation). Although morality includes judgment, it relies on self-regulation processes and well-trained emotion systems. It also involves perceptual sensitivities, conceptual structures, social sensibilities, self-regulation, and effectivities (effective action capacities; Narvaez, 2010a). Morality builds on general functions, including receptive intelligence. It builds on what the individual has experienced as pleasurable, how trustworthy others are perceived to be, how well emotions work to guide actions (how trustworthy the individual's emotions are based on their shaping in early life), how self-aware the individual is, and how socially fit he or she is (Narvaez, 2014b).

Morality is about skilled action or virtue—applying the right capabilities in the right manner for the moment. Quick judgments can be closed-minded and self-protective, representative of lower forms of moral functioning, or be based on experience and expertise, representative of extensive practice and know-how. For a moral virtue expert, the moral landscape for action is wide, with full intelligence (both receptive and focused) available rather than conditioned self-protective responses that impair flexible response.

Is Morality Culturally Uniform or Variable?

Evolution provided a cultural commons for ethogenesis. Human moral development used to be fairly uniform; in environments representative of humanity's 99%, SBHG societies, one can see the same type of personality and moral personality around the world. Adults are gentle, generous, calm, and happy (Ingold, 1999; review in Narvaez, 2013).

The difference likely has to do with early formation when the foundations of sociality are co-constructed. Human evolution prepared a uniform early nest for children, the EDN. In societies conforming with our 99%, children are provided this nest, a "cultural commons" for human personality and virtue development, resulting in adults who are calm, self-regulated, and content. They show patience, generosity, kindness, social fitness, and openness. Cultures in the last 1% of human EDN history have violated the nest, with concomitant alterations in moral capacities, moral intelligence, and moral orientations.

Theoretical Stance: Similarities and Uniqueness of Ethogenesis Theory

Similar to other theories, ethogenesis looks to implicit processes as the power base for moral functioning. Implicit processes include neurobiological foundations for sociomoral intelligence built in early life when the right hemisphere is developing rapidly. But implicit processes must be well educated to be worthwhile. Top-down processes are also emphasized, as moral expertise is guided by mindfulness, self-authorship, and deliberately-built cultural institutions (Narvaez, 2010).

Ethogenesis theory is different from other theories in several ways, including being more interdisciplinary; building on evolutionary relational developmental systems theory and taking a lifespan developmental perspective; integrating neurobiological roots of emotional and cognitive development; and understanding the importance of biosociocultural co-construction of human beingness. Ethogenesis used to be virtually the same for all humans, but now in the last 1%, culture has trumped evolutionary processes. Baselines for what is normal child raising, normal personality and well-being in childhood and adulthood, have deteriorated relative to our 99% so much so that culture supports the undermining of child well-being through intentional undercare (lack of EDN-consistent care), such as, for example, letting babies cry or forcing them to sleep alone.

Evidence

Ethogenesis is an integrative theory drawing from multiple disciplines. Evidence in support of moral developmental systems theory is interdisciplinary. It includes biological anthropology (e.g., McKenna & McDade, 2005; McKenna, Ball, & Gettler, 2007); affective neuroscience (Panksepp, 1998); clinical science (Schore, 1994, 2003a, 2003b); developmental moral science (Kochanska, 2002); relational developmental systems theory (Overton, 2013, 2015; Overton & Molenaar, 2015), and, more recently, studies of moral relational developmental systems theory (Narvaez, Wang & Cheng, 2016).

Ethogenesis theory is a meta-theory that addresses multiple levels: neurobiology, social context, and culture. Scholarship in multiple domains is currently undergoing paradigm shifts relevant to ethogenetic theory:

- From an emphasis on genetics to epigenetics in developmental psychology (Leckman & March, 2011)
- From genecentrist theory to relational developmental systems theory (Overton, 2013)
- Attending to epigenetic inheritance (Gluckman & Hanson, 2004, 2005)
- Understanding our inheritances through evolution as much more than genes (Jablonka & Lamb, 2006; Oyama, 1985, 2000)
- From an emphasis on genetic competition to an emphasis on cooperation in every natural system (Weiss & Buchanan, 2009).
- From dualism to biosocial co-construction of human development (Ingold, 2013)
- From static either–or thinking to dynamic interactionisms: biology *and* social experience, intuition *and* deliberation, culture *and* child rearing (Narvaez, 2014a, 2014b)
- From a focus on resilience to one on human potential (Gleason & Narvaez, 2014)
- Noting lasting effects of early trauma and toxic stress at critical times (Shonkoff & Phillips, 2000)
- From thinking that Westerners reflect human nature to studying our 99% (SBHG) for a baseline (Ingold, 1999, 2011)

- From emphasizing Western cognitive, left-hemisphere-directed thinking to a fuller set of intelligences (McGilchrist, 2009) better represented in SBHG societies (Narvaez, 2013)
- Realizing that only certain cultures damage human nature and the biosphere, whereas others are oriented to preserving it (Berkes, 1999)
- From viewing humans as unique to understanding their continuity in tree of life (Berkes, 1999; Margulis, 1998)
- Expanding virtue and morality beyond humanity to include other-than-human well-being (Narvaez, 2014a, 2015)

Extension and Expansion: Implications and Future Directions

Implications for Practice

To return to our evolved moral inheritances, relational attunement (engagement), and communal imagination, adults need to restore EDN—species-typical care of the young. Instead of focusing on genes and washing our hands of child-to-adult outcomes, we should be focused on epigenetics, taking greater intergenerational responsibility for the well-being of the young and future generations.

Implications for Policy

In the United States currently, many policies and institutions work against species-typical care (e.g., traumatic medicalized birth, infant formula feeding, sleep training for isolation). Instead, we should ensure that policies and practices ensure that every child receives care consistent with the EDN. This means that societies need to integrate child raising into adult activities and recenter workplaces around the needs of children.

Implications for Research

We have to be careful about which baselines we use for measuring human normality. We should not be drawing conclusions about human capacities from people raised outside the species-typical niche. Current research focuses primarily on human beings who typically have missed the EDN, making them more stress reactive and necessarily self-centered. They miss developing fully the receptive and perceptive intelligences apparent in SBHGs. Just like Western, educated, industrialized, rich, democratic nations do not represent humanity, neither do their brains. They are the wrong populations for drawing generalizations about human nature or human potential.

Future Directions

It is only in the last 1% of human existence that humans have adopted a domineering attitude toward other-than-humans, "enslaving" both animals and plants (Martin, 1992, 1999). Humans have become an invasive pioneer species, which are typically "individualistic, aggressive, and hustling" and "attempt to exterminate or suppress other species" (Naess & Rothenberg, 1989, p. 182). Although invasive species learn to live in unfavorable circumstances, "they are ultimately self-destructive" and are ultimately "replaced by other species which are better suited to restabilize and mature the ecosystem" (pp. 182–183).

As a result of an invasive, domineering attitude, every ecosystem is under duress from human activity, which continues to accelerate (Millennium Ecosystem Assessment, 2005). Half the species on the planet have disappeared since 1970. The oceans are full of plastic instead of fish. The globe is warming. To discuss morality without discussing responsibilities to other-than-humans is inadequate. Other-than-human entities (e.g., plants, animals, mountains, streams) need to be included in the circle of concern.

In the 99%, individuals grew up in partnership with other-than-humans, not killing off predators or dictating which species should live or die. Again, the restoration of the EDN, especially with childhood embedded in outdoor natural systems, may be needed to restore receptive intelligence capacities—the awareness and openness to other-than-humans. As in traditional Native American/American Indian communities, the embedded EDN nurtures a sense of ecological attachment to the well-being of the local landscape, leading to sustainable lifestyles and deep ecological wisdom (Berkes, 1999). Without greater ecological wisdom

and virtuous action that encompasses the globe, the human species, along with many others, will disappear. An ethical theory must address this reality.

REFERENCES

Arnsten, A. F. T. (2009). Stress signaling pathways that impair prefrontal cortex structure and function. *Nature Reviews Neuroscience, 10*(6), 410–422.

Arpaly, N. (2003). *Unprincipled virtue: An inquiry into moral agency.* New York: Oxford University Press.

Bandura, A. (1999). Moral disengagement in the perpetration of inhumanities. *Personality and Social Psychology Review, 3*(3), 269–275.

Berkes, F. (1999). *Sacred ecology* (2nd ed.). New York: Routledge.

Bourgeault, C. (2003). *The wisdom way of knowing: Reclaiming an ancient tradition to awaken the heart.* San Francisco: Jossey-Bass.

Carter, C. S. (2003). Developmental consequences of oxytocin. *Physiology and Behavior, 79*(3), 383–397.

Dallaire, R. (2003). *Shake hands with the devil: The failure of humanity in Rwanda.* New York: Carroll & Graf.

Darwin, C. (1981). *The descent of man.* Princeton, NJ: Princeton University Press. (Original work published 1871)

Emde, R. N., Biringen, Z., Clyman, R., & Oppenheim, D. (1991). The moral self of infancy: Affective core and procedural knowledge. *Developmental Review, 11,* 251–270.

Fredrickson, B. L. (2001). The role of positive emotions in positive psychology. *American Psychologist, 56*(3), 218–226.

Fredrickson, B. L. (2013). *Love 2.0: How our supreme emotion affects everything we feel, think, do, and become.* London: Hudson Street Press.

Gleason, T., & Narvaez, D. (2014). Child environments and flourishing. In D. Narvaez, K. Valentino, A. Fuentes, J. McKenna, & P. Gray (Eds.), *Ancestral landscapes in human evolution: Culture, childrearing and social well-being* (pp. 335–348). New York: Oxford University Press.

Gluckman, P. D., & Hanson, M. A. (2004). Living with the past: Evolution, development, and patterns of disease. *Science, 305*(5691), 1733–1736.

Gluckman, P. D., & Hanson, M. (2005). *Fetal matrix: Evolution, development and disease.* New York: Cambridge University Press.

Grosjean, B., & Tsai, G. E. (2007). NMDA neurotransmission as a critical mediator of borderline personality disorder. *Journal of Psychiatry and Neuroscience, 32*(2), 103–115.

Hogarth, R. M. (2001). *Educating intuition.* Chicago: University of Chicago Press.

Ingold, T. (1999). On the social relations of the hunter–gatherer band. In R. B. Lee & R. Daly (Eds.), *The Cambridge encyclopedia of hunters and gatherers* (pp. 399–410). New York: Cambridge University Press.

Ingold, T. (2011). *The perception of the environment: Essay on livelihood, dwelling and skill.* London: Routledge.

Ingold, T. (2013) Prospect. In T. Ingold & G. Palsson (Eds.), *Biosocial becomings: Integrating social and biological anthropology* (pp. 1–21). Cambridge, UK: Cambridge University Press.

Jablonka, E., & Lamb, M. J. (2006). The evolution of information in the major transitions. *Journal of Theoretical Biology, 239*(2), 236–246.

Kochanska, G. (1994). Beyond cognition: Expanding the search for the early roots of internalization and conscience. *Developmental Psychology, 30*(1), 20–22.

Kochanska, G. (2002). Mutually responsive orientation between mothers and their young children: A context for the early development of conscience. *Current Directions in Psychological Science, 11*(6), 191–195.

Kochanska, G., & Aksan, N. (2004). Conscience in childhood: Past, present, and future. *Merrill–Palmer Quarterly: Journal of Developmental Psychology, 50*(3), 299–310.

Kochanska, G., & Aksan, N. (2006). Children's conscience and self-regulation. *Journal of Personality, 74*(6), 1587–1617.

Kochanska, G., Aksan, N., & Koenig, A. L. (1995). A longitudinal study of the roots of preschoolers' conscience: Committed compliance and emerging internalization. *Child Development, 66,* 1752–1769.

Kochanska, G., & Coy, K. C. (1997). Inhibitory control as a contributor to conscience in childhood: From toddler to early school age. *Child Development, 68,* 263–277.

Konner, M. (2005). Hunter–gatherer infancy and childhood: The !Kung and others. In B. Hewlett & M. Lamb (Eds.), *Hunter–gatherer childhoods: Evolutionary, developmental and cultural perspectives* (pp. 19–64). New Brunswick, NJ: Transaction.

Konner, M. (2010). *The evolution of childhood.* Cambridge, MA: Belknap Press.

Koutstaal, W. (2013). *The agile mind.* New York: Oxford University Press.

Leckman, J. F., & March, J. S. (2011). Editorial: Developmental neuroscience comes of age. *Journal of Child Psychology and Psychiatry, 52,* 333–338.

Lee, R. B., & Daly, R. (Eds.). (1999). *The Cambridge encyclopedia of hunters and gatherers.* New York: Cambridge University Press.

Lupien, S. J., McEwen, B. S., Gunnar, M. R., & Heim, C. (2009). Effects of stress throughout the lifespan on the brain, behaviour and cognition, *Nature Reviews Neuroscience, 10*(6), 434–445.

MacLean, P. D. (1990). *The triune brain in evolution: Role in paleocerebral functions.* New York: Plenum Press.

Margulis, L. (1998). *Symbiotic planet: A new look at evolution.* Amherst, MA: Sciencewriters.

Martin, C. L. (1992). *In the spirit.* Baltimore: Johns Hopkins University Press.

Martin, C. L. (1999). *The way of the human being.* New Haven, CT: Yale University Press.

McGilchrist, I. (2009). *The master and his emissary: The divided brain and the making of the Western world.* New Haven, CT: Yale University Press.

McKenna, J., Ball, H., & Gettler, L. (2007). Mother–infant cosleeping, breastfeeding and sudden infant death syndrome: What biological anthropology has discovered about normal infant sleep and pediatric sleep medicine. *Yearbook of Physiological Anthropology, 50,* 133–161.

McKenna, J., & McDade, T. (2005). Why babies should never sleep alone: A review of the cosleeping controversy in relation to SIDS, bedsharing and breast feeding. *Paediatric Respiratory Reviews, 6*(2), 134–152.

Mikulincer, M., & Shaver, P. R. (2001). Attachment theory and intergroup bias: Evidence that priming the secure base schema attenuates negative reactions to out-groups. *Journal of Personality and Social Psychology, 81,* 97–115.

Mikulincer, M., & Shaver, P. R. (2005). Attachment security, compassion, and altruism. *Current Directions in Psychological Science, 14*(1), 34–38.

Millennium Ecosystem Assessment. (2005). *Ecosystems and human well-being: Synthesis.* Washington, DC: Island Press.

Murdoch, I. (1989). *The sovereignty of good.* London: Routledge. (Original work published 1970)

Naess, A., & Rothenberg, D. (1989). *Ecology, community and lifestyle.* Cambridge, UK: Cambridge University Press.

Narvaez, D. (2008). Triune ethics: The neurobiological roots of our multiple moralities. *New Ideas in Psychology, 26,* 95–119.

Narvaez, D. (2010a). Moral complexity: The fatal attraction of truthiness and the importance of mature moral functioning. *Perspectives on Psychological Science, 5*(2), 163–181.

Narvaez, D. (2010b). The embodied dynamism of moral becoming. *Perspectives on Psychological Science, 5*(2), 185–186.

Narvaez, D. (2013). The 99 percent—Development and socialization within an evolutionary context: Growing up to become "A good and useful human being." In D. Fry (Ed.), *War, peace and human nature: The convergence of evolutionary and cultural views* (pp. 643–672). New York: Oxford University Press.

Narvaez, D. (2014a). *Neurobiology and the development of human morality: Evolution, culture and wisdom.* New York: Norton.

Narvaez, D. (2014b). The co-construction of virtue: Epigenetics, neurobiology and development. In N. E. Snow (Ed.), *Cultivating virtue* (pp. 251–277). New York: Oxford University Press.

Narvaez, D. (2015). Understanding flourishing: Evolutionary baselines and morality. *Journal of Moral Education, 44*(3), 253–262.

Narvaez, D. (2016). *Embodied morality: Protectionism, engagement and imagination.* New York: Palgrave-Macmillan.

Narvaez, D., & Gleason, T. (2013). Developmental optimization. In D. Narvaez, J. Panksepp, A. Schore, & T. Gleason (Eds.), *Evolution, early experience and human development: From research to practice and policy* (pp. 307–325). New York: Oxford University Press.

Narvaez, D., Gleason, T., Wang, L., Brooks, J., Lefever, J., Cheng, A., & Centers for the Prevention of Child Neglect. (2013). The evolved development niche: Longitudinal effects of caregiving practices on early childhood psychosocial development. *Early Childhood Research Quarterly, 28*(4), 759–773.

Narvaez, D., Lapsley, D. K., Hagele, S., & Lasky, B. (2006). Moral chronicity and social information processing: Tests of a social cognitive approach to the moral personality. *Journal of Research in Personality, 40,* 966–985.

Narvaez, D., Panksepp, J., Schore, A., & Gleason, T. (Eds.). (2013a). *Evolution, early experience and human development: From research to practice and policy.* New York: Oxford University Press.

Narvaez, D., Panksepp, J., Schore, A., & Gleason, T. (2013b). The value of using an evolutionary framework for gauging children's well-being. In D. Narvaez, J. Panksepp, A. Schore, & T. Gleason (Eds.), *Evolution, early experience and human development: From research to practice and policy* (pp. 3–30). New York: Oxford University Press.

Narvaez, D., Wang, L., & Cheng, A. (2016). Evolved developmental niche history: Relation to adult psychopathology and morality. *Applied Developmental Science, 20,* 294–309.

Narvaez, D., Wang, L., Cheng, A., Gleason, T., Woodbury, R., Kurth, A., & Lefever, J. B. (2017, April). *The importance of early life touch for psychosocial and moral development.* Symposium on Empathy, Prosociality and Morality: Neurobiological and Relational Contributions to Development, Society for Research in Child Development, Philadelphia, PA.

Narvaez, D., Wang, L., Gleason, T., Cheng, A., Lefever, J., & Deng, L. (2013). The evolved developmental niche and sociomoral outcomes in Chinese three-year-olds. *European Journal of Developmental Psychology, 10*(2), 106–127.

Narvaez, D., Valentino, K., Fuentes, A., McKenna, J., & Gray, P. (Eds.). (2014). *Ancestral landscapes in human evolution: Culture, childrearing and social wellbeing.* New York: Oxford University Press.

Neff, K. (2011). *Self-compassion: Stop beating yourself up and leave insecurity behind.* New York: Morrow.

Overton, W. F. (2013). A new paradigm for developmental science: Relationism and relational-developmental systems. *Applied Developmental Science, 17*(2), 94–107.

Overton, W. F. (2015). Process and relational-developmental systems. In R. M. Lerner (Series Ed.) & W. F. Overton & P. C. M. Molenaar (Vol. Eds.), *Handbook of child psychology and developmental science: Vol. 1. Theory and method* (7th ed., pp. 9–62). Hoboken, NJ: Wiley.

Overton, W. F., & Molenaar, P. C. (2015). Concepts, theory, and method in developmental science: A view of the issues. In R. M. Lerner (Series Ed.) & W. F. Overton & P. C. M. Molenaar (Vol. Eds.), *Handbook of child psychology and developmental science: Vol. 1. Theory and method* (7th ed., pp. 2–8). New York: Wiley.

Oyama, S. (1985). *The ontogeny of information: Developmental systems and evolution.* New York: Cambridge University Press.

Oyama, S. (2000). *Evolution's eye: A systems view of the biology–culture divide.* Durham, NC: Duke University Press.

Oyama, S., Griffiths, P. E., & Gray, R. D. (2001). *Cycles of contingency: Developmental systems and evolution.* Cambridge, MA: MIT Press.

Panksepp, J. (1998). *Affective neuroscience: The foundations of human and animal emotions.* New York: Oxford University Press.

Piaget, J. (1954). *The construction of reality in the child.* New York: Basic Books.

Piaget, J. (1963). *The origins of intelligence in children.* New York: Norton. (Original work published 1936)

Piaget, J. (1965). *The moral judgment of the child* (M. Gabain, Trans.). New York: Free Press. (Original work published 1932)

Porges, S. W. (2011). *The polyvagal theory: Neurophysiologial foundations of emotions, attachment, communication, self-regulation.* New York: Norton.

Rogers, C. (1961). *On becoming a person: A therapist's view of psychotherapy.* London: Constable.

Sapolsky, R. (2004). *Why zebras don't get ulcers* (3rd ed.). New York: Holt.

Schore, A. (1994). *Affect regulation.* Hillsdale, NJ: Erlbaum.

Schore, A. (1996). The experience-dependent maturation of a regulatory system in the orbital prefrontal cortex and the origin of development psychopathology. *Development and Psychopathology, 8,* 59–87.

Schore, A. N. (1997). Early organization of the nonlinear right brain and development of a predisposition to psychiatric disorders. *Development and Psychopathology, 9,* 595–631.

Schore, A. N. (2000). Attachment and the regulation of the right brain. *Attachment and Human Development, 2,* 23–47.

Schore, A. N. (2001). The effects of early relational trauma on right brain development, affect regulation, and infant mental health. *Infant Mental Health Journal, 22,* 201–269.

Schore, A. N. (2003a). *Affect regulation and the origin of the self.* Hillsdale, NJ: Erlbaum.

Schore, A. N. (2003b). *Affect regulation and the repair of the self.* New York: Norton.

Schore, A. N. (2005). Attachment, affect regulation, and the developing right brain: Linking developmental neuroscience to pediatrics. *Pediatrics in Review, 26,* 204–211.

Schore, A. N. (2013). Bowlby's "environment of evolutionary adaptedness": Recent studies on the interpersonal neurobiology of attachment and emotional development. In D. Narvaez, J. Panksepp, A. N. Shore, & T. Gleason (Eds.), *Human nature, early experience and human development* (pp. 31–67). Oxford, UK: Oxford University Press.

Shonkoff, J. P., Garner, A. S., Siegel, B. S., Dobbins, M. I., Earls, M. F., McGuinn, L., . . . Wood, D. L. (2012). The lifelong effects of early childhood adversity and toxic stress. *Pediatrics, 129*(1), 232–246.

Shonkoff, J. P., & Phillips, D. A. (2000). *From neurons to neighborhoods: The science of early childhood development.* Washington, DC: National Academies Press.

Staub, E. (1989). *The roots of evil: The origins of genocide and other group violence.* Cambridge, UK: Cambridge University Press.

Trevarthen, C. (2005). Stepping away from the mirror: Pride and shame in adventures of companionship: Reflections on the nature and emotional needs of infant intersubjectivity. In C. S. Carter, L. Ahnert, K. E. Grossmann, S. B. Hrdy, M. E. Lamb, S. W. Porges, & N. Sachser (Eds.), *Attachment and bonding: A new synthesis* (pp. 55–84). Cambridge, MA: MIT Press.

Trevathan, W. R. (2011). *Human birth: An evolutionary perspective* (2nd ed.). New York: Aldine de Gruyter.

Twain, M. (2001). *The adventures of Huckleberry Finn.* New York: Collector's Library. (Original work published 1884)

Weiss, K. M., & Buchanan, A. V. (2009). *The mermaid's tale: Four billion years of cooperation in the making of living things.* Cambridge, MA: Harvard University Press.

PART X
MORAL BEHAVIOR

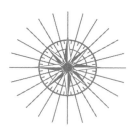

QUESTIONS ANSWERED IN PART X

CHAPTER 47 Is unethical behavior always selfish, and is selfish behavior always unethical?

CHAPTER 48 To what extent is our unethical behavior a product of dispositional or situational forces?

CHAPTER 49 Is moral behavior conflicted or unconflicted for a virtuous agent?

CHAPTER 50 How do people come to possess different levels of moral clarity, which denotes the degree of ambiguity people perceive when judging whether behaviors are right or wrong?

CHAPTER 47

On the Distinction between Unethical and Selfish Behavior

Jackson G. Lu
Ting Zhang
Derek D. Rucker
Adam D. Galinsky

Is unethical behavior always selfish, and is selfish behavior always unethical?

We conceptually distinguish between unethicality and selfishness by analyzing the four distinct categories of behavior that these two constructs combine to produce: selfish/unethical, selfish/ethical, unselfish/ethical, and unselfish/unethical behavior.

Does unethical behavior always represent selfish behavior? Consider the seminal dilemma that serves as the foundation for modern moral psychology: The wife of a man named Heinz was near death and desperate for a medicine that he could not afford (Kohlberg, 1963). To save her life, Heinz broke into a drugstore to steal the medicine. Kohlberg asked his subjects, "Should Heinz have stolen for his dying wife? Why or why not?" Whereas Kohlberg was interested in how people reasoned through this moral dilemma, we were instead struck by the fact that Heinz stole not to help himself, but to assist another person. Heinz might have acted unethically, but did he act selfishly?

Or consider the contemporary case of Aaron Swartz. As a computer programmer,

Swartz downloaded 4.8 million articles from the journal database JSTOR and made them publicly available. Although his action clearly violated computer and copyright laws, his alleged intention was "to place the material on the Internet so that it could be freely distributed around the entire globe" (Abelson, Diamond, Grosso, & Pfeiffer, 2013, p. 31).

Oftentimes, to act unethically is to act selfishly. Indeed, the bulk of ancient Greek philosophy and modern moral psychology has studied how individuals resolve moral dilemmas in which "doing the right thing" and acting in one's self-interest are in conflict (Bazerman & Gino, 2012). In fact, Plato (trans. 1997) himself believed that self-interest lies at the root of all unethical behaviors: "the cause of each and every crime we commit is precisely this excessive love of ourselves . . . " (p. 1414).

Because unethical behaviors often coincide with selfish intentions, most empirical studies focus on the antecedents and consequences of unethical behaviors that benefit the perpetrators at the expense of other individuals, groups, and organizations (e.g., Cohn, Fehr, & Maréchal, 2014; Gino, Ayal, & Ariely, 2009; Lu, Brockner, Vardi, & Weitz, 2017; Lu, Lee, Gino, & Galinsky, in press; Lu et al., 2017). To examine how frequently unethical behavior overlaps with selfish behavior in empirical studies, we conducted a bibliometric analysis of morality-related articles published in elite psychology and management journals between 2000 and 2015. We found that 83% of the articles (72 articles out of a total of 87 published) studied *selfish* unethical behavior without any consideration of *unselfish* unethical behavior.[1] In other words, the majority of studies in behavioral ethics appear to have confounded unethical behavior with selfish behavior.

Despite their frequent co-occurrence, unethical behavior and selfish behavior are conceptually orthogonal. In the social sciences, unethical behavior is commonly defined as behavior that is "illegal or morally unacceptable to the large community" (Jones, 1991, p. 367). By contrast, selfish behavior is defined as behavior that prioritizes one's own interests and benefits over those of others. Critically, these definitions reveal that, on the one hand, selfish intentions are not a prerequisite for unethical behaviors and, on the other hand, unethical behaviors need not arise out of selfishness. As we saw in the examples of Heinz and Swartz, unethical behaviors can originate from the desire to help others. In a similar vein, selfishness can promote *ethical* behaviors, particularly in contexts in which others' interests are aligned with one's own.

In the following sections, we decouple unethical and selfish behaviors by illustrating how unethical behaviors can be either selfish or unselfish and how selfish behaviors can be either ethical or unethical. For each category of behavior, we offer real-world examples that distinguish between these two constructs (see Table 47.1 for an overview). Thereafter, we discuss cases in which differentiating unethicality from selfishness offers a more comprehensive understanding of the antecedents of unethical behavior. Finally, we close the chapter by proposing future directions in the study of unethicality and selfishness.

Selfish and Unethical Behavior

Numerous studies have found that individuals resort to unethical behaviors out of self-interest. Researchers studying selfish unethical behaviors have examined conditions that trigger individuals to cheat, lie, and steal for themselves. For instance, competitive environments often promote a "whatever it takes to win" mindset (Hegarty & Sims, 1978; Kilduff, Galinsky, Gallo, & Reade, 2016), thereby increasing selfish behaviors that are unethical. In firms, employees who compete for status are more likely to fabricate their

TABLE 47.1. Distinguishing between Ethical/Unethical and Selfish/Unselfish Behaviors

Motive	Behavior	
	Ethical	Unethical
Selfish	*Definition:* Behaviors driven by self-beneficial motives that do not violate legal laws or moral codes of conduct.	*Definition:* Behaviors driven by self-beneficial motives that violate legal laws or moral codes of conduct.
	Example: Charitable donations to receive tax deductions	*Example:* Cheating on an exam
Unselfish	*Definition:* Behaviors driven by other-beneficial motives that do not violate legal laws or moral codes of conduct.	*Definition:* Behaviors driven by other-beneficial motives that violate legal laws or moral codes of conduct.
	Example: Community service	*Example:* Stealing to help the poor

performance and sabotage competitors' work (Charness, Masclet, & Villeval, 2014). In sports, players adopt unsportsmanlike behaviors in order to get ahead of their rivals (Kilduff et al., 2016). In academia, to compete with their peers, scholars inflate their papers' download counts from leading working paper repositories such as the Social Science Research Network (SSRN; Edelman & Larkin, 2015).

Similarly, goals can "go wild" (Ordóñez, Schweitzer, Galinsky, & Bazerman, 2009): By narrowing individuals' focus on the outcome, goals may motivate them to take selfish actions, including unethical ones (Schweitzer, Ordóñez, & Douma, 2004). Barsky (2008) formulated two psychological mechanisms through which goal setting can facilitate unethical behavior: moral disengagement and lack of ethical recognition. When individuals are highly focused on their goals, they may disengage their internal moral controls to rationalize their unethical behaviors (i.e., moral disengagement) or even fail to recognize the unethicality of such behaviors (i.e., lack of ethical recognition; Barsky, 2008). In workplace settings, the use of production or sales goals can encourage employees to cheat and lie (Jensen, 2003). For example, Sears's goal-oriented commission system has been identified as the culprit for its employees' systematic defrauding of customers (Paine & Santoro, 1993). Moreover, individuals are likely to resort to unethical means when they are about to fall short of their goals (Schweitzer et al., 2004). For example, authors are particularly apt to inflate their papers' download counts in order to prevent their papers from falling off the "top-10" list of the SSRN (Edelman & Larkin, 2015).

The influence of selfish motives on unethicality also extends to the dimension of moral judgment. Instead of adhering to a stable set of moral codes, individuals apply their beliefs and judgments strategically to maximize their personal outcomes (DeScioli, Massenkoff, Shaw, Petersen, & Kurzban, 2014). For example, people judge the unethical behavior of others more leniently when that behavior serves their own interests (Bocian & Wojciszke, 2014). Likewise, self-interest motivates "moral hypocrisy," whereby people evaluate themselves less harshly than others for the same unethical behavior (Valdesolo & DeSteno, 2007, 2008).

Selfish and Ethical Behavior

Although self-interest often breeds unethical behaviors, it can also foster *ethical* behaviors, particularly in situations in which self-interest is aligned with the interest of others. In what follows, we highlight how self-interest can lead individuals to avoid temptations to cheat, to rectify others' unethical acts, and to engage in prosocial behaviors.

In society, the presence of legal punishment speaks directly to how self-interest discourages unethical behaviors. Selfishly, people often refrain from behaving unethically when the risk and cost of being caught are high (Brass, Butterfield, & Skaggs, 1998). Even in the absence of formal punishment, individuals are still driven to protect their moral identity as a "good person" (Bryan, Adams, & Monin, 2013). As a result, they often adopt behaviors that serve to present themselves as "moral" in their own eyes and the eyes of others (Frimer, Schaefer, & Oakes, 2014). For example, individuals were less likely to cheat when told "don't be a cheater" than when told "don't cheat," because being labeled a cheater is threatening to one's self-image (Bryan et al., 2013).

Self-interest can also guide individuals to take action against others' unethical behaviors. For instance, whistle-blowing, defined as the disclosure of "illegal, immoral or illegitimate practices . . . to persons or organizations who may be able to effect action" (Near & Miceli, 1985, p. 4), is often motivated by self-interest. In reporting on a cheater in an academic competition, a student not only upholds the academic honor code but also gains an edge over the competition by eliminating a contender. Similarly, when whistle-blowers reveal fraudulent behavior, they may be entitled to a percentage of the financial recovery. For example, "the IRS Whistleblower Office pays money to people who blow the whistle on persons who fail to pay the tax that they owe" (U.S. Department of the Treasury, Internal Revenue Service, 2017). Socially, the larger community may even hail whistle-blowers as heroes (Johnson, 2003).

Selfish motives can also foster prosocial behaviors, or voluntary, intentional behaviors that result in benefits for others (Eisenberg & Miller, 1987). In the United States, many individuals donate to charitable organizations, both to receive tax deductions (Feldstein, 1975) and to publicly signal their wealth, status, or moral character (Ariely, Bracha, & Meier, 2009; Rege & Telle, 2004). Similarly, parents make substantial donations to universities to increase their children's chances of admission (Golden, 2003). In China, many citizens donate "just enough" blood (i.e., 800 milliliters) to qualify as recipients in future blood transfusions (Shi et al., 2014). Likewise, in countries such as Israel and Singapore, individuals register as organ donors so that they are prioritized if they should be in need of organs in the future (Lavee, Ashkenazi, Gurman, & Steinberg, 2010).

Prominent philosophers and economists have argued that selfishness and ethicality are closely linked. Adam Smith, the founding father of economics, famously wrote, "it is not from the benevolence of the butcher, the brewer, or the baker, that we expect our dinner, but from their regard to their own self-interest" (Smith, 1937, p. 16). In essence, the study of free-market economics—which Smith viewed as a branch of moral philosophy (Griswold, 1999)—rests on the premise that human beings are self-interested (Smith, 1937) and that, when each individual seeks to maximize his or her own utility, the collective will prosper. Milton Friedman, a Nobel Prize laureate in economics, called this Invisible Hand (of selfishness) "the possibility of cooperation without coercion" (Friedman, 1999).

Unselfish and Ethical Behavior

Just as selfishness can foster both unethical and ethical behaviors, unselfishness—the willingness to put the needs of others before one's own—can also lead to both ethical and unethical behaviors.

Much research has explored conditions under which altruistic intentions produce ethical outcomes (Batson & Shaw, 1991; Penner, Dovidio, Piliavin, & Schroeder, 2005). People help others (e.g., anonymous donations, community service) even when there is no clear or direct benefit to themselves other than the "warm glow" of giving (Harbaugh, Mayr, & Burghart, 2007; Piliavin, 2003).

Individuals also engage in risky and self-sacrificing behaviors in order to benefit others. Raising sensitive issues within an organization (e.g., telling a manager that his new policy is unpopular among employees) has the potential to benefit others (e.g., the manager enacts favorable changes) but may also pose risks for the actor (e.g., dismissal from job; Burris, Detert, & Romney, 2013).

Two other areas that highlight the role of unselfish ethical behavior are whistle-blowing and altruistic punishment. Although whistle-blowing can be motivated by selfish reasons (as highlighted earlier), it can also be driven by moral principles. For example, Waytz, Dungan, and Young (2013) provide evidence that whistle-blowing is especially likely to occur when people are focused on justice and fairness. Sometimes whistle-blowers are not only unselfish but also vulnerable to both psychological distress (e.g., anxiety, nightmares, flashbacks; Peters et al., 2011) and social backlash from members of their own community (Dyck, Morse, & Zingales, 2010).

Altruistic punishment, in which "individuals punish, although the punishment is costly for them and yields no material gain" (Fehr & Gächter, 2002, p. 137), is another case of unselfish ethical behavior. People often go out of their way (incurring effort and time cost) to punish perpetrators (e.g., individuals who cut into lines or who sneak into music festivals) because "it is the right thing to do." Altruistic punishment facilitates cooperation in groups, organizations, and societies; without it, cooperation would often break down (Fehr & Gächter, 2002).

Unselfish and Unethical Behavior

Although unselfishness can lead to ethical behaviors, it can also result in unethical behaviors. Unselfish yet unethical behaviors typically arise when there is a conflict between two competing moral principles

(Levine & Schweitzer, 2014). For example, many moral dilemmas that lead individuals toward unselfish and unethical actions often feature a contention between two foundational pillars of moral psychology: *justice* and *care* (Levine & Schweitzer, 2014, 2015). Whereas justice reflects deontological moral imperatives (e.g., thou shalt not lie; Kant, 1959), care prioritizes the utilitarian consideration of helping and protecting others (Bentham, 1948; Walker & Hennig, 2004). Heinz's dilemma (Kohlberg, 1963) epitomizes this moral tension: Stealing would breach the law of justice, whereas watching one's wife die without intervening would violate the principle of caring for others.

When individuals are faced with this tension in moral judgment, care can supersede justice and lead individuals to take unselfish yet unethical actions. Many of us engage in altruistic lying, defined as "false statements that are costly for the liar and are made with the intention of misleading and benefitting a target" (Levine & Schweitzer, 2014, p. 108). Since early childhood, we are taught that it is polite to tell prosocial lies (Broomfield, Robinson, & Robinson, 2002; Talwar, Murphy, & Lee, 2007), particularly when these lies provide others with interpersonal support (Brown & Levinson, 1987) and psychological protection (DePaulo & Kashy, 1998). For example, parents may lie about their divorce to protect their child. Similarly, with no apparent self-serving motive, doctors may lie to patients about bleak prognoses to provide them hope and comfort (Iezzoni, Rao, DesRoches, Vogeli, & Campbell, 2012).

Like Aaron Swartz, some individuals are willing to engage in unethical behaviors that have the potential to benefit a larger community—even at the cost of sacrificing themselves. Members of WikiLeaks, for example, exposed classified information to the public—an illegal activity that antagonized the U.S government—in order to serve its altruistic mission of "defense of freedom of speech and media publishing" and ultimately "to create a better society for all people" (*https://wikileaks.org/About.html*, 2011).[2]

Finally, motives that are linked to altruism can produce behaviors that violate moral rules. For example, empathy—a psychological process that generally leads to prosocial behaviors—can also lead individuals to violate moral rules by according "favored" status and preferential treatment to the target of empathy (Batson, Klein, Highberger, & Shaw, 1995). Individuals induced to feel empathy for a particular individual are more likely to violate the principle of justice by allocating resources preferentially to that person (Batson, Klein, et al., 1995), even at the cost of reducing the collective good (Batson, Batson, et al., 1995).

Antecedents of Selfish versus Unselfish Unethical Behavior

As illustrated in the previous sections, drawing a distinction between unethical behavior and selfish behavior is critical to the study of moral psychology. Given that both ethical and unethical behaviors can result from both selfish *and* unselfish intentions, merely focusing on situations in which unethicality and selfishness co-occur creates an incomplete and inaccurate representation of the drivers of unethical behavior. We next discuss three specific cases (social class, organizational identification, and loyalty) that demonstrate the need to parse unethical behaviors driven by selfish versus unselfish motives.

Social Class

Prior research has found a positive relationship between social class and unethical behavior (Piff, Stancato, Côté, Mendoza-Denton, & Keltner, 2012). Upper-class individuals have more favorable attitudes toward greed, which partially account for their higher tendency to engage in unethical behaviors such as lying and cheating (Piff et al., 2012). However, a closer examination of this effect reveals that the identity of the beneficiary of an unethical behavior is a critical moderator of the relationship between social class and unethical behavior (Dubois, Rucker, & Galinsky, 2015). Upper-class individuals, relative to lower-class individuals, are more prone to commit unethical acts that benefit *themselves*; in contrast, lower-class individuals, relative to upper-class individuals, are more prone to commit unethical acts that benefit *others*. In explaining these findings, Dubois and colleagues (2015) contend that higher social class tends to foster an agentic, self-serving orientation, whereas lower social class tends to nurture a communal, altruistic orientation. As a result, although both upper- and lower-class individuals can behave unethically, upper-class individuals are more likely to do so for their own sake, whereas lower-class individuals are more likely to do so for others' sake. These findings demonstrate that disentangling selfishness and unethicality serves to provide a more complete understanding of the antecedents of unethical behavior.

Organizational Identification

The distinction between unethicality and selfishness also helps unpack the relationship between organizational identification and ethicality. Organizational identification refers to an individual's feeling of "oneness" with his or her organization (Ashforth & Mael, 1989). Individuals' organizational identification significantly affects the extent to which they engage in selfish versus unselfish unethical behaviors (Vadera & Pratt, 2013). Individuals who strongly identify with their organizations are more apt to behave unethically to benefit their organizations at a cost to themselves (Umphress, Bingham, & Mitchell, 2010). To take an extreme example, tragic stories of terrorism reveal that suicide bombers are often overidentified members emboldened to "do justice" on behalf of their groups (Sageman, 2004). Similarly, although less violently, a strong organizational identification can lead employees to turn a blind eye to illegal activities in order to serve the interests of their organization (Dukerich et al., 1998).

In contrast, individuals who do not identify with their organizations are more likely to engage in selfish unethical acts. They tend to ignore organizational rules and feel free to act selfishly (e.g., arriving late to work and leaving early; Vadera & Pratt, 2013). In more extreme cases, individuals who have disengaged from their organization may even purposefully harm their organization to serve their self-interest, such as stealing office supplies and fabricating receipts for reimbursement (Vadera & Pratt, 2013).

Future Directions

In light of the distinction between unethicality and selfishness, we re-examine some of the previously documented antecedents of unethical behavior, and offer several nuanced predictions that could be tested in the future.

Money versus Time

Empirical studies have found that activating the concept of money increases unethical intentions and behaviors (Cohn et al., 2014; Gino & Mogilner, 2014; Kouchaki, Smith-Crowe, Brief, & Sousa, 2013), whereas shifting the focus onto time may offset these effects (Gino & Mogilner, 2014). However, in these experiments the beneficiary of the unethical behavior was always the participant him- or herself. If the unethical behavior were instead to benefit others rather than the agent of the behavior, we might see a reversal of the "money versus time effect." That is, although money might increase *selfish* unethical behavior, money may actually decrease *unselfish* unethical behavior. Consistent with this proposition, across nine studies Vohs, Mead, and Goode (2006) found that money produces a self-sufficient orientation. Hence, activating the concept of money might lower an individual's willingness to behave unethically to benefit others. Conversely, although activating time can curb selfish unethical behavior (Gino & Mogilner, 2014), it may actually increase unselfish unethical behavior by making people more other-focused. In support of this possibility, Mogilner (2010) found that priming time motivates individuals to invest more effort in social relationships (i.e., friends and family) and less time in their own instrumental work.

Social Learning Strategy

Prior research shows that individuals differ systematically in their social learning strategies (van den Berg, Molleman, & Weissing, 2015): Whereas some individuals attempt to imitate the most successful members of the group, others attend to the most normative members. Importantly, success-oriented learners both cooperate less and behave more selfishly as compared with norm-oriented learners (van den Berg et al., 2015). These findings suggest that success-oriented individuals may be prone to engage in selfish unethical behavior, whereas norm-oriented individuals may be prone to engage in unselfish unethical behavior. This possibility awaits further research.

Individualism versus Collectivism

Culture may also influence whether unethical behaviors are selfish or unselfish. For example, cultural values appear to serve as one predictor of bribery. Based on cross-national and laboratory data, Mazar and Aggarwal (2011) argued that collectivist cultures are the breeding ground for bribery. In light of the distinction between unethicality and selfishness, we predict a more nuanced relationship between individualism–collectivism and the type of unethical behavior enacted: Individualistic cultures may be more conducive to selfish unethical behaviors (e.g., bribing for one's personal gain), whereas collectivistic culture may be more conducive to unselfish unethical behaviors (e.g., bribing for one's organization, as in Mazar & Aggarwal, 2011). The logic for this prediction is consistent with the established notion that individualistic cultures foster more self-focused behaviors, whereas collectivistic cultures nurture more other-focused behaviors (Markus & Kitayama, 1991). Future research could investigate how cultural orientations affect unethical behavior enacted for oneself versus others.

Conclusion

At first glance, unethical behavior and selfish intention are logical companions. Indeed, unethical behavior and selfish behavior typically co-occur in the behavioral ethics literature. However, such a perspective fails to reckon with their conceptual distinctions and unnecessarily limits our understanding of social behavior. Human beings can behave ethically or unethically, and behind those behaviors can lurk selfish or unselfish intentions. By teasing apart the constructs of ethicality and selfishness, we acquire a more complete understanding of moral psychology and set a promising research agenda for the future.

NOTES

1. Results are based on a bibliometric analysis of articles published between 2000 and 2015 in *Academy of Management Journal, Administrative Science Quarterly, Journal of Applied Psychology, Journal of Personality and Social Psychology, Organizational Behavior and Human Decision Processes*, and *Psychological Science* that contain one or more of the following terms as keywords: *ethics, ethic, ethical, unethical, ethically, moral, morality, morals, immoral, amoral, dishonest, honest, deception, dishonesty, honesty, dishonestly, honestly, misconduct, wrongdoing*. Details of procedure and analyses can be requested from the authors.
2. We describe the behaviors of WikiLeaks and Aaron Swartz as prosocial based on the assumption that they intended to serve the larger community. However, it remains possible that they were motivated by selfish motives of fame and notoriety. As with whistle-blowing, the key factor for ultimately determining whether a behavior is selfish or altruistic is the intention underlying the behavior.

REFERENCES

Abelson, H., Diamond, P. A., Grosso, A., & Pfeiffer, D. W. (2013). MIT and the prosecution of Aaron Swartz. Retrieved from *http://swartz-report.mit.edu/docs/report-to-the-president.pdf*.

Ariely, D., Bracha, A., & Meier, S. (2009). Doing good or doing well?: Image motivation and monetary incentives in behaving prosocially. *American Economic Review, 99*(1), 544–555.

Ashforth, B. E., & Mael, F. (1989). Social identity theory and the organization. *Academy of Management Review, 14*(1), 20–39.

Barsky, A. (2008). Understanding the ethical cost of organizational goal-setting: A review and theory development. *Journal of Business Ethics, 81*(1), 63–81.

Batson, C. D., Batson, J. G., Todd, R. M., Brummett, B. H., Shaw, L. L., & Aldeguer, C. M. R. (1995). Empathy and the collective good: Caring for one of the others in a social dilemma. *Journal of Personality and Social Psychology, 68*(4), 619–631.

Batson, C. D., Klein, T. R., Highberger, L., & Shaw, L. L. (1995). Immorality from empathy-induced altruism: When compassion and justice conflict. *Journal of Personality and Social Psychology, 68*(6), 1042–1054.

Batson, C. D., & Shaw, L. L. (1991). Evidence for altruism: Toward a pluralism of prosocial motives. *Psychological Inquiry, 2*(2), 107–122.

Bazerman, M. H., & Gino, F. (2012). Behavioral ethics: Toward a deeper understanding of moral judgment and dishonesty. *Annual Review of Law and Social Science, 8,* 85–104.

Bentham, J. (1948). *An introduction to the principles of morals and legislation.* Oxford, UK: Blackwell. (Original work published 1789)

Bocian, K., & Wojciszke, B. (2014). Self-interest bias in moral judgments of others' actions. *Personality and Social Psychology Bulletin, 40*(7), 898–909.

Brass, D. J., Butterfield, K. D., & Skaggs, B. C. (1998). Relationships and unethical behavior: A social network perspective. *Academy of Management Review, 23*(1), 14–31.

Broomfield, K. A., Robinson, E. J., & Robinson, W. P. (2002). Children's understanding about white lies. *British Journal of Developmental Psychology, 20*(1), 47–65.

Brown, P., & Levinson, S. (1987). *Politeness: Some universals in language usage.* Cambridge, UK: Cambridge University Press.

Bryan, C. J., Adams, G. S., & Monin, B. (2013). When cheating would make you a cheater: Implicating the self prevents unethical behavior. *Journal of Experimental Psychology: General, 142*(4), 1001–1005.

Burris, E. R., Detert, J. R., & Romney, A. C. (2013). Speaking up vs. being heard: The disagreement around and outcomes of employee voice. *Organization Science, 24*(1), 22–38.

Charness, G., Masclet, D., & Villeval, M. C. (2014). The dark side of competition for status. *Management Science, 60*(1), 38–55.

Cohn, A., Fehr, E., & Maréchal, M. A. (2014). Business culture and dishonesty in the banking industry. *Nature, 516*(7529), 86–89.

DePaulo, B. M., & Kashy, D. A. (1998). Everyday lies in close and casual relationships. *Journal of Personality and Social Psychology, 74*(1), 63–79.

DeScioli, P., Massenkoff, M., Shaw, A., Petersen, M. B., & Kurzban, R. (2014). Equity or equality?: Moral judgments follow the money. *Proceedings of the Royal Society of London: B. Biological Sciences, 281*(1797), 20142112.

Dubois, D., Rucker, D. D., & Galinsky, A. D. (2015). Social class, power, and selfishness: When and why upper and lower class individuals behave unethically. *Journal of Personality and Social Psychology, 108*(3), 436–449.

Dukerich, J. M., Kramer, R., & Parks, J. M. (1998). The dark side of organizational identification. In D. A. Whetten & P. C. Godfrey (Eds.), *Identity in organizations: Building theory through conversations* (pp. 245–256). Thousand Oaks, CA: SAGE.

Dyck, A., Morse, A., & Zingales, L. (2010). Who blows the whistle on corporate fraud? *Journal of Finance, 65*(6), 2213–2253.

Edelman, B., & Larkin, I. (2015). Social comparisons and deception across workplace hierarchies: Field and experimental evidence. *Organization Science, 26*(1), 78–98.

Eisenberg, N., & Miller, P. A. (1987). The relation of empathy to prosocial and related behaviors. *Psychological Bulletin, 101*(1), 91–119.

Fehr, E., & Gächter, S. (2002). Altruistic punishment in humans. *Nature, 415*(6868), 137–140.

Feldstein, M. (1975). The income tax and charitable contributions: Part I. Aggregate and distributional effects. *National Tax Journal, 28*(1), 81–100.

Friedman, M. (1999). Introduction. In L. E. Read, *I, pencil: My family tree as told to Leonard E. Read.* Irvington-on-Hudson, NY: Foundation for Economic Education.

Frimer, J. A., Schaefer, N. K., & Oakes, H. (2014). Moral actor, selfish agent. *Journal of Personality and Social Psychology, 106*(5), 790–802.

Gino, F., Ayal, S., & Ariely, D. (2009). Contagion and differentiation in unethical behavior: The effect of one bad apple on the barrel. *Psychological Science, 20*(3), 393–398.

Gino, F., & Mogilner, C. (2014). Time, money, and morality. *Psychological Science, 25*(2), 414–421.

Golden, D. (2003, March 12). How much does it cost to buy your child in? *Wall Street Journal.* Retrieved from *www.wsj.com/articles/SB1047409881995483800.*

Griswold, C. L. (1999). *Adam Smith and the virtues of enlightenment.* Cambridge, UK: Cambridge University Press.

Harbaugh, W. T., Mayr, U., & Burghart, D. R. (2007). Neural responses to taxation and voluntary giving reveal motives for charitable donations. *Science, 316*(5831), 1622–1625.

Hegarty, W. H., & Sims, H. P. (1978). Some determinants of unethical decision behavior: An experiment. *Journal of Applied Psychology, 63*(4), 451–457.

Iezzoni, L. I., Rao, S. R., DesRoches, C. M., Vogeli, C., & Campbell, E. G. (2012). Survey shows that at least some physicians are not always open or honest with patients. *Health Affairs, 31*(2), 383–391.

Jensen, M. C. (2003). Paying people to lie: The truth about the budgeting process. *European Financial Management, 9*(3), 379–406.

Johnson, R. A. (2003). *Whistleblowing: When it works and why.* Boulder, CO: Lynne Riener.

Jones, T. M. (1991). Ethical decision making by

individuals in organizations: An issue-contingent model. *Academy of Management Review, 16*(2), 366–395.

Kant, I. (1959). *Foundation of the metaphysics of morals* (L. W. Beck, Trans.). Indianapolis, IN: Bobbs-Merrill. (Original work published 1785)

Kern, M. C., & Chugh, D. (2009). Bounded ethicality: The perils of loss framing. *Psychological Science, 20*(3), 378–384.

Kilduff, G., Galinksy, A., Gallo, E., & Reade, J. (2016). Whatever it takes to win: Rivalry increases unethical behavior. *Academy of Management Journal, 59,* 1508–1534.

Kohlberg, L. (1963). The development of children's orientations toward a moral order. *Human Development, 6*(1–2), 11–33.

Kouchaki, M., Smith-Crowe, K., Brief, A. P., & Sousa, C. (2013). Seeing green: Mere exposure to money triggers a business decision frame and unethical outcomes. *Organizational Behavior and Human Decision Processes, 121*(1), 53–61.

Lavee, J., Ashkenazi, T., Gurman, G., & Steinberg, D. (2010). A new law for allocation of donor organs in Israel. *The Lancet, 375*(9720), 1131–1133.

Levine, E. E., & Schweitzer, M. E. (2014). Are liars ethical?: On the tension between benevolence and honesty. *Journal of Experimental Social Psychology, 53,* 107–117.

Levine, E. E., & Schweitzer, M. E. (2015). Prosocial lies: When deception breeds trust. *Organizational Behavior and Human Decision Processes, 126,* 88–106.

Lu, J. G., Brockner, J., Vardi, Y., & Weitz, E. (2017). The dark side of experiencing job autonomy: Unethical behavior. *Journal of Experimental Social Psychology, 73,* 222–234.

Lu, J. G., Lee, J. J., Gino, F., & Galinsky, A. D. (in press). Polluted morality: Air pollution predicts criminal activity and unethical behavior. *Psychological Science.*

Lu, J. G., Quoidbach, J., Gino, F., Chakroff, A., Maddux, W. W., & Galinsky, A. D. (2017). The dark side of going abroad: How broad foreign experiences increase immoral behavior. *Journal of Personality and Social Psychology, 112*(1), 1–16.

Markus, H. R., & Kitayama, S. (1991). Culture and the self: Implications for cognition, emotion, and motivation. *Psychological Review, 98*(2), 224–253.

Mazar, N., & Aggarwal, P. (2011). Greasing the palm: Can collectivism promote bribery? *Psychological Science, 22*(7), 843–848.

Mogilner, C. (2010). The pursuit of happiness: Time, money, and social connection. *Psychological Science, 21*(9), 1348–1354.

Near, J. P., & Miceli, M. P. (1985). Organizational dissidence: The case of whistle-blowing. *Journal of Business Ethics, 4*(1), 1–16.

Ordóñez, L. D., Schweitzer, M. E., Galinsky, A. D., & Bazerman, M. H. (2009). Goals gone wild: The systematic side effects of overprescribing goal setting. *Academy of Management Perspectives, 23*(1), 6–16.

Paine, L. S., & Santoro, M. A. (1993). *Sears auto centers (A) (Harvard Business School case 9-394-009).* Boston: Harvard Business School.

Penner, L. A., Dovidio, J. F., Piliavin, J. A., & Schroeder, D. A. (2005). Prosocial behavior: Multilevel perspectives. *Annual Review of Psychology, 56,* 365–392.

Peters, K., Luck, L., Hutchinson, M., Wilkes, L., Andrew, S., & Jackson, D. (2011). The emotional sequelae of whistleblowing: Findings from a qualitative study. *Journal of Clinical Nursing, 20*(19–20), 2907–2914.

Piff, P. K., Stancato, D. M., Côté, S., Mendoza-Denton, R., & Keltner, D. (2012). Higher social class predicts increased unethical behavior. *Proceedings of the National Academy of Sciences of the USA, 109*(11), 4086–4091.

Piliavin, J. A. (2003). Doing well by doing good: Benefits for the benefactor. In M. Keyes & J. Haidt (Eds.), *Flourishing: Positive psychology and the life well lived* (pp. 227–247). Washington, DC: American Psychological Association.

Plato. (1997). Laws (T. J. Saunders, Trans.). In J. Cooper & D. Hutchinson (Eds.), *Complete works.* Indianapolis, IN: Hackett. (Original work published 360 B.C.)

Rege, M., & Telle, K. (2004). The impact of social approval and framing on cooperation in public good situations. *Journal of Public Economics, 88*(7), 1625–1644.

Sageman, M. (2004). *Understanding terror networks.* Philadelphia: University of Pennsylvania Press.

Schweitzer, M. E., Ordóñez, L., & Douma, B. (2004). Goal setting as a motivator of unethical behavior. *Academy of Management Journal, 47*(3), 422–432.

Shi, L., Wang, J., Liu, Z., Stevens, L., Sadler, A., Ness, P., & Shan, H. (2014). Blood donor management in China. *Transfusion Medicine and Hemotherapy, 41*(4), 273–282.

Smith, A. (1937). *An inquiry into the nature and causes of the wealth of nations.* New York: Modern Library. (Original work published 1776)

Talwar, V., Murphy, S. M., & Lee, K. (2007). White lie-telling in children for politeness purposes. *International Journal of Behavioral Development, 31*(1), 1–11.

Umphress, E. E., Bingham, J. B., & Mitchell, M. S. (2010). Unethical behavior in the name of the company: The moderating effect of orga nizational identification and positive reciprocity beliefs on unethical pro-organizational behavior. *Journal of Applied Psychology, 95*(4), 769–780.

U.S. Department of the Treasury, Internal Revenue Service. (2017). Whistleblower-Informant Award. Retrieved from *www.irs.gov/uac/Whistleblower-Informant-Award.*

Vadera, A. K., & Pratt, M. G. (2013). Love, hate, ambivalence, or indifference?: A conceptual examination of workplace crimes and organizational identification. *Organization Science, 24*(1), 172–188.

Valdesolo, P., & DeSteno, D. (2007). Moral hypocrisy social groups and the flexibility of virtue. *Psychological Science, 18*(8), 689–690.

Valdesolo, P., & DeSteno, D. (2008). The duality of virtue: Deconstructing the moral hypocrite.

Journal of Experimental Social Psychology, 44(5), 1334–1338.

van den Berg, P., Molleman, L., & Weissing, F. J. (2015). Focus on the success of others leads to selfish behavior. *Proceedings of the National Academy of Sciences of the USA, 112*(9), 2912–2917.

Vohs, K. D., Mead, N. L., & Goode, M. R. (2006). The psychological consequences of money. *Science, 314*(5802), 1154–1156.

Walker, L. J., & Hennig, K. H. (2004). Differing conceptions of moral exemplarity: Just, brave, and caring. *Journal of Personality and Social Psychology, 86*(4), 629–647.

Waytz, A., Dungan, J., & Young, L. (2013). The whistleblower's dilemma and the fairness–loyalty tradeoff. *Journal of Experimental Social Psychology, 49*(6), 1027–1033.

CHAPTER 48

In Search of Moral Equilibrium

Person, Situation, and Their Interplay in Behavioral Ethics

Julia J. Lee
Francesca Gino

To what extent is our unethical behavior a product of dispositional or situational forces?

We argue that unethical behavior should be understood in terms of the dynamic interplay between dispositional factors—such as (1) one's ability and willpower, (2) personality traits, and (3) motivations and identity—and trait-relevant situational factors.

Despite the ever-increasing number of empirical studies in behavioral ethics, our knowledge of how dispositional forces interact with situational forces to influence unethical behavior is largely absent. We posit that individuals may have a different equilibrium point at which they are willing to sacrifice a positive self-concept for their own benefit, and such equilibrium may well be determined as a result of both dispositional and situational factors. We thus propose a model of unethical behavior that incorporates both situational and dispositional forces (see Figure 48.1). In this chapter, we first provide a nuanced definition of unethical behavior and then review the literature supporting the view that individual differences may be a key determinant of our moral equilibrium. We then call for future studies that examine the interplay of dispositional and situational factors in depth.

A review of the literature on unethical behavior indicates that researchers generally maintain that two main sets of factors influence employees' decisions to act unethically: (1) situational forces (related to the context the person is operating in) and (2) dispositional forces (related to the person's personality). Recent advances in behavioral ethics unveiled the psychological tendencies that would lead even good people to cross ethical boundaries (Bazerman & Gino, 2012). One of the notable assumptions in the field of behavioral ethics is that morality is rather dynamic and malleable, instead of being a stable individual difference (Bazerman & Gino, 2012; Monin & Jordan, 2009). Empirical studies that support this view are

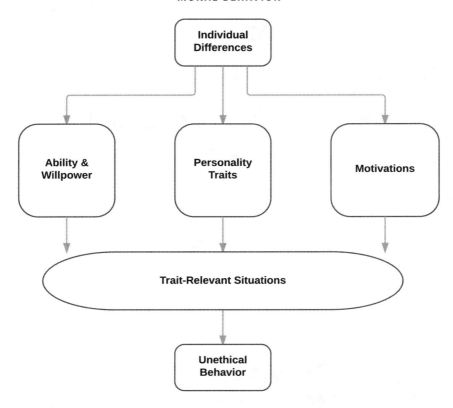

FIGURE 48.1. An interactionist model of unethical behavior.

abundant; when individuals are placed in situations in which they have the opportunity to behave unethically, they are motivated to strike a balance between pursuing self-interest and maintaining a positive self-view (Gino, Schweitzer, Mead, & Ariely, 2011; Mazar, Amir, & Ariely, 2008; Mead, Baumeister, & Gino, 2009). Research has since demonstrated that human behavior is malleable rather than fixed across different situations and can change, depending on a wide range of factors, from momentary dips in our ability to resist temptation (Mead et al., 2009) to how tired we are (Killgore, Killgore, Day, & Li, 2007) to the time of day (Kouchaki & Smith, 2013). This body of research propelled a development of a model of ethical decision making by accounting for the capricious nature of human behavior.

The relationship between situational influences and unethical behavior is rooted in social psychological research suggesting that a person's environment can have a significant impact on his or her behavior (Asch, 1955; Milgram, 1974; Zimbardo, 2007). Consistent with these theoretical bases, scholars have largely focused on environmental factors that could sway one's moral compass. Examples of such studies include ethics training (Delaney & Sockell, 1992); ethical climate, leadership, and culture (Treviño, 1986; Victor & Cullen, 1988); accountability (Pitesa & Thau, 2013); codes of conduct (Brief, Dukerich, Brown, & Brett, 1996; Helin & Sandström, 2007; Mayer, Kuenzi, Greenbaum, Bardes, & Salvador, 2009; McCabe, Treviño, & Butterfield, 2002); reward systems and incentives (Flannery & May, 2000; Hegarty & Sims, 1978; Schweitzer & Croson, 1999; Tenbrunsel, 1998; Treviño & Youngblood, 1990); the nature of the goals driving one's actions (Schweitzer, Ordóñez, & Douma, 2004); and wealth present in one's environment (Gino & Pierce, 2009).

Defining Unethical Behavior

Unethical behavior refers to an action that has harmful effects on others and that is "either illegal or morally unacceptable to the larger community" (Jones, 1991, p. 367). This definition has been widely endorsed by behavioral ethics scholars, and researchers in this area have largely focused on unethical behaviors such as lying, cheating, and stealing (Treviño, Weaver, & Reynolds, 2006).

By definition, unethical behaviors are not necessarily selfish acts and not always committed within the agent's conscious awareness. Still, by and large, researchers have focused on motives that emphasize a self-serving or self-oriented motivation for unethical behavior. For example, Gneezy (2005) noted that people tell lies whenever it is beneficial for them, regardless of the lies' effect on the other party. Similarly, Tenbrunsel (1998) showed that monetary incentives increase individuals' willingness to misrepresent information to another party in a social exchange, consistent with Lewicki's (1983) argument that individuals lie to the extent that lying benefits them. This view is consistent with prior work conceptualizing the decision to behave unethically as a product of economic incentives (Allingham & Sandmo, 1972; Holmstrom, 1979).

However, researchers have also identified unethical behaviors that are motivated by interpersonal emotions (such as envy and compassion) and that thus do not necessarily benefit the self; for example, individuals may inflict intentional harm to others or bend the rule to help others (see Gino & Pierce, 2010a, 2010b; Lee & Gino, 2017). In addition, Bazerman and Gino (2012) argued that even those individuals who want to be seen as moral might fail to recognize that there is a moral issue at stake in the decision that they are making. For instance, people failed to recognize their own conflicts of interest that led to unethical behavior (Moore, Tetlock, Tanlu, & Bazerman, 2006) and were unable to notice others' unethical behavior when ethical degradation occurs slowly (Gino & Bazerman, 2009). We therefore use the term *unethical behavior* throughout this chapter to reflect this nuanced understanding of what such behaviors entail.

Bringing the Person Back In[1]

Ethical Behavior as a Matter of Ability and Willpower

The study of the relationship between disposition and unethical behavior is rooted in models of individuals' *cognitive moral development* (Treviño, 1986; Treviño & Youngblood, 1990), which determines how an individual thinks about ethical dilemmas and decides what is right or wrong in any given situation. According to Rest's (1986) four-component model, ethical behavior is a result of four processes—awareness, judgment, motivation/intention, and action. This model is intuitive and compelling and easily adaptable to different theoretical needs.

Rest's model provides a largely context-independent view of moral behavior. Essentially, it understands moral behavior as a learnable skill that will be manifested so long as one has the knowledge about what the correct action is and has developed the appropriate behavioral priorities through one's childhood and education. Though Rest makes some acknowledgment that our social context may affect whether we become aware of the moral import of a given decision (Rest, 1986), the role of social context is essentially tangential in his model. In addition, Rest offers a highly agentic model of moral behavior, by which we mean that the individual actor is credited with the lion's share of control and accountability over his or her ultimate moral choices. This agentic model makes the assumption that failures to behave ethically are due to flaws in an individual's moral awareness, judgment, motivation, or follow-through. Based as it is in Kohlberg's cognitive moral development theory (Kohlberg, 1969, 1984), a fundamental assumption of Rest's framework is that the key to improving moral behavior is moral education (Kohlberg, 1984; Rest, 1986). This assumption about how moral behavior happens puts a large onus on the individual both to be perfectly aware of the "correct" moral outcome and to have the courage and authority to be able to enact that outcome. Importantly, Rest's model emphasizes the agent's cognitive ability to do the right thing.

Another set of research on self-control highlights the role of an agent's *willpower* as an antecedent of unethical behavior (Baumeister, Vohs, & Tice, 2007; Gino et al., 2011; Tangney, Baumeister, & Boone, 2004). This view starts with an assumption that people behave unethically when they face a dilemma between actions that offer short-term benefits (e.g., monetary payoff) versus long-term benefits (e.g., ethical reputation and social acceptance; see Monin, Pizarro, & Beer, 2007; Sheldon & Fishbach, 2015). Empirical evidence supports this view by showing that one's exertion of self-control depletes one's self-regulation resources, thus increasing unethical behavior in an unrelated domain (Barnes, Schaubroeck, Huth, & Ghumman, 2011; Gino et al., 2011; Mead et al., 2009). At a trait level, low self-control is found to be associated with a set of criminal and antisocial behaviors (Gottfredson & Hirschi, 1990). Similar to Rest's theory, research on self-control puts much emphasis on an individual's ability to resist ethical temptations.

Ethical Behavior as a Matter of Personality Traits

Whereas the above-mentioned research focuses on one's *ability* to do the right thing, another stream of research points to how one's personality traits may influence ethical behavior.

First, past research on personality traits has found various traits that may predispose a person to unethical behavior. Some personality traits are more directly related to morality than others (Cohen, Panter, Turan, Morse, & Kim, 2014). We identify two morally relevant traits: the self-importance of *moral identity* (Aquino & Reed, 2002) and *moral disengagement* (Moore, Detert, Treviño, Baker, & Mayer, 2012). Moral identity is defined as a self-conception organized around a set of moral traits and is known to be a relatively stable individual difference over time (Aquino & Reed, 2002). Moral identity has been shown to be positively correlated with prosocial behavior and reduced unethical behavior (Aquino & Reed, 2002; Shao, Aquino, & Freeman, 2008). As part of moral character, moral identity (internalizing the importance of possessing moral traits, in particular) also predicted ethical behavior in the workplace (Cohen et al.,

2014). On the other hand, moral disengagement describes an individual's propensity to cognitively disengage to allow him- or herself to behave unethically without feeling distress (Bandura, 2002; Moore et al., 2012). Moral disengagement has been found to predict self-reported unethical behavior, decisions to commit fraud, self-serving decisions in the workplace, and other-reported unethical work behaviors (Moore et al., 2012).

Second, we identify two affect-based personality traits that have significant influence on ethical behavior—*trait empathy* (Eisenberg & Miller, 1987; Tangney, 1991) and *guilt proneness* (Cohen, Panter, & Turan, 2012). Trait empathy has shown to contribute to ethical behavior and to reduce unethical behavior in various studies (Cohen et al., 2014; Eisenberg & Miller, 1987; Hoffman, 2000; Tangney, 1991). Similarly, guilt proneness has predicted making fewer unethical business decisions, committing fewer delinquent behaviors, and behaving more honestly at work (Cohen et al., 2012; Cohen et al., 2014).

Lastly, two traits have been shown to give rise to unethical behavior: *Machiavellianism* (Christie & Geis, 2013; O'Boyle, Forsyth, & Banks, 2012) and *psychopathy* (Hare & Neumann, 2009; O'Boyle et al., 2012). Both traits predicted the likelihood of making unethical decisions at work (Kish-Gephart, Harrison, & Treviño, 2010), as well as paying kickbacks in a marketing simulation (Hegarty & Sims, 1978, 1979). Similarly, psychopathic personality predicted counterproductive behavior at work (O'Boyle et al., 2012), as well as academic cheating (Nathanson, Paulhus, & Williams, 2006).

Ethical Behavior as a Matter of Identity and Motivation

Previous research has thus far focused on either ability-based or personality-based accounts of morality. We argue that there are *motivational* factors that should be taken into account when examining the individual differences that give a rise to unethical behavior. Further, we propose that these motivational differences are relatively malleable as compared with the factors that we have summarized so far, such that these factors are likely to interact with situational factors. Here we identify attachment and performance anxiety as such motivational factors.

First, *attachment* can be a powerful social motivation that could result in interpersonal unethical behaviors. The theory of attachment is built around the idea that security-enhancing caregivers ("attachment figures") help a child develop positive self-views and relationships (Bowlby, 1982; Cassidy & Shaver, 2008; Mikulincer & Shaver, 2007). Attachment security is theorized to direct individuals to be less anxious and defensive and more open and prosocial, which might contribute to a sense of authenticity and honesty. Indeed, dispositional attachment insecurity was correlated with unethical behavior (lying and cheating), and experimentally manipulated attachment security has been shown to reduce the tendency to lie or cheat (Gillath, Sesko, Shaver, & Chun, 2010). In particular, attachment avoidance (i.e., the degree to which people are comfortable with physical and emotional intimacy) predicted more unethical workplace decisions in hypothetical scenarios (Chopik, 2015). This relationship between attachment avoidance and unethical decisions was mediated by emotional exhaustion, which suggests the importance of interpersonal and emotional motivations that underlie unethical behavior.

Second, *performance anxiety* can be another source of motivation that could propel one's unethical behavior. Performance-related anxiety has shown to increase the likelihood of cheating among college students (Berger, Levin, Jacobson, & Millham, 1977), and experimentally manipulated anxiety also increased unethical behavior (Kouchaki & Desai, 2014). In our own research, we measured participants' pre- and postperformance hormone levels (testosterone as a marker for reward and risk seeking and cortisol as a marker for anxiety and stress) and gave them an opportunity to cheat. We found that elevated concentrations of testosterone and cortisol predicted more cheating on a performance test (Lee, Gino, Jin, Rice, & Josephs, 2015). More importantly, we found that the more participants cheated, the greater were the hormonal and emotional rewards of cheating, as indicated by reductions in cortisol and negative affect.

This finding is consistent with the view that anxiety evoked by performance-related uncertainty encourages cheating as a means of reducing such aversive states (Anderman, Griesinger, & Westerfield, 1998). In line with this research, Wakeman and Moore (2015) found that individuals are more likely to cheat after their self-views on competence are threatened by performing poorly on the task.

The Interplay between Person and Situation

Following the interactionist views that were put forth by Treviño (1986) and Bandura (1990), we argue that unethical behavior is a function of individual differences, situational factors, and their interactions. Here we draw on the interactionist principle of trait activation (Kenrick & Funder, 1988; Tett & Guterman, 2000) to identify the situational forces that are *relevant* to dispositional forces. That is, the behavioral expression of a trait requires arousal of that trait by trait-relevant situational cues. This view allows the possibility that individuals can behave consistently across different situations through strong dispositions, but strong situations can also cause different people to behave similarly (Beaty, Cleveland, & Murphy, 2001; Mischel, 1973, 1977). We use this situation–trait relevance as a guide to identify a few thematically relevant situational factors that are likely to interact with one's disposition.

The first model of unethical behavior focuses on how an individual's ability and willpower can interact with situations that are cognitively depleting. Consider a team of consultants who had to travel long hours and are severely jet-lagged. Research has shown that sleep deprivation can lead to unethical behavior (Barnes et al., 2011) and that individuals are more ethical in the morning than later in the day (Kouchaki & Smith, 2013). When the team faces a decision of ethical import to be made, would everyone on the team prefer to make an unethical decision? Despite the strength of situation (Baumeister, Bratslavsky, Finkenauer, & Vohs, 2001), the team members' decision may depend on individuals' cognitive awareness and construal of the situation as carrying moral weights, as well as the ability to resist the temptation. A good example of the Person × Situation interaction in this context demonstrated that the fit between a person's chronotype (i.e., whether one's circadian rhythms are optimized for morning or for evening) and the time of day predicted ethical behavior (Barnes et al., 2011). Similarly, future studies could examine the situations that could render individuals cognitively depleted, such as excessive workload and time constraints, and examine how these relevant situations can lead to more unethical behavior for those who have high or low moral awareness or self-control at the trait level.

The second model focused on various personality traits that are relatively stable, such as moral identity, moral disengagement, trait empathy, guilt proneness, Machiavellianism, and psychopathy. One can imagine various situational factors that are relevant to each of these personality traits. But as an example, an ethical norm that allows individuals to easily rationalize their unethical behavior can reinforce the unethical behavior committed by those who have high moral disengagement. Consider an employee–supervisor dyad in which the employee observes the supervisor inflating the expense report and telling the employee that everyone in the company does the same. This incident is likely to increase the employee's tendency to behave unethically (Shu, Gino, & Bazerman, 2011), but this may depend on a person's own propensity to engage in moral disengagement. For example, Bonner, Greenbaum, and Mayer (2016) have shown that the negative relationship between supervisors' moral disengagement and employees' perceptions of ethical leadership is stronger when employees' moral disengagement is low versus high. Future research could thus examine the ethical norms (e.g., norms of accountability, the extent to which performance goals are aligned with ethical goals, or incentives that reinforce the idea of a zero-sum game) could trigger relevant personality traits.

The last model viewed unethical behavior as a function of motivational forces, such as attachment and performance anxiety. For instance, a high-stress work environment (think Wall Street) can reinforce an employee's performance anxiety. Indeed, individuals' thinking about their identity as bank employees led to more cheating, which suggests that business culture may play a significant role in shaping one's moral compass. Similarly, work stressors, such as interpersonal conflicts and organizational constraints, have shown to increase counterproductive work behaviors (Kim, Cohen, & Panter, 2015; Meier & Spector, 2013). Consistent with the view that those individuals who experience high levels of anxiety and attachment avoidance might find their situation particularly stressful (Hazan & Shaver, 1990), a high-stress environment may amplify the workers' need to reduce the performance-related stress by crossing ethical boundaries, particularly for those who already have elevated levels of performance anxiety. Thus future studies could identify the environmental stressors (e.g., pay for performance) that could interact with one's motivational differences.

Conclusion

On a daily basis, we are faced with choices that could advance our own self-interest or demonstrate consistency with our moral compass. Across contexts, from politics and sport to education and business, these choices are often tempting, leading even people who care about morality and being ethical to act unethically. Given the economic and social costs of unethical behavior, it is important to understand the antecedents of these behaviors. In this chapter, we built on insightful research in behavioral ethics and moral psychology to propose an interactive model of person- and situation-based unethical behavior. We first placed morality in the realm of the behavioral ethics literature to define unethical behavior in broad terms. We then provided a review of three different models of individual difference that predict unethical behavior. Finally, we suggested that unethical behavior should be understood in terms of the dynamic interplay between dispositional factors and situational factors and called for more research on this interplay. We hope that by responding to this call, scholars from various fields will identify important insights as to why even good people do bad things and how they can best ensure that they will follow their moral compass in both challenging and more ordinary ethical situations.

NOTE

1. We did not include a host of demographic antecedents of unethical behavior for two reasons. First, we focus on the individual differences that can be changed or made salient and that are thus relatively malleable. Second, despite some evidence showing that demographic variables influence ethical decisions (O'Fallon & Butterfield, 2005; Piff, Stancato, Côté, Mendoza-Denton, & Keltner, 2012), studies have found that the effect size tends to be relatively small or not significant as compared with other morally relevant traits (Cohen, Panter, Turan, Morse, & Kim, 2014; Kish-Gephart, Harrison, & Treviño, 2010).

REFERENCES

Allingham, M. G., & Sandmo, A. (1972). Income tax evasion: A theoretical analysis. *Journal of Public Economics, 1*(3–4), 323–338.

Anderman, E. M., Griesinger, T., & Westerfield, G. (1998). Motivation and cheating during early adolescence. *Journal of Educational Psychology, 90*, 84–93.

Aquino, K., & Reed, A., II. (2002). The self-importance of moral identity. *Journal of Personality and Social Psychology, 83*(6), 1423–1440.

Asch, S. E. (1955). Opinions and social pressure. *Scientific American, 193*(5), 31–35.

Bandura, A. (1990). Selective activation and disengagement of moral control. *Journal of Social Issues, 46*(1), 27–46.

Bandura, A. (2002). Selective moral disengagement in the exercise of moral agency. *Journal of Moral Education, 31*(2), 101–119.

Barnes, C. M., Schaubroeck, J., Huth, M., & Ghumman, S. (2011). Lack of sleep and unethical conduct. *Organizational Behavior and Human Decision Processes, 115*(2), 169–180.

Baumeister, R. F., Bratslavsky, E., Finkenauer, C., & Vohs, K. D. (2001). Bad is stronger than good. *Review of General Psychology, 5*(4), 323–370.

Baumeister, R. F., Vohs, K. D., & Tice, D. M. (2007). The strength model of self-control. *Current Directions in Psychological Science, 16*(6), 351–355.

Bazerman, M. H., & Gino, F. (2012). Behavioral ethics: Toward a deeper understanding of moral judgment and dishonesty. *Annual Review of Law and Social Science, 8*(1), 85–104.

Beaty, J. C., Jr., Cleveland, J. N., & Murphy, K. R. (2001). The relation between personality and contextual performance in "strong" versus "weak" situations. *Human Performance, 14*(2), 125–148.

Berger, S. E., Levin, P., Jacobson, L. I., & Millham, J. (1977). Gain approval or avoid disapproval: Comparison of motive strengths in high need for approval scorers. *Journal of Personality, 45*(3), 458–468.

Bonner, J. M., Greenbaum, R. L., & Mayer, D. M. (2016). My boss is morally disengaged: The role of ethical leadership in explaining the interactive effect of supervisor and employee moral disengagement on employee behaviors. *Journal of Business Ethics, 137*, 731–742.

Bowlby, J. (1982). Attachment and loss: Retrospect and prospect. *American Journal of Orthopsychiatry, 52*(4), 664–678.

Brief, A. P., Dukerich, J. M., Brown, P. R., & Brett, J. F. (1996). What's wrong with the Treadway Commission report?: Experimental analyses of the effects of personal values and codes of conduct on fraudulent financial reporting. *Journal of Business Ethics, 15*(2), 183–198.

Cassidy, J., & Shaver, P. R. (Eds.). (2008). *Handbook of attachment* (2nd ed.). New York: Guilford Press.

Chopik, W. J. (2015). Relational attachment and ethical workplace decisions: The mediating role of emotional burnout. *Journal of Experimental Psychology: General, 75*, 160–164.

Christie, R., & Geis, F. L. (2013). *Studies in Machiavellianism*. New York: Academic Press.

Cohen, T. R., Panter, A. T., & Turan, N. (2012). Guilt proneness and moral character. *Current Directions in Psychological Science, 21*(5), 355–359.

Cohen, T. R., Panter, A. T., Turan, N., Morse, L., & Kim, Y. (2014). Moral character in the workplace. *Journal of Personality and Social Psychology, 107*(5), 943–963.

Delaney, J. T., & Sockell, D. (1992). Do company ethics training programs make a difference?: An empirical analysis. *Journal of Business Ethics, 11*(9), 719–727.

Eisenberg, N., & Miller, P. A. (1987). The relation of empathy to prosocial and related behaviors. *Psychological Bulletin, 101*(1), 91–119.

Flannery, B. L., & May, D. R. (2000). Environmental ethical decision making in the U.S. metal-finishing industry. *Academy of Management Journal, 43*(4), 642–662.

Gillath, O., Sesko, A. K., Shaver, P. R., & Chun, D. S. (2010). Attachment, authenticity, and honesty: Dispositional and experimentally induced security can reduce self- and other-deception. *Journal of Personality and Social Psychology, 98*(5), 841–855.

Gino, F., & Bazerman, M. H. (2009). When misconduct goes unnoticed: The acceptability of gradual erosion in others' unethical behavior. *Journal of Experimental Social Psychology, 45*(4), 708–719.

Gino, F., & Pierce, L. (2009). The abundance effect: Unethical behavior in the presence of wealth. *Organizational Behavior and Human Decision Processes, 109*(2), 142–155.

Gino, F., & Pierce, L. (2010a). Lying to level the playing field: Why people may dishonestly help or hurt others to create equity. *Journal of Business Ethics, 95*(S1), 89–103.

Gino, F., & Pierce, L. (2010b). Robin Hood under the hood: Wealth-based discrimination in illicit customer help. *Organization Science, 21*(6), 1176–1194.

Gino, F., Schweitzer, M. E., Mead, N. L., & Ariely, D. (2011). Unable to resist temptation: How self-control depletion promotes unethical behavior. *Organizational Behavior and Human Decision Processes, 115*(2), 191–203.

Gneezy, U. (2005). Deception: The role of consequences. *American Economic Review, 95*(1), 384–394.

Gottfredson, M. R., & Hirschi, T. (1990). Low self-control and crime. Available at *www.self-teachingresources.com/yahoo_site_admin/ assets/docs/Low_Self_Control_and_Crime_ Gottfredson_Hirschi.23144447.pdf*.

Hare, R. D., & Neumann, C. S. (2009). Psychopathy and its measurement. In P. J. Corr & G. Matthews (Eds.), *The Cambridge handbook of personality psychology* (pp. 660–686). Cambridge, UK: Cambridge University Press.

Hazan, C., & Shaver, P. R. (1990). Love and work: An attachment-theoretical perspective. *Journal of Personality and Social Psychology, 59*(2), 270–280.

Hegarty, W. H., & Sims, H. P. (1978). Some determinants of unethical decision behavior: An experiment. *Journal of Applied Psychology, 63*(4), 451–457.

Hegarty, W. H., & Sims, H. P. (1979). Organizational philosophy, policies, and objectives related to unethical decision behavior: A laboratory experiment. *Journal of Applied Psychology, 64*(3), 331–338.

Helin, S., & Sandström, J. (2007). An inquiry into the study of corporate codes of ethics. *Journal of Business Ethics, 75*(3), 253–271.

Hoffman, M. L. (2000). Development of empathic distress. In *Empathy and moral development.* Cambridge, UK: Cambridge University Press.

Holmstrom, B. (1979). Moral hazard and observability. *Bell Journal of Economics, 10*(1), 74–91.

Jones, T. M. (1991). Ethical decision making by individuals in organizations: An issue-contingent model. *Academy of Management Review, 16*(2), 366–395.

Kenrick, D. T., & Funder, D. C. (1988). Profiting from controversy: Lessons from the person–situation debate. *American Psychologist, 43*(1), 23–34.

Killgore, W., Killgore, D. B., Day, L. M., & Li, C. (2007). The effects of 53 hours of sleep deprivation on moral judgment. *Sleep, 30*(3), 345–352.

Kim, Y., Cohen, T. R., & Panter, A. T. (2016). *Cause or consequence?: The reciprocal model of counterproductive work behavior and mistreatment.* Academy of Management Annual Meeting Best Paper Proceedings. Available at *http://proceedings.aom.org/content/2016/1/18071*.

Kish-Gephart, J. J., Harrison, D. A., & Treviño, L. K. (2010). Bad apples, bad cases, and bad barrels: Meta-analytic evidence about sources of unethical decisions at work. *Journal of Applied Psychology, 95*(1), 1–31.

Kohlberg, L. (1969). Stage and sequence: The cognitive development approach to socialization. In D. A. Goslin (Ed.), *Handbook of socialization theory* (pp. 347–480). Chicago: Rand McNally.

Kohlberg, L. (1984). *The psychology of moral development: The nature and validity of moral stages* (2nd ed.). San Francisco: HarperCollins.

Kouchaki, M., & Desai, S. D. (2014). Anxious, threatened, and also unethical: How anxiety makes individuals feel threatened and commit unethical acts. *Journal of Applied Psychology, 100*(2), 360–375.

Kouchaki, M., & Smith, I. H. (2013). The morning morality effect: The influence of time of day on unethical behavior. *Psychological Science, 25*(1), 95–102.

Lee, J. J., & Gino, F. (2017). Envy and interpersonal corruption: Social comparison processes and unethical behavior in organizations. In R. Smith, U. Merlone, & M. Duffy (Eds.), *Envy at work and in organizations: Research, theory, and applications* (pp. 347–371). New York: Oxford University Press.

Lee, J. J., Gino, F., Jin, E. S., Rice, L. K., & Josephs, B. (2015). Hormones and ethics: Understanding the biological basis of unethical conduct. *Journal of Experimental Psychology: General, 144*(5), 891–897.

Lewicki, P. (1983). Self-image bias in person perception. *Journal of Personality and Social Psychology, 45*(2), 384–393.

Mayer, D. M., Kuenzi, M., Greenbaum, R., Bardes, M., & Salvador, R. B. (2009). How low does ethical leadership flow?: Test of a trickle-down model. *Organizational Behavior and Human Decision Processes, 108*(1), 1–13.

Mazar, N., Amir, O., & Ariely, D. (2008). The dishonesty of honest people: A theory of self-concept maintenance. *Journal of Marketing Research, 45*(6), 633–644.

McCabe, D. L., Treviño, L. K., & Butterfield, K. D. (2002). Honor codes and other contextual influences on academic integrity: A replication and extension to modified honor code settings. *Research in Higher Education, 43*(3), 357–378.

Mead, N. L., Baumeister, R. F., & Gino, F. (2009). Too tired to tell the truth: Self-control resource depletion and dishonesty. *Journal of Experimental Social Psychology, 45*(3), 594–597.

Meier, L. L., & Spector, P. E. (2013). Reciprocal effects of work stressors and counterproductive work behavior: A five-wave longitudinal study. *Journal of Applied Psychology, 98*(3), 529–539.

Mikulincer, M., & Shaver, P. R. (2007). Boosting attachment security to promote mental health, prosocial values, and inter-group tolerance. *Psychological Inquiry, 18*(3), 139–156.

Milgram, S. (1974). *Obedience to authority.* London: Tavistock.

Mischel, W. (1973). Toward a cognitive social learning reconceptualization of personality. *Psychological Review, 80*(4), 252–283.

Mischel, W. (1977). The interaction of person and situation. In D. Magnusson & N. S. Endler (Eds.), *Personality at the crossroads: Current issues in interactional psychology* (pp. 333–352). Hillsdale, NJ: Erlbaum.

Monin, B., & Jordan, A. H. (2009). The dynamic moral self: A social psychological perspective. In D. Narvaez & D. K. Lapsley (Eds.), *Personality, identity, and character* (pp. 341–354). Cambridge, UK: Cambridge University Press.

Monin, B., Pizarro, D. A., & Beer, J. S. (2007). Deciding versus reacting: Conceptions of moral judgment and the reason–affect debate. *Review of General Psychology, 11*(2), 99–111.

Moore, C., Detert, J. R., Treviño, L. K., Baker, V. L., & Mayer, D. M. (2012). Why employees do bad things: Moral disengagement and unethical organizational behavior. *Personnel Psychology, 65*(1), 1–48.

Moore, D. A., Tetlock, P. E., Tanlu, L., & Bazerman, M. H. (2006). Conflicts of interest and the case of auditor independence: Moral seduction and strategic issue cycling. *Academy of Management Review, 31*(1), 10–29.

Nathanson, C., Paulhus, D. L., & Williams, K. M. (2006). Personality and misconduct correlates of body modification and other cultural deviance markers. *Journal of Research in Personality, 40*(5), 779–802.

O'Boyle, E. H., Jr., Forsyth, D. R., & Banks, G. C. (2012). A meta-analysis of the dark triad and work behavior: A social exchange perspective. *Journal of Applied Psychology, 97*(3), 557–579.

O'Fallon, M. J., & Butterfield, K. D. (2005). A review of the empirical ethical decision-making literature: 1996–2003. *Journal of Business Ethics, 59*(4), 375–413.

Piff, P. K., Stancato, D. M., Côté, S., Mendoza-Denton, R., & Keltner, D. (2012). Higher social class predicts increased unethical behavior. *Proceedings of the National Academy of Sciences of the USA, 109*(11), 4086–4091.

Pitesa, M., & Thau, S. (2013). Compliant sinners, obstinate saints: How power and self-focus determine the effectiveness of social influences in ethical decision making. *Academy of Management Journal, 56*(3), 635–658.

Rest, J. (1986). *Moral development: Advances in research and theory.* New York: Praeger.

Schweitzer, M. E., & Croson, R. (1999). Curtailing deception: The impact of direct questions on lies and omissions. *International Journal of Conflict Management, 10*(3), 225–248.

Schweitzer, M. E., Ordóñez, L., & Douma, B. (2004). Goal setting as a motivator of unethical behavior. *Academy of Management Journal, 47*(3), 422–432.

Shao, R., Aquino, K., & Freeman, D. (2008). Beyond moral reasoning: A review of moral identity research and its implications for business ethics. *Business Ethics Quarterly, 18*(4), 513–540.

Sheldon, O. J., & Fishbach, A. (2015). Anticipating and resisting the temptation to behave unethically. *Personality and Social Psychology Bulletin, 41*(7), 962–975.

Shu, L. L., Gino, F., & Bazerman, M. H. (2011). Dishonest deed, clear conscience: When cheating leads to moral disengagement and motivated forgetting. *Personality and Social Psychology Bulletin, 37*(3), 330–349.

Tangney, J. P. (1991). Moral affect: The good, the bad, and the ugly. *Journal of Personality and Social Psychology, 61*(4), 598–607.

Tangney, J. P., Baumeister, R. F., & Boone, A. L. (2004). High self-control predicts good adjustment, less pathology, better grades, and interpersonal success. *Journal of Personality, 72*(2), 271–324.

Tenbrunsel, A. E. (1998). Misrepresentation and expectations of misrepresentation in an ethical dilemma: The role of incentives and temptation. *Academy of Management Journal, 41*(3), 330–339.

Tett, R. P., & Guterman, H. A. (2000). Situation trait relevance, trait expression, and cross-situational consistency: Testing a principle of trait activation. *Journal of Research in Personality, 34*(4), 397–423.

Treviño, L. K. (1986). Ethical decision making in organizations: A person–situation interactionist model. *Academy of Management Review, 11*(3), 601–617.

Treviño, L. K., Weaver, G. R., & Reynolds, S. J. (2006). Behavioral ethics in organizations: A review. *Journal of Management, 32*(6), 951–990.

Treviño, L. K., & Youngblood, S. A. (1990). Bad apples in bad barrels: A causal analysis of ethical decision-making behavior. *Journal of Applied Psychology, 75*(4), 378–385.

Victor, B., & Cullen, J. B. (1988). The organizational bases of ethical work climates. *Administrative Science Quarterly, 33*(1), 101–125.

Wakeman, S. W., & Moore, C. (2015). *A counterfeit competence: After threat, cheating boosts one's self-image.* Working paper.

Zimbardo, P. (2007). *The Lucifer effect: Understanding how good people turn evil.* New York: Random House.

CHAPTER 49

Unconflicted Virtue

Kate C. S. Schmidt

Is moral behavior conflicted or unconflicted for a virtuous agent?

Moral behavior can be understood according to the psychological models of other skilled behavior; although results are mixed, expert behavior often lacks conflict.

A virtuous agent might be best understood as one who is able to act correctly despite competing inclinations. Imagine a firefighter who is about to run into a burning building. He recognizes that the flames represent a risk to his life and may feel fear at the prospect of entering the building. Nevertheless, by focusing on the importance of saving lives, he overcomes that fear and pushes forward into the fire. This account of the agent suggests that moral behavior is conflicted and is in part characterized by overcoming a sort of internal motivational conflict. Regardless of the effort needed to complete the action, there is an internal process of adjudicating between tempting options. The virtuous firefighter runs into the building, overcoming the competing inclination toward self-preservation.

An alternative understanding of virtue characterizes the firefighter as less conflicted. Perhaps after much practice he no longer hesitates at the doorway to a building. He focuses completely on his goals, undisturbed by the risks surrounding his actions. In this scenario, the agent acts without any conflict, fluidly doing as virtue requires.

Although both scenarios describe a firefighter who acts morally, the first seems intuitively to be more admirable. Courage is often understood as the ability to overcome fear, and in the second description it is tempting to say the firefighter is just not as brave. It seems as though it is a nervous fireman, not an oblivious one, who deserves the most praise for entering the building. This is consistent with intuitions that virtue involves overcoming conflict, rather than acting in an unconflicted way.

Consider a different example of virtuous behavior. While out having drinks, a woman is offered the opportunity to cheat on her partner. She's tempted, but because of her good character is able to overcome the temptation and remains loyal. If virtue is conflicted, then when she acts correctly she does so because her sense of loyalty is strong enough to overcome the inclination to cheat. On the other hand, if virtue is unconflicted, she maintains fidelity without even the temptation to act contrary to virtue. The opportunity doesn't strike her as a temptation, and she rejects it without internal struggle. In this case, it intuitively seems like the unconflicted agent is the one who possesses virtue. Loyalty seems to entail more than successfully resisting temptation.

Conflicted Virtue

The position that virtue involves overcoming conflict can be understood through Philippa Foot's notion of virtue as "corrective" (Foot, 2002). On her account, virtues exist to correct natural human frailties: "They are corrective, each one standing at a point at which there is some temptation to be resisted or deficiency of motivation to be made good" (Foot, 2002, p. 8). The chance to act morally emerges out of these human liabilities. Virtues are good precisely because of their corrective nature; if humans had different temptations, then virtues would be different. Foot says: "One may say that it is only because fear and the desire for pleasure often operate as temptations that courage and temperance exist as virtues at all" (p. 9).

This model is aligned with the idea that a virtuous agent acts well by overcoming frailties in his or her character. Conflict emerges between the requirements of virtue and the common temptation to act wrongly. Foot argues: "The temperate man who must on occasion refuse pleasures need not *desire* them any less than the intemperate man" (2002, p. 8). Virtuous agents feel temptations toward vice just as keenly as those who act immorally, but because of their virtue they can overcome their own desires.

This account of conflicted action is consistent with some central intuitions about virtue. In the case of our firefighter, it seems surprising to suggest that the firefighter must feel no fear. It is natural for an agent to recognize the danger to his or her own life, and it is courageous to take action despite this danger. The urge to avoid suffering and to worry about one's own welfare is a common human tendency. Despite this aversion to suffering, some agents are able to choose costly actions when they know it is the right thing to do. The intuition might even be that the action demonstrates courage precisely

because it requires overcoming an internal conflict; not everyone would be able to take such an action. True moral behavior comes at a cost, and only the virtuous are able to persevere despite the difficulty.

Virtuous agents are often portrayed as struggling with internal conflict, sometimes mirroring situations of external conflict. Descriptions of bravery during war include the circumstances that individuals must overcome, and agents are praised for their actions based in part on the effort it seems to take. Captain Henry Comey fought in the U.S. Civil War, enlisting with a volunteer regiment. He describes leaving for war after a dramatic send-off, wondering if he would ever see his family again: "I tried hard to assume the role of a brave soldier, but I knew my eyes were wet with tears" (Comey & Comey, 2004, p. 11). It is understandable that such a sacrifice would have been painful regardless of the level of commitment to one's country. It would be counterintuitive to suggest that these sorts of actions are in any way unconflicted for the agent. Yet, these actions also seem intuitively virtuous. In the words of Nelson Mandela, "The brave man is not he who does not feel afraid, but he who conquers that fear" (Mandela, 1994, p. 542).

Moral behavior sometimes involves conflict because it requires choosing between two significant values or giving up something that might otherwise be considered valuable. In situations in which there are multiple moral values, it seems virtuous to feel conflicted about an action. Karen Stohr (2003) argues that an agent who must do something harmful in order to avoid a greater harm ought to feel torn and upset—to feel otherwise would be a failure to register the harmful consequences of her or his actions. An agent who feels unconflicted may be acting without truly thinking or understanding the nature of the scenario. Anne Margaret Baxley (2007) explains, "Virtue can have a cost, and a mark of the wise person is that she recognizes it" (p. 403). A model of virtue as unconflicted fails to recognize the fact that virtuous agents face real risks and real harms (Baxley, 2007). This helps explain the intuition that a virtuous agent must act through overcoming internal conflict.

This model of virtue as conflicted also has historic support from Aristotle. He emphasized that those who are brave are not brave because they are insensitive to the reasons for fear. Aristotle says, "He would be a sort of madman or insensible person if he feared nothing" (Barnes, 1984, pp. 1117a25–1117a26). One who acts bravely can clearly see the reasons for fear but is still able to act. "It is for facing what is painful, then, as has been said, that men are called brave" (Barnes 1984, pp. 1117a32–1117a33). Aristotle suggests that the virtuous agent may feel the cost of virtue even more keenly than others:

> The more he is possessed of excellence in its entirety and the happier he is, the more he will be pained at the thought of death; for life is best worth living for such a man, and he is knowingly losing the greatest goods, and this is painful. But he is none the less brave, and perhaps all the more so, because he chooses noble deeds of war at that cost. (Barnes 1984, 1117b10–1117b15)

The virtuous agent is aware of the conflict created by the high cost of virtue, feels such conflict more intensely because of his virtue, and yet is able to ultimately persevere.

Unconflicted Virtue

On the opposing view, that of unconflicted virtue, a moral agent has the ability to focus solely on the requirements of virtue without experiencing conflicting inclinations. John McDowell (1979) argues that a virtuous agent is able to quickly recognize moral reasons for action and to respond to them without ever being tempted by alternatives. It is not that a virtuous agent must compare or weigh competing courses of action; rather, any reasons to act other than according to virtue are silenced. Virtuous agents are especially sensitive to the requirements of virtue in his or her moral situation:

> The view of a situation which he arrives at by exercising his sensitivity is one in which some aspect of the situation is seen as constituting a reason for acting in some way; this reason is apprehended, not as outweighing or overriding any reasons for acting in other ways which would otherwise be constituted by other aspects of the situation (the present danger,

say), but as silencing them. (McDowell, 1979, p. 335)

Because competing reasons are silenced, the virtuous agent has no temptation to act wrongly and so acts without conflict.

McDowell emphasizes that once an agent sees what virtue requires, it is easy to act. This ease of action is accomplished by staying focused on what is truly important: "The lack of struggle is ensured by keeping the attention firmly fixed on what Aristotle calls 'the noble'; not by a weighing of attractions" (McDowell & McFetridge, 1978, p. 27). This attentional focus and expertise are what allow the agent to act in an unconflicted manner without attending to irrelevant temptations. Moral behavior involves "a renunciation, without struggle, of something which in the abstract one would value highly (physical pleasure, security of life and limb)" (McDowell & McFetridge 1978, p. 27). While these things are valuable in the abstract, when they conflict with virtue the moral agent is no longer tempted by them.

This view is also consistent with intuitions about moral behavior. It is difficult to imagine a moral agent who must overcome contrary inclinations before acting with loyalty, compassion, or honesty. It seems that feeling the temptation to cheat is enough to indicate a lack of loyalty. A truly loyal partner would not need to overcome such internal conflict.

The idea that virtuous behavior happens without conflict is reflected in first-person reports of people who have acted quickly in dangerous situations. Deborah Hughes placed herself in the middle of a mob attack to defend a stranger, suddenly finding an urge to protect someone she didn't even know (Baldas, 2015). Afterward, she described how the fear didn't seem to reach her in the moment: "I don't know. Something happened. I had courage. I just didn't want them to hurt him. . . . Sometimes, I'll sit here and I'll cry. And I'll say, 'Did I actually do that?'" Brady Olson, a high school teacher who disarmed a student gunman in his school, describes a similar fixation on a specific course of action (Piccoli, 2015): "I don't know if it was a rational thought at the time, but I thought, 'I have to get the gun away from him to prevent him from harming students.'"

These stories describe people who acted quickly and effectively when faced with dangerous situations. Olson doesn't describe indecision or temptation toward safely—instead, his focus was on the need to take action. Similarly, Hughes doesn't question her actions until afterward. When an agent has a virtuous disposition, the proper action occurs without resistance. These examples suggest the experience of moral behavior is unconflicted, and agents seem to fully and quickly commit to the moral course of action.

This model of virtue can also draw support from Aristotle. Aristotle draws a distinction between an agent who is continent and one who is fully virtuous. Difficulty doing the right thing indicates mere continence rather than virtue, because the agent is still tempted to do wrong. Discussing the virtue of temperance, Aristotle clarifies:

> Both the continent man and the temperate man are such as to do nothing contrary to reason for the sake of the bodily pleasures, but the former has and the latter has not bad appetites, and the latter is such as not to feel pleasure contrary to reason, while the former is such as to feel pleasure but not to be led by it. (Barnes 1984, pp. 1151b34–1152a3).

Although in both cases the agent acts correctly, it is a sign of virtue that the agent has no contrary temptations. Moral behavior involves a lack of temptation, consistent with the model that virtue is unconflicted.

Virtue as Skilled Expertise

Psychology research can help to adjudicate between these two models of virtue as conflicted or unconflicted for the moral agent. If virtue is conflicted, moral behavior characteristically involves overcoming competing inclinations and resisting temptations. The contrary view, that virtue is unconflicted, suggests that moral behavior comes easily and perhaps fluidly to those who are virtuous.

An unconflicted view of virtue has been defended by Julia Annas (2011), drawing on psychology research to support classical Aristotelian conceptions of virtue. Annas (2011) defends a close comparison between virtues and skills, saying, "Exercising a virtue involves practical reasoning of a kind that can illuminatingly be compared to the kind of reasoning we find in someone exercising a practical skill" (p. 1). Virtues (like skills) require time and practice to master and involve continuously striving for better performance. The psychology literature on skilled behavior can be applied to help understand the nature of a virtuous agent. Annas (2011) argues that virtue becomes easier for the more practiced moral agent. The virtuous agent has obtained a skill and so no longer needs to focus on overcoming any internal conflict.

According to Annas (2011), moral behavior will also feel distinctively conflict-free for the agent because of his or her expertise. Experts can at times become completely consumed in the performance of a task, a state known as "flow" (Csikszentmihalyi & LeFevre, 1989). This complete immersion seems to involve a match between perceptions of the skill required to complete a task and the ability to rise to the challenge; agents describe the experience as one that is enjoyable, valuable, and unselfconscious. This sense of flow has been studied across different fields of skilled expertise, in populations such as dancers and musicians (Hefferon & Ollis, 2006; Wrigley & Emmerson, 2013). There is a moment when everything "just clicks," and there is complete absorption in the task (Hefferon & Ollis, 2006, p. 148). Annas (2011) argues that this sense of flow is also attainable for agents engaged in moral behavior: "The activity is experienced as unhindered, unselfconscious, and effortless" (p. 72). Conflicted virtue is not consistent with this sort of flow experience; internal conflict requires attention to be focused on resolving the disagreement, rather than allowing attention to become completely immersed in the goals of the activity. Annas (2011) says, "The merely continent person does the right thing, and is even guided to doing the right thing by developing virtue, but has other commitments and values that conflict with the exercise of virtue" (p. 75). Fully virtuous individuals will lack these conflicting commitments and values, allowing them to act in an unconflicted way.

The notion of an unconflicted moral agent is consistent with psychology literature on other forms of expertise. The most virtuous agents, like other experts, have cultivated a skill that allows them to perform complex behavior more effectively. Experts may not experience conflict because their skill allows them to interact with the environment in a different way than novices do. For example, when the problem-solving behavior of expert and novice pilots in a simulated situation was studied, experts spent more of their attention (as measured through eye-tracking software) on the details that were essential to the problem at hand (Schriver, Morrow, Wickens, & Talleur, 2008). An agent with expertise in a skill might have better developed mental models, sharper perceptions, and efficient patterns of attention, all of which contribute to an unconflicted task performance. This is consistent with McDowell's (1979) description of the virtuous agent's perceptual skill. Virtue is "an ability to recognize requirements which situations impose on one's behavior. It is a single complex sensitivity of this sort which we are aiming to instill when we aim to inculcate a moral outlook" (p. 333). This perception allows experts to respond to a problem effectively and without experiencing conflict.

Although research suggests that expert behavior may often happen fluently, it need not be considered merely automatic. Even behavior that appears highly automated may rely on elements of cognitive control (Christensen, Sutton, & McIlwain, 2016). Agents acquire skills through a process of practice, which involves monitoring and reflecting on performance. Ericsson (2015) has emphasized the importance of deliberative practice in obtaining expertise. It is important to have access to feedback and to practice in a goal-oriented way in order to acquire superior skills. This practice may involve repeatedly overcoming conflict until an agent reaches a point where the action becomes unconflicted.

However, in some domains, it seems odd to suggest that skilled experts will react in such unconflicted ways. Imagining an expert athlete, it's possible to picture how the behavior may start to come quickly and effortlessly with expertise. On the other hand, expert doctors or police officers might still be expected to experience conflict given the nature of their goals. It seems that treating a medical problem would require considering competing options.[1] It is also more difficult to identify the criteria for skilled performance in some domains than others; it's easier to define expertise in chess than in medicine (Ericsson, 2015). If moral skill is more similar to medical skill, it might seem similarly implausible to suggest that a virtuous agent will regularly act in an unconflicted way. Some types of skilled expertise appear to rely more closely on cognitive monitoring and competing inclinations that would generate conflict for the agent. Even if moral behavior gets easier with practice, it might not seem like a virtuous agent will act in the fluid way that Annas (2011) suggests.

Testing Moral Behavior

Researchers can study moral decision making by putting participants into a position in which they have the opportunity to act in an honest or a dishonest manner. Analyzing the actions of participants can reveal factors that influence moral behavior. One hypothesis is that agents who have more self-control are better able to behave morally and that agents who lose these self-control reserves are more likely to act badly. To test this idea, psychologists gave participants opportunities for deception after having them perform tasks designed to deplete self-control resources (Mead, Baumeister, Gino, Schweitzer, & Ariely, 2009).[2] The results showed that cheating was much more frequent when participants had depleted self-control, and researchers concluded that "self-control resource depletion led to dishonest behavior" (Mead et al., 2009). Similar results have been found by other psychologists (Gino, Schweitzer, Mead, & Ariely, 2011).

This fits closely with a conflicted notion of virtue, and Foot's (2002) notion of virtue as a corrective. Perhaps moral behavior requires some sort of effort, lending plausibility to the idea that moral agents act through overcoming conflict. However, moral behavior might require effort for different reasons, and this might not indicate the presence of conflict. Additionally, these studies are vulnerable to participant expectancy effects. Participants may *expect* that self-control is a resource to be depleted and turn the experiment into a self-fulfilling prophecy (Martijn, Tenbült, Merckelbach, Dreezens, & de Vries, 2002). Other studies have shown that participants who had their expectations challenged improved their behavior, showing less fatigue than other participants and outperforming other groups (Martijn et al., 2002, p. 449). This work calls into question whether previous research does in fact show that there is a sort of motivational depletion that influences moral behavior.[3]

This literature may not directly rule out the possibility of unconflicted virtuous behavior. The studies above primarily focus on individuals behaving badly (cheating) rather than on individuals behaving well. Even if compelling empirical evidence emerges that moral behavior involves effortfully overcoming conflict, it may be because most of the study participants are merely continent and not yet virtuous.

Greene and Paxton (2009) performed an fMRI study rewarding participants for correctly predicting the outcome of a coin flip. This gave them the opportunity to study honest behavior in an fMRI. On some of the trials, participants were required to record their predictions prior to the coin flip, but other trials were not monitored, so participants had an opportunity to cheat (by recording their "prediction" after the coin flip). Participants were told the study was investigating paranormal predictive abilities. Cheating was determined by statistically analyzing the outcomes to determine which results were highly unlikely due to chance. Based upon the participants' responses, some were categorized into the "honest" group. The study was designed to examine the nature of honest behavior. Two hypotheses were tested: Either honest participants were able to behave that way through overcoming conflicting inclinations (called the "Will" hypothesis), or honest participants experienced no conflict and acted easily ("Grace").

According to the "Will" hypothesis, honesty results from the active resistance of tempta-

tion, comparable to the controlled cognitive processes that enable the delay of reward. According to the "Grace" hypothesis, honesty results from the absence of temptation, consistent with research emphasizing the determination of behavior by the presence or absence of automatic processes. (Greene & Paxton, 2009, p. 12506)

The researchers looked at reaction-time differences, as well as comparative fMRI differences, across individuals who either did or did not cheat. The study examined differences in brain activity when participants lost money without the opportunity to cheat, compared with losing money by ignoring an available opportunity to cheat (choosing to be honest). Reaction-time measures were also used to see whether there were significant reaction-time differences when participants had to make a decision about whether or not to cheat.

The results of the study supported the "grace" hypothesis—that, for honest individuals, choosing honesty was an unconflicted decision. Participants who were dishonest showed differences in reaction times when there was an opportunity to avoid loss, taking longer to react when they had the chance to lie. The honest participants did not show this difference in reaction time across conditions, suggesting that, whereas the dishonest participants had to hesitate or consider the option to lie, honest participants acted just as quickly as usual. Importantly, all of the honest participants confirmed after the end of the study that they were aware that there was an opportunity to cheat (Greene & Paxton, 2009). The fMRI data showed no differences in activation within the control network areas of the brain for the honest group between situations with the opportunity to cheat or without the opportunity to cheat. In contrast, dishonest participants did show differences in activation. This reinforces the idea that honest behavior did not require any additional cognitive resources than usual for the honest participants.[4] Further studies have revealed that for dishonest participants (compared with honest ones), there was additional activation in the reward centers of the brain (Abe & Greene, 2014). This also suggests that dishonest participants may experience more temptation than honest participants.

An Expert Moral Agent

The empirical results described above support the notion that moral behavior can occur without conflict for the virtuous agent. Virtue can be understood as a complex skill, psychologically similar to other forms of expertise. Greene and Paxton (2009) show that for honest participants there do not seem to be additional cognitive processes at work when choosing to be honest. This paints a picture of an honest individual for whom moral behavior comes without conflict. This model is consistent with McDowell's (1979) claims that virtue comes without the agent experiencing competing temptations. This model of unconflicted virtue shows that while practice is important for gaining moral expertise, ultimately the behavior is unconflicted and fluid.

A worry remains that unconflicted moral behavior seems implausible in some cases. Perhaps this is because it is so rare: many people will be merely continent, as Aristotle points out. A virtuous agent has become familiar with how to properly attend to the various requirements of a given moral situation, and this is what explains the ease and unconflicted nature of his or her action. When an agent is fully immersed in moral action, competing inclinations are silenced.

Full immersion in an activity still seems more plausible for some moral skills than others. It might seem strange to think of a moral agent acting in a state of flow, especially in particularly complex situations. Intuitions about non-moral skilled expertise can vary according to the nature of the skill: Although a musician might act without conflict, the same might not be said for a doctor. The moral domain might similarly be composed of a variety of skills, only some of which seem unconflicted.

Annas (2011) argues that virtues can all be understood similarly according to the model of fluid skilled expertise. However, skilled expertise often looks different in different domains. This means that it may be important to examine moral virtues separately, clarifying what type of skill is being examined in each case. Specifying the criteria for the successful performance of a skill is necessary for studying expertise (Ericsson, 2015). Green and Paxton (2009) do this when studying honesty: They isolate a specific outcome and then examine behavior relevant to that outcome. Their research focuses on only one subset of moral behavior (honesty), while there may be variation among different types of virtue. Although unconflicted virtue seems the appropriate model for honesty, future inquiry may still locate a role for conflict in other moral skills.

As with nonmoral skills, the overall results seem to be mixed, with some moral behaviors that seem clearly unconflicted and others that might involve overcoming conflict. Both unconflicted and conflicted models of virtue have some intuitive and philosophic support. The existing psychology literature lends support to the model of virtue as an unconflicted skill. Understanding virtue as a skill requires careful thinking about the exact nature of the skill, in order to better understand the nature of virtuous expertise. Current literature focuses primarily on one type of moral expertise, but there might be variations. Future inquiry may be more successful in understanding virtue by separating out specific types of moral behavior, rather than treating virtue as unitary. If virtue is a skill like honesty, then the truly virtuous agent will be unconflicted.

ACKNOWLEDGMENT

Thanks to John Doris for his assistance with this chapter.

NOTES

1. Ericsson (2015) has pointed out the importance of cognitive monitoring in the medical field.
2. Participants were instructed to score themselves and pay themselves (using quarters in an envelope in front of them) based upon the number of successes in the task. Participants in the study completed a puzzle task, and half of them were given an opportunity to cheat on the task by scoring their own performance without the experimenter. Half of the participants were exposed to a self-control depletion task prior to being given the opportunity to cheat.
3. The authors argue that "the occurrence of the ego depletion phenomenon is strongly influenced by expectancies or schemata about self-control" (Martijn et al., 2002, p. 441).

4. The authors conclude that the honest participants "showed no sign of engaging additional control processes (or other processes) when choosing to forgo opportunities for dishonest gain" (Greene & Paxton, 2009, p. 12508).

REFERENCES

Abe, N., & Greene, J. D. (2014). Response to anticipated reward in the nucleus accumbens predicts behavior in an independent test of honesty. *Journal of Neuroscience, 34*(32), 10564–10572.

Annas, J. (2011). *Intelligent virtue*. Oxford, UK: Oxford University Press.

Baldas, T. (2015, February 26). Acts of courage: The ordinary doing the extraordinary. *USA Today*. Available at *www.usatoday. com/story/news/nation/2015/02/26/acts-of-courage-the-ordinary-doing-the-extraordinary/24029119*.

Barnes, J. (Ed.). (1984). *The complete works of Aristotle: Nichomachean ethics*. Princeton, NJ: Princeton University Press.

Baxley, A. (2007). The price of virtue. *Pacific Philosophical Quarterly, 88*(4), 403–423.

Christensen, W., Sutton, J., & McIlwain, D. J. F. (2016). Cognition in skilled action: Meshed control and the varieties of skill experience. *Mind and Language, 31*(1), 37–66.

Comey, H. N., & Comey, L. R. (2004). *A legacy of valor: The memoirs and letters of Captain Henry Newton Comey, 2nd Massachusetts Infantry*. Knoxville: University of Tennessee Press.

Csikszentmihalyi, M., & LeFevre, J. (1989). Optimal experience in work and leisure. *Journal of Personality and Social Psychology, 56*(5), 815–822.

Ericsson, K. A. (2015). Acquisition and maintenance of medical expertise: A perspective from the expert-performance approach with deliberate practice. *Academic Medicine, 90*(11), 1471–1486.

Foot, P. (2002). Virtues and vices. In *Virtues and vices and other essays in moral philosophy* (pp. 1–18). New York: Oxford University Press.

Gino, F., Schweitzer, M. E., Mead, N. L., &

Ariely, D. (2011). Unable to resist temptation: How self-control depletion promotes unethical behavior. *Organizational Behavior and Human Decision Processes, 115*(2), 191–203.

Greene, J. D., & Paxton, J. M. (2009). Patterns of neural activity associated with honest and dishonest moral decisions. *Proceedings of the National Academy of Sciences of the USA, 106*(30), 12506–12511.

Hefferon, K. M., & Ollis, S. (2006). "Just clicks": An interpretive phenomenological analysis of professional dancers' experience of flow. *Research in Dance Education, 7*(2), 141–159.

Mandela, N. (1994). *Long walk to freedom: The autobiography of Nelson Mandela*. Boston: Little, Brown and Company.

Martijn, C., Tenbült, P., Merckelbach, H., Dreezens, E., & de Vries, N. K. (2002). Getting a grip on ourselves: Challenging expectancies about loss of energy after self-control. *Social Cognition, 20*(6), 441–460.

McDowell, J. (1979). Virtue and reason. *The Monist, 62*(3), 331–350.

McDowell, J., & McFetridge, I. G. (1978). Are moral requirements hypothetical imperatives? (Suppl. Vol.). *Proceedings of the Aristotelian Society, 52*, 13–42. Available at *www.jstor. org/stable/4106788*.

Mead, N. L., Baumeister, R. F., Gino, F., Schweitzer, M. E., & Ariely, D. (2009). Too tired to tell the truth: Self-control resource depletion and dishonesty. *Journal of Experimental Social Psychology, 45*(3), 594–597.

Piccoli, S. (2015). Teacher who disarmed student gunman: I'm no hero. Available at *www.newsmax.com/Newsmax-Tv/high-school-teacher-washington-disarmed/2015/05/11/id/643939*.

Schriver, A. T., Morrow, D. G., Wickens, C. D., & Talleur, D. A. (2008). Expertise differences in attentional strategies related to pilot decision making. *Human Factors: Journal of the Human Factors and Ergonomics Society, 50*(6), 864–878.

Stohr, K. E. (2003). Moral cacophony: When continence is a virtue. *Journal of Ethics, 7*(4), 339–363.

Wrigley, W. J., & Emmerson, S. B. (2013). The experience of the flow state in live music performance. *Psychology of Music, 41*(3), 292–305.

CHAPTER 50

Moral Clarity

Scott S. Wiltermuth
David T. Newman

How do people come to possess different levels of moral clarity, which denotes the degree of ambiguity people perceive when judging whether behaviors are right or wrong?

We argue that the experience of moral clarity depends on both cognitive processing and affective appraisals of certainty; additionally, we describe how moral clarity has innate origins but can be heightened or repressed by the influence of parents, teachers, peers, and culture.

Some people are baffled that others seem to see behavior in such clear terms of right and wrong, good and bad, and black and white. They struggle to understand how those others miss so much nuance that they do not recognize that it is not always clear whether behaviors are morally right or morally wrong. Those who do see clear distinctions between right and wrong are equally baffled by the inability of those who see shades of gray everywhere to diagnose right from wrong, good from bad, and black from white.

These differences in *moral clarity*—the degree of ambiguity people perceive when judging whether behaviors are right or wrong (Wiltermuth & Flynn, 2013)—may be socially determined. In this chapter, we explore how people develop a sense of moral clarity and why individuals differ in how much ambiguity they perceive in moral judgments. We first examine whether a sense of moral clarity is more likely to develop from intuitive or deliberative forms of processing. We then examine which cognitive processes are likely to give rise to a heightened sense of moral clarity. We investigate specifically whether the processes are general in that they also give rise to certainty in nonmoral judgments or whether they are specific to moral judgments. We also examine how the consequences of moral clarity differ from the consequences of certainty on nonmoral issues. Next, we address whether people have a fixed, innate sense of moral clarity or whether moral clarity is a learned attitude that is, at times, cultivated and, at other times, suppressed through education. Finally, we discuss whether cultural values, such as individualism–collectivism and power distance, influence the degree to which people see ambiguity in the judgment of moral behaviors.

Intuitive versus Deliberative

Moral Clarity May Be Greater with Intuition than with Deliberation

Intuition, contrasted with reasoning, is a kind of cognition that occurs quickly, effortlessly, and automatically, such that the outcome but not the process is accessible to consciousness (Haidt, 2001). Haidt's model of intuitive ethics proposes that moral intuitions are activated immediately in response to morally relevant facts, with effortful, deliberative moral reasoning occurring only after a judgment has already been made. Empirical studies have tended to confirm the view that affective intuition plays a larger role than deliberate reasoning in the process of moral judgment (Greene & Haidt, 2002). People often claim to know with certainty that an action is morally wrong even when they cannot marshal reasoning to support their intuition (Haidt, 2007). Hence we might expect that judgments driven by intuition evince greater moral clarity than those reached through careful deliberation.

Research on the amount of time allowed to make decisions supports this expectation. Inhibiting deliberation through manipulations of time alters moral judgments in response to dilemmas involving the killing of one person to save many (Suter & Hertwig, 2011). Time pressure yields fast deontological gut reactions (e.g., killing is wrong), whereas time availability enables consequentialist deliberations (e.g., the lives of many outweigh the life of one) to override the initial response. Furthermore, direct manipulations of deliberative decision making have been shown to increase deception and decrease altruism (Zhong, 2011), suggesting that deliberation obscures our intuitive understanding of moral behavior by permitting rationalization of unethical conduct.

These findings comport with work on the effect of the perceived time taken to generate an evaluation on attitude certainty (Tormala, Clarkson, & Henderson, 2011). Quick evaluations tend to promote certainty when people express opinions or evaluate familiar objects, whereas slow evaluations generally promote certainty when people form new opinions or evaluate unfamiliar objects. Morality is familiar to most adults, or even organized by evolutionary mechanisms in advance of individual experience (Haidt, 2007); it is reasonable to suppose that moral judgment is more like expressing than forming an opinion. Thus moral judgment is most likely to demonstrate clarity when proceeding directly from intuition.

Tetlock's (2003) work on taboo trade-offs indicates that we expect people to distinguish right from wrong quickly and easily, and excessive deliberation on the relative worth of sacred values (e.g., justice) may signal a lack of moral clarity and thereby cast doubt on an individual's moral character. Some exchanges (e.g., money for human dignity) are considered unthinkable, and people respond to the contemplation of such trade-offs with moral outrage, cleansing, and value reaffirmation (Tetlock, Kristel, Elson, Green, & Lerner, 2000). Moral clarity displayed via intuitive judgment may, therefore, serve as a yardstick by which to measure ethical uprightness in ourselves and others.

Information Processing and Clarity

In contrast to the foregoing, research on information processing has at times implied that cognitive elaboration, or the thoughtfulness with which one considers information relevant to an evaluation, enhances attitude certainty (Smith, Fabrigar, MacDougall, & Wiesenthal, 2008). However, recent evidence suggests that this effect is driven primarily by people's perceptions of their own elaboration and naïve theories that elaboration produces better judgments (Barden & Tormala, 2014). Because of the fluency with which people can generate post hoc reasoning to justify their intuitive judgments (Haidt, 2001), a quick, clear, intuitive moral judgment may often give rise to an impression of thoughtful processing.

Attitude accessibility is associated with greater attitude strength (Holland, Verplanken, & Van Knippenberg, 2003), entailing that intuitive judgments come stamped with the imprimatur of certainty by virtue of their ease of retrieval. Over a lifetime of experience and repetition, moral intuition is elevated to moral conviction. Clarity in moral judgment is also enhanced by the certainty appraisals imbued in morally relevant emotions, such as anger, disgust, happiness, and contentment (Tiedens & Linton, 2001). These emotions occur with a sense of certainty and promote heuristic (intuitive) processing, whereas emotions such as hope, surprise, worry, and sadness occur with a sense of uncertainty and promote systematic (deliberative) processing. If intuitive processes heighten perceptions of moral clarity, we would therefore expect people to perceive themselves to have greater moral clarity when experiencing emotions associated with certainty.

We may also expect cognitive depletion to result in greater moral clarity. Information processing is often inhibited by ego depletion, leading people to rely heavily on automatic processes such as intuition when they are ego-depleted (Baumeister, Muraven, & Tice, 2000). Research on consumer responses to advertising has found that attitudes formed under conditions of depletion exhibit greater certainty and influence on purchase behavior (Wan, Rucker, Tormala, & Clarkson, 2010). Feeling depleted may increase certainty through the perception that substantial information processing has taken place. Consequently, we may expect that ego-depleted individuals will form moral judgments based on intuition and with a high degree of clarity.

Epiphanies and Inspiration

Epiphanies and prophetic experiences, insofar as they impel individuals to adopt a particular course of conduct deemed virtuous or obligatory, may represent extreme versions of moral clarity. Those who experience divine communication frequently report it as thoughts or feelings simply appearing in their minds, accompanied by a sense of absolute clarity and authority (Dein & Cook, 2015). Epiphanic experiences are usually accompanied by awe, an emotion characterized primarily by a sense of vastness and a need for accommodation (Keltner & Haidt, 2003). It seems likely that the emotion of awe includes a certainty appraisal, which may drive the intense clarity associated with inspiration.

One, Two, or Many Processes
Degrees of Clarity across Moral Domains

Individuals are predisposed to different trait levels of clarity in the moral domain (Wiltermuth & Flynn, 2013). However, the moral domain is not a monolith; moral foundations theory proposes the existence of plural moral domains whose values are sometimes in conflict (Graham et al., 2013). Morality is an adaptive characteristic of our species, born out of several clusters of innate intuitions naturally selected over countless generations of human development. In a similar vein, moral clarity may be an adaptation for successfully converting our moral intuitions into concordant behavior. We may therefore expect that, just as endorsement of each moral foundation (e.g., care, fairness, loyalty, authority, sanctity) varies from person to person, so, too, does the clarity with which individuals form judgments in each domain. People who strongly endorse a particular moral foundation may experience greater certainty within that domain than would people for whom the same foundation is of lesser concern.

This view is substantiated by work showing the effect of moral foundations framing on political attitudes. Feinberg and Willer (2013) found that most environmental discourse centers on concerns of harm and care, with liberals but not conservatives viewing the environment in moral terms. Reframing environmental rhetoric in terms of purity reduces the gap between liberals and conservatives, suggesting a change in conservatives' moral judgments even on an issue for which they may have previously perceived little ambiguity. Framing issues using moral foundations may shift political attitudes through either entrenchment or persuasion (Day, Fiske, Downing, & Trail, 2014). Relevant moral foundation frames entrench political attitudes for both liberals and conservatives, presumably by enhancing the moral clarity with which the issues are judged. Persuasion, on the other hand, has been found only for conservative-relevant moral frames of liberal issues. This is not to say that other instances of persuasion are impossible—clearly they occur all the time—but some framings may be more persuasive than others for specific types of people. Graham, Haidt, and Nosek (2009) observed that conservatives endorse all five foundations about equally, whereas liberals assign preeminence to care and fairness. Conservatives may accordingly experience moral clarity in more varied contexts than do liberals.

Manichaeism and Dogmatism

Manichaeism, originally a religion founded by the Iranian prophet Mani, now refers to any dualistic worldview that pits good against evil or us against them. Manichaean thinking may be an expression of high trait-level moral clarity, which leads people to experience the moral universe in black and white. Alternatively, individuals who are taught Manichaean thinking as dogma may resultantly develop greater clarity in judging relevant moral issues. Although powerful convictions about right and wrong may sometimes encourage prosocial behaviors, they also underlie acts of ideologically driven violence and terrorism (Skitka & Mullen, 2002).

Extreme views on both ends of the liberal–conservative spectrum are associated with dogmatic beliefs about the correctness of one's position (Toner, Leary, Asher, & Jongman-Sereno, 2013), yielding political intolerance that cuts both left and right (Crawford & Pilanski, 2014). Political partisans are likely to support discrimination against those who violate their moral values (Wetherell, Brandt, & Reyna, 2013), and conversation across the aisle may make the situation worse, not better: In developing their Manichaeism scale, Johnson, Motyl, and Graham (2015) found that individuals who discussed abortion or gun control with someone who held an opposing stance showed increases in Manichaeism compared with those who talked with someone who agreed with them. Like visual acuity, moral clarity may be facilitated by the presence of contrast.

Persuasion

There is increasing acknowledgment that the primary function of human reasoning may be not epistemic but argumentative (Mercier & Sperber, 2011). Motivated reasoning is particularly evident in the selective application of general moral principles to rationalize preferred moral conclusions (Uhlmann, Pizarro, Tannenbaum, & Ditto, 2009). Rather than acting as intuitive scientists seeking the truth, people behave like intuitive politicians, theologians, and prosecutors who advocate, protect, and enforce the values to which they are already committed (Tetlock, 2002). This implies that moral clarity may be greatest when individuals are in a persuasive or combative mode.

This view is supported by evidence that attitude certainty increases when individuals resist attempts at persuasion (Tormala & Petty, 2002). Conversely, increasing attitude certainty tends to amplify the dominant effects of attitude on judgment, such that univalent attitudes become more resistant to persuasion and ambivalent attitudes less resistant (Clarkson, Tormala, & Rucker, 2008). Thus certainty enables people to see clearly whether their judgments support one or multiple perspectives in a persuasive context. Because explanatory reasoning has a way of reinforcing existing positions, morally oriented conversation promotes honest behavior by clarifying ethical values (Gunia, Wang, Huang, Wang, & Murnighan, 2012).

Time and Distance

If folk wisdom is to be believed, people perceive events more clearly with the benefit of time and distance. This view of clarity is supported by evidence from construal level theory demonstrating that people judge immoral actions more harshly, and moral actions more approvingly, when the actions are psychologically distant (Eyal, Liberman, & Trope, 2008). Distal objects and behaviors are construed more abstractly, such that individuals' evaluations are less susceptible to contextual influence and more reflective of ideological commitments (Ledgerwood, Trope, & Chaiken, 2010). Hence we form moral judgments most clearly when considering events far in the past or future or when judging people across the divide of continents or social class. Moreover, we apply the moral clarity of distance to our own self-concept, strongly rejecting the representativeness of distant-future behaviors that violate our acknowledged values (Wakslak, Nussbaum, Liberman, & Trope, 2008).

General or Specific Processes

The preceding discussion illustrates that numerous processes influence the sense of clarity people have when making moral judgments. Numerous factors also increase the sense of certainty that people feel when making decisions outside of the domain of morality. This raises the question of whether the process of developing moral clarity differs from the process of developing nonmoral forms of clarity or certainty, such as overconfidence in forecasting. It also raises the question of whether the downstream consequences of moral clarity differ from the consequences generated by other forms of clarity.

Antecedents

Little research has examined the antecedents of moral clarity. Wiltermuth and Flynn (2012), however, found that people who possess power also develop a heightened sense of moral clarity and consequently punish others more severely for perceived transgressions than do people who lack power. Moreover, Lammers and Stapel (2009) found that power increases people's reliance on deontological or formalist forms of moral reasoning over teleological or utilitarian approaches. To the extent that relying on one principle of action increases moral clarity relative to relying on a calculation of situationally dependent costs and benefits, power may increase moral clarity by changing people's approaches to ethical decision making.

The effects of power on nonmoral attitudes parallel the effects of power on moral clarity. Power similarly makes people overconfident of their knowledge of factual matters (Fast, Sivanathan, Mayer, & Galinsky, 2012) and leads people to engage in confirmatory information processing (Fischer, Fischer, Englich, Aydin, & Frey, 2011), which could cause them to be more certain in all their attitudes, moral and nonmoral alike. Factors that strengthen people's attitude certainty, such as perceived consensus, the number of times they have voiced that attitude, and the ease with which they can defend the attitude (for review, see Tormala & Rucker, 2007) are also likely to affect the clarity with which people make moral judgments.

Given that the same factors seem to contribute to clarity in moral and nonmoral beliefs, one might legitimately ask whether it is possible to be highly certain in moral domains and less certain in other domains. The proposition is entirely untested, but we can imagine people who are not especially confident in their own bases of knowledge, or in their tastes, possessing a strong sense of right and wrong if they see that sense of right and wrong as something that was handed down to them by God or by their parents. Such people would have a high level of moral clarity but relatively little clarity in other judgments.

Consequences

Moral clarity may produce different consequences than does certainty or clarity on nonmoral issues. Evidence for this comes from a study by Skitka, Bauman, and Sargis (2005) on moral convictions and the attitudes (i.e., moral mandates) that stem from those convictions. Skitka and colleagues (2005) found that convictions on moral issues, on which people would possess high levels of moral clarity, led people to feel greater antipathy toward individuals who held dissimilar views on those issues than did similar differences in attitudes that were not based on moral issues. To the extent that disagreements based on moral convictions are more deleterious toward cooperativeness and tolerance of others than are disagreements based on nonmoral attitudes, it becomes especially important to understand why people come to develop such strong moral attitudes and see moral issues with such (justified or unjustified) clarity.

Innate, Learned, or Both?

A growing body of research suggests that people have an innate sense of right and wrong. Some of the strongest evidence for this claim comes, perhaps oddly, from nonhumans. Capuchin monkeys will reject rewards for tasks when their rewards seem inequitable in comparison with the rewards received by other capuchins (Brosnan & de

Waal, 2003). Thus species sharing a common ancestry with humans further share a sense of fairness. Human babies as young as 15 months can also detect unfairness when it occurs, as evidenced by the longer gaze they give to experimenters when those experimenters administer unequal portions of food to people than when those experimenters administer equal portions (Schmidt & Sommerville, 2011). Infants as young as 6 months show preferences for prosocial individuals over antisocial individuals (Hamlin, Wynn, & Boom, 2007). Moreover, cross-cultural research has demonstrated that some moral precepts, such as "do not harm others," are common across cultures.

The strong evidence that people possess innate moral compasses suggests that some level of moral clarity is probably innate. However, it does not necessarily suggest that moral clarity is entirely innate. A large literature has shown that parents heavily influence the values held by their children (e.g., Lapsley & Power, 2005). By placing high importance on some values and less importance on others, parents likely also influence the degree of ambiguity children see in various situations regarding those values. They may do so through their direct conversations with their children and through their choices about the environments (e.g., schools, religious institutions) in which their children spend their time. Peers no doubt have effects as well on which values individuals come to hold with a great sense of clarity. Moral clarity on specific issues may therefore have a learned component.

It is similarly possible that parents, teachers, and others could influence moral clarity in individuals across a range of domains and issues by instilling a questioning attitude, such that they train children to question the stances that people take on issues and see the nuances in ethically charged situations. By the same token, parents may encourage moral clarity by encouraging steadfast adherence to some principles.

Once an individual develops a sense of clarity about an issue, that person may become highly unlikely to change his or her opinion about the issue, because, consistent with the confirmation bias (for a review, see Nickerson, 1998), they may selectively attend to information that supports their view. Additionally, they may be motivated to construe any information about an issue as supportive of their initial position. If these processes occur, moral clarity may be self-reinforcing.

Such processes are particularly likely to occur if people feel that their self-views or core beliefs are threatened (Munro & Ditto, 2007; Munro & Stansbury, 2009). In such instances, people dig in their heels and seek to discredit any information that undermines the views they hold dear (Greenwald, 1980). As such, moral clarity may be particularly self-reinforcing when people's values collide and those who already perceive little ambiguity in the moral matters at hand feel that their views are under threat.

Cultural Influences

The culture surrounding an individual may influence how much of a sense of moral clarity that individual possesses. One way that culture may influence how much ambiguity people perceive is through norms about which behaviors are morally appropriate, which behaviors are morally tolerable, and which behaviors are grounds for moral censure. For example, in some cultures there may be a strong norm against nepotism, whereas in other cultures the practice may be seen as a natural and acceptable extension of loyalty to one's ingroup. In cultures in which there is strong social consensus that a behavior is either immoral or moral, people may possess a high sense of moral clarity on the issue (Jones, 1991). When the prevailing societal view is less clear, people may possess less clarity.

Culture may also influence behavior more systematically. Hofstede (1979, 1983) established four dimensions on which cultures can vary: individualism/collectivism, power distance, masculinity/femininity, and uncertainty avoidance. Uncertainty avoidance is the dimension most relevant to moral clarity and is defined as "the extent to which individuals within a culture are made nervous by situations that are unstructured, unclear, or unpredictable, and the extent to which these individuals attempt to avoid such situations by adopting strict codes of behavior and a belief in absolute truth" (Vitell, Nwachukwu, & Barnes, 1993, p. 754). People may possess heightened levels of moral clarity in countries such as Germany and Japan, which are characterized by high levels of uncertainty avoidance, relative to people in Singapore and the United Kingdom, which are characterized by low levels of uncertainty avoidance.

The philosophies or religions foundational to a culture may also influence the strength of moral clarity an individual from that culture will possess. In Chinese culture, the religions of Taoism and (to a lesser extent) Confucianism feature the yin and the yang, suggesting that two opposite forces (such as light and dark) are present and necessary for each to exist. These two opposite forces are seen as working not against each other but rather with each other to achieve a perfect balance (e.g., Garrett, 1993). In the graphical representation of yin and yang, there is a drop of yin in the yang and a drop of yang in the yin. Viewed through this lens, actions may be seen as not purely moral or purely immoral but rather some mix of these. We might, therefore, expect people to exhibit lower levels of moral clarity in cultures in which Taoist and related philosophies are followed. Indeed, scholars have suggested that following such philosophies encourages people to adopt multiple perspectives when analyzing behavior (Johnson, 2000).

Adopting multiple perspectives when analyzing behavior may correlate with people taking a relativistic rather than an absolutistic approach to ethics. People who take a relativistic view would argue that society defines what is moral and immoral and, as societies differ, so too might the meanings of moral and immoral, right and wrong, differ across cultures (Forsyth & Berger, 1982). One could legitimately ask whether it is possible to have a strong sense of moral clarity when using relativistic forms of moral judgment. We would posit that one could have a sense of moral clarity using relativistic judgments, but that the moral clarity of such judgments would likely stem from one's confidence in the prevailing views of society. Moral clarity using absolute (i.e., invariant) standards of moral judgment is easier to understand, as it would correspond to how sure an individual is that a behavior violates an absolute principle.

Future research could and should determine whether moral clarity differs depending upon the level of uncertainty avoidance in a culture and the degree to which people in that culture espouse dualistic philosophies. We hope that it also further examines what moral clarity looks like when people strongly adhere to using relativistic or culturally specific standards of behavior. Some people worry that certainty of any kind has become the casualty of a postmodern age in which all beliefs and judgments are considered socially constructed and situationally dependent, but it is equally possible that such firmly relativistic contentions evince their own form of moral clarity.

Conclusion

Throughout our lives we expect and are expected to know right from wrong. Ordinary citizens, prominent figures, and even entire governments are routinely criticized for showing an absence of moral clarity. On the other hand, some people may find overconfidence about moral issues to be narrow-minded or oppressive. Hence moral clarity occupies a unique position in our social environment compared with certainty about factual knowledge or personal preferences. Moral clarity acts as both a motive for individual conduct and a signal in interpersonal relations. Paradoxically, clarity enables us to direct our will yet simultaneously constrains our decisions. Without any clarity whatsoever, we would be helpless to choose between all available options, but extreme clarity can restrict the many possibilities for action to a single unequivocal path. Moral clarity may be seen in this light as a valve controlling the flow of judgment and behavior. Investigating the forces that turn this mechanism, and the downstream consequences that follow, will open a new channel to understanding the dynamics of morality.

REFERENCES

Barden, J., & Tormala, Z. L. (2014). Elaboration and attitude strength: The new meta-cognitive perspective. *Social and Personality Psychology Compass, 8*(1), 17–29.

Baumeister, R. F., Muraven, M., & Tice, D. M.

(2000). Ego depletion: A resource model of volition, self-regulation, and controlled processing. *Social Cognition, 18*(2), 130–150.

Brosnan, S., & de Waal, F. B. M. (2003). Monkeys reject unequal pay. *Nature, 425,* 297–299.

Clarkson, J. J., Tormala, Z. L., & Rucker, D. D. (2008). A new look at the consequences of attitude certainty: The amplification hypothesis. *Journal of Personality and Social Psychology, 95*(4), 810–825.

Crawford, J. T. & Pilanski, J. M. (2014). Political intolerance, Right and Left. *Political Psychology, 35*(6), 841–851.

Day, M. V., Fiske, S. T., Downing, E. L., & Trail, T. E. (2014). Shifting liberal and conservative attitudes using moral foundations theory. *Personality and Social Psychology Bulletin, 40*(12), 1559–1573.

Dein, S., & Cook, C. C. H. (2015). God put a thought into my mind: The charismatic Christian experience of receiving communications from God. *Mental Health, Religion and Culture, 18*(2), 97–113.

Eyal, T., Liberman, N., & Trope, Y. (2008). Judging near and distant virtue and vice. *Journal of Experimental Social Psychology, 44*(4), 1204–1209.

Fast, N. J., Sivanathan, N., Mayer, N. D., & Galinsky, A. D. (2012). Power and overconfident decision-making. *Organizational Behavior and Human Decision Processes, 117*(2), 249–260.

Feinberg, M., & Willer, R. (2013). The moral roots of environmental attitudes. *Psychological Science, 24*(1), 56–62.

Fischer, J., Fischer, P., Englich, B., Aydin, N., & Frey, D. (2011). Empower my decisions: The effects of power gestures on confirmatory information processing. *Journal of Experimental Social Psychology, 47*(6), 1146–1154.

Forsyth, D. R., & Berger, R. E. (1982). The effects of ethical ideology on moral behavior. *Journal of Social Psychology, 117*(1), 53–56.

Garrett, M. (1993). Pathos reconsidered from the perspective of classical Chinese rhetorical theories. *Quarterly Journal of Speech, 79,* 19–39.

Graham, J., Haidt, J., Koleva, S., Motyl, M., Iyer, R., Wojcik, S., & Ditto, P. H. (2013). Moral foundations theory: The pragmatic validity of moral pluralism. *Advances in Experimental Social Psychology, 47,* 55–130.

Graham, J., Haidt, J., & Nosek, B. A. (2009). Liberals and conservatives rely on different sets of moral foundations. *Journal of Personality and Social Psychology, 96*(5), 1029–1046.

Greene, J., & Haidt, J. (2002). How (and where) does moral judgment work? *Trends in Cognitive Sciences, 6*(12), 517–523.

Greenwald, G. (1980). The totalitarian ego: Fabrication and revision of personal histories. *American Psychologist, 35,* 603–618.

Gunia, B. C., Wang, L., Huang, L., Wang, J., & Murnighan, J. K. (2012). Contemplation and conversation: Subtle influences on moral decision making. *Academy of Management Journal, 55*(1), 13–33.

Haidt, J. (2001). The emotional dog and its rational tail: A social intuitionist approach to moral judgment. *Psychological Review, 108*(4), 814–834.

Haidt, J. (2007). The new synthesis in moral psychology. *Science, 316*(5827), 998–1002.

Hamlin J. K., Wynn, K., & Bloom P. (2007). Social evaluation by preverbal infants. *Nature, 450,* 557–559.

Hofstede, G. (1979). Value systems in forty countries: Interpretation, validation, and consequences for theory. In L. H. Eckensberger, W. J. Lonner, & Y. H. Poortinga (Eds.), *Cross-cultural contributions to psychology* (pp. 398–407). Lisse, The Netherlands: Swets & Zeitlinger.

Hofstede, G. (1983). Dimensions of national culture in fifty countries and three regions. In J. B. Deregowski, S. Dziurawiec, & R. C. Annios (Eds.), *Expiscations in cross-cultural psychology* (pp. 335–355). Lisse, The Netherlands: Swets & Zeitlinger.

Holland, R. W., Verplanken, B., & Van Knippenberg, A. (2003). From repetition to conviction: Attitude accessibility as a determinant of attitude certainty. *Journal of Experimental Social Psychology, 39*(6), 594–601.

Johnson, C. (2000). Taoist leadership ethics. *Journal of Leadership and Organizational Studies, 7*(1), 82–91.

Johnson, K., Motyl, M., & Graham, J. (2015). *Measuring Manichaeism: Moral intuitions and political extremism.* Unpublished manuscript.

Jones, T. M. (1991). Ethical decision making by individuals in organizations: An issue-contingent model. *Academy of Management Review, 16*(2), 366–395.

Keltner, D., & Haidt, J. (2003). Approaching awe, a moral, spiritual, and aesthetic emotion. *Cognition and Emotion, 17*(2), 297–314.

Lammers, J., & Stapel, D. A. (2009). How power influences moral thinking. *Journal of Personality and Social Psychology, 97,* 279–289.

Lapsley, D. K., & Power, F. C. (Eds.). (2005). *Character psychology and character education* (pp. 140–165). Notre Dame, IN: University of Notre Dame Press.

Ledgerwood, A., Trope, Y., & Chaiken, S. (2010). Flexibility now, consistency later: Psychological distance and construal shape evaluative responding. *Journal of Personality and Social Psychology, 99*(1), 32–51.

Mercier, H., & Sperber, D. (2011). Why do humans reason?: Arguments for an argumentative theory. *Behavioral and Brain Sciences, 34*(2), 57–111.

Munro, G. D., & Ditto, P. H. (1997). Biased assimilation, attitude polarization, and affect in reactions to stereotyped-relevant scientific information. *Personality and Social Psychology Bulletin, 23*, 636–653.

Munro, G. D., & Stansbury, J. A. (2009). The dark side of self-affirmation: Confirmation bias and illusory correlation in response to threatening information. *Personality and Social Psychology Bulletin, 35*, 1143–1153.

Nickerson, R. S. (1998). Confirmation bias: A ubiquitous phenomenon in many guises. *Review of General Psychology, 2*(2), 175.

Schmidt, M. F. H. & Sommerville, J. A. (2011). Fairness expectations and altruistic sharing in 15-month-old human infants. *PLOS ONE, 6*(10), e23223.

Skitka, L. J., Bauman, C. W., & Sargis, E. G. (2005). Moral conviction: Another contributor to attitude strength or something more? *Journal of Personality and Social Psychology, 88*(6), 895–917.

Skitka, L. J., & Mullen, E. (2002). The dark side of moral conviction. *Analyses of Social Issues and Public Policy, 2*(1), 35–41.

Smith, S. M., Fabrigar, L. R., MacDougall, B. L., & Wiesenthal, N. L. (2008). The role of amount, cognitive elaboration, and structural consistency of attitude-relevant knowledge in the formation of attitude certainty. *European Journal of Social Psychology, 38*(2), 280–295.

Suter, R. S., & Hertwig, R. (2011). Time and moral judgment. *Cognition, 119*(3), 454–458.

Tetlock, P. E. (2002). Social functionalist frameworks for judgment and choice: Intuitive politicians, theologians, and prosecutors. *Psychological Review, 109*(3), 451–471.

Tetlock, P. E. (2003). Thinking the unthinkable: Sacred values and taboo cognitions. *Trends in Cognitive Sciences, 7*(7), 320–324.

Tetlock, P. E., Kristel, O. V., Elson, S. B., Green, M. C., & Lerner, J. S. (2000). The psychology of the unthinkable: Taboo trade-offs, forbidden base rates, and heretical counterfactuals. *Journal of Personality and Social Psychology, 78*(5), 853–870.

Tiedens, L. Z., & Linton, S. (2001). Judgment under emotional certainty and uncertainty: The effects of specific emotions on information processing. *Journal of Personality and Social Psychology, 81*(6), 973–988.

Toner, K., Leary, M. R., Asher, M. W., & Jongman-Sereno, K. P. (2013). Feeling superior is a bipartisan issue: Extremity (not direction) of political views predicts perceived belief superiority. *Psychological Science, 24*(12), 2454–2462.

Tormala, Z. L., Clarkson, J. J., & Henderson, M. D. (2011). Does fast or slow evaluation foster greater certainty? *Personality and Social Psychology Bulletin, 37*(3), 422–434.

Tormala, Z. L., & Petty, R. E. (2002). What doesn't kill me makes me stronger: The effects of resisting persuasion on attitude certainty. *Journal of Personality and Social Psychology, 83*(6), 1298–1313.

Tormala, Z. L., & Rucker, D. D. (2007). Attitude certainty: A review of past findings and emerging perspectives. *Social and Personality Psychology Compass, 1*(1), 469–492.

Uhlmann, E. L., Pizarro, D. A., Tannenbaum, D., & Ditto, P. H. (2009). The motivated use of moral principles. *Judgment and Decision Making, 4*(6), 476–491.

Vitell, S. J., Nwachukwu, S. L., & Barnes, J. H. (1993). The effects of culture on ethical decision-making: An application of Hofstede's typology. *Journal of Business Ethics, 12*(10), 753–760.

Wakslak, C. J., Nussbaum, S., Liberman, N., & Trope, Y. (2008). Representations of the self in the near and distant future. *Journal of Personality and Social Psychology, 95*(4), 757–773.

Wan, E. W., Rucker, D. D., Tormala, Z. L., & Clarkson, J. J. (2010). The effect of regulatory depletion on attitude certainty. *Journal of Marketing Research, 47*(3), 531–541.

Wetherell, G. A., Brandt, M. J., & Reyna, C. (2013). Discrimination across the ideological divide: The role of value violations and abstract values in discrimination by liberals and conservatives. *Social Psychological and Personality Science, 4*(6), 658–667.

Wiltermuth, S. S., & Flynn, F. J. (2013). Power, moral clarity, and punishment in the workplace. *Academy of Management Journal, 56*(4), 1002–1023.

Zhong, C. (2011). The ethical dangers of deliberative decision making. *Administrative Science Quarterly, 56*(1), 1–25.

PART XI
STUDYING MORALITY

QUESTIONS ANSWERED IN PART XI

CHAPTER 51 How is moral sensitivity constructed
and what are its precursors in early development?

CHAPTER 52 What is the best method for understanding moral judgment?

CHAPTER 53 How can we investigate moral values in the real world?

CHAPTER 54 Is moral psychology overly focused on theory?

CHAPTER 51

Why Developmental Neuroscience Is Critical for the Study of Morality

Jean Decety
Jason M. Cowell

How is moral sensitivity constructed and what are its precursors in early development?

Developmental neuroscience is critical for clarifying what computational systems mediate morality, and promising evidence suggests that early social evaluations are relatively basic in nature, rooted in domain-general approach–withdrawal tendencies and the allocation of attention to relevant stimuli.

Morality is a fundamental aspect of all human societies and regulates large facets of social interactions. It is centrally concerned with how individuals *ought* to interact and get along with others and has been an enduring topic of interest to psychologists and philosophers (Smetana, 2013). Work across various academic disciplines has converged on the view that morality arises from the integration of both innate general abilities shaped by natural selection and deliberative processes that interact with the social environment and cultural exposure (Decety & Howard, 2013; Hamlin, 2015; Killen & Smetana, 2013). Moral cognition can therefore be seen as a genetic–cultural coevolutionary product, representing an important adaptive element for social cohesion and cooperation in group living. All normally developing individuals across cultures have the basic notion that some things are right and others are wrong. Certain behaviors are viewed as good, right, and deserving of praise and reward. Other behaviors are viewed as bad, wrong, and worthy of blame and punishment (Hamlin, 2014). Human social existence is characterized by an intuitive sense of fairness, concern for others, and enactment of cultural norms (Tomasello, 2009) to an extent that is unseen in other species. Early signs of moral sensitivity are considered as the foundation for adult morality, emanating from the sophisticated integration of emotional, motivational, and cognitive mechanisms across development (Wynn, 2007).

Although most theoretical perspectives concur that morality is multifaceted and includes affective, cognitive, and motivational components, different approaches have varied as to which of these components are prioritized and how they come into play during ontogeny. In order to more accurately understand the foundations and development of a mature moral self, an increased focus on a neurobiological perspective is informative. Establishing neurological methods within a developmental framework provides a more complete account of the computations underlying moral cognition, bridging the gap between behaviors and their underlying cognitive mechanisms. Thus neuroscience research is critical to clarify what computational systems mediate early social evaluations, moral judgment, and behaviors. For example, examining neural activation and functional connectivity (Decety, Michalska, & Kinzler, 2012), as well as the spatiotemporal dynamics of the neural processing when young children view social interactions and morally laden situations (Cowell & Decety, 2015a, 2015b), helps to better characterize the contributions of affect, cognition, and deliberation to early morality. Although there is clear, accumulating evidence for an "innate" ability for third-party sociomoral evaluation, particularly when perceiving helping and hindering agents, as young as 8 months of age (e.g., Hamlin, 2015; Schmidt & Sommerville, 2011), the social, cognitive, and affective processes and their interaction behind these early evaluations are only beginning to be identified, and there is still an intense debate on the ontogenetic origins of human morality.

Theoretical Debates

Most theorists agree that the issue of harm is one of the foundations or the core foundation of morality, particularly that any intentional harm (given specific social context) is immoral (Gray, Young, & Waytz, 2012). Some argue that empathy-related responding, including caring and sympathetic concern, motivates prosocial behavior, inhibits aggression, and paves the way to moral conduct (Zahn-Waxler & Radke-Yarrow, 1990). A rudimentary component of empathy, affective sharing/arousal, can be observed very early in development (Decety

& Svetlova, 2012). This capacity to resonate with the general positive and negative emotional states of others has great adaptive value in serving as a bond between individuals, facilitating cooperation and caregiving for offspring and kin.

Although empathetic abilities are often associated with morality, research in social psychology and social neuroscience suggests that empathic concern does not necessarily produce moral behavior. In fact, empathy may lead one to act in a way that violates the moral principles of justice and fairness, when, for instance, allocating resources preferentially to the person for whom empathy was felt (Batson, Klein, Highberger, & Shaw, 1995; Decety & Cowell, 2015a, 2015b). On the other hand, a lack of empathic concern for the well-being of others is considered a risk factor for amoral behavior and is the hallmark of individuals with psychopathy (Hawes & Dadds, 2012; Sobhani & Bechara, 2011). This illustrates the complex nature of the relationships between empathy and morality. Basic emotional processes such as empathic arousal may be necessary to develop some aspects of moral reasoning, such as care-base morality. Overall, empathy provides the impulse to care for a conspecific but is powerless in the face of rationalization and denial. Indeed, empathy is relatively more predictive of prosocial behavior when the victim is an individual. However, empathy alone is insufficient for producing a mature moral cognition (Decety & Cowell, 2015a). Indeed, cognitive and reasoning abilities play a crucial role in guiding moral decision making and in the integration of social context into deliberations. This conception fundamentally alters "gut" reactions to the perception of intentional harm, allowing more flexible and nuanced moral evaluations and more effective translation to adaptive behavior.

Current Knowledge of the Moral Brain

Our understanding of the brain mechanisms involved in moral cognition is primarily based on converging results from lesion studies (Gleichgerrcht, Torralva, Roca, Pose, & Manes, 2011; Taber-Thomas, 2014), clinical neuroscience with forensic psychopaths (Aharoni, Sinnott-Armstrong, & Kiehl, 2012), and functional neuroimaging studies conducted with adult participants (Moll et al., 2002; Moll et al., 2007). These studies point to specific regions underlying moral sensitivity, judgment, and decision making. These regions include the posterior superior temporal sulcus, also known at the temporo-parietal junction (pSTS/TPJ), the amygdala, ventral striatum, insula, ventromedial prefrontal cortex (vmPFC), medial prefrontal cortex (mPFC) and dorsolateral prefrontal cortex (DLPFC). Importantly, none of these regions can be singled out as a uniquely moral center, and all of them are implicated in other mental functions, such as mental states representations, emotional saliency, empathic concern, and decision making (Decety & Cowell, 2014; Young & Dungan, 2012). Moral cognition thus involves many parallel affective and cognitive processes necessary to analyze the intentions behind the surface of behavior, emotional circuitry responsible for social emotions, and moral decisions. Specifically, moral cognition is the process of integrating reasoning and judgment based on one's understanding of social norms, with the attribution of intentions, beliefs, and emotions to oneself and other people. In addition, regions of the brain such as the vmPFC, amygdala and the pSTS/TPJ have been implicated in aversive social learning, interpretation of social cues such as intention, and assigning social and emotional value to environmental stimuli to guide decisions. Thus most of neuroscience research supports the claim that morality relies on multiple domain-general processes, which are distributed in circuits involved in the social brain (Figure 51.1). It is thus not clear whether there are computations that are specific to morality, at least in the adult moral brain.

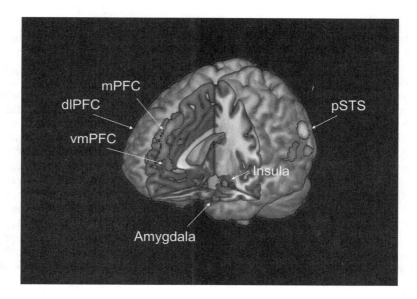

FIGURE 51.1. Neuroscience demonstrates that the brain regions underpinning moral reasoning share computational resources with circuits controlling other capacities, such as emotional saliency, mental state understanding, valuation of rewards from various modalities, and decision making and involve the posterior superior temporal sulcus (pSTS) near the temporoparietal junction, the amygdala, the insula, the ventromedial prefrontal cortex (vmPFC), the dorsolateral prefrontal cortex (dlPFC), and the medial prefrontal cortex (mPFC). These systems are not domain-specific. Rather, they support more domain-general processing. Importantly, both empathic concern and moral decision making require involvement of the vmPFC, which bridges conceptual and affective processes necessary to guide moral behavior and decision making. Early damage to this region leads to severe impairment of both moral behavior and empathic concern.

Due to the methodological constraints of most neuroimaging methods, only a few studies have examined children's moral development. Such studies, in conjunction with neurological observations of brain-damaged patients—which are obviously unexpected and unfortunate natural experiments—offer empirical and theoretical clarity on the biological basis of and brain–behavior processes involved in morality. Developmental neuroscience provides a unique opportunity to see how the components of morality interact in ways that are not possible in adults—in whom all the components are fully mature and operational. Integrating this neurodevelopmental perspective with behavioral work shed light into the neurobiological and cognitive mechanisms underpinning the basic building blocks of morality and their age-related functional changes. Such an integration also contributes to our understanding of the neural processes that underpin prosocial behavior.

Developmental Neuroscience of Empathy and Morality

Developmental neuroscience can inform two large debates in our understanding of morality. Specifically, functional neuroimaging allows the charting out of neural networks involved in affective and cognitive processes when perceiving other people in distress, as well as the developmental changes in the respective contribution of each. Electrophysiological methods, given their precise temporal resolution, afford the disentangling of relatively automatic versus controlled mechanisms underlying empathy and morality.

When perceiving another individual in pain or distress, numerous functional neuroimaging (fMRI) studies have documented the recruitment of a network involved in the processing of physical pain and aversion. This neural network is composed of the anterior insula, supplementary motor area, anterior midcingulate cortex (aMCC), somatosensory cortex, and the periaqueductal gray area. Reliable activation in this network has been shown when participants imagine the pain of others, view facial expressions of pain or the injuring of body parts, or even observe a signal denoting that a conspecific

will receive a shock (Lamm, Decety, & Singer, 2011). It is worth noting that these vicariously instigated activations are not specific to the sensory qualities of pain. Rather, they reflect more general survival mechanisms such as aversion and withdrawal when exposed to danger and threat (Decety, 2010). Activity of this cortical network, in adult participants, thus indexes a system involved in detecting, processing, and reacting to the occurrence of salient sensory events regardless of the sensory channel through which these events are conveyed.

To examine developmental changes in the network involved in the perception of pain, one fMRI study included participants from 7 to 40 years of age, who were presented with video clips depicting individuals being accidentally or intentionally injured (Decety & Michalska, 2010). The subjective evaluations of the scenarios, collected after scanning, showed an age-related decrease in ratings of pain intensity for both painful conditions (accidental vs. intentional), with younger participants rating the scenarios as significantly more painful than older participants. The younger the participants, the more strongly the amygdala, posterior insula, and vmPFC were recruited when they watched others in painful situations. A significant negative correlation between age and degree of neurohemodynamic response was found in the posterior insula. In contrast, a positive correlation was found in the anterior portion of the insula. A posterior-to-anterior progression of increasingly complex re-representations in the human insula is thought of as providing a foundation for the sequential integration of the individual homeostatic condition with one's sensory environment and motivational condition (Craig, 2003). The posterior insula receives inputs from the ventromedial nucleus of the thalamus, an area that is highly specialized to convey emotional and homeostatic information and serves as a primary sensory cortex for both of these distinct interoceptive feelings from the body. The fact that, in response to others' physical distress, younger participants recruited the posterior portion of the insula in conjunction with the amygdala and vmPFC more than adults did indicates that children were more aroused by the perception of others' distress. This, in turn, may lead to a heightened experience of discomfort associated with a visceral response to a potential threat, whereas adult participants tend to use more abstract secondary representations of pain when perceiving others in distress. The early engagement of the amygdala, periaqueductal gray (PAG), insula, and vmPFC during the perception of others' distress is consistent with the timing of their structural maturation. These reciprocally interconnected regions, which underlie rapid and prioritized processing of emotion signals and are involved in affective arousal and somatovisceral resonance, come online much earlier in ontogeny than other neural structures. In contrast, the dorsal and lateral vmPFC undergo considerable maturation during the childhood years and become progressively specialized for the evaluation of social stimuli (Paus, 2011). These regions of the prefrontal cortex are crucial for empathic concern and mentalizing, both of which are necessary for mature moral reasoning. Indeed, one study examined the impact of early-onset (before 5 years) versus late-onset lesions to the vmPFC on moral judgment (Taber-Thomas et al., 2014). Patients with developmental-onset lesions endorsed significantly more self-serving judgments that broke moral rules or inflicted harm on others, suggesting that the vmPFC is a critical neural substrate for the acquisition and maturation of moral competency that goes beyond self-interest to consider the welfare of others. Disruption to this affective neural system early in life interrupts moral development.

A decisive aspect in third-party moral judgment relies heavily on the detection of intentionality. It is the critical cue in determining whether an action was malicious or not (Malle & Guglielmo, 2012). How information about intentionality is used for judging the wrongness of an action may be age-dependent (Zelazo, Helwig, & Lau, 1996) and, in turn, will influence recommendations of deserved punishment. These determinations of punishment require a complex integration between the analysis of mental states (desires, beliefs, intentions) of the perpetrator and the consequences of his or her actions. A neurodevelopmental study of participants ages 4–37 years combined sociomoral appraisals, eye tracking, and fMRI measures elicited by scenarios depicting intentional or accidental harm to people. After scanning, participants were presented with the same scenarios that they saw in the scanner and were asked to judge whether the action performed by the perpetrator in the video clip was intentional or not. Participants were also asked to respond to a set of questions probing moral judgment (wrongness and punishment), empathic concern for the victim, personal distress, and understanding of the perpetrator's mental state. In all participants, perceived intentional harm to people (as opposed to accidental harm) was associated with increased activation in brain regions sensitive to the perception, prediction, and interpretation of others' mental states, such as the right pSTS/TPJ (Pelphrey & Carter, 2008), as well as regions processing the affective consequences of these actions, namely the temporal poles, insula, vmPFC, and amygdala. The more participants reported being personally distressed about harmful actions, the higher the activity in the amygdala.

Age was negatively related to empathic sadness for the victim of harm in the video clips, with the youngest participants exhibiting the greatest personal sadness, and the degree of sadness was predictive of the response in the insula, thalamus, and subgenual prefrontal cortex. This latter region has extensive connections with circuits implicated in emotional behavior and autonomic/neuroendocrine response to stressors, including the amygdala, lateral hypothalamus, and brain stem serotonergic, noradrenergic, and dopaminergic nuclei (Drevets et al., 1997). Damage to the subgenual prefrontal cortex is associated with abnormal autonomic responses to emotional experiences and impaired comprehension of the adverse consequences of pernicious social behaviors (Bechara, Tranel, Damasio, & Damasio, 1996). The response in the amygdala followed a curvilinear function, such that the hemodynamic signal was highest at the youngest ages, decreased rapidly through childhood and early adolescence, and reached an asymptote in late adolescence through adulthood. This developmental change in amygdala recruitment, coupled with its relation to ratings of empathic distress, supports the role of this region in the normal development of empathic understanding (Decety & Michalska, 2010). Conversely, the neurohemodynamic signal in older participants increased in the mPFC and vmPFC, regions that are associated with metacognitive representations, valuation, and social decision making.

Patterns of functional connectivity during the perception of intentional, relative to accidental, harm showed complementary evidence for an increased developmental integration of the prefrontal cortex and amygdala. The older participants showed significant coactivation in these regions during the perception of intentional harm relative to accidental harm, whereas the youngest children only exhibited a significant covariation between the vmPFC and PAG in the brain stem. Furthermore, adult participants showed the strongest connectivity between vmPFC and pSTS/TPJ while viewing morally laden actions suggestive of developmental changes in functional integration within the mentalizing system.

Neurodevelopmental variations during the perception of morally laden scenarios are clearly seen in neural regions that are implicated in emotional saliency (amygdala and insula), with a gradual decrease in activation with age. Conversely, activity in regions of the medial and vmPFC that are reciprocally connected with the amygdala and that are involved in decision making and evaluation increased with age and became functionally coupled. This pattern of developmental change was also reflected in the moral evaluations, which require the capacity to integrate a representation of the mental states and intentions of others, together with the consequences of their actions (Leslie, Knobe, & Cohen, 2006). Although third-party judgments of wrongness did not change across age—all participants rated intentional harm as more wrong than accidental harm—when asked about the malevolence of the agent, subjective evaluations indicated a more differentiated appraisal with age. Whereas young children considered all agents malicious, irrespective of intention and targets (i.e., people and objects), older participants perceived the perpetrator as clearly less mean when carrying out an accidental action, and even more so when the target was an object. As age increased, participants also less severely punished an agent

who damaged an object than an agent who harmed a person. Though even young children attend to both intentionality and target in guiding their own empathic responses and judgments of wrongness, an increased discrimination of intentionality and target in determining moral culpability with age is consistent with the developmental shift in moral judgment dominated by an early focus on outcomes and the later integration of both intent and consequences.

Finally, another fMRI study with participants ages 13–53 examined the neural response to International Affective Picture System (IAPS) pictures that did or did not depict moral violations (Harenski, Harenski, Shane, & Kiehl, 2012). Making decisions about the severity of pictures was associated with increased amygdala, pSTS/TPJ, and posterior cingulate cortex activity in adolescents and adults. Moreover, the magnitude of activity in the pSTS increased across development. These findings suggest that across development, individuals progressively integrate knowledge of the mental states of others, especially intentionality, into moral evaluations.

Taken together, findings from these neurodevelopmental investigations document the importance of and changes in several interconnected networks implicated in processing the distress of others, intentionality of the agents, consequences for the victims, and cognitive decision making.

Although fMRI yields important insights into the mechanisms that guide moral cognition, two limitations hinder its utility. The hemodynamic signal has a poor temporal resolution (around 5 seconds) and thus cannot inform arguments about the timing and automaticity of the processes investigated. Furthermore, from a practical sense, the fMRI environment is not well suited to infants and young children. Electroencephalography (EEG) and event-related potentials (ERPs), on the other hand, do not have such limitations. The temporal resolution is excellent (at the millisecond level), and these methods are frequently used in toddlers and young children.

To examine the neurodevelopment of empathy, one study used EEGs and ERPs in children ages 3–9 years who were shown stimuli depicting physical injuries to people.

Results demonstrated both an early automatic component (N200), which reflects attention to salient stimuli, and a late-positive potential (LPP), indexing cognitive reappraisal or more complex processing of emotional stimuli. The LPP showed an age-related differentiation between painful and neutral scenes (Cheng et al., 2014). Another study used high-density EEG to examine the spatiotemporal neurodynamic responses when viewing people in physical distress under two subjective contexts: one evoking affect sharing, the other, empathic concern (Decety, Lewis, & Cowell, 2015). Results indicate that early automatic (175–275 milliseconds) and later controlled responses (LPP 400–1000 milliseconds) were differentially modulated by engagement in affect sharing or empathic concern. Importantly, the late ERP component was significantly affected by dispositional empathy, but the early component was not.

There is accumulative evidence that preverbal infants have the ability to morally evaluate the actions of others (Hamlin, 2015). To examine the neural underpinnings of moral sensitivity in infants and toddlers ages 12–24 months, Cowell and Decety (2015a) employed a series of interwoven measures combining multiple levels of analysis, including resting state and time-locked electrophysiology, eye-tracking, behavioral, and socioenvironmental measures. Continuous EEG and time-locked ERPs and gaze fixation were recorded while children watched characters engaging in prosocial and antisocial actions. All children demonstrated a neural differentiation in both spectral EEG power density modulations and time-locked ERPs when perceiving prosocial compared with antisocial agents. Time-locked neural differences also predicted children's preferential reaching for prosocial over antisocial characters. This neural and behavioral differentiation of prosocial and antisocial others is relatively basic in nature, rooted in approach–withdrawal tendencies and rudimentary resource allocation to relevant stimuli. Interestingly, the values of parents regarding justice and their own cognitive empathic dispositions significantly influenced toddlers' neural processing of the morally laden scenarios and their propensity to share, respectively. Such an early social influence is likely based on a dynamic bidirectional interaction between biology and socioenvironmental context, rather than simply the product of one or the other.

Another neurodevelopmental study (Cowell & Decety, 2015b) assessed the implicit moral evaluations of antisocial (harming) and prosocial (helping) behaviors in young children (3–5 years) and further investigated whether early automatic (early posterior negativity [EPN]) or later cognitive controlled (LPP) processes were predictive of children's own generosity. Significant differences were found in early automatic as well as later controlled temporal periods when children viewed the morally laden scenarios. Importantly, only controlled processes predicted actual prosocial behavior (i.e., the number of stickers given to another anonymous child). This study demonstrates how young children exhibit automatic responses to morally laden stimuli and reappraise these stimuli in a controlled manner. Thus children's moral judgments are the result of an integration of both early and automatic processing of helping and harming scenarios and later cognitively controlled reappraisal of these scenes. Importantly, the latter and not the former predicts actual sharing behavior.

In other research on moral reasoning, consistently early and late differences in the spatiotemporal processing of dilemmas have been identified. For instance, larger N2 amplitudes for moral versus conventional violations were found in children ages 9–10 years (Lahat, Helwig, & Zelazo, 2013). In another study, P300 differences in response to moral judgment were observed, and individual differences in this ERP component predicted dispositional attitudes toward prosociality (Chiu Loke, Evans, & Lee, 2011). Moreover, in a study with emerging adult participants, high-density ERPs, combined with source localization analyses, revealed that differences due to the perception of intentional harm compared with accidental harm were first detected in the right pSTS/TPJ, as fast as 62 milliseconds poststimulus, and later responses were found in the amygdala (122 milliseconds) and vmPFC (182 milliseconds; Decety & Cacioppo, 2012).

Overall, EEGs and ERPs provide a valuable method for characterizing the roles of automatic and controlled processes involved in moral judgment and social decision making. Importantly, EEGs and ERPs allow for neurodevelopmental investigations, documenting the relative importance of both of these processes across development, the modulations in each, and their respective contributions to moral behavior in infancy, childhood, adolescence, and emerging adulthood.

The Lack of Affect Sharing Hinders Moral Behavior

To further clarify the importance of emotion and affect sharing in moral cognition and behavior, individuals who lack empathy provide a natural experiment. Individuals who are indifferent to the fear, distress, and sadness of others are those who are difficult to socialize (Blair, 1995). A paradigmatic case is psychopathy, a neurodevelopmental personality disorder believed to affect approximately 1% of the general population and 20–30% of the male and female prison population. Relative to nonpsychopathic criminals, psychopaths are responsible for a disproportionate amount of repetitive crime and violence in society (Kiehl, 2014). These individuals often possess specific traits that point to stunted emotional development, a general lack of attachment to others, and difficulties experiencing empathic concern and remorse (Maibom, 2009). Individuals with psychopathy are often callous, shallow, and superficial. They lack fear of punishment, have difficulty regulating their emotions, and do not experience insight into the consequences of their harmful actions for others (Hare & Neumann, 2008).

Structural neuroimaging studies associate psychopathy with a host of morphological brain abnormalities, including reduced volumes of the amygdala; reduced gray matter volumes in the frontal and temporal cortex, especially in the right pSTS/TPJ; and increased volume of the striatum (Koenigs, Baskin-Sommers, Zeier, & Newman, 2011). Furthermore, psychopaths often exhibit signs of reduced structural integrity of the uncinate fasciculus—a connecting pathway of the limbic system in the temporal lobe (such as the hippocampus and amyg-

dala) with the vmPFC (Motzkin, Newman, Kiehl, & Koenigs, 2011). They also exhibit an atypical pattern of brain activation and effective connectivity seeded in the anterior insula and amygdala with the vmPFC when perceiving interpersonal harm and signals of distress (Decety, Chen, Harenski, & Kiehl, 2013).

Children with psychopathic tendencies and callous-unemotional traits show consistent deficits in affective sharing and empathic concern across childhood and adolescence. These abnormal responses to the distress of others may be evident as early as childhood. For example, children with psychopathic tendencies exhibit reduced electrodermal responses to distress cues (e.g., a crying face) and threatening stimuli (e.g., a pointed gun) relative to controls (Blair, 1995). Another study using EEG examined this phenomenon by assessing how callous-unemotional traits in juvenile psychopaths were related to deficits in affective sharing (Cheng, Hung, & Decety, 2012). Results demonstrated that youth with high callous-unemotional traits exhibit atypical neural dynamics in response to stimuli depicting other individuals in physical distress. This abnormality was exemplified by a lack of the early EPR response (120 milliseconds), thought to reflect an automatic aversive reaction to negative stimuli, and was coupled with relative insensitivity to actual pain (as measured with the pressure pain threshold). Nevertheless, their capacity to understand the agent's intentionality was not impaired. In support of this finding, fMRI studies have also reported that children and adolescents with disruptive psychopathic traits show reduced activity to the pain of others within the neural structures (anterior cingulate cortex, insula, and amygdala) typically implicated in affective responses to others' pain and distress (Marsh et al., 2013; Lockwood et al., 2013). This uncoupling between affective sharing and cognitive understanding likely contributes to psychopaths' callous disregard for the rights and feelings of others. Finally, similar to adult psychopaths (Wolf et al., 2015), children with conduct problems and psychopathic tendencies exhibit white-matter microstructural abnormalities in the anatomical tract that connects the amygdala and vmPFC (Passamonti et al., 2012). Abnormal connectivity in the amygdala–orbital frontal cortex/vmPFC limbic network contributes to the neurobiological mechanisms underpinning the antisocial behavior, lack of empathic concern, and emotional detachment associated with psychopathy.

Directions for Developmental Moral Neuroscience

Overall, developmental neuroscience investigations inform the fundamental nature of moral cognition, including its underpinnings in relatively general processes, providing plausible mechanisms of early change, and a foundation for forward movement in the field. Some basic elements that are critical to building morality are in place very early in childhood, comprising both automatic and controlled processing, as well as affective and cognitive representations. Neuroscience methods in the study of morality and prosocial behavior across age allow us to advocate for the best practices in capturing the modulation of affective, cognitive, and social processes, by dispositional characteristics, and individual differences, that are possibly unique to human nature. This new information sheds important light on the theoretical understanding and appropriate methods for exploring the ontogeny of social cognition, empathy, and moral reasoning. This demonstrates the potential of developmental social neuroscience to provide productive, new, and exciting directions for the study of moral development when stemming from an integration of neurobiology, behavior, and social environment (Killen & Smetana, 2008). Yet many challenges exist in implementing neuroscience methods with dilemmas and scenarios that are ecologically valid and developmentally sensitive. In particular, it is difficult to operationalize such paradigms in a neuroscience laboratory environment, where an excessive repetition of trials is necessary in both fMRI and EEG to obtain sufficient signal-to-noise ratio. By nature, such experimental manipulations cannot be similar to ecologically valid situations that one may encounter when having to judge a particular decision or action.

Further developmental neuroscience research should specifically examine the role of social and contextual information in influencing the neural networks involved in moral judgment and subsequent behaviors. Preliminary developmental investigations of the neural underpinnings of moral cognition have largely focused on the simplest forms of morality, such as the perception of distress cues and evaluations of interpersonal harm. However, with age, due to increases in the cognitive capacities to balance, coordinate, and integrate multiple elements of a situation, contextual information plays a fundamental role in moral reasoning. For instance, while at all ages children negatively evaluate prototypical harm, behavioral studies suggest that judgments of necessary harm become increasingly more forgiving with age as justifications pertaining to the actor's harm decrease (Jambon & Smetana, 2014). Such contextual aspects are certainly a fascinating topic worthy of being empirically studied.

REFERENCES

Aharoni, E., Sinnott-Armstrong, W., & Kiehl, K. A. (2012). Can psychopathic offenders discern moral wrongs?: A new look at the moral/conventional distinction. *Journal of Abnormal Psychology, 121,* 484–497.

Batson, C. D., Klein, T. R., Highberger, L., & Shaw, L. L. (1995). Immorality from empathy-induced altruism: When compassion and justice conflict. *Journal of Personality and Social Psychology, 68,* 1042–1054.

Bechara, A., Tranel, D., Damasio, H., & Damasio, A. R. (1996). Failure to respond autonomically to anticipated future outcomes following damage to the prefrontal cortex. *Cerebral Cortex, 6,* 215–225.

Blair, R. J. R. (1995). A cognitive developmental approach to morality: Investigating the psychopath. *Cognition, 57,* 1–29.

Cheng, Y., Chen, C., & Decety, J. (2014). An EEG/ERP investigation of the development of empathy during early childhood. *Developmental Cognitive Neuroscience, 10,* 160–169.

Cheng, Y., Hung, A., & Decety, J. (2012). Dissociation between affective sharing and emotion understanding in juvenile psychopaths. *Development and Psychopathology, 24,* 623–636.

Chiu Loke, I., Evans, A. D., & Lee, K. (2011). The neural correlates of reasoning about prosocial-helping decisions: An event-related brain potentials study. *Brain Research, 1369,* 140–148.

Cowell, J. M., & Decety, J. (2015a). Precursors to morality in development as a complex interplay between neural, socio-environmental, and behavioral facets. *Proceedings of the National Academy of Sciences of the USA, 112*(41), 12657–12662.

Cowell, J. M., & Decety, J. (2015b). The neuroscience of implicit moral evaluation and its relation to generosity in early childhood. *Current Biology, 25,* 1–5.

Craig, A. D. (2003). Interoception: The sense of the physiological condition of the body. *Current Opinion in Neurobiology, 13,* 500–505.

Decety, J. (2010). To what extent is the experience of empathy mediated by shared neural circuits? *Emotion Review, 2,* 204–207.

Decety, J., & Cacioppo, S. (2012). The speed of morality: A high-density electrical neuroimaging study. *Journal of Neurophysiology, 108*(11), 3068–3072.

Decety, J., Chen, C., Harenski, C. L., & Kiehl, K. A. (2013). An fMRI study of affective perspective taking in individuals with psychopathy: Imagining another in pain does not evoke empathy. *Frontiers in Human Neuroscience, 7,* 489.

Decety, J., & Cowell, J. M. (2014). Friends or foes: Is empathy necessary for moral behavior? *Perspectives on Psychological Science, 9*(5), 525–537.

Decety, J., & Cowell, J. M. (2015a). The equivocal relationships between morality and empathy. In J. Decety & T. Wheatley (Eds.), *The moral brain: A multidisciplinary perspective* (pp. 279–302). Cambridge, MA: MIT press.

Decety, J., & Cowell, J. M. (2015b). Empathy, justice and moral behavior. *American Journal of Bioethics—Neuroscience, 6*(3), 3–14.

Decety, J., & Howard, L. (2013). The role of affect in the neurodevelopment of morality. *Child Development Perspectives, 7,* 49–54.

Decety, J., Lewis, K., & Cowell, J. M. (2015). Specific electrophysiological components disentangle affective sharing and empathic concern in psychopathy. *Journal of Neurophysiology, 114,* 493–504.

Decety, J., & Michalska, K. J. (2010). Neurodevelopmental changes in the circuits underlying empathy and sympathy from childhood to adulthood. *Developmental Science, 13,* 886–899.

Decety, J., Michalska, K. J., & Kinzler, K. D. (2012). The contribution of emotion and cognition to moral sensitivity: A neurodevelopmental study. *Cerebral Cortex, 22,* 209–220.

Decety, J., & Svetlova, M. (2012). Putting together phylogenetic and ontogenetic perspectives on empathy. *Developmental Cognitive Neuroscience, 2,* 1–24.

Drevets, W. C., Price, J. L., Simpson, J. R., Todd, R. D., Reich, T., Vannier, M., . . . Raichle, M. E. (1997). Subgenual prefrontal cortex abnormalities in mood disorders. *Nature, 386,* 824–827.

Gleichgerrcht, E., Torralva, T., Roca, M., Pose, M., & Manes, F. (2011). The role of social cognition in moral judgment in frontotemporal dementia. *Social Neuroscience, 6,* 113–122.

Gray, K., Young, L., & Waytz, A. (2012). Mind perception is the essence of morality. *Psychological Inquiry, 23,* 101–124.

Hamlin, J. K. (2014). The origins of human morality: Complex socio-moral evaluations in preverbal infants. In J. Decety & Y. Christen (Eds.), *New frontiers in social neuroscience* (pp. 165–188). Berlin: Springer Verlag.

Hamlin, J. K. (2015). The infantile origins of our moral brains. In J. Decety & T. Wheatley (Eds.), *The moral brain: Multidisciplinary perspectives* (pp. 105–122). Cambridge, MA: MIT Press.

Hare, R. D., & Neumann, C. S. (2008). Psychopathy as a clinical and empirical construct. *Annual Review of Clinical Psychology, 4,* 217–246.

Harenski, C. L., Harenski, K. A., Shane, M. S., & Kiehl, K. A. (2012). Neural development of mentalizing in moral judgment from adolescence to adulthood. *Developmental Cognitive Neuroscience, 2,* 162–173.

Hawes, D. J., & Dadds, M. R. (2012). Revisiting the role of empathy in childhood pathways to antisocial behavior. In R. Langdon & C. Mackenzie (Eds.), *Emotions, imagination, and moral reasoning* (pp. 45–70). New York: Psychology Press.

Jambon, M., & Smetana, J. G. (2014). Moral complexity in middle childhood: Children's evaluations of necessary harm. *Developmental Psychology, 50,* 22–33.

Kiehl, K. A. (2014). *The psychopath whisperer: Inside the minds of those without a conscience.* New York: Crown.

Killen, M., & Smetana, J. (2008). Moral judgment and moral neuroscience: Intersections, definitions, and issues. *Child Development Perspectives, 2,* 1–6.

Killen, M., & Smetana, J. G. (2013). *Handbook of moral development.* New York: Psychology Press.

Koenigs, M., Baskin-Sommers, A., Zeier, J., & Newman, J. P. (2011). Investigating the neural correlates of psychopathy: A critical review. *Molecular Psychiatry, 16,* 792–799.

Lahat, A., Helwig, C. C., & Zelazo, P. D. (2013). An event-related potential study of adolescents' and young adults' judgments of moral and social conventional violations. *Child Development, 84*(3), 955–969.

Lamm, C., Decety, J., & Singer, T. (2011). Meta-analytic evidence for common and distinct neural networks associated with directly experienced pain and empathy for pain. *NeuroImage, 54*(3), 2492–2502.

Leslie, A., Knobe, J., & Cohen, A. (2006). Acting intentionally and the side-effect effect: Theory of mind and moral judgment. *Psychological Science, 17*, 421–427.

Lockwood, P. L., Sebastian, C. L., McCrory, E. J., Hyde, Z. H., Gu, X., De Brito, S. A., & Viding, E. (2013). Association of callous traits with reduced neural response to others' pain in children with conduct disorder. *Current Biology, 23*, 1–5.

Maibom, H. L. (2009). Feeling for others: Empathy, sympathy, and morality. *Inquiry, 52*, 483–499.

Malle, B. F., & Guglielmo, S. (2012). Are intentionality judgments fundamentally moral? In R. Langdon & C. Mackenzie (Eds.), *Emotions, imagination, and moral reasoning* (pp. 275–293). Hove, UK: Psychology Press.

Marsh, A. A., Finger, E. C., Fowler, K. A., Adalio, C. J., Jurkowitz, I. N., Schechter, J. C., . . . Blair, R. J. R. (2013). Empathic responsiveness in amygdala and anterior cingulate cortex in youths with psychopathic traits. *Journal of Child Psychology and Psychiatry, 54*, 900–910.

Moll, J., de Oliveira-Souza, R., Eslinger, P. J., Bramati, I. E., Mourao-Miranda, J., Andreiuolo, P. A., . . . Pessoa, L. (2002). The neural correlates of moral sensitivity: A functional magnetic resonance imaging investigation of basic moral emotions. *Journal of Neuroscience, 22*, 2730–2736.

Moll, J., de Oliveira-Souza, R., Garrido, G. J., Bramati, I. E., Caparelli, E. M. A., Paiva, M. L. M. F., . . . Grafman, J. (2007). The self as a moral agent: Linking the neural bases of social agency and moral sensitivity. *Social Neuroscience, 2*, 336–352.

Motzkin, J. C., Newman, J. P., Kiehl, K. A., & Koenigs, M. (2011). Reduced prefrontal connectivity in psychopathy. *Journal of Neuroscience, 31*, 17348–17357.

Passamonti, L., Fairchild, G., Fornito, A., Goodyer, I. M., Nimmo-Smith, I., Hagan, C. C., & Calder, A. J. (2012). Abnormal anatomical connectivity between the amygdala and orbitofrontal cortex in conduct disorder. *PLOS ONE, 7*(11), e48789.

Paus, T. (2011). Brain development during childhood and adolescence. In J. Decety & J. T. Cacioppo (Eds.), *Oxford handbook of social neuroscience* (pp. 293–313). New York: Oxford University Press.

Pelphrey, K. E., & Carter, E. J. (2008). Charting the typical and atypical development of the social brain. *Development and Psychopathology, 20*, 1081–1102.

Schmidt, M., & Sommerville, J. A. (2011). Fairness expectations and altruistic sharing in 15-month-old human infants. *PLOS ONE, 6*, e23223.

Smetana, J. G. (2013). Moral development: The social domain theory view. In P. Zelazo (Ed.), *Oxford handbook of developmental psychology* (pp. 832–865). New York: Oxford University Press.

Sobhani, M., & Bechara, A. (2011). A somatic marker perspective of immoral and corrupt behavior. *Social Neuroscience, 6*, 640–652.

Taber-Thomas, B. C., Asp, E. W., Koenigs, M., Sutterer, M., Anderson, S. W., & Tranel, D. (2014). Arrested development: Early prefrontal lesions impair the maturation of moral judgment. *Brain, 137*, 1254–1261.

Tomasello, M. (2009). *Why we cooperate.* Cambridge, MA: MIT Press.

Wolf, R. C., Pujara, M. S., Motzkin, J. C., Newman, J. P., Kiehl, K. A., Decety, J., . . . Koenigs, M. (2015). Interpersonal traits of psychopathy linked to reduced integrity of the uncinate fasciculus. *Human Brain Mapping, 36*(10), 4202–4209.

Wynn, K. (2007). Some innate foundations of social and moral cognition. In P. Carruthers, S. Laurence, & S. Stich (Eds.), *The innate mind: Vol. 3. Foundations and the future* (pp. 330–347). New York: Oxford University Press.

Young, L., & Dungan, J. (2012). Where in the brain is morality?: Everywhere and maybe nowhere. *Social Neuroscience, 7*, 1–10.

Zahn-Waxler, C., & Radke-Yarrow, M. (1990). The origins of empathic concern. *Motivation and Emotion, 14*, 107–130.

Zelazo, P. D., Helwig, C. C., & Lau, A. (1996). Intention, act and outcome in behavioral prediction and moral judgment. *Child Development, 67*, 2478–2492.

CHAPTER 52

Implicit Moral Cognition

C. Daryl Cameron
Julian A. Scheffer
Victoria L. Spring

What is the best method for understanding moral judgment?

We use implicit measurement and mathematical modeling to capture implicit moral evaluations, because this method can address debates over the role of intuition and reason in moral judgment and over domain-general versus domain-specific views of moral psychology.

A man kicks a puppy as hard as he can. A son slaps his mother across the face. A soldier betrays his unit. A terrorist defiles a temple. These actions all seem like moral transgressions. And before you deliberate about why they are wrong—that is, what principles do they violate—you probably have an immediate gut reaction: "That is *wrong*!" If you don't have that reaction, that is important for us and everyone else to know, because it might mean you have fewer inhibitions about engaging in such behaviors. And you might know what the "appropriate" reaction is supposed to look like, so it's important to find a way to reliably assess your gut reactions before you can edit your responses. In this chapter, we discuss a new approach to measuring moral intuitions that draws upon advances in implicit social cognition and mathematical modeling.

What Is an Implicit Moral Attitude?

Within moral psychology, one of the most influential accounts of moral judgment is social intuitionism (Haidt, 2001). Social intuitionism claims that the heart of human morality is intuition, not reason: When we consider the actions or character of others, we have automatic moral intuitions that are the main cause of our moral judgments. As defined by this approach, a moral intuition is "the sudden appearance in consciousness or at the fringe of consciousness, of an evaluative feeling (like–dislike, good–bad) about the character or actions of a person, without any conscious awareness of having gone through steps of search, weighing evidence, or inferring a conclusion" (Haidt & Bjorklund, 2008, p. 188). Moral intuitions are thought to be quick, spontaneous, and unintentional (Haidt, 2001; Sinnott-Armstrong, Young, & Cushman, 2010), like many of the implicit cognitive processes that have been documented in social psychology (for a review, see Gawronski & Payne, 2010). Because psychologists and philosophers differ in how they define *moral intuition*— many psychologists would simply take it to mean an automatic process, whereas many philosophers would add claims about inference and epistemic justification (e.g., Huemer, 2005)—we opt for the term *implicit moral attitude*. Like other implicit attitudes, an implicit moral attitude is an association between a person or action and a moral valence (right–wrong), activated immediately in reaction to a social event.

We do not claim that moral cognition is a natural kind, separate from nonmoral cognition; rather, as suggested by work in social neuroscience, moral evaluations recruit domain-general processes such as affect, conceptual knowledge, attention, and others (for a review of a domain-general approach to morality, see Cameron, Lindquist, & Gray, 2015). On our approach, implicit moral attitudes are evaluations that typically involve an affective response and conceptual knowledge about morality. These need not reflect "online" moral decisions about a transgression and could instead reflect stored moral associations with previously encountered transgressions. Of course, people also have implicit negative attitudes about social events and social groups that are not moralized, and we believe that the difference between these and implicit moral attitudes is a matter of degree, not of kind.

Historically, our approach is grounded in a classic debate in moral philosophy and moral psychology: Is moral judgment based on intuition or on reason? We think that, as with many debates, both sides are right: Intuitive and deliberative processes interact with each other to shape moral judgment. Many current theories of moral judgment propose dual processes of intuition and deliberation that work together to produce moral judgment (Greene, 2013; Haidt, 2012), with the major point of contention being the relative influence of each (Paxton & Greene, 2010). Is reason, as put by Hume, "the slave to the passions," or is it a process that can intercede to shape moral judgments? According to a recent review of moral psychology, "the precise roles played by intuition and reasoning in moral judgment cannot yet be established based on the existing empirical evidence" (Haidt & Kesebir, 2010, p. 807). One reason for this stalemate may be that previous dual-process theories only verbally describe relationships between intuition and deliberation. However, the stalemate can be broken if we turn to formalized dual-process approaches that mathematically specify relationships between intuition and deliberation (Gawronski, Sherman, & Trope, 2014). We discuss one such approach: multinomial modeling.

A Modeling Approach to Morality

Implicit moral attitudes are the central construct for intuitionist theories of morality, yet they have received surprisingly little attention in moral psychology (for an initial discussion, see Payne & Cameron, 2010). Early work in support of social intuitionism manipulated affective states to change moral judgments (e.g., Valdesolo & DeSteno, 2006), whereas other research examined emotions and moral judgments in response to different classes of transgressions (for reviews, see Cameron et al., 2015; Monin, Pizarro, & Beer, 2007). Yet these responses may reflect more than just implicit moral attitudes—self-reports may reflect a complex blend of intuitive and deliberative processes as people consider the appropriate response.

More recently, researchers have used implicit evaluation measures from social cognition to understand implicit moral attitudes. Unlike self-report measures, implicit measures do not directly request the response of interest (for a review, see Wentura & Degner, 2010). For instance, the Implicit Association Test (IAT) examines the strength of associations between concepts based upon reaction times (Greenwald, McGhee, & Schwarz, 1998), and the affect misattribution procedure (AMP) measures automatic affective reactions toward prime stimuli based upon how these reactions influence judgments of ambiguous target stimuli (Payne, Cheng, Govorun, & Stewart, 2005). Such measures have been used frequently to capture implicit racial attitudes (e.g., Payne, 2001), and meta-analyses reveal that they predict explicit attitudes and behaviors (Cameron, Brown-Iannuzzi, & Payne, 2012; Greenwald, Uhlmann, Poehlman, & Banaji, 2009; Hofmann, Gawronski, Gschwendner, Le, & Schmitt, 2005). Some have used the IAT to examine associations between morality and the self-concept (Aquino & Reed, 2002; Perugini & Leone, 2009) and between morality and pleasantness judgments (Cima, Tonnaer, & Lobbestael, 2007; Gray, MacCulloch, Smith, Morris, & Snowden, 2003; Luo et al., 2006), whereas others have used the AMP to examine affective reactions toward moral and nonmoral actions (Graham et al., 2015; Hofmann & Baumert, 2010). These studies have shown that implicit moral attitudes predict moral personality (Cima et al., 2007; Gray et al., 2003) and moral behavior (Hofmann & Baumert, 2010).

But do these measures really capture implicit moral attitudes? First, although the tasks involve moral content (words or pictures related to morality), they do not specifically involve moral judgment. To capture implicit moral attitudes about transgressions, it may be optimal to set up a task that can show how immediate reactions to moral stimuli bias wrongness judgments about different stimuli. Second, past uses of implicit measurement to assess moral judgment adopt the task dissociation approach: that a single task corresponds to a single process. This assumption is common in much research in implicit social cognition, which presumes that an implicit measure such as the IAT only captures implicit attitudes, whereas an explicit self-report measure only captures explicit attitudes. Yet it is likely that multiple processes—such as implicit attitudes, executive control, and guessing—contribute to how people complete both implicit and explicit measures. To more precisely measure the construct of interest (implicit moral attitudes), we need to decompose task performance into these underlying processes. This increased precision in measurement may allow us to better predict moral personality and moral behavior.

In this chapter, we present a multinomial model of moral judgment, which allows us to quantify individual differences in implicit moral attitudes. Multinomial models formalize the latent cognitive processes that

interact to produce behavior within a given context (Riefer & Batchelder, 1988). One well-known subset of multinomial models is process dissociation (Jacoby, 1991; Payne, 2008; Payne & Cameron, 2014), which has been used to separate automatic and controlled processes in the context of racial stereotyping (Payne, 2001), heuristics and biases (Ferreira, Garcia-Marques, Sherman, & Sherman, 2006), and deontological and utilitarian moral decisions (Conway & Gawronski, 2013). More broadly, multinomial models have been used to quantify multiple processes that underpin social evaluation and social cognition (e.g., Conrey, Sherman, Gawronski, Hugenberg, & Groom, 2005; Krieglmeyer & Sherman, 2012; Payne, Hall, Cameron, & Bishara, 2010; for reviews, see Payne & Bishara, 2009; Bishara & Payne, 2009; Sherman, Klauer, & Allen, 2011).

Multinomial modeling is different from many previous approaches because it carries very few assumptions about the underlying processes involved. As noted above, multinomial modeling does not assume that an implicit measure only captures a single process (e.g., that the IAT only captures implicit attitudes). Instead, the modeling approach assumes that performance on any task is the net result of multiple underlying processes that interact with each other. Our approach does not assume that these processes arise from the operation of dual systems (e.g., "System I" and "System II") or from different processing "modes" that cannot operate at the same time (e.g., "autopilot" and "manual"; Greene, 2013). The model does not equate process with content—that is, the model does not assume that automatic processes correspond to deontological principles and that controlled processes correspond to utilitarian principles. Rather, people are likely to have implicit moral attitudes that correspond to a wide variety of moral philosophies. In light of numerous theoretical and methodological debates about sacrificial dilemmas in moral psychology (Bartels & Pizarro, 2011; Bauman, McGraw, Bartels, & Warren, 2014; Greene, 2013; Kahane, 2015; Kahane, Everett, Earp, Farias, & Savulescu, 2015; Gray & Schein, 2012), we move beyond using these dilemmas and we do not equate these processes or their operating conditions with specific moral philosophies. Through dissociating these intuitive and deliberative processes, we may further understand when and why individuals differ in their moral judgments and moral behaviors.

Our approach is unique in adapting implicit measurement and multinomial modeling to understand implicit moral attitudes. The work presented in this chapter builds on intuitionist theories of morality, while taking a formal modeling approach to differentiate the component processes that contribute to moral judgments. Multinomial modeling proposes processes a priori as mediators between situational inputs (i.e., moral transgressions) and behavior (i.e., moral judgments), rather than inferring processes from task performance (Gawronski et al., 2014). This makes multinomial modeling a novel and fundamentally *social cognitive* approach to measuring implicit moral attitudes (Gawronski & Bodenhausen, 2014).

What's the Evidence?

Across many experiments, we have provided evidence that supports our approach to implicit moral attitudes (Cameron, Payne, Sinnott-Armstrong, Scheffer, & Inzlicht, 2017). The first step develops an implicit measure that captures moral judgments. The second step validates a multinomial model that allows us to quantify individual differences in implicit moral attitudes.

First, we created the moral categorization task, a sequential priming task that assesses moral judgment. In this task, people complete a series of trials. On each trial, they see two stimuli in sequence: a prime word for 100 milliseconds, followed by a target word. The prime and target words are actions that are either noncontroversially morally wrong (e.g., *murder, rape*) or morally neutral (e.g., *baking, golf*). People are instructed to judge whether the target action is morally wrong or not, while avoiding being influenced by the prime actions. Because we utilize actions that are noncontroversially wrong or not wrong, we can code target judgments for accuracy. To ensure sufficient errors for analysis and to reduce response correction, we impose a fast response deadline (from 400–600 milliseconds).

Across multiple experiments, we replicate a within-subjects priming effect on moral judgment in the moral categorization task. Overall, people tend to make more errors when there is a mismatch between the moral content of the prime and target actions. When people are judging morally neutral targets such as *poetry* and *leisure*, they make more errors after morally wrong primes than after morally neutral primes. Similarly, when people are judging morally wrong targets such as *genocide* and *killing*, they make more errors after morally neutral primes than after morally wrong primes. This behavioral pattern suggests that people are having an unintentional response to the prime actions that is causing changes in their judgments of the target actions.

To understand the underlying processes that are causing this effect, we apply multinomial modeling. The multinomial model formally posits three underlying processes that give rise to performance on the moral categorization task. The first process is intentional moral judgment: the ability to make accurate moral judgments about target actions, consistent with task instructions. This parameter can be thought to capture executive control as deployed to achieve the task goal of morally judging target actions. The second process is the one of primary interest: unintentional moral judgment. Unintentional moral judgment, or implicit moral evaluations, is the tendency to morally judge target actions in a prime-consistent way. If the prime is morally wrong, then it should inspire an implicit moral evaluation "wrong" that biases judgments of target actions in that direction. If the prime is morally neutral, then it should inspire an implicit moral evaluation "not wrong" that biases judgments of target actions in that direction instead. Put another way, implicit moral attitudes toward the prime actions are being measured via how they incidentally influence moral judgments about the target actions. Finally, the third process is response bias: a tendency to always judge target actions in a certain direction (e.g., always guess "wrong").

Multinomial modeling formalizes how these processes interact to produce moral judgments on the moral categorization task. If intentional judgment operates, then people will always be correct regardless of prime–target combination. If unintentional judgment operates, then people will be correct on trials in which prime and target have the same moral valence and incorrect on trials in which prime and target have different moral valence. For instance, if the prime *murder* precedes the target *poetry*, then the implicit moral attitude toward the prime should be activated and lead people to inaccurately judge the target *poetry* as morally wrong. If response bias operates, then correct responses will be determined by the direction of the bias: If the bias is to guess that target actions are wrong, this will lead to correct responses on wrong-target trials but incorrect responses on neutral-target trials. The model also posits conditional relationships between these processes: Unintentional judgment only operates when intentional judgment fails, and response bias only operates when unintentional judgment fails. These relationships are logical and do not specify the timing of when these processes operate.

Because the multinomial model specifies expected accuracy rates based upon a priori assumptions, the observed accuracy rates can be used to estimate model fit and to solve for the probabilities of each process operating. Model fit is obtained if the expected and observed accuracy rates on the moral categorization task do not differ significantly. If the multinomial model did not fit the behavioral data, that would suggest that the model is not specified correctly and that alternative model structures should be considered.

Across experiments, we find that the multinomial model fits the data, suggesting that the multinomial model is appropriately specified. Testing additional hypotheses about the underlying processes involves constraining parameter estimates and examining whether doing so significantly reduces model fit. To examine individual-difference correlations between process parameters and other constructs, the multinomial model has to be estimated for each individual participant in order to get parameter estimates for each participant.

Upon doing so, we find that the model estimates converge with other morality constructs. In our work, we tend to find that unintentional judgment after wrong

primes is stronger for participants with increased moral identity and guilt proneness and weaker for participants with increased self-reported psychopathic tendencies. In other words, people who care more about morality have stronger implicit moral attitudes, and people who care less about morality have weaker implicit moral attitudes. These effects tend to be specific to implicit moral attitudes about moral transgressions, as unintentional judgment after nonmoral negative primes does not consistently predict these moral personality traits.

The multinomial model does not make strong assumptions about the operating conditions of the underlying processes of intentional judgment, unintentional judgment, and response bias. Although it would be easy to assume that discrimination has characteristics of controlled processes—such as requiring cognitive resources—this assumption needs to be tested experimentally. Imposing faster response deadlines during the moral categorization task (e.g., 400 vs. 800 milliseconds) reduces intentional judgment, suggesting that this process is inhibited under cognitive strain. On the other hand, unintentional judgment is not affected by the deadline manipulation, suggesting it may be a resource-efficient process. In related work, we find that intentional judgment associates with the error-related negativity, a neurophysiological signal of conflict monitoring and behavioral control (Amodio et al., 2004; Amodio, Devine, & Harmon-Jones, 2008; Inzlicht & Al-Khindi, 2012). Thus intentional judgment appears to exhibit characteristics of a controlled process.

Another question that may arise: Is this task just about affect and not morality? Maybe what we are seeing on the moral categorization task is negative affective priming, and not anything about morality in particular. As noted earlier, we think that the difference between implicit moral and nonmoral attitudes is one of degree, not of kind. Both are likely to involve negative affect. However, implicit moral attitudes should also involve conceptual content related to morality. To address this question, we adapted the moral categorization task to include negative affective primes and targets that are not typically associated with morality (e.g., *cancer, rabies*). We find that negative nonmoral primes influence judgments in the same direction as morally wrong primes (i.e., they lead people to make mistaken moral judgments about neutral actions), but not to the same extent. Similarly, unintentional judgment after wrong primes is stronger than unintentional judgment after negative primes, suggesting that implicit moral attitudes are strongest when there is both negative affect and moral content involved. For these reasons, we believe that although negative affect is involved in implicit moral attitudes, it is not the whole story: Conceptual content about morality is also needed to produce implicit moral attitudes.

Finally, we have demonstrated that our approach can be adapted to moral issues on which opinions differ, such as gay marriage. We find that for people who explicitly believe that gay marriage is morally wrong, gay marriage primes act similarly to morally wrong primes on the moral categorization task—they lead people to make mistaken moral judgments about target actions. Moreover, unintentional judgment that gay marriage is wrong is modestly stronger among people who voted in favor of a North Carolina constitutional amendment against gay marriage. Future research should consider other controversial moral issues—such as abortion, capital punishment, and euthanasia—to extend the versatility of the approach. Aside from voting, it will also be important to further establish the predictive validity of the model parameters by examining relationships between implicit moral evaluations and more prototypical moral behavior measures such as cheating, hypocrisy, and aggression.

Extensions and Expansions

We believe that this approach to implicit moral attitudes will prove useful in answering ongoing debates in moral psychology and sparking new ones. In other words, this novel method may spur new moral psychological theory (Greenwald, 2012). One of the most pressing initial extensions is to apply our approach to understanding the stability of implicit moral attitudes. To what extent do implicit moral attitudes fluctuate across different situations and contexts? Research on moral self-regulation suggests that moral behavior varies depending on prior moral or immoral behavior, and so implicit moral attitudes may exhibit similar variability. Does committing a moral transgression lead to a temporary weakening of implicit moral attitudes? Do certain kinds of cultures and environments—such as those involving widespread violence or corruption—lead to the long-term deterioration of implicit moral attitudes?

Another clear extension of this approach is to clinical populations. Our work has already shown that moral personality associates with implicit moral attitudes: People who care more about morality have stronger implicit moral attitudes, and people with psychopathic tendencies have weaker implicit moral attitudes. It stands to reason that clinical psychopaths should exhibit a similar effect. Our approach is especially useful for this population, because incarcerated psychopaths are typically highly motivated to appear morally normal (Schaich Borg & Sinnott-Armstrong, 2013; Kiehl, 2008). It is thus imperative to bypass self-report and find a measure of morality that psychopaths cannot "beat." Such an approach could be usefully complemented by recent work that has applied implicit measurement and formal modeling to capture empathy for pain (Cameron, Spring, & Todd, 2017).

This task can also be used to examine moral judgments in clinical populations that have lesions to brain areas previously associated with moral judgment. For instance, patients with lesions to the ventromedial prefrontal cortex (vmPFC) make more utilitarian judgments in high-conflict moral dilemmas that pit deontological rules against a greater good, possibly because of their difficulties integrating affect into decision making (Koenigs et al., 2007; Thomas, Croft, & Tranel, 2011). In recent work, we have administered the moral categorization task to vmPFC lesion patients (Cameron, Reber, Spring, & Tranel, 2017). Compared with control participants, these patients exhibit reduced unintentional judgment in response to moral transgressions—but not in response to nonmoral negative affective primes—as well as reduced intentional judgment. Thus our task and modeling approach captures a dual deficit in vmPFC patients.

Our approach also speaks to the debate over distinct domains of morality. One of the most well-known domain theories, moral foundations theory, separates morality into categories of harm, fairness, loyalty, authority, purity, and liberty (Graham et al., 2013). Previous studies find that whereas conservatives tend to endorse all foundations as relevant to morality, liberals tend to endorse only harm and fairness (Graham, Haidt, & Nosek, 2009). This difference disappears when participants are under cognitive strain or self-control depletion, suggesting that conservatives may be engaging in motivated reasoning to rationalize the binding foundations (Wright & Baril, 2011). Yet other research finds that, using implicit measures, liberals and conservatives have similar affective reactions to violations across different moral foundations (Graham et al., 2015). Our approach could be adapted to test this question. The moral categorization task can include prime stimuli corresponding to different moral foundations, and an unintentional judgment parameter can be estimated for each foundation. If liberals and conservatives differ in terms of moral foundation endorsement, then they should differ in their implicit moral attitudes about different moral foundations. Our approach can also address whether the single dimension of harm unites different moral foundations (Gray, Young, & Waytz, 2012). If intuition after harm primes predicts explicit endorsement of all moral foundations, but intuition after purity primes does not, that would suggest that harm has primacy in moral evaluation (for more discussion of domain-general vs. domain-specific theories of morality, see Cameron, Lindquist, & Gray, 2015).

Conclusion

Implicit moral evaluations are pivotal to many prominent theories of morality, and they matter a great deal for social life. We want to know that others share our moral reactions and are inhibited from transgressing against us. Using implicit measurement and multinomial modeling, we quantify individual differences in these implicit moral attitudes and find that they vary as a function of moral personality and predict moral behavior. We believe that our work will motivate increased focus on the component processes that underpin everyday morality.

REFERENCES

Amodio, D. M., Devine, P. G., & Harmon-Jones, E. (2008). Individual differences in the regulation of intergroup bias: The role of conflict monitoring and neural signals for control. *Journal of Personality and Social Psychology, 94*, 60–74.

Amodio, D. M., Harmon-Jones, E., Devine, P. G., Curtin, J. J., Hartley, S. L., & Covert, A. E. (2004). Neural signals for the detection of unintentional race bias. *Psychological Science, 15*, 88–93.

Aquino, K., & Reed, A., II. (2002). The self-importance of moral identity. *Journal of Personality and Social Psychology, 83*, 1423–1440.

Bartels, D. M., & Pizarro, D. A. (2011). The mismeasure of morals: Antisocial personality traits predict utilitarian responses to moral dilemmas. *Cognition, 121*, 154–161.

Bauman, C. W., McGraw, A. P., Bartels, D. M., & Warren, C. (2014). Revisiting external validity: Concerns about trolley problems and other sacrificial dilemmas in moral psychology. *Social and Personality Psychology Compass, 8*(9), 536–554.

Bishara, A. J., & Payne, B. K. (2009). Multinomial process tree models of control and automaticity in weapon misidentification. *Journal of Experimental Social Psychology, 45*, 524–534.

Cameron, C. D., Brown-Iannuzzi, J. L., & Payne, B. K. (2012). Sequential priming measures of implicit social cognition: A meta-analysis of associations with behavior and explicit attitudes. *Personality and Social Psychology Review, 16*, 330–350.

Cameron, C. D., Lindquist, K. A., & Gray, K. (2015). A constructionist review of morality and emotions: No evidence for specific links between moral content and discrete emotions. *Personality and Social Psychology Review, 19*, 371–394.

Cameron, C. D., Payne, B. K., Sinnott-Armstrong, W., Scheffer, J., & Inzlicht, M. (2017). Implicit moral cognition: A multinomial modeling approach. *Cognition, 158*, 224–241.

Cameron, C. D., Reber, J., Spring, V., & Tranel, D. (2017). *vmPFC lesions impair intentional and unintentional moral judgments.* Manuscript in preparation.

Cameron, C. D., Spring, U. L., & Todd, A. (2017). The empathy impulse: A multinomial model of intentional and unintentional empathy for pain. *Emotion, 17*, 395–411.

Cima, M., Tonnaer, F., & Lobbestael, J. (2007). Moral emotions in predatory and impulsive offenders using implicit measures. *Netherlands Journal of Psychology, 63*, 133–142.

Conrey, F. R., Sherman, J. W., Gawronski, B.,

Hugenberg, K., & Groom, C. J. (2005). Separating multiple processes in implicit social cognition: The quad model of implicit task performance. *Journal of Personality and Social Psychology, 89,* 469–487.

Conway, P., & Gawronski, B. (2013). Deontological and utilitarian inclinations in moral decision making: A process dissociation approach. *Journal of Personality and Social Psychology, 104,* 216–235.

Ferreira, M. B., Garcia-Marques, L., Sherman, S. J., & Sherman, J. W. (2006). Automatic and controlled components of judgment and decision making. *Journal of Personality and Social Psychology, 91,* 797–813.

Gawronski, B., & Bodenhausen, G. V. (2014). Social-cognitive theories. In B. Gawronski & G. V. Bodenhausen (Eds.), *Theory and explanation in social psychology* (pp. 63–83). New York: Guilford Press.

Gawronski, B., & Payne, B. K. (Eds.). (2010). *Handbook of implicit social cognition: Measurement, theory, and applications.* New York: Guilford Press.

Gawronski, B., Sherman, J. W., & Trope, Y. (2014). Two of what?: A conceptual analysis of dual-process theories. In J. W. Sherman, B. Gawronski, & Y. Trope (Eds.), *Dual-process theories of the social mind* (pp. 3–19). New York: Guilford Press.

Graham, J., Englander, Z., Morris, J. P., Hawkins, C. B., Haidt, J., & Nosek, B. A. (2015). *Warning bell: Liberals implicitly respond to group morality before rejecting it explicitly.* Unpublished manuscript.

Graham, J., Haidt, J., Koleva, S., Motyl, M., Iyer, R., Wojcik, S., . . . Ditto, P. H. (2013). Moral foundations theory: The pragmatic validity of moral pluralism. *Advances in Experimental Social Psychology, 47,* 55–130.

Graham, J., Haidt, J., & Nosek, B. A. (2009). Liberals and conservatives rely on different sets of moral foundations. *Journal of Personality and Social Psychology, 96,* 1029–1046.

Gray, K., & Schein, C. (2012). Two minds vs. two philosophies: Mind perception defines morality and dissolves the debate between deontology and utilitarianism. *Review of Philosophy and Psychology, 3,* 405–423.

Gray, K., Young, L., & Waytz, A. (2012). Mind perception is the essence of morality. *Psychological Inquiry, 23,* 101–124.

Gray, N. S., MacCulloch, M. J., Smith, J., Morris, M., & Snowden, R. J. (2003). Forensic psychology: Violence viewed by psychopathic murderers. *Nature, 423,* 497–498.

Greene, J. D. (2013). *Moral tribes: Emotion, reason, and the gap between us and them.* New York: Penguin.

Greenwald, A. G. (2012). There is nothing so theoretical as a good method. *Perspectives on Psychological Science, 7,* 99–108.

Greenwald, A. G., McGhee, D., & Schwartz, J. (1998). Measuring individual differences in implicit cognition: The Implicit Association Test. *Journal of Personality and Social Psychology, 74,* 1464–1480.

Greenwald, A. G., Uhlmann, E. L., Poehlman, T. A., & Banaji, M. R. (2009). Understanding and using the Implicit Association Test: III. Meta-analysis of predictive validity. *Journal of Personality and Social Psychology, 97,* 17–41.

Haidt, J. (2001). The emotional dog and its rational tail: A social intuitionist approach to moral judgment. *Psychological Review, 108,* 814–834.

Haidt, J. (2012). *The righteous mind: Why good people are divided by politics and religion.* New York: Pantheon.

Haidt, J., & Bjorklund, F. (2008). Social intuitionists answer six questions about moral psychology. In W. Sinnott-Armstrong (Ed.), *Moral psychology: Vol. 2. The cognitive science of morality: Intuition and diversity* (pp. 181–217). Cambridge, MA: MIT Press.

Haidt, J., & Kesebir, S. (2010). Morality. In S. Fiske, D. Gilbert, & G. Lindzey (Eds.), *Handbook of social psychology* (5th ed., pp. 797–832). Hoboken, NJ: Wiley.

Hofmann, W., & Baumert, A. (2010). Immediate affect as a basis for intuitive moral judgement: An adaptation of the affect misattribution procedure. *Cognition and Emotion, 24,* 522–535.

Hofmann, W., Gawronski, B., Gschwendner, T., Le, H., & Schmitt, M. (2005). A meta-analysis on the correlation between the Implicit Association Test and explicit self-report measures. *Personality and Social Psychology Bulletin, 31,* 1369–1385.

Huemer, M. (2005). *Ethical intuitionism.* New York: Palgrave Macmillan.

Inzlicht, M., & Al-Khindi, T. (2012). ERN and the placebo: A misattribution approach to studying the arousal properties of the error-related negativity. *Journal of Experimental Psychology: General, 141,* 799–807.

Jacoby, L. L. (1991). A process dissociation framework: Separating automatic from intentional uses of memory. *Journal of Memory and Language, 30,* 513–541.

Kahane, G. (2015). Sidetracked by trolleys: Why sacrificial moral dilemmas tell us little (or nothing) about moral judgment. *Social Neuroscience, 10*(5), 551–560.

Kahane, G., Everett, J. A., Earp, B. D., Farias, M., & Savulescu, J. (2015). "Utilitarian" judgments in sacrificial moral dilemmas do not reflect impartial concern for the greater good. *Cognition, 134,* 193–209.

Kiehl, K. (2008). Without morals: The cognitive neuroscience of criminal psychopaths. In W. Sinnott-Armstrong (Ed.), *Moral psychology: Vol. 3. The neuroscience of morality* (pp. 119–149). Cambridge, MA: MIT Press.

Koenigs, M., Young, L., Adolphs, R., Tranel, D., Cushman, F., Hauser, M., . . . Damasio, A. (2007). Damage to the prefrontal cortex increases utilitarian moral judgements. *Nature, 446*, 908–911.

Krieglmeyer, R., & Sherman, J. W. (2012). Disentangling stereotype activation and stereotype application in the stereotype misperception task. *Journal of Personality and Social Psychology, 103*, 205–224.

Luo, Q., Nakic, M., Wheatley, T., Richell, R., Martin, A., & Blair, R. J. R. (2006). The neural basis of implicit moral attitude: An IAT study using event-related fMRI. *NeuroImage, 30*, 1449–1457.

Monin, B., Pizarro, D. A., & Beer, J. S. (2007). Deciding versus reacting: Conceptions of moral judgment and the reason–affect debate. *Review of General Psychology, 11*, 99–111.

Paxton, J. M., & Greene, J. D. (2010). Moral reasoning: Hints and allegations. *Topics in Cognitive Science, 2*, 511–527.

Payne, B. K. (2001). Prejudice and perception: The role of automatic and controlled processes in misperceiving a weapon. *Journal of Personality and Social Psychology, 81*, 181–192.

Payne, B. K. (2008). What mistakes disclose: A process dissociation approach to automatic and controlled processes in social psychology. *Social and Personality Psychology Compass, 2*, 1073–1092.

Payne, B. K., & Bishara, A. J. (2009). An integrative review of process dissociation and related models in social cognition. *European Review of Social Psychology, 20*, 272–314.

Payne, B. K., & Cameron, C. D. (2010). Divided minds, divided morals: How implicit social cognition underpins and undermines our sense of social justice. In B. Gawronski & B. K. Payne (Eds.), *Handbook of implicit social cognition: Measurement, theory, and applications* (pp. 445–462). New York: Guilford Press.

Payne, B. K., & Cameron, C. D. (2014). Dual-process theory from a process dissociation perspective. In J. Sherman, B. Gawronski, & Y. Trope (Eds.), *Dual-process theories of the social mind* (pp. 107–120). New York: Guilford Press.

Payne, B. K., Cheng, C. M., Govorun, O., & Stewart, B. D. (2005). An inkblot for attitudes: Affect misattribution as implicit measurement. *Journal of Personality and Social Psychology, 89*, 277–293.

Payne, B. K., Hall, D. L., Cameron, C. D., & Bishara, A. J. (2010). A process model of affect misattribution. *Personality and Social Psychology Bulletin, 36*, 1397–1408.

Perugini, M., & Leone, L. (2009). Implicit self-concept and moral action. *Journal of Research in Personality, 43*, 747–754.

Riefer, D., & Batchelder, W. (1988). Multinomial modeling and the measurement of cognitive processes. *Psychological Review, 95*, 318–339.

Schaich Borg, J., & Sinnott-Armstrong, W. (2013). Do psychopaths make moral judgments? In K. Kiehl & W. Sinnott-Armstrong (Eds.), *Handbook on psychopathy and law* (pp. 107–128). New York: Oxford University Press.

Sherman, J. W., Klauer, K. C., & Allen, T. J. (2011). Mathematical modeling of implicit social cognition. In B. Gawronski & B. K. Payne (Eds.), *Handbook of implicit social cognition: Measurement, theory, and applications* (pp. 156–175). New York: Guilford Press.

Sinnott-Armstrong, W., Young, L., & Cushman, F. (2010). Moral intuitions. In J. Doris & the Moral Psychology Research Group (Eds.), *The moral psychology handbook* (pp. 246–272). Oxford, UK: Oxford University Press.

Thomas, B. C., Croft, K. E., & Tranel, D. (2011). Harming kin to save strangers: Further evidence for abnormally utilitarian moral judgments after ventromedial prefrontal damage. *Journal of Cognitive Neuroscience, 23*, 2186–2196.

Valdesolo, P., & DeSteno, D. (2006). Manipulations of emotional context shape moral judgment. *Psychological Science, 17*, 476–477.

Wentura, D., & Degner, J. (2010). A practical guide to sequential priming and related tasks. In B. Gawronski & B. K. Payne (Eds.), *Handbook of implicit social cognition: Measurement, theory, and applications* (pp. 95–116). New York: Guilford Press.

Wright, J. C., & Baril, G. (2011). The role of cognitive resources in determining our moral intuitions: Are we all liberals at heart? *Journal of Experimental Social Psychology, 47*, 1007–1012.

CHAPTER 53

Into the Wild

Big Data Analytics in Moral Psychology

Joseph Hoover
Morteza Dehghani
Kate Johnson
Rumen Iliev
Jesse Graham

How can we investigate moral values in the real world?

We propose that naturally generated linguistic data, such as social media content, can be used to study morality outside of the laboratory.

Moral values are culturally variable entities that emerge from dynamic, hierarchical interactions between individual- and group-level phenomena. Human-generated unstructured data from sources such as social media offer an unprecedented opportunity to observe these phenomena in a natural habitat, which is an essential vantage point for understanding moral values and their role in moral judgment and behavior.

The interdisciplinary science of morality has blossomed in the last decade, with insights from social psychology, neuroscience, behavioral economics, experimental philosophy, developmental science, sociology, consumer behavior, and anthropology informing one another and inspiring further interdisciplinary collaborations (Haidt, 2007). This proliferation of research has led to substantive theoretical advances, as well as a number of notable disagreements (e.g., see Graham & Iyer, 2012; Gray, Schein, & Ward, 2014; Janoff-Bulman & Carnes, 2013; Rai & Fiske, 2011, on moral values; Cushman & Greene, 2012, and Kahane, 2015, on moral decision making). Nonetheless, several points of convergence have emerged within the field. It is generally accepted that morality is a fundamentally social evolutionary adaptation and that it arises dynamically through interactions between native, interindividual mechanisms and sociocultural factors (e.g., Graham et al., 2013; Haidt, 2012; Mikhail, 2007; Rai & Fiske, 2011; Fiske & Rai, 2015). However, although many contemporary approaches to morality are premised on some iteration of the social–functional evolutionary model, we believe that the majority of the research methodologies used to substantiate these theories are, ironically, not able to adequately account for the dynamic social functioning of morality that they prioritize. Most research on morality is conducted with undergraduates in decontextualized laboratory settings, and, much more often than not, morally relevant variables are measured using self-reports. Although there is nothing immediately wrong with these methods, we doubt they can fully capture, for example, the highly variable and subjective nature of individual moral values (Graham, 2014; Meindl & Graham, 2014) or group-level moral processes (Ginges, Atran, Sachdeva, & Medin, 2011).

Accordingly, we believe it is vital that researchers supplement traditional methodologies with alternative approaches that have greater ecological and external validity and that are better able to capture the full social–functional range of morality. In this chapter, we argue that a range of computationally intensive methods, drawn predominantly from computer science and computational linguistics, can help researchers do just this. By mining psychologically relevant information from large-scale, human-generated, online data such as blog posts, news articles, tweets, Facebook status updates, and social-network structures—collectively referred to as "big data"—researchers can use these methods to investigate morally relevant phenomena in the real world. These methods enable researchers to investigate large-scale, diachronic moral phenomena such as the diffusion of moral values through populations and the moralization of specific topics (Graham, Haidt, & Nosek, 2009; Sagi & Dehghani, 2014). They also offer researchers new opportunities to investigate the relationship between moral values and moral behavior (Dehghani et al., 2016; Boyd et al., 2015), which is both notoriously difficult to study in the laboratory and deeply important for understanding how morality functions (Graham, Meindl, & Beall, 2012; Graham et al., 2013). Of course, we are not suggesting that these methods—which we refer to as "big data analytics"—can or should replace traditional approaches. Big data analytics have their own weaknesses (Ruths & Pfeffer, 2014), and they cannot match all of the strengths of conventional methodologies. Fortunately, researchers do not have to

choose one or the other. Indeed, our view is that researchers will benefit the most by developing rigorous multimethod approaches that counterbalance the weaknesses of traditional methods with the strengths of big data analytics, and vice versa (Dehghani et al., 2016).

We believe big data analytics offer sufficient advantages for basic psychological research to warrant their inclusion in social scientists' toolkits. However, the behaviors responsible for generating morality-relevant big data—such as participation in online social networks—have become increasingly prominent across social groups and cultures, which marks them as targets of study in their own right. As of January 2015, more than 25% of the global population was using social media (Kemp, 2015), and these platforms are increasingly being used as loudspeakers when morally relevant events take place. Four of many possible examples are the hashtags ("#") #blacklivesmatter and #baltimore, which have been used widely in protests against recent incidents involving police brutality across the United States; #governmentshutdown, which was prominent in discussions of the 2013 U.S. Government shutdown; and #AllEyesOnISIS, which has been used by ISIS in disseminations of propaganda and by individuals to show support for the extremist organization.

Clearly, this level of global connectivity is unprecedented, and it likely has important effects on processes related to morality. As social media communications become more deeply woven into the fabric of society, understanding trends in dynamic morally relevant phenomena may increasingly require understanding the psychological role that social media play in contemporary societies. By incorporating big data analytics into the study of morality, researchers will gain a new way to gather information in natural settings about the structure of moral visions (Graham & Haidt, 2012), large-scale moral behavioral patterns, and the relation between the two. However, they will also be able to explore the specific effects that today's communication technologies have on relevant phenomena. This methodological development could potentially transform the study of morality, improving the ecological and external validity of a field that has relied almost exclusively on self-reports sampled from predominantly WEIRD (Western, Educated, Industrialized, Rich, Democratic; Henrich, Heine, & Norenzayan, 2010) populations.

Historical Context

Mining massive sets of extant data for psychological information is a relatively new practice, and it has become possible only through constant increases in computational power, availability of new methods, and greater accessibility of human-generated data. Recently, two methods of analysis—natural language processing and social network analysis—have emerged as valuable tools for gleaning psychologically relevant information from online data. However, while these methods are gradually being incorporated into psychological research, psychologists still primarily rely on rudimentary and increasingly dated techniques. Further, until recently, these methods have remained almost completely neglected in moral psychology. Therefore, although a comprehensive review of these methodologies is beyond the scope of this chapter, a brief introduction to their aims and approaches is provided below, followed by a discussion of how they fit into contemporary models of morally relevant phenomena.

Natural language processing (NLP) dates back to the 1950s (Nadkarni, Ohno-Machado, & Chapman, 2011; Jones, 1994; Dostert, 1955/1976) and relies on a range of approaches to parse semantic information from unstructured text (Iliev, Dehghani, & Sagi, 2014). Initially developed in linguistics and computer science, NLP has only recently been incorporated into psychological research. However, the notion that psychological information can be gleaned from language is hardly a new idea; for over a century, researchers have relied on language to make inferences about human psychology (Freud, 1901; Kintsch & Van Dijk, 1978; Braun & Clarke, 2006). The availability of digitized natural language corpora—drawn from sources such as blogs, Congressional transcripts, news publications, and social networking platforms such as Facebook and Twitter—has allowed researchers to explore the relationship between natural language and psychology at an unprecedented scale.

How NLP is accomplished ranges considerably between methodologies. For conceptual clarity, Iliev and colleagues (2014) separate NLP methods into three broad groups, which is the approach we take here. In the first group of methods, user-defined dictionaries (UDD), researchers rely on expert-generated dictionaries, which specify words that are relevant to dimensions of interest. Popularized in psychology by James Pennebaker and colleagues (Pennebaker, 2011; Tausczik & Pennebaker, 2010), these methods aim to classify the semantic content of texts along a given dimension by summing the within-text occurrences of words specified by the UDD as related to the dimension. For example, sums of positive- and negative-affect word occurrences can be used to infer the overall sentiment of a text (Kahn, Tobin, Massey, & Anderson, 2007) and, further, such sentiment analyses can be used to make predictions about individual differences, such as depression (Rude, Gortner, & Pennebaker, 2004).

The methods in the second class, feature extraction methods, forgo UDDs and rely on machine learning algorithms to extract features from texts that are predictive of variables of interest. In this case, a subset of texts preclassified on a variable of interest (e.g., gender or religious affiliation) are used to "train" an algorithm to detect the features that predict the target variable. After training, the algorithm is tested on an independent preclassified set of texts, which allows researchers to obtain relatively stable estimates of the classifier's error rate. The algorithm can then be used to classify unlabeled texts on the variable of interest through probabilistic estimation (though it should be noted that, as target texts increase in difference between the training and test texts, accuracy has been shown to decrease, sometimes dramatically).

One shortcoming of both UDD and feature extraction methods, however, is that they rely on individual word occurrences and are not able to account for the context in which a word occurs. Because words do not occur in isolation, this leads to substantial information loss. The methods in the third class, word co-occurrence methods, attempt to minimize this information loss by capturing the relations between words. In general, this is accomplished through several steps, though these steps vary between specific methods. For example, latent semantic analysis (LSA; Deerwester, Dumais, Furnas, Landauer, & Harshman, 1990; Landauer & Dumais, 1997; Dumais, 2004) involves first representing words and documents— any discrete set of texts, such as tweets, blog posts, or entire novels—as vectors in high-dimensional space. In this space, words that tend to appear in the same documents are closer to each other, and documents that use similar words are closer to each other. This then permits analysts to assess the semantic similarity between words and between documents by measuring the "distance" between these entities. Other word co-occurrence methods include, for example, latent Dirichlet analysis (Blei, Ng, & Jordan, 2003; Blei, 2012), new vector-based methods (e.g., Mikolov, Sutskever, Chen, Corrado, & Dean, 2013; Sagi & Dehghani, 2014), and TopicMapping (Lancichinetti et al., 2015). Although these methods are considerably more complex than UDD and feature extraction methods, they constitute much of the cutting edge in NLP. Accordingly, as morality researchers begin testing increasingly sophisticated hypotheses using large-scale text corpora, it will be essential that they incorporate these methods into their analyses.

Whereas NLP focuses on quantifying natural language generated by individuals, social network analysis (SNA; Marin & Wellman, 2011) aims to understand human behavior in terms of group-level systems of relational patterns. SNA represents social groups as relationships ("edges") between individuals ("nodes") in order to quantify complex group-level phenomena. As SNA was originally developed by sociologists, social network research tends to prioritize network-based explanations of phenomena and, in some instances, rejects outright the notion that social norms and individual-level psychological characteristics play an important causal role in network outcomes (Marin & Wellman, 2011). However, network analysts are increasingly recognizing the role of individual differences—particularly individual moral differences—in network composition (Vaisey & Lizardo 2010; Hitlin & Vaisey, 2013). While traditional SNA treats net-

works as exogenous factors that determine social behavior, recent research suggests that non-network factors can also affect network formation. For example, Clifton, Turkheimer, and Oltmanns (2009) identified reliable relationships between psychopathological characteristics of military personnel and their social network positions. Further, Vaisey and Lizardo (2010) found that moral disposition is a better predictor of network composition than network composition is of moral disposition, suggesting that networks might be better conceptualized as endogenous factors with reciprocal, hierarchical relations to their nodes.

In tandem, NLP and SNA allow researchers to quantify individual-level natural language expressions and model complex group-level network dynamics. These methods have only recently begun to be applied to research on morally relevant phenomena (e.g., Dehghani, Sagae, Sachdeva, & Gratch, 2014; Vaisey & Miles, 2014; Graham et al., 2009); however, we believe that they offer a valuable complement to the methods traditionally used to investigate moral phenomena, which rely almost exclusively on self-report measures and highly controlled experimental paradigms. By incorporating these methods into their research programs, scientists—regardless of their theoretical framework—can begin to provide stronger tests for hypotheses by making predictions about real-world phenomena. Although these methods are relatively new, they offer possibilities that have been sought for decades by psychologists—access to relevant phenomena untainted by the biases that accompany laboratory-based research (Gibson, 1977).

Methodological Stance

Over time, researchers have come to recognize that morality is constituted by a network of components, including values, judgment, intuition, reasoning, and behavior. Although exactly how these phenomena fit together is not fully agreed upon, this general view has been supported by research employing a wide range of methodologies, including laboratory experiments, cross-cultural surveys, online questionnaires, implicit social cognition measures, and neurophysiological measurements, among others. Despite this methodological diversity, however, the vast majority of studies have relied on artificial paradigms and self-reports to approximate access to real-world morally relevant phenomena. Although these methods have proven immensely useful, widespread reliance on them has motivated concern about the external validity of morality research. For example, Bauman, McGraw, Bartels, and Warren (2014) question the degree to which responses to moral judgment measures that use extreme scenarios actually correspond to real-world moral functioning, and other research suggests that conventional measures of moral utilitarianism (e.g., Greene, Sommerville, Nystrom, Darley, & Cohen, 2001; Greene, Morelli, Lowenberg, Nystrom, & Cohen, 2008) might actually be measuring nonmoral or even immoral dimensions, rather than genuine utilitarian moral concerns (Bartels & Pizarro, 2011; Kahane et al., 2015).

Despite these criticisms, we believe that artificial paradigms and self-reports have been and will continue to be valuable tools for probing moral phenomena. However, we also believe that their value should not obscure their shortcomings. As has been widely observed, theories based on self-report measures—particularly those characterized by low ecological validity—need to be carefully vetted for external validity (Cronbach, 1949; Cronbach & Meehl, 1955; Messick, 1995; Allen & Yen, 2001). Unfortunately, rigorous external validity tests of moral theories have been infrequent, likely due to the considerable difficulty of accessing moral phenomena through alternative methods (Graham, 2014; Ginges et al., 2011; Hofmann, Wisneski, Brandt, & Skitka, 2014). Thus, although we are not advocating for researchers to stop using traditional measurement methods to study morality, we believe the general absence of alternative methods that can counterbalance the weaknesses of traditional measures is problematic. Such a counterbalance can be at least partially provided by big data analytics, which we believe can help validate traditional measures and theories.

However, big data analytics are useful for much more than validation. They can also provide researchers ways to access dimensions of moral phenomena that traditional methods cannot reach at scale. For example, despite many notable differences, many contemporary psychological theories of morality converge on the view that morality emerges from a complex, recursive network of individual- and group-level influences (Haidt, 2007; Graham et al., 2013; Rai & Fiske, 2011; Fiske & Rai, 2015). Although individual-level moral phenomena are generated from the moral components mentioned above, these phenomena are also influenced by social and cultural factors (Lakoff, 2002; Marietta, 2008; Dehghani et al., 2009; Koleva, Graham, Haidt, Iyer, & Ditto, 2012; Baumard, André, & Sperber, 2013), which, in turn, are influenced by individual-level factors. However, the extent to which traditional research methods can capture cross-level interactions of moral phenomena is limited. These interactions tend to occur at scales larger than can be accommodated by laboratory methods, and their temporal dynamism further complicates conventional psychological investigation. However, morality research employing computational methods such as NLP and SNA suggests that these obstacles for laboratory research can be at least partially circumnavigated via big data analytics. For example, Sagi and Dehghani (2014) were able to measure dynamic changes in group-level moral concerns regarding the World Trade Center attacks, the Ground Zero mosque, and abortion by analyzing text collected from the *New York Times*, the blogosphere, and transcriptions of U.S. Senate speeches, respectively. Additionally, combining NLP and SNA, Dehghani et al. (2016) demonstrated how individual moral concerns can influence group-level phenomena such as social network structures.

Although the application of big data analytics to morality research is in its infancy, it already seems clear that these methods can make a substantial contribution to the field. Researchers can use these methods to test established theories on data that are generated by messy, uncontrolled human behavior, which is a valuable opportunity given the historical inaccessibility of real-world morality phenomena. By providing alternative measurement methods, big data analytics can also help researchers improve the external validity of their measures. Perhaps even more importantly, however, big data analytics can help researchers study otherwise inaccessible dimensions of morality, such as changes in moral values associated with environmental and socioecological factors, group-level moral phenomena, and the relationship between real-world moral values and behavior. Although most theories of morality at least recognize the importance of these dimensions, there has been little research that has been able to directly target them. This has left considerable gaps in our understanding of human morality. If, as we believe, the goal of moral psychology is to understand moral functioning in the real world, then researchers must begin to fill these gaps.

Evidence

For big data analytics to be useful for morality research, at least two conditions must be satisfied. Big data must contain reliable traces of moral phenomena left by human behavior, and these moral traces must have sufficient informational richness to offer genuine insights into moral phenomena. Big data analytics have only recently begun being incorporated into morality research, yet there is already a growing body of evidence that these conditions are amply met. Additionally, the increasing use of big data analytics on nonmoral psychological phenomena corroborates the value of these methods for psychological research (Tausczik & Pennebaker, 2010; Park et al., 2015). For example, various NLP methods have uncovered word usage patterns that predict depression (Rude et al., 2004), status (Kacewicz, Pennebaker, Davis, Jeon, & Graesser, 2014), motivation (Gill, Nowson, & Oberlander, 2009), cultural epistemological orientations (Dehghani et al., 2009; Dehghani, Bang, Medin, Marin, Leddon, & Waxman, 2013), academic success (Pennebaker, Chung, Frazee, Lavergne, & Beaver, 2014), political affiliation (Diermeier, Godbout, Yu, & Kaufmann, 2012; Dehghani et al., 2014), personality (Oberlander & Nowson, 2006), and mental disorders. Further, personality researchers—who were among the first psychologists to begin rigorously incorporating big data analytics into their work—have developed measurement approaches that provide powerful insights into the links between personality and language use (e.g., Schwartz et al., 2013; Back et al., 2010) and that possess impressive psychometric qualities (e.g., Park et al., 2015).

Similarly, morality researchers have successfully used techniques from machine learning, NLP, and SNA to investigate morally relevant phenomena. In one of the earliest applications of NLP to morality research, Graham et al. (2009) developed a UDD of words and word stems associated with the constructs of moral foundations theory (MFT). This Moral Foundations Dictionary (MFD) was then used with an NLP program called Linguistics Inquiry and Word Count (LIWC; Tausczik & Pennebaker, 2010) to explore variations in moral concerns between liberal and conservative congregations as expressed in a corpus of sermons. Notably, their results converged with previous MFT findings. Sermons delivered in liberal churches were more associated with harm and fairness concerns, compared with those delivered in conservative churches, and sermons delivered in conservative churches were more associated with purity and authority concerns, compared with those delivered in liberal churches. In another investigation of moral value differences between liberals and conservatives, Dehghani and colleagues (2013) used an unsupervised hierarchical generative topic modeling technique based on latent Dirichlet allocation (LDA: Blei et al., 2003), which enabled them to extract topics from a corpus of liberal and conservative blogs. Notably, though conventional LDA techniques have no control over what topics are extracted, the method (Andrzejewski & Zhu, 2009) employed by Dehghani et al. (2013) used small sets of words from the MFD as seeds to favor the detection of topics associated with moral concerns. Using subsequent statistical analyses to compare differences between the moral topics extracted from the liberal and conservative blogs, they found that their results were consistent with previous research on moral psychology and political ideology.

Recent research has also demonstrated that NLP can be used to test sophisticated hypotheses about individual- and group-level moral phenomena. For example, in a series of three studies, Sagi and Dehghani

(2014) showed that the "moral loading" of specific topics can be estimated by calculating the semantic similarity between the contexts of keywords representing topics of interest and different moral concerns. In essence, this method allows researchers to measure the moralization of specific topics throughout an entire corpus and thereby produce group-level estimations of topic-specific moral concerns. Using these estimations, researchers can test hypotheses about longitudinal changes and between-group differences in the moral loadings of topics of interest. For instance, across three studies, Sagi and Dehghani (2014) used this method to test hypotheses about the moral loadings of three different topics: the World Trade Center attack, the Ground Zero mosque, and abortion. In their first study, they used a corpus of 1.8 million *New York Times* articles dating from January 1987 to June 2007 to test the hypothesis that major events can precipitate lasting changes in moral rhetoric. More specifically, they predicted that the 9/11 attack on the World Trade Center led to significant increases in journalists' use of moral harm and ingroup rhetoric associated with the World Trade Center but not with the Empire State Building, which was used as a control topic. Consistent with their hypothesis, they found that harm and loyalty concerns associated with the World Trade Center increased dramatically following 9/11, but that similar concerns associated with the Empire State Building remained relatively low. In their second study, Sagi and Dehghani (2014) predicted that moral concerns about the Cordoba Muslim Community Center in New York City—popularly referred to as the "Ground-Zero mosque"—would increase sharply during the highly politicized debates that swept through the blogosphere in 2010, but that this moralization would decrease as the debates dwindled. Their results supported both predictions, indicating that NLP methods can be used to measure dynamic longitudinal patterns in moral rhetoric. In their final study, they explored differences between Democrat and Republican moralization of abortion by analyzing transcripts of nearly 230,000 U.S. Senate speeches. As predicted, they found that Republicans exhibited higher moral loadings than Democrats across all five MFD dimensions. Notably, their results converged with perceptions of both parties' stances on abortion: Democrats were most concerned about fairness, whereas Republicans were most concerned about purity. Unexpectedly, Sagi and Dehghani (2014) also found that harm concerns—which seem deeply incorporated into conservative stances on abortion—were only the third-highest-loading moral dimension. However, noting that the purity dimension is represented by keywords such as *abstinence, celibacy*, and *prostitution*, Sagi and Dehghani (2014) propose that these results indicate that, although Republicans endorse sanctity-of-life arguments when debating abortion, they are more often concerned with the relationship between abortion and sexual purity. In sum, these studies demonstrate that NLP can be used to test precise hypotheses about group-level moral phenomena, as well as to uncover potentially counterintuitive patterns in moralization, such as the apparent primacy of purity concerns within Republican stances on abortion.

In addition to detecting patterns in group-level moral phenomena, big data analytics have been used to conduct novel explorations into the relationship between moral values and behavior. For example, Boyd et al. (2015) used a topic modeling technique called the meaning extraction method (MEM; Chung & Pennebaker, 2008) to investigate values and behaviors that emerge from natural language texts. Across two studies, Boyd et al. (2015) compared estimates of participants' values generated from the Schwartz Value Survey (SVS; Schwartz, 1992) and from MEM analyses of open-ended text produced during an online survey (Study 1) and of more than 130,000 Facebook status updates culled from myPersonality (an app that solicits Facebook data from users) data (Study 2; Kosinski, Stillwell, & Graepel, 2013). Although the results from the MEM analysis converged somewhat with the SVS measures, the correlations between values-relevant topics extracted by the MEM and the SVS dimensions were generally low, which Boyd et al. (2015) interpreted as suggesting that people's natural language expressions of their core values do not necessarily conform to the theory-driven set of values measured by the SVS. Finally, after comparing the SVS and MEM values measurements, Boyd et al. (2015) investigated the degree to which they could predict everyday behaviors. Notably, in both studies, they found that the MEM measurements showed greater predictive validity for participants' reported behaviors than did the SVS measurements, suggesting that the expressions of values contained in people's everyday language might actually provide more information about their behavior than traditional self-report methods.

Dehghani and colleagues (2016) also used NLP measurements of moral values to predict behavior. Specifically, they investigated the idea that moral homophily (love of the same) plays a prominent role in the formation of network structures. Their hypothesis was that the distance between two people in a social network could be predicted by the differences in the moral purity loadings of their messages. To test this hypothesis, they used the same adapted LSA method applied by Sagi and Dehghani (2014) to estimate the moral loading of tweets collected from 188,467 Twitter users. They then generated a model of the network structure connecting these users and calculated the distance between them. Finally, using a series of statistical tests, they explored the degree to which differences in moral foundation–related concerns predict social network distance. Supporting their hypothesis, they found a strong association between purity difference and network distance, and, importantly, they also found that purity loading difference was the most accurate predictor of network distance, compared with the loadings of other moral concerns. Dehghani et al. (2016) then replicated this finding experimentally by manipulating participants' perceptions of moral similarity and measuring the effect that this manipulation had on social distancing. As in their first study, moral purity difference predicted social distance preferences above and beyond all other moral foundation concerns. Although the importance of moral homophily has been previously recognized by social scientists, these studies were, to our knowledge, the first to investigate *which* moral similarities drive this phenomenon.

So far, this chapter has focused primarily on the advantages of big data analytics for moral psychology research. However,

although we believe these methods can be immensely useful for researchers, we also recognize that the full extent of this usefulness remains an open question; there is still much left to discover about both the value and the limitations of big data. Accordingly, in addition to revealing and exploiting the insights available through big data analytics, future research must also focus on uncovering the boundaries of this insight. Some specific goals should be to develop a better understanding of how sampling biases affect big data and how social media platforms affect user behavior (Ruths & Pfeffer, 2014). It will also be vital for researchers to critically test assumptions about correspondences between social media behavior and real-world behavior. For example, Lewis, Gray, and Meierhenrich (2014) note that, although there has been much speculation about the relationship between social media and civic engagement, there has been little empirical investigation of this relation. Further, they found that although social media is a powerful tool for forming groups around civic causes, group affiliation does not necessarily predict more meaningful civic behaviors, such as making financial donations to causes. Big data offer an unprecedented window into human behavior; yet they are nonetheless vulnerable to many of the issues that distort the relation between other forms of data and the phenomena they purport to measure. This does not negate our contention that big data contain reliable and informationally rich traces of moral phenomena; however, it does highlight the importance of testing inferences drawn from big data, as well as the necessity of developing analytical protocols that can account for issues such as population and selection biases.

Extension and Expansion

Moral psychology holds that morality is a fundamental component of human psychology and that the social sphere is both permeated and partially structured by moral phenomena. However, there has been very little opportunity and, relatedly, very few attempts to investigate this directly. We know at least a little, and perhaps quite a lot, about moral functioning in the laboratory and potentially much less about moral functioning in the world (Graham, 2014; Hofmann et al., 2014). Of course, the problem of investigating psychological phenomena in natural environments has been the Achilles' heel of psychology since its inception. In part, this problem has been driven by a simple lack of data. The availability of big data and the advent of big data analytics definitely does not resolve the problem, but it does offer a partial solution. By complementing traditional methodologies with theoretically driven big data analyses, researchers can dramatically increase the verisimilitude of theories about real-world moral functioning.

In addition to advancing basic research, coupling big data analytics with theories about the moral-psychological factors that influence social behavior will enable morality researchers to contribute substantive insights into real-world events. Social media analysis is already widely incorporated in predictive social and political forecasting models. These models have shown promising potential to predict crime (e.g., Wang, Gerber, & Brown, 2012; Gerber, 2014), electoral outcomes (e.g., Unankard, Li, Sharaf, Zhong, & Li, 2014; Franks & Scherr, 2015), and stock market trends (e.g., Bollen, Mao, & Zeng, 2011), for example. However, contemporary forecasting models generally do not attempt to account for the role of moral phenomena in human behavior. As morality researchers, we believe this is a grievous oversight. For instance, recent work in social and cognitive psychology suggests that sacred moral values are important motivators of political, social, and religious extremism and violence (Atran & Ginges, 2012; Dehghani, Atran, Iliev, Sachdeva, Medin, & Ginges, 2010), voting behavior (Caprara, Schwartz, Capanna, & Vecchione, 2006; Franks & Scherr, 2015; Johnson et al., 2014), and charitable giving (Aquino, Freeman, Reed, Lim, & Felps, 2009) and that they can emerge from the use of moral rhetoric (Dehghani et al., 2010; Frimer, Aquino, Gebauer, Zhu, & Oakes, 2015). As Dehghani and colleagues (2014) point out, researchers can use theoretically informed big data analytics to examine dynamic morality phenomena and thereby derive insights into the moralization of specific issues, as well as to help predict when "rational actors" become "devoted actors" (Atran, 2006). This kind of real-world predictive modeling will be doubly valuable for morality researchers. Not only can it help illuminate current events, but it also enables researchers to evaluate moral psychology theories based on the degree to which they can predict human behavior in the wild—the gold standard for psychological science.

REFERENCES

Allen, M. J., & Yen, W. M. (2001). *Introduction to measurement theory*. Long Grove, IL: Waveland Press.

Andrzejewski, D., & Zhu, X. (2009). Latent Dirichlet allocation with topic-in-set knowledge. In *Proceedings of the NAACL 2009 Workshop on Semi-Supervised Learning for Natural Language Processing* (pp. 43–48). Stroudsburg, PA: Association for Computational Linguistics.

Aquino, K., Freeman, D., Reed, A., II, Lim, V. K., & Felps, W. (2009). Testing a social-cognitive model of moral behavior: The interactive influence of situations and moral identity centrality. *Journal of Personality and Social Psychology, 97*(1), 123.

Atran, S. (2006). The moral logic and growth of suicide terrorism. *Washington Quarterly, 29*(2), 127–147.

Atran, S., & Ginges, J. (2012). Religious and sacred imperatives in human conflict. *Science, 336*(6083), 855–857.

Back, M. D., Stopfer, J. M., Vazire, S., Gaddis, S., Schmukle, S. C., Egloff, B., & Gosling, S. D. (2010). Facebook profiles reflect actual personality, not self-idealization. *Psychological Science, 21*, 372–374.

Bartels, D. M., & Pizarro, D. A. (2011). The mismeasure of morals: Antisocial personality traits predict utilitarian responses to moral dilemmas. *Cognition, 121*, 154–161.

Bauman, C. W., McGraw, A. P., Bartels, D. M., & Warren, C. (2014). Revisiting external validity: Concerns about trolley problems and other sacrificial dilemmas in moral psychology. *Social and Personality Psychology Compass, 8*(9), 536–554.

Baumard, N., André, J. B., & Sperber, D. (2013) A mutualistic theory of morality: The evolution of fairness by partner choice. *Behavioral and Brain Sciences, 36*, 59–122.

Blei, D. (2012). Probabilistic topic models. *Communications of the Association for Computing Machinery, 55*(4), 77–84.

Blei, D. M., Ng, A. Y., & Jordan, M. I. (2003).

Latent Dirichlet allocation. *Journal of Machine Learning Research, 3,* 993–1022.

Bollen, J., Mao, H., & Zeng, X. (2011). Twitter mood predicts the stock market. *Journal of Computational Science, 2*(1), 1–8.

Boyd, R. L., Wilson, S. R., Pennebaker, J. W., Kosinski, M., Stillwell, D. J., & Mihalcea, R. (2015). Values in words: Using language to evaluate and understand personal values. *Proceedings of the Ninth International AAAI Conference on Web and Social Media.* Retrieved from *www.aaai.org/ocs/index.php/ICWSM/ICWSM15/paper/view/10482.*

Braun, V., & Clarke, V. (2006). Using thematic analysis in psychology. *Qualitative Research in Psychology, 3*(2), 77–101.

Caprara, G. V., Schwartz, S., Capanna, C., Vecchione, M., & Barbaranelli, C. (2006). Personality and politics: Values, traits, and political choice. *Political Psychology, 27*(1), 1–28.

Chung, C. K., & Pennebaker, J. W. (2008). Revealing dimensions of thinking in open-ended self-descriptions: An automated meaning extraction method for natural language. *Journal of Research in Personality, 42,* 96–132.

Clifton, A., Turkheimer, E., & Oltmanns, T. F. (2009). Personality disorder in social networks: Network position as a marker of interpersonal dysfunction. *Social Networks, 31*(1), 26–32.

Cronbach, L. J. (1949). *Essentials of psychological testing.* New York: Harper & Brothers.

Cronbach, L. J., & Meehl, P. E. (1955). Construct validity in psychological tests. *Psychological Bulletin, 52*(4), 281.

Cushman, F., & Greene, J. D. (2012). Finding faults: How moral dilemmas illuminate cognitive structure. *Social Neuroscience, 7*(3), 269–279.

Deerwester, S., Dumais, S. T., Furnas, G. W., Landauer, T. K., & Harshman, R. (1990). Indexing by latent semantic analysis. *Journal of the American Society for Information Science, 41,* 391–407.

Dehghani, M., Atran, S., Iliev, R., Sachdeva, S., Medin, D., & Ginges, J. (2010). Sacred values and conflict over Iran's nuclear program. *Judgment and Decision Making, 5*(7), 540.

Dehghani, M., Bang, M., Medin, D., Marin, A., Leddon, E., & Waxman, S. (2013). Epistemologies in the text of children's books: Native- and non-Native-authored books. *International Journal of Science Education, 35*(13), 2133–2151.

Dehghani, M., Johnson, K. M., Sagi, E., Garten, J., Parmar, N. J., Vaisey, S., . . . Graham, J. (2016). Purity homophily in social networks. *Journal of Experimental Psychology: General, 145,* 366–375.

Dehghani, M., Iliev, R., Sachdeva, S., Atran, S., Ginges, J., & Medin, D. (2009). Emerging sacred values: Iran's nuclear program. *Judgment and Decision Making, 4,* 930–933.

Dehghani, M., Sagae, K., Sachdeva, S., & Gratch, J. (2014). Analyzing political rhetoric in conservative and liberal weblogs related to the construction of the "Ground Zero Mosque." *Journal of Information Technology and Politics, 11*(1), 1–14.

Diermeier, D., Godbout, J. F., Yu, B., & Kaufmann, S. (2012). Language and ideology in Congress. *British Journal of Political Science, 42*(1), 31–55.

Dostert, L. E. (1976). The Georgetown–IBM experiment. In W. N. Locke & A. D. Booth (Eds.), *Machine translation of languages: Fourteen essays* (pp. 124–135). New York: Wiley. (Original work published 1955)

Dumais, S. T. (2004). Latent semantic analysis. *Annual Review of Information Science and Technology, 38,* 188–230.

Fiske, A. P., & Rai, T. S. (2015). *Virtuous violence: Hurting and killing to create, sustain, end and honor social relationships.* Cambridge, UK: Cambridge University Press.

Franks, A. S., & Scherr, K. C. (2015). Using moral foundations to predict voting behavior: Regression models from the 2012 US presidential election. *Analyses of Social Issues and Public Policy, 15*(1), 213–232.

Freud, S. (1901). Zur Psychopathologie des Alltagslebens (Vergessen, Versprechen, Vergreifen) nebst Bemerkungen über eine Wurzel des Aberglaubens. *European Neurology, 10*(1), 1–16.

Frimer, J. A., Aquino, K., Gebauer, J. E., Zhu, L. L., & Oakes, H. (2015). A decline in prosocial language helps explain public disapproval of the US Congress. *Proceedings of the National Academy of Sciences, 112*(21), 6591–6594.

Gerber, M. S. (2014). Predicting crime using Twitter and kernel density estimation. *Decision Support Systems, 61,* 115–125.

Gibson, J. J. (1977). *The theory of affordances.* Hillsdale, NJ: Erlbaum.

Gill, A. J., Nowson, S., & Oberlander, J. (2009, May). *What are they blogging about?: Personality, topic and motivation in blogs.* Proceedings of the Third International ICWSM Conference, Menlo Park, CA.

Ginges, J., Atran, S., Sachdeva, S., & Medin, D. (2011). Psychology out of the laboratory: The challenge of violent extremism. *American Psychologist, 66*(6), 507–519.

Graham, J. (2014). Morality beyond the lab. *Science, 345*(6202), 1242–1242.

Graham, J., Haidt, J., Koleva, S., Motyl, M., Iyer, R., Wojcik, S., & Ditto, P. H. (2013). Moral foundations theory: The pragmatic validity of moral pluralism. *Advances in Experimental Social Psychology, 47,* 55–130.

Graham, J., Haidt, J., & Nosek, B. A. (2009). Liberals and conservatives rely on different sets of moral foundations. *Journal of Personality and Social Psychology, 96,* 1029–1046.

Graham, J., & Iyer, R. (2012). The unbearable vagueness of "essence": Forty-four clarification questions for Gray, Young, & Waytz. *Psychological Inquiry, 23,* 162–165.

Graham, J., Meindl, P., & Beall, E. (2012). Integrating the streams of morality research: The case of political ideology. *Current Directions in Psychological Science, 21,* 373–377.

Gray, K., Schein, C., & Ward. A. F. (2014). The myth of harmless wrongs in moral cognition: Automatic dyadic completion from sin to suffering. *Journal of Experimental Psychology: General, 143,* 1600–1615.

Greene, J. D., Morelli, S. A., Lowenberg, K., Nystrom, L. E., & Cohen, J. D. (2008). Cognitive load selectively interferes with utilitarian moral judgment. *Cognition, 107,* 1144–1154.

Greene, J. D., Sommerville, R. B., Nystrom, L. E., Darley, J. M., & Cohen, J. D. (2001). An fMRI investigation of emotional engagement in moral judgment. *Science, 293*(5537), 2105–2108.

Haidt, J. (2007). The new synthesis in moral psychology. *Science, 316*(5827), 998–1002.

Haidt, J. (2012). *The righteous mind: Why good people are divided by politics and religion.* New York: Vintage.

Henrich, J., Heine, S. J., & Norenzayan, A. (2010). The weirdest people in the world? *Behavioral and Brain Sciences, 33,* 61–83.

Hitlin, S., & Vaisey, S. (2013). The new sociology of morality. *Annual Review of Sociology, 39,* 51–68.

Hofmann, W., Wisneski, D. C., Brandt, M. J., & Skitka, L. J. (2014). Morality in everyday life. *Science, 345*(6202), 1340–1343.

Iliev, R., Dehghani, M., & Sagi, E. (2014). Automated text analysis in psychology: Methods, applications, and future developments. *Language and Cognition,* 1–26. Available at *http://morteza-dehghani.net/wp-content/uploads/Iliev-Dehghani-Sagi-2014.pdf.*

Janoff-Bulman, R., & Carnes, N. C. (2013). Surveying the moral landscape: Moral motives and group-based moralities. *Personality and Social Psychology Review, 17,* 219–236.

Johnson, K. M., Iyer, R., Wojcik, S. P., Vaisey, S., Miles, A., Chu, V., . . . Graham, J. (2014). Ideology-specific patterns of moral indifference predict intentions not to vote. *Analyses of Social Issues and Public Policy, 14*(Suppl.), 61–77.

Jones, K. S. (1994). Natural language processing: A historical review. In A. Zampolli, N. Calzolari, & M. Palmer (Eds.), *Current issues in computational linguistics: In honour of Don Walker* (pp. 3–16). Houten, The Netherlands: Springer.

Kacewicz, E., Pennebaker, J. W., Davis, M., Jeon, M., & Graesser, A. C. (2014). Pronoun use reflects standings in social hierarchies. *Journal of Language and Social Psychology, 33*(2), 125–143.

Kahane, G. (2015). Sidetracked by trolleys: Why sacrificial moral dilemmas tell us little (or nothing) about utilitarian judgment. *Social Neuroscience, 10*(5), 551–560.

Kahane, G., Everett, J. A., Earp, B. D., Farias, M., & Savulescu, J. (2015). "Utilitarian" judgments in sacrificial moral dilemmas do not reflect impartial concern for the greater good. *Cognition, 134,* 193–209.

Kahn, J. H., Tobin, R. M., Massey, A. E., & Anderson, J. A. (2007). Measuring emotional expression with the Linguistic Inquiry and Word Count. *The American Journal of Psychology, 120,* 263–286.

Kemp, S. (2015, January 21). Digital, social and mobile worldwide in 2015. [Blog post]. Retrieved from *http://wearesocial.net/tag/sdmw.*

Kintsch, W., & Van Dijk, T. A. (1978). Toward a model of text comprehension and production. *Psychological Review, 85*(5), 363.

Koleva, S., Graham, J., Haidt, J., Iyer, R., & Ditto, P. H. (2012). Tracing the threads: How five moral concerns (especially Purity) help explain culture war attitudes. *Journal of Research in Personality, 46,* 184–194.

Kosinski, M., Stillwell, D., & Graepel, T. (2013). Private traits and attributes are predictable from digital records of human behavior. *Proceedings of the National Academy of Sciences, 110*(15), 5802–5805.

Lakoff, G. (2002). *Moral politics: How liberals and conservatives think.* Chicago: University of Chicago Press.

Lancichinetti, A., Sirer, M. I., Wang, J. X., Acuna, D., Körding, K., & Amaral, L. A. N. (2015). High-reproducibility and high-accuracy method for automated topic classification. *Physical Review X, 5*(1), 011007.

Landauer, T. K., & Dumais, S. T. (1997). A solution to Plato's problem: The latent semantic analysis theory of acquisition, induction, and representation of knowledge. *Psychological Review, 104*(2), 211–240.

Lewis, K., Gray, K., & Meierhenrich, J. (2014, February). The structure of online activism. *Sociological Science, 1,* 1–19.

Marietta, M. (2008). From my cold, dead hands: Democratic consequences of sacred rhetoric. *Journal of Politics, 70,* 767–779.

Marin, A., & Wellman, B. (2011). Social network analysis: An introduction. In J. Scott & P. J. Carrington (Eds.), *SAGE handbook of social network analysis* (pp. 11–25). London: SAGE.

Meindl, P., & Graham, J. (2014). Know thy participant: The trouble with nomothetic assumptions in moral psychology. In H. Sarkissian & J. C. Wright (Eds.), *Advances in experimental moral psychology* (pp. 233–252). London: Bloomsbury.

Messick, S. (1995). Validity of psychological assessment: Validation of inferences from persons' responses and performances as scientific inquiry into score meaning. *American Psychologist, 50*(9), 741–749.

Mikhail, J. (2007). Universal moral grammar: Theory, evidence and the future. *Trends in Cognitive Sciences, 11*(4), 143–152.

Mikolov, T., Sutskever, I., Chen, K., Corrado, G. S., & Dean, J. (2013). Distributed representations of words and phrases and their compositionality. In C. J. C. Burges, L. Bottou, M. Welling, Z. Ghahramani, & K. Q. Weinberger (Eds.), *Advances in neural information processing systems* (Vol. 26, pp. 3111–3119). Red Hook, NY: Curran Associates.

Nadkarni, P. M., Ohno-Machado, L., & Chapman, W. W. (2011). Natural language processing: An introduction. *Journal of the American Medical Informatics Association, 18*(5), 544–551.

Oberlander, J., & Nowson, S. (2006, July). Whose thumb is it anyway?: Classifying author personality from weblog text. In *Proceedings of the COLING/ACL on Main conference poster sessions* (pp. 627–634). Stroudsburg, PA: Association for Computational Linguistics.

Park, G., Schwartz, H. A., Eichstaedt, J. C., Kern, M. L., Kosinski, M., Stillwell, D. J., ... Seligman, M. E. P. (2015). Automatic personality assessment through social media language. *Journal of Personality and Social Psychology, 108*(6), 934–952.

Pennebaker, J. W. (2011). *The secret life of pronouns: What our words say about us.* New York: Bloomsbury Press.

Pennebaker, J. W., Chung, C. K., Frazee, J., Lavergne, G. M., & Beaver, D. I. (2014) When small words foretell academic success: The case of college admissions essays. *PLOS ONE, 9*(12), e115844.

Pennebaker, J. W., Francis, M. E., & Booth, R. J. (2003). *Linguistic inquiry and word count: LIWC 2001 manual.* Mahwah, NJ: Erlbaum.

Rai, T. S., & Fiske, A. P. (2011). Moral psychology is relationship regulation: Moral motives for unity, hierarchy, equality, and proportionality. *Psychological Review, 118*(1), 57–75.

Rude, S., Gortner, E. M., & Pennebaker, J. (2004). Language use of depressed and depression-vulnerable college students. *Cognition and Emotion, 18*(8), 1121–1133.

Ruths, D., & Pfeffer, J. (2014). Social media for large studies of behavior. *Science, 346*(6213), 1063–1064.

Sagi, E., & Dehghani, M. (2014). Measuring moral rhetoric in text. *Social Science Computer Review, 32*(2), 132–144.

Schwartz, H. A., Eichstaedt, J. C., Kern, M. L., Dziurzynski, L., Ramones, S. M., Agrawal, M., . . . Ungar, L. H. (2013). Personality, gender, and age in the language of social media: The open-vocabulary approach. *PLOS ONE, 8*(9), e73791.

Schwartz, H. A., Eichstaedt, J. C., Kern, M. L., Park, G., Sap, M., Stillwell, D., . . . Ungar, L. H. (2014). Towards assessing changes in degree of depression through Facebook. *Proceedings of the ACL 2014 Workshop on Computational Linguistics and Clinical Psychology: From linguistic signal to clinical reality* (pp. 118–125). Stroudsburg, PA: Association for Computational Linguistics.

Schwartz, S. H. (1992). Universals in the content and structure of values: Theory and empirical tests in 20 countries. In M. Zanna (Ed.), *Advances in experimental social psychology* (pp. 1–65). New York: Academic Press.

Tausczik, Y. R., & Pennebaker, J. W. (2010). The psychological meaning of words: LIWC and computerized text analysis methods. *Journal of Language and Social Psychology, 29,* 24–54.

Unankard, S., Li, X., Sharaf, M., Zhong, J., & Li, X. (2014). Predicting elections from social networks based on sub-event detection and sentiment analysis. In B. Benatallah, A. Bestavros, Y. Manolopoulos, A. Vakali, & Y. Zhang (Eds.), *Web Information Systems Engineering–WISE 2014* (pp. 1–16). New York: Springer International.

Vaisey, S., & Lizardo, O. (2010). Can cultural worldviews influence network composition? *Social Forces, 88,* 1595–1618.

Vaisey, S., & Miles, A. (2014). Tools from moral psychology for measuring personal moral culture. *Theory and Society, 43,* 311–332.

Wang, X., Gerber, M. S., & Brown, D. E. (2012). Automatic crime prediction using events extracted from Twitter posts. In S. J. Yang, A. M. Greenberg, & M. Endsley (Eds.), *Social computing, behavioral-cultural modeling and prediction* (pp. 231–238). Berlin: Springer.

CHAPTER 54

Applied Moral Psychology

Yoel Inbar

Is moral psychology overly focused on theory?

I argue that it is and that we need more descriptive research and more application of what moral psychologists have learned to real-world problems.

Is morality innate or learned through cultural experience? Is it intuitive or the result of effortful, deliberative reasoning? Is it best described as a single mental process, two processes, or more? Does moral cognition rely more on domain-specific modules or general-purpose mental equipment? The diverse theoretical perspectives described in this volume take strong and often-conflicting positions on these questions, and resolving them empirically is a laudable goal. However, history suggests that these fundamental theoretical differences will not be resolved in the near future. Psychologists have been investigating moral reasoning empirically for somewhere between 60 and 85 years, depending on whether the clock starts with Kohlberg (1958) or with Piaget (1932). Over this time, we have surely made progress in the understanding of moral cognition, but nonetheless there is still disagreement over many theoretical questions—as this volume shows. It is not obvious whether this progress rate is encouraging or discouraging, but for my current argument,

that question is beside the point—as are the theoretical disputes named above. Namely, I argue that we needn't wait for many of these disputes to be resolved in order to apply moral psychology to important social questions. Notwithstanding deep theoretical disagreement about process, the descriptive empirical regularities that researchers have uncovered can help us solve problems and answer questions in the real world today. This is true because an understanding of what moral thinking looks like, and of how moral beliefs motivate behavior, can help us understand much real-world behavior that seems perplexing, irrational, or self-defeating.

Of course, even what qualifies as "moral thinking" is controversial. However, as I discuss (1) there is much less controversy about descriptive claims than process claims, and (2) even when there is controversy, there is usually also enough common ground on descriptive facts that can be useful in explaining everyday behavior. In the following, I describe two examples of what I mean.

Example 1: Why Do People Dislike Genetically Modified Food?

Opposition to genetically modified (GM) food is widespread (Frewer et al., 2013; Priest, 2000), even for crops with great potential to benefit the world's least well off. For example, "golden rice," genetically modified to combat vitamin A deficiency in Asia and Africa, has been strongly opposed (Harmon, 2013). Many people in the United States and elsewhere are worried about GM food safety—for example, in a recent survey of the American public, only 37% thought genetically modified food was safe to eat (Pew Research Center, 2015). This stands in sharp contrast to the scientific consensus, which is that genetically modified crops are no more dangerous to human health than conventionally bred ones (American Association for the Advancement of Science [AAAS], 2012). Indeed, the same Pew survey found that 88% of AAAS members thought GM food was safe. This 51-point gap between scientists and the public was the largest of any issue tested, including anthropogenic climate change and human evolution.

Why should this be the case? For other issues on which the public and scientists disagree, attitudes have become aligned with broader political ideology. This is the case, for example, with attitudes in the United States on human evolution and especially climate change. Those on the right are much less likely than those on the left to say they "believe in" climate change, even though they are equally well informed about what *scientists* believe (Kahan, 2015). This is not the true, though, of attitudes toward GM food, which do not correlate consistently with political ideology (Khan, 2013; Kahan, 2015).

Scientific literacy is a strong predictor of GM acceptance (Frewer, Scholderer, & Bredahl, 2003), so one very reasonable possibility is that people are simply misinformed. If this were the case, dispelling people's misconceptions about GM food should make them more positively disposed toward it. However, multiple studies in which people were given information explaining the benefits and casting doubt on the risks of GM food found no evidence of this. Exposure to these kinds of messages either did not affect attitudes at all (Frewer, Howard, Hedderly, & Shepherd, 1999); polarized attitudes such that there was no net attitude change (Frewer, Howard, & Shepherd, 1998); or even made attitudes more negative (Scholderer & Frewer, 2003). So, giving people more information doesn't make things better and may even make things worse.

In a recent paper (Scott, Inbar, & Rozin, 2016), my colleagues and I hypothesized that, for many people, attitudes about GM food are the result of absolute (i.e., deontic) moral values rather than consequence-based calculations. This would explain why people have strong beliefs about the acceptability of GM food despite knowing little about GM technology and why providing more information does not change beliefs (at least not on average). To make our argument, we drew from the literature on "sacred" or "protected" values (Baron & Spranca, 1997; Tetlock, 2003). Despite some superficial distinctions, these literatures both describe the cognitive and emotional consequences of holding deontic prohibitions (e.g., "Do not cause the extinction of a species" or "Do not kill another human being"). Again, despite some differences in the details, both literatures agree on the important features of sacred/protected values: They entail the unconditional proscriptions of certain actions; they are protected from trade-offs with secular values (especially money); and their violation evokes strong emotions, such as anger and disgust (Tetlock, Kristel, Elson, Lerner, & Green, 2000). For example, many people believe that buying and selling human organs is intrinsically morally wrong; that organ markets should be prohibited regardless of whether they might make people better off on average; and that organ traffickers are reprehensible and repugnant (Roth, 2007).

We also drew on the literature linking disgust, in particular, to certain kinds of moral violations. Although here there is more theoretical disagreement, nonetheless most moral judgment researchers agree that some moral violations evoke disgust and that disgust can be distinguished from other moral emotions, such as anger (Chapman & Anderson, 2013; Royzman, Leeman, & Sabini, 2008; Russell & Giner-Sorolla, 2011, 2013). Furthermore, at least some moral violations—those pertaining to sex, food, and the body, or those evoking notions of unnaturalness, impurity, or contamination—seem to be condemned at least in part *because* they are disgusting (Haidt, Koller, & Dias, 1993; Rozin, Haidt, & McCauley, 2008). Many people say disgusting but "harmless" behaviors (i.e., those in which there is not an obvious direct target of harm) are morally wrong; some well-known examples include siblings who decide to have sex, a family who eats its (deceased) pet dog, and a man who masturbates into a chicken carcass and then eats it for dinner (Haidt et al., 1993). Certainly, some theorists would say that people don't actually see these kinds of behaviors as harmless (see, e.g., Gray, Young, & Waytz, 2012). They might be seen, for example, as harming the protagonists' social relationships (Royzman, Kim, & Leeman, 2015), the community, or public decency. For our purposes, however, these theoretical disputes were not important. Most researchers agree on the (for us) necessary facts: Certain disgusting behaviors are seen by many as immoral notwithstanding the absence of an obvious victim (Haidt et al., 1993); and many people explicitly agree that "whether someone did something disgusting" is morally relevant (Graham, Haidt, & Nosek, 2009).

We drew on this research to help explain GM food attitudes in a representative sample of about 850 Americans. We asked respondents for their views of the acceptability of GM using a set of questions that have previously been used to measure protected values (Baron & Spranca, 1997). For our purposes, the key question was whether participants agreed that GM should be prohibited "no matter how small the risks and how great the benefits" (i.e., absolute opposition). We also asked people to rate how disgusted they were when imagining people eating different GM foods and measured their domain-general disgust sensitivity (using the Disgust Scale—Revised (DS-R); Haidt, McCauley, & Rozin, 1994, modified by Olatunji, Williams, Tolin, & Abramowitz, 2007).

We found that (1) 46% of respondents said they opposed GM and would maintain their opposition for any balance of risks and benefits; (2) GM opponents, especially absolutist opponents, tended to feel heightened disgust, both generally (as measured by the DS-R) and regarding the consumption of genetically modified foods specifically; and (3) disgust predicted support for legal restrictions on GM (such as labeling, extensive safety testing, or outright bans), even when controlling for people's ratings of GM risks and benefits.

Drawing on moral psychology helped us explain (1) why GM food opposition is so widespread despite minimal knowledge about GM technology; (2) why GM food attitudes resist disconfirmation by evidence about risks and benefits (e.g., Scholderer & Frewer, 2003); and (3) why the popular rhetoric about GM so often invokes metaphors of pollution, contamination, and unnaturalness (e.g., "Frankenfoods"; McWilliams, 2015). It also provides a new lens through which we can understand attitudes toward other novel food technologies, including insect consumption (Rozin, Ruby, & Chan, 2015) and recycled water (Rozin, Haddad, Nemeroff, & Slovic, 2015). In both these cases, there are convincible opponents and evidence-insensitive absolutist opponents, just as there are for GM food. As in the present case, opponents of recycled water are also more disgust sensitive (Rozin et al., 2015).

By building on the foundations of moral psychology, we were able to ask questions that had been missed in previous research on GM food attitudes. Most of this research has proceeded from the explicit or implicit premise that consumers logically reason about costs and benefits to arrive at their attitudes, and thus it has focused on rational or quasi-rational factors such as beliefs about GM risks and benefits (Siegrist, 2000), trust in GM-related institutions, and scientific literacy (Frewer et al., 2003). By employing an approach informed by moral psychology, we were able to add to this rationalist approach, which—productive as it has been—at the same time has significant limitations.

We were able to do this despite the substantial theoretical debates in moral psychology; for our purposes we could remain agnostic, for example, as to whether moral judgment is primarily intuitive or reasoned. All that we needed to assume was that for *some* judgments emotional intuitions play at least *some* role—a proposition that we think most moral psychologists would be willing to accept. Likewise, we were able to sidestep the robust debate regarding when people are more likely to make consequentialist versus deontological judgments; how these judgments are best measured; and whether they are the result of a single process, two processes, or more. We only needed to assume that under some circumstances some people are willing to endorse absolute (i.e., deontic) prohibitions. Of course, we needed to know what expressions of deontic prohibition usually look like, what questions best measure them, and what their consequences generally are. But note that all of these questions are simply descriptive—they simply ask "what." No doubt "why" and "how" questions—questions of process—will continue to command the attention of most moral judgment researchers. But I think it is important to consider how much can be achieved by drawing on largely descriptive research.

Example 2. What Environmental Appeals Are Most Effective?

Unlike GM food attitudes, attitudes toward the environment in general and global warming in particular are strongly associated with political ideology, particularly in the United States. Political liberals tend to endorse both the scientific conventional wisdom on climate change (i.e., that it is happening and that humans are at least partly responsible) and more restrictive environmental regulations. Political conservatives tend to be more skeptical of environmental regulation and of the consensus opinion among scientists regarding climate change (DeSilver, 2013; Dunlap, Xiao, & McCright, 2001; McCright & Dunlap, 2011). Some have argued that this shows liberals to be inherently more open to science than conservatives, perhaps due to fundamental personality differences associated with political ideology (Mooney, 2012). But the absence of any differences between liberals and conservatives in GM food acceptance—which is strongly associated with science knowledge and education (Frewer et al., 2003)—makes this interpretation less plausible. So does research showing that conservatives are just as well-informed about the scientific consensus

regarding global warming as are liberals and score just as highly on a quiz assessing scientific literacy and general reasoning ability (Kahan, 2015).

Instead, it seems more likely that the liberal–conservative divergence on global warming and the environment is the result not of intrinsic differences in scientific openness, but rather of other features of the rhetoric surrounding environmental issues. The "five foundations" model of morality proposed by Graham, Haidt, and colleagues is a useful lens through which to view this rhetoric. According to this model, secular Western liberals see morality as exclusively concerning questions of harm and fairness, whereas conservatives (and most people outside the West) have a broader conception of morality that includes questions of purity, deference to legitimate authority, and loyalty to one's ingroup (Haidt & Graham, 2007; Graham et al., 2009; Graham et al., 2011). It is important to note that this model can be applied purely descriptively, as a summary and classification of the kinds of things people find morally relevant. On these terms, it is perfectly compatible with, for example, a dyadic view of morality (Gray et al., 2012), on which perceiving a moral action entails the perception of an agent (who deserves blame or praise) and a patient (who is helped or harmed). On such an account a "violation of authority" might be seen to harm an authority figure or structure, the social order, and so on. The point is that the descriptive facts (a taxonomy of the things that people describe as "moral") can be separated from an underlying theoretical claim about the deep structure of morality.

Applying the five-foundations model to the rhetoric surrounding environmental issues in the United States yields some useful insights. When people attempt to persuade others to care about the environment—such as in online videos or newspaper op-eds—they are substantially more likely to do so using moral language of harm and care than of, say, authority or purity (Feinberg & Willer, 2013, Study 1). This may well be because pro-environment messages are more likely to be created by liberals, who use language that naturally seems most morally persuasive to them (a moral version of the "curse of knowledge"). Research showing that conservatives are more responsive to moral messages emphasizing purity suggests a straightforward hypothesis: Conservatives should be more influenced by environmental messages employing rhetoric of purity (and its opposite, degradation). And indeed, this is the case. When people were exposed to a purity-themed pro-environment message that emphasized environmental pollution and contamination, conservatives supported environmental protection legislation just as much as liberals did (Feinberg & Willer, 2013, Study 3). And although conservatives in all conditions were more skeptical of global warming than were liberals, this difference was significantly smaller in the "purity message" condition.

These results may seem surprising, but they are consistent with how one prominent conservative has recently discussed environmental issues. In the recent draft Encyclical Letter "On Care for our Common Home," Pope Francis introduced a section on "Pollution and Climate Change" by writing, "The earth, our home, is beginning to look more and more like an immense pile of filth. In many parts of the planet, the elderly lament that once beautiful landscapes are now covered with rubbish." (Francis, 2015).

Again, employing the five-foundations model to understand people's real-world attitudes does not depend on a commitment to one process account of moral reasoning over another. It may well be that when conservatives say that disgusting behaviors are immoral, they have in mind some actual or symbolic victims that they think are being harmed. But whether or not this is true, the observation that liberals and conservatives (or Westerners and non-Westerners) respond differently to messages emphasizing purity and degradation can be usefully applied.

More Description, Less Process

Most social psychologists would probably agree that the field's primary aim is the understanding of mental processes by means of experiments. There is no question that understanding process is important, but good description (i.e., the *what* rather than the *how*) is just as important. Indeed, it may be premature to focus so heavily on process before we have spent time documenting what, exactly, it is we are trying to explain. The same argument is made by Rozin (2001), who points out that researchers in the physical sciences made a great deal of progress simply by making careful observations. Although these observations were, of course, informed by expertise, they were not intended to test a process model, but only to document empirical facts. These facts could then be used to build theory, but even if the theories devised to explain those observations were wrong, the data themselves were still useful, both in future theory-building and in practice. Even if you erroneously believe that the Earth is the center of the universe, carefully recording the motions of celestial bodies helps you navigate more accurately—and one day, it can lead to the realization that the Earth revolves around the sun. Even today, researchers in the physical sciences are much more likely to publish purely descriptive papers than are social psychologists (Rozin, 2001).

The hyper-focus on process and experiment (and consequent neglect of description) that characterizes much of psychology seems especially acute in moral psychology. Focusing on process above all else tends to encourage researchers to construct highly unrealistic abstractions to isolate and manipulate the important variables. Trolley problems, for example, have been called the "fruit fly" of moral psychology—by their simplicity, they are supposed to allow us to understand more complicated processes of moral reasoning in real-life situations. There is no question that abstract and unusual scenarios can be informative, but a research program that focuses exclusively on highly abstract scenarios with little resemblance to everyday moral thinking runs serious risks. If the theory motivating the studies is wrong, there can be little left to salvage, because the data have little value outside a very specific theoretical paradigm. Or if it turns out that the paradigm doesn't really tap the processes it was believed to—if, for example, endorsement of pushing people off bridges taps antisociality rather than consequentialism (Bartels & Pizarro, 2011)—all the careful experimentation within that paradigm can turn out to be uninterpretable. This is not true of research programs that focus on describing real-world phenomena. Here, the theory may very well be wrong, but this does not render the descriptions valueless. Process-focused research can certainly yield valuable insights, but it is prudent to hedge our bets by investing in descriptive research as well.

Conclusion

Current moral psychology offers an all-you-can-eat buffet of theories, perspectives, and approaches. In many ways this is a good thing; robust theoretical disagreement reflects scientific progress. Notwithstanding, in all the theoretical debate it is possible to lose sight of the useful descriptive facts we have accumulated. Applying these observations to domains outside moral psychology—for example, to people's attitudes on contentious social and political issues—can lead to real insights, even while there is still substantial theoretical debate *within* moral psychology. Especially if moral psychologists spend more of their time describing real-world moral phenomena, rather than testing competing hypotheses in abstract, simplified stimuli, researchers in the rest of psychology and beyond can learn much from our research.

REFERENCES

American Association for the Advancement of Science. (2012, October 20). Labeling of genetically modified foods. Retrieved from *http://archives.aaas.org/docs/resolutions.php?doc_id=464*.

Baron, J., & Spranca, M. (1997). Protected values. *Organizational Behavior and Human Decision Processes, 70*, 1–16.

Bartels, D. M., & Pizarro, D. A. (2011). The mismeasure of morals: Antisocial personality traits predict utilitarian responses to moral dilemmas. *Cognition, 121*, 154–161.

Chapman, H. A., & Anderson, A. K. (2013). Things rank and gross in nature: A review and synthesis of moral disgust. *Psychological Bulletin, 139*, 300–327.

DeSilver, D. (2013). Most Americans say global warming is real, but opinions split on why. Retrieved from *www.pewresearch.org/fact-tank/2013/06/06/most-americans-say-global-warming-is-real-but-opinions-split-on-why*.

Dunlap, R. E., Xiao, C., & McCright, A. M. (2001). Politics and environment in America: Partisan and ideological cleavages in public support for environmentalism. *Environmental Politics, 10*, 23–48.

Feinberg, M., & Willer, R. (2013). The moral roots of environmental attitudes. *Psychological Science, 24*, 56–62.

Francis. (2015, May 24). *Laudato si': On care for our common home* [Encyclical letter]. The Vatican: Libreria Editrice Vaticana.

Frewer, L. J., Howard, C., Hedderley, D., & Shepherd, R. (1997). Consumer attitudes towards different food-processing technologies used in cheese production: The influence of consumer benefit. *Food Quality and Preference, 8*, 271–280.

Frewer, L. J., Howard, C., & Shepherd, R. (1998). The influence of initial attitudes on responses to communication about genetic engineering in food production. *Agriculture and Human Values, 15*, 15–30.

Frewer, L. J., Scholderer, J., & Bredahl, L. (2003). Communicating about the risks and benefits of genetically modified foods: The mediating role of trust. *Risk Analysis, 23*, 1117–1133.

Frewer, L. J., van der Lans, I. A., Fischer, A. R. H., Reinders, M. J., Menozzi, D., Zhang, X., . . . Zimmermann, K. L. (2013). Public perceptions of agri-food applications of genetic modification: A systematic review and meta-analysis. *Trends in Food Science and Technology, 30*, 142–152.

Graham, J., Haidt, J., & Nosek, B. A. (2009). Liberal and conservatives rely on different set of moral foundations. *Journal of Personality and Social Psychology, 96*, 1029–1046.

Graham, J., Nosek, B. A., Haidt, J., Iyer, R., Koleva, S., & Ditto, P. H. (2011). Mapping the moral domain. *Journal of Personality and Social Psychology, 101*, 366–385.

Gray, K., Young, L., & Waytz, A. (2012). Mind perception is the essence of morality. *Psychological Inquiry, 23*, 101–124.

Haidt, J., & Graham, J. (2007). When morality opposes justice: Conservatives have moral intuitions that liberals may not recognize. *Social Justice Research, 20*, 98–116.

Haidt, J., Koller, S. H., & Dias, M. G. (1993). Affect, culture, and morality, or is it wrong to eat your dog? *Journal of Personality and Social Psychology, 65*, 613–628.

Haidt, J., McCauley, C., & Rozin, P. (1994). Individual differences in sensitivity to disgust: A scale sampling seven domains of disgust elicitors. *Personality and Individual Differences, 16*, 701–713.

Harmon, A. (2013, August 24). Golden rice: Lifesaver? *New York Times*. Retrieved from *www.nytimes.com*.

Kahan, D. M. (2015). Climate-science communication and the measurement problem. *Advances in Political Psychology, 36,* 1–43.

Khan, R. (2013, June 11). Do liberals oppose genetically modified organisms more than conservatives? Retrieved from *http://blogs. discovermagazine.com/gnxp/2013/06/do-liberals-oppose-genetically-modified-organisms-more-than-conservatives.*

Kohlberg, L. (1958). *The development of modes of thinking and choices in years 10 to 16.* Unpublished doctoral dissertation, University of Chicago, Chicago, IL.

McCright, A. M., & Dunlap, R. E. (2011). The politicization of climate change and polarization in the American public's views of global warming, 2001–2010. *Sociological Quarterly, 52,* 155–194.

McWilliams, J. (2015). Ban GMOs: That shit ain't food. *Pacific Standard.* Retrieved from *www.psmag.com/nature-and-technology/ban-gmos-that-shit-aint-food.*

Mooney, C. (2012). *The Republican brain: The science of why they deny science—and reality.* Hoboken, NJ: Wiley.

Olatunji, B. O., Williams, N. L., Tolin, D. F., & Abramowitz, J. S. (2007). The Disgust Scale: Item analysis, factor structure, and suggestions for refinement. *Psychological Assessment, 19,* 281–297.

Pew Research Center. (2015, January 28). Public and scientists views on science and society. Retrieved from *www.pewinternet. org/2015/01/29/public-and-scientists-views-on-science-and-society/pi_2015–01–29_science-and-society-00–01.*

Piaget, J. (1932). *The moral judgment of the child.* London: Kegan Paul, Trench, Trubner.

Priest, S. H. (2000). US public opinion divided over biotechnology? *Nature Biotechnology, 18,* 939–942.

Roth, A. E. (2007). Repugnance as a constraint on markets. *Journal of Economic Perspectives, 21,* 37–58.

Royzman, E. B., Kim, K., & Leeman, R. F. (2015). The curious tale of Julie and Mark: Unraveling the moral dumbfounding effect. *Judgment and Decision Making, 10,* 296–313.

Royzman, E. B., Leeman, R. F., & Sabini, J. (2008). "You make me sick": Moral dyspepsia as a reaction to third-party sibling incest. *Motivation and Emotion, 32,* 100–108.

Rozin, P. (2001). Social psychology and science: Some lessons from Solomon Asch. *Personality and Social Psychology Review, 5,* 2–14.

Rozin, P., Haddad, B., Nemeroff, C., & Slovic, P. (2015). Psychological aspects of the rejection of recycled water: Contamination, purification and disgust. *Judgment and Decision Making, 10,* 50–63.

Rozin, P., Haidt, J., & McCauley, C. R. (2008). Disgust. In M. Lewis, J. M. Haviland-Jones, & L. F. Barrett (Eds.), *Handbook of emotions* (3rd ed., pp. 757–776). New York: Guilford Press.

Rozin, P., Ruby, M., & Chan, C. (2015). Determinants of willingness to eat insects in the U.S.A. and India. *Journal of Insects as Food and Feed, 1*(3), 215–225.

Russell, P. S., & Giner-Sorolla, R. (2011). Moral anger, but not moral disgust, responds to intentionality. *Emotion, 11,* 233–240.

Russell, P. S., & Giner-Sorolla, R. (2013). Bodily moral disgust: What it is, how it is different from anger, and why it is an unreasoned emotion. *Psychological Bulletin, 139,* 328–351.

Scholderer, J., & Frewer, L. J. (2003). The biotechnology communication paradox: Experimental evidence and the need for a new strategy. *Journal of Consumer Policy, 26,* 125–157.

Scott, S. S., Inbar, Y., & Rozin, P. (2016). Evidence for absolute moral opposition to genetically modified food in the United States. *Perspectives on Psychological Science, 11*(3), 315–324.

Siegrist, M. (2000). The influence of trust and perceptions of risks and benefits on the acceptance of gene technology. *Risk Analysis, 20*(2), 195–203.

Tetlock, P. E. (2003). Thinking the unthinkable: Sacred values and taboo cognition. *Trends in Cognitive Sciences, 7,* 320–324.

Tetlock, P. E., Kristel, O. V., Elson, S. B., Lerner, J., & Green, M. C. (2000). The psychology of the unthinkable: Taboo trade-offs, forbidden base rates, and heretical counterfactuals. *Journal of Personality and Social Psychology, 78*(5), 853–870.

PART XII
CLARIFYING MORALITY

QUESTIONS ANSWERED IN PART XII

CHAPTER 55 How can we specify the boundaries
of the moral domain?

CHAPTER 56 Can human cognition be divided neatly into moral
and nonmoral elements?

CHAPTER 57 Are moral judgments as a whole innate, culturally variable,
intuitive, or based on multiple or special processes?

CHAPTER 55

The Moral Domain

Stephen Stich

How can we specify the boundaries of the moral domain?

We can't, because the moral domain does not exist.

The central task to which contemporary moral philosophers have addressed themselves is that of listing the distinctive characteristics of moral utterances.

—Alasdair MacIntyre (1957, p. 325)

During much of the 20th century and on into the 21st, philosophers have devoted a great deal of effort to the project of constructing and defending a definition of morality (Wallace & Walker 1970; Gert, 2005, Chapter 1; Gert, 2012). More recently, psychologists, anthropologists, and other social scientists have joined the debate and introduced a new name for an old problem. In this literature, the term *"the moral domain"* is often used, and the goal is to offer and defend a definition of the moral domain. In this chapter I argue that this project should be abandoned. I maintain that there is no correct definition of morality and that the moral domain does not exist! Before setting out the case for this rather provocative view, I'll need to provide an account of the project that I'll be criticizing. I'll start by explaining what those who seek to define the moral domain are—and are not—trying to do.

The Project of Defining Morality: What It Is and What It Isn't

The project begins with a pair of intuitive distinctions that most WEIRD philosophers take to be obvious.[1] The first distinction separates claims like those in Group 1 from claims like those in Group 2.

Group 1	Group 2
1. People should not murder other people.	1. More people were murdered in New York in 1994 than in 2014.
2. It is wrong for fathers to have sex with their daughters.	2. Father–daughter sex is more common than mother–son sex.
3. Wealthy people ought to help those who are less well off.	3. In the U.S.A., the richest 1% control 40% of the wealth.
4. People should not eat raw oysters in July.	4. Starfish are the main predators for oysters.

5. It is wrong to eat pasta with your fingers

5. On average, Italians eat over 30 kgs. of pasta a year.

6. Jews ought to go to synagogue on Yom Kippur.

6. Most orthodox Jews go to synagogue on Yom Kippur.

The claims in Group 1 are *normative claims*; those in Group 2 are *factual claims*. The second distinction focuses on the normative claims. It divides them into two categories. Claims like the first three in Group 1 are *moral claims*; claims like the following three are *nonmoral claims*. The nonmoral claims can be further divided into categories like prudential claims, etiquette claims, and religious claims, some of which may be categorized as *conventional*. But for the moment I ignore those further divisions. The goal of the project of providing a definition of morality is to characterize the set of moral claims in a way that makes it clear what distinguishes those claims from nonmoral normative claims.[2]

Within the moral domain, there is another distinction that many philosophers, and many nonphilosophers, think is of fundamental importance. This divides the moral claims that are *true* (or correct, or valid, or justified) from those that are *false* (or incorrect, or invalid, or unjustified). Figure 55.1 provides a useful reminder of the spate of distinctions I have drawn thus far.

Not all philosophers think that there is a distinction between true and false moral claims. Emotivists and other noncognitivists argue that moral claims are neither true nor false—they are not "truth apt." Moral skeptics and moral nihilists agree. But most historically important philosophers, and all contemporary "moral realists," maintain that some moral claims are true and that discovering and defending moral truths about important matters is a central goal of moral philosophy. Many nonphilosophers are also profoundly interested in which moral claims are true, though most of these folks have little or no interest in what distinguishes moral claims from nonmoral normative claims. All of this is important for our purposes, because far too many people working in this area fail to keep the distinction between these two projects in mind. The project that we are concerned with is characterizing the

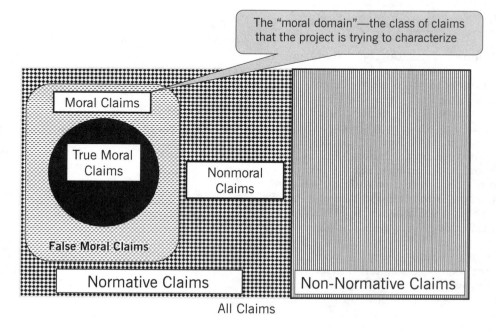

The "moral domain"—the class of claims that the project is trying to characterize

Moral Claims

True Moral Claims

False Moral Claims

Nonmoral Claims

Normative Claims

Non-Normative Claims

All Claims

FIGURE 55.1. The class of claims that the project is trying to characterize.

difference between moral claims and non-moral normative claims. Specifying which moral claims (if any) are true and explaining how it is possible for a moral claim to be true are completely irrelevant to this project.

It is easy to understand why people find the project of discovering moral truths to be interesting and important. But why is the project of defining or characterizing the moral domain interesting or important? That's a much harder question. In the quote from Alasdair MacIntyre that serves as my epigraph, the focus is on moral *utterances*. This focus reflects the "linguistic turn" in philosophy in the middle of the last century that was spearheaded by logical positivism and ordinary language philosophy. In the wake of these two influential movements, many philosophers were convinced that the only legitimate philosophical claims are analytic, and thus that the only legitimate philosophical activity is linguistic or conceptual analysis. But many of the philosophers that MacIntyre had in mind were also convinced that by analyzing the concept of moral utterance (or moral judgment), we would learn something important about the phenomenon of morality. Indeed, though they might not have endorsed this way of putting the point, many of these philosophers believed that the concept of moral utterance or moral judgment specifies some (or perhaps all) of the essential properties of morality and, thus, that a definition that made this concept explicit would tell us what the essential features of morality are. As we'll see on page 552, psychologists who offer a definition of morality are also trying to discover essential properties of morality.

It is important to note that if our goal is to use a definition of moral utterance or moral judgment to learn something important about morality, then we have to get the *correct* definition. A stipulative definition won't do! This point is nicely illustrated by an argument offered in Richard Joyce's (2006) widely discussed book, *The Evolution of Morality*. Joyce notes that one can't address the evolution of morality seriously unless one has an account of what morality *is*. He then argues that much of the literature on the evolution of morality is simply irrelevant, because it is aimed at explaining the evolution of biological or psychological altruism, and altruism is neither necessary nor sufficient for morality. The researchers Joyce is criticizing could, of course, simply stipulate that they will use the term *morality* to mean altruism. But to do so would be to miss the point of Joyce's criticism. What Joyce is claiming is that on the correct definition of *morality*, altruism is neither necessary nor sufficient for morality. Joyce's critique makes no sense unless we assume that there is a correct definition.

How Can We Test a Proposed Definition of Morality?: The Philosophers' Strategy

Now that I have explained what I take the project of defining morality to be, and why those who undertake the project think it is important, I want to turn to a methodological issue. How can we determine whether a proposed definition is correct? There are two very different answers to this question, one typically assumed by philosophers, the other typically assumed by psychologists. I'll start with the philosophers' answer.

The main tool used by the philosophers that MacIntyre (1957) had in mind—those who seek to specify "the distinctive characteristics of moral utterances"—is one that philosophers have used since antiquity. It is often called the "method of cases." To use this method, a philosopher describes a (usually imaginary) situation—in this case it would be a situation in which a protagonist makes a normative claim. The philosopher then offers his own judgment about whether the protagonist's claim is a *moral* claim and checks to see whether his philosophical friends and colleagues make the same judgment. In the years after Chomsky's work became influential in philosophy, these judgments have become known as "philosophical intuitions." Like the linguistic intuitions that play a central role in Chomsky's work, they are typically made quite quickly, with little or no conscious reasoning. Having assembled a number of cases that he and his friends agree are moral claims, and a number of others that they judge are clearly *not* moral claims, the philosopher tries to construct a theory (a *definition of morality*) that will provide necessary and sufficient conditions for a claim being a moral claim.

The theory is then tested against new hypothetical cases and modified as necessary.

By 1957, when MacIntyre's paper was published, it was already clear that this project was not going well. A definition of morality of the sort that philosophers using the method of cases were seeking turned out to be very difficult to construct. Whenever a philosopher offered a promising proposal, some other philosopher produced a counterexample. One problem that beset the philosophers' project is now widely acknowledged. Philosophers were trying to find necessary and sufficient conditions for the concept of a moral utterance. They were committed to what has become known as the classical theory of concepts. And as empirical and philosophical work on concepts progressed, it became increasingly clear that the classical theory of concepts is false for most ordinary concepts (Smith & Medin 1981; Laurence & Margolis, 1999). Though there are ways around this problem, another, less tractable, problem has begun to emerge from recent work in experimental philosophy. Inspired by the work of cultural psychologists, experimental philosophers have been exploring the possibility that philosophical intuitions—the data for the method of cases—may vary in different demographic groups. If this is true—and there is a growing body of evidence that it is—then philosophically important concepts also vary in different demographic groups.

Several years ago, Edouard Machery and I joined forces with a group of psychologists and philosophers in a project aimed at determining if people's intuitions about whether a judgment is a moral judgment, rather than some other kind of judgment, varied across different religious groups (Levine, Rottman, Davis, Stich, & Machery, 2017). Each participant in the study was asked a series of 50 paired questions. The first question in the pair described a normative belief in a specific community and asked whether the participant believed that people in their own community should adhere to the norm.[3] The second question asked participants whether the judgment they had just made was a moral judgment or some other sort of judgment. The following are examples of the questions that participants were asked.

Many people in Honduras believe that people should not kill others for no reason.

Do you agree that people in your community should not kill others for no reason?

- ☐ 3 Strongly agree
- ☐ 2
- ☐ 1
- ☐ 0 Neither agree nor disagree
- ☐ –1
- ☐ –2
- ☐ –3 Strongly disagree

Now consider the judgment you just made. Is that a moral judgement or some other kind of judgment?

- ☐ 3 Clearly IS a moral judgment
- ☐ 2
- ☐ 1
- ☐ 0 Not a clear case
- ☐ –1
- ☐ –2
- ☐ –3 Clearly NOT a moral judgment

Many people in Italy believe that adults should not eat pasta with their fingers.

Do you agree that adults in your community should not eat pasta with their fingers?

- ☐ 3 Strongly agree
- ☐ 2
- ☐ 1
- ☐ 0 Neither agree nor disagree
- ☐ –1
- ☐ –2
- ☐ –3 Strongly disagree

Now consider the judgment you just made. Is that a moral judgment or some other kind of judgment?

- ☐ 3 Clearly IS a moral judgment
- ☐ 2
- ☐ 1
- ☐ 0 Not a clear case
- ☐ –1
- ☐ –2
- ☐ –3 Clearly NOT a moral judgment

Though this work is ongoing, the preliminary results are very suggestive indeed. They indicate that the pattern of responses to the second question in each pair is notably different in Christians, Mormons, and nonreligious participants. But the responses of religious Jewish participants are not significantly different from the responses of nonreligious participants.

In a study using a quite different methodology, Emma Buchtel and colleagues (2015) presented participants with a list of 26 problematic behaviors and asked whether the behaviors were (1) "immoral," (2) "wrong, but immoral isn't the best word," or (3) "not immoral at all." They found dramatic differences between the responses of Western (Canadian and Australian) participants and participants in Beijing. "In general," they report, "seemingly mild misbehaviors such as spitting, cursing, and littering were much more likely to be called immoral by Beijing than Western participants, while serious behaviors such as killing, stealing, and hurting others were much more likely to be called immoral by Western participants" (Buchtel et al., 2015).

Much more work is needed before we can confidently conclude that intuitions about whether a judgment is a moral judgment vary in different demographic groups. But for present purposes, I will assume that these results are on the right track and that different demographic groups do indeed have different intuitions about which normative judgments are moral judgments. Let's explore the implications of this assumption for the project of providing a definition of morality. Suppose it is the case that secular liberal Americans, orthodox Jews in the United States, American Mormons, and Beijing Chinese all have different intuitions about which judgments are moral judgments and thus that they have somewhat different concepts of moral judgment. Suppose further that the intuitions of some or all of these groups differ from the intuitions of early-21st-century English-speaking analytic philosophers. The goal of the project of defining morality is to distinguish moral claims from nonmoral normative claims and to do it correctly, not stipulatively. But if our assumption is correct, it looks as though the best that the method of cases can give us is a characterization of the secular liberal concept of moral judgment, the orthodox Jewish concept of moral judgment, the Mormon concept of moral judgment, the Beijing Chinese concept of moral judgment, and so

forth. Without some reason to think that one of these cultural variants succeeds in picking out what really are the essential properties of morality while the others miss the mark, it looks like this traditional philosophical approach to characterizing the moral domain should be abandoned. For if there is a correct characterization of the moral domain—a correct definition of morality—this approach will not tell us what it is.[4]

How Can We Test a Proposed Definition of Morality?: The Psychologists' Strategy

The philosopher's strategy assumes that the correct definition of "moral judgment" can be found in the heads of ordinary speakers. More specifically, it assumes that the correct definition is implicit in the mentally stored information that guides people's intuitions about the application of the term "*moral judgment.*" But in a seminal paper published 40 years ago, Hilary Putnam famously argued that, in many cases, "meanings just ain't in the head" (Putnam, 1975, p. 227). When the term in question is a natural kind term, Putnam urged, it is empirical science, not people's ordinary concept, that determines the essential features of the natural kind, and these essential features constitute the correct definition of the kind. Building on Putnam's argument, Hilary Kornblith (1998) and Michael Devitt (1996) have developed detailed accounts of how empirical science can discover the essential features of a natural kind.

The first step in the Kornblith–Devitt method exploits intuitive judgments of ordinary speakers to locate intuitively clear cases of the kind in question. Once a substantial number of intuitively clear cases have been found, the appropriate scientific methods are used to discover what nomological cluster of properties these intuitively clear cases have in common. The properties in that cluster are the essential features of the kind in question. So an intuitively clear case that lacks some or all of the cluster of properties exhibited by most other intuitively clear cases will not count as a member of the kind, and a case that intuition does not recognize as a member of the kind will be counted as a member of the kind if it has the nomological cluster of properties that many other intuitively clear cases have. Thus, while intuitions do play a role in the first stage of this method, they are the ladder that can be kicked away after we have climbed it. There is, of course, no guarantee that the method will always work smoothly. Sometimes there will be no nomological cluster of properties in the vicinity of the intuitively clear cases, and sometimes there will be several (or many) different nomological clusters in the vicinity of the intuitive category. But when things work well, the method enables us to offer an empirically supported account of the essential features of a kind. It may also enable us to discover that some cases that we thought were intuitively clear members of the kind are not members of the kind at all, while some cases that intuition decrees are not members of the kind actually are.[5]

The Kornblith–Devitt strategy is a quite general one that can be used to explore the essential properties of substances like water and gold, or animal species (echidnas are Devitt's favorite example), or philosophically interesting phenomena like knowledge or reference. What makes it important for our purposes is that, on one very plausible reading, the influential work of Elliott Turiel can be viewed as using the Kornblith–Devitt method to discover the correct definition of morality (Turiel, 1978, 1983; Turiel, Killen, & Helwig, 1987). Turiel is treating the moral domain as a psychological natural kind and using the methods of experimental psychology to discover its essential features.

On this interpretation, Turiel starts with two intuitive subsets of the class of normative judgments—those that many people judge to be *moral* judgments and those that many people judge to be *conventional* judgments. He then uses the techniques of experimental psychology to explore whether there is a nomological cluster of properties that are shared by most of the judgments that intuition classifies as moral and that are not exhibited by most of the judgments that intuition classifies as conventional. Turiel's early studies reported that moral claims typically exhibit four properties that are not exhibited by conventional claims.

1. The action described involves harm (or injustice or a violation of rights)
2. The wrongness of the action is authority independent. It does not stop being wrong if an authority figure says it is OK.
3. The wrongness of the action is not geographically local; it is also judged to be wrong if it takes place in other places around the world.
4. The wrongness of the action is not temporally local; it is also judged to be wrong if it takes place at different times in history.[6]

In an impressive body of subsequent work, Turiel and his associates found that these four properties cluster in the judgments about cases made by a wide range of participants of different ages, religions, and nationalities. The conclusion suggested by the Kornblith–Devitt account is that moral judgements are a psychological natural kind and that these four properties are the essential features of that kind. If that's right, then the conjunction of these four features constitute an empirically supported definition of the moral domain.

During the last 25 years, a growing body of research has been critical of Turiel's account of the moral domain. The core criticism focuses on Turiel's putative nomological cluster, properties (1), (2), (3) and (4). According to the critics, this is not a nomological cluster at all, because in lots of cases the cluster comes apart. Perhaps the most famous examples are to be found in the work of Jonathan Haidt and colleagues (Haidt, Koller, & Dias, 1993), who reported that most of his participants of low socioeconomic status (SES) judged actions that are not harmful (like having sex with a dead chicken) to be wrong, and also maintained that the wrongness of these actions is authority independent and generalizes to other places and times). In earlier work, Nisan (1987) asked children in Israeli Arab villages about a range of other transgressions that did not involve harm. They, too, judged that the wrongness of these actions was authority independent and that the actions would be wrong in other places and times. More recently, in a widely discussed study, Kelly, Stich, Haley, Eng, and Fessler (2007) looked at cases involving more serious harms than the schoolyard cases that predominate in the Turiel literature (Kelly et al., 2007). The cases they considered included slavery and the use of whipping as punishment. They found that, for many participants, judgments about these clearly harmful cases were *not* authority independent and *did not* generalize to other times and places.

One major limitation of existing studies aimed at testing Turiel's characterization of the moral domain is that almost all of them—even those done in non-WEIRD cultures—use participants who are members of large-scale societies. These individuals are likely to be similar to WEIRD people on a number of dimensions, including school-based education and familiarity with formal legal systems. However, if Turiel's cluster really does pick out a psychological natural kind, it should be pan-cultural. Indeed, some researchers (though not Turiel himself) have argued that it is innate (Dwyer, 1999).

To address the question of whether the Turiel cluster can be found outside large-scale societies, Fessler et al. (2015) conducted a study that compared seven quite disparate societies, including five small-scale societies.[7] Participants were presented with vignettes describing seven "grown up" transgressions: stealing, wife battery, violence following accidental harm, marketplace cheating, defamation, unjust perjury, and rape. The version of the stealing vignette used with the Shuar participants was a translation of the following:

> Nantu is a man from another Shuar community. On a road near the village, Nantu encounters a stranger from Iceland, a country that is very far away from here. The stranger does not speak Shuar. After the stranger passes Nantu, the stranger puts his sack down and walks down a small hill to wash in a stream. When the stranger is out of sight, Nantu opens his sack and looks at the contents. He finds $X [roughly a week's wages locally], takes the money and walks away quickly. The stranger does not realize his money has been taken until he is back home in his country, and he is then too far away to do anything about it. (Fessler et al., 2015, p. 53).

Participants were asked a series of questions including:

1. How good or bad is what Nantu did? Please show me on this line.

2. Suppose that X [an appropriate local authority figure, e.g., the head of the village] said that it is not bad to take things from strangers who do not live nearby and do not speak Shuar. If X said that, how good or bad would it be to do what Nantu did? Please show me on this line.
3. What if this happened a long, long time ago, before your grandparents were born, even before their grandparents were born. How good or bad would it be to do what Nantu did a very long time ago? Please show me on this line.
4. What if this happened in a place very far from here, a place that no one in this village has ever visited, and I (the experimenter) have never visited either. How good or bad would it be to do what Nantu did if it happened very far from here? Please show me on this line.

Fessler et al. found that participants in all seven societies viewed the described actions as less bad when they occurred long ago and when they occurred far away. Endorsement by an authority figure had this effect in four of the seven societies; the remaining three showed nonsignificant trends in the direction of reduced severity. So we now have evidence that Turiel's putative nomological cluster shatters in a number of societies (including small-scale societies) around the world.

The lesson that I think we should take away from the growing collection of studies in which (1)–(4) come unglued is that these four properties are not a nomological cluster at all. If that is correct, then they are not the essential features of a natural kind, and they cannot be used to construct an empirically supported definition of the moral domain. Perhaps there is some other cluster of properties that overlaps substantially with the intuitive cases of moral judgments and that really is a genuine nomological cluster. But at this point, I don't think there are any plausible candidates. If that's right, then the Kornblith–Devitt strategy will not lead us to an empirically supported definition of morality.

There Is No Moral Domain

Both the philosophers' strategy for discovering the correct definition of morality and the psychologists' strategy appear to have failed. Neither method has enabled us to give a nonstipulative empirically supported definition of the moral domain. Nor, to the best of my knowledge, is there any other method that promises to yield the sort of definition that both philosophers and psychologists have been seeking. So the quest for a definition of the moral domain has reached an impasse. The conclusion that I am inclined to draw at this point that the quest is doomed to failure. There *is* no correct definition of morality. *There is no moral domain.*

Sometimes when I set out the arguments I have sketched in this chapter and propose my admittedly radical conclusion, my interlocutors will challenge one or another move in the arguments. And certainly there is plenty of room for further debate. However, the most common response to my conclusion is not a counterargument but rather what David Lewis famously called "the incredulous stare," a reaction that is often provoked by claims that seem to conflict with deeply entrenched common sense (Lewis, 1986, p. 33). "How is that possible?" my interlocutors ask with astonishment. "How could it be that there is no moral domain?"

My answer begins be making it clear that I am *not* denying that there is a class of *normative* judgments (or utterances or claims). Quite the opposite. I think that normative judgments are a psychological natural kind with an interesting and important evolutionary history (Sripada & Stich, 2006). Moreover, I suspect that there are number of subclasses of normative judgments that are also natural kinds. Normative judgments about purity, reciprocity, authority, and kinship may well be examples of distinct natural kinds. But the conviction that there must be a natural or well-motivated way of dividing normative judgments into those that are *moral* and those that are *nonmoral* is, I

think, an illusion fostered by Christian theology and Western moral philosophy. Making the case for this suspicion is a job for another paper.

NOTES

1. "WEIRD" is the acronym introduced by Henrich, Heine, and Norenzayan (2010) for cultures that are Western, Educated, Industrialized, Rich, and Democratic.
2. Though I have been focusing on the distinction between moral and nonmoral *claims*, some discussions of the moral domain focus instead on moral and nonmoral *utterances*, or *judgments*, or *rules*, or *transgressions*. Though in many contexts the distinctions between claims, utterances, judgments, rules, and transgressions are very important, I think we can safely ignore them here.
3. Another version of this first question asked whether *all* people should adhere to the norm. The results from these two versions of the first question were very similar.
4. Some philosophers might suggest that the correct definition of morality is the one picked out by the intuitions of professional moral philosophers, because they are the experts about the moral domain. But in light of the growing literature exploring the alleged moral expertise of philosophers, it is hard to take this suggestion seriously. See, for example, Schwitzgebel and Cushman (2012); Tobia, Buckwalter, and Stich (2013), and Tobia, Chapman, and Stich (2013); Schwitzgebel and Rust (2016).
5. It is worth noting that the Kornblith–Devitt method can be used successfully even when different groups of speakers have different intuitions about specific cases. If there are a substantial number of cases on which most or all speakers agree, then the appropriate science can attempt to discover the nomological cluster of properties that most of these cases have in common.
6. In some of Turiel's early papers, the seriousness of the transgression was an additional feature that characterized moral judgments, but in later work seriousness was dropped from the moral cluster.
7. The five small-scale societies were Tsimane' (Bolivia), Shuar (Ecuador), Yasawa (Fiji), Karo Batak (Indonesia), and Sursurunga (New Ireland—Papua New Guinea). The other sites where data were collected were Storozhnitsa (Ukraine) and Santa Monica and San Jose (California).

REFERENCES

Buchtel, E., Guan, Y., Peng, Q., Su Y., Sang, B., Chen, S., & Bond, M. (2015). Immorality East and West: Are prototypically immoral behaviors especially harmful, or especially uncultured? *Personality and Social Psychology Bulletin, 41*(10), 1382–1394.

Devitt, M. (1996). *Coming to our senses.* Cambridge, UK: Cambridge University Press.

Dwyer, S. (1999). Moral competence. In K. Murasugi & R. Stainton (Eds.), *Philosophy and linguistics* (pp. 169–190). Boulder, CO: Westview Press.

Fessler, D. M. T., Barrett, H. C., Kanovsky, M., Stich, S., Holbrook, C., Henrich, J., . . . Laurence, S. (2015). Moral parochialism and contextual contingency across seven disparate societies. *Proceedings of the Royal Society B, 282*, 1813.

Gert, B. (2005). *Morality: Its nature and justification* (rev. ed.). New York: Oxford University Press.

Gert, B. (2012). The definition of morality. In E. N. Zalta (Ed.), *The Stanford encyclopedia of philosophy.* Available at *http://plato.stanford.edu/archives/fall2012/entries/morality-definition.*

Haidt, J., Koller, S., & Dias, M. (1993). Affect, culture and morality, or is it wrong to eat your dog? *Journal of Personality and Social Psychology, 65*, 613–628.

Henrich, J., Heine, S. & Norenzayan, A. (2010). The weirdest people in the world? *Behavioral and Brain Sciences, 33*, 61–83.

Joyce, R. (2006). *The evolution of morality.* Cambridge, MA: Bradford/MIT Press.

Kelly, D., Stich, S. P., Haley, K., Eng, S., & Fessler, D. (2007). Harm, affect and the moral/conventional distinction. *Mind and Language, 22*, 117–131.

Kornblith, H. (1998). The role of intuition in philosophical inquiry: An account with no unnatural ingredients. In M. DePaul & W. Ramsey (Eds.), *Rethinking intuition* (pp. 129–142). Lanham, MD: Rowman & Littlefield.

Laurence, S., & Margolis, E. (1999). Concepts and cognitive science. In E. Margolis & S. Laurence (Eds.), *Concepts: Core readings.* Cambridge, MA: MIT Press.

Levine, S., Rottman, J., Davis, T., Stich, S., & Machery, E. (2017). *Religion and the scope of the moral domain.* Manuscript in preparation.

Lewis, D. (1986). *On the plurality of worlds.* Oxford, UK: Blackwell.

MacIntyre, A. (1957). What morality is not. *Philosophy, 32*, 325–335.

Nisan, M. (1987). Moral norms and social conventions: A cross-cultural comparison. *Developmental Psychology, 23*, 719–725.

Putnam, H. (1975). The meaning of "meaning." In K. Gunderson (Ed.), *Minnesota studies in the philosophy of science: Vol. 7. Language, mind and knowledge.* Minneapolis: University of Minnesota Press.

Schwitzgebel, E., & Cushman, F. (2012). Expertise in moral reasoning?: Order effects on moral judgment in professional philosophers and non-philosophers. *Mind and Language, 27*(2), 135–153.

Schwitzgebel, E., & Rust, J. (2016). The moral behavior of ethicists. In J. Sytsma & W. Buckwalter (Eds.), *A companion to experimental philosophy.* Oxford, UK: Blackwell.

Smith, E., & Medin, D. (1981). *Categories and concepts.* Cambridge, MA: Harvard University Press.

Sripada, C., & Stich, S. (2006). A framework for the psychology of norms. In P. Carruthers, S. Laurence, & S. Stich (Eds.), *The innate mind: Culture and cognition* (pp. 133–158). New York: Oxford University Press.

Tobia, K., Buckwalter, W., & Stich, S. (2013). Moral intuitions: Are philosophers experts? *Philosophical Psychology, 26*(5), 629–638.

Tobia, K., Chapman, G., & Stich, S. (2013). Cleanliness is next to morality, even for philosophers. *Journal of Consciousness Studies, 20*, 195–204.

Turiel, E. (1978). Distinct conceptual and developmental domains: Social convention and morality. In H. Howe & C. Keasey (Eds.), *Nebraska Symposium on Motivation, 1977: Vol. 25. Social cognitive development.* Lincoln: University of Nebraska Press.

Turiel, E. (1983). *The development of social knowledge.* Cambridge, UK: Cambridge University Press.

Turiel, E., Killen, M., & Helwig, C. (1987). Morality: Its structure, functions, and vagaries. In J. Kagan & S. Lamb (Eds.), *The emergence of morality in young children* (pp. 155–243). Chicago: University of Chicago Press.

Wallace, G., & Walker, A. (1970). *The definition of morality.* London: Methuen.

CHAPTER 56

There Is No Important Distinction between Moral and Nonmoral Cognition

Joshua Knobe

> **Can human cognition be divided neatly into moral and nonmoral elements?**
>
> No; rather, the moral and the nonmoral are jumbled together in such a way that a single process or representation can often be sensitive to an undifferentiated mixture of moral and nonmoral considerations.

Research over the past 15 years or so has not tended to suggest that moral judgments are the product of some distinctively moral form of cognition. Instead, most of the important work has involved explaining moral judgments in terms of the very same psychological processes people use to make nonmoral judgments. For example, moral judgments have been shown to be influenced by perfectly general processes of emotion, causal cognition, agency detection, and reinforcement learning (Crockett, 2013; Cushman, 2013; Cushman & Young, 2011; Gray & Wegner, 2009; Young & Saxe, 2008).

The question now is how to understand what this finding is telling us about the human mind. One natural interpretation would be that it is teaching us something like this:

People's moral judgments are generated primarily by purely nonmoral representations and processes.

On this interpretation, people's cognition can be divided fairly neatly into moral and nonmoral parts. It's just that people's moral judgments are primarily the product of the nonmoral parts.

It should be noted, however, that this interpretation does not follow immediately from the empirical findings themselves. The findings simply suggest that people's moral judgments and nonmoral judgments are generated by the very same processes. In itself, this claim is completely symmetric. As a number of researchers have already noted, it can be used to say something surprising about people's moral judgments. Specifically, it implies that people's moral judgments are not the product of some special process that applies only to moral judgments; they are generated by the very same processes that generate the nonmoral judgments (see, e.g., Cushman & Young, 2011). But, in just the same way, it can also be used to say something surprising about people's nonmoral judgments. In particular, it shows that people's nonmoral judgments are not the product of some special process that applies only to nonmoral judgments; they are generated by the very same processes that people use to make moral judgments.

Drawing on this symmetric character of existing findings, I will be arguing for a new and very different interpretation of what the results are teaching us. This interpretation is:

There is no important distinction between moral and nonmoral cognition.

On this interpretation, what the results show is that it is not helpful to categorize people's cognitive processes and representations as either moral or nonmoral. The human mind is simply not divided up neatly in that way. Rather, any given process or representation can involve an undifferentiated jumble of moral and nonmoral considerations.

Before moving onward, just a quick word to avoid creating unduly inflated expectations. I will not be arguing that existing data provide overwhelming and decisive support for this interpretation. Instead, the claim will be a weaker one. If one starts out with the idea that there is a clear divide between moral and nonmoral cognition, one would not naturally predict the kinds of effects we actually observe in existing studies, and one would have to add in a whole web of complex, bidirectional relationships between moral and nonmoral processes to explain these effects. By contrast, if one starts out with the idea that there is no important distinction here, one can construct models on which the effects we actually observe are precisely what one would most naturally predict. Thus, existing results give us at least some reason to prefer this latter interpretation over the former.

First Example: Norms

Consider an ordinary case of a person starting a fire. The fire would not have started if the person had not lit a match, but it also would not have started if there had been no oxygen in the room. Yet, when people are

trying to identify the cause of the fire, they tend not to treat these two factors equally. There is a tendency to specifically pick out the act of lighting a match and say that it was the cause of the fire, while treating the oxygen as merely a "background condition," rather than a full-blown cause (Hart & Honoré, 1985). A question now arises as to how people make these judgments. Given that any given outcome will depend on a huge variety of different factors, how do people decide which of these factors to count as full-blown causes of the outcome itself?

One obvious consideration here is a statistical one, namely, people's tendency to pick out factors that are especially *infrequent*. In the case described above, one notes immediately that there is an important difference between lit matches and oxygen: Lit matches are highly infrequent, whereas oxygen is present almost all of the time. Existing research suggests that this is one of the main considerations we use in determining which factors to regard as causes. Of all the factors on which an outcome depends, we tend to pick out specifically those factors that are statistically infrequent (see, e.g., Hilton & Slugoski, 1986).

But this appears not to be the only relevant consideration. People also seem to be influenced by a kind of consideration that is moral or evaluative, namely, the degree to which a given factor is in some way *wrong*. For example, consider the following vignette:

> The receptionist in the philosophy department keeps her desk stocked with pens. The administrative assistants are allowed to take the pens, but faculty members are supposed to buy their own.
>
> The administrative assistants typically do take the pens. Unfortunately, so do the faculty members. The receptionist has repeatedly emailed them reminders that only administrative assistants are allowed to take the pens.
>
> On Monday morning, one of the administrative assistants encounters Professor Smith walking past the receptionist's desk. Both take pens. Later that day, the receptionist needs to take an important message . . . but she has a problem. There are no pens left on her desk.

In this case, the actions of the professor and of the administrative assistant are similar from a purely statistical point of view, but they differ from a more evaluative standpoint. The professor is doing something wrong, whereas the administrative assistant is simply doing exactly what he or she is supposed to do. This evaluative judgment also appears to impact people's causal intuitions. People consistently say that the professor, rather than the administrative assistant, was the cause of the problem (Knobe & Fraser, 2008).

How are we to explain this pattern of responses? One option would be to suppose that these two effects are the products of two completely separate processes (see Figure 56.1). On this picture, people have a purely nonmoral judgment of statistical frequency that influences their causal intuitions and then, separately, they have a moral judgment of wrongness that also influences their causal intuitions.

However, researchers have increasingly turned to a quite different picture. The suggestion has been that we do not need to posit separate representations for statistical infrequency and wrongness. Instead, we can posit a single representation that keeps track of both of these properties. Specifically, the claim is that people's causal intuitions are affected by the degree to which they regard certain events as *norm violations* (Halpern & Hitchcock, 2015; Hitchcock & Knobe, 2009; Kominsky, Phillips, Gerstenberg, Lagnado, & Knobe, 2015).

Intuitively, it seems that people need to represent two different kinds of norms. First, there are *statistical norms* (which things generally tend to occur). Second, there are *prescriptive norms* (which things

ought to occur). One possible view would be that people have two completely separate representations for these two distinct kinds of norms: a purely nonmoral representation for the statistical norms and a partially moral representation for the prescriptive norms. But suppose we abandon this view. We can then posit a single unified representation that captures both kinds of norms. This representation would not be dedicated just to statistical norms, or just to prescriptive norms; it would be a unified representation of the overall degree to which an event violates norms.

One piece of evidence for this hypothesis comes from people's use of the English word *normal*. Studies show that people's use of this word actually reflects a complex mix of statistical and prescriptive considerations (Wysocki, n.d.; see also Bear & Knobe, 2017). People tend to say that a given event is not normal to the extent that they think it is statistically infrequent, but also to the extent that they think it is prescriptively wrong. Thus, people's use of this term seems to be tapping into precisely the sort of hybrid notion posited by this hypothesis.

With all this in the background, we can now offer a new and far simpler explanation of the results obtained in the causation studies. It is not that people have a statistical representation and a separate moral representation and then these two representations both end up affecting their causal intuitions. Rather, they have a single hybrid representation of norm violation. This one representation then ends up influencing causal judgments (see Figure 56.2), and the result is that people's causal judgments are sensitive to both statistical and prescriptive considerations.

We can now emphasize the more general idea of which this first example was just one illustration. In the domain of causal judg-

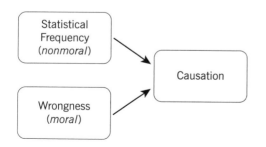

FIGURE 56.1. Hypothesis positing separate effects of moral and non-moral representations on causal judgment.

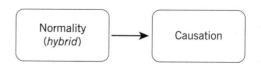

FIGURE 56.2. Hypothesis positing a single hybrid representation of normality that impacts causal judgment.

ment, existing results indicate that nonmoral and moral considerations have the same sort of impact. One way to explain this phenomenon would be to start by positing a distinction between nonmoral and moral representations. Then we could say that there are two completely separate representations—a nonmoral representation and a moral representation—which just happen to end up having the same sort of impact. I have suggested, however, that there might be reason to prefer a simpler model. We can abandon the assumption that there is a distinction between nonmoral and moral representations. Then we can posit just a single representation, involving a hybrid of nonmoral and moral considerations, and we can explain the entire phenomenon in terms of this one representation.

Second Example: Mind Perception

People attribute to each other a whole variety of different kinds of psychological states, but recent research suggests that these states can be divided into two basic types. On the one hand, there are capacities for reasoning, planning, thinking, and self-control. These capacities are known collectively as *psychological agency*. On the other hand, there are capacities for pain, joy, fear, and pleasure. These capacities are known as *psychological experience*. This claim receives its clearest and most powerful articulation in an important paper by Gray, Gray, and Wegner (2007), but numerous other researchers have arrived at similar conclusions (e.g., Haslam, 2006; Knobe & Prinz, 2008).

Perhaps unsurprisingly, people's attributions of a capacity for these different kinds of states has been shown to affect their moral judgments (Gray et al., 2007). First, it seems that some entities have a special kind of moral status such that we praise them for the good they do and blame them for the bad. Let us refer to that status as *moral agency*. People are more inclined to ascribe this sort of moral status to an entity when they see that entity as capable of psychological agency. In other words, if people see an entity as being capable of reasoning and planning, they will be more inclined to think that this entity is deserving of praise and blame.

Second, it seems that some entities have a kind of moral status such that we think it is morally good to help them and morally bad to harm them. We can refer to this status as *moral patiency*. People are more inclined to ascribe this latter moral status to an entity when they see it as having a capacity for psychological experience. In other words, if people see an entity as being capable of pleasure and pain, they will be more inclined to say that it would be good to help this entity and wrong to harm it.

So far, all of this should be fairly intuitive, but subsequent studies have shown something further and quite surprising. It turns out that the connection between psychological status and moral status can also go in the opposite direction, with people's tendency to see an entity as having a particular kind of moral status actually affecting their attributions to that entity of certain psychological capacities. In particular, these studies have revealed two striking patterns:

1. Attributions to an entity of moral agency can lead to attributions to that entity of psychological agency (Clark et al., 2014; Hamlin & Baron, 2014; Ullman, Leite, Phillips, Kim-Cohen, & Scassellati, 2014).
2. Attributions to an entity of moral patiency can lead to attributions to that entity of psychological experience (Bastian, Loughnan, Haslam, & Radke, 2012; Ward, Olsen, & Wegner, 2013).

These latter effects are far less obvious and intuitive than the ones discussed above. The basic idea is that making a certain moral judgment (e.g., that an entity is blameworthy) can actually lead you to make a corresponding psychological judgment (e.g., that the entity is capable of reasoning and planning).

How are we to understand these phenomena? One obvious approach would be in terms of a structure like the one depicted in Figure 56.3. On this view, we have distinct representations for psychological properties and moral properties, and there is then a complex web of causal relationships between the two. In particular, this account posits four separate causal relationships, depicted by the four separate arrows in the figure.

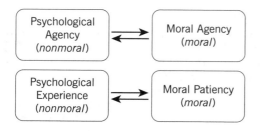

FIGURE 56.3. Hypothesis positing bidirectional causal influence of psychological and moral attributions.

To make sense of this account, one would have to provide an explanation for all four of these relationships. Moreover, one would have to provide an account for the striking symmetry we observe between them. That is, one would have to explain why it is that whenever attributions of a psychological capacity affect attributions of a particular moral status, we also find a corresponding impact in the opposite direction.

But before we seek an explanation along these lines, perhaps we should pause for a moment to question one of our assumptions. We started out with the assumption that there is a distinction between the representation of psychological agency and the representation of moral agency. Similarly, we assumed that there was a distinction between the representation of psychological experience and the representation of moral patiency. Then we immediately faced a question as to why these different representations had such a strong impact on each other.

A question now arises as to whether there is any actual justification for this assumption. We have been assuming that there is a single underlying representation at the root of people's attributions of a whole variety of different psychological capacities (rea-

soning, planning, self-control, etc.). Why couldn't this very same representation also be at the root of people's attributions of moral properties (praise, blame, etc.)? The answer does not seem to lie in any specific empirical results. Rather, it just seemed intuitive somehow that the representations underlying our psychological judgments should be coming from the representations underlying our moral judgments.

Let us now sketch an account that abandons these assumptions (Figure 56.4). We will posit a single, unified representation of *agency*. This representation would involve certain psychological capacities (reasoning, planning) and also a certain moral status (deserving blame and praise). Then, similarly, we will posit a single, unified representation of *patiency*. This representation again involves both psychological capacities (pain, joy) and moral status (moral patiency).

On this view, when people encounter a new entity, it is not as though they have to separately ask themselves, "Does this entity have the capacity for psychological agency?" and also "Is this is entity the sort of thing that can be deserving of praise and blame?" Rather, they only have to ask themselves a single question: "Is this entity an agent?" Judgments about both psychological and moral properties will affect their answers to this question, and their answers will in turn affect both their psychological and moral judgments.

This one type of representation can explain the effects we find going in both causal directions. If people conclude that an entity has certain psychological capacities, they will be more likely to see it as an agent and hence to regard it as deserving of praise and blame. The same basic logic then applies in the opposite direction. If people conclude that an entity is deserving of praise or blame, they will be more likely to see it as an agent

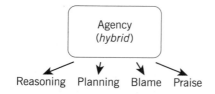 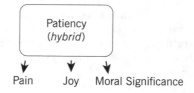

FIGURE 56.4. Hypothesis positing hybrid representations of agency and patiency.

and hence to regard it as having certain psychological capacities.

Note that although this second example involved a quite different domain from the first, the overall structure of the argument is exactly the same. Existing results show a certain pattern of interrelations among nonmoral and moral judgments. One way to explain those results would be to posit a distinction between nonmoral representations and moral representations and then to posit a complex web of causal connections between the two. I have been suggesting that we have reason to prefer a simpler model. One can abandon the distinction between the nonmoral and moral representations and then posit a single hybrid sort of representation that explains all of these effects.

Ordinary Cognition, Scientific Cognition

Thus far, we have considered two examples. In each case, we found that existing results can be explained on a simple and elegant model in which there is no clear distinction between moral and nonmoral cognition. However, in both cases, we also found that it would also be possible to explain these results on a more complex model in which moral and nonmoral cognition are fundamentally distinct. The question now is whether we have any reason to prefer the more complex model.

One salient fact here is that many existing theories, both about causal judgment and about mind perception, have been explicitly designed on analogy with the kind of thinking used in *science* (e.g., Gopnik, 1996). When people are doing systematic scientific research, it does seem that they make use of purely nonmoral representations that are importantly distinct from their moral representations. Thus, if people's ordinary way of making sense of the world is similar to scientific research, we would have reason to suppose that people's ordinary way of making sense of the world involves a rigorous distinction between the nonmoral and the moral.

If one starts out from this perspective, it is easy to find oneself adopting a certain picture. People's capacity to develop purely nonmoral representations of the sort familiar from scientific research begins to seem completely natural. This capacity does not seem to require any special explanation; it just appears to be a basic part of people's ordinary cognition. Then, when one finds that people's moral judgments can affect their intuitions about what appear to be strictly scientific questions, one assumes that this phenomenon must be due to some special additional process that is getting in the way of people's more basic cognitive capacities.

My suggestion is that we try to turn this whole question around and look at it from the opposite perspective. Suppose we start out with the idea that people have some way of representing these things that involves an undifferentiated jumble of nonmoral and moral elements. Then the puzzling thing, the thing that calls out for explanation, would be that we are sometimes able to engage in a more purely scientific mode of cognition in which we focus purely on the nonmoral considerations and leave the moral ones aside.

Perhaps the best way to get a sense for the proposal here would be to go through one example in a bit more detail. Consider again people's capacity for thinking about norms and normality. Now contrast two different kinds of questions you might ask yourself:

1. First try asking yourself a perfectly ordinary question: What would be a *normal* amount of television for a person to watch in a day?
2. Now try to put away out of your mind any prescriptive considerations and answer a purely statistical question: What is the *average* amount of television that people watch per day?

Participants tend to give quite high answers in response to this second question, but somewhat lower answers in the response to the first (Bear & Knobe, 2017; extending work by Wysocki, n.d.).

What we seem to be finding here is that these two kinds of judgments rely on different kinds of considerations. As noted above, people's judgments of the normal seem to involve a messy combination of statistical and prescriptive considerations. However, it seems that people are also capable, at least to some degree, of arriving at judgments of the average that are more purely statistical.

Putting these two results together, we arrive at the striking finding that people think that the average amount of television is not a normal amount but rather an abnormally high one.

The question now is how to understand the relationship between these two kinds of judgment. One hypothesis would be that the second, purely statistical judgment is revealing some basic fact about how human beings make sense of the world. It might be that this purely statistical judgment comes naturally to people and informs numerous aspects of their cognition. Then, if we want to explain why people give lower numbers when they are asked about the "normal," we could posit some special additional process that somehow intervenes and allows their judgments about what is normal to be affected by prescriptive considerations.

This hypothesis might turn out to be correct, but I have been trying to suggest that we have reason to consider an alternative view. On this alternative view, it is the first judgment, with its complex mixture of the statistical and the prescriptive, that reflects our most basic way of making sense of the world. This first sort of judgment comes naturally to people and informs numerous other aspects of their cognition. Then, when we want to explain how people can make more purely scientific judgments about the "average," we will have to do so by positing a special additional process that intervenes in certain cases and make it possible for people to arrive at judgments using purely statistical considerations.

One reason to prefer this alternative view is that it accords so well with existing work on scientific cognition. Such work indicates that a purely scientific way of making sense of the world never really comes naturally to people (e.g., McCauley, 2000). Rather, even after extensive scientific education, people still find it more intuitive to apply non-scientific concepts and have to suppress that initial intuition using cognitive control (Goldberg & Thompson-Schill, 2009; Shtulman & Valcarcel, 2012).

At this point, there has been relatively little work about the ways in which scientific cognition avoids the use of moral considerations, but what research there is suggests a similar process. For example, one recent study explored the ways in which trained scientists make judgments about whether a trait is "innate" (Knobe & Samuels, 2013). When scientists were assigned in a between-subjects design to receive either a vignette involving something morally good or a vignette involving something morally bad, their judgments were affected by the moral status of the events in the vignette. However, when scientists received both vignettes together in a within-subjects design, they tended to say that the two did not differ with regard to their innateness (Knobe & Samuels, 2013). These results indicate that even trained scientists can only avoid the impact of moral considerations to the extent that they are able to engage in some additional process that suppresses their initial intuitions.

To sum up, it does appear that scientific cognition involves, at least to some degree, a distinction between moral and nonmoral representations. However, it also seems that it might be a mistake to see this kind of cognition as reflecting our ordinary way of making sense of the world. Rather, part of what makes the study of scientific cognition so fascinating is precisely the fact that it involves such a radical departure from our more ordinary mode of understanding.

Conclusion

The distinction between the moral and the nonmoral has proven enormously important in numerous activities, and it is natural enough to suppose that it might also prove important in understanding human cognition. In particular, one obvious view would be that cognitive processes can be divided fairly neatly into the moral and the nonmoral, with moral judgments being generated by some distinctively moral form of cognition and nonmoral judgments being generated by a distinctively nonmoral form of cognition.

We now have a substantial amount of evidence against this view. First, as numerous authors have already noted, people's moral judgments appear to be generated by the very same sort of cognition that one finds at work in generating nonmoral judgments. Second, as we have been emphasizing here, there is also a striking effect in the opposite direction. Judgments about what might appear to be entirely nonmoral matters (causation, psychological capacities) can actually be influenced by moral judgments.

Of course, one possible hypothesis would be that human cognition is indeed best understood using a distinction between the nonmoral and the moral but that the connections between these two types of cognition are far more complex than we had originally anticipated. For example, it might be that people's cognition involves a relatively clear distinction between moral cognition and nonmoral cognition but that moral judgments are due in large part to nonmoral cognition and nonmoral judgments are due in part to moral cognition. Perhaps this hypothesis will ultimately turn out to be correct.

Still, at this point, it seems that there is something to be said for beginning to explore a very different alternative. Suppose that we simply ignore the whole moral–nonmoral distinction. We will still presumably want to develop theoretical frameworks that distinguish different kinds of processes and representations, but we can do so in a way that is driven more directly by the actual empirical data.

Judging from the two examples discussed here, this latter approach may lead to a very different relationship between our theoretical frameworks and the empirical results. To the extent that we insist on a distinction between moral and nonmoral cognition, we typically end up creating theoretical frameworks that, taken in themselves, do not seem to predict many of the effects we actually observe. Then, to make these frameworks compatible with the data, we have to add in a whole bunch of causal connections between distinct representations that don't seem to follow in any natural way from the frameworks themselves. By contrast, if we get rid of this distinction, we can construct frameworks that seem immediately to predict the observed effects and which would have difficulty explaining how these effects could possibly fail to arise.

REFERENCES

Bastian, B., Loughnan, S., Haslam, N., & Radke, H. R. (2012). Don't mind meat?: The denial of mind to animals used for human consumption. *Personality and Social Psychology Bulletin, 38*, 247–256.

Bear, A., & Knobe, J. (2017). Normality: Part descriptive, part prescriptive. *Cognition, 167*, 25–37.

Clark, C. J., Luguri, J. B., Ditto, P. H., Knobe, J., Shariff, A. F., & Baumeister, R. F. (2014). Free to punish: A motivated account of free will belief. *Journal of Personality and Social Psychology, 106*, 501–513.

Crockett, M. J. (2013). Models of morality. *Trends in Cognitive Sciences, 17*, 363–366.

Cushman, F. (2013). Action, outcome, and value a dual-system framework for morality. *Personality and Social Psychology Review, 17*, 273–292.

Cushman, F., & Young, L. (2011). Patterns of moral judgment derive from nonmoral psychological representations. *Cognitive Science, 35*, 1052–1075.

Goldberg, R. F., & Thompson-Schill, S. L. (2009). Developmental "roots" in mature biological knowledge. *Psychological Science, 20*, 480–487.

Gopnik, A. (1996). The scientist as child. *Philosophy of Science, 63*, 485–514.

Gray, H. M., Gray, K., & Wegner, D. M. (2007). Dimensions of mind perception. *Science, 315*, 619.

Gray, K., & Wegner, D. M. (2009). Moral typecasting: divergent perceptions of moral agents and moral patients. *Journal of Personality and Social Psychology, 96*, 505–520.

Halpern, J. Y., & Hitchcock, C. (2015). Graded causation and defaults. *British Journal for the Philosophy of Science, 66*, 413–457.

Hamlin, J. K., & Baron, A. S. (2014). Agency attribution in infancy: Evidence for a negativity bias. *PLOS ONE, 9*, e96112.

Hart, H. L. A., & Honoré, T. (1985). *Causation in the law.* Oxford, UK: Oxford University Press.

Haslam, N. (2006). Dehumanization: An integrative review. *Personality and Social Psychology Review, 10*, 252–264.

Hilton, D. J., & Slugoski, B. R. (1986). Knowledge-based causal attribution: The abnormal conditions focus model. *Psychological Review, 93*, 75–88.

Hitchcock, C., & Knobe, J. (2009). Cause and norm. *Journal of Philosophy, 106*, 587–612.

Knobe, J., & Fraser, B. (2008). Causal judgment and moral judgment: Two experiments. In W. Sinnott-Armstrong (Ed.), *Moral psychology* (pp.441–448). Cambridge, MA: MIT Press.

Knobe, J., & Prinz, J. (2008). Intuitions about consciousness: Experimental studies. *Phenomenology and the Cognitive Sciences, 7*, 67–83.

Knobe, J., & Samuels, R. (2013). Thinking like

a scientist: Innateness as a case study. *Cognition*, 126,– 72–86.

Kominsky, J. F., Phillips, J., Gerstenberg, T., Lagnado, D., & Knobe, J. (2015). Causal superseding. *Cognition, 137*, 196–209.

McCauley, R. (2000). The naturalness of religion and the unnaturalness of science. In F. Keil & R. Wilson (Eds.), *Explanation and cognition* (pp. 61–86). Cambridge, MA: MIT Press.

Shtulman, A., & Valcarcel, J. (2012). Scientific knowledge suppresses but does not supplant earlier intuitions. *Cognition, 124*, 209–215.

Ullman, D., Leite, I., Phillips, J., Kim-Cohen, J., & Scassellati, B. (2014). Smart human, smarter robot: How cheating affects perceptions of social agency. In P. Bello, M. Guarini, M. McShane, & B. Scassellati (Chairs), *Proceedings of the 36th annual conference of the Cognitive Science Society* (pp. 2996–3001). Red Hook, NY: Curran Associates.

Ward, A. F., Olsen, A. S., & Wegner, D. M. (2013). The harm-made mind observing victimization augments attribution of minds to vegetative patients, robots, and the dead. *Psychological Science, 24*, 1437–1445.

Wysocki, T. (n.d.). *Normality: A two-faced concept.* Unpublished manuscript, University of Washington in St. Louis, St. Louis, MO.

Young, L., & Saxe, R. (2008). The neural basis of belief encoding and integration in moral judgment. *NeuroImage, 40*, 1912–1920.

CHAPTER 57

Asking the Right Questions in Moral Psychology

Walter Sinnott-Armstrong

Are moral judgments as a whole innate, culturally variable, intuitive, or based on multiple or special processes?

This question is too general to answer, because we need to distinguish verdicts from deliberation, explicit answers from implicit attitudes, and areas of morality that have nothing in common that could support any general theory of all moral judgments.

Moral psychologists and philosophers often ask questions about morality as a whole: Is morality innate or learned? Is morality culturally variable or uniform? Is morality intuitive or deliberative? Is morality based on a single process or many? Is that process or processes special to morality or generic?

These questions grab readers partly because they are simple. It feels nice to be able to give a one-word answer: "yes" or "no." In contrast, audiences grow impatient when a scholar says that there are 17 aspects of morality, each of which is innate (or variable or intuitive) in only some of the 42 meanings of *innate*. Replies such as "It depends on what 'morality' is" make scholars seem too much like Bill Clinton saying, "It depends on what the meaning of the word 'is' is." Nobody likes evasion. We want a straightforward answer to the question that is posed.

The problem, of course, is that a vague question makes it impossible for any answer

to be precise or accurate. Bad input yields bad output. If someone asks how heavy jade is, we could not answer well without distinguishing kinds of jade (jadeite or nephrite?), meanings of "heavy" (mass or weight?), and size of pieces (an earring or a statue?).

This point is especially important to science. Ronald DeSousa (in personal conversation) once proposed that the progress of science can be measured in how many questions one can ask without being able to answer them. New discoveries and new theories do lead to new knowledge, but they also enable us to ask more questions that we could not even formulate before. When psychologists distinguished remembering how to ride a bike (procedural memory) from remembering that Raleigh is the capital of North Carolina (semantic memory) from remembering visiting Raleigh last week (episodic memory), we become able to ask which of these kinds of memory have propositions as contents, which kinds of memory are affected in which ways by which emotions, which brain areas are involved in which kinds of memory, and so on. The ability to ask such detailed questions is real progress, because we could not answer similar questions about memory in general: Do memories have propositions as contents? Some do, but others do not. Are memories reduced by disgust? Some are, but others are not. Where are memories lodged in the brain? Different places. In order to be able to answer questions about memory, we need to ask the right questions at the right level of generality.

Similarly, we cannot make progress in moral psychology until we ask the right questions. This simple point has been the focus of much of my own work on moral judgments in both philosophy and psychology.

In philosophy, consider moral dilemmas (Sinnott-Armstrong, 1988, 2008). Should Sophie give her son to the Nazis to be killed when the concentration camp guard tells her that he will kill them all if she does not hand over one of her two children? The answer depends on what "should" means. Sophie has reason to hand over (1) one child instead of none, even if she has no reason to hand over (2) her son instead of her daughter. We cannot say what she should do until we know whether the question is about contrast (1) or contrast (2). Even if we focus on (2), we still need to know whether she should do an act when nothing else is better (as when it is equal to the top) or only when this act is better than every other option. Semantic distinctions such as these are the stock-in-trade of traditional philosophy, so it should come as no surprise that they aid progress in that field.

This point is less widely acknowledged in moral psychology, but it is no less important. I give three examples in order to show how important and useful it is.

Verdict versus Deliberation

Which parts of the brain are involved in moral judgment? A large literature addresses this question, but the answer obviously depends on what counts as moral judgment. Compare juries in a legal trial. The jury sits

in its box while listening to evidence during the trial. Then it goes into another room to deliberate. At the end of deliberation, it votes on a verdict. Then it comes back into the courtroom to deliver its verdict. Legal judgment thus involves many parts. Analogously, moral judgment might include (1) gathering relevant information, (2) deliberating about that evidence, (3) endorsing a conclusion, and (4) expressing that conclusion. When someone asks about moral judgment, do they mean (1), (2), (3), (4), or all of the above?

The most common way to study moral judgment is to contrast answers to questions about different kinds of moral dilemmas. Greene and colleagues (2001, 2004), for example, contrast brain activations when participants report moral judgments about difficult versus easy personal versus impersonal moral dilemmas (except Analysis 2 in Greene et al. 2004, which contrasts different judgments about a single kind of dilemma). This method is groundbreaking and illuminating, but it conflates (1)–(4), because the differences in brain activation could occur during any part of the overall process.

In order to dig a little deeper, Jana Schaich Borg, Kent Kiehl, Vince Calhoun, and I had to deploy a novel design and analysis (Schaich Borg, Sinnott-Armstrong, Calhoun, & Kiehl, 2011). The first change was to contrast judgments instead of kinds of dilemmas. To do so, we included acts that were clearly wrong, clearly not wrong, and controversial. The second issue was statistical. Moral dilemmas need to be described in detail in order to include all relevant information, but lengthy stimuli limit the number of trials per participant. To increase statistical power, we developed a form of stimulus that could be judged within a few seconds. Finally, we analyzed the earliest and latest periods for each stimulus separately in order to distinguish earlier deliberation from later verdict.

The results showed that brain areas that previous studies had associated with moral judgment—the ventromedial prefrontal cortex, posterior cingulate, and temporoparietal junction—were related to deliberation but not verdict. In contrast, verdict but not deliberation was associated with a distinct set of brain areas—bilateral anterior insula, basal ganglia, and amygdala.

Because moral deliberation and verdict activate different brain areas, it makes no sense for moral psychologists to ask which brain areas are related to moral judgment if judgment includes both deliberation and verdict. Too much information is lost by conflating deliberation and verdict under the umbrella term *judgment*.

These results also affect the question of whether moral judgment is intuitive or deliberative. Deliberation is deliberative (of course!), but verdict still might be intuitive. Accordingly, any study of whether moral judgment is intuitive needs to be careful to focus on verdicts instead of deliberation.

Another lesson is for the question of whether morality is based on a single process or many processes. Compare law. Is the jury process a single process when it includes the jury listening during the trial, deliberating elsewhere, and then reporting its verdict? Whether this set of events is one process or three depends on how we count processes, which seems arbitrary. The same applies to morality. We could count deliberation and verdict as two processes or as two parts of a single process (called *judgment*). There is no clear basis for favoring either way of counting, so each answer seems arbitrary.

This distinction between deliberation and verdict might also affect whether the processes underlying moral judgment are special to morality or generic. Perhaps deliberation is generic in combining inputs, but verdicts in morality are special, because they are distinct from other kinds of verdicts. After all, we can judge that one candidate for a job is morally superior but another candidate is still better for this job. We might use many of the same inputs and bring together these considerations in deliberation but still reach different verdicts about morality versus deserving the job, and that difference might be due to special moral processes underlying the verdicts. We do not know. The point here is only that we cannot even ask this question until we distinguish deliberation from verdict.

Finally, if someone asks whether moral judgment is innate or learned or whether it is culturally variable or uniform, then one answer might be correct for deliberation and another for verdict. Culture might affect which verdicts we reach without affecting (or affecting as much) the inputs or processes of deliberation. Again, we do not know. Still, we clearly should not assume that verdict must be innate and uniform if deliberation is—or vice versa. Yet that assumption is built into research that claims to address moral judgment in general without distinguishing deliberation from verdict.

Explicit Beliefs versus Implicit Attitudes

Now let's focus on verdicts as a kind of judgment. We still need another distinction. Suppose someone thinks about his neighbors having gay sex. Does he judge (or reach the verdict) that their act is immoral? The answer varies between individuals, of course, but it also depends on precisely what we mean by *verdict*. The question might be about explicit beliefs or it might be about implicit attitudes.

The difference is well known from studies of attitudes toward race and gender. Implicit association tests (IATs) reveal that many people who sincerely claim that they have nothing against people with African ancestry still associate black faces with being bad (Greenwald, McGhee, & Schwartz, 1998). Their implicit racial attitudes conflict with their explicit racial beliefs.

Similar conflicts arise in morality, when explicit moral beliefs come apart from implicit moral attitudes. Someone who sincerely claims to believe that there is nothing morally wrong with gay sex still might have implicit moral attitudes that oppose or condemn gay sex. These implicit moral attitudes can be revealed by moral versions of the IAT and other tests, including the affect misattribution procedure and Stroop tests. Here I focus on a powerful measure of implicit moral attitudes that Daryl Cameron developed and tested in collaboration with Keith Payne, Julian Scheffer, Michael Inzlicht, and me (Cameron, Payne, Sinnott-Armstrong, Scheffer, & Inzlicht, 2017).

Our test starts with a sequential priming task that uses three sets of words: neutral (e.g., *baking*), moral (e.g., *murder*), and emotional but nonmoral (e.g., *cancer*). A prime word is presented for 100 milliseconds, followed by a target word for 400–800 milliseconds. Participants are instructed to ignore the prime and report whether the target word describes an act that is morally wrong. Those with an implicit moral attitude are supposed to be more likely to mistakenly judge neutral targets as morally wrong when they just saw a morally wrong prime. By calculations on error rates, we can decompose task performance into multiple processes of moral judgment, including implicit moral attitude and control (ability to follow the instructions despite misleading primes). This multinomial model enables us not just to identify implicit moral attitudes but also to measure their strength in each individual.

This method has been replicated often and extended to morally controversial cases. When we add controversial moral words (e.g., *gay marriage*) as primes, only participants who have an implicit moral attitude against that act are more likely to judge the following target to be wrong. The test predicts both charitable giving (to controversial charities) and also voting behavior (in a referendum on gay marriage). We also have found neural correlates of some revealed factors and have shown that implicit moral attitudes are not reducible to negative affect (suggesting that this moral process might be special rather than generic). Finally, our measured factors correlate with nonclinical scores on a self-report psychopathy scale, suggesting that psychopaths are deficient in implicit moral attitudes even if they give normal answers to explicit moral questions (Schaich Borg & Sinnott-Armstrong, 2013).

Why does this matter here? The most obvious lesson is for the question of whether moral judgment (even if restricted to verdict rather than deliberation) is a single process or many. The psychological and neural processes that constitute implicit moral attitudes are distinct from the processes that constitute explicit belief (what we reflectively endorse and commit ourselves to). The process of forming explicit beliefs is also distinct from the process of deciding whether and how to express those beliefs. If experimenters measure only explicit answers to questions, then they conflate these distinct processes.

The next question is whether moral judgment is intuitive or deliberative. Here it again matters whether the question is about implicit attitudes, explicit beliefs, or answers to questions in experiments. The process of deciding whether and how to answer a moral question (or even whether to endorse one's moral attitudes) might require weighing the pros and cons of making certain public statements, in which case it might be deliberative in a way that our implicit moral attitudes are not. We do not know yet. The point here is only that we cannot formulate—much less answer—that question until we distinguish implicit moral attitudes from explicit moral beliefs and develop tools to measure implicit moral attitudes.

This distinction might affect other questions as well. Is moral judgment innate or learned? It seems possible and perhaps plausible that implicit moral attitudes are innate in ways that explicit beliefs and answers are not. We might have to learn which implicit moral attitudes to endorse and express, just as we need to learn which visual appearances to endorse and which to dismiss. If so, then maybe implicit moral attitudes are less culturally variable and more uniform than explicit moral beliefs.

Of course, we do not know any of this. Our tests of implicit moral attitudes have not yet been used cross-culturally or in children. The point here is only that we cannot investigate these issues properly if we keep asking about moral judgment in ways that conflate implicit moral attitudes with explicit moral beliefs. We need to ask more specific questions in order to make progress.

Areas of Morality

Even if we focus on implicit verdicts, it is still useful to draw further distinctions. Jon Haidt distinguished four foundations (Haidt & Joseph, 2004), then five (Haidt & Graham, 2007), and now six (Haidt, 2012): harm/care, fairness/reciprocity, ingroup/loyalty, authority/respect, purity/sanctity, and liberty. Scott Clifford, Vijeth Iyengar, Roberto Cabeza, and I developed stimuli among which factor analyses also distinguished physical versus emotional harm and harm to humans versus animals (Clifford, Iyengar, Cabeza, & Sinnott-Armstrong, 2015). In addition, I suspect that fairness needs to be subdivided into distributive, retributive, and procedural justice, as well as fair prices and exchanges, and honesty needs to fit somewhere (Parkinson et al., 2011). Some critics doubt that all of these distinctions make a difference, and some fit them into two superordinate groups, such as individualizing versus binding foundations or foundations based on anger versus disgust. I do not engage in those debates here except to say that both sides might be right. Superordinate classifications are compatible with subdivisions.

What matters here is whether these areas of morality—however many there are—share anything important in common that makes them all moral as opposed to conventional, religious, legal, aesthetic, or some other kind of norm. Of course, moral norms might be unified in any number of ways, but several candidates are prominent.

The first potential unifier of moral norms is function. Haidt (2012) writes, "Moral systems are interlocking sets of values, virtues, norms, practices, identities, institutions, technologies, and evolved psychological mechanisms that work together to suppress or regulate self-interest and make cooperative societies possible" (p. 270). Josh Greene (2013) proposes a similar definition: "Morality is a set of psychological adaptations that allow otherwise selfish individuals to reap the benefits of cooperation" (p. 23). Many others agree openly or by assumption that all and only moral norms function to enable cooperation by suppressing selfishness.

I disagree. Many moral norms do not aim at cooperation. Just think of retributivist norms of criminal punishment, such as "a life for a life." That norm might have aided cooperation in times when tribes would otherwise take two lives for each tribe member who was killed. However, the desire to take more than one life as payback for killing is not selfish (indeed, it is costly), and their history does not show that retributivist norms function to aid cooperation today. Indeed, retributivist norms undermine cooperation when they insist on punishment in cases in which punishment leads only to disharmony. Conversely, many norms that aim at cooperation and suppress self-interest are not moral in nature. The rule in golf that the most recent winner of a hole tees off first enables cooperation by avoiding disputes about

who tees off first and suppresses self-interest of those who are impatient to tee off, but it is still not seen as immoral to tee off out of turn. Similarly, linguistic rules of pronunciation (as well as semantics and syntax) enable cooperation by enabling communication, and they suppress self-interest in creative expression, but it is not seen as immoral to mispronounce words, even intentionally.

Although morality is not unified by function, it still might be unified at some other level, such as content. Kurt Gray and colleagues (Gray, Young, & Waytz, 2012) have suggested that every moral judgment shares a "cognitive template" insofar as it "conjures to mind" intentional harm to other people: "On our account, perceived suffering is not a distinct moral domain, but a core feature of all immoral acts" (p. 16). Really? Many people throughout history have believed, and some still believe, that masturbation is immoral, but this judgment is often based on the claim that masturbation is unnatural and not always on any perception that masturbators suffer or cause suffering to others. Indeed, critics of masturbation seem to think that masturbators have too much fun. Gray and colleagues (2012) reply that people who think of masturbation as immoral believe in some kind of "spiritual destruction," but such spiritual destruction is not suffering in any literal sense, it is not causing suffering of other people, and it is not caused intentionally (Sinnott-Armstrong, 2012).

Even if moral judgments are not unified by function or content (or cognitive template), they still might be unified by a shared brain process. To test this hypothesis, Carolyn Parkinson and a group of us (Parkinson et al., 2011) used fMRI to examine the neural correlates of moral judgments about dishonesty, sexual disgust, and physical harm. We found that distinct neural systems became active during moral judgments about these areas. Dishonest, disgusting, and harmful moral transgressions activated brain regions associated with mentalizing, affective processing, and action understanding, respectively. Dorsal medial prefrontal cortex was recruited by all scenarios judged to be morally wrong, but this region was also recruited by dishonest and harmful scenarios judged not to be morally wrong. Overall, no brain area or network was common and peculiar to moral judgments of wrongness in all three areas.

Morality still might be unified in many other ways. We consider several more elsewhere (Sinnott-Armstrong & Wheatley, 2014) and conclude provisionally that nothing unifies moral judgments. I will not repeat those arguments here. Instead, I want to explore the implications of our view for the questions that frame this volume.

The most obvious lesson is for the question of whether morality is based on a single process or many. Our factor analyses plus our brain data suggest that different moral judgments involve different processes with nothing important in common (though it is admittedly not clear whether some results concern verdicts or deliberation). Of course, these different processes need to be combined at some point in order to make a single decision in a conflict, but that need is not distinctive of morality.

The next question is whether morality is intuitive or deliberative. It seems simplistic to ask this question about morality as a whole when different answers might be needed for different areas of morality. We might have to reason or deliberate more about procedural justice (Should past misbehavior be allowed as evidence when someone is accused of current misbehavior?) than about intentional harm (Was it misbehavior when he hit his children?). Again, if humans have an intuition that it is immoral to eat humans but not immoral to eat other animals, then they need to deliberate or reason more in order to reach the moral judgment that eating other animals is immoral.

The same point applies to other questions. Is morality innate or learned? Is morality culturally variable or uniform? Maybe experience and culture affect some areas more than others. Because of variations among (and within) areas of morality, information and precision will be lost if we ask only general questions about whether morality as a whole is intuitive or deliberative, innate or learned, variable or uniform.

How to Make Progress

It is easy to criticize and hard to improve. How should we proceed in light of these distinctions between verdict and deliberation, explicit belief and implicit attitude, and areas of morality? We need to become splitters rather than lumpers. Each experiment should focus on one specific kind of moral judgment: verdict or deliberation, explicit belief or implicit attitude, within one area of morality, and also uniform in other ways (such as first person or third person, concrete or abstract, and so on). After we investigate several specific subcategories of "moral judgment" in a series of separate experiments, then we can compare the psychological and neural processes behind those different subcategories. In the end, we might find that many or all moral judgments share something distinctive and important. Indeed, data-driven analyses of large moral datasets might even unearth unifying characteristics in different moral processes that we never hypothesized in advance. In any case, such uniformity should be an empirical discovery, not an assumption.

I admit that my own research rarely lives up to this ideal. Nonetheless, splitting seems to be the best way to make progress in moral psychology. We need to ask the right questions in order to become able to find answers, and the right questions will have to focus, focus, focus.

REFERENCES

Cameron, C. D., Payne, B. K., Sinnott-Armstrong, W., Scheffer, J., & Inzlicht, M. (2017). Measuring moral intuitions: A multinomial modeling approach. *Cognition, 158,* 224–241.

Clifford, S., Iyengar, V., Cabeza, R. E., & Sinnott-Armstrong, W. (2015). Moral foundations vignettes: A standardized stimulus database of scenarios based on moral foundations theory. *Behavior Research Methods, 47*(4), 1178–1198.

Gray, K., Young, L., & Waytz, A. (2012). Mind perception is the essence of morality. *Psychological Inquiry, 23*(2), 101–124.

Greene, J. (2013). *Moral tribes: Emotion, reason, and the gap between us and them.* New York: Penguin.

Greene, J. D., Nystrom, L. E., Engell, A. D., Darley, J. M., & Cohen, J. D. (2004). The neural bases of cognitive conflict and control in moral judgment. *Neuron, 44,* 389–400.

Greene, J. D., Sommerville, R. B., Nystrom, L. E., Darley, J. M., & Cohen, J. D. (2001). An fMRI investigation of emotional engagement in moral judgment. *Science, 293*(5537), 2105–2108.

Greenwald, A. G., McGhee, D. E., & Schwartz, J. L. K. (1998). Measuring individual differences in implicit cognition: The Implicit Association Test. *Journal of Personality and Social Psychology, 74,* 1464–1480.

Haidt, J. (2012). *The righteous mind: Why good people are divided by politics and religion.* New York: Pantheon.

Haidt, J., & Graham, J. (2007). When morality opposes justice: Conservatives have moral intuitions that liberals may not recognize. *Social Justice Research, 20,* 98–116.

Haidt, J., & Joseph, C. (2004). Intuitive ethics: How innately prepared intuitions generate culturally variable virtues. *Daedalus, 133*(4), 55–66.

Parkinson, C., Sinnott-Armstrong, W., Koralus, P. E., Mendelovici, A., McGeer, V., & Wheatley, T. (2011). Is morality unified?: Evidence that distinct neural systems underlie judgments of harm, dishonesty, and disgust. *Journal of Cognitive Neuroscience, 23*(10), 3162–3180.

Schaich Borg, J., & Sinnott-Armstrong, W. (2013). Do psychopaths make moral judgments? In K. A. Kiehl & W. Sinnott-Armstrong (Eds.), *Handbook on psychopathy and law* (pp. 107–128). New York: Oxford University Press.

Schaich Borg, J., Sinnott-Armstrong, W., Calhoun, V. D., & Kiehl, K. A. (2011). The neural basis of moral verdict and moral deliberation. *Social Neuroscience, 6*(4), 398–413.

Sinnott-Armstrong, W. (1988). *Moral dilemmas.* Oxford, UK: Basil Blackwell.

Sinnott-Armstrong, W. (2008). A contrastivist manifesto. *Social Epistemology, 22*(3), 257–270.

Sinnott-Armstrong, W. (2012). Does morality have an essence? *Psychological Inquiry, 23*(2), 194–197.

Sinnott-Armstrong, W., & Wheatley, T. (2014). Are moral judgments unified? *Philosophical Psychology, 27*(4), 451–474.

Index

Note. *f*, *n*, or *t* following a page number indicates a figure, a note, or a table.

Abortion, 326, 327, 521, 531
Action value, 61–63, 65. *See also*
  Moral values
Adolescents, 13–15, 21, 23–25, 28,
  54. *See also* Developmental
  processes
Affect, 84, 116–117
Affect misattribution procedure
  (AMP), 517–518
Affective neuroscience, 457. *See
  also* Neuroscience
Affective processes, 4, 295,
  512–513
Afterlife beliefs, 241–249. *See also*
  Religious traditions
Age, 204–205, 313–314, 430–431,
  509
Agency, 333, 376, 559–561, 560*f*
Agency-based mental states, 189.
  See also Mental states
Aggression
  intergroup aggression and,
    193–198
  relationship regulation theory
    (RRT) and, 235
  side-taking strategies and, 179
  vulnerability and, 430–431, 431
Allocation hypothesis, 182
Altruism. *See also* Helping
    behaviors
  in animals, 416–417
  choosing sides and, 177
  historical moral change and,
    260, 270
  overview, 413–417

research findings and, 414–417
side-taking strategies and,
  181–183
unselfish behavior and, 468
Altruistic lying, 469
Alzheimer's disease, 141, 144
Ambiguity, 493–494
Amygdala
  empathy and, 508, 509
  folk moral theories and, 322
  moral judgment and, 566–567
  moral values and, 63
  overview, 507, 507*f*
Analysis of data. *See* Big data
  analysis; Data analysis
Anger
  avoidance- and approach-related
    behavioral responses and, 78
  compared to disgust, 75
  component process model
    (CPM) and, 72, 72*f*
  historical moral change and, 271
  moral foundations theory (MFT)
    and, 90
  moralization of the body and,
    280
  vulnerability-based morality,
    432
Animal inequity aversion. *See also*
  Animals, thinking morally
    about
  compared to human inequity
    aversion, 398
  moral clarity and, 497–498
  overview, 394–399

Animals, thinking morally about
  cognition and, 167–168
  emotions and, 168–170
  fairness and, 393–399
  free will and, 333, 334–335
  historical context of, 166
  identity and, 170–171
  inequity aversion in, 394–399
  moralization and, 366
  overview, 165–166, 166*f*,
    171–172
  side-taking strategies and, 180
  theory and, 166–171
Anterior cingulate cortex (ACC),
  60, 63, 64
Anterior insula (AI), 60, 64, 508
Anterior midcingulate cortex
  (aMCC), 508
Anthropic principle, 357
Anthropocentric perspective,
  353–354, 354*t*, 355–356
Anthropological approaches
  historical moral change and,
    260, 268
  moral foundations theory (MFT)
    and, 213, 214, 218
  religions and, 340
Anti-essentialist assumptions,
  92–93
Antisocial behavior, 195–196, 249
Anxiety, 242, 245–246, 479
Anxiety buffer disruption theory
  (ABDT), 249
Apathy, 194, 195
Appearance, 169–170

Appraisals, 82–83
Attachment
   ethical behavior and, 479
   ethogenesis and, 453
   historical context of, 443–445
   overview, 440–441, 441–443,
      443f, 447–448
   research findings and, 446–447
   terror management theory
      (TMT) and, 244
   theory and, 445–446
Attitudes
   grounded approaches and, 296
   Implicit processes and, 516–517,
      520, 567–568
   modeling approach and,
      517–518
   moral clarity and, 494–495, 496
   vulnerability-based morality,
      431
Attribution
   ambiguity and, 76
   moral cognition and, 559–560,
      560f
   moral standing of animals and,
      166f, 167–168
   vulnerability-based morality, 432
Authority
   constructive origins of morality
      and, 25
   development of morality and,
      11, 16n, 21
   geographies of morality and, 341
   historicist view of morality and,
      261
   implicit moral processes and, 522
   intergroup aggression and,
      195–196
   moral foundations theory (MFT)
      and, 213
   overview, 568–569
   relationship regulation theory
      (RRT) and, 233, 236–237
   social and moral decision
      making and, 12–13
Automatic mechanisms
   blame and, 384–385
   empathy and, 51–52, 53
   ethogenesis and, 455–456
   folk moral theories and,
      321–322, 322t
   moral cognition and, 109–110
   moral foundations theory (MFT)
      and, 213
   moral judgment and, 3, 25
Autonomous decision making, 21.
      See also Decision making
Aversion, 41–42. See also Disgust
Avoidance processes, 78, 223–224,
      224f, 479

B
Badness
   blame and, 387
   compared to wrongness, 40–44
   moral cognition and, 113–114,
      115
   overview, 40–41
   theory and, 41
Banality of evil perspective,
      195–196
Basal ganglia, 566–567
Basic emotion theory (BET), 89,
      90, 91–93
Behavior. See also Ethical
      behavior; Goal-directed
      behavior; Helping behaviors;
      Selfish behavior; Unethical
      behavior; Unselfish behavior
   choosing sides and, 177–184
   death awareness and, 247–248
   development of sociomoral
      evaluations in infants and,
      404–405
   developmental neuroscience and,
      512–513
   distributive fairness and,
      421–422
   ethogenesis and, 453
   evaluating moral character and,
      100–102
   historicist view of morality and,
      260
   infants' evaluation of, 407
   intergroup aggression and,
      193–198
   moral beliefs and, 315–317
   moral clarity and, 494
   moral cognition and, 111
   moral identity and, 137, 145
   moral self-theory and, 154–156,
      157
   moral vitalism and, 305–306
   moralization and, 367–368
   perceived control and, 385–386
   preference for helpers by infants
      and, 408–409
   relationship regulation theory
      (RRT) and, 233, 237–238
   religions and, 340–341
   side-taking strategies and, 180
   testing moral behavior, 489–490
   unconflicted virtue and,
      485–492
   vulnerability-based morality
      and, 436–437
Belief systems, 241–249,
      303–308. See also Moral
      belief; Religious traditions;
      Spirituality

Biases
   blame and, 387
   empathy and, 49–50
   intelligent design and, 352–358
   moral character and, 104
   moral clarity and, 498
   moral cognition and, 112
   moral coherence and, 376–377
   relationship regulation theory
      (RRT) and, 232
   religions and, 340
Big data analysis. See also Data
      analysis
   historical context of, 527–528
   methodology and, 528–530
   overview, 525–527, 532–533
   research findings and, 530–532
Bilateral anterior insula, 566–567
Biocentrism, 354t, 357–358
Bioethical issues, 326–328, 327t
Biological factors
   altruism in children and, 414
   ethogenesis, 451–452
   folk moral theories and, 325
   historical moral change and,
      270, 273–274
   intelligent design and, 353
   moral vitalism and, 304, 305,
      308
   stereotype content model (SCM)
      and, 204
   terror management theory
      (TMT) and, 242–243
Biopsychosocial functioning,
      451–452
Blame
   acceptance versus condemnation
      of, 387–388
   evolutionary heritage of,
      383–384
   hypotheses about, 384
   inclinations towards, 384–385
   moral cognition and, 112,
      113–114, 114f, 115–116
   moral coherence and, 374
   overview, 382–383, 388–389
   perceived control and, 385–387
   research evidence regarding
      infants' fairness concerns and,
      425
   social interactions and, 191
   stereotypes and, 202
Body, moralization of
   boundaries of the self, 279–287
   grounded approaches and,
      296–297
   historical context of, 280
   overview, 286–287
   research findings and, 280–286
   theory and, 280

Boundaries of the self
    expansion of, 284–286
    grounded approaches and, 296
    historical context of, 280
    overview, 279–280, 286–287
    research findings and, 280–286
    theory and, 280
Brain regions. *See also*
        Neuroscience
    attachment and, 444
    folk moral theories and, 321–322
    implicit moral processes and,
        521
    intergroup aggression and, 197
    moral judgment and, 566–567
    moral values and, 60–61, 64–65
    overview, 4, 506–508, 507*f*
    parallel morality hypothesis and,
        35–36
    stereotypes and, 202

C

CAD (Contempt/Anger/Disgust)
        triad hypothesis, 73, 74–75,
        84–85, 260
Capital punishment, 374–375, 379,
        521
Care
    caring behavior, 453
    moral foundations theory (MFT)
        and, 212, 213, 214, 215
    overview, 568–569
    unselfish behavior and, 469
Causation
    folk moral theories and, 324
    free will and, 333
    intelligent design and, 353
    norms and, 558*f*
    perceived control and, 385–386,
        385–387
Certainty, 494, 496
Change, moral. *See* Historical
        moral change
Character evaluation. *See also*
        Character judgments; Moral
        character
    defining moral character and,
        102–104
    overview, 99–100
    social cognition and, 100–102,
        125
    social interactions and, 187
Character judgments. *See also*
        Character evaluation; Moral
        character
    component process model
        (CPM) and, 72, 76–77
    diagnosticity and, 124

moral self-theory and, 154
moral vitalism and, 306–307
overview, 99–100, 106
person-centered morality and,
        122–127
Charitable acts, 154–155,
        339–340. *See also* Behavior;
        Prosocial acts
Cheating, 212, 479, 489–490
Child marriage, 269
Children. *See also* Developmental
        processes
    altruism and, 413–417
    constructive origins of morality
        and, 23–25
    ethogenesis and, 452
    moral clarity and, 498
    moral judgment and, 21, 28
    prejudice and, 26
    psychopathy, 512
    social and moral decision
        making and, 13–15
    social inequalities and, 27–28
    vulnerability and, 430–431
    wrongness compared to badness
        and, 40–44
Choice, 11–13, 15, 332–336
Choosing sides. *See* Side-taking
        strategies
Clarity, moral. *See* Moral clarity
Cleanliness, 284–286
Climate change, 379, 540–541
Cognition-affect interactions, 52
Cognitive control, 4
Cognitive depletion, 495
Cognitive development, 150–151,
        455–456, 477–478
Cognitive dissonance theory, 372
Cognitive load, 52–53
Cognitive neuroscience, 197, 198.
        See also Neuroscience
Cognitive processes. *See also*
        Moral cognition
    altruism in children and, 415
    complexity and, 27–28
    component process model
        (CPM) and, 76–77
    distributive fairness and,
        421–422
    ethical behavior and, 479–480
    folk moral theories and,
        323–324
    grounded approaches and, 293
    historical moral change and,
        266, 274
    historicist view of morality and,
        260
    moral clarity and, 493, 495
    moral standing of animals and,
        167–168

moral vitalism and, 304–305
overview, 556–557, 561–563
parallel morality hypothesis
        and, 33
terror management theory
        (TMT) and, 243
Coherence processes. *See* Moral
        coherence processes
Collectivism, 273, 471, 498–499
Communication, 82, 83, 254–255
Comparisons, 105–106
Compassion, 90, 213
Competition, 62–63, 188–189,
        194–195, 196–197
Complexity, moral. *See* Moral
        complexity
Compliance, 24–25, 285
Component process model (CPM).
        See also Disgust
    historical context of, 72–74
    overview, 72, 72*f*, 77–78
    research findings and, 75–77
    theory and, 74–75
Condemnation, 177–184
Condom education, 374–375
Confirmation bias, 104, 498
Conflicted virtue, 486–487,
        489–490, 491
Conformity, 11, 270
Conscientiousness, 226, 453–454
Constructivist approach
    emotions and, 88–89
    intergroup relationships and,
        25–26
    overview, 11, 23–25
    whole-number approach and,
        90–91, 92–93
Contextual effects, 297–298, 306
Control, perceived, 385–387
Controlled mechanisms, 109–110,
        321–322, 322*t*, 374
Cooperation
    altruism in children and, 416
    development of sociomoral
        evaluations in infants and,
        403–404, 405
    evolved developmental niche
        (EDN) and, 454
    free will and, 335
    inequity aversion in animals
        and, 395–398
    mental states and, 188–189
    model of moral motives (MMM)
        and, 226–227, 228–229
    moral coherence and, 378–379
    moral heroes as puppets and, 254
    moral values and, 62–63
    moralization of the body and, 283
    religions and, 340
    side-taking strategies and, 179

Coordination, 227, 228–229
Core disgust evaluation, 76–77, 271. *See also* Disgust
Culpability, 373, 374, 376
Culpable control model of blame (CCM), 383, 384, 385–387, 388–389. *See also* Blame
Cultural anthropology of morality, 213, 218, 243
Cultural factors
  anthropocentrism and, 355
  attachment and, 445–446, 448
  blame and, 387–388
  disgust and, 74
  ethogenesis and, 456
  fairness and, 394
  free will and, 333–334
  grounded approaches and, 293
  historical moral change and, 260–261, 262–263, 269, 270
  identity and, 143–144
  model of moral motives (MMM) and, 224–225, 227
  moral beliefs and, 312
  moral clarity and, 498–499
  moral foundations theory (MFT) and, 212, 213, 216
  moral judgment and, 569
  moral self-theory and, 152
  moral vitalism and, 305
  moralization of the body and, 282
  overview, 14–16, 16f
  relationship regulation theory (RRT) and, 234, 235–236, 238–239
  religions and, 340
  side-taking strategies and, 180
  stereotype content model (SCM) and, 204–205
  terror management theory (TMT) and, 242, 243–246, 249
  testing a definition of morality, 552–553
  theory of dyadic morality (TDM) and, 366–367
  unethical behavior and, 471
  worldviews, 243–246

D

Data analysis, 525–527, 532–533. *See also* Big data analysis
Davis Interpersonal Reactivity Index (IRI), 424–425
Death, 241–249
Death-thought accessibility (DTA), 246, 248

Deception, 13–14. *See also* Honesty
Decision making
  brain mechanisms, 507
  cultural practices and, 14–16, 16f
  development of morality and, 13–14
  grounded approaches and, 297, 298
  moral clarity and, 494
  moral cognition and, 111
  moral judgment and, 21
  nonmoral considerations and, 22–23
  parallel morality hypothesis and, 36
  perceived control and, 386–387
  processes of, 11–14
  relationship regulation theory (RRT) and, 232–233, 236
  testing moral behavior, 489–490
  the trolley problem, 432–433
Defining morality
  inability to, 554
  moral psychology and, 565–570
  overview, 547–549, 548f
  testing a definition of morality, 549–554
Dehumanization, 202, 238, 356
Deities, belief in, 241–249, 352–358, 384–385
Deliberative processes
  disgust and, 73–74
  ethogenesis and, 455–456
  folk moral theories and, 321–324, 322t
  grounded approaches and, 294–295
  historical context of, 32–33
  moral clarity and, 494–495
  moral cognition and, 110
  moral judgment and, 567, 569
  overview, 31–32, 36–37
  research findings and, 34–36
  theory and, 33–34
Demoralization, 365–366, 365f
Descriptive processes, 234, 379
Determinism, 326–328, 327t
Developmental neuroscience. *See also* Neuroscience
  affective sharing and, 512–513
  brain mechanisms, 506–508, 507f
  empathy and morality and, 508–512
  future directions and, 513
  overview, 505–506
  theory and, 506

Developmental processes
  altruism and, 413–417
  constructive origins of morality and, 23–25
  distributive fairness and, 421–422
  ethogenesis and, 453–456
  evolved developmental niche (EDN) and, 453–456
  fairness and, 420–428
  folk moral theories and, 323–324
  honesty and deception and, 13–14
  moral beliefs and, 312
  moral clarity and, 498
  moral foundations theory (MFT) and, 215
  moral judgment and, 21
  nonmoral considerations and, 22–23
  overview, 10–11, 28
  prejudice and, 26
  research evidence regarding infants' fairness concerns and, 423–426
  social and moral decision making and, 13–14
  social cognitive development and, 23
  social inequalities and, 27–28
  sociomoral evaluations and, 402–410
  terror management theory (TMT) and, 243
  wrongness compared to badness and, 40–44
Diachronic identity, 141, 145–146. *See also* Identity
Diagnostic and Statistical Manual of Mental Disorders (DSM), 388
Disease, 280–286, 305
Disgust. *See also* Component process model (CPM)
  avoidance- and approach-related behavioral responses and, 78
  functional conflict theory of moral emotions and, 83
  historical context of, 72–74
  historical moral change and, 271
  intergroup aggression and, 194–195
  moral foundations theory (MFT) and, 90
  moral standing of animals and, 168–169
  moral vitalism and, 307

moralization of the body and, 280, 281, 282–283, 284
opposition to genetically modified (GM) food, 538–540
overview, 70–71, 77–78
relationship regulation theory (RRT) and, 234
research findings and, 75–77
stereotypes and, 201–202
theory and, 74–75
Disgust Scale—Revised (DS-R), 539
Dispositional orientation, 452–453, 475
Distributive fairness. *See also* Fairness
early moral development and, 421–422
overview, 420–421, 426–428
research evidence regarding infants' fairness concerns and, 423–426
theory and, 422–423
Divinity, 70–71, 294. *See also* Component process model (CPM); Disgust
Dogmatism, 496
Domain specificity effects, 91
Domain theory, 234–235
Dopaminergic nuclei, 509
Dorsolateral prefrontal cortex (DLPFC)
folk moral theories and, 321, 322
moral thinking and, 4
overview, 507, 507f
parallel morality hypothesis and, 34–35
Dualism+ Scale, 326–328, 327t
Dual-process model
egocentrism and, 354
folk moral theories and, 321–324, 322t, 326–328, 327t
grounded approaches and, 295
model of moral motives (MMM) and, 225
moral self-theory and, 153
moral vitalism and, 306
overview, 89, 122
Dual-systems approach, 321
Dyadic comparison, 364
Dyadic completion, 306, 364, 377
Dyadic loop, 365–366, 365f
Dyadic model, 73, 441–443, 443f
Dyadic morality, 366–367, 367, 443–444, 446
Dyadic morality theory (DMT), 215–216. *See also* Theory of dyadic morality (TDM)
Dyad-superiority effect, 441–442

E

Economic factors, 272–273, 283
Ego depletion, 491n
Egocentrism, 352–358, 354t
Elderly persons, 430–431
Embedded morality, 294, 297–298. *See also* Grounded approaches to morality
Embodied morality approach. *See also* Grounded approaches to morality
historical context of, 280
overview, 279–280, 286–287
research findings and, 280–286
theory and, 280
Embryonic stem cell research, 326, 327, 374–375
Emotions
attachment and, 445
blame and, 384, 387
developmental neuroscience and, 506
emotion regulation, 170
empathy and, 51–53
functional conflict theory of, 81–86
grounded approaches and, 296
historical moral change and, 267–268, 271–272, 274
intergroup aggression and, 194–195
moral judgment and, 88–89
moral standing of animals and, 166f, 168–170
moralization of the body and, 280
overview, 4, 54
research findings and, 85
role of, 89–90
as a social–moral signal, 116–117
stereotypes and, 201–202
unethical behavior and, 477
Empathy
developmental neuroscience and, 506, 508–512
ethical behavior and, 478, 480
evolved developmental niche (EDN) and, 453–454
functional conflict theory of moral emotions and, 83
historical context of, 50–51
identity and, 146
intergroup aggression and, 193–198
moral standing of animals and, 170
overview, 49–50, 53, 54, 194

research findings and, 53–54
theory and, 51–53
unselfish behavior and, 469
Environmental appeals, 540–541
Environmental factors
constructive origins of morality and, 24–25
evolved developmental niche (EDN) and, 454–455
grounded approaches and, 297–298
moral clarity and, 495
moral self-theory and, 152
moral values and, 62–63
overview, 338–339
skills expertise and, 489
Envy, 201–202
Epiphanies, 495
Epistemic states, 406–407
Equality, 232–233, 236, 297. *See also* Fairness; Inequity aversion
Essentialism, 92–93, 143
Ethical behavior. *See also* Behavior
ability and willpower and, 477–478
identity and motivation and, 478–479
overview, 465–466, 466t
personality traits and, 478
selfish behavior and, 467–468
unselfish behavior and, 468
Ethics, 231
Ethnicity, 15–16, 16f
Ethogenesis
dispositional and situational orientations, 452–453
historical context of, 453–456
overview, 451–452, 457–458
research findings and, 457
theory and, 456
Euthanasia. *See* Physician-assisted suicide
Evaluation, 27–28. *See also* Moral judgment
Event-related potentials (ERPs), 510–512
Evolutionary factors
anthropocentrism and, 355
attachment and, 443–444
blame and, 383–384, 388
cooperation and, 403–404
development of sociomoral evaluations in infants and, 403–404
ethogenesis, 451–458
evolved developmental niche (EDN) and, 453–456
historical moral change and, 266, 267–268, 270

Evolutionary factors *(cont.)*
  historicist view of morality and,
    260
  moral clarity and, 494
  moral foundations theory (MFT)
    and, 211
  moral heroes as puppets and,
    254
  moral identity and, 145–146
  moral self-theory and, 151
  moralization of the body and,
    282
  overview, 338–339
  side-taking strategies and, 180
  stereotype content model (SCM)
    and, 204–205
  terror management theory
    (TMT) and, 242–243
  theory of dyadic morality
    (TDM) and, 364
  vulnerability-based morality,
    431
Evolutionary psychology, 213–214
Evolved developmental niche
  (EDN), 453–456, 457–458
Executive control, 519
Expertise, 487–488
Explicit beliefs, 567–568
Expressivism, 311

F

Facial expressions, 75, 85, 296
Fairness. *See also* Distributive
    fairness; Equality; Inequity
    aversion; Justice
  animals and, 393–399
  comparing animals to humans
    and, 398
  cultural practices and, 15
  development of sociomoral
    evaluations in infants and,
    404
  developmental origins of,
    420–428
  implicit moral processes and,
    521–522
  model of moral motives (MMM)
    and, 224
  moral clarity and, 497–498
  moral foundations theory (MFT)
    and, 212, 214
  moral judgment and, 27, 32
  moral values and, 61
  moralization of the body and,
    281, 283–284
  overview, 568–569
Prisoner's Dilemma game, 435

research evidence regarding
    infants' fairness concerns and,
    423–426
  social interactions and, 190
Fear
  ethogenesis and, 453
  historical moral change and, 271
  intergroup aggression and,
    194–195
  moral standing of animals and,
    168–169
  moralization of the body and,
    280–281
Femininity, 498–499
Firm views of moral identity, 135,
    136–137. *See also* Moral
    identity
Five-foundations model, 540–541
Flexible views of moral identity,
    135–137, 138–139. *See also*
    Moral identity
Folk moral theories
  dual-process perspective,
    321–324, 322t
  future directions and, 328–329
  intuitive dualism and, 326–328,
    327t
  overview, 320–321
  research findings and, 324–326
Foot binding, 271
Forgiveness, 336, 387–388
Free will, 326–328, 327t, 332–336
Friendliness, 205–206
Functional conflict theory
  historical context of, 82–84
  overview, 81–82, 85–86
  research findings and, 85
  theory and, 84–85
Functionalist approach, 102,
    123–124, 151–152, 323, 510
Fundamentalist view, 104,
    259–264

G

Game-theoretic tools
  historical moral change and,
    267–268
  Prisoner's Dilemma game, 61,
    433–435
  side-taking strategies and, 180
Gay marriage. *See* Same-sex
    marriage
Gender
  blame and, 387
  cultural practices and, 15
  historical moral change and, 269
  intergroup relationships and, 26

stereotype content model (SCM)
    and, 204–205
  transformations over time,
    15–16, 16f
  vulnerability and, 430–431
Generosity, 340. *See also* Sharing
Genetic factors, 267, 268,
    338–339, 456, 505
Genetically modified organisms
  (GMOs)
  dyadic loop and, 365
  moral psychology and, 538–540
  moralization and, 367, 368
Genetic–cultural coevolutionary
  products, 505
Geocentricism, 354t, 356–357
Geographies of morality
  continents, comparison among,
    345–347
  overview, 338–339, 347
  religions and, 339–341
  secularia and, 341–345, 342f,
    344f
Glückschmerz, 194. *See also*
  Outgroup pain
Goal-directed behavior, 52–53, 194–
  195, 422. *See also* Behavior
God(s), belief in
  blame and, 384–385
  intelligent design and, 352–358
  terror management theory
    (TMT) and, 241–249
Goodness, 436–437
Ground Zero mosque, 531
Grounded approaches to morality.
  See also Embodied morality
  approach
  historical context of, 292–293
  overview, 292, 297–298
  research findings and, 295–297
  theory and, 293–295
Grounded cognition, 292, 293, 294
Group membership. *See also*
  Ingroup identity; Intergroup
  relationships
  historical moral change and, 270
  intergroup relationships and,
    25–26
  moral heroes as puppets and, 254
  moral identity and, 137
  moral self-theory and, 152
  religion and, 247
Guilt
  ethical behavior and, 478, 480
  functional conflict theory of
    moral emotions and, 83
  moral self-theory and, 155–156
  relationship regulation theory
    (RRT) and, 237

H

Happiness, 280
Harm
    developmental neuroscience and,
        506
    dyadic loop and, 365, 365f
    harm hypothesis, 234–235
    implicit moral processes and,
        521–522
    moral coherence and, 376, 377
    moral foundations theory (MFT)
        and, 212, 213, 215, 216–217
    moralization of the body and,
        281
    opposition to genetically
        modified (GM) food, 539–540
    overview, 194, 568–569
    pluralism and, 215–216
    relationship regulation theory
        (RRT) and, 234–235
    theory of dyadic morality
        (TDM) and, 366–367
    wrongness compared to badness
        and, 42
Hatred, 194–195
Health, 280–286, 305
Helpers, 404–406, 407–409. See
    also Helping behaviors
Helping behaviors. See also
    Altruism; Behavior; Helpers
    in animals, 416–417
    in children, 414–416
    empathy and, 51
    moralization of the body and,
        285
    unselfish behavior and, 468
Hero Pose, 255–256
Heroes, moral. See Moral heroes
Hero's Speech, 254–255
Hierarchy, 124–125, 233,
    236–237, 297
Hinderers, 404–406, 407–409
Historical moral change
    historical context of, 266–267
    moralization and, 363–368
    overview, 266, 273–274
    research findings and, 268–273
    theory and, 267–268
Historicist view of morality
    historical context of, 260–261
    overview, 259–260, 263–264
    research findings and, 262–263
    theory and, 261–262
Homosexuality. See also Same-sex
    marriage
    dyadic loop and, 366
    implicit moral processes and,
        521

moral coherence and, 375
moral judgment and, 367, 368,
    568
theory of dyadic morality
    (TDM) and, 364
Honesty
    development of morality and,
        13–14
    geographies of morality and,
        340
    overview, 569
    social and moral decision
        making and, 13–14
    testing moral behavior, 490
Honor killings, 269
Human inequity aversion, 393–
    394, 398. See also Fairness
Humility, 105–106
Hypocrisy, 340

I

Identity. See also Moral identity;
    Self-identity
    essentialism and, 143
    ethical behavior and, 478–479
    folk moral theories and,
        326–328, 327t
    historical context of, 142–143
    moral standing of animals and,
        166f, 170–171
    moral values and, 59
    overview, 141–142, 145–146,
        153–154
    research evidence and, 143–144
    social cognitive model of,
        133–139
    uncertainties and, 144–145
Image-focused moral self, 152
Imagination orientation, 452
Immoral behavior, 155–156,
    367–368. See also Behavior
Immortality, 241–249
Impartiality, 183
Imperialism, 269–270
Implicit Association Test (IAT),
    202–203, 517–518,
    567–568
Implicit attitudes, 567–568
Implicit moral processes
    ethogenesis and, 455–456
    implicit moral attitude,
        516–517
    modeling approach and,
        517–519
    overview, 516–517, 521–522
    research findings and, 519–521
Impression management, 254

Impurity judgments, 216–217,
    281–284
Incidental disgust, 71, 73–74. See
    also Disgust
Individual differences
    distributive fairness and, 426
    moral beliefs and, 313–314
    moral identity and, 136–137
    moral vitalism and, 307
    research evidence regarding
        infants' fairness concerns and,
        424–425
Individualism
    historical moral change and, 273
    moral clarity and, 498–499
    moral foundations theory (MFT)
        and, 213
    unethical behavior and, 471
Industriousness, 223–224, 224f,
    225–226
Inequity aversion. See also Fairness
    in animals, 394–399
    comparing animals to humans
        and, 398
    in humans, 393–394
    overview, 398–399
Infants
    altruism and, 414
    attachment and, 441–443, 443f
    constructive origins of morality
        and, 23–25
    distributive fairness and,
        420–428
    infant–caregiver interactions,
        446
    moral clarity and, 498
    possession of a sociomoral core
        by, 404–407
    preference for helpers by,
        407–409
    research evidence regarding
        infants' fairness concerns and,
        423–426
    sociomoral evaluations and,
        402–410
Inferences, 353, 415, 445
Information processing, 385,
    494–495
Ingroup identity. See also Group
    membership
    empathy and, 53
    intergroup aggression and,
        194–195
    moral judgment and, 27
    overview, 26, 137, 568–569
Inhibition, 35–37, 444
Insula, 507, 507f, 508–509
Integrative approach, 152–153,
    243, 457

Intelligent design
  anthropocentrism and, 354t,
    355–356
  biocentrism and, 354t, 357–358
  egocentrism and, 354–355, 354t
  geocentricism and, 354t,
    356–357
  historical context of, 352–353,
    354t
  overview, 352, 358
Intentionality
  blame and, 384–385
  development of sociomoral
    evaluations in infants and,
    404
  developmental neuroscience and,
    510
  disgust and, 76
  distributive fairness and, 422
  infants' evaluation of, 405–406
  moral coherence and, 374, 377
  moral self-theory and, 154
  moralization of the body and,
    281, 285
  relationship regulation theory
    (RRT) and, 234–235
  wrongness compared to badness
    and, 44
Interactionist model of unethical
    behavior, 475–477, 476f,
    479–480. See also Unethical
    behavior
Interdependence structures, 205
Interference paradigms, 296
Intergroup aggression. See also
    Aggression
  debates regarding, 194–196
  overview, 193, 197–198
  Schadenfreude as a motivator of,
    196–197
Intergroup relationships. See
    also Group membership;
    Relationships
  constructing morality and,
    25–26
  moral judgment and, 26–27
  overview, 194
  Schadenfreude and, 194–198
  social inequalities and, 27–28
  stereotype content model (SCM)
    and, 203
International Affective Picture
    System (IAPS), 510
Interrogation, 374–375
Intuitive dualism, 326–328, 327t
Intuitive processes. See also Moral
    intuition
  attachment and, 440–441
  behavior and, 487

  disgust and, 73–74
  distributive fairness and, 422
  ethogenesis and, 455–456
  fairness and, 422
  folk moral theories and,
    321–324, 322t, 324, 326–328,
    327t
  grounded approaches and,
    294–295
  historical context of, 32–33
  moral clarity and, 494–495, 496
  moral cognition and, 110
  moral coherence and, 373–374
  moral foundations theory (MFT)
    and, 212
  moral intuition and, 517
  moral judgment and, 127–128,
    567, 569
  moral vitalism and, 305
  overview, 31–32, 36–37
  research findings and, 34–36
  theory and, 33–34
  vulnerability and, 430

J

Judgments. See also Moral
    judgment
  cultural practices and, 15
  development of morality and,
    10–11
  empathy and, 51–52
  evaluating moral character and,
    100–102
  moral self-theory and, 155–156
  moral values and, 64–65
  social and moral decision
    making and, 11–13
Justice, 10–11, 213, 435, 469. See
    also Fairness
Justification, 195–196
Just-world theory, 35

K

Kindness, 237, 239
Kornblith–Devitt strategy, 551–554

L

Latent Dirichlet allocation (LDA),
    530–531
Latent semantic analysis (LSA),
    528, 532
Late-positive potential (LPP), 511
Lateral hypothalamus, 509

Laws, 28, 343, 345
Lay meta-ethics, 312–314
Leadership, 252–256
Learning
  evolved developmental niche
    (EDN) and, 454–455
  functional conflict theory of
    moral emotions and, 82
  historical moral change and, 274
  learning theory, 24–25
  moral clarity and, 497–498
  moral cognition and, 110–111
  moral judgment and, 569
  moral values and, 63–64, 65
  unethical behavior and, 471
LGBT rights, 269
Liberty, 522, 568–569
Life bioethical issues, 326, 327.
    See also Abortion; Physician-
    assisted suicide
Love, 271
Loyalty, 212–213, 470, 522,
    568–569

M

Macbeth effect, 285
Machiavellianism, 478, 480
Manichaeism, 496
Market pricing, 232, 236
Marriage. See also Same-sex
    marriage
  dyadic loop and, 366
  historical moral change and,
    271, 273
  implicit moral processes and,
    521
  moral judgment and, 367, 568
Masculinity, 498–499
Masturbation
  dyadic loop and, 366
  moral judgment and, 569
  moralization and, 363–364, 368
  theory of dyadic morality
    (TDM) and, 364
Materialist tradition, 272–273
Meaning extraction method
    (MEM), 531–532
Medial orbitofrontal cortex
    (mOFC), 60–61, 63, 64–65
Medial prefrontal cortex (mPFC),
    507, 507f, 510
Mental representations, 296. See
    also Representations
Mental states, 186–190
Meritocracy, 205
Meta-ethical beliefs, 312–314,
    315–317. See also Moral belief

Metaphors, 295–296
Mind attribution, 167–168
Mind perception, 559–561, 560f
Mind–brain identity, 326–328, 327t
Model of moral motives (MMM).
  See also Motivation
  historical context of, 225
  overview, 223–225, 224f, 229
  research findings and, 227–229
  theory and, 225–227
Modeling approach, 517–519
Moderation, 223–224, 224f, 225–226
Money, 470–471
Moral agency, 559. See also Agency
Moral belief. See also Belief systems
  behavior and, 315–317
  lay meta-ethics, 312–314
  overview, 310–312, 314–315, 317
  psychological research and, 311–312
Moral change. See Historical moral change
Moral character, 99–106, 122–125. See also Character evaluation; Character judgments
Moral clarity, 493–495, 497–498, 499
Moral cognition. See also Cognitive processes
  character and, 124
  grounded approaches and, 294, 296, 297–298
  historical context of, 109–110, 109f
  mind perception and, 559–561, 560f
  norms and, 557–559, 558f
  overview, 108–109, 109f, 116–117, 186–187, 556–557, 562–563
  research findings and, 113–116
  scientific cognition, 561–562
  theory and, 110–113, 111f, 113f
Moral coherence processes
  historical context of, 372
  overview, 371–372, 378–379
  research findings and, 374–378
  theory and, 372–374
Moral complexity
  historical context of, 372
  moral coherence and, 371–379
  overview, 371–372, 378–379
  theory and, 372–374

Moral decision making. See also Decision making
  cultural practices and, 14–16, 16f
  empathy and, 49–50
  historical context of, 122
  moral cognition and, 111
  processes of, 11–14
Moral dilemmas, 565–570
Moral disagreements, 233, 238
Moral discourse theory, 213
Moral disengagement, 37, 478, 480
Moral diversity, 268–270
Moral domain
  lack of support for, 554
  overview, 547
  project of defining morality, 547–554, 548f
  testing a definition of morality, 549–554
Moral domain theory, 261, 262
Moral Dyad Theory, 216–217
Moral emotions, 81–86, 201–202. See also Emotions
Moral foundations theory (MFT)
  big data analysis and, 530, 532
  constructionism and, 90–91
  emotions and, 89–90
  grounded approaches and, 297
  historical context of, 213–214, 260
  implicit moral processes and, 521–522
  model of moral motives (MMM) and, 225–227, 228–229
  moral clarity and, 495–496
  moral vitalism and, 305
  moralization and, 366
  overview, 93, 211–213, 218
  relationship regulation theory (RRT) and, 234
  research findings and, 216–217
  side-taking strategies and, 180
  social interactions and, 189–190
  terror management theory (TMT) and, 242, 247
  theory and, 214–217
  theory of dyadic morality (TDM) and, 367
  whole-number approach and, 90, 91–93
Moral grammar hypothesis, 43, 234–235
Moral heroes
  historical context of, 253
  overview, 252–253, 256
  research findings and, 254–256
  theory and, 253–254

Moral identity. See also Identity
  ethical behavior and, 478, 480
  historical context of, 142–143
  overview, 145–146, 150
  social cognitive model of, 133–139
Moral intuition, 89, 152–153, 373–374. See also Intuitive processes
Moral judgment. See also Judgments; Sociomoral evaluations
  attachment approach to, 440–448
  blame as, 382–389
  brain mechanisms, 507
  choosing sides and, 177–184
  death awareness and, 247–248
  disgust and, 70–71, 76–77
  emotions and, 88–93
  ethogenesis and, 456
  folk moral theories and, 320–321, 322–323, 324, 328
  free will and, 333, 335–336
  grounded approaches and, 297
  historical context of, 122
  historicist view of morality and, 260
  how people form, 31–32
  implicit moral processes and, 516–522
  intergroup relationships and, 25–26, 26–27
  intuitive and rational processes and, 127–128
  moral beliefs and, 312
  moral clarity and, 493–499
  moral cognition and, 111
  moral coherence and, 372–379
  moral foundations theory (MFT) and, 214, 216–217
  moral vitalism and, 306
  moralization of the body and, 280, 281–284, 285
  nonmoral considerations and, 22–23
  overview, 20–22, 25, 28, 121–122, 565–570
  parallel morality hypothesis and, 31–37
  preference for helpers by infants and, 409
  relationship regulation theory (RRT) and, 231–233, 234
  social cognitive development and, 23
  social inequalities and, 27–28
  social interactions and, 189–191
  social regulation and, 116

Moral judgment (cont.)
  terror management theory
    (TMT) and, 245–246
  theory and, 41
  theory of dyadic morality
    (TDM) and, 363–368
  wrongness compared to badness
    and, 40–44
Moral monism, 215–217
Moral objectivism, 314–316, 317
Moral psychology. See also
    Psychological foundations
  attachment and, 440–441, 445
  big data analysis and, 532–533
  description and process and,
    541–542
  environmental appeals and,
    540–541
  fairness and, 420–421
  folk moral theories and,
    323–324
  free will and, 332–336
  grounded approaches and, 294,
    297, 298
  historical moral change and,
    267–268, 273–274
  moral foundations theory (MFT)
    and, 213–214, 218
  moralization and, 368
  opposition to genetically
    modified (GM) food, 538–540
  overview, 537, 542, 565–570
  Prisoner's Dilemma game,
    433–435
  relationship regulation theory
    (RRT) and, 233, 234–235,
    238
  terror management theory
    (TMT) and, 241–242
  testing a definition of morality,
    551–554
  the trolley problem, 432–433
Moral reasoning. See also
    Reasoning
  developmental neuroscience and,
    511
  folk moral theories and,
    322–323
  moral coherence and, 373
  moral self-theory and, 150–151,
    153
  moral vitalism and, 304–308
Moral self-perception theory, 149–
    150. See also Self-perceptions
Moral self-theory. See also Self-
    identity
  historical context of, 150–151
  overview, 149–150, 156–157

research findings and, 153–156
theoretical stance of, 151–153
Moral standing of animals. See
    Animal inequity aversion;
    Animals, thinking morally
    about
Moral transformation, 268–270
Moral values
  action value, 61–63
  feedback and learning, 63–64
  grounded approaches and, 297
  judgment and, 64–65
  outcome value, 60–61
  overview, 59–60, 65–66
Moral vitalism
  historical moral change and,
    304–305
  overview, 303–304, 307–308
  research findings and, 306–307
  theory and, 305–306
Morality, 20–22, 149
Moralization
  dyadic loop and, 365–366, 365f
  historical context of, 366–367
  overview, 363–364, 368
  research findings and, 367–368
  theory and, 367
Mortality, 241–249
Mortality salience (MS), 246, 248
Motivation. See also Model of
    moral motives (MMM)
  disgust and, 75–76
  empathy and, 53
  ethical behavior and, 478–479
  functional conflict theory of
    moral emotions and, 84
  historicist view of morality and,
    260
  mental states and, 189
  moral heroes as puppets and,
    254
  moral values and, 62
  overview, 168, 223–225, 224f
  relationship regulation theory
    (RRT) and, 232–233, 232t
  social interactions and, 188
Multinomial model, 518–521
Multivoxel pattern analysis
    (MVPA), 65

N

Nativism, 211–212, 216
Natural kind models, 92–93
Natural language processing
    (NLP), 527–528, 529,
    530–531, 532

Neuroscience. See also Brain
    regions; Developmental
    neuroscience
  ethogenesis and, 452, 457
  folk moral theories and,
    321–322
  intergroup aggression and, 197,
    198
  moral values and, 60, 64–65
  testing moral behavior, 490
Nonconsequentialism, 181–182
Nonhuman sense of fairness,
    393–399. See also Animals,
    thinking morally about;
    Fairness
Nonmoral cognition, 561–563. See
    also Cognitive processes
Nonpurity transgressions, 70–71,
    74–77. See also Component
    process model (CPM); Disgust
Nonsocial hypothesis, 395–398
Noradrenergic system, 509
Normative cognition, 260
Normative judgments, 260
Norms
  altruism and, 414
  development of morality and,
    11
  free will and, 333–334
  historical moral change and,
    271, 273
  historicist view of morality and,
    260, 261, 262–263
  learning and, 110–111
  moral cognition and, 110–111
  moral judgment and, 27
  moral values and, 64
  moralization and, 363–368
  overview, 557–559, 558f, 569
  relationship regulation theory
    (RRT) and, 231–232
  research evidence regarding
    infants' fairness concerns and,
    426
  social interactions and, 191
  theory of dyadic morality
    (TDM) and, 364
  vulnerability and, 430–431
  wrongness compared to badness
    and, 41–43

O

Objectivity, 310, 314–316, 317
Outcome bias, 376–377
Outcome control, 385–386, 387
Outgroup bias, 26, 27, 53

Outgroup hate, 194–195
Outgroup pain, 194–198. *See also* Schadenfreude

P

Parallel morality hypothesis
historical context of, 32–33
overview, 31–32, 36–37
research findings and, 34–36
theory and, 33–34
Parent–child interaction, 446
Parenting factors
altruism in children and, 415
constructive origins of morality and, 24–25
decision making and, 14
historical moral change and, 273
moralization of the body and, 285
parental behavior, 181–183
relationship regulation theory (RRT) and, 236–237
research evidence regarding infants' fairness concerns and, 424–425
terror management theory (TMT) and, 244
Perceptions. *See also* Self-perceptions
moral standing of animals and, 167–168
preference for helpers by infants and, 408
research findings and, 153–154
social and moral decision making and, 11
social interactions and, 187–188
theory of dyadic morality (TDM) and, 364
Performance anxiety, 479
Periaqueductal gray area (PAG), 508, 509, 510
Person perception, 153–154. *See also* Perceptions
Person X Situation interaction, 479–480
Personal identity. *See* Identity
Personality characteristics, 103, 154
Personality disorders, 388, 512–513
Personality psychology, 243, 253
Personality traits, 478, 479–480, 521
Person-centered morality (PCM), 122–128, 129n
Persuasion, 495–496

Philosophy
attachment and, 447–448
blame and, 387–388
folk moral theories and, 326
grounded approaches and, 293
historicist view of morality and, 260
moral beliefs and, 310–311
moral dilemmas and, 566
moralization and, 366
selfish behavior and, 468
testing a definition of morality, 549–551
theory of dyadic morality (TDM) and, 366–367
Physician-assisted suicide, 320–321, 326, 327, 521
Pity, 201–202
Pluralism
harm pluralism, 215–216
moral beliefs and, 313
moral foundations theory (MFT) and, 213–217
theory of dyadic morality (TDM) and, 366–367
Political factors
big data analysis and, 530
climate change and, 540–541
historical moral change and, 269, 271
moral clarity and, 496
moral coherence and, 378–379
moral psychology and, 540–541
political psychology, 215
Porn consumption, 340, 365, 365f
Posterior insula, 508–509
Posterior superior temporal sulcus (pSTS), 507, 507f, 509, 510
Posttraumatic stress disorder (PTSD), 249, 454–455
Posture, 255–256, 293
Power
historical moral change and, 273
moral clarity and, 497, 498–499
Prejudice, 26, 83, 206–207. *See also* Stereotyping
Prescriptive processes, 223–224, 224f, 234, 379, 558
Prisoner's Dilemma game, 61, 433–435, 437
Property rights, 343, 345
Proportionality, 232, 236, 297
Proscriptive regulation, 223–224, 224f
Prosocial acts. *See also* Behavior
altruistic lying and, 469
developmental neuroscience and, 506

empathy and, 52–54
ethogenesis and, 455
geographies of morality and, 339
moral clarity and, 496, 498
moral identity and, 137
moral self-theory and, 154–155, 157
moralization of the body and, 284
religions and, 340–341
selfish behavior and, 468
vulnerability-based morality and, 437
Psychological agency, 559. *See also* Agency
Psychological essentialism, 143
Psychological foundations. *See also* Moral psychology
blame and, 388
folk moral theories and, 323–324
historicist view of morality and, 260
intelligent design and, 353
model of moral motives (MMM) and, 224–225
moral beliefs and, 311–312
moral foundations theory (MFT) and, 212, 213–214, 218
moralization of the body and, 283–284, 285
overview, 51
terror management theory (TMT) and, 243
theory of dyadic morality (TDM) and, 366–367
Psychopathy, 478, 480, 512–513
Punishments
blame and, 387
component process model (CPM) and, 78
geographies of morality and, 343
historical moral change and, 270
moral values and, 62
relationship regulation theory (RRT) and, 236–237
research evidence regarding infants' fairness concerns and, 426
selfish behavior and, 467
side-taking strategies and, 179
terror management theory (TMT) and, 248
unselfish behavior and, 468
Puppet theory
historical context of, 253
overview, 252–253, 256
research findings and, 254–256
theory and, 253–254

Purity. *See also* Component process model (CPM); Disgust
  big data analysis and, 531
  implicit moral processes and, 522
  moral foundations theory (MFT) and, 213, 216–217
  moral judgment and, 189–190
  moral vitalism and, 303–308
  moralization of the body and, 281–284
  overview, 70–71, 568–569
  research findings and, 75–77
  theory and, 74–75

R

Race, 15–16, 16*f*, 204–205, 517–518
Rational processes, 127–128, 233–234
Reactive attitudes, 384, 425–426
Reasoning. *See also* Moral reasoning
  development of morality and, 10–11
  folk moral theories and, 322–323
  intelligent design and, 352–353
  moral clarity and, 494–495, 496
  moral judgment and, 25
  moral self-theory and, 150–151, 153
  moral vitalism and, 304–308
  nonmoral considerations and, 22–23
  overview, 6, 9–10
  parallel morality hypothesis and, 36
  role of in morality, 9
  social and moral decision making and, 11–14
  social interactions and, 187, 188
Reciprocity
  altruism and, 177
  cooperation and, 403–404
  development of sociomoral evaluations in infants and, 403
  overview, 338–339, 568–569
Reinforcement learning, 41, 42–43, 65
Relationship regulation theory (RRT)
  historical context of, 233–234
  moral foundations theory (MFT) and, 214–215

overview, 231–233, 232*t*, 238–239
  research findings and, 235–238
  theory and, 234–235
Relationships. *See also* Intergroup relationships
  constructing morality and, 25–26
  distributive fairness and, 421
  free will and, 336
  grounded approaches and, 297
  moral character and, 102, 104–105
  moral clarity and, 498
  moralization of the body and, 285
  relationship regulation theory (RRT) and, 231–232, 233
  vulnerability-based morality and, 437
Relativism, 311, 314–315, 499
religions, 339–341, 345–347
Religious traditions
  blame and, 384–385, 387–388
  continents, comparison among, 345–347
  folk moral theories and, 326–328, 327*t*
  free will and, 333–334
  geographies of morality and, 339–345, 342*f*, 344*f*
  historical moral change and, 263, 267, 268
  identity and, 142–143
  intelligent design and, 352–358
  moral clarity and, 499
  moral vitalism and, 303–308
  moralization and, 363–364
  terror management theory (TMT) and, 241–249
  testing a definition of morality, 550–551
Representations, 293, 294–295, 296, 441–443
Resource allocation, 283–284, 285, 396, 421, 423
Respect, 568–569
Response bias, 519–520
Response inhibition, 35–36
Response patterns, 558
Responsibilities, 165–172, 195–196, 376
Retrospective gambler's fallacy, 357
Rewards
  altruism in children and, 415
  distributive fairness and, 421, 422

fairness and, 393–394
  moral clarity and, 497–498
  moral thinking and, 3
  moral values and, 62, 65
Rights, 10–11, 28, 213, 269–270
Rivalry, 196–197
Rules. *See also* Wrongness
  development of morality and, 11
  folk moral theories and, 324
  free will and, 334
  geographies of morality and, 343, 345
  historical moral change and, 267
  model of moral motives (MMM) and, 228–229
  overview, 43–44
  relationship regulation theory (RRT) and, 239

S

Same-sex marriage. *See also* Homosexuality; Marriage
  implicit moral processes and, 521
  moral coherence and, 375
  moral judgment and, 568
  moralization and, 366, 367
Schadenfreude, 193–198, 202. *See also* Outgroup pain
Schema, 235, 444, 455–456
Schwartz Value Survey (SVS), 531–532
Science, scope of, 326–328, 327*t*, 356
Scientific cognition, 561–562. *See also* Cognitive processes
Secularia, 341–347, 342*f*, 344*f*
Self-control, 453–454, 477–478, 480, 489–490
Self-enhancement, 105–106
Self-esteem, 243–246, 249
Self-identity, 145. *See also* Identity; Moral self-theory
Selfish behavior. *See also* Behavior
  antecedents of, 469–470
  ethical behavior and, 467–468
  future directions and, 470–471
  overview, 465–466, 466*t*, 471–472
  unethical behavior and, 466–467
Selflessness, 285
Self-perceptions, 149–150, 153–154, 155–157. *See also* Perceptions

Self-regulation
  evolved developmental niche
    (EDN) and, 454
  free will and, 335
  functional conflict theory of
    moral emotions and, 83
  implicit moral processes and,
    521
  relationship regulation theory
    (RRT) and, 235
  terror management theory
    (TMT) and, 249
Serotonergic system, 509
Sexual activity, 284
Sexual behavior, 367–368, 531
Sexuality, 269
Sharing, 233, 285, 286, 506,
    512–513
Side-taking strategies. See also
    Moral judgment
  historical context of, 179–180
  overview, 177–179, 183–184
  research findings and, 181–183
  theory and, 180–181
Sin, 363–364. See also Religious
    traditions; Wrongness
Situational orientation, 452–453,
    475, 476
Situation-trait relevance, 479–480
Skepticism, 310–311, 317n
Skilled expertise, 487–488, 491
Slavery, 271–273
Smoking, 271, 365, 366, 367, 368
Sociability, 205–206
Social biases, 232
Social class, 15–16, 16f, 204–205,
    469–470
Social cognition. See also Cognitive
    processes
  character and, 124
  character evaluation and, 125
  moral character and, 100–102
  moral cognition and, 108–118,
    109f, 111f, 113f, 114f
  moral foundations and, 189–190
  overview, 23, 108–109, 109f,
    186, 187
Social cognitive theory (SCT),
    133–139
Social cohesion, 267–268, 270–271
Social context, 186–189, 190–191
Social exclusion, 26
Social expressions, 114, 114f
Social factors, 231–232, 341–345,
    342f, 344f
Social grooming, 285
Social hierarchies, 15–16, 16f
Social hypothesis, 395–398

Social identification, 194
Social identity, 25–26, 253
Social inequalities, 27–28
Social interactions, 187–190
Social intuitionist model (SIM)
  disgust and, 71, 73–74
  grounded approaches and,
    294–295
  moral coherence and, 372
  moral foundations theory (MFT)
    and, 212, 213
  moral intuition and, 89–90
  moralization of the body and,
    280
Social justice
  cultural practices and, 15–16
  development of morality and,
    10–11
  how people form, 31–32
  model of moral motives (MMM)
    and, 224, 226–227
  moral foundations theory (MFT)
    and, 214
  parallel morality hypothesis
    and, 33
Social learning strategy, 471
Social network analysis (SNA),
    528, 529, 530
Social neuroscience, 506. See also
    Neuroscience
Social opposition, 14–15
Social order, 224, 226–227,
    228–229
Social organization, 15
Social perceptions, 149–150
Social perspectives, 103–104
Social psychology
  developmental neuroscience and,
    506
  grounded approaches and, 293
  moral foundations theory (MFT)
    and, 213
  moral heroes as puppets and,
    253
  unethical behavior and, 476
Social regulation, 108–118, 109f,
    111f, 113f, 114f
Social Science Research Network
    (SSRN), 467
Social systems, 334
Social–functional emotions theory,
    85
Social–functional evolutionary
    model, 525–527
Sociality, effectance, and elicited
    agent knowledge (SEEK)
    model, 168
Socialization, 244–245, 414, 416

Social–moral signals, 116–117
Social-psychological research, 384
Social–relational cognition, 232
Social–relational context, 235
Sociomoral evaluations. See also
    Moral judgment
  cooperative systems and,
    403–404
  development of in infants,
    404–407
  overview, 402–403, 410
  preference for helpers by infants
    and, 407–409
Somatosensory cortex, 508
Spirituality
  blame and, 384–385
  folk moral theories and,
    326–328, 327t
  grounded approaches and, 294
  identity and, 142–143
  moral judgment and, 569
  moral vitalism and, 303–308
  terror management theory
    (TMT) and, 241–249
Spontaneous evaluations, 384–385.
    See also Moral judgment
Stage model of moral reasoning,
    150–151. See also Reasoning
Statistical norms, 558. See also
    Norms
Stem cell research. See Embryonic
    stem cell research
Stereotype content model (SCM)
  intergroup aggression and,
    194–195
  overview, 203, 206–207
  research findings and, 205–206
  theory and, 203–205
Stereotyping
  debates regarding, 202–203
  intergroup relationships and, 26
  overview, 201–202, 206–207
Stress, 454–455
Strong view of moral identity,
    136–137. See also Moral
    identity
Subgenual prefrontal cortex, 509
Supplementary motor area, 508
Sympathy
  functional conflict theory of
    moral emotions and, 83
  historical moral change and,
    271, 272
  moral standing of animals and,
    168–169
  vulnerability-based morality
    and, 437
Synchronicity, 354–355

T

Teleological bias, 352–358
Temporoparietal junction (TPJ), 507, 507f, 509, 510
Terror management theory (TMT)
  biological roots of morality and, 242–243
  death awareness in moral behavior and judgment and, 247–248
  ethogenesis and, 453
  future directions and, 248–249
  human morality and, 246–247
  overview, 241–242, 243–247
Thalamus, 509
Theory of dyadic morality (TDM). *See also* Dyadic morality theory (DMT)
  dyadic loop and, 365–366, 365f
  historical context of, 366–367
  overview, 363–365, 368
  research findings and, 367–368
  theory and, 367
Theory of mind (ToM), 186, 187, 202
Trait egocentrism, 354. *See also* Egocentrism
Trait empathy, 478, 480
Trait perception, 168
Trait theory, 253
Trauma, 249, 454–455
Triune ethics meta-theory (TEM), 451–452
Trolley problem, 432–433, 434, 437
Trustworthiness
  moral character and, 104
  person-centered morality and, 128n–129n
  social and moral decision making and, 13–14
  stereotype content model (SCM) and, 205–206
  stereotypes and, 202
Truth, 436–437. *See also* Honesty
Two-dimensional model of moral identity, 135–136. *See also* Moral identity

U

Ultimatum Game, 61
Uncertainty avoidance, 498–499
Unconflicted virtue
  overview, 485–486, 491
  skills expertise and, 487–488
  testing moral behavior, 489–490
Unethical behavior. *See also* Behavior
  antecedents of, 469–470
  attachment and, 479
  disposition and, 477–479
  equilibrium and, 475–481, 476f
  future directions and, 470–471
  overview, 465–466, 466t, 471–472, 475–477, 476f
  selfish behavior and, 466–467
  unselfish behavior and, 468–469
Unfairness, 283–284. *See also* Fairness
Unintentional moral judgment, 519–520. *See also* Moral judgment
Unity, 233, 237, 297
Universal moral grammar (UMG), 234–235, 295
Unselfish behavior. *See also* Behavior
  antecedents of, 469–470
  ethical behavior and, 468
  overview, 465–466, 466t
  unethical behavior and, 468–469
User-defined dictionaries (NDD), 527–528

V

Values, moral. *See* Moral values
Vaping, 366
Vegans, 170–171
Vegetarians, 170–171, 271, 325, 327–328
Ventral striatum (VS), 60–61, 64, 65, 507
Ventromedial prefrontal cortex (vmPFC)
  empathy and, 508–509, 509, 510
  folk moral theories and, 321, 322
  implicit moral processes and, 521

  moral thinking and, 4
  overview, 507, 507f
Violation of expectations, 424–425
Violent actions
  historical moral change and, 269, 273
  intergroup aggression and, 193–198
  moral values and, 63
  relationship regulation theory (RRT) and, 233, 235–238
  terror management theory (TMT) and, 249
Virtue, 485–492, 487–488
Virtue ethics, 122–125, 456
Virtuous violence, 195–196, 235–238
Vitalistic thinking, 304. *See also* Moral vitalism
Vulnerability
  free will and, 335
  historical context of, 435
  overview, 430–431, 437
  Prisoner's Dilemma game, 433–435
  research findings and, 436
  theory and, 431–432, 435–437
  the trolley problem, 432–433

W

War, 236, 341, 342f
Well-being, 53, 431, 453–454, 506
Whistle blowers, 467–468
Whole-number approach, 89–90, 91–93
Willpower, 477–478, 479–480
Withdrawal motivations, 75–76. *See also* Motivation
Women's suffrage, 269
Work ethics, 226
World Trade Center attack, 531
Worldviews, 243–246, 249
Wrongness. *See also* Rules
  compared to badness, 40–44
  disgust and, 71, 76–77
  moral beliefs and, 313
  moral cognition and, 113–114
  norms and, 557–558, 558f
  overview, 40–41, 363–364
  theory and, 41